MW00973817

BK

ENGLISH

COMMUNICATION SKILLS IN THE NEW MILLENNIUM

GRADE 8

Annotated Teacher's Edition

J.A. Senn
Carol Ann Skinner

Barrett Kendall Publishing
Austin, Texas

Critical Readers

Lisa Adkins
Pflugerville ISD,
Pflugerville, TX

Jan Graham
Cobb Middle School,
Tallahassee, FL

Lisa Joyner
McDougal Middle School
Chapel Hill, NC

Eddie Martinez
Bailey Middle School,
Austin, TX

Jeri Putnam
Pflugerville Middle
School, Pflugerville, TX

Project Manager
Sandra Stucker Blevins

Editorial Director
Sandra Mangurian

Editorial Staff
Marianne Murphy
Marlene Greil
Donna Laughlin
Susan Sandoval
Vicki Tyler
Catherine Foy
Michelle Quijano
Elizabeth Wenning
Cheryl Duksta
Margaret Rickard

Production Directors
Gene Allen
Pun Nio

Photo Research and Permissions
Laurie O'Meara

Art and Design
Pun Nio
Leslie Kell
Rhonda Warwick

Production
Bethany Powell
Isabel Garza
Rhonda Warwick

Cover
Leslie Kell Designs
Pun Nio
Images © Photodiscs, Inc.

Editorial and Production Services
Book Builders, Inc.
Gryphon Graphics
Inkwell Publishing Solutions, Inc.
NETS

Printed in the United States of America.

ISBN 1-58079-116-6 2 3 4 5 6 7 RRD 06 05 04 03 02 01

Senior Consultants

Tommy Boley, Ph.D.
Director of English Education
The University of Texas at El Paso
El Paso, TX

Deborah Cooper, M.Ed.
Coordinating Director of PK-12 Curriculum
Charlotte-Mecklenburg Public Schools
Charlotte, NC

Susan Marie Harrington, Ph.D.
Associate Professor of English,
Director of Writing, Director of Placement and Assessment, and Adjunct Assistant Professor of Women's Studies
Indiana University-Purdue University, Indianapolis
Indianapolis, IN

Carol Pope, Ed.D.
Associate Professor of Curriculum and Instruction
North Carolina State University
Raleigh, NC

Rebecca Rickly, Ph.D.
Department of English
Texas Tech University
Lubbock, TX

John Simmons, Ph.D.
Professor of English Education and Reading
Florida State University
Tallahassee, FL

John Trimble, Ph.D.
University Distinguished Teaching Professor of English
The University of Texas
Austin, TX

Contributing Writers

Jeannie Ball

Grace Bultman

Richard Cohen

Elizabeth Egan-Rivera

Laurie Hopkins Etzel

Bobbi Fagone

Lesli Favor

Nancy-Jo Hereford

Susan Maxey

Linda Mazumdar

Elizabeth McGuire

Shannon Murphy

Carole Osterink

Michael Raymond

Duncan Searl

Jocelyn Sigue

Lorraine Sintetos

James Strickler

Diane Zahler

Kathy Zahler

Table of Contents COMPOSITION

Chapter 3 Writing Well-Structured Paragraphs

CHAPTER 4 Writing Effective Compositions

Chapter 5 Personal Writing: Self-Expression and Reflection

Chapter 6 Using Description: Observation

Chapter 7 Creative Writing: Stories, Plays, Poems

Chapter 8 Writing to Inform and Explain

Chapter 9 Writing to Persuade

Chapter 12 Letters

Communication Resource • Planning Guide . . C438a

Chapter 16 Library and Media Center

Table of Contents LANGUAGE

Grammar

CHAPTER 1 The Sentence

CHAPTER 2 Nouns and Pronouns

Chapter 3 Verbs

Chapter 4 Adjectives and Adverbs

Chapter 5 Other Parts of Speech and Review

CHAPTER 6 Complements

CHAPTER 7 Phrases

CHAPTER 8 Verbals and Verbal Phrases

Usage

CHAPTER 11 Using Verbs

CHAPTER 12 Using Pronouns

CHAPTER 13 Subject and Verb Agreement

CHAPTER 14 Using Adjectives and Adverbs

Mechanics

CHAPTER 15 Capital Letters

CHAPTER 16 End Marks and Commas

CHAPTER 17 Italics and Quotation Marks

CHAPTER 18 Other Punctuation

Spelling

Chapter 19 Spelling Correctly

Study and Test-Taking Skills Resource

COMPOSITION

Exploring Writer's Craft

PLANNING GUIDE This chart will help you create a flexible instructional plan that addresses the individual needs of all your students in the new millennium.

LEARNING TO KNOW

A Foundation of Knowledge	CHAPTER 1 Using Your Writing Process	CHAPTER 2 Developing Your Writing Style
PE **Communication Models**	Reading with a Writer's Eye, p. C2 "Eighth Book of Junior Authors and Illustrators" by Caroline Cooney, pp. C3–C4 Thinking as a Writer, p. C5 **Grammar in the Writing Process** • Sentence Fragments, p. C39	Reading with a Writer's Eye, p. C44 "Man Eats Car" by Natalie Goldberg, pp. C45–C47 Thinking as a Writer, p. C48 **Grammar in the Writing Process** • Subject and Verb Agreement, pp. C61–C62
TE **Skills Instruction**	Lesson 1: Writing Process Lesson 2: Drafting, Revising Lesson 3: Editing, Publishing	Lesson 1: Specific and Sensory Words Lesson 2: Combining Sentences, Coordinating and Subordinating Lesson 3: Varied Sentence Beginnings Lesson 4: Focused, Concise Sentences
PE **Skills Practice**	**Practice Your Skills** • Interest Inventory, p. C9 • Freewriting, p. C11 • Writing in Your Journal, p. C13 • Learning More About a Subject, p. C14 • Tracking Errors, p. C14 • Limiting a Subject, p. C17 • Occasions, Audiences, and Purposes, p. C18 • Writers' Voices, p. C19 • Observing, p. C21 • Brainstorming for Ideas p. C23 • Cluster Diagram, p. C24 • Inquiring, p. C25 • Organizing Details, p. C28 • Drafting from Notes, p. C30 • Drafting a Title, p. C31 • Studying a Revision, pp. C33–C34 • Editing with Proofreading Symbols, p. C38 **Writing Is Thinking** • Classifying, p. C26	**Practice Your Skills** • Revising with Specific Words, p. C50 • Showing, Not Telling, p. C53 • Combining Sentences with Specific Details, p. C54 • Combining Sentences by Coordinating, p. C57 • Combining Sentences by Subordinating, p. C58 • Varying Sentence Beginnings, p. C60 • Revising Rambling Sentences, pp. C63–C64 • Eliminating Unnecessary Words, p. C65 **Writing Is Thinking** • Comparing, p. C55
PE **Independent Application**	**In the Media** • Photo Essay, p. C15	**In the Media** • Tourist Brochure, p. C51 **Connection Collection** • Representing, p. C69 • In Everyday Life, p. C70 • In the Workplace, p. C70
Assessment and Evaluation	PE Pretest PE Checklist for Writing Process, p. C43 + I Chapter Test	PE Time Out to Reflect, p. C58 PE Checklist for Writing Style, p. C66 PE A Writer Writes, pp. C67–C68 PE Assess Your Learning, p. C71 + I Chapter Test

PE PUPIL'S EDITION TE TEACHER'S EDITION + ANCILLARIES I INTERNET

ADDITIONAL RESOURCES

- Composition Skills Practice
- Language Skills Practice
- Assessment
- Assessment Resources
- Standardized Test Preparation
- ESL Practice and Test Preparation
- Transparency Tools
- Writing Prompts
- Writers at Work

CHAPTER 3 Writing Well-Structured Paragraphs	CHAPTER 4 Writing Effective Compositions
Reading with a Writer's Eye, p. C72 "The Case for Short Words" by Richard Lederer, p. C73 Thinking as a Writer, p. C74 **Grammar in the Writing Process** • Adverbs, p. C87	Reading with a Writer's Eye, p. C98 "The Fixed" by Annie Dillard, pp. C99–C101 Thinking as a Writer, p. C102 **Grammar in the Writing Process** • Conjunctions, p. C118
Lesson 1: Paragraph Structure and Elements Lesson 2: Supporting Sentences Lesson 3: Unity, Coherence, and Concluding Sentence	Lesson 1: Subjects and Supporting Details Lesson 2: Drafting
Practice Your Skills • Topic Sentences, p. C78–C79 • Using a Pyramid to Write, p. C82 • Deleting Unrelated Ideas, pp. C84–C85 • Improving Paragraph Coherence, p. C86 **Writing Is Thinking** • Generalizing, p. C80	**Writing Is Thinking** • Inferring, p. C110
In the Media • Movie Review, p. C83 **Communicating Your Ideas** • Topic Sentence, p. C79 • Body of Your Paragraph, p. C82 • Concluding Sentence, p. C88 • Unity and Coherence, p. C89 • Editing, Publishing, p. C90 **Connection Collection** • Representing, pp. C94-C95 • In Everyday Life, p. C96 • Oral Communication, p. C96	**In the Media** • Television, p. C119 **Communicating Your Ideas** • Subject Inventory, p. C106 • Subject, p. C107 • Supporting Details, p. C109 • Arrangement of Details, p. C111 • Introduction, p. C112 • Body of the Composition, p. C113 • Conclusion and Title, p. C115 • Revising, p. C116 • Editing, Publishing, p. C117 **Connection Collection** • Representing, p. C123 • In the Workplace, p. C124 • Oral Communication, p. C124
PE Time Out to Reflect, p. C89 PE Checklist for Writing a Well-Structured Paragraph, p. C91 PE A Writer Writes, pp. C92–C93 PE Assess Your Learning, p. C97 + I Chapter Test	PE Checklist for Writing Effective Composition, p. C120 PE A Writer Writes, pp. C121–C122 PE Assess Your Learning, p. C125 + I Chapter Test TE Evaluating Compositions, pp. C125a–C125b

LEARNING TO DO

Competencies for the World of Work

Basic Skills
Reads, writes, performs arithmetic and mathematical operations, listens, and speaks
- Reading
- Writing
- Arithmetic/Mathematics
- Listening
- Speaking

Thinking Skills
Thinks creatively, makes decisions, solves problems, visualizes, knows how to learn, and reasons
- Creative Thinking
- Decision Making
- Problem Solving
- Seeing Things in the Mind's Eye
- Knowing How to Learn
- Reasoning

Personal Qualities
Displays responsibility, self-esteem, sociability, self-management, and integrity and honesty
- Responsibility
- Self-Esteem
- Sociability
- Self-Management
- Integrity/Honesty

LEARNING WITH TECHNOLOGY

Tools for the Information Age

I **http://www.bkenglish.com**
- BK English Online (password required)
- Chapter Tests
- Skill Practice
- Writing Prompts
- Standardized Tests

Teaching Suggestions

Essential Knowledge and Skills

- Writing to express, discover, record, develop, reflect on ideas, and to problem solve
- Selecting and using voice and style appropriate to audience and purpose
- Writing in complete sentences
- Generating ideas and plans for writing using prewriting strategies such as brainstorming, graphic organizers, notes, and logs
- Developing drafts by categorizing ideas
- Proofreading his/her own writing and that of others
- Evaluating how different media forms influence and inform
- Selecting, organizing, and producing visuals to complement and extend meanings

CHAPTER 1

Using Your Writing Process

"Anyone who doesn't write," proclaimed Anne Frank in her journal, "doesn't know how wonderful it is." When she composed these words in her personal diary, she could have had no idea how many people would read them. Yet her thoughts eventually traveled far beyond her own circle of family and friends. For Anne Frank, putting words on paper turned out to be a rich process of discovering, creating, shaping, and communicating.

When you write you communicate ideas, opinions, feelings, and observations. The need to write springs up in all aspects of your life. In school you write compositions. On a job you will write reports and business letters. In your personal life, you write letters and E-mails to friends. As you learn about each stage of writing, you will develop and refine your writing process by creating a composition. Throughout this book you will be reminded to employ your writing process as you write different types of paragraphs and compositions.

Reading with a Writer's Eye

In the following article, writer Carol Bruce Cooney discusses her love of books as well as her own experience of writing. Read the article once for pleasure. As you read for a second time, pay attention to what the author says about her writing process.

BLOCK SCHEDULING

- If your schedule requires that you cover the chapter in a **shorter time**, use Reading with a Writer's Eye and Developing Your Writing Process.
- If you want to take advantage of **longer class time**, add any or all of the following: In the Media, Writing Is Thinking, and Editing Workshop.

FROM

EIGHTH BOOK of Junior Authors and Illustrators

Caroline Cooney

I love books. I love reading, borrowing, buying, shelving, and writing them. I can't go more than a week without visiting at least two libraries and a bookstore. A few years ago I covered one entire room with bookshelves and painted it all fire engine red and indigo blue. It holds hundreds of books, and they look like jewels against these colors.

I read everything. At the library I go to New Books and read travel and essays and economics and birding and autobiography and especially history. My first eight books (not one of which was ever published) were set in ancient Rome, and I am always reading at least one book about the ancient Mediterranean. (I tend to read many books at once, and I keep little book depositories for every bed, chair and sofa.) At the bookstore I just wander, awestruck by how much there is and how much I want to read it all. Although I write fiction, for my own reading I'm more attracted to nonfiction. I do love mysteries—I like action. I like the good guys to win.

Writing comes easily to me. I enjoy mostly stages. I write three books a year, so I'm always daydreaming about a distant

FOR INCREASING STUDENT ACHIEVEMENT

GUIDED READING

Text Analysis

- This text is an example of **autobiography,** an account of one's own life. Cooney describes her love of reading, her method of writing, and her experiences with writing fiction.
- Cooney uses lists that include **specific examples** and **details.** For example, in the first paragraph, she identifies things she loves about books. In later paragraphs, she lists the types of topics about which she has witten.
- **Anecdotes** show readers important points in Cooney's life. She recalls writing a story about a missing child because she was influenced by a poster she saw in an airport. These incidents remained with Cooney and influenced her writing career.
- **Transitions** link ideas and help the reader follow the flow of events. Start sentences with "A few years ago," "Although," and "But."

SELECTION AMENDMENT
Description of change: excerpted
Rationale: to focus on the process of writing presented in this chapter

GUIDED READING

Strategy: Previewing

Before reading the excerpt, have volunteers read the first sentence of each paragraph aloud. Discuss what students expect to read about in this excerpt.

REACHING ALL STUDENTS

Struggling Learners

Ask students to list the various topics about which Cooney has written. Then have students list the types of books Cooney likes to read. Ask students to consider why Cooney prefers to read and write different types of books. For example, she prefers to write fiction, but she enjoys reading nonfiction.

Advanced Students

Encourage students to do research on Cooney to find out more about her life, her attitudes, and her writings. Have students share what they learn with the class.

READER RESPONSE

You may want to use the following questions to elicit students' personal responses to the selection.

1. Explain whether you have ever thought, as Cooney sometimes does, that you had to read, buy, shelve, and write books.
2. What is the highest number of drafts you have ever written of any paragraph, essay, report, or story? Explain whether you felt this was a high number.
3. How did you feel when Cooney described the fictional account of her music teacher's house fire?
4. Cooney felt that she had to write a story about a missing child. Have you ever felt that you "must" write a particular story? Explain.
5. How would you describe Cooney based on the information in this excerpt?

one, plotting the next, halfway through writing the current story, and probably re-writing one I thought was finished. Having an editor is like having your own personal life-long English teacher. No matter how well you write, she thinks you can do better, and mails the story back to be improved.

Many of my ideas came from one of my three children: Louisa became an EMT at sixteen and inspired *Flight #116 Is Down.* Harold wanted to live abroad, so we went to London, which led to *The Terrorist.* Once I forced Sayre to be in beauty contests so I could get background information for *Twenty Pageants Later.*

The Face on the Milk Carton was entirely fiction. I was shocked to see a homemade missing child poster in an airport and read that the child had been missing for 15 years! Nobody could recognize her from her toddler photography . . . unless, of course, she recognizes herself. I did not expect to write a sequel to this book. It was a book about worry and I wanted my readers to go on worrying. But for me and for my readers, it became very intense, and I found I had many more things to say about what happened to Janie. So now there are two more books, and I am planning a fourth!

My newest book, *Burning Up,* is based upon a fire in which my junior high music teacher lost his home. Nothing in my book happened in real life, and yet there's memory in it: my own seventh and eighth grade is there. It's the first time I've really used my own childhood for a story, although the time travel books *(Both Sides of Time, Out of Time, Prisoner of Time)* really take place in Old Greenwich, at its beach, Tod's Point.

ADDITIONAL RESOURCES

Composition Skills Practice. . . . . pages 1–6
Transparency Tools GO2, GO8
ESL Practice and Test Preparation . . . . . pages 1–7
Writers at Work . . . . 8•1–8•10
Assessment: Pretest . . . . pages 1–15
Assessment: Chapter Test. . . . . pages 30–34
Assessment Resources . . . . pages 1–10, 13–44

Thinking as a Writer

Analyzing a Writer's Process

- Caroline Cooney writes that she reads everything. How do Cooney's reading habits affect her writing?
- How do you think Cooney uses what she knows to write about things that never happened in real life?

Reading for Inspiration

Oral Expression

- Form a small group and, following Cooney's example, select books on a variety of subjects from the classroom or school library.
- Have each member of the group select at least one paragraph from a book to read aloud. Take turns reading your passages aloud. Then brainstorm about the kinds of stories the information might inspire.

Seeing a Story

Viewing

Cooney was inspired to write a novel after seeing a poster about a missing child.

- Look at the following photograph. What kind of story would you write about it? Jot down your ideas. Then write a brief summary of your story. What additional material would you need to complete your story?

Using *Thinking as a Writer*

You may choose to have students respond to the questions orally or in writing.

LITERARY CONNECTION

You might want to explore the writing process in the following works, which appear in literature textbooks at this grade level.

- "Camp Harmony" by Monica Stone
- *I Know Why the Caged Bird Sings* by Maya Angelou
- "The Million-Pound Bank Note" by Mark Twain
- *The Right Stuff* by Tom Wolfe

FOR DEVELOPING SKILLS

LESSON 1 *(pages C6–C28)*

OBJECTIVES

- **To understand the five basic stages in the writing process**
- **To practice such prewriting techniques as exploring interests, freewriting, brainstorming, and organizing ideas logically**

Create Interest

Ask students to recall something they have written that they liked. They might think of a report they wrote for a class, a letter or an E-mail they sent to a friend, a story they made up for fun, a poem that expressed their feelings, or any other written material. Ask students to talk about the process they used to write it. Point out similarities in how students work. Use student comments to begin to identify the various stages that a writer goes through in developing a piece of writing.

REACHING ALL STUDENTS

Struggling Learners

If students have difficulty grasping the stages of the writing process and how one may move back and forth among them, ask them to describe another process they use. Then compare the steps they go through with the stages involved in writing. For example, in making chili, checking the recipe and gathering the ingredients are like prewriting. Putting the basic ingredients together and starting to cook is like drafting. Adding more of various ingredients is like revising. Adjusting the seasoning is like editing. Serving is like publishing. At any point in the process, the cook might have to return to the cookbook, gather more ingredients, or add more of something, just as a writer may go back to a stage in the writing process at any point.

Developing Your Writing Process

"Once you've got some words looking back at you, you can take two or three—throw them away and look for others," wrote novelist Bernard Malamud. No matter what writing task is before you—a book report, an E-mail message to a distant relative, or a poem about a sunset—you will want to write well in order to communicate exactly what you mean. Writing well means writing something once and then writing it again. Writing is a process that is different for every writer. Even so, there is a general process that you can use to find your way to your own unique process of writing.

Your **writing process** is the series of stages that you go through when developing your ideas and discovering the best way to express them.

Writing is a creative process. As a writer you can shift from one stage to another or change the order of the stages you follow. For example, you may choose to revise your writing as you draft it, or edit your writing as you revise it. Each stage has its own distinct characteristics. The diagram on the following page illustrates and describes these stages and shows the relationship between them. As you review the diagram, think about the stages you go through when you create a piece of writing.

You will notice this icon throughout this book as you work through the stages of writing various paragraphs and compositions. It will remind you to save your work in a convenient place so you can return to it and continue to work on it, or simply use it later for inspiration. You may wish to use a manila folder or a pocket in your binder to store your work. If you usually work on a computer, you will probably want to create a folder on your hard drive, along with some kind of backup copy on a removable storage disk. Use whatever kind of storage system will be most convenient for you.

Guide Instruction

By Connecting Ideas

Ask students to compare the traits of reading and writing. Both use words, both transmit information and ideas, both are essential to success in school and in most jobs. However, reading is a way to gather information, while writing is a means of expressing it. Reading is, generally, more linear: the reader starts at the beginning and goes to the end. Writing is much more circular: the writer may loop back to earlier stages and passages very frequently.

Consolidate Skills

Through Guided Practice

Have students practice identifying their interests by writing a list of traits they had five years ago and a list of traits they hope to have ten years in the future. Students should compare the two lists and note similarities and differences. Point out that as they change, so will their writing style.

Process of Writing

The following diagram illustrates the stages writers go through as they create. Notice that the diagram loops back and forth. This looping shows how you often move back and forth among various stages of writing instead of going step-by-step from beginning to end. You can go back to any stage at any point until you are satisfied with the quality of your writing.

Prewriting includes the invention you do before writing your first draft. During prewriting you find and develop a subject, purpose, and audience; collect ideas and details; and make a basic plan for presenting them.

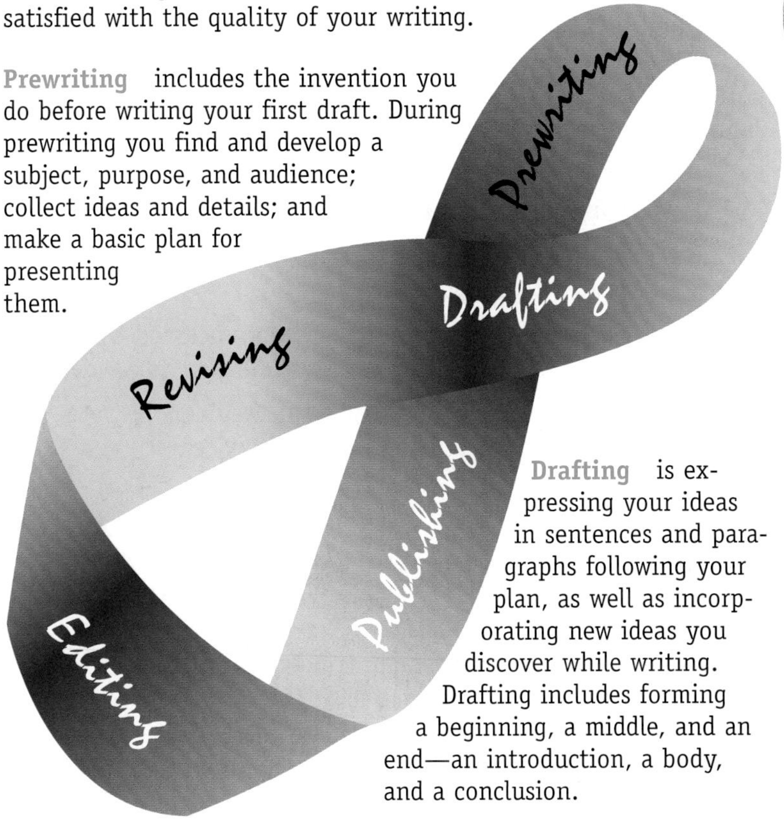

Drafting is expressing your ideas in sentences and paragraphs following your plan, as well as incorporating new ideas you discover while writing. Drafting includes forming a beginning, a middle, and an end—an introduction, a body, and a conclusion.

Revising means rethinking what you have written and reworking it to increase its clarity, smoothness, and power.

Editing involves checking and reworking sentences and sentence structure. It also includes looking for and correcting errors in grammar, usage, spelling, and mechanics and proofreading your final version before making it public.

Publishing is sharing your work with an audience.

YOUR IDEAS

For the Writing Process

Apply to Communication

Through Independent Writing

Have students write a one- or two-page essay on how they feel about writing. They should indicate both what they like and what they dislike about writing, and they should include specific examples when possible. Encourage them to keep this essay, and to refer back to it later in the chapter to see if their attitudes have changed.

Transfer to Everyday Life

By Evaluating Writing

As student complete various **Practice Your Skills** activities and discuss the text, encourage them to notice items they read that they think are well-written. Have them be as specific as pos-sible about what appeals to them in the writing, and to consider if they can use a similar technique in their own writing.

REACHING ALL STUDENTS

Advanced Students

Have students recall the time they started attending the school building they are currently in. What should they have known that no one told them? Then ask them to write a humorous "Guide to School" for incoming students. Invite students to read their advice aloud to the class.

GETTING STUDENTS INVOLVED

Cooperative Learning

Divide students into groups. In each group, students should discuss what they would say in a three-minute presentation about life in their school. They should explain how they would vary the speech for these audiences:

- students in the same grade at another school ten miles away
- students of the same age in a school in Japan
- students who are in the first grade
- people who attended school in the same community but are now in their seventies

After each group has described how they might vary their speeches, have students share the results with the class.

Your Writer's Portfolio

Saving your written work—short stories, poems, plays, or other completed works—is a good way to keep track of your development as a writer.

PORTFOLIO This icon is a reminder to place your work in your portfolio. The portfolio displays your progress as a writer and your ability to express yourself on a broad range of topics and in many different styles. When you add to your portfolio, be sure to include the date of your entry and a summary of the piece.

Guidelines for Including Work in Your Portfolio

- Date each piece of writing so that you can see where it fits into your progress.
- Write a note to yourself about why you included each piece—what you believe it shows about you as a writer.
- Unfinished works may be included if they demonstrate something meaningful about you as a writer.

Prewriting

Writing Process

Some event or problem usually triggers the act of writing: your teacher gives you a research assignment or your cousin sends you an urgent E-mail. Once you decide to write something, you set in motion a writing process. Where do you begin? The answer is almost always with prewriting. **Prewriting** is all of the planning and thinking that takes place from the moment you decide to write up to the time you begin the first draft.

A beginning writer is sometimes tempted to skip the prewriting stage, but that is a temptation that should be avoided. Like an athlete warming up before a match or a musician practicing for a concert, you must prepare before writing. Thinking, planning, and organizing are all essential before starting to draft.

Pull It All Together
By Summarizing
Review the five stages of the writing process. Write the stages on the board as students suggest them. The try to create a colorful name for each stage. For example, Prewriting could also be Getting Ready to Rumble.

Check Understanding
By Making Associations
Ask students to list five verbs, or phrases starting with verbs, for each stage of the writing process. Each verb should describe an action commonly taken in that stage. After students have completed their lists, ask students to read some of the verbs they used. Note whether any verbs are used to describe actions in more than one writing process stage.

Strategies for Finding a Subject

Finding a good subject—one that will truly interest you and your readers—is your first task. You may discover good ideas through your own experiences, through reading or watching movies, or through listening to the radio. The following strategies will help you discover ideas for writing.

Taking an Inventory of Your Interests Much of the writing you do will grow out of your own interests, experiences, and knowledge. One way to find a writing subject is to concentrate on topics that are most familiar to you. Focus on yourself and some of your interests and experiences. Try to identify some of your interests by doing the inventory exercise below.

Practice Your Skills

Taking an Interest Inventory

Use the following phrases to take a personal interest inventory. Write as many items as you can for each sentence.

1. My positive role models are . . .
2. My favorite subjects in school are . . .
3. My friends and I like to . . .
4. I could teach someone how to . . .
5. My least favorite things are . . .
6. My favorite places are . . .
7. I often dream of . . .
8. I would like to know more about . . .
9. I wish . . .
10. I enjoy reading (or watching) . . .
11. I often see . . .
12. I sometimes hear . . .

USING STUDENTS' STRENGTHS

Multiple Intelligences: Musical

Students who have tried to compose music can compare their process of writing with notes and with words. Ask them to share with the class the similarities and differences.

HOME WORK

Assign students to explore their own interests by listing five words that they think describe their personality. They should try to see themselves as they think others see them.

USING STUDENTS' STRENGTHS

Multiple Intelligences: Intrapersonal

Remind students that writing in a journal is a good way to promote self-understanding. Ask students to describe any excerpts from journals they have read. For example, they may have read excerpts from the journals of explorers, soldiers, scientists, musicians, or travelers. They may have also read excerpts from fiction written as journals, such as the Henry Reed series by Keith Robertson.

Freewriting Another strategy for discovering possible subjects for writing is freewriting. Just as the word implies, **freewriting** means writing freely about whatever comes to mind, without stopping and without worrying about making mis-takes. If you get stuck, look around you at an object or person and write about that. You can start writing without any idea in mind, or you can do **focused freewriting**, in which you have a specific idea or word in mind before beginning. Remember: write freely and let your thoughts spill onto your paper. The following example shows how potential subjects come to the surface through freewriting.

MODEL: Freewriting from Scratch

It's raining outside and I think my feet are getting colder and colder. Why didn't I wear my boots? I'm wondering what to write about. What if I can't think of anything? My mind feels blank. Sometimes I like my mind to go blank, like when I'm trying to relax before a game. Then I let my muscles go and stare up at the sky. I don't try to remember anything about what the coach said for a few minutes. Then I bring myself back to earth and go over a few plays. We have a great team. I like sports, even though I don't play too much. We've had a pretty good season, but then we've lost a fair number of games. I try not to think about losing or even winning for those few moments before a game. Just about how to relax and get my mind prepared.

As the student wrote, several thoughts—enjoying sports and preparing for a game—started to emerge. Freewriting can result in different ideas that can be related to one another or lead to distinct subjects or ideas.

By freewriting on the subject, another student found herself imagining a story about a turtle that teaches.

MODEL: Focused Freewriting

Turtles-what am I to write about turtles? I don't know a thing about turtles. I never had one as a pet, except in my Kindergarten class. I remember imagining that Otto, our turtle, would become our teacher. He wouldn't teach us how to read or write. Instead, he would teach us how to swim, eat, and live as a turtle. He would teach us about the different places he's lived. Maybe that's what I can write about. I can write a story about a turtle that takes over a classroom.

PRACTICE YOUR SKILLS

Freewriting

Freewrite for five minutes by writing down everything that comes to mind. Keep your pencil or pen on the paper and write as far as your thoughts lead you. When you have finished, review what you have written. Underline any ideas that interest you and see if they can be developed further into a story, poem, or composition.

Freewriting with a Focus

Freewrite again, but this time focus on any of the subjects or passages you underlined from the prior exercise. Try to develop the idea or passage as fully as you can. Afterward, decide which of the freewriting exercises worked better and compare the ideas that resulted from each.

Keeping a Journal An excellent way to explore your thoughts and discover subjects is through journal writing. A **journal** is a daily notebook in which you record your thoughts, feelings, and observations. You may keep more than one journal. You may want to keep a *personal journal*. Your teacher might ask you to keep a *writing journal* of responses to stories, poems, and other literature. Since both journals contain what is

HOME WORK

Have students try freewriting for two minutes in a quiet setting, such as a library, and for two minutes in a noisy, public place, such as a shopping mall or on a street corner. Ask them to compare the results to see how the setting affected what they wrote.

important to you, your entries can be a collection of ideas for writing.

Throughout this book you will find several journal-writing activities. These activities will help you improve the flow of your writing. The activities, however, are only suggestions. The following excerpts show the many different kinds of journal writing.

> April 14, 1804
>
> Rained the fore part of the day . . . I set out at 4 oClock P.M., in the presence of many of the neighboring inhabitents, and proceeded on under a jentle brease up the Missourie . . . a heavy rain this after-noon.
>
> —*William Clark*
> *from the journals of Captains Meriwether Lewis and William Clark*
>
> December 21st, 1915
>
> Good-bye France, you have given me some sleepless nights, and many a hard day's work. I very much regret leaving you for foreign parts, but some day I shall return to you and go over all the ground again; no doubt it will recall many sad recollections.
>
> —*E. E. Jones*
> *from the war diary of Edwin Jones*
>
> Nairobi, Kenya
> Thursday, September 10, 1998
>
> Woke up to sunbirds singing outside my window at 4:00 A.M. Four trips later and I'm still overwhelmed by the tremendous sense of belonging I feel in Africa—with the people, the animals, the landscape. Perhaps this truly is the cradle of humankind.
>
> —*Evelyn Gallardo*
> *children's writer and wildlife photographer*

It's important to choose a notebook you enjoy writing in and to date each entry. You are always free to write about whatever you want in your **journal.** You may write about whatever is on your mind, or you may help yourself to the activities offered in this book.

Practice Your Skills

Writing in Your Journal

Think of a favorite book or story. Imagine yourself within the action of the story and think of how the plot would be different if you were a character. Would the story come to the same conclusions or resolutions? How would your presence affect the other, already existing characters? In your journal, list the plot changes that result from inserting yourself, or other people, as characters within the story.

Keeping a Learning Log A Learning Log is a section of your **journal** that can be used to write ideas and information on subjects that interest you. The Learning Log can help you organize your thoughts, discover new topics of interest, or inspire you to look at a subject differently. Your entry may look like this.

Model: Learning Log Entry

A new photography exhibit opened at the museum. I saw an exhibit on antique furniture last week, and one on sculpture the week before. I wonder what it would be like to work at a museum. Seems like you have to keep your mind open to different kinds of artworks. What kind of art would I need to study? What experience would I need to work in a museum? Maybe the museum curator could give me some advice, or I can search the Internet for some schools that offer classes in art history and museum studies.

HOME WORK

Have students remove a character from their favorite book or story, and explain how the absence of that character would change the plot. They should note whether other characters could pick up the role performed by the character.

PRACTICE YOUR SKILLS

Learning More About a Subject

Create a new section in your journal labeled Learning Log. Use this section to write about topics that interest you and could help you in developing a story idea. Use stories from newspapers, magazines, television, movies, radio, or conversations to help generate topics. Write a Learning Log entry identifying the subject, what you already know about it, what you would like to find out about it, and where you could find additional information.

Creating a Personalized Editing Checklist A **Personalized Editing Checklist** is a section of your **journal** where you can catalog errors that you frequently make in your writing, such as misspellings, usage mistakes, and mechanical errors. When you edit your writing, you should refer to this checklist.

PRACTICE YOUR SKILLS

Keeping Track of Errors

Create another section of your journal called Personalized Editing Checklist. Add to it as you work on the writing assignments in this book.

COMPUTER TIP

If you keep your **journal** entries on your computer, you can organize your documents in a way that works best for you. For instance, you can create a single document, a folder containing three separate documents (one for personal entries, one for your Learning Log, and one for your Personalized Editing Checklist), or folders within a main folder. Use the File menu to create folders that will help you organize your **journal.**

HOME WORK

Assign students to add five topics to their Learning Log. As they do, they should note where they found the idea.

HOME WORK

Have students write three items in their Personalized Editing Checklist. They should list items that have been difficult for them in the past.

FYI

How to Use with Windows™ To create a new folder, open the File menu and select Save As. One of the options in the window that appears is to create a new folder. Reorganizing existing folders—by combining existing folders, dividing one folder into two, or moving files from one folder to another—can be done using the program Windows Explorer™, which can be opened by clicking on Start, and looking at the listing under Programs.

How to Use with Macintosh™ From the File menu, choose New Folder. You can also create a new folder by pressing the Command key and the N key at the same time.

Photo Essay

Photographs convey a message instantly. Newspapers, magazines, and television news programs all use photos to interest people in their stories. Photographs seem to represent the truth, but in reality photographs are quite subjective. The photographer imposes a point of view as soon as he or she chooses what will be in the frame of the picture and what will be left out. The way in which a photo is printed also affects how we see it—darker colors make a photograph seem somber, while brighter colors may appear cheerful. A photographer may choose to heighten the contrast between colors in order to emphasize different aspects of a photo. The size of a photograph and its placement affect how we see it as well—a large photo will appear more important than a small one, but a small picture surrounded by a great deal of empty space may seem especially important.

Media Activity

When pictures and text appear together to tell a story, the result is called a photo essay.

- Working in groups of three, brainstorm a list of topics that would make good photo essays.
- Using magazines and newspapers, choose several photos and arrange them so that they tell a story.
- If you can, use a photocopy machine to crop some of the images and make others larger.
- Work together to create captions that make the story even clearer.

How do the changes you made affect the story your pictures tell? Display and discuss your completed photo essays.

IN THE MEDIA

Using *In the Media*

Objective

- **To analyze how photo essays convey information**

Group Project

- Divide students into small groups, and have each group create a photo essay about their class. They might include photos of individual students, of groups of students, of activities in which many students participate, or of aspects of the school or community that influence the students. Each photo essay should include between six and twelve photos. Have each group present its essay to the class, and discuss how they differ.

FYI

Websites to Visit Photo essays from TimeLife on influential African Americans, activists for women's rights, the Oscars, and other topics are available at http://www.pathfinder.com/photo/essay/essays.htm. The site http://www.dbstamps.com/html/gallery.html includes photo essays on several topics, including winter, Cape Cod, and tall ships. A Library of Congress site, http://memory.loc.gov/ammem/ammemhome.html, includes historical photo essays on topics ranging from baseball cards to pioneer settlements on the Great Plains.

REACHING ALL STUDENTS

English Language Learners

Have students write about another class they are taking. Suggest that they write about something they have just learned in the class. Encourage them to use vocabulary from that subject so that they can better learn those terms.

IDENTIFYING COMMON STUMBLING BLOCKS

Problem

- Not recognizing subjects that are not individuals

Solution

- Review with students the variety of forms a subject can take. List on the board items that can be subjects: people, animals, forces of nature, machines, items of fantasy, personal qualities, etc. Then have students write short sentences with non-human subjects. For example, Honesty is the best policy, and, Green ideas sleep furiously. Have students read the sentences and discuss what the subject is.

Choosing and Limiting a Subject

Making an inventory of your interests, freewriting, exploring the Internet, and reading literature are all activities that can be helpful in generating new writing ideas. You can review everything you have written to develop ideas or add new details to previous subjects. You can use other media such as television, film, radio, newspapers, magazines, and other publications to find a new subject. The following guidelines will help you choose a subject.

Guidelines for Choosing a Subject

- Choose a subject that genuinely interests you.
- Choose a subject that will interest your readers.
- Choose a subject that you know something about or can research with reasonable effort.

Limiting a Subject The subject you choose may be very broad. Subjects such as "sports" or "school" are too general to cover completely in a single composition. Focusing on a detail or smaller aspect of the subject can help you narrow the scope of your search and make your writing more concise. To limit your subject, use the strategies listed below.

Strategies for Limiting a Subject

- Focus on one person or one example that represents the subject.
- Limit your subject to a specific time or place.
- Focus on a particular event or person.
- Choose one effect or one purpose of your subject.

Consider the subject of sports. The following model shows how this broad subject can be limited.

Model: Limiting a Subject

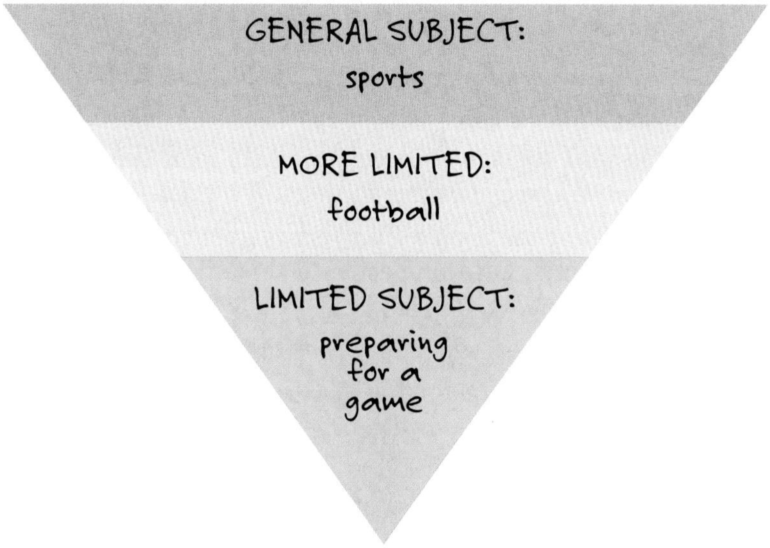

GENERAL SUBJECT:
sports

MORE LIMITED:
football

LIMITED SUBJECT:
preparing for a game

Practice Your Skills

Limiting a Subject

Using the preceding strategies, limit each of the following broad subjects into smaller, more focused subjects.

Example:

General	pets
Limited Subjects	my dog Baxter, how to clean a fish tank, caring for hamsters

1. television
2. cars
3. school
4. families
5. marine life
6. computers
7. music
8. chores
9. books
10. Internet

HOME WORK

Ask students to list three more subjects that are too broad, and identify three smaller, more focused subjects under each one.

Practice Your Skills Sample Answers

1. the effect on children's behavior, the ethics of advertising, the best televisions to purchase
2. why used cars are a better value than new cars, how to change the oil, who invented the car
3. the hectic start to each day, the schedule for eating lunch, the feelings of students at the end of the day
4. why aunts and uncles are important, how cousins get along, who cares for the grandparents
5. the diet of a shark, the migratory habits of whales, the development of coral reefs
6. the history of the Internet, the development of home computers, the effects of computers on communication
7. why people still listen to the Beatles, how to listen to Beethoven, who listens to blues music today
8. selecting household jobs for seven-year-olds, debating whether to pay children for chores, dividing jobs among several children
9. the best books for children, the industry of publishing, the future of the book
10. how the Internet was developed, using the Internet for research, fun on the Internet

HOME WORK

Have students describe situations in which they would write to explain or inform, to describe, to entertain, to create, to persuade, and to express thoughts and feelings.

PRACTICE YOUR SKILLS Sample Answers

1. to persuade
2. to entertain
3. to create
4. to explain or inform
5. to explain or inform

PRACTICE YOUR SKILLS

Writing for Different Occasions, Audiences, and Purposes

Decide which writing purpose or combination of purposes you would use for each of the following situations.

1. You visit the zoo and decide to help raise funds to improve the conditions in the bird house.

2. Your aunt tells you a funny story about when she was a child, and you decide to share it with others.

3. You imagine a story about a robot that wants to become a great chef.

4. You study the history of the Underground Railroad and decide to share with other students what you have learned.

5. You take a course on computers and want to show your parents how to create a Website.

Developing Your Voice

In writing it is helpful to discover and develop your voice and the ability to adapt your voice to different situations. **Voice** in writing is the particular sound and rhythm of the language the writer uses. Voice is an important part of your writing that has to do with word choice. There are times, however—for example, if you were to write a dialogue—when it would be helpful to imitate someone else's voice.

Your voice can and should vary, depending on the occasion, audience, and purpose. In speaking you probably use a different voice when asking your teacher to clarify an assignment than when you are joking with a friend. Similarly, your voices should vary when writing. In your **journal** you might use a different voice when you are in a good mood than when you are recording frustration.

Practice Your Skills

Recognizing a Writer's Voice

1. Reread aloud the first paragraph in Caroline Cooney's piece. Focus on the tone of your voice as you read. Afterward, choose from the list below the word that best describes the feeling conveyed by Cooney. Write a sentence explaining your choice.

a. cheerful **c.** emotional

b. enthusiastic **d.** mechanical

2. Reread the third paragraph in Cooney's article and compare the feeling conveyed with the feeling in the final paragraph of the piece. Choose which words would apply to both passages.

a. reflective **c.** solemn

b. sad **d.** angry

Developing Different Voices

Write freely from three to five minutes on each of the following.

- Your best friend is moving to live elsewhere. You want to write a farewell letter expressing your thoughts and feelings about your friendship.
- You disagree with a grade you received on a project. You want to ask why you received the grade and to persuade your teacher to reconsider the mark. How would you express yourself in writing?
- You have been accepted to study at the school of your choice. What do you write in an acceptance letter?
- You are preparing a pamphlet for children explaining the dangers of playing with matches. What would you write?

HOME WORK

Have students bring in a sample of writing in which the author has a clear voice. Students should be prepared to read the excerpt and describe the voice.

Practice Your Skills Sample Answers

1. b. Cooney enthusiastically shares her passion for books, even telling how she painted her book room "fire engine red and indigo blue."

2. a. reflective

REACHING ALL STUDENTS

Struggling Learners

Have students choose one subject in nature that they can observe firsthand, such as a bird that comes to a feeder, a plant in the park, a tree, or a rock. Have students brainstorm a list of everything they see when they look at their subject. Then have them use their notes to write up their observations to share with their classmates.

Reading your work aloud will help you hear whether your writing voice sounds the way you want it to sound. The work becomes a slightly different piece, and you will detect features that you missed in a silent reading.

Read your work aloud to evaluate your written **voice.**

Strategies for Developing Your Subject

After you have chosen and limited your subject—and you have considered your occasion, audience, and purpose—you should collect specific details that develop your writing. **Main ideas** are the points you want to get across. **Supporting details** are the facts, examples, incidents, reasons, or other specific points that back up your ideas. Following are some pre-writing strategies for improving your powers of observation.

Observing Observation is an important tool for collecting information and for developing your own view and interpretation of a subject. **Observing** involves using your senses to describe the sights, sounds, smells, tastes, and feelings associated with your subject. Through practice a writer tries to be aware of details that present the subject in a particular way. The following techniques will help you observe.

Techniques for Observing

- Be aware of why you are observing. Keep your purpose in mind as you decide what and how to observe.
- Use all your senses. Look, listen, smell, touch, and taste.
- Use your mind. Think about what your observations mean.

- Observe from different viewpoints. Look at your subject from all angles: near and far, above and below, and inside and out.
- Sketch your subject. Make a drawing of what you observe. Take notes to keep a record of your observations.

It is important to know how to collect the information you get from observing in a way that is easy to organize. Taking notes using note cards or computer files is a way of collecting information so that it can easily be arranged and rearranged when drafting. The following note card shows how a student took notes on the piece by Caroline Cooney.

SUMMARIES OF MAIN IDEA:

YOUR NOTES RECORD THE WRITER'S MAIN MESSAGE AND FACTS.

Caroline Cooney

Cooney writes about her love of books. She also writes about being a writer and how she gets her ideas for writing.

PRACTICE YOUR SKILLS

Observing

Look carefully at the photograph. Use the Techniques for Observing to place yourself in the scene. Using all of your senses, record ten or more details that you could use to describe the scene.

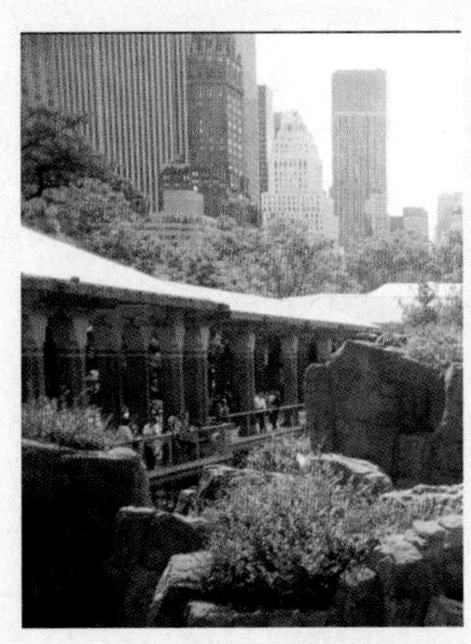

HOME WORK

Assign students to select a photograph from a book or magazine and repeat the **Practice Your Skills** activity.

YOUR IDEAS

For Developing the Subject

REACHING ALL STUDENTS

Advanced Learners

Point out to students that conversations sometimes sound like brainstorming sessions. Have students work with a partner, and tape record or videotape a five-minute conversation. Then have them review the conversation, taking notes on how the topic of the conversation shifted and what triggered the change.

IDENTIFYING COMMON STUMBLING BLOCKS

Problem

- Not feeling free to roam from topic to topic while brainstorming

Solution

- Have students play the game "Makes Me Think." Begin by having each student write down two topics on separate pieces of paper. They should exchange one piece of paper with one neighbor, and the other with another neighbor. Then they must try to connect the two topics on their new sheets of paper. For example, if they received tigers and toast as their topics, they might think: Tigers make me think of India, which makes me think of spicy food, which makes me think of spices, which makes me think of cinnamon, which makes me think of toast.
- After students have completed one round of "Makes Me Think," have volunteers share how they made the connections.

Brainstorming for Details **Brainstorming** is the process of writing everything that comes to mind when thinking about a particular subject. Once you have chosen and limited a subject, brainstorming can help you discover details when you work with a group or partner. Sometimes, one idea will lead to another, or result in a new subject or perspective.

Guidelines for Brainstorming

- Set a time limit, such as 15 minutes.
- Write the subject on a piece of paper and assign one group member to record ideas.
- Brainstorm for details—facts, examples, reasons, connections, and associations.
- Build on the ideas of other group members. Add or modify the ideas until they can be used as supporting details.
- Keep your mind open and avoid criticizing others.

When you have finished brainstorming, you should get a copy of all the supporting details from the group recorder. Select details that support your subject or use the details to generate new ideas.

Look at the following sample brainstorming list on how a sports player prepares for a big game.

Model: Brainstorming

Preparing for a Game

— Practice long and hard ahead of time

— Remember to bring a bottle of water!

— Visualize the big play

— End-around; fake pass; defense-heavy formation; study other special plays

— Team meetings

Practice Your Skills

Brainstorming for Ideas

With a group, brainstorm for ideas on the subject of preserving the tropical rain forest. Follow the preceding Guidelines for Brainstorming.

Clustering Another strategy for developing your subject is clustering. **Clustering** is a visual form of brainstorming in which you not only jot down details as you think of them, but also make connections among those details. Often, writers use clustering to help organize their thoughts

A cluster can look like a wheel. At the hub, or center, is your subject. Each idea that supports or explains your subject is connected to the hub by a line, like a spoke in a wheel. Sometimes supporting ideas become hubs of their own, with new spokes coming out of them.

Model: Clustering

HOME WORK

Have students make a list of ten general ideas that they will brainstorm later. Encourage students to use a range of areas from their lives; from personal interests to current events.

HOME WORK

Have students create a pictorial cluster based on one of their brainstorming ideas. They can either cut-out pictures from a magazine or create their own drawings.

REACHING ALL STUDENTS

Advanced Learners

Encourage students to make mind maps. These are freer than clusters. Have them use just key words, or images that represent those key words. They should start from the center of the page and work outward. As in cluster, they can make sub-areas as they think of related groupings. Tell them that the things that stand out on the page will probably be the things that stand out in the composition. Encourage them to use colors, icons, arrows, and other visual tools to show relationships. There are no hard and fast rules except students should include every idea that occurs to them and place it where it most logically seems to fit. For more information on a mind map, visit http://www.peterussel.com/mindmap1.html.

PRACTICE YOUR SKILLS

Clustering

Use your brainstorming notes on preserving the tropical rain forest to create a cluster. Or create a cluster using your own topic or the ones provided below.

1. What makes a good movie?
2. What makes my neighborhood unique?
3. What is wrong with television advertising?
4. What makes someone a hero?

Inquiring Another strategy for exploring a subject is to ask yourself questions concerning that subject. *Who, what, where, when, why,* and *how* questions can provide answers and help generate ideas that are helpful in developing the details for a composition. Suppose, for example, that you are asked to write a report on studying insects. You might start with the following questions.

MODEL: Inquiring

Studying Insects

Who	are some of the experts in the field of studying insects?
What	specific details do people look for when they study different insects, and what tools are used?
Where	are the best places to look for insects?
Why	is gaining knowledge about insects helpful to people?
When	did people first begin to study insects?
How	are insects captured, named, and observed?

Practice Your Skills

Inquiring

Use the strategy of inquiring to develop supporting details on two of the following topics.

1. a memorable vacation
2. a concert or a performance
3. an exciting, adventurous experience
4. a smart decision
5. an inspiring person
6. a favorite hobby

Strategies for Organizing Details

Prewriting strategies such as freewriting, brainstorming, inquiring, observing, and clustering help you search for subjects and details for your writing. Once you have collected details, you need to organize them in logical order. The following strategies will help you do that.

Focusing Your Subject To best organize your details and ideas, first determine the focus, or main points, of your writing. To do this, ask yourself, "What exactly do I want to say about my subject?" To help you answer this question, use the following guidelines.

Guidelines for Deciding on a Focus

- Look over your details. Can you draw meaningful ideas from some or all of the details? If so, the ideas could be the focus of your writing.
- Choose a main idea that intrigues you.
- Choose a main idea that suits your purpose and audience.

HOME WORK

Have students develop supporting details on two topics of their own choice.

USING STUDENTS' STRENGTHS

Multiple Intelligences: Spatial

To help student classify, order, and organize details, have them write down their notes on notecards. Then they can sort the cards by putting them into related piles and experiment with various orders.

Practice Your Skills Sample Answers

2. a concert, a performance
   Who? three friends and me
   What? a concert by the Frightening Four, a group that does parodies of popular songs
   Where? at the school auditorium
   When? the Friday before Halloween
   Why? to support the local food pantry and to have fun
   How? we met at my house and walked to the school together
4. a smart decision
   Who? George Washington
   What? decided not to run for a third term as president
   Where? at Mount Vernon, Virginia
   When? around 1800
   Why? he was tired of serving as president
   How? he analyzed his personal attitudes

Using *Writing Is Thinking*

Objective

- **To practice grouping ideas into meaningful categories**

A DIFFERENT APPROACH

Kinesthetic Have students stand in a group in the front of the room. Discuss different ways to classify students. For example, students wearing orange should move to one side of the room, those not wearing orange should move to the other. Follow up with other classifications, and have the students rearrange themselves based on them. Choose attributes and attitudes that will not embarrass students. For example, divide students according to whether they prefer to watch baseball, basketball, or hockey; whether they think it likely, possible, or unlikely that people will travel to Mars in their lifetimes; and whether they are left-handed or right-handed.

Select some classifications in which the response groups can be further divided. For example, students who drank milk this morning. Divide the Yes group into those who drank milk by itself and those who drank it with something else, such as cereal. Discuss what value the classification might have. For example, an advertising company working for the milk industry might want to know about milk consumption among school students.

Writing Is Thinking

Classifying

The process of grouping ideas into categories is called **classifying.** Classifying allows you to see connections among details or information that at first may seem unrelated. Suppose, for example, you are writing about the opportunities your school offers to students. You have brainstormed the following list of details.

- basketball teams for boys and girls
- variety of classes students can take
- intramural program in sports
- tutoring available in all subjects

The first step in classifying is to ask whether any of the details are alike. When you look closely at the list of your school's opportunities, you can see that two of the details are alike in that they relate to sports. You can also see that the remaining two details are alike in that they relate to studying and learning. By looking for similarities, you have discovered two large groupings into which these details can be classified.

SPORTS LEARNING OPPORTUNITIES	STUDYING AND OPPORTUNITIES
• basketball teams for boys and girls	• variety of classes students can take
• intramural program in sports	• tutoring available in all subjects

THINKING PRACTICE

Classify the following sports into at least two separate groups.

hockey baseball swimming tennis skiing football

Classifying Your Details Many of the supporting details you develop can be organized into different groups or categories. For example, if you are writing about a bakery, your details may fall into the following groups: smells, sights, and tastes. If you are discussing the similarities and differences between elementary and middle school, you might list similarities in one group and differences in another.

Ordering Your Details Once you have classified your details, you need to place them in an order that will not only support your subject, but also help you achieve your purpose and make sense to your readers.

WAYS TO ORDER DETAILS

Types of Order	Definition	Examples
Chronological	The order in which events occur	story, explanation, history, biography, drama
Spatial	Location or physical arrangement	description (top to bottom, near to far, left to right, etc.)
Order of Importance	Degree of importance, size, or interest	persuasive writing, description, explanation
Logical	Logical progression, one detail leads to another	classifications, definitions, comparison and contrast

Choose the type of order most appropriate to your writing purpose. For example, if you were writing to persuade, you might choose to use order of importance, whereas if you were to write about a past vacation or trip, you might choose to use chronological or spatial order.

Tactile Have each student bring to class three objects that are each small enough to hold in one hand, such as an eraser, a paper clip, and a wooden spoon. Then divide students into groups. Have all the students in a group place their objects on a table and create four different ways to classify the items. They might group items by size, color, shape, function, texture, or other criteria. Have one student from each group explain one of the sets of categories they created.

THINKING PRACTICE Evaluation Guidelines
Check to make sure that students' categories are valid and result from adequate thinking. They should be able to back up their groupings.

Thinking Skills	
Classifying	**Analyzing**
Comparing	**Hypothesizing**
Generalizing	**Synthesizing**
Inferring	**Summarizing**
Imagining	**Setting Goals**
Observing	**Evaluating Audience**
Predicting	

DEVELOPING WORKPLACE COMPETENCIES

Thinking Skills: Reasoning

Tell students that many jobs require workers to use their reasoning skills to classify, organize, and order information. Lawyers and accountants often must decide which of several competing regulations or principles applies in a situation. Investment counselors and human resource specialists often try to help individuals order their various, and often conflicting, goals for their investments or their careers. Advertisers and consultants try to organize information so that people, either consumers or clients, can make efficient decisions.

Ask students to imagine that they are in one of the careers mentioned in the previous paragraph. Have them write an imaginary situation in which they would reason about what to do.

HOME WORK

Assign students to find three stories in books, magazines, or newspapers, and to decide what type of organization is used in each.

PRACTICE YOUR SKILLS Sample Answers

1. order of importance
2. chronological or spatial
3. chronological
4. chronological
5. logical

The following is a list of details compiled by a student who is writing about training for a marathon race.

MODEL: Ordering Details

Before running
- get plenty of rest
- maintain a healthful diet
- stretch and exercise your muscles
- study the route of the race
- wear suitable clothes, good sneakers

Running
- train for distance
- train for time
- run on a track, at a park, or to the side of the road
- drink plenty of fluids
- run with a friend, someone else to motivate you

PRACTICE YOUR SKILLS

Organizing Details

Explain which method of organization you would use to organize the details of the subjects listed below. Write *chronological, spatial, order of importance,* or *logical* after each of them.

1. reasons people should vote
2. history of space exploration
3. story of the first time you rode a bicycle
4. description of a humorous experience
5. similarities and differences between elementary and middle school

LESSON 2 *(pages C29–C35)*

OBJECTIVES

- **To write a first draft using prewriting notes**
- **To use a revision checklist to revise the first draft**

Create Interest

Ask students to identify an activity that they enjoy, and what specific part of it is the core of what it means to do the activity. For example, in playing the piano, one might collect music, practice scales, and give recitals, but the most important part of the activity is sitting at the piano and playing music for one's own enjoyment. Tell students they are going to focus on the two core steps in writing: drafting and revising. Without drafting, and, to a lesser extent, without revising, one cannot claim to be writing.

Drafting

Writing Process

Drafting is the stage in writing where all your ideas from prewriting are put into complete sentences, forming a beginning, a middle, and an end—or an introduction, a body, and conclusion. Your first draft is just a rough sketch that allows you to see how your details and ideas fit on paper. You will most likely have to write several complete drafts. The following strategies will help you prepare a first draft.

Strategies for Drafting

- Write an introduction that will capture the reader's interest and express your main idea.
- After you write your introduction, use your organized prewriting notes as a guide. Depart from those notes, however, when a good idea occurs to you.
- Write fairly quickly without worrying about spelling or phrasing. You will have the opportunity to go back and fix your writing when you revise.
- Stop frequently and read aloud what you have written. This practice will help you move logically from one thought to the next.
- Return to the prewriting stage whenever you find that you need to clarify your thinking. You can always stop and freewrite, brainstorm, or cluster to collect more ideas.
- Write a conclusion that drives home the main point of the composition.

The following draft was written from the previous brainstorming, clustering, and organizing activities on the subject of preparing for a football game. Notice that the writer did not take the time to correct mistakes. The errors will be corrected later.

INTEGRATING TECHNOLOGY

Computer

Help students understand both the strengths and weaknesses of spell-checkers. They can help catch obvious spelling errors. However, they are not able to point out words that are used in the wrong context. Write the following sentence on the board to demonstrate the point. *Mark finished his hole composition in one day.*

Ask students what the spell-checker would have to say about the sentence. (It would not notice the incorrect use of *hole* instead of *whole*.) Encourage students to experiment with the other editing tools in their software to learn their strengths and weaknesses.

Guide Instruction

By Modeling Strategies

Dim the lights of the room. Have students close their eyes and look into the future. Suggest that they try to focus on themselves and catch a glimpse of what they might be doing forty years from now. After about two minutes, have them take out pencil and paper and write freely for five minutes. Remind students that since this is the drafting stage, their piece of writing should be more constructed than in the pre-writing stage. Encourage students to share what they have written, and point out well-written or creative ideas in each student's vision. Ask students to note ideas that they would expand, shorten, or otherwise revise if they had more time.

Consolidate Skills

Through Guided Practice

Through the **Practice Your Skills** activities, students will develop their skills of drafting and revising. To extend these activities, have students write additional short compositions on topics of their choice. Have them revise the

YOUR IDEAS

For Monitoring Students' Growth

MODEL: First Draft

I am often asked how us players prepare for a big game. One thing is having team meetings, these help build team spirit and make you want to do good for all the other players. The fans are also counting on you. It also helps to concentrate only on the game and the game plan. If you let your mind wander, you can forget or make a mistake on a important play. Team meetings also help you get all the plays straight. Even more important, though, is the long, hard practice you put in all season long. nothing can take the place of practice. Practice makes perfect. Maybe the most important thing is visualizing, or picturing, victory or a big play. That's how we prepare for a big game.

PRACTICE YOUR SKILLS

Drafting from Notes

Use the prewriting notes below to write the first draft of a paragraph. The first and last sentences are given.

FIRST SENTENCE: One cold night my family went to the university observatory to look through the telescope.

NOTES:
- — temperature was 17 degrees
- — arrived and saw line of people waiting outside
- — winding stairway to viewing area jammed with people waiting their turn; no heat
- — so cold I wanted to forget the whole thing
- — telescope fixed on Saturn; people ahead of me gasped when they saw it
- — my turn finally came; could understand their excitement—Saturn a beautiful sight

compositions to increase their familiarity with the Checklist for Revising.

Apply to Communication

Through Independent Writing
Comedians, reviewers, and others often make lists, such as the ten best movies of the year, or ten reasons to wear a bow tie. Have students find a list about a topic that interests them. Then have them use the list to draft and revise a composition.

Transfer to Everyday Life

By Evaluating Writing
Ask students to bring to class examples of paragraphs that they found confusing or boring. They might look in news stories, textbooks, novels, or anything else that they read. Have students read these paragraphs aloud in class, and discuss how they could be improved. Then have students revise the paragraphs to make them clearer and more interesting.

— rings of Saturn looked near enough to touch

LAST SENTENCE: The wonder and beauty of Saturn on that cold night warmed me inside and out.

Drafting a Title When you have written a complete draft of your composition, take some time to come up with a title for it. Whichever title you create, you should try to choose one that captures your reader's interest and suggests the main idea of your composition.

PRACTICE YOUR SKILLS

Drafting a Title

Review the draft on preparing for a football game and write three possible titles for it. You may also want to brainstorm for ideas with your classmates.

COMPUTER TIP

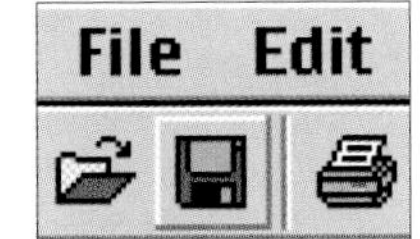

One of the more important steps in using a word-processing program is to save your work—often. Errors and power outages happen easily, so get in the habit of using the Save command whenever you pause in your writing. You can also let your computer do the remembering for you: program it to save your work every fifteen minutes.

Revising

Writing Process

When asked if he ever rewrote his stories, writer Frank O'Connor replied, "Endlessly, endlessly, endlessly." In some ways, writing is never completely finished. It can always be improved just a little bit more. When you revise, you rework your draft as often as needed until it is the very best you can make it.

HOME WORK

Ask students to create one title that can be used for three different occasions, such as the title of a composition, of a picture, and of a toy. Or, the title of a drawing, the theme of a dance, and a short story. Allow them to bring examples in writing (their own or from another source), in pictures, or as props.

FYI

How to Use with Windows™ To save a file, choose the File menu, and select Save or Save As. The first time you save a file, and anytime you select Save As, a dialog box will ask you to name the file and to identify which folder you want to save it in. You can also save a file by pressing the Control key and the S key at the same time.

How to Use with Macintosh™ To save a file, choose the File menu and select Save. Or press the Command key and the S key at the same time. The first time you save a file, a dialog box will ask you to name the file and to identify which folder you want to save it in.

Pull It All Together

By Sharing

Ask students whether their attitudes toward revising have changed since they began studying the drafting and revising stages. Highlight comments from students who note that they now place more emphasis on revising than they did before. Also note students who have a broader idea of what revising means.

Check Understanding

By Reviewing

Ask students to review the stages of the writing process and what is involved in each. Focus on the drafting and revising stages. Then ask what might trigger moving from the drafting or revising stage back to the prewriting stage. Point out that some ideas become hard to develop and must be dropped, and others must be found to replace them.

IDENTIFYING COMMON STUMBLING BLOCKS

Problem

- Feeling uncomfortable with a messy first draft

Solution

- With the writer's permission, show to the class examples of a messy first draft prepared by one of the students in the class. Point out that each erasure, cross-out, and insert indicates that the student has explored other writing choices for better expressing their ideas. If you know anyone who writes for a living, ask him or her to save samples of first drafts showing the changes made.

FYI

How to Use with Windows™ Pressing the Control key and the Z key at the same time will undo the last typing commands.

How to Use with Macintosh™ Pressing the Control key and the Z key at the same time will undo the last typing command.

Strategies for Revising

Before you revise your work, set it aside for a while. When you come back to it, you will be able to see both its strengths and its weaknesses with a fresh eye. You can then use the following strategies to improve your work.

Adding Details and Information If your composition seems weak and empty, ask yourself whether you need to **elaborate** to explain your subject clearly. Brainstorm or cluster to come up with additional details, and add whatever seems to be missing.

Deleting Unnecessary Words or Ideas Deleting means removing. If you find that you have included details that stray from your subject, cross them out. Also delete repetition that does not serve a useful purpose.

Substituting Words and Sentences Read your writing aloud. Are there places where you have used a weak, vague word instead of a strong one? Are there any places where your sentences sound monotonous? Substitute more lively words and more varied sentences.

Rearranging Look carefully at the organization of your words, sentences, and ideas. Are any out of place? Rearrange any part of your draft that is out of order.

COMPUTER TIP

You can use the Undo command to make a change in your draft from the earlier version. The Undo command reverses whatever action you have most recently taken.

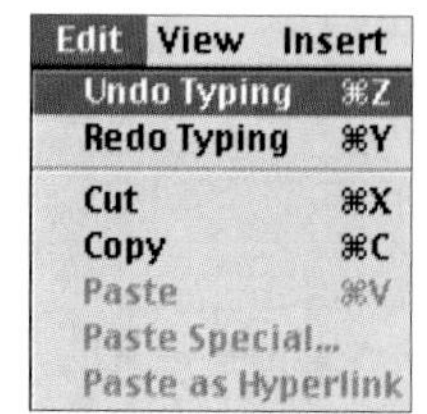

Revising challenges you as a writer to look at the style and content of your work. Using a checklist will help you evaluate your writing to see whether your latest draft includes the features of a good composition. The checklist below will help you keep track of the revisions you have made and identify some changes you will need to make. Throughout this book you will find several evaluation checklists to guide you during the revising stage.

Evaluation Checklist for Revising

- ✓ Did you clearly state your main idea?
- ✓ Does your composition have a strong introduction, body, and conclusion?
- ✓ Did you elaborate, or support your main idea with enough details?
- ✓ Do your details demonstrate what you want to say?
- ✓ Did you present your ideas in logical order?
- ✓ Do any of your sentences stray from the main idea?
- ✓ Are your ideas clearly explained?
- ✓ Are your words specific?
- ✓ Are any words or ideas repeated unnecessarily?
- ✓ Are your sentences varied and smoothly connected?
- ✓ Is the purpose of your composition clear?
- ✓ Is your writing suited to your audience?
- ✓ Is your title interesting and does it capture the main idea?

Practice Your Skills

Studying a Revision

Study the following revision of the paragraph on preparing for a football game. (Errors in spelling, capitalization, and usage will be corrected in the editing and publishing stage.) Be prepared to explain which revision strategy the writer used to make each change.

INTEGRATING TECHNOLOGY

Internet

Students can view revisions that Thomas Jefferson made to the rough draft of the Declaration of Independence at the Library of Congress website that includes Jefferson's papers. Go to http://memory.loc.gov/ammemhome.html and select the Search option. Search for "Declaration of Independence Rough Draft."

I am often asked how us *football* players prepare for a big game. One ~~thing~~ *important part of preparing* is having team meetings, these help build team spirit and make you want to do ~~good~~ *your best* for all the ~~other players~~ *your teammates*. ~~The fans are also counting on you.~~ *Team meetings also help you get your plays straight.* It also helps to concentrate only on the game and the game plan If you let your mind wander, you can ~~forget or~~ make a mistake on a important play. Team meetings also help you get all the plays straight. Even more important. though, ~~is~~ *are* the long *hours of* hard practice you put in all season ~~long~~. Nothing can take the place of practice *for making sure that you know what to do on each play.* ~~Practice makes perfect~~. Maybe the most important thing is visualizing, or picturing, victory or a big play. *You have to picture yourself making an interception or tackling a runner or else you won't suceed.* That's how we prepare for a big game.

COMPUTER TIP

Suppose you named your main character "Jim" in the first draft of a short story and then, while revising, decide you want to name him "Bob" instead. You can do this with ease by using the global search-and-replace function of your word processing software. Pull down the Edit menu, and click Replace. Do this for words, phrases, or even punctuation marks that you want to change throughout an entire story.

FYI

How to Use with Windows™ You can also call up the Find and Replace feature by pressing the Control key and the H key at the same time.

How to Use with Macintosh™ You can click on Command and the H key to access the Replace feature.

Conferencing

When you are fairly pleased with the changes you have made, you may wish to conference. **Conferencing** means sharing your writing with a "test reader" to see if there are any other ways you could improve your work. Listen carefully to what your partner has to say. Keep in mind, however, that your partner's comments are suggestions only. You are the final judge of what needs to be changed in your composition.

LESSON 3 *(pages C35–C43)*

OBJECTIVES

- **To edit a composition before recopying**
- **To prepare a composition for others to read**

Create Interest

Read to students sample passages that include a glaring error. Start with a line students are likely to recognize, such as, "Oh say can you see, by the dawn's early light . . ." but change *you* to *we*. Ask students what they notice about the line. Then read a less famous line, such as Abraham Lincoln's "I claim not to have controlled events, but confess plainly that events have controlled me," changing the second *controlled* to *control*. Ask students to respond to each statement. Point out how the simple mistakes cause readers to focus on those errors rather than the meaning of the sentence. Explain that editing and publishing are important in order to minimize distractions to the reader.

Peer Conferencing Another way to conference is to form a group with several other students and exchange drafts for review. Then take turns reading and discussing each person's written work. During this time, offer praise, constructive criticism, and suggestions for improvement. The following guidelines will help get the most out of conferencing as a revising technique.

Guidelines for Conferencing

Guidelines for the Writer

- List some questions for your classmate. What aspects of your writing most concern you?
- Try to be grateful for your critic's honesty rather than being upset or defensive. Keep in mind that the criticism you are getting is well-intended.

Guidelines for the Reader

- Read your partner's work carefully. What is the writer's purpose?
- Point out strengths as well as weaknesses. Start your comments by saying something positive like, "Your opening really captured my interest."
- Be specific. Refer to a specific word, sentence, or section of the compostion when you comment.
- Be sensitive to your partner's feelings. Phrase your criticisms as questions. You might say, "Do you think your details might be stronger if . . . ?"

Editing

Writing Process

During the prewriting, drafting, and revising stages, you have concentrated your efforts on the substance and structure of your draft. Once you are satisfied with your draft, you should begin to polish your work by correcting mechanical errors.

GETTING STUDENTS INVOLVED

Reciprocal Teaching

To help students make balanced, constructive comments during peer conferencing, suggest that they start their comments with, "What I really liked about this paper was . . ." and then follow up with "What could be strengthened in this paper is . . ."

HOME WORK

Have students evaluate a story in a newspaper using the Guidelines for Conferencing, and write what they would say to the writer in a conference.

Guide Instruction

By Modeling Strategies

Ask students to bring in examples of books or news articles so poorly designed that they were hard to read. Students may find the type size too small, the font hard to read, the visuals interfering with the text, or other design problems. Discuss how proper presentation helps readers rather than hinders them.

Consolidate Skills

Through Guided Practice

Divide students into pairs. Each student should write a paragraph that contains at least five different types of mistakes that should be caught with proofreading. Have students proofread their partner's paper, marking it with commonly used proofreading symbols.

Apply to Communication

Through Independent Writing

Assign students to write five sentences in which adding or leaving out punctuation changes the meaning of the sentence. Consider the sentence: "Bill said he came with us." It could mean that Bill admitted that he went with the

IDENTIFYING COMMON STUMBLING BLOCKS

Problem

- Not seeing errors in drafts

Solution

- If the schedule allows enough time, encourage students to take a break from working on their composition for at least one day before proofreading it. The longer they can wait, the fresher they will be when they read if for the last time, and the more errors they will catch.

Using an Editing Checklist When you edit you should go over your work at least three times, each time looking for a different kind of problem. For example, the focus of one reading might be misspellings. During another reading, focus on usage errors, such as subject-verb agreement. The last reading can be reserved for identifying and fixing errors in punctuation or capitalization. The Editing Checklist below will help you.

Editing Checklist

✓ Are sentences free of errors in grammar and usage?

✓ Did you punctuate each sentence correctly?

✓ Did you spell each word correctly?

✓ Did you use capital letters where needed?

✓ Did you indent paragraphs as needed?

Creating a Personalized Editing Checklist As you work through the editing stage, reserve a section in your **journal** to use as a Personalized Editing Checklist. Write the following headings on every other page: *Grammar Problems; Usage Problems; Spelling Problems;* and *Mechanical Problems.* Use these pages to record your errors. Add to this checklist throughout the year and refer to it each time you edit your writing.

Proofreading You may become so familiar with your work during the revising stage that you skip over mistakes. Proofreading during the editing stage gives you the distance to pick up on mistakes that you missed earlier. **Proofreading** is the process of carefully rereading one's work and marking corrections in grammar, usage, spelling, and mechanics. The following techniques may help.

Proofreading Techniques

- Focus on one line at a time.
- Exchange your work with a partner and check each other's work.

group, or that Bill declared that some other male went with the group.

Transfer to Everyday Life

By Reading Headlines

Read to students examples of news headlines that are humorous because they are unclear. For example, "Kids Make Nutritious Snacks" or "Residents Can Drop Off Trees." Several other ones can be found at the Website http://www.public.iastate.edu/~bbehle/headlines.html. Discuss how ambiguity may be deliberate or may show lack of editing. Ask students to bring in ambiguous headlines.

- Read your composition backward, word by word. By changing the way you read your work, you will find errors you may have missed earlier.
- Read your writing aloud, very slowly.
- Use a dictionary and a handbook to check spelling, grammar, usage, and mechanics.

Proofreading symbols are convenient shorthand notations that writers frequently use during the editing stage. The most commonly used proofreading symbols are shown below.

Proofreading Symbols

Symbol	Meaning	Example
∧	insert	We completed an journey. (went on; eventful)
∧,	insert comma	Meg enjoys hiking, skiing and skating.
⊙	insert period	Gary took the bus to Atlanta
ℓ	delete	Refer back to your notes.
¶	new paragraph	¶Finally Balboa saw the Pacific.
no ¶	no paragraph	no ¶The dachshund trotted away.
. . .	let it stand	I appreciated her sincere honesty.
#	add space	She will be downhere in a moment.
⁀	close up	The airplane waited on the run way.
∽	transpose	They only have two dollars left.
≡	capital letter	We later moved to the south.
/	lowercase letter	His favorite subject was Science.
(SP)	spell out	I ate 2 oranges.
∨∨	insert quotes	I hope you can join us, said my brother.
=	insert hyphen	I attended a school related event.
∨	insert apostrophe	The ravenous dog ate the cats food.
⤻	move copy	I usually on Fridays go to the movies.

HOME WORK

Have students photocopy the Proofreading Symbols chart from their textbook. Then have students use the symbols to proofread a newspaper article at home. Students should save their Proofreading Symbols chart to use throughout the year.

Pull It All Together

By Reflecting

Ask students to think about how they view writing now compared to when they started this chapter. List on the board key ideas they have learned or become more familiar with. Discuss how writing is a multi-faceted skill, one that develops over time.

Check Understanding

By Using the Literary Selection

Ask students to reread the article on page C3 by Caroline Cooney. They should review her comments on how she writes and compare them to how they have learned to write. Discuss the importance she places on rewriting, noting that this is a comment made by many writers.

PRACTICE YOUR SKILLS Sample Answers

1. we and delete *us*
2. meetings . and delete comma
3. These
4. play.
5. Nothing
6. delete, or *picturing, victory or*
7. correct
8. correct
9. delete *else* and *be*
10. delete one *able*

PRACTICE YOUR SKILLS

Editing with Proofreading Symbols

Write the correction for each numbered error in the paragraph below.

I am often asked how (1) us football players prepare for a big game. One important part of preparing is having team meetings (2), these help build team spirit and make you want to do your best for all (3) the your teammates. Team meetings also help you get the plays straight. It also helps to concentrate on only the game and the game plan. If you let your mind wander, you can make a mistake on (4) a important play (5) Even more important are the long hours of hard practice you put in all season. (6) Nothing can take the place of practice for making sure that each player knows exactly what to do on each play. Maybe the most important thing, though, is visualizing, or picturing, victory or a big play. You have to (7) picture (8) yourself yourself making an interception or tackling a runner or else you won't (9) be succeed. (10) Thats how we prepare for a big game.

Grammar in the Writing Process

Prewriting Workshop
Drafting Workshop
Revising Workshop
Editing Workshop
Publishing Workshop

Sentence Fragments

When you edit your writing, be sure you have used complete sentences. A sentence has a subject and a verb, and it expresses a complete thought. One common sentence error is called a **sentence fragment,** a group of words that does not express a complete thought. Study the sentence fragments below.

No Subject	Made a model of a ship. (Who made a model?)
Sentence	**Fred** made a model of a ship.
No Verb	The players on our baseball squad. (What do the players do?)
Sentence	The players on our baseball squad **practice** every afternoon.

Some phrases are mistaken for sentences, but, because a phrase has no subject or verb, it is not a sentence.

Prepositional Phrase	Near the white fence.
Sentence	**We waited** near the white fence.
Participial Phrase	The cat hiding in the tree.
Sentence	**I saw** the cat hiding in the tree.

Editing Checklist

✓ Are your sentences free of errors in grammar and usage?
✓ Did you spell each word correctly?
✓ Did you use capital letters where needed?
✓ Did you punctuate each sentence correctly?

Using *Editing Workshop*

Objective

- **To practice identifying and correcting sentence fragments**

A DIFFERENT APPROACH

Visual Ask three students to come to the board. Together they will write a sentence. They should take turns, each writing one word at a time. They can add their word before, after, or in between any words members of their group have already written. The class should stop them when they have written a sentence. Repeat with other groups of students.

Auditory Have students write down three groups of words. One should be a complete sentence, the others should be fragments. Have students take turns reading one of their three statements, and discuss with the class whether it is a fragment or a sentence.

INTEGRATING TECHNOLOGY

Computer

Tell students to print the final version of their essay in a font that is easy to read. To make the title stand out, they can use larger type and a different font, one that contrasts with the text font. For example, if the text is in a font with serifs, the small additional lines designed into the letters, they might choose a sans serif font, one that does not include additional lines. Some common serif fonts are Times Roman and Bookman. Common sans serif fonts include Helvetica and Avant Garde.

Publishing

Writing Process

Most of the writing you do is meant to be shared with others. Publishing, the final stage of the process, involves presenting your completed work in a final form to an audience. You may submit your work to your teacher or seek to gain a larger audience by having it published in a newspaper, magazine, or Web page.

Ways to Publish Your Writing

In School

- Read your work aloud to a small group in your class.
- Display your final draft on a bulletin board in your classroom or school library.
- Read your work aloud to your class or present it in the form of a radio program or videotape.
- Create a class library and media center to which you submit your work. The class media center could be a collection of folders or files devoted to different types of student writing and media presentations.
- Create a class anthology to which every student contributes. Share your anthology with other classes.
- Submit your work to your school literary magazine, newspaper, or yearbook.

Outside School

- Submit your written work to a newspaper or magazine.
- Share your work with an interested professional.
- Present your work to an appropriate community group.
- Send a video based on your written work to a local cable television station.
- Enter your work in a local, state, or national writing contest.

Using Standard Manuscript Form The appearance of your composition may be almost as important as its content. A marked-up paper with inconsistent margins is difficult to read. A neat, legible paper, however, makes a positive impression on your reader. Use the following guidelines for standard manuscript form to help you prepare your final draft. The model that follows the guidelines shows how the writer used these guidelines to prepare his final draft on preparing for a game.

Standard Manuscript Form

- Use standard-sized 8½-by-11-inch white paper. Use one side of the paper only.
- If handwriting, use black or blue ink. If using a word-processing program or typing, use a black ink cartridge or black typewriter ribbon and double-space the lines.
- Leave a 1.25-inch margin at the left and right. The left margin must be even. The right margin should be as even as possible.
- Put your name, the course title, the name of your teacher, and the date in the upper right-hand corner of the first page. Follow your teacher's specific guidelines for headings and margins.
- Center the title of your composition two lines below the date. Do not underline or put quotation marks around your title.
- If using a word-processing program or typing, skip four lines between the title and the first paragraph. If handwriting, skip two lines.
- If using a word-processing program or typing, indent the first line of each paragraph five spaces. If handwriting, indent the first line of each paragraph 1 inch.
- Leave a 1-inch margin at the bottom of all pages.
- Starting on page 2, number each page in the upper right-hand corner. Begin the first line 1 inch from the top. Word-processing programs allow you to insert page numbers.

INTEGRATING TECHNOLOGY

Electronic Publishing

You may want to refer students to *A Writer's Guide to Electronic Publishing* on pages C520–C545 for suggestions on using resources for publishing.

YOUR IDEAS
For Word-Processing Final Drafts

MODEL: Final Draft

Omar Byrne
English: Ms. Weymouth
September 13, 2000

Preparing for a Game

I am often asked how we football players prepare for a big game. One important part of preparing is having team meetings. These help build team spirit and make you want to do your best for all your teammates. Team meetings also help you get the plays straight. It also helps to Concentrate only on the game and the game plan. If you let your mind wander, you can make a mistake on an important play. Even more important are the long hours of hard practice you put in all season. Nothing can take the place of practice for making sure that each player knows exactly what to do on each play. Maybe the most important thing, though, is visualizing, or picturing, victory or a big play. You have to picture yourself making an interception or tackling a runner or else you won't succeed. That is how we prepare for a big game.

1.25 INCHES

1.25 INCHES

1 INCH

Writing Process Checklist

Remember that writing is a process. You move back and forth among the stages of the process to achieve your purpose. The numbers in parentheses refer to pages where you can get help with your writing.

PREWRITING

✓ Find a subject to write about by taking an inventory of your interests, freewriting, exploring the Internet, keeping a journal, and reading and thinking about literature. *(pages C9–C14)*
✓ Choose and limit a subject. *(pages C16–C18)*
✓ Consider your occasion, audience, and purpose. Be aware of the voice you choose. *(pages C18–C20)*
✓ Develop your subject by observing, brainstorming for details, clustering, and inquiring. *(pages C20–C25)*
✓ Organize your material by focusing your subject, classifying your details, and ordering your details. *(pages C25–C28)*

DRAFTING

✓ Write a first draft and choose a title that will capture your reader's attention. *(pages C29–C31)*

REVISING

✓ Elaborate by using facts, details, quotations, or examples to develop an idea or support a statement.
✓ Rearrange or delete needless words and ideas, and substitute words and sentences. *(pages C31–C34)*
✓ Use the Evaluation Checklist for Revising as a guide. *(page C33)*
✓ Use conferencing to help you revise your draft. *(pages C34–C35)*
✓ Revise your draft as often as needed. Repeat some of the prewriting and drafting strategies if necessary.

EDITING

✓ Use the Editing Checklists to look for errors in grammar, usage, spelling, capitalization, and punctuation. *(pages C36 and C39)*
✓ Use proofreading symbols to correct errors. (*page C37*)

PUBLISHING

✓ Follow standard manuscript form and make a neat final copy of your work. Share your work with others. *(pages C40–C42)*

EXPANDING THE LESSON

Using Technology

You will find additional **instructional** and **practice** materials for this chapter at http://www.bkenglish.com.

...G SUGGESTIONS

Essential Knowledge and Skills

- Using effective rate, volume, pitch, and tone for audience and setting
- Writing to influence such as to persuade, argue, and request
- Writing in complete sentences, varying the types such as compound and complex sentences
- Using verb tenses appropriately and consistently
- Describing how illustrator's choice of style, elements, and media help to represent or extend the text's meaning
- Selecting, organizing, or producing visuals to complement and extend meanings

CHAPTER 2

Developing Your Writing Style

One goal of effective writing is to capture the interest of readers and make them feel involved. Exact words and well-shaped sentences can breathe life into writing. In the following passage, notice how you can experience the scene as if you were in it yourself.

> It was a soft, reposeful summer landscape, as lovely as a dream, and as lonesome as Sunday. The air was full of the smell of flowers, and the buzzing of insects and the twittering of birds, and there were no people, no wagons, there was no stir of life, nothing going on.
>
> —*Mark Twain*, A Connecticut Yankee in King Arthur's Court

Words like *buzzing, twittering,* and *reposeful* help you picture this summer scene easily. The sentence structure suggests the quiet laziness of a summer afternoon.

This chapter will help you breathe life into your writing by choosing fresh, vivid words that leave a strong impression in the reader's mind. It will also help you shape your words into smooth, varied, and lively sentences.

Reading with a Writer's Eye

Natalie Goldberg is an author who frequently writes about the writing process. In the following article, she discusses the role the imagination plays in writing. Read "Man Eats Car" first to acquaint yourself with its content. Then, as you read it again, look for the words the author uses and the way she puts her sentences together.

BLOCK SCHEDULING

- If your schedule requires that you cover the chapter in a **shorter time**, use Reading with a Writer's Eye, Choosing Vivid Words, Sentence Combining Strategies, Creating Sentence Variety, and Writing Concise Sentences.
- If you want to take advantage of **longer class time**, add any or all of the following: Writing Is Thinking and the Editing Workshop.

FROM WRITING DOWN THE BONES

Man Eats Car

Natalie Goldberg

There was an article in the newspaper several years ago—I did not read it, it was told to me—about a yogi in India who ate a car. Not all at once, but slowly over a year's time. Now, I like a story like that. How much weight did he gain? How old was he? Did he have a full set of teeth? Even the carburetor, the steering wheel, the radio? What make was the car? Did he drink the oil?

I told this story to a group of third-graders in Owatonna, Minnesota. They were sitting on the tile blue carpet in front of me. The students looked confused and asked the most obvious question, "Why did he eat a car?," and then they commented, "Ugh!" But there was one bristling, brown-eyed student, who will be my friend forever, who just looked at me and burst into tremendous laughter, and I began laughing too. It was fantastic! A man had eaten a car! Right from the beginning there is no logic in it. It is absurd.

In a sense, this is how we should write. Not ask-

FOR INCREASING STUDENT ACHIEVEMENT

GUIDED READING

Text Analysis

- An **anecdote** provides a strong opening to the excerpt. First, Goldberg uses it to grab the attention of the readers. Besides providing a catchy title, it gives her a chance to raise the questions that many readers will raise in their minds about the story. Second, the anecdote leads to the main point of the excerpt: people should let their minds eat up everything and spew it out on paper.
- Goldberg writes in the **first person style.** She tells the reader what has happened to her. Then when she shifts to giving advice, the reader still feels that Goldberg writes from her own experience and convictions.
- The style is very **forceful**. Goldberg tells readers what they will be able to do: to see that ants are elephants, to see the transparency of all forms. She also tells readers what not to do: don't worry about metaphors, don't be literary, don't make your mind do anything.
- Goldberg **varies sentence structure** effectively. Most sentences are organized with a subject followed by a verb. To change the rhythm, though, she starts some sentences with introductory phrases or clauses. She also adds clauses or phrases after the main verb.

SELECTION AMENDMENT
Description of change: excerpted
Rationale: to focus on stylistic devices presented in this chapter

GUIDED READING

Strategy: Reviewing

Ask students to count the number of words in each sentence. How many have seven words or fewer? How many have eight to fifteen words? How many have sixteen words or more? Discuss how Goldberg varies sentence length for effect.

REACHING ALL STUDENTS

Struggling Learners

Students who have difficulty understanding Goldberg's belief that all life is connected might try creating diagrams of where energy comes from. You may find a well-designed diagram in a science textbook, or you can construct your own. Human energy for growth and movement comes from food, food comes from plants and animals, animal energy comes from plants, and plants get energy by converting sunlight. Ultimately, then, all life relies upon the sun for energy.

Advanced Students

Encourage students who are curious about Goldberg's belief that all life is connected to find out what various religious and philosophical belief systems say about the issue. Ask students to share what they find out with the class.

ing "Why?," not delicately picking among candies (or spark plugs), but voraciously, letting our minds eat up everything and spewing it out on paper with great energy. We shouldn't think, "This is a good subject for writing." "This we shouldn't talk about." Writing is everything, unconditional. There is no separation between writing, life, and the mind. If you think big enough to let people eat cars, you will be able to see that ants are elephants and men are women. You will be able to see the transparency of all forms so that all separations disappear.

This is what metaphor is. It is not saying that an ant is *like* an elephant. Perhaps; both are alive. No. Metaphor is saying the ant *is* an elephant. Now, logically speaking, I know there is a difference. If you put elephants and ants before me, I believe that every time I will correctly identify the elephant and the ant. So metaphor must come from a very different place than that of the logical, intelligent mind. It comes from a place that is very courageous, willing to step out of our preconceived ways of seeing things and open so large that it can see the oneness in an ant and in an elephant.

But don't worry about metaphors. Don't think, "I have to write metaphors to sound literary." First of all, don't be literary. Metaphors cannot be forced. If all of you does not believe that the elephant and the ant are one at the moment you write it, it will sound false. If all of you does believe it, there are some who might consider you crazy; but it's better to be crazy than false. But how do you make your mind believe it and write metaphor?

Don't "make" your mind do anything. Simply step out of the way and record your thoughts as they roll through you. Writing practice softens the heart and mind, helps to keep us flexible so that rigid distinctions between apples and milk, tigers and celery, disappear. We can step through moons right into bears. You will take leaps naturally if you follow your thoughts, because the mind spontaneously takes great leaps. You know. Have you ever been able to just stay with one thought for very long? Another one arises.

Your mind is leaping, your writing will leap, but it won't be artificial. It will reflect the nature of first thoughts, the way we see the world when we are free from prejudice and can see the underlying principles. We are all connected. Metaphor knows this and therefore is religious. There is no separation between ants and elephants. All boundaries disappear, as though we were looking through rain or squinting our eyes at city lights.

READER RESPONSE

You may want to use the following questions to elicit students' personal responses to the selection.

1. How did you feel when you read the first two sentences?
2. Do you think Goldberg is curious about why the man ate the car?
3. Explain what you think Goldberg means when she says, "Writing is everything."
4. Have you ever just recorded your thoughts as they rolled through your mind? Explain.
5. Do you see the world as connected the way Goldberg sees the world?

LITERARY CONNECTION

You might want to explore writing style in the following works, that appear in literature textbooks at this grade level.

- "Mrs. Flowers" by Maya Angelou
- *One Writer's Beginnings* by Eudora Welty
- "Sorry, Right Number" by Stephen King
- *Still Me* by Christopher Reeve

ADDITIONAL RESOURCES

Composition Skills Practice. . . . . pages 7–14
Transparency Tools GO2, VR1
Connection Collection . . . . pages C69–C70
ESL Practice and Test Preparation . . . . . pages 8–14
Writers at Work . . . . 8•1–8•10
Assessment: Chapter Test. . . . . pages 35–40
Assessment Resources . . . . pages 1–10, 13–44

Using *Thinking as a Writer*

You may choose to have students respond to the questions either orally or in writing.

YOUR IDEAS

For Thinking as a Writer

Thinking as a Writer

Evaluating Stylistic Devices

In "Man Eats Car," Natalie Goldberg offers fresh, lively inspiration to writers about using their imaginations.

- Think about the words Goldberg chooses and how she uses them. How do these choices contribute to the overall effect?
- Find a sentence in the article that puzzles or pleases you. What is it about the sentence that stands out?

Analyzing Art Style

Viewing Elements of art—such as line, color, shape, and texture—are to a visual artist what words are to a writer. Both the artist and the writer use these means to communicate their thoughts and feelings. Both are also concerned with principles of design—the thoughtful arrangement and ordering of parts of their compositions. Pattern, variety, and rhythm are to the artist what sentences and paragraphs are to the writer. They dictate the way the elements are used to communicate ideas and feelings.

- What ideas and feelings does this painting suggest to you? How does the artist's style—his unique treatment of the elements—shape your interpretation of his subject?

Romare Bearden. *Morning of the Rooster,* 1980.
Collage on board, 18 by 13¾ inches. Bearden Foundation/Licensed by VAGA, New York, NY.

Using Metaphors

Oral Expression Goldberg gives a personal definition for the concept of metaphors.

- Think of another metaphor that fits this article and discuss with your classmates why you chose this metaphor.

FOR DEVELOPING SKILLS

LESSON 1 *(pages C49–C53)*

OBJECTIVES

- **To use specific words to express meaning exactly**
- **To use words that appeal to the senses**

Create Interest

Ask students to copy the words on movie posters or advertisements that are written to attract people to the movie. Have students read in class what they have copied. Discuss whether the language is precise and whether it appeals to the senses.

Guide Instruction

By Modeling Strategies

Tell students that you are reading an edited text of a document with which they are familiar. Ask students to raise their hands when they can identify it. "We believe some things are true, that

Developing Stylistic Skills

The novelist John Gardiner once wrote, "Between these extremes, the endless sentence and the very short sentence, lies a world of variation, a world every writer must eventually explore." As Gardiner suggests, writing is choice and exploration. As a writer you choose words, phrases, and sentence structures to communicate your ideas. Your choices create your writing style.

Your writing **style** is the distinctive way you express yourself through the words you choose and the way you shape your sentences.

Your Writer's Journal

Think about a summer scene that brings back pleasant memories. Then re-create the scene in your journal. Include sights, sounds, feelings, smells, and tastes. Read your description aloud. Does it flow smoothly?

Choosing Vivid Words

Mountain climbers need secure footholds to keep from slipping. In the same way, readers need something concrete to support their understanding of a passage. Vivid words that communicate exactly what you mean will give your readers a firm footing.

Specific Words

Read the following movie reviews. Which one gives you a better idea of the film?

FOR INCREASING STUDENT ACHIEVEMENT

GETTING STUDENTS INVOLVED

Cooperative Learning

Divide students into small groups. Write the following words on the board: *small animal, unusual sound, pretty flower, long trip, many people.* Each group should list three other words or phrases that are similar to the words on the board, but more specific and vivid. Have each group share part of its list with the class.

REACHING ALL STUDENTS

English Language Learners

Encourage students to keep a word list of descriptive phrases they hear used by people in conversation or that they read. In addition to the phrases, they should note the source and the context.

How to Use with Windows™ To access the thesaurus feature, press the Shift key and the F7 key at the same time.

How to Use with Macintosh™ To access the thesaurus, press the Command, Option, and R keys at the same time. Or you can find Thesaurus on the pull-down Tools menu under Language.

SELECTION AMENDMENT
Description of change: excerpted
Rationale: to focus on the concept of writing style as presented in this chapter

everyone is the same, that God made it so everyone could live, and do what they wanted, and try to be happy." Then read the passage from the *Declaration of Independence* on which this was based: "We hold these truths to be self-evident, that all men are created equal, that they are endowed by their Creator with certain unalienable rights, that among these are life, liberty, and the pursuit of happiness."

Discuss how the language of the original is sharper and more forceful than that of the edited version.

Consolidate Skills

Through Guided Practice

The **Practice Your Skills** activities on revising with specific words will help students learn to replace general words with more precise ones. To extend this activity, have the class make a list of ten general words. Then have each student write two more specific words for each general one.

HOME WORK

Assign students to revise one or two paragraphs from a history textbook or a newspaper article, adding detail and precision. Discuss in class why the writers of the original paragraphs may have deliberately left out some of the detail and precision that the students added.

PRACTICE YOUR SKILLS Sample Answers

scout camp: majestic Poweshiek Creek Scout Camp

counselors: underpaid college students who are employed to keep us out of trouble

things: rugged hikes through the woods, close investigations of animal habitats, and hotly contested swimming races

deer: scared-looking white-tailed deer

take: paddle, row, or sail

rules: camp regulations that are drilled into us the first day

bad: dumber than trying to catch a grizzly bear barehanded

make: nurture from nearly nothing

put it out: to extinguish it completely

good: more in touch with the earth than a worm

The movie was very good. The actors were good. The special effects were great. The story was interesting.

Star Base is thrillingly entertaining. The young cast performed sensitively. The special effects were dazzling. The story throbbed with action and conflict and concluded with a surprise ending.

The first review uses only general words. Since general words can mean different things to different people, they do not communicate precisely. The second review replaces the general words with specific words that call precise images to mind.

PRACTICE YOUR SKILLS

Revising with Specific Words

The following paragraph contains too many general words. On separate paper, revise the paragraph, substituting specific words for each word that is underlined.

Summer Camp

Every year I go to <u>camp</u>. The <u>people</u> plan many <u>things</u> for us to do. On nature walks we sometimes see a <u>deer</u> running for cover. Once a day we can pair up and <u>take</u> boats out on the lake. The <u>rules</u> require partners because going swimming or boating without a companion is <u>bad</u>. The counselors teach us how to <u>make</u> a fire and <u>put it out</u>. At night we sometimes cook marshmallows over the embers. After two weeks in the woods, I return home feeling <u>good</u>.

Apply to Communication

Through Independent Writing

Have students bring to class objects for their classmates to describe. Set the objects on a desk or table where everyone can see them. Each student should write a description of one of the objects without naming it. Other students should try to identify the object. As they do, discuss which clues in writing were most helpful to them.

Transfer to Everyday Life

By Describing a Personal Story

Have students write a story describing an event they remember from when they were younger. Have students revise it to make the writing precise and appealing to the senses.

Pull It All Together

By Sharing

Ask students to write an advertisement for your school. Have students share what they have written. Point out good examples of engaging writing.

IN THE MEDIA

Tourist Brochure

All forms of advertising have a target audience that they are trying to reach. Whether it is a toy commercial geared to children or a billboard intended for middle-aged men, each advertisement is created with particular groups in mind. The words, pictures, and colors used are all chosen for a specific intended effect: to interest the targeted consumer.

In targeting consumers so specifically, advertisers work hard to find the right words and images that will attract people. A sports car speeding around curves makes the car seem exciting. A picture of a meadow full of flowers on a shampoo bottle makes the shampoo seem natural and wholesome. The words "Just Do It" suggest that anything is possible if you have the right athletic shoes. Advertisers find out what is important to the people they are selling to and then create ads that promise to deliver those qualities—excitement, wholesomeness, or other endless possibilities.

Media Activity

Suppose you are on the city council for the city or town in which you live. You need to attract tourists to your town and are creating a brochure toward that end.

- Working in groups brainstorm a list of attractions in your town.
- Target a brochure to each of the following audiences: football fans, poets, and naturalists.
- Feature the same attractions from your list for each group, but change what you emphasize about each attraction to appeal to your target audience.

How does your brochure change depending on what group you are targeting?

Using *In the Media*

Objective

- **To understand how travel brochures target particular audiences**

Group Project

- As a class, select a tourist site that appeals to a wide range of people. Students might choose a large museum, a zoo, or an amusement park. Divide the students into small groups. Each group should design a tourist brochure that appeals to a particular group of people to visit that site. Groups might target adolescents, parents with young children, senior citizens, females, males, or others. Groups do not need to find the actual images they would use, but they should write clear descriptions of them, and sketch a design for their brochure. Have groups share their brochures with the class, and explain how they appealed to their targeted audience.

FYI

Website to Visit The site http://www.wwb.com/ shows the covers of travel brochures from around the world. This site, and many others, offers to send copies of the brochures to anyone requesting them.

Check Understanding

By Studying the Literary Selection
Ask students to reread the first paragraph of "Man Eats Car." Ask them to evaluate how well Goldberg uses precise words and details to appeal to the reader.

GETTING STUDENTS INVOLVED

Cooperative Learning

Divide students into pairs. The students should take turns suggesting adjectives. For each adjective, the other student should respond with three nouns that it might describe. For example, if one suggests *blazing*, the other student might respond with *fire, furnace,* or *sun*. To help students get started, you might write other adjectives on the board, such as *bitter, clanging, dazzling, sour, whining,* and *rough.*

HOME WORK

Have students create a cluster diagram consisting of sensory words to describe the best book they have read in the past year. Then use the details to write five sentences that describe the book.

Appealing to the Senses

Most of the impressions you gather come to you through your five senses. Your experiences are based on what you see, hear, smell, taste, or touch. You can share these experiences in writing by using words that appeal to your readers' senses. Compare the following two sentences.

> Josie felt **sad.**
>
> Josie **slumped** in the big, **overstuffed** chair, resting her **downcast** head on her **fist** and **sighing.**

The first sentence tells a reader that Josie is sad. The second sentence shows the sadness. A reader can see Josie's posture and hear her sighing. These sensory details communicate more clearly than does the adjective *sad* in the first sentence.

When you are writing, take time during the prewriting stage to think of vivid sensory details you will be able to use in your composition. The techniques of clustering and brainstorming will help you come up with details that will appeal to your readers' senses. The following cluster shows a number of sensory words that could be used to describe a peach.

Model: Sensory Detail Cluster

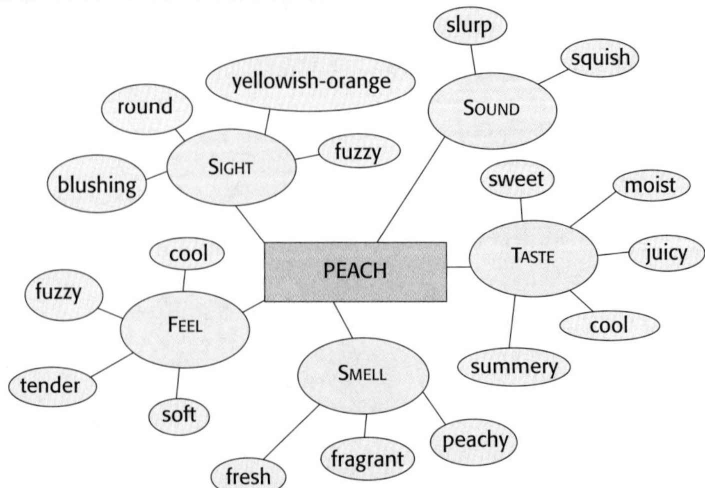

LESSON 2 *(pages C53–C58)*

OBJECTIVES

- **To combine short, choppy sentences to achieve sentence variety**
- **To use coordinating and subordinating words correctly**

Create Interest

Read to the class a book written for children learning to read. Discuss how students feel about the book and how the writing differs from writing in books for their age group. Among the differences they may notice are that the sentences in the children's book are uniformly short. Discuss how this makes the book less interesting to more proficient readers.

Guide Instruction

By Modeling Strategies

Have students select a story written for beginning readers and rewrite it for students their own age. Encourage them to use longer sentences, as well

PRACTICE YOUR SKILLS

Revising Using Sensory Detail

Rewrite each of the following sentences. Use details that appeal to the senses.

EXAMPLE	Bill was happy.
POSSIBLE ANSWER	Bill whistled as he raced home.

1. My dog is beautiful.
2. Katrina was angry.
3. The pancake breakfast was delicious.
4. Mary seemed nervous.
5. The beach was breathtaking.

Describing with Sensory Words

Think of a specific food that you particularly like. Then make a cluster like the one shown on the previous page. Think of as many sensory words as you can that describe the food you chose. When you have finished, use your cluster to write five sentences that describe the food without naming it. Then exchange papers with a classmate. Try to guess the kind of food your partner has described.

Sentence Combining Strategies

A good mix of sentence types and structures will help keep your readers interested. Sentence combining is one way to vary the patterns of your sentences.

Combining with Specific Details

One good strategy for creating sentence variety is to combine specific details from short, choppy sentences into one interesting sentence. Study the following example.

REACHING ALL STUDENTS

Advanced Learners

Have students use language creatively by inventing alliterative descriptive phrases, several words that start with the same sound, such as "nattering nabob of negativity." Ask students to write phrases describing each of five current celebrities or people in the news.

HOME WORK

Have students create five more sentences and revise them to include more details. Suggest that students make their original sentences short and general so that revising them will be easier.

PRACTICE YOUR SKILLS Sample Answers

1. The black and white fur on Lulu, my border collie, looks like a drift of brilliant fresh snow blown up against a pile of coal.
2. After stomping to the kitchen table, Katrina glared even as she read the comics.
3. I smiled as I recalled how the sweet and tangy cranberries accented the hearty flavor of the pancakes we had for breakfast.
4. Edging toward the door, Mary looked like a dog that sensed a cat nearby.
5. Like they were part of the flag of some mythical country, the hot tan sand, the smooth dark water, and the soft blue sky formed three perfect bands.

as more precise words. Ask volunteers to read their revised stories to the class.

Consolidate Skills

Through Guided Practice

The **Practice Your Skills** activity on combining sentences with specific details allows students to practice revising choppy sentences into longer, smoother ones. To extend this activity, discuss whether students think the original or the revised versions of the sentences are easier to understand and which sentences show relationships among ideas more clearly.

Apply to Communication

Through Independent Writing

Have students write a long paragraph about an animal of their choice. They should circle the words they use to coordinate or subordinate ideas.

HOME WORK

Have students write six short sentences about one topic of their choice. Then have them combine the sentences into two or three longer ones.

Practice Your Skills Sample Answers

1. The *Viking* spacecraft was an enormous, sophisticated robot.
2. *Viking* was sent on a mission to the surface of Mars.
3. *Viking* relayed information to Earth.
4. *Viking* also took photographs of the red, dusty surface of Mars.
5. *Viking* had complex instruments aboard for measuring Marsquakes.
6. Over a period of years, *Viking* sent back useful information.

Choppy Sentences	The robot squeaked. The robot was metallic. It squeaked continually. It squeaked at its hinges.
Combined Sentence	The metallic robot squeaked continually at its hinges.

If your combined sentence contains two or more adjectives in a row, remember to separate the adjectives with commas. Study the following example.

Choppy Sentences	The museum has a robot. It is metallic. It is squeaky.
Combined Sentence	The museum has a metallic, squeaky robot.

Practice Your Skills

Combining Sentences with Specific Details

Combine each group of short sentences into one longer one.

1. The *Viking* spacecraft was a robot. It was enormous. It was sophisticated.
2. It was sent on a mission. The mission was to the surface of Mars.
3. *Viking* relayed information. The information went to Earth.
4. It also took photographs. They were of the surface of Mars. The surface was red and dusty.
5. *Viking* had instruments aboard. The instruments were complex. They were for measuring Marsquakes.
6. Over a period of years, *Viking* sent back information. The information was useful.

Writing Is Thinking

Comparing

Comparisons are based on similarities. Sometimes similarities are immediately obvious. For example, the similarities between blue jeans and sweatpants are easy to spot. Many similarities—such as those between blue jeans and houses—are far less obvious. Some of the most original thinking you can do is to find similarities between two things that are different in most ways. The following examples show comparisons between very different objects.

> His eyes are like lasers.
>
> The moon is a pearl in the velvet night sky.

The two things being compared are alike in only one way. The eyes and lasers are alike because of their piercing quality. The moon and pearl are alike because they are both shining white spheres.

THINKING PRACTICE

For each of the following subjects, think of something completely different with which to compare it. Write a complete sentence expressing the comparison. Try to be original. Avoid such overused comparisons as "busy as a bee" or "sheepish grin."

EXAMPLE	flowers
POSSIBLE ANSWER	Flowers are the embroidery of the earth.

1. winter
2. friends
3. mountains
4. loneliness
5. thunderstorms
6. telephones

Using *Writing Is Thinking*

Objective

- **To practice creating striking comparisons**

A DIFFERENT APPROACH

Kinesthetic Divide students into pairs. Have each pair act out scenes that involve the words for which they are trying to find comparisons. As they create their scene, tell them to note comparisons that come to mind.

THINKING PRACTICE

Sample Answers

1. Winter is a gazelle, jumping unpredictably.
2. Friends are the chewy centers of lollipops.
3. Mountains are truth and honesty shaped out of rock and dirt.
4. Loneliness is the single note from a broken banjo.
5. Thunderstorms are the popcorn of summer.
6. Telephones are flies, necessary yet pesky.

Thinking Skills	
Classifying	Analyzing
Comparing	Hypothesizing
Generalizing	Synthesizing
Inferring	Summarizing
Imagining	Setting Goals
Observing	Evaluating Audience
Predicting	

Transfer to Everyday Life

By Analyzing an Editorial

Have students select a newspaper editorial. They should circle the words used to coordinate or subordinate ideas. Then they should analyze how someone with a perspective different from the writer's might disagree with the relationships indicated by the circled words.

Pull It All Together

By Summarizing

Write on the board as many coordinating and subordinating words as students can think of without looking at their textbook. Suggest that they think about the possible relationships between any two ideas.

Check Understanding

By Studying the Literary Selection

Have students select a five-sentence section of "Man Eats Car" and list the coordinating and subordinating words Goldberg uses in that section. Discuss how the writing would be harder to understand without these words.

DEVELOPING WORKPLACE COMPETENCIES

Thinking Skills: Reasoning

Explain to students that coordinating and subordinating words often show the relationships between two ideas. To show the correct relationship requires reasoning skills. For example, consider these two statements:

A. The company increased its advertising budget last quarter.

B. Sales increased sharply last quarter.

What is the relationship between these two statements? Maybe A caused B: the increase in advertising causes sales to increase. Maybe B caused A: the increase in sales allowed the company to spend more money on advertising. Maybe the two are unrelated: advertising may need longer time to have an impact on sales. Whether these two sentences are combined with *as a result,* or *because* or *also* will reflect the writer's analysis of the relationship between the two statements. Investment advisers, lawyers, insurance agents, and others who analyze the causes of events need solid reasoning skills and the ability to write about causation.

Ask students to imagine they are analyzing why a sports team is more successful one year than in a previous year. List five changes that occurred between the years. Then write a paragraph showing the relationships among these reasons.

Writing Tip

Be open to finding striking **comparisons**—similarities between two things that are different in most ways. Fresh comparisons will make your writing more specific, sensory, and interesting to readers.

Combining by Coordinating

You can also combine choppy sentences by **coordinating,** or linking ideas of equal importance. Use the coordinating conjunctions *and, but, or,* and *yet* to combine subjects, to combine verbs, and to combine parts of sentences.

CHOPPY	Two huge tusks are one characteristic of the walrus. A mustached upper lip is another characteristic.
COMBINED SUBJECTS	Two huge tusks **and** a mustached upper lip are characteristics of the walrus.
CHOPPY	Scientists have observed the walrus for many years. Scientists still have much to learn.
COMBINED VERBS	Scientists have observed the walrus for many years **but** still have much to learn.
CHOPPY	The walrus is a powerful member of the seal family. The walrus is timid.
COMBINED PARTS OF SENTENCES	The walrus is a powerful **yet** timid member of the seal family.

PRACTICE YOUR SKILLS

Combining Sentences by Coordinating

The sentences in the following paragraph are clumsy and repetitious. Revise the paragraph, combining sentence parts by coordinating. Use the words *and, but, or,* or *yet* to combine the sentences. The first sentence is done for you.

Walruses

Scientists have observed the walrus for many years. and ~~Scientists have~~ have recorded much information. Walruses belong to the seal family. They differ from seals in many ways. The air sacs in its neck make the walrus unique. Its huge tusks make it unique. The inflatable air sacs help keep the walrus's head above water. These air sacs allow the walrus to take a nap in the ocean. Their huge ivory tusks serve as helpful tools in the ice. These long, curved teeth can become dangerous weapons during a fight. The walrus is a timid animal. It will fight for the protection of its young. Many mysteries about these fascinating sea animals have been solved. Scientists still have much to learn about them.

Combining by Subordinating

If the ideas in two short sentences are of unequal importance, you can combine them by subordinating. This technique turns one of the sentences into a clause that becomes part of another sentence. The following are some words that can be used to combine by subordinating.

who	after	if
which	although	because
that	unless	until

INTEGRATING TECHNOLOGY

Internet

A Website operated by Seaworld provides excellent background information on walruses: http://www.seaworld.org/walrus/walrus.html. The information is presented in numbered lists, with most items being only one or two sentences. Interested students may wish to combine these facts into longer sentences and paragraphs and present a report to the class.

HOME WORK

The practice activity gives students an opportunity to use words such as *and, but, or,* and yet to make writing smoother. To extend the lesson, have students write pairs of short sentences that could be combined with these pairs of words or phrases: *both/and, either/or, just as/so, not only/but also,* and *neither/nor.*

PRACTICE YOUR SKILLS Sample Answers

Scientists have observed walruses for many years and recorded much information about them. Walruses belong to the seal family, but differ from seals in many ways. The air sacs in its neck and its huge tusks make the walrus unique. The inflatable air sacs in its neck keep its head above water and allow the walrus to take a nap in the ocean. Their huge ivory tusks are helpful tools in the ice, and can become dangerous weapons during a fight. The walrus is a timid animal, yet it will fight for the protection of its young. Many mysteries about these fascinating sea animals have been solved, but scientists still have much to learn about them.

HOME WORK

The practice activity gives students an opportunity to use words such as *if, which, because, unless,* and *which* to make writing smoother. To extend the lesson, have students write pairs of short sentences that could be combined with these words: *as, before, since, than,* and *while.*

PRACTICE YOUR SKILLS Sample Answers

You can learn a lot about people's feelings if you study their body language. Shrugging the shoulders, which can mean a lack of knowledge, is a common body signal. Because the head houses memory, many people touch their foreheads to show forgetfulness. If you are sitting alone at a cafeteria table, your eyes can signal to a new arrival that you want to be left alone. Unless you look down, the new arrival will assume you want some company and conversation. Understanding others, which is a goal of human societies, is aided by understanding body language.

PRACTICE YOUR SKILLS

Combining Sentences by Subordinating

In the following paragraph, each pair of choppy sentences can be improved through combining by subordinating. Use the subordinating word in parentheses to create the combined sentence. Be sure to use commas where needed.

EXAMPLE Lifting an eyebrow may show disbelief. It may also show surprise. (although)

ANSWER Although lifting an eyebrow may show disbelief, it may also show surprise.

Body Language

You can learn a lot about people's feelings. You study their body language. (if) Shrugging the shoulders can mean a lack of knowledge. Shrugging the shoulders is a common body signal. (which) The head houses memory. Many people touch their foreheads to show forgetfulness. (because) You are sitting alone at a cafeteria table. Your eyes can signal to a new arrival that you want to be left alone. (if) You look down. The new arrival will assume you want some company and conversation. (unless) Understanding others is aided by understanding body language. Understanding others is a goal of human society. (which)

Time Out to Reflect

Meet with a partner and exchange a piece of writing you have done this year. Read each other's writing aloud, slowly. Listen carefully to your own writing as your partner reads. What words do you notice? What sentences seem clear and interesting? Together, review the criteria for word choice and combining sentences presented so far in this chapter. Write the criteria in the Learning Log section of your **journal.**

Lesson 3 *(pages C59–C60)*

OBJECTIVE

- **To write sentences with varied beginnings**

Create Interest

Write two column heads on the board: Boring and Interesting. Write activities that students suggest belong in each category. Then discuss the differences. Point out that one trait of most boring activities is dull repetition, while interesting activities usually include variety. Tell students that writing also needs variety to be interesting.

Guide Instruction

By Connecting Ideas

Discuss with students how repetition in writing—having the same length and structure of sentences—is boring to readers. Ask students to imagine how

Creating Sentence Variety

You have learned how to use sentence combining to vary the length and structure of your sentences. Another way to add variety to your writing is to begin your sentences in different ways.

Sentence Beginnings

The most natural way to begin a sentence is with the subject. For variety, experiment with other sentence beginnings.

Subject	Chi Cheng was a very fast runner in her high school days.
Phrase	In her high school days, Chi Cheng was a very fast runner.

The following sentences show just a few of the ways you can begin your sentences.

Prepositional Phrase	At the age of 16, she represented Taiwan in the 1960 Olympics.
Adjective	Steadfast, she kept up her running even though she hurt her leg during the second Olympic match.
Adverb	Altogether Cheng broke or matched seven world records during the next five years.

Writing Tip

Vary sentence beginnings by moving phrases from the end to the beginning.

USING STUDENTS' STRENGTHS

Multiple Intelligences: Musical

Ask students who play the piano to describe ways that composers link sounds together on the piano. For example, they tie notes together into phrases, they use the sustenuto pedal to allow notes to linger, and they have one hand hold notes longer while the other plays shorter notes. If you have access to a keyboard in the classroom, ask students to play a well-known piece, such as *Lullaby* by Johannes Brahms with short, choppy phrases, and again with longer, smoother phrases.

music would sound if the tempo never changed, if the dynamics never changed, if the notes never changed.

Consolidate Skills

Through Guided Practice

After students have completed the **Practice Your Skills** activity on varying sentence beginnings, ask them to evaluate a paragraph in this textbook. They should decide whether the paragraph includes sufficient variety in sentence beginnings.

Apply to Communication

Through Independent Writing

Have students write two or three paragraphs summarizing the history of a topic they know well. Then they should count how many sentences start with a subject and how many start with a phrase.

Transfer to Everyday Life

By Evaluating a News Article

Ask students to bring a news story to class. They should evaluate how many

HOME WORK

Assign students to find a passage of at least ten sentences in a book, newspaper, or magazine. Have them identify which sentences start with a prepositional phrase, participial phrase, adverb, or adverb clause.

Practice Your Skills Sample Answers

1. Surprising his bosses, Watson sold many, many machines.
2. At 35 years of age, Watson became the sales manager of the National Cash Register Company.
3. After five years Watson left NCR and became president of the Computer-Tabulating-Recording-Company.
4. Tirelessly, Watson worked year after year to build up the struggling company.
5. To reflect its growing foreign business, Watson changed the company's name to International Business Machines (IBM) before long.
6. Under Watson's direction, IBM grew steadily.
7. Undoubtedly, Watson's belief in the value of expert sales people was one reason for the company's huge success.
8. By printing up signs that said "THINK," Watson stressed the importance of careful thought for his workers.

Practice Your Skills

Varying Sentence Beginnings

Add variety to the following passage by beginning each sentence with the opener suggested in parentheses. Remember to follow the rules for using commas with introductory elements.

EXAMPLE William J. Watson went to work for the National Cash Register Company in 1894. (prepositional phrase)

ANSWER In 1894, William J. Watson went to work for the National Cash Register Company.

1. Watson sold many, many machines, surprising his bosses. (participial phrase)

2. Watson became the sales manager of the National Cash Register Company at 35 years of age. (prepositional phrase)

3. Watson left NCR and became president of the Computer-Tabulating-Recording-Company after five years. (prepositional phrase)

4. Watson worked tirelessly year after year to build up the struggling company. (adverb)

5. Watson changed the company's name to International Business Machines (IBM) before long to reflect its growing foreign business. (prepositional phrase)

6. IBM grew steadily under Watson's direction. (prepositional phrase)

7. One reason for the company's huge success was undoubtedly Watson's belief in the value of expert sales people. (adverb)

8. Watson stressed the importance of careful thought for his workers by printing up signs that said "THINK." (prepositional phrase)

sentences start with the subject and how many start with a phrase.

Pull It All Together

By Reflecting

Ask students to suggest reasons a writer might create a character in a story that always uses the same sentence structure. Discuss what this might say about the personality of the character.

Check Understanding

By Working with a Partner

Divide students into pairs. Have students write three sentences and exchange them with their partner. Have the partners revise the three so they start differently. Return the sentences to the original writer, who should decide if the revisions have the same meaning as the original versions.

Grammar in the Writing Process

Prewriting Workshop
Drafting Workshop
Revising Workshop
Editing Workshop
Publishing Workshop

Subject and Verb Agreement

In all sentences the verb must agree in number with the subject. **Number** is the term used to indicate whether the subject or verb is singular (one) or plural (more than one). The following examples, based on sentences from "Man Eats Car," illustrate subject and verb agreement.

A singular subject takes a singular verb and a plural subject takes a plural verb.

Singular	Your mind **is** leaping.
Plural	Their minds **are** leaping.

Subject-Verb Agreement in Compound Subjects

A **compound subject** is formed when two or more subjects take the same verb. Compound subjects are joined together by the conjunctions *and* or *or*, or by one of the pairs *both...and, either...or,* and *neither...nor.* When a compound subject is joined together by *and*, the verb is plural.

Compound Subject, Plural Verb	Ants, elephants, moons, and bears **are** equal in the writer's mind.

When a compound subject is joined together by the conjunctions *or, nor, either...or,* or *neither...nor,* the verb agrees with the subject that is closest to it in the sentence.

Compound Subject, Singular Verb	*Neither* the celery stalks *nor* the moonbeam **walks** upright except in writing.

Using *Editing Workshop*

Objective

- **To understand how to make subjects and verbs agree in number**

A DIFFERENT APPROACH

Visual Have students draw sketches of the subjects in the sentences. If they sketch one item, then the verb should be singular. If they sketch more than one, then the verb should be plural. Discuss how to handle subjects that are a group, such as a team. Since a team is just one item, use it with singular verbs.

Auditory Have students write sentences using both singular and plural subjects, but leaving the verb blank. Ask them to read aloud sentences in a small group. The group should decide whether a singular or a plural verb should be inserted. Many students find that listening will help them identify correct usage.

YOUR IDEAS
For Subject and Verb Agreement

COMPOUND SUBJECT, PLURAL VERB	*Either* the yogi *or* the bears **are** feasting on cars.
COMPOUND SUBJECT, SINGULAR VERB	*Neither* the carburetor *nor* the car radio **was** working.

You and *I* as Subjects

You is always used with a plural verb—whether *you* refers to one person or more than one person.

You **take** leaps naturally if you **follow** your thoughts.

Although *I* refers to one person, it takes a plural verb. The only exceptions are the *be* verb forms *am* and *was*.

I **am** not saying an ant is an elephant. I **know** the difference.

Subject-Verb Agreement in Combined Sentences

When you combine sentences, you may change the number of the subject. If so, you must change the verb so that it agrees with the subject.

CHOPPY SENTENCES	The yogi has teeth. The bear has teeth. (two singular subjects, two singular verbs)
COMBINED SENTENCE	Both the yogi and the bear have teeth. (compound subject, plural verb)

Editing Checklist

✔ Have you combined two or more sentences correctly?
✔ Does the verb agree with the subject?

LESSON 4 *(pages C63–C66)*

OBJECTIVES

- **To write sentences that are focused rather than rambling**
- **To write concise sentences that include no unnecessary words**

Create Interest

Challenge students to each write a sentence with more than fifty words. Ask volunteers to read the sentences aloud. Discuss whether or not the sentences are easy to follow.

Guide Instruction

By Modeling Strategies

Ask students how to revise the sentences they wrote for **Create Interest.** Discuss whether dividing these long sentences into shorter ones makes them easier to read.

Writing Concise Sentences

When you shop, you want the most value for your dollar. When you write, you want the most value for each word you use. Avoid bulky writing. Be economical and concise when you write.

Rambling Sentences

One cause of bulky writing is throwing too many ideas into one sentence. The result, called a **rambling sentence,** is hard to read and difficult to understand.

RAMBLING SENTENCE: About seven million people in the United States do not eat meat, but they find protein in other types of food, and they combine certain kinds of food, such as rice and beans, to make sure they eat complete proteins, or they sometimes eat such dairy products as cheese, milk, and yogurt for protein.

REVISED SENTENCES: About seven million people in the United States do not eat meat. Instead, they find protein in other types of food. They also combine certain kinds of food, such as rice and beans, to make sure they eat complete proteins. Others eat such dairy products as cheese, milk, and yogurt for protein.

PRACTICE YOUR SKILLS

Revising Rambling Sentences

On a separate sheet of paper, revise the following paragraph to eliminate the rambling sentences.

IDENTIFYING COMMON STUMBLING BLOCKS

Problem

- Writing as one speaks, in rambling sentences

Solution

- Ask pairs of students to tape-record a serious, animated conversation. They might discuss a sporting event, a musical group, or any other topic about which they both feel strongly. Then they should play the tape and listen to the sentence structure in their conversation. They may notice that their sentences start with one subject and shift to another before finishing. Explain that such shifts may reflect how one thinks. However, when writing, people have time to reflect on, to organize, and to clarify their statements.

Problem

- Breaking all long sentence into shorter ones

Solution

- Have students try to write a long sentence that does not ramble. Remind students that a sentence can be long and still be easy to read if it has only one main idea.

Consolidate Skills
Through Guided Practice
Have students complete the **Practice Your Skills** activity on revising rambling sentences. Then ask students why they revised some sentences but left others as they were. They should focus on how many ideas were in a sentence rather than how many words were in it.

Apply to Communication
Through Independent Writing
Have students write a paragraph in which they include ten words they consider unnecessary. Have students trade papers with a partner and circle the words they consider unnecessary. After they return the papers to their partners, students should discuss whether they identified the same words as unnecessary.

Transfer to Everyday Life
By Evaluating Writing
Ask students to bring to class examples they find of writing that includes unnecessary words. Suggest to them that writings by insurance companies

HOME WORK

Have students work with a partner. Each student should write three rambling sentences for their partner to revise into shorter sentences.

USING STUDENTS' STRENGTHS

Multiple Intelligences: Linguistic
Have students write two sentences in which they repeat words or an idea for a good reason, and two sentences in which they repeat words or an idea unnecessarily. Have students read their sentences aloud, and discuss them with the class. Try to develop a guideline for when repetition is useful and when it is not. Repetition may be useful for clarifying unusual terms, for emphasizing points, and for providing a sentence with a pleasing rhythm. When a sentence seems to define a well-known term, though, the repetition is not needed.

PRACTICE YOUR SKILLS Sample Answers

Sunlight passing through and reflecting dust particles explains the sometimes brilliant colors we see in the sky. One of the sources of this dust is volcanic explosion. A single blast can send tons of dust into the sky. Another source of dust is the ocean, from which salt is sprayed and then evaporated into salty dust. Plants also give off billions of grains of pollen and spores. Dust particles by the ton also enter Earth's atmosphere from outer space, but no one knows exactly where these come from. Around the house dust looks gray and dingy, but in the skies dust glimmers with some of the most beautiful colors ever seen.

Dusty Skies

Sunlight passing through and reflecting dust particles explains the sometimes brilliant colors we see in the sky, and one of the sources of this dust is volcanic explosion, and a single blast can send tons of dust into the air. Another source of dust is the ocean, from which salt is sprayed and then evaporated into salty dust, and plants also give off billions of grains of pollen and spores. Dust particles by the ton also enter Earth's atmosphere from outer space, but no one knows exactly where these come from. Around the house dust looks gray and dingy, but in the skies dust glimmers with some of the most beautiful colors ever seen.

Repetition

Sometimes without thinking you may repeat an idea unnecessarily. As you revise check your sentences to be sure you have not included unnecessary words and phrases.

REPETITIVE	I resolved to **try again** and **not give up.**
CONCISE	I resolved to **try again.**
REPETITIVE	Sam's face looked **pale** and **colorless.**
CONCISE	Sam's face looked **pale.**
REPETITIVE	The **hungry** guests were **eager to eat.**
CONCISE	The guests were **eager to eat.**

Empty Expressions

Empty expressions are wasted words that add no real meaning to a sentence. Notice how they can be deleted or replaced when you revise.

and by lawyers are often cited as having more words than necessary.

Pull It All Together

By Reflecting

Ask students to describe how they write differently now from when they began this chapter. Discuss whether they read any differently as well.

Check Understanding

By Studying the Literary Selection

Have student reread "Man Eats Car." Ask them to note any words Goldberg uses that she could leave out. Discuss these in class to see if other students agree.

EMPTY	**What I mean is,** I learned a difficult lesson.
CONCISE	I learned a difficult lesson.
EMPTY	The Girl Scouts met their fund-raising goal **due to the fact that** cookie sales were high.
CONCISE	The Girl Scouts met their fund-raising goal because cookie sales were high.

PRACTICE YOUR SKILLS

Revising to Eliminate Unnecessary Words

Revise the following paragraph to eliminate unnecessary words or empty expressions. Change the wording and use commas as needed. The first sentence is done for you.

Pets and Health

Pets are good for more than just fun ~~and good times~~. As a matter of fact, stroking an animal can even reduce blood pressure. People who own dogs also exercise more regularly because they take their dogs for walks, which gives the people exercise too. Because of the fact that pets help sick people recover from their illness, pets are sometimes even brought to hospitals. There is this natural bond that forms between humans and pet animals, and due to this fact senior citizens should be allowed to have pets in their housing.

COMPUTER TIP

Use the Delete, Cut, and Paste functions of your word-processing program to help you revise your writing. Delete unnecessary words. Cut and paste words and phrases to vary sentence beginnings.

HOME WORK

Have students quickly write a paragraph of at least fifty words on a topic of their choice. Then have them cut at least ten words out of it. They should eliminate the words that are least essential to conveying the main idea of the paragraph.

PRACTICE YOUR SKILLS Sample Answers

Pets are good for more than just fun. Stroking an animal can even reduce blood pressure. People who own dogs also exercise more regularly because they need to take their dogs for walks. Because pets help sick people recover from their illness, pets are sometimes even brought to hospitals. Because this natural bond forms between humans and pet animals, senior citizens should be allowed to have pets in their housing.

FYI

How to Use with Windows™ Besides using the commands under the Edit menu to cut and paste, one can also move text using the mouse. Highlight the text to be moved. Click on it, and before releasing, move the text to where it is to go. Release, and the text will move to the new location.

How to Use with Macintosh™ Besides using the commands under the Edit menu to cut and paste, one can also move text using the mouse. Highlight the text to be moved. Click on it, and before releasing, move the text to where it is to go. Release, and the text will move to the new location.

HOME WORK

Have students write five short, clear sentences. Then have them rewrite the sentences adding at least three more words in each sentence, but without adding any significant information. Ask students to read one of their revised sentences to the class, and have other students identify which words were added.

Your Writing Style Checklist

CHOOSING VIVID WORDS

✓ Use specific words to convey your meaning exactly. *(pages C49–C51)*

✓ Choose words whose connotations match your meaning.

✓ Use descriptive words that appeal to your reader's senses. *(pages C52–C53)*

SENTENCE COMBINING STRATEGIES

✓ Combine short, choppy sentences into longer, more interesting ones. *(pages C53–C54)*

✓ Use the coordinating conjunctions *and*, *but*, *or*, and *yet* to combine ideas of equal importance. *(page C56)*

✓ Combine by subordinating when you are joining two sentences of unequal importance. *(page C57)*

CREATING SENTENCE VARIETY

✓ Use sentence combining to vary the lengths of your sentences. *(pages C53–C55)*

✓ Vary the beginnings of your sentences. *(page C59)*

WRITING CONCISE SENTENCES

✓ Break up long, rambling sentences into shorter ones. *(page C63)*

✓ Avoid unnecessary repetition. *(page C64)*

✓ Eliminate empty expressions. *(pages C64–C65)*

A Writer Writes

A Radio Advertisement

Purpose: **to persuade listeners to buy your product**

Audience: **teen-age radio listeners**

Prewriting

Using clustering, brainstorming, or freewriting, think of products you use often and genuinely like. When you have thought of between 10 and 20 products, choose the one you like the most. Brainstorm a list of all the reasons you like that product. Also make a cluster to think of sensory words that could describe your product. Write one general statement that sums up in your mind why that product is so good.

Drafting

Use the statement you wrote as the first sentence in a short advertisement. Refer to your other notes to expand on the virtues of the product with specific reasons and sensory words. Remember you are trying to persuade people. Add a strong conclusion, possibly in the form of a slogan.

Revising

Remember that your audience will be listening to rather than reading your advertisement. Read it aloud to see if it conveys enough power to persuade. Are your words specific and lively? Do they appeal to the senses? Are your sentences varied? Do any sound choppy? If so, combine sentences to improve the flow.

Using *A Writer Writes*

Objective

- **To write a persuasive advertisement**

EXPANDING THE LESSON

Using Technology

You will find additional **instructional** and **practice** materials for this chapter at http://www.bkenglish.com.

YOUR IDEAS
For Media In the Classroom

Then read your ad to a "test" listener. Ask that person whether he or she would be "sold." As appropriate, use your listener's comments to improve your ad.

Editing

Check your work for errors in grammar or usage. Use the **Editing Checklist** on page C62 as a guide.

Publishing

Practice reading your ad with all the expression a good radio actor would use. Then deliver your ad to the class.

Connection Collection

Representing in Different Ways

From Print . . .

Dear Rocío,

Guatemala is amazing! For the last two days I have been staying in Panajachel, a beautiful village that rests on the shore of Lake Atitlán. From where I'm sitting on the shore, Lake Atitlán seems as expansive as the sea. As I write I am distracted by the cries of the local men and women who are selling blankets woven with brilliant red and orange thread. The smell of fresh tortillas carried in the air is making my stomach rumble. I have to go!

Sincerely,
Roberto

Rocío Marcos
3444 Path Way
Lubbock, TX 79401

. . . to Visuals Draw a picture, or find a photograph from a newspaper or magazine, that represents the details and style of the postcard above.

From Visuals . . .

. . . to Print

You have just spent a hot summer day at the beach. Write a postcard to a friend that captures the style of the photograph above.

- **Which strategies can be used for creating both written and visual representations? Which strategies apply to one, not both? Which type of representation is more effective?**
- **Draw a conclusion and write briefly about the differences between written ideas and visual representations.**

FOR REVIEWING SKILLS

Using *Connection Collection*

Representing in Different Ways

Consider using these print and visual activities to make students aware of the benefits of using different media to suit particular purposes. Help students understand when a visual medium, for example, is better suited to their purpose than a print medium, or the reverse.

YOUR IDEAS

For Viewing and Representing

Using *Connection Collection*

Consider using these writings prompts as independent or small-group activities.

GETTING STUDENTS INVOLVED

Cooperative Learning

After organizing students into groups, thoroughly explain the task to be accomplished and establish a time frame. Make sure that each group member is responsible for a given task. Have each group share its project with the class and discuss the process the group used to carry out the assignment.

YOUR IDEAS

For Writing Prompts

Writing in Everyday Life

Postcard to a Friend

Your father has recently taken a knitting course and is proud of his new ability—so proud that he has knitted matching sweaters for you and your sister. Unfortunately, the sweaters are hideous-looking. Nevertheless, you and your sister wore them to school yesterday because you appreciate his effort.

Write a postcard to a friend describing the sweaters in vivid details. Appeal to all five senses—sight, smell, sound, touch, and taste—in this description. Use specific details, and include at least one comparison into your description.

What strategies did you use to help your friend see the sweaters as vividly as possible?

Writing in the Workplace

Poster for a Picnic

The large company you work for is having its annual picnic, and you are on the publicity committee. In previous years the company has had trouble getting employees to come to the picnic. This year the publicity committee is putting all its energy into a poster with an appealing photograph of a big field surrounded by huge trees.

Write the text for the committee's poster aimed at persuading your fellow employees to attend the picnic. List the main events of the picnic and describe them using sensory language and specific details. Be sure to vary your sentence structure by beginning your sentences in different ways. Check your work for subject-verb agreement.

What strategies did you use to make the picnic sound attractive to your coworkers?

A DIFFERENT DELIVERY SYSTEM

For formal assessment print the composition chapter test from the *BK English* Test Bank at http://www.bkenglish.com.

Assess Your Learning

The day was bright outside. The sun was shining. The birds were singing. I walked along, thinking of all the things I was going to do that day. In the afternoon I was going to a game with my sister, and then we were going out to eat. That night there was a party at this one boy's house. But before all that I had to do this school project that involved some complicated things. So even though the day was nice, I could not really enjoy it.

▶ **Twenty general words and phrases are underlined in the passage above. Revise the passage by replacing each general word or phrase with a specific noun, verb, adjective, or adverb. In addition, vary the sentences by combining specific details and using conjunctions and subordinate clauses.**

Before You Write **Consider the following questions:**
What is the ***subject?***
What is the ***occasion?***
Who is the ***audience?***
What is the ***purpose?***

After You Write **Evaluate your work using the following criteria:**

- Have you substituted interesting, vivid words for bland ones?
- Have you provided specific details to illustrate the general words and phrases?
- Have you appealed to all of the reader's senses—sight, smell, sound, touch, and taste?
- Have you varied your sentence structure?
- Do you have subject-verb agreement in all your sentences?
- Have you proofread for spelling, capitalization, and punctuation errors?

Write briefly on how well you did. Point out your strengths and areas for improvement.

FOR ASSESSING LEARNING

Using *Assess Your Learning*

This writing prompt will help you and your students informally assess their developing writing abilities, using the accompanying primary trait rubrics, which list the key features and qualities of vivid, clear writing taught in this chapter. You may want to have students maintain their self-assessment in their portfolios as a record of their individual progress throughout the year.

YOUR IDEAS

For Informal Assessment

TEACHING SUGGESTIONS

Essential Knowledge and Skills

- Comparing oral traditions across regions and cultures
- Writing to express, discover, record, develop, reflect on ideas, and to problem solve
- Producing cohesive and coherent texts by organizing ideas, using effective transitions, and choosing precise wording
- Using adverbs appropriately to make writing vivid or precise
- Applying criteria to evaluate writing
- Using media to compare ideas and points of view

CHAPTER 3

Writing Well-Structured Paragraphs

When you write a paragraph, think of yourself as a builder: each of your words is a brick, and your sentences are the lines of bricks that become walls. Writing one paragraph is like building a little room of words. Write a story with many paragraphs and you create a whole castle.

Both writing and building require careful planning. You cannot build a castle by stacking bricks any which way; its walls will not stand if they are not properly constructed. A paragraph also needs a certain structure to support it.

Like buildings, paragraphs are the unique ideas of their creators. As each building has a certain look and mood and purpose, so will every paragraph that you create.

Reading with a Writer's Eye

The following excerpt from *The Miracle of Language* by Richard Lederer is a composition about using short words. Read the excerpt once through to grasp the author's point. As you reread, ask yourself if Lederer puts his arguments into practice.

BLOCK SCHEDULING

- If your schedule requires that you cover the chapter in a **shorter time,** use the selection from *The Miracle of Language,* Thinking as a Writer, and Developing Your Paragraph Writing Skills.
- If you want to take advantage of **longer class time,** use Grammar in the Writing Process and A Writer Writes in addition to the foregoing features.

FROM

The Miracle of Language

The Case for Short Words

Richard Lederer

When you speak and write, there is no law that says you have to use big words. Short words are as good as long ones, and short, old words—like *sun* and *grass* and *home*—are best of all. A lot of small words, more than you might think, can meet your needs with a strength, grace, and charm that large words do not have.

Big words can make the way dark for those who read what you write and hear what you say. Small words cast their clear light on big things—night and day, love and hate, war and peace, and life and death. Big words at times seem strange to the eye and the ear and the mind and the heart. Small words are the ones we seem to have known from the time we were born, like the hearth fire that warms the home.

Short words are bright like sparks that glow in the night, prompt like the dawn that greets the day, sharp like the blade of a knife, hot like salt tears that scald the cheek, quick like moths that flit from flame to flame, and terse like the dart and sting of a bee.

Here is a sound rule: Use small, old words where you can. If a long word says just what you want to say, do not fear to use it. But know that our tongue is rich in crisp, brisk, swift, short words. Make them the spine and the heart of what you speak and write. Short words are like fast friends. They will not let you down.

FOR INCREASING STUDENT ACHIEVEMENT

GUIDED READING

Text Analysis

- This example of **exposition** uses **strong, specific verbs** such as *cast, glow, scald,* and *flit.* Though each word is short, it is very concrete.
- The writer uses **similes** to describe the impact of small words. He compares small words to hearth fires, sparks, the dawn, a knife, salt tears, moths, and bees.
- He uses **contrasts** in the beginnings of the sentences in the second paragraph. The first and third sentences begin "Big words." The second and fourth sentences begin "Small words."
- The first two sentences and the last two sentences of the excerpt express the **main point** clearly.

Strategy: Rereading

Ask students to read the passage twice: the first time reading for understanding, the second time reading for a specific purpose. Ask students to find the longest word in the selection (paragraph 1– *strength*).

SELECTION AMENDMENT
Description of change: excerpted
Rationale: to focus on the concept of paragraph structure as presented in this chapter

ADDITIONAL RESOURCES

Composition Skills Practice. . . . . pages 15–20
Transparency Tools VR2
Connection Collection . . . . pages C94–C96
ESL Practice and Test Preparation . . . . . pages 15–21
Writers at Work . . . . 8•1–8•10
Assessment: Chapter Test. . . . . pages 41–46
Assessment Resources . . . . pages 1–10, 13–44

Using *Thinking as a Writer*

You may choose to have students respond to the questions either orally or in writing.

READER RESPONSE

You may want to use the following questions to elicit students' personal responses to the selection.

1. What examples can you think of from music, advertising, or other areas that show the power of short words?
2. Who are some people, particularly writers, who you think should read this excerpt from Lederer?

LITERARY CONNECTION

You might want to explore writing well-structured paragraphs in the following works, which appear in literature textbooks at this grade level.

- "Choice: A Tribute to Dr. Martin Luther King, Jr." by Alice Walker
- "Finding America" by A. C. Greene
- "The Old Grandfather and His Little Grandson" by Leo Tolstoy
- *Undaunted Courage* by Stephen E. Ambrose

REACHING ALL STUDENTS

English Language Learners

Pair one student who is learning English with another student who is proficient in English. Have the two compare the words they know that identify and describe the images in the picture.

Thinking as a Writer

Evaluating Structure

Richard Lederer limited himself to short words in writing about short words—a clever structural idea.

- What is the main idea of each paragraph?
- How has Lederer tried to prove each main idea?
- Was Lederer successful in proving his overall main idea? Why or why not?

Developing Main Ideas

Oral Expression

- Brainstorm with a small group to come up with a main idea for a paragraph. Take turns saying aloud sentences that support this main idea. Try to have each sentence build on the one before it. Listen as others speak.
- How successful was your group at developing its main idea? Were examples and descriptions used effectively?

Connecting Words and Images

Viewing

- Study this photograph. Then write a list of every one-syllable word you can think of that the photograph brings to mind. Then do the same with two-syllable words.
- Using your lists, describe what you see. Do your words match the feeling of the photograph?

FOR DEVELOPING SKILLS

LESSON 1 *(pages C75–C79)*

OBJECTIVES

- **To understand paragraph structure and its components of topic sentences, supporting sentences, and concluding sentences**
- **To practice writing topic sentences**

Create Interest

Ask each student to make a list of four items, three of which go together. Ask students to read their lists to the class, and have other students determine which of the items does not belong with the others. For example, in the list *cat, dog, turtle,* and *lion,* three of the animals are common pets, but the lion is not. Explain how well-written paragraphs include only those items that go together.

Developing Your Paragraph Writing Skills

"Good writing is clear thinking made visible," says the writer Bill Wheeler. Readers appreciate it when a writer has made his or her thoughts clear. A paragraph is a unit of thought. It can be part of a long composition, or it can stand alone as a short composition, complete within itself. However it is used, a paragraph always sticks to one main idea—the general point the paragraph is trying to make.

A **paragraph** is a group of related sentences that present and develop one main idea.

Paragraph Structure

Most paragraphs that stand alone consist of three main types of sentences. These are the topic sentence, the supporting sentences, and the concluding sentence. Each type of sentence performs a special function in a paragraph. Review the chart below.

STRUCTURE OF A PARAGRAPH	
TOPIC SENTENCE	states the main idea
SUPPORTING SENTENCES	expand on the main idea with specific facts, examples, details, or reasons
CONCLUDING SENTENCE	provides a strong ending

In the paragraph on the following page, notice how all the other sentences relate directly to the main idea stated in the topic sentence.

USING STUDENTS' STRENGTHS

Multiple Intelligences: Musical

Musical works are often structured like paragraphs. They frequently begin with a general statement of the main theme of the piece. The middle section then develops on the main theme. It is usually the longest part of the piece. The end of the piece provides a conclusion, often with a dramatic flourish. You may wish to ask students who have a portable keyboard and can play it well to perform a sample of music organized like a paragraph for the class.

GETTING STUDENTS INVOLVED

Reciprocal Teaching

Have students work with a partner to develop their understanding of topic, supporting, and concluding sentences. Each student should write five sentences about a specific topic and read them to a partner. The partner should explain whether each sentence would work well as a topic, supporting, or concluding sentence and answer these questions:

1. If it is a topic sentence, what information would they expect to read in the rest of the paragraph?
2. If it is a supporting sentence, what would the topic sentence of the paragraph be?
3. If it is a concluding sentence, what information would it follow?
4. Point out to students that some sentences will work well in more than one category.

Guide Instruction

By Modeling Strategies

Give students a sample topic sentence and discuss what information would fit in the same paragraph. An example topic sentence might be, "Our school is the best one in the region." Students could discuss the academic program, extra-curricular activities, student achievements, qualifications of the faculty, the building's physical structure, or other aspects of the school.

Consolidate Skills

Through Guided Practice

The **Practice Your Skills** activity on choosing a topic sentence gives students opportunities to identify topic sentences. To give students additional practice, ask them to find paragraphs in other parts of this book. Take turns reading the paragraphs aloud. Help students identify the topic sentence in each one. Discuss how each topic sentence indicates the main idea of the paragraph. Point out that the other sentences in each paragraph support the idea in the topic sentence.

USING STUDENTS' STRENGTHS

Multiple Intelligences: Spatial

Have students sketch pie graphs representing what portions of the paragraph "The Man Who Rode the Thunder" are the topic sentence, the supporting sentences, and the concluding sentence. The diagrams might take the shape of a circle, with a large section and two small sections. Help students understand that these proportions are common in paragraphs.

REACHING ALL STUDENTS

Struggling Learners

If students have difficulty picking out topic sentences, ask them to choose the one sentence in the paragraph they would memorize if they wanted to recall all of the details of the paragraph. Usually, this will be the topic sentence because it is the sentence that best summarizes the paragraph's main idea.

Model: Paragraph Structure

The Man Who Rode the Thunder

TOPIC SENTENCE

SUPPORTING SENTENCES

CONCLUDING SENTENCE

Marine pilot William Rankin made history in 1959 when he survived a nine-mile fall from the sky. Over Norfolk, Virginia, Rankin had engine trouble and had to eject himself from his plane. After he had fallen for about eight minutes, his parachute opened perfectly. To his dismay, however, he found himself in the middle of a thunderstorm. The strong winds kept driving him up instead of down toward the earth. For forty minutes Rankin was tossed by fierce winds and surrounded by blasts of thunder and sheets of lightning. Finally he reached the ground, frostbitten and injured, but alive. Soon after, newspapers all around the world honored "the man who rode the thunder."

The main idea in this paragraph is that William Rankin survived a nine-mile fall. The rest of the paragraph backs up that main idea by providing the startling details. Each time you write a paragraph that stands alone, you will be going through the writing process—planning, drafting, and polishing. The result, a well-structured paragraph with vivid words and smooth, concise sentences, should be as satisfying to read as it was to write.

Your Writer's Journal

Write freely about typical scenes of your everyday life that you would like to capture in words and remember in future years. When you have finished, go back and circle specific details, examples, or experiences that could best be used as supporting details if you were going to write a paragraph about any of these scenes.

Apply to Communication

Through Independent Writing

The **Communicate Your Ideas** activity on topic sentences prompts students to generate topic sentences for a "cheer-up" booklet. Have them review their topic sentences to make sure that they can think of several supporting concepts for each one. If they cannot, then they should consider revising the topic sentence to make it broader.

Transfer to Everyday Life

By Evaluating News Reports

Ask students to bring to class examples of articles in newspapers or magazines. Identify topic sentences in the paragraphs. Ask students how they would read the story if the topic sentences were omitted. Discuss whether these sentences convey information and whether they make other sentences easier to understand. Note that topic sentences often provide the context for information presented in the rest of the paragraph.

Topic Sentence

The topic sentence is usually more general than the other sentences in a paragraph. It may be at the beginning, at the end, or in the middle of a paragraph. The purpose of the topic sentence is to focus the reader's attention on the main idea.

The **topic sentence** states the main idea of the paragraph.

Although a topic sentence is usually more general than the other sentences, it also serves to limit a paragraph to one specific subject. The following paragraph begins with a very general sentence. The second sentence, which is the topic sentence, limits the broad subject to one specific aspect.

Model: Topic Sentence

The Emperor's Feet

The bitterly cold climate of Antarctica is hostile to many forms of life. Even the emperor penguin, which thrives in the cold, has had to develop unusual behaviors to hatch a chick. If an egg were allowed to touch the frozen ground, the developing chick inside would not survive. To protect the chick, the male penguin carries the egg on his feet, tucking it under the feathers on his body. For two months, while the female penguin is away storing food in her belly, the male goes nowhere without the egg on his feet. Cuddled securely in the male's warmth, the chick can survive until hatching. At that time the mother returns and takes over the care of her newborn chick. Even then the down-covered chick needs its mother's feet and feathers to shield it from the frigid weather of Antarctica.

Topic Sentence

IDENTIFYING COMMON STUMBLING BLOCKS

Problem

- Finding the topic sentence, particularly if it is not the first sentence

Solution

- Ask students to edit the paragraph down to five key words. Then identify which sentence best expresses those words.

YOUR IDEAS

For Identifying Topic Sentences

Pull It All Together

By Sharing

Have students work with partners to write a summary of what they know about topic sentences. Students should discuss the function of topic sentences as well as the qualities that make a good topic sentence. Ask students to present their summaries to the class.

Check Understanding

By Evaluating Topic Sentences

Read excerpts from various library books or textbooks. Ask students to identify the topic sentence in each paragraph. Discuss whether students think the topic sentences work well. After students have heard several excerpts from various books, discuss whether they noticed any patterns. Which book used topic sentences most effectively?

HOME WORK

Ask students to write one-paragraph biographies of people they admire. Students may choose famous people, family members, or people from history. Each paragraph should begin with a topic sentence that expresses the student's perspective of the individual.

Practice Your Skills Sample Answers

1. c. Rapid transit systems are more efficient than expressways in moving great numbers of people.
2. a. The day the sound barrier was broken was a milestone in aviation history.

Practice Your Skills

Choosing a Topic Sentence

Read each paragraph. Choose the sentence that would be the best topic sentence.

1. *Moving People*

A city train system can move 60,000 people an hour on each line. Expressways can manage only about 2,000 cars an hour in each lane. If the average number of passengers in each car is one and a half, the total number of people moved is only 3,000 an hour in each lane. Rapid transit systems, then, can move 20 times more people in the same amount of space.

a. More and more people are riding subways.

b. Many cities are encouraging people to join car pools in order to cut down on traffic.

c. Rapid transit systems are more efficient than expressways in moving great numbers of people.

2. *Breaking the Sound Barrier*

On October 14, 1947, test pilot Chuck Yeager was ready to fly a new jet to see if it could travel faster than the speed of sound. Until then many people had believed that a plane would be destroyed if it tried to go faster than the speed of sound. Yeager took off confidently. Before long a thunderous blast was heard. The sound barrier had been broken, and Yeager brought the plane down safely.

a. The day the sound barrier was broken was a milestone in aviation history.

b. When a plane accelerates beyond the speed of sound, a loud roar can be heard.

c. High-speed jet transport is taken for granted today.

LESSON 2 *(pages C79–C84)*

OBJECTIVES

- **To understand the role of supporting sentences in the body of a paragraph**
- **To practice writing sentences that support a topic sentence**

Create Interest

Write these two topic sentences on the board: 1. Young people today have it easier than did young people thirty years ago. 2. Growing up is harder today than it was thirty years ago. Have students brainstorm facts, opinions, or anecdotes that support one of these two topic sentences. Write them under the sentence they support.

Guide Instruction

By Connecting Ideas

Ask students to think of other examples of support. For example, a foundation supports a building, fans support a team, taxpayers support schools. Note that often the number of people or the

Writing Topic Sentences

Write one other possible topic sentence for each paragraph in the preceding activity.

Communicate Your Ideas

PREWRITING *Topic Sentence*

Imagine that a classmate had his appendix out and will miss school for a week. You and your classmates have decided to write him a "cheer-up" booklet. Think of times when you were sick and had to stay in bed. Also scan your memory for what you know about patients who have been hospitalized. Brainstorm, cluster, or freewrite to think of things that would cheer up your friend. After reviewing your notes, write a general statement that connects and clarifies your ideas. Use your general statement to write the topic sentence of a paragraph. Save your work in your writing folder to continue developing into a paragraph later.

SAVE YOUR WORK

Writing Tip

Check the **topic sentences** in your paragraphs to make sure they express the most meaningful generalizations possible from the specifics you include.

Supporting Sentences

Supporting sentences make up the body of a paragraph. Their purpose is to back up the main idea in the topic sentence with specific information.

Supporting sentences explain or prove a topic sentence with specific details, facts, examples, or reasons.

PRACTICE YOUR SKILLS Sample Answers

1. Citizens concerned about congestion should support construction of rapid transit systems.
2. Chuck Yeager's bravery won him a place in the history books.

TIMESAVER *QuickCheck*

Have students read their topic sentences and make sure they create a single overall impression. Ask students whether their sentences are broad enough to cover the sentiments they want in their letter. Also note whether sentences are clear enough to provide a focus for a paragraph.

amount of material providing support is greater than what is supported. Point out that in a well-constructed paragraph, a topic sentence provides the main idea, but that several sentences provide support for it.

Consolidate Skills

Through Guided Practice

The **Practice Your Skills** activity about writing supporting sentences provides students an opportunity to brainstorm ideas and write supporting sentences. You can expand this activity by asking students to suggest additional topic sentences for the class to work on. To challenge students, propose a topic sentence that many students may disagree with, such as, "Intelligent life exists on other planets," or "Schools should give more homework."

Using *Writing Is Thinking*

Objective

- **To understand and practice creating generalizations**

A DIFFERENT APPROACH

Auditory Ask students to listen to a radio station that plays music that they do not usually listen to. Ask them to listen to at least three different selections, and try to write a generalization about the music they hear. They should try to identify specific traits of the music that characterize it, such as the rhythm, lyrics, or instruments.

THINKING PRACTICE Evaluation Guidelines
Strong responses will make the connection between too much sugar on breakfast cereal and health problems. Average responses will mention cereals, sugar, weight gain, and tooth decay. Weak responses will mention only some of these points.

Thinking Skills	
Classifying	Analyzing
Comparing	Hypothesizing
Generalizing	Synthesizing
Inferring	Summarizing
Imagining	Setting Goals
Observing	Evaluating Audience
Predicting	

Writing Is Thinking

Generalizing

The topic sentence you write in a paragraph is a kind of generalization. A **generalization** is an overall idea that explains specific facts, examples, or instances. You have been forming generalizations all your life. For example, the first time you roller-skated over a crack in the sidewalk, you may have fallen down. Without previous experience, you might not know that there is a relationship between the crack in the sidewalk and losing your balance. Then you begin to notice that your friends sometimes fall when they try to go over a crack. Maybe you try it again and fall again. By this time you might conclude from your experience that skating over cracks is dangerous. That general idea guides you to avoid big sidewalk cracks.

The general idea in a paragraph is the topic sentence. Its purpose is to explain the specific facts, examples, or instances you relate in the rest of the paragraph. As a general statement, it clarifies the details by stating a broad idea that connects them.

THINKING PRACTICE

Read the following facts. Then write a general statement that connects them in a meaningful way.

- Many breakfast cereals contain sugar.
- People often add even more sugar.
- Sugar adds calories but no nutrients.
- Excess calories lead to unhealthy weight gain.
- Sugar promotes tooth decay.

Apply to Communication

Through Independent Writing

Write a topic sentence on the board. Have students work independently to write supporting sentences to develop a paragraph. Encourage them to create a range of supporting sentences, including facts, opinions, examples, and anecdotes, for the topic sentence.

Transfer to Everyday Life

By Describing a Place

Have students practice developing supporting sentences by describing a place about which they have a strong feeling. The place might be a city, a park, or a room. The topic sentence should summarize their attitude toward the place. The supporting sentences should describe each element of the place.

Pull It All Together

By Reflecting

Ask students how their writing skills have improved over the last five years. To help them recall how they wrote years ago, students with younger brothers or sisters might be able to

Writing Tip

Check the topic sentence in your paragraph to make sure it expresses the most meaningful **generalization** possible from the specifics you include.

Supporting sentences also provide answers to questions that readers might have about the topic sentence. Read the following topic sentence. Think of questions that you would expect the supporting sentences to answer.

TOPIC SENTENCE People who lived in pioneer days would never have believed that world news could be received as quickly as it is today.

Most readers would probably want to know how news traveled during pioneer days and how news travels today. The supporting sentences answer these questions. They provide facts and examples that relate to the main idea.

MODEL: Supporting Sentences

Changes in News Communication

TOPIC SENTENCE

People who lived in pioneer days would never have believed that world news could be received as quickly as it is today.

SUPPORTING SENTENCES

In early days newspapers were often several months old by the time they reached a settlement. Letters were carried by travelers who happened to be going in the right direction and often were received months after they were sent, or not at all. Today by radio, television, newspapers, and the Internet, we get world news almost at once. Letters are carried to distant countries overnight.

CONCLUDING SENTENCE

It is hard to believe that such changes have taken place in less than 100 years.

DEVELOPING WORKPLACE COMPETENCIES

Thinking Skills: Knowing How to Learn

Tell students that although receiving news instantly via E-mail, telephone, fax, television, Internet, and radio does not astound us now, we might well be astounded by the advances of the future. Ask students what the people of 2200 might be able to do that seems impossible to us today. Ask students to think of all the technology they use on a day-to-day basis that didn't exist 100 years ago. As technology continues to progress, businesses will continue to require employees who can use the latest technology. Point out that employees in the workplace must be able to use advanced technology.

describe how their siblings write. A short essay by a third-grade student may read like a collection of topic sentences: general assertions with few specifics or examples to support them. Help students understand that one way they have improved is that as they have gotten older, they have learned to support their ideas more fully.

Check Understanding

By Using a Newspaper Editorial

Read students a newspaper editorial. Ask them to identify the topic sentence and supporting ideas. Discuss whether the support is strong or weak. Ask students to suggest other supporting information.

TIMESAVER *QuickCheck*

Ask students to exchange papers and assess the work of one of their peers. Have students note whether the topic sentence expresses the main idea of the paragraph.

HOME STUDY

Have students find an example of a well-written paragraph in a book, newspaper, magazine, or catalog. They should write a brief analysis of the paragraph, identifying its topic sentence and explaining how the other sentences support it. They should also suggest any revisions that they think would strengthen the paragraph.

HOME WORK

Have students imagine that they are food critics for the newspaper, and they are evaluating a meal at their home. Their review should include a topic sentence and at least four supporting sentences describing the food and the atmosphere of the meal.

PRACTICE YOUR SKILLS Sample Answers

1. **The common cold has several annoying symptoms.**

   A sore throat is often the first sign of a cold.

   Sneezing keeps you grabbing for the tissues.

   It is hard to sleep because of sinus congestion.

2. **Many forms of exercise are good for the heart and lungs.**

   Running is vigorous, demanding exercise.

   Swimming is excellent, particularly for

PRACTICE YOUR SKILLS

Using a Pyramid to Write Supporting Sentences

Write each topic sentence. Then develop at least three supporting sentences for each one. Using a pyramid like the one below, brainstorm a list of specific facts, examples, or details that expand on each general statement. Use these details to write the supporting sentences.

1. The common cold has several annoying symptoms.
2. Many forms of exercise are good for the body.
3. My favorite holiday is . . .

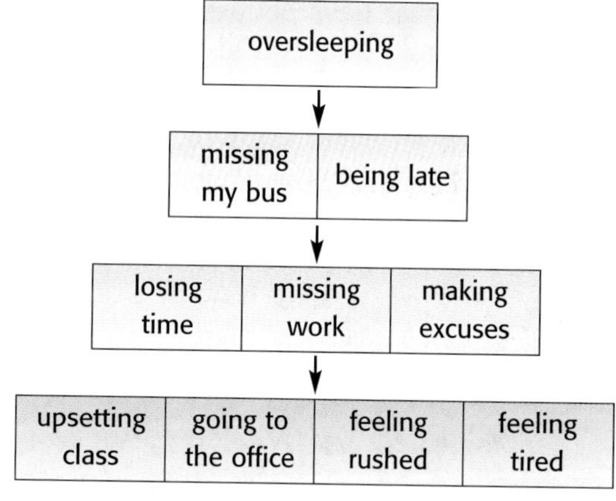

Communicate Your Ideas

DRAFTING *Body of Your Paragraph*

Review the topic sentence you wrote for your "cheer-up" booklet. Also review your prewriting notes. Write the topic sentence, indented, on the first line of a fresh piece of paper. Then draft the body of your paragraph, adding supporting sentences to back up your main idea. Save your work for later use.

Movie Review

Movie reviews can be excellent examples of well-structured writing because they tend to follow a predictable pattern. First they tell you what the movie is about without giving away the ending. Then they point out aspects of the film that the reviewer felt either worked or did not. They might also discuss the actors' performances or the way the movie was filmed or edited. Movie reviews can be crucial in persuading people whether they should see a movie.

Media Activity

Choose a movie from the media center or rent one from a video store. Then write a movie review using the guidelines below.

Give a basic plot description. Be very careful not to give too much away or even to hint at some event that should remain a secret to the audience. Then use the following guidelines to help you.

Guidelines for Movie Criticism

- Was the movie fast-paced or slow?
- What lighting or camera angles were used? Were they effective?
- Were the actors' performances moving? Why or why not?
- How did the setting affect the feeling of the movie?
- Was the script well written? Did you believe what people were saying?
- Describe the use of special effects.

The last few sentences of the review should sum up your overall evaluation of the movie in a way that lets the reader know if they should see it. Share your review with your classmates.

IN THE MEDIA

Using *In the Media*

Objective

- **To evaluate what makes a good movie review**

Group Project

- Divide students into small groups. Each group should select a movie to review collectively. They might select a movie from the school collection or from a rental store. After all students in the group have seen the movie, members of the group should discuss what they want to say in their review and write it. Then they should watch the movie again, revise their review if needed, and complete a final version to share with the class.

FYI

Website to Visit The Movie Review Query Engine at http://www.mrqe.com/ includes links to a wide range of movie reviews, including some from outside the United States. The site is easy to use. It can be searched by movie title and often includes links to more than 100 reviews for a movie. It includes recent mass-market releases, classics, and independent films.

HOME WORK

Ask students to copy a paragraph from another book or from a magazine, and add two more sentences to it. The new sentences should relate directly to the topic sentence. They might add new information or expand on existing information in the paragraph.

Practice Your Skills Sample Answers

"The Red Cross offers classes in emergency techniques."

"Computers are also used by doctors to help make diagnoses."

The topic sentence discusses Medic Alert bracelets, but neither of these sentences mentions these bracelets.

Unity

A paragraph has unity when all of the supporting sentences relate directly to the main idea. Paragraphs without unity include unrelated ideas that distract readers from the main point. Suppose you are writing a paragraph about tricks your dog can do. In the process of writing, you can sometimes lose your focus. You may be led to include other details about your dog, such as where and when you got him, or what his favorite foods are. Although these relate to your dog generally, they probably do not belong in a paragraph about the tricks your dog can do.

Achieve **unity** by making sure all the supporting sentences relate directly the topic sentence.

Practice Your Skills

Deleting Unrelated Ideas

In the following paragraph, two sentences do not relate directly to the topic sentence. Write these sentences. Then write a statement that tells why you believe the additional two sentences do not support the main idea.

Medic Alert Saves Lives

The Medic Alert bracelet was designed to help people with medical problems in emergency situations. If the wearer of the bracelet is unconscious or otherwise unable to talk, the bracelet can tell medical workers what they need to know about the patient. On the back of the Medic Alert bracelet are listed the patient's medical problem, an identification number, and an

LESSON 3 *(pages C85–C91)*

OBJECTIVES

- **To practice using transitional words to create unity and coherence in a paragraph**
- **To understand the value of a strong concluding sentence in a paragraph**

Create Interest

Ask each student to write a sentence about basketball. They might write about a player, a game, a rule, or a feeling. Collect the sentences and read them aloud. As you read them, begin to group them into related topics. Point out that while they are all related to basketball, they would not all fit into the same paragraph.

emergency number. The Red Cross offers classes in emergency techniques. By dialing this telephone number, the medical workers can find out about the patient's special condition from a computer. Computers are also used by doctors to help make diagnoses. Knowing the patient's medical background can help the workers decide which treatment to provide and what kind of medication to give. In an emergency, a Medic Alert bracelet can become a lifesaver.

Coherence

Coherence in a paragraph is the quality that makes each sentence seem connected to all the others. One way to achieve coherence is to present ideas in a logical order. Another way is to use transitions. **Transitions** are words and phrases that show how ideas are related.

Achieve **coherence** by presenting ideas in logical order and using transitional words and phrases.

The following chart shows some common types of logical order and the transitions often used with them.

TRANSITIONS FOR DIFFERENT TYPES OF ORDER

Types of Order	Definition	Transitions
Chronological	The order in which events occur	first, second, third, before, after, next, on Tuesday, later, finally

IDENTIFYING COMMON STUMBLING BLOCKS

Problem

- Starting every sentence in a paragraph with the same transitional word or phrase

Solution

- Ask students to read their paragraph aloud. Listening to their sentences may remind them of the importance of variation in word choice and sentence structure. For example, instead of starting with *Then*, they could insert a short transitional sentence such as "The next step is crucial."

INTEGRATING TECHNOLOGY

Video

Have students videotape someone performing a simple action that includes several steps, such as making a sandwich or tying a knot. Each student should watch the videotape and describe the action in writing. After each individual is done, students can compare their paragraphs to see how each one explained the actions. You can find information on creating a video in A Writer's Guide to Electronic Publishing on pages C520–C545.

Guide Instruction

By Connecting Ideas

Discuss the difference between *unity* and *coherence* in a paragraph. Explain that unity of a paragraph means that all sentences relate directly to the main idea. Coherence in a paragraph means that each sentence is related to all the others. Discuss whether a paragraph could have one of these traits without the other. Can students imagine a paragraph in which all sentences relate to the topic sentence, but not to each other? Can students imagine a paragraph in which all sentences relate to each other, but some do not relate to the topic sentence?

Consolidate Skills

Through Guided Practice

The **Practice Your Skills** activity on improving coherence in a paragraph gives students opportunities to analyze a paragraph for coherence. For additional practice, ask students to bring to class books or magazines that they are reading. Instruct each student to select

REACHING ALL STUDENTS

Struggling Learners

Write the following words and phrases on the board:

Briefly	*Straight ahead*
Suddenly	*In the distance*
For instance	*Meanwhile*

Have students work in pairs. Instruct one student in each pair to write a sentence. Then have the partner write a follow-up sentence that begins with one of the words on the board. Students should take turns writing the initial sentence.

HOME WORK

Have students write a paragraph using order of importance, interest, or degree. They should use at least four transitions in their paragraph and underline each one.

PRACTICE YOUR SKILLS Sample Answers

Since fire engines must rush to arrive at a fire, all possible warning measures must be used to alert other drivers. For example, the siren is a warning measure. It is probably the other drivers' first clue that an emergency vehicle is approaching. Another warning device is the flashing light. Finally, very important in spotting a fire engine is its color. Although red trucks are the tradition, lime yellow fire trucks may ultimately prove to be safer. Firefighters in Detroit, Newark, and Kansas City have lime yellow fire trucks. Their accident rate is less than half that of firefighters in Miami, San Francisco, and other cities where red fire engines are used.

Spatial	Location or physical arrangement	left, right, in front of, behind, next to, to the south of
Order of Importance	Degree of importance, size, or interest	first, finally, in addition, smallest, largest, more/most important

Chronological order is used with events or stories to tell what happened first, next, and so on. It is also used when giving directions or the steps in a process. **Spatial order** is used in descriptions to show how objects are related in location. **Order of importance** is often used in paragraphs that explain or persuade.

PRACTICE YOUR SKILLS

Improving Paragraph Coherence

The following paragraph lacks transition words. It also presents some details out of order. On a separate paper, revise the paragraph to improve its coherence.

Spotting Fire Engines

Since fire engines must rush to arrive at a fire, all possible warning measures must be used to alert other drivers. Firefighters in Detroit, Newark, and Kansas City have lime-yellow fire trucks. Their accident rate is less than half that of firefighters in other cities where red fire engines are used. The siren is a warning measure. It is probably other drivers' first clue that an emergency vehicle is approaching. The flashing light is a warning device. Very important in spotting a fire engine is its color. Although red trucks are the tradition, lime-yellow fire trucks may ultimately prove to be safer.

a paragraph that includes at least six sentences. Students should identify the topic sentence and decide whether the paragraph has unity and coherence. Have students discuss their paragraph with a partner.

Apply to Communication

Through Independent Writing
Ask students to write a paragraph in spatial order describing a room in their home. Encourage them to consider various positions for viewing the room. How would the room look to someone entering a doorway? to a spider on the ceiling? to a mouse on the floor? Remind students to use words and phrases that will help the reader keep track of location.

Transfer to Everyday Life

By Writing a Story
Ask students to write a paragraph in chronological order describing the first time they attended school. Students may focus on the entire first day of

Adverbs

Many of the transitional words you use for paragraph coherence function as adverbs. An adverb is a word that modifies a verb, an adjective, or another adverb. Adverbs answer the questions *Where? When? How?* and *To what extent?*

EXAMPLES **Outside** the rain pattered **softly** against the windows. *(where?)*

Yesterday Ella had a great surprise. *(when?)* *(how?)*

Adverb Clauses

By using an adverb clause to extend the descriptive range of a simple adverb, you can vary the rhythm of your writing and enhance its expressive power. An **adverb clause** is a subordinate clause that modifies a verb, an adjective, or an adverb. Like an adverb, an adverb clause answers the questions *How? When? Where?* and *To what extent?* An adverb clause also answers the question *Under what condition?* or *Why?* The following examples, from Richard Lederer's "The Case for Short Words," illustrate the effective use of adverb clauses.

WHEN?	**When you speak and write,** there is no law that says you have to use big words.
WHERE?	Use small, old words **where you can.**
UNDER WHAT CONDITION?	**If a long word says just what you want to say**, do not fear to use it.

Using *Editing Workshop*

Objective

- **To understand the value of using adverbs effectively to make paragraphs more coherent**

A DIFFERENT APPROACH

Kinesthetic Ask students to list the adverbs they find in an article describing a physical activity, such as a dance step or a technique used in a sport. They should prepare to demonstrate how they would perform the activity differently if the adverbs were omitted from the description.

Visual Have students view a painting, poster, or other work of art, and describe in writing the order in which they viewed each part. Encourage them to use adverbs to make clear the path their eye traveled from element to element in the piece.

school, an activity, or a particular incident. Remind students to use words and phrases that help the reader keep the events in order.

Pull It All Together

By Summarizing

Divide students into groups of three or four. Ask students to write three topic sentences that could be supported with chronological order, three with spatial order, and three with order of importance. Have students discuss how they would organize the sentences in each set for coherence.

Check Understanding

By Using the Literary Selection

Return to the excerpt from *The Miracle of Language* by Richard Lederer. Ask students whether they think each of the paragraphs in the excerpt have unity and coherence.

GETTING STUDENTS INVOLVED

Group Discussion

Invite students to bring in examples of paragraph-long jokes they can share with the class. Ask students to read their jokes aloud. Discuss the structure of the jokes. Does the first line serve as a topic sentence? Do the middle sentences follow from the first sentence? Does the last line make the message complete? To emphasize the importance of the last line—the punch line—try reading some of the jokes, but omitting the last line.

Website to Visit For links to sites about the Rubik's cube, including several that have cubes to work on-screen and explanations of solutions, go to http://www.math.brown.edu/~reid/rubik/.

TIMESAVER *QuickCheck*

Ask students to read the first and last sentence of their paragraph. Students should see a clear connection between them. If none is evident, then encourage students to rewrite one or both sentences.

Concluding Sentence

Every good composition has a clear beginning, middle, and ending. In a single paragraph, the concluding sentence serves as the ending. It wraps up the ideas and makes the reader feel that the message is complete.

A **concluding sentence** adds a strong ending to a paragraph by summarizing, referring to the main idea, or adding an insight.

MODEL: Concluding Sentence

Solving the Rubik's Cube

TOPIC SENTENCE — Students at the University of Illinois invented the final answer to solving the Rubik's Cube.

SUPPORTING SENTENCES — Their invention is Robbie Rubik, a robot that can solve the cube in two-tenths of a second. Robbie's computer works very fast, but his mechanical hands work much slower. It takes Robbie about five to six minutes to make the 75 to 160 twists and turns needed to unscramble a cube.

CONCLUDING SENTENCE — Despite slow hand movements, Robbie can still solve the puzzle faster than any of its human inventors.

Communicate Your Ideas

DRAFTING *Concluding Sentence*

Return to the draft of the paragraph you have written. Add a strong concluding sentence to wrap up your thoughts. Save your work for later use. 

Time Out to Reflect

Review other paragraphs you have written and check them for unity and coherence. Is there anything you would like to change? Can you better organize your ideas? Have you always been able to make your "clear thinking" visible? What have you learned that will help you write better paragraphs in the future? Record your thoughts in your **journal**.

Communicate Your Ideas

REVISING *Unity and Coherence*

Use the checklist below to revise your paragraph. Look over your paragraph. Does it have unity? If not, cross out ideas that stray. Is your paragraph coherent? If not, add transitional words or rearrange ideas so that the flow of your ideas is smooth. Save your work.

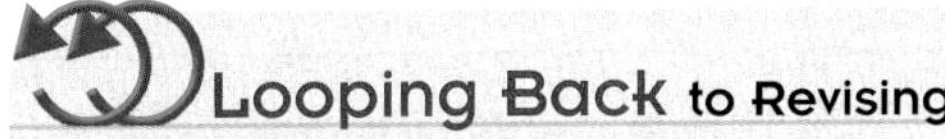

Adverbs add precision. Using them well also adds variety to the rhythm of your writing. Take this opportunity to experiment with adverbs to make your writing more expressive.

Evaluation Checklist for Revising

✓ Does your topic sentence introduce the subject and suggest your overall impression of it? *(page C77)*

✓ Do your supporting sentences supply specific details and sensory words that bring your subject to life? *(pages C79–C82)*

IDENTIFYING COMMON STUMBLING BLOCKS

Problem

- Writing a concluding sentence that sounds like it is repeating the topic sentence

Solution

- Have students rewrite their topic sentence twice. The first time, they should write it using one-half as many words. The second time, they should write it using twice as many words. After they have tried to condense and expand the topic sentence, they should be better prepared to write a concluding sentence that does not sound exactly like the topic sentence.

HOME WORK

Ask students to write a paragraph describing the importance of an activity they do. They might choose activities common to everyone, such as attending school or brushing teeth, or more specialized activities, such as playing chess or singing in a choir. Be sure their paragraphs include a strong concluding sentence.

TIMESAVER *QuickCheck*

Ask students to point out the transitional words in their paragraph. Students should be able to identify them easily. If they are not aware of which words are transitional, have them read their paragraph without these words.

TIMESAVER *QuickCheck*
Read students' paragraphs and make sure they have a topic sentence and a concluding sentence. A well-done paragraph will also include transitional words, as well as pertinent supporting sentences.

FYI

How to Use with Windows™ Highlight the text you wish to format, pull down the Format menu, and select either Font or Paragraph.

How to Use with Macintosh™ Highlight the text you wish to format, and then pull down the Format menu or the Font menu.

- ✓ Does your paragraph have unity of ideas and coherence? *(pages C84–C86)*
- ✓ Do you use adverbs to create smoother-flowing sentences? *(page C87)*
- ✓ Does your concluding sentence summarize and add meaning to your paragraph? *(pages C88–C89)*

Communicate Your Ideas

EDITING, PUBLISHING

Carefully edit your paragraph for errors in spelling, grammar, punctuation, and usage. Experiment with word choice to create a more vivid picture in your readers' minds. Pay attention to the use of adverbs for smoother-flowing sentences. When you are satisfied that you have found all your errors, prepare a neat final copy of your paragraph.

COMPUTER TIP

Use the Format feature on your word-processing program to set up line spacing, font type, and type size in your paragraph. Experiment with different layouts to find the one that creates an easy-to-read version of your work.

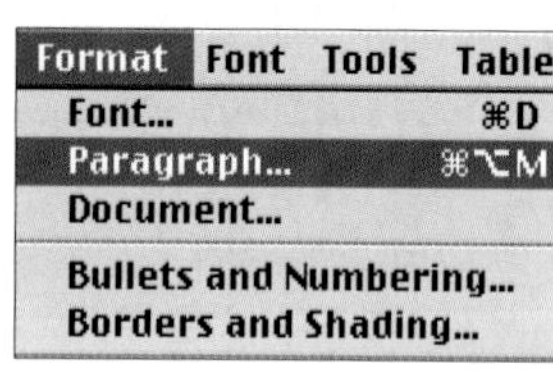

Process of Writing a Well-Structured Paragraph

Remember that the writing process is recursive—you can move back and forth among the stages of the process to achieve your purpose. For example, during editing, you may wish to return to the revising stage to add details that have occurred to you while editing. The numbers in parentheses refer to pages where you can get help with your writing.

- Choose a topic that interests you.
- Decide whether you are writing for yourself or another audience.
- Determine your purpose for writing.
- State the main idea of the paragraph in a topic sentence. *(page C77)*
- Use supporting sentences to back up the main idea with specific details and form the body of the paragraph. *(page C81)*
- Achieve unity by making sure all the supporting sentences relate directly to the topic sentence. *(page C84)*
- Achieve coherence by presenting ideas in a logical order and by using transitional words and phrases. *(page C85)*
- Add a strong statement to conclude your paragraph by summarizing, referring to the main idea, or adding an insight. *(page C88)*

YOUR IDEAS

For Using the Writing Process

Using *A Writer Writes*

Objectives

- **To write a news story that informs an audience about an event**
- **To write a fully developed paragraph that includes a topic sentence, supporting sentences, and a concluding sentence**

IDENTIFYING COMMON STUMBLING BLOCKS

Problem

- Thinking that no event a student has witnessed is worthy of community attention

Solution

- Students should list events they have seen or participated in that made them happy, sad, or angry. If they had a strong emotional reaction to an event, others probably did as well, and the event is appropriate to write about.

A Writer Writes

A News Story

Purpose: to inform

Audience: readers of your local paper

Prewriting

Imagine that you have been asked to report on an event that received community attention. It could be a fire, an accident, or a planned event, such as a fireworks display on the Fourth of July or a parade. Scan your memory through clustering, brainstorming, or freewriting to think of an event you have actually witnessed. Choose one you think holds the greatest interest for your readers. Assume that the event just happened yesterday. Think about what the event meant to you. Then develop a list of supporting details you would use in explaining why the event was important. These would include events, descriptive details, and any necessary background information. When you have finished developing your details, arrange them in a logical order.

Drafting

Look over your supporting ideas. Then write a general statement that serves as the topic sentence for your news story. In that statement, generalize about the importance or meaning of the event. Then write a fully developed paragraph, using your details in supporting sentences. Add a concluding sentence to make the story complete and wrap up your report.

Revising

Exchange papers with a classmate. Comment on your partner's work using the Evaluation Checklist for Revising on pages C89 and C90. Then use your reader's comments and your own judgment to improve your news story. Add, delete, substitute, and rearrange as needed.

Editing

Read your story again checking for errors in spelling, punctuation, grammar, and usage.

Publishing

Prepare a neat final copy of your story. Display your work as part of a bulletin board spread titled "News Around the Town."

YOUR IDEAS

For Publishing Students' News Stories

EXPANDING THE LESSON

Using Technology

You will find additional **instructional** and **practice** materials for this chapter at http://www.bkenglish.com.

FOR REVIEWING SKILLS

Using *Connection Collection*

Representing in Different Ways

Consider using these print and visual activities to make students aware of the benefits of using different media to suit particular purposes. Help students understand when a visual medium, for example, is better suited to their purpose than a print medium, or the reverse.

REACHING ALL STUDENTS

Struggling Learners

To help students who find designing a logo difficult, suggest they look at the advertisements in a magazine for ideas. Ask them to identify why certain logos catch their attention. Students should use these traits in their own logo.

Connection Collection

Representing in Different Ways

From Visuals . . .

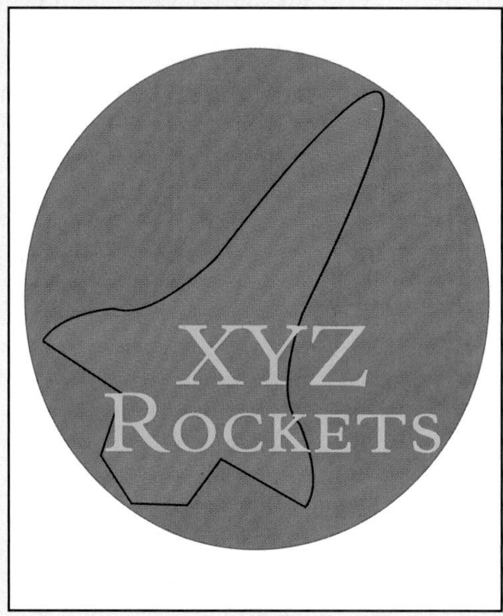

. . . to Print

This is a logo for the company XYZ Rockets, a manufacturer of spaceships. You have just designed this logo and have to present it to the board of directors for their approval. Write a paragraph explaining why this would be a good logo for the company. Remember to use a topic sentence, supporting sentences, and a concluding sentence.

From Print . . .

Here at Squiggly Marshmallows, we are not afraid to go against current trends. Instead of following the crowd, we have designed a line of marshmallows for cooking that come in a myriad of animal shapes and colors. We use only natural food coloring and pure unrefined sugar in all our products. Best of all, our standard-size White Zebras cost less than the standard sizes of Puffy Pillow and Silky White brands! Pick up a bag of Squiggly Marshmallows today!

. . . to Visuals

From the information in the above paragraph, design a logo for this company. Name the company anything you like. You are also free to make up a different product for the company to produce. Include that product in your logo if you wish.

- **Which strategies can be used for creating both written and visual representations? Which strategies apply to one, not both? Which type of representation is more effective?**
- **Draw a conclusion and write briefly about the differences between written ideas and visual representations.**

GETTING STUDENTS INVOLVED

Cooperative Learning

After organizing students into groups, thoroughly explain the task to be accomplished and establish a time frame. Make sure that each group member is responsible for a given task. Have each group share its project with the class and discuss the process the group used to carry out the assignment.

Using *Connection Collection*

Consider using these writing prompts as independent or small-group activities.

USING STUDENTS' STRENGTHS

Multiple Intelligences: Spatial

Invite students to create a Venn diagram comparing the benefits of participating in drama and in pottery making by drawing two circles that partly overlap. In one circle, list the benefits of joining the drama group; in the other list the benefits of taking a pottery class. List benefits of both in the area where the circles overlap.

GETTING STUDENTS INVOLVED

Cooperative Learning

Students could develop their oral presentation as part of a group. Each student in the group might research different countries within a region, such as countries in western Africa, eastern Europe, or southeastern Asia. Students should share information with one another and attempt to cover some of the same topics. For example, all students might research the languages and religions of their country. Then when presenting their oral report, groups could compare and contrast the countries.

Writing in Everyday Life

E-mail to a Friend

Your friend who lives in Texas is trying to decide between taking a pottery class or acting in the drama club's productions after school. You have been a member of both groups at different times but have enjoyed drama more. Knowing your friend's interests, you think she will probably enjoy the drama group, too.

Compose an E-mail to your friend, persuading her in one paragraph to join the drama group. Make sure you include a topic sentence, supporting sentences, and a concluding sentence.

What strategies did you use to persuade your friend?

You can find information on writing E-mails in A Writer's Guide to Using the Internet.

Writing for Oral Communication

Presentation

You have returned from a trip to the island of Sippa Moka, where you studied the ancient people called the Zippygenes. The principal of Mable Maplepost Middle School has asked you to give a presentation to the students describing your adventures.

Prepare a report to be delivered to the Mable Maplepost Middle School students. Include information about the culture and any regional sayings that would be interesting to your audience.

What strategies did you use to present your adventures to the students?

You can find information on making presentations on pages C411–C424.

A DIFFERENT DELIVERY SYSTEM

For formal assessment print the composition chapter test from the *BK English* Test Bank at http://www.bkenglish.com.

Assess Your Learning

An online magazine and Website called *Techno Wizard* is looking for submissions for a new project called "How to Do Just About Anything." Your class has decided to vote on its three best paragraphs to send to *Techno Wizard*. Each student has been asked to write about how to perform a task he or she can do well. The winning paragraph will be published online!

- **Write a paragraph to send to *Techno Wizard,* in which you explain how to do a specific activity. It can be playing a sport or game, creating a craft project, building a model or a Website, or performing an experiment. Present your information in a clear, logical manner with smooth transitions.**
- **Be sure to organize your thoughts and sentences so that they flow smoothly and make sense.**

Before You Write **Consider the following questions:**
What is the ***subject?***
What is the ***occasion?***
Who is the ***audience?***
What is the ***purpose?***

After You Write **Evaluate your work using the following criteria:**

- Did you write a clear topic sentence, supporting sentences, and a conclusion that sums up your main ideas?
- Have you expanded on the topic sentence with specific facts, examples, details, and reasons?
- Have you made smooth transitions from one idea to the next?
- Did you keep your audience in mind as you wrote your paragraph?
- Did you organize your ideas and present them in a logical order?
- Does your paragraph have unity and coherence?

Write briefly on how well you did. Point out your strengths and areas for improvement.

FOR ASSESSING LEARNING

Using *Assess Your Learning*

This writing prompt will help you and your students informally assess their developing writing abilities, using the accompanying primary trait rubrics, which list the key features and qualities of writing well-structured paragraphs taught in this chapter. You may want to have students maintain their self-assessments in their portfolios as a record of their individual progress throughout the year.

Teaching Suggestions

Essential Knowledge and Skills

- Clarifying and supporting spoken ideas with evidence, elaboration, and examples
- Writing to inform such as to explain, describe, report, and narrate
- Using conjunctions to connect ideas meaningfully
- Developing drafts by categorizing ideas, organizing them into paragraphs, and blending paragraphs within larger units of text
- Applying criteria to evaluate writing
- Interpreting and evaluating the various ways visual image makers represent meanings
- Assessing how language, medium, and presentation contribute to the message

CHAPTER 4

Writing Effective Compositions

Think of one of your favorite topics and imagine discussing it with someone who knows nothing about it. Suppose you are fascinated with traditional African music. You know a great deal about the different kinds of musical instruments, the way musical styles vary from country to country, and the names of bands that play this music.

You probably cannot explain all this to someone in a few minutes. Similarly, if you were to write about it, even the longest paragraph would probably be too short to contain all the information and points that you want to make. A composition would be more suitable. This chapter will give you the tools you need to write a strong composition.

Reading with a Writer's Eye

"The Fixed" by Annie Dillard is a composition about a personal experience. After you read the composition once, read it again, noting to yourself how the author builds her sentences into paragraphs and her paragraphs into an effective piece of writing.

BLOCK SCHEDULING

- If your schedule requires that you cover the chapter in a **shorter time**, use Reading with a Writer's Eye, Developing Your Writing Skills, and Using the Writing Process.
- If you want to take advantage of **longer class time**, use Thinking as a Writer, Writing Is Thinking: Inferring, and In the Media.

FROM *Pilgrim at Tinker Creek*

THE FIXED

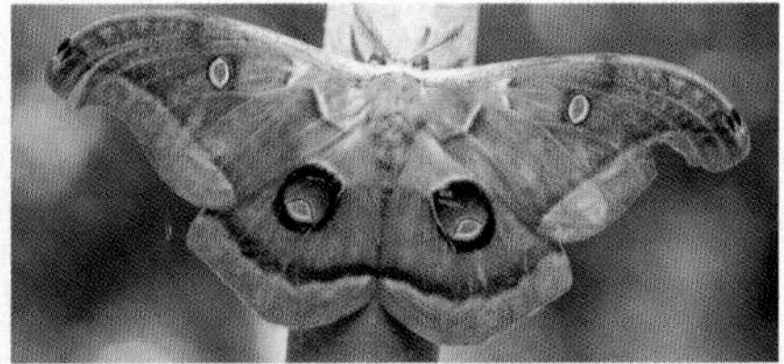

ANNIE DILLARD

Once, when I was ten or eleven years old, my friend Judy brought in a Polyphemus moth cocoon. It was January; there were doily snowflakes taped to the schoolroom panes. The teacher kept the cocoon in her desk all morning and brought it out when we were getting restless before recess. In a book we found what the adult moth would look like; it would be beautiful. With a wingspread of up to six inches, the Polyphemus is one of the few huge American silk moths, much larger than, say, a giant or tiger swallowtail butterfly. The moth's enormous wings are velveted in a rich, warm brown, and edged in bands of blue and pink delicate as a watercolor wash. A startling "eyespot," immense, and deep blue melding to an almost translucent yellow, luxuriates in the center of each hind wing. The effect is one of a masculine splendor foreign to the butterflies, a fragility unfurled[1] to strength. The Polyphemus moth in the picture looked like a mighty wraith,[2] a beating essence of the hard-

[1] **unfurled** (ŭn fûrld′) *v.*: Opened or spread out; unrolled.

[2] **wraith** (rāth) *n.*: An apparition or a ghost.

FOR INCREASING STUDENT ACHIEVEMENT

GUIDED READING

Text Analysis

- **Vocabulary** Ask a student to read the first paragraph aloud. Have students listen to the rhythm and the descriptive words that Dillard uses for the moth. Discuss any words that students may be unfamiliar with, such as *velveted, wash, melding, translucent, luxuriates,* or *wraith*.
- **Verbs** Ask students to notice the strong verbs that Dillard uses. Words such as *trapped, unfurled, jerk, heaving, banging, hardened*, and *crumpled* help convey a conflict between confinement and liberty. Students might try replacing these verbs with less specific, less concrete ones to help them see how important they are.
- **Focus** Ask students to identify the main focus of each paragraph. The first four paragraphs are almost entirely about the moth; the last paragraph focuses on Dillard. The shift in focus at the end highlights the significance of the story.
- **Tense** In the last sentence, Dillard switches to the present tense. Discuss with students why Dillard does this. Note how this switch makes this sentence stand out and how it provides a sense that the story still has an impact on Dillard today.

SELECTION AMENDMENT
Description of change: excerpted
Rationale: to focus on the features of an effective composition as presented in this chapter

GUIDED READING

Strategy: Previewing and Predicting

Before students read the entire selection, ask them to read just the first sentence. Have students make predictions about what will happen. Ask them whether they think a story about a moth will interest them.

IDENTIFYING COMMON STUMBLING BLOCKS

Problem

- Not recognizing similarities between the moth's and Dillard's desire for freedom.

Solution

- Ask students to list words and phrases that suggest struggle or force. Most, such as, "It was coming" and "thing's struggle to be a moth or die trying" are about the moth. Some, though, refer to Dillard. "The bell rang twice; I had to go" and "I ran inside" suggest that Dillard was also under compulsion.

wood forest, alien-skinned and brown, with spread, blind eyes. This was the giant moth packed in the faded cocoon. We closed the book and turned to the cocoon. It was an oak leaf sewn into a plump oval bundle; Judy had found it loose in a pile of frozen leaves.

We passed the cocoon around; it was heavy. As we held it in our hands, the creature within warmed and squirmed. We were delighted, and wrapped it tighter in our fists. The pupa began to jerk violently, in heart-stopping knocks. Who's there? I can still feel those thumps, urgent through a muffling of spun silk and leaf, urgent through the swaddling of many years, against the curve of my palm. We kept passing it around. When it came to me again it was hot as a bun; it jumped half out of my hand. The teacher intervened. She put it, still heaving and banging, in the ubiquitous Mason jar.

It was coming. There was no stopping it now, January or not. One end of the cocoon dampened and gradually frayed in a furious battle. The whole cocoon twisted and slapped around in the bottom of the jar. The teacher fades, the classmates fade, I fade: I don't remember anything but that thing's struggle to be a moth or die trying. It emerged at last, a sodden crumple. It was a male; his long antennae were thickly plumed, as wide as his fat abdomen. His body was very thick, over an inch long, and deeply furred. A gray, furlike plush covered his head; a long, tan furlike hair hung from his wide thorax over his brown-furred, segmented abdomen. His multijointed legs, pale and powerful, were shaggy as a bear's. He stood still, but he breathed.

He couldn't spread his wings. There was no room. The chemical that coated his wings like varnish, stiffening them permanently, dried, and hardened his wings as they were. He was a monster in a Mason jar. Those huge wings stuck on his back in a torture of random pleats and folds, wrinkled as a dirty tissue, rigid as leather. They made a single nightmare clump still wracked with useless, frantic convulsions.

The next thing I remember, it was recess. The school was in Shadyside, a busy residential part of Pittsburgh. Everyone was playing dodgeball in the fenced playground or racing around the concrete schoolyard by the swings. Next to the playground a long delivery drive sloped downhill to the sidewalk and street. Someone—it must have been the teacher—had let the moth out. I was standing in the driveway, alone, stock-still, but shivering. Someone had given the Polyphemus moth his freedom, and he was walking away.

He heaved himself down the asphalt driveway by infinite degrees, unwavering. His hideous crumpled wings lay glued and rucked on his back, perfectly still now, like a collapsed tent. The bell rang twice; I had to go. The moth was receding down the driveway, dragging on. I went; I ran inside. The Polyphemus moth is still crawling down the driveway, crawling down the driveway hunched, crawling down the driveway on six furred feet, forever.

READER RESPONSE

You may want to use the following questions to elicit students' personal responses to the selection.

1. How easily could you imagine being in the classroom that Dillard describes?
2. Evaluate whether the teacher was correct to allow the children to handle the cocoon.
3. How did you feel when you read that someone had let the moth out?
4. Explain whether you found this story either sad or uplifting.
5. Explain whether you think Dillard is comparing herself to the moth.

LITERARY CONNECTION

You might want to explore writing effective compositions in the following works, which appear in literature textbooks at this grade level.

- *All Things Bright and Beautiful* by James Herriot
- "The Deserter" by Irene Hunt
- "Flying" by Reeve Lindbergh
- "Lights in the Night" by Annie Dillard

ADDITIONAL RESOURCES

Composition Skills Practice	pages 21–24
Transparency Tools	VR3
Connection Collection	pages C123–C124
ESL Practice and Test Preparation	pages 22–28
Writers at Work	8•1–8•10
Assessment: Chapter Test	pages 47–51
Assessment Resources	pages 1–10, 13–44

Using *Thinking as a Writer*

You may choose to have students respond to the questions either orally or in writing.

REACHING ALL STUDENTS

Advanced Learners

Have students write a paragraph describing this story from the perspective of the moth. How did it feel about going into the classroom, struggling out of its cocoon, finding itself still trapped, and being released?

GETTING STUDENTS INVOLVED

Reciprocal Teaching

Ask students to bring in photographs of nature scenes. Have them explain to each other what details they think are significant in the images. As they do, encourage them to consider other ways to interpret the same details.

Thinking as a Writer

Analyzing Author's Purpose

- Think about Annie Dillard's purpose in writing this piece. Does she express her purpose as a main idea? When did you realize what the main idea is?
- Does the author give specific facts in the body of the composition to support the main idea? How does she use personal experience to support the facts?

Observing Changes

Viewing • Study the photograph below. Compare this image of a cocoon to the image of a moth on page C99. What do the two images suggest to you about the process of a moth changing its form? Support your response with examples from the photographs.

- Might pictures taken over time help you understand the process better than a text description? Why or why not?

Recognizing Tone

Oral Expression • With a partner, take turns reading the article aloud. Notice how the use of pronouns, such as *he* and *it,* helps create smooth-sounding sentences. What is the over-all feeling of the composition?

FOR DEVELOPING SKILLS

LESSON 1 *(pages C103–C111)*

OBJECTIVES

- **To understand the structure of a composition**
- **To choose a subject and to list and arrange supporting details**

Create Interest

Ask each student to write a few notes describing an incident that happened to them within the past week that they can describe to the class. Have a few students relate their incidents. Then discuss the structure of their descriptions. Did they usually start off with a sentence describing the setting and the main point of the story? Did they then describe the incident in more detail? Did they close with a strong ending that summed up the main

The Power of Effective Compositions

In the last few chapters, you learned the process of writing single paragraphs. Sometimes, however, your ideas will need more development than a single paragraph. In history class, for example, you may be asked to write a composition about the system of checks and balances built into the government of the United States. In science class you may be asked to write a composition explaining the life cycle of a moth. A paragraph is too short to contain all of these ideas. An composition would be more suitable.

Uses of Composition

Here are some situations for which you or your classmates may write compositions.

- **The editor of your school newspaper asks you to write about the class trip** for students who did not participate.
- **On an application for a volunteer tutoring program, you write about your interest** in helping young children learn to read.
- **To broaden your cultural experiences, you and your classmates put together a proposal** for a foreign-exchange program.
- **To win a computer for your classroom, you and your friends work together on an explanation** of how the class will use the computer.

USING STUDENTS' STRENGTHS

Multiple Intelligences: Intrapersonal

Ask students if they have ever received a personal letter in the mail. If they have, ask them to analyze how they felt about it. Push students to clarify their feelings beyond that it made them happy. Encourage students who have enjoyed receiving a letter to return the pleasure by writing a letter back to the sender.

REACHING ALL STUDENTS

English Language Learners

Discuss with students who are learning English the names of the three main sections of a composition. The introduction is sometimes called the intro, the beginning, or the opening. Students may be familiar with the biological meaning of body, but not its use in describing part of a composition. The conclusion is the end of the composition. *Con-* means with or together, *-clusion* means to close or to shut.

point of the story? Tell students that compositions typically have an introduction, body, and conclusion.

Guide Instruction

By Modeling Strategies

Ask students to read aloud the first sentence and the last paragraph of "Messages into Space." Help students recognize the relationship between these two parts of the composition, and discuss what information they would expect to find in between them. Then, after they have read the entire composition, ask them to evaluate the first sentence and the last paragraph.

Consolidate Skills

Through Guided Practice

Students can select and narrow a subject by using the instruction on limiting a subject on pages C106–C107. Ask students to take a subject and write four additional focus points for it. Have volunteers read their lists aloud.

USING STUDENTS' STRENGTHS

Multiple Intelligences: Visual

Ask students to draw a timeline for the trip of Pioneer 10. Besides the dates mentioned in the composition, include these dates:

c. 100,000 B.C.	First humans move out of Africa
c. 30,000 B.C.	First humans reach the Americas
c. A.D. 1000	First Europeans visit North America
A.D. 1969	First humans visit the moon

SELECTION AMENDMENT

Description of change: excerpted

Rationale: to focus on the organization of a composition as presented in this chapter

Process of Writing Effective Compositions

In his composition "Letter Writing," Andy Rooney says: "Some of my most precious possessions are letters that have been written to me sometime in the past. I don't have a single memorable phone call stored in a box in my attic or basement." Too often, people find it easier to make a phone call or send an E-mail rather than to take the time to express their thoughts on paper. To use your precious time to communicate something in writing shows that you must care about your subject and, most likely, your readers.

A **composition** presents and develops one main idea in three or more paragraphs.

Like paragraphs, compositions have three main parts. In the following composition, the three main parts are labeled at the left.

MODEL: Composition

Messages into Space

MAIN IDEA

INTRODUCTION: PROVIDES BACKGROUND INFORMATION AND CAPTURES READER'S ATTENTION

Two space missions from recent years are carrying our messages into interstellar space. *Pioneer 10* is carrying a plaque with a drawing of a man and a woman plus some information about Earth and its inhabitants. *Voyager* is carrying a "cosmic LP" a two-hour phonograph record. Encoded on the record are photographs, diagrams, and drawings that represent life on this planet. It also contains greetings from Earth spoken in 53 languages, musical selections, sounds of our animal life, the roar of the

Apply to Communication

Through Independent Writing

Communicate Your Ideas activity can help students develop their skill at selecting a focus point. To extend it, have students write their reasons for choosing one focus point over others.

Transfer to Everyday Life

By Using Media

Ask students to bring in automobile advertisements from magazines. They should find ads targeted to people according to age, gender, income, ethnicity, and interests. Discuss how the focus point varies depending on the audience.

Pull It All Together

By Summarizing

Tell students that selecting the right focus point and details will make the rest of the composition much easier to write. Encourage them to take time to think about their choices so that they feel comfortable with them.

surf, the cry of a baby, and the soft thump of the human heartbeat. Thirty-two thousand years will pass before *Pioneer 10* draws close to a star. After that approach a million years will go by before there is another close approach, and still another million years will elapse before a third occurs.

BODY: PROVIDES SPECIFIC INFORMATION

Because of the emptiness of interstellar space, the spacecraft's ancient hulk will probably never be seen by alien eyes. In fact, the messages aboard the *Pioneer* and *Voyager* spacecraft were composed with little hope that anyone would ever discover them. They were only bottles thrown in a cosmic ocean, a symbol of our deep desire to communicate with a civilization other than our own.

CONCLUSION: ADD A STRONG ENDING

Millions of years from now, those messages will still be journeying through the universe. They may never be found. They will, however, be a solid piece of evidence that a tiny inhabited planet exists, or once existed, in the suburbs of a small galaxy with the odd name *Milky Way*.

—Margaret Poynter and Michael J. Klein, Cosmic Quest

Your Writer's Journal

Compositions often convey the writer's unique viewpoints. As you study this chapter, record *your* views in your journal. For example, consider the saying, "Beauty is in the eye of the beholder." Then think of places where you see beauty even if others do not. Write about these places in your journal. In the process, you may discover several good subjects for compositions.

IDENTIFYING COMMON STUMBLING BLOCKS

Problem

- Students will choose a topic that is too broad or too narrow for their composition.

Solution

- Ask students to make a set of five concentric circles. They should write their idea in the third circle. Then, they should write broader topics in the outer two circles and narrower topics in the inner two circles. After students have written their five ideas, have them discuss with a partner how many pages they would need to write a composition on each one. Help students see that too narrow topics will not produce enough pages for a composition, while too broad topics will produce too many pages.

Check Understanding
By Analyzing
Divide students into small groups and ask them to analyze the details used in "Messages into Space." Each group should appoint a spokesperson to report on the group's general impression of how well details support the main idea of this composition.

TIMESAVER *QuickCheck*
Have students describe to a partner three possible subjects they are considering. As students listen, they should evaluate which of the three subjects the speaker describes with the most enthusiasm. This feedback may help the speaker decide which subject to pursue.

HOME STUDY
You may assign students to call or E-mail each other to discuss subjects they might want to write about. Point out that professional writers have editors with whom they can discuss ideas, and that many find talking about their ideas helps them to clarify their thoughts.

Prewriting
Writing Process

Choosing a good subject is one of the most important prewriting activities. If you choose a subject you are not genuinely interested in, your composition will lack fire. If you care about your subject, however, your writing will crackle with interest.

Communicate Your Ideas

PREWRITING *Subject Inventory*

Using freewriting, clustering, or brainstorming, continue to explore your interests and knowledge in search of a subject you can develop into a composition. Save your work in your writing folder. SAVE YOUR WORK

Choosing and Limiting a Subject

After exploring your interests, the next step is to choose one subject and refine it for development in a composition.

Determining Your Purpose As a first step, think about your purpose for writing. Ask yourself "Do I want to provide information? Do I want to give directions? Do I want to persuade my readers?"

Determining Your Audience Once you have decided on a purpose, consider your audience. Develop an audience profile to help you understand your readers' knowledge, attitudes, and beliefs.

You may want to refer to page C18 for help in identifying your audience.

Listing Focus Points As a final step, list several possible focus points. Focus points are specific aspects of your general subject. In the example on the following page, the subject of snorkeling is too large for a short composition. Any of the focus points, however, would be a suitably limited subject.

SUBJECT	snorkeling (underwater exploring)
PURPOSE	to explain
AUDIENCE	people who do not know much about it
FOCUS POINTS	• what equipment is needed • how to control breathing and clear snorkel • what someone can do while snorkeling • how to make different kinds of surface dives

Communicate Your Ideas

PREWRITING *Subject*

Look over your prewriting work regarding subjects for compositions. Then decide on your purpose, determine your audience, and list focus points suitable for your purpose and audience. Finally, choose one focus point as your limited subject and put a circle around it. Save your work for later use.

Listing Supporting Details

During your writing process, you move back and forth between controlling your thoughts carefully and letting them run freely. First, you narrowed your subject and brought it under control. The next stage, listing supporting details, calls for letting your ideas run freely. The kinds of supporting details you should use will depend on your purpose for writing.

HOME WORK

Have students write down two more subjects, identify the purpose and audience for each, and list four focus points for each one.

TIMESAVER *QuickCheck*

Review each student's focus points to see if he or she has chosen one that supports the purpose. If not, suggest that the student consider other focus points.

HOME STUDY

Students can check their focus point at home by asking themselves these questions:

- Does this focus point support my purpose?
- Will the audience for this composition understand this focus point?
- Do I enjoy talking about this focus point?

REACHING ALL STUDENTS

Struggling Learners

Students who have difficulty letting their ideas run freely might try asking themselves the following questions about each supporting detail in order: *Who? What? When? Where? Why? How?* Depending on the type of detail, some of these questions will be more helpful than others, but each one may prompt the student to think of other details.

SUPPORTING DETAILS

Purpose	Kinds of Details
To inform	• details that relate causes and effects or likenesses and differences
To explain	• facts, examples, reasons
To give directions	• steps in a process
To persuade	• reasons, based on fact, to support an opinion
To create	• details that develop characters and incidents

Brainstorming One way to think of supporting details is to brainstorm. Write down everything that comes to mind when you think about your subject. One idea will lead to another.

LIMITED SUBJECT	things to do while snorkeling
BRAINSTORMING IDEAS	• collecting shells • feeding fish • mastering basic snorkeling techniques • shells are on the seafloor, sometimes hidden in sea grasses • fish will eat bread or cheese • carry the food in a bag you can close • taking pictures • need waterproof camera equipment • if collecting shells, watch for dangerous animals that could be hiding nearby

In addition to brainstorming, you could also use the strategies of freewriting and clustering to develop details.

You can find more information on freewriting and clustering on pages C9–C10 and C23.

Communicate Your Ideas

PREWRITING *Supporting Details*

Return to your focused subject. Then use brainstorming or any other prewriting strategy to develop a list of details that will support your focus point. Save your work for later use.

Arranging Details in Logical Order

After brainstorming, arrange your ideas in a logical order.

TYPES OF ORDER	
Chronological	• Items are arranged in time order.
Spatial	• Items are arranged in location order.
Importance or Degree	• Items are arranged in order of least to most or most to least important.
Sequential	• Steps in a process are arranged in their proper sequence.

As you group your ideas, you may find that some do not fit in neatly. Save these for possible use later. Notice the order of the notes about things to do while snorkeling.

LEAST DIFFICULT	• feeding fish • fish will eat bread or cheese • carry the food in a bag you can close
NEXT IN DIFFICULTY	• collecting shells • shells are on the seafloor, sometimes hidden in sea grasses • look out for dangerous animals that could be hiding near shells
MOST DIFFICULT	• taking pictures • need waterproof camera equipment
USE ELSEWHERE?	• mastering basic snorkeling techniques

TIMESAVER *QuickCheck*

Divide students into small groups. As each student presents his or her focus point, the other students should brainstorm details that support it. When possible, students should provide specific anecdotes, facts, or sources of information.

HOME STUDY

To help students brainstorm details that support a focus point, suggest that they visit relevant Websites. They might see a variety of information related to their focus point that they could use.

INTEGRATING TECHNOLOGY

Internet

The Southeast Florida Library Information Network, a non-profit organization of libraries in Broward, Dade, Palm Beach, Martin, and Monroe counties, maintains a site on snorkeling adventures at http://www.seflin.org/snorkel/snklsite.mnu.html. One avid snorkeler has set up a Website for those who share this interest and has invited people to send in stories about snorkeling in places all over the world. The site address is http://www.lrsm.upenn.edu/~ghosh/. The site also includes links to other sites on snorkeling.

Using *Writing Is Thinking*

Objectives

- **To understand the process of inferring**
- **To infer conclusions from information**

A DIFFERENT APPROACH

Tactile

Supply items with distinctive textures. Have students take turns touching an item and trying to determine what it is. Discuss how they are reasoning from what they know to what they do not know.

THINKING PRACTICE Sample Answers

1. This cannot be inferred.
2. This cannot be inferred.
3. This can be inferred from the statement "if collecting shells, watch for dangerous animals that could be hiding nearby."
4. This cannot be inferred.
5. This can be inferred from the statement "need waterproof camera equipment."

Thinking Skills	
Classifying	Analyzing
Comparing	Hypothesizing
Generalizing	Synthesizing
Inferring	Summarizing
Imagining	Setting Goals
Observing	Evaluating Audience
Predicting	

Writing Is Thinking

Inferring

Inferring means using your reasoning powers to draw a meaningful conclusion, or inference, from given information or situations. A sound inference should be stated in the introduction of your composition.

How do you form an inference? You do it all the time without realizing it. For example, if you call a friend and get no answer, you may infer that no one is home. You have used specific information—the fact that no one answered the phone—and drawn a larger conclusion from it. Is your conclusion necessarily true? Maybe someone was home but could not get to the phone in time. Maybe the phone was out of order. Maybe you dialed the wrong number by mistake.

A good inference accounts for as many details as possible. For example, if you called and got no answer, and then drove past your friend's house and saw it was dark, you would have another piece of evidence to back up your inference that no one is home.

THINKING PRACTICE

Decide which of the following could be inferred from the specific information provided on pages C108–C109 about snorkeling. After each statement, explain why it can or cannot be inferred from the details.

1. Snorkeling is easy.
2. Snorkeling is for professionals only.
3. Snorkeling carries some risks.
4. So many people are snorkeling today that the underwater wildlife is disturbed.
5. Snorkeling requires special equipment.

Lesson 2 (pages C111–C117)

OBJECTIVES

- **To develop skill in writing a main idea statement**
- **To practice writing a strong introduction**
- **To understand the steps in drafting a composition**
- **To practice drafting a composition**

Create Interest

Read this list of five numbers to students: 27, 81, 243, 729, 2187. Then ask a student to repeat the list back. Most students will have difficulty recalling all five numbers. Then explain that you are going to read a list of numbers, each of which is three times greater than the first. Reread the same list of five numbers, and again ask a student to tell you what the numbers are. Given a few seconds to compute the numbers, most students will be able to reconstruct the list. Discuss how presenting the main idea at first provided

Communicate Your Ideas

PREWRITING *Arrangement of Details*

Look over your work. Do you have enough details to develop into a solid essay? If and when you are satisfied with your details, arrange them in logical order.

Drafting Writing Process

When your notes are organized, you are ready to begin the second stage of the writing process—drafting. Remember that your goal in writing is to turn your prewriting notes into connected sentences and paragraphs.

Introduction of a Composition

The introduction to a composition should accomplish two main goals. The first is to arouse your reader's interest and make him or her want to read on. The second is to state clearly the main idea of the composition.

In the following introduction on the subject of snorkeling, the sentence stating the main idea is highlighted.

Model: Introduction

INTRODUCTION

Imagine the feeling of suddenly having all of your weight lifted from you. You glide along almost without effort. You feel the coolness of water around you. You see the brilliant colors of fish swimming past you, and the sounds of the world outside are muffled. These are just a few of the pleasures of snorkeling. For those who have mastered the basic techniques, how-

USING STUDENTS' STRENGTHS

Multiple Intelligences: Logical

To give students practice making inferences, give them a logic puzzle to solve. For example, imagine that Hercules, Odysseus, Robin Hood, and William Tell had an archery contest:

- Hercules hit the bullseye more often than Odysseus did.
- Robin Hood hit the bullseye more often than Hercules did.
- William Tell hit the bullseye less often than Odysseus did.

Who was the best archer that day? Robin Hood. Similar problems can be found in puzzle books by Martin Gardner, Raymond M. Smullyan, and others.

GETTING STUDENTS INVOLVED

Cooperative Learning

Have students bring in examples of paragraphs in which details are arranged using chronological order, spatial order, or order of importance or degree. Group the paragraphs according to the type of logical order they use. Discuss any patterns that students notice. For example, do most paragraphs describing historical events use chronological order? Do most paragraphs from persuasive essays use order of importance or degree? Do paragraphs using spatial order frequently come at the beginning of a piece of writing, when the writer is describing the setting for an event?

the context that enabled listeners to understand better. Similarly, a well-crafted introduction to a composition will help readers understand the writing more effectively.

Guide Instruction

By Connecting Ideas

Ask students to read the definition of inferring given in the text. Point out the use of the word *conclusion.* Raise the question: If an inference is like a conclusion, why it is being taught in connection with the thesis statement, something that usually appears in the first paragraph of a composition? Discuss the connection between the first and last paragraphs of a composition.

Consolidate Skills

Through Guided Practice

Students can consolidate their understanding of the traits of a strong introduction by using the **Communicate Your Ideas** on improving a weak introduction. Have students extend the activity by comparing how students changed the paragraph and recogniz-

GETTING STUDENTS INVOLVED

Reciprocal Teaching

Divide students into small groups. Each student should write three main idea statements on one topic of the student's choice. Then, as a group, the students should rank each student's three statements according to which would make the best main idea statement.

HOME WORK

Explain to students that a thesis statement expresses a writer's point of view. If a writer takes a different position, then the thesis statement will change. Have students write thesis statements that express a contradictory point of view from those they have just written.

MAIN IDEA

ever, the pleasures are even greater. Instead of simply gliding and observing, an experienced snorkeler can keep busy underwater with several interesting activities.

Writing an Introduction

A strong introduction

- captures the reader's attention with an interesting fact, detail, incident, or description.
- gives background information if needed.
- includes a sentence expressing the main idea.
- does not include such empty expressions as *In this composition I will . . .* or *This composition will be about . . . .*

Communicate Your Ideas

DRAFTING *Introduction*

Write several possible introductions to your composition based on the prewriting work you completed. Try out different approaches to beginning a composition. In one version, start with an interesting fact or detail. In another, start by telling an incident that got you interested in your subject in the first place. In a third, start with some lively description, just as the model essay introduction about snorkeling begins. In each version include a statement that expresses the main idea of the composition.

Read each version aloud to a classmate, who will listen carefully. After each ask your partner to tell what he or she expects in the rest of the composition. After you have read all three, ask your partner which would make him or her most interested in reading on.

ing that it could be strengthened in several different ways.

Apply to Communication

Through Independent Writing

Students can use the **Communicate Your Skills** activity on page C112 to develop their skills at drafting the introduction of a composition. As they work, ask them to consider how they might shape their introduction for various groups of readers.

Transfer to Everyday Life

By Reading the Newspaper

Have students bring in editorials, essays, and other opinion pieces from newspapers or magazines. Evaluate the relationship between the opening paragraphs and the body of the text. Identify strengths and discuss ways to improve weaknesses. As students identify words or phrases they would like to change, ask them to consider if they think the writer would agree with the changes. Ask students to identify the audience the writer was targeting.

Body of a Composition

As you write the body of your composition, keep your reader in mind. Try to make your message as clear as possible. Use your prewriting notes to write complete, varied sentences with vivid words. Use transitions to connect your thoughts smoothly.

Compare the following composition body with the prewriting notes on pages C107–C108. The transitions are printed in **bold** type. Refer to pages C85–C86 for a list of transitions.

MODEL: Body

One of the easiest and most enjoyable underwater activities is feeding fish. Fish particularly like bread or cheese. If you want to feed fish, carry the food in a bag you can close. **In that way** you can keep hungry fish from swimming inside your food bag. **Another** activity, shell collecting, requires slightly **more** skill. A good shell collector must know where to look for shells that might be hidden in grasses on the seafloor. He or she must also recognize dangerous animals that might be hiding near the shells. **A third activity,** taking pictures underwater, requires the **most** skill and equipment. The camera and gear must all be made specially for working underwater.

Communicate Your Ideas

DRAFTING *Body of the Composition*

Using your prewriting work and the version of the introduction that you chose, draft the body of your composition. Be sure to use transitions where appropriate. Remember to work fairly quickly, rereading every now and then to keep your thoughts on track. Do not worry about mistakes at this point. Just write to put your ideas down on paper in a coherent form.

TIMESAVER *QuickCheck*

Read students' main idea statements. If one does not express a main idea, suggest that the student revise it.

HOME STUDY

Students can write their main idea statements at home. They may wish to write several versions of it in order to prompt themselves to think of it in varying ways.

TIMESAVER *QuickCheck*

See that students used their list of details from the previous exercise on page C109. If they have strayed from this list, ask them to justify why they added these new details.

Pull It All Together

By Summarizing

Ask students if they have ever read a book or seen a movie, and then thought that its title did not fit it very well. Discuss why a writer may write the title of composition last. Point out that some writers feel that they do not know what they want to say until they see it on paper.

Check Understanding

By Analyzing Literature

Have students reread the excerpt from *Pilgrim at Tinker Creek* by Annie Dillard. Ask them to evaluate the structure of the excerpt. Students should note the divisions between the introduction, body, and conclusion, and the general flow of ideas.

USING STUDENTS' STRENGTHS

Multiple Intelligences: Spatial

Have students create a Venn diagram showing the similarities and differences between a good introduction and a good conclusion.

HOME WORK

Assign students to find examples of well-written conclusions in books, magazines, or newspaper articles. Ask them to be prepared to compare the conclusion against the guidelines in the Writing a Conclusion box.

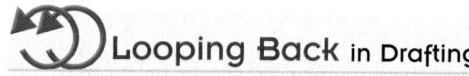

Looping Back in Drafting

Adding Personal Experience

Reread the excerpt from *Pilgrim at Tinker Creek* (pages C99–C101). Note how Dillard uses personal experience to show how she learned the value of nature's creatures. Is there a new way that you can add personal experience to support your main idea?

Conclusion of a Composition

A conclusion to a composition is like a farewell. It wraps up the ideas in the composition and provides a strong ending.

Model: Conclusion

> Almost anything you do while snorkeling is a pleasure. The nearness to sea creatures, the beauty of a coral reef, and the feel of the water all add up to an unforgettable experience. When you actually interact with the life below by feeding fish, collecting empty shells, or taking action pictures, you will feel even more a part of the mysterious sea.

Use the guidelines below when writing a conclusion.

Writing a Conclusion

A strong concluding paragraph

- emphasizes the main idea without restating it exactly.
- may refer to ideas in the introduction.
- does not introduce a completely new idea.
- does not use such empty expressions as *I have just told you about . . .* or *Now you know about . . . .*

Writing a Title

A title should give the reader an idea of what the composition will be about. It might come from some element of your composition—the main subject, an important event, or, when appropriate, where your action takes place. Whatever the inspiration behind your title is, it should make your reader curious enough to want to read the entire composition. What titles can you think of to go with the composition on snorkeling?

Communicate Your Ideas

DRAFTING *Conclusion and Title*

Refer to the guidelines on the previous page to write a conclusion to your composition. Then look over your entire composition. Are the three parts of your compo-sition smoothly connected? If not, smooth them out. When you are satisfied with the flow of your composition, think of an accurate and lively title for it. Save your work.

Revising

Writing Process

Once your ideas are down on paper, you can stand back and look at them to see how they can be improved. The following checklist will help you improve your composition.

Evaluation Checklist for Revising

Checking Your Composition

✓ Do you have an interesting introduction that states the main idea of the composition? *(pages C111–C112)*

DEVELOPING WORKPLACE COMPETENCIES

Thinking Skills: Decision Making

Tell students that making decisions is a skill we use as students, as friends, as parents, and as professionals. Every job requires employees to make decisions: a lawyer must decide which strategy will be most effective in a particular case; a farmer must decide what portion of his or her income should be used to buy new farming tools; an architect must decide how to maximize parking in a limited space.

Selecting a title is an important decision students make when writing a composition. Suggest that students adapt a general decision-making procedure for choosing a title:

1. Identify the purpose of the title and any limits on its length or content.
2. Propose several possible titles.
3. List the strengths and weaknesses of each possible title.
4. Evaluate the strengths and weaknesses, deciding how significant each one is.
5. Choose the best title for the composition.

TIMESAVER *QuickCheck*

Have students assess their conclusions by asking them to read the first and last paragraphs in succession. They should see a clear connection between them. The main idea presented in the first paragraph should be summarized in the last paragraph.

IDENTIFYING COMMON STUMBLING BLOCKS

Problem

- Not revising a composition because students are unable to think of alternate ways to express their thoughts

Solution

- Have students identify the verbs in each sentence, and propose alternative words for each one. Then have them identify whether they want to use an adverb to modify each verb. As they focus on verbs and adverbs, they may also find other changes they want to make in the composition.

✓ Do all your sentences relate to the main idea? In other words, does your composition have unity? *(page C113)*

✓ Are your ideas arranged logically with transitions? In other words, is your composition coherent? *(page C113)*

✓ Do you have a strong conclusion? *(page C114)*

Checking Your Paragraphs

✓ Does each paragraph in the body of your composition have a topic sentence? *(pages C77–C79)*

✓ Is each paragraph unified? *(page C84)*

✓ Is each paragraph coherent? *(page C85)*

Checking Your Sentences and Words

✓ Did you eliminate short, choppy sentences by combining related sentences? *(pages C53–C57)*

✓ Did you vary the length and beginnings of your sentences? *(pages C53-C55)*

✓ Did you eliminate rambling sentences? *(page C63)*

✓ Are your sentences free of repetition and empty expressions? *(pages C64–C65)*

✓ Are your words fresh and vivid? *(pages C49–C53)*

Communicate Your Ideas

REVISING

Use the Evaluation Checklist for Revising above to improve the first draft of your composition. Save your work for further revising and for editing.

Editing — Writing Process

When you are satisfied with your ideas and organization, you are ready to check your composition carefully for errors. Use the proofreading symbols on page C37 when you edit.

Editing Checklist

- ✔ Are your sentences free of errors in grammar and usage?
- ✔ Did you spell each word correctly?
- ✔ Did you use capital letters where needed?
- ✔ Did you punctuate sentences correctly?
- ✔ Did you indent each paragraph?

Publishing — Writing Process

The appearance of your composition is important. A neat paper makes a positive impression on your reader. Prepare your final copy. When you are satisfied with the results, share your composition with family or friends.

Communicate Your Ideas

EDITING, PUBLISHING

Use the **Editing Checklist** to edit your composition. Then make a final copy of your composition using the proper form and present it to an interested reader.

PORTFOLIO

TIMESAVER *QuickCheck*

Review with students the Editing Checklist. Discuss why each question is important.

HOME STUDY

Students can use the Evaluation Checklist for Revising when working at home.

Have students ask another household member to read the final copy of their composition. The household member should focus on the appearance rather than the content.

Using *Editing Workshop*

Objective

- **To understand the value of creating sentence variety through sentence combining**

A DIFFERENT APPROACH

Visual

Have students create a bar chart showing the number of words in each sentence. Ask them to evaluate whether they have enough variety in sentence length. Remind students to consider carefully whether any of their sentences are too long or whether they have too many short sentences in row.

TIMESAVER *QuickCheck*

Scan student papers, noting short sentences that might be better connected with a conjunction. Point out any such places to students.

HOME STUDY

Ask students to find examples from other written materials of well-used conjunctions.

Grammar in the Writing Process

Prewriting Workshop
Drafting Workshop
Revising Workshop
Editing Workshop
Publishing Workshop

Conjunctions

When editing your composition, try reading your sentences aloud. Do they sound too short and choppy? You can join them into a single sentence through the use of conjunctions.

If the ideas in two short sentences are of equal importance, you can combine them into a single sentence by using a **coordinating conjunction** such as *and, but,* or *and.*

CHOPPY SENTENCES	Someone had given the Polyphemus moth his freedom. He was walking away.
COMBINED SENTENCE	Someone had given the Polyphemus moth his freedom, **and** he was walking away.

If the ideas in two short sentences are of unequal importance, you can combine them by changing the less important idea into an abverb clause. Adverb clauses begin with a **subordinating conjunction** such as *when, since, after, because,* or *although.*

CHOPPY SENTENCES	I was 10 or 11 years old. My friend Judy brought in a moth cocoon.
COMBINED SENTENCE	**When** I was 10 or 11 years old, my friend Judy brought in a moth cocoon.

Editing Checklist

✓ Do you use *and, but,* or *or* to join two short sentences of equal importance?

✓ Did you use an adverb clause to join two short sentences of unequal importance?

Television

Thinking about your audience is an important part of any communication—oral, written or visual. Cartoons, for example, are produced for several different audiences. Once viewed as children's entertainment, animation has become popular with all age groups. Cartoons often reflect the culture in which we live. Cartoons on television, particularly those on prime time, often deal in surprising depth with serious subjects in a light-hearted way. These cartoons are more than just entertainment for young people. They regularly comment on and explore the values of our culture.

Media Activity

Select a cartoon that appears on television and, if possible, videotape several episodes. As you watch, take notes on any aspect of American culture that the show presents. What is the action of the plot? How do characters react to it? Is the setting rural? Urban? Watch once again with the sound off. What messages are strictly visual?

Once you have done some research, write a paragraph evaluating cartoons as a statement about our culture. Answer the following questions in your paragraph.

- What is the actual subject of the cartoon? Is it simply presenting the antics of animals or superheroes, or is it offering bigger ideas?
- What happens in the cartoon itself? Give a brief description of the plot. What, if anything, does the cartoon say about life in America today?

Share your paragraph about cartoons with your classmates.

IN THE MEDIA

Using *In the Media*

Objective

- **To evaluate what makes a good animation or claymation feature**

Group Project

- Divide students into small groups. Each group should select a classic work of animation or claymation. They might select one featuring a landmark character such as Mickey Mouse, Bugs Bunny, or Wallace and Grommit. Or, they may want to review an innovative use of animation or claymation, such as the movie *Fantasia* or *Toy Story.* You may wish to encourage groups to look at works from different eras so that the class can see how techniques evolved. Students should view the work selected and take notes on it. Then, as a group, they should write a review of it and prepare to read it to the class.

FYI

Websites to Visit A scholarly site for the study of animation, http://www.chapman.edu/animation/, include links to many other sites. One of these is http://lcweb2.loc.gov/ammem/oahtml/oahome.html, a Library of Congress site that includes clips from animations made between 1900 and 1921.

EXPANDING THE LESSON

Using Technology

You will find additional **instructional** and **practice** materials for this chapter at http://www.bkenglish.com.

Process of Writing an Effective Composition

PREWRITING

- Make a list of possible subjects by exploring your interests. *(page C106)*
- Choose one subject from your list. *(page C106)*
- Limit your subject by deciding on your purpose, audience, and focus point. *(pages C106–C107)*
- Freewrite, brainstorm, or cluster to develop supporting details. *(pages C107–C108)*
- Organize your list into a logical order. *(page C109)*

DRAFTING

- Write an introduction that includes a sentence stating your main idea. *(pages C111–C112)*
- Use your notes to write the body of your composition with transitions between ideas. *(page C113)*
- Add a concluding paragraph that wraps up the ideas and provides a strong ending. *(page C114)*
- Add an interesting title that will capture your reader's attention. *(page C115)*

REVISING

- Put your first draft aside for a while. Then use the Evaluation Checklist for Revising on pages C115–C116 to improve your first draft. Use the revision strategies of adding, deleting, substituting, and rearranging.

EDITING

- Use the Editing Checklists on pages C36 and C117 to polish your work.

PUBLISHING

- Use the guidelines for correct manuscript form on page C41 to prepare a final copy of your composition. Present your finished work to an interested reader.

A Writer Writes

A Persuasive Composition

Purpose: **to convince people to go to the movies rather than rent a movie to watch at home.**

Audience: **people in your town**

Prewriting

Suppose that you are the owner of a movie theater in your town. Business has been slow lately because many people in your town are renting videotaped movies to watch at home. Videotaped movies are very inexpensive to rent, often costing less than it would cost to buy one movie theater ticket.

You want to write a persuasive composition to be printed in the local newspaper. First think of as many possible reasons as you can why people should go out to the movies instead of watching them at home. Include specific details about what makes the movie-going experience better than watching movies at home. Then, in a logical order, organize your details so that they effectively support your main idea.

Drafting

Use your prewriting notes to write the introduction, body, and the conclusion of your composition. At this point, do not worry about mistakes in grammar, usage, or spelling. You can correct any errors and polish your work later in your writing process. Just write quickly to get your ideas down on paper smoothly.

Using *A Writer Writes*

Objective

- **To write a persuasive composition for a local newspaper**

TIMESAVER *QuickCheck*

In the revising stage, encourage students to exchange their persuasive papers with a partner. Partners should read the papers and share their ideas for improvements.

INTEGRATING *Writers at Work*

For more opportunities to stimulate students' persuasive writing, look at *Writers at Work.*

REACHING ALL STUDENTS
Advanced Learners

As students work on revising, encourage them to research the writing habits of a writer whose work they enjoy reading. Does the writer:

- work at the same time each day?
- work for a certain length of time?
- create a draft quickly or slowly?
- revise often or rarely?
- enjoy the process of writing?

Revising

Exchange papers with a classmate. Ask your reader to tell whether he or she would be convinced. If not, try to develop arguments that *would* persuade your reader. Then, using your reader's response and the **Evaluation Checklist for Revising** on pages C115–C116, revise your composition carefully, adding punch and liveliness wherever you can. Go over your draft several times, each time looking for a different kind of problem.

Editing

Use the **Editing Checklists** on pages C36 and C117 to find and correct errors in your composition. Again, go over your paper several times. If you try to find everything at once you might miss a mistake.

Publishing

Oral Expression

Create a clean copy of your composition. Then practice reading your composition aloud to try to match your tone of voice and hand gestures to the meaning of the words. Finally, read your composition aloud to the class.

Connection Collection

Representing in Different Ways

From Print . . .

. . . to Visuals

Choose a photograph from a newspaper or magazine or make a drawing to accompany this newspaper article.

COMMUNITY SNEEZES

PEPPERVILLE, P.A.—Yesterday in a freak accident, all but one of the townspeople in Pepperville sneezed at the exact same moment. The community sneeze caused three houses to collapse.

Sneezing is a reflex of the human body's respiratory system. It is the body's way of expelling dust and other foreign matter. Sneezes often occur when people are around an area where small particles have become airborne, such as when dusting or vacuuming.

No one in Pepperville can explain why so many people in the same area would sneeze at the same time. The local police department is looking into the incident but has not yet come up with any leads.

Only one citizen escaped the mass sneeze—Mr. Salt. Ironically, Mr. Salt was also one of the victims of the incident, having lost his home to the sneeze. "I woke up to a loud noise," he said, "the next thing I knew my house fell down around me." When asked what he did next, Mr. Salt replied, "What could I do? I said, 'Gesundheit,' and went back to sleep."

From Visuals . . .

. . . to Print

Using the photograph above, write a short composition about the steps Mr. Salt had to take to rebuild his house in Pepperville. Be sure to include an introduction, body, and conclusion. Present your ideas in a logical order.

- **Which strategies can be used for creating both written and visual representations? Which strategies apply to one, not both? Which type of representation is more effective?**
- **Draw a conclusion, and write briefly about the differences between written ideas and visual representations.**

FOR REVIEWING SKILLS

Using *Connection Collection*

Representing in Different Ways

Consider using these print and visual activities to make students aware of the benefits of using different media to suit particular purposes. Help students understand when a visual medium, for example, is better suited to their purpose than a print medium, or the reverse.

Using *Connection Collection*

Consider using these writing prompts as independent or small-group activities.

YOUR IDEAS

For Viewing and Representing

Writing in the Workplace

Magazine Article

You work at the local telephone company. Your boss has asked you to write for other employees about your experience with a customer who tried to pay his telephone bill with a truckload of carrots.

Write a composition for the company magazine about your experience with the carrot-paying customer. Consider the audience of the magazine as you write. Provide a beginning that will capture reader's attention. Use specific details when describing the customer and the event. Include dialogue and make sure you tell how the situation was resolved.

What strategies did you use to describe the situation for your co-workers?

Writing for Oral Communication

Descriptive Presentation

As the set designer for a community theater, you have been asked to come up with a plan for a design of the theater company's latest production—*Romeo and Juliet's Excellent Adventure.* You need to present your ideas orally to producers before you begin sketching out your plans.

Prepare a composition describing the set of *Romeo and Juliet's Excellent Adventure*. Include sensory words and specific details in your description. Use spatial order to arrange your details into a logical order. Present the description to your class, who will act as the producers of the play.

What strategies did you use to describe your proposed set design to the play's producers?

You can find information on preparing oral presentations on pages C411–C118.

A DIFFERENT DELIVERY SYSTEM

For formal assessment print the composition chapter test from the *BK English* Test Bank at http://www.bkenglish.com.

Assess Your Learning

You are helping your pesky little brother with his homework when he remembers that his first-grade class is holding show-and-tell tomorrow. Since he looks up to you so much, he wants to bring in a picture of you. You are flattered—he is such a sweet kid.

- **Write a composition about yourself for your brother to read to his class when he shows your picture during show-and-tell. As you write, remember the age of your audience as well as the occasion.**
- **Focus your subject and include an introduction that will capture the audience's attention. Remember to include lively details and use precise wording in your composition. Vary sentence beginnings to give the composition an interesting structure. Your conclusion should leave the audience with a memorable image.**

Before You Write **Consider the following questions:**
What is the ***subject?***
What is the ***occasion?***
Who is the ***audience?***
What is the ***purpose?***

After You Write **Evaluate your work using the following criteria:**

- Does the composition address a specific audience and purpose?
- Is your subject focused?
- Does your composition include an introduction, body, and conclusion?
- Is the length of your sentences suited to your audience?
- Are your ideas presented in a logical order that young children can understand?
- Have you used vivid descriptive language?
- Have you chosen vocabulary that suits your audience?

Write briefly on how well you did. Point out your strengths and areas for improvement.

FOR ASSESSING LEARNING

Using *Assess Your Learning*

This writing prompt will help you and your students informally assess their developing writing abilities, using the accompanying primary trait rubrics, which list the key features and qualities of writing effective compositions taught in this chapter. You may want to have students maintain their self-assessment in their portfolios as a record of their individual progress throughout the year.

Evaluating Compositions

In writing compositions, students often need to concentrate on

- **developing a clear main idea**
- **making sure that all body paragraphs support this idea**
- **finding a tone suited to the composition's purpose and audience.**

Self-evaluation and peer evaluation at the revision stage can help students to improve in these areas.

Self-evaluation

After students have finished their first drafts, distribute copies of the Evaluation Checklist for Writing Effective Compositions. (See the Evaluation Checklists in BK English Language and Composition Assessment.) As students read their drafts for the first time, tell them to focus on content, with special attention to the traits numbered below.

Peer evaluation

An alternative strategy is for students to work in pairs or small groups to evaluate one another's paragraphs. Suggest that each author read at least part of his or her composition aloud and that the listener or listeners concentrate on identifying the main idea, purpose, or tone of the composition.

1 A thesis statement in the introduction makes clear the essay's main idea and purpose.
2 Each paragraph presents an idea that supports the main idea statement.
3 Each paragraph has a topic sentence, body, and conclusion.
4 The tone suits the composition's subject, purpose, and audience.
5 The conclusion reinforces the main idea.

Teacher evaluation

Primary Traits

The following introductory paragraph of a composition exhibits a clear main idea statement and suitable tone and suggests a plan for adding supporting paragraphs; it can be used as a model for evaluating students' compositions.

MODEL FOR EVALUATION

Excellent examples

A basketball star is arrested for using illegal drugs. A local citizen is awarded for volunteering countless hours to a homeless shelter. Who is the better role model? Today's society places too much importance on sports stars as role models, leading children to believe that they should behave as the athletes do. Unfortunately, many celebrity athletes do not exhibit appropriate conduct, and too many children are following their example. Over the years America's children have seen many instances of athletes behaving poorly. One involves an athlete arrested for drug use, one involves an athlete driving while intoxicated, and another involves an athlete arrested for illegal gambling.

Interesting thesis

Slightly angry tone suits topic

Good lead into supporting paragraphs

Teacher Evaluation

Primary Trait Evaluation

For primary trait assessment of students' compositions, the following chart lists key features.

	EXCELLENT	ACCEPTABLE	NEEDS IMPROVEMENT
Main Idea Statement	The introduction clearly states an interesting main idea that can be broken into topics and developed with details.	The introduction states a main idea that may be somewhat too broad or narrow to develop.	The essay does not have a recognizable main idea statement.
Organization	Each paragraph in the body of the composition develops an idea related to the main idea statement. Paragraphs are organized in a logical order suited to the topic.	Not all paragraphs relate clearly to the main idea statement. Some paragraphs or parts of paragraphs do not follow logical order.	The information presented is either irrelevant to the main idea statement, not in logical order, or both.
Supporting Details	Each paragraph has a topic sentence supported with facts, examples, reasons, or incidents.	Some topic sentences are well supported, but some are not.	Topic sentences are either lacking or poorly supported.
Tone	The tone of the composition is well suited to its subject, purpose, and audience.	The composition's tone is basically appropriate, and some transitions are used.	The composition's tone is unidentifiable or unsuitable. Transitional techniques are absent.
Conclusion	The composition has a strong conclusion that reinforces the main idea.	The conclusion at least affirms the main idea.	A conclusion either is lacking or does not reinforce the main idea.

Teacher Evaluation

Holistic Evaluation

The following criteria may be used to evaluate students' compositions holistically, using a rating scale of
- 4 (excellent)
- 3 (good)
- 2 (acceptable)
- 1 (needs improvement)
- 0 (unscoreable)

4	3	2	1
The main idea is contained in an interesting introductory statement and can be developed with details.	The main idea is clear and capable of being developed with details.	The main idea is not subject to much development.	The composition has either no main idea or none that can be developed.
The composition employs interesting, plentiful, and logically ordered supporting facts, examples, reasons, or incidents.	Supporting material generally is sufficient and well ordered.	The composition contains some supporting details that are relevant to the main idea.	Details are irrelevant or lacking.
The composition is well organized. An appropriate tone is set in the introduction and carried throughout the composition. The body offers well-developed supporting paragraphs in logical order. A strong conclusion reinforces the main idea.	The composition is basically well organized, but a few supporting paragraphs or sentences are out of logical order or unneeded.	The composition is in introduction-body-conclusion form, but the relation of its parts to the main idea and to one another is hard to follow.	The composition is not organized into a recognizable introduction, body, and conclusion.

Achieving Writer's Purpose

PLANNING GUIDE This chart will help you create a flexible instructional plan that addresses the individual needs of all your students in the new millennium.

LEARNING TO KNOW

A Foundation of Knowledge	CHAPTER 5 Personal Writing: Self-Expression and Reflection	CHAPTER 6 Using Description: Observation	CHAPTER 7 Creative Writing: Stories, Plays, and Poems
PE **Communication Models**	Reading with a Writer's Eye, p. C126 "The House on Mango Street" by Sandra Cisneros, pp. C127–C129 Thinking as a Writer, p. C130 **Grammar in the Writing Process** • Pronouns, pp. C145-C146	Reading with a Writer's Eye, p. C154 "Rascal" by Sterling North, pp. C155–C164 Thinking as a Writer, p. C165 **Grammar in the Writing Process** • Adjectives, p. C180	Reading with a Writer's Eye, p. C188 "Pauses" by Lee Bennett Hopkins, pp. C189–C190 Thinking as a Writer, p. C191 **Grammar in the Writing Process** • Dialogue Punctuation, p. C213
TE **Skills Instruction**	Lesson 1: Narrative Structure Lesson 2: First and Third Person Styles Lesson 3: Writing a Narrative Paragraph	Lesson 1: Descriptive Structure Lesson 2: Specific Details, Sensory Words, and Spatial Order Lesson 3: Writing a Descriptive Paragraph	Lesson 1: Structure and Elements of the Short Story Lesson 2: Writing a Short Story Lesson 3: Play Scene with Setting, Dialogue, and Stage Directions Lesson 4: Elements and Writing of Humorous Poems
PE **Skills Practice**	**Practice Your Skills** • Chronological Order, pp. C136–C137 • Transitions, pp. C139–C140 • First Person and Third Person Narratives, p. C141 • Adequate Development, p. C143 **Writing Is Thinking** • Imagining, p. C134	**Practice Your Skills** • Topic Sentences, p. C169 • Sensory Details, p. C172 • Types of Spatial Order, pp. C174–C175 **Writing Is Thinking** • Developing Skills of Observation, p. C171	**Practice Your Skills** • Short Story, p. C201 • Thinking of Subjects, p. C202–C203 • Different Points of View, p. C204 • Characters, p. C205 • Settings, p. C206 • Dialogue, p. C209 • Choosing a Conflict or Problem, p. C219 • Characters, p. C220 • Settings, p. C220 • Dialogue, p. C221 • Stage Directions, p. C222 • Ideas for a Humorous Poem, p. C226 • Free Verse Poems and Sound Devices, p. C230 **Writing Is Thinking** • Predicting, p. C200
PE **Independent Application**	**Communicating Your Ideas** • Chronological Order, p. C137 • Transitions, p. C141 • Adequate Development, p. C143 • Unity, Coherence, and Clarity, p. C144 **Connection Collection** • Representing, pp. C151–C152	**In the Media** • Sound Bites, p. C176 **Communicating Your Ideas** • Topic Sentence, p. C169 • Drafting, p. C172 • Spatial Order and Transitions, p. C175 **Connection Collection** • Representing, p. C185 • In Everyday Life, p. C186 • In Academic Areas, p. C186	**In the Media** • Evaluating Performances, p. C211 **Communicating Your Ideas** • Subject Choice, p. C203 • Story Element Grid, p. C207 • Story Beginning, p. C208 • Story Middle, p. C209 • Story Resolution, p. C210 • Evaluation Checklist for Revising Short Stories, p. C212 • Editing, p. C214 • Read Aloud, p. C214 • Scene From a Play, p. C223 • Poem, p. C231 **Connection Collection** • From Print to Visuals, p. C235 • Representing, p. C236
Assessment and Evaluation	PE Time Out to Reflect, p. C146 PE Checklist for Writing a Narrative, p. C148 PE A Writer Writes, pp. C149–C150 PE Assess Your Learning, p. C153 + I Chapter Test TE Evaluating Personal Essays, pp. C153a–C153b	PE Time Out to Reflect, p. C175 PE Assess Your Learning, p. C187 + I Chapter Test	PE Time Out to Reflect, p. C231 PE Checklist for Creative Writing, p. C232 PE A Writer Writes, pp. C233–C234 PE Assess Your Learning, p. C237 + I Chapter Test TE Evaluating Creative Writing, pp. C237a–C237b

PE PUPIL'S EDITION TE TEACHER'S EDITION + ANCILLARIES I INTERNET

ADDITIONAL RESOURCES

- Composition Skills Practice
- Language Skills Practice
- Assessment
- Assessment Resources
- Standardized Test Preparation
- ESL Practice and Test Preparation
- Transparency Tools
- Writing Prompts
- Writers at Work

CHAPTER 8 Writing to Explain or Inform	CHAPTER 9 Writing to Persuade	CHAPTER 10 Writing About Literature
Reading with a Writer's Eye, p. C238 "Where a Hurricane Gets Its Force" by Time Magazine, pp. C239–C241 Thinking as a Writer, p. C242 **Grammar in the Writing Process** • Colorful Verbs, p. C265	Reading with a Writer's Eye, p. C276 "Homeless" by Anna Quindlen, pp. C277–C280 Thinking as a Writer, p. C281 **Grammar in the Writing Process** • Predicate Nominatives and Adjectives, p. C295	Reading with a Writer's Eye, p. C304 "Checkouts" by Cynthia Rylant, pp. C305–C309 Thinking as a Writer, p. C310 **Grammar in the Writing Process** • Participles, p. C333
Lesson 1: Informative Structure and Prewriting Strategies Lesson 2: Drafting Lesson 3: Revising, Editing	Lesson 1: Persuasive Structure Lesson 2: Facts and Opinions Lesson 3: Writing Persuasive Paragraphs	Lesson 1: Personal and Literary Responses Lesson 2: Prewriting Lesson 3: Drafting, Revising, Editing, Publishing
Practice Your Skills • Limiting Subjects, p. C250 • Audience Questions, pp. C251–C252 • Arranging Details in Logical Order, pp. C255–C256 • Topic Sentences, pp. C258–C259 • Unity and Coherence, p. C262 **Writing Is Thinking** • Analyzing, p. C253	**Practice Your Skills** • Recognizing Facts and Opinions, Clustering, Writing Persuasive Topic Sentences, and Revising a Paragraph with Facts, pp. C285–C289 **Writing Is Thinking** • Hypothesizing, p. C290	**Practice Your Skills** • Responding from Personal Experience, p. C314 • Prewriting Plot Diagram, p. C316 • Choosing Subjects, p. C318 • Limiting Subjects, p. C321 **Writing Is Thinking** • Synthesizing, p. C319
In the Media • Create a "How-to" Show, p. C267 **Communicating Your Ideas** • Subject Inventory, p. C247 • Choosing a Subject, p. C248 • Supporting Details, p. C252 • Idea Organization, p. C256 • Topic Sentence, Body, and Concluding Sentence, p. C261 • Conference, p. C263 • Editing, Publishing, p. C264 **Connection Collection** • Representing, p. C273 • In the Workplace, p. C274 • In Academic Areas, p. C274	**In the Media** • Radio Advertising, p. C287 **Communicating Your Ideas** • Reasons, p. C289 • Prewriting, Drafting, p. C292 **Connection Collection** • Representing, p. C301 • In Academic Areas, p. C302 • Oral Communication, p. C302	**In the Media** • Adapting Literature, p. C335 **Communicating Your Ideas** • Personal Response, p. C315 • Subject, p. C320 • Limited Subject, p. C321 • Thesis, p. C322 • Evidence, p. C325 • Supporting Details, p. C327 • Writing About Literature, p. C330 • Conferencing, p. C332 • Editing, p. C334 • Publishing, p. C336 **Connection Collection** • Representing, p. C341 • In the Workplace, p. C342 • Oral Communication, p. C342
PE Time Out to Reflect, p. C269 PE Checklist for Writing to Inform and Explain, p. C270 PE A Writer Writes, pp. C271–C272 PE Assess Your Learning, p. C275 + I Chapter Test TE Evaluating Informative Writing, pp. C275a–C275b	PE Time Out to Reflect, p. C297 PE Checklist for Revising, p. C297 PE Checklist for Writing a Persuasive Paragraph, p. C298 PE A Writer Writes, pp. C299–C300 PE Assess Your Learning, p. C303 + I Chapter Test TE Evaluating Persuasive Writing, pp. C303a–C303b	PE Time Out to Reflect, p. C337 PE Checklist for Writing About Literature, p. C338 PE A Writer Writes, pp. C339–C340 PE Assess Your Learning, p. C343 + I Chapter Test TE Evaluating Compositions About Literature, pp. C343a–C343b

LEARNING TO DO

Competencies for the World of Work

Basic Skills
Reads, writes, performs arithmetic and mathematical operations, listens, and speaks
- Reading
- Writing
- Arithmetic/Mathematics
- Listening
- Speaking

Thinking Skills
Thinks creatively, makes decisions, solves problems, visualizes, knows how to learn, and reasons
- Creative Thinking
- Decision Making
- Problem Solving
- Seeing Things in the Mind's Eye
- Knowing How to Learn
- Reasoning

Personal Qualities
Displays responsibility, self-esteem, sociability, self-management, and integrity and honesty
- Responsibility
- Self-Esteem
- Sociability
- Self-Management
- Integrity/Honesty

LEARNING WITH TECHNOLOGY

Tools for the Information Age

I **http://www.bkenglish.com**
- BK English Online (password required)
- Chapter Tests
- Skill Practice
- Writing Prompts
- Standardized Tests

TEACHING SUGGESTIONS

Essential Knowledge and Skills

- Producing cohesive and coherent written texts by organizing ideas, using effective transitions, and choosing precise wording
- Employing standard English usage in writing for audiences, including pronoun referents, and parts of speech
- Revising selected drafts by adding, elaborating, deleting, combining, and rearranging texts
- Revising drafts for coherence, progression, and logical support of ideas
- Selecting, organizing, or producing visuals to complement and extend meanings

CHAPTER 5

Personal Writing: Self-Expression and Reflection

One of the most important parts of planning a composition is knowing your purpose for writing. If your purpose is to tell a story, you will be writing a narrative. On a history test, for example, you might write a narrative telling the story of Paul Revere's midnight ride. In an E-mail to a friend or relative, you might tell what happened at your team's first volleyball practice. Whenever you are writing a story, you are writing a narrative.

A personal narrative can stir up a range of feelings within you—joy, sorrow, excitement, sympathy, even frustration. A well-written personal narrative can help you better understand an event, whether you are reading about it for the first time or writing about something that happened to you.

Reading with a Writer's Eye

The House on Mango Street is a real-life memoir by the writer Sandra Cisneros. Read through the excerpt once, just to understand what's going on. As you read for a second time, take note of the images Cisneros describes. What words does she use to describe her homes? How do these images come together to create a portrait of the houses and neighborhoods she and her family lived in?

BLOCK SCHEDULING

- If your schedule requires that you cover the chapter in a **shorter time**, use Reading with a Writer's Eye, Thinking as a Writer, and Process of Writing a Personal Narrative.
- If you want to take advantage of **longer class time**, add any or all of the following: Writing Is Thinking, Grammar in the Writing Process, and a Writer Writes.

FROM

THE HOUSE ON MANGO STREET

Sandra Cisneros

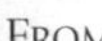

We didn't always live on Mango Street. Before that we lived on Loomis on the third floor, and before that we lived on Keeler. Before Keeler it was Paulina, and before that I can't remember. But what I remember most is moving a lot. Each time it seemed there'd be one more of us. By the time we got to Mango Street we were six—Mama, Papa, Carlos, Kiki, my sister Nenny and me.

The house on Mango Street is ours, and we don't have to pay rent to anybody, or share the yard with the people downstairs, or be careful not to make too much noise, and there isn't a landlord banging on the ceiling with a broom. But even so, it's not the house we'd thought we'd get.

We had to leave the flat on Loomis quick. The water pipes broke and the landlord wouldn't fix them because the house was too old. We had to leave fast. We were using the washroom next door and carrying water over in empty milk gallons. That's why Mama and Papa looked for a house, and that's why we moved into the house on Mango Street, far away, on the other side of town.

FOR INCREASING STUDENT ACHIEVEMENT

GUIDED READING

Text Analysis

- **Narrative** is the primary mode of this fiction selection. Cisneros is part of the events, so she tells the story in the first person narrative style. She writes most of the selection in the plural. To highlight her personal reaction to events, she switches to the singular for one sentence in the first paragraph and for the last several sentences of the excerpt.
- **Repetition** provides emphasis. In the second and third sentence of the first paragraph, Cisneros uses *before* four times in the first two sentences to emphasize the movement of time. In the next to the last paragraph, she uses *there* five times to emphasize that the house was separate from her psychologically as well as physically.
- **Variation** in the sentence structure makes the story pleasing to listen to. The sentences with the most emotional power are the short ones, such as "We didn't always live on Mango Street," and, "We had to leave fast." The entire last paragraph is made up of short sentences and fragments. This increases the tempo of the writing and leads to a climax in the last sentence.

SELECTION AMENDMENT
Description of change: excerpted
Rationale: to focus on concept of using specific details and sensory words

GUIDED READING

Strategy: Noting Important Details

Ask students to notice the two times that Cisneros lists her family members. Each time, she sets their names off from the rest of the sentence with a dash. Discuss whether students think Cisneros did this on purpose. She may have been trying to focus attention on her family as a unit, separate and distinct in the world, all struggling together.

YOUR IDEAS

For Guided Reading

They always told us that one day we would move into a house, a real house that would be ours for always so we wouldn't have to move each year. And our house would have running water and pipes that worked. And inside would have real stairs, not hallway stairs, but stairs inside like the houses on T.V. And we'd have a basement and at least three washrooms so when we took a bath we wouldn't have to tell everybody. Our house would be white with trees around it, a great big yard and grass growing without a fence. This was the house Papa talked about when he held a lottery ticket and this was the house Mama dreamed up in the stories she told us before we went to bed.

But the house on Mango Street is not the way they told it at all. It's small and red with tight steps in the front and windows so small you'd think they were holding their breath. Bricks are crumbling in places, and the front door is so swollen you have to push hard to get in. There is no front yard, only four little elms the city planted by the curb. Out back is a small garage for the car we don't own yet and a small yard that looks smaller between two buildings on either side. There are stairs in our house but they're ordinary hallway stairs, and the house has only one washroom. Everybody has to share a bedroom—Mama and Papa, Carlos and Kiki, me and Nenny.

Once when we were living on Loomis, a nun from my school passed by and saw me playing out front. The laundromat downstairs had been boarded up because it had been robbed two days before and the owner had painted on the wood YES WE'RE OPEN so as not to lose business.

Where do you live? she asked.

There, I said pointing to the third floor.

You live *there*?

There. I had to look to where she pointed—the third floor, the paint peeling, wooden bars Papa had nailed on the windows so we wouldn't fall out. You live *there*? The way she said it made me feel like nothing. *There.* I lived *there*. I nodded.

I knew then I had to have a house. A real house. One I could point to. But this isn't it. The house on Mango Street isn't it. For the time being, Mama says. Temporary, says Papa. But I know how those things go.

READER RESPONSE

You may want to use the following questions to elicit students' personal responses to the selection.

1. How do you think you would have reacted to moving into the house on Mango Street?
2. What is your impression of Cisneros's parents?
3. How did you feel towards Cisneros when she described talking with the nun?
4. Based on this excerpt, what would you predict would happen to Cisneros in the future?

LITERARY CONNECTION

You might want to explore personal writing in the following works, which appear in literature textbooks at this grade level.

- "Achieving the American Dream" by Mario Cuomo
- *All But My Life* by Gerda Weissmann Klein
- "The Dogs Could Teach Me" by Gary Paulsen
- "My Two Dads" by Marie G. Lee

ADDITIONAL RESOURCES

Composition Skills Practice	pages 25–28
Transparency Tools	VR4
Writing Prompts	pages 1, 12, 16, 23, 27, 40
Connection Collection	pages C151–C152
ESL Practice and Test Preparation	pages 29–35
Standardized Test Preparation	Units 7, 14, 15
Writers at Work	8•1–8•10
Assessment: Chapter Test	pages 52–55
Assessment Resources	pages 1–10, 13–44, 46–53

Using *Thinking as a Writer*

You may choose to have students respond to the questions either orally or in writing.

YOUR IDEAS

For Thinking as a Writer

Thinking as a Writer

Identifying Narrative Purpose

People often choose subjects that are very meaningful to them when writing personal narratives. Part of what makes *The House on Mango Street* so interesting is the importance of the main idea to its author.

- Why do you think Sandra Cisneros chose to write about her childhood homes? What do you think might have been different about her personal narrative had she written about a visit to an amusement park?

Exploring Subjects for a Personal Narrative

Oral Expression

- Think of something that happened to you that brought up strong feelings. It could be an event from long ago or from last week.
- In a small group, talk about the experience that you chose, and compare it to those of your classmates. Whose story was the most moving, funny, or enjoyable?

Contrasting Narrative Style

Viewing The two houses below are very different, both in setting and in style.

- Using your imagination as your guide, write a paragraph about the people who live in each of these houses.
- Exchange papers with a classmate. How do your paragraphs compare?

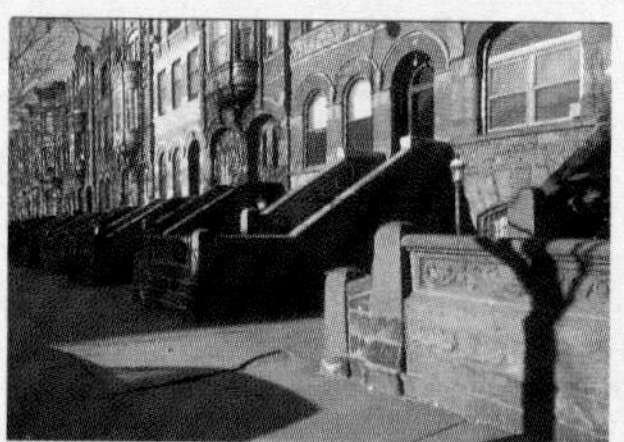

FOR DEVELOPING SKILLS

LESSON 1 *(pages C131–C140)*

OBJECTIVES

- **To recognize that the purpose of narrative writing is to tell a story**
- **To use chronological order with appropriate transitions**

Create Interest

Ask students to volunteer to tell their favorite stories. These might be fairy tales, movie plots, historical anecdotes, or jokes. Ask students to identify the similarities in the structure of these stories. Usually, they have three identifiable sections: beginning, middle, and end. In addition, something or some character changes between the beginning and the end, and that is often what makes the story memorable. Point out that stories are narratives.

The Power of Personal Writing

You have already read an example of a personal narrative—Sandra Cisneros's account of her childhood homes. A personal narrative is one kind of narrative writing.

Uses of Personal Writing

Here are just a few examples of the ways in which narrative writing is used to relay thoughts, feelings, and events.

- **A presidential candidate makes a speech** to convince voters that her background has shaped her for this important office.
- **Your grandmother writes you an E-mail message** telling you how much your visit means to her.
- **A filmmaker makes a documentary** on the real-life stories of hurricane survivors.
- **You keep a journal** recording your amazing experiences exploring the mountains of Peru.

CAREERS AND COMMUNICATION

Historian

One profession in which people often write narratives is history. The English word history comes from the Greek word *historia*, which means finding out. The job of a historian is to find out what happened in the past and to tell about it.

Many people trained as historians are employed by colleges or universities. In these positions, they usually combine writing about their research with teaching students. Other historians work for historical societies or research institutes, positions in which their subjects for research are determined by their employer. Some people with degrees in history work for private companies, documenting and explaining the history of the company.

Historians often write reflective accounts of the lives of individuals. Sometimes, they write a book-length biography of one person. Often, though, they incorporate the story of an individual into a larger work. These stories may come from their own research or be based on the research of others.

Ask students to write a one-page summary of the life story of an elderly relative or neighbor. The student should interview the individual and write about the key points in the person's life.

Guide Instruction

By Modeling Strategies

Ask students to evaluate the topic sentence in "A Surprise Visitor" on page C135. Tell students that the writer of this paragraph could have chosen topic sentences that fulfill other purposes. She could have set the scene: "Sounds drifted into my tent from the African Serengeti plains as I tried to sleep." Or, she could have tried to capture the reader's attention with drama. "What is that sound? I wondered fearfully as I lay in my bed." Discuss whether students think either of these sentences would have worked well with this story.

Consolidate Skills

Through Guided Practice

The **Practice Your Skill** activity on adding transitions on page C139 will provide students an opportunity to use transitions in a paragraph. To extend the activity, discuss what other transitions could fit into each of the blanks.

INTEGRATING TECHNOLOGY

Internet

Several Websites include first person narratives about historical events. A Library of Congress site, at http://memory.loc.gov/ammem/cbhtml/cbhome.html, includes a collection "'California as I Saw It:' First-Person Narratives of California's Early Years, 1849-1900." The University of Virginia has a site that includes several slave narratives collected in the 1930s, many with audio: http://xroads.virginia.edu/~HYPER/wpa/wpahome.html. A collection of first-hand accounts available on the Internet is at http://www.justpublications.org/linklib/index.cgi.

Process of Writing a Personal Narrative

Whenever your purpose in writing is to tell what happened, you will be writing a narrative. Although narrative paragraphs differ from informative paragraphs, the process of writing them is similar. In both cases you begin by exploring your storehouse of memories and experiences for ideas and continue by shaping your ideas into an organized plan for writing. In both cases you use your plan to help you write a first draft. After drafting you look at your work critically. You ask yourself which parts seem to work well and which need further work. Finally, in both cases you add the finishing touches to your writing by correcting your mistakes, making a neat copy, and presenting your work to a reader.

As always, however, you may find that a technique that works well for one writing activity may not work as well for another. As you work your way through writing various narrative paragraphs, try to judge which strategies work best for you.

Narrative writing tells a real or imaginary story that has a clear beginning, middle, and end.

The following narrative paragraph describes a woman's visit to the Serengeti, a large wildlife preserve in northern Tanzania. The writer begins with a topic sentence that makes a general statement. The concluding sentence summarizes the events. As you read the paragraph, notice how the story unfolds event by event.

Apply to Communication

Through Independent Writing

The **Communicate Your Ideas** activity on transitions will help students develop their skill by showing when events happen. Ask volunteers to read their drafts to the class. Encourage students to provide constructive comments about how well the sentences flow into each other. Point out places where a change in a transition might help.

Transfer to Everyday Life

By Discussing

Ask students to bring in newspaper articles. Discuss whether they tell a story. If they do, note whether the first sentence summarizes the main points of the article, and whether the last sentence provides a conclusion. Save the articles for the next activity.

Your Writer's Journal

Many imaginary stories take shape when a writer asks "What would happen if . . . ?" To help you think of subjects for stories, choose one of the following *what if* questions. In your journal, write a story that answers the question you've chosen.

- What would happen if two mind readers became roommates?
- What would happen if your dog began to talk?
- What would happen if a person who did not speak the same language as you came to stay with you for a month?
- What would happen if your town flooded after a large storm?

Narrative Paragraph Structure

The following chart shows how each part of a narrative paragraph helps to tell a story.

Structure of a Narrative Paragraph

- The **topic sentence** introduces the story by making a general statement, setting the scene, or capturing the reader's attention.
- The **supporting sentences** tell the story event by event and answer the questions *Who? What? Where? Why? When?* and *How?*
- The **concluding sentence** ends the story by summarizing the events or making a point about the story.

IDENTIFYING COMMON STUMBLING BLOCKS

Problem

- Students may have difficulty creating a narrative on their own that includes several elements of a good story, such as a clear conflict, characters, symbolism, and theme.

Solution

- Have students revise a story created by someone else. Ask students to choose a familiar story, such as a fairy tale, a movie plot, or a nursery rhyme, and write freely for about five minutes, noting all the aspects of the original story they don't like. Then have the students rewrite the whole story as they would like.

Pull It All Together

Evaluating News Stories

Evaluate the newspaper articles that students have brought in. Note whether they use transitions effectively to tell readers when events happened.

Check Understanding

By Using the Literary Selection

Have students make a time line for the excerpt from *The House on Mango Street*. Discuss why Cisneros may have decided to present some of the information out of chronological order.

Using *Writing Is Thinking*

Objective

- **To understand the significance of imagination in writing**

A DIFFERENT APPROACH

Auditory Have students make a list of five sounds they hear in their home: the ring of a telephone, the buzz of an alarm clock, the beep of a microwave, the creak of the stairs, the drip of a faucet, etc. Then ask them to write down an imaginative use of each sound in a narrative about themselves.

Kinesthetic Ask students to describe in writing a gesture or movement, and then explain how this motion might be used in various settings. For example, a boy suddenly raising his right hand might be responding to a teacher's question, trying to grab a fly, gesturing toward a shooting star, waving to a passing celebrity, or performing a dance.

Thinking Skills	
Classifying	Analyzing
Comparing	Hypothesizing
Generalizing	Synthesizing
Inferring	Summarizing
Imagining	Setting Goals
Observing	Evaluating Audience
Predicting	

Writing Is Thinking

Imagining

When you write a narrative, you can tell a true story like the one Joy Adamson told about her surprise visitor. By using the skill of imagining, however, you can also write a narrative about events that *could* have happened but did not. **Imagining** means creating new situations and events out of your memory and experience. Through imagining you can enter new worlds and take your reader with you. Edgar Allan Poe, author of "The Raven" and many other stories and poems about the dark side of life, knew the power of the imagination. He wrote: "If you cannot conveniently tumble out of a balloon, or be swallowed up in an earthquake, or get stuck fast in a chimney, you will have to be contented with simply imagining some similar misadventure."

THINKING PRACTICE

Look at the picture on this page. Use your imagination to answer one of the following questions through freewriting. Save your ideas in case you would like to use them in developing an imaginative narrative.

- Imagine you are one of the people in the cage. How did you get there? What are you doing? Why are you doing it? How do you get back to safety?
- Imagine you are one of the polar bears in the picture. What do you make of this thing and the creatures in it? How do you feel about it? How do you respond?

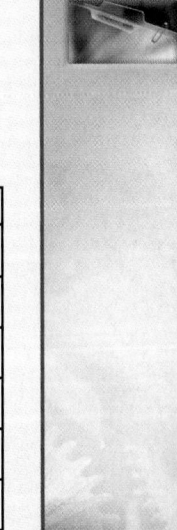

MODEL: Narrative Paragraph

A Surprise Visitor

TOPIC SENTENCE — My nights in camp were often exciting.

SUPPORTING SENTENCES — I could hear lions prowling around. I even came to recognize the voices of most of them. Once I awoke to hear lapping noises. Being half asleep, I listened for some time before I realized that a lioness was inside my tent drinking out of my basin. I shouted at her to go away, which finally she did. I reported this incident to the park warden. He told me that lions of the Serengeti were known occasionally to go into tents and take a look around to see what was going on.

CONCLUDING SENTENCE — I shall never forget the night that nothing but a table stood between me and Africa.

–*Joy Adamson,* Forever Free

Prewriting

Writing Process

During the prewriting stage, your mind should be free to wander as you search your memories for possible subjects for narrative paragraphs. This is the time to take the opportunity to jot down any ideas that come to mind, using prewriting techniques such as brainstorming, clustering, and freewriting to help get ideas to start flowing. Before long you will find that you have a good subject for a personal narrative.

Chronological Order

Most narrative paragraphs are arranged in **chronological order.** In chronological order, or time order, events are arranged in the order in which they happened.

REACHING ALL STUDENTS

Struggling Learners

Ask students to bring in examples of stories that are only one or two paragraphs long. Such short stories can be found in books of fables, anecdotes, and jokes. Have volunteers read their story to the class, and discuss the structure of each one. Point out the introduction, body, and conclusion.

GETTING STUDENTS INVOLVED

Cooperative Learning

Have students work together in small groups to create a story. One student should start by speaking the first line of the story, and a transition word to start the second sentence. The next student should complete the sentence and give the transition to start the next. Students should continue until everyone has contributed at least three sentences. Each student should take notes to remember what he or she said. Ask a group to volunteer to tell their story to the class.

SELECTION AMENDMENT
Description of change: excerpted
Rationale: to focus on the concept of narrative writing presented in this chapter

PRACTICE YOUR SKILLS Sample Answers

1. **being locked out of the house**

   assuring my parents in the morning that I would remember to take my keys to school with me

   arriving home after my student council meeting and realizing I had left my keys in my school locker

   remembering with relief that my neighbors had a set of keys to my house

2. **auditioning for the school musical**

   signing up for the audition

   rehearsing for weeks to master the songs for the part I wanted

   being called to audition

   searching for my name on the list of people who made the cast

   seeing my name next to the part I wanted

3. **power blackout caused by electrical storm**

   last Tuesday severe thunderstorm occurred at 9:20 P.M.

   power out in six-block area near my home

   workers from the power company began tracing problem immediately

   located a power line that had been hit by lightning

   workers continued for three more hours to repair damage

The following paragraph is in chronological order.

MODEL: Chronological Order

Anything but Trotting

I had often dreamed of riding a horse. I imagined myself sailing smoothly along, horse and rider as one. This was my day! Here I was, perched on top of a beautiful gray horse. Everything was fine. The lead horse led us slowly down the forest path. We came to a clearing and the horses broke into a canter, a smooth and easy-to-ride gait. They sped into a gallop, a thunderous pace that was surprisingly easy to ride. Everything went fine until the lead horse started to trot and my dream of riding smoothly vanished. I was bouncing wildly and could hardly catch my breath. After minutes that seemed like hours, the lead horse finally headed back to the stable at a slow walk. I knew very well what it meant to be saddle sore. The only place I wanted to be for the next few days was in a very soft chair.

PRACTICE YOUR SKILLS

Arranging Events in Chronological Order

Write each subject. Then list the events in chronological order.

1. SUBJECT being locked out of the house

EVENTS

- remembering with relief that my neighbors had a set of keys to my house
- assuring my parents in the morning that I would remember to take my keys to school with me
- arriving home after my student council meeting and realizing I had left my keys in my school locker

2. Subject auditioning for the school musical

Events

- being called to audition
- rehearsing for weeks to master the songs for the part I wanted
- signing up for the audition
- searching for my name on the list of people who made the cast
- seeing my name next to the part I wanted

3. Subject power blackout caused by electrical storm

Events

- workers continued for three more hours to repair damage
- power out in six-block area near my home
- last Tuesday severe thunderstorm occurred at 9:20 P.M.
- located a power line that had been hit by lightning
- workers from power company began tracing problem immediately

Communicate Your Ideas

PREWRITING *Chronological Order*

Use freewriting, clustering, or any other prewriting strategy to think of a good subject for a personal narrative. (You may wish to use your work from Writing Is Thinking, page C134, for ideas.) Then develop a list of all the events that will be included in your narrative paragraph. Finally, arrange your list of events in chronological order. Save your work in your writing folder for later use. SAVE YOUR WORK

HOME WORK

Have students describe an event that occurs to them during the evening. They should use chronological order in their description.

TIMESAVER *QuickCheck*

Have students review each other's work. They should check that the other student has chosen a clear subject, created a list of relevant events, and arranged the events in chronological order.

HOME STUDY

Students can do this activity at home with a partner. Particularly when trying to list all the events for a story, students may find it helpful to work with someone else.

REACHING ALL STUDENTS

English Language Learners

Ask students learning English to create pairs of transitions that have similar meanings. For example, *next* and *afterward* are similar. Encourage students to use a dictionary for words they do not know.

USING STUDENTS' STRENGTHS

Multiple Intelligences: Kinesthetic

Remind students that time lines show the relative length of time between events. Divide students into small groups. Each group should create a human time line in which each student represents an event. They should stand in a line, with the distance between them corresponding to how far apart in time each event occurred.

Multiple Intelligences: Intrapersonal

Have students create a time line showing change in one aspect of their life. They might note landmarks in their development of a particular skill such as swimming, in their shifting tastes in music, or in their growing awareness of politics. Discuss how these events could be incorporated into a personal narrative.

Drafting

Writing Process

Writing the first draft of your personal narrative is a matter of transforming your ideas first into sentences and then into a paragraph. As with other kinds of paragraphs, your narrative paragraph should include a topic sentence, a body, and a concluding sentence. Keep your readers' interests in mind as you write.

Transitions

Presenting your ideas in chronological order will help your readers follow the events in narrative writing. Use transitional words and phrases to make sure that the order is clear. **Transitions** are words and phrases that show how ideas are related. In chronological order, transitions point out the passing of time.

The following transitions are useful in showing chronological order in narrative writing.

TRANSITIONS FOR CHRONOLOGICAL ORDER

after	during	afterward	immediately
later	until	just as	while
next	first	meanwhile	then
when	second	suddenly	the next day
before	at last	finally	after a while

Following is a version of the paragraph that you read on page C136. This version, however, contains transitions, which appear in blue type.

LESSON 2 *(pages C140–C143)*

OBJECTIVES

- **To use first person narrative style appropriately**
- **To use third person narrative style appropriately**

Create Interest

Tell students that the way a particular behavior is described often reflects the person doing the behavior. For example, a two-year old playing with food is cute; a thirteen-year-old playing with food is childish. On the board, make two columns, *I am* and *He* or *She is*. Ask students to suggest pairs of words that both might describe the same action. For example, *I am courageous, he is reckless; I am cautious, she is indecisive; I am fast, he is careless; I am honest, she is rude.* Help students understand the importance of point of view in writing.

MODEL: Transitions

I had often dreamed of riding a horse, of sailing smoothly as if horse and rider were one. **Today** was my day. Here I was perched on top of a huge gray horse. **At first** everything was fine. The horses in my group were walking slowly down the forest path. **Before long** we came to a clearing and the horses broke into a canter, a smooth and easy-to-ride gait. **Then** the lead horse sped into a gallop, a thunderous gait that was surprisingly easy to ride. Everything went fine **for the rest of the morning** until the lead horse started to trot. **With the first** trot, my dream of horse and rider as one vanished. I was bouncing wildly and could hardly catch my breath. **After** minutes that seemed like hours, we **finally** headed back to the stable at a slow walk. **By then** I knew very well what it meant to be saddle sore. The only place I wanted to be for the next few days was in a very soft chair.

PRACTICE YOUR SKILLS

Adding Transitions

As you write the following paragraph, replace each blank with a transition. Use the transitions listed below.

after	the next morning	last summer
until	before they left	for two hours

My Gardening Days Are Over

I will never be a gardener again. I was a gardener for two days ■ when my parents went away on vacation. ■ , they told me to water the fruit trees every morning without fail. ■ I was about to water the trees when I had a great idea. I pushed the hose

HOME WORK

Have students write another paragraph using the same six transitions as in the **Practice Your Skills** activity on transitions.

PRACTICE YOUR SKILLS Sample Answers

I will never be a gardener again. I was a gardener for two days **last summer** when my parents went away on vacation. **Before they left**, they told me to water the fruit trees every morning without fail. **The next morning** I was about to water the trees when I had a great idea. I pushed the hose down into the ground so the water would reach the roots more quickly. My idea worked **until** I tried to pull the hose back out. It would not budge. **After** tugging at it **for two hours**, I had to cut it off. I ended up spending my whole allowance on a new hose.

Guide Instruction

By Modeling Strategies

With students, review a well-known story, such as "Little Red Riding Hood" or the ride of Paul Revere, that is usually told in third person style. Retell the story in first person style. Discuss how this change affects the emotional impact of the story.

Consolidate Skills

Through Guided Practice

Have students compare the models of first person and third person narrative style about the boys fishing. Discuss the advantages of each style. First person may have more immediacy, but third person may seem more objective.

Apply to Communication

Through Independent Writing

Have students write a one-paragraph personal story in first person style, and then rewrite it in third person style. Discuss whether they felt one style was more effective than the other.

REACHING ALL STUDENTS

Struggling Learners

If students have difficulty organizing their paragraph, have them write their information in a list. They should start each sentence on a separate line, and number the sentences in the order they occurred. After they have the chronology correct, they can replace the numbers with transitions and make other revisions as needed to transform their list into a paragraph.

down into the ground so the water would reach the roots more quickly. My idea worked ■ I tried to pull the hose back out. It would not budge. ■ tugging at it ■ , I had to cut it off. I ended up spending my whole allowance on a new hose.

First Person and Third Person Narratives

In personal narratives, the person telling the story is a character in the story. In this type of narrative, the first person pronouns *I, we, me, us, my,* and *our* are used. These narratives are called **first person narratives.**

Model: First Person Narrative

Mike and **I** were just packing away **our** gear after a successful day of fishing when the trouble began. As storm clouds started to gather, **we** headed for the shore. Suddenly . . . .

Some narratives do not involve the writer at all. Writers telling a story about other people will refer to them with third person pronouns. These stories are called **third person narratives.**

Model: Third Person Narrative

The boys were just packing away **their** gear after a successful day of fishing when the trouble began. As storm clouds started to gather, **they** headed for shore. Suddenly . . . .

Transfer to Everyday Life

By Listening to the News

Ask students to listen to a radio newscast and take notes on whether the reporters use first person or third person narrative style. Longer stories, such as those on National Public Radio newscasts, often use both. These newscasts are available on the Internet at http://www.npr.org.

Pull It All Together

By Sharing

Ask students to tell about favorite books or stories they have read. Discuss whether they were written in first person or third person narrative style.

Check Understanding

By Using Well-Known Literature

Read the opening lines from famous works, such as the "Gettysburg Address" and *Moby-Dick,* or famous quotations. Ask students to identify whether they are in first person or third person narrative style.

Writing Tip

As you plan your narrative, decide which **point of view** suits your story and then use it consistently.

Practice Your Skills

Recognizing First Person and Third Person Narratives

Read each story beginning. Then write *first person* or *third person* to tell what type of narrative is used.

1. My last birthday was truly a day to remember.

2. Edison proposed to his wife in an unusual way.

3. Mary hoped that the important letter would come today.

4. I had to admit it: I was lost.

5. Martin, a sailor, wearily stood his turn at watch.

Communicate Your Ideas

DRAFTING *Transitions*

Return to the chronological list of events you made in the previous activity. Using the list, write a draft of your personal narrative. Begin with a topic sentence that makes a general statement, sets the scene, or captures attention. As you draft your narrative, be sure to add transitions that clearly show when each event happened. Decide which point of view you will use. Finish your story with a strong concluding sentence. Save your work in your writing folder for later use.

HOME WORK

Ask students to write four more story beginnings using first person style and four more using third person style.

Practice Your Skills Sample Answers

1. first person
2. third person
3. third person
4. first person
5. third person

TIMESAVER *QuickCheck*

Review students' work to see if they were consistent in using either first person or third person narrative style.

DEVELOPING WORKPLACE COMPETENCIES

Personal Qualities: Self-Management

Tell students that self-management is a quality that is important for them to continue developing as they go from school out into the world. As employees or self-employed adults, they will be required to set goals for themselves and monitor their own progress. Sales people often set a higher sales goal for themselves than their company requires in order to challenge themselves to excel; teachers evaluate their own effectiveness in the classroom by comparing their style and lessons from one year to the next.

Writing reflective narratives encourages students to recall and evaluate how they have acted in the past. It stimulates their awareness of their own values and their ability to act according to those values. Ask students to write a narrative describing an incident in which they or someone else was excluded from a group or discriminated against. As they relate the events, they should also indicate how they felt about what was happening.

REACHING ALL STUDENTS

Advanced Learners

Ask students to bring in news stories reported in third person style. Have them rewrite the stories in the first person style. Tell them to invent and add plausible details as appropriate to make the story seem realistic.

Revising

Writing Process

Once you have turned your thoughts and reflections into a rough draft, you can start revising. Revising a personal narrative involves attention to three important points.

- Have you developed your personal narrative in enough detail?
- Have you made your ideas and feelings clear?
- Have you maintained a consistent voice?

Checking for Adequate Development

Check to make sure you have included enough specific supporting details to make your reader clearly see and hear what you want to share. The following strategies will help you do that.

STRATEGIES FOR REVISING FOR ADEQUATE DEVELOPMENT	
Events	Close your eyes and visualize the experience you are writing about. Write down the details that you "see" in your mind's eye.
People	Visualize each person you are writing about. Visualize the head and face of each person and slowly move down to the feet. Write down details as you "see" them.
Places	Visualize the place you are describing. Visualize that place from left to right and from top to bottom, as well as from the foreground to the background.
Feelings	Imagine reliving the experience that you are writing about. As you relive the experience, focus on your thoughts and feelings.

LESSON 3 *(pages C143–C148)*

OBJECTIVE

- **To write narrative paragraphs using the writing process**

Create Interest

Ask students to summarize a book, a movie, or a television show that they consider funny. Note that the humor often comes from something unexpected: someone falls in love with the wrong person, someone tries to fill the wrong role, someone says the wrong thing. The unexpected action creates tension that draws the reader or viewer into the story. Discuss with students how they can use this technique in writing narratives.

PRACTICE YOUR SKILLS

Revising for Adequate Development

Revise the following paragraph by adding details that would help readers visualize or understand the experience.

I got off of my bike to look at the bird. It was on the ground, under a plant. It flapped its wings and tried to scare me away as soon as I started to approach it. I was surprised that a bird would try to scare a person away, but that's exactly what it did.

Communicate Your Ideas

REVISING *Adequate Development*

Return to the draft of your personal narrative and revise it. Check for adequate development, using the strategies on the previous page for guidance. Save your work for later use.

Checking for Unity, Coherence, and Clarity

After you have revised your writing to be sure you have developed your ideas adequately, check for unity, coherence, and clarity. A paragraph in which all of the sentences support the main idea has **unity.** A paragraph with **coherence** is well organized and tightly written. A paragraph with **clarity** is easy to understand and is enjoyable to read.

You can learn more about unity, coherence, and clarity on pages C84–C85.

IDENTIFYING COMMON STUMBLING BLOCKS

Problem

- Not recalling events that seemed unexpected when they occurred

Solution

- Create imaginary events where something unexpected happens. Ask each student to write down the names of five famous people, alive or from history, and five common events or settings. Then, ask the student to imagine that one of the famous people has suddenly appeared in one of the settings. The student should then write a story about what happened. For example, a student might write about what happened when Ghengis Khan showed up at a family's Thanksgiving dinner.

Guide Instruction

By Connecting Ideas

Discuss with students whether narratives are similar to other works of art. Can paintings tell a story? Do sculptures or buildings have beginnings, middles, and ends? Does instrumental music have a narrative flow? Encourage students to express their beliefs.

Consolidate Skills

Through Guided Practice

To help students write drafts of a joke, you might bring to class books of jokes for them to read. Students can select a joke they enjoy, noting whether it is written in first person or third person narrative style.

Apply to Communication

Through Independent Writing

Writing first and third person narratives will give students practice in developing these skills. Encourage students to think about how their writing would change if they used a different point of view.

FYI

Spell Check/Grammar Check

The Spell Check and Grammar Check features can be turned off in order to encourage students to thoroughly edit compositions themselves.

How to Use with Windows™ Click on Tools and scroll down to Options. Select Options and click on the Spelling and Grammar tab. Then uncheck the boxes for Spelling and Grammar.

How to Use with Macintosh™ Click on Tools and scroll down to Preferences. Select Preferences and click on the Spelling and Grammar tab. Then uncheck the boxes for Spelling and Grammar.

Communicate Your Ideas

REVISING *Unity, Coherence, and Clarity*

Continue revising your personal narrative. Be sure to check for unity, coherence, and clarity. Save your work for later use.

COMPUTER TIP

Spell Check will alert you if you have spelled a word incorrectly, but will not tell you if you have used the wrong word. When using your word-processing program's Spell Check feature, be especially aware of homonyms, such as *their/they're* and *to/too,* or words that are commonly misused such as *farther/further, effect/affect,* and *bring/take*.

Looping Back to Prewriting

Look over your freewriting notes from Writing Is Thinking, on page C134. If you answered the questions from the perspective of the person in the photographic prompt, go back and answer the questions from the point of view of the animal. If you answered from the point of view of the animal, now freewrite from the person's perspective. Compare your freewriting notes for each point of view. How are they alike? Different? Which one would you choose to develop into a narrative? Why?

Transfer to Everyday Life
By Listening to Stories
Ask students to take notes on the stories they hear during a day from classmates, teachers, or family members. Examine the structure of each story. Does it have a clear beginning, middle, and end? What makes it memorable?

Pull It All Together
By Sharing
Ask students to recall the first time they met someone they now consider a friend. Discuss how they learned about each other. Highlight examples in which students recall telling each other stories about themselves. First person narratives that reflect personal experience are often the building blocks of friendships.

Pronouns

Pronouns can add variety and clarity to your writing. Whether you use first person or third person narrative point of view in your paragraphs, be sure that the pronouns you use agree in number (singular or plural) and gender (masculine, feminine, or neuter) with their antecedents. Otherwise, your reader will be confused. The following examples, adapted from *The House on Mango Street*, illustrate the proper agreement of pronouns and their antecedents.

Singular

MASCULINE SINGULAR — My **father** held the lucky lottery ticket. **He** said it would bring us luck. (The pronoun *he* is masculine singular and refers back to *father*.)

My **father** displayed **his** lottery ticket and talked about the house. (The pronoun *his* agrees in gender and number with *father*, its antecedent.)

FEMININE SINGULAR — A **nun** from my school passed by. **She** saw me playing in front of the house. (The feminine singular pronoun *she* agrees with its antecedent *nun* in gender and number.)

Mama told **her** children about the house of **her** dreams. (The singular possessive pronouns *her* refer to their antecedent *Mama*.)

NEUTER — Our **house** would be white with trees around **it**. (The pronoun *it* refers back to the neuter singular antecedent *house*.)

Using *Revising Workshop*

Objective

- **To understand how pronouns relate to their antecedents**

A DIFFERENT APPROACH

Visual Have students copy the sample sentences onto a sheet of paper. Then ask them to color code each pronoun and its antecedent. Use a separate color for each antecedent-pronoun set. After they have coded the sample sentences, have them find and code five other sentences from other writings.

Tactile Encourage students to place their left index finger on an antecedent and their right index finger on the pronoun that refers to it. After they have practiced on the examples in the book, have them try it on a passage they find in a newspaper or magazine.

Check Understanding

By Summarizing

After students have written a first person narrative and a third person narrative, ask them to summarize each one in a single sentence. The sentence should tell the main idea of the story they have written.

INTEGRATING TECHNOLOGY

Video

Ask for students to volunteer to make three-minute videotapes of specific events. They should choose events that have clear beginnings and endings, such as athletic contests, musical concerts, or political debates. Select one of the videos to show to the class. Have students write a story explaining what the video shows. Compare the stories, noting how students emphasized different elements in their writing.

Plural

The plural forms *they, them,* and *their* have no gender. They can have masculine, feminine, or neuter antecedents. Their antecedent can also be a combination of masculine and feminine as in the following examples.

PLURAL

My **parents** promised that **they** would buy a real house with running water and pipes that worked. (The plural pronoun *they* refers back to its antecedent *parents* and agrees in number.)

Mama and Papa did not have a basement in **their** house. (The plural pronoun *their* agrees with its antecedent in number.)

Papa told the **children** about the house. Mama told **them** stories. (The plural pronoun *them* agrees with its antecedent children.)

Time Out to Reflect

Review the notes you made as you read your classmates' writing or your own narratives. Think about the narratives you have read in this chapter, too. What has worked well in the narrative paragraphs you have read? What areas have needed improvement? Make a list of each. What patterns do you notice? In a statement in your **journal,** summarize any patterns you find.

The following checklist will help you identify areas for improvement when you revise your personal narrative.

Evaluation Checklist for Revising

Checking Your Paragraph

✓ Does your topic sentence introduce the story by making a general statement, setting the scene, or capturing attention? *(page C133)*

✓ Do your supporting sentences tell the story event by event and answer the questions *Who? What? Where? Why? When?* and *How? (page C133)*

✓ Does your paragraph have unity, coherence, and clarity? *(page C143)*

✓ Did you use chronological order with appropriate transitions to give your paragraph coherence? *(pages C135–C139)*

✓ Did you use first person if you are a character in the story? Did you use third person if your story is about something that happened to others? *(pages C140–C141)*

✓ Does your concluding sentence end the story by summarizing the events or making a point about the story? *(page C133)*

Checking Your Sentences

✓ Did you combine related sentences to avoid too many short, choppy sentences in a row? *(pages C53–C57)*

✓ Did you vary the length and beginnings of your sentences? *(pages C53–C59)*

✓ Did you avoid rambling sentences? *(page C63)*

✓ Did you avoid unnecessary repetition and empty expressions? *(pages C64–C65)*

Checking Your Words

✓ Did you use specific words? *(pages C49–C51)*

✓ Did you use words that appeal to the senses? *(pages C52–C53)*

YOUR IDEAS

For Revising

GETTING STUDENTS INVOLVED

Reciprocal Teaching

Have students exchange papers, allowing them to offer suggestions, editorial advice, and recommendations. This is a good opportunity for students to use their skills critically, as well as have some distance from their own work so that they will be able to look at it with fresh eyes when it is returned to them.

Process of Writing a Narrative

Remember that the writing process is recursive—you can move back and forth among the stages of the process to achieve your purpose. For example, during drafting you may wish to refine the list of details you developed in prewriting, adding the things you remember as you begin writing. The numbers in parentheses refer to pages where you can get help with your writing.

PREWRITING

- Use your own experiences or your imagination to think of possible stories to tell. *(pages C9–C14)*
- Make a list of subjects and choose one that interests you and your readers. *(page C16)*
- Limit your subject so that it can be covered in a short narrative. *(pages C16–C18)*
- Write down everything that comes to mind when you think about your subject. *(pages C20–C24)*
- Arrange your notes in chronological order. *(pages C135–C139)*

DRAFTING

- Write a topic sentence. *(pages C77–C79)*
- Use your prewriting notes to write supporting sentences with transitions where needed. *(pages C79–C82)*
- Add a concluding sentence. *(page C88)*

REVISING

- Put your paper aside for a while. Then use the Evaluation Checklist for Revising to improve your first draft. *(page C147)*

EDITING

- Use the Editing Checklist on page C36 to check your work for errors.

PUBLISHING

- Prepare a neat, polished copy of your work and present it to a reader. *(page C40–C41)*

A Writer Writes

A Personal Reflection

Purpose: to tell a story about a time you were careless

Audience: a person younger than you who looks to you for guidance

Prewriting

Think back over times in your life when you were careless. Use brainstorming, freewriting, or clustering to think of ideas. When you have five or six good ideas, choose the one that seems most promising for developing into a narrative. List all the little events that made up the incident. Also list details of time and place that would add interest to your story. Arrange the events in chronological order.

Drafting

Using your prewriting notes, write a draft of your narrative. Take care to start your narrative effectively. Use transitions to help your story unfold smoothly. Conclude with a sentence that highlights what you learned from the experience.

Revising

Divide into small groups to share and respond to one another's work. Instead of reading the papers silently, listen while each writer reads his or her story. Practice your listening skills by paying close attention to everything you hear. Are the events told in a logical order? Are the transitions smooth? What colorful details linger in your mind? Offer

Using A Writer Writes

Objective

- **To practice telling a story of personal reflection**

TIMESAVER QuickCheck

After students have written a draft of their story, review their use of transitions. Check that they have moved from one idea to the next smoothly.

INTEGRATING Writers at Work

For more opportunities to inspire and stimulate students' personal writing, look at *Writers at Work.*

EXPANDING THE LESSON

Using Technology

You will find additional **instructional** and **practice** materials for this chapter at http://www.bkenglish.com.

INTEGRATING TECHNOLOGY

Electronic Publishing

You may want to refer students to *A Writer's Guide to Electronic Publishing* on pages C520–C539 for suggestions on using resources for publishing.

YOUR IDEAS

For Publishing Student's Personal Narratives

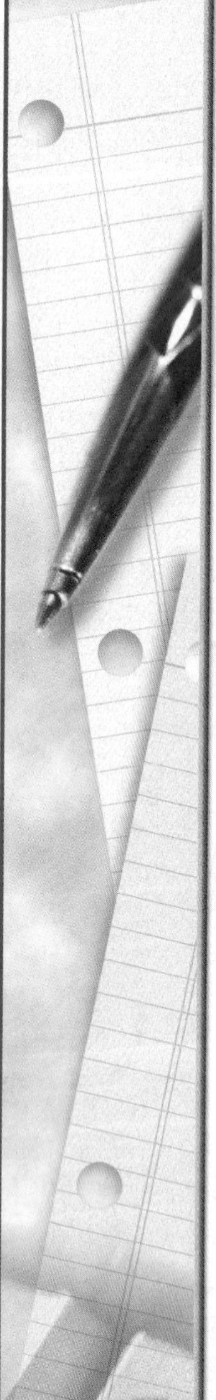

comments to each writer about what worked well in the story and what could be improved. Then, using your listeners' comments and your own judgment, revise your work. Use the **Evaluation Checklist for Revising** on page C147 to make your narrative the best it can be.

Editing

Use the **Editing Checklist** on page C36 and the list in your **journal** of your own common mistakes to check your work for errors. Use proofreading marks to correct your mistakes.

Publishing

Make a neat final copy of your narrative. Through a friend, family member, or your teacher, arrange a way to present your work to a younger person. You may, for example, be able to loan the papers written by you and your classmates to a sixth- or seventh-grade class.

Connection Collection

Representing in Different Ways

From Visuals . . .

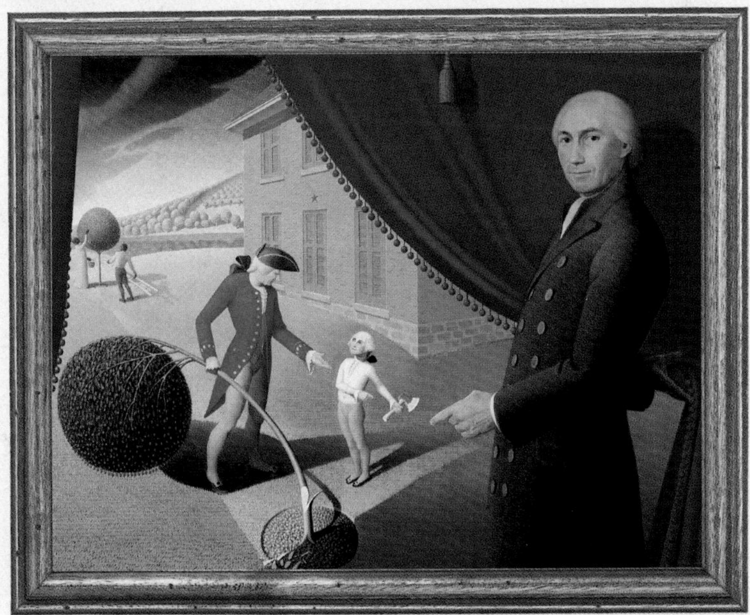

Grant Wood, *Parson Weems' Fable*, 1939. Oil on canvas. 38⅝ by 50⅛ inches.

. . . to Print

"A picture is worth a thousand words"—or so goes the cliché. Consider the painting *Parson Weems' Fable* by Grant Wood. What story does it suggest to you? Write a letter to a friend telling him or her a 'story' of this painting. Put your narrative in chronological order and use third person point of view.

FOR REVIEWING SKILLS

Using *Connection Collection*

Representing in Different Ways

Consider using these print and visual activities to make students aware of the benefits of using different media to suit particular purposes. Help students understand when a visual medium, for example, is better suited to their purpose than a print medium, or the reverse.

YOUR IDEAS

For Viewing and Representing

From Print . . .

337 Contada Avenue
Fresno, CA 92849
February 15, 2000

Dear Otis,

Would you believe I've turned into an eighth-grade entrepreneur? It all began when I offered to prune Ms. Lauer's tea roses next door. They were growing like crazy, and she kept getting pricked by the thorns every time she walked to her garage. Then she told Mr. Arkady about my work; he hired me to trim back his lilacs and weed his flowerbeds every week. Soon I was getting calls from all over the neighborhood—word had gotten around about my gardening expertise. I even have a commission to design a perennial bed for Eunice Washington, our local weather anchor! I'm looking forward to seeing you in a month, but don't expect the guy in shorts and a T-shirt. I have a green coverall with my name embroidered right above the pocket.

Your friend,
Steve
Steve

. . . to Visuals

You are Otis and wish to draw a picture of Steve in his new role as an eighth-grade garden expert. You may choose any aspect of this story to draw—Steve pruning tea roses, weeding a flowerbed, designing a flowerbed, or any other scene that this story suggests.

- **Which strategies can be used for creating both written and visual representations? Which strategies apply to one, not both? Which type of representation is more effective?**
- **Draw a conclusion and write briefly about the differences between written ideas and visual representations.**

A DIFFERENT DELIVERY SYSTEM

For formal assessment print the composition chapter test from the *BK English* Test Bank at http://www.bkenglish.com.

Assess Your Learning

You are a member of the school band and have earned quite a reputation as a top-notch tuba player. Last weekend the band played at the school's first football game of the season. You wore brand new uniforms, royal blue with gold braid. The first half of the game passed uneventfully; you all played the school fight song without missing a note and you marched into your various formations without a misstep. But in the last half of the game, nearly everything went wrong! The scene was such a disaster that you have decided to write a reflective letter to Bill, a friend who used to live in your town, to tell him about the events of the night.

- **Write the letter to Bill that describes the episode at the football game. Decide whether to make the narrative hilarious or horrible. Put the events in chronological order and first person point of view, with a topic sentence and concluding sentence for each paragraph. Tell your friend not only what happened at the game, but also what the experience meant to you. Remember to use specific and colorful details in describing the disaster and be sure to use transitions to help your narrative flow smoothly.**

Before You Write **Consider the following questions:**
What is the ***subject?***
What is the ***occasion?***
Who is the ***audience?***
What is the ***purpose?***

After You Write **Evaluate your work using the following criteria:**

- Is your narrative about the events at the football game in chronological order and first person?
- Have you written each topic sentence to accurately reflect what you talk about in the rest of your paragraph?
- Have you thought about the experience at the football game, and then reflected on what the experience meant to you?
- Is your letter written in a voice and style appropriate to the audience and purpose?

Write briefly on how well you did. Point out your strengths and areas for improvement.

FOR ASSESSING LEARNING

Using *Assess Your Learning*

This writing prompt will help you and your students informally assess their developing writing abilities, using the accompanying primary trait rubrics, which list the key features and qualities of personal narrative writing taught in this chapter. You may want to have students maintain their self-assessment in their portfolios as a record of their individual progress throughout the year.

Evaluating Personal Essays

In writing personal essays or compositions, many students need special help in

- **developing a main idea through the use of sufficient interesting details**
- **organizing these details logically**
- **maintaining a smooth flow, consistent tone, and individual voice. Self-evaluation and peer evaluation can help students improve their compositions in these areas during revision.**

Self-evaluation

After students have finished their first drafts, have them evaluate their compositions for the purpose of revising. Give them copies of the Evaluation Checklist for Personal Writing. (See the Evaluation Checklists in BK English Language and Composition Assessment.) Tell them to focus on content and tone as they read their compositions, with special attention to the traits numbered below.

Peer evaluation

An alternative method for evaluating personal compositions is for students to work in pairs to evaluate each other's work. Each partner should read his or her composition aloud. This allows both students to hear how the composition sounds and identify areas that need changing, especially in tone.

1 The main idea is elaborated with sufficient details.
2 Related details are vivid and are organized into paragraphs.
3 The details within each paragraph are ordered logically.
4 The paragraphs are unified and the conclusion reinforces or adds a new dimension to the main idea.
5 The composition maintains a consistent tone and an individual voice.

Teacher evaluation

Primary Traits

The following opening of a personal composition shows excellent use of details and tone in developing a main idea; it can be used as a model for students' introductory paragraphs.

MODEL FOR EVALUATION

Pleasant tone – clear and warm

It was years ago, but I remember the three of us sitting in the living room, my parents facing me from across the room. I remember being excited and a little nervous. When you're a kid, adults do not usually invite you to listen to them make an important announcement. That night, my Mom and Dad told me to sit down in the living room because they needed to tell me something important. After sitting quietly for a few moments, my parents announced that soon I was finally going to have a brother or sister. My parents were adopting a child from Russia. Suddenly it was as if we were all beginning a new adventure; only now there weren't three of us—there were four.

Main idea very well put

Good preparation for following paragraphs

TEACHER EVALUATION

Primary Trait Evaluation

The following chart lists key features and qualities to look for in primary trait assessment of personal compositions.

	EXCELLENT	ACCEPTABLE	NEEDS IMPROVEMENT
Introduction	Introduces a subject based on personal insights that can be developed through the use of details and sets an appropriate tone.	Introduces a personal subject or some aspect of it, with some success in setting a tone.	Fails to establish a clear subject or a recognizable tone.
Details	The composition is developed through the use of vivid, interesting details throughout.	Some good details are used in developing the composition.	Few or no supporting details appear in the composition.
Organization	In each paragraph, the details are arranged in an appropriate logical order. The paragraphs also follow a logical order.	Details and paragraphs basically are arranged logically, with occasional deviations.	Neither details nor paragraphs are clearly organized.
Style	Ample vivid details and consistent, natural tone are employed throughout.	Some strong details are used, and tone is basically consistent.	Details are few, tone inconsistent or wooden.
Conclusion	The conclusion reinforces or adds a new dimension to the main theme.	The conclusion has some bearing on the main idea.	The conclusion is irrelevant or nonexistent.

TEACHER EVALUATION

Holistic Evaluation

The following criteria may be used to evaluate students' personal compositions holistically, using a rating scale of

- 4 (excellent)
- 3 (good)
- 2 (acceptable)
- 1 (needs improvement)
- 0 (unscoreable)

4	3	2	1
Personal insights are reflected in an interesting main theme that lends itself to development through the use of details.	There is a main theme based on personal insights and capable of development through the use of details.	The main theme is unclear, uninteresting, or both, and does not lend itself to development.	The composition does not state or develop a main theme.
Vivid, interesting, logically ordered details develop the main theme, and a consistent and appropriate tone is maintained throughout.	Use of details is adequate and the tone is basically consistent and appropriate.	Some supporting details are present in some form of order, and an overall tone is detectable.	The composition offers few or no details and has no clear tone.
The composition is well organized. The main theme is introduced in a way that catches reader interest and sets the tone. The body develops this theme in several logically ordered paragraphs linked by suitable transitions. The conclusion reinforces or adds a new dimension to the main idea.	The composition is basically well organized, with occasional lapses.	The composition has an introduction that sets forth the main theme, a body that contains some developmental details, and a conclusion related to the main theme.	The work does not follow composition form.

Teaching Suggestions

Essential Knowledge and Skills

- Monitoring his/her own understanding of the spoken message and seek clarification as needed
- Writing to inform such as to explain, describe, report, and narrate
- Use adjectives appropriately to make writing vivid or precise
- Evaluating how different media forms influence and inform
- Producing communications using technology or appropriate media such as video reports

CHAPTER 6

Using Description: Observation

Have you ever been lost—in a book? Did the characters, setting, and mood seem so real that you felt part of the story? How could that be?

Writers paint pictures with words. Vivid description makes the difference between writing that just sits on the page and writing that dances off the page straight into the reader's imagination. A good writer can make you feel, touch, taste, hear, and see; a good writer stimulates your senses.

Description is part of narrative writing; it provides the details that complete the picture. In this chapter, you will learn that concise word choice is the secret to good description and writing that is fresh and exciting.

Reading with a Writer's Eye

The following selection is the opening chapter from *Rascal* by Sterling North. You will meet Sterling; his friend Oscar; Sterling's Saint Bernard, Wowser; and Rascal, the baby raccoon. While reading, think about the ways the author describes the setting and the characters. Do you get a clear picture of what boyhood in the early 1900s was like for this character? Which images seem familiar? Which seem unfamiliar?

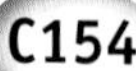

BLOCK SCHEDULING

- If your schedule requires that you cover the chapter in a **shorter time**, use Reading with a Writer's Eye, Thinking as a Writer, The Power of Description, and Process of Writing a Descriptive Paragraph.
- If you want to take advantage of **longer class time**, add any or all of the following: Writing Is Thinking, In the Media, and Grammar in the Writing Process.

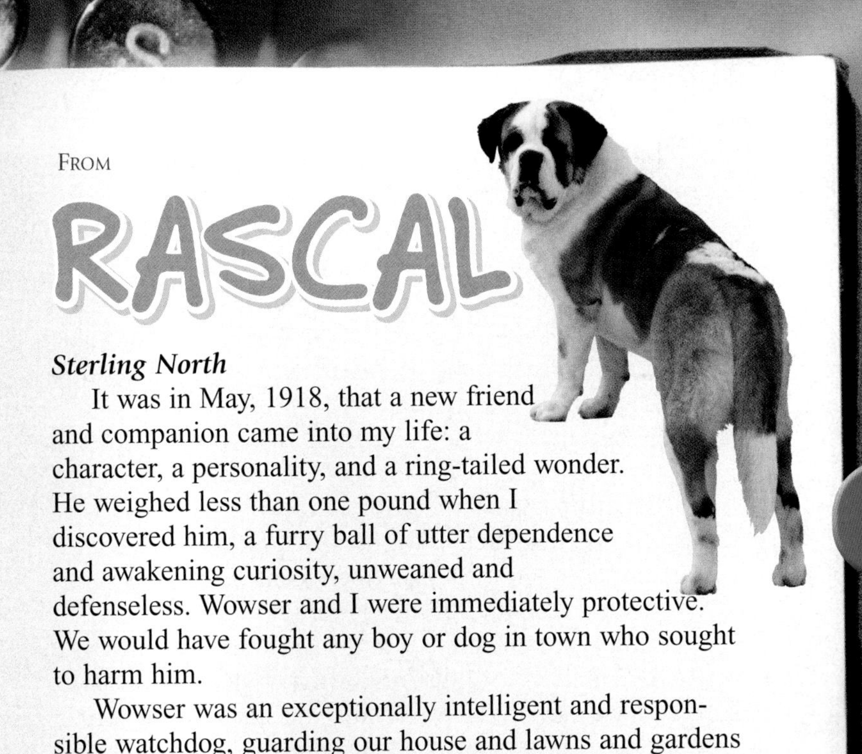

FROM

RASCAL

Sterling North

It was in May, 1918, that a new friend and companion came into my life: a character, a personality, and a ring-tailed wonder. He weighed less than one pound when I discovered him, a furry ball of utter dependence and awakening curiosity, unweaned and defenseless. Wowser and I were immediately protective. We would have fought any boy or dog in town who sought to harm him.

Wowser was an exceptionally intelligent and responsible watchdog, guarding our house and lawns and gardens and all my pets. But because of his vast size—one hundred and seventy pounds of muscled grace and elegance—he seldom had to resort to any violence. He could shake any dog on the block as a terrier shakes a rat. Wowser never started a fight, but after being challenged, badgered, and insulted, he eventually would turn his worried face and great sad eyes upon his tormentor, and more in sorrow than in anger, grab the intruder by the scruff of the neck, and toss him into the gutter.

Wowser was an affectionate, perpetually hungry Saint Bernard. Like most dogs of his breed he drooled a little. In the house he had to lie with his muzzle on a bath towel, his eyes downcast as though in slight disgrace. Pat Delaney, a saloonkeeper who lived a couple of blocks up the street,

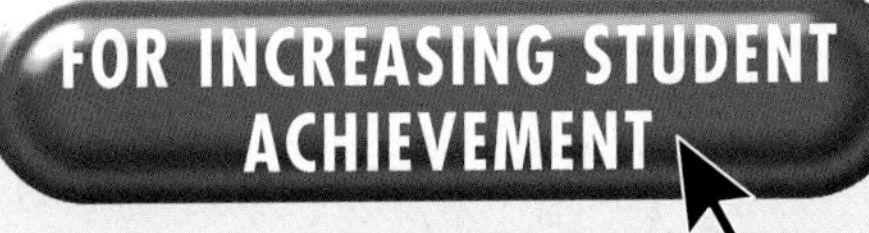

GUIDED READING

Text Analysis

- **Description** gives the story its power. For example, the various details about Wowser, from his muscled grace to his downcast eyes, provide the reader with a clear portrait of the dog. Likewise, each of the human characters is well drawn.
- The **first person narrative style** means that the story is told form the viewpoint of one of the participants. In this case, it is from Sterling's viewpoint. Through Sterling's comments on others, such as Oscar's parents, readers get a sense of his values and situation in life.
- The story of capturing the raccoon is captivating, even though the reader knows what the outcome will be. In the first line, North says that a raccoon entered his life. The drama comes from wondering how the boys will accomplish the task, and what they will do with the raccoon once they capture it.
- North develops characters through **dialogue**. For example, readers develop a clear sense of the personality of Oscar's mother through what she says. Her sympathy for Sterling, her success in handling her husband, and her wisdom in feeding the little raccoon all reflect her strength and compassion.

GUIDED READING

Strategy: Making Predictions

Ask students to predict how Sterling's relationship with the raccoon will develop. They should identify passages on which they base their predictions. Encourage students to read the whole book to see if their predictions are accurate.

said that Saint Bernards drool for the best of all possible reasons. He explained that in the Alps these noble dogs set forth every winter day, with little kegs of brandy strapped beneath their chins, to rescue wayfarers lost in the snowdrifts. Generations of carrying the brandy, of which they have never tasted so much as a blessed drop, have made them so thirsty that they continuously drool. The trait has now become hereditary, Pat said, and whole litters of bright and thirsty little Saint Bernards are born drooling for brandy.

On this pleasant afternoon in May, Wowser and I started up First Street toward Crescent Drive where a semicircle of late Victorian houses enjoyed a hilltop view. Northward lay miles of meadows, groves of trees, a winding stream, and the best duck and muskrat marsh in Rock County. As we turned down a country lane past Bardeen's orchard and vineyard, the signature of spring was everywhere: violets and anemones in the grass; the apple trees in promising bud along the bough.

Ahead lay some of the most productive walnut and hickory trees I had ever looted, a good swimming hole in the creek, and, in one bit of forest, a real curiosity—a phosphorescent stump which gleamed at night with foxfire, as luminescent as all the lightning bugs in the world—ghostly and terrifying to boys who saw it for the first time. It scared me witless as I came home one evening from fishing. So I made it a point to bring my friends that way on other evenings, not wishing to be selfish about my pleasures.

Oscar Sunderland saw me as I passed his bleak farmhouse far down that lane. He was a friend of mine who knew enough not to talk when we went fishing. And we were trapping partners on the marsh. His mother was a gentle Norwegian woman who spoke English with no trace of an accent, and also her native language. His father Herman Sunderland was another kettle of hasenpfeffer[1]—German on his mother's side and Swedish on his father's—with a temper and dialect all his own.

Oscar's mother baked delicious Norwegian pastries, particularly around Christmastime. Sometimes in placing before me a plate of her delicacies she would say something tender to me in Norwegian. I always turned away to hide the shameful moisture in my eyes. As Mrs. Sunderland knew, my mother had died when I was seven, and I think that is why she was especially kind to me.

Oscar's tough old father presented no such problem. I doubt that he had ever said anything kind to anyone in his life. Oscar was very much afraid of him and risked a whipping if he were not home in time to help with the milking.

No one was concerned about the hours *I* kept. I was a very competent eleven-year-old. If I came home long after dark, my father would merely look up from his book to greet me vaguely and courteously. He allowed me to live my own life, keep pet skunks and woodchucks in the back yard and the barn, pamper my tame crow, my many cats, and my faithful Saint Bernard. He even let me build my eighteen-foot canoe in the living room. I had not entirely completed the framework, so it would take another year at least. When we had visitors, they sat in the easy chairs surrounding the canoe, or skirted the prow to reach the great shelves of books we were continuously lending. We lived alone and liked it, cooked and cleaned in our own fashion, and paid little attention to indignant housewives who told my father that this was no way to bring up a child.

[1] **hasenpfeffer (hä′zən-fĕf′ər) n.:** A seasoned stew of rabbit meat.

YOUR IDEAS

For Guided Reading

USING STUDENTS' STRENGTHS

Multiple Intelligences: Naturalistic

Ask students to discuss the wisdom of trying to capture an adult raccoon, and of taking a baby raccoon home. Point out that the behavior of characters in stories should be believable, though it is often not the most appropriate behavior. Students may wish to do some research on the habits and characteristics of raccoons, and whether they make good pets.

My father agreed amiably that this might well be true, and then returned to his endless research for a novel concerning the Fox and Winnebago Indians, which for some reason was never published.

X X X

"I'm headed for Wentworth's woods," I told Oscar, "and I may not start home before moonrise."

"Wait a minute," Oscar said. "We'll need something to eat."

He returned so swiftly with a paper sack filled with coffee cake and cookies that I knew he had swiped them.

"You'll get a licking when you get home."

"Ishkabibble,[2] I should worry!" Oscar said, a happy grin spreading across his wide face.

We crossed the creek on the steppingstones below the dam. Pickerel[3] were making their seasonal run up the stream, and we nearly caught one with our hands as he snaked his way between the stones. Kildeer[4] started up from the marshy shallows, crying "kildeer, kildeer" as though a storm were brewing.

Wowser had many virtues, but he was not a hunting dog. So we were much surprised when in Wentworth's woods he came to a virtual point. Oscar and I waited silently while the Saint Bernard, on his great paws, padded softly to the hollow base of a rotten stump. He sniffed the hole critically, then turned and whined, telling us plainly that something lived in that den.

"Dig 'em out, Wowser," I shouted.

"He won't dig," Oscar predicted. "He's too lazy."

---

[2] **ishkabibble (ĭsh′ka-bib-əl)** ***n.:*** Nonsense.

[3] **pickerel (pĭk′ər-əl)** ***n.:*** Small freshwater fishes, especially found in eastern and southern United States.

[4] **kildeer (kĭl′dîr)** ***n.:*** A wading bird with a distinctively noisy cry.

"You just watch," I said loyally. But I wasn't betting any glass marbles.

In another minute Wowser was making dirt fly, and Oscar and I were helping in a frenzy of excitement. We scooped the soft earth with our hands, and used our pocket knives when we came to old decaying roots.

"I'll bet it's a fox," I panted hopefully.

"Probably an old woodchuck," Oscar said.

But we couldn't have been more surprised when a furious mother raccoon exploded from her lair screaming her rage and dismay. Wowser nearly fell over backward to avoid the flying claws and slashing little teeth. A moment later the big raccoon had racked her way up a slender oak tree. Thirty feet above us she continued to scream and scold.

In plain sight now, within the den, we found four baby raccoons, a month old perhaps. The entire litter of kits might easily have fitted within my cap. Each tail had five black rings. Each small face had a sharp black mask. Eight bright eyes peered up at us, filled with wonder and worry. And from four inquiring little mouths came whimpered questions.

"Good old Wowser," I said.

"That's a pretty good dog you've got there," Oscar admitted, "but you better hold him back."

"He wouldn't hurt them; he takes care of all my pets."

In fact the big dog settled down with a sigh of satisfaction, as near to the nest as possible, ready to adopt one or all of these interesting little creatures. But there was one service he could not render. He could not feed them.

"We can't take them home without their mother," I told Oscar. "They're too young."

"How do we catch the mother?" Oscar asked.

"We draw straws."

YOUR IDEAS

For Reading Strategies

YOUR IDEAS
For Increasing Comprehension

"And then what?"

"The one who gets the short straw shinnies up the tree and catches her."

"Oh, no," Oscar said. "Oh no you don't. I ain't that crazy."

"Come on, Oscar."

"No siree."

But at just this moment the four little raccoons set up such a plaintive quavering that we all felt miserable. We *had* to catch that mother raccoon. Wowser was as sad as I was. He pointed his big muzzle toward the evening sky and howled mournfully.

"Well," Oscar said, kicking his shoe into the fresh earth, "I'd better be getting home to help with the milking."

"Quitter," I taunted.

"Who's a quitter?"

"You're a quitter."

"Well, OK, I'll draw straws; but I think you're loony."

I held the straws and Oscar drew the long one. Naturally I had to live up to my bargain. I looked far above me. In the fading glow of the sunset there she still was, twenty pounds of ring-tailed dynamite. I patted Wowser as though for the last time and began my tough scramble up that slender trunk.

As I shinnied up the tree, in no great hurry to tangle with the raccoon, I had one piece of good fortune. The full moon began to rise above an eastern hill giving me more light for my dangerous maneuver. Far out on the first limb, the outraged animal took a firm stance, facing me, her eyes glowing balefully in the moonlight.

"I'm going to cut off the branch with my jackknife," I told Oscar.

"And then what?"

"You're supposed to catch her when she falls in the hazel brush."

Oscar suggested that I had bats in my belfry. But he took off his corduroy jacket and prepared to throw it over the raccoon in a do-or-die effort for which he had little enthusiasm.

Whittling through two-and-one-half inches of white oak with a fairly dull jackknife is a laborious process, as I soon discovered. I was in a cramped position, holding on with my left hand and hacking away at the wood with my right. And I feared the raccoon might try to rush me when the limb began to break.

The moon rose slowly through the trees as blisters rose slowly on my right hand. But I couldn't weaken now. From far below came the whimpering of the raccoon kits, and an occasional mournful howl from Wowser. Tree toads and frogs in the swamp began their chorus, and a little screech owl, sounding almost like another raccoon, added an eerie tremolo.

"How are you coming?" Oscar asked.

"Coming fine. Get ready to catch her,"

"Count on me," Oscar said, his voice sounding less convincing than his brave words.

The tasseled limb of the white oak sighed at last, broke with a snap, and drifted down to the hazel brush below.

Oscar tried. I will give him credit for that. He tangled for five seconds with that raccoon, and then retreated with a damaged jacket. Three of the little raccoons, hearing their mother's call, trundled with amazing swiftness into the hazel brush to follow her, and were gone. Oscar, however, was quick enough to cup one kit in his cap, our only reward for our labor—but reward enough, as time would prove. As nearly as we could tell, the handsome,

REACHING ALL STUDENTS

Advanced Learners

Ask students to compare Sterling and Oscar. Their family situations, their comments when Wowser detected something living at the base of the rotten stump, and their attitudes toward catching the mother raccoon all differ sharply. Discuss with students how these differences affected or reflected the outlooks of the two boys.

HOME WORK

Direct students to the definitions at the bottom of this page. Have students use a dictionary to write an additional definition for *crawdads.* Then have students make a quick sketch of a crawdad.

sharply marked little animal was covered only with soft gray underfur, having few of the darker guard hairs which later gleam on the adult raccoon.

He was the only baby raccoon I have ever held in my hands. And as he nestled upward like a quail chick, and nuzzled like a puppy seeking its mother's milk, I was both overwhelmed with the ecstasy of ownership and frightened by the enormous responsibility we had assumed. Wowser romped beside us through the moonlight, often coming to sniff and lick the new pet we had found—this bit of masked mischief which had stolen his heart as well as my own.

"He's yours," Oscar said sadly. "My old man would never let me keep him. He shot a 'coon in the chicken house just a few weeks ago."

"You can come and see him," I suggested.

"Sure, I can come and see him."

We walked in silence for a time, thinking of the injustices of the world that made so few allowances for the nature of raccoons and boys of our age. Then we began talking about all the raccoons we had ever seen, and how we would feed this kit and teach him all the things he would have to learn.

"I seen a raccoon mother once with five kits," Oscar said.

"What were they doing?"

"She was leading them along the edge of the stream. They did everything she did."

"Like what?"

"Feeling around with their front paws hunting for crawdads,[5] I guess."

[5] **crawdads:** A crayfish; a small crustacean resembling a lobster.

On the horizon there were flashes of distant lightning and a low rumbling of thunder, sounding like artillery many miles away. It reminded us that the war[6] was still raging in France, and that maybe my brother Herschel was being moved up to the front. I hated to think about that terrible war which had been killing and wounding millions of men ever since the year my mother died. Here we were, safe and remote from the war, and worrying about such small and unimportant things as whether Oscar would get a whipping when he got home, and how to feed and raise a little raccoon.

As we came up to the lane toward the Sunderland's farmhouse, Oscar began saying, "Ishkabibble, I should worry." But he acted worried to me. When we reached his farm yard he dared me and double-dared me to go up and knock on the door. Meanwhile he hid behind a flowering spirea bush and waited to see what might happen.

Oscar was wise to let me do the knocking. Herman Sunderland came out, swearing in German and Swedish. He was certainly angry with Oscar, and he didn't seem to like me very much either.

"Vere is dot no-goot son of mine?"

"It wasn't Oscar's fault," I said. "I asked him to come for a walk with me, and . . . "

"Vere iss he now?"

"Well," I said.

"Vell, vell, vell! Vot do you mean, vell?"

"We dug out a den of raccoons," I said, "and here is the one we brought home."

"Coons," shouted Sunderland, "*verdammte* varmints."

I was afraid that Mr. Sunderland might flush Oscar from behind the spirea bush, but at just this moment

[6] **war:** World War I.

YOUR IDEAS
For Using Description

READER RESPONSE

You may want to use the following questions to elicit students' personal responses to the selection.

1. How would you describe the relationship between Sterling and his father?
2. Do you think you would like Sterling if you met him? Explain.
3. How did you feel when you read the description of how Sterling felt when he held the raccoon in his hand?
4. What was your favorite passage in the excerpt?

LITERARY CONNECTION

You might want to explore descriptive writing in the following works, which appear in literature textbooks at this grade level.

- "The Battleground" by Elsie Singmaster
- "The Choice" by Dorothy Parker
- "The Cremation of Sam McGee" by Robert W. Service
- *Travels with Charley* by John Steinbeck

Oscar's gracious mother came out on the front porch, the moonlight shining on her silvering hair.

"Go to bed, Herman," she said quietly. "I will take care of this. Come out, Oscar, from behind that bush."

To my surprise, Oscar's father meekly obeyed, taking a lamp up that long, dark parlor stairway—his shadow much taller than himself. And Oscar's mother took us to the kitchen where she fed us a warm supper and began to heat a little milk to the temperature that would be right for a human baby.

"It is hungry, the little one," she said, petting the small raccoon. "Go fetch a clean wheat straw, Oscar."

She filled her own mouth with warm milk, put the wheat straw between her lips, and slanted the straw down to the mouth of the little raccoon. I watched, fascinated, as my new pet took the straw eagerly and began to nurse.

"Look how the little one eats," Oscar's mother said. "This is the way you will have to feed him, Sterling."

ADDITIONAL RESOURCES

Composition Skills Practice	pages 29–32
Transparency Tools	GO15, VR5
Writing Prompts	pages 1, 2–7, 8–11, 13, 14–18, 20–23, 25–34, 36–39
Connection Collection	pages C185–C186
ESL Practice and Test Preparation	pages 36–42
Standardized Test Preparation	Units 2, 9, 15
Writers at Work	8•1–8•10
Assessment: Chapter Test	pages 56–59
Assessment Resources	pages 1–10, 13–44, 54–60

Thinking as a Writer

Evaluating Description

- Describe each of these story elements in a single sentence: the setting, Wowser, Rascal, the mother raccoon, and one other character.
- Which senses does the author focus on to bring you into the story? Which senses are not called upon?
- Do you think the elements of the story were adequately described? Were you confused by anything? What would you do to clarify parts that were unclear?

Matching Reading Style with Writing Style

Oral Expression

- The narrator of this selection is reminiscing with humor and affection. Review the chapter, finding three good examples of this narrative tone.
- Pick two paragraphs from the chapter to read aloud with a partner. Try to match your reading style with the author's writing style. As your partner reads aloud, listen for the appropriate voice and pacing.

Describing the Images and Impressions of Art

Viewing Look at the photograph below. Using vivid, expressive words, describe what you see. Think about the sounds you would hear if you could step into the picture. Imagine the smells. What things could you touch and how would they feel? After writing, read what you have written. Does your descriptive language give any indication how you feel about the photograph?

Using *Thinking as a Writer*

You may choose to have students respond to the questions either orally or in writing.

REACHING ALL STUDENTS

English Language Learners

Students learning English may benefit from describing the photograph in their first language, and then translating their description into English. This process may lead them to expand their English vocabulary by teaching them new English words and provide them a visual image to associate with these words.

FOR DEVELOPING SKILLS

LESSON 1 *(pages C166–C169)*

OBJECTIVES

- **To state that the purpose of a descriptive paragraph is to create a vivid picture in words of a person, an object, or a scene**
- **To identify the function of the topic sentence, supporting sentences, and concluding sentence in a descriptive paragraph**

Create Interest

Tell students to imagine that a movie director who is making a movie about school life is considering using your school for the setting. Have students discuss how they would describe the school to the director. They should describe both the traits that make the school typical of all schools as well as traits that make it distinctive from most schools.

CAREERS AND COMMUNICATION

Social Workers

Social workers help individuals and families work through problems. To keep track of their clients' progress, social workers usually keep a file on each one. Often they include descriptive passages in their files. A social worker might make a careful description of the clothing, manners, and speech patterns of a client. After visiting a home, a social worker might try to write an accurate description of the environment in the home. In writing these descriptive comments, social workers note details that may prove useful in understanding the attitudes and behaviors of the client.

Divide students into groups of three. One student should interview another student in the group, and the third student should take notes. After each student has had an opportunity to take notes, all three students should write one-page summaries of the interviews in which they describe the student, the setting, and the content of the interview.

The Power of Description

The author of *Rascal* re-created the mood of a specific time and place through the careful description of both the characters and setting of his story. This type of description is used in a number of print media, including books, newspapers, and magazine articles.

Uses of Description

Below are some examples of places where you might find descriptive writing in your daily life.

- **A coin collector creates a classified ad** to sell coins.
- **A travel agent creates a colorful brochure** describing a new package tour.
- **A journalist describes the lastest fashions** appearing in the stores that season.
- **A detective observes and writes down every detail** to re-create the scene of a crime.
- **An inventor carefully describes her invention** in an application for a protective patent.

Guide Instruction

By Modeling Strategies

Have the class work together to outline a paragraph describing your classroom. Start by asking students to describe details about the room. Write notes about these details on the board. Encourage students to be specific and creative in their selection of details. Then use student suggestions and comments to develop a topic sentence for the paragraph. Write this sentence on the board. Finally, develop a concluding sentence for the paragraph, and write it on the board.

Consolidate Skills

Through Guided Practice

The **Practice Your Skills** activity on writing topic sentences on page C169 provides students practice on that skill. You can extend the activity by having students volunteer to read their sentences out loud, and discuss what information readers would expect to follow.

Developing Your Skills of Description

"When writing, I think of myself as a tour guide at a large museum," says writer Stephanie Coontz. Sometimes your purpose for writing will be to describe. You may describe the pyramids in Mexico in a composition for your history class, or the tiny organisms you see through a microscope in your biology class. In a letter you may describe the scenery you saw on your vacation. Whenever your purpose is to help your reader see what you have seen and feel what you felt, you will be writing a description.

Descriptive writing is not only about what you see. Good descriptive writing employs all the senses: sight, sound, taste, touch, and smell. The words that you use must be precise and well organized to create as clear a picture as possible. Remember, as the writer you are responsible for pointing out all the details you want your readers to see and feel.

Descriptive writing uses words to create a vivid picture of a person, an object, or a scene.

Your Writer's Journal

Your journal is a good place to develop ideas for subjects to describe. Write about what you know. You might think back to important events in your life. Flip through your memory as you would through a photo album, glancing at highlights from your life like pictures captured on film. Each day, select a memory that brings a clear "photo" to mind. Study it in your mind's eye. Look at it closely—see it as if it were an actual photo (or series of photos). Then write about it, recording everything you see in your mental picture. Include sights, sounds, tastes, and anything else that animates the experience.

GETTING STUDENTS INVOLVED

Cooperative Learning

Divide students into small groups. Assign each group a place to describe that everyone has seen, such as the school gymnasium, the local library, or a park. Each individual in the group should write down ten words or phrases describing that place. Then group members should share their descriptions, noting similarities and differences. As a class discuss whether students relied upon different senses. Note whether any students made descriptions that were unusual, but that all agreed were accurate.

USING STUDENTS' STRENGTHS

Multiple Intelligences: Musical

As students write in their journals, encourage them to note songs and other sounds they associate with their memories. Suggest that they write down some of their favorite songs, and then describe the specific events or feelings that the song prompts them to recall.

Apply to Communication

Through Independent Writing

Students can use their journal notes to help them complete the **Communicate Your Ideas** activity on topic sentences. Have students discuss with a partner the topic sentence they have written. As they read it to their partner and explain what would be in the paragraph, they should begin to clarify what they want to write.

Transfer to Everyday Life

By Showing Rather than Telling

Have students take a statement that tells them something simply and revise it into a longer sentence or a paragraph that makes the same basic point. For example, a writer could tell the reader, *Mark's room was messy.* Or the writer could show the reader by writing, *Each morning, Mark blazed a trail through the dirty clothes, half-read magazines, and assorted gizmos that hid the floor of his room.*

Have students write five simple statements that they hear during the day. Then have them write a paragraph that makes the basic point of each.

IDENTIFYING COMMON STUMBLING BLOCKS

Problem

- Not recognizing the topic sentence, particularly when it does not come first in the paragraph

Solution

- Have students draw a pyramid diagram for the paragraph on the Jack Gore Baygall. They are to put the topic sentence at the top of the pyramid, because it is the one that all other sentences will fall under. They should experiment with different sentences at the top, and decide how well each one supports the others.

Descriptive Paragraph Structure

Like other paragraphs that stand alone, a descriptive paragraph has a topic sentence, a body of supporting sentences, and a concluding sentence. The following chart shows how each part helps to complete the picture.

Structure of a Descriptive Paragraph

- The **topic sentence** introduces the subject and often suggests an overall impression or generalization.
- The **supporting sentences** supply specific details that appeal to the senses to bring the subject to life.
- The **concluding sentence** summarizes the subject.

The following paragraph paints a dynamic picture.

MODEL: Descriptive Paragraph

The Jack Gore Baygall

TOPIC SENTENCE — The Jack Gore Baygall is a junglelike region about three miles wide and four miles long.

SUPPORTING SENTENCES — Sunlight filters through one-hundred-foot-tall tupelos and cypresses, reaching the thick undergrowth in eerie green shafts. By night the sounds of animals moving, calling, warning others of their kind, fill the recesses of the baygall. It is the home of alligators, otters, beavers, hawks, owls, roadrunners, snakes, fox squirrels, and whitetail deer. Oaks growing out of the muck to heights of 135 feet sprouted from acorns in the days when America was only a British colony.

CONCLUDING SENTENCE — The Jack Gore Baygall is a wild piece of the Big Thicket National Preserve.

—*Howard Peacock,* The Big Thicket of Texas

Pull It All Together

By Reflecting

Ask students to explain how their descriptive writing skills have changed over time. They may mention changes over the past few years or focus on changes in the past few weeks. Point out that developing writing skills is an ongoing process that never ends. Ask them to predict how their writing will improve over the coming years.

Check Understanding

By Comparing

Ask students to compare descriptive writing with other genres of writing. Note both the differences in purpose and the similarities in organization. If students mention the importance of specific details in descriptive writing, tell them that they will be focusing on this concern in the next section of the chapter.

The topic sentence of this paragraph gives the reader a clue about the kind of place the Jack Gore Baygall is: "a junglelike region." The descriptions of the eerie shafts of sunlight and the nighttime sounds of animals support this overall impression. The concluding sentence summarizes the impression by calling this area a "wild piece" of land.

Practice Your Skills

Writing Topic Sentences

For each descriptive subject, write a topic sentence that suggests an overall impression.

EXAMPLE a swimming pool

POSSIBLE ANSWER The empty pool looked forsaken with the dead leaves and branches lying at its bottom.

1. a wolf
2. the night sky
3. a carnival
4. a grandparent
5. a forest
6. a pet
7. a hayride
8. your kitchen
9. a fancy cake
10. a spaceship

Communicate Your Ideas

PREWRITING *Topic Sentence*

Look over some of the subjects you have listed in your **journal**. Choose one that you think would make a good subject for a descriptive paragraph. Then brainstorm, freewrite, or cluster to think of the elements you want to use in your description. Write a topic sentence for your paragraph. Save your work for later use.

HOME WORK

Have students write additional descriptive sentences for five of the words in the **Practice Your Skills** activity. Tell students that the additional sentences should describe the words in very different ways than did their first sentences.

Practice Your Skills Answers

1. The wolf was an angry gray charge of energy pacing back and forth.
2. The huge stretches of the night sky are like endless bolts of black velvet.
3. The carefree atmosphere of the carnival caught me up completely.
4. My grandmother is one of the most determined women I know.
5. After the hubbub of city life, the forest was a peaceful paradise.
6. Red-Eye the parrot likes to play practical jokes on me.
7. The crisp fall air was perfect for an old-fashioned hayride.
8. Your kitchen looks as if a herd of buffalo has stampeded through it.
9. His four-layer birthday cake was smothered in nine colors of frosting.
10. The saucer-shaped spacecraft hovered noisily over the small town-square.

LESSON 2 (pages C170–C176)

OBJECTIVES

- **To use specific details and sensory words in developing a descriptive paragraph**
- **To use spatial order with transitions in a descriptive paragraph**

Create Interest

Ask students to mention their favorite advertising slogans. Write these slogans on the board, and discuss whether they include specific details. Try revising the slogans to make them more vague. Ask students if they think the slogans would be as effective if they were vague rather than specific.

Tell students that in the next part of the chapter they will focus on using specific details and sensory words in developing a descriptive paragraph.

TIMESAVER *QuickCheck*

Have students volunteer to read their topic sentences to the class. Discuss whether the topic sentences are broad enough to introduce a paragraph. Then have students review their own sentences to see if they think they are appropriate.

HOME STUDY

To help students develop elements to use in their description, suggest that they draw a picture of the scene they are describing. As they do, have them note what information they are showing—the shapes they draw, the colors they use, the relationships they portray—and how they will express that in their writing.

IDENTIFYING COMMON STUMBLING BLOCKS

Problem

- Using general comments rather than specific details in descriptions

Solution

- On the board write general descriptive terms, and ask students to suggest more specific words that could replace them. For example, *pretty* could be replaced by *cute, elegant, lovely,* or *captivating.*

Specific Details and Sensory Words

In a descriptive paragraph, your topic sentence tells your readers your overall impression of the subject. Your supporting sentences should then help them see what you see.

Writing Tip

Use **specific details** and **sensory words** to bring your description to life.

As you read the following descriptive paragraph, look for specific details and words that appeal to the senses.

MODEL: Specific Details and Sensory Words

The Square Dance

TOPIC SENTENCE — Stepping into the school auditorium on Tuesday nights is like traveling through time to the colorful days of the frontier barn dance.

SENSORY DETAILS — On the stage at the front of the hall, musicians in overalls and red bandanas stomp out the tunes for the dances. The middle of the floor creaks under the weight of the twirling dancers in their squares. The colors of the women's full skirts blur into a mosaic as partners swing around and around. From the back of the hall, the smells of popcorn being made in the kitchen tell the dancers that a break is coming up. Within minutes the tables set up along the back of the hall will be brimming with pitchers of ice-cold lemonade and bowls of popcorn.

CONCLUDING SENTENCE — For a few short minutes, the dancers will cool off, but before long they will be back on the floor, reliving the fun of old time dancing.

Guide Instruction

By Connecting Ideas

Discuss with students how the senses are connected. For example, smell and taste are closely connected. Have students noticed that food has less taste when they have a cold stopping up their nasal passages? Have they ever felt the vibrations of a booming bass in music they are listening to? Other connections may require more imagination. Have they ever heard a sight? Or seen a sound? Encourage students to think of connections among the senses. Even if they do not see any connection, this process may sharpen their skills at observation and description.

Consolidate Skills

Through Guided Practice

Students can use the **Practice Your Skills** activity on identifying types of spatial order on page C174 to improve their awareness of how descriptive paragraphs are organized. You can extend this activity by asking students to bring to class other examples of

Writing Is Thinking

Observing

When developing intense sensory details for descriptive writing, you can call on your skills of **observation**. Observing something is different from simply seeing it. When you observe a scene, you notice not only separate things that make it up, but also the relationships among those things. For example, while at the beach, you might see water lapping at the shore and sunbathers on blankets. With focused observation you may also be aware of the striking contrast between the natural landscape of water, sky, and sand, and the numerous objects such as boats, planes, and people that cover it. Careful observation allows the separate details of the scene—the seagulls, the wind and waves, the smells of suntan lotion—to form a whole, complete picture in your mind.

THINKING PRACTICE

Use a chart like the one below to record your observations about a scene of your choosing.

SENSE	OBSERVATIONS
Sight	sand, colorful beach blankets
Touch	hot sand, hot sun, cool water
Sound	birds, lapping waves, wind, music
Smell	suntan lotion, sea air, sizzling hot dogs
Taste	salty water, lemonade

Using *Writing Is Thinking*

Objective

- **To practice the skill of observation**

A DIFFERENT APPROACH

Auditory Have students listen to a piece of music that does not include words and complete a chart like the one used in the Writing Is Thinking activity. Ask students to write down the name of the piece of music they listened to. Discuss which rows of the chart were easiest for them to fill in.

THINKING PRACTICE Sample Answers

What is being observed: beach

Sight: sand, colorful beach blankets

Touch: hot sand, hot sun, cool water

Sound: birds, lapping waves, wind, music

Smell: suntan lotion, sea air, sizzling hot dogs

Taste: salty water, lemonade

Thinking Skills	
Classifying	Analyzing
Comparing	Hypothesizing
Generalizing	Synthesizing
Inferring	Summarizing
Imagining	Setting Goals
Observing	Evaluating Audience
Predicting	

descriptive paragraphs for their classmates, either in small groups or as an entire class, to analyze.

Apply to Communication

Through Independent Writing

After students complete the **Communicate Your Ideas** activity on spatial order and transitions, ask them to count the number of transitions they used in their paragraph. On the board create a bar graph showing the number of transitions. Ask students to analyze the data on the graph. Discuss what a typical number of transitions is for the paragraphs written by their classmates. Students who lack confidence in their writing may feel more comfortable if they know that their paragraphs share some similarities with those of their classmates. Discuss with students the range shown in the graph, noting that either a low or a high number may be appropriate depending on the paragraph.

PRACTICE YOUR SKILLS Sample Answers

Sight: overalls and red bandanas, twirling dancers, colors of women's full skirts, tables set up with lemonade and bowls of popcorn

Sound: tunes for dances, floor creaking

Taste: lemonade, popcorn

Smell: popcorn

Touch: musicians stomping, the weight of the dancers, the dancers cool off

1. **Thanksgiving**
   aroma of turkey cooking
   table set with sparkling china
   taste of pumpkin pie
   plates clattering
   voices of relatives
2. **a wedding**
   bridesmaids' colorful gowns
   songs sung during the wedding
   scent of flowers
   music and dancing at the reception
   taste of wedding cake
3. **a football game**
   football kicked for a field goal
   blue and gold uniforms
   cool autumn air
   taste of hot dogs
   cheering

PRACTICE YOUR SKILLS

Identifying Sensory Details

List all the details in the paragraph on page C170 that appeal to the five senses: sight, sound, taste, smell, and touch.

Developing Sensory Details

Choose five of the following subjects. Under each one, write five sensory details you could use in a description.

1. Thanksgiving
2. a wedding
3. a football game
4. an old book
5. a horse
6. a workshop
7. a mountain lake
8. a newborn kitten
9. a run-down car
10. a pickle

Communicate Your Ideas

PREWRITING *Drafting*

Return to the topic sentence you wrote to begin your descriptive paragraph. Look over your prewriting notes to create a list of specific details and sensory words to use in your description. Write a draft of your descriptive paragraph. Save your work for later use.

Spatial Order and Transitions

One way to organize the details in a description is spatial, or location, order. Transitions used with spatial order tell how the details are related in space. They are like pointers that lead a reader's eye from spot to spot.

Spatial order arranges details according to their location. **Transitions** show the relationship of the details.

Transfer to Everyday Life

By Analyzing Advertising

Advertisements often describe products in memorable, but incomplete, ways. Companies may leave out information, hoping that the potential consumer will not notice what is missing, or will assume the most favorable interpretation. Have students bring in advertisements for breakfast cereals, clothes, automobiles, and other products. Discuss which details the advertisements emphasize and which ones it avoids, and how people might interpret the information.

Pull It All Together

By Summarizing

Review with students the four basic types of spatial order and some of the transitions commonly used with each one. Encourage students to consider all four types as they begin to write descriptive paragraphs.

As a writer of description, you can decide the direction in which you want to lead your reader's eye. The following chart shows four directions commonly used with spatial order and the transitions associated with each one.

SPATIAL ORDER	TRANSITIONS
near to far (or reverse)	close by, beyond, around, farther, across, behind, in the distance
top to bottom (or reverse)	at the top, in the middle, lower, below, at the bottom, above, higher
side to side	at the left (right), in the middle, next to, at one end, to the west
inside to outside (or reverse)	within, in the center, on the inside (outside), the next layer

In the following descriptive paragraph, the details are arranged in spatial order from top to bottom. The transitions are printed in **bold** type.

MODEL: Spatial Order

Yoda's Face

Every detail in the face of Yoda, the Jedi master in *The Empire Strikes Back*, suggests his wisdom and intelligence. His green body is dwarfed by his huge head. His high forehead gives the impression of a large, busy brain. **Beneath** his forehead his expressive eyes show both disappointment and hope at his young pupil's progress. His huge pointed ears that reach **the**

4. **an old book**
   binding of old red leather
   musty smell
   yellowed pages
   silk ribbons for place markers
   original owner's name in faded ink
5. **a horse**
   mane flowing in breeze
   rhythmic galloping
   whinnying
   sleek appearance of well-brushed coat
   sound of hooves on ground

HOME WORK

Have students write five details about each of five items they find around their home. They can select common items, although encourage them to try to describe one item that might be unusual.

REACHING ALL STUDENTS

Struggling Learners

Students can practice using spatial order by revising the description of Yoda's face, beginning at the bottom and moving to the top. Students can use the same information, but they should change the order of the sentences and the transitions.

Check Understanding

By Analyzing the Literary Selection

Divide the class into pairs. Assign each a section of *Rascal* to evaluate. Students should identify the type of spatial order used in descriptive paragraphs in their section, and point out details that made the writing clear and engaging.

USING STUDENTS' STRENGTHS

Multiple Intelligences: Spatial

Have students draw diagrams that show the four directions commonly used with spatial order. Tell them their diagrams should show the location of the observer, and how five items could be arranged in each of the four ways.

Practice Your Skills Answers

1. side to side
2. outside to inside
3. top to bottom

same level as his eyes show his ability to take in sounds that others would miss. **Below** his eyes, a smallish nose twitches in response to events around him. **At the bottom** of his face, a mouth that knows how to stay shut reveals his ability to concentrate. At first sight, Yoda may appear ugly, but as you see his great intelligence at work, his face begins to show the wisdom of the Jedi masters.

Practice Your Skills

Identifying Types of Spatial Order

Identify the type of spatial order used by writing *top to bottom, side to side, near to far,* or *outside to inside.*

1. The Animal Shelter

As I looked at the row of puppies, I wanted to adopt them all. In a cage to my left was a single black puppy, peacefully curled up with her nose warmed by her tail. Next to her was a litter of twelve-week-old beagle puppies, playfully pawing the cage and yelping with excitement. In the cage directly in front of me were two white, fluffy pups with wildly wagging tails. To my right, in the biggest cage, were a mother dog and her litter of four-week-old puppies who would stay with her for another month before being adopted. How would I ever choose?

2. The Piñata

Piñatas are a tradition at parties in my family. The piñata is a papier-mâché form, often in the shape of a burro, that is colorful on the outside and filled with surprises inside. The outside of the piñata is covered with brightly colored short strips of paper to suggest a burro's hair. Inside the piñata is a hollow space filled with small presents such as yo-yos, balls, twirlers, and other trinkets. The piñata is hung by twine from the ceiling. Near the end of the party, guests take turns hitting the piñata with a stick, eagerly waiting for it to split and the presents to come tumbling down.

3. My Sister Gwen

My five-year-old sister Gwen looks as mischievous as she usually is. A stubborn cowlick rises out of her sandy-colored hair, imitating Gwen's own strong will. Her bangs are cut straight across her forehead, but somehow they always seem to part in a funny spot on the left side. Her blue eyes always flash with humor when she tells a joke, while her long curly eyelashes give her an innocent look she sometimes hides behind. Gwen's cheeks are usually flushed, mainly because of her energetic dashing around the house and yard. Her delicate lips are often turned up in a tricky smile. Gwen looks like one of the family, but her own impish personality always shines through.

Communicate Your Ideas

REVISING *Spatial Order and Transitions*

Try rewriting your description with the details arranged in spatial order. Be sure to include the transitions you need to guide the reader from point to point in the description.

Time Out to Reflect

You have read several examples of descriptive writing in this chapter. Each piece has had a unique subject and purpose. Think about where you have seen or used descriptive writing in your own life. Then make your own list of the different ways descriptive writing is used. You might want to compare lists with your classmates. As you think of additional uses of description, add them to your list.

HOME WORK

Have students find three paragraphs in books or other written materials that use spatial order. Ask volunteers to read their paragraphs, and have the class identify which type of spatial order is used in each.

GETTING STUDENTS INVOLVED

Cooperative Learning

Working in small groups, students should develop three examples of descriptions that would use each of the four directions commonly used with spatial order. Have groups share their lists with the class.

Using *In the Media*

Objective

- **To analyze sound bites used in the media**

Group Project

- Assign class members to write down sound-bites they hear during a two-day period. Each student should list at least three soundbites. They might hear them on radio or television or read them in newspapers. Have students read some of their soundbites in class, and discuss which ones are most effective at summarizing issues or positions in a memorable way.

FYI

Websites to Visit Students can listen to soundbites, and sometimes full speeches, at the site of the Historic Audio Archives, http://www.webcorp.com/sounds/; at the site of the Vincent Voice Library at Michigan State University, http://www.lib.msu.edu/vincent/; and the History and Politics Out Loud site, http://www.hpol.org/. Several famous clips from movies can be heard at http://www.moviesounds.com/.

IN THE MEDIA

Sound Bites

We have all heard about sound bites, but what are they exactly? A **sound bite** is a short video clip that has been extracted from a larger piece of footage and used by television or radio stations to capture the interest of the viewer. The phrase is used to summarize the most sensational or interesting ideas from a speech or document of some kind. Often it is a phrase used by a public figure that is used in this way. For example, when former President George Bush indicated in the early 1990s that he would never raise taxes, he said, "Read my lips, no new taxes." This became a sound bite—a familiar phrase that has been shortened over time to "Read my lips." Today the news media are in constant competition for our attention, and sound bites are used more and more to grab the viewer or listener and to get them to watch a news program, log on to a Website, or listen to the radio.

Media Activity

Make an audio or video recording of yourself or a partner describing something you see every day, on your way to school, or in your classroom, or at home. Be sure to discuss as many details of the object as you can. Then listen to or watch the tape to find a phrase or sentence you or your partner used that somehow sums up the object. If you can edit the tape, create your own sound bite. Play it for the class and ask them to tell you what it brings to mind.

LESSON 3 *(pages C177–C182)*

OBJECTIVE

- **To follow the steps of the writing process to develop a descriptive paragraph**

Create Interest
Divide the class into small groups. Give each group a picture, or at least the name, of a person whose face most people will recognize, such as George Washington, Martin Luther King, Jr., or Marilyn Monroe. Ask each group to write a description of the face to read to the class. The rest of the class should try to guess the person based on the description. Discuss the difficulties of describing the features of a person accurately.

Guide Instruction
By Modeling Strategies
Have the class work together to create an accurate description of the two figures in the painting *American Gothic*

Process of Writing a Descriptive Paragraph

Writing a descriptive paragraph is like making a movie. Like a set designer, you must create striking visual images. Like a sound operator, you must include sounds that go along with the scene. Finally, like a director, you must put all the details together to create an overall impression. Through prewriting, drafting, revising, and editing you will be able to shape your words into a moving picture.

Describing a Person

Prewriting When you are deciding on a subject to write about, it is best to pick someone you know. A friend, neighbor, or family member would be a good choice for the subject of a description. Limit your description to an aspect that you consider unique to that individual. You may wish to consider the following questions:

- What are your subject's facial features?
- What are your subject's facial expressions?
- What is your subject's hair like?
- How old is your subject?
- What kind of clothing does your subject like to wear?
- What is your subject's posture like?

Look through some photographs and choose a picture of a member of your family. Then develop a list of details, such as facial features, facial expression, hair, clothing, and posture. Arrange your details in a logical order.

Drafting Without mentioning your subject's name, write a description of the family member exactly as he or she appears in the photograph. Your purpose is to describe the person's

IDENTIFYING COMMON STUMBLING BLOCKS

Problem

- Feeling uncomfortable commenting on the features and clothing of a friend or family member

Solution

- Ask students to bring in a picture of someone shown in an advertisement and to write a description of that person.

by Grant Wood. You may wish to bring in art books that include the painting, or direct students to a Website where they can see the painting, such as one of the Art Institute of Chicago, http://www.artic.edu/aic/collections/20c/73pc wood.html. Students may also enjoy visiting a site devoted to parodies of the painting, http://www.bcpl.lib.md.us/~glake/am.html.

Consolidate Skills

Through Guided Practice

To give students additional practice using adjectives, have them select a section about five sentences long from *Rascal* and repeat the activity described in **Grammar in the Writing Process.**

Apply to Communication

Through Independent Writing

Have students write a paragraph describing someone writing a paragraph following the writing process. In their paragraph, students should use at least ten adjectives.

INTEGRATING TECHNOLOGY

Internet

Encourage students to use a thesaurus in book form. They can also access the best-known thesaurus, Roget's, at http://web.cs.city.ac.uk/text/roget/thesaurus.html. This site is maintained by City University of London. A thesaurus organized on current psycholinguistic theories is available at http://www.cogsci.princeton.edu/~wn/, a site at Princeton University.

appearance so well that other members of your family will be able to recognize who it is.

Revising Conferencing Ask someone who knows your subject well to review your description. Ask your reviewer these questions: *Are you able to name the person I have described? What clues helped you to decide who it is? What other details might I have included?* Use the **Evaluation Checklist for Revising** on page C181 and the feedback from your reviewer to revise your work.

COMPUTER TIP

The revision process is a good time to use the Thesaurus in your computer's Tools menu. If you are typing your paragraph in Word, highlight a word you are thinking of replacing, go to Thesaurus, and read the list of synonyms to choose from.

Creating and Describing a Scene

Prewriting The items listed below appeal to the sense of smell. Think of a scene that goes along with each one. Then write freely about each item using the questions that follow. Complete your work by drawing a sketch of each scene.

- pine
- popcorn
- campfire
- hay
- soap

1. What sights go along with this smell?
2. What sounds would I hear when I smell this?
3. What tastes, if any, go with this smell?
4. What might appeal to my sense of touch?

Transfer to Everyday Life

By Reading Catalogs

Ask students to bring to class examples of catalogs that provide lavish descriptions of items for sale. Then have students write a similar description of an article of clothing, a household utensil, or some other object.

Pull It All Together

By Sharing

When students have gone over their descriptive paragraph using the **Evaluation Checklist for Revising,** ask volunteers to read their paragraphs to the class. Then ask the students to describe some of the decisions they made in writing the paragraph, such as how they developed their topic sentence, how they decided which details to include and which to omit, and what alternatives they considered to their concluding sentence.

Check Understanding

By Applying to Reading

Ask students how the study of descriptive writing has affected their reading.

Drafting Choose one item from the preceding list. Use your freewriting notes and your sketch to write a descriptive paragraph that creates your scene in words. Be sure to include details that appeal to at least four of the five senses.

Looping Back to Prewriting

Look at your draft. What sensory words have you used? Make a list. Then try to expand the list of words that are related just to the sense of smell. Pair up with a classmate who is writing about the same subject you are. Compare your lists of sensory words. What words do you have in common? What words are unique to your list? Save your list to refer to as you revise your paragraph.

Revising Conferencing Take turns reading your descriptive paragraphs out loud with a partner. When it is your turn to listen, take note of the words and phrases you hear that appeal to your senses. Are there enough sensory words to create a vivid picture? Share your comments with your partner. Use your partner's comments and your own judgment to revise your paragraph.

COMPUTER TIP

You can investigate different fonts and point sizes to enhance your paragraph. It is fun to do, but do not allow the print and size to distract the reader from your writing.

GETTING STUDENTS INVOLVED

Cooperative Learning

Divide the class into groups of five or six. Each student should write one short descriptive sentence on a piece of paper. Students then pass their paper to the person on their left, who must then change or add one or two words to enliven the sentence. Students keep passing the papers until they get their original back. Each student can then read the sentence they started with, and what the group created. For example, a student may start with *The room was dark.* The sentence may become *The frigid dungeon was without light or hope.*

USING STUDENTS' STRENGTHS

Multiple Intelligences: Linguistic

Have students work with a partner. Ask each pair to write a noun on their paper, and then to write one word or phrase that describes it for each letter of the alphabet. For example, if they start with *dog* as their noun, they might list *active, barking*, and *chummy*.

FYI

How to Use with Windows™ To change a font size, click on the Format menu, and select Font.

How to Use with Macintosh™ To change a font or point size, click on the Format menu or the Font menu.

Do they read descriptive passages more carefully? Are they more aware of sensory details? Do they note the type of spatial organization used? Are they critical of misuse of adjectives? Help students understand the close relationship between writing and reading skills.

Using *Revising Workshop*

Objective

- **To practice using adjectives**

A DIFFERENT APPROACH

Tactile Have students write five words describing a surface they like to touch, such as a soft cloth or a smooth piece of wood. Then have them write five words about a surface they find unpleasant, such as a piece of sandpaper. Ask if any words would describe both surfaces.

Grammar in the Writing Process

By using vivid adjectives, a writer can paint a verbal masterpiece. A single descriptive word can sometimes speak volumes about a character, a place, a mood, or an event. In the following excerpt from *Rascal* note how the author uses adjectives to intensify the action.

> But we couldn't have been more surprised when a **furious** mother raccoon exploded from her lair screaming her rage and dismay. Wowser nearly fell over backward to avoid the **flying** claws and **slashing little** teeth. A moment later the **big** raccoon had racked her way up a **slender** oak tree.

The boldfaced words in this passage are **adjectives**, words that modify nouns and pronouns. The following examples from *Rascal* show how adjectives can transform a vague, uninteresting description into a vivid and expressive portrait.

VAGUE	He turned and looked at the racoon. (The reader cannot relate to how Wowser is feeling.)
VIVID	After being challenged, badgered, and insulted, he eventually would turn his worried face and great sad eyes upon his tormentor. (The reader can relate to Wowser's anxiety and sadness— human qualities.)
VAGUE	Wowser was a dog. (What kind of dog?)
VIVID	Wowser was an affectionate, perpetually hungry Saint Bernard.

Writing Tip

Use **adjectives** to help bring your descriptions to life, and make each adjective count. Be precise.

Evaluation Checklist for Revising

Checking Your Paragraph

✓ Does your topic sentence introduce the subject and suggest your overall impression of it? *(pages C168–C169)*

✓ Do your supporting sentences supply specific details and sensory words that bring your subject to life? *(pages C168–C170)*

✓ Does your paragraph have unity? *(page C84)*

✓ Did you arrange your details in spatial order (or another logical order) with transitions to give your paragraph coherence? *(pages C172–C174)*

✓ Does your concluding sentence summarize your overall impression of the subject? *(pages C168–C169)*

Checking Your Sentences

✓ Are your sentences varied? *(pages C53–C59)*

✓ Are commas in the correct place?

Checking Your Words

✓ Did you use specific words and well-chosen adjectives? *(pages C170 and C180)*

TIMESAVER *QuickCheck*

Have students review their lists of details to see how many senses they have appealed to. Ask them to consider whether they want to add words that appeal to any senses they are missing.

INTEGRATING *Writers at Work*

For more opportunities to inspire and stimulate students' descriptive writing, look at *Writers at Work.*

EXPANDING THE LESSON

Using Technology

Use Barrett Kendall ancillary **Instructional** and **practice** materials located at http://www.bkenglish.com.

Process of Writing a Descriptive Paragraph

Remember that the writing process is recursive—you can move back and forth among the stages of the process to achieve your purpose. For example, during drafting you may decide to return to the prewriting phase to brainstorm more details. The numbers in the parentheses refer to pages where you can get help with your writing.

PREWRITING

- Think of possible subjects by looking at pictures and searching your memory.
- Make a list of subjects and choose one that interests you and your readers.
- Limit your subject so that it can be covered in one paragraph.
- Write down all the sensory details that come to mind when you think about your subject. *(pages C170–C172)*

DRAFTING

- Arrange your notes in spatial order or in some other logical order. *(pages C172–C174)*
- Write a topic sentence that suggests an overall impression. *(pages C77–C79)*
- Use your prewriting notes to write supporting sentences with transitions where needed. *(pages C79–C82)*
- Add a concluding sentence that summarizes the overall impression. *(page C88)*

REVISING

- Put your paper aside for a while. Then use the Evaluation Checklist for Revising on page C181 to revise your paragraph.
- Give your work to a test reader for comments.

EDITING

- Use the Editing Checklist on page C36 to check your work for errors.

PUBLISHING

- Prepare a neat, polished copy of your work and present it to a reader. *(pages C40–C41)*

A Writer Writes

A Description

Purpose: to describe the majesty of the California condor

Audience: wildlife lovers

Read the following passage about a wolf pup's birth. As you read, note how the author uses specific details and sensory words to describe the scene of the newly born wolf pup and his mother.

> The world he entered was bare and cold. He lay on sand; a cool breeze passed over him. Somewhere in the darkness of the cavern his mother's panting came to his ears. He opened his mouth and whimpered a tiny, high-pitched whine. A large tongue sloshed across his face as his mother began to wash him. Fore and aft, belly and back, the tongue slobbered over him.
>
> *–Robert Gray,*
> The Natural Life of North American Wolves

Prewriting

Use the picture on the next page to develop a list of details you could use to describe the California condor in flight. Try to think of striking, original comparisons you could use in your description. List sensory words and specific details that describe the condor. Then sort through your prewriting notes to choose the best ideas. Arrange these details in a logical order.

Using *A Writer Writes*

Objective

- **To convey emotion through descriptive writing**

TIMESAVER *QuickCheck*

In the revising stage, encourage students to exchange their descriptive writing with a partner. Partners should read the papers and share their ideas for improvements.

INTEGRATING *Writers at Work*

For more opportunities to stimulate students' descriptive writing, look at *Writers at Work.*

YOUR IDEAS

For the Writing Process

Drafting

Use your prewriting work to help you draft a paragraph describing a California condor in flight. Refer to Structure of a Descriptive Paragraph on page C168 to help you develop your paragraph.

Revising

Exchange papers with a classmate. Ask your partner specific questions about your draft. Have you added enough adjectives? Have you used precise and stimulating language? Are there clear transitions between ideas? Listen to any comments your classmate might have about how your description could be improved. Then, using your own judgment, add, delete, rearrange, and substitute to improve your draft. Finally, use the Evaluation Checklist for Revising on page C181 to check your work.

Editing and Publishing

Correct any errors in your descriptive paragraph. Make a neat final copy of your work to present to a reader.

Connection Collection

Representing in Different Ways

From Print . . .

. . . to Visuals

Use the information in the advertisement to create a logo for Mighty Munch Snack Company. Consider the image Mighty Munch wants to promote, and be sure to include the product name on your logo.

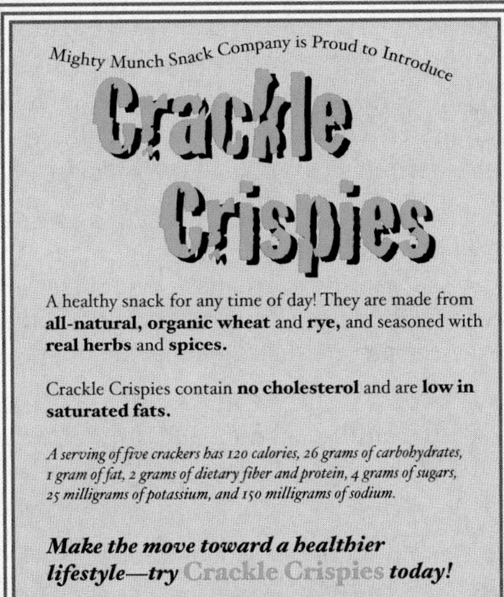

Mighty Munch Snack Company is Proud to Introduce
Crackle Crispies
A healthy snack for any time of day! They are made from **all-natural, organic wheat** and **rye,** and seasoned with **real herbs** and **spices.**
Crackle Crispies contain **no cholesterol** and are **low in saturated fats.**
A serving of five crackers has 120 calories, 26 grams of carbohydrates, 1 gram of fat, 2 grams of dietary fiber and protein, 4 grams of sugars, 25 milligrams of potassium, and 150 milligrams of sodium.
Make the move toward a healthier lifestyle—try Crackle Crispies today!

From Visuals . . .

Nutrition Facts
Chewer's Fruit Chewies
Serving Size: 20 Chewies (85g)
Amount Per Serving
Calories 300
Total Fat 5g
Cholesterol 20mg
Sodium 500mg
Potassium 140mg
Total Carbohydrates 33g
Dietary Fiber 0g
Sugars 20g
Protein 5g
Vitamin C: 50% Daily Value

. . . to Print

From the information in the nutrition label, write an advertisement describing Chewer's Fruit Chewies.

- **Which strategies can be used for creating both written and visual representations? Which strategies apply to one, not both? Which type of representation is more effective?**
- **Draw a conclusion and write briefly about the differences between written ideas and visual representations.**

FOR REVIEWING SKILLS

Using *Connection Collection*

Representing in Different Ways

Consider using these print and visual activities to make students aware of the benefits of using different media to suit particular purposes. Help students understand when a visual medium, for example, is better suited to their purpose than a print medium, or the reverse.

YOUR IDEAS

For Writing Prompts

Writing in Everyday Life

E-mail Message

Your family has decided to host an exchange student from Kenya named Sulia. Culture Swap is the agency that runs the exchange program, and they have asked you for a short E-mail message with specific details about your family, school, and community. They will pass on your description to Sulia and send you her comments about her family, school, and village in Kenya.

Write an E-mail message to Sulia in care of Culture Swap explaining what makes your "homeland" unique. Include specific details and sensory words to create a vivid picture. Brainstorm for ideas first, and edit your message for coherence. Remember that Sulia may not be completely fluent in English.

What strategies did you use to describe your family, school, and hometown to Sulia?

You can find information on writing E-mail messages in A Writer's Guide to the Internet.

Writing in Academic Areas

Informal Note

The year is 3508, and you are a scientist at Lunar State University. You are visiting Earth on a field trip and you have found the ruins of an ancient city from the early 2000s. Your boss has asked you for a brief update on your discovery. Among the ruins, you see a household object, like an iron, a telephone, a television, or a personal computer. Although you pick the object up and observe it closely, you have no idea what it is or how it was used.

Write an informal note to your boss at Lunar State, describing your relic. Use sensory words and specific details to help your boss imagine the object. You may share your writing with a classmate if you like. Was your classmate able to guess the item you described?

What strategies did you use to describe the object to your boss?

A DIFFERENT DELIVERY SYSTEM

For formal assessment print the composition chapter test from the *BK English* Test Bank at http://www.bkenglish.com.

Assess Your Learning

Your grandfather is organizing a large family reunion, and he has asked you to help him. He wants to create a large book with a short biography and picture of each family member who is planning to attend the reunion. Your first task is to describe someone in your family. You may choose your mother, father, brother, sister, cousin, aunt, uncle, or grandparent.

- **Prewrite to create a list of the person's characteristics or traits. Then limit your subject to one aspect of this person's life. You may try conferring with someone else who knows the person well. Keep track of your notes and use them to draft a one-paragraph biography. In revising your draft, be sure to use a topic sentence, supporting details, and a conclusion that summarizes and expands on your topic.**
- **Try to make your writing so clear and vivid that your family will be able to imagine every detail about their relative, whether or not they know that person. Use specific details, sensory words, and transitions. Remember that your family will be your audience, and the person's picture will appear next to your piece. Try to use a small number of powerful adjectives.**

Before You Write **Consider the following questions:**
What is the ***subject?***
What is the ***occasion?***
Who is the ***audience?***
What is the ***purpose?***

After You Write **Evaluate your work using the following criteria:**

- Does your topic sentence give an impression of the person you chose to describe?
- Do your supporting sentences include specific details and sensory words?
- Have you organized your biography in logical order and used appropriate transitions?
- Did you use a variety of sentence structures to make your writing flow together and make sense?
- Have you used the right number of adjectives, neither too few nor too many?

Write briefly on how well you did. Point out your strengths and areas for improvement.

FOR ASSESSING LEARNING

Using *Assess Your Learning*

This writing prompt will help you and your students informally assess their developing writing abilities, using the accompanying primary trait rubrics, which list the key features and qualities of descriptive writing taught in this chapter. You may want to have students maintain their self-assessment in their portfolios as a record of their individual progress throughout the year.

Teaching Suggestions

Essential Knowledge and Skills

- Adapting spoken language such as word, choice, diction, and usage to the audience, purpose, and occasion
- Presenting dramatic interpretations of experiences, stories, poems, or plays to communicate
- Writing to entertain such as to compose humorous poems or short stories
- Using literary devices effectively such as suspense, dialogue, and figurative language
- Generating ideas and plans for writing by using prewriting strategies such as brainstorming, graphic organizers, notes, and logs
- Analyzing published examples as models for writing

CHAPTER 7

Creative Writing: Stories, Plays, and Poems

The world of plays, stories, and poems has been built by creative writers. Think of the complete freedom a writer has to invent plots and characters. The author can manipulate characters and situations any which way to examine human foibles and strengths. This may cause the reader to ask questions about the author: What made the author think of this? What does this work reveal about the author? The reader may marvel at the writer's skill in using language. In this chapter you will have a chance to use your imagination to write a story, a scene for a play, and poems that will allow others to peek into unique worlds of your own creation. You may be surprised to find what the creative process reveals about you.

Reading with a Writer's Eye

Many writers' ideas come from an experience or from a person in their lives. Writers use their imaginations to elaborate and change facts. Creative writing affords a great deal of freedom to play with reality and come up with something quite different. Read the following selection first to see what the author E. B. White says about writing. Read it a second time and compare his creative process to your own.

BLOCK SCHEDULING

- If your schedule requires that you cover the chapter in a **shorter time,** use Reading with a Writer's Eye, Thinking as a Writer, The Power of Creative Writing, and Process of Writing a Short Story.
- If you want to take advantage of **longer class time,** add any or all of the following: In the Media, Grammar in the Writing Process, Process of Writing a Play, and Writing a Poem.

FROM

PAUSES

Lee Bennett Hopkins

Inspired by questions from his students, poet and teacher Lee Bennett Hopkins interviewed hundreds of authors and illustrators to find out how the people who have shaped the world of children's books use their inspirations to write. In the following excerpt, Hopkins presents the reflections of E.B. White, whose popular novels include Stuart Little *and* Charlotte's Web.

Many years ago I went to bed one night in a railway sleeping car, and during the night I dreamed about a tiny boy who acted rather like a mouse. That's how the story of Stuart Little got started. It took about twelve years to do Stuart, but most of the time I did not think I was writing a book. I was busy with other matters.

I like animals and my barn is a very pleasant place to be, at all hours. One day when I was on my way to feed the pig, I began feeling sorry for the pig because, like most pigs, he was doomed to die. This made me sad. So I started thinking of ways to save a pig's life. I had been watching a big gray spider at her work and was impressed by how clever she was at weaving. Gradually I worked the spider into *Charlotte's Web*, a story of friendship and salvation on a farm.

Before attempting the book, I studied spiders and boned up on them. I watched Charlotte at work, here on my place, and I also read books about the life of spiders, to inform myself about their habits, their capabilities, their temperament. Having finished the book, I was dissatisfied with it, so instead of submitting it to my publisher, I laid it aside for a while, then rewrote it introducing Fern and other characters. This took a year, but it was a year well spent. Three

FOR INCREASING STUDENT ACHIEVEMENT

GUIDED READING

Text Analysis

- The **narrative** expresses White's recollections. He uses first person narration, almost every sentence includes *I* or *my.* This emphasizes for the readers that they are getting his perspective.
- White uses short sentences, simple sentence structure, and common vocabulary in talking as well as writing. These traits make his works easy to read for children as well as adults.

Strategy: Noting Writer's Style

Ask students to stop after reading the first paragraph. Ask them if they notice anything unusual about the writer's style. Guide them to the idea that White writes as if he is talking rather than writing an essay. Ask them to look for examples of this kind of "speaking writing" as they continue to read the selection. He shifts topics often, rather than presenting each topic in depth before leaving it. For example, he starts by explaining how he developed the ideas for two of his books, changes topics, and then discusses another book.

SELECTION AMENDMENT
Description of change: excerpted
Rationale: to focus on the creative process of writing as presented in this chapter

IDENTIFYING COMMON STUMBLING BLOCKS

Problem

- Not being familiar with *Charlotte's Web* or other books by E. B. White

Solution

- Ask for volunteers to summarize several of White's books for the class. Students might find summaries of his works in reviews, in studies of children's literature, or in articles on White. Ask one student to find out more about White's life and career. A Website on Maine authors, http://www.umcs.maine.edu/~orono/projects/samm/samm.html includes a short biography of White and some interesting background on several of his books. The E. B. White Homepage at http://www.winsor.edu/library2/ebwhite.htm includes a collection of comments on his books.

READER RESPONSE

You may want to use the following questions to elicit students' personal responses to the selection.

1. Imagine you are a publisher and an author has submitted an idea for book about how to save the life of a pig. How would you react?
2. How did you feel when you read White's comment that children often find pleasure and satisfaction in trying to set their thoughts down on paper?
3. Do you agree with White that real life is only one kind of life? Explain.

years after I started writing *Charlotte's Web*, it was published. (I am not a fast worker, as you can see.)

Sometimes I'm asked how old I was when I started to write, and what made me want to write. I started early—as soon as I could spell. In fact, I can't remember any time in my life when I wasn't busy writing. I don't know what caused me to do it, or why I enjoyed it, but I think children often find pleasure and satisfaction in trying to set their thoughts down on paper, either in words or in pictures. I was no good at drawing, so I used words instead. As I grew older, I found that writing can be a way of earning a living.

My stories are imaginary tales, containing fantastic characters and events. In *real* life, a family doesn't have a child who looks like a mouse; in *real* life, a spider doesn't spin words in her web. In *real* life, a swan doesn't blow a trumpet. But real life is only one kind of life—there is also the life of the imagination. And although my stories are imaginary, I like to think that there is some truth in them, too—truth about the way people and animals feel and think and act.

I don't know how or when the idea for *Trumpet of the Swan* occurred to me. I guess I must have wondered what it would be like to be a Trumpeter Swan and not be able to make any noise.

There is a difference between writing for children and adults. I am lucky, though, as I seldom seem to have my audience in mind when I am at work. It is as though they didn't exist.

Children are the most attentive, curious, eager, observant, sensitive, quick, and generally congenial readers on earth. They accept, almost without question, anything you present them with, as long as it is presented honestly, fearlessly, and clearly.

My own vocabulary is small, compared to most writers, and I tend to use the short words. So it's no problem for me to write for children. We have a lot in common.

ADDITIONAL RESOURCES

Composition Skills Practice	pages 33–40
Transparency Tools	GO2, VR6
Writing Prompts	pages 10, 15, 21, 26, 37, 43–45
ESL Practice and Test Preparation	pages 43–49
Writers at Work	8•1–8•10
Assessment: Chapter Test	pages 60–63
Assessment Resources	pages 1–10, 13–44, 61–69

Thinking as a Writer

Analyzing a Writer's Creative Process

In the description of his creative process, E.B. White says that "real life is only one kind of life—there is also the life of the imagination."

- What does he mean when he says that although his stories are imaginary, he thinks they contain some truth about the way people and animals feel, think, and act? How can your observations of people and animals help you create characters for a short story or a play?

Extending Real-Life Experiences

Oral Expression E. B. White finds inspiration in closely observing the behavior of animals. Cartoonists also find inspiration in animal behavior and create entire story lines based on those animals.

- Choose an animal you know well or have seen, perhaps a pet or a friend's pet. Who does this animal remind you of? Does the animal have a special way of moving or an interesting look in its eye? If the animal could speak, how might it sound?
- In a group of three or four of your classmates, improvise a conversation among your animal characters. How does your dialogue reflect the personality you imagine your animal character has? How did discussing the character help you to construct dialogue?

Blending Experience and Imagination to Create Character

Viewing Many visual artists have been inspired by works of literature. In the Central Park children's zoo in New York City, there is a bronze sculpture of characters from Lewis Carroll's *Alice's Adventures in Wonderland,* a

Using *Thinking as a Writer*

You may choose to have students respond to the questions either orally or in writing.

After learning about E. B. White's creative process and using their own creative skills, students might enjoy learning about how other authors create their stories. Have students write letters or E-mail to authors and inquire about their creative processes. Students can find information on writing E-mail messages in *A Writer's Guide to Using the Internet* on pages C545–C576.

REACHING ALL STUDENTS

Advanced Learners

Ask students to write a description of their own creative process. They might describe writing a story, drawing a picture, or solving a problem. Have students share their descriptions with the class.

LITERARY CONNECTION

You might want to explore creative writing in the following works, which appear in literature textbooks at this grade level.

- "Paul Bunyan" by Shel Silverstein
- "Paul Bunyan of the North Woods" by Carl Sandburg
- "The Raven" by Edgar Allan Poe
- "The Woman in the Snow" retold by Patricia McKissack

book that combines a real character (a young nineteenth-century English girl named Alice) with imaginary animal characters such as the March Hare (a rabbit) and the dormouse (a sleepy mouse). These animal characters all talk to Alice, and exhibit human characteristics.

- How has the sculptor captured these characters from one of the most famous fantasy/adventure books ever written? Has he successfully conveyed the fantasy elements of the story?
- Do you think seeing illustrations of a story can help you visualize the characters more accurately, or do you think illustrations simply limit the imagination?

Alice in Wonderland, José de Creeft. Central Park, New York City, NY.

FOR DEVELOPING SKILLS

LESSON 1 *(pages C193–C201)*

OBJECTIVE

- **To identify the structure and elements of a short story**

Create Interest

Write the names *Bart, Princess, Wendy, Jeff*, and *Dad* on the board. Then tell students that you are going to read the start of a story about these characters and that students will write an ending to the story. The story begins as follows: *Just as the guest of honor entered, Bart stepped on Princess's tail. Princess let out a pained yelp, and Bart dropped the tray of olives he was carrying. As olives started peppering the furniture and the guests, Wendy rushed to help Bart, upsetting a glass of lemonade. Jeff, seeing Wendy's plight, bounded toward the scene of disaster.*

The Power of Creative Writing

Creative writing takes many forms. In addition to stories, authors may choose to write plays, poems, movie scripts, songs, or comic strips. Creative writing does not have to be serious; it can be humorous, tragic, suspenseful, or whimsical. Whatever you can imagine, you can create.

Uses of Creative Writing

Here are some examples of ways you can use creative writing in your daily life.

- **The creator of a comic strip writes humorously** about life in his neighborhood.
- **A poet uses special rhythms and rhymes** to tell about a visit to a new country.
- **Comedians write funny sketches** about current events.
- **A songwriter uses rhyming lyrics and music** to tell about a beautiful autumn afternoon.
- **A short story writer tells** about the discovery of a new planet.
- **A playwright tells** about the courageous pioneers who traveled across the country to find a new life.

CAREERS AND COMMUNICATION

Scriptwriter

For a handful of writers, scriptwriting is a lucrative and glamorous job. The writers who create the stories that end up as major motion pictures, successful television shows, or widely performed plays may earn great amounts of money and respect. With the development of cable television, the demand for television scriptwriters has increased in recent years.

However, the market for Hollywood movies, television scripts, and Broadway plays is much smaller than the market for educational videos. These videos are produced by organizations to use in schools to teach students, by nonprofit organizations to explain their mission to potential donors, and, most significantly, by corporations to train or inspire workers. Writing and editing scripts for industrial training videos is steady and valued work. Writers must set up scenes, develop characters, and tell stories just as other writers do. As in other types of creative writing, scriptwriters need excellent skills in describing details and writing dialogue.

Divide students into small groups. Have each group develop a short script for a video that teaches some skill or technique. Students should then prepare to act out their script for the class.

"Watch out for the lamp!" cried Dad. You may wish to read the story more than once. Students should end the incident in two or three paragraphs. When they are done, ask students to summarize what they wrote. Discuss the elements that make a good story.

Guide Instruction

By Modeling Strategies

On the board write headings for four columns: *Characters, Traits, Settings, Reasons*. Under the first, write characters from books or movies that students find interesting. Under the second, write the traits that students believe make these characters interesting. Under the third, write the settings that students associate with good stories. Under the fourth, write the reasons these settings are intriguing. After completing the lists on the board, discuss with students how various characters might react in various settings. Note which combinations seem likely to produce good stories.

GETTING STUDENTS INVOLVED

Reciprocal Teaching

Select three students to read "Thank You, M'am" out loud. One should be the narrator, one the woman, and one the boy. At the following points in the story, stop the reading and ask students to write down what they think will happen next:

- After the third sentence in the first paragraph
- After the woman asks, "If I turn you loose, will you run?"
- After the woman says, "You ought to be my son. I would teach you right from wrong."
- After the boy asks, "You gonna take me to jail?"
- After the woman says, 'I were young once and I wanted things I could not get.'
- After the woman says, "Eat some more, son."

Discuss how well students were able to foretell the action of the story. Then have them reread the story and decide whether any of the actions seemed unrealistic.

Developing Your Creative Writing Skills

The screenwriter Mel Brooks once said, "Every human being has hundreds of separate people living under his skin. The talent of a writer is his ability to give them their separate names, identities, personalities and have them relate to other characters living with him." Though the characters you create are only one aspect of a short story, an interesting character thrust into a threatening, confusing, or desperate situation always makes a good basis for a short story.

A **short story** is a well-developed fictional story about characters facing a conflict or problem.

Read the following short story by Langston Hughes and think about how the author has created a vivid scene and lively characters.

Model: Short Story

Thank You, M'am

She was a large woman with a large purse that had everything in it but hammer and nails. It had a long strap and she carried it slung across her shoulder. It was about eleven o'clock at night, and she was walking alone, when a boy ran up behind her and tried to snatch her purse. The strap broke with the single tug the boy gave it from behind. But the boy's weight, and the weight of the purse combined, caused him to lose his balance so, instead of taking off full blast as he had hoped, the boy fell on his back on the sidewalk, and his legs flew up. The large woman simply turned around and kicked him right square in his blue-jeaned sitter. Then she reached down,

Consolidate Skills

Through Guided Practice

The **Practice Your Skills** activity on analyzing a short story on page C201 provides students with questions to respond to in analyzing "Thank You M'am." Ask students to find another short story and answer the same questions for it. Students may find short stories in anthologies or on the Internet. Stories from many well-known authors can be reached through the Online Text section of the Internet Public Library, http://www.ipl.org/. The site is operated by the University of Michigan School of Information.

Apply to Communication

Through Independent Writing

Have students write a review of a short story they have read. In their review they should comment on at least seven of the following items: narrator, setting, characters, conflict, triggering event, climax, resolution, outcome, dialogue, and description. They should also comment on the overall effectiveness of

picked the boy up by his shirt front, and shook him until his teeth rattled.

After that the woman said, "Pick up my pocketbook, boy, and give it here."

She still held him. But she bent down enough to permit him to stoop and pick up her purse. Then she said, "Now ain't you ashamed of yourself?"

Firmly gripped by his shirt front, the boy said, "Yes'm."

The woman said, "What did you want to do it for?"

The boy said, "I didn't aim to."

She said, "You a lie!"

By that time two or three people passed, stopped, turned to look, and some stood watching.

"If I turn you loose, will you run?" asked the woman.

"Yes'm," said the boy.

"Then I won't turn you loose," said the woman. She did not release him.

"I'm very sorry, lady, I'm sorry," whispered the boy.

"Um-hum! And your face is dirty. I got a great mind to wash your face for you. Ain't you got nobody home to tell you to wash your face?"

"No'm," said the boy.

"Then it will get washed this evening," said the large woman starting up the street, dragging the frightened boy behind her.

He looked as if he were fourteen or fifteen, frail and willow-wild, in tennis shoes and blue jeans.

The woman said, "You ought to be my son. I would teach you right from wrong. Least I can do right now is to wash your face. Are you hungry?"

"No'm," said the being-dragged boy. "I just want you to turn me loose."

"Was I bothering *you* when I turned that corner?" asked the woman.

"No'm"

"But you put yourself in contact with *me*," said the woman. "If you think that contact is not going to last

YOUR IDEAS
For Guided Reading

the story and what types of readers they would recommend it to.

Transfer to Everyday Life

By Evaluating an Incident

Point out to students that each day holds several events that could be the basis of a short story. Have students analyze an incident from their life that they think could be infused with enough tension to make a good short story.

Pull It All Together

By Reflecting

Ask students to reread the story "Thank You M'am." Discuss how they react to it now and if the reaction is different from the first time they read it. Discuss how their understanding and appreciation of short stories has changed.

Check Understanding

By Evaluating Short Story Elements

Review with students the elements of a short story. Discuss whether they think some of these elements are more important than others in creating a good short story. Have students identify which elements they think are most significant.

USING STUDENTS' STRENGTHS

Multiple Intelligences: Interpersonal

Ask students to consider the boy's perspective. Have students explain why they think the boy told the woman that he wanted a pair of blue suede shoes. She did not ask him directly why he had tried to steal her pocketbook, but he admitted his motive anyway. Discuss what this suggests about the boy's personality.

awhile, you got another thought coming. When I get through with you, sir, you are going to remember Mrs. Luella Bates Washington Jones."

Sweat popped out on the boy's face and he began to struggle. Mrs. Jones stopped, jerked him around in front of her, put a half nelson about his neck, and continued to drag him up the street. When she got to her door, she dragged the boy inside, down a hall, and into a large kitchenette-furnished room at the rear of the house. She switched on the light and left the door open. The boy could hear other roomers laughing and talking in the large house. Some of their doors were opened, too, so he knew he and the woman were not alone. The woman still had him by the neck in the middle of her room.

She said, "What is your name?"

"Roger," answered the boy.

"Then, Roger, you go to that sink and wash your face," said the woman, whereupon she turned him loose—at last. Roger looked at the door—looked at the woman—looked at the door—*and went to the sink.*

"Let the water run until it gets warm," she said. "Here's a clean towel."

"You gonna take me to jail?" asked the boy, bending over the sink.

"Not with that face, I would not take you nowhere," said the woman. "Here I am trying to get home to cook me a bite to eat and you snatch my pocketbook! Maybe you ain't been to your supper either, late as it be. Have you?"

"There's nobody home at my house," said the boy.

"Then we'll eat," said the woman. "I believe you're hungry—or been hungry—to try to snatch my pocketbook."

"I wanted a pair of blue suede shoes," said the boy.

"Well, you didn't have to snatch *my* pocketbook to get some suede shoes," said Mrs. Luella Bates Washington Jones. "You could of asked me."

"M'am?"

The water dripping from his face, the boy looked at her. There was a long pause. A very long pause. After he had dried his face and not knowing what else to do dried it again, the boy turned around, wondering what next. The door was open. He could make a dash for it down the hall. He could run, run, run, run, *run!*

The woman was sitting on the daybed. After a while she said, "I were young once and I wanted things I could not get."

There was another long pause. The boy's mouth opened. Then he frowned, but not knowing he frowned.

The woman said, "Um-hum! You thought I was going to say *but*, didn't you? You thought I was going to say, *but I didn't snatch people's pocketbooks*. Well, I wasn't going to say that." Pause. Silence. "I have done things, too, which I would not tell you, son—neither tell God, if he didn't already know. So you set down while I fix us something to eat. You might run that comb through your hair so you will look presentable."

In another corner of the room behind a screen was a gas plate and an icebox. Mrs. Jones got up and went behind the screen. The woman did not watch the boy to see if he was going to run now, nor did she watch her purse which she left behind her on the daybed. But the boy took care to sit on the far side of the room where he thought she could easily see him out of the corner of her eye, if she wanted to. He did not trust the woman *not* to trust him. And he did not want to be mistrusted now.

"Do you need somebody to go to the store," asked the boy, "maybe to get some milk or something?"

"Don't believe I do," said the woman, "unless you just want sweet milk yourself. I was going to make cocoa out of this canned milk I got here."

"That will be fine," said the boy.

She heated some lima beans and ham she had in the icebox, made the cocoa, and set the table. The woman did not ask the boy anything about where he lived, or his

USING STUDENTS' STRENGTHS

Multiple Intelligences: Linguistic

Have students concentrate on the dialogue Hughes uses to help readers better understand the character of the woman. For example, what do readers learn from phrases she uses, such as "Maybe you ain't been to your supper either, late as it be" and "I were young once . . ."? Have students share their ideas about the woman's background and educational level by focusing on her dialogue.

YOUR IDEAS
For Using Writer's Journal

folks, or anything else that would embarrass him. Instead as they ate, she told him about her job in a hotel beauty shop that stayed open late, what the work was like, and how all kinds of women came in and out, blondes, redheads, and brunettes. Then she cut him a half of her ten-cent cake.

"Eat some more, son," she said.

When they were finished eating she got up and said, "Now, here, take this ten dollars and buy yourself some blue suede shoes. And next time, do not make the mistake of latching on to *my* pocketbook *nor nobody else's*—because shoes come by devilish like that will burn your feet. I got to get my rest now. But I wish you would behave yourself, son, from here on in."

She led him down the hall to the front door and opened it. "Good night! Behave yourself, boy!" she said, looking out into the street.

The boy wanted to say something else other than, "Thank you, m'am," to Mrs. Luella Bates Washington Jones, but he couldn't do so as he turned at the barren stoop and looked back at the large woman in the door. He barely managed to say, "Thank you," before she shut the door. And he never saw her again.

—Langston Hughes

Your Writer's Journal

Langston Hughes has written a sharp tale of a young boy who learns a lesson. In your journal, note any stories that come to mind in which you or someone you know learned an important lesson. At the end of a week, look over your journal entries. In the margin next to your ideas, jot down further ideas that will give your stories a twist to make them more interesting. You may want to use these ideas later as you begin to write stories.

Short Story Structure

All short stories have three main parts. The **beginning** introduces the characters and the problem or conflict. The **middle** tells the events in the order in which they happened. The **ending** shows how the problem was finally resolved.

Short stories also have other elements. The following chart shows the other elements most short stories have.

ELEMENTS IN A SHORT STORY	
NARRATOR	the person telling the story; may be first person (if he or she is in the story) or third person (if he or she is telling what happened to others)
SETTING	the time and place in which the story takes place
CHARACTERS	the people involved in the story
CONFLICT	the problem at the heart of the story
TRIGGERING EVENT	the event that starts the story rolling
CLIMAX	the point in the story where the conflict or problem is most serious
RESOLUTION	how the problem or conflict is solved
OUTCOME	the way the story ends
DIALOGUE	words spoken by the characters
DESCRIPTION	writing that helps the reader see, hear, feel, taste, or smell what is happening

GETTING STUDENTS INVOLVED

Cooperative Learning

Have students use the **Elements in a Short Story** chart on page C199 as they work with a partner. Students should take turns providing an example for each element in the list. Students' examples should come from stories or plays they have read or viewed in the past. Students may also use examples from their literature textbooks or from a novel they are currently reading.

Using *Writing Is Thinking*

Objective

- **To understand how people use information to make predictions about what will come next**

A DIFFERENT APPROACH

Auditory Prediction plays a key role in music. For example, tap the first five sounds of the classic rhythm–"shave and a haircut, two bits" –long, short, short, long, long, rest, long, long. See if students can predict what will follow. Or, play a recording of the Franz Joseph Haydn's Symphony No. 94 in G Major. This symphony is nicknamed "The Surprise" because it does not fulfill the expectations of the listener. Invite students with musical skills to perform other examples.

Thinking Skills	
Classifying	Analyzing
Comparing	Hypothesizing
Generalizing	Synthesizing
Inferring	Summarizing
Imagining	Setting Goals
Observing	Evaluating Audience
Predicting	

Writing Is Thinking

Predicting

All the different elements in a short story help readers predict how a story will end. **Predicting** means using available information to foretell a future outcome. Before football games, for example, sports announcers often make predictions about who will win the game. They base their predictions on what they know about the players on each team, the players' drive to win, injuries that may give one team an advantage over another, and other factors related to the teams' past performances. The only worthwhile predictions are those based on available information.

As readers, you probably make predictions more often than you realize. On what do you base your predictions? Partly you base them on other stories you have read—all the way back to fairy tales that end "happily ever after." Partly you base your predictions on the details, or clues, in the story you are reading. Good writers know they can shape their readers' expectations with well-chosen details.

THINKING PRACTICE

Explore your predictions in writing as you read "Checkouts" by Cynthia Rylant on pages C305–C309. Stop reading after the eighth paragraph. Then write your impressions of the story so far and briefly tell the situation. Using information in the story and your past reading experiences, write a prediction about how the story will end. Then finish reading the story. Afterward return to your prediction and, in writing, tell whether or not your prediction came true. If it did come true, explain how you guessed that it would. If it did not come true, explain why you thought it would.

Practice Your Skills

Analyzing a Short Story

Reread "Thank you, M'am" on pages C194–C198. Then write answers to the following items.

1. What is the setting of this narrative? (Where and when does the story take place?)
2. List all the characters in the story.
3. Is the narrator a character in the story or does the narrator only tell what happens to other people?
4. What is the conflict or problem in this story?
5. In your own words, summarize the events in this story.
6. How can you recognize which parts are dialogue?
7. Choose one sentence of description from the story and write it on your paper.

HOME WORK

After students have completed the **Practice Your Skills** activity on analyzing a short story, ask them to predict what might happen to Roger after the story was over. Have them share their predictions and discuss them.

Practice Your Skills Sample Answers

1. The story is set on a street and in a house at about eleven o'clock at night.
2. The characters are a woman named Luella Bates Washington Jones and a boy named Roger.
3. The narrator tells only what happens to other people.
4. The main conflict is between the woman and the boy.
5. Roger tries to steal Jones' pocketbook. He fails, and she takes him to her home, where she feeds him, gives him the money he wanted, and sends him home.
6. The parts that are dialogue are in quotation marks.
7. Answers will vary. Students may choose the first sentence: *She was a large woman with a large purse that had everything in it but hammer and nails.*

LESSON 2 *(pages C202–C214)*

OBJECTIVES

- **To begin a short story by thinking of a subject, determining a point of view, sketching characters, and creating a setting**
- **To draft, revise, edit, and publish a short story**

Create Interest

Discuss with students the old newspaper adage: "When a dog bites a man, that is not news, but when a man bites a dog, that's news." Ask students to describe something unusual that has happened to them. Even small occurrences, if they are surprising, can be noteworthy and can provide the start of a good story.

Guide Instruction

By Connecting Ideas

Ask students to think of comparisons that express what makes a short story different from other forms of writing. For example, a short story is usually

HOME WORK

Have students freewrite on any one of the answers from the **Practice Your Skills** activity for fifteen minutes.

Process of Writing a Short Story

Short stories, like other kinds of writing, usually do not spring out of a writer's imagination fully completed and ready to write down. Most writers follow a process of prewriting, drafting, revising, and editing to shape their ideas into meaningful stories.

Prewriting

Writing Process

Many good stories tell about events that are out of the ordinary. Unusual happenings, such as a celebrity moving next door, keep readers interested. When choosing a subject, search your memory and imagination for experiences that stand out as unusual or especially important.

PRACTICE YOUR SKILLS

Thinking of Subjects

Answer each question with as many items as you can.

1. What has happened to me in the last year that I will probably never forget?
2. What experiences have taught me a valuable lesson?
3. What events in history would I like to have witnessed?
4. Who are my personal heroes? What have they done that would make a good story?
5. At what times in my life have I overcome a problem?
6. What funny things have happened to me?
7. At what times in my life have I felt in danger?

shorter than a novel, has fewer characters, and fewer settings. If a novel is like a house, then a short story is like a one-room apartment. Students might develop comparisons between short stories and other forms of writing, such as poems, essays, reports, and jokes.

Consolidate Skills

Through Guided Practice

The **Practice Your Skills** activity on thinking of subjects on page C202 prompts students to analyze their own experiences. To extend this activity, have them interview a neighbor or relative using similar questions.

Apply to Communication

Through Independent Writing

Have students use the information they collected in the previous activity to write a narrative in a third person point of view. Ask students to note how they think their presentation of the story differs from what others might present based on the same information. Point out that narrators are sometimes neu-

8. What embarrassing moments have I experienced?

9. What stories do my family members like to tell?

10. What unusual things have happened to me when I have been away from home?

Communicate Your Ideas

PREWRITING *Subject Choice*

Circle the incident from the above activity that is most memorable or unusual. Save your work for later use.

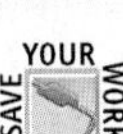

Determining Point of View

Every story has a narrator, the person whose written "voice" is telling the story. Readers see the story unfolding through the eyes, or **point of view**, of the narrator. If the narrator takes part in the story, the narrative is said to have a **first person** point of view. If the narrator tells what happens to others and is not a character in the story, the narrative has a **third person** point of view.

Compare the two story openers below. Both introduce the same narrative. Each, however, is told from a different point of view. Notice the different pronouns used in each.

First Person Point of View	Last year, on an early spring evening, **I** was looking forward to having the house to **myself. My** parents were going out to dinner, and **my** younger sister was staying overnight at a friend's house. For about four hours, **I** would be alone in the house. **I** could play **my** CDs as loudly as **I** wanted.
Third Person Point of View	Last year, on an early spring evening, **Mark** was looking forward to having the

REACHING ALL STUDENTS

English Language Learners

Students who are learning English may have difficulty knowing which verb forms to use in first person and third person point of view. In the past tense, the verbs are often the same in both: compare *I talked* and *he talked.* In the present tense, though, they often differ: compare *I talk* to *he talks.* Pair an English language learner with a student who is proficient in English. Have them work together to change text written in one point of view to the other point of view.

TIMESAVER *QuickCheck*

Review students' selections to be sure that they have chosen a topic that has potential for a good story.

HOME STUDY

Students may wish to talk to their parents or others who might recall incidents that would make good topics for a story.

tral observers and sometimes representatives of the author's own viewpoint.

Transfer to Everyday Life

By Narrating a News Story

Have students write a one-page story based on an item in the news. Encourage students to select a story with only two main characters, one setting, and one basic theme. Since they are basing it on a news item rather than reporting the actual item, they can make up dialogue and other elements of the story.

Pull It All Together

By Sharing

Have students read a short story that they like. Ask students to explain why they like the short story.

Check Understanding

By Asking Questions

As each student reads aloud the story he or she has created, have other students point out the strengths of the story. Students should identify the structure and elements of the story and compliment the writer.

PRACTICE YOUR SKILLS Sample Answers

1. I will always remember the day I met my best friend. I was standing in the hallway at school, trying to open my locker. The door was jammed, and I could not budge it. Suddenly I heard a voice behind me saying, "Need some help?" Before long, Susan had the locker open, and we have been friends since then. (look for first person pronouns)
2. For the third morning in a row, Robert woke up with a numbness in his leg. During the day the numbness went away, but he was starting to become worried. Because he thought he might be sleeping in a strange position, he asked his parents to look in on him during the night to see if they noticed anything strange. The next morning he had his answer. His dog, Max, who was supposed to sleep in the dog bed on the floor, was sprawled all over Robert's leg, sound asleep. (look for third person pronouns)
3. Saturdays are the worst. I see hundreds and hundreds of people walk by me. Their arms are usually loaded with bags and boxes. Sometimes a person will stop and feel the fabric of the outfit I am wearing. I do not really mind that. What I do mind are the comments like, "You'll never see me in an outfit like that!" My favorite sight is the blue uniform of the security officer. When he comes by at closing time, I know I can soon relax. (look for first person pronouns)

house to **himself. His** parents were going out to dinner, and **his** younger sister was staying overnight at a friend's house. For about four hours, **he** would be alone in the house. **He** could play **his** CDs as loudly as **he** wanted.

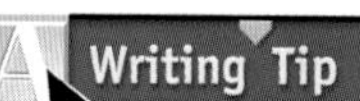

Use the **first person point of view** if the narrator is a character in the story. Use the **third person point of view** if the narrator is telling what happened to others.

PRACTICE YOUR SKILLS

Writing from Different Points of View

1. Write a short paragraph telling how you met your best friend. Use the first person point of view.
2. Write a short paragraph telling about something unusual that happened to a friend or family member. Use the third person point of view. Call the person by name and use third person pronouns.
3. Write a short paragraph telling what a mannequin in a store would see if it were alive. Pretend you are the mannequin and use the first person point of view.

Sketching Characters

Draw upon your own personality mix of traits and habits when sketching, or describing, characters. You might create a story character by mixing together details of yourself and other people, such as the determined way you approach challenges, the way your third-grade teacher walked, the color of your best friend's hair, and the laugh of your great-aunt Matilda. Below are sketches of the characters created by Langston Hughes in "Thank you, M'am." Notice how the description includes both physical and personality traits.

LUELLA BATES WASHINGTON JONES	Urban, large, physically strong, stern, intimidating, kind, no-nonsense, uses *ain't* in speech, hardworking, works in a hotel beauty shop, middle-aged, may have a "past"
ROGER	Urban, skinny, fourteen or fifteen, speech reflects urban street culture, probably poor and feeling defeated, desperately wants blue-suede shoes, a good kid inside

PRACTICE YOUR SKILLS

Sketching Characters

Write a brief character sketch of the following people:

1. yourself **3.** an older relative

2. a friend **4.** someone you just met

Creating a Setting

Once you have chosen a subject and a point of view, you can plan the details of your story's setting. First determine the location and time of your story. Then add details that will bring the setting to life. Notice how the following details give the setting a vivid mood in "Thank you, M'am."

HOME WORK

Have students write a paragraph on one of the following topics: a person trapped inside someone's computer, a secret romance between the children of owners of rival businesses, or a wrestling match between two best friends.

PRACTICE YOUR SKILLS Sample Answers

1. thirteen-year-old rural girl, stocky build, brown hair, freckles, shy, from middle class family, likes telling jokes
2. twelve-year-old urban girl, small build, red hair, outgoing, funny, thoughtful and loving
3. elderly grandmother, white hair, large build, very religious, wears dresses all the time, enjoys telling jokes to grandchildren
4. middle-aged man, brown hair, small build, acts suspicious and uncomfortable, eyes shift frequently, talks rapidly, plays with hands

Assign students to write a brief character sketch of a familiar literary figure such as Jo March, Huckleberry Finn, or Harry Potter. You may wish to have students do this assignment in pairs. Have students choose which point of view they will use before they write.

HOME WORK

Assign students to select three more settings and to write three details for each one.

Practice Your Skills Sample Answers

1. a big city—crowded downtown area; modern office building; top-floor office

   autumn—noon hour; Monday; chilly, windy day
2. a zoo—modern zoo with natural habitats; wolf enclosure made to include dens; hay inside one of the wolf dens

   night—midnight; first day of winter; full moon
3. a hospital—new, huge hospital with lots of glass; crowded waiting area of the emergency room; view from the receptionist's desk

   morning—5 A.M.; sun just rising; hot summer day
4. a school cafeteria—long line; tables already filled with people; a mess everywhere you look

   noon—Tuesday; the first day of school; after a long morning that began at 6 A.M.

SETTING OF "THANK YOU, M'AM"	
WHERE	**WHEN**
city	evening
a quiet street	recent past
a rooming house	11:00 P.M.
large kitchenette-furnished room	probably summer

Create a **setting** by determining the time and location of your story. Add details to bring the setting to life.

Practice Your Skills

Creating Settings

Use your imagination to add at least three details to the following locations and times for stories.

1. Location: a big city

Time: autumn

2. Location: a zoo

Time: night

3. Location: a hospital

Time: morning

4. Location: a school cafeteria

Time: noon

Listing Events in Chronological Order

The last step before writing your short story is to list all the events that make up the story. When listing events answer the following questions. Your list will then be in chronological order, the order in which the events occurred. This order will help your readers follow the story as it unfolds.

Listing Events in Chronological Order

- What happens to start the story rolling?
- What happens next? Next? Next?
- What is the climax of the story?
- What finally happens to resolve the conflict?
- How does the story end?

List all the events in your story in **chronological order**. Include the event that starts the story in motion, the climax of the story, the resolution of the conflict, and the outcome.

Communicate Your Ideas

PREWRITING *Story Element Grid*

 Using your subject choice, complete the following story element grid for your story. Save your work.

Setting		
Characters		
Situation or Conflict		

Good stories draw readers into the action and make them feel involved. Before you begin writing your short story, think about what you enjoy most as you read stories. Do you like characters with whom you can identify? Do you like a lot of action, humor, or suspense?

TIMESAVER *QuickCheck*

Review students' maps, providing feedback on the story elements.

HOME STUDY

Students may complete their story element map at home.

IDENTIFYING COMMON STUMBLING BLOCKS

Problem

- Not knowing if a detail will be interesting to readers or if it will slow down the story.

Solution

- Have students be prepared to explain the significance of every detail. If they find that explaining this connection is difficult for them, then the detail is probably not needed. Any detail that does not relate to the main point of the story is probably not needed.

REACHING ALL STUDENTS

Struggling Learners

Ask students to bring in the first few lines of favorite stories. Have students read these openings to the class. Discuss what elements make these effective beginnings to stories.

YOUR IDEAS

For Drafting Story Beginnings

As you work on the first draft of your short story, keep your audience in mind. Add details that will make your narrative more interesting to readers and leave out unnecessary details that slow the story down or lead your readers to false predictions.

Drafting the Beginning

The beginning of a short story introduces where and when the story takes place, the main characters, and what the story will be about. You can begin your story any way you like, but remember the beginning is the place where you "hook" your readers and draw them into the world you have created. Make your beginning provocative enough so that your readers will want to read on.

When writing your story beginning, include all of the elements shown in the following box.

Guidelines for Beginning a Story

- Set the time and place of the story, adding details that capture the reader's attention.
- Introduce the characters in the story.
- Provide any background information needed.
- Include the event that starts the story in motion.

DRAFTING *Story Beginning*

Refer back to your story element grid. Then use the guidelines above to write a beginning for your story. Decide whether you will use first person or third person point of view. Save your work for later use.

Drafting the Middle

The middle of your narrative tells the story, event by event. The following guidelines will help you present your story smoothly and dramatically.

Guidelines for Drafting the Middle

- Tell the events in chronological order, using transitions to show the passing of time.
- Build on the conflict, or problem, until the action reaches a climax, or high point.
- Use dialogue to show what the characters are thinking.
- Use description to bring the events to life.

PRACTICE YOUR SKILLS

Writing Dialogue

Write about ten lines of dialogue between you and a friend. Choose a subject for your conversation, such as whether or not to try out for the school play. Try to make your dialogue true to life by reflecting your region and culture in the spelling of words. Refer to Mechanics in the Writing Process on page C213 for further information.

Communicate Your Ideas

DRAFTING *Story Middle*

Return to your story beginning. Now write the middle of your story, telling the events in chronological order. Be sure to use transitions where needed. Also add dialogue where appropriate and include descriptions that bring your story to life.

TIMESAVER *QuickCheck*

As students develop their short story have them share drafts with each other. Students should provide constructive comments and use the Evaluation Checklist.

PRACTICE YOUR SKILLS Evaluation Guidelines

Check students' work to be sure the dialogues reflect the words and phrases particular to students' regions and cultures. Also check that the dialogues have been punctuated correctly.

HOME STUDY

Students might want to keep a list of alternative elements for their stories. For example, they might note different conversations, different events, and different endings that they could have used in their story. After they have completed the story, they should write a brief explanation of why they rejected the alternatives that they did not use.

Drafting the Ending

The ending of your story should make readers feel satisfied that the conflict or problem reached an appropriate conclusion. Chances are you felt the conclusion of "Thank you Ma'am" brought that story to a meaningful close.

End your short story by telling how the conflict was **resolved.** Tell the final **outcome** of the events.

Communicate Your Ideas

DRAFTING *Story Resolution*

Add a strong ending to your short story that brings resolution to the conflict. Save your work for revising and editing later.

Writing Tip

When reading short stories, draw on your **previous reading experience** and the **details** in the story to predict how the story will come out. When writing short stories, be aware that readers will be using the details you include to make predictions about the outcome.

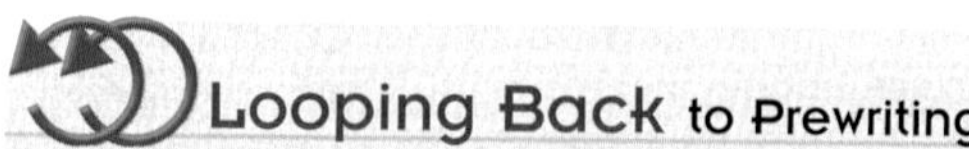

Looping Back to Prewriting

Writing the Ending of a Story

Look at the story you are writing. Is there any way to improve upon your ending? Brainstorm different ways your story might end. Freewrite on each idea. Try to add a surprising twist to your ending.

Evaluating Performances

Some literary works are wonderful when they are performed. This process can in fact help the audience understand the work more fully. Books on tape, poetry readings on the radio, and literary television shows attract faithful audiences.

How can you tell if a performance is effective? Here is a list of criteria that may help you evaluate artistic performances:

Guidelines for Evaluating Performances

- Does the performance move you?
- Does the performance make confusing parts clearer?
- Did the performers communicate using their bodies as well as voices?
- Do the performers use vocal variety to express the work's underlying meanings?
- Does the performance use the stage effectively, with variety of pacing and use of space?
- Are camera angles, lighting, sequencing, and music used effectively? How do they contribute to the overall effect?

Media Activity

Use the criteria above to evaluate the following:

- A poem such as "Like Scales" on page C229 or another of your choice that you perform for your class.
- A short story from "Collected Shorts" on NPR: **http://www.npr.org/programs/entertainment.html.**
- A video presentation of a literary work.

Share your evaluation with your classmates.

IN THE MEDIA

Using *In the Media*

Objective

- **To appreciate the value of performing readings of literary works**

Group Project

- Divide students into pairs. Each pair should select a scene from a play or from a story, and prepare to present it to the class. Encourage them to select scenes that other students will recognize or that audiences can appreciate without knowing the entire story. They should also select a scene that is developed primarily through dialogue. Volunteer to serve as the narrator or as a minor third character if the scene requires it. After students have practiced, ask them to present their reading to the class.

FYI

Websites to Visit Several Websites include readings of poetry and stories. Wired for Books, a site operated by the Ohio University Telecommunications Center at http://www.tcom.ohiou.edu/books/ includes works by Shakespeare, Poe, Twain, and many others. A site designed for students learning to speak English, http://www.mnsinc.com/richardx/listen3.html, includes several ghost stories. Candlelight Stories, at http://www.candlelightstories.com/defaultnew.asp includes fifteen classic children's tales, such as *Little Red Riding Hood* and *Tales of Peter Rabbit.*

HOME STUDY
Students might want to read their short stories to family members. Have students ask their listeners for one suggestion to improve the story. Students may choose whether to incorporate the suggestions.

Revising

Writing Process

The following checklist will help you revise your short story.

Evaluation Checklist for Revising

✓ Does the beginning of your story give the setting, capture attention, introduce characters, and include the triggering event? *(pages C204–C206 and C208)*

✓ Does the middle tell the events in chronological order with transitions? *(pages C206–C207 and C209)*

✓ Does your story build on the conflict until the action reaches a climax? *(pages C206–C207 and C209)*

✓ Did you use dialogue and description to bring your story to life? *(pages C209 and C213)*

✓ Does the ending show how the conflict was resolved and bring the story to a close? *(pages C206–C207 and C210)*

✓ Did you choose the appropriate point of view and stick to it throughout the story? *(pages C203–C204)*

Communicate Your Ideas

REVISING

Use the checklist above to revise your short story. Save your work for later use.

Editing

Writing Process

When you are satisfied with your short story, read through one more time for errors in grammar, spelling, usage, and mechanics. As you edit check for commonly misspelled words such as *their, they're,* and *there*. Also make sure you have always used complete sentences.

Mechanics in the Writing Process

Prewriting Workshop
Drafting Workshop
Revising Workshop
Editing Workshop
Publishing Workshop

Dialogue Punctuation

When writing dialogue you must distinguish a person's exact words with quotation marks. The following example shows how dialogue should look on the page.

> The woman said, "You ought to be my son. I would teach you right from wrong. Least I can do right now is to wash your face. Are you hungry?"
>
> "No'm," said the being-dragged boy. "I just want you to turn me loose."

The following guidelines will help you present clear dialogue.

- Use quotation marks to enclose a person's words.
- Capitalize the first word of a direct quotation.
- Use a comma to separate a direct quotation from a speaker tag, such as *the woman said* or *he replied.*
- Place punctuation inside the closing quotation marks when the end of the quotation comes at the end of the sentence.
- When writing dialogue, begin a new paragraph each time the speaker changes.

A direct quotation can appear before or after a speaker tag. A speaker tag can also interrupt a direct quotation. The quotation marks enclose only the speaker's words.

Editing Checklist

✔ Have you used a new paragraph for each change of speaker?

✔ Have you enclosed exact quotes in quotation marks?

✔ Have you used commas to separate direct quotations from speaker tags?

Using *Editing Workshop*

Objective

- **To use correct punctuation of dialogue**

A DIFFERENT APPROACH

Tactile To help students remember that they should use quotation marks in pairs, have them draw a line between the opening and closing set of marks around each piece of dialogue.

Auditory Have two students volunteer to read the parts of the two characters in "Thank You, M'am." Have the rest of the class follow the text in their books and listen to the reading, noting where quotation marks are needed.

SELECTION AMENDMENT
Description of change: excerpted
Rationale: to focus on punctuating dialogue as presented in this section

FYI

How to Use with Windows™ You do not need to choose Select All to change a word that appears throughout a story. You can use the Replace command under the Edit menu, or press Control H.
How to Use with MacIntosh™ You do not need to use Select All to change a word that appears throughout a story. You can use the Replace command under the Edit menu. Click Find Next to go to the next occurrence of the word you wish to change.

TIMESAVER *QuickCheck*
As students complete their final drafts and prepare to read them aloud to the class, review them for neatness. A clean, legible paper will be easier to read than one with proofreading marks and messy writing.

HOME STUDY
Encourage students to have someone else in their household read their final draft. Someone who has not read earlier drafts may catch mistakes the writer overlooked.

COMPUTER TIP

Most word-processing programs have an easy way to change a word that appears many times in your story. For example, if a character's name is Sam and you want to change it to Bob, you can use Select All in the Edit menu. Then use Find and Replace, also in the Edit menu, to type in the old word and the word you want to replace it with.

Communicate Your Ideas

EDITING

Carefully edit your narrative, checking for usage and mechanics errors that could distract your readers. The Editing Checklist on the previous page will help you polish your final draft. Use the proofreading symbols on page C37 as you edit.

Publishing

Writing Process

After you have read your edited version over several times, prepare a neat final copy that is either typed or in cursive writing to share with a classmate. (See page C41.)

Communicate Your Ideas

PUBLISHING *Read Aloud*

Practice reading your finished story aloud. Try to match the tone of your voice, your hand gestures, and your posture to the changing events in your story. Rehearse your oral reading in front of family members or friends. Then read your story to the class.

LESSON 3 *(pages C215–C223)*

OBJECTIVES

- **To begin a play by finding ideas for a play scene, selecting a setting, writing dialogue, and writing stage directions**
- **To complete a play and present a reading to the class**

Create Interest

Write on the board a list of plays that students have seen. The list might include school plays as well as commercial theater productions. Ask students how watching a live performance differs from watching a movie.

Guide Instruction

By Modeling Strategies

Before students read the excerpt from *Romeo and Juliet*, ask them to note how the organization of the text differs from that of a short story. The text is

Process of Writing a Play

A play is a special form of creative writing. It differs from a short story because it is performed by actors on a stage. A play has many things in common with the short story—both use character, setting, and plot. However, a playwright uses dialogue and action alone to tell the story without using narrative to explain the plot.

Modern playwrights provide the dialogue in a script along with information about how the characters should perform. This information is called **stage directions**. William Shakespeare, a 16th century English playwright, did not use many stage directions; he expected his actors to understand the characters well enough to interpret his words effectively. Shakespeare himself was an actor and wrote his plays for a company of actors who were familiar with his style of writing.

A **play** is a piece of writing intended to be performed on a stage by actors.

The following scene is from one of Shakespeare's most famous plays, *Romeo and Juliet*. In this scene, Juliet, a girl from a wealthy family, anxiously asks her nurse for news of her fiancé, Romeo. (In Shakespeare's time, a nurse was like a nanny.) As you read the scene, imagine how you would say the dialogue. Does the language give you clues about the characters? What can you tell about the relationship between Juliet and her nurse from the way they speak to one another?

MODEL: Play Scene

from *Romeo and Juliet*

JULIET The clock struck nine when I did send the nurse;
In half an hour she promised to return.
Perchance she cannot meet him. That's not so.
O, she is lame! Love's heralds should be thoughts

GETTING STUDENTS INVOLVED

Reciprocal Teaching

Have volunteers read the parts of Juliet and the Nurse. Tell the students that each character should be sincere and serious. Discuss what interpretation the writer, William Shakespeare, intended.

SELECTION AMENDMENT
Description of change: excerpted
Rationale: to focus on the features of a play as presented in this section

set almost entirely as dialogue, with a few stage directions added. This difference reflects the greater importance of character development and of spoken word in plays.

Consolidate Skills

Through Guided Practice

The activity on finding ideas for a play scene on page C219 prompts students to write about conflicts. You can also assign them to write about conflicts they see in their lives: between siblings, between athletic teams, or between children and their parents.

Apply to Communication

Through Independent Writing

Some writers revise classic plays by adapting them to modern settings. Assign students to take a famous play they have seen or read, such as *A Midsummer Night's Dream*, and describe how they might transfer it to a contemporary setting. Tell students to

IDENTIFYING COMMON STUMBLING BLOCKS

Problem

- Not knowing who Shakespeare is

Solution

- Discuss William Shakespeare in class. Ask for volunteers to find out additional information on his background and accomplishments.

which ten times faster glide than the sun's beams
Driving back shadows over low'ring hills.
Therefor do nimble-pinioned doves draw love,
And therefor hath the wind-swift Cupid wings.
Now is the sun upon the highmost hill
Of the day's journey, and from nine till twelve
Is three long hours; yet she is not come.
Had she affections and warm youthful blood,
She would be as swift in motion as a ball;
My words will bandy her to my sweet love,
And his to me.
But old folks, many feign as they were dead—
Unwieldy, slow, heavy and pale as lead.

[Enter Nurse and Peter.]

O God, she comes! O honey nurse, what news?
Hast thou met with him? Send thy man away.

NURSE Peter stay at the gate. *[Exit Peter.]*

JULIET Now, good sweet nurse—O Lord, why lookest thou sad?
Though news be sad, yet tell them merrily;
If good, thou shamest the music of sweet news
By plating it to me with such a sour face.

NURSE I am aweary, give me leave awhile.
Fie, how my bones ache. What a Jaunce have I had!

JULIET I would thou hadst my bones, and I thy news.
Nay, come, I pray thee speak. Good, good nurse, speak.

NURSE Jesu, what haste! Can you not stay awhile?
Do you not see that I am out of breath?

JULIET How art thou out of breath when thou hast breath
To say to me that thou art out of breath?

keep the main conflict and the personalities of the leading characters, but to change other elements as needed.

Transfer to Everyday Life

By Recording Dialogue

Students can practice their skill at writing dialogue by trying to write down an actual conversation they have with a friend or family member. They should try to capture the flavor of the conversation as well as specific words and phrases.

Pull It All Together

By Reflecting

Ask students to discuss what they learned from trying to write a scene from a play. Note in particular any comments that highlight the differences students noticed between playwriting and other types of writing.

The excuse that thou dost make in this delay
Is longer than the tale thou dost excuse.
Is thy news good or bad? Answer to that
Say either, and I'll stay the circumstance.
Let me be satisfied, is't good or bad?

NURSE Well, you have made a simple choice; you know not to choose a man. Romeo? No, not he. Though his face better than any man's, yet his leg exels all men's; and for a hand and a foot, and a body, though they not be talked on, yet they are past compare. He is not the flower of courtesy, but, I'll warrant him, as gentle as a lamb. Go thy ways, wench; serve God. What, have you dined at home?

JULIET No, no. But all this did I know before.
What says he of our marriage? What of that?

NURSE Lord how my head aches! What a head have I!
It beats as it would fall in twenty pieces.
My back a t'other side—ah, my back, my back!
Beshrew your heart for sending me about
To catch my death with jauncing up and down.

JULIET I' faith, I am sorry that thou art not well
Sweet, sweet, sweet nurse, tell me, what says my love?

NURSE Your love says, like an honest gentleman, and a courteous, and a kind, and a handsome, and I warrant, a virtuous—where is your mother?

JULIET Where is my mother? Why, she is within.
Where should she be? How oddly thou repliest!
'Your love says, like an honest gentleman,
"Where is your mother?"'

IDENTIFYING COMMON STUMBLING BLOCKS

Problem

- Having difficulty understanding words, terms, and dialogue in Shakespeare's plays

Solution

- Tell students that the language and words William Shakespeare used in his writing seem archaic and difficult for many readers to understand today. Point out that his usage represents English language usage of his day (1500s). Ask students to use a dictionary to look up such difficult words as *perchance, hath, bandy, thou, beshrew, hast.* Also discuss the juxtaposition of Shakespeare's words within sentences like " . . . when I did send the nurse," and "What a head have I!" Have students paraphrase some of these sentences that are difficult to understand. Remind them to use context clues to help them understand.

Check Understanding

By Self-Evaluating

Have students write an evaluation of their play scene. Students should decide how well they think the scene will capture the interest of an audience and whether they think they would enjoy watching it themselves.

YOUR IDEAS
For Writer's Journal

NURSE O God's Lady dear!
Are you so hot? Marry come up, I trow.
Is this the poultice for my aching bones?
Henceforward do your messages yourself.

JULIET Here's such a coil! Come what says Romeo?

NURSE Have you got to leave to go to shrift to-day?

JULIET I have.

NURSE Then hie you to friar Lawrence' cell;
There stays a husband to make you a wife.
Now comes the wanton blood upon your cheeks:
They'll be in scarlet straight at any news.
Hie you to church; I must another way,
To fetch a ladder, by the which your love
Must climb a bird's nest soon when it is dark.
I am the drudge, and toil in your delight;
But you shall bear the burden soon at night.
Go; I'll to dinner; hie you to the cell.

JULIET Hie to high fortune! Honest nurse farewell.

Your Writer's Journal

This scene from Shakespeare's famous tragedy *Romeo and Juliet* shows Juliet and her nurse in a conversation that has Juliet very anxious. In your journal, note conversations you have had or overheard in which someone withheld information. See how many such conversations you can remember over the next week. Then read over your notes to decide which ones may make a good scene for a play.

Choosing a Conflict or Problem

Like stories, plays are based on conflict. A conflict may be between two or more people, as when Juliet tries to get her nurse to hurry and tell her about Romeo. A conflict may also exist within a single person, as when Juliet talks to herself before the nurse returns. For a conflict to be interesting in a play, it must be seen and heard onstage.

Practice Your Skills

Choosing a Conflict or Problem

Freewrite about the following conflicts. Save your work.

1. What historical event has captured your interest?
2. What current news event has affected you strongly?
3. What is the most surprising thing that has ever happened to you? How did you react? How did this event change you?
4. Who are the three most interesting people you know, and why? What might happen if they disagreed over an important issue? Would two of them side together against the third?

Sketching Characters

As in a story, the characters are usually the most important element of a play. In drama the characters are brought to life by actors—people who use gestures, facial expressions, and tones of voice to capture the essence of a particular character in a unique way.

USING STUDENTS' STRENGTHS

Multiple Intelligences: Naturalistic

Many stories include a conflict between humans and nature. In such stories, nature is often portrayed as violent–a dangerous animal, a deadly storm, or a devastating earthquake. Ask students to think of conflicts between people and nature in which nature is not treated as violent. Forces of nature might represent purity, timelessness, or peacefulness.

HOME WORK

Have students freewrite about a conflict similar to one that occurs in a song that they like. They should not describe the actual song. Rather, they should adapt the song's conflict, placing it with different characters in another setting.

HOME WORK

Assign students to write a sketch of a character in a movie. In addition to describing traits, students should describe some activity that shows how the character acts. In some cases, the character might be not be a person. It could be an animal, an invented creature, or an inanimate object, such as a computer.

USING STUDENTS' STRENGTHS

Multiple Intelligences: Linguistic

Tell students to write a description of an imaginary place that could be a setting for a play. For example, they might describe a planet in outer space, a fairy tale world, or a utopian community. In their description, they should provide enough details so that a reader can envision the place.

Practice Your Skills

Sketching Characters

Return to your answer to question 1 in the previous activity. For each person involved in the event, write a character sketch. Each sketch should be a paragraph describing the important facts and details about the person. An actor preparing to play the role of the character should be able to learn a lot from the sketch.

Deciding on a Setting

In a book or movie, the writer can create scenes that move from setting to setting. One scene might take place inside an apartment, and the next might be in the middle of a forest. In contrast, most plays have only a few scenes with different settings. Because of the difficulty of changing sets quickly and easily between scenes, an entire play might take place inside one room. It is the playwright's job to create an interesting, dramatic story that can be shown physically on a stage. For example, in the scene between the nurse and Juliet, the action takes place entirely in one room, probably Juliet's bedroom.

Practice Your Skills

Deciding on Settings

Make a list of five places that would make good settings for a play. For each location, state your reason for thinking it would make a good stage setting. Be sure your settings are specific enough to be physically shown on a stage.

Using Dialogue

Action and dialogue give information about the characters, the **plot**–or story, and the set. When writing dialogue, the author carefully chooses words for the character to speak so as to reveal information such as level of education, culture, and personality. Just as the dialogue in stories must seem believable and natural, so must the speech in plays.

Because plays consist of live action, and the audience is not reading descriptions of what is going on, most plays contain a lot of dialogue. Dialogue is the medium through which the playwright shows the plot development, expresses the characters' emotions, and creates conflict. As in a story, the dialogue in a play should seem real. Each character should have his or her own way of speaking. In addition, the dialogue in plays needs to deliver information to the audience. Everything the audience learns about the characters must be shown through action or dialogue. For example, we learn about Juliet's impatience when she says, "...from nine till twelve is three long hours; yet she is not come." And we learn of the nurse's exasperation with Juliet when she replies, "...what haste! Can you not stay awhile? Do you not see that I am out of breath?" The need to express information and characterization at the same time makes the dialogue in plays particularly rich in content.

Practice Your Skills

Writing Dialogue

Write a conversation between two strangers who get stuck together in an elevator. They are applicants competing for the same job: a computer trainee for a new Internet company in this building. One of them is claustrophobic, or afraid of confined spaces. Write at least five separate lines for each character. Save your work.

DEVELOPING WORKPLACE COMPETENCIES

Personal Qualities: Sociability

Students may not view friendliness, understanding, and politeness as important job skills; reassure them that these qualities are key to succeeding in any profession. A successful interview is the essential first step on any career path. Interviewers look among qualified candidates for people who are able to express themselves clearly, confidently, and politely. For sales people, customer service representatives, and food servers, among others, sociability is especially important after the interview, as well. Everyone has had the unpleasant experience of being served food by a rude person, and the pleasant experience of being served by a friendly person. Employers are looking for people who can provide customers and coworkers with that pleasant experience.

Ask students to practice writing a dialogue between a food server and a customer. Encourage them to use the dialogue to develop their characters, giving them backgrounds, appearances, and characteristics.

HOME WORK

Have students write a conversation between two historical figures who were opponents, such as Civil War generals Ulysses S. Grant and Robert E. Lee. Students might choose figures who never actually met, but would likely have had conflicting ideas, such as the French emperor Napoleon and the Indian pacifist Gandhi. The conversation should reflect the distinctive opinions of the two figures and should reach a logical conclusion.

You may expand the above activity by sssigning students to write stage directions for the conversation they wrote for the historical figures. The stage directions should provide additional information about the personalities or beliefs of the two main characters.

Using Stage Directions

Playwrights usually supply stage directions for the reader (and the actor and the director) about how the characters speak and move. Stage directions are usually found in *italic* print. Because the dialogue itself often conveys what the audience learns about the characters, most modern playwrights like to keep their stage directions brief. As you can see in the scene from Romeo and Juliet, some playwrights use very few, if any, stage directions.

Shakespeare's stage directions tend to be directions to enter or exit the stage or, as he jokingly wrote in his play *Pericles, Prince of Tyre,* "Exit, pursued by a bear." Some stage directions are necessary, however. They express meaningful actions, such as one character pushing another character. At the beginning of the play, there is usually a brief description of the set. When a new character appears, there is usually a brief physical description of the character, perhaps including how the character is dressed. **Props**—short for properties, the physical objects important to a scene—are also mentioned in stage directions.

Practice Your Skills

Writing Stage Directions

Return to the dialogue you wrote about the two strangers stuck in an elevator. Write at least two stage directions for each character. Be sure your stage directions express action or emotion.

Communicate Your Ideas

SCENE FROM A PLAY

Write a scene on one of the following subjects or choose a subject of your own.

- a teenager and a younger sibling get lost
- two teenagers at a sports event
- a teenage student and his/her foreign pen pal meet for the first time

Decide on the setting—the time and place in which the action takes place. Use the suggestions on subjects, characters, setting, dialogue, and stage directions to help you create your scene. Write a first draft, then have two friends read the dialogue aloud to make sure it sounds real. Also have them perform your stage directions. Are the actions easy to carry out? Do the emotions convey the feelings you want? Then revise your script, cutting or adding lines in the dialogue. Make your stage directions more specific and descriptive.

Make a final copy, using a script from your library or classroom as a model for the play script format. Remember that Shakespeare often used verse when he wrote his plays. Most modern playwrights use prose when they write, so the lines of dialogue are punctuated the same way they would be in a story or novel.

Make extra copies of your script and give them to students who want to portray the characters. Have them perform the scene for the class.

TIMESAVER *QuickCheck*

Review the setting for the play scene to be sure that it is both clear and simple enough for a stage production.

HOME STUDY

Have students write a play scene that uses some of the other ideas from their journal or from the home work assignments they have done during this chapter.

USING STUDENTS' STRENGTHS

Multiple Intelligences: Musical

Have students select music to go with their play scene. They should choose music that conveys the emotions that they want to emphasize. Students might consider having a musical theme for each character.

LESSON 4 *(pages C224–C232)*

OBJECTIVES

- **To recognize how writers use rhythm, rhyme, and imagery to create poetry**
- **To write a humorous poem**

Create Interest

Read to the class the following limerick or other examples of humorous poetry.

There once was a young girl named June,
Who sang through the house, night and noon.
She'd do-re-mi as she cleaned,
And tra-la-la as she dreamed,
Until even the dishes could croon.

Then discuss with students what makes a poem funny.

Guide Instruction

By Modeling Strategies

Read the first four lines of "Jabberwocky" using intonation that suggests a mysterious and ominous

GETTING STUDENTS INVOLVED

Collaborative Learning

Divide students into pairs. Have each pair interpret the meaning of the word *poetry.* Then combine partners and have each group of four students share their interpretations. In each group of four, students should try to reach a consensus on what poetry is. Then have the whole class discuss the meaning of poetry.

REACHING ALL STUDENTS

Struggling Learners

Ask students to suggest types of writing that they do not consider poetry. Write the suggestions on the board, and discuss whether other class members agree. To help students evaluate the definition of poetry, encourage them to refer to the Elements of Poetry listed in the book on pages C227–C228.

Writing a Poem

When you feel strongly about something you may find yourself inspired to write a poem. Poetry allows you to say something in an imaginative way. It allows you to dig deeper and to speak more eloquently. In this section you will learn how to use language in special ways to express special feelings; you will learn how to write a poem.

Poems are an expression of your thoughts and feelings. They can be serious, sad, or silly. They can be whatever you imagine. The writer Lewis Carroll wrote the following poem, "Jabberwocky," as part of his fantasy novel, *Through the Looking Glass.* In the poem he makes up many of the words to achieve a particularly humorous effect. Read the poem aloud to hear how such words as *brillig, slithy, whiffling, burbled, galumphing,* and *mimsy* add to the humorous tone of the poem. Some of the words that Carroll coined, or invented, are words we use today, such as *galumphing*, or "moving clumsily." Others are words he formed by combining two other words: *slithy* combines "slimy" and "lithe".

As you read this poem, notice how the made-up words create humorous sounds when you say them aloud. Lewis Carroll used **onomatopoeia**—the use of words whose sounds suggest their meaning—to create a whimsical, nonsensical mood.

MODEL: Onomatopoeia

Jabberwocky

'Twas brillig, and the slithy toves
  Did gyre and gimble in the wabe:
All mimsy were the borogoves,
  And the mome raths outgrabe.

setting. Then read the same lines to suggest a pleasant, light-hearted setting. As students read sections, encourage students to modify their tone to match the text.

Consolidate Skills

Through Guided Practice

The **Practice Your Skills** activity on using a word web on page C226 will provide students an opportunity to think of comical details for particular topics. Ask students to create similar webs for four words of their choice.

Apply to Communication

Through Independent Writing

Have students write a paragraph explaining Lewis Carroll's reasons for using nonsense words in "Jabberwocky." Why might a poet use words that readers cannot understand? Have students think of reasons and explain why in a paragraph.

"Beware the Jabberwock, my son!
The jaws that bite, the claws that catch!
Beware the Jubjub bird, and shun
The frumious Bandersnatch!"

He took his vorpal sword in hand:
Long time the manxome foe he sought—
So rested he by the Tumtum tree,
And stood awhile in thought.

And, as in uffish thought he stood,
The Jabberwock, with eyes of flame,
Came whiffling through the tulgey wood,
And burbled as it came!

One, two! One, two! And through and through
The vorpal blade went snicker-snack!
He left it dead, and with its head
He went galumphing back.

"And hast thou slain the Jabberwock?
Come to my arms, my beamish boy!
O frabjous day! Callooh! Callay!"
He chortled in his joy.

'Twas brillig, and the slithy toves
Did gyre and gimble in the wabe:
All mimsy were the borogoves,
And the mome raths outgrabe.

—*Lewis Carroll*

Lewis Carroll enables his readers to come up with their own definitions of his nonsense words. In doing this he involves the reader intimately in his creation. When you read this poem, you are helping to create its meaning for yourself. What does the phrase *manxome foe* suggest to you? Since foe means "enemy," perhaps manxome means "fearful." What do you think?

REACHING ALL STUDENTS

English Language Learners

Students learning English may not be aware that a number of words in "Jabberwocky" were created by Carroll. Trying to find them in a dictionary may be frustrating. Encourage English Language Learners to practice reading the poem aloud without trying to understand each word. Carroll used normal patterns of spelling and pronunciation in the words he created.

Transfer to Everyday Life
By Writing Poetry
Have students write a short, lighthearted poem about a topic in their life. They may wish to write a limerick, a type of poetry in which lines 1, 2, and 5 rhyme, and lines 3 and 4 rhyme.

Pull It All Together
By Sharing
Have students bring to class examples of humorous poetry. Ask volunteers to read what they have found. Books, magazines, and the Internet are all possible sources for students to check.

Check Understanding
By Evaluating Poetry
Ask students to read "Jabberwocky" again. Discuss the elements that make it a good poem.

USING STUDENTS' STRENGTHS

Multiple Intelligences: Linguistic

Divide students into groups. Have each group select five words in "Jabberwocky" that they suspect Carroll made up. Each group should write a definition for the word and explain how they arrived at that definition.

HOME WORK

Suggest that students use a thesaurus to help them think of words to add to their word webs. If their thesaurus does not include the topics as entries, they should look up related words. For example, for modes of transportation, they might look for words such as *boat, train, airplane, travel,* and *car.*

Your Writer's Journal

Look through your journal notes on your thoughts and experiences. Make a new entry about the ideas, descriptions, and individual words and phrases that seem especially powerful to you. You will be able to use this entry as a starting point when you search for a subject for a poem.

Finding Ideas for Poems

Poetry depends on the thoughts and emotions of the writer. You can choose any subject about which you have strong feelings. For a humorous poem, your subject may be a joke that made you laugh so hard that you cried. It may be a hilarious comedy routine you recently saw performed. Or it may be a whimsical take on something serious, like "Jabberwocky."

PRACTICE YOUR SKILLS

Finding Ideas for a Humorous Poem

Copy and complete the following word web. Add funny or unusual humorous examples.

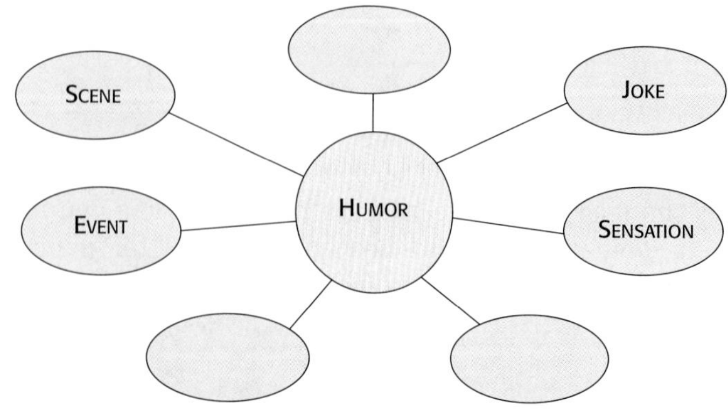

Using Sound Devices

The sound of language is extremely important in poetry. In fact, the full effect of a poem comes through only when it is read aloud. Not only can the sounds of the words be beautiful, interesting, or strange, but they can make interesting connections among ideas in the poem. The sounds of the words can emphasize the poem's meaning. Poets use particular sound devices to achieve special effects and to stir the reader's emotions. You have already seen how onomatopoeia works in the poem "Jabberwocky." Here are some other sound devices you can use when you write a poem.

SOUND DEVICES	
ALLITERATION	Repetition of a consonant sound or sounds at the beginning of a series of words **B**aa, **B**aa, **b**lack sheep
CONSONANCE	Repetition of a consonant sound or sounds, used with different vowel sounds, usually in the middle or at the end of words the pa**tt**er of li**tt**le fee**t**
RHYME	Repetition of accented syllables with the same vowel and consonant sounds The woods are lovely, dark, and **deep,** But I have promises to **keep**, And miles to go before I **sleep** *–Robert Frost, "Stopping by Woods on a Snowy Evening"*

USING STUDENTS' STRENGTHS

Multiple Intelligences: Spatial

Ask students to draw an illustration for "Stopping by Woods on a Snowy Evening." Provide a copy of the entire poem for students to read. They might draw a realistic setting, emphasizing the setting that Frost describes. Or, they may try to create a more abstract image that reflects the general impression and mood that Frost creates.

REACHING ALL STUDENTS

Struggling Learners

Students who have difficulty creating couplets might start by finding words that rhyme. To be systematic, they can try each letter of the alphabet with the ending sound. If they are writing about a dog, for example, they might list words that rhyme with *dog,* such as *bog, cog, fog, hog,* etc. They can then develop a sentence ending in a one of those words.

HOME WORK

Assign students to create rhyming couplets about five different objects in their house. Encourage them to make the couplets humorous.

Using Rhyme

A rhymed poem usually has a pattern, or rhyme scheme, that can be shown by letters.

Sally, will you come out to **play?**	*a*
Yes, my dearest **friend.**	*b*
I'll play with you till the sky turns **gray**	*a*
And the day has reached its **end.**	*b*

Notice that the rhyme pattern for the poem above is **ABAB**. The first line rhymes with the third, and the second line rhymes with the last. You may also write poetry with other patterns, such as **AABB**. In this pattern, the first two lines rhyme and then the next two.

Using Stanzas

A stanza is a division of a poem separated by spacing. It is a group of lines standing together, apart from other such groups. Stanzas are defined according to the number of lines they contain: couplets (two lines), triplets (three lines), quatrains (four lines), etc. Poetry containing specific patterns of rhyme and rhythm (meter) usually also contain a specific stanza pattern.

Writing Free Verse

A free-verse poem is a poem without a regular pattern of rhyme or rhythm. Instead, it creates a pattern with repeated phrases and uses the rhythms of everyday speech. Free-verse poetry uses imagery to recreate a vivid scene or memory.

In "Like Scales," the poet Julia Mishkin uses imagery to create a scene comparing nature (sheep in a field) to art (scales played on a piano).

Like Scales

The lamb in my neighbor's pasture
has caught her shaggy wool
on a fence and can't pull free.
All night we heard the frightened bleating,
low and intermittent. We were playing
a game about trivia made
specifically for my generation:
the babies of the post-war boom,
music lessons and ballet.
Luckily, it did not rain.
The stars wheeled overhead in that slow
design determined in another time.
What Persian astronomer-poet wrote
a celebrated collection of quatrains?
What does the name 'Zapruder' signify?
How many flamboyant musicians soared
before the age of thirty, plummeted
and died? And all the while
the gentle wind blowing blades
of grass in the field where the sheep graze.
When I was eight I was taken
to study piano in another town,
to a house between two meadows.
I fed the lamb small crusts
of bread. Sheep and Scarlatti!
Who tells them when it's time
to retire? Relentless, they move
toward the shed, one after another,
each evening. Has someone called them in?
Or do they just know, with a lucky affinity,
the day's end? And who
will free the lamb from her wiry bed?

—Julia Mishkin

YOUR IDEAS

For Guided Reading

HOME WORK

Have students create their own words that they could use in describing someone. Encourage them to start with syllables from words they know and to add commonly used endings, such as *-er* and *-ish.*

Practice Your Skills

Writing Free Verse Poems

Write a free verse poem, comparing and contrasting one person to another. After you have chosen a subject, jot down your answers to these questions.

1. What makes each of these people unique?
2. What main feelings do these people give you?
3. How would you recognize these people by sound? List two or three details.
4. How would you recognize these people by sight? List two or three details.

Then write your poem, using the details you have listed to help you come up with vivid images to compare and contrast the two people. To decide where your lines should end, read your poem aloud. Listen for places where the thought seems to break naturally. Create an ending for your poem that ties up the images and thoughts you have expressed.

Developing Sound Devices

Write a poem about a humorous event you recall. Choose two sound devices from page C227 to use in your poem.

Communicate Your Ideas

APPLY TO WRITING *Poem*

Prepare to write a poem on a subject of your choice. Your poem may be sad, serious, funny, or even silly. Use your **journal** and your notes from the practice activity on page C226. Then use the suggestions on pages C227 and C228 to develop sound devices. Write a free verse poem, or choose a rhyme scheme for your poem—ABAB or AABB. Read your poem aloud as you work. Finally, read the draft aloud to your classmates and friends.

Time Out to Reflect

In this chapter you have experienced writing creatively in three forms: stories, plays, and poems. Which form is the most natural for you to write? Which form would you like to try again? Have you learned anything surprising about any of these forms? Elaborate on your answers to these questions.

TIMESAVER *QuickCheck*

As students work with partners to evaluate the poems, circulate through the room to read and listen to the poems. Note the students who are having difficulty and arrange for individual conference times or for peer tutoring.

HOME STUDY

Have students create their own personal booklet of poetry. They could include several poems that they have written, as well as copies of some of their favorite poems.

EXPANDING THE LESSON

Using Technology

You will find additional **instructional** and **practice** materials for this chapter at http://www.bkenglish.com.

Process of Creative Writing

Writing a Short Story

PREWRITING

- List memorable events. Then choose a subject. *(page C16)*
- Determine the point of view. *(page C203)*
- Write a brief character sketch for every person in your story.
- Create a setting for your story. *(pages C205–C206)*
- List the events in your story in chronological order. *(pages C206–C207)*

DRAFTING

- Write a beginning that introduces characters and the setting. *(pages C204–C206 and C208)*
- Tell events in chronological order with transitions. Use dialogue and description to bring the events to life. *(pages C206–C207 and C209)*
- Write an ending that tells how the conflict is resolved and that brings the story to a close. *(page C210)*

REVISING

- Use the Evaluation Checklist for Revising on page C212 to check all the elements of your story.

EDITING

- Use the Editing Checklist on page C213 to polish your story.

PUBLISHING

- Prepare a final copy and share it with an interested reader.

Writing a Play Scene

- Develop characters with dramatic conflicts. *(page C219)*
- Select a setting that can be shown onstage. *(page C220)*
- Use dialogue to show character's feelings. *(page C221)*
- Use stage directions appropriately. *(page C222)*

Writing a Poem

- Choose a subject that inspires you. *(page C224)*
- Use sound devices. *(pages C227–C228)*
- Write rhymed verse or free verse. *(pages C228–C229)*

A Writer Writes

A Suspense-Filled Short Story

Purpose: **to entertain**

Audience: **your classmates**

Prewriting

Think of the climax, or high point, of a story you would like to write. A suspenseful climax might include a scene in which a car driven by your main character hangs over the edge of a cliff. Use your imagination to list the events leading up to this point, the resolution, and the outcome. Use the techniques of freewriting, brainstorming, or clustering to help you think of as many lively details as you can to include in your story. To help organize your thoughts, complete a story element grid like the one on page C207. Then list all the events of the story in chronological order.

Drafting

With your story grid at hand, draft your story. Follow the suggestions on pages C208, C209, and C210 for writing the beginning, middle, and ending of your story.

Revising

Exchange papers with a classmate. Read your partner's work carefully, noting whether or not it succeeds in its purpose of entertaining through suspense. If you can, suggest ways that your partner could heighten the suspense in his or her story. After hearing your partner's response to your story, make any changes you think would improve your story. Then use the Evaluation Checklist for Revising on page C212 to make a thorough revision of your story.

Using A Writer Writes

Objective

- **To write a suspense-filled short story using the writing process**

TIMESAVER *QuickCheck*

Have students self-check their work at various points. After the prewriting, ask if they feel their climax is dramatic enough. After drafting, ask if they feel the story has an engaging beginning and a satisfying ending. After revising, ask if they agreed with their reader's suggestions.

INTEGRATING ***Writers at Work***

For more opportunities to inspire and stimulate students' writing of stories, plays, and poems, look at *Writers at Work.*

YOUR IDEAS
For Publishing

INTEGRATING TECHNOLOGY
Electronic Publishing

You may want to refer students to *A Writer's Guide to Electronic Publishing* on pages C520–C544 for suggestions on using resources for publishing.

Editing

When you edit your work, check to make sure you have accurately punctuated and indented all dialogue. Use the Editing Checklist on page C213.

Publishing

When you are satisfied you have caught all the errors in your work, prepare a neat final copy of your story and share it with an interested reader.

Connection Collection

Representing in Different Ways

From Visuals . . .

. . . to Print

You have recently been hired as the creative director for a play company. The photograph above shows the theater's stage where you will bring your ideas to life. Write a letter to the owner of the theater about the play you want to produce. Make the letter as descriptive as possible, including details about the story and how the set will be used. Give your play a title, list the characters, and include details about the action in each scene.

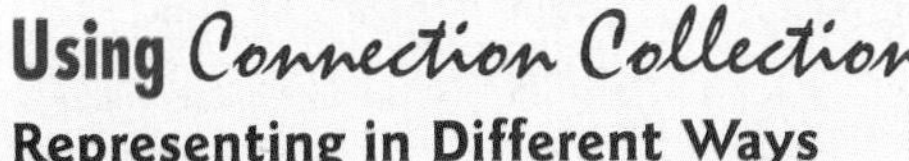

FOR REVIEWING SKILLS

Using *Connection Collection*

Representing in Different Ways

Consider using these print and visual activities to make students aware of the benefits of using different media to suit particular purposes. Help students understand when a visual medium, for example, is better suited to their purpose than a print medium, or the reverse.

YOUR IDEAS
For Writing Prompts

From Print . . .

1 Director Street
Dramatic, IA 78678
July 18, 2000

Plays, Incorporated
7867 Theater Row
Dramatic, IA 78678

Dear Creative Director:

I would like you to produce my award-winning play, Lost on the Stormy Seas, at your theater. I have heard about your qualities as both a playwright and set designer, and would like you to take creative control of the project if you agree to produce it.

Sincerely,

Ann Gables

Ann Gables

. . . to Visuals

You have agreed to produce *Lost on the Stormy Seas*—a play about a group of sailors and the mishaps that befall them during a terrible storm. Sketch a set design that can fit the stage in the photograph on page C235. Include descriptive notes that point out the aspects of your design. Consider the different entrances and exits, and explain any elements of the set that have special properties.

- **Which strategies can be used for creating both written and visual representations? Which strategies apply to one, not both? Which type of representation is more effective?**
- **Draw a conclusion and write briefly about the differences between written ideas and visual representations.**

A DIFFERENT DELIVERY SYSTEM

For formal assessment print the composition chapter test from the *BK English* Test Bank at http://www.bkenglish.com.

Assess Your Learning

It is the beginning of the new year, and your teacher is preparing events to help your school celebrate the upcoming holidays of President's Day and Martin Luther King, Jr.'s birthday. You have chosen to write an original short story that celebrates the life and accomplishments of either Abraham Lincoln, George Washington, or Martin Luther King, Jr.

▶ **Write a short story that fits the theme of this upcoming school event. Your story will be read by an audience of students and teachers. Invent your own details and characters, but also use reference sources to find facts to include in your story. Base your story on a main conflict that will be resolved at the end. Be sure to tell the events in chronological order, using transitions to show the passing of time, and supply enough vivid description to bring the story's events to life.**

Before You Write **Consider the following questions:**
What is the ***subject?***
What is the ***occasion?***
Who is the ***audience?***
What is the ***purpose?***

After You Write **Evaluate your work using the following criteria:**

- Does the beginning of your story introduce the characters and add details that capture the reader's attention?
- Have you used reference sources to find facts to include in your story?
- Have you developed a draft of the story by organizing and reorganizing the content to suit your audience and purpose?
- Does your story build on the conflict until the action reaches a climax or high point?
- Have you produced a legible story that uses accurate spelling and correct punctuation and capitalization?
- Does your story include lively, vivid description and dialogue?

Write briefly on how well you did. Point out your strengths and areas for improvement.

FOR ASSESSING LEARNING

Using *Assess Your Learning*

This writing prompt will help you and your students informally assess their developing writing abilities, using the accompanying primary trait rubrics, which list the key features and qualities of creative writing taught in this chapter. You may want to have students maintain their self-assessment in their portfolios as a record of their individual progress throughout the year.

Evaluating Creative Writing

In writing fiction, students often have difficulty in

- **establishing a central conflict**
- **bringing the characters to life**
- **developing a plot naturally**
- **maintaining a consistent point of view.**

Self-evaluation and peer evaluation can help students to improve their stories in these areas in revision.

Self-evaluation

When students have finished their first drafts, help them evaluate their work for the purpose of revising. Hand out copies of the Evaluation Checklist for Creative Writing. (See the Evaluation Checklists in BK English Language and Composition Assessment.) As students read their stories, have students focus on content and pay special attention to the traits numbered below.

Peer evaluation

It may be helpful for students to work in small groups to evaluate one another's stories. All members of a group will read the others' stories, but have each reader focus on only one of the listed traits and evaluate it for the group, with discussion. Emphasize to students that constructive criticism is the goal when evaluating creative writing.

1 The story unfolds around a clear conflict and the plot unfolds naturally.

2 Details, dialogue, action, and description are used effectively to give the characters life.

3 The ending reveals a believable thematic outcome or resolution of the conflict.

4 The writer maintains a consistent point of view.

Teacher evaluation

Primary Traits

The following represents the beginning and end of a short story on the theme of the unexpected. It exhibits excellent attention to the basics of story development and can be used as a model for evaluation.

MODEL FOR EVALUATION

The day the aliens landed, I was playing with some of my friends in the crater in my backyard. Suddenly one of my friends yelled, "Look at that!" And here they came, floating out of the darkness in that large white cocoon of theirs. Some of my friends hid behind some moon rocks, but most of us just stared. A couple creatures came out of the ship and headed right for us. They were wearing protective suits and helmets and were attached to their ship by large cords.

Excellent attention-getter

Good to state natural series of events

Effective conflict between the familiar and the unknown

One of them stuck a pole with a flowing piece of fabric on it into our moon. Another made some sounds, not like our language. It sounded like "One small step for man...." After a while, they left, leaving their red, white, and blue fabric sticking out of the ground. I wonder if they will ever be back.

Effective twist!

TEACHER EVALUATION

Primary Trait Evaluation

The following chart lists the key features and qualities for primary trait assessment of compositions.

	EXCELLENT	ACCEPTABLE	NEEDS IMPROVEMENT
Opening	Captures the reader's interest while establishing the setting and/or introducing the main characters or conflict.	Establishes a believable setting or characters.	Does not establish any key story element, such as setting or conflict.
Details	Details of description, narration, dialogue, and action believably bring the events and characters to life.	More details could be used, but those that do appear generally help to develop the story.	There are few details that support the story.
Organization	The plot unfolds naturally, in chronological order or with an occasional flashback, toward a climax. Transitional words and phrases smoothly connect events.	The plot generally follows chronological order, and most events are smoothly linked.	Events are disordered and unrelated.
Point of View	The writer consistently maintains a point of view suited to the story.	An identifiable point of view is maintained with a few lapses.	No identifiable point of view is established.
Conclusion	The ending reveals an interesting, believable, thematic outcome or resolution of the conflict.	The ending is plausible and in some way reflects the theme.	There is no clear ending or resolution, or the one that is there is implausible or irrelevant.

TEACHER EVALUATION

Holistic Evaluation

The following criteria may be used to evaluate holistically the stories students will write in this chapter, using a rating scale of
- 4 (excellent)
- 3 (good)
- 2 (acceptable)
- 1 (needs improvement)
- 0 (unscoreable)

4	3	2	1
The story unfolds around a clearly expressed central conflict that is developed through details of plot and characterization.	The story has an identifiable central conflict that can be developed through plot and characterization.	The central conflict is vague or otherwise hard to develop.	There is no identifiable central conflict.
Plot and characterization develop naturally and strongly, with effective use of description, narration, dialogue, and action.	Plot and characters are for the most part solidly developed, with adequate use of details.	Enough details are used to present an identifiable plot and recognizable characters.	Plot and characters are developed poorly or not at all.
The beginning of the story captures interest and introduces key elements. The middle develops the plot chronologically and builds the central conflict toward a climax. Transitions connect events. The conclusion tells the resolution of the conflict.	The story basically follows the beginning-middle-end form, although a few ideas or details may be disconnected or out of place.	The story has a beginning, middle, and end, but there are numerous lapses of connection and chronological order.	The story is disorganized, and parts do not fulfill the roles of beginning, middle, and end.
Point of view is apparent and consistent throughout story.	Point of view is established and consistent with a few lapses.	Point of view is not well established or is inconsistent throughout story.	Point of view is not established and therefore lacks consistency throughout story.

Essential Knowledge and Skills

- Demonstrating effective communications skills that reflect such demands as providing information
- Writing to inform, such as to explain, describe, report, and narrate
- Producing cohesive and coherent written texts by organizing ideas, using effective transitions, and choosing precise wording
- Using available technology to support aspects of creating, revising, editing, and rearranging
- Interpreting important events and ideas gathered from maps, charts, graphics, video segments, or technology presentation
- Assessing how language, medium, and presentation contribute to the message

CHAPTER 8

Writing to Inform and Explain

Instructions that show you how to put together a piece of furniture, an atlas that tells you about continents and oceans, or the recipes in a cookbook are all examples of writing that informs and explains.

It is easy to see why everyone relies on this type of writing. Let us say you want to plant your first vegetable garden. You buy the seeds but wonder what to do next. What you need now is a very specific type of writing. A novel or a play about seeds won't help you. A dictionary of seed names or the biography of botanist Louis Burbank won't work either. What you need is a gardening book with information about starting seeds, climate zones, soil, watering, sun, and shade. In other words, you need a book written to inform and explain.

Reading with a Writer's Eye

In the following article from *Time* magazine, many writers have shared their knowledge and research to give a well-rounded picture of a hurricane. Notice how the information is given in the article. How are the facts presented? What is the best way to explain something as complicated as a hurricane?

BLOCK SCHEDULING

- If your schedule requires that you cover the chapter in a **shorter time**, use Reading with a Writer's Eye, The Power of Writing, and Developing Your Skills.
- If you want to take advantage of **longer class time**, add any or all of the following: Writing Is Thinking, Editing Workshop, and Process of Writing.

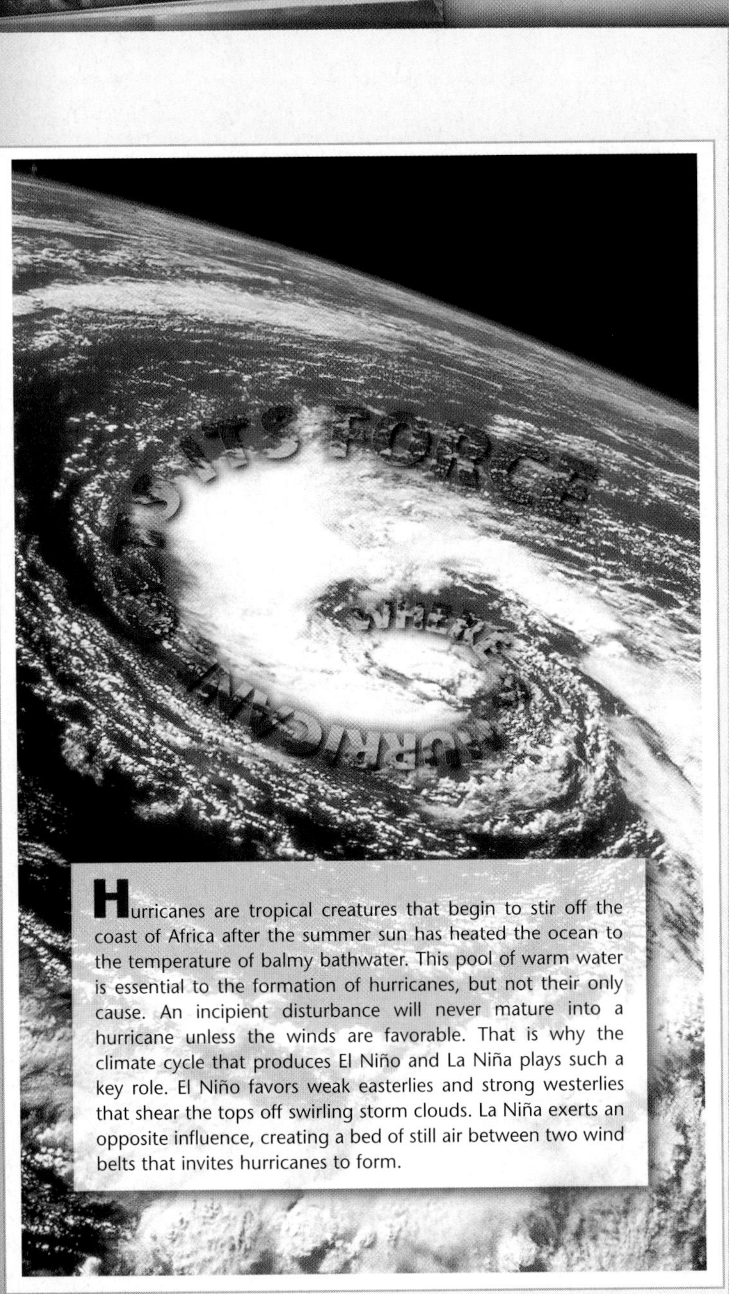

Hurricanes are tropical creatures that begin to stir off the coast of Africa after the summer sun has heated the ocean to the temperature of balmy bathwater. This pool of warm water is essential to the formation of hurricanes, but not their only cause. An incipient disturbance will never mature into a hurricane unless the winds are favorable. That is why the climate cycle that produces El Niño and La Niña plays such a key role. El Niño favors weak easterlies and strong westerlies that shear the tops off swirling storm clouds. La Niña exerts an opposite influence, creating a bed of still air between two wind belts that invites hurricanes to form.

FOR INCREASING STUDENT ACHIEVEMENT

GUIDED READING

Text Analysis

- The *Time* article presents the information in **third person style**. That is, the narrator rather than a participant describes the events leading up to a hurricane. This is the style most commonly used in **expository writing,** such as news reporting. Journalists usually relate what happened to others rather than to themselves. This lends to the objectivity of the story.
- The information unfolds in **chronological order** and the writers use **cause and effect** to explain the steps in the formation of a hurricane, which creates a sense of drama.
- **Precise words** make the writing strong. For example, the verbs in the first sentence are *tropical, summer,* and *balmy.* A flatter, duller sentence might have been: *Hurricanes are storms that begin to stir off the coast of Africa after the sun has heated the ocean to a warm temperature.*

SELECTION AMENDMENT
Description of change: excerpted
Rationale: to focus on the elements of writing to inform and explain as presented in this chapter

GUIDED READING

Strategy: Previewing

Have students read the first sentence in each paragraph of the *Time* article about hurricanes. Discuss what the article is about, and list on the board what other information students expect to get from it when they read the rest of it. After students have read the entire article, see if it fulfilled their expectations.

EYE
EYE WALL
DESCENDING AIR
RISING WARM AIR
COUNTER CLOCKWISE WINDS
Storm surge
Cooler air
Warm humid air
Condensation
Low pressure
1 Winds from different directions converge over waters that have warmed to more than 81°F. Water evaporates. The lighter warm air rises above the cooler air like steam from a boiling pot.
2 As the warm, moist vapor rises, it expands and cools, condensing into cloud droplets and then into rain. The process releases heat locked within the vapor and lowers air pressure, fueling additional showers and thunderstorms.

JET STREAM
Air currents sent hurricane northward
Warm water and still air provided ideal conditions for a hurricane's development
Hurricane path
HIGH-ALTITUDE WINDS
La Niña creates favorable conditions for hurricanes
81°F
88°F
Spiral bands of rain
Spiraling wind

3 Picking up the direction of the earth's rotation, the winds in these thunderstorms circulate counterclockwise (clockwise in the Southern Hemisphere). Collectively they form a churning mass known as a tropical cyclone.

4 When the spiraling winds reach 74 m.p.h. the storm is called a hurricane. At its core is a chimney-like column of calm air (the eye) around which multiple thunderstorms swirl. The storms that form the eye wall are the most ferocious.

READER RESPONSE

You may want to use the following questions to elicit students' personal responses to the selection.

1. How well did this article capture your interest?
2. What part does condensation play in the formation of a hurricane?
3. Does this article address the fears people have about hurricanes? Explain why or why not.
4. How does the use of cause and effect and of chronological order help you to better understand hurricanes?

LITERARY CONNECTION

You might want to explore writing to inform and explain in the following works, which appear in literature textbooks at this grade level.

- "Always to Remember: The Vision of Maya Ying Lin" by Brent Ashabranner
- "The Naming of Cats" by T. S. Eliot
- *On the Road with Charles Kuralt* by Charles Kuralt
- "The Story of an Eyewitness" by Jack London

ADDITIONAL RESOURCES

Composition Skills Practice	pages 41–46
Transparency Tools	VR7
Writing Prompts	pages 4, 13, 17, 24, 31, 41
Connection Collection	pages C273–C274
ESL Practice and Test Preparation	pages 50–56
Standardized Test Preparation	Units 2, 3, 8, 11, 13
Writers at Work	8•1–8•10
Assessment: Chapter Test	pages 64–67
Assessment Resources	pages 1–10, 13–44, 70–77

Using *Thinking as a Writer*

You may choose to have students respond to the questions either orally or in writing.

REACHING ALL STUDENTS

Struggling Learners

Students may not understand how devastating hurricanes can be. Encourage students to find books in the library, Internet sites, and video clips that describe or show the destructive power of hurricanes. Ask students to share what they have learned with the class. Your class may want to form a table showing the number of deaths caused by various hurricanes.

Thinking as a Writer

Analyzing Writing That Informs or Explains

The selection about hurricanes is part of an article published in a magazine. Magazines are one source for informative writing.

- Why does informative writing use facts and examples?
- How does informative writing use illustration?

Speaking Informatively

Oral Expression Imagine that you are a television weather reporter for a weekly show. Take turns with a partner, reading the article aloud. Before you begin, consider the following questions.

- What kind of voice does a reporter use?
- How do you react to a reporter's voice?

Interpreting Informative Illustrations

Viewing This article uses illustrations and text to explain how hurricanes form and where they get their force. With a partner or in a small group discuss the following questions.

- How do the text and illustrations work together to explain how a hurricane occurs?
- Why would it be much harder to explain this topic with text or illustration alone?

FOR DEVELOPING SKILLS

LESSON 1 *(pages C243–C256)*

OBJECTIVE

- **To follow prewriting steps that shape a general idea into an organized plan for an expository paragraph—choosing and limiting a subject, listing details, and arranging them in a logical order**

Create Interest

List on the board the steps that students mention in planning a party. Discuss how they will decide the purpose of the party, whom to invite, when to have it, and other basic issues. Remind students that effective planning is the first step in having a successful party.

Guide Instruction

By Modeling Strategies

Bring a newspaper to class. Go through it with the class, identifying the various sections and types of sto-

The Power of Informative Writing

The *Time* magazine reporters used facts and examples from news and weather reports to give information about hurricanes. Another way to write an informative paragraph is to list directions or to show how something happens.

Uses of Informative Writing

Here are some common examples of writing that explains or informs.

- **An encyclopedia entry provides general facts and information** about Alaska.
- **You present a report on hermit crabs** to your science class.
- **A newspaper article features a profile** of a famous inventor.
- **A magazine illustrator draws a diagram** of a solar eclipse.
- **A family creates their geneology tree on their own Internet home page.**

CAREERS AND COMMUNICATION

Technical Writer

Explain to students that many people write informative or explanatory reports for work. Those who specialize in it are called technical writers. For example, in a glass company that is developing a new, energy-efficient window, the top executives might want regular reports of the progress the team is making and the problems they are facing. Providing these reports may be a responsibility of the leading chemist on the team, or of a full-time technical writer. Either one might write quarterly reports for the executives. In addition, someone on the team might be responsible for documenting the procedures used and their results. To be an effective technical writer usually requires both specialized training in a field, such as chemistry, biology, or engineering, as well as excellent writing skills.

Have students write a report of an experiment they have done in science class, on a card trick they have learned, or some other multistep process. They should identify how the process works and what difficulties may prevent it from working well.

ries in it. As you do, list on the board ideas for subjects students would like to write about. Some of the subjects might be taken directly from stories; others might be ones that pop into their minds as a result of what you are showing them.

Consolidate Skills

Through Guided Practice

Divide students into groups. Have each group list as many subjects as they can for paragraphs that inform or explain something about school in one minute. See which group can list the most subjects. Repeat several times, replacing the category of school with books, sports, animals, and other broad areas of interest.

Apply to Communication

Through Independent Writing

Have groups of students take one of the lists they created in the previous activity and think about the audience that each would appeal to. They

IDENTIFYING COMMON STUMBLING BLOCKS

Problem

- Having difficulty thinking of subjects for an informative or explanatory paragraph

Solution

- Have students keep a list of the activities they do during an evening. While they can list common activities, such as washing the dishes, they should particularly note any activities that they suspect not everyone does or that they do in a distinctive way. For example, they might have a special game they play with their dog or a certain ritual they go through when setting the table.

Developing Your Informative Writing Skills

Having information at your fingertips is as important now as it was in the 1st century A.D. when the Roman statesman Seneca said, "If one does not know to which port one is sailing, no wind is favorable." We would all be at sea without informative writing. There would be no reference materials, instructional manuals, cookbooks, textbooks; the whole idea is hard to imagine. For those who love facts and trivia, this is a favorite type of writing. This chapter will help you develop the invaluable skills of writing informatively.

Informative writing presents information using facts and examples by giving directions or listing steps in a process.

Your Writer's Journal

Sometimes the details you use to develop an informative paragraph will be causes and effects. An effect is *what* happened. A cause is *why* it happened. Experiment with writing about causes and effects in your journal. Keep a running list of events that have happened. For example: I forgot to return my library books *(what)* because they were buried under some other books in my locker *(why)*. My grandmother did not recognize me *(what)* because I dyed my hair for the school play *(why)*. Save your work for further use.

should consider variations in age, gender, residence, and other factors as appropriate. Remind students that any predictions they make about what appeals to a particular group are only generalizations. A well-written paragraph may appeal to people in a wide range of categories.

Transfer to Everyday Life

By Making a Schedule

Explain to students that planning a composition is similar to making a schedule. In both, one is deciding what to focus on and what goals to achieve. In both, one tries to be realistic in setting goals, recognizing limitations of time and resources.

Pull It All Together

By Summarizing

Ask students to summarize the main activities in prewriting. List them on the board, and discuss what is involved in each. After you have completed the list, ask students if they think any other activities should be included.

Informative Paragraph Structure

The purpose of the following paragraph is to inform the reader how a computer can "smell."

Model: Paragraph That Informs

An Electronic Nose

Topic Sentence / Supporting Sentences / Concluding Sentence

Computers can be programmed to do many things, even tell the difference between roses and lilacs. Computers, of course, need a special kind of "nose" to do this. This electronic nose samples the air and sends signals to a memory chip in the computer. The signals are compared to information stored in the memory chip. If the signals match the information for rose, the computer identifies the smell. Because of clever programming, the computer nose knows!

—*Seymour Simon,* Computer Sense, Computer Nonsense

The following informative paragraph gives information by providing directions.

Model: Paragraph That Gives Directions

How to Take Action Photos

Topic Sentence / Supporting Sentences

Capturing an exciting moment on film requires planning and coordination. First, make sure that the lighting for your picture is suitable. Whenever possible, try to stand with your back toward the source of light. Next, try

YOUR IDEAS

For Informative Paragraph Structure

SELECTION AMENDMENT

Description of change: excerpted

Rationale: to focus on informative paragraph structure

Check Understanding

By Considering Alternatives

Ask students if they have ever tried to write without prewriting. Some students may suggest that they always do at least a few minutes of thinking before they begin drafting. Discuss what would happen if they tried to write without planning at all.

Help students recognize that in writing, as in many activities, a little planning can make the rest of the process much smoother.

YOUR IDEAS

For Informative Paragraphs

SUPPORTING SENTENCES

to anticipate the exact location of the action so that you can arrange an attractive frame for your picture. Finally, when the moment of action arrives, be ready to press the shutter button with your finger. Although you might be caught up in the excitement, press the button calmly and firmly. Hitting the button too hard can cause the camera to move, and the picture may come out blurred. Taking good

CONCLUDING SENTENCE

action photos requires practice, but even beginners can capture a picture worth a thousand words if proper care is taken.

Structure of an Informative Paragraph

- The **topic sentence** states a main idea based on fact.
- The **supporting sentences** provide facts, examples, or steps in a process.
- The **concluding sentence** summarizes the main idea and adds a strong ending.

Prewriting

Writing Process

When you go on a trip, you do not simply walk out the door and take off. Instead, you plan the trip in advance. In the same way, when you write, you do not simply sit down and write a composition. You must first plan what you want to say. The planning stage of the writing process is called the prewriting stage.

Discovering Subjects to Write About

Ideas for paragraphs that inform or explain can come from many different sources. Use the following techniques to think of possible subjects.

Strategies for Thinking of Informative Subjects

- Look through your **journal**, particularly your Learning Log and interest inventory, for ideas you could explain.
- Think about books, magazines, or newspaper articles you have read lately on subjects of special interest to you.
- Think about an interesting television show or movie you have watched recently.
- Think about a conversation you had recently that made you stop and think.
- Browse through the Media Center.
- Think about what interests you in your other classes.
- Talk to friends and family members and find out what they would like to know more about.
- Start freewriting and see what is on your mind.
- Use the clustering technique starting with the phrase *things I can explain*.

Communicate Your Ideas

PREWRITING *Subject Inventory*

Use any or all of the above strategies to think of at least five possible subjects for a paragraph that informs or explains. Remember that your writing purpose is to explain or give directions. As you search for ideas, try to focus on subjects that are unique to you. What in your background gives you a special understanding of something that you could explain to others? Save your notes for later use.

SAVE YOUR WORK

TIMESAVER *QuickCheck*

Review the possible subjects that students have listed to see if they have selected ideas that are suitable for explaining or giving directions. If they are not, suggest that students develop other possible subjects.

HOME STUDY

Students may want to talk with classmates about the possible subjects they are considering. In talking, they may develop other ideas.

TIMESAVER *QuickCheck*
Divide students into pairs. Each student should explain to the other why the subject he or she selected would make a good subject. If he or she cannot do so convincingly, then the student should consider changing subjects.

HOME STUDY
Students can continue to add to their knowledge of their subjects by doing a search on the Internet or by visiting a library/media center.

Considering Your Audience

Decide who your audience will be by using the following Audience Profile Chart.

Audience Profile Chart
- Who will read my work?
- What subjects would interest them?
- Which subject is the most suitable for my audience?

Choosing a Subject

Now that you have several possible subjects and a good idea of who your readers will be, you can select the subject that seems most promising. You may find when you start working on that subject, however, that it was not as good as you thought. In that case, you can always return to your prewriting ideas and try another subject. Use the following guidelines to choose a promising subject.

Choosing an Informative Subject
- Choose a subject that interests you.
- Choose a subject that will interest your audience.
- Choose a subject you know enough about to explain accurately.

Now it's time to turn your subject into a topic sentence. As you plan your topic sentence, keep your readers' needs and interests in mind.

Communicate Your Ideas

PREWRITING *Choose a Promising Subject*

 Refer to the five possible subjects you selected. Leave about ten lines under each one. Then, on the blank lines under each subject, list what you know

about that subject. Circle the subject that comes closest to following all three guidelines for choosing an informative subject. Be prepared to explain why you think that subject would make a good composition.

Limiting a Subject

Some subjects are too broad for one paragraph. The subject of baseball, for example, could fill an entire book. Within this general subject, however, are several smaller subjects. These may include how to throw a curve ball or the meaning of the term *double play*. As part of planning your work, be sure to limit your subject so that it can be adequately covered in one paragraph.

The following examples shows broad, general subjects that have been narrowed down to a more manageable size.

General Subject	More Limited	Limited Subject
Nature	waterfalls	Niagara Falls
Hobbies	crafts	working with clay
Courses	science	using a microscope

One good way to discover the smaller subject is to ask yourself questions about it. Among the many possible questions you can ask, try the following.

Strategies for Limiting a Subject

- Who are some of the people associated with my subject?
- What are some specific examples of my subject?
- Where is my subject usually done or found?
- Why should people know about my subject?
- When was my subject first discovered? When did it become popular?

USING STUDENTS' STRENGTHS

Multiple Intelligences: Spatial

Have students draw a large, upside down triangle on a sheet of paper. In the middle of the triangle, students should write a topic that they think would be appropriate for a one-page composition. Above it, they should write three topics, each one larger than the one beneath it, suitable for longer papers. Below it, they should write three topics, each one more focused than the one above it, suitable for shorter papers.

Multiple Intelligences: Logical

Have students create branching diagrams showing how possible topics are related to each other. Students should place a broad topic at the top. Branching off it should be three more limited topics. Branching off each of these should be three even more limited topics.

HOME WORK

Assign students to write a list of five general subjects, and to list two limited subjects under each one. They should consider topics they might write about for a class in school.

PRACTICE YOUR SKILLS Sample Answers

1. parakeets, gerbils
2. history class, drama club
3. steam engines, commuter trains
4. early sports cars, car safety
5. computerized special effects, casting
6. taking fingerprints, training to be a police officer
7. radio telescopes, the electric light
8. Washington's cabinet, Washington at Valley Forge

Focusing Your Subject The final step in limiting a subject is to focus your thoughts by expressing the main idea in a phrase.

LIMITED SUBJECT	Niagara Falls
QUESTION	What is unique about Niagara Falls?
FOCUS	Niagara Falls is the place where the boat *The Maid of the Mist* takes passengers.

PRACTICE YOUR SKILLS

Limiting Your Subject

Write two limited subjects for each general subject listed below.

1. pets
2. school
3. trains
4. cars
5. movies
6. the police
7. inventions
8. George Washington

Listing Details

Now that you have a more focused, limited subject, you can begin listing the details that will help you explain that subject to readers. The kinds of details will depend on your main idea and your purpose for writing. If your purpose is to inform, you will probably use facts and examples. If your purpose is explain or to give directions, your details will be the steps in a process.

The following main idea (limited subject) is one that calls for facts and examples. The writer's purpose is to explain.

Limited Subject	tarpits at Rancho la Brea
Focus	how prehistoric animals were trapped in pits
Fact	rainwater gathered on surface of tar pools and gave appearance of lake
Fact	animals came to drink and got caught in tar
Fact	their dead bodies attracted scavenging animals who also became trapped
Fact	tar helped preserve bones of animals
Examples	animals trapped include mammoths, saber-toothed tigers, and mastodons

To help you think of details, first make a list of questions that readers might have about your subject. Then jot down any details that will help you answer those questions. Your final list should include three to five details.

Practice Your Skills

Questioning to Create Details

Write each focused subject. Then under each one, write at least three questions that might occur to readers about it.

Focused Subject	prehistoric animals trapped in tarpits at Rancho la Brea
Questions	How did they get trapped? What animals are trapped there? Can people still see their remains?

HOME WORK

Have students create cluster diagrams about topics of their choice. Encourage them to think of topics that would appeal to members of their class.

Practice Your Skills Sample Answers

1. How is a friend unlike a family member?
   What do friends do?
   Who are examples of friends in literature?
2. What is the goal of the game?
   What are the rules?
   What is the best strategy for winning?
3. What skills do teenagers have?
   What are the laws about working?
   How much should teenagers expect to earn?
4. What are the symbols of our school?
   How long have the symbols been in use?
   How do students feel about the symbols?

TIMESAVER *QuickCheck*
Review the final lists that students have created. Be sure that they include enough information so that students can easily write a paragraph from them.

HOME STUDY
Students can complete this **Communicate Your Ideas** activity at home. To generate questions, they might ask other members of their household what they would like to know about the topic.

FOCUSED SUBJECT

1. the meaning of friendship
2. how to play your favorite game
3. ways teenagers can earn money
4. the symbols of your school

Communicate Your Ideas

PREWRITING *Supporting Details*

Return to your focused subject. Think of questions about it that might occur to readers. For each question, list one or more details that will help you answer your readers' questions. Then compile all your details into a final list you can use to develop your paragraph. Save your work for later use.

Arranging Details in Logical Order

The final step in the prewriting stage is arranging your list of supporting details in a logical order. A logical order is an arrangement that makes sense—an arrangement your readers will be able to follow clearly. The guidelines below will help you organize your brainstorming notes.

Strategies for Organizing Details

- Group related items together through classifying.
- If your purpose is to give information, arrange your details in the order of importance, interest, size, or degree.
- If your purpose is to give directions or to explain a process, arrange your details in the order in which they occur.

Writing Is Thinking

Analyzing

If you are writing an informative paragraph to give directions or to explain a process, analyzing your subject will help you come up with the details you need. **Analyzing** means breaking something down into its parts to better understand it.

Suppose, for example, you are writing about how to release a bowling ball. You go bowling so often that releasing the ball is second nature to you. When you try to explain it clearly to someone else, however, you may need to analyze the action; or break it down into its parts, so the other person can understand it.

As you analyze the way you release the ball, you see that you are actually following several different steps. You take a series of steps. As you move, your arm straightens and swings the bowling ball back behind you. The opposing hand and arm follow through in a smooth motion as you release the ball. What seemed like one continuous motion was actually a series of smaller, intermediate steps that can be explained. Analyzing helps you recognize the smaller parts, or steps, within a whole so that you can explain them clearly to your reader.

THINKING PRACTICE

Think of a physical motion that is second nature to you. It may be jumping into a double rope, doing a somersault, or simply skipping. Analyze the motion by breaking it down into its parts. Then team up with a partner and explain the steps so that your partner can easily understand them.

Using *Writing Is Thinking*

Objective

- **To understand how to analyze a procedure**

A DIFFERENT APPROACH

Visual Have students sketch each stage in a process with which they are familiar. In their sketches, students should focus on the significant details the viewer needs to know rather than the overall merit of the image. After they have drawn each stage, they should add captions that explain the process in words.

Kinesthetic Have students act out each stage in a process with which they are familiar as another student videotapes them. Then, the student should write a description of each stage to accompany the video.

Thinking Skills	
Classifying	Analyzing
Comparing	Hypothesizing
Generalizing	Synthesizing
Inferring	Summarizing
Imagining	Setting Goals
Observing	Evaluating Audience
Predicting	

DEVELOPING WORKPLACE COMPETENCIES

Thinking Skills: Problem Solving

Analyzing is a key skill in solving problems. The ability to break down a process into its steps or stages, to distinguish among the elements of a situation, and to separate information into useful segments are all valued analytical skills. Businesses often expect employees to analyze a situation to see how to resolve problems that develop. For example, if one branch bank is losing money while all the other branches are making money, the central office of the bank may send a team to investigate and report on the one poorly performing branch. A hospital considering the purchase of new software may send several employees to a convention so they can talk with potential vendors. The employees then may write a summary of the options available for the hospital. A manufacturing company may send representatives to its factories around the world to find out how each one has solved various production problems.

Assign students to write a report on a company, explaining whether they think the company will increase or decrease its profits in the coming year. Besides using what they know about companies, markets, and changing demand, students can find information about companies in the business section of newspapers, in magazines, and on the Internet. Encourage students to begin looking for information before they select a company.

If your paragraph calls for order of importance, interest, size, or degree, you may list your details in the **order of least to most** or **most to least.** In the following paragraph, the details are arranged in order of least to most.

Model: Order of Degree

Hungry Mammals

TOPIC SENTENCE

DETAILS IN ORDER OF LEAST TO MOST

CONCLUDING SENTENCE

Different animals have different food requirements depending on their body weight, activity, and chemistry. The relatively small chimpanzee, for example, eats an average of 4.5 pounds of food each day. The lion needs about 15 pounds of food, while the African elephant requires about 350 pounds. The recordholder for amount of food eaten daily is the blue whale. It eats about one ton of food each day. Despite this enormous amount, the whale actually consumes a smaller percentage of its body weight than does the chimpanzee.

If you are giving directions or explaining a process, your details should be arranged in the proper sequence, the order in which they are carried out. This type of order, called **sequential order,** is similar to chronological order. The following paragraph about mountain climbing uses sequential order.

Model: Sequential Order

Using Your Feet

TOPIC SENTENCE

DETAILS IN SEQUENTIAL ORDER

The natural tendency of beginning climbers is to look for handholds, but you must begin your climbing education by learning to look down for footholds. In the beginning tell yourself repeatedly, "Look down; look down!" Once you have the habit of looking down, you must learn to see footholds. They may be very small or steeply sloping. The next step is to test the foothold by trying to stand on it. While you are learning, expect to slide off holds quite a bit. With more and more experience, you will learn to recognize footholds that you can stand on safely.

CONCLUDING SENTENCE

—*Michael Loughman,* Learning to Rock Climb

PRACTICE YOUR SKILLS

Arranging Details in Logical Order

Write each focused subject. Then list the details in a logical order, numbering them consecutively. Under each list write the method you used to organize the details. Indicate your answer by writing *least to most, most to least,* or *sequential.*

1. Focused Subject how a dolphin is trained

Details
- dolphin soon begins to connect fish reward with behavior it just performed
- trainer waits for dolphin to perform desired stunts, such as jumping into air
- later fish reward is postponed until after a whistle signal is given
- trainer sees desired behavior and immediately rewards dolphin with fish
- knowing that fish reward will follow, dolphin eventually performs whenever it hears a whistle signal

2. Focused Subject astronomical distances

Details
- Earth to nearest planet (Venus): 25 million miles

GETTING STUDENTS INVOLVED

Cooperative Learning

When arranging details in order of importance, people may disagree on which details are most important. Divide students into groups. Each group should select a topic on which to develop a paragraph. Each student should contribute two details about the topic. Then, as a group, the students should decide on the order of importance of the details.

PRACTICE YOUR SKILLS Sample Answers

1. how a dolphin is trained (sequential)
   - trainer waits for dolphin to perform desired stunts, such as jumping into air
   - trainer sees desired behavior and immediately rewards dolphin with fish
   - dolphin soon begins to connect fish reward with behavior it just performed
   - later fish reward is postponed until after a whistle signal is given
   - knowing that fish reward will follow, dolphin eventually performs whenever it hears a whistle signal
2. astronomical distances (least to most)
   - Earth to moon: 240,000 miles
   - Earth to nearest planet (Venus): 25 million miles

SELECTION AMENDMENT

Description of change: excerpted

Rationale: to focus on the concept of logical order as presented in this chapter

- Earth to sun: 93 million miles
- Earth to nearest star other than the sun: 4.3 light years
- sun to limits of Milky Way galaxy: 30,000 light years (Note: 1 light year equals 5.9 trillion miles)

3. why many skating teams are make up of a brother and a sister (least to most)
   - appearance when skating together is good because body types tend to be similar
   - more important, similar body types have similar striding motions on ice so that unison work matches
   - most important is ability to predict each other's movements

HOME WORK

Assign students to write a focused subject and five details about an aspect of their home, such as the layout of a room, the colors used on the walls, or the styles of the windows. Students should identify which method of organizing the details they used.

TIMESAVER *QuickCheck*

Have students self-check the order of their facts. Ask them to be sure that the facts are listed in the logical order that they intended to use.

- sun to limits of Milky Way galaxy: 30,000 light years (Note: 1 light year equals 5.9 trillion miles.)
- Earth to moon: 240,000 miles
- Earth to nearest star other than sun: 4.3 light years
- Earth to sun: 93 million miles

3. Focused Subject why many skating teams are made up of a brother and a sister

Details
- appearance when skating together is good because body types tend to be similar
- most important is ability to predict each other's movements
- more important, similar body types have similar striding motions on ice so that unison work matches

Plotting Cause and Effect

Causes	Effects
1. →	

Pick one or more of the *cause-and-effect* situations you have been writing about in your journal and plot it in a grid like the one above.

Communicate Your Ideas

PREWRITING *Idea Organization*

Return to the details you developed for your informative paragraph. Arrange your ideas in an order that is logical for your paragraph and number them consecutively. Save your work in your writing folder for later use.

LESSON 2 *(pages C257–C260)*

OBJECTIVE

- **To write the first draft of an expository paragraph, including the topic sentence, body, and concluding sentence**

Create Interest

Have students draft a paragraph using one of the following proverbs as a topic sentence:

- The brightest of all things, the sun, has its spots.
- A little neglect may breed great mischief.
- A good word costs no more than a bad one.
- Wise people change their minds; fools never do.
- Understand your opponents before you answer them.

Ask volunteers to share their paragraphs. Discuss how much time students took for prewriting, revising, and editing.

Writing Tip

In paragraphs that provide information, use **order of importance** or **size** with appropriate transitions. Arrange the details in the order of **least to most** or **most to least**. In paragraphs that explain, use **sequence order** with transitions.

Drafting

Writing Process

Through prewriting you have explored your topic and examined what you know about it. You have also jotted down ideas and arranged them in a logical order. At this stage you are ready to write a first draft. The first draft need not be polished. It should, however, contain the basic parts of a paragraph—a topic sentence that states the main idea, a body of supporting sentences, and a concluding sentence.

Topic Sentence

A good way to begin drafting is to focus on your main idea—the point you want to make about your subject. During the prewriting stage, you expressed your main idea in a phrase. Now your task is to express that idea in a complete sentence. Your final topic sentence should be broad enough to cover all of the supporting details that you plan to include in your paragraph. To make sure your topic sentence is appropriate, refer often to your prewriting notes.

If you had decided to write a paragraph about students in Japan, your prewriting notes might look like the following.

FOCUSED SUBJECT student attitudes in Japanese classrooms

HOME STUDY

Assign students to review their idea organization at home, and check for any missing information. They may want to add additional information to bolster their explanation or to fill in more information.

USING STUDENTS' STRENGTH

Multiple Intelligences: Spatial

Ask students to compare how they write with how they draw. Drafting might be similar to sketching: both are an initial effort to get a basic idea onto paper so that it can be revised and improved with more work.

Guide Instruction

By Connecting Ideas

Discuss with students the function that a topic sentence has in a paragraph. It is the point a writer wants to make about a subject. Ask students to compare a topic sentence in a paragraph with other items. For example, a topic sentence is like the main character in a play, the entree in a meal, or the theme in a piece of music.

Consolidate Skills

Through Guided Practice

After students have completed the **Practice Your Skills** activity on writing topic sentences, have them try the activity in reverse. Students should write three intriguing topic sentences for paragraphs that inform or explain, and then list four details under each one. Ask them which process was easier: finding the details first or writing the topic sentence first.

Apply to Communication

Through Independent Writing

Encourage students to try drafting while in different moods. Some people write best when they are very calm

REACHING ALL STUDENTS

Struggling Learners

If students are having difficulty writing topic sentences that are broad enough, have them each find a well-written paragraph in another book, magazine, or newspaper. They should identify the topic sentence. Have students read the paragraph aloud to the class without the topic sentence. The rest of the class should then write a topic sentence they think goes with the paragraph. Compare the sentences proposed by students with the one actually used in the printed version of the paragraph.

PRACTICE YOUR SKILLS Sample Answers

1. Besides being fun, dancing has several additional benefits.
2. Computers come in many sizes to suit many purposes.
3. Following basic safety rules makes owning a dog more enjoyable.

HOME WORK

Assign students to write three topic sentences, and to list three notes that could be used to write the rest of a paragraph for that sentence.

DETAILS

- students are taught to respect those with knowledge and to treat them as teachers
- students are taught to listen carefully and to be humble when learning something
- students are eager to ask questions to increase their knowledge
- students believe that studying in a group can increase their knowledge

After reading over the notes, you might write the following topic sentence.

Students in Japan are humble about learning.

This sentence, however, is not broad enough to cover all the supporting details. It does not, for example, suggest anything about students working in groups. A revised, broader statement makes a better topic sentence.

Students in Japan are encouraged to respect those with knowledge and to take advantage of all opportunities to learn.

PRACTICE YOUR SKILLS

Writing Topic Sentences

Read each set of prewriting notes for a paragraph that informs or explains. Then write a topic sentence for each one.

1. Focused Subject the benefits of dancing

Details
- is good exercise
- allows you to let off steam
- opportunities to make new friends
- helps build confidence and coordination

and focused. Others prefer to write while excited or angry. Ask students to share their experiences with the class.

Transfer to Everyday Life

By Recognizing the Importance of Drafting

Point out to students that for much of the writing they will do in their life, drafting is the key stage. For example, when they write a letter or send an E-mail to a friend, they will probably spend less time in the prewriting, revising, editing, and publishing stages than they do in the drafting stage. However, when they want to produce their best writing, they will spend more time in all of the other stages of writing.

Pull It All Together

By Reflecting

Ask students how they feel about drafting. For many students, this is the stage they enjoy most. It is more concrete than the prewriting stage and less precise than the later stages. It offers a

2. Focused Subject there are many different computers to suit specific needs

Details
- small, portable personal computers
- mid-sized home computers
- large business computers
- gigantic mainframe computers

3. Focused Subject safety rules for dogs

Details
- dogs should not be left alone in yard
- dogs should not be allowed to wander around neighborhood
- when walking a dog, owners should use leash
- dogs should not be left in closed cars

Paragraph Body

The body of an informative paragraph is made up of flowing, connected supporting sentences. Once again, use your prewriting notes to help you with the first draft.

Tips for Drafting the Body

- Try to work fairly quickly. Do not worry about mistakes.
- Follow the order you placed your supporting details in during prewriting.
- Every now and then, pause to read over what you have written. That process will help you keep track of the flow of your writing.
- When needed, add transitional words and phrases to help one sentence lead smoothly into the next.

The following draft of an informative paragraph is about students in Japan. Compare the supporting sentences in the

IDENTIFYING COMMON STUMBLING BLOCKS

Problem

- Feeling unable to write the first sentence when drafting

Solution

- Have students set a goal for how many words they want to write each minute. Help students figure out a reasonable goal. Ask them to estimate how long it takes them to write a typical paragraph, and how many words are in one. Use this information to determine an average writing speed per minute. After figuring their goal, students should set a timer for one minute at a time and try to meet their goal each minute.

clear product—a first draft—that is substantial. Others may find drafting the most difficult part of writing. It includes more uncertainty than the other stages, and some students will find this hard. Remind them that many professional writers feel the same way.

Check Understanding

By Comparing Stages

Ask students to clarify how drafting differs from the other stages of the writing process. You may wish to write the stages on the board to help students review them.

IDENTIFYING COMMON STUMBLING BLOCKS

Problem

- Not being able to write a strong concluding sentence

Solution

- Have students read effective concluding sentences in paragraphs in speeches. Often, these lines are written to generate applause when delivered. Northwestern University maintains a Website named for Frederick Douglass that includes classic American speeches at http://douglass.speech.nwu.edu/index.html#go. The periodical *Vital Speeches of the Day* and its Website http://www.votd.com/ are excellent sources of contemporary speeches.

body with the prewriting notes at the top of page C258. Notice the transitions that were added to improve the flow.

MODEL: Draft of an Informative Paragraph

TOPIC SENTENCE — Students in Japan are encouraged to respect those with knowledge and to take advantage of all opportunities to learn.

SUPPORTING SENTENCES — By far the most important attitude Japanese students bring to their learning is a respect for anyone with knowledge. That person is always regarded as the teacher. Related to this respect is the students' humble attitude toward learning. This attitude allows them to listen carefully in class and to ask questions eagerly to increase their knowledge.

CONCLUDING SENTENCE — Finally, Japanese students are taught to respect what they can learn from classmates when working together in groups.

Concluding Sentence

The concluding sentence brings your paragraph to a strong close. Without it, your paragraph may leave your readers hanging. To write a concluding sentence, first read over what you have written. Then write a sentence that serves one or more of the following purposes.

Writing a Concluding Sentence

A concluding sentence may

- restate the main idea in a different way.
- summarize the paragraph, picking up key ideas or terms.
- evaluate the details.
- add an insight that shows new understanding of the main idea.

LESSON 3 *(pages C261–C270)*

OBJECTIVES

- **To revise the draft for unity and coherence and to use a revision checklist**
- **To edit the paragraph and prepare a final draft**

Create Interest

Ask students to mention activities they do that they can never do correctly the first time they try. List these on the board. For example, learning a new piece of music, acting in a play, and training a dog all require more than one attempt. Point out that just as these activities require continued efforts for success, so does writing.

Guide Instruction

By Modeling Strategies

Write on the board a topic sentence for a paragraph. For example, *Thomas Edison was the greatest inventor in the history of the United States.* Discuss different directions the writer could

Communicate Your Ideas

DRAFTING *Topic Sentence, Body, and Concluding Sentence*

Return to your prewriting work. Keeping your notes handy, write the first draft of your informative paragraph. Start off by drafting a topic sentence that states the main idea of your paragraph. Be sure that it covers all the details you intend to include in your paragraph. Then draft the body of supporting sentences. Work to achieve a smooth flow by using transitions. As you write you are free to add new ideas that occur to you as long as they relate directly to your main idea. Keep your readers in mind. Remember the questions you listed that may occur to readers. Strive to answer these questions in your draft. Finally, add a strong concluding sentence that serves one of the purposes listed on the preceding page.

Revising

Writing Process

If you are like most writers, your first draft will not be the best you can do. In the revising stage of the writing process, you have a chance to improve your writing in a second or third draft. When revising look at your draft as if you were the reader instead of the writer.

Checking for Unity and Coherence

One way to improve your draft is to check it carefully for unity. A paragraph has unity when all of the supporting sentences in the body relate directly to the main idea stated in the topic sentence. Sentences that stray from the main idea cause readers to become confused and distracted.

TIMESAVER *QuickCheck*

Have students exchange drafts with a partner. Each student should provide encouragement and feedback to their partner on their drafts.

HOME STUDY

Tell students to read their topic sentence to another member of their household, and to ask the listener what they would expect to hear in the rest of the paragraph. If the listener expects something other than what the writer expected, he or she should consider revising the topic sentence.

take the rest of the paragraph. For example, the writer might list some of Edison's inventions. Or, the writer might compare Edison with other inventors. While each direction might work, combining both would be awkward.

Consolidate Skills

Through Guided Practice

The **Practice Your Skills** activity on revising for unity and coherence helps students develop their revising skills. To extend this activity, have students find a paragraph in another book or magazine. They should copy it, but leave out all transitions. Then have students trade paragraphs and add transitions as needed.

Apply to Communication

Through Independent Writing

Have students bring to class copies of letters to the editor that inform or explain written in newspapers. Ask students to read them aloud, and discuss

Practice Your Skills Sample Answers

Snow can actually help plants and animals keep warm in cold weather. Snow on the ground is actually warmer than the air above it. You can test this fact with a simple experiment. Borrow a thermometer from your parents. First take a reading of the temperature near the surface of a pile of snow. Then take a reading in the middle of the pile. Finally, take a reading of the temperature near the ground. You will find that the closer you get to the ground, the warmer the temperature will be. Because it stays warmer than the sometimes sub-zero air around it, snow can help keep plants and animals alive all through the winter months.

HOME WORK

Revise the information in the paragraph "A Blanket of Snow" to create a new paragraph. Instead of focusing on snow as a blanket, focus on how parents and their children can do science experiments together. Write a new title, a new topic sentence, and a new concluding sentence, and revise the other sentences as needed.

Another way to improve a first draft is to make sure that it is coherent. In a paragraph with coherence, the ideas are presented in a logical order with clear transitions. While drafting you paid attention to presenting your ideas in a clear order and using transitions to help with the flow of your writing. As you revise check your writing to see if any idea got out of place, or if additional transitions could improve the flow even more.

Practice Your Skills

Revising for Unity and Coherence

On separate paper, revise the following paragraph. Be sure that

- no ideas wander off the main point.
- the ideas are presented in their most logical order.
- transitions, if necessary, are added.

A Blanket of Snow

Snow can actually help plants and animals keep warm in cold weather. The reason is that snow on the ground is warmer than the air above it. You can test this fact with a simple experiment. Take a reading of the temperature near the surface of a pile of snow. Borrow a thermometer from your parents. Read the temperature at ground level. You will see that it is warmer there than near the surface at the top of the pile. You could also take a temperature reading in the middle of the pile of snow if you want. The temperature there will be cooler than at ground level but warmer than at surface level. Because it stays warmer than the sometimes sub-zero air around it, snow can help keep plants and animals alive all through the winter months.

how they would revise and edit them. Encourage students to focus on whether the paragraphs in the letters have unity and coherence.

Transfer to Everyday Life

By Writing Letters

Have students write a letter to a friend or relative informing the recipient how the student has changed in the past year. Revise and edit the letter using the checklists in the text.

Pull It All Together

By Reflecting

Ask students how their understanding and use of the writing process has changed during this unit. Discuss specific examples of how students think their writing has improved. Students may note that as they study writing, they become more sophisticated readers as well.

Check Understanding

By Defining

Ask students to write definitions of *revising* and *editing.*

Use the checklist below to help you revise your writing.

Evaluation Checklist for Revising

Checking Your Paragraph

✓ Does your topic sentence state your main idea and cover all your supporting details? *(pages C27–C29)*

✓ Does your paragraph have unity? *(page C84)*

✓ Did you use a logical order and transitions to give your paragraph coherence? *(pages C85–C86)*

✓ Does your concluding sentence provide a strong ending? *(page C88)*

Checking Your Sentences

✓ Did you combine related sentences to avoid too many short, choppy sentences in a row? *(pages C53–C54)*

✓ Did you vary the length and beginnings of your sentences? *(pages C53–C55)*

✓ Did you avoid rambling sentences? *(page C63)*

✓ Did you avoid unnecessary repetition and empty expressions? *(pages C64–C65)*

Checking Your Words

✓ Did you use clear, specific words? *(pages C49–C51)*

Communicate Your Ideas

REVISING *Conference*

As a final step in revising your informative paragraph, rework your writing until you are ready to share it with a partner. Add, substitute, delete, and rearrange to achieve a stronger paragraph. Use the Evaluation Checklist for Revising above to revise your partner's paragraph. Ask your classmate to read your paragraph to be sure you have expressed your ideas clearly and logically. Save your paper for editing later.

TIMESAVER *QuickCheck*

Read the first and last sentence of each student's paragraph. Decide if they work well together or if one needs further revision.

HOME STUDY

Encourage students to read their paragraph aloud at home. This will allow them to hear phrases that need revision.

GETTING STUDENTS INVOLVED

Reciprocal Teaching

You may wish to reproduce an unedited, anonymous student paper and distribute it to the class. Then work, as a group, through the editing process and the use of proofreading symbols.

TIMESAVER *QuickCheck*

Have students check another classmate's paragraph using the Editing Checklist.

HOME STUDY

If time allows, students should set their paragraph aside for one day or more. Then, when they return to it again, they will be able to read it with a fresher eye and increase their chances of catching mistakes.

Editing

Writing Process

When you are satisfied with the content of your paragraph, you can move on to editing, correcting mistakes in grammar, usage, mechanics, or spelling. Use proofreading symbols as a shorthand way of showing corrections.

Editing Checklist

- ✓ Did you read through your work to identify mistakes in grammar, spelling, or mechanics?
- ✓ Did you use the proofreading symbols on page C37 to edit your work?

Communicate Your Ideas

EDITING, PUBLISHING

Use the Editing Checklist to catch any mistakes in grammar, spelling, usage, and mechanics you might have made. Prepare a neat final copy of your work when you have finished editing.

Grammar in the Writing Process

Prewriting Workshop
Drafting Workshop
Revising Workshop
Editing Workshop
Publishing Workshop

Colorful Verbs

At school some day, watch how different people walk down the hall. If you were to write a description of this scene, you might include overused verbs such as *walk*. However, if you searched your imagination, a dictionary, or thesaurus, you might find more colorful verbs to make lively word pictures for your readers. Some students shuffle along, stroll, or saunter at a leisurely pace. Others stride confidently, strut arrogantly, or march briskly as though they are intent on important business. The expressive power of colorful verbs is limitless.

Newspaper and magazine writers use colorful language to transport readers right into the scene they are covering. The following example shows how colorful verbs can add drama and excitement to an otherwise ho-hum presentation of facts.

WITHOUT COLORFUL VERBS

Still, the storm, **going along** the coast all the way to Massachusetts, **brought** punishing rains from Florida to Maine and **caused** widespread flooding.

WITH COLORFUL VERBS

Still, the storm, **skirting** the coast all the way to Massachusetts, **dumped** punishing rains from Florida to Maine and **triggered** widespread flooding.

It is easy to see how colorful verbs bring clarity and definition to a word picture. The verbs *dumped* and *triggered* give a sense of the crushing weight and sudden disaster brought by hurricanes. Colorful verbs can transform a rainstorm into a natural disaster.

Using *Editing Workshop*

Objective

- **To practice using precise, colorful verbs rather than general, overused verbs**

A DIFFERENT APPROACH

Visual Have students write ten verbs scattered across a sheet of white paper. They should include examples of both general and precise verbs. Then, using colored pencils, markers, or paints, have them place colored dots by each verb. They should use pale, bland colors for the general verbs, and richer, brighter colors for the more precise verbs. As they work on their own writing, they should strive to use verbs to which they would give rich, bright colors.

Auditory Have students write ten verbs, including both general and precise verbs. Then have them read the list aloud, using a stronger voice for the more precise verbs and a weaker voice for the more general verbs. As they work on their writing, they should strive to use verbs that they would shout out if they were reading them.

REACHING ALL STUDENTS

English Language Learners

Encourage students to associate specific verbs with specific nouns. This will help them use the verbs in appropriate contexts. For example, *broke* might apply to both a pane of glass and a clock. However, *shatter* is more likely to be used with *glass* than with *clock*.

YOUR IDEAS

For Informative and Explanatory Writing

Process of Writing Informative Paragraphs

The activities in this section of the chapter will help you write clear informative paragraphs. Use the strategies and process that work best for you. During prewriting, however, be sure to consider the needs of your audience as you plan your explanations. During drafting put your thoughts in flowing sentences. As you revise and edit your work, look for any weaknesses or errors in your writing and correct them. The result should be an explanation that is easy for your intended reader to follow.

Writing That Informs

When you are writing informatively, you can write from personal experience or outside your experience by using research.

Prewriting Think of a tradition your family follows for a holiday, birthday, or a family celebration. Make as many notes as you can about your family celebration: who is involved, how long this has been celebrated, when celebrated, special foods, and other pertinent information.

Drafting Use the details from your notes to draft sentences that inform and explain. Write a topic sentence that introduces your subject, and write a conclusion.

Revising Conferencing Pair off with a partner. Have your partner read your paragraph aloud, then read your partner's. Decide if any of the information presented is confusing.

Use your partner's comments and the Evaluation Checklist for Revising on page C263 to help you revise your paragraph. You do not have to incorporate all of your partner's comments.

Editing Check over your paragraph for errors, using the Editing Checklist on page C264.

Create a "How-to" Show

It can be a challenge to write to inform without being dull in your presentation. Since the advent of cable television, shows that cover cooking, home improvement, arts and crafts, and sewing have become very popular. One reason for this is that television producers have made these shows interesting and fun to watch. There are also more informational commercials (known as *infomercials*) on television. These are usually shorter shows that sell specific products: make-up, hair care, and exercise machines using "ordinary" people to demonstrate the wide appeal and use of their products.

"How-to" shows work well when they are clear and easy to follow. They can make complex tasks seem simple by showing how they are done, step by step. In addition, they might include helpful hints and other applications of the skills demonstrated. A show about making chocolate chip cookies might include shots of the cook, the audience, the dough, the oven, and tips for making other cookies.

Media Activity

Watch several how-to shows on television. Choose one and, if possible, videotape several episodes so that you can watch them several times. Use the following questions to analyze the how-to shows as you watch.

Questions for Viewing a "How-to" Show

- Was the script thorough?
- Did you learn something?
- Was it fun to watch?
- Did the props work in the show?
- Would you watch another show in the series?

IN THE MEDIA

Using *In the Media*

Objective

- **To evaluate "how-to" shows**

Group Project

- Divide students into groups of three. In each group, one person should be the director and camera operator, while the other two demonstrate how to do some activity. Have students show their video to the class.

Website to Visit The website http://food.epicurious.com/run/EpiTV/main includes eighty "how-to" videos demonstrating cooking techniques.

Publishing Make a neat final copy referring to the publishing suggestions on page C40.

Giving Directions

Any time you explain how to do something or get somewhere you are giving directions.

Prewriting How would you make an omelette? List all the steps, ingredients, and utensils needed to make an omelette.

Drafting Use your list to draft an explanatory paragraph giving directions on how to make an omelette.

Revising Conferencing Exchange your paragraph with a partner. Pantomime the directions as your partner reads them to you. Let your partner know if any parts of the directions are confusing.

Use your partner's comments and the Evaluation Checklist for Revising on page C263 to help you revise your directions. Incorporate only the comments that you agree on with your partner.

Editing Check over your paragraph for errors, using the Editing Checklist on page C264.

Publishing Make a neat final copy referring to the publishing suggestions on page C40.

COMPUTER TIP

All computers offer menu items and arrow icons that allow you to sort information. The Sort feature in the Table menu allows for specific organization of lists or text.

FYI

How to Use with Windows™ The Sort command allows text to be sorted in alphabetical order, numerical order, or date order, either in ascending or descending order.

How to Use with Macintosh™ The Sort command allows text to be sorted alphabetically, numerically, or by date, in either ascending or descending order.

Explaining Cause and Effect

Cause is why something happened and **effect** is the result. Start out by explaining the situation, then explain the cause for it, and its effects.

Prewriting Brainstorm these questions: What was the wisest choice you ever made? What made you make this wise choice? What was the effect on you and on the people around you? Jot down some quick notes, keeping the events in order.

Drafting Refer to your notes while drafting your cause-and-effect paragraph.

Revising Conferencing Exchange your paper with a classmate. Ask your partner if the causes and effects are clear. Use your classmate's comments and the Evaluation Checklist for Revising to revise your paragraph.

Editing Check over your paragraph for errors, using the Editing Checklist on page C264.

Publishing Make a neat final copy using the suggested form for publishing on page C40.

Time Out to Reflect

What have you learned about informative writing? In your **journal** make a list of five ideas to remember when writing informatively. Add to the list or change it each time you learn more about this type of writing. Use your list the next time you write to inform or explain.

EXPANDING THE LESSON

Using Technology

You will find additional **instructional** and **practice** materials for this chapter at http://www.bkenglish.com.

INTEGRATING TECHNOLOGY

Electronic Publishing

You may want to refer students to *The Writer's Guide to Electronic Publishing* on pages C520–C544 for suggestions on using resources for publishing.

Process of Writing to Inform and Explain

Remember that you can move back and forth among the stages of the writing process. For example, during editing, you may wish to return to the drafting stage to add some details. The page numbers in the parentheses refer to pages where you can get help with your writing.

PREWRITING

- Decide on a writing purpose and think about who will be reading your work.
- Make a list of possible subjects and choose one.
- Limit your subject so that it can be covered in one paragraph.
- If your purpose is to provide information, list facts and examples. If your purpose is to give directions, list steps in the process. If your purpose is cause and effect, tell what happened and the result of the situation. *(pages C250–C252)*
- Arrange your notes in a logical order. *(pages C252–256)*

DRAFTING

- Write a topic sentence suited to your purpose. *(pages C257–C259)*
- Use your prewriting notes to write the supporting sentences. *(pages C259–C260)*
- Add a concluding sentence. *(pages C260–C261)*

REVISING

- Put your paragraph aside for a while. Then use the Checklist for Revising on page C263 to make it as clear as possible.

EDITING

- Is your paragraph free of errors in grammar, usage, and spelling?
- Did you use capital letters where needed?
- Did you punctuate your sentences correctly?

PUBLISHING

- If you are typing your paragraph refer to Correct Form for a Composition on page C41. If you are handwriting:
  - Did you indent your paragraph?
  - Are your margins even?
  - Is your handwriting neat?

A Writer Writes

A Paragraph Giving Directions

Purpose: **to give directions on how to play a game**

Audience: **fourth graders**

Prewriting

You have been asked to contribute a one-paragraph composition to a book about party games for children. Your paragraph should give the directions to a game so clearly that fourth graders would be able to play the game after reading your paragraph. Scan your memory for possible games to write about, or use one of the strategies on page C274 for thinking of ideas. Try to come up with several different games you could explain. Choose the one you think fourth graders would enjoy the most. Then use what you have learned about prewriting to plan your composition. The end result should be clearly organized notes from which you can draft your composition.

Drafting

Use your notes to write the first draft of your paragraph of directions. As you write, pause every now and then to see how your ideas are flowing. Remember that you do not need to worry about mistakes at this point.

Revising

Exchange papers with a classmate. Ask the classmate to read your work and then tell you in his or her own words how to play the game. Did your paragraph succeed in giving the directions in the proper order? Are all necessary directions given? Ask your partner if there are

Using *A Writer Writes*

Objective

- **To write an explanatory paragraph**

TIMESAVER *QuickCheck*

Students may need help thinking of games fourth graders might play. Have students work in small groups to share memories of parties they attended when they were in fourth grade. Together they can come up with games like pin-the-tail-on-the-donkey, three-legged race, memory, breaking open a pinãta, or hide-and-seek.

You might choose to have students who wrote direction for the same game exchange papers with one another.

INTEGRATING *Writers at Work*

For more opportunities to inspire and stimulate students' informative and explanatory writing, look at *Writers at Work.*

YOUR IDEAS
For the Writing Process

any questions that are not fully answered in your paragraph. Use your partner's comments to improve your work. Also use the Evaluation Checklist for Revising on page C263.

Editing

Give your paragraph a title. Then use the Editing Checklist on page C264 to look for and correct any mistakes.

Publishing

Finally, through friends or family members, find a fourth-grade class that might be interested in your book about games. Decide with the rest of the class how to publish the book about games. Consider these questions:

1. In what order should the paragraphs be presented?
2. Should there be illustrations?
3. Should the book be bound by a cardboard cover, a ring binder, or by staples?

Connection Collection

Representing in Different Ways

From Visuals . . .

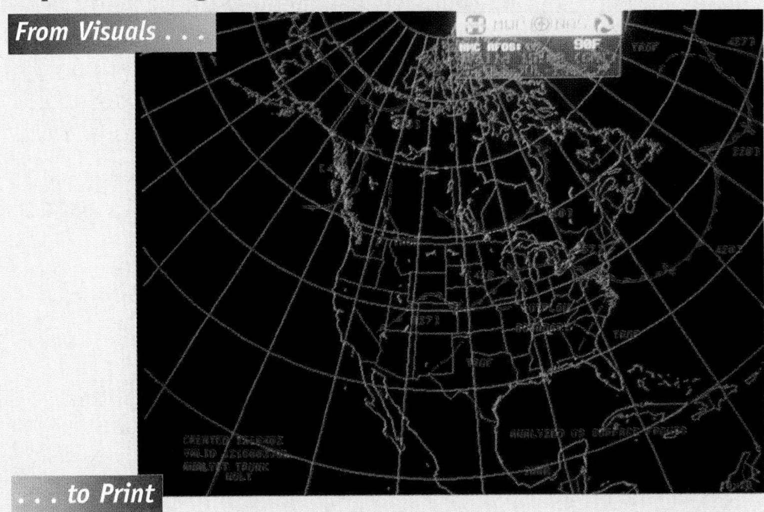

. . . to Print

From the accompanying weather map, prepare a national forecast.

From Print . . .

A winter storm warning is in effect for Hot Town, Blazing Brook, and Summer Village, due to storms forming off the western coast over Warm Weather Sea.

. . . to Visuals

Create a weather map from the information in the above weather forecast notes. Use your imagination to create the exact shape of the area and placement of the locations mentioned. Be sure your map does not contradict the information given.

- **Which strategies can be used for creating both written and visual representations? Which strategies apply to one, not both? Which type of representation is more effective?**
- **Draw a conclusion and write briefly about the differences between written ideas and visual representations.**

FOR REVIEWING SKILLS

Using *Connection Collection*

Representing in Different Ways

Consider using these print and visual activities to make students aware of the benefits of using different media to suit particular purposes. Help students understand when a visual medium, for example, is better suited to their purpose than a print medium, or the reverse.

YOUR IDEAS

For Viewing and Representing

Using *Connection Collection*

Representing in Different Ways

Consider using these print and visual activities to make students aware of the benefits of using different media to suit particular purposes. Help students understand when a visual medium, for example, is better suited to their purpose than a print medium, or the reverse.

GETTING STUDENTS INVOLVED

Cooperative Learning

After organizing students into groups, thoroughly explain the task to be accomplished and establish a time frame. Make sure that each group member is responsible for a given task. Have each group share its project with the class and discuss the process the group used to carry out the assignment.

YOUR IDEAS

For Writing Prompts

Writing in the Workplace

Informative E-mail

You are an inventor and you have just completed your newest invention—the Watchamawhozit. You mailed your model to Miss Chaching, a prospective investor. The investor has sent you an E-mail message because she does not know how to get your invention to work. She is not even sure what it is supposed to do.

Compose a reply E-mail message to the investor explaining how the gadget works and what it does. Give a step-by-step process for operating the invention. Be sure you are clear and exact in your explanation—you don't want Miss Chaching to get frustrated and give up.

What strategies did you use to explain the gadget to Miss Chaching in the E-mail message?

You can find information on writing E-mail messages in A Writer's Guide to Using the Internet.

Writing in Academic Areas

Informative Instructions

You are in charge of public relations at the zoo. The zoo has agreed to participate in an exchange program with a local school. Students will come to the zoo and live in cages while animals take their places in homes and classrooms. The first animal to be placed is Tux the penguin. Tux needs to bring instructions for his care to the school with him on his first day.

Write an informative paragraph for Tux to bring with him. In the paragraph include some general information about penguins and give instructions on how to care for them. Keep your audience and purpose in mind as you write. Make sure your paragraph is clear and progresses logically. Use transitions between ideas.

What strategies did you use to inform Tux's caretakers about penguins?

You can find information about writing paragraphs on pages C75–C88.

A DIFFERENT DELIVERY SYSTEM

For formal assessment print the composition chapter test from the *BK English* Test Bank at http://www.bkenglish.com.

Assess Your Learning

You are a writer for the national magazine, *Egoist*. Your column, entitled "What I Know," is a big hit—at least you think so.

- **Write an informative magazine article about a subject you know well.**
- **Limit your subject to what can be covered in a short article. Keep the audience, purpose, and occasion in mind as you write and gear your voice and style toward them. Your article should contain an introduction with a topic sentence, a body with supporting sentences, and a conclusion. Check your work for unity and coherence.**

Before You Write **Consider the following questions:**
What is the ***subject?***
What is the ***occasion?***
Who is the ***audience?***
What is the ***purpose?***

After You Write **Evaluate your work using the following criteria:**

- Was the style of the writing appropriate to the occasion, audience, and purpose?
- Was the subject sufficiently limited?
- Did the introduction include a topic sentence?
- Did the body contain supporting details and examples that adequately supported the topic sentence?
- Were the supporting details arranged in logical order?
- Did the conclusion summarize the main points?
- Was the work unified and coherent?
- Overall, was the work informative?

Write briefly on how well you did. Point out your strengths and areas for improvement.

FOR ASSESSING LEARNING

Using *Assess Your Learning*

This writing prompt will help you and your students informally assess their developing writing abilities, using the accompanying primary trait rubrics, which list the key features and qualities of expository writing taught in this chapter. You may want to have students maintain their self-assessments in their portfolios as a record of their individual progress throughout the year.

Evaluating Informative Writing

In writing compositions to inform or explain, many students need special help in

- **developing a main idea statement with sufficient ideas and details**
- **organizing these details and ideas logically**
- **presenting this information clearly and coherently.**

Self-evaluation and peer evaluation can help students improve their compositions in these areas as they revise.

SELF-EVALUATION

After students have finished their first drafts, have them evaluate their compositions for the purpose of revising. If you choose, hand out copies of the Evaluation Checklist for Writing Essays to Inform or Explain. (See the Evaluation Checklists in BK English Language and Composition Assessment.) Suggest that students focus on content as they read their compositions, with special attention to the traits numbered below.

PEER EVALUATION

Some students may find it helpful to work in pairs to evaluate each other's work. Having the writers read their compositions aloud will help both students detect strengths and flaws. The writer also might quiz the listener to see how well he or she has understood the composition's content.

1 The main idea statement is supported by paragraphs in the body of the composition.
2 Each topic relates to the main idea.
3 Topics are fully developed with details.
4 The body paragraphs follow a logical order and the conclusion reinforces the main idea.
5 All information is presented clearly and coherently.

TEACHER EVALUATION

Primary Traits

The following introductory paragraph of an expository composition can serve as a model for students' introductory paragraphs. It presents a main idea statement and suggests a plan for developing the main idea in the body of the composition.

MODEL FOR EVALUATION

KIDNAPPED BY ALIENS. You probably have seen newspaper headlines or television stories like this. What you may not realize is how old such tales are. Hoaxes and rumors about space creatures began many years ago. One famous example occurred in 1835 when the New York Sun printed a sensational series claiming that an astronomer had spotted winged men on the moon. Another example occurred in 1938 when the radio program "War of the Worlds" reported that Martians were invading our planet. The broadcast created panic all across America. A look at these old stories may shed some light on modern-day hoaxes.

Effective attention-getter

Good to state that these are hoaxes in topic sentence

Interesting supporting examples

Good to develop the examples as topics of body paragraph

TEACHER EVALUATION

Primary Trait Evaluation

For primary trait assessment of expository compositions, the following chart lists key traits and features.

	EXCELLENT	ACCEPTABLE	NEEDS IMPROVEMENT
Main Idea Statement	Clearly states an interesting informative or explanatory main idea that can be broken into topics and developed with details.	States an expository main idea too narrow or too broad for adequate development.	Does not state a recognizable main idea.
Organization	Each paragraph has a topic sentence that relates to the main idea. Paragraphs are organized in a logical order.	Not all paragraphs relate clearly to the main idea. Logical order of topic paragraphs is not always apparent.	The information presented does not relate clearly to the main idea and is not clearly organized into paragraphs.
Supporting Details	Each topic sentence is supported with facts, examples, reasons, or incidents.	Some topic sentences are well supported, but some are not.	Where topic sentences exist, they are supported either poorly or not at all.
Transitions	Appropriate transitions enhance the composition's flow by guiding the reader between topic paragraphs as well as details.	Some transitions are used.	Transitions are lacking.
Conclusion	The composition has a strong conclusion that reinforces the main idea.	The conclusion at least affirms the main idea, although not as forcefully as possible.	The conclusion either is lacking or does not support the main idea.

TEACHER EVALUATION

Holistic Evaluation

The following criteria may be used to evaluate students' expository compositions holistically, using a rating scale of

- 4 (excellent)
- 3 (good)
- 2 (acceptable)
- 1 (needs improvement)
- 0 (unscoreable)

4	3	2	1
The main idea is contained in an interesting explanatory statement that can be developed with details.	The main idea is capable of being developed with details.	The main idea is not subject to much development.	There is either no expository main idea or none capable of being developed.
The composition employs interesting, plentiful, and logically ordered supporting facts, examples, details, or incidents.	Supporting details are sufficient and generally well ordered.	The composition contains some supporting details that are relevant to the topics under discussion.	Details are irrelevant or lacking altogether.
The composition is well organized. The introduction sets the tone and captures attention while stating the main idea. The body offers several well-developed supporting paragraphs in logical order. A strong conclusion reinforces the main idea.	The composition is basically well organized, but some supporting paragraphs or sentences are out of logical order or are unnecessary.	The composition is in introduction-body-conclusion form, but the relation of the paragraphs to the main idea and to one another is hard to follow.	The composition is not orga-nized into a recognizable introduction, body, and conclusion.

Teaching Suggestions

Essential Knowledge and Skills

- Writing to influence and persuade
- Producing cohesive and coherent written texts by organizing ideas, using effective transitions, and choosing precise wording
- Analyzing a speaker's persuasive techniques and credibility
- Producing communications using technology or appropriate media such as multimedia reports
- Assessing how language, medium, and presentation contribute to the message
- Distinguishing between the speaker's opinion and verifiable fact

CHAPTER 9

Writing to Persuade

Why are some laws passed while others are voted down? Why do some products sell while others sit on store shelves? Why are some people awarded desirable positions while others are left behind? One important factor in all of these situations is the power of persuasion. The ability to persuade others is important in many areas of life. It also plays a part in sharpening thinking skills.

A big part of writing persuasively is taking a stand. You need to know what you think about a topic in order to be able to persuade others that your ideas are correct. Believing strongly in your position is vital to persuasive writing. No matter what the issue—great or small—you need to be sure of your own opinion. Then, by applying various persuasive strategies, you can attempt to convince others. This chapter will help you build your powers of persuasion through writing persuasive paragraphs.

Reading with a Writer's Eye

Read the following selection by Anna Quindlen at least twice. The first time just read for an overall understanding of what the author is trying to convey. Then read it through again. What was the author's purpose for writing the composition? What persuasive strategies did she use? Was the composition effective? Why or why not?

BLOCK SCHEDULING

- If your schedule requires that you cover the chapter in a **shorter time,** use the selection "Homeless" with Thinking as a Writer and Developing Your Skills of Persuasion.
- If you want to take advantage of **longer class time,** add any or all of the following: The Process of Writing Persuasive Paragraphs, In the Media, and A Writer Writes.

FROM LIVING OUT LOUD

HOMELESS

Anna Quindlen

Her name was Ann, and we met in the Port Authority Bus Terminal several Januarys ago. I was doing a story on homeless people. She said I was wasting my time talking to her; she was just passing through, although she'd been passing through for more than two weeks. To prove to me that this was true, she rummaged through a tote bag and a manila envelope and finally unfolded a sheet of typing paper and brought out her photographs.

They were not pictures of family, or friends, or even a dog or cat, its eyes brown-red in the flashbulb's light. They were pictures of a house. It was like a thousand houses in a hundred towns, not suburb, not city, but somewhere in between, with aluminum siding and a chain-link fence, a narrow driveway running up to a one-car garage and a patch of backyard. The house was yellow. I looked on the back for a date or a name, but neither was there. There was no need for discussion. I knew what she was trying

FOR INCREASING STUDENT ACHIEVEMENT

GUIDED READING

Text Analysis

- This **persuasive composition** uses elements of **description, observation,** and **reflection** to support its main idea. It is a work of **participatory journalism** in which the journalist describes her own process of discovering her material.
- The essay is narrated from the **first-person point of view** of the journalist.
- **Word choice,** or **diction,** is simple and concrete, both to appeal to the general reader and to emphasize the stark bareness of the lives of homeless people.
- The **varied sentence structure** in this essay uses strings of short sentences punctuated with longer ones.

GUIDED READING

Strategy: Previewing

First have students look at the accompanying photograph and the title. Then have students skim the first and last sentence of each paragraph in the composition. Ask volunteers to state their hypotheses on what the composition is going to be about, and what opinion or position the author is going to try to persuade the reader to share. Then have students read the entire composition carefully in order to verify or revise their initial impressions.

REACHING ALL STUDENTS

Struggling Learners

To reinforce comprehension, have students make a numbered list summarizing each paragraph in the composition in one or two sentences.

Advanced Learners

To connect the selection to larger issues, ask students to discuss the question, "What, if anything, does Anna Quindlen's article contribute to the goal of solving the problem of homelessness?"

to tell me, for it was something I had often felt. She was not adrift, alone, anonymous, although her bags and her raincoat with the grime shadowing its creases had made me believe she was. She had a house, or at least once upon a time she had had one. Inside were curtains, a couch, a stove, potholders. You are where you live. She was somebody.

I've never been very good at looking at the big picture, taking the global view, and I've always been a person with an overactive sense of place, the legacy of an Irish grandfather. So it is natural that the thing that seems most wrong with the world to me right now is that there are so many people with no homes. I'm not simply talking about shelter from the elements, or three square meals a day, or a mailing address to which the welfare people can send the check—although I know that all these are important for survival. I'm talking about a home, about precisely those kinds of feelings that have wound up in cross-stitch and French knots on samplers over the years.

Home is where the heart is. There's no place like it. I love my home with a ferocity totally out of proportion to its appearance or location. I love dumb things about it; the hot-water heater, the plastic rack you drain dishes in, the roof over my head, which occasionally leaks. And yet it is precisely those dumb things that make it what it is—a place of certainty, stability, predictability, privacy, for me and for my family. It is where I live. What more can you say about a place than that? That is everything.

Yet it is something that we have been edging away from gradually during my lifetime and the lifetimes of my parents and grandparents. There was a time when where you lived often was where you worked and where you grew the food you ate and even where you were buried. When that era passed, where you lived at least was where your parents had lived and where you would live with your children when you became enfeebled. Then suddenly, where you lived was where you lived for three years, until you could move on to something else and something else again.

And so we have come to something else again, to children who do not understand what it means to go to their rooms because they have never had a room, to men and women whose fantasy is a wall they can paint a color of their own choosing, to old people reduced to sitting on molded plastic chairs, their skin blue-white in the lights of a bus station, who pull pictures of houses out of their bags. Homes have stopped being homes. Now they are real estate.

People find it curious that those without homes would rather sleep sitting up on benches or huddled in doorways than go to shelters. Certainly some prefer to do so because they are emotionally ill, because they have been locked in before and they are damned if they will be locked in again. Others are afraid of the violence and trouble they may find there. But some seem to want something that is not available at shelters, and they will not compromise, not for a cot, or oatmeal, or a shower with special soap that kills bugs. "One room," a woman with a baby who

IDENTIFYING COMMON STUMBLING BLOCKS

Problem

- Seeing sentence fragments like "No drawer that holds the spoons" and "No window to look out upon the world" in literary selections

Solution

- Remind students that authors sometimes deliberately use sentence fragments for dramatic, emotional, or rhetorical effect. Authors also use sentence fragments when they are conveying the sound of speech, as in dialogue. Quindlen is using sentence fragments in order to convey her emotions of shock and compassion about the life of a homeless person. Although her sentence fragments are not dialogue, they sound like words that might come into someone's mind in the form of silent speech.

READER RESPONSE

You may want to use the following questions to elicit students' personal responses to the essay.

1. What is the message or main point of "Homeless"?
2. What is distinctive about this author's view of homelessness?
3. What images of homelessness do you think will remain with you from reading this essay? Why?
4. If you were Ann, the homeless woman at the bus terminal, how would you feel about this composition?

LITERARY CONNECTION

You might want to explore persuasion in the following works, which appear in literature textbooks at this grade level.

- "Saving the Wetlands" by Barbara A. Lewis
- "A Tragedy Revealed: A Heroine's Last Days" by Ernst Schnabel
- "Wait Till Next Year" by Doris Kearns Goodwin

was sleeping on her sister's floor, once told me, "painted blue." That was the crux of it; not size or location, but pride of ownership. Painted blue.

This is a difficult problem, and some wise and compassionate people are working hard at it. But in the main I think we work around it, just as we walk around it when it is lying on the sidewalk or sitting in the bus terminal—the problem, that is. It has been customary to take people's pain and lessen our own participation in it by turning it into an issue, not a collection of human beings. We turn an adjective into a noun; the poor, not poor people; the homeless, not Ann or the man who lives in the box or the woman who sleeps on the subway grate.

Sometimes I think we would be better off if we forgot about the broad strokes and concentrated on the details. Here is a woman without a bureau. There is a man with no mirror, no wall to hang it on. They are not the homeless. They are people who have no homes. No drawer that holds the spoons. No window to look out upon the world. My God. That is everything.

ADDITIONAL RESOURCES

Composition Skills Practice	pages 47–50
Transparency Tools	GO2, VR8
Writing Prompts	pages 8, 14, 19, 25, 35, 42
Connection Collection	pages C301–C302
ESL Practice and Test Preparation	pages 56–62
Standardized Test Preparation	Units 1, 4, 5, 6, 10, 12
Writers at Work	8•1–8•10
Assessment: Chapter Test	pages 68–71
Assessment Resources	pages 1–10, 13–44, 78–85

Thinking as a Writer

Analyzing Intent

Viewing • Do you think the photograph on page C277 that accompanies the essay, "Homeless," is being used as a persuasive tool? How so?

- Imagine you are the editor of "Homeless." Does the photograph below match the content and intent of Quindlen's composition? Why or why not?

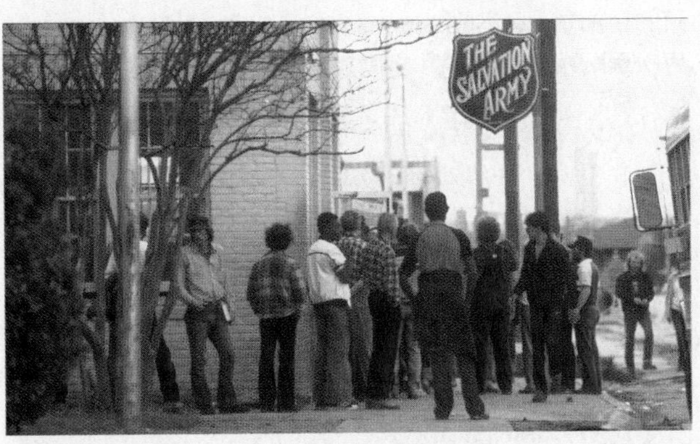

Evaluating Persuasive Strategies

- Anna Quindlen uses various descriptive details and examples. How are these details persuasive?
- What were your feelings about the homeless before you read the composition? How did the composition change your view?

Listening for Persuasive Tone

Oral Expression Quindlen describes a few simple things she loves about her home, although she admits it may not seem like much to an outsider.

- Think of something you like about the place you live. Describe it to a partner, explaining why you like it.
- When your partner is speaking, listen for voice. How does the tone aid in the description?

Using *Thinking as a Writer*

You may choose to have students respond to the questions either orally or in writing.

YOUR IDEAS

For Thinking as a Writer

FOR DEVELOPING SKILLS

LESSON 1 *(pages C282–C289)*

OBJECTIVES

- **To recognize persuasive language and the structure of a persuasive paragraph**
- **To distinguish between fact and opinion**
- **To recognize appeals to emotion and appeals to logic**

Create Interest

Ask students to brainstorm a list of words and phrases that come to mind when they think about homelessness. Write students' ideas on the chalkboard, or have a volunteer do so. Then point out that some of the words and phrases have positive shades of meaning, while others have negative shades of meaning, even though the topic is the same.

CAREERS AND COMMUNICATION

Lawyer

Persuasion is the bread-and-butter skill of the legal profession. Lawyers must learn to write and speak persuasively, constructing solid arguments based on the facts of cases and on the precedents of previous cases. Lawyers' persuasive techniques shape their oral arguments to juries, their questionings of witnesses, and their written briefs for judges. Judges, in turn, use persuasion when they write opinions explaining their rulings on cases; and law professors use the same skills in writing articles that develop legal theories.

Invite students to discuss the view of the legal profession that they have acquired from seeing it portrayed on television and in movies and books. Discuss to what extent persuasive power is part of their image of the law. If you or any students have lawyers in your family, or have had experience with lawyers, compare and contrast the view of lawyers in the media with the reality of legal work. (It is safe to say that the media concentrate on the most dramatic, unusual kinds of legal cases, and that media lawyers rely more on rousing speeches and courtroom heroics than do lawyers in real life, where persuasion is built on painstaking research.)

The Power of Persuasion

Persuasive strategies are used every day to convince, argue, and request. Whenever you want to get someone to think a certain way, you use persuasive tactics.

Uses of Persuasion

Here are just a few examples of the ways in which persuasion can affect your everyday life.

- **You give a speech** telling your classmates why you are qualified to be class president.
- **Advertisers write television commercials** convincing people to buy their products.
- **A citizen writes a letter to his state representative** asking her to support a particular issue.
- **A doctor talks to her patients** about living healthful lives.
- **Film critics write reviews of movies** convincing readers of their point of view.

Guide Instruction

By Modeling Strategies

Tell students that good persuasive writers are skilled at choosing words that help writers influence readers' opinions. Then select two words or phrases from students' brainstorming: one positive and one negative. Compose a sentence about homelessness using the positive word or phrase, and another sentence using the negative word or phrase; lead students to see that the first might be found in a paragraph sympathetic to the homeless, while the other might be found in an unsympathetic paragraph. Point out to students how this language colors the facts the writer is putting forth.

Consolidate Skills

Through Guided Practice

You can use the **Practice Your Skills** activity on clustering (page C286) to give students extra practice at finding persuasive language. Have each student independently choose one topic idea developed in the clusters. Ask him or her to make a new cluster containing words or phrases associated with that topic and to put a plus sign next to each

Developing Your Skills of Persuasion

"I delight in argument, not because I want to convince, but because argument itself is an end," said the newspaperman H. L. Mencken. Although Mencken states he was not interested in convincing, a good argument does just that—a good argument persuades others to take your point of view.

The ability to persuade others is important in many areas of life. Persuasion can be the reason one candidate wins an office over another. It is the reason a product becomes popular even though it may not be the best. Sharpening your thinking skills will help you to master the ability to persuade. You must be able to "see all the angles" in order to form a convincing argument. This chapter will help you build your powers of persuasion through sharpening your thinking skills and writing persuasive paragraphs.

Persuasive writing states an opinion and uses facts, examples, and reasons to convince readers.

Your Writer's Journal

Journal writing can help you discover opinions you can develop into persuasive paragraphs. A good way to explore your opinions is to think carefully about how your views have changed over time. Each day as you work through this chapter, use the following starter line to write freely in your journal. Fill in the blanks with different words each day to discover various opinions you hold and why you hold them. Be sure to explain what changed your mind and why.

I used to think that _____, but now I think that ___________.

REACHING ALL STUDENTS

English Language Learners

In the quote from Mencken, make sure students understand that the word *end* means "goal, purpose" rather than "finish, completion."

IDENTIFYING COMMON STUMBLING BLOCKS

Problem

- Distinguishing between writing an opinion and writing persuasively

Solution

- Remind students that an opinion is simply a view that a person holds; but persuasion involves convincing someone else to share an opinion. Many opinions are matters of personal taste and do not involve proving anything or convincing others. For example, an opinion might be, "I used to like vanilla ice cream best, but now I prefer chocolate." In contrast, an opinion on a persuasive subject might be, "I used to think that young people don't need to care about nutrition; now I think they do." In their journals, students may write any opinions, but when selecting topics for paragraphs later, students should focus on topics suitable for persuasive writing.

word or phrase with a positive meaning and a minus sign next to each word or phrase with a negative meaning.

Apply to Communication

Through Independent Writing

You can use the **Communicate Your Ideas** prewriting activity on page C289 as a springboard for further exploration of persuasive language. Have students review the reasons they listed for supporting a certain song as a class theme song. Ask students to underline any words or phrases in their reasons that they feel express positive shades of meaning about the song. Then ask students to write one more sentence supporting the song, containing a positively persuasive word or phrase they did not use previously. Remind students to support their ideas with facts, not opinions.

Transfer to Everyday Life

By Analyzing Advertisements

Tell students that they encounter language used in persuasive ways every day in advertisements. Ask students to suggest examples of words or phrases

USING STUDENTS' STRENGTHS

Multiple Intelligences: Linguistic

Ask pairs of students to role play a conversation in which one partner tries to convince a dubious member of his or her family that fire drills should be held in the home. Students in the persuasive role should use all the points made in the model paragraph and may add other persuasive points of their own. Students in the dubious role should come up with reservations, doubts, or objections. Partners should switch roles after a given time such as three minutes. Encourage students to use realistic tones of voice.

Persuasive Paragraph Structure

When you write a persuasive paragraph, you should assume that your audience does not agree with your opinion. To convince your readers, your topic sentence, supporting sentences, and concluding sentence must work together logically and forcefully. The purpose of the following paragraph is to persuade readers that they should have fire drills at home. Notice how each sentence works toward this goal.

Model: Persuasive Paragraph

Fire Drills at Home

TOPIC SENTENCE — Fire drills should be conducted in homes as well as in schools and other public buildings.

SUPPORTING SENTENCES — First of all, having regular fire drills at home would allow all family members to practice what to do in an emergency. This practice would reduce panic during a fire and perhaps make the difference between escaping safely and being trapped. Second, having home fire drills would set a good example in the neighborhood. Nearby families may be encouraged to have their own drills. Most important, having fire drills at home would probably lead people to be more safety-conscious so that fires would not get started in the first place.

CONCLUDING SENTENCE — A few minutes a few times a year can help save lives.

In a well-structured persuasive paragraph, each sentence should have a specific purpose. Each sentence should flow logically from the sentence before and add to your argument. The role of each part of a persuasive paragraph is summarized in the following chart.

used often in advertising that have powerful persuasive implications. Invite students to share their examples and to elaborate on the implications of the words and phrases.

Pull It All Together

By Reflecting

Invite students to think about the question, *How can a writer learn to improve his or her skill at using language persuasively?* Encourage specific answers such as, *look for synonyms in a dictionary or thesaurus, ask for feedback from readers,* and *read the works of persuasive writers.*

Check Understanding

By Using the Literary Selection

Return to Anna Quindlen's "Homeless" and ask students to find examples of words and phrases that the author has chosen for shades of meaning that would persuade or move the reader. Ask them whether they feel Quindlen is using facts or opinions to persuade or move the reader. Discuss the examples.

Structure of a Persuasive Paragraph

- The **topic sentence** states an opinion.
- The **supporting sentences** use facts, examples, and reasons to back up the opinion.
- The **concluding sentence** makes a strong point or a final appeal to persuade readers.

Facts and Opinions

If you intend to change someone's mind, you must provide a convincing argument. Sticking to the facts is essential to building a strong case. Opinions have their place, but they cannot be used as proof. Learn to recognize opinions by watching for words such as *should, must, ought, better, best,* and *worst.*

Facts are statements that can be proved. **Opinions** are judgments that vary from person to person.

Use **facts** and examples to convince readers. Do not use **opinions** to support your position.

Practice Your Skills

Recognizing Facts and Opinions

For each statement write *F* if it is a fact or *O* if it is an opinion.

1. Schools should allow students more say in which classes they take.

2. In July of 1985, musicians donated their talents to the Live Aid concert to raise money for hungry Africans.

IDENTIFYING COMMON STUMBLING BLOCKS

Problem

- Not knowing if every paragraph needs a topic sentence

Solution

- Tell students that at times, the topic of a paragraph can be implied rather than stated in a sentence of its own. However, stated topic sentences are more commonly found in persuasive writing than in narrative or descriptive writing, because in persuasive writing the author's purpose involves making a clearcut point.

Practice Your Skills Answers

1. O
2. F
3. O
4. F
5. F
6. O
7. O
8. F
9. O
10. F

HOME WORK

Have students select a letter to the editor in today's newspaper and identify one fact and one opinion in it.

PRACTICE YOUR SKILLS Evaluation Guidelines

Have students add more ideas for category 1 and create clusters with at least three ideas for each of the remaining categories.

HOME WORK

Ask students to do about fifteen minutes' research on the item from the Practice Your Skills clustering list that interests them most, and to add at least three more ideas to that item's cluster. Suggest the use of an almanac—or recent news articles, if applicable—as a research tool for category 2 and an encyclopedia for the other categories.

INTEGRATING TECHNOLOGY

Internet

Encourage students researching their clusters for the **Practice Your Skills** activity to search the Internet for sources of information.

3. Dolphins are beautiful creatures.

4. Dolphins use sonar to locate objects underwater.

5. Many companies in the United States now use recycled paper.

6. Everyone should use recycled paper.

7. The movie ratings should include more categories than the four it currently has.

8. The rating PG-13 means that parts of the movie may be unsuitable for viewers under the age of 13.

9. Old science fiction movies, despite their clumsy special effects, are better than recent ones.

10. Some guitars have six strings.

Clustering

A cluster diagram can be a helpful tool in brainstorming with someone and choosing a topic for writing. Fill in organizers with topic ideas for each of the following general categories. The first one has been started for you.

1.

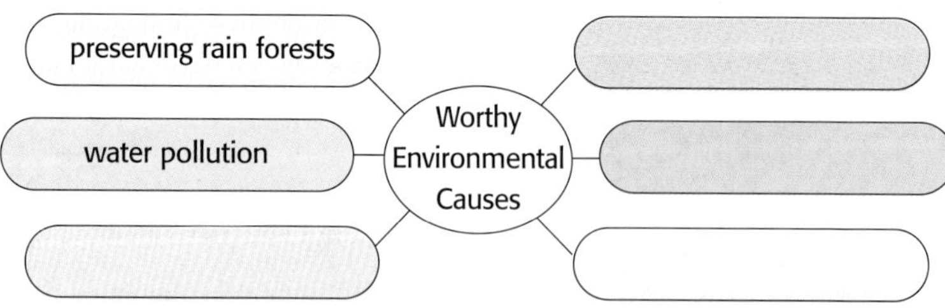

2. Best Actor/Actress of the Year

3. Best Breed of Dog

4. Easiest Way to Save Money

5. Greatest Book of All Time

6. Worst Way to Spend a Summer

7. Funniest Movie Ever

Radio Advertising

Advertising companies spend an enormous amount of time and money researching the age groups and income levels of their customers. Companies that create radio advertising also research the listening habits of the customers they want to attract. They have become clever about using music as a tie-in to a product.

Music can instantly evoke a mood or a feeling. Hundreds of hip-hop, country, and rock and roll songs have been used to sell burgers, trucks, khaki pants, running shoes, and computers. An old rock and roll song may make someone in her fifties long for her youth. An advertiser selling a car to someone in that age group may use a rock and roll song together with a slogan that says "Age is a state of mind." The combination suggests that owning that car will make the buyer feel young.

Similarly, a hip-hop song evokes a feeling of "cool." If an advertiser has decided that the best potential market for the athletic shoes it is selling is young people, then a hip-hop song may just do the trick. Such an ad blends seamlessly into the music being played on the radio station that young people listen to all afternoon.

Media Activity

Rock and roll, hip-hop, and country radio stations all have specific audiences. To practice your persuasive writing skills, form three groups, one for each kind of station. Then write a radio ad selling a spatula to your target audience. What is the average age of your listeners? Are they male or female? Select a song that ties in to your product. Then think of a slogan that works with the song. Write a script, and, if possible, make a recording of your ad and play it for the class.

IN THE MEDIA

Using *In the Media*

Objective

- **To analyze radio commercials**

Group Project

- Divide the class into small groups. Each group should select a radio station and analyze the types of commercials it airs. Encourage groups to select stations besides those that they usually listen to. Each student should listen to the commercials during a different twenty-minute time period. Students should note the products or services advertised, the types of music used, and the tone of each appeal. Then each group should compile its results and write a short evaluation of the audience they think listens to the station.

FYI

Websites to Visit Thirteen classic radio ads can be heard at the Sound Bites section of the Library of American Broadcasting Website of the University of Maryland libraries, http://www.lib.umd.edu/UMCP/LAB/. Another ten classic commercials are available at The Radio Sounds Showcase at http://earthstation1.simplenet.com/radio.html.

HOME WORK
For each statement of opinion, have students find one fact that backs it up.

Practice Your Skills Sample Answers

1. Good eating habits should be everyone's highest priority.
2. Use of computers will improve students' school grades.
3. Television news is oversimplified.
4. City life is more exciting than life in the country.
5. We should do the utmost to preserve endangered species.
6. Commercials are a nuisance.
7. A good book is better entertainment than a good movie.
8. Schools in the United States today place too much emphasis on sports.
9. Curfews should be abolished.
10. Popular music today is neither better nor worse than it ever was.

Writing Persuasive Topic Sentences

For each subject write a topic sentence that states an opinion.

1. eating habits
2. grades in school
3. television news
4. city life
5. endangered species
6. commercials
7. good books
8. school sports
9. curfews
10. popular music

Revising a Paragraph with Facts

The following persuasive paragraph uses only opinions to support its position. Read the paragraph and the facts that follow it. Then use some of the facts to revise the paragraph.

A Throw-away Culture

The people of the United States should learn to use things over and over instead of simply throwing them away. First of all, too much trash could harm the environment. Second, disposing of things so easily might lead to an overall throw-away attitude. Perhaps the reason that so many dogs and cats are put to sleep in animal shelters is that we have a throw-away attitude toward them too. Finally, throwing away so many things is expensive. Why not spend a little more money to buy a pen that could last a lifetime instead of buying many cheaper pens that you throw away after a month? This fairly new throw-away attitude has become the worst problem of our time.

Facts to use in revision

- Plastics in disposable items remain in the environment for many years after the items have been thrown away.

- Americans throw out 3 to 5 pounds of garbage per day; this is more than half a ton of garbage per person each year.
- Each year 15 million dogs and cats are put to sleep in humane societies.
- Americans spend about $2 billion each year on disposable plastic and paper plates.
- Americans spend nearly $3 billion each year on disposable diapers.
- Other disposable items, such as pens, lighters, and razors, cost another $2 billion.

Communicate Your Ideas

PREWRITING *Reasons*

Imagine that you are entering a contest to choose a theme song for your class. The song will be played at all school dances and at graduation. Use freewriting, brainstorming, or clustering to think of a number of popular songs that may be suitable. Choose one among them that seems the best. Then use any of the prewriting techniques that work for you to develop a list of at least three reasons why your song would make a good theme song for your class. Save your work.

SAVE YOUR WORK

HOME WORK

Have students read an editorial in the newspaper and highlight expressions of fact and expressions of opinion, using separate highlighting methods.

PRACTICE YOUR SKILLS Sample Answers

The people of the United States should learn to use things over and over instead of simply throwing them away. First, too much trash could harm the environment. **Plastics in disposable items remain in the environment for many years after the items have been thrown away.** In spite of this, **Americans throw out 3 to 5 pounds of items per day**; this is more than half a ton of garbage per person per year. Second, disposing of things so easily might lead to an overall throw-away attitude. **Each year 15 million dogs and cats are put to sleep in humane societies.** Perhaps the reason that so many dogs and cats are put to sleep in animal shelters is that we have a throw-away attitude toward them too. Finally, throwing away so many things is expensive. Each year, **Americans spend about 2 billion dollars on disposable plastic and paper plates, nearly 3 billion dollars on disposable diapers, and another 2 billion dollars on such disposable items as pens, lighters, and razors.** Why not spend a little more money to buy a pen that could last a lifetime instead of buying many cheaper pens that you throw away after a month? This fairly new throw-away attitude has become the worst problem of our time.

LESSON 2 *(pages C290–C298)*

OBJECTIVES

- **To recognize ways of supporting a hypothesis through facts, examples, and reasons**
- **To use transitions to show connections between points**
- **To use the tools of persuasion in order to write a cohesive, convincing paragraph**

Create Interest

Tell students that you have a hypothesis: The earth is flat. Invite students to respond. (Sample responses: It *is* a hypothesis, but it is wrong; it is an outdated hypothesis.) Then ask how we know that the hypothesis is false. (It has been proven false by observations from outer space, by travel around the globe, and by mathematical calculations.)

Guide Instruction

By Connecting Ideas

Tell students that a hypothesis is an excellent starting point for a work of persuasive writing, but that the hypothesis on its own is basically just an

Using *Writing Is Thinking*

Objectives

- **To understand the skill of hypothesizing**
- **To form a hypothesis**
- **To use discussion to critique or refine a hypothesis**

A DIFFERENT APPROACH

Interpersonal In the **Thinking Practice** activity, students form hypotheses individually and critique them as a group. You may also wish to have them form groups at the beginnings of the activity in order to brainstorm and select possible hypothesesis. Assign one of the three problems to each group. Groups should then remain intact for the critique phase.

THINKING PRACTICE Evaluation Guidelines

Ask groups or individuals to discuss their hypothesizing processes in conference with you. Make sure that each individual's or group's work process has resulted in a genuine hypothesis that offers potential for further exploration.

Thinking Skills	
Classifying	Analyzing
Comparing	Hypothesizing
Generalizing	Synthesizing
Inferring	Summarizing
Imagining	Setting Goals
Observing	Evaluating Audience
Predicting	

Writing Is Thinking

Hypothesizing

Many times the opinion stated in a persuasive paragraph will be a hypothesis. A **hypothesis** is a possible explanation for how or why something is happening, has happened, or will happen. A hypothesis tries to explain something that cannot be known for certain.

In the persuasive paragraph about our throw-away culture on page C288, for example, the writer hypothesizes about the destruction of pet dogs and cats. In trying to explain why so many animals are destroyed each year, the writer suggests that the throw-away attitude applies to animals as well as things. Although there is no certain way to measure the truth of this idea, it is offered as a possible explanation worth further thought. When you form a hypothesis, you search for explanations that seem reasonable and that can be supported with as much evidence as possible.

THINKING PRACTICE

Form a hypothesis about how a throw-away attitude might be related to one of the following issues.

1. treatment of elderly people
2. endangered species
3. the dwindling supply of mineral energy resources

Then form small groups with others who have chosen the same issues you chose. Discuss your hypothesis about problems related to the issue, as well as possible solutions. Save your hypothesis in your writing folder in case you want to develop it later into a persuasive composition.

opinion. In order to persuade readers, the hypothesis must be backed up by evidence. Ask students to suggest different kinds of evidence. List students' suggestions on the board. The following categories of evidence should be supplied either by students or by you.

- **Facts**—pieces of information or data that can be verified, such as, "Many sports records are broken every year." Some facts are **statistics**—data that can be expressed numerically.
- **Examples**—Specific cases that illustrate a point, such as, "Mark McGwire and Sammy Sosa have both surpassed Roger Maris's record 61 home runs."
- **Reasons**—Statements that support a point by means of logic, such as, "If sports medicine keeps discovering new facts about exercise and nutrition, athletes should continuing reaping the benefits."

Order of Importance and Transitions

A logical presentation of ideas helps you convince your readers. Placing the most important point at the end of a paragraph can give you a special advantage. For one thing, the last point tends to stick longer in a reader's mind. For another, placing your most persuasive point last gives your argument more impact.

Writing Tip

Arrange **supporting points** in the order of least to most (or most to least) important. Use **transitions** to show the connection between the points.

TRANSITIONS FOR ORDER OF IMPORTANCE			
also	another	for example	more important
first	besides	furthermore	most important
second	moreover	similarly	to begin with
third	finally	in addition	in conclusion

The following paragraph was written by a student to persuade readers that Jack London's book is more than just a story about a dog named Buck. Read the paragraph. Notice that the writer has arranged the supporting points from least to most important.

MODEL: Order of Importance

Lessons from *Call of the Wild*

TOPIC SENTENCE: OPINION

Although many people look at *Call of the Wild* as a fast-moving adventure story about a dog, I think of it as something more. **One**

USING STUDENTS' STRENGTHS

Multiple Intelligences: Spatial

Suggest that students use graphic organizers of their choice, such as outlines, idea pyramids, or flow charts, to arrange their points in order of importance when prewriting.

Multiple Intelligences: Linguistic

Suggest that students say their points aloud to themselves during prewriting, in order to hear whether the order seems natural and logical to them, and in order to rearrange the points in a better order if necessary. In addition, when drafting and revising, students might read their paragraphs aloud in order to see whether there are enough, and appropriate, transitions between points.

Consolidate Skills

Through Guided Practice

Students can use the **Practice Your Skills** activity on writing persuasive topic sentences (page C288) to hone their skills of providing different types of evidence. Have each student select one of the topic sentences he or she wrote, and suggest how the three types of evidence could be provided to support the sentence.

Apply to Communication

Through Independent Writing

The **Communicate Your Ideas** activity on page C289 can be used as the basis for an exercise in types of evidence. Ask students to review their revised paragraphs and to revise further by supplying one of the types of evidence listed above. It should be a type of evidence not already present in the paragraph.

Transfer to Everyday Life

By Connecting Cross-Curriculum Ideas

Ask students to search in their science textbooks for examples of hypotheses that were proposed by scientists and

TIMESAVER *QuickCheck*

Have partners read and assess each other's drafts, using the following guidelines:

- The paragraph contains a topic sentence clearly recommending a specific song.
- The recommendation is supported by well-ordered reasons.
- The writer uses transitions where appropriate.
- The paragraph ends with a strong concluding sentence.

HOME STUDY

Either prewriting, drafting, or both can be done at home, depending on your time schedule.

SUPPORTING POINTS: ORDER OF LEAST TO MOST IMPORTANT

reason I do is that it shows how it is possible to adapt to a new environment even when conditions are extremely bad. Buck changed his habits and a way of life in order to survive. Along with exciting action, I **also** saw how inhuman and uncivilized people can be, not only to dogs but also to each other. Men stole from one another, fought one another, and killed one another. **The most important reason** for considering this as more than just an ordinary action story is the lesson I learned from the way the story ended. Buck went off to become the leader of a pack of wolves because civili-zation in the Klondike was worse than life in the wild. More than just an adventure story, *Call of the Wild* presents worthwhile lessons for us today.

CONCLUDING SENTENCE: FINAL APPEAL

COMPUTER TIP

With a word-processing program, you can easily cut and paste text. Use this function to rearrange your ideas as you decide their proper order of importance.

Communicate Your Ideas

PREWRITING, DRAFTING *Persuasive Paragraph*

Return to your list of reasons and put them in order of importance. Then draft a paragraph recommending your chosen song. Be sure your topic sentence states your opinion and use transitions. End your paragraph with a strong concluding sentence. Use the Evaluation Checklist for Revising on page C297 to revise your work.

PORTFOLIO

ultimately proven true. Have students tell about the kinds of evidence that were used to prove these scientific hypotheses. Then discuss the difference between a scientific hypothesis and a persuasive hypothesis: a scientific hypothesis (such as whether the world is round or flat) can be proven or disproven, but a persuasive hypothesis (such as whether a certain defendant should be found guilty of a murder) remains ultimately an opinion that is supported more or less strongly by evidence.

Pull It All Together

By Summarizing

One at a time, write the headings *Facts*, *Examples*, and *Reasons* on the chalkboard, and ask volunteers to explain these categories.

Process of Writing Persuasive Paragraphs

Think of a time when you won an argument. What finally convinced the other person? From time to time, you have probably used all of the following tools of persuasion.

Tools of Persuasion

- Use solid reasons and examples that are based on fact.
- Refer to experts who agree with you.
- Think about other viewpoints and offer strong counter-arguments.
- Use polite, reasonable language.

To present your argument effectively in writing, follow the writing process that works best for you. Remember that the writing process is not static. You can move between the stages as they suit you, even revisiting stages when necessary. Explore your opinions—as well as the facts you can use to back them up—through such prewriting strategies as freewriting, brainstorming with others, or clustering. With your ideas arranged logically, draft your paragraph. Then put it aside for a while so you can come back to it and revise it with a fresh eye. Finally, polish your paragraph through the editing process, and share it with an interested reader. The following activities will give you practice in developing your opinions into sound persuasive paragraphs that are backed up by facts and reasons. As you write, remember to keep your audience in mind—think about what techniques would be most effective in persuading them. Use the tools of persuasion that you think are appropriate for your particular audience and purpose.

GETTING STUDENTS INVOLVED

Cooperative Learning

Have students prewrite in groups of three or four using a roundtable method. Each student takes a clean sheet of paper and writes a list of persuasive subjects inspired by a photograph you have provided. Students should list as many subjects as there are members of the group. After writing the subjects, students pass their papers to the partner on their left. Each student writes his or her opinion, with a reason, for one item on the list he or she has received. After a given time, such as a minute, students pass their papers to the left again and repeat the process for a subject that is still available on the papers they have just received. Continue the process until each member of the group has had a chance to write an opinion on each sheet of paper, including his or her own. Then have students share all their papers in order to select subjects, opinions, and reasons to include in their paragraphs.

Check Understanding

By Using the Literary Selection

Offer students the following hypothesis from Anna Quindlen's "Homeless": "It has been customary to take people's pain and lessen our own participation in it by turning it into an issue, not a collection of human beings." Ask students what evidence Quindlen supplies for this view and what categories of evidence it belongs to.

YOUR IDEAS

For Revising Conferencing

Persuading with Facts

Prewriting

Imagine that your science teacher has asked you to write a prediction based on current scientific knowledge. You have decided to write about athletes of the future. From your reading you have learned the following facts about athletes of today. Use these notes to form an opinion about athletes of the future.

- continue to break records
- use scientific studies to increase athletic ability
- use latest knowledge of nutrition to develop sound bodies
- use scientific training techniques

Once you have your hypothesis, freewrite and brainstorm ideas with a partner for a persuasive paragraph supporting your opinion. Be sure to include arguments that defend your opinion against opposing ones. Remember to base your arguments on facts instead of opinions.

Drafting

Using your notes and the facts given, draft your persuasive paragraph. Use adverb clauses to present opposing viewpoints without weakening your own stance. Make sure your points are presented in a logical order.

Revising Conferencing

Reread your paper and revise it if necessary. Then exchange papers with a classmate. If the opinion in your partner's topic sentence differs from yours, are you convinced by the facts provided? Tell your partner what you like about the paragraph and what could be improved. Make any changes you think would improve your composition.

Grammar in the Writing Process

Prewriting Workshop
Drafting Workshop
Revising Workshop
Editing Workshop
Publishing Workshop

Predicate Nominatives and Adjectives

A **predicate nominative** is a noun or a pronoun that follows a linking verb and identifies, renames, or explains the subject. A predicate nominative is linked to the subject by a linking verb. A **predicate adjective** is an adjective that follows a linking verb and modifies a subject.

Predicate nominatives and predicate adjectives are especially useful when you are writing definitions. The linking verb connects the subject and the predicate. In the following examples from "Homeless," Anna Quindlen uses predicate nominatives and adjectives to question unchallenged assumptions and unquestioned definitions, and to redefine ideas about identity.

PREDICATE NOMINATIVES	She was **somebody.** Homes have stopped being **homes**. Now they are **real estate**. They are **people** who have no homes.
PREDICATE ADJECTIVES	The house was **yellow.** She was not **adrift, alone, anonymous**, although her bags and her raincoat with the grime shadowing its creases had made me believe she was.

Sometimes a noun clause can take the place of a noun or adjective.

PREDICATE NOUN CLAUSE	Home is **where the heart is**. You are **where you live**.

Using *Drafting Workshop*

Objective

- **To identify and use predicate nominatives and predicate adjectives in presenting viewpoints**

A DIFFERENT APPROACH

Linguistic Encourage students to brainstorm a list of predicate nominatives and predicate adjectives. Have students use each one in a sentence that balances two opposing viewpoints. Have students read their sentences aloud.

REACHING ALL STUDENTS

Struggling Learners

Some students may have a difficult time distinguishing between a fact and an opinion, particularly if the persuasive argument reflects a feeling or emotion the student has. Remind students that facts are verifiable; one can find a source that states the fact. Often an opinion can be started with *I think, I believe,* or *I feel.* If the student can place one of these phrases in front of the statement in question, it is most likely to be an opinion, not a fact.

Persuading with Reasons

Prewriting

You just heard that your favorite television show may be canceled after this season. The network that carries the show has decided that the hosts are overpaid and that the show has no social merit. You've decided to write a letter requesting that they keep the show. Brainstorm with someone a list of reasons why the network executives should keep the show on the air. Remember to address their particular concerns.

Drafting

Using your list of reasons, draft a letter requesting that the network decide in favor of keeping the show on the air. Use compelling reasons and wording. Be sure to use logical order and transitions as well as polite, reasonable language. You can acknowledge opposing viewpoints without taking away from your own reasoning.

Revising Conferencing

When you are done drafting your letter, exchange papers with a classmate. Read your partner's letter carefully and give him or her suggestions for making it more persuasive. Tell your partner whether or not you agree with the support given to each reason. When your paper is returned, use your partner's suggestions and the Evaluation Checklist for Revising to revise your work.

PORTFOLIO

Evaluation Checklist for Revising

Checking Your Paragraph

✓ Does your topic sentence state an opinion? *(pages C27–C29)*

✓ Did you use facts and examples instead of opinions to support your topic sentence? *(C79–C82)*

✓ Did you think about other viewpoints and offer strong counter arguments?

✓ Does your paragraph have unity? *(page C84)*

✓ Did you use order of importance with clear transitions to give your paragraph coherence? *(pages C85–C86)*

✓ Does your concluding sentence make a strong point or a final appeal? *(page C88)*

Checking Your Sentences and Words

✓ Did you combine related sentences to avoid too many short, choppy sentences in a row? *(pages C53–54)*

✓ Did you vary the length and beginnings of your sentences? *(pages C53–C55)*

✓ Did you position your viewpoints in contrast to those of your readers?

✓ Did you avoid unnecessary repetition and empty expressions? *(pages C64–C65)*

✓ Did you use specific words? *(page C49–C53)*

✓ Did you use polite, reasonable language?

Time Out to Reflect Look back at some persuasive writing you did before starting this chapter. How is it different from your recent work? Is there anything you still need to improve upon? Record your thoughts in the Learning Log section of your **journal**.

YOUR IDEAS

For Using the Evaluation Checklist for Revising

EXPANDING THE LESSON

Using Technology

You will find additional **instructional** and **practice** materials for this chapter at http://www.bkenglish.com.

Process of Writing a Persuasive Paragraph

PREWRITING

- Explore your opinions on subjects you feel strongly about through freewriting, clustering, or brainstorming. *(pages C293–C294)*
- Choose a subject that interests you and that suits your purpose and audience. *(pages C293–C294)*
- Limit your subject so that it can be adequately covered in one paragraph. *(page C284)*
- Brainstorm a list of facts or examples that support your opinion. If necessary, find additional facts and figures in the library. *(page C285)*
- Arrange your notes in order of importance. *(pages C291–C292)*

DRAFTING

- Write a topic sentence that states an opinion. *(page C285)*
- Use your prewriting notes to add supporting sentences with transitions. Remember to stick to the facts. *(page C285)*
- Add a concluding sentence that makes a final appeal or a strong point. *(page C285)*

REVISING

- Put your paper aside for a while. Then pretend you disagree with your own opinion as you read the paper over. Use the **Evaluation Checklist for Revising** to make your paper more persuasive. *(page C297)*

EDITING

- Prepare a final polished paragraph. *(page C293)*

PUBLISHING

- Present your finished work to an interested reader. *(page C293)*

A Writer Writes

A Persuasive Evaluation

Purpose: to persuade fellow judges to vote for your choice in a school poster contest

Audience: fellow judges

You are a judge for the school poster contest. The theme of this year's contest is "Keeping Your Neighborhood Clean." The finalists' posters are shown below. Choose the one that you think deserves to win. Write a paragraph persuading other judges to vote for your choice.

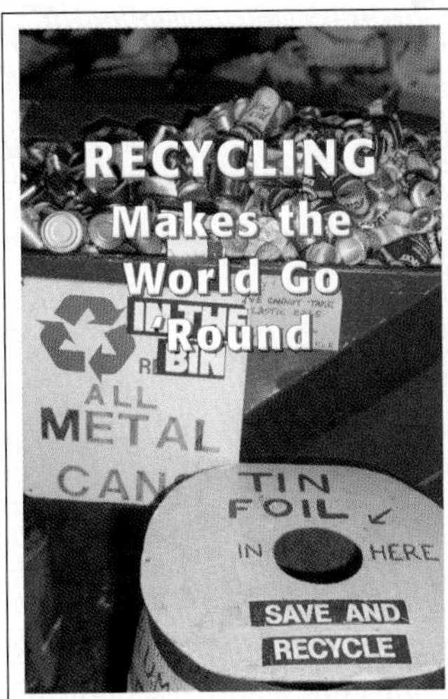

Prewriting

Brainstorm a list of reasons, including specific details from the poster, that support your opinion about which poster deserves to win. Then arrange your reasons in order of importance.

Using A Writer Writes

Objective

- **To write a paragraph persuading the judges of a contest**

TIMESAVER QuickCheck

Allow students to prewrite and draft independently. Read students' final drafts and assess them with reference to the instruction in this chapter, the Evaluation Checklist for Revising, and the Editing Checklist on page C297.

INTEGRATING Writers at Work

To find more opportunities to inspire and stimulate students' persuasive writing, look at *Writers at Work*.

INTEGRATING TECHNOLOGY

Electronic Publishing

You may want to refer students to *The Writer's Guide to Electronic Publishing* on pages C520–C544 for suggestions on using resources for publishing.

Drafting

Write a topic sentence expressing your opinion, supporting sentences to back it up, and a strong concluding sentence.

Revising

Use the **Evaluation Checklist for Revising** on page C297 to revise your paragraph.

Editing

Edit your work for errors in grammar, mechanics, and usage.

Publishing

Turn your paper in to your teacher for evaluation.

Connection Collection

Representing in Different Ways

From Print . . .

Skateboarding is a healthy, exciting way to spend time. Some people complain that kids watch too much television, or play too many video games. Many kids are developing strong muscles, quick reflexes, and healthy lungs and hearts by skateboarding. The Surgeon General recommends that people exercise every week. Skateboarding is an excellent exercise that can be done almost anywhere. Any sidewalk or parking lot can be an excellent place to ride. Finally, skateboarding provides kids with a healthy alternative to the kinds of trouble that idleness can bring about. All in all, a skateboard is a good investment in any kid's health and future.

. . . to Visuals

Find a photo in a magazine or newspaper that could be used to create a poster using the above text. Persuade your viewers that skateboarding is a healthy, useful, and exciting way for kids to spend time.

From Visuals . . .

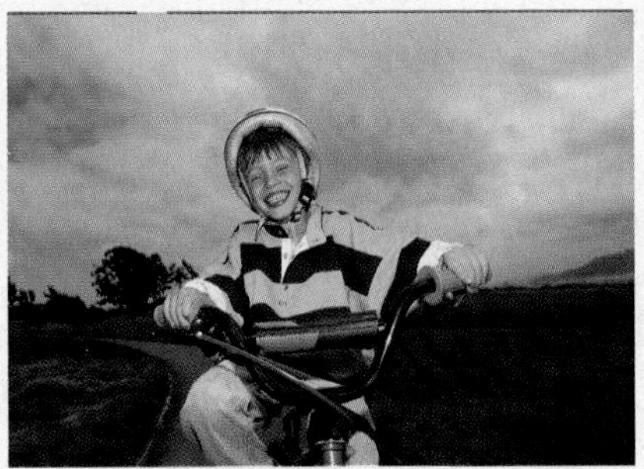

. . . to Print

Write the text to appear on a poster with the picture above. Persuade your viewers that bicycle riding is a healthy activity for kids.

- **Which strategies can be used for creating both written and visual representations? Which strategies apply to one, not both? Which type of representation is more effective?**
- **Draw a conclusion and write briefly about the differences between written ideas and visual representations.**

FOR REVIEWING SKILLS

Using *Connection Collection*

Representing in Different Ways

Consider using these print and visual activities to make students aware of the benefits of using different media to suit particular purposes. Help students understand when a visual medium, for example, is better suited to their purpose than a print medium, or the reverse.

Using *Connection Collection*

Consider using these writing prompts as independent or small-group activities.

GETTING STUDENTS INVOLVED

Cooperative Learning

After organizing students into groups, thoroughly explain the task to be accomplished and establish a time frame. Make sure that each group member is responsible for a given task. Have each group share its project with the class and discuss the process the group used to carry out the assignment.

YOUR IDEAS

For Oral Communication

Writing in Academic Areas

Persuasive Report

As a health professional, you are worried about the amount of time that young people spend wearing hats. You have noticed some ill-effects due to frequent hat wearing. Ill-effects include hair loss, difficulty seeing (when a brim is pulled low), and overheating of the brain. In your opinion this is scientific evidence and should not be taken lightly. You worked long and hard gathering data—hats off to you!

Write a persuasive report about your concerns to share with school principals nationwide. Persuade them to enact and enforce school rules against hats. Begin your report with a statement of your opinion, and support it with facts and examples. Arrange your points in a logical order.

What strategies did you use to persuade the principals that hats are dangerous?

You can find information on writing reports on pages C344–C379.

Writing for Oral Communication

Persuasive Speech

Your class has just nominated you to be Spring Festival Chairperson. It is a prestigious position—you will be in charge of the pie booth and get pies thrown at you all day. You do not believe you deserve such an honor. You are sure there is someone more worthy of the position.

Prepare a speech to deliver to your classmates persuading them not to vote for you. Keep your audience and purpose in mind as you write and gear your argument toward them. Offer reasons, facts, and examples to convince them. Use transitions to connect ideas.

What strategies did you use to persuade your classmates not to vote for you?

You can find information on preparing speeches on pages C404–C437.

A DIFFERENT DELIVERY SYSTEM

For formal assessment print the composition chapter test from the *BK English* Test Bank at http://www.bkenglish.com.

Assess Your Learning

Your school marching band has organized a half-time show for the big football game against your rival. At the very end of the show, a giant warthog, covered with sparklers will march onto the field. The band will light the sparklers so that the warthog blazes for several seconds. You do not feel that this is a very good use of the school's money, especially considering that your school mascot isn't even a warthog. It's a panther, but the warthog costume was on sale.

- **Write a persuasive composition to submit to the school newspaper persuading students to protest this frivolous use of the school's money.**
- **The composition should state your opinion and contain facts, examples, and reasons to support it. Think of possible objections to your opinion and address them. Transitions can be used to place your opinion in contrast to those objections. Be sure to end your composition with a strong concluding statement. Check your work for errors in grammar, mechanics, spelling, and usage that may weaken your authority in the eyes of your readers.**

Before You Write **Consider the following questions:**
What is the ***subject?***
What is the ***occasion?***
Who is the ***audience?***
What is the ***purpose?***

After You Write **Evaluate your work using the following criteria:**

- Does the topic sentence state an opinion?
- Are facts and examples used instead of opinions to support the topic sentence?
- Are opposing viewpoints addressed with strong counter-arguments?
- Did you contrast your opinions to those of your readers?
- Were order of importance and clear transitions used to give the work coherence?
- Does the concluding sentence make a strong point or a final appeal?

Write briefly on how well you did. Point out your strengths and areas for improvement.

FOR ASSESSING LEARNING

Using *Assess Your Learning*

This writing prompt will help you and your students informally assess their developing writing abilities, using the accompanying primary trait rubrics, which list the key features and qualities of persuasive writing taught in this chapter. You may want to have students maintain their self-assessment in their portfolios as a record of their individual progress throughout the year.

Evaluating Persuasive Writing

The three areas in which many students need special help in writing persuasive compositions are

- supporting or elaborating a main idea statement with sufficient reasons and facts
- organizing the reasons logically
- presenting the reasons and evidence clearly

Self-evaluation and peer evaluation can help students improve their compositions in these areas as they revise.

Self-Evaluation

After students have finished their first drafts, have them evaluate their compositions for the purpose of revising. Give them copies of the Evaluation Checklist for Writing Compositions to Persuade. (See the Evaluation Checklists in BK English Language and Composition Assessment.) Suggest that students focus on content as they read their compositions, with special attention to the traits numbered below.

Peer Evaluation

An alternative method of evaluating persuasive compositions for revision is for students to form pairs and evaluate each other's work. In each pair, one student should read his or her composition aloud while the other listens. Doing so will help both writer and listener to detect things that need changing.

1 The main idea statement is supported by several reasons.
2 Each reason is supported by several facts.
3 Each reason is explained clearly.
4 The reasons are organized logically with effective use of transitions.
5 The paragraphs are unified and the conclusion pulls the composition's ideas together.

Teacher Evaluation

Primary Traits

The following represents the first paragraph of a persuasive composition with excellent use of evidence; it can be used as a model.

MODEL FOR EVALUATION

Throughout history the twentieth century will be known for its remarkable advances in technology. From the invention of the automobile and the TV to laser surgery and space exploration, technology changed the way of life for Americans. Though no one can deny the importance of modern medicine or space exploration, those advances cannot be counted as the most important technological breakthrough. That honor goes to the worldwide network known as the Internet—the most influential technological invention of the century. The Internet holds this place of honor for a number of reasons.

Effective use of details

Good transition for persuasion

Excellent preparation for body

TEACHER EVALUATION

Primary Trait Evaluation

For primary trait assessment of persuasive compositions, the following chart lists the key features and qualities of such compositions.

	EXCELLENT	ACCEPTABLE	NEEDS IMPROVEMENT
Main Idea Statement	Clearly states an arguable proposition that can be defended with facts and examples.	States an arguable proposition too narrow to be defended.	Does not state an arguable proposition.
Supporting Points	Facts, examples, and reasons are used throughout to support each main point.	Some points are well supported by facts, examples, or reasons.	There is no use of facts, examples, or logical reasoning to support main points.
Organization	Each supporting point is discussed in a paragraph with a topic sentence and details. The argument is easy to follow.	There are paragraphs, but each one does not necessarily develop a point related to the main idea. The argument is hard to follow at points.	Ideas are not clearly organized in paragraphs. The argument is hard to follow throughout.
Transitions	Transitions are used frequently to guide the reader through the argument.	Some transitions are used.	Transitions are lacking.
Conclusions	A concluding paragraph pulls the composition's ideas together and restates the thesis in an interesting way.	The conclusion pulls together some of the composition's ideas.	A conclusion does not exist or fails to pull together the composition's ideas.

TEACHER EVALUATION

Holistic Evaluation

The following criteria may be used to evaluate students' persuasive compositions holistically, using a rating scale of

- 4 (excellent)
- 3 (good)
- 2 (acceptable)
- 1 (needs improvement)
- 0 (unscorable).

4	3	2	1
The arguable proposition states an interesting opinion that can be supported by facts or authoritative opinions.	The arguable proposition is clearly supportable by facts or authoritative opinions.	The arguable proposition is weak and difficult to support.	There is no supportable arguable proposition.
Strong supporting evidence is used. The logic of the argument is easy for the reader to follow.	Sufficient supporting evidence is used and the reasoning is sound.	Some relevant supporting evidence is included and presented logically.	No relevant evidence or logical reasoning is used to support the main idea.
The composition is well organized. An introductory paragraph states the thesis and builds interest. The body includes several well-developed supporting paragraphs in a logical order. Ideas are connected with transitional words or phrases. The conclusion summarizes the main points and restates the main idea in an interesting way.	The composition is basically well organized, but a few ideas are not logically connected or are out of place.	There is an introductory paragraph that states the main idea, a body that includes some supporting points, and a conclusion that restates the main idea.	The composition is not organized into an introduction, a body, and a conclusion.

Teaching Suggestions

Essential Knowledge and Skills

- Writing to express, discover, record, develop, reflect on ideas, and problem solve
- Choosing the appropriate form for his/her own purpose for writing, including reviews, journals, letters, poems, memoirs
- Refining selected pieces frequently to "publish" for general and specific audiences
- Evaluating how well his/her own writing achieves its purposes
- Comparing and contrasting print, visual, and electronic media such as film with written story
- Selecting, organizing, or producing visuals to complement and extend meanings

CHAPTER 10

Writing About Literature

Reading and writing often go hand in hand. You can sometimes read, for example, to help you through a tough spot in your own writing. You might research books or articles to gather information that you need, or search other writers' compositions, stories, or poems to get ideas for your own writing. In a similar way, writing can help you with your reading. You can write freely about a poem, story, play, or novel in order to explore your responses to it, or to try to puzzle out parts that confuse you. You can also use a more formal piece of writing—such as a composition—to share your understanding of a literary work with readers. In this chapter you will learn and practice the skills you need to write about literature.

Reading with a Writer's Eye

The following story by Cynthia Rylant is about a girl who moves to a new town. Read the story once for your own enjoyment. As you reread, consider what the overall feeling, or mood, of the selection is. What details does the writer focus on to create this mood? How is the mood of the story related to the overall message the writer is sending?

BLOCK SCHEDULING

- If your schedule requires that you cover the chapter in a **shorter time**, use Reading with a Writer's Eye, Thinking as a Writer, Power of Writing About Literature, and the Revising Workshop.
- If you want to take advantage of **longer class time**, add any or all of the following: In the Media, Process of Writing about Literature, and A Writer Writes.

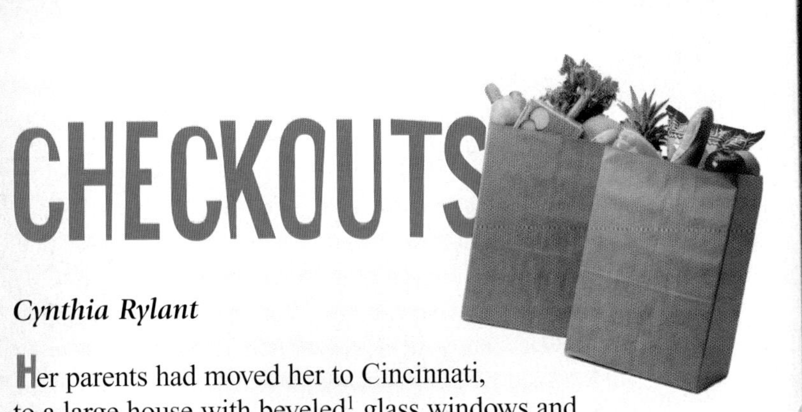

CHECKOUTS

Cynthia Rylant

Her parents had moved her to Cincinnati, to a large house with beveled[1] glass windows and several porches and the *history* her mother liked to emphasize. You'll love the house, they said. You'll be lonely at first, they admitted, but you're so nice you'll make friends fast. And as an impulse tore at her to lie on the floor, to hold to their ankles and tell them she felt she was dying, to offer anything, anything at all, so they might allow her to finish growing up in the town of her childhood, they firmed their mouths and spoke from their chests and they said, It's decided.

They moved her to Cincinnati, where for a month she spent the greater part of every day in a room full of beveled glass windows, sifting through photographs of the life she'd lived and left behind. But it is difficult work, suffering, and in its own way a kind of art, and finally she didn't have the energy for it anymore, so she emerged from the beautiful house and fell in love with a bag boy at the supermarket. Of course, this didn't happen all at once, just like that, but in the sequence of things that's exactly the way it happened.

She liked to grocery shop. She loved it the way some people love to drive long country roads, because doing it she

[1] **beveled** (bĕv′əld) *adj.*: Having two planes that meet at a sloping edge.

FOR INCREASING STUDENT ACHIEVEMENT

GUIDED READING

Text Analysis

- In this **narrative** piece, the verb in the first sentence is in **passive voice**. This emphasizes that the girl did not choose to move. Using the passive voice immediately sets the girl up as a victim. In general, though, Rylant uses **active voice** verbs in the selection.
- Between paragraphs two and three, the story **jumps back in time**. In the second paragraph, Rylant tells the reader that the girl fell in love with a bag boy at the supermarket. Then she goes back to explain.
- Rylant uses **comparisons** to make main points about the inner lives of people. She compares the girl to a Tibetan monk, humans in general to cats, and the girls in a bookstore to honeybees. The last line compares the girl and the bag boy to strangers on a bus.
- Rylant frequently starts sentences with *And*. This gives a sense that she is adding something she just thought of, a **spur of the moment quality** that enhances the feeling that this is a story about young people who are reacting to the environment rather than carefully planning events and making decisions.

SELECTION AMENDMENT
Description of change: excerpted
Rationale: to focus on how the writer creates a mood, one of the topics for literary analysis presented in this chapter

GUIDED READING

Strategy: Reviewing

After students have read the selection from "Checkouts," ask them to review how Rylant shows the change in the girl from the beginning to the end of the selection. Ask them to compare how she reacts to the move and how she reacts to not checking out in the boy's line. Compare her ability to control the event, her emotional response, and the length of time it took her to get over the experience.

could think and relax and wander. Her parents wrote up the list and handed it to her and off she went without complaint to perform what they regarded as a great sacrifice of her time and a sign that she was indeed a very nice girl. She had never told them how much she loved grocery shopping, only that she was "willing" to do it. She had an intuition which told her that her parents were not safe for sharing such strong, important facts about herself. Let them think they knew her.

Once inside the supermarket, her hands firmly around the handle of the cart, she would lapse into a kind of reverie[2] and wheel toward the produce. Like a Tibetan monk in solitary meditation, she calmed to a point of deep, deep happiness; this feeling came to her, reliably, if strangely, only in the supermarket.

Then one day the bag boy dropped her jar of mayonnaise and that is how she fell in love. He was nervous—first day on the job—and along had come this fascinating girl, standing in the checkout line with the unfocused stare one often sees in young children, her face turned enough away that he might take several full looks at her as he packed sturdy bags full of food and the goods of modern life. She interested him because her hair was red and thick, and in it she had placed a huge orange bow, nearly the size of a small hat. That was enough to distract him, and when finally it was her groceries he was packing, she looked at him and smiled and he could respond only by busting her jar of mayonnaise on the floor, shards of glass and oozing cream decorating the area around his feet.

She loved him at exactly that moment, and if he'd known this perhaps he wouldn't have fallen into the brown

---

[2]**reverie:** A daydream.

depression he fell into, which lasted the rest of his shift. He believed he must have looked the jackass in her eyes, and he envied the sureness of everyone around him: the cocky cashier at the register, the grim and harried store manager, the bland butcher, and the brazen bag boys who smoked in the warehouse on their breaks. He wanted a second chance. Another chance to be confident and say witty things to her as he threw tin cans into her bags, persuading her to allow him to help her to her car so he might learn just a little about her, check out the floor of the car for signs of hobbies or fetishes[3] and the bumpers for clues as to her beliefs and loyalties.

But he busted her jar of mayonnaise and nothing else worked out for the rest of the day.

Strange, how attractive clumsiness can be. She left the supermarket with stars in her eyes, for she had loved the way his long nervous fingers moved from the conveyor belt to the bags, how deftly (until the mayonnaise) they had picked up her items and placed them into her bags. She had loved the way the hair kept falling into his eyes as he leaned over to grab a box or a tin. And the tattered brown shoes he wore with no socks. And the left side of his collar turned in rather than out.

The bag boy seemed a wonderful contrast to the perfectly beautiful house she had been forced to accept as her home, to the *history* she hated, to the loneliness she had become used to, and she couldn't wait to come back for more of his awkwardness and dishevelment.

Incredibly, it was another four weeks before they saw each other again. As fate would have it, her visits to the

[3] **fetishes:** An object of too much attention or reverence.

YOUR IDEAS
For Guided Reading

USING STUDENTS' STRENGTHS

Multiple Intelligences: Interpersonal

Have students write a brief version of this story from the point of view of the bag boy. They can use what Rylant says about him, but they should expand it to explain more fully why he was attracted to the girl, why he dropped the mayonnaise, and why he changed jobs.

supermarket never coincided with his schedule to bag. Each time she went to the store, her eyes scanned the checkouts at once, her heart in her mouth. And each hour he worked, the bag boy kept one eye on the door, watching for the red-haired girl with the big orange bow.

Yet in their disappointment these weeks there was a kind of ecstasy. It is reason enough to be alive, the hope you may see again some face which has meant something to you. The anticipation of meeting the bag boy eased the girl's painful transition into her new and jarring life in Cincinnati. It provided for her an anchor amid all that was impersonal and unfamiliar, and she spent less time on thoughts of what she had left behind as she concentrated on what might lie ahead. And for the boy, the long and often tedious hours at the supermarket which provided no challenge other than that of showing up the following workday . . . these hours became possibilities of mystery and romance for him as he watched the electric doors for the girl in the orange bow.

And when they finally did meet up again, neither offered a clue to the other that he, or she, had been the object of obsessive thought for weeks. She spotted him as soon as she came into the store, but she kept her eyes strictly in front of her as she pulled out a cart and wheeled it toward the produce. And he, too, knew the instant she came through the door—though the orange bow was gone, replaced by a small but bright yellow flower instead—and he never once turned his head in her direction but watched her from the corner of his vision as he tried to swallow back the fear in his throat.

It is odd how we sometimes deny ourselves the very pleasure we have longed for and which is finally within our reach. For some perverse reason she would not have been able to articulate, the girl did not bring her cart up to the bag boy's checkout when her shopping was done. And the bag boy let her leave the store, pretending not to notice her.

This is often the way of children, when they truly want a thing, to pretend they don't. And then they grow angry when no one tries harder to give them this thing they so casually rejected, and they soon find themselves in a rage simply because they cannot say yes when they mean yes. Humans are very complicated. (And perhaps cats, who have been known to react in the same way, though the resulting rage can only be guessed at.)

The girl hated herself for not checking out at the boy's line, and the boy hated himself for not catching her eye and saying hello, and they most sincerely hated each other without ever having exchanged even two minutes of conversation.

Eventually—in fact, within a week—a kind and intelligent boy who lived very near her beautiful house asked the girl to a movie and she gave up her fancy for the bag boy at the supermarket. And the bag boy himself grew so bored with his job that he made a desperate search for something better and ended up in a bookstore where scores of fascinating girls lingered like honeybees about a hive. Some months later the bag boy and the girl with the orange bow again crossed paths, standing in line with their dates at a movie theater, and, glancing toward the other, each smiled slightly, then looked away, as strangers on public buses often do, when one is moving off the bus and the other is moving on.

READER RESPONSE

You may want to use the following questions to elicit students' personal responses to the selection.

1. Have your parents ever forced you to make a major change that you felt you had no choice but to accept? Explain how you felt.
2. Do you have activities that you enjoy doing that other people think well of you for doing?
3. Rylant says that children will go into a rage when they cannot say yes when they mean yes. Describe any incidents you have observed that suggest Rylant is correct.
4. Did you like how the story ended? Explain whether Rylant provides a satisfying conclusion to the relationship between the girl and the bag boy.

ADDITIONAL RESOURCES

Composition Skills Practice	pages 51–54
Transparency Tools	GO4, VR9
Writing Prompts	pages 12–37
Connection Collection	pages C341–C342
ESL Practice and Test Preparation	pages 57–63
Writers at Work	8•1–8•10
Assessment: Chapter Test	pages 72–75
Assessment Resources	pages 1–10, 13–44, 86–92

Using *Thinking as a Writer*

You may choose to have students respond to the questions either orally or in writing.

LITERARY CONNECTION

You might want to explore writing about literature in the following works, which appear in literature textbooks at this grade level.

- "The Lady, or the Tiger" by Frank R. Stockton
- "Raymond's Run" by Toni Cade Bambara
- "There Will Come Soft Rains" by Ray Bradbury
- "Debbie" by James Herriot

Thinking as a Writer

Interpreting Theme in Fiction

- What message is the author relaying to the reader in this story? What details from the story support your interpretation?
- How realistic is this story? What elements make it seem believable? How does its realism affect its message?

Identifying Narrative Clues

Oral Expression

- What do you think the girl might say to her parents, given the chance to express herself? Write a dialogue between the girl and her parents.
- Read your dialogue aloud to your classmates. Then explain which narrative clues in the story helped you decide what to say in your letter.

Interpreting Visual Clues in Art

Viewing

- Look closely at this photo. How would you describe the relationships that are pictured? What details support your ideas?
- Write a caption for the picture. What visual clues did you use in writing your caption?

FOR DEVELOPING SKILLS

LESSON 1 *(pages C311–C316)*

OBJECTIVES

- **To respond to literature using personal experience**
- **To respond to literature using literary knowledge**

Create Interest

Ask each student to write down the names of three favorite works of literature. Have students quickly read off their lists. Write on the board the names of any works that are mentioned more than once. If no book is mentioned more than once, list some of the ones that you think several students have read. As you discuss what makes the listed works good, encourage students to provide specific examples rather than just general impressions.

The Power of Writing About Literature

Works of literature include novels, plays, poems, and short stories. You have probably read many works of literature. You have probably also written book reports. You may have shared your opinion of a book with a friend or written a review of a school play.

Uses of Writing About Literature

Some examples for writing about literature in everyday life are listed below.

- **Book critics write about literature in their reviews** for print and for electronic media.
- **Publishers issue catalogs and other promotional materials** that convey information about their publications.
- **Educators write about literature for scholarly journals and books** as well as in preparation for lectures and classes.
- **Students write about literature in book reports.**

CAREERS AND COMMUNICATION

Literary Critic

The success of literary works is shaped by thoughtful responses of literary critics. In book reviews and articles in newspapers and literary magazines, literary critics shape the public reaction to new novels, short stories, and collections of poetry. Few people make their entire living by commenting on the literature of others. Most literary critics have another job in the book world. They might be also be a writer of literature, a book review editor for a newspaper or journal, an editor for a publishing company, a literary agent who links writers with publishers, a writing instructor at a writers' workshop, or a literature professor at a college or university. All of these fields reward people with skill in reading and reacting to literature.

Encourage students to read several reviews of one book. They can find reviews in newspapers, magazines and journals, and on the Internet. Students can read excerpts from reviews at the major Internet booksellers. An excellent place to begin finding book reviews is *Book Review Digest*. You may also wish to introduce students to collected works of literary criticism, such as *Twentieth Century Literary Criticism*. After students have read examples of book reviews and literary criticism, ask them to write a critical analysis of a work of literature they have read.

Guide Instruction

By Modeling Response

Tell students about your personal response to a literary work. Choose a work that has been significant to you, either one you read when you were your students' age or one you have read more recently. Explain how and why the work affected you. Focus on the circumstances in your life that conditioned your response to the book.

Consolidate Skills

Through Guided Practice

Have students complete the **Practice Your Skills** activity on responding from personal experience on page C314. To extend this activity, ask students to read the specific excerpts from "Thank You, M'am" on page C194 that shaped their responses to the questions.

Apply to Communication

Through Independent Writing

Have students write a response to a poem in which they draw upon their previous reading experience. They can select a new or familiar work. Encourage them to compare it to others, particularly by the same poet, on the same topic, or in the same form.

REACHING ALL STUDENTS

English Language Learners

Students learning English may not have read many of the literary works that other students in the class have read. Have these students select and read a book that others in the class have enjoyed. Also assign a helper who is familiar with the book to assist the student learning English. The helper should talk with the student regularly to answer any questions about plot and to help analyze the book when the student has finished it.

USING STUDENTS' STRENGTHS

Multiple Intelligences: Musical

Ask students to compare reading a book to listening to a piece of music. Emphasize how they are both interactive experiences. The reader/listener brings experience to the book/music that shapes the response to it. As the experiences of the reader/listener change, so will the reaction to the work.

Developing Your Skills of Writing About Literature

"Literature," wrote author Roland Barthes, "is the question minus the answer." Writing about a particular piece of literature is often the closest you can come to providing the answer to its question. The form in which you write about a work of literature can range from the informal to the formal. An informal piece of writing about literature might take the form of something as simple as quick notes jotted in your **journal**. Creating a carefully developed composition requires not only more thought, but also clear and concise writing.

A **literary analysis** presents an interpretation of a work of literature and supports that interpretation with appropriate details and quotations from the work.

Your Writer's Journal

Begin the practice of keeping a record of your reactions to works you are reading. Start today, beginning with the following suggestions. You can use any story you are currently reading, or write in response to "Checkouts."

- Tell what you liked or disliked about what you read.
- Write about anything that left a strong impression or that puzzled you.
- Keep track of how your feelings about the characters change.
- Make predictions about what you think will happen next.

Transfer to Everyday Life

By Connecting Events and Literature

Have students keep a list of events that remind them of a story or poem. Each student should list between four and eight examples. A student who encounters a stern but loving adult might remember "Thank You M'am."

Pull It All Together

By Sharing

Ask students if they have ever read a book more than once. If so, ask them how their response to it differed each time and what caused the difference. Highlight comments that indicate that the difference reflected changes in the student's life or literary knowledge.

Check Understanding

By Predicting the Future

Ask students to predict how they might react to "Thank You, M'am" as adults: how their perspective on the world will change, how they might evaluate behavior differently, and how their identification with a character might change.

Responding from Personal Experience

The American writer Ralph Waldo Emerson wrote: "'Tis the good reader that makes the good book." By that he probably meant that the reader helps create the meaning in a poem, story, novel, or play. Readers do not simply curl up in a comfortable chair and let the writer do all the work. Instead, each reader brings all of his or her own past experiences and uses them to "fill out" and make sense of the writer's world. Good readers learn to be aware of how their unique experiences help shape their responses to literary works. Developing this awareness is one of the most important parts of prewriting.

One way a reader responds to literature is by drawing on personal memories and associations. Responding in this way means letting a work of literature trigger memories and feelings from your own life. For example, if you are reading a story about a circus, and you once had a fun experience at a circus, chances are those pleasant memories will be rekindled as you read the story and color your reaction to the work.

Writing Tip

Literary works mean different things to different readers. Responding from **personal experience** will help you discover what a literary work means to you.

Personal Response Strategies

1. In your **journal**, freewrite answers to the following questions:
   - Where in the poem, story, novel, or play do you see yourself? What character(s) do you identify with? Are there characters that remind you of people you know?
   - How does the work make you feel? Why?

IDENTIFYING COMMON STUMBLING BLOCKS

Problem

- Not wanting to discuss embarrassing or private memories triggered by literature

Solution

- Remind students that they should not feel pressure to say or write things for class that they do not want to share with others. However, students may find that writing about issues they think are embarrassing or private will help them put past events into perspective. Encourage students to write about these memories and to keep these writings to themselves.

REACHING ALL STUDENTS

English Language Learners

Students learning English may have difficulty expressing their responses to literature using a limited English vocabulary. Remind these students that the freewriting they do in their journals is an excellent time to practice their English, since they are not expected to focus on grammar, usage, or mechanics. It is also a place where they can move back and forth between languages.

HOME WORK

After students have answered the personal response questions, have them consider why Langston Hughes wrote this story. Students should write a paragraph explaining whether they think they were part of the audience that Hughes had in mind when he wrote it.

- If you were a character in the work, would you have behaved differently? What behaviors in the story puzzle you?
- What experiences from your own life come to mind as you read this work? How did those experiences make you feel?

2. Write a personal response statement. In this statement, explain what the work means to you.
3. In small discussion groups, share your various reactions to the previous questions. Feel free to adjust your reactions if your classmates suggest ideas that make sense to you. After the discussion write freely about how, if at all, your ideas about the work changed after talking with your classmates.

PRACTICE YOUR SKILLS

Responding from Personal Experience

Read "Thank You, M'am" by Langston Hughes on page C194. Then complete the following questions and activities.

1. What do you think of the boy in "Thank You, M'am"? Does he remind you of anyone you know? How would you describe him? What do you think of the woman in the story? Does she remind you of anyone you know?
2. When you were reading the story, did you predict the outcome? If not, why did you think the story would end differently?
3. Write about events in your life that came to mind when you read the story.

Communicate Your Ideas

PREWRITING *Personal Response*

Reread "Checkouts" on pages C305–C309. Use the Personal Response Strategies to explore your reactions to the story. Then write a personal response statement explaining what the story means to you. Save your work for later use.

YOUR SAVE WORK

Responding from Literary Knowledge

In addition to responding from personal experience, good readers also use all their previous reading experiences to help them interpret a work of literature. When you respond in this way, you use your knowledge of literature (based on other stories, poems, or novels you have read) to identify and appreciate the various literary elements in the work you are currently reading. In contrast to responding personally, you pay more attention to the work itself than to your personal reactions.

You may wish to review the elements of fiction on page C199.

The following strategies will help you understand the elements in a literary work. Writing and small group discussions will help you carry out these strategies.

Literary Knowledge Strategies

Fiction

- Examine the plot (sequence of events) of the story. Identify the key events in the story and the meaning or significance of each one. Identify the major conflict in the story.
- Look closely at the main character. What is his or her motivation, or reason, for behaving as he or she does?

TIMESAVER *QuickCheck*

Ask students to show you the one sentence that best summarizes their response to the story. Check that students have given a personal response rather than a general comment on the story.

HOME STUDY

Students can write their personal response to "Checkouts" at home. Remind students to use precise verbs to describe how they felt.

REACHING ALL STUDENTS

Advanced Learners

Encourage students to find out more about the author of "Thank You, M'am," Langston Hughes. James Madison University maintains a Website with links to several excellent sites on Hughes at http://falcon.jmu.edu/~ramseyil/hughes.htm.

Struggling Learners

Students who have difficulty recognizing the meter of a poem may try clapping the rhythm as they read the poem. As they clap they should listen for which words or syllables they feel like clapping louder. These accented points provide the meter for the poem.

- Look closely at the setting. What are the most important details in the setting? What overall feeling do they convey?
- Express in your own words what you think the theme (message) of the story is. Use details from the story, including the title, to help explain the theme.

Poetry

- Identify the speaker in the poem.
- Describe the meter of the poem and explain how it adds to the feeling the poem conveys.
- Describe the rhyme scheme, if any, of the poem and explain how it contributes to the poem's overall effect.
- Identify any figures of speech and explain their purpose.

PRACTICE YOUR SKILLS

Prewriting Plot Diagram

Review the prewriting work you have done so far. Use the Literary Knowledge Strategies to further react to the story, this time from your prior knowledge of literature. You may wish to use a plot diagram to help you organize your thoughts. The one below is started for you. Use your completed diagram to help you evaluate the importance of each event.

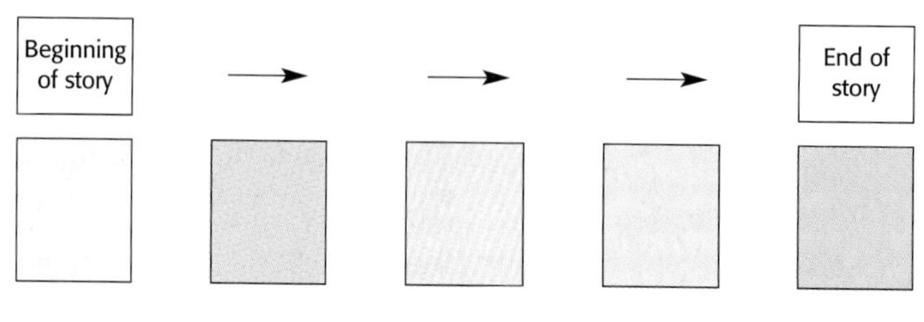

PLOT

LESSON 2 *(pages C317–C326)*

OBJECTIVE

- **To follow prewriting steps in writing a literary analysis, such as choosing a subject, limiting a subject, developing a thesis, gathering evidence, and creating an informal outline**

Create Interest

Read to students a very short literary work, such as one of Aesop's fables. As a class, plan a literary analysis of the work. Take notes on the board of information that students think should be in the literary analysis.

Guide Instruction

By Modeling Strategies

Explain to students that a more systematic way to prepare to write a literary analysis would be to follow these steps: choose a specific subject, limit the subject, develop a thesis, gather evidence, and create an informal outline.

Process of Writing About Literature

At this point you have read and responded to a work of literature, calling on both your personal experiences and literary knowledge. You have also explored these responses in writing.

Prewriting Writing Process

The prewriting stage is probably the most important stage in preparing a literary analysis. Careful planning and choosing of a subject is the best preparation for drafting.

Choosing a Subject

You can now draw on your previous work to develop a subject for writing about literature. In some cases you will be assigned a subject for writing about literature. In other cases, however, you may be expected to choose your own subject. The questions below will help you think of subjects of personal interest.

Questions for Choosing a Subject

- What parts of the work puzzle me? What would I like to understand better?
- What parts of the work move me especially? Why do they have that effect on me?
- What images or details made a strong impression on me? What do they contribute to the overall work?

USING STUDENTS' STRENGTHS

Multiple Intelligences: Logical

Compared to personal response strategies, literary knowledge strategies depend more on analytical skills. Suggest that students create a three-column table to help them organize information about a literary work. In the first column on the left, list the type of information needed. These types can be based on those described in the Literary Knowledge Strategies box in the text. In the middle column, students can list references to specific lines in the literary work that provide the information needed. In the third column, students can list their interpretation of that information.

Multiple Intelligences: Interpersonal

In addition to analyzing the main character, students can analyze the relationships among characters. In "Thank You M'am" and many other literary works, the interaction between two characters is what drives the plot and what determines the theme.

Consolidate Skills
Through Guided Practice
The **Practice Your Skills** activity on choosing subjects gives students practice in thinking of possible subjects for literary analysis. You can extend the activity by having students share their ideas in class. Help students realize that they can explore one literary element in one literary work from many perspectives.

Apply to Communication
Through Independent Writing
After students complete the **Communicate Your Ideas** activity on limiting subjects, have students write an explanation of how they decided to limit their subject. They should explain how they concluded that their topic was narrow enough but not too narrow for their literary analysis.

Transfer to Everyday Life
By Discussing Limits
Ask students how they limit their focus in other areas of their life. For example,

HOME WORK
Assign students to respond to the questions in the **Practice Your Skills** activity for another work of literature. They can select a novel, short story, or a poem that they like.

Practice Your Skills Sample Answers
1. character: the character of Mrs. Jones
2. theme: the power of compassion in affecting behavior
3. writer's style: the effective use of dialogue
4. images and repeated details: Mrs. Jones's pocketbook

- With which character do I identify, and why?
- What message does the work convey to me?
- How do the characters in the work differ? What makes each one "tick"?

You will probably find the answers to some of these questions in the responses you have already made in your **journal**. Carefully review your written responses looking for aspects of the literary work that hold the most interest for you. It is also a good idea to reread the literary work to see if you have any fresh, new responses now that you have had a chance to become better acquainted with the work. One of your new insights, or one of the answers to the questions above, could become the subject for a composition about literature.

Practice Your Skills

Choosing Subjects

Review "Thank You, M'am" on page C194. For each of the following literary elements, think of a possible subject for writing about "Thank You, M'am."

Example	theme
Possible Answer	the importance of choice in everyday relationships

1. character
2. theme
3. writer's style
4. images and repeated details

if they like music, how many instruments are they learning to play? If they want to go to college, how many classes are they taking designed to prepare them for college? If they have a part-time job, how many hours a week do they work?

Pull It All Together

By Sharing

Ask students to share examples of notes they have written. As students read them, discuss why the student wrote each one down, and how each may be useful later.

Check Understanding

By Reviewing Thesis Sentences

Ask five students to suggest possible main idea statements for a literary analysis. Write each one on the board. As a class, discuss the strengths and weakness of each one, and consider ways to improve each.

Writing Is Thinking

Synthesizing

When you are choosing a subject for a composition about literature on your own, it is helpful to use the skill of synthesizing. **Synthesizing** means combining, or bringing together. In your search for a meaningful subject, you can combine your personal response with your literary response.

To see how this process works, begin by reading the story "Thank You, M'am" by Langston Hughes on page C194. Then write a personal response statement to the story like the following:

> Everyone makes mistakes, and some mistakes are bigger than others. I like the way this story makes the point that important lessons can be learned from the mistakes you make—I know I've learned some! Mrs. Jones cares about teaching Roger what's right. My aunt talks to me the same way. She believes I'm a good kid, just like Mrs. Jones believes Roger is a good kid.

THINKING PRACTICE

Reread "Checkouts" on page C305. Using the Elements in a Short Story chart on page C199, write a paragraph that combines your personal response to the short story with your literary response. Use the sample response paragraph above as your model.

Using Writing is Thinking

Objective

- **To practice combining personal experience with literary response in writing a literary analysis**

A DIFFERENT APPROACH

Visual

Have students respond to pieces of literature with a drawing. They might sketch a representational scene from the work, or they might create a more abstract visual that shows the emotions the literature caused them to feel.

Kinesthetic

Have students respond to pieces of literature with three-dimensional works of art. They might use clay, paper maché, or other materials. Their works might be representational or more abstract. Either way, they should write one or two paragraphs to help viewers interpret their work.

Thinking Skills	
Classifying	Analyzing
Comparing	Hypothesizing
Generalizing	Synthesizing
Inferring	Summarizing
Imagining	Setting Goals
Observing	Evaluating Audience
Predicting	

TIMESAVER *QuickCheck*

Ask students to self-check their work. Ask them

- if they have identified one clear subject.
- whether they have drawn upon their personal response.
- whether they have drawn upon their literary response.

HOME STUDY

Have students extend this activity by discussing the subject they have selected with another member of their household. The process of explaining it may help them analyze their response to "Checkouts."

Communicate Your Ideas

PREWRITING *Subject*

Carefully review both your personal and literary responses to "Checkouts." Synthesize your personal and literary responses to help you think of a personally meaningful subject. *(You may wish to look over the Questions for Choosing a Subject on page C317 to give you ideas.)* Write your subject on a piece of paper and save it for later use.

Limiting a Subject

If you have followed the process of synthesizing your personal and literary responses to choose a subject, chances are good that the subject you have come up with is suitably limited. A clearly focused, limited subject will keep your analysis from meandering aimlessly through a general discussion of the literary work.

To test whether your subject is suitably limited, ask yourself whether you can express your subject in a phrase rather than a single word. If you can express your subject only in a single word, then ask yourself "What about [my subject] do I want to say?" until you can express your subject in a phrase. Here is an example of how one student limited a subject for the story "Checkouts."

Too General	the supermarket
Ask Yourself	What about the supermarket do I want to say?
Possible Answer	the importance of the supermarket
Suitably limited	what the supermarket symbolizes to the girl

PRACTICE YOUR SKILLS

Limiting Subjects

Each of the following subjects is too broad for a brief composition about "Thank You, M'am." Write a suitably limited subject for each one.

EXAMPLE	Mrs. Jones
POSSIBLE ANSWER	what Mrs. Jones stands for in the story

1. choice
2. learning a lesson
3. making mistakes
4. speaking with actions
5. Roger

Communicate Your Ideas

PREWRITING *Limited Subject*

Review the subject you chose for writing about the story "Checkouts." If you have expressed your subject in a single word, ask yourself, "What about my subject?" until you have a clearly focused phrase. Save your limited subject for later use.

Developing Your Thesis

Like other kinds of compositions, writing about literature develops one main idea, or **thesis**. Your clearly focused subject is just a step away from your thesis. In fact, your focused subject is like the subject of a sentence without the verb. To complete the "sentence," you need to pin down the exact statement you want to make about your subject. In the

HOME WORK

Have students write three more subjects for a literary analysis on "Thank You, M'am." They should select subjects that are limited enough for a brief analysis.

PRACTICE YOUR SKILLS Sample Answers

1. choice: Roger's choice not to run out of Mrs. Jones's room
2. learning a lesson: the lesson that Mrs. Jones had learned when she was young
3. making mistakes: the learning that came from Roger's mistake
4. speaking with actions: how Mrs. Jones demonstrated her concern for Roger
5. Roger: how Roger changed by the end of the story

TIMESAVER *QuickCheck*

Review students' work to see that they have written a clearly focused phrase. Students who have only one word or have a long sentence should rework their subject.

IDENTIFYING COMMON STUMBLING BLOCKS

Problem

- Writing a vague main idea statement

Solution

- Ask students to write a main idea statement that is specific enough that other people could disagree with it. A main idea statement that no one could disagree with is probably too general or too vague to be useful in shaping a composition.

TIMESAVER *QuickCheck*

Ask students to self-check their work. They should be sure that they have written a well-focused, complete sentence.

HOME STUDY

Have students read their sentence aloud. They should be sure that it is a clear, well-written sentence.

following example, notice how the thesis goes one step further and makes a complete statement about the subject.

FOCUSED, LIMITED SUBJECT	how the story uses mother-son imagery
THESIS	In "Thank You, M'am," mother-son imagery is used to stress the importance of Roger's encounter with Mrs. Jones.

In the limited subject, there is not a complete statement about how the story uses mother-son imagery. In the thesis, the statement is completed with the addition of the phrase "to stress the importance of Roger's encounter with Mrs. Jones."

To develop your thesis, cast your focused, limited subject into the form of a complete sentence. Pin your subject down by saying something definite and concrete about it. Once again, you can ask yourself, "What *about* my subject?" until you have a statement that is expressed in a complete sentence.

Remember you can adjust and improve your thesis statement during drafting and revising. Even in its rough form, however, your thesis statement will help you develop the rest of your composition.

Communicate Your Ideas

PREWRITING *Thesis*

Review your focused, limited subject. To develop your thesis, cast your limited subject in the form of a complete sentence and write it in your **journal**. Save your work for later use.

Gathering Evidence

After clearly expressing your composition's thesis, you can move on to gathering evidence to support it. In most cases the evidence you use will be specific parts of the literary work's dialogue, description, and events, as well as your interpretation of them.

When developing a list of supporting details for your analysis, skim the literary work from start to finish looking for any and all details that help support your thesis statement. For example, if you were writing about how mother-son imagery is used to stress the importance of Roger's encounter with Mrs. Jones in "Thank You, M'am," you would look for details that show how Roger's encounter with Mrs. Jones is an important one. You would also look for any references to mother-son imagery.

On separate pieces of paper or note cards, jot down each detail as you come across it, and put a page reference beside it so you can return easily to that spot if you need to read it again. You may also want to make a brief note to yourself about why you think the detail is important in supporting your thesis.

The note cards that follow show how a writer gathered evidence to support the thesis that mother-son imagery in "Thank You, M'am" is used to stress the importance of Roger's encounter with Mrs. Jones. Notice that the evidence is drawn from the story's narration as well as the dialogue.

GETTING STUDENTS

Cooperative Learning

After students have written their main idea statements, divide them into small groups. Have students take turns reading their main idea sentences and discussing with the other students what support they find in the story.

YOUR IDEAS

For Gathering Evidence

Model: Gathering Evidence

Thesis: In "Thank You, M'am," by Langston Hughes, mother-son imagery is used to stress the importance of Roger's encounter with Mrs. Jones.

After that the woman said, "Pick up my pocketbook, boy, and give it here." She still held him. But she bent down enough to permit him to stop and pick up her purse. Then she said, "Now ain't you ashamed of yourself?"

Firmly gripped by his shirt front, the boy said, "Yes'm."

The woman said, "You ought to be my son. I would teach you right from wrong. Least I can do right now is to wash your face. Are you hungry?"

"No'm," said the being-dragged boy. "I just want you to turn me loose."

"Was I bothering *you* when I turned that corner?" asked the woman.

"No'm."

"But you put yourself in contact with *me*," said the woman. "If you think that that contact is not going to last awhile, you got another thought coming. When I get through with you, sir, you are going to remember Luella Bates Washington Jones."

1. the woman said, "Pick up my pocketbook, boy, and give it here," and "Now ain't you ashamed of yourself?" (page C195)
—shows Mrs. Jones as strong disciplinarian set on teaching

Roger a lesson, seems to be treating him as a disappointed mother would treat a son; Roger reacts by saying he is ashamed.

2. Mrs. Jones tells Roger plainly "you ought to be my son." says she would teach him right from wrong, and to wash his face; asks if he is hungry; declares he won't forget the fact that he chose to put himself in contact

with her (page C195)
—actions and words show that she treats him as she would a misbehaving child, with firmness but with compassion and concern for his well being; makes clear statement that

this encounter will be one the boy will remember for a long time

"Eat some more, son," she said.

When they were finished eating she got up and said, "Now, here, take this ten dollars and buy yourself some blue suede shoes. And next time, do not make the mistake of latching onto *my* pocketbook *nor nobody else's*—because shoes come by devilish like that will burn your feet. I got to get my rest now. But I wish you would behave yourself, son, from here on in.

She led him down the hall to the front door and opened it. "Good night! Behave yourself, boy!" she said, looking out into the street.

The boy wanted to say something else other than, "Thank you, m'am," to Mrs. Luella Bates Washington Jones, but he couldn't do so as he turned at the barren stoop and looked back at the large woman in the door. He barely managed to say, "Thank you," before she shut the door. And he never saw her again.

3. Mrs. Jones calls Roger "son" and "boy", she feeds him, gives him money to buy shoes, tells him to behave himself; Roger reacts by wanting to "say something else" (page C198)

—Language and actions work to reinforce mother-son imagery; Mrs. Jones gives Roger food, money and more discipline. Roger reacts by feeling that he wants to say something—he

is changed now, and Mrs. Jones's large body filling the doorframe indicates she has taken on a larger meaning in boy's eyes

Communicate Your Ideas

PREWRITING *Evidence*

Skim the story "Checkouts" looking for details that support your thesis. Jot the details on note cards, along with the page number and a note telling how the detail supports your thesis.

TIMESAVER *QuickCheck*

Ask several students to tell the class how many details they found to support their work. Discuss with students how many details they need to write a strong paragraph. If students have too few details, they may want to read "Checkouts" more closely to find more details. Or, they may want to revise their main idea statement to make it broader.

HOME STUDY

Encourage students to talk about their main idea statement with a partner from the class. They can discuss possible details that support each other's main idea.

INTEGRATING TECHNOLOGY

Internet

Several Internet sites include poetry. The Academy of American Poets at http://www.poets.org/ is an excellent resource for poems, information about poets, and audio clips of poetry readings. The Favorite Poem Project at http://www.favoritepoem.org/ includes poems and commentary submitted by a wide variety of Americans.

Organizing Supporting Details into an Informal Outline

After you have collected as many supporting details as you can find, think carefully about the best order in which to present them. The nature of your thesis will help determine the best order for your supporting details. For example, if your thesis involves comparison and contrast, you may begin by showing all the aspects that are alike, and then move on to showing all the aspects that are different. Or if your thesis involves analyzing a character's motivation, you may present your details in order of importance *(See page C109)*. In some cases, you may even present the details in the order in which they appear in the story. This type of order, related to chronological order, would be useful to show how a character changes over time, for example *(See page C109)*.

After deciding on a logical order for your details, make a simple list, chart, or informal outline showing the order. An informal outline is a quick way to show the organizational plan of your composition. The following is an informal outline for a composition about "Thank You, M'am." The details are arranged in order of importance, as judged by the writer.

Model: Informal Outline

1. Introduction to include thesis statement: In "Thank You, M'am" mother-son imagery is used to describe the encounter between the characters.
2. Body

   1st detail: Mrs. Jones disciplines Roger, yet at same time tells him she will make sure he washes his face, Roger reacts by saying "Yes m'am" and saying he is ashamed of his behavior

LESSON 3 *(pages C327–C338)*

OBJECTIVES

- **To draft and revise a literary analysis**
- **To edit and publish a literary analysis**

Create Interest

Have students identify the literary work that they have been using for their prewriting activities in this chapter. Ask students to share with the class why they like the literary work and whether they think others in the class would enjoy it.

Guide Instruction

By Connecting Ideas

Point out to students that the final four stages of the writing process—drafting, revising, editing, and publishing—are closely connected to the prewriting stage. Prewriting provides the basis for the rest of the stages, just as the base of a building provides the foundation

2nd detail: Mrs. Jones's own words ("you ought to be my son")

3rd detail: Mrs. Jones feeds Roger, calls him "son" and "boy," gives him money, tells him to "behave"

4th detail: Mrs. Jones's own words "you are going to remember Luella Bates Washington Jones"

5th detail: Roger wants to say something other than thank you, encounter with Mrs. Jones has taken larger meaning for him

3. Conclusion

Communicate Your Ideas

PREWRITING *Supporting Details*

Return to your prewriting work. Decide on an appropriate order for your supporting details and create an informal outline showing an organizational plan for your composition. Save your work for later use.

Drafting

Writing Process

With your informal outline as a guide, drafting your composition about literature is a matter of putting your ideas into flowing sentences. The following guidelines will help you draft the introduction, body, and conclusion of your composition.

TIMESAVER *QuickCheck*

Check to see that students have used outline form. They should have the main divisions clearly apparent, with the appropriate details under each one.

HOME STUDY

Students can create their outline on a computer. Word processing programs often include assistance, such as special templates, for making outlines.

on which a building is constructed. The later stages of the writing process include all of the details and final touches that make the final product both useful and pleasing.

Consolidate Skills

Through Guided Practice

Have each student make a list of four types of changes he or she might make in a literary analysis during the last four stages of the writing process. For example, students might list adding transitions, revising topic sentences, checking spellings, and making a clean copy. Have students take turns reading items from their list. Ask other students which stage would be the most appropriate place in which to make that change.

IDENTIFYING COMMON STUMBLING BLOCKS

Problem

- Limiting one's analysis to whether the student liked the piece of literature or not

Solution

- If students cannot answer the question why they like the piece or not, ask them to focus on one particular aspect of the work that affected them, either a character they could identify with, an environment they are familiar with, or an event that is similar to one they have experienced.

  Using this one aspect, they can develop their ideas about character, setting, or plot to write an analysis of this aspect.

Guidelines for Drafting a Composition About Literature

- In the introduction be sure to identify the title and the author of the work you are discussing.
- Include your thesis statement somewhere in the introduction, revised if necessary, and worked in as smoothly as possible.
- In the body of your composition, include clearly organized supporting details. Be sure to use transitions to show how one detail relates to another. Throughout your composition, use direct quotes from the work if they strengthen the points you are trying to make. Always enclose direct quotes in quotation marks.
- In the conclusion draw together, or synthesize, the details you have included to reinforce the main idea of your literary analysis.
- Add a title that suggests the focus of your composition.

As you read the following model of a composition about literature, notice how each part of the composition works to clarify or support the main idea. Your first draft will no doubt be less polished than this finished analysis. Just use this model to help you include all the necessary parts of your first draft.

MODEL: Composition About Literature

TITLE: SUGGESTS FOCUS OF COMPOSITION

Thank You, Mom: Mother-Son Imagery in "Thank You, M'am"

INTRODUCTION: IDENTIFIES TITLE, AUTHOR, AND THESIS

In Langston Hughes's short story "Thank You, M'am," mother-son imagery is used throughout the story to stress the lasting importance of the encounter between the two main characters. When a young man named

Transfer to Everyday Life

Reading Movie Reviews

Ask students to read a movie review of a movie they have seen and feel strongly about (negatively or positively). They can find reviews in newspapers, online and in movie anthologies. Ask them whether they agree or disagree with the reviewer concerning the movie. Even if they disagree, ask the student whether they can acknowledge the line of reasoning of the movie reviewer.

Pull It All Together

By Reflecting

Ask students if they feel differently about the literary piece they wrote an analysis on. Many times after a closer, more analytic look, a person has a different feeling about the piece. Encourage students that this feeling is normal, and shows how much they have learned.

Roger attempts to steal a purse from a large woman named Luella Bates Washington Jones, not only does the "frail and willow-wild" Roger not get Mrs. Jones's purse, but she publicly disciplines him. Mrs. Jones quickly turns the dynamics of their relationship from victim and criminal to angry mother and regretful son—teaching Roger a lesson he will never forget.

FIRST BODY PARAGRAPH

From the moment Mrs. Jones and Roger encounter one another, Mrs. Jones is portrayed as a strong disciplinarian set on teaching a misbehaving child an important lesson. After Roger falls to the ground while trying to steal her purse, Mrs. Jones holds on to him, demanding, "Now ain't you ashamed of yourself?" She reacts to Roger as a disappointed mother would react to her own son: not only with firmness but also with compassion and concern for his well-being. And Roger reacts in kind, acknowledging that he is, in fact, ashamed of his behavior.

SECOND BODY PARAGRAPH

As the story develops, other words and actions work to reinforce the mother-son imagery established in the story's opening scene. Even as Mrs. Jones lectures Roger, she tells him she has a "great mind to wash [his] face for [him]." Later, Mrs. Jones says to Roger directly, "You ought to be my son. I would teach you right from wrong." She takes Roger to her home, fixes him dinner, and asks that he comb his hair so he will look "presentable." After they eat Mrs. Jones gives Roger money so that he can buy a pair of shoes, and, calling him "son," admonishes him to "behave...from here on in."

YOUR IDEAS

For Writing About Literature

Check Understanding

By Self-Evaluating

Encourage students to consider publishing their literary analysis. How do they feel their piece of work would be useful to understanding the work of literature? Do they feel they have provided some insight to the work? Perhaps you can suggest collecting the analyses and producing a literary review kept in the school library.

TIMESAVER *QuickCheck*

Ask students to self-check their drafts. Ask them if they have used topic sentences and concluding sentences in each paragraph.

HOME STUDY

After students complete their drafts, encourage them to make a list of additional information that would be helpful to making their point. They might list information they could find in the story or in research about the author.

Third Body Paragraph

The relationship between Mrs. Jones and Roger is, of course, surprising. Although these two people have just met under negative circumstances, an immediate, positive, nurturing relationship has formed. There is perhaps no relationship more important than the relationship between a parent and a child. Mrs. Jones tells Roger that his contact with her will "last awhile....When I get through with you, sir, you are going to remember Luella Bates Washington Jones." Roger's contact with Mrs. Jones is, in fact, relatively brief.

Conclusion: Reinforces thesis statement

But when he sees Mrs. Jones's large body filling the doorframe in the last scene of the story, and feels that he *wants* to say something—something other than just "thank you"—it is clear that the impact will be permanent.

Communicate Your Ideas

DRAFTING *Writing About Literature*

Using the guidelines on page C328 and your prewriting work, write your first draft about "Checkouts." Remember to stop every now and then and read over what you have written to keep your ideas on track. Save your draft for revising later.

Revising

Writing Process

Before revising your writing about literature, you may wish to share it with peers to see what they think is good about your writing and what they think could be improved. After receiving their comments, try to improve your composition to make it the best it can be. The following checklist will help you revise your writing about literature.

Evaluation Checklist for Revising

Checking Your Composition

✓ Do you have a strong introduction that identifies the author and work you will discuss? *(pages C317–C318)*

✓ Does your introduction contain a clearly worded thesis statement? *(pages C321–C322)*

✓ Does the body of your composition provide ample details and evidence from the work to support your thesis? *(pages C323–C325)*

✓ Did you use quotes from the work to strengthen your points? *(page C323)*

✓ Does your conclusion synthesize the details in the body of your composition and reinforce your thesis statement? *(pages C326–C327)*

✓ Does your composition have unity and coherence? *(pages C327–C328)*

✓ Did you add a title showing the focus of your composition? *(pages C328)*

Checking Your Paragraphs

✓ Does each paragraph have a topic sentence? *(page C328)*

✓ Is each paragraph unified and coherent? *(page C328)*

Checking Your Sentences and Words

✓ Are your sentences varied and concise? *(pages C53–C55)*

✓ Did you use lively, specific words? *(pages C49–C53)*

YOUR IDEAS

For Revising

TIMESAVER *QuickCheck*

Check with students as they are commenting on each other's drafts. Remind students to be positive and supportive, even as they suggest ways to improve the other student's paper.

HOME STUDY

Students can ask someone else in their household to read their draft. Students should tell readers that they are looking at a first draft that will be revised, and request that readers focus on the general content rather than on specific problems with grammar, usage, or mechanics.

FYI

How to Use with Windows™ To save revisions to a file, press the Control key and the S key at the same time. Encourage students to develop the habit of saving their work often, at least every ten minutes and after every major change they make to the text.

How to Use with Macintosh™ To save revisions to a file, press the Command key and the S key at the same time. To save a new version of the file, press F12 and select a new name fo the file.

COMPUTER TIP

You can use the Save As feature on your computer to save different versions of your composition. During the revision process you may wish to return to a previous version to review or reevaluate the changes you have made. Give each version a different file name to avoid overwriting files. You can find the Save As feature under the File heading on your toolbar.

File	Edit	View	Insert	Format
New...				⌘N
Open...				⌘O
Open Web Page...				
Close				⌘W
Save				⌘S
Save As...				
Save as HTML...				
Versions...				
Page Setup...				
Print Preview				
Print...				⌘P
Send To				▶
Properties...				

Communicate Your Ideas

REVISING *Conferencing*

Exchange papers with a partner. Comment on the strengths and weaknesses of your partner's paper and make suggestions for improvement. Be very specific in your suggestions. Keep your partner's comments in mind as you use the Evaluation Checklist for Revising to improve your draft. Save your work for later use.

Grammar in the Writing Process

Participles

Participles are particularly versatile and expressive forms that a writer can use for a variety of purposes. A **participle** is a word that is formed from a verb but acts like an adjective by modifying a noun. A participle also has characteristics of a verb—it can be turned into a **participial phrase** by joining it with a complement or a prepositional phrase, and it can be modified by an adverb. Participles are especially useful for creating a vivid sense that several things are happening at once. Consider the following sentence from "Checkouts."

> Some months later the bag boy and the girl with the orange bow again crossed paths, **standing** in line with their dates at a movie theater, and, **glancing** toward the other, each smiled slightly, then looked away, as strangers on public buses do, when one is moving off the bus and the other is moving on.

By using participial phrases, the author vividly relates—in a single sentence—the circumstances, the underlying emotions, and the delicate tension of this brief, final meeting. The following example shows how you can use participial phrases to combine simple sentences and highlight the relationship between ideas.

Two Sentences	The bag boy let her leave the store. He pretended not to notice her.
Combined	The bag boy let her leave the store, **pretending not to notice her.**

Using *Editing Workshop*

Objective

- **To practice using participial phrases**

A DIFFERENT APPROACH

Visual Have students draw sketches to illustrate each example sentence at the bottom of page C333. Then have students paraphrase to tell about their sketches. Remind students to use participial phrases in their sentences.

TIMESAVER *QuickCheck*
Glance at student papers to be sure they are neat and easy to read. Have students redo any papers that are not.

HOME STUDY
Students can make their final copy of their literary analysis at home. The final copy should be as neat as possible.

Editing

Writing Process

When you are satisfied that your composition clearly conveys your interpretation of the work you have chosen to write about, you can move on to polishing it and presenting it to readers. The following checklist will help you edit your work. In the process of editing, use the proofreading marks on page C37.

Editing Checklist

- ✓ Are your sentences free of errors in grammar and usage?
- ✓ Did you spell each word correctly?
- ✓ Did you capitalize and punctuate correctly?
- ✓ Did you use quotation marks around all direct quotations from the work?
- ✓ Did you check your Personalized Editing Checklist to make sure you have avoided errors you sometimes make?

Communicate Your Ideas

EDITING

Use the Editing Checklist and your Personalized Editing Checklist to catch any errors you might have made in your final draft of your composition about "Checkouts."

Screenplay

In a book everything must be described. The setting, plot, and characters are all determined by words. In a movie, images, scenery, costumes, music, and actors can show in an instant something that in a book may have taken pages to describe. In a book the words on the page create images in your imagination. In a movie the images are created for you.

Media Activity

Reread the scene from *Romeo and Juliet* on pages C215–C218 and write a paragraph telling how you would turn it into a screenplay. Remember there are many differences between these two forms. One offers a story in words alone, while the other uses visual aids, actors, music, and dialogue to tell the story. Writing a screenplay means taking out words that do not further the action of the story and including images that invoke the atmosphere on the page. Be sure to include information about the camera angles, sets, and props you want to include. Then change the scene into a script. Here is an example.

> Jane *(a small, dark-haired woman, exotic)*: I don't know what happened to my purse. I have been in the store for an hour and I had it when I walked in. I realized just now that it is gone.
>
> Police Officer *(Tall, imposing figure in full uniform, holding a pad of paper)*: Ma'am, I'll need to take down your name, address, and phone number. I know you are in shock, but we will find the perpetrator—don't you worry."

Share your paragraph with a partner. Take turns evaluating one another's ideas. Will your suggestions make a good film?

IN THE MEDIA

Using *In the Media*

Objective

- **To understand how stories change when they are transferred from a book to a movie**

Group Project

- Have each student work with a partner to compare the book and movie versions of a popular story. Most fairy tales and classic works of children's literature, including *Little Women; Huckleberry Finn; Mary Poppins; Dr. Doolittle; Charlotte's Web; The Lion, the Witch, and the Wardrobe;* and *James and the Giant Peach,* have been made into at least one movie. Students should study movie reviews and other news articles published at the time the movie was released to decide how the book and the movie version of the story differ. Each pair of students should report their findings to the class. Discuss any patterns that emerge.

FYI

Website to Visit The Website for the Playwriting Seminar at Virginia Commonwealth University at http://www.vcu.edu/artweb/playwriting/ analyzes topics such as how to adapt a novel to a screenplay, the differences between screenwriting and playwriting, and how to read professional screenplays.

YOUR IDEAS
For Publishing

Publishing

Writing Process

One of the most satisfying parts of the writing process is sharing your work with readers. When you have corrected all your errors, prepare a neat final copy of your literary analysis to present to readers. Some ways of publishing your composition about literature are listed below.

Ways to Publish Your Composition About Literature

- Enter your composition in a literary contest. Write to the National Council of Teachers of English (1111 Kenyon Road, Urbana, IL 61801) for information.
- Publish a class anthology, or collection, of compositions on literary works. Decide how to organize, illustrate, bind, and circulate your anthology.
- Hold a Reader's Roundtable. At this meeting each participant reads his or her literary analysis aloud. The rest of the group responds with questions and/or shares other interpretations of the same work.

Communicate Your Ideas

PUBLISHING

Make a neat final copy of your composition and publish it in one of the ways listed above.

PORTFOLIO

Time Out to Reflect

A thorough evaluation of a work of literature requires vigorous critical thinking, clear organization, and precise writing—in other words, hard work! What are the rewards of doing a careful, thoughtful analysis? Consider how your understanding and enjoyment of "Checkouts" was positively affected by your analysis of the work. In the Learning Log section of your **journal**, write a summary of your thoughts.

DEVELOPING WORKPLACE COMPETENCIES

Personal Qualities: Integrity/Honesty

Tell students that one way people benefit from studying literature is that it helps them think about ethical choices. For example, in *Huckleberry Finn*, readers can follow Huck as he wrestles with his conscience about whether to help his friend Jim escape slavery. In their work life, people often have to make ethical choices. For example, if they have business expenses that the company will reimburse them for, they must decide whether to report the expenses truthfully. Or, in dealing with customers, they will have to decide how much information to give out that may not be favorable to their company's products. Maybe the most difficult decisions that employees face is when they think a fellow employee is being unfairly criticized, discriminated against, or otherwise mistreated by a supervisor. Standing up to defend the rights of others requires great integrity, particularly when doing so might cost a person his or her job.

Divide students into small groups. Have each group role play a situation in which one employee is mistreated by a supervisor in some way as other employees watch. Ask groups to role-play their situation for the class.

EXPANDING THE LESSON

Using Technology

You will find additional **instructional** and **practice** materials for this chapter at http://www.bkenglish.com.

Process of Writing About Literature

Remember that the writing process is recursive and personal. You can return to an earlier part of the process at any time to add, change, or delete details and ideas as you see fit.

PREWRITING

- Read the work carefully and respond to it from both personal experience and literary knowledge. *(pages C313–C316)*
- By synthesizing your personal and literary responses, choose and limit a subject for your composition. *(pages C317–C321)*
- Shape your limited subject into a thesis statement that will guide you as you write. *(pages C321–C322)*
- Skim the work again, looking for details that will support your thesis statement. On separate paper jot down each detail with a page reference after it. *(pages C323–C325)*
- Organize your supporting details into an informal outline. *(pages C326–C327)*

DRAFTING

- Use the guidelines on page C328 to help you draft your composition about literature.

REVISING

- After peer conferencing use the Evaluation Checklist for Revising to help you make a thorough revision of your composition about literature. *(page C331)*

EDITING

- Use the editing checklist to check your grammar, spelling, usage, and mechanics. *(page C334)*

PUBLISHING

- Prepare a neat final copy of your work and present it to an interested reader in an appropriate way. *(page C336)*

A Writer Writes

Literary Analysis of a Poem

Purpose: to explain your understanding of a poem

Audience: your classmates

Read the poem "Like Scales" by Julia Mishkin on page C229. Respond both personally and critically to the poem in your **journal**. When responding personally, be sure to think about your own impressions of the sound of a lamb bleating and sheep in a field. Then use the guidelines that follow to write a composition about your understanding of the poem to share with readers.

Prewriting

Synthesize your personal and literary responses to the poem as you search for a good subject to write about. Review your personal response to see what aspect of the poem strikes you as most important. Then review your critical response, looking for a match between the special interests you have already identified and the elements of poetry you could write about in a composition. Shape your subject first into a focused, limited subject, and then develop a complete thesis statement for your composition. Gather supporting details for your composition by skimming the poem and noting each and every detail you can use to support your thesis. Arrange your details in a logical order, and make an informal outline of your composition.

Drafting

Using your informal outline as a guide, draft your composition about "Like Scales". *(You may wish to refer to*

Using *A Writer Writes*

Objective

- **To practice interpreting a poem**

TIMESAVER *QuickCheck*

Review each student's main idea statement. Check to see that it is clear and that it can be supported with details.

INTEGRATING *Writers at Work*

For more opportunities to stimulate students' critical writing, look at *Writers at Work*.

the guidelines on page C328 before beginning your draft.) Remember to stop every now and then and reread what you have written.

Revising

Exchange papers with a classmate. Read one another's papers, and comment on the following:

- Is the thesis clear?
- Does each detail work to support the thesis?
- Does the composition have unity and coherence?

After receiving your partner's comments, revise your work as you see fit. Use the Evaluation Checklist for Revising on page C331 as a guide.

Editing and Publishing

When you are satisfied with your final draft, prepare a neat final copy. You may wish to make and publish a booklet titled "Like Scales" in which you include the following:

- a copy of the poem by Julia Mishkin
- a copy of your literary analysis of the poem
- pictures of sheep and fields clipped from magazines or drawn by you

When all the booklets in your class are complete, you may wish to share them with another class or display them in the school library.

Connection Collection

Representing in Different Ways

From Print . . .

. . . to Visuals

Read the poem by William Carlos Williams aloud. Consider the images the poet uses to evoke his mood and describe his feelings. Then search through magazines to find pictures that best illustrate the poem for you. Create a collage of these images to accompany the text of the poem.

The Red Wheelbarrow

so much depends
upon

a red wheel
barrow

glazed with rain
water

beside the white
chickens

—William Carlos Williams

From Visuals . . .

Leonora Carrington,
Red Cow, 1989.
Oil on canvas, 24 by 36 inches
Private collection.

. . . to Print

Write a poem that you think represents the subject, mood, and theme of *Red Cow* by Leonora Carrington. Consider how the rhythm, images, and words you use in the poem can express the mood of the painting.

- **Which strategies can be used for creating both written and visual representations? Which strategies apply to one, not both? Which type of representation is more effective?**
- **Draw a conclusion and write briefly about the differences between written ideas and visual representations.**

FOR REVIEWING SKILLS

Using *Connection Collection*

Representing in Different Ways

Consider using these print and visual activities to make students aware of the benefits of using different media to suit particular purposes. Help students understand when a visual medium, for example, is better suited to their purpose than a print medium, or the reverse.

Using *Connection Collection*

Consider using these writings prompts as independent or small-group activities.

GETTING STUDENTS INVOLVED

Cooperative Learning

After organizing students into groups, thoroughly explain the task to be accomplished and establish a time frame. Make sure that each group member is responsible for a given task. Have each group share its project with the class and discuss the process the group used to carry out the assignment.

YOUR IDEAS

For Writing Prompts

Writing for Oral Communication

Book Review E-mail

You really like to read, and your friends and classmates trust your careful evaluation of the positive and negative qualities of books and stories. Your good friend Clara recently E-mailed you to ask your opinion on what book she should read for an upcoming book report at school.

Write an E-mail message to Clara about the book you recommend. Organize your thoughts before you write, and begin your message with a topic sentence. Give a thorough literary analysis of the book in your E-mail, describing why the book is important, expressing in your own words what you think the theme, or message, is. Use details from the book to support your points.

What strategies did you use to inform Clara of the details of the book?

You can find information on writing E-mail messages in A Writer's Guide to Using the Internet.

Writing in the Workplace

Analytical Composition

You have just accepted a job as assistant editor at *Dandelion*, a journal devoted to creative expression among junior high school students. The upcoming issue will feature poetry by famous writers as well as students such as yourself. Ida Nelson, the editor of the journal, has asked you to find a poem to reprint in *Dandelion*. As a test of your editing skills, Ms. Nelson also wants you to write a composition that analyzes the poem's meaning.

Find a poem that you like and write a composition analyzing the meaning of the poem. Discuss how the speaker in the poem relates to the subject, mood, and theme of the poem. Also analyze what images the words create and what feelings those images suggest.

What strategies did you use to analyze the poem you chose?

You can find information on responding to poetry on pages C316.

A DIFFERENT DELIVERY SYSTEM

For formal assessment print the composition chapter test from the *BK English* Test Bank at http://www.bkenglish.com.

Assess Your Learning

Your eighth-grade teacher is taking a much-needed vacation. In her place is Mr. Hayfever, a substitute notorious for his controversial teaching ideas. Today he announced that he will require students only to see movies from now on. He has decided that works of literature such as poems, short stories, and novels are "lesser forms of knowledge" because they are not as entertaining as movies. Although some of your classmates are excited by his proposed changes, you disagree with Mr. Hayfever and wish to write a composition to express your opinion.

▶ **Write a composition for your school newspaper about why literature should still be taught to eighth graders. Consider examples of literature that you think are just as entertaining, or more entertaining, than movies. Respond from personal experience in your composition, explaining why your chosen poem, story, novel, or play has special meaning for you. Narrow your subject, focus on a specific thesis, and be sure to quote direct lines and images from the work.**

Before You Write **Consider the following questions:**
What is the ***subject?***
What is the ***occasion?***
Who is the ***audience?***
What is the ***purpose?***

After You Write **Evaluate your work using the following criteria:**

- Have you included a strong introduction that identifies the author and the work you will discuss?
- Have you narrowed your subject and focused on a specific thesis for your discussion of the importance of studying literature?
- Have you quoted direct lines and images from the work to support your main idea?
- Does your conclusion draw together your details to reinforce your opinion in the composition for the newspaper?

Write briefly on how well you did. Point out your strengths and areas for improvement.

FOR ASSESSING LEARNING

Using *Assess Your Learning*

This writing prompt will help you and your students informally assess their developing writing abilities, using the accompanying primary trait rubrics, which list the key features and qualities of critical writing taught in this chapter. You may want to have students maintain their self-assessment in their portfolios as a record of their individual progress throughout the year.

Evaluating Compositions About Literature

In writing compositions about literature, many students need help in

- **supporting a main idea statement with enough details and quotations**
- **organizing this evidence logically**
- **presenting the argument as a clear and coherent whole.**

Self-evaluation and peer evaluation can help students improve their compositions in these areas as they revise.

Self-evaluation

When students have finished their first drafts, help them evaluate their work for the purpose of revising. Hand out copies of the Evaluation Checklist for Writing about Literature. (See the Evaluation Checklists in BK English Language and Composition Assessment.) Tell them to focus on content as they read their compositions, with special attention to the traits numbered below.

Peer evaluation

Another approach to evaluating compositions about literature is for students to work in pairs to evaluate each other's work. You might pair students whose compositions treat similar subjects, express conflicting opinions, or are otherwise related.

1 The main idea statement is supported by details and quotations.
2 The supporting material is ordered logically.
3 Each point related to the main idea is clearly stated.
4 The argument forms a coherent whole.
5 There is a balance of personal and literary responses in the interpretation.

Teacher evaluation

Primary Traits

The following opening paragraphs from "Thank You, M'am" state a main idea, give some supporting material, and suggest a direction for the rest of the composition. They can serve as a model for evaluating students' composition openings.

MODEL FOR EVALUATION

No relationship is more important than the relationship between a parent and a child. In "Thank You, M'am," Langston Hughes emphasizes the importance of this relationship by creating a story filled with mother-son imagery. A young boy Roger attempts to steal a purse from a woman named Luella Bates Washington Jones, a forthright and commanding woman. Roger does not succeed in robbing Ms. Jones; instead he his publicly disciplined by his intended victim. Although Roger's relationship with Ms. Jones is brief, her care and advice have an impact on the frail child, as was Ms. Jones intention saying, "When I get through with you, sir, you are going to remember Luella Bates Washington Jones."

General point with which reader will agree

Effective evidence supports thesis

Quotation supports point

TEACHER EVALUATION

Primary Trait Evaluation

The following chart lists the key features and qualities to look for in primary trait assessment of compositions about literature.

	EXCELLENT	ACCEPTABLE	NEEDS IMPROVEMENT
Main Idea Statement	Clearly states an interesting insight about the work that can be supported by the use of details and quotations from the work.	States a main idea that is either somewhat narrow for textual support or overly general.	Fails to state a supportable main idea.
Supporting Points	Uses details and quotations from the work to support each main point.	Supports some points with details and quotations.	Uses few or no supporting details or quotations.
Organization	Each main point relates to the main idea and is discussed in a paragraph with a topic sentence and supporting material. Development of the discussion is easy to follow.	Some main points are difficult to relate to the main thesis. The flow of the discussion breaks down at some points.	Ideas may not be organized into paragraphs, and they relate only vaguely, if at all, to the main idea. The flow of the discussion is unclear.
Transitions	Transitions are used to enhance the flow of discussion.	Some helpful transitions are used.	Transitions are lacking.
Synthesis	The interpretation of the literary work uses a balance of personal and literary responses.	The interpretation uses both personal and literary responses, although one (usually the personal) predominates.	The interpretation does not synthesize personal and literary responses.

TEACHER EVALUATION

Holistic Evaluation

The following criteria may be used to evaluate students' critical compositions holistically, using a rating scale of

4 (excellent)
3 (good)
2 (acceptable)
1 (needs improvement)
0 (unscoreable).

4	3	2	1
The main idea statement presents an interesting and original insight that can be supported by details and quotations from the work.	The main idea statement is supportable by details and quotations from the work.	The main idea statement is trite, vague, or difficult to support with material from the work.	The composition fails to state a supportable main idea statement.
Main points are relevant to the main idea, supported by ample details and quotations, and easy to follow.	Main points are adequately supported and most points are relevant to the main idea.	Some supporting material from the work appears, presented in a manner relevant to the main idea.	Supporting material from the work is scanty or lacking; the discussion does not relate to the main idea.
The composition is well organized. The introductory paragraph names the work and author and states the main idea. The body includes paragraphs that support the main idea. Ideas are connected by transitions. The conclusion restates the main idea.	The composition is basically well organized, with only a point or two logically out of place or unrelated to the main idea.	An introductory paragraph states the main idea, one or more body paragraphs include some supporting material, and a conclusion restates the main idea.	The composition is not organized into an introduction, body, and conclusion.
There is a balance between personal and literary responses.	The interpretation uses more personal responses than literary responses.	Almost every response is personal.	Every response in the interpretation is personal.

Applying Communication Skills

PLANNING GUIDE

This chart will help you create a flexible instructional plan that addresses the individual needs of all your students in the new millennium.

LEARNING TO KNOW

A Foundation of Knowledge	CHAPTER 11 Reports	CHAPTER 12 Letters
PE Communication Models	Reading with a Writer's Eye, p. C344 "Birth of a Legend" by G.K. Chesterton, pp. C345–C348 Thinking as a Writer, p. C349 **Grammar in the Writing Process** • Punctuation of Titles, p. C370	Reading with a Writer's Eye, p. C380 "America's First Woman Soldier" a letter from Paul Revere, pp. C381–C383 Thinking as a Writer, p. C384 **Grammar in the Writing Process** • Commas, p. C392
TE Skills Instruction	Lesson 1: Structure of a Report, Prewriting Lesson 2: Drafting, Listing Sources Lesson 3: Revising, Editing, Publishing	Lesson 1: Friendly and Social Letters Lesson 2: Business Letters and Forms
PE Skills Practice	**Practice Your Skills** • Researching and Limiting Subjects, pp. C352–C353 • Creating Source Cards, p. C356 • Taking Notes, p. C358 • Outlining, p. C361 • Preparing a Sources Page, p. C367 • Editing a Paragraph, p. C369 **Writing Is Thinking** • Summarizing, p. C359	
PE Independent Application	**In the Media** • Documentary, p. C372 **Communicating Your Ideas** • Subject, p. C353 • Source Cards, p. C356 • Notes, Outline, p. C362 • Introduction, Body, Conclusion, Title, p. C366 • Sources Page, p. C367 • Conferencing, p. C368 • Publishing, p. C371 **Connection Collection** • Representing, pp. C376-C377 • In Everyday Life, p. C378 • In the Workplace, p. C378	**In the Media** Write a Letter, p. C387
Assessment and Evaluation	PE Time Out to Reflect, p. C371 PE Checklist for Writing a Report, p. C373 PE A Writer Writes, pp. C374–C375 PE Assess Your Learning, p. C379 + I Chapter Test TE Evaluating Reports, pp. C379a–C379b	PE A Writer Writes, p. C402 PE Assess Your Learning, p. C403 + I Chapter Test

PE PUPIL'S EDITION TE TEACHER'S EDITION + ANCILLARIES I INTERNET

ADDITIONAL RESOURCES

- + Composition Skills Practice
- + Language Skills Practice
- + Assessment
- + Assessment Resources
- + Standardized Test Preparation
- + ESL Practice and Test Preparation
- + Transparency Tools
- + Writing Prompts
- + Writers at Work

CHAPTER 13
Directions and Speeches

Reading with a Writer's Eye, p. C404
"Commencement Speech" by Jerry Greenfield, pp. C405–C406
Thinking as a Writer, p. C407
Grammar in the Writing Process
- Prepositional Phrases, p. C419

Lesson 1: Informal and Formal Speeches
Lesson 2: Preparing a Speech

Practice Your Skills
- Improving Directions, pp. C409–C410
- Finding, Choosing, and Limiting a Subject, p. C413
- Delivering a purpose of a Speech, pp. C414–C415
- Gathering Information with Note Cards, pp. C416–C417
- Determining the Order of a Formal Speech, p. C421
- Listening to Enjoy and Appreciate, pp. C425–C426
- Listening, Taking Notes, and Following Directions, p. C428
- Understanding Fact and Opinion, p. C429
- Evaluating for Misleading Information, p. C430

Writing Is Thinking
- Evaluating Audience, p. C412

In the Media
- Political Speech, p. C424

Communicating Your Ideas
- Subject, p. C413
- Purpose, p. C415
- Research, Outline, p. C417
- Practice, p. C418
- Delivering, p. C422

Connection Collection
- Representing, pp. C434–C435
- In the Workplace, p. C436
- Oral Communication, p. C436

PE Time Out to Reflect, p. C422
PE Checklist for Presenting a Speech, p. C423
PE A Speaker Speaks, pp. C432–C433
PE Assess Your Learning, p. C437
+ I Chapter Test
TE Evaluating Speeches and Presentations, pp. C437a–C437b

LEARNING TO DO

Competencies for the World of Work

Basic Skills:
Reads, writes, performs arithmetic and mathematical operations, listens, and speaks
- Reading
- Writing
- Arithmetic/Mathematics
- Listening
- Speaking

Thinking Skills:
Thinks creatively, makes decisions, solves problems, visualizes, knows how to learn, and reasons
- Creative Thinking
- Decision Making
- Problem Solving
- Seeing Things in the Mind's Eye
- Knowing How to Learn
- Reasoning

Personal Qualities:
Displays responsibility, self-esteem, sociability, self-management, and integrity and honesty
- Responsibility
- Self-Esteem
- Sociability
- Self-Management
- Integrity/Honesty

LEARNING WITH TECHNOLOGY

Tools for the Information Age

I **http://www.bkenglish.com**
- BK English Online (password required)
- Chapter Tests
- Skill Practice
- Writing Prompts
- Standardized Tests

TEACHING SUGGESTIONS

Essential Knowledge and Skills

- Demonstrating effective communication skills that reflect such demands as reporting
- Writing to inform such as to explain, describe, report, and narrate
- Framing questions to direct research
- Taking notes from relevant and authoritative sources such as periodicals and online searches
- Following accepted formats for writing research, including documenting sources
- Interpreting and evaluating the various ways visual image makers such as documentary filmmakers represent meanings
- Evaluating the purposes and effects of varying media such as film

CHAPTER 11

Reports

You are sure to have many interests throughout your life. You will probably want to know more about your interests and hobbies. You may not, however, be able to explore all of your interests first-hand. In that case you can turn to a report. A report is a storehouse of information—a collection of facts presented in a pleasing and meaningful way. Many of the facts that you know, you know because you read them in some kind of report. Reports are all around us—in books, magazines, E-mail messages, newspapers, newsletters, and on the Internet. If you have ever watched the evening news, you have seen an oral report.

We live in a time when information is becoming increasingly available. This new availability may make researching facts easier, but it also means we have to choose our facts carefully and be able to present them in a manner that is logical and easy to understand. A good report does just that.

Reading with a Writer's Eye

The following report from the television series *Nova* deals with the origins of the Loch Ness Monster mystery. Read over the report to gain a general understanding of the material. Then read it again, paying close attention to how the report is organized. How do you think the author went about getting the facts on which the report is based?

BLOCK SCHEDULING

- If your schedule requires that you cover the chapter in a **shorter time,** use Reading with a Writer's Eye, Process of Writing a Report, and A Writer Writes.
- If you want to take advantage of **longer class time,** add any or all of the following: Writing Is Thinking, Editing Workshop, and In the Media.

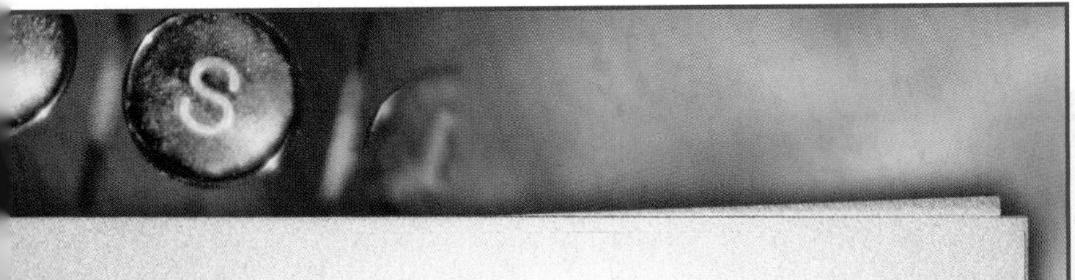

"Birth of a Legend"

BY STEPHEN LYONS

Many a man has been hanged on less evidence than there is for the Loch Ness Monster.
—G. K. Chesterton

When the Romans first came to northern Scotland in the first century A.D., they found the Highlands occupied by fierce, tattoo-covered tribes they called the Picts, or painted people. From the carved, standing stones still found in the region around Loch Ness, it is clear the Picts were fascinated by animals, and careful to render them with great fidelity. All the animals depicted on the Pictish stones are lifelike and easily recognizable—all but one. The exception is a strange beast with an elongated beak or muzzle, a head locket or spout, and flippers instead of feet. Described by some

FOR INCREASING STUDENT ACHIEVEMENT

GUIDED READING

Text Analysis

- In this piece of **expository** writing, Lyons presents information in **chronological order.** He tells about the Romans and the Picts in the first century A.D., describes an incident with Saint Columba in A.D. 565, **summarizes** pre-twentieth century references, and then describes events in the 1930s.
- **Transitions** between sentences link ideas together. Lyons starts sentences with words such as *Then, From,* and *These.* These words help the reader follow the information, and make the writing flow smoothly.
- Lyons presents the information in a **neutral tone.** He reports both local legends and the comments of scientists without ridiculing either one. Lyons presents the information, and allows the reader to form conclusions.
- Each paragraph, except the first one, starts with a **topic sentence.** The first paragraph ends with the main topic for the entire selection: the idea that Loch Ness is home to a mysterious aquatic animal.

SELECTION AMENDMENT
Description of change: excerpted

GUIDED READING

Strategy: Previewing

Before students read the selection, ask them what they know about the legend of the Loch Ness monster. Discuss whether the members of the class are a representative sample of the likely readers of the story in terms of their knowledge of the topic. Point out that writers have to make assumptions about the level of knowledge of their audience.

scholars as a swimming elephant, the Pictish beast is the earliest known evidence for an idea that has held sway in the Scottish Highlands for at least 1,500 years—that Loch Ness is home to a mysterious aquatic animal.

In Scottish folklore, large animals have been associated with many bodies of water, from small streams to the largest lakes, often labeled Lock-na-Beistie on old maps. These water-horses, or water-kelpies, are said to have magical powers and malevolent intentions. According to one version of the legend, the water-horse lures small children into the water by offering them rides on its back. Once the children are aboard, their hands become stuck to the beast and they are dragged to a watery death, their livers washing ashore the following day.

The earliest written reference linking such creatures to Loch Ness is in the biography of Saint Columba, the man credited with introducing Christianity to Scotland. In A.D. 565, according to this account, Columba was on his way to visit a Pictish king when he stopped along the shore of Loch Ness. Seeing a large beast about to attack a man who was swimming in the lake, Columba raised his hand, invoking the name of God and commanding the monster to "go back with all speed." The beast complied, and the swimmer was saved.

When Nicholas Witchell, a future BBC correspondent, researched the history of the legend for his 1974 book *The Loch Ness Story,* he found about a dozen pre-20th-century references to large animals in Loch Ness, gradually shifting in character from these clearly mythical accounts to something more like eyewitness descriptions.

But the modern legend of Loch Ness dates from 1933, when a new road was completed along the shore, offering the first clear views of the loch from the northern side. One April afternoon, a local couple was driving home along this road when they spotted "an enormous animal rolling and plunging on the surface." Their account was written up by a correspondent for *The Inverness Courier*, whose editor used the word "monster" to describe the animal. The Loch Ness Monster has been a media phenomenon ever since.

Public interest built gradually during the spring of 1933, then picked up sharply after a couple reported seeing one of the creatures on land, lumbering across the shore road. By October, several London newspapers had sent correspondents to Scotland, and radio programs were being interrupted to bring listeners the latest news from the loch. A British circus offered a reward of £20,000 for the capture of the beast. Hundreds of boy scouts and outdoorsmen arrived, some venturing out in small boats, others setting up deck chairs and waiting expectantly for the monster to appear.

The excitement over the monster reached a fever pitch in December, when *The London Daily Mail* hired an actor, film director, and big-game hunter named Marmaduke Wetherell to track down the beast. After only a few days at the loch, Wetherell reported finding the fresh footprints of a large, four-toed animal. He estimated it to be 20 feet

INTEGRATING TECHNOLOGY

Internet

Two Websites with extensive details, and some images, about the Loch Ness mystery are http://www.lochness.co.uk/ and http://www.nessie.co.uk/.

READER RESPONSE

You may want to use the following questions to elicit students' personal responses to the selection.

1. Why do you think the Picts carved images of an animal that no one recognizes today?
2. How did you feel when you read about the fresh footprints Wetherell reported finding?
3. Who benefits from keeping the mystery of the Loch Ness monster alive?
4. Would you like to visit Loch Ness and search for a mysterious animal in it? Explain.

LITERARY CONNECTION

You might want to explore report writing in the following works, which appear in literature textbooks at this grade level.

- *Anne Frank: The Diary of a Young Girl* by Anne Frank
- *Harriet Tubman: Conductor on the Underground Railroad* by Ann Petry
- "O Captain! My Captain!" by Walt Whitman
- "The Pilgrims' Landing and First Winter" by William Bradford

long. With great fanfare, Wetherell made plaster casts of the footprints and, just before Christmas, sent them off to the Natural History Museum in London for analysis. While the world waited for the museum zoologists to return from holiday, legions of monster hunters descended on Loch Ness, filling the local hotels. Inverness was floodlit for the occasion, and traffic jammed the shoreline roads in both directions.

The bubble burst in early January, when museum zoologists announced that the footprints were those of a hippopotamus. They had been made with a stuffed hippo foot— the base of an umbrella stand or ashtray. It wasn't clear whether Wetherell was the perpetrator of the hoax or its gullible victim. Either way, the incident tainted the image of the Loch Ness Monster and discouraged serious investigation of the phenomenon. For the next three decades, most scientists scornfully dismissed reports of strange animals in the loch. Those sightings that weren't outright hoaxes, they said, were the result of optical illusions caused by boat wakes, wind slicks, floating logs, otters, ducks, or swimming deer.

ADDITIONAL RESOURCES

Composition Skills Practice. . . . . pages 55–60
Transparency Tools GO4, VR10
Writing Research Reports . . . . pages 1–56
Connection Collection . . . . pages C376–C378
ESL Practice and Test Preparation . . . . . pages 64–70
Writers at Work . . . . 8•1–8•10
Assessment: Chapter Test. . . . . pages 76–81
Assessment Resources . . . . pages 1–10, 12–28

Thinking as a Writer

Evaluating Reporting Technique

- How was the report organized? Was this organization helpful to you as a reader? Why or why not?
- There are many facts included in this report, but the report is not simply a "dry" list of facts. What techniques does the author use to present the facts in an interesting way?
- Did you find the report to be clear? Were there any questions left unanswered?

Conveying Tone

Oral Expression — Read aloud the section of the report that deals with the "Loch-na-Beistie" of Scottish folklore.

- What tone do you hear expressed in this section? Why do you think the author chose this tone?
- Retell this section of the report to a partner in your own words, using a different tone. Remember that you cannot change the facts, only the tone.
- Have your partner tell you what tone he or she heard conveyed. Was this the tone you intended to express?

Analyzing Visual Sources

Viewing — This photograph of an eel was taken by an underwater camera below the surface of Loch Ness.

- What would you think if you saw this photo and only knew that it was taken below the surface of Loch Ness?
- What questions would you ask to get more information about this photo?

USING THINKING AS A WRITER

You may choose to have students respond to the questions either orally or in writing.

USING STUDENTS' STRENGTHS

Multiple Intelligences: Naturalistic

Ask students to list animals that might share a resemblance to Nessie. Ask whether similarities with known animals make the existence of a Loch Ness creature more or less believable. Consider that if Nessie looks like known animals, people who claim to have sighted Nessie might actually have seen one of the known animals. On the other hand, the existence of a mysterious animal might be harder to accept if it looks like no other animal in existence.

Multiple Intelligences: Linguistic

Ask students how using the word *monster* might affect how people think of the Loch Ness mystery. Have them consider the emotions attached to the term *monster,* and how people might react differently to terms such as *animal, fish,* or *water-horse*. Discuss how language shapes perceptions.

FOR DEVELOPING SKILLS

LESSON 1 *(pages C350–C361)*

OBJECTIVES

- **To define a research report as a composition of three or more paragraphs that uses information from books, magazines, and other sources**
- **To follow the prewriting steps—which include choosing and limiting a subject, gathering information, taking notes, and outlining—to shape a subject idea into an organized plan for a report based on research**

Create Interest

Ask students what they would like to know. You might throw out some questions to get them started. Why does the moon look bigger when it is near the horizon? When did the first people arrive in the Americas? What's the difference between a horse and pony? A student could answer any of

DEVELOPING WORKPLACE COMPETENCIES

Thinking Skills: Decision Making

People in many different jobs are expected to write reports to help companies, schools, and governments make decisions. Policy analysts report on how a proposed tax increase will affect citizens. Market researchers report on changes in demographics, consumer attitudes, and economic conditions that might influence demand for a company's products. Purchasing department researchers report on new products, from software to office equipment, that the company is considering buying. Stock analysts for an investment firm report on the products, finances, and management of a company that the firm is considering advising its clients to invest in. Writers of these reports need to be clear and concise, and they need to document their information carefully. After summarizing and analyzing information, the writer often recommends a course of action.

Assign students to write a report on how demand for a product will change in coming years. They should select a product they are familiar with, think about who uses it, and consider whether more or fewer people will desire it and be able to afford it in the future. Then they should recommend whether a company should increase, decrease, or otherwise adjust the production of that product.

Process of Writing a Report

When you write compositions, you often draw on your own knowledge and experience for ideas. When you write research reports, on the other hand, you draw on the knowledge and experience of others. You acquire this knowledge by doing research—reading books, magazines, and encyclopedias, and viewing Web pages.

A **report** is a factual composition of three or more paragraphs that uses information from books, magazines, the Internet, and other sources.

Your Writer's Journal

Subject ideas for reports can come from many different places, including the Learning Log section of your journal. Look over the entries you have made in your Learning Log. Over the next few days, write freely in your journal about each subject represented there. In your freewriting you may wish to include your feelings about the subject, what you already know about the subject, what else you would like to know about the subject, and where you could probably find more information. Your freewriting may help you decide which subjects would be most worthwhile for a research report.

Structure of a Report

The three main parts of a report are the **introduction**, the **body**, and the **conclusion**. In addition, a report ends with a page that lists your sources of information.

these or other questions by doing research to find out what others already know. The student could pass the information along to others by writing a report.

Guide Instruction

By Modeling Strategies

Select some of the questions that students raised in the previous activity. Write them on the board and discuss how they would find the answer. Besides looking in encyclopedias and library books, students could use magazines and journals. They could also use resources on the Internet: Websites devoted to the topic, Websites on general research, Websites of news organizations that have stories about the topic in their archives, and E-mails to people with special knowledge about the topic.

STRUCTURE OF A REPORT	
TITLE	• suggests the subject of the report
INTRODUCTION	• captures the reader's attention • provides any background information that the reader may need to know • contains a sentence expressing the main idea of the report
BODY	• supports the main idea stated in the introduction • follows the order of your outline • includes specific information from your sources
CONCLUSION	• brings the report to a close • summarizes the main idea • includes a comment that shows the importance of your subject
SOURCES PAGE	• lists your sources of information • appears at the end of the report

Prewriting

Writing Process

Planning a research report requires some detective work to find the library materials you need. *(See Chapter 16.)* The right supplies will help you keep track of your information as you collect it. These supplies include a folder with pockets, index cards, paper clips, and rubber bands.

Choosing and Limiting a Subject

A subject for a research report must pass three tests. The first is *Are you genuinely interested in learning more about*

YOUR IDEAS

For Choosing and Limiting Subjects

Consolidate Skills

Through Guided Practice

The various **Practice Your Skills** activities help students develop their prewriting skills, particularly their ability to gather information. To extend these activities, read a news story of contemporary interest to the class. Ask students to take notes on it as you read. You may wish to read the story a second time to give students a chance to check and revise their notes.

Apply to Communication

Through Independent Writing

Have students use their notes from the previous activity to write a one-paragraph summary of the story. Have students compare summaries with one another to see how they vary. Point out that each student brings particular interests and skills to their writing, and, as a result, the summaries will not turn out identical.

Practice Your Skills Answers

1. research
2. personal experience
3. research
4. research
5. personal experience
6. research
7. personal experience *or* research
8. personal experience
9. research
10. research

HOME WORK

Have students write five more subjects that are suitable for research reports and five more that are not.

the subject? The second is *Does your subject require research in books, magazines, and other sources?* The third is *Does your library have enough information on your subject?* If you can answer *yes* to all three questions, you have found a good subject to write about.

Once you have chosen a general subject, the next step is to limit it. Your subject should be limited enough to allow you to cover it thoroughly in a short report.

WAYS TO LIMIT A SUBJECT

1. Divide the general subject into its smaller parts.

Example	training guide dogs for the blind
Parts	basic obedience training
	training for crossing streets
	training for around the house

2. Limit the subject to a certain time, place, or person.

Example	training guide dogs for the blind
Place	how dogs are trained at San Rafael, California
Person	how Dorothy Eustis helped found the guide dog program in the United States

Practice Your Skills

Identifying Subjects That Need Research

Decide whether each subject is suitable for a research report. Indicate your answer by writing *personal experience* or *research* after the proper number.

1. robots
2. popular spots in your neighborhood
3. the history of your neighborhood
4. efforts to protect the wildlife in the Everglades
5. your trip to the Everglades
6. differences among wide-bodied airplanes

Transfer to Everyday Life

By Comparing Everyday Notetaking to Report Notetaking

Make a list on the board of circumstances in which students take notes. They may write down phone messages, record assignments in class, or take notes during lectures. Ask them how the skills involved in taking these notes compare to those used in taking notes for a report. Both require the writer to summarize and to select key details.

Pull It All Together

By Reflecting

Ask students to review the progress they have made in the prewriting stage and to consider whether they feel ready to write their reports. Point out that they can return to the prewriting stage at any point in the writing process. In particular, they may wish to do more research about specific points in their report.

7. clubs at your school
8. packing a picnic lunch
9. what causes thunder and lightning
10. how to keep safe in a thunderstorm

Limiting a Subject

For each general subject, write two limited subjects that would be suitable for a short report.

1. trains
2. music
3. deserts
4. police
5. the moon
6. the Grand Canyon
7. polar bears
8. the circus
9. telephones
10. volleyball

PRACTICE YOUR SKILLS Sample Answers

1. the Orient Express; trains in India
2. how a CD is made; how Beethoven composed after he became deaf
3. kinds of plant life that grow in the desert; Death Valley
4. training for police officers; Scotland Yard
5. how the men who landed on the moon were able to take off again; what the moon is made of
6. how the Grand Canyon was formed; how the Grand Canyon became a national park
7. feeding habits; relationship between mother and offspring
8. how the Ringling Brothers circus got started; circus animal trainers
9. how satellites are used to relay telephone messages; early telephones
10. volleyball rules; today's star volleyball players

Communicate Your Ideas

PREWRITING *Subject*

Review your **journal.** Also look over your Learning Log. What ideas seem worth developing into a report? Make a list of ten possible subjects for a report. Then decide which one you will write a research report about. Limit your subject so that you can adequately cover it in a short report. Save your work. SAVE YOUR WORK

TIMESAVER *QuickCheck*

Review the subjects students have selected. Check to see if they are limited enough for a short report.

HOME STUDY

Have students bring to class three articles in newspapers or magazines that interest them. They should write the limited subject for each of the articles.

Gathering Information

After you have limited your subject, think about what you need to learn to write about the subject. A good way to plan your research is to jot down some questions that you want your report to answer. Suppose you had chosen the subject of sightings of UFOs. Your research questions might appear as follows.

Check Understanding

By Reviewing

Ask students what they think are the most important elements in prewriting. While all students will not agree on what is most important, they should recognize that the stage includes many elements, all of which are useful in preparing to write a first draft.

IDENTIFYING COMMON STUMBLING BLOCKS

Problem

- Having difficulty developing research questions

Solution

- Have students talk about their subject with another classmate. As they talk, the listening student should take notes about what questions arise or about aspects of the subject that particularly fascinate them. Students can use their classmate's notes to guide their research. Also, remind students that they should find sources to document the information that they believe is true. They should not rely upon their memory, except for the most basic information.

FYI

Search Engines When using a search engine for the first time, students should read the advice on how to use it. Some engines have features that will help improve a search. For example, whether one puts the search terms in quotation marks or connects them with *and* or *or* can make a difference in the types of results the engine produces.

- What different kinds of sightings are there?
- How do scientists classify these sightings?
- What is a close encounter?
- How many kinds of close encounters are there?

The strategies below will help you find the answers.

Strategies for Gathering Information

- Begin by checking an encyclopedia in print, online, or on CD-ROM. This will give you an overview of your subject. It may also contain a list of books and other references with more information.
- Use the card catalog to find more books on your subject.
- Check *The Readers' Guide to Periodical Literature* and a news index such as *Facts on File* for magazine and newspaper articles.
- Use an Internet search engine to search for Websites related to your subject.
- Make a *source card* for each of your sources. Use a 3- by 5-inch index card to record the necessary information. For each source record the proper information in the proper format.

COMPUTER TIP

When you are searching the Web, different search engines may give you different results. Try using some of the specialized search engines available. One engine that specializes in sites of particular interest to young adults is Yahooligans: www.yahooligans.com.

The following examples show how you can prepare source cards so they contain all the necessary information. Note that if you cannot find full information for a source, include just the information you have.

ENCYCLOPEDIA

J. Allen Hynek, "Unidentified Flying Objects," World Book Encyclopedia, 1985 ed.

BOOK

The UFO Handbook by Allen Hendry, New York, Doubleday & Company, 1979, 523 HE

MAGAZINE

Science Digest, November 1981, pps. 86–88, "Scientists Who Have Seen UFOs," by P. Huyghe

CD-ROM

"UFO." Encarta 98 Deluxe Encyclopedia. CD-ROM. Redmond: Microsoft Corporation, 1999.

WEBSITE

"Hall of UFO Mysteries." Museum of Unnatural Mystery. 10 Nov. 1999. 8 Dec. 1999 <http://www.unmuseum.mus.pa.us>

(The last update to this Website was November 10, 1999. The material was accessed on December 8, 1999.)

INTEGRATING TECHNOLOGY

Internet

Several Internet sites provide excellent starting points for research. Students can access the Encyclopedia Britannica, as well as links to articles and Websites, at http://www.britannica.com. The Internet Public Library, which is based at the University of Michigan, has a special section for youths and teens: http://www.ipl.org. An excellent collection of links for students can be found at http://www.awesomelibrary.org.

GETTING STUDENTS INVOLVED

Cooperative Learning

Students can help each other learn about the variations in search engines. Divide students into groups. Each group should agree on one topic to research on the Internet. Each member should perform the search for that topic using a different search engine. Students should then compare results. After discussing the results in their small groups, have a class discussion on how search engines differ.

REACHING ALL STUDENTS

Struggling Learners

Students may be confused about what information needs to go on source cards. Ask them what information they need to identify exactly what source was used. The source card should include all of the details they would need to find a source a second time in case they needed to recheck something or that a reader would need to locate the source.

HOME WORK

Have students find five more sources on a subject of their choice. At least one of the sources should be a magazine.

TIMESAVER *QuickCheck*

Have students trade source cards with a partner. Students should check their partner's cards to see if they include all of the necessary information.

PRACTICE YOUR SKILLS

Creating Source Cards

Use the library or media center to find three sources for each subject below. At least one source should be a magazine. Use source cards like the ones shown to record your findings.

1. formations on Mars

"Mars, Water, and Life." NASA. 6 Dec. 1999. 7 Dec. 1999 <http://polarlander.jpl.nasa.gov/why.html>

Uncovering the Secrets of the Red Planet: Mars by Paul Raeburn, Washington, D.C.: National Geographic Society, 1998, 523.43 R

2. creating Web pages
3. the goals of the Sierra Club
4. guide dogs for the blind
5. Old Faithful in Yellowstone Park

Communicate Your Ideas

PREWRITING *Source Cards*

Use the Strategies for Gathering Information on page C354 to find the information you need for the subject you chose. Your sources should include at least one article from both a magazine and an encyclopedia. Check your source cards to be sure you have accurately recorded the necessary information. The call number is especially important, since it will help you find your source again quickly if you need to refer to it many times. Save your source cards for future use.

Taking Notes

After finding sources, check the table of contents and index for information you need. If you are using a magazine article, skim it. Then read the sections about your subject and take notes in your own words on note cards.

The following excerpt is from a book on UFOs. Read it, then study the sample note card and guidelines that follow it.

> **Close Encounter (CE): a sighting of a UFO within five hundred feet of the witness.** With the introduction of Close Encounters, we arrive at some of the most convincing reports—those sightings that are so close to the witness that the possibility of misinterpretation is reduced. *Close Encounters of the First Kind (CE I's)* are those encounters in which the UFO does not influence the environment in any way. Following are some common features of UFOs as described in accounts of CE I's.
>
> Appearance: variety of shapes; many disks, ovals, footballs; some domes and other appendages
>
> Behavior: hovering; rotating; rapid acceleration; very steep ascent/descent; silence even though near observer

SAMPLE NOTE CARD

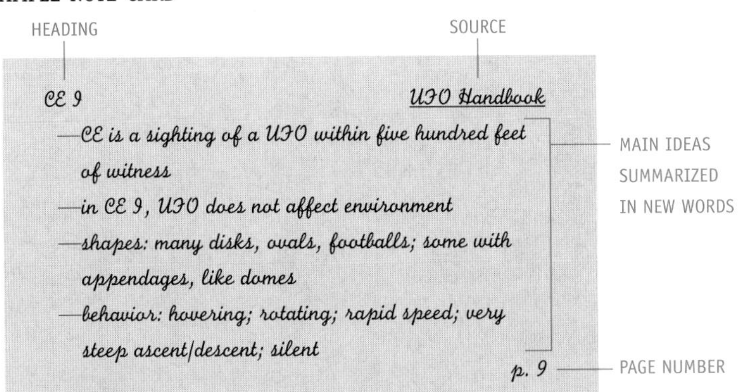

HEADING
SOURCE
CE I
UFO Handbook
—CE is a sighting of a UFO within five hundred feet of witness
—in CE I, UFO does not affect environment
—shapes: many disks, ovals, footballs; some with appendages, like domes
—behavior: hovering; rotating; rapid speed; very steep ascent/descent; silent
p. 9
MAIN IDEAS SUMMARIZED IN NEW WORDS
PAGE NUMBER

HOME STUDY

Have students try to find a Website on the Internet that is useful for the subject they have chosen. If students do not have access to the Internet at home, encourage them to visit a library/media center that does.

GETTING STUDENTS INVOLVED

Reciprocal Teaching

Ask students to share in class the types of resources they used for their report. List the types on the board. Students may suggest books, magazines, newspapers, Internet Websites, movies, museums, interviews, and other sources. Highlight examples of unusual sources or creative ways to gather information.

REACHING ALL STUDENTS

Struggling Learners

All students need to understand that the notes they take represent the viewpoint of the writer. Since writers have different viewpoints, students may find that two sources provide conflicting information. Some students may struggle to reconcile these differences. Ask students who come across clearly conflicting information to bring it to the attention of the class. Discuss whether the conflict reflects differences in the values, interests, or data of the two writers.

REACHING ALL STUDENTS

English Language Learners

Students who are learning English may want to practice taking notes using a textbook from another class. This will provide them with additional help in learning the vocabulary of that discipline.

PRACTICE YOUR SKILLS Sample Answers

benefits of underwater parks
Coral Reef Fishes
—tourists bring prosperity to parts of the Caribbean and the Maldives
—heavily exploited species have a place to grow and reproduce before moving outside the conservation area where fisherman can catch them
—they provide food, recreation, education, and economic development

HOME WORK

Tell students to take notes on a paragraph in a book or magazine and bring both the source and their notes to class. Have students show their source and notes to a partner. Partners should provide feedback on how well the student took notes.

SELECTION AMENDMENT
Description of change: excerpted
Rationale: to focus on the skill of taking notes as presented in this chapter

Taking Notes

- Write the title of your source in the upper right-hand corner of your index card.
- Identify the part of the subject being discussed with a heading in the upper left-hand corner.
- Begin a new card for each new part of your subject.
- Summarize main points in your own words.
- Record the page number(s) containing the information.
- Clip together all cards from the same source.

PRACTICE YOUR SKILLS

Taking Notes

Using an index card, take notes on the following information from pages 20 and 21 of *Coral Reef Fishes* by Eswald Lieske and Robert Myers.

In many parts of the world there are underwater parks where marine life is protected. In the Caribbean and the Maldives, the economic prosperity of entire nations depends on their underwater parks and the tourists they attract. Underwater parks and marine conservation areas also benefit the fishermen by offering a refuge for heavily exploited species to grow and reproduce so that the species' continued presence outside conservation areas is ensured. The key to the future well-being of many of the world's coral reef fish resources is clear. The establishment of underwater parks is a necessity if the maximum and well-balanced benefits of food, recreation, education, and economic development of marine resources are to be realized.

Writing Is Thinking

Summarizing

Summarizing will help you take notes. When you summarize, you use your own words to record the writer's most important points, leaving out unnecessary details. Much of your final research report will be a summary of the information you have read and digested in the course of your research. However, you will not simply be repeating the words from your sources, but will instead put the information into your own words. Omit details that do not relate directly to your topic.

THINKING AND WRITING PRACTICE

Read the paragraph below. Then summarize it by completing the activities that follow it.

THE HUMAN EAR

The human ear consists of three parts—the external ear, the middle ear, and the internal ear—each of which performs different functions. The *external ear* receives sound waves traveling through the air and directs them toward the middle ear. The *middle ear* concentrates sound waves and conducts them to the internal ear. The *internal ear* converts sound vibrations to nervous impulses that are then carried by the acoustic nerve to the brain. Only when nerve impulses reach the brain do we hear sound.

—Joan Elma Rahn, Ears, Hearing, and Balance

1. Look up any unfamiliar words and define them in your own words.
2. Write the main idea of this paragraph in your own words.
3. Write three or more sentences summarizing the rest of the paragraph.

Using *Writing Is Thinking*

Objective

- **To practice the skill of summarizing information**

A DIFFERENT APPROACH

Visual Have students create a visual representation showing the relative importance of words in a paragraph. If they have a computer, have them type a paragraph, either "The Human Ear" or one of their choice. Then have them adjust the size, font, and color of words and phrases so that important words stand out.

THINKING PRACTICE Sample Answers

2. Each of the three parts of the human ear has a distinct role in helping us hear.
3. The external ear moves sound from the air to the middle ear. The middle ear concentrates sound and moves it to the internal ear. The internal ear converts sound to nerve impulses.

Thinking Skills	
Classifying	Analyzing
Comparing	Hypothesizing
Generalizing	Synthesizing
Inferring	Summarizing
Imagining	Setting Goals
Observing	Evaluating Audience
Predicting	

GETTING STUDENTS INVOLVED

Reciprocal Teaching

Assign all students to take notes on the same article. You might pass out photocopies of an article, or, if all students have easy access to the Internet, select an article they can find on a Website. In class, have students compare the notes they have taken. Encourage them to consider why other students took different notes than they did.

Outlining

Once your research is completed, you can begin to outline your report. First, use the headings on your note cards to organize your information into categories. Next, arrange your categories in a logical order. Assign a Roman numeral to each category, or main topic. Finally, add subtopics under the Roman numerals by finding related ideas in your notes. Notes that do not fit into the categories can be saved for possible use in your introduction or conclusion.

The categories on UFO sightings can be arranged logically in order of degree.

MODEL: Topic Outline

SUBJECT	Types of UFO sightings
STATEMENT OF MAIN IDEA	I. Distant sightings
MAIN TOPIC	A. Nocturnal lights
SUBTOPICS	B. Daylight disks
	C. Radar-visuals
MAIN TOPIC	II. Close encounters with UFOs
SUBTOPICS	A. First type
	B. Second type
MAIN TOPIC	III. Close encounters with alien creatures
SUBTOPICS	A. Third type
	B. How scientists view third type

Outline Form

- Include a title and a statement of the main idea.
- Use Roman numerals for main topics.
- Use capital letters for subtopics.
- Always include at least two subtopics under each main topic.
- Indent as shown in the model above.
- Capitalize the first word of each entry.

Practice Your Skills

Outlining

Use the notes below to complete the following outline.

SUBJECT Police technology

STATEMENT OF MAIN IDEA There have been many developments in police technology throughout the years.

I. Ancient forerunners of police technology
   A.
   B.
II. Advances in the nineteenth century
   A.
   B.
   C.
III. Modern developments
   A.
   B.
   C.
   D.

SUBTOPICS
- Use of fingerprints, handwriting, and detailed word descriptions by ancient crime fighters
- Adoption of fingerprint classification system by Scotland Yard in 1901
- Telegraph first used by British bobbies in 1849
- Use of unscientific lie-detector tests in ancient societies
- Telephone first used by Washington, D.C., police in 1878
- 1950 invention of transistor and police transmitter-receivers
- Automobile first used by Ohio police in 1899
- Bugs and wiretaps introduced after World War II
- Use of computers currently on the rise

PRACTICE YOUR SKILLS Sample Answers

I. A. Use of fingerprints, handwriting, and detailed word descriptions by ancient crime fighters
   B. Use of unscientific lie detector tests in ancient societies
II. A. Telegraph first used by British bobbies in 1849
   B. Telephone first used by Washington, D.C., police in 1878
   C. Automobile first used by Ohio police in 1899
III. A. Adoption of fingerprint classification system by Scotland Yard in 1901
   B. Bugs and wiretaps introduced after World War II
   C. 1950 invention of transistor and police transmitter-receivers
   D. Use of computers currently on the rise

HOME WORK

Have students create an outline based on a story in the newspaper. Students should follow the guidelines for outline form presented in the text.

LESSON 2 *(pages C362–C367)*

OBJECTIVES

- **To write the first draft of a report, including the main idea statement, introduction, body, and conclusion**
- **To use and list sources accurately**

Create Interest

Ask students how they know that France exists. If students have been to France, they can claim personal knowledge. Others, though, probably rely upon what they are told, what they read, and what they see on television. Evaluate the reliability of these resources. Encourage students to understand that within each category, not all sources are equally reliable. For example, highly educated experts are more reliable than other people; regular newspapers are more reliable than supermarket tabloids; and some television reporters are more reliable than others.

TIMESAVER *QuickCheck*

Review students' outlines to be sure that they have used proper form. If they have not, ask them to make revisions as needed.

HOME STUDY

Students may wish to create their outline using a word processing program on a computer. One advantage of using a computer is that it makes moving items from one part of the outline to another fairly easy.

Communicate Your Ideas

PREWRITING *Notes, Outline*

Review the sources you identified for your chosen subject. With your index cards handy, follow the guidelines for taking notes on page C358. Then use your note cards—and your skill at classifying—to organize your information and outline your report. Save your work.

Drafting

Writing Process

After outlining your report, you are ready to write the first draft. Your first draft should include all three parts of the report—the introduction, body, and conclusion.

Drafting the Introduction

Think about your readers as you write the introduction. Remember that they have not done the research you have just completed. They will not even know what your report is about until they begin reading. Use the following guidelines to write a strong introduction.

Writing an Introduction

A strong introduction

- captures the reader's attention.
- provides any necessary background information.
- contains a sentence expressing the main idea of the report.

Guide Instruction

By Modeling Strategies

Bring to class, or ask students to bring to class, a variety of news accounts about a story in the news. Besides standard newspapers, newsmagazines, and stories printed from Internet sites, bring in a copy of a supermarket tabloid. Point out how the sources treat the news differently. Have students discuss how much they trust each account and the basis for their opinion.

Consolidate Skills

Through Guided Practice

As students draft their reports, they should refer to their notes frequently. As they use their notes, have them write down anything they would do differently next time they were taking notes. For example, some students may wish they had written in more detail or had included more direct quotations. Tell students to use what they learn to help them the next time they write a report.

The following introduction shows how all three items in the preceding chart can be smoothly worked into the opening paragraph of a report on the subject of UFO sightings.

MODEL: Introduction of a Report

STRONG INTRODUCTION

MAIN IDEA

Have you ever noticed something unusual in the night sky? If so, you are not alone. Thousands of people have reported seeing unidentified flying objects (UFOs) over the years. One expert, J. Allen Hynek, has devised a way to classify the thousands of sightings that are regularly reported to the authorities. His system is based on the distance between the UFO and the witness.

Drafting the Body

When you are satisfied with your introduction, you can use your outline to help you draft the body of your report. Follow the order of your outline and write complete sentences and paragraphs. Use transitions to guide your readers from idea to idea. *(Refer to pages C85–C86.)*

Compare the following body of a report on UFO sightings to the outline on page C360.

MODEL: Body of a Report

FROM ROMAN NUMERAL I IN OUTLINE

The first main category of UFOs in Hynek's system may be called distant sightings. Any sighting in which the witness is more than five hundred feet away from the UFO falls into this group. Within this group there are three main types of sightings. One is the nocturnal light, which is any light seen in the night sky that cannot be explained. A second is the daylight disk. Into this group fall any unidentified ob-

IDENTIFYING COMMON STUMBLING BLOCKS

Problem

- Writing the draft using the information word-for-word from the source

Solution

- Have students explain the essence of their report aloud to a partner or a small group of students. As they do so, they are more likely to express their ideas in their own words.

Problem

- Assuming that readers know more than they do and failing to provide background information that many readers will need

Solution

- Ask students to pretend they are writing their introduction for young children. They should explain all terms and relationships that their readers may not understand.

Apply to Communication

Through Independent Writing

Remind students that the introduction may be a report's most important paragraph. Have students write two sharply different introductions. Share both with a partner, and ask the partner for comments on which one is stronger. Point out that professional writers go through different openings before selecting one.

Transfer to Everyday Life

By Using Notetaking for Writing Letters

The skills involved in drafting a report—writing a full version based on notes and an outline—can be used in other contexts. When writing a letter to a friend, for example, a few minutes jotting down notes on what to include and sketching an outline can make the letter easier to write and to read.

Pull It All Together

By Sharing

Ask students to explain what they have learned about doing research. In particular, have them comment on how

REACHING ALL STUDENTS

Advanced Learners

Writers often open or close a report with a strong quotation from an expert or someone with first-hand knowledge. Some quotations are short enough and dramatic enough to be used in titles. If used in a conclusion, a quotation should summarize what has been presented rather than introduce new information.

jects of any shape seen during the daytime. The last type of distant sighting is the radar-visual. This group includes UFOs that are seen by a witness and recorded on radar at the same time.

FROM ROMAN NUMERAL II

The second main group of UFO sightings is made up of those that occur within five hundred feet of a witness. These are called close encounters. This group is also divided into three smaller groups. The Close Encounter of the First Kind is a sighting in which the witness sees a UFO but feels no effects from it. No trace of the UFO is left after a Close Encounter of the First Kind. A Close Encounter of the Second Kind, however, does involve evidence of the encounter. The evidence may include scorch marks on grass, footprints, odors, headaches, or electrical disturbances.

FROM ROMAN NUMERAL III

All UFO sightings are controversial. None is more so than the last type of close encounter, the Close Encounter of the Third Kind. In this kind of sighting, a witness reports seeing occupants in the UFO. Sometimes the occupants are short; sometimes they are human size. Some people claim to have been taken aboard a craft. Because people's accounts are often fantastic, many scientists disregard these reports.

Drafting the Conclusion

Use the strategies below to write a strong conclusion.

Writing a Conclusion

- Restate your main idea in new words.
- Add a comment that shows the importance of your subject or an insight about it.

comfortable they feel about gathering and organizing information. Discuss whether they have become more sensitive to reliability of sources, the point of view of various writers, and the need for accuracy in taking notes.

Check Understanding

By Looking Ahead

Have students review the draft of the report they have written. Then they should make a list of five aspects of the report they want to change. They might list things such as developing a stronger introduction, adding more information about a specific point, clarifying a topic sentence, improving the transitions between paragraphs, and writing a better closing sentence. Remind them that they should expect to make extensive changes to a draft. They should feel that each change is a worthwhile improvement.

- Round out the report by referring to an idea in the introduction without repeating it exactly.
- Avoid introducing a new, unrelated idea.
- Avoid such phrases as *Now you have seen . . .* or *I have just told you about . . .*

The following conclusion to the report on UFO sightings reinforces the main idea and shows its importance.

Model: Conclusion of a Report

Conclusion

Many distant UFO sightings can eventually be explained as weather balloons, comets, meteors, or even hoaxes. Close encounters are more difficult to explain, since the nearness of the witness leaves little room for mistaking the object. Some scientists dismiss all close encounters as figments of the witnesses' imaginations. Others are keeping an open mind. With the help of Hynek's system of classifying UFOs, they continue to collect reports. They hope someday an explainable pattern will emerge.

Writing a Title

Once you have finished your first draft, give your report an interesting title. Your title should catch your readers' interest and indicate what your report is about.

YOUR IDEAS

For Writing a Title

TIMESAVER *QuickCheck*

Ask students to work with a partner in evaluating their titles. Students should discuss how well each title fits what was written.

HOME STUDY

Students can write several possible titles for their draft. Then they can try the titles out on other members of their household to see which best captures the interest of the readers.

IDENTIFYING COMMON STUMBLING BLOCKS

Problem

- Not knowing whether to include a source in the list if it was perused but not used in the report

Solution

- Remind students that the list of sources tells the reader where the writer got the information used in the report so that the reader can evaluate the reliability of the report. In addition, it can also provide leads to sources for someone who is writing about, or is just curious about, the topic. If in doubt, students should include the source in their list.

Communicate Your Ideas

DRAFTING *Introduction, Body, Conclusion, Title*

Use your outline to draft your report. Then reread your report and give it a title. Save your draft for later use.

Listing Sources

The final page of your report should contain a list of your sources. Center the word *Sources* at the top. Then list each source in alphabetical order according to the author's last name. If the name is not given, use the first word in the title. The following examples show the correct form and punctuation for different kinds of sources.

Correct Form for Sources

BOOKS	Hendry, Allen. *The UFO Handbook*. New York: Doubleday & Company, 1979.
MAGAZINES	Huyghe, P. "Scientists Who Have Seen UFOs." *Science Digest*. November 1981: 86-88.
ENCYCLOPEDIAS	Hynek, J. Allen. "Unidentified Flying Objects." *World Book Encyclopedia*. 1985 ed.
CD-ROMs	"UFO." Encarta 98 Deluxe Encyclopedia. CD-ROM. Redmond: Microsoft Corporation, 1999.
WEBSITES	"Hall of UFO Mysteries." Museum of Unnatural Mystery. 10 November 1999; 8 December 1999 http://www.unmuseum.mus.pa.us.

LESSON 3 *(pages C367–C373)*

OBJECTIVES

- **To revise a report using a revision checklist**
- **To edit a report for grammar, mechanics, and usage**
- **To publish a final version of a report for others to read**

Create Interest

Ask students to share with the class the topic of the report they have been writing and one bit of interesting information they have learned. Help students recognize how much they have learned about their topic, and highlight any comments that express the enjoyment of learning new information.

Guide Instruction

By Connecting Ideas

Ask students what the purpose of writing is. In particular, discuss the purpose of writing a report. While people sometimes write primarily for their own

PRACTICE YOUR SKILLS

Preparing a Sources Page

The following sources are on the subject of theatrical makeup. Prepare a sources page in correct form.

1. an article in *Horizon* magazine by Donald Chase entitled "The Godfather of Movie MakeUp," appearing in the May–June issue of 1982 on pages 14–19

2. a book named *The American Movies: A Pictorial Encyclopedia* by Paul Mitchell, published in 1979 by Galahad Publishing Co. in New York

3. an article called "Motion Pictures" by Arthur Knight in the 1985 edition of *World Book Encyclopedia*

5. a section "hairstyles" on the CD-ROM "Cosmopolitan Virtual Makeover Style Pack 1" by Mindscape, in Novato, California

6. an area on an Internet Web page called "Southern Illinois University," www.siue.edu/PROJECT2000, entitled "The International Theatre Design Archive" which you found today. It was updated three days ago.

Communicate Your Ideas

DRAFTING *Sources Page*

Prepare a sources page for your report, listing sources in the correct form. Save your work. 

Revising — Writing Process

A report should flow smoothly and be easy to follow. Before revising, set your report aside for a while. Later, imagine you are a reader seeing it for the first time. Then use the checklist on the following page to improve your first draft.

PRACTICE YOUR SKILLS Answers

Chase, Donald. "The Godfather of Movie Make Up." *Horizon.* May/June 1982: 14-19.

"Hairstyles." Cosmopolitan Virtual Makeover Style Pack 1. CD-ROM. Novato: Mindscape.

"The International Theatre Design Archive." Southern Illinois University. 10 February 2001 www.siue.edu/PROJECT2000.

Knight, Arthur. "Motion Pictures." *World Book Encyclopedia*. 1985 ed.

Mitchell, Paul. *The American Movies: A Pictorial Encyclopedia.* New York: Galahad Publishing Co., 1979.

HOME WORK

Have students prepare a source page that includes a magazine article, a book, an encyclopedia article, a CD-ROM, and an Internet Web page about a subject of their choice.

TIMESAVER QuickCheck

Review students' source pages. Be sure they have listed their sources in alphabetical order and included all the necessary information for each source.

HOME STUDY

Have students review the sources listed in a book or a magazine article. They should note whether the sources have followed the guidelines presented in the text. Have students bring the source and their analysis to class.

interests, reports are usually written in order to transmit information to others. In that way, reports are a way of connecting with others. Ask students if they ever feel a connection with a writer who shares an interest with them.

Consolidate Skills

Through Guided Practice

The **Practice Your Skills** activity on editing a paragraph helps students develop their editing skills. You can extend this activity by having each student trade two paragraphs from their report with a partner. Each partner should edit the paragraph of the other student. After returning them, the students should discuss the changes each one suggested.

Apply to Communication

Through Independent Writing

Have students write down how they would revise the paragraph from the report on bicycles to make it twice as

TIMESAVER *QuickCheck*

As students review each other's work, remind everyone to point out what they like about the report they are reading. Writers need to know what not to change, as well as what to change.

HOME STUDY

After students have received suggestions on their report, they can revise their work at home. They should use their judgment about which suggestions to follow.

Evaluation Checklist for Revising

Checking Your Report

✓ Does your introduction contain a statement expressing the main idea of the report? *(pages C362–C363)*

✓ Does the body support the main idea with specific information and examples? *(pages C363–C364)*

✓ Did you use your own words?

✓ Does your report have unity?

✓ Does your report have coherence?

✓ Does your conclusion add a strong ending? *(pages C364–C365)*

✓ Does your report have a title? *(page C365)*

✓ Does your report have a sources page? *(page C366)*

Checking Your Paragraphs

✓ Does each paragraph in the body have a topic sentence?

✓ Is each paragraph unified and coherent?

✓ Does one paragraph lead smoothly into the next?

Checking Your Sentences

✓ Did you vary the length and beginnings of your sentences? *(pages C58–C59)*

✓ Did you avoid rambling sentences? *(page C63)*

✓ Are your sentences free of repetition and empty expressions? *(pages C64–C65)*

✓ Did you use specific, vivid words? *(pages C49–C53)*

Communicate Your Ideas

REVISING *Conferencing*

Use the checklist above to revise the report you wrote. Then exchange work with a classmate and give

long as it is. Students should indicate what additional information they would look for in order to expand the paragraph in a meaningful way.

Transfer to Everyday Life

By Checking Styles

After students have completed the **Editing Workshop,** have them find five examples of titles printed in books, newspapers, or other sources. Have them decide whether they follow the conventions described in the text. Discuss why some may follow their own style guidelines. Emphasize the importance of consistency within a report. Inconsistency will confuse the reader.

Pull It All Together

By Summarizing

Ask each student to summarize his or her report and explain to the class how its focus has changed since the beginning of the writing process. In particular, note students who were at first unclear about a topic but came to a clear position after doing research.

each other suggestions for further revision. Save your work.

Editing

Writing Process

One of the final stages in writing a report is to edit your work for proper grammar, mechanics, spelling, and usage.

PRACTICE YOUR SKILLS

Editing a Paragraph

Edit the following paragraph from a report about bicycles.

The high wheel bicycle first attracted the attention of americans at the 1876 philadelphia centennial exposition. They featured a large wheel in the front and a much more smaller wheel in the rear. Because of the large wheel, a rider could pedal faster. And go farther with less effort. Sitting atop the big wheel, the bicycle provided a surprisingly plesant and comforable ride, a few riders even acheived a speed of 20 miles an hour. Between 1883 and 1890 the bicycle reached it's peek of popularity. Two years later however american manufacturers ended production for safty reasons during a sudden stop the light rear wheel would fly upward. Throwing the rider over the handelbars. The need for a safer bicycle eventualy led to the development of the modern safty bicycle. With the end of production in 1892. A period in bicycle history comes to a close.

PRACTICE YOUR SKILLS Sample Answers

The high wheel bicycle first attracted the attention of Americans at the 1876 Philadelphia Centennial Exposition. It featured a large wheel in the front and a much smaller wheel in the rear. Because of the large wheel, a rider could pedal faster and go farther with less effort. Sitting atop the big wheel, the rider enjoyed a surprisingly pleasant and comfortable ride. A few riders achieved a speed of 20 miles an hour. Between 1883 and 1890, the bicycle reached its peak of popularity. Two years later, however, American manufacturers ended production for safety reasons. During a sudden stop, the light rear wheel would fly upward, throwing the rider over the handlebars. The need for a safer bicycle eventually led to the development of the modern safety bicycle. With the end of production in 1892, a period in bicycle history came to a close.

HOME WORK

After students have completed editing the paragraph on bicycles, have them write feedback to the writer of the paragraph. Remind them to point out the strengths as well as the weaknesses that they noticed.

Check Understanding

By Reflecting

Ask students what the best and worst parts of writing a report were. Remind them that many of the details that they might find difficult at first, such as using proper form in listing sources or remembering what information to put on their notecards, will become much easier with practice.

Using *Editing Workshop*

Objective

- **To learn the conventions for setting off titles with underlining, italics, or quotation marks**

A DIFFERENT APPROACH

Kinesthetic Have each student write down a title on a slip of paper, and a description of whether it is the title of a book, magazine, encyclopedia, or article. Collect the papers and put them in a hat. Draw out one at a time. Students who think the title should be underlined or printed in italics should stand up. If students disagree, have them explain their reasons for standing or sitting. Continue drawing titles until students are, without discussion, consistently in agreement.

Mechanics in the Writing Process

Prewriting Workshop
Drafting Workshop
Revising Workshop
Editing Workshop
Publishing Workshop

Punctuation of Titles

Remember that titles of books, magazines, magazine articles, and other works need italics and quotation marks. Substitute underlining for italics in handwritten work.

The following guidelines will help you determine which to underline and which to enclose in quotation marks.

Underline the titles of long works. These include books, magazines, newspapers, long plays, movies, very long poems, operas, symphonies, ballets, and compact discs. Also underline the titles of paintings and sculptures.

> I want to read the rest of Sterling North's Rascal.
>
> Have you ever tried the puzzle in the Ames Herald?
>
> Our drama club is working on Wilson's Fourth of July.

Use quotation marks for the titles of chapters, articles, stories, one-act plays, short poems, and songs.

> Most of the words in "Jabberwocky" are made up!
>
> I just finished reading the article "Man Eats Car."
>
> I loved "The Case for Short Words" in Richard Lederer's *The Miracle of Language*.
>
> "Try a Little Tenderness" is among my favorite classic songs.

Editing Checklist

✔ Have you enclosed titles of short poems, stories, articles, and songs in quotation marks?

✔ Have you underlined the titles of books, newspapers, movies, and long poems?

Publishing

Writing Process

An important part of report writing is publishing—the purpose of writing in this form is to present information. During the process of writing a research report, the writer learns about his or her subject in order to pass the information on to an interested reader. When deciding how to publish a research report, keep in mind the subject and who might benefit from reading about it.

Communicate Your Ideas

PUBLISHING

Present a final copy of your research report to an interested reader. With your teacher's permission, you and your classmates might display your reports on a table in your school library or media center.

Time Out to Reflect

In what ways have your research and report-writing skills improved after going through this chapter? Find a report that you wrote earlier in the year. Is it different from the one you just wrote? How? What did you do differently in this recent report? What report-writing skills would you like to improve upon? Record your thoughts in the Learning Log section of your **journal.**

TIMESAVER *QuickCheck*

Glance at each student's paper to be sure that it is neat and easy to read. If the report is messy, if the margins are too small, or if other problems exist, ask the student to make changes.

HOME STUDY

Before making their final copy, students should read their report aloud. This will help them catch many minor errors that they may overlook in reading it.

Using *In the Media*

Objective

- **To evaluate what makes a good documentary**

Group Project

- Divide the class into small groups. Have each group arrange to watch a documentary together. Students might watch a film that is owned by the school, rented from a video store, or shown on television. After watching the documentary, they should discuss its strengths and weaknesses. One student should summarize the feelings of members of the group and report them to class.

FYI

Websites to Visit Among the best-known documentaries are those in the POV series shown on the Public Broadcasting System. For information about these works, see http://www.pbs.org/pov. The Website http://www.documentaryfilms.net includes information on documentaries, clips from several, including ones on *Star Trek* fans, and links to other sites about documentaries. The International Documentary Filmfestival Amsterdam Website at http://www.damocles.nl/idfa/9909/uk/index.html is a wide-ranging site, including clips from many documentaries.

IN THE MEDIA

Documentary

A documentary is a research report on film. It uses images, narration, interviews, and sound to tell a story about different subjects. Unlike a newspaper or TV news report, a documentary does not have space constraints. As a result, documentaries are able to cover their subjects more in depth. A documentary can be about a wide variety of subjects—women's baseball leagues, insects, civil-rights leaders, a particular town—anything that has an interesting story.

Like other journalistic media forms, documentaries may seem at first like they are objective presentations of the truth. In fact they are just as biased as any other type of media. They reflect the values and biases of the individuals who make them. Camera angles, editing, lighting—all of these factors affect how the story gets told. Michael Moore, a documentary filmmaker, brought this issue into national discussion when he released his 1989 documentary *Roger & Me,* about his attempt to speak to the head of General Motors. Critics complained that Moore was obviously biased in his presentation of the story. Supporters argued that documentaries are always biased and that at least it was easy to tell what Moore's perspective was.

Media Activity

Start by watching at least two documentaries to get a feel for how they are structured. Then pick a topic that you think would make a good documentary. Write an outline for it that states the topic, what the issues are, and how you plan on presenting them. Think about whom you would need to interview, as well as what images and sounds you could use to support your story.

When you have finished, trade outlines with a classmate to give one another feedback. If you have access to video equipment, use A Writer's Guide to Electronic Publishing.

Process of Writing a Report

Remember you can move back and forth among the stages of the writing process to achieve your purpose. For example, during editing you may wish to return to the revising stage to add details that have occurred to you while editing. The numbers in parentheses refer to pages where you can get help with your writing.

PREWRITING

- Choose a subject that you can research and limit it. *(pages C351–C353)*
- Prepare a source card for each of your sources. *(page C355)*
- Gather information from varied print and electronic sources. *(pages C353–C356)*
- Take notes on note cards. *(pages C357–C358)*
- Organize your notes into categories and use them to outline the body. *(pages C360–C361)*

DRAFTING

- Write an introduction that includes a sentence expressing your main idea. *(pages C362–C363)*
- Use your outline to write the body in your own words. *(pages C363–C364)*
- Add a concluding paragraph. *(pages C364–C365)*
- Add a title. *(page C365)*
- Prepare a list of sources as your final page. *(pages C366–C367)*

REVISING

- Use the Evaluation Checklist for Revising on page C368 to improve your first draft.

EDITING AND PUBLISHING

- Polish your work by checking for errors in grammar, mechanics, and usage. Prepare a final copy for presentation to an interested reader.

EXPANDING THE LESSON

Using Technology

You will find additional **instructional** and **practice** materials for this chapter at http://www.bkenglish.com.

INTEGRATING TECHNOLOGY

Electronic Publishing

You may want to refer students to *A Writer's Guide to Electronic Publishing* on pages C520–C544 for suggestions on using resources for publishing.

Using *A Writer Writes*

Objective

- **To practice writing an I-search report**

TIMESAVER *QuickCheck*

At each stage, check to be sure that students are both reporting on their individual quest for information and leaving out any personal stories not related to the topic. One way to describe the I-search report is as a travelogue, where the journey is one of discovery of knowledge about a topic.

A Writer Writes

An I-Search Report

Purpose: to inform and explain

Audience: your classmates

Generally, research reports for school are formal and impersonal. There is a special type of report, however, in which the author takes a more personal approach—the I-search report. An I-search report is about a topic of personal interest or importance to you—about your individual quest for knowledge on a subject. An I-search report is usually written in the first person and is less formal than a research report. An I-search report still contains solid facts, but they are not presented in the same way as a typical research report. It is more like a magazine article than an official document. In other words, the author or reporter appears personally in the report.

Prewriting

In order to write an I-search report, choose a topic that is of personal interest to you—a topic that you really want to know more about. Brainstorm with someone, using your **journal** entries and notes to help you find a topic. Next, make a list of possible sources of information. In preparing this special kind of report, you can use all the traditional research report sources as well as interviews, personal reflections, and prior knowledge. People you interview may include those you know personally—family, friends, and neighbors, as well as people you are not as familiar with such as experts you contact via E-mail, telephone, or mail.

Drafting

As with a research report, your I-search report will have an introduction, body, conclusion, and title. Your introduction might state why you chose your particular topic. The body of your report could tell about your research process and what you learned. Your conclusion might state how your process and the information you found helped you to discover more about the topic you chose than you previously knew.

Just as with a research report, your I-search report should have a list of sources. Review the guidelines on page C366 before you prepare your list to be sure you have the correct format.

Revising

Revise your I-search report using the **Evaluation Checklist for Revising** on page C368. Share your paper with a classmate and ask for any suggestions he or she may have on how to improve it. A classmate who is interested in the topic of your paper or who has knowledge of your subject will be especially useful in giving suggestions. That person will be able to tell you what else he or she would like to learn, what questions remain unanswered, and if any explanations were unclear.

Editing

Edit your report for grammar, mechanics, spelling, and usage.

Publishing

Prepare a final copy of your report and share it with interested readers. You may want to send copies of your report to specialists on your topic or publish your paper on a Website devoted to your topic.

INTEGRATING *Writers at Work*

For more opportunities to stimulate students' report writing, look at *Writers at Work*.

FOR REVIEWING SKILLS

Using *Connection Collection*

Representing in Different Ways

Consider using these print and visual activities to make students aware of the benefits of using different media to suit particular purposes. Help students understand when a visual medium, for example, is better suited to their purpose than a print medium, or the reverse.

Connection Collection

Representing in Different Ways

From Print . . .

To: Front Page News Network Graphics Department
From: Clyde Tolson, President
Date: 12/09/01

Subject: New Background Slides

This week there are several breaking news stories that Channel 2 will be following closely. We will need two new background slides with captions to run during these segments of our broadcast. Here is a brief description of the top stories:

- **Amazon Rain Forest on the Move:** Brazil is losing thousands of square miles of rain forest every year as it creeps further north. Scientists expect the Amazon rain forest to have moved as far north as Georgia by early this century.
- **Dow Jones at Record High:** The Dow Jones may hit a record one and a half trillion points this week, topping its previous record of one trillion points.

Thank you.

. . . to Visuals

While television newscasters read stories, background slides are usually shown behind them. The slides illustrate the story and capture the viewers' attention. Illustrate the two breaking stories from the memo with background slides of your own.

From Visuals . . .

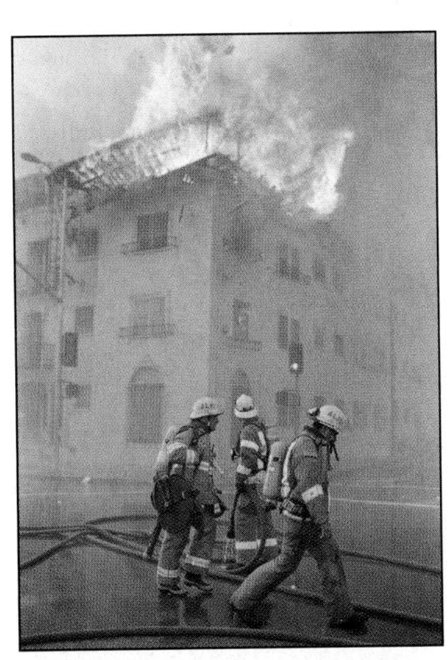

Downtown Fire

. . . to Print

Write a short news story for the background slide above. Remember that news stories are supposed to be clear and concise. They should begin with a topic sentence that answers the questions *who*, *what*, *when*, and *where* and include a quote from either a witness of the event or an expert on it.

- **Which strategies can be used for creating both written and visual representations? Which strategies apply to one, not both? Which type of representation is more effective?**
- **Draw a conclusion and write briefly about the differences between written ideas and visual representations.**

YOUR IDEAS

For Viewing and Representing

GETTING STUDENTS INVOLVED

Cooperative Learning

After organizing students into groups, thoroughly explain the task to be accomplished and establish a time frame. Make sure that each group member is responsible for a given task. Have each group share its project with the class and discuss the process the group used to carry out the assignment.

YOUR IDEAS

For Writing Prompts

Writing in Everyday Life

E-mail Report of Research

Your yearbook advisor wants you to find out what was popular this year among the students. The yearbook publishes photographs and descriptions of the fads and trends at your school annually, as it has done ever since your advisor, Mr. Ramspott, was a student. "In my day," he tells you, "the kids wore leather headbands and bell-bottoms. Rallies for the Equal Rights Amendment and ending the Vietnam War were popular, and Greg Brady and Evel Knievel were my heroes."

Write an E-mail to your advisor that reports at least five trends, fads, or ideas that are currently popular at your school. Observe your fellow students and listen to their conversations. Take notes on what they are wearing and discussing. You may also want to survey some of your classmates about what they think is important and fashionable.

What strategies did you use to report the trends to your yearbook advisor?

You can find information on writing E-mail in A Writer's Guide to Using the Internet.

Writing in the Workplace

Developing Research Subjects

You work for the quiz show *Beats Me!* and you need to write questions for the show every week. This week the host, Dale Dooley, has some special requests. He wants one easy question and one hard one for each of the following subjects: Chinese cuisine, popular music of the 1980s, squirrels, and bicycles.

Write two questions (one easy, one hard), along with their answers, for each of these subjects. Since the show has to award money for every correct answer, you must make sure that your questions are fair and clear and the answers are well researched. Remember to consult reliable research sources to obtain your questions and answers.

What strategies did you use to develop your questions and answers?

You can find information on choosing research subjects on pages C351–C353.

A DIFFERENT DELIVERY SYSTEM

For formal assignment print the composition chapter test from the *BK English* Test Bank at http://www.bkenglish.com.

Assess Your Learning

You are a reporter for *Young Consumers Newsletter* and you have been assigned a story on the worst deal of the year. Your editor wants you to investigate purchases that you, your friends, or your family have made that were disastrous.

- **Write a short report on a disastrous purchase that you have investigated. As a story in a newsletter, your report should be informative, fun to read, and it should warn people not to make a similar purchase.**
- **In trying to convince others of your ideas, be sure to identify your audience. Begin your report with a topic sentence that identifies the subject of your story and the main points that you want to make about it. Your report should include evidence that supports your point, and it should be organized to ensure coherence and logical progression.**

Before You Write **Consider the following questions:**
What is the ***subject?***
What is the ***occasion?***
Who is the ***audience?***
What is the ***purpose?***

After You Write **Evaluate your work using the following criteria:**

- Did you include a topic sentence?
- Did you support your point with evidence?
- Were your ideas organized in a coherent and logical progression?
- Have you used connecting devices so that your report is sensible and easy to read?
- Have you evaluated your research sources to make sure that they are reliable?
- Does your conclusion round out the report by referring to an idea in the introduction without repeating it exactly?
- Have you checked for grammatical, spelling, and punctuation errors that might weaken your authority in the eyes of your audience?

Write briefly on how well you did. Point out your strengths and areas for improvement.

FOR ASSESSING LEARNING

Using *Assess Your Learning*

This writing prompt will help you and your students informally assess their developing writing abilities, using the accompanying primary trait rubrics, which list the key features and qualities of report writing taught in this chapter. You may want to have students maintain their self-assessment in their portfolios as a record of their individual progress throughout the year.

Evaluating a Research Report

In writing research reports, many students need special help in

- **arriving at a suitable main idea statement**
- **supporting this main idea with information drawn from research**
- **presenting supporting data clearly and logically**

Self-evaluation and peer evaluation can help students improve their research papers in these areas during revision.

Self-evaluation

When students have finished their first drafts, help them evaluate their work for the purpose of revising. Hand out copies of the Evaluation Checklist for Writing Research Reports. (See the Evaluation Checklists in BK English Language and Composition Assessment.) As students read their drafts a first time, have them focus on content, with special attention to the traits numbered below.

Peer evaluation

An alternative approach to evaluating research papers is for students to work in pairs or small groups, preferably selected on the basis of similar or related report topics. In that way, after reading the drafts silently or hearing them read aloud, peers can make suggestions concerning not only content, but also sources of more or better information.

1 The subject is of interest and is suited to a 3–5 page research paper.

2 The introduction clearly states the main idea, and subsequent paragraphs cover topics related to the main idea.

3 The research paper contains sufficient and accurate details with data effectively incorporated and clearly cited.

4 Paragraphs are logically ordered, and transitional expressions are used effectively.

5 The concluding paragraph pulls all the information together to reinforce the main idea.

Teacher evaluation

Primary Traits

The following opening paragraphs of a research paper exhibit excellent use of information drawn from research and can serve as a model in evaluating students' research papers.

MODEL FOR EVALUATION

Effective use of direct address

At the next election, will you wear a button for your favorite candidate? Wearing political buttons is a tradition in America that is more than a century old. The familiar pin-back kind we wear today was first worn in the presidential election of 1896 where citizens wore buttons for their favorite candidate, either William McKinley or William Jennings Bryan ("Buttons" 1194). The popularity of these buttons has led the nation to the joke and slogan buttons we wear today. Buttons, however, were worn long before the election of 1896.

Research data well cited and incorporated

Thesis is well suited for short report

Decorated buttons are "almost as old as clothes" (Haymaker 3). The first buttons appeared in France in the 1700s.

Teacher Evaluation

Primary Trait Evaluation

The following chart lists the key features and qualities for primary trait assessment of research papers.

	EXCELLENT	ACCEPTABLE	NEEDS IMPROVEMENT
Main Idea Statement	Clearly states an interesting main idea that lends itself to support by information drawn from research.	States a main idea that is at least supportable by information drawn from research.	Does not state a main idea supportable by researched information.
Supporting Information	The research paper contains ample information from current, accurate, and objective books, periodicals, and interviews with experts, all of which are properly cited.	The research paper contains adequate information from relatively recent and reliable sources, most of them properly cited.	The research paper uses little or no researched information; the information used is from outdated or unreliable sources. Citations are wrong or absent.
Organization	Each paragraph develops a topic related to the main idea, and the topics are presented in a logical order.	Topics are organized in paragraphs, but not all topics clearly relate to the main idea or follow a logical order.	Clear topic paragraphs are lacking; the information presented has little internal order or relation to the main idea.
Style	Transitions are used to enhance the flow of information, and quotations and other details drawn from research are woven smoothly into the text.	Some transitions are used, and an effort is made to fit quotations and details into the text.	Transitions are lacking and quotations and details are used disconnectedly.
Conclusion	A concluding paragraph pulls all the information together in restating or otherwise reinforcing the main idea.	The conclusion recaps some of the information in the main idea.	There is either no conclusion or none clearly related to the main idea and data presented.

Teacher Evaluation

Holistic Evaluation

The following criteria may be used to evaluate research papers holistically, using a rating scale of

4 (excellent)
3 (good)
2 (acceptable)
1 (needs improvement)
0 (unscoreable).

4	3	2	1
The main idea statement clearly states an interesting idea or opinion supportable by information drawn from research.	The main idea statement is clearly supportable by information drawn from research.	The main idea statement is either too obvious or difficult to support.	The research paper has no main idea statement supportable by researched information.
The supporting information is interesting, ample, related to the main idea, well integrated and properly cited.	The supporting information is adequate, basically related to the main idea, integrated with the text, and properly cited.	Some relevant supporting information is given, with an attempt at citation.	Little or no relevant supporting information drawn from research is used.
The research paper is well organized. An introductory paragraph gives background information and states the main idea. The body includes ordered paragraphs developed with supporting information. Ideas are connected by transitional words. A conclusion pulls the research together and reinforces the main idea.	The research paper is generally well organized, although a few ideas or supporting points are out of place or unrelated.	An introductory paragraph states the main idea; a body contains some supporting information; and a conclusion restates the main idea.	The research paper is poorly organized, with no recognizable introduction, body, and conclusion.

Essential Knowledge and Skills

- Demonstrating effective communications skills that reflect such demands as reporting
- Selecting and using voice and style appropriate to audience and purpose
- Choosing the appropriate form for his/her own writing purpose including letters and editorials
- Writing legibly by selecting cursive or manuscript as appropriate
- Capitalizing and punctuating correctly to clarify and enhance meaning such as capitalizing titles, using hyphens, semicolons, and colons
- Corresponding with peers or others via E-mail and conventional mail
- Using media to compare ideas and points of view

CHAPTER 12

Letters

When friends or relatives move away, how do you keep from missing them so much? One way to keep in touch is by writing letters. Sometimes you need to write letters to invite people to a special occasion, to thank someone for doing something for you, or to express regret at not being able to attend an event to which you are invited. Letters can also help you collect information you may need while working on research reports. You will also write letters to order merchandise or conduct other kinds of business. This chapter will show you the correct form for various kinds of letters.

Reading with a Writer's Eye

Letters sometimes provide insights into history that facts and figures cannot provide. Some time after the Revolutionary War, Paul Revere wrote the following letter to a member of Congress. As you read, notice how the letter's style, spelling, and other writing conventions have changed since the time of Paul Revere.

BLOCK SCHEDULING

- If your schedule requires that you cover the chapter in a **shorter time**, use the core lesson in Developing Everyday Writing Skills.
- If you want to take advantage of **longer class time**, use one or more of the following: In the Media, Writing Is Thinking, or A Writer Writes.

Paul Revere to William Eustis on Deborah Sampson Gannett,

AMERICA'S FIRST WOMAN SOLDIER

Despite faithfully serving in the Continental Army for several years, Robert Shurtliff did not receive the pension guaranteed to all veterans. The situation, however, was unique: Robert Shurtliff was, in fact, Deborah Sampson, believed to be the first American woman to fight as a soldier for her country. Dressed as a man Sampson enlisted in the army and was assigned to the Fourth Massachusetts Regiment. In June of 1782, during a battle in New York, Sampson was shot in the leg but returned to her regiment after a brief recuperation. Soon after, her regiment was ordered to march several hundred miles through blizzards, and Sampson was eventually hospitalized for pneumonia. Again, she recovered and went back to fight. After the war Sampson was honorably discharged and eventually married Benjamin Gannett, had children, and worked on a farm. But as the years went on, working became difficult, owing in part to her injuries and hospitalizations, and her family slipped into poverty. Paul Revere, a neighbor who sympathized with Gannett's plight, assisted her in her efforts to receive a pension. In 1804 he wrote the following letter to William Eustis, a Massachusetts representative in Congress.

FOR INCREASING STUDENT ACHIEVEMENT

GUIDED READING

Text Analysis

- This **letter of request** by a famous Revolutionary War figure is **persuasive** in purpose and mode. Have students identify the primary reason for writing the letter.
- Because the letter is addressed to someone in a position of power, the language of the letter is **formal** and the **tone** is serious.
- The **organization** of the letter is designed to present the request in a cogent, logical way. The writer begins with an introduction of the problem, includes **reasons** and **examples** to support his opinion, and ends with a specific request.

GUIDED READING

Strategy: Self-Questioning

Suggest that as students read Paul Revere's letter, they ask themselves questions to monitor their own understanding. Model this strategy by asking some preliminary questions before they begin to read: Why would Paul Revere have bothered to intervene in Deborah Gannett's case? How did the two people know each other? Have students read to find the answer to these and other questions they have as they read.

Sir—

Mrs. Deborah Gannett of Sharon informed me, that she has inclosed to your care a petition to Congress in favour of Her. My works for manufacturing Copper, being at Canton, but a short distance from the neighbourhood where she lives; I have been induced to enquire her situation, and character, since she quitted the Male habit, and Soldier's uniform, for the more decent apparel of her own sex; and since she has been married and become a Mother:—Humanity, and Justice obliges me to say, that every person with whom I have conversed about Her, and it is not a few, speak of Her as a woman of handsom talents, good morals, a dutifull Wife, and an affectionate parent. She is now much out of health. She has several Children, her Husband is a good sort of man, 'tho of small force in business; they have a few acres of poor land which they cultivate, but they are really poor.

She told me, she had no doubt that her ill health is in consequence of her being exposed when she did a Soldier's duty; and that while in the army, she was wounded.

We commonly form our idea of the person whom we hear spoken of, whom we have never seen, according as their actions are described. When I heard her spoken of as a Soldier, I formed the idea of a tall, masculine female, who had a small share of understanding, without education, and one of the meanest of her sex.—When I saw and discoursed with her I was agreeably surprised to find a small, effeminate, and conversable Woman, whose education entitled her to a better situation in life.

I have no doubt your humanity will prompt you to do all in your power to get her some relief. I think her cause much more deserving than the hundreds to whom Congress has been generous.

I am sir with esteem and respect your humble servant.

Paul Revere

A short time later Congress added to the Massachusetts Pension Rolls the name "Deborah Sampson Gannett, who served as a soldier in the Army of the United States during the late Revolutionary War, and who was seriously wounded therein."

READER RESPONSE

You may want to use the following questions to elicit students' personal responses to the letter.

1. If you were in charge of pensions, which of Revere's arguments would have helped to persuade you to add Deborah Gannett to the rolls? Which arguments could Revere have left out, in your opinion?
2. How does Revere attempt to touch his reader through specific description? through an appeal to his character?
3. What makes this letter one of historical interest? Is it a good letter to use as a model for persuasive letters? Why or why not?

LITERARY CONNECTION

You may wish to explore letter writing using one or more of the following works, which appear in literature textbooks at this grade level.

- *E-Mail from Bill Gates* by John Seabrook
- "Letter to Harriet Tubman" by Frederick Douglass
- *Letters from Rifka* by Karen Hesse
- "Paul Revere's Ride" by Henry Wadsworth Longfellow

ADDITIONAL RESOURCES

Composition Skills Practice. . . . . pages 61–66
ESL Practice and Test Preparation . . . . . pages 71–77
Standardized Test Preparation . . . . Units 1, 4, 10, 12
Writers at Work . . . . 8•1–8•10
Assessment: Chapter Test. . . . . pages 82–86
Assessment Resources . . . . pages 1–10, 13–44

Using *Thinking as a Writer*

You may choose to have students respond to the questions either orally or in writing.

REACHING ALL STUDENTS

English Language Learners

Use the **Viewing** exercise to enable English Language Learners to expand their oral communication skills and their vocabulary. As students suggest words to describe the female soldier, list them on the chalkboard. Help students come up with synonyms or words with more precise shades of meaning for some of the words suggested.

Thinking as a Writer

Evaluating a Persuasive Argument

In this letter, the author's purpose is to persuade his reader that Deborah Sampson is worthy of a pension.

- What argument does he use to persuade his reader? Do you think his strategy is effective?
- If you were writing a similar letter today, would you present your argument differently? If so, how?

Assessing Tone

Oral Expression Read aloud Paul Revere's letter with a partner. While you read, have your partner listen. Then switch roles.

- Identify words or phrases that sound old-fashioned.
- How would you characterize the tone of Revere's letter? Is it formal or informal?

Finding Words to Describe Visual Images

Viewing Revere pictured Deborah Sampson one way before meeting her. He admits that this impression was proved wrong upon meeting her.

- Look at the photograph of a female soldier. What words would you use to describe this soldier? Focus on her expression as well as her clothes.
- How might Paul Revere and Deborah Sampson react to this picture? Would they describe her in the same way? If not, why not?

FOR DEVELOPING SKILLS

LESSON 1 *(pages C385–C393)*

OBJECTIVES

- **To identify tone in letters**
- **To recognize the connection among audience, purpose, and tone in various types of letters**

Create Interest

Read aloud the letter by Paul Revere and the model of a friendly letter on page C386. Explain that these letters were written centuries apart, with different purposes in mind, and for different audiences. Although they have some things in common, they differ in language and tone.

Developing Your Everyday Writing Skills

Even though writing E-mails is becoming more common, there are still occasions when you can write a letter. What distinguishes one type of letter from another is its purpose.

Friendly Letters

Sometimes you write just to keep in touch and share news. These kinds of letters are friendly letters.

A **friendly letter** is an informal letter that you write to a friend or relative.

PARTS OF A FRIENDLY LETTER	
HEADING	This includes your full address with zip code. Use the full name of your state or the abbreviation. *(See page C396.)* Always include the date after your address. Follow the rules of capitalization and using commas.
SALUTATION	This is your personal greeting. Always capitalize the first word and all proper nouns. Use a comma after the salutation. **D**ear **A**unt **S**ally, **D**ear **D**ad,
BODY	This is your conversational message. Remember to indent each paragraph.
CLOSING	This is followed by a comma. Capitalize the first word only. **Y**our nephew, **L**ove always,
SIGNATURE	Sign your name below the closing.

REACHING ALL STUDENTS

Struggling Learners

Review with students the capitalization rules for proper nouns. Remind students that names of particular people, places, and things begin with capital letters, as do titles with names and abbreviations of place names and titles. Write these examples on the board and have students capitalize them correctly.

ms. roberta chavez (Ms. Roberta Chavez)

los angeles, california (Los Angeles, California)

254 monterey blvd. (254 Monterey Blvd.)

Guide Instruction

By Connecting Ideas

Define tone as a writer's attitude toward his or her subject matter and audience. Remind students that Paul Revere's tone was formal and serious, which suited his purpose and audience. Ask students to describe the tone of the example on page C386 (polite, interested, caring).

Consolidate Skills

Through Guided Practice

Have students imagine that the model letter on page C386 is written for a different audience; for example, a close teenage friend who has just attended a family gathering. Discuss how the tone of the letter would be likely to change or have students rewrite the letter to express the change in audience.

USING STUDENTS' STRENGTHS

Multiple Intelligences: Kinesthetic

Ask students to use their fingers to locate indentations in the body of the letter and identify the number of paragraphs written.

REACHING ALL STUDENTS

Advanced Learners

Analyze those elements that make this letter especially appealing to its audience. Point out that the language is appropriate for writing to an older person, and that the attitude of the writer toward her audience shines through. In addition, the content of the letter is of special interest to the recipient, and the writer is careful to address her audience in a conversational tone.

Friendly Letter Form The following model shows the correct form for a friendly letter. All friendly letters have the following five main parts, as shown in the chart.

MODEL: Friendly Letter

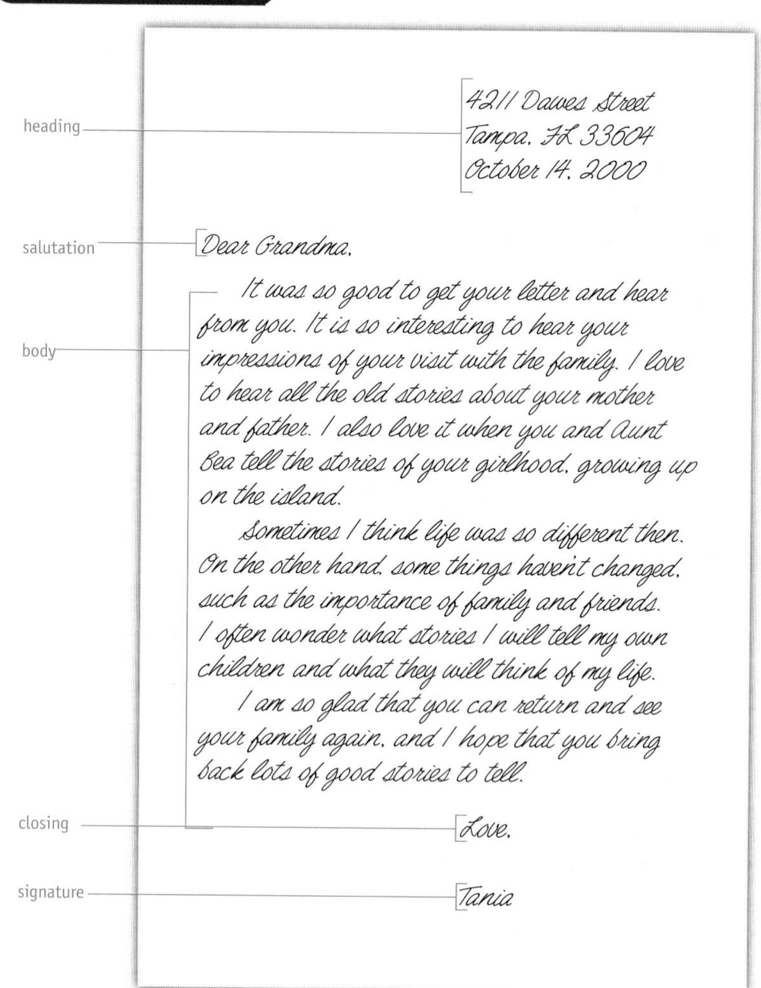
heading — 4211 Dawes Street
Tampa, FL 33604
October 14, 2000

salutation — Dear Grandma,

body — It was so good to get your letter and hear from you. It is so interesting to hear your impressions of your visit with the family. I love to hear all the old stories about your mother and father. I also love it when you and Aunt Bea tell the stories of your girlhood, growing up on the island.

Sometimes I think life was so different then. On the other hand, some things haven't changed, such as the importance of family and friends. I often wonder what stories I will tell my own children and what they will think of my life.

I am so glad that you can return and see your family again, and I hope that you bring back lots of good stories to tell.

closing — Love,

signature — Tania

Apply to Communication

Through Independent Writing

Letter-writing activities can be used to extend students' understanding of tone. Help them decide whether their purpose and audience suit a tone that is chatty or erudite, comic or serious.

Transfer to Everyday Life

By Analyzing Others' Letters

Ask students to choose a letter from an anthology of letters and to analyze the letter for tone. Suggest that they first identify the letter's purpose and audience and then determine whether the tone suits that purpose and audience.

Pull It All Together

By Sharing

Ask students to read the letter they chose for the **Transfer to Everyday Life** activity aloud to the class. Have them take questions from the class about the letter's purpose, audience, and tone.

IN THE MEDIA

Write a Letter

Before E-mail and telephone messages were invented, letter writing was the only way to communicate over large distances. Letters were so important that Thomas Jefferson used a primitive printing machine to copy all of the letters he ever wrote. Letters also have a long legacy as a tool for social change. During the Great Depression, hundreds of Americans sent letters to First Lady Eleanor Roosevelt asking for help. Those letters helped to determine government policy. The trend continues: when politicians receive a number of letters regarding a certain topic, it can help them decide what to do about it.

One use for a formal letter is to reach a wider audience. Letters to the editor are a regular feature of almost every magazine and newspaper. These letters provide private citizens with a public forum, and publicize other points of view. Not all letters to the editor are published, but editors usually print a variety of letters that are well written and offer a fresh perspective.

Media Activity

Read through the "letters to the editor" section in your local newspaper. What sort of things do people write about? Now, pick a topic covered by your school newspaper that concerns you and write your own letter to the editor. Be clear in defining the topic. Use examples that clearly illustrate what is going on, and offer solutions. How is this different from writing an E-mail message to a friend or talking on the phone? Did you have to organize your thoughts differently? Send your letter and see if it gets published!

Using *In the Media*

Objective

- **To analyze the significance of letters to the editor**

Group Project

- As a class, analyze the traits of letters to the editor. Each student should select five different letters to the paper. For each letter, the student should estimate the number of words in the letter, decide whether the letter supports or opposes a viewpoint expressed in an earlier article in the paper, and categorize the tone of the letter as reasonable, angry, or humorous. Compile the results from the class, and decide what length, viewpoint, and tone of letters are most likely to be published in that paper.

Websites to Visit The Internet Public Library has an extensive and easy-to-use collection of links to newspapers around the world at http://www.ipl.org/reading/news/. Another large collection of newspaper links is http://www.concentric.net/~stevewt/.

Check Understanding

By Discussing

Have students work in small groups to determine an appropriate tone for a friendly letter

- written to cheer up an ailing friend
- sent as a holiday greeting to a distant cousin
- written to console an elderly neighbor on a death in the family

DEVELOPING WORKPLACE COMPETENCIES

Personal Qualities: Responsibility

Explain to students that one requirement of being a responsible worker and adult is timely, polite communication. In the business world, this involves writing memos and business letters. In everyday life, it involves writing social letters.

The timing of social letters is key. Thank-you letters and notes must be sent shortly after the receipt of any gift or favor. Invitations must be sent enough in advance of an event for the recipient to make appropriate plans. Letters of regret must be sent as soon as possible following the receipt of an invitation.

In many social circles, only handwritten social letters are considered polite. Some occasions, such as weddings, may call for a more formal, printed invitation. In any case, getting into the habit of writing social letters promptly can help develop personal responsibility.

Have students work in small groups to draft sample social letters for these situations:

- a thank-you letter to a friend's parent for recommending you for a job
- a letter inviting a co-worker to join your family and friends on a boat ride
- a letter of regret declining an invitation to attend a lecture at a local university

Social Letters

Social letters have a more formal tone than friendly letters. However, a social letter is written using the same form as a friendly letter. Social letters have a specific purpose such as to thank someone for something, to invite someone to an event, or to inform someone that you cannot accept an invitation.

Invitations An invitation informs someone about an occasion you would like him or her to attend. It includes the time and place and any other details your guests might need to know. You can use smaller paper for invitations.

Model: Invitation

46 Alexis Lane
Santa Clara, CA 95050
December 1, 2000

Dear Janine,

I know it has been a while since we spoke, so I hope you are doing well. Our family has been busy, but I want to let you know that you are invited to my Holiday Party on Friday, December 22, at 8 p.m. at the above address. The dress code will be informal but festive. Please feel free to bring a friend. R.S.V.P.

Sincerely,

Wanda Reckhaus

Thank-you Letters A thank-you letter expresses your gratitude or appreciation. The following model shows the correct form for a thank-you letter.

Model: Thank-you Letter

711 Country Mile Drive
Houston, TX 7701
November 26, 2000

Dear Uncle Pete,

Thank you very much for the computer encyclopedia. It is fantastic! I have already used it to do some research for a school report on one-celled animals. It is great to be able to do my research right from my computer at home instead of having to go to the library. I know I will use it often in the future.

Thanks again for the perfect gift. I am looking forward to seeing you at the holidays.

Your favorite nephew,

Tony

REACHING ALL STUDENTS

Struggling Learners

Ask students to review the model to locate the date and time of the party, the location of the party, and special information for the guests. Have students tell about similar invitations they have received. Encourage students to bring to class examples of invitations they have received.

HOME WORK

Have students write an invitation to a real or imaginery party. Have students check their invitations for the following: all five letter parts, information that tells when and where, and specific information relating to dress or locale.

USING STUDENTS' STRENGTHS

Multiple Intelligences: Interpersonal

Have students recall an event to which they received an invitation but were unable to attend. Have students write a letter of regret. Remind students that a tone of sincerity is important in a letter of regret. The writer should sound genuinely sorry. Ask students to read their drafts aloud so that their classmates can comment on the tone.

Letters of Regret A letter of regret informs someone that you will be unable to attend an event to which you have been invited. The following model shows the correct form for a letter of regret.

Model: Letter of Regret

22 Salamander Drive
Albuquerque, NM 87111
January 5, 2000

Dear Elsie,

I am so sorry that I will be unable to attend your potluck dinner party next week. My grandfather has taken ill in Cincinnati, and my whole family is going there to be with him. Thank you for thinking of me, and I hope you have a nice party. I'll talk to you when I get back.

Sincerely,

Lucas Martinez

Business Letters

Most of the business letters you write will ask the receiver to do something. You may write a letter requesting information about some research that you are doing. You may order merchandise from a catalog, asking the receiver to send the desired items. You may write a letter requesting a form that you need to fill out in order to register for a service. To ensure you get the results you want, keep your letter brief and state your business clearly.

A **business letter** is a formal letter that requires action on the part of the receiver.

Things to Remember When Writing a Business Letter:

- Use white stationery when you write a business letter, preferably 8½ by 11 inches.
- Leave margins at least 1 inch wide on all sides.
- Be sure to keep a copy of every business letter you send. You can keep an electronic copy on your computer, but you should also keep a hard copy.

There are many styles for writing business letters. The **block style** puts each part of the letter at the left margin of the page. A blank line is left between each paragraph in the body of the letter. The paragraphs are not indented.

In the **modified block style,** the heading, closing, and signature are on the right. The inside address, salutation, and body all start at the left margin. Paragraphs are indented. All business letters in this chapter use the modified block style.

Business Letter Form Business letters have six main parts, one part more than friendly letters. This extra part is called the inside address. The inside address includes all the information about the receiver that you will put on the envelope.

INTEGRATING TECHNOLOGY

Internet

Tell students that locating the mailing addresses of businesses around the world is possible using the Internet. They may use a search engine to locate the home page of the business whose address they require; most businesses post their addresses right on the home page. Alternatively, they may use an online telephone directory to find the information they require. You may also direct students to *A Writer's Guide to the Internet* on pages C545–C576.

Using *Editing Workshop*

Objective

- **To understand and use commas correctly in letters**

A DIFFERENT APPROACH

Auditory Remind students that commas often signify a pause, as in a compound sentence. Have them listen as you read the examples on this page aloud. Point out that in normal speech, the voice lifts slightly as it approaches the comma. Then it drops off following the comma. By reading addresses and dates aloud, students may often be able to tell where commas belong.

Visual Write these dates and addresses on the chalkboard and have students determine why each comma is needed. Explain that commas, like other forms of punctuation, are used to improve communication by eliminating potential confusion.

January 20 2000
January 20, 2000
Morgantown West Virginia
Morgantown, West Virginia

Mechanics in the Writing Process

Prewriting Workshop
Drafting Workshop
Revising Workshop
Editing Workshop
Publishing Workshop

Commas

Like all other kinds of interactions among people, letters carry with them their own rules for polite behavior. Especially when writing business letters, be sure to follow the accepted form. A letter in proper form signals to the receiver that you know and respect the rules for polite correspondence.

One important part of the correct form of letters is the correct use of commas.

Using Commas in Dates

When writing the date, use commas to separate the day of the month from the year.

Commas Separating Day from Year	September 21, 2000 February 14, 2000 August 8, 2001

Using Commas in Addresses

Also remember to use commas to separate parts of addresses that appear on the same line. The only exception is in the final line of the address. Do not use a comma to separate the state from the zip code. This rule applies to both the heading and the inside address.

Commas Separating Parts of Address	111 Koster Avenue, Apt. 12B Evanston, IL 60201

Editing Checklist

- ✔ Did you use commas to separate the day from the year?
- ✔ Have you used commas to separate parts of an address that appear on the same line?

PARTS OF A BUSINESS LETTER	
Heading	The heading is the same as the heading of a friendly letter. Include your full address and the date. Follow the rules for capitalizing proper nouns and using commas. Use the full name of your state or the abbreviation. *(page C396)* If you use the abbreviation, be sure to abbreviate the state in the inside address too.
Inside Address	Start two to four lines below the heading. Write the name of the person who will receive the letter, if you know it. Use *Mr.*, *Ms.*, *Mrs.*, *Dr.*, and so on, before the name. If the person has a title, like *General Manager*, write it on the next line. Then write the receiver's address.
Salutation	Start the salutation, or greeting, two lines below the inside address. In a business letter, use a colon after the salutation. *Dear Mrs. Walters:* *Dear Sir or Madam:*
Body	Two lines below the salutation, begin the body or message of the letter. Skip a line between paragraphs and indent each new paragraph.
Closing	In a business letter, use a formal closing. Start two or three lines below the body. Line up the closing with the left-hand edge of the heading. Capitalize the first word only and use a comma. *Sincerely,* *Yours truly,* *Sincerely yours,* *Very truly yours,*
Signature	In the signature of a business letter, your name appears twice. First type or print your name four or five lines below the closing. Then sign your name in the space between the closing and your typed name. Do not use *Mr.* or *Ms.* to refer to yourself.

IDENTIFYING COMMON STUMBLING BLOCKS

Problem

- Leaving out the inside address

Solution

- Remind students that business letters differ from friendly letters in four main ways: their tone is more formal; they use a colon instead of a comma after the salutation; they include a handwritten and a typed signature; and they list both the address of the sender and the address of the recipient. Suggest that students review their business letters and ask themselves: "Could I address an envelope completely based on the information in this letter?" If they have included both a heading and an inside address, the answer should be yes.

LESSON 2 *(pages C394–C401)*

OBJECTIVES

- **To distinguish between formal and informal language in letters**
- **To practice writing formal and informal English**

Create Interest

Tell students that you plan to write to the superintendent of schools suggesting a Master Teacher Plan. Read aloud this excerpt from your "first draft": *Hey, man, you'd better get with the program. Master Teaching is like the wave of the future, and it's totally the way we should go.* Have students suggest the response you might receive. (You would not be taken seriously because your language was inappropriate.)

Guide Instruction

By Connecting Ideas

Explain that English is malleable; we alter it depending on our audience and purpose. When we talk to friends, we

USING STUDENTS' STRENGTHS

Multiple Intelligences: Spatial

Ask students with good visual and spatial sense to create a grid that shows the class how to line up a letter properly, including indentations and numbers of lines to skip between letter parts. They may create the grid on graph paper to be photocopied for general use.

HOME WORK

Have students read their local newspaper or a magazine that comes to their home and draft a business letter to the editor, making a request or stating an opinion.

Notice that the model business letter shown below is a letter of request. A letter of request is a kind of business letter that requests information or requires some kind of response from the receiver.

MODEL: Business Letter (Letter of Request)

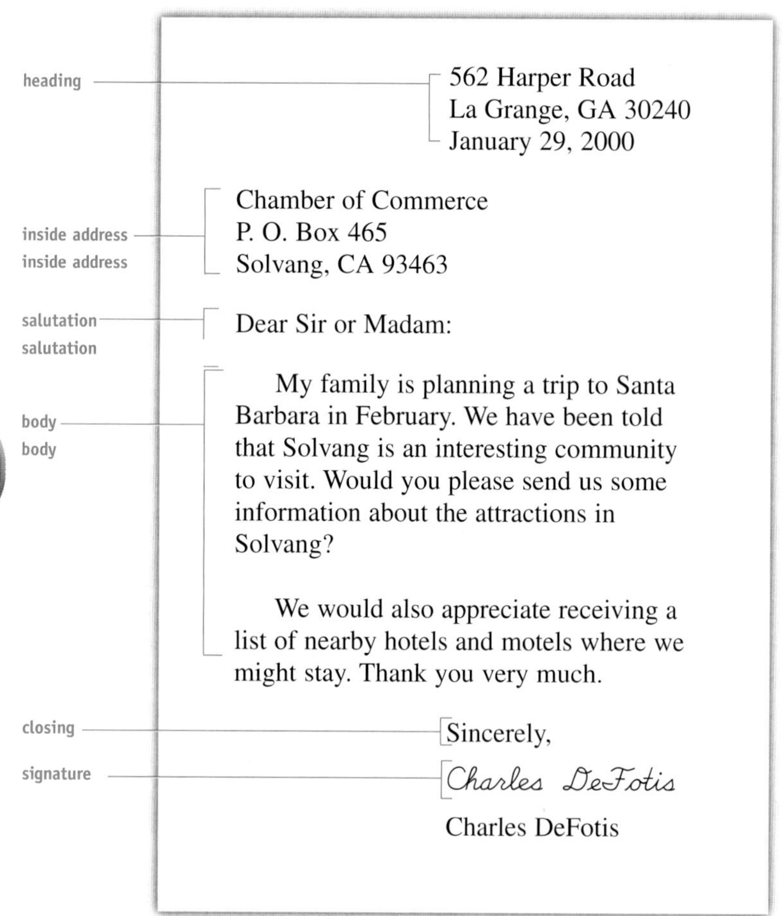

562 Harper Road
La Grange, GA 30240
January 29, 2000

Chamber of Commerce
P. O. Box 465
Solvang, CA 93463

Dear Sir or Madam:

My family is planning a trip to Santa Barbara in February. We have been told that Solvang is an interesting community to visit. Would you please send us some information about the attractions in Solvang?

We would also appreciate receiving a list of nearby hotels and motels where we might stay. Thank you very much.

Sincerely,

Charles DeFotis

Charles DeFotis

use one kind of language. When we talk to people in positions of power, we use another. Similarly, when we write a personal letter, we may use informal language. When we write a business letter, the language should always be formal. Informal language may include slang, dialect, contractions, and so on. Formal language follows the rules of English grammar to the letter.

Consolidate Skills

Through Guided Practice

Use the model business letter on page C394 to extend students' understanding of formal versus informal language. Point out that there are no contractions used, and that formal phrases such as, "We would appreciate" and "Would you please" contribute to the overall serious tone. Next, have students imagine that the writer is communicating with a former classmate who has just moved to Santa Barbara, California. Ask them to work in small groups to rewrite the letter as a personal letter asking for information about Santa Barbara. Have a volunteer

Envelopes The model below shows the correct form for an envelope. Print or type your own name and address in the upper left-hand corner. The receiver's address is the same as the inside address. It is centered on the envelope. Use the abbreviation for the state and remember to include the zip code.

Model: Envelope

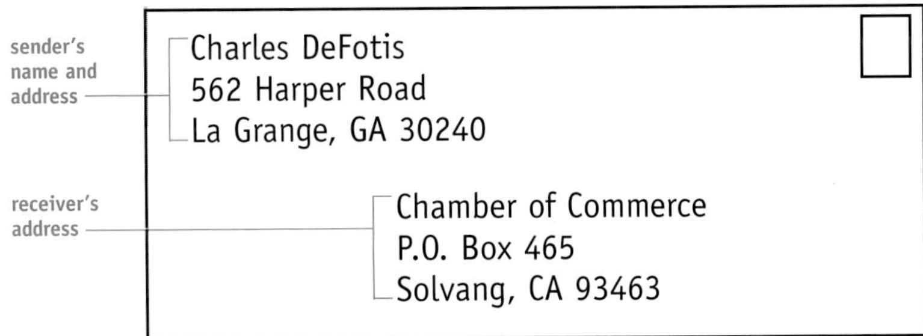

sender's name and address
Charles DeFotis
562 Harper Road
La Grange, GA 30240
receiver's address
Chamber of Commerce
P.O. Box 465
Solvang, CA 93463

The way you fold your letter depends on the size of your envelope. If you use envelopes that are as wide as your stationery, fold the letter in thirds as shown in the diagram below.

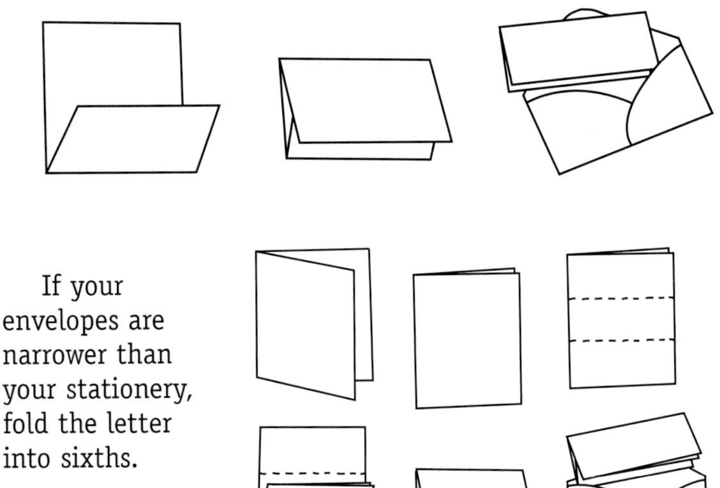

If your envelopes are narrower than your stationery, fold the letter into sixths.

IDENTIFYING COMMON STUMBLING BLOCKS

Problem

- Writing illegibly

Solution

- Students must understand that the delivery of any letter depends in large part on the legibility of the address. Students must follow the standard three- or four-line format:

  NAME
  COMPANY
  STREET ADDRESS
  CITY, STATE, ZIP

They must also make sure that their writing can be read by postal workers. If students' cursive writing is hard to read, suggest that they use simple block letters when handwriting an envelope. Alternatively, they may type the return and receiver's addresses, lining them up as shown.

HOME WORK

Ask students to look at an envelope they or another family member received and then to imagine writing back to the sender. Have them prepare an envelope that would suit the purpose.

from each group read the revision aloud. Discuss the informal language used and its effect on the overall tone of the letter.

Apply to Communication

Through Independent Writing

As students revise their own business letters, have them note places where they might replace informal language with language that is more appropriate to the purpose and audience of the letter.

Transfer to Everyday Life

By Evaluating Letters to the Editor

Supply an op-ed page from your local newspaper and ask students to work in groups to evaluate the appropriateness of the language used in letters to the editor. Tell them that some newspapers edit readers' letters to conform to the newspaper's style.

REACHING ALL STUDENTS

English Language Learners

This chart may be used to help students learn state names as well as abbreviations. Work with a map of the United States. Challenge students to locate each state on the map as they read the name on the chart. Then ask students to name the states that border your state and to use the chart to spell those states' abbreviations.

STATE ABBREVIATIONS

Alabama	AL	Montana	MT
Alaska	AK	Nebraska	NE
Arizona	AZ	Nevada	NV
Arkansas	AR	New Hampshire	NH
California	CA	New Jersey	NJ
Colorado	CO	New Mexico	NM
Connecticut	CT	New York	NY
Delaware	DE	North Carolina	NC
District of Columbia	DC	North Dakota	ND
Florida	FL	Ohio	OH
Georgia	GA	Oklahoma	OK
Hawaii	HI	Oregon	OR
Idaho	ID	Pennsylvania	PA
Illinois	IL	Puerto Rico	PR
Indiana	IN	Rhode Island	RI
Iowa	IA	South Carolina	SC
Kansas	KS	South Dakota	SD
Kentucky	KY	Tennessee	TN
Louisiana	LA	Texas	TX
Maine	ME	Utah	UT
Maryland	MD	Vermont	VT
Massachusetts	MA	Virginia	VA
Michigan	MI	Washington	WA
Minnesota	MN	West Virginia	WV
Mississippi	MS	Wisconsin	WI
Missouri	MO	Wyoming	WY

Pull It All Together

By Summarizing

Have students use their own words to write a rule that explains why formal language should be used in business letters.

Check Understanding

By Finding Examples

Have students skim anthologies of letters to find examples of formal and informal language used in letter writing.

Order Letters If you want to order an item from a catalog, you can use a business letter form. An order letter includes the six parts of a business letter. The model below shows the correct form for an order letter.

MODEL: Order Letter

4333 West Silvestre Avenue
Bluff Dale, TX 76433
March 10, 2000

Hollywood Heaven
643 Baker Road
Detroit, MI 48222

Dear Sir or Madam:

Please send me the following items from your 2000 winter catalog:

quantity and description of item — 1 poster (36 x 24) of Paul Newman and Robert Redford from *The Sting*,
Order # 45-H-112
price for each item — $9.95
size and color — 1 *Wizard of Oz* T-shirt, blue, size small,
order number — Order # 41-T-33588
$14.95
total amount of order — Total $24.90

I have enclosed a check for $27.40 to cover the cost of the merchandise, plus $2.50 for shipping and handling.

Sincerely,
Raphaela Gomez
Raphaela Gomez

GETTING STUDENTS INVOLVED

Cooperative Learning

Have students work in pairs using catalogs of all kinds—electronic, clothing, housewares, and so on. Ask them to take turns finding an item and having their partners locate the kind of information mentioned on page C401—description of item, size and color, order number, and price. Discuss those qualities that make a catalog easy to use.

HOME WORK

Ask students to find a catalog or circular at home and draft an order letter ordering an item they find in that catalog. Remind them to include all the pertinent information: description, size and color, order number, price, quantity, and total amount of order.

IDENTIFYING COMMON STUMBLING BLOCKS

Problem

- Omitting information

Solution

- Business forms often appear as charts, which means that information may be required both across and down the page. Tell students always to preview the entire form before beginning to write, making a note in their heads of the information required. This can prevent simple errors such as printing instead of signing a form, putting a street address on the wrong line, or leaving out a piece of necessary information.

Business Forms

You will need to fill out business forms for a variety of reasons. Subscribing to a magazine, applying for a library card, or joining a book club are just a few examples. The following guidelines will help you in filling out business forms.

Completing Business Forms

- Read all of the directions carefully before you begin to fill out the form.
- Check both sides of the form to make sure you do not miss any questions written on the back.
- Do not leave blanks. If a question does not apply to you, write *N/A* (not applicable).
- Always use blue or black pen.
- Be sure to print neatly and clearly.
- Remember to sign the form.
- Read over the form when you are finished to be sure your answers are accurate and complete.

Writing Tip

If the form you are filling out is long, you may want to write the answers on a separate sheet of paper first. Then copy the answers onto the form in ink.

Most banks have different savings accounts to suit the various needs of its customers. The form used to open a savings account and the savings deposit slip used to put money into the account are shown on the next page. Both of these forms can be obtained and filled out at your local bank.

The form below is used when you are opening a savings account at the bank.

Savings Bank Application Form

Tri-Town Savings Bank

Type of Account: *Savings*

Customer's Name: *Karen Kelly*

Home Address (Street): *16 River Drive*

(City): *Hanover* (State): *NH* (Zip): *03755*

Phone: *646-1212* Date of Birth: *4/24/77*

Social Security: *184-46-4380*

Initial Deposit: *$10.00* Branch: *Hanover*

Signature: *Karen Kelly* Date: *2/18/00*

When you want to put money into your account, you fill out a savings deposit slip.

Deposit Slip

Tri-Town Savings Bank **Date** *3/17/00*

Karen Kelly
NAME ON ACCOUNT (PLEASE PRINT)

ACCOUNT NUMBER
8 8 5 - 9 3 3

CASH	15	00
CHECKS (LIST SEPARATELY)	10	00
	7	50
TOTAL	32	50

HOME WORK

Ask students to visit a bank and ask for various types of application forms. Have students fill them out completely at home and bring them to class for discussion.

USING STUDENTS' STRENGTHS

Multiple Intelligences: Visual/Kinesthetic

Help students set goals as part of prewriting their letters. Have students identify goals in a letter. Tell students that creating a time line is a good way to visualize goals. A time line might include the starting point and the finished product. Then students might include steps along the path to the goal. For example, a time line for a letter of request to a food processing company might look like this:

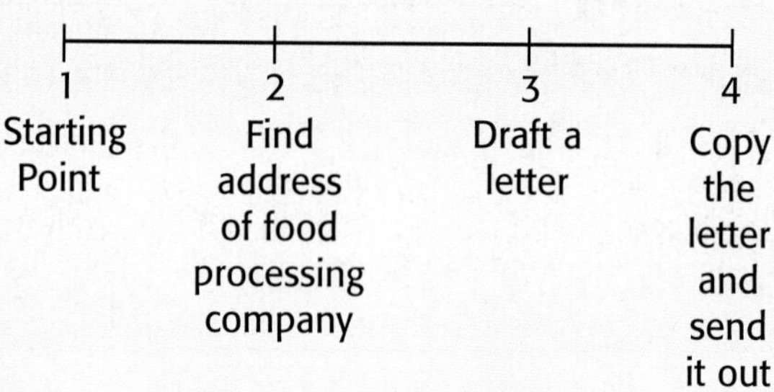

Writing Different Kinds of Letters

Writing Social Letters

The following exercises will give you practice in writing various types of social letters. Remember to use the proper form for each letter you write.

Writing a Thank-you Letter Imagine that you have just received a gift from a friend who lives in a foreign country. Write a thank-you note to your friend. Be sure to use the correct form for a thank-you letter.

Writing an Invitation You are giving a New Year's Eve party. Where and when will it be given? What details might you want to tell your guests? Write the invitation to your party, using the invitation letter format.

Writing a Letter of Regret Imagine that a friend of yours has asked you and a few others to go to the theater for her birthday. Decide what show they are going to see. Then write a letter of regret explaining why you cannot go.

Writing Business Letters

Writing a Letter of Request You want to explore your family history, so you decide to write to Elmer Branch, the president of Family Trees Incorporated. Draft a letter to Mr. Branch, asking him to send you some ideas for making a family tree. His company is at 5 Oak Street in Maplewood, Missouri, and the zip code is 63143. Be sure to use the proper form for a letter of request.

Writing an Order Letter Use the following information to write an order letter. Be sure to include all the pertinent details about the items you want to order.

ADDRESS:	Order Department, Sports City, 1789 Juneway Place, Scranton, PA 18510
ORDER:	1 baseball jacket, blue, size medium, Order # 880-3G, $22.00; 1 medium-weight Home Run King baseball bat, Order # 670-2E, $8.00; $3.75 for shipping and handling

COMPUTER TIP

Before you print a letter, you can check to see what it will look like on the page. Go to Print Preview under the File pulldown menu to check the page layout.

How to Use with Windows™ The Print Layout is accessed by clicking the Print Layout button or by choosing File and then Print Layout.

How to Use with Macintosh™ Print Preview is accessed by pulling down the File menu and clicking Print Preview, or by pressing Command-Option-I.

EXPANDING THE LESSON

Using Technology

You will find additional **instructional** and **practice** materials for this chapter at http://www.bkenglish.com.

Using *A Writer Writes*

Objectives

- **To write a personal letter expressing an opinion**
- **To write a business letter requesting information**

INTEGRATING *Writers at Work*

For more opportunities to inspire and stimulate students' letter writing, look at *Writers at Work.*

TIMESAVER *QuickCheck*

Have pairs of students exchange letters for peer evaluation. Suggest that students use this checklist:

- Do the letters contain all friendly/business letter parts?
- Are capitalization and punctuation used correctly?
- Does the friendly letter express an opinion about the three most important things on Earth? Is support given for this opinion?
- Does the business letter request information about the zoo animals' living environment? Are the letter's tone and language appropriate?

A Writer Writes

A Personal Letter

Purpose: to collaborate with other writers to create a common message

Audience: possible intelligent life on other planets

Team up with two or more partners. Imagine that you as a team have been asked to write a letter that will be carried aboard a spacecraft. The spacecraft will travel for hundreds of thousands of years until it reaches another intelligent civilization. Collaborate with your team to write a message telling what you think are the three most important things about life on Earth. Use a personal letter form.

A Business Letter

Purpose: to request information

Audience: zoo official

Write a letter to a major zoo in the United States requesting information on the animals' living quarters. Your goal is to find out to what extent the zoo tries to imitate the animals' natural surroundings. Also request any free materials the zoo might have. Below are the addresses of two well-known zoos.

- Education Department, San Diego Zoo, P.O. Box 551, San Diego, CA 92112
- Publicity Manager, Cincinnati Zoo, 3400 Vine Street, Cincinnati, OH 45220

A DIFFERENT DELIVERY SYSTEM

For formal assessment print the composition chapter test from the *BK English* Test Bank at http://www.bkenglish.com.

Assess Your Learning

The Town Council in your town is designing a new community center and is asking for input from residents. So far they have decided to include a wading pool for toddlers, a large playground, and a bike path. You and your friends would like to see a skateboarding park built because there are no other places in the town to skateboard. The downtown area is crowded with pedestrian traffic and too many cars make it dangerous to skateboard elsewhere.

- **Write a persuasive business letter to the Town Council persuading them to include a skateboard park in their design for the community center.**
- **To make a strong argument, be sure to make your main point clear and support it with several reasons why the skating park would be good not just for you and your friends, but for the town as a whole. Organize your ideas to ensure coherence and logical progression. Remember to include all six parts of a business letter. Choose either block or modified-block format. Do not forget to proofread for spelling, capitalization, and punctuation errors.**

Before You Write **Consider the following questions:**
What is the ***subject?***
What is the ***occasion?***
Who is the ***audience?***
What is the ***purpose?***

After You Write **Evaluate your work using the following criteria:**

- Do you clearly set out the purpose of your letter in the first paragraph?
- Do you provide several reasons why the skateboard park is a good idea?
- Have you acknowledged and answered objections to the project?
- Have you written in a voice and style appropriate to your audience and purpose?
- Have you used the correct business letter format?
- Have you used conjunctions to connect ideas meaningfully?
- Have you proofread for spelling, capitalization, and punctuation errors?

Write briefly on how well you did. Point out your strengths and areas for improvement.

FOR ASSESSING LEARNING

Using *Assess Your Learning*

This writing prompt will help you and your students informally assess their developing writing abilities, using the accompanying primary trait rubrics, which list the key features and qualities of letter writing taught in this chapter. You may want to have students maintain their self-assessment in their portfolios as a record of their individual progress throughout the year.

Teaching Suggestions

Essential Knowledge and Skills

- Determining the purposes for listening such as to gain information, to solve problems, or to enjoy and appreciate
- Eliminating barriers to effective listening
- Understanding the major ideas and supporting evidence in spoken messages
- Listening to learn by taking notes, organizing, and summarizing spoken ideas
- Evaluating a spoken message in terms of its content, credibility, and delivery
- Using effective rate, volume, pitch, and tone for the audience and setting
- Selecting and using voice and style appropriate to audience and purpose

CHAPTER 13

Directions and Speeches

You have probably seen and heard countless conversations—in real life, on television, or in the movies. No doubt you focused on *what* was being said, but what about *how* it was said—and received? Did the speaker look relaxed, excited, or nervous? Did the listener look interested, distracted, or bored? Were the two people really speaking with and listening to each other?

Most of your speaking and listening take place under informal circumstances. There are times, however, that require formal speeches.

How well do you speak? How well do you listen? You can study, practice, and improve your speaking and listening like any other skill. This chapter will help you sharpen your speaking and listening skills so that you can communicate your ideas more effectively.

Reading with a Writer's Eye

When Ben Cohen and Jerry Greenfield were invited to speak at a graduation, they arrived with an unusual story delivered in an informal style that reflects who they are. Before reading Greenfield's speech, try to predict how he and Cohen got into the ice-cream business. Is your prediction anything like the real story?

BLOCK SCHEDULING

- If your schedule requires that you cover the chapter in a **shorter time,** use the core lesson in Developing Your Informal Speaking Skills.
- If you want to take advantage of **longer class time,** use the selection and one or more of the following: In the Media, Writing Is Thinking, or A Speaker Speaks.

Commencement Speech

Southampton College, May 21, 1995

Jerry Greenfield

Graduation is a time for words of wisdom, thought-provoking words, challenging words. And that is why we have Ben with us today. I'll be speaking to you about how we reached our august positions as true ice-cream magnates.

Ben and I are old friends from junior high school. We met at Merrick Avenue Junior High School in the seventh grade, when we were the two slowest, fattest kids running around the track together. Coach Phelps was yelling at us, "Gentlemen, you have to run the mile in under seven minutes. If you don't run the mile in under seven minutes, you're gonna have to do it again!" And there were Ben and I in this little pack way behind the rest of the pack, and Ben would yell back, "Gee, Coach, if I don't run it in under seven minutes the first time, I'm certainly not going to run it in under seven minutes the second time!" And that's when I first realized that Ben was someone I wanted to get to know.

We went through school together and graduated in 1969. It was time to go to college. Ben didn't really want to go to college. But his parents wanted him to go, so his father and his older sister filled out his applications for him and he ended up going to Colgate in upstate New York. Because they had fireplaces in the dorms and

FOR INCREASING STUDENT ACHIEVEMENT

GUIDED READING

Text Analysis

- This graduation **speech** by a famous entrepreneur is **informative,** but it is primarily meant to **entertain.**
- Because the speech is addressed to young college students at a joyous turning point in their academic lives, the language of the letter is **informal** and the **tone** is humorous.
- The speech is filled with **personal anecdotes** that cheerfully illustrate the speaker's points—that one's goals may constantly change; that one failure doesn't end one's career; that there are many paths to take in life.

Strategy: Evaluating

As students read Jerry Greenfield's speech, have them ask themselves how they would feel if they were hearing it at their own graduation. Is the speaker's message conveyed well? What do they like best about the speech? What, if anything, do they dislike about it?

SELECTION AMENDMENT
Description of change: excerpted
Rationale: to focus on the purpose and audience of a speech as presented in this chapter

READER RESPONSE

You may want to use the following questions to elicit students' personal responses to the speech.

1. What is Jerry Greenfield saying about people who plan their lives and careers at an early age?
2. Is this speech appropriate for its audience? How did the speaker keep his audience in mind as he spoke? Which aspects of the speech do you think would appeal most to college students?
3. If you met Jerry Greenfield after hearing this speech, what question would you like to ask him?

LITERARY CONNECTION

You may wish to explore speeches using one or more of the following works, which appear in literature textbooks at this grade level.

- "Cub Pilot on the Mississippi" by Mark Twain
- "Emancipation" by Russell Freedman
- "The First Americans" by The Grand Council Fire of American Indians
- "The Gettysburg Address" by Abraham Lincoln
- "I Have a Dream" by Martin Luther King Jr.
- *Roughing It* by Mark Twain

Ben thought that was really cool. Ben soon dropped out of Colgate, signed up with another school, soon dropped out of there, and then he joined up with a program called University Without Walls, a progressive, unstructured program where you don't have to go to class. The world is your campus, and you get credit for learning. And Ben dropped out of there too. Still a little too much structure.

Ben worked at various jobs: as a taxi driver in New York, a short-order cook, a night mopper, a security guard, a phone book delivery person. I, on the other hand, went to Oberlin College in Ohio, finished in four years straight, tried to get into medical school, didn't get in, got a job as a lab technician in a biochemistry research lab, reapplied to medical school, didn't get in again, and took another job as a lab technician since I already had the experience.

This is how we found each other facing the world. Gee, we thought, why don't we do something fun? We could be our own bosses, and hang out together. We thought we'd do something with food since we both liked to eat quite a bit. We picked ice cream. We didn't know anything about ice cream so we decided to continue our formal education by taking a correspondence course in ice cream. It was a five-dollar course from Penn State University that we split, so it was two-fifty apiece. They sent us a textbook in the mail. You read through the chapters of the textbook; you have tests at the end of every chapter. You're allowed to look up the answers at the end of every chapter. You mail them to your professors. They grade them and mail them back. We got a hundred percent on every test!

So we had finally found the type of education that was really suited to our learning. And we've gone on from there. . . .

ADDITIONAL RESOURCES

Composition Skills Practice	pages 67–72
Transparency Tools	VR11
Connection Collection	pages C434–C436
ESL Practice and Test Preparation	pages 78–84
Standardized Test Preparation	Unit 6
Writers at Work	8•1–8•10
Assessment: Chapter Test	pages 87–90
Assessment Resources	pages 1–11, 13–44

Thinking as a Writer

Analyzing a Speech

- How did Jerry Greenfield and Ben Cohen get into the ice cream business? Was the speech clear as to how that happened? Why or why not?
- From the opening of the speech, did you know what the speaker was going to speak about? How?
- What new understanding did you have by the end of the speech? What things did the speaker say to help develop that understanding?

Matching the Tone to the Content

Oral Expression

- Take turns with a partner reading aloud and listening to parts of the speech. Discuss the ways the speaker uses language to engage the listener. Are there any special words or phrases that stand out?
- Try to match your style of reading to the tone of the speech. Do you think the speech invites a special tone to come through? What is it?

Engaging an Audience

Viewing

- Compare the two photos below. How would you describe the classroom audience shown in each photo?
- What type of speech or presentation do you think the audience is listening to? Explain your answer.

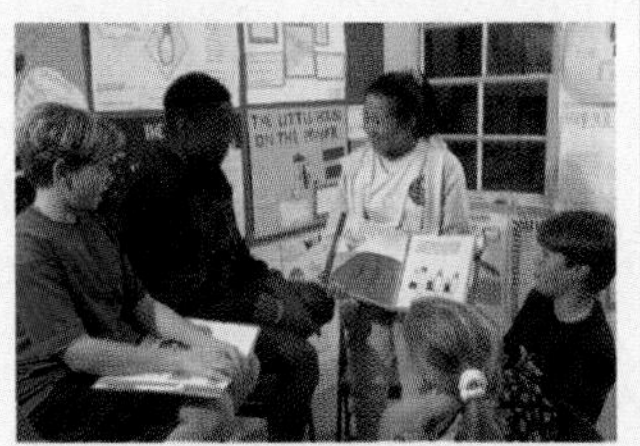

Using *Thinking as a Writer*

You may choose to have students respond to the questions either orally or in writing.

GETTING STUDENTS INVOLVED

Cooperative Learning

Arrange for students to work in pairs to read and listen to parts of the speech. Have them work together to share their ideas about the speaker's use of language and generate a list of words and phrases they find most effective. Provide class time for pairs to share their observations with the class.

USING STUDENTS' STRENGTHS

Multiple Intelligences: Spatial

Have students explore how shifting around components of the ads would alter the message. Would the ads be more or less effective if elements of them were enlarged or moved?

FOR DEVELOPING SKILLS

LESSON 1 *(pages C408–C423)*

OBJECTIVE

- **To use effective rate, volume, pitch, and tone for a particular audience and setting**

Create Interest

Remind students that Jerry Greenfield was speaking to an audience of college students. He delivered the speech in a large forum, possibly outdoors or in an auditorium. Ask students to imagine that he was instead giving a speech for an audience of elderly residents of a nursing home in a small lunchroom. What might he have done differently?

Guide Instruction

By Connecting Ideas

Tell students that part of a speaker's job is to choose an appropriate rate, volume, pitch, and tone for the presentation of a speech. Define rate as

REACHING ALL STUDENTS

English Language Learners

Review time-order words with which students can improve their skills at giving directions. On the board write *first, next,* and *last.* Ask students to explain how such words might be used when giving directions. Have students brainstorm additional time-order words that might prove useful. (Possibilities include *then, afterward, finally.*)

Developing Your Informal Speaking Skills

In one of his most famous songs, "Sound of Silence," Paul Simon wrote the lyrics "People talking without speaking. People hearing without listening, . . ." Even when you are speaking informally, it is important to be clear and exact. This section of the chapter will help you sharpen your informal speaking skills so that even in everyday speech, you will be better understood by your listeners. It is also important, as Paul Simon wrote, to *listen* and not just *hear.* Listening skills will be discussed later on in the chapter, but keep them in mind as you go through this section.

Informal speaking is a form of speech that is suitable for everyday use or for casual occasions.

Giving Directions

Giving directions is an important type of informal speech. Clear directions show organized thinking. Clear directions are also easier to listen to and to follow. Read the two sets of directions below. Then compare them to determine why the second set of directions would be clearer to a listener who is unfamiliar with the area.

UNCLEAR — The football stadium. Yes, follow this road for a while until you come to a light. Then go west. The stadium should be near there.

CLEAR — To get to the football stadium, continue on Maple Street until you come to the second traffic light. That is Spring Street. You will see a gas station on one corner and a medi-

the speed of delivery. Define volume as the loudness of delivery. Define pitch as the highness or lowness of a sound. Define tone as the style and manner of speaking. Explain that a good speaker maintains a volume that can be heard throughout the venue and chooses a tone appropriate to the subject matter of the speech. To add interest to a speech, a speaker should vary the rate and pitch used. The rate should never be excessive, but the speaker might speed up through lists or examples and slow down to emphasize main ideas and major details. Similarly, the speaker might pitch his or her voice higher to emphasize points or to express emotion.

Consolidate Skills

Through Guided Practice

As students practice their speeches, tell them to take several run-throughs to focus on rate, volume, tone, and pitch. Have them determine whether a friendly, grave, jocular, or serene tone best suits their subject matter and adjust their voices accordingly. Have them think about the room in which

cal building on another corner. Turn left on Spring Street and go half a mile. The stadium will be on your right.

The second set of directions would be clearer to a listener because it includes a specific distance, street names, and landmarks. The first set of directions does not provide clear information.

Following are some important steps to keep in mind when you give directions.

Guidelines for Giving Directions

- Use *right, left,* or *straight* rather than *north, south, east,* or *west.*
- Use names of streets if you know them.
- Mention landmarks whenever possible.
- Include the approximate number of miles if you know this information.
- If possible, draw a map.
- Do not give directions for a difficult shortcut.
- If you are unsure of the correct directions, direct the person to someone who might know.
- Repeat the directions or have the other person repeat the directions to you.
- Speak clearly.
- Look directly at the person as you give them directions.
- Pay attention to nonverbal clues that might indicate he or she does not understand.

PRACTICE YOUR SKILLS Sample Answers

Improving Directions

The aquarium is near the East River. To get there, go north for two miles. When you see a railroad crossing ahead, take a right on Autumn Parkway. Drive three blocks, and the parkway ends at the Selma Shoe Factory. Take that right onto Riverside Road. After four stoplights, you will see the aquarium on your left.

Giving and Following Directions

Students' directions should follow the bulleted rules from the lesson.

they intend to deliver the speech and adjust their volume to fit that setting. If they wish, they might annotate their speeches to indicate where their pitch might rise or fall, or their rate might vary.

Apply to Communication

Through Evaluation

As students deliver their speeches and listen to each other's presentations, have them evaluate what they hear in terms of rate, volume, tone, and pitch.

Transfer to Everyday Life

By Analyzing a News Broadcast

Have students watch a newscast and evaluate the various speakers on their rate, volume, tone, and pitch. Ask them to watch for the speakers' use of pitch and rate to emphasize certain points and to determine whether the speakers' tones were suited to their subject matter.

HOME WORK

Ask students to imagine that they are directing someone from their house to the nearest grocery store. Have them write directions that include specific details.

PRACTICE YOUR SKILLS

Improving Directions

Read the set of directions on the following page. Then rewrite the directions to make them more specific. Use the guidelines above and your imagination to help you include necessary details. After you have written the directions, draw a map to accompany them.

I think the aquarium is near the river. To get there, go north for several miles. You will come to a railroad crossing. Before the crossing take a right. Soon you will see a big building. Take another right and you should come to the river in a little while. Down the road a bit, you will see the aquarium.

Giving and Following Directions

Write directions from your classroom to the following places in your school. Include as many specific details as possible. If time permits read some of the directions aloud. Then have other students list ways the directions could be improved.

1. the library
2. the office
3. the baseball field
4. the cafeteria
5. the principal's office
6. the gymnasium

Pull It All Together

By Sharing

Have students share their analyses of newscasts from the **Transfer to Everyday Life** activity. Discuss the effect of using a tone that does not match the subject matter and the importance of varying rate and pitch.

Check Understanding

By Using the Literary Selection

Ask students to reread Jerry Greenfield's speech and to suggest some places where he might have slowed down his rate of speaking or varied his pitch. Ask them to speculate on the tone he used to deliver the speech.

Developing Your Formal Speaking Skills

A formal speech is different from an informal speech in two basic ways. A **formal speech** is prepared in advance and is usually longer than an informal speech. A formal speech may be anything from a science or book report, given in front of a class, to a guided tour of the school for parents at an open house.

Preparing Your Speech

The preparation of a formal speech is similar to the preparation of a written report. (See pages C344–C379.) The main difference is that you will practice your speech and deliver it orally rather than write it.

Choosing and Limiting a Subject

To choose a subject, first make a list of topics you know something about. Then choose one that will interest both you and your audience. For example, if you were speaking to parents about your school's need for new athletic equipment, you might inform them about your school's athletic programs and explain the need for new equipment. If, however, you were speaking to your classmates, you could persuade them to help raise money for the new equipment.

After deciding on a subject, you need to consider the amount of time you have to deliver your speech. If you have only ten minutes, you may not be able to cover all the athletic programs your school offers. Instead, you could limit your subject to the athletic programs that attract the largest number of participants.

USING STUDENTS' STRENGTHS

Multiple Intelligences: Logical

Students who think logically may enjoy limiting their subject using an inverted pyramid graphic organizer. Model choosing and limiting a subject with a pyramid like this one:

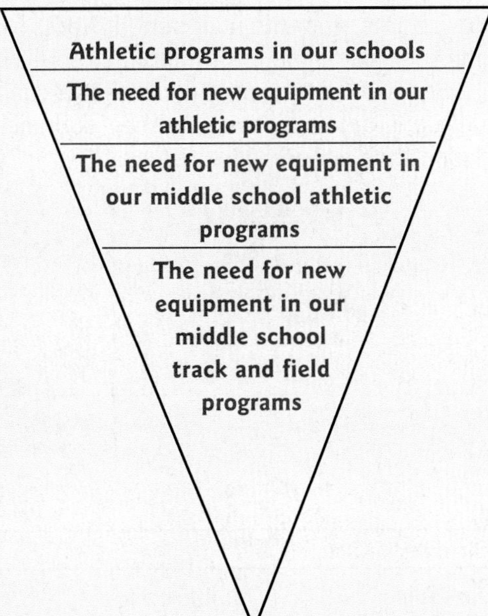

Once they understand the logic of the organizer, have students make their own organizers to choose and limit their subjects.

Using *Writing Is Thinking*

Objectives

- **To evaluate potential audiences for a speech**
- **To tailor a speech to a specific audience**

A DIFFERENT APPROACH

Visual Some students may benefit from seeing their audience information laid out in a chart. Suggest that these students use a chart like the one below to evaluate their audience and plan their speech.

MY AUDIENCE

Who They Are	What They Know	What They Might Like to Learn

Thinking Skills	
Classifying	Analyzing
Comparing	Hypothesizing
Generalizing	Synthesizing
Inferring	Summarizing
Imagining	Setting Goals
Observing	Evaluating Audience
Predicting	

Writing Is Thinking

Evaluating

Before selecting a subject for your speech, think about who your audience will be. In most situations your audience will be classmates who share your interests and experiences. At other times, however, your audience might be teachers, parents, families in your community, or students from another school.

When choosing a subject for a speech, ask yourself the following questions about your audience. The answers to these questions will help you decide upon a subject that will suit your audience. The answers will also help you determine what information you should include in your speech to make your subject clear to your listeners.

KNOWING YOUR AUDIENCE

- What are the interests of my audience? Are they similar to mine?
- What will my audience already know about the subject?
- Is my audience listening to learn, to be persuaded, or to be entertained?

THINKING PRACTICE

Use the questions above to list information about the audience you might expect for the following speeches.

1. Accepting a school honor
2. Introducing the mayor of your town before she speaks to your school assembly
3. Making a presentation to your after-school chess club

PRACTICE YOUR SKILLS

Finding a Subject

Write the subject of a speech that could be included under each area.

1. personal experiences
2. current events
3. how to do something
4. experiences of others
5. past events
6. how to make something

Choosing and Limiting a Subject

Limit each subject so that it is suitable for a ten-minute speech.

EXAMPLE	trees
POSSIBLE ANSWER	the giant redwoods in California

1. Spanish explorers
2. elephants
3. television
4. comets
5. China
6. the Great Lakes
7. household pets
8. the solar system
9. baseball
10. inventions

Communicate Your Ideas

PREWRITING *Subject*

You will be presenting a ten-minute speech to your class. The topic will be "My Favorite Sport or Hobby." Brainstorm, cluster, or freewrite to choose a subject that is appropriate to the length and audience of your speech. Jot down the subject as well as any initial ideas you may have about it. Save your work for later use.

SAVE YOUR WORK

PRACTICE YOUR SKILLS Sample Answers

Finding a Subject

1. Why I Would Recommend Taking Latin
2. How We Can Help Our Senators Understand School Issues
3. Some Basics of Calligraphy
4. Our Exchange Student's First Day at School
5. Why We Should Celebrate Martin Luther King Day
6. Making Doll House Furniture

Choosing and Limiting a Subject

1. The Legacy of Coronado
2. What Is an Elephant Graveyard?
3. Should Your Parents Control What You Watch?
4. Comets and Medieval Beliefs
5. My Aunt's Visit from China
6. Cleaning Up Lake Erie
7. Chocolate Labs: The Best Pets
8. A Failed Mission to Mars
9. How Baseball Came to Japan
10. The Elevator's Effect on Urban Growth

HOME WORK

Ask students to read their local newspapers to find three newsworthy subjects that interest them. Have them limit each subject so that it could be discussed in a ten-minute speech.

TIMESAVER *QuickCheck*

Evaluate students' ideas to make sure they are both limited enough and meaty enough for a ten-minute speech.

HOME STUDY

Students may do their brainstorming, clustering, or freewriting at home, but they should bring their ideas in for evaluation before proceeding further.

REACHING ALL STUDENTS

Advanced Learners

Advanced learners might enjoy skimming an anthology of famous speeches to locate and read one of each kind—an informative speech, a persuasive speech, and an entertaining speech. Ask them to analyze the speeches they find to see whether they encompass more than one purpose.

PRACTICE YOUR SKILLS Sample Answers

1. to inform
2. to entertain
3. to persuade
4. to inform
5. to entertain
6. to inform
7. to inform
8. to persuade
9. to inform
10. to entertain

Understanding Your Purpose

Once you have chosen and limited your subject, you should think about the purpose of your speech. Most speeches have one of the following three purposes.

PURPOSES OF SPEECHES

Purpose	Examples
To Inform	• to explain about the effect of the moon on ocean tides • to explain the structure of icebergs
To Persuade	• to encourage students to join after-school volleyball games • to encourage the school administration to sponsor a school newspaper
To Entertain	• to tell about the first time you made Thanksgiving dinner for your family • to tell about the first and only time you tried to ice-skate

PRACTICE YOUR SKILLS

Determining a Purpose for a Speech

Label the purpose of each speech *to inform, to persuade,* or *to entertain.*

1. to explain a solar eclipse
2. to tell about a picnic involving 25 people and a rainstorm
3. to encourage students to try out for the school play
4. to explain the difference between a marathon and a triathlon
5. to tell about the first time you tried to sail a boat
6. to explain how penicillin was discovered

LESSON 2 *(pages C415–C431)*

OBJECTIVES

- **To gather and organize information for a speech**
- **To identify verbal and nonverbal signals**
- **To deliver and listen to speeches**

Create Interest

Read aloud paragraphs 4 and 5 of Jerry Greenfield's speech, using gestures and facial expressions and varying your rate and pitch where it seems natural to do so. Remind students that listening to a speech requires certain skills on the part of the listener. Have volunteers recap Jerry Greenfield's main point in giving this speech to a class of graduating seniors.

Guide Instruction

By Connecting Ideas

Remind students that they have learned that a good speaker outlines a speech to make sure that main ideas and details get across as planned. A good listener should be able to

7. to trace the history of the National Football League
8. to encourage your school to plan more field trips
9. to explain how Sacajawea helped Lewis and Clark explore the West
10. to tell about the time squirrels got into your attic

Communicate Your Ideas

PREWRITING *Purpose*

Look back at the subject you chose for your speech. Decide on the purpose for your speech. Note your purpose. Save your work for later use.

Gathering and Organizing Your Information

After choosing and limiting your subject and deciding on your purpose, you should begin to gather and organize information. These stages are similar to those you follow when writing a report. *(See page C354.)* Following are some suggestions to help you gather and organize your information.

Gathering Information

- List what you already know about your subject.
- Gather more information in the library or through an interview.
- Find interesting examples and quotations to include.
- Write your information on note cards.

Organizing Information

- Make an outline of your speech. Unlike an outline for a report, an outline for a speech should include your introduction and your conclusion.

HOME WORK

Have students take the subject "The School Play" and limit it in three ways: first as the title of a speech to inform, second as the title of a speech to persuade, and third as the title of a speech to entertain.

TIMESAVER *QuickCheck*

Have students answer this question to evaluate their own decisions about purpose: Can I think of three details about this subject that would suit the purpose I chose? If they cannot, they might consider changing the purpose they selected.

HOME STUDY

Students may do this activity as homework. Remind them to save all their ideas in their writing portfolios.

USING STUDENTS' STRENGTHS

Multiple Intelligences: Intrapersonal

Tell students that using a KWL chart is a good way to assess what they know and what they would like to know about a subject. Write this example on the board and have students use it as a model if they like.

K: What I KNOW About the Subject	W: What I WANT to Learn About the Subject	L: What I LEARNED as I Studied the Subject

recognize the structure used by the speaker and use it to get the most out of the speech. Speakers often give verbal clues to meaning, using words or phrases that point out key ideas or transitions between ideas. In addition, speakers may use body language, facial expressions, rate, and pitch to emphasize what is important.

Consolidate Skills

Through Guided Practice

The boxed feature **Taking Notes on Speeches** (page C426) gives students a plan for analyzing the structure of a speech they hear. As students complete the **Practice Your Skills** exercise on listening, taking notes, and following directions (page C428), have them listen to see how each explanation is constructed. Suggest that they listen for verbal clues such as *next, for example,* or *finally* and that they watch for nonverbal clues that indicate the speaker's attitude toward his or her words.

REACHING ALL STUDENTS

Struggling Learners

Some students will benefit from a review of outlining skills (page C360). Give these students practice in outlining before asking them to outline their own speeches.

PRACTICE YOUR SKILLS Sample Answers

Source: www.altculture.com
–first franchise, 1981
–out-of-state distribution, 1983
–went public, 1984

Source: www.altculture.com
–growth
–$150 million, 1994
–around 100 ice cream shops
–groceries and delis
–equals Häagen-Dazs

- The *introduction* of your speech should capture the attention of your audience. It should also include the main idea of your speech.
- The *body* of your speech should include the supporting points. Arrange your points in a logical order. Use transitions to connect your ideas.
- The *conclusion* of your speech should summarize your main idea.

PRACTICE YOUR SKILLS

Gathering Information with Note Cards

Use index cards to take notes on the following paragraph from www.altculture.com. This will make it easy to rearrange and organize your notes as you prepare your outline. Use a new card for each new idea. Be sure to note the source for your information in case you need to find it again. An example card has been filled out for you.

Superpremium, socially conscious ice cream. Founded in 1978 by Ben (Bennett R.) Cohen (b. 1950) and Jerry Greenfield (b. 1951), who started their empire in a vacant Vermont gas station with a $12,000 investment and the resolution to stay in business one year. Their first franchise opened in 1981, with a distribution outside Vermont beginning in 1983. After going public in 1984, Ben & Jerry's Homemade Inc. sales grew to an annual revenue, in 1994, of some $150 million worth of Wavy Gravy, Maple Walnut, White Russian, and numerous other flavors in grocery stores, delis, and its approximately 100 "scoop shops." It thus equals Häagen-Dazs in superpremium ice cream market share.

Apply to Communication

Through Speaking and Listening

As students prepare their own explanations, have them consider how they might use verbal and nonverbal clues to get their meaning across to their audience.

Transfer to Everyday Life

By Watching a Talk Show

Ask students to tune in to the beginning of a local or syndicated talk show. (Use your local TV listings to find one or two examples that are low in controversy and whose topics are appropriate.) Tell students to listen carefully to the host's introduction of the day's subject. Ask them to take notes and to assess (1) how the host feels about the subject and (2) what the host considers important for the audience to understand about the subject. Discuss how structure, verbal clues, and nonverbal clues helped them understand the host's point of view.

Source: www.altculture.com
—Started by Ben Cohen and Jerry Greenfield
—began in vacant gas station in Vermont—1978
—$12,000 initial investment

Communicate Your Ideas

PREWRITING, DRAFTING *Research, Outline*

Look back at the subject and purpose you chose for your speech. Write what you know about it on note cards. Next, go to the library and find information for at least four more note cards. Then organize your cards and write an outline of your speech. Save your work for later use.

Practicing Your Speech

Practicing aloud is a necessary step in delivering a successful speech. You may want to use a tape recorder to hear yourself. Then, if possible, practice in front of a friend or a family member and ask for suggestions. The list shown on the next page will help you as you practice your speech.

HOME WORK

Have students find a short article in an encyclopedia, either print or online, or in another reference book. Ask them to use index cards to take notes on the article.

TIMESAVER *QuickCheck*

Review students' outlines for coherence and completeness.

HOME STUDY

Students may complete their research at the school or public library, or online at school or at home. If you assign this activity as homework, make sure students are able to check out books and take them home as needed.

Pull It All Together

By Reflecting

Invite students to reflect on these questions:

- How can nonverbal clues help you better understand a speech?
- Why is it important for a listener to understand a speech's structure?

Check Understanding

By Evaluating a Speech

Play a video of a famous speech (a variety of good ones are found in Wilson's *In Their Own Words* series, including *The Speeches of Famous Women, The Speeches of Our Founding Fathers, The Speeches of Sitting Bull,* and *The Speeches of Nelson Mandela*). Ask students to listen for structure and verbal clues and to watch for nonverbal clues. When the speech is over, have them write a three-sentence summary that expresses its main idea.

TIMESAVER *QuickCheck*

Ask partners to use these questions to assess the speeches they hear:

- Can I tell what the purpose of the speech is? Can I name the main idea?
- Is the speech well-organized? Is there material that doesn't fit the subject? Is there anything missing?
- Is the speech too long or too short?
- Was the speech presented well? Could I understand the words? Did the speaker use an appropriate rate, volume, pitch, and tone?

HOME STUDY

If students practice their speeches at home, suggest that they ask a family member to listen and make recommendations for improvement.

Practicing Your Speech

- Read your complete outline several times until you are familiar with all the information.
- Make only a few notes to use as you begin to practice aloud. You want to talk about your subject, not read about it.
- Practice in front of a long mirror so that you will be aware of your facial expressions and gestures, such as biting your lips or clenching your hands.
- Practice looking around the room as you talk. Good eye contact is important.
- Time the length of your speech. If it is too long, decide what information you can omit. If it is too short, you should find more information.
- Practice over a period of several days.

Each time you practice your speech, you will feel more confident. The more confident you are, the less nervous you will be when you deliver your speech in front of an audience.

Writing Tip

Edit your speech for correct **personal pronoun** use.

Communicate Your Ideas

REVISING, EDITING *Practice*

Take out the speech you have prepared. Choose a partner and take turns practicing your speech in front of each other. Listen to your classmate's speech and discuss how it might be improved. If needed, revise and edit your speech. Save your work.

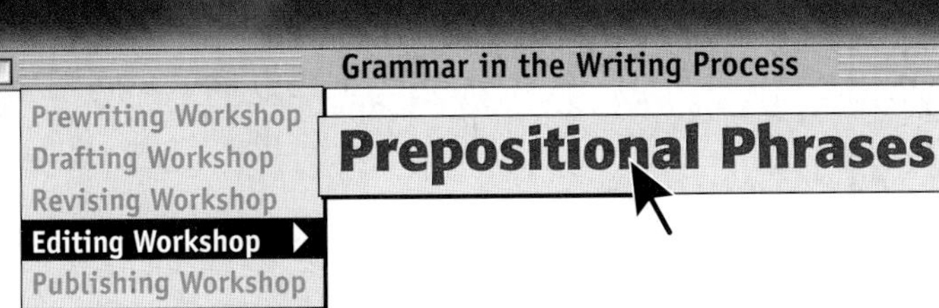

Prepositional Phrases

Because they can serve as adjectives or adverbs, prepositional phrases are handy for adding information to your sentences. An **adjective phrase** is a prepositional phrase that is used to modify a noun or a pronoun. An **adverb phrase** is a prepositional phrase that is used to modify a verb, an adjective, or an adverb. The following examples are from Jerry Greenfield's commencement speech at Southampton College.

Like a single adjective, an adjective phrase answers the questions *Which one(s)?* or *What kind?*

Adjective Phrase	Ben and I are old friends **from junior high school.** (answers the question *What kind?*)
Adjective Phrase	I will give a speech **about our success in the ice cream industry.** (Both adjective phrases answer the question *What kind?*)
Adjective Phrase	We didn't know anything **about ice cream.** (answers the question *What kind?*)
Adjective Phrase	We took the tests **in every chapter.** (answers the question *Which one(s)?*)

Like a single adverb, an adverb phrase answers the questions *Where? When? How? To what extent?* or *To what degree?*

Using *Editing Workshop*

Objective

- **To identify adjective phrases and adverb phrases used correctly in a speech**

Auditory Have students listen carefully as you read these sentences aloud from entrepreneur Jerry Greenfield's commencement speech. Students should first identify the prepositional phrases and tell whether each is an adjective phrase or an adverb phrase. Remind students to use the questioning strategies listed on pages C419 and C420 to identify each phrase.

- *Graduation is a time for words of wisdom, thought-provoking words, challenging words.* (for words of wisdom, thought-provoking words, challenging words: adjective phrase)
- *Gentlemen, you have to run the mile in under seven minutes.* (in under seven minutes: adverb phrase)
- *We both thought we'd do something with food since we both liked to eat quite a bit.* (with food: adjective phrase; since we both liked to eat quite a bit: adverb phrase)

IDENTIFYING COMMON STUMBLING BLOCKS

Problem

- Dropping out essential syllables or sounds

Solution

- Remind students that pronunciation and enunciation are key when delivering a speech. If they have any doubts about the pronunciation of a word, they should look it up in a dictionary ahead of time. They might go through their speech, using a colored marker to underline particularly difficult words, and writing their pronunciations phonetically in the margins. Have students work in pairs to practice saying these tricky words: *asked, February, comfortable, history, length, recognize, usually.* Have their partners alert them if they leave out a sound or syllable.

ADVERB PHRASE	I'll be speaking to you **about how we reached our august positions as ice cream magnates.** (answers the question *How?*)
ADVERB PHRASE	Coach Phelps was yelling **at us.** (answers the question *Where?*)
	We were the two slowest, fattest kids running **around the track together.** (answers the question *Where?*)

Editing Checklist

✓ Have you used prepositional phrases to add information to your sentences?

Delivering Your Speech

It is important to be well prepared before a speech. Following are some guidelines for delivering your speech.

Guidelines for Delivering a Speech

- Be well prepared and have all the necessary materials.
- Wait until your audience is quiet and settled.
- Take a deep breath and begin.
- Stand with your weight evenly divided between both feet. Avoid swaying back and forth.
- Speak slowly, clearly, and loudly enough to be heard.

- Use rehearsed gestures and facial expressions to emphasize your main points.
- Look directly at the people in your audience, not over their heads. Try to make eye contact.
- Use pictures and other audiovisual aids to increase the attention of your audience.

COMPUTER TIP

The size of the letters that your computer prints is called the font size. You can print the outline of your speech in a slightly larger font size than usual. This way, you can more easily read your outline as you give your speech. You can find the font controls on your tool bar under Font or Format. Try a 14- or 15- point size.

PRACTICE YOUR SKILLS

Preparing a Formal Speech

Read the following steps for preparing a formal speech. Then write them in the correct order.

1. Gather and organize information about your subject.

2. Deliver your speech.

3. Determine the purpose of your speech.

4. Practice your speech.

5. Choose and limit your subject.

6. Know your audience.

Fonts If you would like to use a font size in between the sizes listed on your computer, simply highlight the word or words you want to change, click on the font size that appears in the window, and type in a new size. Then click on Enter or Return to complete the change.

PRACTICE YOUR SKILLS Sample Answers

6. Know your audience; 5. Choose and limit your subject; 3. Determine the purpose of your speech; 1. Gather and organize information about your subject; 4. Practice your speech; 2. Deliver your speech

HOME WORK

Ask students to write a how-to paragraph informing a student who has been absent how to prepare a formal speech.

TIMESAVER *QuickCheck*

If you wish, work with students to create an evaluation checklist for students' speeches. Evaluation should concentrate on achievement of purpose, organization, supporting details, confident delivery, enunciation, adequate volume, and variety of pitch and rate.

HOME STUDY

Students may do their self-evaluations at home and may or may not bring them in to share with you.

Communicate Your Ideas

PUBLISHING *Delivery*

Present the speech you have been practicing before a group of classmates. In your **journal** list parts that you think you did well and others you would like to improve in your next speech. Save your speech for future reference.

Time Out to Reflect

Join with your classmates to compare and contrast the different speeches. What makes one speech stand out? What skills do each of the students need to work on? You may want to use the Oral Assessment Form on page C431. Record this information in the Learning Log section of your **journal**.

Process of Presenting a Speech

Remember that while preparing a speech, you can move back and forth among the stages of the process. For example, during editing, you may wish to return to the revising stage to add further details. The numbers in parentheses in the list below refer to pages where you can get help with your preparation.

PREPARING YOUR SPEECH

- Identify a subject that suits the purpose and audience for your speech. *(page C411)*
- Limit your subject to fit the purpose, audience, and length of your speech. *(page C411)*
- Make a list of what you know about your subject along the lines of a general speech structure. *(page C415)*
- Research your material and write it on note cards. *(page C415)*
- Organize your note cards so that your ideas follow a logical order. *(page C415)*

GATHERING AND ORGANIZING YOUR INFORMATION

- Make an outline from your note cards. *(page C415)*

PRACTICING YOUR SPEECH

- Practice your speech and make notes. *(page C417)*
- Practice your speech in front of others and listen to their suggestions. *(page C418)*
- Make changes as needed.

DELIVERING YOUR SPEECH

- Remember that you are presenting your speech orally, not in writing.
- Use the Guidelines for Delivering a Speech to make your presentation as effective as possible. *(page C420)*
- Use the Oral Presentation Assessment Form for you and others to assess your speech so that you can improve your skills. *(page C431)*

YOUR IDEAS

For Presenting a Speech

Using *In the Media*

Objectives

- **To use listening and speaking skills to deliver a famous political speech**
- **To use peer review to critique speech delivery**

Group Project

- After students have located Nixon's "Checkers" speech on the Internet, divide them into small groups. Within their groups, students should use listening and speaking skills they have learned to deliver the "Checkers" speech. As students practice in their groups, partners should critique the delivery, enunciation, and body language of the speaker. Have each group choose one speaker from their group to deliver the speech to the class.

FYI

Websites to Visit Students can find additional political speeches to practice and deliver at the following Websites. At http://www.wfu.edu/~louden/SPEECHES.html students can find the inaugural speeches of U.S. presidents from George Washington to George Bush. Additional famous political speeches are archived at http://www.web.co.nz/govtweb/0050.html.

IN THE MEDIA

Political Speech

One of the most famous political uses of television is Richard Nixon's "Checkers" speech. When he was running for Vice President in 1952, Nixon was discovered accepting monetary "gifts" from campaign contributors. Many thought that Nixon's political career was over, but in a brilliant display of speechmaking, Nixon went before an audience of 30 million TV viewers and made an appeal that was so successful it allowed him to remain in the race.

Media Activity

Using the Internet, locate the text of Nixon's speech. (www.pbs.org/wgbh/amex/presidents/nf/resource/nixon/primdocs/checkers.html). Then answer the following questions.

- What issues does Nixon address?
- Can you tell from the content of the speech what type of audience Nixon is addressing? How?
- What sort of appeal does Nixon make in the speech?
- Do you think the speech was successful? Why or Why not?
- Why is the speech known as the "Checkers" speech?
- Do you think this speech would have had the same impact if it had been printed in the newspaper or heard on the radio? Why or why not?

Developing Your Listening Skills

Listening is more than just hearing words. It involves understanding what another person has said. It also requires using critical thinking skills. You must evaluate what a speaker is saying by separating fact from opinion. Listening, like speaking, is a skill that can be practiced and improved. This section will help you improve your listening skills.

Listening to Enjoy and Appreciate

One of the most important aspects of listening is enjoying and appreciating the subject. You will remember more about a presentation you enjoyed than one you did not enjoy. Some speakers use humor or descriptions to solidify their points and keep their speech interesting. Paying attention and listening carefully will help you enjoy the speech. You will also better appreciate what the speaker is trying to say.

Practice Your Skills

Listening to Enjoy and Appreciate

Take turns with a partner reading the poem on the following page aloud. While you are listening to your partner read, simply listen to the poem. Close your eyes if that helps you focus. Take the time to enjoy and appreciate what you are listening to. When you have each heard the poem, answer the following questions.

- Did you enjoy the poem? Why or why not?
- Even if you did not enjoy the poem, did you appreciate what the author was trying to convey?

INTEGRATING TECHNOLOGY

Audio

Remind students that many poems and novels are now available on audiotape. Recorded books allow people to listen to literature as they drive to work or lie in bed. The only prerequisite for using an audiobook is the ability to listen.

PRACTICE YOUR SKILLS Sample Answers

Students' answers will vary but all should be supported with explanations or examples.

HOME WORK

Have students find a poem in an anthology and read it silently. Then have them read it aloud. In class, discuss the difference they noticed between the two readings.

The Dream Keeper

Bring me all of your dreams,
You dreamers,
Bring me all of your
Heart melodies
That I may wrap them
In a blue-cloth
Away from the too-rough fingers
Of the world.

—*Langston Hughes*

Listening for Information and Taking Notes

Taking notes is one way to focus your attention while listening to a speech. Taking notes requires you to listen carefully for important points and to organize the information. The following guidelines will help you take clear notes while listening to a speech.

Guidelines for Taking Notes on Speeches

- Write the main idea presented in the introduction of the speech.
- Write the main topics, using Roman numerals (I, II, III) in an outline form.
- Under each main topic, write the subtopics, or supporting points, using capital letters (A, B, C). Listen for clues to the supporting points, such as "There are three main reasons why . . ." or "I will explain the four main causes of . . ."
- In the conclusion of the speech, write the restatement of the main idea.

When you take notes, do not write down everything. If you do, you probably will miss important points. Write only the information that is necessary to remember the most important points accurately. Your notes will then help you remember the other details. Following is an outline of a ten-minute speech about the development of gymnastics.

Model: Outline of a Speech

Main Idea	Gymnastics, a sport in which physical feats are performed in an artistic manner, has a long history.
Main Topic Subtopics	I. Began in ancient Greece A. Greeks had gymnasiums with fields for throwing discuses and javelins B. Romans adopted Greek ideas; added them to their military training II. Died out between 392 A.D. and the 1700s A. Revived in Germany by Frederick Jahn B. He added side bar with pommels, horizontal bars, parallel bars, balance beams, jumping standards III. Brought to the U.S. in the 1800s by immigrants A. Americans participated in first international competition in 1881 B. Four Americans won first gold medals in gymnastics in USA in 1904 Olympics
Summary Statement	Gymnastics started in ancient Greece but died out for many centuries until it was revived in the 1700s. Americans did not become involved in gymnastics until the 1880s. They have participated in international competition since then.

DEVELOPING WORKPLACE COMPETENCIES

Basic Skills: Listening

Tell students that there are very few careers that do not require good listening skills. Whether you are a politician responding to constituents' concerns, a teacher determining your students' abilities, or a snow-plow operator getting your assignment for the day, you listen for information. The ability to determine a speaker's main idea is vital. Paying attention to major details helps you understand what the speaker considers important. Listening for verbal signals such as "remember that," "on the other hand," "I want to stress," or "in conclusion" can help any listener better understand a speaker's organization.

Have students work in small groups to suggest reasons and examples that prove that listening skills are critical for these people: surgeon, logger, auto mechanic, firefighter, ballerina, and judge.

Practice Your Skills

This exercise requires the listeners to evaluate the speaker. Make sure all students participate in taking notes, summarizing, asking questions, and comparing notes.

HOME WORK

Have students watch a how-to program on television, perhaps a cooking show or a show on building furniture. Ask them to take notes on the program, summarize it, and evaluate it for clarity and simplicity.

Practice Your Skills

Listening, Taking Notes, and Following Directions

Prepare a brief explanation of how to do something, such as how to do a certain dance step or how to make a pizza. Present your explanation to the class.

- Take notes as each student presents an explanation to the class.
- When the explanation is complete, summarize it in one complete sentence.
- Clarify with the speaker any points about which you are unclear.
- If there were something you didn't know how to do before, use what you heard to try to do it. Were the directions clear enough for you to follow?
- Compare notes with your classmates to see if you have included the same topics.

Listening Critically

When listening and taking notes, it is important to listen carefully and evaluate what is being said.

Fact and Opinion

A **fact** is a statement that can be proved, but an **opinion** is a personal feeling or judgment. Because opinions are often stated as facts, you must listen carefully to tell them apart.

Fact	Dogs belong to the canine family.
Opinion	Dogs are people's best friends.

Practice Your Skills

Understanding Fact and Opinion

Label each statement *fact* or *opinion*.

1. All books by Mark Twain are interesting.
2. Halloween is always the last day of October.
3. Tiger gasoline is the best gasoline to buy.
4. My sister is three years younger than I am.
5. *Rumble Fish* was written by S. E. Hinton.
6. Baseball is the best sport in the world.
7. My sister should be an artist.
8. Gasoline is more expensive than it was 20 years ago.
9. Betsy's costume was the most unusual one.
10. Pete Rose broke Ty Cobb's record for base hits.

Bandwagon

Commercials and advertisements sometimes include a bandwagon statement. A **bandwagon** statement is one that leads you to believe that everyone is using a certain product. In other words, everyone is "jumping on the bandwagon." A bandwagon statement can be misleading because it suggests that, if you do not jump on the bandwagon, you will be different from everyone else.

Bandwagon Statement	Don't be left out. Join the healthy generation and take Peak-of-Health vitamins.

Testimonial

In a **testimonial** a famous person encourages you to buy a certain product. A testimonial can be misleading because it suggests that, if a famous person uses the product, it must be worth buying.

Practice Your Skills Sample Answers

1. opinion
2. fact
3. opinion
4. fact
5. fact
6. opinion
7. opinion
8. fact
9. opinion
10. fact

HOME WORK

Ask students to write one fact and one opinion about each of the following topics:

1. basketball
2. zoos
3. E-mail
4. marching bands
5. potatoes

GETTING STUDENTS INVOLVED

Collaborative Learning

Divide students into three groups and assign each group one of the techniques listed: bandwagon, testimonial, or loaded words. Have members of that group skim old magazines and newspapers to find and clip examples of advertisements that use the technique they were assigned. Groups should discuss and evaluate the ads they found and then use them to teach the rest of the class about their assigned technique.

Practice Your Skills Sample Answers

1. bandwagon
2. testimonial
3. loaded words
4. bandwagon
5. testimonial
6. bandwagon
7. bandwagon
8. testimonial

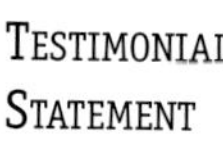

TESTIMONIAL STATEMENT	Hi! I'm baseball star Bob Mose. Bran Buds gives me the energy I need to hit the ball out of the park!

Loaded Words

Another type of misleading statement is one that contains loaded words. **Loaded words** are ones that are carefully chosen to appeal to your hopes or fears rather than to reason or logic. In the following advertisement, the word *embarrassment* was chosen to stir up the listener's emotions.

LOADED WORD	When standing close to that special person, avoid embarrassment by using Why Worry Antiperspirant.

Practice Your Skills

Evaluating for Misleading Information

Label each statement *bandwagon, testimonial,* or *loaded words.*

1. All beautiful people wear Glow cosmetics.
2. A hardworking basketball player like me, Dan Dunk, needs Hi-Jumps on his feet to win the game.
3. Eliminate unsightly blemishes with Freshface.
4. All cats, even a gourmet like André, prefer Kavier Katmeal.
5. I'm Gloria Glitter, the star of *Life Goes On*. I drink only No-Cal juice. You should too.
6. Successful people always choose Executive Airlines.
7. Everyone with good taste has Regal Rugs.
8. I'm Mitchel Judson. A star like me knows that Sparkle works better than any other toothpaste.

Listening to Evaluate

After you have listened to a speech in class, you can assess it for its effectiveness. Through self-assessment and sharing others' assessments, you can improve your listening and speaking skills and help your classmates improve theirs.

ORAL PRESENTATION ASSESSMENT FORM

SUBJECT ____________________

Speaker ____________________ **Date** ____________

Content

____ Was the subject appropriate for the audience?
____ Was the length of the speech appropriate?
____ Was the main point clear?
____ Was the purpose clear?
____ Did all the ideas clearly relate to the subject?

Organization

____ Was the introduction clear and interesting?
____ Did the introduction include the main idea?
____ Did the ideas in the body follow a logical order?
____ Were transitions used between ideas?
____ Did the conclusion summarize the main idea?

Presentation

____ Was the speaker well prepared?
____ Did the speaker speak loudly and clearly enough?
____ Did the speaker pace the delivery well?
____ Did the speaker make eye contact with the audience?
____ Were the speaker's pitch and tone appealing?
____ Did the speaker use gestures and pauses well?
____ If there were audiovisual aids or other props, were they used well?
____ Were cue cards or an outline used well?

Comments / Added Criteria ____________________

____

____

____

HOME WORK

Have students select a magazine or television advertisement and analyze it for technique. Ask them to describe the ad and label it *band-wagon, testimonial,* or *loaded words.*

USING *A Speaker Speaks*

Objective

- **To write and deliver a speech that shares knowledge about the writer's cultural background**

TIMESAVER *QuickCheck*

If the class has created an evaluation checklist for students' speeches, use that to evaluate these speeches. Evaluation should concentrate on achievement of purpose, organization, supporting details, confident delivery, enunciation, adequate volume, and variety of pitch and rate.

Oral Presentation

Purpose: to share information about your cultural traditions

Audience: your classmates

Preparing

After reading Jerry Greenfield's speech *(page C405)* and the paragraph about Ben & Jerry's *(page C416)*, we can see that Ben and Jerry decided not to follow the mainstream. Instead they decided to form their own work ethic. In many ways, this is what culture is all about—the way people do things. Your own cultural background is a big part of who you are, what you believe, and how you do things.

Think about your family's origins. Are there any traditions or holidays that your family celebrates? Choose one to share with your class in a ten-minute speech. As you prepare your speech, keep in mind the length of the speech, the audience, and your purpose. Make notes about what you already know about this tradition. Talk to older family members. When you have enough information, organize it into a logical order.

Use your organized notes to outline your speech. Be sure to include an introduction, a body, and a conclusion. If necessary, transfer the outline to index cards that you will use during the speech. As you prepare your speech, keep in mind that certain words or sayings you use may be directly related to your background. Your audience may not understand these phrases unless you explain their meaning.

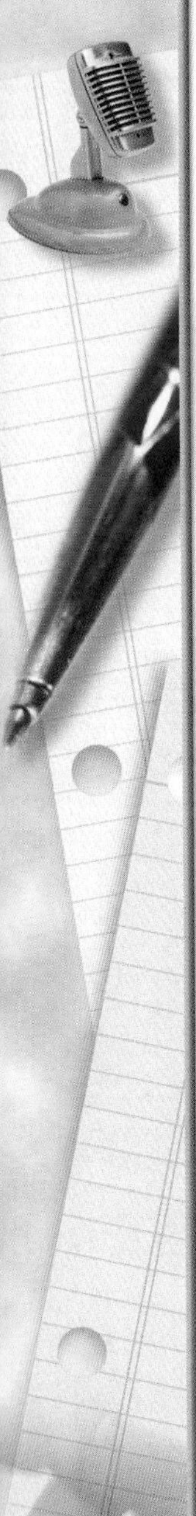

Practicing

Practice your speech over a few days. Watch yourself in a mirror and use body language and gestures to reinforce important ideas. Experiment with pauses. Time your speech, then add or remove material as necessary. When you are reasonably comfortable with it, practice your speech in front of friends who can give you advice. Use their suggestions to revise. Prepare any visuals you plan to use.

Delivering

When it is time to deliver your speech to your class, relax and take your time. Deliver the speech as you practiced it, using rehearsed gestures and pauses. Remember to display any visuals you have prepared. When you are finished, remember to thank your audience.

As your classmates deliver their speeches, use the following guidelines in listening.

- Listen carefully while your classmates speak.
- See if any of your own ideas and insights on culture are similar to those expressed in the speeches. Perhaps you share some element of culture, or maybe your cultural background is very different from theirs.
- Be attentive. Enjoy and appreciate what your classmates are sharing with you.
- If you have questions or comments on something, wait until the speech is over and then approach the speaker with your thoughts.
- Speak with the rest of the audience about what you heard, comparing perceptions of the speeches.

EXPANDING THE LESSON

Using Technology

You will find additional **instructional** and **practice** materials for this chapter at http://www.bkenglish.com.

FOR REVIEWING SKILLS

Using *Connection Collection*

Representing in Different Ways

Consider using these print and visual activities to make students aware of the benefits of using different media to suit particular purposes. Help students understand when a visual medium, for example, is better suited to their purpose than a print medium, or the reverse.

Connection Collection

Representing in Different Ways

From Visuals . . .

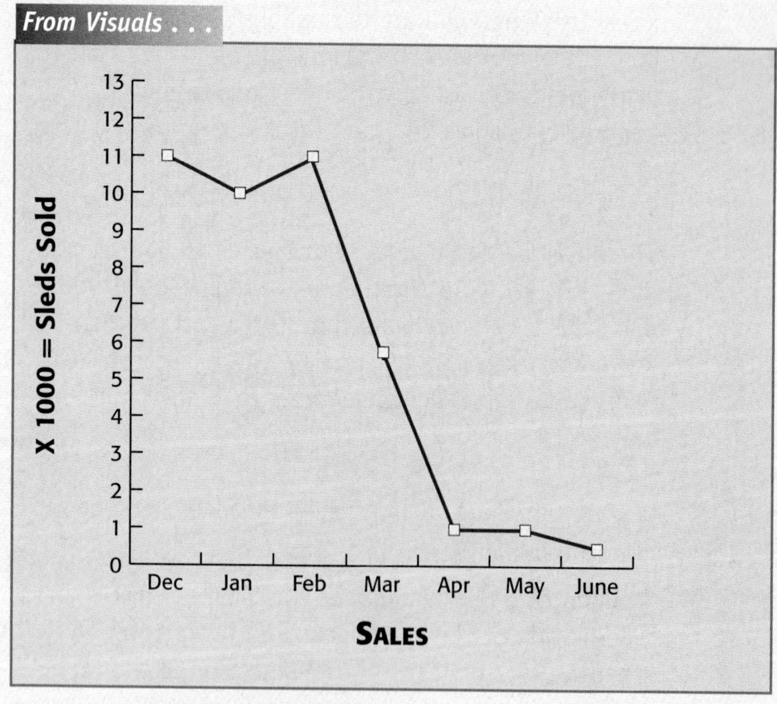

. . . to Print

Based on the chart, prepare a speech for the next board of directors meeting of Sink or Sled Inc. Be sure to explain the cause behind the dropping figures and suggest possible solutions.

From Print . . .

INTRODUCTION

Welcome to Sink or Sled Inc. stockholders

I. Decline in nationwide sales figures
   A. Poor dividends paid on stock
   B. Share price dropping

II. Steady sales in Anchorage, Alaska
   A. Sales figures holding at 800 sleds per month from November—January and in May
   B. 850 sleds per month February—March
   C. 825 sleds per month April

III. Steady sales in Anchorage due to extensive advertising
   A. Increase advertising budget nationwide
   B. Place more billboards on beaches during summer (high traffic areas)

CONCLUSION

—Nationwide sales will rise if we follow Anchorage model

—Thank you to stockholders for attending

. . . to Visuals

Based on the speech outline, create a line graph showing the sales of Sink or Sled Inc. in Anchorage, Alaska. Remember to label your graph.

- **Which strategies can be used for creating both written and visual representations? Which strategies apply to one, not both? Which type of representation is more effective?**
- **Draw a conclusion and write briefly about the differences between written ideas and visual representations.**

YOUR IDEAS

For Viewing and Representing

GETTING STUDENTS INVOLVED

Cooperative Learning

After organizing students into groups, thoroughly explain the task to be accomplished and establish a time frame. Make sure that each group member is responsible for a given task. Have each group share its project with the class and discuss the process the group used to carry out the assignment.

YOUR IDEAS

For Writing Prompts

Writing in the Workplace

Persuasive Speech

Last year's company picnic was a dud. The only activities were thumb wrestling and head scratching. A kazoo band provided the music and the only food served was dry toast and evaporated milk. You work hard at your job and deserve to have some fun.

Prepare a speech for your boss on the kind of picnic you would like to attend. Choose and limit your subject and understand your purpose. Be persuasive in your points and present them in a clear order. Practice your speech before presenting it to a classmate who will listen as your boss.

What strategies did you use to persuade your boss?

You can find information on preparing speeches on pages C411–C423.

Writing for Oral Communication

Clear Directions

The first prize in your school's Winter Raffle is 10 million dollars. You just heard that you won the raffle. Unfortunately you won second prize—a year's supply of calendars.

Prepare directions from your school to your house for the prize delivery person. Be sure the directions are clear and mention street names and landmarks whenever possible. Draw a map if the directions are complicated. Read the directions to a classmate who will act as the delivery person.

What shapes, objects, or graphic elements did you use to complete the directions for your classmate?

You can find information on giving directions on page C409.

A DIFFERENT DELIVERY SYSTEM

For formal assessment print the composition chapter test from the *BK English* Test Bank at http://www.bkenglish.com.

Assess Your Learning

You are the mayor of your city. Saturdays are the only day you get to sleep late. Last Saturday morning you were awakened at 5 A.M. by a singing bluebird. You have decided to rally for a law that would ban singing (by birds and humans) before noon on weekends. A fine would be imposed on all those who did not comply.

- **Prepare a speech persuading the city council to vote for your new "Bluebird" law.**
- **Be sure to have a strong introduction and a compelling conclusion. Be clear in your supporting points and use specific examples when necessary. Practice the delivery of your speech, experimenting with different gestures and body language. Deliver your speech to classmates who will listen as town council members. Remember to make eye contact and to speak slowly and clearly.**

Before You Write **Consider the following questions:**
What is the ***subject?***
What is the ***occasion?***
Who is the ***audience?***
What is the ***purpose?***

After You Write **Evaluate your work using the following criteria:**

- Is the speech written with a specific audience and purpose in mind?
- Are ideas organized to ensure coherence and logical progression?
- Does the introduction capture the attention of the audience?
- Are the supporting points clear and are specific examples given?
- Does the conclusion summarize the main ideas?
- Was the speech presented clearly with a tone suitable to your content and audience?
- Were rehearsed gestures and body language used to emphasize points?

Write briefly on how well you did. Point out your strengths and areas for improvement.

FOR ASSESSING LEARNING

Using *Assess Your Learning*

This writing prompt will help you and your students informally assess their developing writing abilities, using the accompanying primary trait rubrics, which list the key features and qualities of speech writing and listening taught in this chapter. You may want to have students maintain their self-assessment in their portfolios as a record of their individual progress throughout the year.

Evaluating Speeches and Presentations

In presenting speeches and dramatic performances, many students need special help in

- **appearing calm and confident**
- **using body language and gestures effectively**
- **preparing materials**
- **using visual aids effectively**

Self-evaluation and peer-evaluation can help students to improve their speaking skills.

Self-evaluation

After students have finished making their presentations, distribute copies of the Speech Evaluation Checklist. (See the Evaluation Checklists in BK English Language and Composition Assessment.) Have students carefully consider each standard to determine their level of proficiency. Students might have a more objective view of their own presentation if they complete their evaluation after seeing others' presentations.

Peer evaluation

Presentations also may be evaluated by students working in pairs or small groups. After hearing the presentations, listeners should be able to use the Speech Evaluation Checklist to provide feedback to each presenter. Remind students how to provide constructive and respectful comments to their peers.

Teacher evaluation

Speech Evaluation Checklist

The following checklist can be used by the teacher as students give their presentations or for peer or self-evaluations.

EVALUATION CHECKLIST

4 = Always 3 = Sometimes 2 = Seldom 1 = Never

______ Speaker was prepared.

______ Speaker's materials were organized.

______ Speaker appeared confident.

______ Speaker stayed focused on topic.

______ Speaker used the appropriate rate and volume of voice.

______ Speaker made eye contact with audience.

______ Speaker used nonverbal communication to reinforce spoken words.

______ Speaker used graphic aids effectively.

TEACHER EVALUATION

Primary Trait Evaluation

For primary trait assessment of speeches and presentations, the following chart lists the key features taught in this chapter.

	EXCELLENT	ACCEPTABLE	NEEDS IMPROVEMENT
Preparation	Speaker appears to have all materials organized and to have thorough knowledge of topic. There is evidence that the student has practiced the presentation.	Speaker has most materials ready and spends little time searching for materials. Some evidence is present that speaker practiced the presentation.	Speaker does not have materials ready and spends time during the presentation searching for materials. No evidence is present that the speaker practiced the presentation.
Verbal Communication	Speaker uses appropriate rate and volume of voice. Speaker's words are clear and easily understood.	Speaker's rate and volume are appropriate with little variance. Most of speaker's words are clear and easily understood.	Speaker's rate and volume are not appropriate to the audience or situation. Speaker's words are not clear and not understood.
Nonverbal Communication	Speaker uses appropriate nonverbal communication such as gestures and eye contact. Speaker's nonverbal communication reinforces the spoken words and does not distract from the speech.	Speaker uses nonverbal communication during most of the presentation, distracting very little from the presentation.	Speaker does not use nonverbal communication at all, or if nonverbal communication is present, it is inappropriate and distracts from the presentation.
Confidence and Focus	Speaker appears confident, in voice as well as body language. Speech has a focused topic and speaker stays on topic and avoids rambling.	Speaker appears confident during most of the presentation. The presentation's topic is somewhat focused with little rambling.	Speaker does not appear confident, evidenced by a soft voice and nervous behavior such as fidgeting. Topic of presentation is not focused and speaker appears to ramble from one topic to another.
Graphic Aids	Speaker uses graphic aids effectively and only uses graphics that extend or clarify the meanings in the speech.	Speaker uses graphic aids, distracting little from the presentation. The graphic aids lend some meaning to the presentation.	Speaker does not use graphic aids or uses graphic aids that do not lend meaning to the presentation.

TEACHER EVALUATION

Holistic Evaluation

The following criteria may be used to evaluate speaker's presentations for the various activities in the chapter, using a rating scale of
- 4 (excellent)
- 3 (good)
- 2 (acceptable)
- 1 (needs improvement)
- 0 (unscoreable).

4	3	2	1
Speaker is well prepared for the presentation. Speaker appears to have practiced the presentation prior to giving it.	Speaker has most materials ready for the presentation and spends little time searching for materials. There is evidence that the speaker practiced somewhat for the presentation.	Speaker does not have all needed materials, or they are not properly organized, and speaker spends a large amount of time looking for materials. Speaker does not appear to have practiced the presentation.	The speaker has no materials prepared and does not exhibit any evidence of having practiced the presentation.
Speaker uses appropriate verbal and nonverbal communication, including rate, volume, pitch, and clarity of spoken words. Use of graphic aids is appropriate and does not distract from the presentation.	Speaker's verbal communication is clear most of the time and nonverbal communication does little to distract from the presentation.	Speaker either uses no nonverbal communication, or uses nonverbal communication that is frequently distracting to the audience. Verbal communication is often inappropriate or unclear.	Speaker's verbal communication is unclear and inappropriate, and speaker's nonverbal communication is very distracting.
Speaker appears confident and aware of the audience. Topic of the speech is focused.	Speaker appears confident most of the time with little nervous behavior present. Topic of the speech is clear.	Speaker frequently appears nervous and exhibits behaviors that distract from the presentation. Topic of the speech is not clear.	Speaker seems only to ramble from one topic to another.

Communication Resource

Planning Guide

This chart will help you create a flexible instructional plan that addresses the individual needs of all your students in the new millennium.

Learning to Know

A Foundation of Knowledge	CHAPTER 14 Vocabulary	CHAPTER 15 Dictionary
PE Communication Models	Reading with a Writer's Eye, p. C438 "Words We Need" by Richard Lederer, pp. C439–C441 Thinking as a Writer, p. C442	Reading with a Writer's Eye, p. C468 "Order Out of Chaos" by Bill Bryson, pp. C469–C472 Thinking as a Writer, p. C473
TE Skills Instruction	Lesson 1: The English Language Lesson 2: Word Meanings	Lesson 1: Structure of the Dictionary Lesson 2: Homographs and Word Origins
PE Skills Practice	**Practice Your Skills** • Looking Up Word Origins, p. C445 • Identifying Dialects, p. C448 • Identifying Informal Language, p. C449 • Identifying Denotations and Connotations, p. C451 • Using Sentence and Paragraph Context Clues, pp. C454–C455 • Finding Roots, p. C456 • Combining Prefixes and Roots, pp. C457–C458 • Combining Suffixes and Roots, pp. C459–C460 • Recognizing Synonyms, pp. C461–C462 • Recognizing Antonyms, pp. C463–C464 • Recognizing Analogies, p. C465	**Practice Your Skills** • Using Guide Words, p. C476 • Alphabetizing Words and Entries, pp. C476–C477 • Correcting Spelling Errors, p. C479 • Dividing Words into Syllables, pp. C480–C481 • Marking Pronunciation, p. C482 • Placing Accent Marks, p. C483 • Identifying Different Uses of Words, p. C485 • Using a Dictionary for Improving Writing, pp. C486–C487 • Matching Old and New Words, p. C488 • Finding Word Origins, p. C489 • Finding Unusual Origins, p. C491
PE Independent Application	**In the Media** • Advertising Vocabulary, p. C467	**In the Media** • Media Messages, p. C492
Assessment and Evaluation	PE Time Out to Reflect, p. C466 + I Chapter Test	PE Time Out to Reflect, p. C491 PE Assess Your Learning, p. C493 + I Chapter Test

PE PUPIL'S EDITION TE TEACHER'S EDITION + ANCILLARIES I INTERNET

ADDITIONAL RESOURCES

- Composition Skills Practice
- Language Skills Practice
- Assessment
- Assessment Resources
- Standardized Test Preparation
- ESL Practice and Test Preparation
- Transparency Tools
- Writing Prompts
- Writers at Work

CHAPTER 16 Library and Media Center	A Writer's Guide to Electronic Publishing pp. C520–C545	A Writer's Guide to the Internet pp. C546–C576
Reading with a Writer's Eye, p. C494 "The Alexandria Project Homepage" from The First Alexandria Library, pp. C495–C498 Thinking as a Writer, p. C499	Desktop Publishing, pp. C521–C529 Nonprint Media–Audio and Video, pp. C530–C540 Publishing on the World Wide Web, pp. C540–C545	How Does the Internet Work? pp. C547–C550 Why Use the Internet? pp. C551–C557 How to Communicate on the Internet, pp. C558–C562 How to Do Research on the Internet, pp. C563–C576
Lesson 1: Locating Works Lesson 2: Card Catalogs Lesson 3: Reference Materials		
Practice Your Skills • Arranging Fiction and Solving Shelving Problems, pp. C501–C502 • Using the Dewey Decimal System, pp. C503–C504 • Searching Online, Using and Writing Card Catalogs, pp. C508–C509 • Using the *Readers' Guide,* pp. C512–C513 • Using General Biographical References, p. C515 • Using Specialized Reference Material, pp. C517–C518		
PE Time Out to Reflect, p. C519 + I Chapter Test		

LEARNING TO DO

Competencies for the World of Work

Basic Skills:
Reads, writes, performs arithmetic and mathematical operations, listens and speaks
- Reading
- Writing
- Arithmetic/Mathematics
- Listening
- Speaking

Thinking Skills:
Thinks creatively, makes decisions, solves problems, visualizes, knows how to learn, and reasons
- Creative Thinking
- Decision Making
- Problem Solving
- Seeing Things in the Mind's Eye
- Knowing How to Learn
- Reasoning

Personal Qualities:
Displays responsibility, self-esteem, sociability, self-management, and integrity and honesty
- Responsibility
- Self-Esteem
- Sociability
- Self-Management
- Integrity/Honesty

LEARNING WITH TECHNOLOGY

Tools for the Information Age

I http://www.bkenglish.com
- BK English Online (password required)
- Chapter Tests
- Skill Practice
- Writing Prompts
- Standardized Tests

Teaching Suggestions

Essential Knowledge and Skills

- Identifying how language use such as labels and sayings reflect regions and cultures
- Understanding the influence of other languages and cultures on the spelling of English words
- Spelling derivatives correctly by applying the spelling of bases and affixes
- Employing standard English usage in writing for audiences
- Evaluating how different media forms influence and inform
- Assessing how language, medium, and presentation contribute to the message

CHAPTER 14

Vocabulary

If someone called you *persistent*, would you be flattered or insulted? If a teacher asked you to *elaborate* after answering a question, what would you do? If a book you are reading describes a character as *meek*, what image would come to mind? In conversation, in school, and in your reading you are likely to come across many unfamiliar words. Take the time to learn them—you will gradually build your vocabulary.

This chapter will help you understand the origins and development of the English language. It will also give you strategies for deciphering the meanings of new words and enlarging your vocabulary. The more words you have at your command, the more precisely you will be able to express your meaning in speech and in writing—choosing vocabulary that is appropriate to your situation, your audience, and your purpose.

Reading with a Writer's Eye

In the following selection, Richard Lederer discusses concepts for which the English language has yet to invent vocabulary. He provides some humorous insight into how words are introduced into language. As you read, think about times in your own life when there simply was not a word to express exactly what you meant. Have you ever been at a loss for words because you just did not have the proper words available to you?

BLOCK SCHEDULING

- If your schedule requires that you cover the chapter in a **shorter time**, use the core lesson: Growth of the English Language, Varieties of the English Language, and Word Meaning.
- If you want to take advantage of **longer class time**, include the selection "Words We Need" and its accompanying material.

FROM *THE MIRACLE OF LANGUAGE*

Words We Need

Richard Lederer

Choconivorous is "the tendency when eating a chocolate Easter bunny, to bite off the head first." The *hozone* is "the place where one sock in every laundry load disappears to." And a *charp* is "the green, mutant potato chip found in every bag."

Welcome to the world of sniglets, the series of pop dictionaries that attempt to describe the hitherto indescribable. Author (and actor-comedian) Rich Hall defines a sniglet as "any word that doesn't appear in a dictionary but should," which makes *sniglet* itself a sniglet. Hall's wiggy lexicons dazzle us with an inherent shortcoming of all vocabularies: No language has a net wide enough to throw over all of reality. There will always be more things and ideas than there are words.

At St. Paul's School I frequently ask my seniors to make up sniglets about our lives together in a boarding school community. As Rich Hall's sniglets books demonstrate again and again, granting something a name helps us to look at it through new eyes and to become more aware of its existence. I hoped that, in the process of fabricating their own sniglets, my students will better understand the realities, dreams, fears, and joys of their lives at residential school nestled in a valley in Concord, New Hampshire:

cryptocarnophobic (adj.) How one feels when mystery meat is placed on the table at evening seated meal.

FOR INCREASING STUDENT ACHIEVEMENT

GUIDED READING

Text Analysis

- This piece of exposition is partly **informational,** but its main purpose seems to be to **entertain.** Have students differentiate between facts and details that are meant to inform and opinions and examples that are meant to entertain.
- The subject matter—concepts that lack words to name them—is addressed in a humorous **tone.**
- The writer sprinkles his writing with personal **anecdotes** and **examples** from books and from real life to support his thesis that there are more things and ideas than there are words.

SELECTION AMENDMENT
Description of change: excerpted
Rationale: to focus on vocabulary skills presented in this chapter

GUIDED READING

Strategy: Evaluating

As students read, ask them to evaluate the author's message and his means of expressing that message. Have them consider these questions: *Do I like this essay? Do the author's examples support his main idea? Is the essay well-organized and easy to read?* Convene the class when everyone has read the essay independently, and discuss the students' views.

gastro-optimize (v.) To go out to the cafeteria for more food in order to stay and talk with the ultimate scope. (In St. Paul's School slanguage a scope is a gorgeous member of the opposite sex.)

postpost (v.) To check your post office box five times a day even on Sunday when you know there can't be anything there.

SATarrhea (n.) The urge to go to the bathroom while taking the Scholastic Aptitude Test.

shmoffles (n.) The crud that accumulates on your cleats and falls off in the shape of waffles.

stud-ups (n.) The special kind of sit-ups executed by members of the football team while the field hockey team jogs by.

Blessed with the wealthiest vocabulary in the history of humankind, many English speakers feel that they have a word for everything. But, as the saga of sniglets illuminates, not even the English language can cast its net over all the things and ideas of life. As wondrously vast as our English vocabulary may be, there remain a surprisingly large number of concepts for which we still do not have good and serviceable words.

We have now embarked on a decade we call the Nineties. With varying emotions, we look back on previous decades—the Twenties, Thirties, Forties, Fifties, Sixties, Seventies, and Eighties.

But after the Nineties, what? When the twenty-first century dawns, what are we going to call its first decade? The Zeros? Too dismal. The Noughts or Naughts? Too negative. The Aughts or Oughts? Too ambiguous, too prescriptive. Surely we can launch the next century with something more cheerful—perhaps the Ohs, an exultant exclamation that conveys the sense of wonder and infinite potential that awaits us.

And what about the decade after that, the one beginning with the year 2010?[1] The Teens leap to mind, but three of those years—2010, 2011, and 2012—will not include numbers in the teens.

When we reach the year 2020, we shall again be equipped with familiar decade names for the next eighty years, but the year 2026 will call out for another word we need but don't have. That year, of course, will mark the 250th anniversary of American independence. In 1876 we celebrated our centennial, in 1926 our sesquicentennial (from the Latin *sesqui* and English *centennial:* "one and a half hundred"), and in 1976 our bicentennial. What shall we call our 250th in 2026? When the town of Epsom, New Hampshire, attained its 250th year of incorporation in 1975, one of its leading citizens, Al Norris, invented the word *quatrimillennial,* literally "a quarter of a thousand." Perhaps our nation in 2026 will take its cue from Mr. Norris.

And what do we call ourselves as citizens of that nation? We say *Americans* and *the American people,* but an American identifies anyone in this hemisphere, from North to Central to South America, and the designation has historically rankled Latin Americans and Canadians. In *The American Language,* H. L. Mencken lists the many alternatives that have been proposed—*Unisians, Unitedstatesians, Columbards,* and the like—but none has earned a thumbs-up from the American people, or whatever it is we are.

---

[1]Purists will fault me on these dates, pointing out that Christ was one year old at the end of the first year A.D. and that the first decade A.D. was not over until the end of the year 10. Each new decade, therefore, begins with the start of a year ending with the number one, not zero, and the second decade of the next century will begin with the year 2011, not 2010. These precise chronologists will stay home on the night of December 31, 1999, while we yahoos are dancing in the streets to celebrate the arrival of the new millennium. One year later, around midnight, the literalists will go out to ring in the twenty-first century and find only a small gathering of themselves.

READER RESPONSE

You may want to use the following questions to elicit students' personal responses to the selection.

1. Do you think the nation should take its cue from Mr. Norris of New Hampshire and call 2026 the country's quatrimillennial? If not, what word would you invent to name that date?
2. Which of the examples of invented words do you think you yourself might use? Why?
3. Do your friends or family have any invented words of your own? What are they and what do they mean?
4. Do you agree with the author that the naming of the American people is problematic? How would you like to see this issue resolved?

ADDITIONAL RESOURCES

Composition Skills Practice. . . . . pages 73–76
Writers at Work . . . . 8•1–8•10
Assessment: Chapter Test. . . . . pages 91–93
Assessment Resources . . . . pages 1–10, 13–44

Using *Thinking as a Writer*

You may choose to have students respond to the questions either orally or in writing.

REACHING ALL STUDENTS

Struggling Learners

Make sure students recognize the connections between the sniglets in Richard Lederer's article and existing words. Write these two on the board and discuss their word parts:
choconivorous: *choco* from *chocolate*; *nivourous* as in *carnivorous* or *omnivorous*, meaning "eater of"
cryptocarnophobic: *crypto* meaning "mysterious," as in *cryptic*; *carno* meaning "meat," as in *carnivore*; *phobic* meaning "afraid of." As students create their own sniglets, have them try to include word parts that already exist in English.

Thinking as a Writer

Suggesting Vocabulary

In his article, Richard Lederer, mentions several concepts over which there is a vocabulary debate.

- What concepts does the author mention as needing words to convey them?
- Why is it important to have words to express these particular concepts? Could the concepts just go "unnamed"? Why or why not?
- What words would you suggest to convey these as yet "unnamed" concepts? Explain your answers.

Creating Sniglets

Oral Expression In the selection, Lederer refers to Rich Hall's work on *sniglets*. The concept of sniglets is that "there will always be more things and ideas than there are words." Have you found this to be true in your own life?

- In a small group, discuss things and ideas in your everyday life for which there is no known word.
- Each person should come up with a sniglet-like suggestion.
- Vote on the words and record the outcomes to share with the class.

Naming Objects by Sight

Viewing Often, simply the way something looks will bring to mind feelings, sounds, and words. Think of a kitten. Doesn't the word *fur* sound exactly like the softness of the cuddly creature?

- Look at the objects shown on the opposite page. Name them according to the feelings and sounds that come to mind when you see them. Why did you choose the names you chose?

DEVELOPING WORKPLACE COMPETENCIES

Thinking Skills: Creative Thinking

Point out that the ability to think creatively—to come up with new uses for existing objects, to invent new objects to fulfill new needs, and to name new objects that have yet to be named—is key to success in today's technological world of work. In advertising and manufacturing, people may sit around a room and brainstorm names for new products. Movies and television shows often go through many preliminary names before the "perfect" name is chosen.

Have students work in pairs to think of (1) a product and (2) a movie or television show that they think have the perfect names. Discuss why those particular names are so effective. Are there any other names they can think of that might be equally good?

FOR DEVELOPING SKILLS

LESSON 1 *(pages C446–C452)*

OBJECTIVES

- **To become familiar with the history of the Modern English language through its origins, development, and usage**
- **To become familiar with varieties of the English language and their usage in everyday life**

Create Interest

Write these words from Richard Lederer's composition on the chalkboard: *serviceable, prescriptive, exultant,* and *rankled.* After discussing their meanings, have students substitute a more informal word *i.e. serviceable–useable, prescriptive–old-timer, exultant–rad, rankled–bugged.*

REACHING ALL STUDENTS

Advanced Learners

Have students look up these words in the dictionary to find their definitions and their Old English and Middle English derivations: *knell, breach, groats,* and *threshhold.* Discuss the changes in spelling over the years.

Growth of the English Language

Just like people, languages are born and then develop. Many different factors can influence the development of a language. Immigration, technology, and popular culture are some examples of things that have greatly influenced our own English language. *(See page C489 for a list of some of the words that American English has borrowed from other languages.)* A language grows and changes along with the people who use it. English is constantly changing and in order to better understand the vocabulary we use, we need to understand where our language comes from and what changes it has gone through over time.

Origins

The English language and all other languages come from a single language that was spoken thousands of years ago. At some point in history, a form of English branched off as a separate language. The growth of English through time is divided into three major stages: *Old English, Middle English,* and *Modern English*. If you were to hear Old or Middle English spoken, they would probably sound like foreign languages and not at all like the English we speak today. This is because English has developed over the centuries—words were added, and spellings, meanings, and pronunciations changed. In fact, our language is still in the process of developing even today.

Spelling and Pronunciation

The spellings and pronunciations of many English words have changed over the centuries. These changes in pronunciations can sometimes help explain what might

Guide Instruction

By Connecting Ideas

Write the following words on the board: *mug, green, class, figure, hero.* Write next to each word all the different meanings and connotations each word brings to students' minds. Without using a dictionary, have students discuss which meanings come from a dictionary, which are slang usage, which are regional, and the positive and negative connotations of any of the meanings.

Consolidate Skills

Through Guided Practice

Working in small groups, have each student in the group choose a word that the group will discuss. Have each group look up the word in the dictionary, note the number of definitions, note the origin of the word, and contribute an informal use of the word the group might know.

otherwise seem like odd spellings of words and vice versa. For example, the silent *k* in many Modern English words is left over from the time when words, such as *knee* and *knight,* used to be pronounced with hard *c* or strong *k* sounds at their beginnings. Gradually, the pronunciations of the words changed, but the spellings remained, reflecting the words' history.

Meaning

The meanings of words have also changed over the years. In recent times, for example, the need for a vocabulary to describe computer-related concepts and ideas has prompted the addition of new definitions to old words. A *mouse* used to be mainly "a small rodent." Now it is also "a device that moves a cursor on a computer screen." The verb *surf* used to refer just to the water sport until the Internet came along. Now *surf* also refers to exploring different Websites. The word *computer* also has a past. Before it came to mean "an electronic machine," it had always meant "a person who computes."

PRACTICE YOUR SKILLS

Looking Up Word Origins

Look up the following words in the dictionary to find each of their origins. You can find more information on how to use the dictionary to find word origins on pages C487–C490.

1.	room	**8.**	swoop
2.	werewolf	**9.**	cold
3.	eel	**10.**	reveal
4.	retain	**11.**	broil
5.	restore	**12.**	analogy
6.	sanitary	**13.**	shed
7.	dunce	**14.**	gear

PRACTICE YOUR SKILLS Sample Answers

1. Middle English *roum* from Old English *rūm*
2. Middle English from Old English *werewulf*
3. Middle English *ele* from Old English *āel*
4. Middle English *retainen* from Old French *retenir* from Latin *retinēre*
5. Middle English *restoren* from Old French *restorer* from Latin *restaurāre*
6. French *sanitaire* from Latin *sanitas*
7. from John *Duns* Scotus, whose once accepted writings were ridiculed in the 16th century
8. Middle English *swopen* from Old English *swāpan*
9. Middle English from Old English *ceald*
10. Middle English *revalen* from Old French *revaler*
11. Middle English *broilen* from Old French *bruler*
12. Middle English *analogie* from Old French from Latin *analogia* from Greek *analogos*
13. Middle English from Old English *scēaden*
14. Middle English *gere* from Old Norse *gervi, gorvi,* akin to Old English *gaerwe*

HOME WORK

Have students use each of the words in items 1-14 in an original sentence that demonstrates its meaning.

Apply to Communication

Through Independent Writing

Have students select a piece of writing from their portfolios that might benefit from improved vocabulary. Have them highlight those words, making a list, and work independently during this chapter to find and use more precise, lively vocabulary.

Transfer to Everyday Life

By Using Cross-Curricular Connections

As students read homework assignments in science, math, or social studies, have them list any words which appear in more than one class in their journals. Ask them to explain the different usages for each class. For instance, in English class the word *composition* refers to a certain type of writing, while in science class it refers to the make-up of an organism or element.

Pull It All Together

By Sharing

Have students read aloud the words they found in reading assignments for other classes. Have students share

INTEGRATING TECHNOLOGY

Video

A useful video that accentuates appreciation of North American languages, accents, and dialects is *National Geographic*'s "Languages" (1993), from the *Celebrating Our Differences* series.

Varieties of the English Language

Although English is one language, there are many varieties of it. There are variations in the way it is spoken, differences in the way it is used, in varieties of sayings, and in meanings of the same words.

American Dialects

The English language is made up of almost a million words and it is spoken in many different counties around the world. Not all English-speaking people speak the language in the same way. Even across our own country, because of the rich mix of people, there are differences in the way words are pronounced from place to place. These different ways of speaking are called **dialects**. Americans tend to speak two kinds of dialects: regional dialects and ethnic dialects. Dialects can be different from one another in vocabulary, pronunciation, and even grammar. Remember, this is not to say that all people from a particular place or ethnic group speak in the same way, simply that people who live close to each other or have similar backgrounds tend to share similar ways of speaking.

Regional Dialects

People from different parts of the same country tend to speak alike. In the United States, English varies among three main regional dialects: Eastern, Southern, and General American. For example, New Englanders are said to speak with a twang and Southerners with a drawl. Each of these dialects may contain many subdialects. In Philadelphia, Pennsylvania, for instance, a large sandwich may be called a *hogie*, and in Boston, Massachusetts, that same sandwich may be called a

their findings with each other, comparing and adding to the meanings they discovered.

Check Understanding

By Developing Formal Language From Informal Language

Using a visual image of your choice, have students freewrite a list of words that the image provokes in them. Then ask them to write a paragraph in reaction to the image using the list of words. Finally, have students revise their paragraph, substituting the informal language (probably resulting from freewriting) with standard language.

submarine. A similar sandwich in the South is called a *po'boy*. Dialects add color and richness to our language.

Ethnic Dialects

A person's cultural background can also be a factor in how he or she speaks. A variety of English spoken by a large number of members of a particular ethnic group is called an **ethnic dialect**. Some of the most widely spoken ethnic dialects in the United States are black, Hispanic, and Asian-influenced English.

Ethnic dialects have a great influence on the general American vocabulary in that they often add new words, meanings, and pronunciations. *(See pages C487–C491 for a list of words that were added to the English language from other languages and cultures.)* These words became part of our language in part because members of particular ethnic groups immigrated to America and introduced words from their own languages and experiences into the English language through ethnic dialects.

Practice Your Skills

Identifying Dialects

Different people use different words for the same thing. With a small group of classmates, discuss the words you use for items in your home and how you pronounce them. For example, do you say *sofa, lounge, davenport, couch,* or *settee*? Do you say *soda, pop,* or *tonic*? Do you carry a *pail* or a *bucket*? Are the words and pronunciations you use the same words and pronunciations that you hear spoken on television?

Writing Tip

Use **standard English** when writing for school and for a large general audience.

YOUR IDEAS

For Discussing Ethnic Dialects

PRACTICE YOUR SKILLS Evaluation Guidelines

Circulate to help students chart the differences they find among dialects. Reconvene the class to discuss groups' results.

HOME WORK

Point out that when adults in a household come from different places, regional differences may exist even within a single family. Have students write these words on index cards and have their family members pronounce them: *water, tomato, February*, and *roof*. Ask them to record any differences they hear.

IDENTIFYING COMMON STUMBLING BLOCKS

Problem

- Using forms of *be* incorrectly

Solution

- Tell students that the words *be* and *been* are never used in standard English unless they are accompanied by a helping verb. In other words, "I been sleeping" is nonstandard English; "I have been sleeping" is standard English. Tell students to make sure they use a helping verb with *be* and *been* whenever they are in a situation that requires standard English.

Standard American English

Standard American English is the most widely used and accepted form of English. It is the variety of English used in newspapers, scholarly writings, and in most nonfiction books. It is the formal kind of English that is expected in your schoolwork and in most business situations. This is not to say that other forms of English are wrong, just that different forms are appropriate to different situations. Using standard English helps people of different regions and cultures to communicate clearly with one another.

Nonstandard American English

Nonstandard American English is English that does not follow the rules and guidelines of standard American English. It is not incorrect or wrong, but simply language that is inappropriate in certain situations, with some audiences, or on occasions where standard English is expected. Nonstandard English is the variety of English you probably use when speaking to friends and family members or when you write fiction, journal entries, or personal letters. It has a conversational tone and is very informal.

Colloquialisms

Colloquialisms are informal phrases or colorful expressions that are not meant to be taken literally but are understood to have particular nonliteral meanings. They can be used when nonstandard English is appropriate. Colloquialisms are appropriate for conversation and informal writing but not for formal writing.

COLLOQUIALISMS	As soon as Dan and Luis met, they **hit it off.** (got along well together)
	That horror movie sure **gave me the creeps.** (scared me)

Slang

Slang consists of nonstandard English expressions that are developed and used by particular groups. For example, teenagers often come up with their own slang expressions. Such expressions are highly colorful, exaggerated, and often humorous. Although most slang goes out of fashion quickly, a few slang expressions—such as those that follow—have become a permanent part of the language.

SLANG EXPRESSIONS	Simone earned ten **bucks** by mowing the Henshaws' lawn. (dollars)
	I'm going to **hang out** with Sheila and Marcus. (spend time)

PRACTICE YOUR SKILLS

Identifying Informal Language

Each sentence below contains informal language. Rewrite each sentence using standard English.

1. Let's stop and grab some grub before the movie.
2. She leaped at the chance to go to the concert.
3. My mom keeps bugging me to clean my room.
4. The library has tons of books on space travel.
5. I ain't gonna go to the park with them on Sunday.
6. There are lots of things to do at the amusement park.
7. It can be difficult and time-consuming to score a good part-time summer job.
8. A rainy summer day can be a bummer.
9. That's a really cool pair of pants.
10. The band's last song brought the house down.

USING STUDENTS' STRENGTHS

Multiple Intelligences: Musical

Have students work in pairs to brainstorm a list of slang they and their friends use. Ask them to incorporate the slang into an original rap that demonstrates the meaning of the slang words. They may then perform it for the class.

PRACTICE YOUR SKILLS Sample Answers

1. Let's stop and eat something before the movie.
2. She was eager to go to the concert.
3. My mom keeps insisting that I clean my room.
4. The library has many books on space travel.
5. I am not going to the park with them on Sunday.
6. There are many things to do at the amusement park.
7. It can be difficult and time-consuming to obtain a good part-time summer job.
8. A rainy summer day can be depressing.
9. That's a very nice pair of pants.
10. The band's last song ended in rousing applause.

HOME WORK

Have students use each of these informal words and phrases in a sentence and then rewrite the sentence in standard English.

1. chill out
2. megabucks
3. totally creepy
4. give me a break
5. a real sicko

GETTING STUDENTS INVOLVED

Cooperative Learning

Give pairs of students magazines or newspapers and ask them to work together to locate and revise tired words and clichés in an article of their choice. Tell students to use one of these methods to work cooperatively:

- As one student reads the article aloud, the other identifies tired words and clichés. The first student approves or disapproves of the choices. Then both brainstorm words and phrases to replace the tired words and clichés.
- Students photocopy the article and individually circle any tired words and clichés they find, replacing them with livelier choices. Then the pairs get together to compare notes and vote on the better corrections.

When students have edited the article, have them rewrite it and compare it to the original.

Tired Words and Clichés

A **tired word** is a word that has been so overused that it has been drained of meaning. Take, for example, the word *wonderful*. This word literally means "full of wonder." Now, through overuse, the word means "good."

A **cliché** is a tired expression. These are also bland and powerless due to overuse. Some examples of clichés follow.

good as gold	light as a feather
heavy as a rock	cold as ice
as rich as Midas	bright and early

We often use tired words and clichés when we speak. We call sunsets "pretty," movies "fabulous," and sweaters "cute." We say a baby is "cute as a button." None of these words conveys precise information, however.

Writing Tip

Avoid **tired words** and **clichés**. Your writing will be fresher, more precise, and more interesting to read.

Denotations and Connotations

The **denotation** of a word means the *specific* definition of a word—the definition you will find in the dictionary. However, sometimes through usage a word takes on additional meanings; this is the **connotation** of a word. For example, although *lazy* and *idle* have similar denotative meanings, they have very different connotative meanings. *Lazy* has come to mean "not willing to work," while *idle* means "not working." The difference in connotative meanings of words is important to consider when choosing vocabulary to use in writing.

The **connotation** of a word can have an emotional impact; as a writer, you should be aware of this impact and use it wisely.

PRACTICE YOUR SKILLS

Identifying Denotations and Connotations

Read the following list of words. Each pair shares a denotative meaning. Which word in each pair do you think has more of a connotative meaning?

1. thrifty; stingy
2. nosy; curious
3. decline; reject
4. childish; playful
5. mature; aged
6. historic; old
7. economical; cheap
8. picky; selective
9. dark; unlit
10. scrawny; thin

Jargon

Jargon is specialized vocabulary used by a particular group of people. It is usually shared among group members who engage in the same activity or profession. For example, photographers use the word *zoom*, meaning "to move the camera's lens in toward the subject." The word *zoom* might not be understood to have that meaning outside a group of photographers.

REACHING ALL STUDENTS

Advanced Learners

One way to witness the additional meanings of a word is to look at particular place names. Rightly or wrongly, many places have a reputation that colors even the mention of their names. Have students work in small groups to discuss the images conjured up by these place names: *Hollywood, Paris, Calcutta, New York City, the South*, and *New Orleans*.

PRACTICE YOUR SKILLS Answers

1. stingy
2. nosy
3. reject
4. childish
5. aged
6. historic
7. cheap
8. picky
9. dark
10. scrawny

HOME WORK

Have students use these synonyms in sentences that demonstrate their different connotations.

bony, slender
amateur, dabbler
foolish, harebrained
corrupt, dishonest
friend, sidekick

Jargon can be useful when you are speaking to a group of people who are sure to understand it. It should not be used, however, when you are speaking to or writing for a general audience who may not be familiar with a specialized meaning.

COMPUTER TIP

E-mail users often use emoticons as a form of shorthand to transmit emotion to an unseeing correspondent. For example, if a person is being sarcastic, she may convey that sentiment with a sideways winking smiley face constructed with a semicolon and a single parenthesis: **;)**

Or, if a person is having a bad day, he may construct a sideways sad face: **: (**

Emoticons are easy ways to add a connotation to an E-mail message, but they are poor substitutes for language. To truly convey emotion and ideas, use precise vocabulary.

LESSON 2 *(pages C453–C466)*

OBJECTIVES

- **To determine meaning through context clues, root words, prefixes, and suffixes**
- **To expand vocabulary through synonyms, antonyms, and analogies**

Create Interest

Write these words on the chalkboard: *doctor, documents*, and *docile*. Explain that all three words have something in common. They all derive from the same Latin root, *docere*, meaning "to teach." A doctor was once a particular kind of teacher, and the word *doctorate* describes a degree for people who have received advanced training. *Documents* can be considered teaching tools, and someone who is *docile* is easily taught or trained. When words share a root, we say that they are part of a *word family*. Knowing a little about the roots of words can help you decipher the meaning of related words.

Word Meaning

If you come across a word that is new to you, what do you do? For example, suppose you came across this sentence.

> Mario was indecisive when it came to choosing which hat to wear.

Perhaps you already know that *indecisive* means "prone to indecision" or "hesitant," but more likely it is a new word to you. One way to learn its meaning is to look it up in a dictionary. In this chapter you will learn several additional ways to unlock the meaning of an unfamiliar word.

Context Clues

One of the ways you can learn the meaning of a word is through context clues. The **context** of a word is the sentence, the surrounding words, or the situation in which the word occurs. The following examples show the three most common kinds of context clues.

DEFINITION	Objects in space that emit strong radio signals are **quasars**. (The word *quasars* is defined within the sentence.)
EXAMPLES	**Fossil fuels**, such as coal, oil, and natural gas, are nonrenewable resources. (The words *fossil fuels* are followed by examples that are known to readers and listeners.)
SYNONYM	Much of our knowledge about Norse explorers comes from **sagas**. These long stories were recited and passed from one generation to the next. (A synonym for the word *saga* is used in the sentence that follows it.)

REACHING ALL STUDENTS

English Language Learners

Review these three common kinds of context clues with English Language Learners. Then have them apply them to a reading passage from another textbook. As they come to a word they do not recognize, help them assess whether the word is defined in the sentence, followed by examples, or provided with a synonym. If none of these is the case, demonstrate how to use other clues to determine the word's part of speech and likely meaning. Have students check their guesses with a dictionary.

Guide Instruction

By Modeling Strategies

Write the words *insignia, signature*, and *design* on the chalkboard, and have students locate the root word (sign). Explain that knowing this root can help you determine that all three words must have something to do with the word *sign*. Have a volunteer look up the words in a dictionary and read the primary definitions. Discuss what each word has to do with the root word. Also, discuss how knowing the root word helps to understand meanings from words students might not know.

Consolidate Skills

Through Guided Practice

As they complete the **Practice Your Skills** exercises on roots, prefixes, and suffixes, students will gain more expertise in using roots to determine meaning. Ask them to write another word in the word family for each word in the exercise entitled **Finding Roots.**

PRACTICE YOUR SKILLS Sample Answers

1. D
2. C
3. B
4. E
5. A
6. A
7. B
8. B
9. E
10. C

barren: bare and without life
parched: dried out
camouflaged: disguised
pursue: chase or follow
hazard: danger
misjudged: underestimated
exceed: surpass
falter: stumble
deprived: gone without
yearn: wish

PRACTICE YOUR SKILLS

Using Sentence Context Clues

Write the letter of the answer that is closest in meaning to the underlined word.

1. The doctor was pleased to announce that the patient had made a complete recovery, for no signs of illness were present.
(A) setback (B) operation (C) diagnosis
(D) return to normal (E) reversal

2. The exterior of the house was run-down, but the inside was beautifully kept up.
(A) roof (B) paint (C) outside
(D) porch (E) basement

3. Something is missing in the egg salad; I must have omitted an ingredient.
(A) doubled (B) left out (C) mixed up
(D) chopped (E) added to

4. Deep-sea divers keep warm by wearing suits that water cannot penetrate.
(A) shrink (B) make wet (C) loosen
(D) stretch (E) come into

5. To avoid being scalded while taking a shower, always use your hand to test the water before entering the shower to make sure it is not too hot.
(A) burned (B) wet (C) punished
(D) cold (E) surprised

6. Sheryl was meek and shy, while her sister Tanya was proud and outgoing.
(A) humble (B) tired (C) talkative
(D) honest (E) slow

7. After paying all our expenses, our club has a surplus of $45, which we are going to donate to charity.
(A) unpaid bill (B) extra amount (C) surprise
(D) prize (E) loss

Apply to Communication

Through Independent Writing

Ask students to skim the dictionary to find word families that include one of these Latin roots: *manus*, meaning "hand," *opus*, meaning "a work," or *crescere*, meaning "to grow." Have them write five original sentences that include five members of the word families they chose.

Transfer to Everyday Life

By Using Brochures and Other Written Materials

Collect brochures, fliers, and forms from banks, insurance companies, and other semi-technical organizations. Have students skim the materials and highlight or circle words they do not

8. Animals often mimic humans; most are great copycats.
(A) understand (B) copy (C) oppose
(D) dislike (E) recall

9. I try to retain my sense of humor even in hard times; those are the times a sense of humor really helps!
(A) give up (B) lose (C) relax with
(D) restore (E) keep

10. Sylvester became frustrated and gave up quickly, but Ben was persistent and, after hours of work, finally solved the brainteaser.
(A) lucky (B) clever (C) determined
(D) lazy (E) grateful

Using Paragraph Context Clues

Write each underlined word and its meaning. Use the context of the paragraph to help you. Then check your answers in a dictionary.

The explorers found themselves in a barren land, with no signs of life anywhere. The hot desert sun parched the earth. Water was nowhere to be found. Suddenly they heard the frightening rattle of a snake. The snake was so well camouflaged that the men could not see it against the rocks, stumps, and sand. They fled quickly for safety, hoping that the snake would not pursue them. During the long, hot weeks of exploration, snakes were only one kind of hazard these newcomers would have to face. One day they misjudged the difficulty of the trail and did not exceed one mile. On another day an explorer began to falter. He stumbled as he walked, having been deprived of nourishment for too long. Soon the weary travelers began to yearn for the cool shade and the safety of their homes far away.

HOME WORK

Ask students to locate three unfamiliar words in a textbook or magazine article. Have them apply context clues to determine the meanings of the words. They may check their guesses in a dictionary.

recognize. Ask them to work in pairs to use roots and word families to help them guess the meaning of the unfamiliar words.

Pull It All Together

By Sharing

Have pairs of students share the words they found and their educated guesses at the words' meaning. Ask them to explain how using roots and word families helped them determine the meanings of the words.

Check Understanding

By Finding Examples

Have students locate five words in the same family as the word *vocal.* Ask them to use the words they find in original sentences.

PRACTICE YOUR SKILLS Answers

1. unlawful	11. unteachable
2. cartoonist	12. independence
3. fearless	13. submarine
4. semicircle	14. persistence
5. react	15. unnaturally
6. disappear	16. irresistible
7. preview	17. speechless
8. restless	18. disagreement
9. coworker	19. interstate
10. displeasure	20. bimonthly

HOME WORK

Have students find ten words from a book they are reading for class whose root they can identify.

Prefixes and Suffixes

In addition to using context clues, you can also unlock the meanings of unfamiliar words by breaking words down into their parts.

A word may have as many as three parts: a prefix, a root, and a suffix. For example, you might come across the word *rename*. You probably recognize one part of this word, *name*. This part is called the root. A **root** is the part of the word that carries the basic meaning.

ROOT	mis**read**	un**touch**able
	re**appear**ance	**wish**ful

PRACTICE YOUR SKILLS

Finding Roots

Write each word and underline the root.

1. unlawful	**11.** unteachable
2. cartoonist	**12.** independence
3. fearless	**13.** submarine
4. semicircle	**14.** persistence
5. react	**15.** unnaturally
6. disappear	**16.** irresistible
7. preview	**17.** speechless
8. restless	**18.** disagreement
9. coworker	**19.** interstate
10. displeasure	**20.** bimonthly

Prefixes

The part of the word that comes before the root is called the **prefix**. A prefix can be one syllable or more than one. In the word *rename*, the prefix is *re-*. If you know that *re-* means "again," you can figure out that *rename* means "name again." Following are some common prefixes and their meanings.

PREFIX	MEANING	EXAMPLE
bi-	two	bi + weekly = biweekly
co-	together	co + author = coauthor
de-	remove, from	de + plane = deplane
in-	not	in + secure = insecure
il-	not	il + legal = illegal
mis-	incorrect	mis + place = misplace
pre-	before	pre + historic = prehistoric
re-	again	re + gain = regain

Practice Your Skills

Combining Prefixes and Roots

Write the prefix that has the same meaning as the underlined word. Then write the complete word defined after the equal sign.

EXAMPLE before + view = to see beforehand
ANSWER pre-, preview

1. together + operate = work together
2. remove + fog = to clear away the fog
3. not + logical = lacking in clear thinking
4. before + determine = to figure out beforehand
5. incorrect + pronounce = to use the wrong pronunciation
6. two + annually = twice a year
7. again + organize = to set up a new order
8. not + appropriate = not appropriate
9. remove + forest = to clear away trees
10. not + legible = unreadable

IDENTIFYING COMMON STUMBLING BLOCKS

Problem

- Using the wrong prefix meaning "not"

Solution

- Tell students that certain spelling rules can help them determine whether a word should begin with the prefix *im-, in-, il-,* or *ir-*. If the root begins with *l*, use *il-*, as in *illegal*. If the root begins with *r*, use *ir-*, as in *irregular*. If the root begins with *b, m,* or *p,* use *im-*, as in *imbalance, immobile,* and *impossible*. In most other cases, use *in-*.

Practice Your Skills Sample Answers

Combining Prefixes and Roots

1. co-, cooperate
2. de-, defog
3. il-, illogical
4. pre-, predetermine
5. mis-, mispronounce
6. bi-, biannually
7. re-, reorganize
8. in-, inappropriate
9. de-, deforest
10. il-, illegible

Using Prefixes to Form Words

1. coexist, costar, copilot, coworker
2. mistrial, misprint, misjudge, misname, miscount, mismatch
3. pretrial, preexist, pretest, preprint, preheat, prejudge
4. retrial, retest, reprint, reheat, rename, recount, rematch

HOME WORK

Have students use the dictionary to find two unfamiliar words with each of the prefixes *co-*, *mis-*, *pre-*, and *re-*. Have them write the words and their definitions.

IDENTIFYING COMMON STUMBLING BLOCKS

Problem

- Failing to drop the final *e* before a suffix beginning with a vowel

Solution

- Tell students that roots that end in *e* keep the final *e* before a suffix that begins with a consonant (Examples: *careless*, *hopeful*). However, most roots that end in *e* drop the *e* before a suffix that begins with a vowel (Examples: *unimaginable*, *grievance*). The exception is for some roots that end in *ce* or *ge*, which keep the final *e* to retain the soft sound of the *c* and *g* (Examples: *peaceable*, *courageous*).

Using Prefixes to Form Words

Write as many words as you can by combining each prefix with as many roots as possible. Use a dictionary to be sure you have made real words.

PREFIXES	mis-, pre-, re-		
ROOTS	trial	heat	name
	test	judge	count
	print	match	trust

Suffixes

The part of the word that comes after the root is called a **suffix.** Suffixes, like prefixes, can have one or more syllables. Unlike prefixes, however, many suffixes can change a word from one part of a speech to another.

COMMON SUFFIXES		
Noun Suffixes	**Meaning**	**Examples**
-ance, -ence	state of	correspond + ence
-ment	state of	govern + ment
-ist	one who or that	art + ist
-ness	state of	well + ness
Verb Suffixes	**Meaning**	**Examples**
-en	make, become	bright + en
-ize	make, cause to be	material + ize
Adjective Suffixes	**Meaning**	**Examples**
-able, -ible	capable of	flex + ible
-less	without	pain + less
Adverb Suffix	**Meaning**	**Example**
-ly	in a certain way	careful + ly

Practice Your Skills

Combining Suffixes and Roots

Write the suffix that has the same meaning as the underlined words. Then write the complete word defined after the equal sign.

Example	fear + without = free from fear
Answer	-less, fearless

1. resent + state of = state of displeasure

2. nervous + in a certain way = in an anxious way

3. work + capable of = likely to work

4. gruff + state of = rough quality

5. journal + one who = a newspaper writer

6. cloud + without = clear

7. jubilant + in a certain way = with great joy

8. weak + make, become = to lose strength

9. persist + state of = able to stick with something

10. capital + make = to make big letters

Using Suffixes to Form Words

Write each word with two different suffixes. Then write the part of speech of each one.

Example	light
Possible Answers	lighten-verb, lightly-adverb

1. deep	**6.** rough	**11.** employ	**16.** respectful
2. depend	**7.** plain	**12.** accept	**17.** manage
3. firm	**8.** mean	**13.** visual	**18.** youthful
4. weak	**9.** motor	**14.** light	**19.** irritable
5. final	**10.** rapid	**15.** vocal	**20.** hopeful

Practice Your Skills Sample Answers

Combining Suffixes and Roots

1. -ment, resentment
2. -ly, nervously
3. -able, workable
4. -ness, gruffness
5. -ist, journalist
6. -less, cloudless
7. -ly, jubilantly
8. -en, weaken
9. -ence, persistence
10. -ize, capitalize

Using Suffixes to Form Words

1. deeply-adverb, deepen-verb
2. dependence-noun, dependable-adjective
3. firmly-adverb, firmness-noun
4. weakly-adverb, weakness-noun
5. finally-adverb, finalist-noun
6. roughness-noun, roughly-adverb
7. plainness-noun, plainly-adverb
8. meanness-noun, meanly-adverb
9. motorist-noun, motorize-verb
10. rapidly-adverb, rapidness-noun
11. employable-adjective, employment-noun
12. acceptance-noun, acceptable-adjective
13. visualize-verb, visually-adverb
14. lighten-verb, lightly-adverb
15. vocalize-verb, vocalist-noun

16. respectfully-adverb, respectfulness-noun
17. management-noun, manageable-adjective
18. youthfulness-noun, youthfully-adverb
19. irritableness-noun, irritably-adverb
20. hopefulness-noun, hopefully-adverb

Using Prefixes and Suffixes

1. B
2. C
3. A
4. C
5. A
6. C
7. B
8. B
9. B
10. B

HOME WORK

Have students look up these words with unfamiliar roots and use their understanding of suffixes to use each word in a sentence that demonstrates its meaning.

tangible
deist
cauterize
placable
spryness

Using Prefixes and Suffixes

Write the letter of the phrase that is closest in meaning to the word in capital letters. The prefixes and suffixes you have learned in this chapter will help you figure out the meanings of the capitalized words.

1. INFORMAL: (A) formal beforehand (B) not formal (C) without form

2. REASSURE: (A) not assure (B) without (C) assure again

3. COINCIDENT: (A) happening together (B) not happening (C) happening again

4. INDEFINITE: (A) removal of certainty (B) certain before (C) not certain

5. MISJUDGE: (A) judge incorrectly (B) judge beforehand (C) without judgment

6. PREFERENCE: (A) prefer in a certain way (B) one who prefers (C) state of preferring

7. VOCALIST: (A) singing in a certain way (B) one who sings (C) state of singing

8. VOCALIZE: (A) one who sings (B) to make vocal (C) singing in a certain way

9. PRECISELY: (A) state of being exact (B) in an exact way (C) condition of exactness

10. HEIGHTEN: (A) high in a certain way (B) make higher (C) one who makes higher

Synonyms

When you write or speak, you want to express your meaning exactly. English is so rich in words that you can often choose among words with similar meanings to find just the right one. A word that has nearly the same meaning as another word is called a **synonym**.

Although synonyms mean *about* the same thing, they often convey slightly different shades of meaning. In the following sentences, for example, the word *padded* paints a more precise picture.

The wolf **walked** through the deep forest
The wolf **padded** through the deep forest.

Dictionaries often include synonyms for words. A special dictionary called a **thesaurus** lists only synonyms.

Writing Tip

When you write, search for the word that conveys your meaning exactly. Use a dictionary or thesaurus to help you, but avoid using words that you do not fully understand. You should write in your own voice and style, and with your own words.

PRACTICE YOUR SKILLS

Recognizing Synonyms

Write the letter of the word that is closest in meaning to the word in capital letters. Then check your answers in a dictionary.

1. NOURISH: (A) restore (B) punish (C) feed (D) fill (E) disappear

2. DESOLUTE: (A) quiet (B) barren (C) teeming (D) angry (E) ordinary

3. EVIDENT: (A) sad (B) harmful (C) proud (D) weary (E) obvious

4. ABUNDANT: (A) repetitious (B) plentiful (C) ripe (D) glorious (E) scarce

5. FORETELL: (A) spy (B) reveal (C) predict (D) guess (E) refuse

REACHING ALL STUDENTS

English Language Learners

Exploring synonyms and their shades of meaning is a good way to improve the vocabulary and oral language skills of your limited English proficient students. Write these words on the board and ask students to give you a synonym for each one. Then discuss the subtle differences between the words in each synonym pair.

polite
funny
smart
run
shout
cry

PRACTICE YOUR SKILLS Answers
Recognizing Synonyms

1. C
2. B
3. E
4. B
5. C
6. A
7. C
8. C
9. D
10. B

Choosing the Better Word

1. disguise
2. reduce
3. leftover
4. feed
5. change
6. laugh
7. fragments
8. exceeding

6. OBLIGATION: (A) duty (B) celebration (C) ritual (D) penalty (E) fine

7. FALTER: (A) accuse (B) interrupt (C) stumble (D) release (E) dismiss

8. RARITY: (A) eagerness (B) healthfulness (C) oddity (D) fairness (E) honesty

9. IMPOSE: (A) relax (B) enclose (C) capture (D) force (E) pry

10. BAN: (A) recommend (B) prohibit (C) call (D) follow (E) win

Choosing the Better Word

Write the synonym in parentheses that fits the meaning of each sentence. Use a dictionary for help.

EXAMPLE Everyone in the room admired Stephen's (persistence, stubbornness).

ANSWER persistence

1. What (disguise, camouflage) are you going to wear to Jenna's party?

2. By counting calories, Kitty was able to (lessen, reduce) her weight by 12 pounds.

3. What shall we do with the (leftover, surplus) mashed potatoes?

4. While we are on vacation, our next-door neighbor will (nourish, feed) the fish.

5. Bill went home to (change, modify) his clothes before going out to play softball.

6. Here is a great joke that everyone in the audience is sure to (scoff, laugh) at!

7. When the glass hit the floor, it shattered into hundreds of tiny (fractions, fragments).

8. Michael's older brother got a ticket for (outdoing, exceeding) the speed limit.

Antonyms

An **antonym** is a word that means the opposite of another word. Dictionaries list antonyms for many words.

ANTONYMS		
	abundant:scarce	ban:allow
	negative:positive	drab:colorful
	precise:inexact	exterior:interior
	descendent:ancestor	effect:cause
	temporary:permanent	meek:bold

COMPUTER TIP

Many word-processing programs have a Thesaurus feature. It can be found in the Tools menu, or combined with the Spell Check feature. It will give you a list of synonyms (and sometimes antonyms) for any word with just a click of the mouse.

PRACTICE YOUR SKILLS

Recognizing Antonyms

Write the letter of the answer that is most nearly opposite in meaning to the word in capital letters. Then check your answers in a dictionary.

1. ELABORATE (A) fancy (B) complicated (C) untruthful (D) simple (E) long

2. ANXIETY (A) fearfulness (B) eagerness (C) satisfaction (D) shyness (E) calmness

3. DEPRIVE (A) give (B) cry (C) take (D) withhold (E) punish

4. PACIFY (A) calm (B) relax (C) upset (D) hinder (E) touch

5. MYSTIFY (A) evaporate (B) clarify (C) confuse (D) scarce (E) startle

HOME WORK

Have students use each of these synonyms in a sentence that demonstrates its precise meaning: *dull, colorless, depressed, blunt,* and *unimaginative*.

FYI

How to Use with Windows™ Press Shift-F7.

How to Use with Macintosh™ Press either Shift-F7 or Command-Option-R, or pull down the Tools menu and select Language, then Thesaurus.

To find *Roget's Thesaurus* online, go to http://humanities.uchicago.edu/formsunrest/ROGET.html.

PRACTICE YOUR SKILLS Sample Answers

Recognizing Antonyms

1. D
2. E
3. A
4. C
5. B

Thinking of Words Between Antonyms

1. like, dislike
2. chill, warm
3. chuckle, whimper
4. damp, moist
5. slim, plump
6. delayed, prompt
7. pleased, dismayed
8. unassuming, confident
9. large, small

HOME WORK

Have students copy five descriptive sentences from a book or magazine. Then have them rewrite the sentences, using antonyms wherever possible.

Thinking of Words Between Antonyms

Write at least two words that lie between each pair of antonyms.

EXAMPLE	hot:cold
POSSIBLE ANSWERS	warm, cool
1. love:hate	**6.** tardy:early
2. freeze:burn	**7.** happy:sad
3. laugh:cry	**8.** meek:bold
4. wet:dry	**9.** enormous:tiny

Analogies

Your knowledge of words will be tested several times throughout your years in school. There are many types of vocabulary tests. One type of vocabulary test asks you to identify relationships between pairs of words. These relationships are called **analogies.**

DRAB:DULL : : (A) wealth:poverty (B) joy:sorrow (C) wisdom:intelligence

The first step in answering this test item is to identify the relationship between the two words in capital letters. In this item the words are synonyms, since *drab* and *dull* have similar meanings. The next step is to find the other pair of words that have the same relationship. The first pair of words, *wealth* and *poverty*, have opposite meanings, so they are antonyms. The next pair of words, *joy* and *sorrow*, are also opposites, or antonyms. The final pair, *wisdom* and *intelligence*, is the correct answer. Like *drab* and *dull, wisdom* and *intelligence* are synonyms.

The capitalized words may also be words with opposite meanings, as in the following test item. As you study it, see if you can choose the other pair of antonyms.

LATTER:FORMER : : (A) old:ancient (B) close:open (C) handsome:attractive

The pairs in (A) and (C) are both synonyms, so they are not correct. The correct answer is (B) since *close* and *open*, like *latter* and *former*, are antonyms.

Practice Your Skills

Recognizing Analogies

Write *synonyms* or *antonyms* to tell how the words in capital letters are related. Then write *A, B,* or *C* to tell which pair of words is related in the same way.

EXAMPLE WHISPER:SHOUT : : (A) foretell:predict (B) lessen:increase (C) wish:desire

ANSWER antonyms—B

1. SHIMMER:SHINE : : (A) smile:grin (B) cry:laugh (C) walk:ride

2. CUNNING:SLYNESS : : (A) beauty:ugliness (B) bravery:courage (C) emptiness:fullness

3. FLEXIBLE:RIGID : : (A) black:white (B) similar:alike (C) reliable:trustworthy

4. CONFIDENTIAL:SECRET : : (A) nervous:calm (B) rainy:dry (C) lifeless:dead

5. MAXIMUM:MINIMUM : : (A) far:distant (B) ill:sick (C) youthful:mature

6. INQUIRY:QUESTION : : (A) cup: saucer (B) cup:mug (C) cup:milk

7. JUBILANT:SAD : : (A) gruff:rough (B) drab:dull (C) tall:short

8. CONSUMER:SELLER : : (A) student:teacher (B) boy:male (C) animal:pet

9. ABOLISH:RESTORE : : (A) leave:depart (B) come:arrive (C) go:come

10. PHASE:STAGE : : (A) television:radio (B) photograph:picture (C) record:phonograph

Practice Your Skills Sample Answers

1. synonyms–A
2. synonyms–B
3. antonyms–A
4. synonyms–C
5. antonyms–C
6. synonyms–B
7. antonyms–C
8. antonyms–A
9. antonyms–C
10. synonyms–B

HOME WORK

Have students create an analogy test of five questions featuring synonyms and antonyms. In class, students may exchange papers and take each other's tests.

USING STUDENTS' STRENGTHS

Multiple Intelligences: Logical

In most tests of analogies, all of the answer choices are word pairs that have a logical relationship, but only one expresses a relationship that parallels the one expressed by the capitalized pair. Students who do well with logic might like to help create analogies with these various relationships, which are the most common types found on standardized tests.

X is a kind of Y
Example: TURTLE:REPTILE
X is a part of Y
Example: TIRE:AUTOMOBILE
X is characteristic of Y
Example: COURAGE:HERO
Lack of X is characteristic of Y
Example: COURAGE:COWARD
X is a large Y
Example: TORRENT:FLOW
X is the tool of Y
Example: AX:WOODSMAN
X is a place where Y is found
Example: AVIARY:BIRD
X is evidence of Y
Example: BLUSH:EMBARRASSMENT

EXPANDING THE LESSON

Using Technology

You will find additional **instructional** and **practice** materials for this chapter at http://www.bkenglish.com.

In this chapter, you have learned ways to expand your vocabulary. You have also learned strategies for identifying unfamiliar words. How might these strategies help you in future writing? Have you been in a situation where these strategies might have been useful? Do you feel your vocabulary skills have improved? In the Learning Log section of your **journal**, make a list of the vocabulary skills you feel you would like to improve upon.

Your Writer's Journal

Build your vocabulary by writing in your journal any unfamiliar words that you read or hear. Look up new words in a dictionary. Then include a brief definition of each word and an example of its appropriate context or use. Begin by listing any of the words from the following list that are unfamiliar to you. Then, whenever you are revising your work, look over your list and include in your writing as many new words as possible. Use your word list as a resource for choosing words that are vivid, appropriate, and precise.

Advertising Vocabulary

Advertising messages have their own vocabulary in addition to words—the vocabulary of sounds and images. The editing, camera angles, music, and lighting are all vital in influencing how we feel about the product being advertised. Advertisers spend a lot of time and money researching the elements to which different markets—groups of likely buyers—will respond. For example, if advertisers learn that professional women in their late twenties to mid-thirties buy a lot of aspirin, they will target their ads to appeal to those women.

The ad may feature a young lawyer working late, talking about how glad she is that her headache is finally gone. It might show her earlier in the day in a harsh office light looking harried with wild office sounds pounding away at her and then later, after she has taken the aspirin, in a soft, relaxing light, looking competent and assured.

Media Activity

Working in groups of three, brainstorm a list of video vocabulary. This list may include lighting, editing, age, gender and ethnic background of actors, setting, music and so on. Then, watch (or tape, if possible) the commercials on Saturday morning cartoons. What do you notice about the ads that you see? Are there any ads that seem geared to boys? Girls? Do you notice anything about where the action of the different ads take place? What about the lighting and sound? What are the predominant colors in the different ads? What do you think the advertisers are saying in these ads? Write a paragraph explaining your findings and discuss it with your class.

IN THE MEDIA

Using *In the Media*

Objective

- **To analyze and critique advertising rhetoric and vocabulary**

Group Project

- Divide the class into small groups. Each group should select an advertisement from television or from a magazine to critique and research. Each student within the group should research the topic or product in the ad using a different reference material. Students should take notes on the vocabulary and main ideas presented in the ads. Students should verify the information using reference material. Then students should compare information and discuss the accuracy of the ad's claims. As a class, discuss how vocabulary contributes to or takes away from an ad's claims about a product.

FYI

Websites to Visit Two Websites that include links to many online reference books, including both general knowledge encyclopedias and specialized ones, are http://www.ipl.org and http://www.refdesk.com/index.html.

Teaching Suggestions

Essential Knowledge and Skills

- Spelling frequently misspelled words correctly
- Using resources to find correct spellings
- Understanding the influences of other languages and cultures on the spelling of English words
- Selecting and using reference materials and resources as needed for writing, revising, and editing final drafts
- Presenting information in various forms using available technology
- Describing how illustrators' choice of style, elements, and media help to represent or extend the text's meaning
- Assessing how language, medium, and presentation contribute to the message

CHAPTER 15

Dictionary

Words are the most important part of writing. In order to uphold the credibility of your writing, you must use and spell words correctly. A perfectly good piece of writing can be ruined by misspellings or improperly used words. A reader will quickly become distracted by these kinds of mistakes. One aid in avoiding this writing pitfall is a dictionary. Many writers work with a dictionary close at hand. They use it most often to check spellings and meanings of words. In addition a dictionary can tell you how to pronounce a word, where to divide it into syllables, and how the word developed throughout history.

Dictionaries come in varied forms, but all dictionaries are organized in the same general manner. This chapter will review the information available in a dictionary and show how to use a dictionary efficiently. Dictionaries can be valuable research and reference writing tools if you know how to use them properly.

Reading with a Writer's Eye

Have you ever thought about how many words you know? In the following selection, the author attempts to make sense out of the different studies that have been done to find out how many words people know. As you read, think about your own writing. Do you actually use all the words you know?

BLOCK SCHEDULING

- If your schedule requires that you cover the chapter in a **shorter time,** begin at Developing Your Dictionary Skills (page C474), omitting the selection "Order out of Chaos" and its associated features.
- If you want to take advantage of **longer class time,** use the entire chapter including the selection and Thinking as a Writer.

FROM

The Mother Tongue: English & How It Got That Way

by Bill Bryson

How big is the English language? That's not an easy question. Samuel Johnson's dictionary contained 43,000 words. The unabridged *Random House* of 1987 has 315,000. Webster's *Third New International* of 1961 contains 450,000. And the revised *Oxford English Dictionary* of 1989 has 615,000 entries. But in fact this only begins to hint at the total.

For one thing, meanings in English are much more various than a bald count of entry words would indicate. The mouse that scurries across your kitchen floor and the mouse that activates your personal computer clearly are two quite separate entities. Shouldn't they then be counted as two words? And then what about related forms like *mousy, mouselike,* and *mice?* Shouldn't they also count as separate words? Surely there is a large difference between something that is a mouse and something that is merely mousy.

And then of course there are all the names of flora and fauna, medical conditions, chemical substances,[1] laws of

[1] One of which, incidentally, is said to be the longest word in the English language. It begins *methianylglutaminyl* and finishes 1,913 letters later as *alynalalanylthreonilarginylserase.* I don't know what it is used for, though I daresay it would take some rubbing to get it out of the carpet.

FOR INCREASING STUDENT ACHIEVEMENT

GUIDED READING

Text Analysis

- This **expository composition** gives information in an entertaining way.
- The introduction begins with a **question,** and **varied sentence types** involve the reader in the composition by encouraging **active reading.**
- The writer includes a variety of interesting **examples** from scientific and linguistic studies to support his **main idea** that we can never really know the size of a person's vocabulary.

SELECTION AMENDMENT
Description of change: excerpted
Rationale: to focus on the concept of words and meanings as presented in this chapter

GUIDED READING

Strategy: Summarizing

Ask students to pause after each paragraph to summarize the main idea on paper or in their heads. Remind them that summarizing or retelling is a good way to make sure they understand what the composition is about. Summarizing paragraph by paragraph ensures that they grasp the main points the author is trying to make.

physics, and all the other scientific and technical terms that don't make it into ordinary dictionaries. Of insects alone, there are 1.4 million named species. Total all these together and you have—well, no one knows. But certainly no less than three million.

So how many of these words do we know? Again, there is no simple answer. Many scholars have taken the trouble (or more probably compelled their graduate students to take the trouble) of counting the number of words used by various authors, on the assumption, one supposes, that that tells us something about human vocabulary. Mostly what it tells us is that academics aren't very good at counting. Shakespeare, according to Pei and McCrum, had a vocabulary of 30,000 words, though Pei acknowledges seeing estimates putting the figure as low as 16,000. Lincoln Barnett puts it at 20,000 to 25,000. But most other authorities—Shipley, Baugh and Cable, Howard—put the number at a reassuringly precise 17,677. The King James Bible, according to Laird, contains 8,000 words but Shipley puts the number at 7,000, while Barnett confidently zeroes in on a figure of 10,442. Who knows who's right?

One glaring problem with even the most scrupulous[2] tabulation is that the total number of words used by an author doesn't begin to tell us the true size of his vocabulary. I know the meanings of *frangible, spiffing,* and *cutesy-poo,* but have never had occasion to write them before now. A man of Shakespeare's linguistic versatility must have possessed thousands of words that he never used because he didn't like or require them. Not once in his plays can you find the words *Bible, Trinity,* or *Holy Ghost,* and yet that is not to suggest that he was not familiar with them.

---

[2] **scrupulous:** With extreme care for detail; painstaking.

Estimates of the size of the average person's vocabulary are even more contentious.[3] Max Müller, a leading German philologist[4] at the turn of the century, thought the average farm laborer had an everyday vocabulary of no more than 300 words. Pei cites an English study of fruit pickers, which put the number at no more than 500, though he himself thought that the figure was probably closer to 30,000. Stuart Berg Flexner, the noted American lexicographer,[5] suggests that the average well-read person has a vocabulary of about 20,000 words and probably uses about 1,500 to 2,000 in a normal week's conversation. McCrum puts an educated person's vocabulary at about 15,000.

There are endless difficulties attached to adjudging how many words a person knows. Consider just one. If I ask you what *incongruent* means and you say, "It means not congruent," you are correct. That is the first definition given in most dictionaries, but that isn't to say that you have the faintest idea what the word means. Every page of the dictionary contains words we may not have encountered before—*inflationist, forbiddance, moosewood, pulsative*—and yet whose meanings we could very probably guess.

At the same time there are many words that we use every day and clearly know and yet might have difficulty proving. How would you define *the* or *what* or *am* or *very?* Imagine trying to explain to a Martian in a concise way just what *is* is. And then what about all those words with a variety of meanings? Take *step. The American Heritage Dictionary* lists a dozen common meanings for the word, ranging from the act of putting one foot in front of the

---

[3] **contentious:** Arguable, quarrelsome.

[4] **philologist:** A person who studies speech and language, especially as they relate to literature.

[5] **lexicographer:** A person who compiles a dictionary.

YOUR IDEAS

For Guided Reading

READER RESPONSE

You may want to use the following questions to elicit students' personal responses to the selection.

1. Do you agree that the total number of words a person uses doesn't tell the true size of his or her vocabulary? Can you cite an example from your own life?
2. Which of the studies cited by the author do you find the most interesting? the silliest? Why?
3. Try the author's test: List all the meanings you can think of for *step.* Then check your list against a dictionary. Is he right when he says, "It is hard to remember what we remember"?

other to the name for part of a staircase. We all know all these meanings, yet if I gave you a pencil and a blank sheet of paper could you list them? Almost certainly not. The simple fact is that it is hard to remember what we remember, so to speak. Put another way, our memory is a highly fickle thing. Dr. Alan Baddeley, a British authority on memory, cites a study in which people were asked to name the capital cities of several countries. Most had trouble with the capitals of countries like Uruguay and Bulgaria, but when they were told the initial letter of the capital city, they often suddenly remembered and their success rate soared. In another study people were shown long lists of random words and then asked to write down as many of them as they could remember. A few hours later, without being shown the list again, they were asked to write down as many of the words as they could remember then. Almost always the number of words would be nearly identical, but the actual words recalled from one test to another would vary by 50 percent or more. In other words, there is vastly more verbal information locked away in our craniums than we can get out at any one time. So the problem of trying to assess accurately just how much verbal material we possess in total is fraught with difficulties.

ADDITIONAL RESOURCES

Thinking as a Writer

Analyzing Word Choice

In "Order Out of Chaos," the author mentions that people usually know many more words than they actually use. As a writer you are always choosing words from your own vocabulary to use in your writing.

- How do you decide which words you will use in your writing?
- Have you ever used a dictionary to help you choose a word? If so, how was the dictionary helpful?
- The author also mentions that a dictionary entry for one word might list a number of different meanings. How might it be helpful to you as a writer to know the various meanings of a word?

Evaluating a Dictionary Illustration

Viewing Following is a dictionary entry for the word *fluke*.

- How does the illustration clarify the written definition?
- Would one be useful without the other? Why or why not?

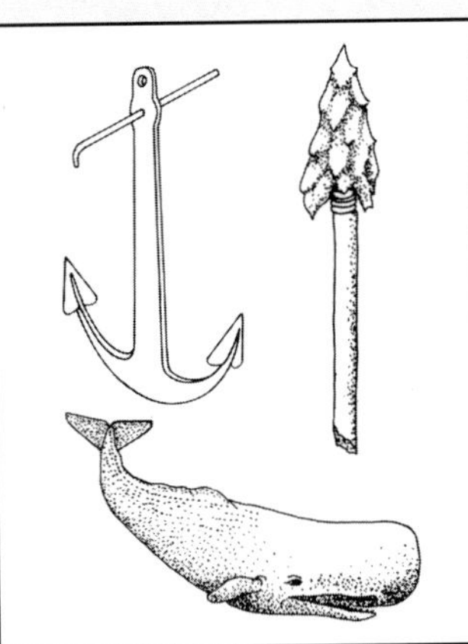

fluke[2] (flo͞ok) *n.* **1.** The triangular blade at the end of either arm of an anchor, designed to dig into the ocean bottom to hold the anchor in place. **2.** The barbed head of a harpoon, a lance, or an arrow. **3.** Either of the two flattened fins of a whale's tail. [First written down in 1561 in Modern English, possibly from *fluke,* flatfish.]

Using *Thinking as a Writer*

You may choose to have students respond to the questions either orally or in writing.

FOR DEVELOPING SKILLS

LESSON 1 *(pages C474–C483)*

OBJECTIVES

- **To understand the structure of a dictionary in order to use it correctly**
- **To identify and use the different parts of the entry word**

Create Interest

Ask students to imagine that they heard this unfamiliar word on a television show: *quagmire.* The word interests them, but they don't know its meaning. Ask students to think about how many times a day they hear a word they don't know the meaning of. Do they have strategies for learning new word meanings or do they just figure it out?

Guide Instruction

By Independent Learning

Have students write down every word they come across in a day that is unfamiliar to them. Each day of studying this chapter, have students choose one

REACHING ALL STUDENTS

Struggling Learners

Review these rules for alphabetizing two words:

- Look at the first letter of the words. Which letter comes first in the alphabet? Put that word first.
- If the first letters are the same, look at the second letters. Which letter comes first in the alphabet? Put that word first.
- If the first two letters are the same, look at the third letters. If those are the same, look at the fourth letters, and so on.

Advanced Learners

Challenge students to name a word that might appear on the same page after *neat* in a dictionary. (Possibilities include *Nebraska, nebula, necessary.*)

Developing Your Dictionary Skills

Whenever you need to confirm the spelling, definition, pronunciation, or part of speech of a word, you will use a dictionary. You can also use the dictionary to research the origin or history of a word. Some dictionaries also provide **synonyms** (similar words) and **antonyms** (opposite words).

A **dictionary** is a reference source that gives the pronunciations, definitions, parts of speech, and other information about the words of a particular language.

Dictionary Structure

Most dictionaries are organized similarly. Dictionaries are structured so that you will be able to quickly and easily find the information you are looking for. The words in a dictionary are listed in alphabetical order.

As you look over the following dictionary entries, notice how the information is organized. Especially notice that the entries are listed in alphabetical order.

MODEL: Dictionary Entries

Ne The symbol for the element **neon.**

abbreviation **NE** *abbr.* An abbreviation of: **1.** Northeast. **2.** Nebraska. **3.** New England.

Ne•a[illegible]de[illegible]thal (nē[illegible]n′[illegible]r th[illegible]) [illegible] N[illegible]erthal

capitalization

Near East (nîr). A region of southwest Asia generally thought to include Turkey, Lebanon, Israel, Iraq, Jordan, Saudi Arabia, the other countries of the Arabian Peninsula, and sometimes Egypt and Sudan.

of those words to research in the dictionary, learning its spelling, pronunciation, usage, and meaning. Each new class day, have students share their new word with the class by reading a sentence with the word in it. Let the rest of the class figure out the meaning. Have the class guess the word that would follow it in the dictionary.

Consolidate Skills

Through Guided Practice

Give students these unfamiliar words orally, and have them jot down the phonetic spelling: *phlegmatic, cerise,* and *gentian.* Then have them use their dictionary's pronunciation guide or table of English spellings to find the entry word and record the definitions.

Apply to Communication

Through Independent Writing

Have students use each of the words they located in the dictionary in an original sentence that illustrates its meaning.

spelling — definitions — pronunciation — related forms — part of speech — word origin — synonyms — antonyms

near•ly (nîr′lē) *adv.* 1. Almost but not quite: *That coat nearly fits.* 2. Closely or intimately: *The two girls are nearly related.*

near•sight•ed (nîr′sī′tĭd) *adj.* Unable to see distant objects clearly; myopic. —**near′sight′ed•ly** *adv.* —**near′sight′ed•ness** *n.*

neat (nēt) *adj.* **neat•er, neat•est.** 1. Orderly and clean; tidy: *a neat room; neat handwriting.* 2. Orderly, as in appearance; not careless or messy: *a neat person.* 3. Performed with precision and skill: *a neat, graceful takeoff.* 4. *Slang.* Wonderful; fine: *a neat party.* [First written down in 1542 in Modern English, from Latin *nitidus,* elegant, gleaming.] —**neat′ly** *adv.* —**neat′ness** *n.*

Synonyms: neat, tidy, trim, shipshape. These adjectives mean marked by good order and cleanliness. **Neat** means pleasingly clean and orderly: *Marcia pulled back her hair into a neat ponytail.* **Tidy** suggests precise arrangement and order: *Even their closets and drawers were kept tidy.* **Trim** stresses a smart appearance because of neatness, tidiness, and pleasing proportions: *The trim little boat was all ready to set sail.* **Shipshape** means both neat and tidy: *We'll have the kitchen shipshape in no time.* **Antonyms: messy, sloppy.**

Word Location

All dictionaries list words in alphabetical order so you can find the information you need quickly. Guide words tell you at a glance which words are on each page.

Guide Words

Guide words are the words printed in **boldface** type at the top of each dictionary page. They show you the first and last words defined on that page. The guide words *pinch/pioneer,* for example, show you that *pine* and *pinto bean* are listed on that page. The words *pistachio* and *pit,* however, would appear on a later page.

REACHING ALL STUDENTS

Advanced Learners

Challenge students to name other words that might appear on a page with the guide words *pinch/pioneer.* (Possibilities include *pink, pinnacle, pint, pinwheel.*)

Transfer to Everyday Life

By Using Listening Skills

As students listen to the radio or television, have them take notes on words they don't know by writing down the phonetic spellings. Once the program is over, they should attempt to find the unfamiliar words in the dictionary and record the definitions.

Pull It All Together

By Summarizing

Have students write a step-by-step explanation of how they located the entry for one word they didn't know how to spell and the meaning they acquired from looking it up in the dictionary.

Check Understanding

By Answering Questions Independently

Students should no longer ask you how to spell a word or what a word means. Students' spelling should improve by using the dictionary. They should be able to answer their own questions regarding dictionary use.

PRACTICE YOUR SKILLS Answers need not be in alphabetical order.

glider/gnaw	**gnome/golf**
gluey	gold
globetrot	golden eagle
gnat	gobble
glory	go-cart
glimpse	goatskin
glutton	goalie
gnarl	goggles
glowworm	goblet
glitter	goldfish
glossary	goal post

HOME WORK

Have students use a dictionary at home and turn to a page at random. Ask them to list the guide words, write down the page number, close the book, and write five words that might be found on that page. They can check their answers by looking back at the page they selected.

PRACTICE YOUR SKILLS

Using Guide Words

Make two columns on a piece of paper. Write the guide words *glider/gnaw* at the top of the first column and *gnome/golf* at the top of the second column. Then write each word in the proper column.

gold	gluey	globetrot	golden eagle
gobble	gnat	go-cart	glory
glimpse	goatskin	glutton	gnarl
goalie	glowworm	glitter	goggles
glossary	goblet	goldfish	goal post

Alphabetical Order

A dictionary includes many different kinds of entries. Notice the strict letter-by-letter alphabetical order.

SINGLE WORD	valentine
TWO-WORD COMPOUND	vampire bat
HYPHENATED COMPOUND	Venus's-flytrap
PREFIX	vice-
PHRASE	vice versa
ABBREVIATION	V.I.P.

A compound word is alphabetized as if there were no space or hyphen between each part of the word. An abbreviation is alphabetized letter by letter, not by the word it stands for.

PRACTICE YOUR SKILLS

Alphabetizing Words

Following are the first lines of famous poems. Arrange the underlined words in each line in alphabetical order.

EXAMPLE: When to the sessions of sweet silent thought (Shakespeare)

ANSWER: sessions, silent, sweet

Famous Firsts

1. A slumber did my spirit seal (Wordsworth)
2. Booth led boldly with his big bass drum (Lindsay)
3. Full fathom five thy father lies (Shakespeare)
4. I sing of brooks, of blossoms, birds, and bowers (Herrick)
5. O Western wind when wilt thou blow (Anonymous)
6. The Soul selects her own society (Dickinson)
7. As I was walking all alone (Anonymous)
8. She told the story and the whole world wept (Dunbar)
9. He clasps the crag with crooked hands (Tennyson)
10. Do not go gentle into that good night (Thomas)

Alphabetizing Different Kinds of Entries

Make three columns on a piece of paper. Then write the words in each column in alphabetical order.

1.	2.	3.
Labor Day	jackpot	nickname
ladyfinger	janitor	New Jersey
Lab.	Japanese	numero uno
labor-saving	jack-o'-lantern	no-show
labor	javelin	N.Y.C.
lady-in-waiting	January	non-
ladybug	jack rabbit	news conference
La.	Jack Frost	Nobel Prize
lace making	Jan.	N.J.
laboratory	jackknife	nitty-gritty

REACHING ALL STUDENTS

Struggling Learners

To make sure they understand the terms, help students come up with other examples of two-word compounds, hyphenated compounds, and prefixes.

PRACTICE YOUR SKILLS Answers

1. seal, slumber, spirit
2. bass, big, boldly, Booth
3. father, fathom, five, Full
4. birds, blossoms, bowers, brooks
5. Western, wilt, wind
6. selects, society, Soul
7. all, alone, As
8. She, story, wept, whole, world
9. clasps, crag, crooked
10. gentle, go, good

PRACTICE YOUR SKILLS Answers

1.	2.
La.	Jack Frost
Lab.	jackknife
labor	jack-o'-lantern
laboratory	jackpot
Labor Day	jack rabbit
labor-saving	Jan.
lace making	janitor
ladybug	January
ladyfinger	Japanese
lady-in-waiting	javelin

3. New Jersey
   news conference
   nickname
   nitty-gritty
   N. J.
   Nobel Prize
   non-
   no-show
   numero uno
   N.Y.C.

HOME WORK

Ask students to find a poem they like in an anthology and to alphabetize all the words in the first line of the poem.

GETTING STUDENTS INVOLVED

Reciprocal Teaching

As students learn about the different parts of an entry, have them work in pairs to instruct each other. Ask each student to pick an unfamiliar word from the dictionary and teach his or her partner the pronunciation of the word, its definition(s), and its origin. To check for understanding, partners should use the word in an oral sentence. After both students have had a turn as teacher and learner, students may share their new vocabulary with the class.

Information in an Entry

The dictionary presents a wealth of information about each word. All of the information for each word is called the **entry**. The four most important parts of the entry are the entry word, pronunciation, definitions, and word origin. The following entry for the word *disk* shows these four main parts.

pronunciation

entry word **disk** also **disc** (dĭsk) *n.* **1.** A thin, flat, circular object, such as a plate or coin. **2.** Something that resembles such an object: *the moon's disk reflected in the pond.* **3.** Often **disc. a.** A phonograph record. **b.** A round flat plate coated with a magnetic substance on which computer data is stored. **c.** An optical disk, especially a compact disk. [First written down in 1664 in Modern English, from Greek *diskos,* quoit, from *dikein,* to throw.]

definitions

word origins

The Entry Word

A quick glance at the entry word will give you three pieces of useful information. It shows you (1) how to spell a word, (2) whether a word should be capitalized, and (3) where a word should be divided into syllables.

Spelling The entry word shows how to spell a word correctly. Some words have more than one correct spelling. The most common spelling is called the **preferred spelling**. The second spelling is called the **variant spelling**. Always use the preferred spelling in your writing.

preferred spelling variant spelling

the·a·ter or **the·a·tre**

A dictionary also shows you how to spell the plurals of nouns, the principal parts of verbs, and the comparative and superlative degrees of adjectives and adverbs. These are given only if the form or spelling is irregular.

pronunciation

principal parts — **com · mute** (kə myōōt′) *v.* **com · mut · ed, com · mut · ing, com · mutes.**
mouse (mous) *n.*, pl. **mice.**
rust · y (rŭs′ tē) *adj.* **rust · i · er, rust · i · est.**
adjective forms

Words formed by adding a prefix or a suffix to the entry word are often shown at the end of the entry. These related forms are called **derived words.**

nois•y (noi′zē) *adj.* **nois•i•er, nois•i•est. 1.** Making a lot of noise: *a noisy engine.* **2.** Full of, characterized by, or accompanied by noise: *noisy streets.*
derived words —**nois′i•ly** *adv.* —**nois′i•ness** *n.*

Practice Your Skills

Correcting Spelling Errors

The following words are misspelled. Using a dictionary, write the correct spelling for each of the following words.

1. oxes
2. sopranoes
3. qualifyed
4. friendlyest
5. acquited
6. hoofs
7. procesing
8. dazzleing
9. harmonise
10. skiming
11. thiner
12. whinnyed
13. choosen
14. growed
15. shelfs
16. prefered
17. blury
18. happyest
19. sillyness
20. patrioticly

INTEGRATING TECHNOLOGY

Computer

Remind students that spell-check software is designed to pick up spelling errors during word processing, but (1) it is only as good as the dictionary that accompanies it, and (2) it cannot differentiate between homophones. In other words, the spell-check may count a word as misspelled simply because it is an unfamiliar word, and it may count a word as spelled correctly even though the writer has used *there* instead of *their* or *find* instead of *fined.* When in doubt, it is always worth checking spelling with a dictionary.

USING STUDENTS' STRENGTHS

Multiple Intelligences: Linguistic

To make sure the class is up to speed, have students define, explain, and give examples of principal parts of verbs and comparative and superlative degrees of adjectives and adverbs.

Practice Your Skills Answers

1. oxen
2. sopranos
3. qualified
4. friendliest
5. acquitted
6. hooves
7. processing
8. dazzling
9. harmonize
10. skimming
11. thinner
12. whinnied
13. chosen
14. grown
15. shelves
16. preferred
17. blurry
18. happiest
19. silliness
20. patriotically

HOME WORK

Send the students on a dictionary scavenger hunt to find the spelling of these items.

1. the past tense of *bury* (buried)
2. the plural of *moose* (moose)
3. the comparative form of *slim* (slimmer)
4. the past tense of *trot* (trotted)
5. a derived form of *milky* (milkiness)

REACHING ALL STUDENTS

Struggling Learners

Review rules of capitalization with students. Have them give examples of proper adjectives and of proper nouns that name people, places, and things.

Capitalization The entry word will be printed with a capital letter. If a word is not always capitalized, the word will be shown with a capital letter near the appropriate definition.

web (wĕb) *n.* **1.** A woven fabric, especially one on or just removed from a loom. **2.** A latticed or woven structure: *A web of palm branches formed the roof of the hut.* **3.** A structure of fine silky strands woven by spiders or by certain insect larvae. **4.** Something that traps or snares by or as if by entangling: *a web of deceit.* **5.** A fold of skin or thin tissue connecting the toes of certain water birds or other animals. **6.** **Web.** World Wide Web. —*tr.v.* **webbed, web•bing, webs.** To provide with a web or webs. [First written down about 725 in Old English and spelled *webb.*]

capital letter

Syllables Sometimes when you are writing a composition, you need to divide a word at the end of a line. The dictionary shows you where each syllable ends.

as·tro·naut **I·tal·ian** **pri·va·cy**

PRACTICE YOUR SKILLS

Dividing Words into Syllables

Find each word in a dictionary and write it with a dot between syllables.

EXAMPLE	patriotic
ANSWER	pa·tri·ot·ic
1. dishonor	**6.** regrettable
2. loyalty	**7.** regularly

3. twentieth	**8.** sandpiper
4. hypnotic	**9.** nationally
5. audacity	**10.** intriguing

Pronunciation A phonetic spelling is shown in parentheses after each entry word. The phonetic spelling shows how to pronounce the word correctly.

knee (nē) **ra · di · o** (rā′dēō)

A complete pronunciation key at the beginning of the dictionary explains all the symbols used in the phonetic spellings. In addition, most dictionaries provide a shortened form of the key on every other page for easy reference.

PARTIAL PRONUNCIATION KEY

Symbols	Examples	Symbols	Examples
ă	pat	o͞o	boot
ā	pay	*th*	this
âr	care	ŭ	cut
ä	father	ûr	urge, term, firm, word, heard
ĕ	pet	zh	vision, pleasure, garage
ē	bee	ə	about, item, edible, gallop, circus
hw	whoop	ər	butter
ĭ	pit		
ī	pie, by		
îr	dear, deer, pier		
ŏ	pot		
ō	toe		
ô	caught, paw, for		
o͝o	took		

Foreign Symbols

œ	*French*	feu
ü	*French*	tu
KH	*Scottish*	loch
N	*French*	bon

PRACTICE YOUR SKILLS Answers

1. dis•hon•or
2. loy•al•ty
3. twen•ti•eth
4. hyp•not•ic
5. au•dac•i•ty
6. re•gret•ta•ble
7. reg•u•lar•ly
8. sand•pi•per
9. na•tion•al•ly
10. in•trigu•ing

HOME WORK

Ask students to skim a textbook to find five multisyllabic words. Have them write the words, using dots to divide them into syllables. Then have them check their work in a dictionary.

DEVELOPING WORKPLACE COMPETENCIES

Basic Skills: Speaking

Tell students that many politicians have been ridiculed for mispronouncing words in speeches. Words such as *nuclear* and *preferable* are often stumbling blocks for otherwise well-educated people. Before you speak in public, it is wise to make sure that you know how to pronounce every word in your speech, whether it's an oral report for eighth-grade history, an advertising presentation for a multimillion-dollar client, or the State of the Union Address.

Suggest that students practice their pronunciation of these often-mispronounced words, using a dictionary to check their speaking skills.

accept	irreparable
athlete	library
candidate	mischievous
comparable	municipal
docile	perform
everybody	probably
further	pronunciation
futile	recognize
genuine	strength
hundred	theater
infamous	vehicle

Diacritical Marks In the pronunciation key on the preceding page, there are marks over some of the vowels. They are called diacritical marks. Diacritical marks are used to show the different sounds a vowel can make. For example, the different sounds of the vowel *a* are shown in the following ways.

DIACRITICAL MARKS — **ă** as in hat **ā** as in age **ä** as in far

The Schwa Sometimes vowels are pronounced like the sound *uh*. Dictionaries use the symbol **ə** to represent this sound. This symbol is called a schwa.

a·bove (ə **bŭv′**) **lem·on** (**lĕm′** ən) **to·ken** (**tō′** kən)

PRACTICE YOUR SKILLS

Marking Pronunciation

Find each word in the dictionary and write the pronunciation. Include all of the diacritical marks.

EXAMPLE ahead

ANSWER (ə **hĕd′**)

1. take	**6.** lit
2. find	**7.** approach
3. circus	**8.** tapestry
4. please	**9.** lemon
5. evil	**10.** petty

Accent Marks An accent mark (′) in a phonetic spelling tells you which syllable should be pronounced with the most stress.

LESSON 2 *(pages C483–C491)*

OBJECTIVES

- **To identify different uses of a word**
- **To use a dictionary to improve writing and vocabulary**

Create Interest

Write these sentences on the chalkboard: *The bubble gum stuck to my gum. I placed my palm on the trunk of the palm. The dogs got into a scrap over a tiny scrap of liver.* Ask students to locate and define the words that are spelled the same in each sentence *(gum, trunk, scrap).* Point out that although these words are spelled exactly the same way, they have nothing in common when it comes to their meanings. Keep the sentences on the chalkboard for students to use as models for the **Apply to Communication** exercise.

fa · mous (fā′məs) **in · jus · tice** (ĭn **jŭs′**tĭs)

Some words have two accent marks. The darker one, called the **primary accent,** receives the most stress. The lighter one, called the **secondary accent,** receives slightly less stress.

PRIMARY ACCENT **in · ex · pen · sive** (ĭn′ĭk **spĕn′**sĭv)

SECONDARY ACCENT

PRACTICE YOUR SKILLS

Placing Accent Marks

Using the dictionary, write the pronunciation of each word. Put dots between syllables and mark both primary and secondary accent marks.

1. influential
2. googol
3. democratic
4. exploration
5. conservatory
6. reservation
7. marshmallow
8. pliability
9. subplot
10. impossibility

Definitions Many words have more than one definition. Look at the entry for the word *program*. Notice that eight definitions are given. When looking for the meaning of a word, be sure to read all of the definitions and examples carefully. Then decide which meaning makes sense in your sentence.

PRACTICE YOUR SKILLS Sample Answers

Diacritical marks may vary depending on the dictionary used.

1. tāk
2. fīnd
3. sûr′k′ əs
4. plēz
5. e′vəl
6. lĭ̌t
7. ə-prōch′
8. tăp′ĭ-strē
9. lĕm′ən
10. pĕt′ē

HOME WORK

Ask students to use the diacritical marks in their dictionaries to write the pronunciation of their own names—first, middle, and last.

USING STUDENTS' STRENGTHS

Multiple Intelligences: Musical

Ask students to use their dictionaries to make lists of ten words that follow the same accent pattern. Then have them arrange their words in a way that seems pleasing and clap the rhythm while reading the words. Students may work in pairs, with each finding words with a different pattern and then the pair collaborating on a rhythmic list.

Guide Instruction

By Connecting Ideas

Explain that many words have multiple meanings. These meanings are generally listed as numbered definitions in a single entry. Occasionally, two or three words have the same spelling but different meanings and different origins. These words are called homographs. They are usually listed as different entries in the dictionary, with a superscript number following the entry word. A few homographs have different pronunciations, as is true of *lead/lead.*

Consolidate Skills

Through Guided Practice

As they complete the **Practice Your Skills** exercise on identifying different uses of a word, make sure that students understand the difference between a word with multiple meanings and homographs. Have them compare the entry for cast to the two entries for case, noting especially the different word origins for each homograph.

Practice Your Skills Answers

1. in′flu•en′tial
2. goo′•gol′
3. dem′•o•crat′•ic
4. ex′•plo•ra′•tion
5. con•ser′•va•tor′•y
6. res′er•va′tion
7. marsh′•mal′•low
8. pli′•a•bil′•i•ty
9. sub′•plot′
10. im•pos′•si•bil′•i•ty

HOME WORK

Have students find a related word for five of the words above. Ask them to write the words with dots between syllables and accent marks where they belong. In class discuss how the accent often moves when suffixes are added to the root word.

pro•gram (prō′grăm′ *or* prō′grəm) *n.* **1.** A list of the order of events and other information for a public presentation or entertainment: *a printed program of the concert.* **2.** A public performance, presentation, or entertainment: *We presented a program of folk music.* **3.** A radio or television show. **4.** An ordered list of activities, courses, or procedures; a schedule: *arranged her program so that she could have Mondays off.* **5.** A course of academic study or extracurricular activities: *an excellent African studies program.* **6.** A system of services or projects designed to achieve a goal: *the space program.* **7.a.** The set of steps necessary for a computer to solve a problem, including the collection and processing of data and the presentation of results. **b.** The set of instructions that a computer must execute in carrying out these steps. —*tr.v.* **pro•** ...

Parts of Speech Labels To indicate what **part of speech** a word is, most dictionaries use the following abbreviations.

n.	noun	*pron.*	pronoun
v.	verb	*prep.*	preposition
adj.	adjective	*conj.*	conjunction
adv.	adverb	*interj.*	interjection

tug (tŭg) *v.* **tugged, tug•ging, tugs.** —*tr.* **1.** To pull at vigorously; strain at: *The puppy was tugging the leash.* **2.** To move by pulling with great effort or exertion; drag: *I tugged a chair across the room.* See Synonyms at **pull. 3.** To tow by a tugboat. —*intr.* To pull hard: *kept tugging until the boot came off.* —*n.* **1.** A strong pull or pulling force. **2.** A tugboat. [First written down before 1200 in Middle English and spelled *toggen,* from Old English *tēon.*]

Apply to Communication

Through Independent Writing

Ask students to use their dictionaries to locate the homographs below. Challenge them to use each homograph pair in a single sentence, as in the **Create Interest** activity.

calf/calf
date/date
hide/hide
keen/keen
nap/nap
refrain/refrain
shed/shed
tender/tender
wag/wag
yard/yard

Transfer to Everyday Life

By Using Cross-Curricular Connections

Ask students to skim a chapter in a social studies or science text and record ten words that have more than one meaning. Have them write one sentence for each meaning in the dictionary. Also have them write one synonym for each meaning of the word.

Many words may be used as more than one part of speech. Notice that the word *cast* can be used as either a verb or a noun. Be sure to find the right part of speech when searching for the definition of a word.

Practice Your Skills

Identifying Different Uses of a Word

Look up the word *cast* in the dictionary. Write the number of the definition and the part of speech used in each sentence.

1. On Tuesday I will cast my vote for Debbie.
2. During an eclipse the moon takes on a copper cast.
3. Rhonda has to wear the cast on her arm for six weeks.
4. The teacher cast her eyes on the whispering students.
5. We cast our lines into the trout-filled lake.
6. Many astrologers cast horoscopes each month.
7. Steven Spielberg casts many young people in his films.
8. Reindeer cast their antlers yearly and grow new ones.
9. Bruce and Eddie cast the rope across the stream.
10. The cast of the play received a standing ovation.
11. My grandmother will only make pancakes in her cast-iron skillet.
12. His first day in Hollywood he went to every casting agent listed in the phone book.
13. We collected cast-off clothing from people in the neighborhood for the homeless shelter.

REACHING ALL STUDENTS

English Language Learners

Write this sentence on the board and tell students that it includes all eight parts of speech. Ask them to identify the part of speech of each word.

Wow!	The	tiny	baby	almost	walked—	and	to	me!
int.	art.	adj.	n.	adv.	v.	conj.	prep.	pron.

Practice Your Skills Answers

Numbers of definitions will vary, depending on the dictionary used.

1. verb
2. noun
3. noun
4. verb
5. verb
6. verb
7. verb
8. verb
9. verb
10. noun
11. adjective
12. adjective
13. adjective

HOME WORK

Have students write sentences using the word *fake* as three different parts of speech.

Pull It All Together

By Sharing

Have students share the cross-curricular words they found with the rest of the class by writing the words on the board and giving their definitions and word origins.

Check Understanding

Have students use their dictionaries to find three words in "Order out of Chaos" that they wish to know the origins of. Have them look these words up and share their findings with the class.

REACHING ALL STUDENTS

English Language Learners

Exploring synonyms and their shades of meaning is a good way to improve the vocabulary and oral language skills of your ELL students. Write these words on the board and ask students to give you a synonym for each one. Then discuss the subtle differences between the words in each synonym pair.

sad
clever
large
make
speak
walk

Synonyms At the end of some entries, the dictionary will list synonyms. Synonyms are words that have similar definitions.

> **glad** (glăd) *adj.* **glad•der, glad•dest. 1.** Experiencing or showing joy and pleasure: *We were so glad to get your letter.* **2.** Providing joy and pleasure: *The wedding was a glad occasion.* **3.** Pleased; willing: *I would be glad to help.* **—glad′ly** *adv.* **—glad′ness** *n.*

synonyms

> Synonyms: **glad, happy, cheerful, lighthearted, joyful.** These adjectives mean being in or showing good spirits. **Glad** often means satisfied with immediate circumstances: *I am so glad we finally met.* **Happy** can mean feeling pleasurable contentment, as from a sense of fulfillment: *Jane is happy with her new job.* **Cheerful** means having good spirits, as distinct from being pleased: *Leroy tried to remain cheerful while he was in the hospital.* **Lighthearted** means free of cares and worries: *Summertime always puts you in a lighthearted mood.* **Joyful** means having great happiness and liveliness: *Their wedding was a joyful occasion*

Aside from the synonyms that are sometimes provided in a regular dictionary, there is another type of dictionary that features synonyms. It is called a **thesaurus.**

PRACTICE YOUR SKILLS

Using a Dictionary for Improving Writing

Using the dictionary, rewrite the following paragraph according to the directions on the following page.

Weather Watch

(1) Meteorologists are sceintists who study the weather. (2) Part of the job is to predict wether the sky

will be blue or grey by studying the layer of air that surrounds the Earth. (3) Meteorologists have a veriaty of instruments desined to help them determine weather patterns. (4) A anemometer measures wind speed, a barometer measures air pressure, and a hygrometer measures the amount of moisture in the air. (5) Altho meteorologists are well trained and expe-rienced, the forecasts are not allways acurrate. (6) Changes in weather happen suddenly and unpredictablely.

1. Correct the misspelling in sentence 1.
2. Correct the misspelling in sentence 2.
3. Use the preferred spelling of *grey* in sentence 2.
4. Correct the capitalization error in sentence 2.
5. Correct two misspellings in sentence 3.
6. Correct the article in sentence 4.
7. Use the preferred spelling of *altho* in sentence 5.
8. Correct the hyphen error in sentence 5.
9. Correct two misspellings in sentence 5.
10. Correct the misspelling in sentence 6.

Word Origins

Over the centuries the English language has gone through many changes, from Old English to Modern English. The following examples show how the words we use today have changed over time.

OLD ENGLISH	MODERN ENGLISH
moder	mother
faeder	father

PRACTICE YOUR SKILLS Answers

Meteorologists are scientists who study the weather. Part of the job is to predict whether the sky will be blue or gray by studying the layer of air that surrounds the earth. Meteorologists have a variety of instruments designed to help them determine weather patterns. An anemometer measures wind speed, a barometer measures air pressure, and a hygrometer measures the amount of moisture in the air. Although meteorologists are well-trained and experienced, the forecasts are not always accurate. Changes in weather happen suddenly and unpredictably.

HOME WORK

Ask students to select a piece of writing from their portfolios that could use some revision. Have them use their dictionaries to make at least three improvements in the piece.

PRACTICE YOUR SKILLS Answers

1. boc
2. cele
3. eorthe
4. fleogan
5. steorra
6. andswaru
7. sweoster
8. waeccan
9. scofl
10. freond

HOME WORK

Have students write ten words they use every day and then find their earlier forms in the dictionary.

weorold	world
eage	eye
buttorfleoge	butterfly

The dictionary provides information about the history of words in the English language. This information, called the **word origin**, is generally found in brackets at the end of an entry. The following entry shows that the word *compute* comes from two Latin words meaning "to reckon together."

com•pute (kəm pyo͞ot′) *v.* **com•put•ed, com•put•ing, com•putes.** —*tr.* **1.** To work out (a result, an answer, or a solution) by mathematics; calculate: *The bank computes the interest on savings accounts.* **2.** To determine by use of a computer: *compute the most efficient design of a sailboat.* —*intr.* **1.** To determine an amount or a number. **2.** To use a computer. [First written down in 1631 in Modern English, from Latin *computāre* : *com-*, together + *putāre*, to reckon.]

word origin

Many of the words we use come from Latin and Greek. The English language, however, also contains words from many other languages.

PRACTICE YOUR SKILLS

Matching Old and New Words

Write the Old English word in group 2 that matches the Modern English word in group 1.

Group 1	Group 2
1. book	eorthe
2. chill	flēogan

3.	earth	scofl
4.	fly	bōc
5.	starboard	cele
6.	answer	sweostor
7.	sister	stēorbord
8.	watch	wæccan
9.	shovel	frēond
10.	friend	andswaru

Words from Other Languages

The English language is constantly growing as well as changing. Although there are many different sources for new words, over half of the words in the English language have been borrowed from other languages. Many come from Greek and Latin, while others have been adopted from a wide variety of sources. Following are some examples.

WORDS FROM OTHER LANGUAGES			
Greek	astronaut	ocean	comedy
Latin	colony	missile	senate
Spanish	breeze	poncho	mustang
Scottish	clan	glen	slogan
French	cartoon	dentist	liberty
Dutch	buoy	landscape	skipper
Irish	bog	leprechaun	shamrock
Italian	zero	spaghetti	violin
Arabic	algebra	candy	magazine

Practice Your Skills

Finding Word Origins

Use the dictionary to write the origin of each of the following words.

HOME WORK

Have students skim their dictionaries to find five words, each with a different country of origin. Ask them to bring their lists to class for discussion.

PRACTICE YOUR SKILLS Answers

1. Italian
2. German
3. Spanish
4. Middle English, from Middle French, from Latin, from Greek
5. Italian, from Old Portuguese
6. French
7. Norwegian
8. Dharuk (Australian dialect)
9. Dutch, from Malay, from Chinese
10. Middle English, from Old French, from Latin

1. confetti
2. loaf
3. tornado
4. pirate
5. zero
6. row
7. yak
8. boomerang
9. teach
10. alien

Words with Unusual Origins

Borrowing words from other languages is only one way our language grows. New words come into our language in a variety of other ways. Some words, called compounds, are formed by combining two words.

COMPOUNDS	fingerprint	raincoat	houseboat

Some words are a blend of two words.

BLENDS	
	television + broadcast = telecast
	squirm + wiggle = squiggle
	fry + sizzle = frizzle

Some words are shortened forms of longer words.

SHORTENED FORM		
	ad	advertisement
	lunch	luncheon
	sitcom	situation comedy

Some words imitate sounds.

SOUNDS			
	crunch	plunk	strum
	yap	whiff	

Some names of people have also become words.

PEOPLE'S NAMES	
	Adolf Sax: Belgian inventor of the **saxophone**
	Earl of Sandwich: English creator of the **sandwich**

Rudolf Diesel: German inventor of the **diesel** engine

Some words are acronyms. Acronyms are words that are formed by the first letters or syllables of other words.

ACRONYMS

SAT: **S**cholastic **A**ptitude **T**est
SONAR: **so**und **na**vigation **r**anging
LORAN: **lo**ng-**ra**nge **n**avigation

PRACTICE YOUR SKILLS

Finding Unusual Origins

Tell how each of the following words came into the English language by writing *compound, blend, shortened form, sound, person's name,* or *acronym.* Use a dictionary to help you.

1. fizz	**6.** deli	**11.** slosh	**16.** moonbeam
2. ACT	**7.** watt	**12.** birdseed	**17.** guesstimate
3. fan	**8.** radar	**13.** OPEC	**18.** pasteurize
4. gym	**9.** NASA	**14.** brunch	**19.** motorcycle
5. smog	**10.** gurgle	**15.** downtown	**20.** Ferris wheel

Time Out to Reflect

In this chapter, you learned how to navigate your way around a dictionary. Before reading this chapter, what kinds of things did you use a dictionary for? Have you learned new uses for the dictionary? Are you completely comfortable using the dictionary or are there still dictionary skills you need to work on? Record your thoughts in the Learning Log section of your **journal**.

PRACTICE YOUR SKILLS Answers

1. sound
2. acronym
3. shortened form
4. shortened form
5. blend
6. shortened form
7. person's name
8. acronym
9. acronym
10. sound
11. sound
12. compound
13. acronym
14. blend
15. compound
16. compound
17. blend
18. person's name
19. compound
20. person's name

HOME WORK

Ask students to invent a word of their own and create a dictionary entry for it, including information about its derivation.

Using *In the Media*

Objective

- **Analyze word meanings in various types of media ads**

Group Project

- With the class, brainstorm a list of ten familiar and unfamiliar words. Then assign each group a word and have them look it up in an online dictionary and in a print dictionary. Ask groups to report on the similarities and differences between the listings and the similarities and differences between the processes of looking something up. Which dictionary did they find easier to use? Why? Have students use these two sources to find words they find in various types of media ads. How successful were students in finding these media terms? Have students share their results.

FYI

Websites to Visit Students may visit the Barrett Kendall Website at http://www.bkenglish.com or use the online dictionary at http://www.m-w.com.

EXPANDING THE LESSON

Using Technology

You will find additional **instructional** and **practice** materials for this chapter at http://www.bkenglish.com.

IN THE MEDIA

Media Messages

NEW AND IMPROVED!

Value Added!!!

As Seen on TV!

Have you ever seen words like these in an ad or commercial? What do you think they mean? If something is new, is it necessarily better? What kind of value has been added? What does seeing a product on TV have to do with its being good?

Media messages create their own meaning. A lot of the time, we are so used to seeing them, we don't even stop to think about what they are actually saying. Advertising slogans don't really make sense on their own—but in the context of an entire advertising campaign, they can take on meaning that goes far beyond the words themselves.

Media Activity

Working in groups of three, make a list of at least ten different word combinations used in ads. These ads can be from any type of media—newspapers, commercials, movie trailers, Websites, magazines—anything intended to be viewed or read. How many of these phrases make sense outside the context of their particular ad? How do the elements of the ad (setting, actors, music, graphics, lighting, type face) give the words meaning? Do you think the meaning is the same for different age groups? Using a thesaurus, look up a few key words and replace them with synonyms. Do the phrases still work as well? Share your findings with your classmates.

A DIFFERENT DELIVERY SYSTEM

For formal assessment print the chapter test from the *BK English* Test Bank at http://www.bkenglish.com.

Assess Your Learning

Your local word-collector club is preparing to launch a Website dedicated to finding new words and understanding the origins of words. The president of the club, Nora Webster, has asked you to contribute a paragraph to be placed on the Website telling how to get this information from a dictionary.

▶ **Look over your work from this chapter and study a dictionary to brainstorm ideas for what you will write. Be sure to include information on pronunciation, guide words, alphabetical order, parts of speech, and word origins. Use several dictionaries and ask your librarian or media center specialist for help. Also be sure to check some dictionaries on the Internet to see how these topics are handled in those dictionaries, since your audience is likely to be people who use the Web. Then organize your information into a paragraph with a topic sentence, supporting details, and a conclusion.**

Before You Write **Consider the following questions:**
What is the ***subject?***
What is the ***occasion?***
Who is the ***audience?***
What is the ***purpose?***

After You Write **Evaluate your work using the following criteria:**

- Have you organized your ideas to ensure coherence and logical progression in your paragraph?
- Have you used several dictionaries and thesauruses to find information for your paragraph?
- Have you enlisted the help of your librarian or media specialist?
- Is your writing accurate, informative, and meaningful?
- Does the information you have researched show accurate spelling and correct punctuation and capitalization?

Write briefly on how well you did. Point out your strengths and areas for improvement.

FOR ASSESSING LEARNING

Using *Assess Your Learning*

This writing prompt will help you and your students informally assess their developing abilities, using the accompanying primary trait rubrics, which list the key features and qualities of dictionary skills taught in this chapter. You may want to have students maintain their self-assessment in their portfolios as a record of their individual progress throughout the year.

TEACHING SUGGESTIONS

Essential Knowledge and Skills

- Selecting and using reference materials and resources as needed for writing, revising, and editing final drafts
- Framing questions to direct research
- Taking notes from relevant and authoritative sources such as periodicals and online searches

CHAPTER 16

Library and Media Center

Libraries and media centers can be some of the most valuable resources available to writers. They are storehouses of information. They are places where knowledge spanning centuries has been gathered. A library not only holds the answers to questions you already have, but also inspires you to ask new questions.

You have probably written many research reports over your school years. Writing research reports is not the only time you utilize your researching and library skills. Maybe you would like to write a short story about two fly fishermen fishing along the banks of the Delaware River. In the library you could research fly fishing and the Delaware to give your story an authentic touch.

Libraries and media centers can be informative, exciting, and entertaining. This chapter will help you to find materials in the library quickly and easily, allowing you access to worlds of knowledge.

Reading with a Writer's Eye

The following selection tells the history of the Alexandrian Library, in Alexandria, Egypt, the greatest known repository of ancient wisdom, which was destroyed around A.D. 415. As you read, consider why collecting vast amounts of knowledge into one central repository was so important to these ancient people. Why do you think we still collect and catalog knowledge into libraries today?

BLOCK SCHEDULING

- If your schedule requires that you cover the chapter in a **shorter time**, use Reading with a Writer's Eye and Developing Your Reference Skills.
- If you want to take advantage of **longer class time**, add Time Out to Reflect.

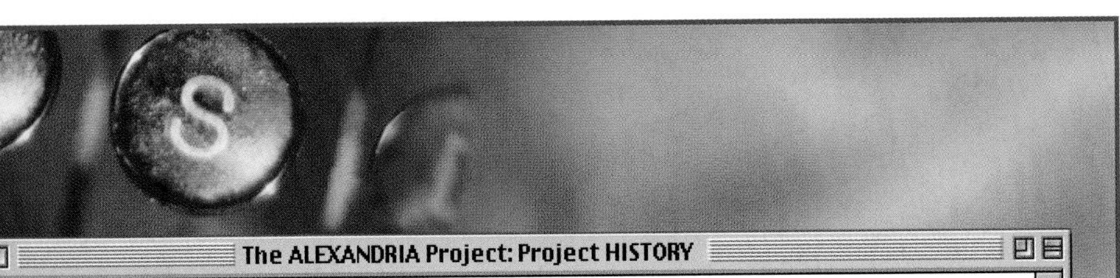

The ALEXANDRIA Project: Project HISTORY

FROM

THE ALEXANDRIA PROJECT HOMEPAGE

www.acs.oakland.edu/~macuenca/alexandria/alexwhy.htm

THE FIRST ALEXANDRIAN LIBRARY

The city of Alexandria was named after Alexander the Great, who founded the city at the delta of the Nile River in Egypt in the early third century B.C. Alexander encouraged the open-minded pursuit of knowledge, and when Ptolemy Soter assumed power, he asked Demitrius Phalerus, a follower of Aristotle, to found a library at Alexandria that would rival that of the library in Athens. Much effort and resource was put into this project, and the Alexandrian Library soon far surpassed its Greek prototype. The library at Alexandria quickly became the greatest collection of literature and scientific information in the ancient world.

The Ptolemies had voracious appetites for knowledge; they bought and borrowed books from libraries and merchants all around the world, and had them meticulously copied by hand. The aim of the library at Alexandria soon became to house a complete collection of every known existing book under one roof, and, legend has it they succeeded in this goal. As one might

FOR INCREASING STUDENT ACHIEVEMENT

GUIDED READING

Text Analysis

- Most of this expository text is written in **third person style.** Occasionally, though, the writer changes to first person. For example, the writer comments on what "we" know today about the accuracy of Eratosthenes' estimate of the earth's diameter and concludes with what memories "we" have about the library. In these two places, the shift gives the writing more emotional punch.
- The writer frequently uses **passive voice verbs,** starting with the first sentence. Students may find passive voice more common in writings about ancient history or other topics in which the writer is unsure whom to credit for an action, or where the writer wants to focus on events rather than on who participated in them.
- The writing is **fact-dense.** That is, the writer provides a great deal of information, rather than a great deal of interpretation or commentary. The last paragraph is the only one in which the balance between facts and commentary is tilted toward commentary.

SELECTION AMENDMENT
Description of change: excerpted
Rationale: to focus on the significance of libraries as presented in this chapter

GUIDED READING

Strategy: Previewing

Have students read the title and the heads in this excerpt. Ask them what questions they expect the article to answer. Write their ideas on the board. They might raise questions such as:

- What was so special about the first Alexandrian Library that an ALEXANDRIA Project exists today?
- Why should students today know about the Alexandrian Library?
- Who and what led to the destruction of the library? Why was that significant?

The ALEXANDRIA Project: Project HISTORY

expect, this collection grew quite large—at its zenith the Alexandrian Library reportedly consisted of more than 400,000 papyrus scrolls.

The library at Alexandria was the first place where human beings seriously and systematically collected and attempted to understand the accumulated knowledge of the race. A succession of famous scholars headed and made use of this library, and it quickly became renowned for the scholarly studies it supported, and the important discoveries that were made within its walls, as well as for its vast collection of knowledge.

THE LEGACY OF ALEXANDRIA

The astronomer, historian, geographer, mathematician, philosopher, and poet Eratosthenes had the honor of, at one point, being the chief librarian at Alexandria. It was he who used only two sticks, the sun, and his mind to determine the Earth was actually round, and to measure its diameter, more than 15 centuries before Copernicus and Galileo were even born. Eratosthenes estimated the size at 7,850 miles, and today we know that this figure was only about 0.5% off!

The mathematician Euclid developed his theories of what has come to be known as Euclidean geometry in the Alexandria Library during the reign of Ptolemy II Philadelphus. It was also from the vast Alexandrian collection of literature that Dionysius carried out his study of language, which helped him define for us the parts of speech.

The ALEXANDRIA Project: Project HISTORY

In the library, the first studies of conic sections, Elipses, Parabola, and Hyperbola were carried out by Appolonius of Perga. It was from the library observatory that the astronomer Hipparchus mapped the constellations and accurately estimated the brightness of stars. It was research in this great library that led the mechanical genius Heron to invent gear trains, steam engines, and the first robots.

Another scholar at the Alexandria Library was Aristarchus of Samos, and it was he who first suggested, in the third century B.C., that the Earth and the planets revolve around the Sun, instead of the universe revolving around the Earth. In the early years A.D., two of the greatest of the late Greek mathematicians also flourished in Alexandria. One, Diophantus, was active around A.D. 230 and produced his long-reaching work "Arithmetica" at this time. Several generations later, Pappus also did his mathematical work at the library.

The research and writing at the great library continued for more than 700 years, and then came to an abrupt ending in the year A.D. 413. The mathematician and philosopher Theon was the last person to have been known as the head of the library at Alexandria, and his daughter, Hypatia, has come to be remembered as a symbol of its great work and destruction. Hypatia was the first woman recorded as a great mathematician and philosopher. She is remembered as an eminent teacher, highly respected scholar, and was described as being charismatic and highly sought after for her opinion on scientific issues.

YOUR IDEAS
For Guided Reading

READER RESPONSE

You may want to use the following questions to elicit students' personal responses to the selection.

1. Explain what you knew about the Library at Alexandria before you read this selection.
2. How much did the collection of the Library at Alexandria, and the achievements of those who worked there, impress you?
3. Did you find the writing engaging? Explain.
4. How does the writer make you feel about the loss of the Library at Alexandria?

The ALEXANDRIA Project: Project HISTORY

THE END OF THE LIBRARY

In A.D. 412, Cyril, who later became St. Cyril, became a bishop of Alexandria. Under his leadership, the city that had once symbolized tolerance and learning began to erupt into religious violence. All of the centers of culture and learning were destroyed one by one, burned to the ground during riots led by the Nitrian monks, a fanatical sect of Christians who were supporters of Cyril. It was one such destructive tirade that destroyed the great library at Alexandria, and led to Hypatia's brutal death at the hands of a Christian lynch-mob.

The library at Alexandria was destroyed not by neglect over time, nor by foreign invaders, or by looters or plunderers, or in error by people who were oblivious to what was contained within. The greatest collection of knowledge in human history was very swiftly and very deliberately destroyed by fanatical people who knew exactly what work was going on inside, who knew the power that information held, and who wanted to see the scientific discovery end.

For what they thought was saving the soul of humankind, these people tore out its brain, and reduced many scholars, and nearly half a million handwritten scrolls to ashes. We now have only passed-down reports and fantastic dreams of the wonderful things that might have been collected in the great library at Alexandria. Oppression and the fear of learning obliterated all proof and almost all memory of what had once been achieved there.

ADDITIONAL RESOURCES

Composition Skills Practice . . . . pages 83–86
Writers at Work . . . . 8•1–8•10
Assessment: Chapter Test . . . . pages 97–100
Assessment: End of Course Test . . . . pages 214–229
Assessment Resources . . . . pages 1–10, 13–44

Thinking as a Writer

Analyzing the Importance of Libraries

- Why do you think that people go through the trouble and expense of creating libraries?
- In what ways do you think the Alexandrian Library helped the advance of science?
- What would it mean to you as a writer if there were no libraries?

Matching Tone

Oral Expression

- What do you think the author's feelings are toward the library? Explain your answer.
- Are there any words or phrases that you find particularly powerful or persuasive?
- How would you describe the tone the author uses?
- Read the selection aloud, matching the tone of your voice to the tone of the article.

Evaluating a Visual Image

Viewing

- Study this photo of a library. What does the design of the library tell you about how its builders felt about libraries?
- What might have been the purpose for choosing this particular style and design?

Using *Thinking as a Writer*

You may choose to have students respond to the questions either orally or in writing.

GETTING STUDENTS INVOLVED

Collaborative Learning

According to its Website, the goal of The ALEXANDRIA Project is "to identify the greatest accomplishments of humanity, and then to collect and preserve them for an uncertain posterity." Have each student nominate three books to include in this collection. Discuss the lists in class, and then have students revise and expand their lists to include five items.

FOR DEVELOPING SKILLS

LESSON 1 *(pages C500–C504)*

OBJECTIVES

- **To locate works of fiction in alphabetical order by the authors' names**
- **To use the Dewey decimal system**

Create Interest

Ask students how their families have organized the books in their home. If they have little or no organization for their books, ask students how they might be arranged so that any particular book could be found easily. As students suggest various principles of organization, write them on the board. Students might organize books by author's name, by subject, by reading level, by which person in the family is likely to read the book, by how recently the book was purchased, or by size. Point out that one can be more flexible when organizing dozens or even hundreds of books than when

DEVELOPING WORKPLACE COMPETENCIES

Thinking Skills: Knowing How to Learn

Libraries and media centers have amazing amounts of information. Skill at acquiring and using this information is valuable in many jobs. To design a project for a client who wants a "classical" look, a graphic designer might want images of women during the Golden Age in Greece. To advise tourists considering a special vacation, a travel agent might want to find background information about a specific island in Indonesia. To prepare a speech for the board of directors, an executive might want examples of how the structure of business enterprises has changed in response to changes in technology. Each of these people needs to know how to get the information they want.

Tell students to write down odd facts, stories, or mysteries that they think could be found in the school or local library. Have students pass in their papers, and then pass them out again. Each student should try to find the information on the paper, and document it in the library.

USING STUDENTS' STRENGTHS

Multiple Intelligences: Spatial

Have students draw a sketch of the school library, including the locations of the major parts of the collection, as well as the various stations for librarians.

Developing Your Reference Skills

Lord Samuel once said, "A library is thought in cold storage." Developing your library and media center skills will help you unlock the storage room so that the information will thaw into a usable form.

The volume of information available in a library can be overwhelming if you are not sure how it is organized. Finding one book amid shelves and shelves of materials can be difficult if your library skills are not sharp.

This chapter will introduce you to the materials available in most libraries and media centers and tell you how to use them. Remember that different establishments may have different materials available. Not all libraries have everything. Some are specialized. For example, there are law libraries—libraries that deal exclusively in law-related materials—and performing arts libraries, full of information on the performing arts as well as archived performances, like a videotape of a play. There are also general libraries that have a broad range of materials. For almost all of the research you will do for school, you will be able to use a general community or school library. Keep in mind however, that other materials may be available elsewhere.

Library Arrangement

Libraries can contain thousands of books. Finding one from among all of them would be impossible without a clear system of arrangement. The books in a library are organized so that you can easily find what you are looking for. In most libraries works of fiction are filed separately from nonfiction books.

organizing tens of thousands, or millions, of books.

Guide Instruction

By Modeling Strategies

Point out how books are organized in the classroom. They may be grouped on bookshelves by use or subject area. Within each group, they might be arranged by title or author. Ask students if they think the books in the classroom are organized well.

Consolidate Skills

Through Guided Practice

Point out to students that books often cover more than one classification. Ask students to consider which Dewey classifications might include each of the following books:

Living Thoughts: Philosophical Foundations of Biology
Believing in the Past: Religious Influences in Russian History
Talking Money: The Economic Advantages of Bilingualism

Fiction

A book or story that is based on imaginary people and events is called fiction. Works of fiction are shelved in alphabetical order according to the author's last name. For special cases, most libraries follow the shelving rules listed below.

Two-part names are alphabetized by the first part of the name.

DeCosta **O'**Casey **La**Salle **Van** Allen

Names beginning with *Mc* or *St.* are shelved as if they began with *Mac* or *Saint.*

Books by the same author are arranged in alphabetical order by title, skipping *a, an,* and *the* at the beginning.

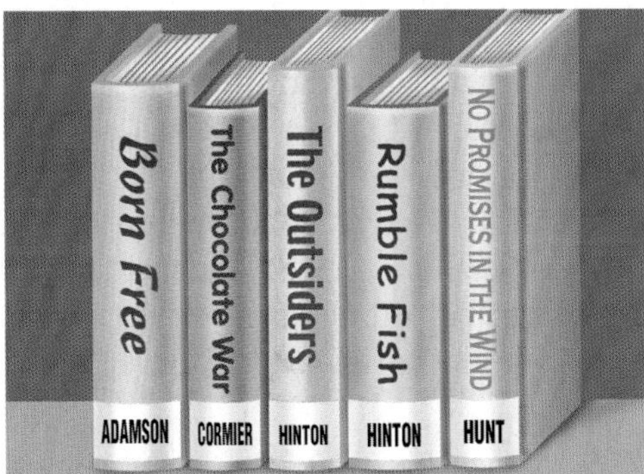

Practice Your Skills

Arranging Fiction

List the novels in the order they should be placed on the shelf.

Words by Heart by Ouida Sebestyen
Athabasca by Alistair MacLean
Island of the Blue Dolphins by Scott O'Dell
Great Expectations by Charles Dickens
The Riddle-Master of Hed by Patricia McKillip
David Copperfield by Charles Dickens
A Formal Feeding by Zibby O'Neal

REACHING ALL STUDENTS

English Language Learners

Libraries often file books in languages other than English in special sections. Have each student check libraries in and near your community to see if they include collections in the student's native language.

IDENTIFYING COMMON STUMBLING BLOCKS

Problem

- Trying to find a book using a different spelling for a translated name or a part of a name other than that which the library uses

Solution

- Remind students that classification of books can vary based on how libraries decide to translate names into English, to modernize spellings, to interpret cultural practices, and to treat pennames. For example, the great Persian poet who lived in the 900s is today known by several English names, including Firdawsi, Ferdowsi, Firdusi, and Firdousi. The English explorer in the 1500s and 1600s who is commonly known today as Walter Raleigh usually spelled his name Ralegh. Books by the Japanese writer Kimtake Hiraoka might be classified under either name, depending on the library; or, they might be classified by either of the names in the penname by which he is better known, Mishima Yukio.

Sound Medicine: Using Musical Therapy to Promote Good Health
Commenting on Compilations: Critiquing Reference Works as Literature

Apply to Communication

Through Independent Writing

Ask students to make up five titles for books. Encourage them to write humorous titles, ones that include puns, alliterations, or odd combinations of content. If your school allows it, provide a prize for the student who creates the title the class considers the most humorous. After students have written their titles, divide them into small groups. Have each group decide how they would classify the book according to the Dewey decimal system.

Transfer to Everyday Life

By Noting Books

Ask students to keep track of book titles that they read or hear about during a day. They might hear an interview with an author on the radio, listen to a news story that mentions a book, see a book review in a newspaper, or

PRACTICE YOUR SKILLS Answers

Arranging Fiction

David Copperfield by Charles Dickens
Great Expectations by Charles Dickens
Flowers for Algernon by Daniel Keyes
The Riddle-Master of Hed by Patricia McKillip
Athabasca by Alistair MacLean
Grandpa and Frank by Janet Majerus
Island of the Blue Dolphins by Scott O'Dell
A Formal Feeding by Zibby Oneal
Words by Heart by Onida Sebestyen
It's Crazy to Stay Chinese in Minnesota by Eleanor Wong Telemaque

Solving Shelving Problems

Dan D'Amelio	Theodore DuBois
Paula Danziger	Rosamund Du Jardin
Paxton Davis	Alexandre Dumas
Duane Decker	Daphne Du Maurier
Adele De Leeuw	Lois Duncan

REACHING ALL STUDENTS

Struggling Learners

Students may have difficulty separating fiction from nonfiction. They might ask how libraries classify a novel based on a real person or poems of all sorts. Divide students into small groups and have them make lists of types of books that would be classified as fiction and a list of books classified as non-fiction. Have groups share their lists with the class, and discuss any differences among the lists.

It's Crazy to Stay Chinese in Minnesota by Eleanor Wong Telemaque
Flowers for Algernon by Daniel Keyes
Grandpa and Frank by Janet Majerus

Solving Shelving Problems

List the following fiction authors in the order that their books would appear on the shelves.

Duane Decker	Paula Danziger
Adele De Leeuw	Rosamund Du Jardin
Lois Duncan	Daphne Du Maurier
Theodore DuBois	Dan D'Amelio
Paxton Davis	Alexandre Dumas

Nonfiction

In contrast to fiction, nonfiction books are about real people and events. Most libraries use the **Dewey decimal system** to arrange nonfiction books on shelves. This system was created more than 100 years ago by an American librarian named Melvil Dewey. In the Dewey decimal system, each book is assigned a number according to its subject. The following chart shows the ten categories in the Dewey decimal system.

DEWEY DECIMAL SYSTEM	
000-099	General Works (reference books)
100-199	Philosophy
200-299	Religion
300-399	Social Science (law, education, economics)
400-499	Language
500-599	Science (mathematics, biology, chemistry)
600-699	Technology (medicine, inventions)
700-799	Fine Arts (painting, music, theater, sports)
800-899	Literature
900-999	History (biography, geography, travel)

see an advertisement for a book somewhere. Each student should bring at least three titles to class. As a class, discuss how each book is probably classified in the Dewey decimal system.

Pull It All Together

By Reflecting

Ask students if they think the Dewey decimal system works well and if they think it should be modified in any way. For example, students might consider combining categories, such as Philosophy and Religion or combining Language and Literature. They might want to further divide Science or Fine Arts into specific subject areas. Or, they might want to reorder categories so that Language and Literature are next to each other or so that Social Sciences and History are next to each other.

Each of the ten main classes is broken up into smaller divisions. In the social science class, for example, the numbers 390-399 are reserved for books about customs and folklore. These smaller groups can be divided even further by using decimal points.

The number assigned to a book is the **call number**. The call number is written on the spine of the book. On the shelf, books are arranged in numerical order according to their call numbers.

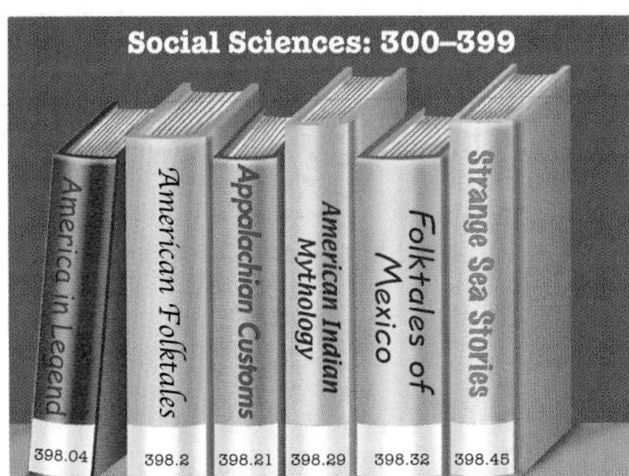

Biographies and Autobiographies

Biographies and autobiographies are usually shelved in a special section. Many libraries label each book with a *B* for biography or with the Dewey decimal number *920*. They are arranged in alphabetical order by the last name of the subject, not the author.

Practice Your Skills

Using the Dewey Decimal System

Write the range of numbers and the category each subject falls under in the Dewey decimal system.

EXAMPLE *The Sports Medicine Book*

ANSWER 600-699 Technology

1. *Computer Games and Puzzles*

2. *The Life of Martin Luther King, Jr.*

GETTING STUDENTS INVOLVED

Cooperative Learning

Divide students into small groups and assign each group one of the ten major classes in the Dewey decimal system, such as the numbers 400 to 499. By exploring the books in the library, students should determine the topic for each group of ten digits (400 to 409, 410 to 419, etc.) Have students share their findings with the class.

USING STUDENTS' STRENGTHS

Multiple Intelligences: Logical

Have students draw a branching diagram showing the major categories of the Dewey decimal system and some of the major topics covered under each one. They can use information collected in the above **Getting Students Involved** activity or from the Website described in the following **Integrating Technology** activity.

INTEGRATING TECHNOLOGY

Internet

The home page for the Dewey decimal classification system is http://www.oclc.org/oclc/fp/index.htm. Among the information it provides is a "Level 3 Summary" of the system, which describes the types of books classified under each whole number used in the system. The site http://www.bccls.org/reference/dewey/TheDeweyIndex.shtml organizes links to Websites according to the Dewey decimal system numbers.

Check Understanding

By Reviewing

As a class, try to list the ten basic categories of the Dewey decimal system without looking them up. Point out to students that they will soon know the basic categories, and some specific smaller categories, if they do much research in the library.

PRACTICE YOUR SKILLS Sample Answers

Using the Dewey Decimal System

1. 600-699 Technology
2. 900-999 History
3. 900-999 History
4. 700-799 Fine Arts
5. 100-199 Philosophy
6. 500-599 Science
7. 200-299 Religion
8. 900-999 History
9. 800-899 Literature
10. 400-499 Language

Solving Shelving Problems

4. 522.6 Eavesdropping on Space
9. 523.5 Mars, The Red Planet
5. 530.3 Your World in Motion
1. 535.6 Color–From Rainbows to Lasers
8. 542.4 Chemistry Magic!
3. 549.1 Rocks, Gems, and Minerals
6. 550.9 The Earth and Its Satellite
10. 551.4 Exploring American Caves
7. 553.8 The World of Diamonds
2. 560.9 Tales Told by Fossils

HOME WORK

Assign students to make up one book title that they think would be in each of the ten major categories of the Dewey decimal system, beginnings with the range from 000 to 099.

3. *A Climber's Guide to Glacier National Park*
4. *The History of Jazz*
5. *The Philosophy of Gandhi*
6. *Algebra in Easy Steps*
7. *Religions of America*
8. *Geography of American Cities*
9. *The Poems of Robert Frost*
10. *Learning Basic Spanish*

Solving Shelving Problems

Write the following Dewey decimal numbers and book titles in the order that the books would appear on the shelves.

1. 535.6 *Color—From Rainbows to Lasers*
2. 560.9 *Tales Told by Fossils*
3. 549.1 *Rocks, Gems, and Minerals*
4. 522.6 *Eavesdropping on Space*
5. 530.3 *Your World in Motion*
6. 550.9 *The Earth and Its Satellite*
7. 553.8 *The World of Diamonds*
8. 542.4 *Chemistry Magic!*
9. 523.5 *Mars, The Red Planet*
10. 551.4 *Exploring American Caves*

Types of Card Catalogs

In order to find a book on the shelves of the library, you need to know the book's call number. You find the call number of a book in the library's card catalog. There are two types of card catalogs: the online catalog and the traditional card catalog.

LESSON 2 *(pages C505–C509)*

OBJECTIVE

- **To use author, title, subject, cross-reference, and guide cards in the card catalog to find books**

Create Interest

Ask students how they find a book. List on the board the types of information that students suggest. They might look for books by title, author, subject, publication year, or length. Discuss how to set up a system that allows readers to search for books using each of these types of information.

Guide Instruction

By Connecting Ideas

Ask students to think of lists that are designed to help people find information efficiently, such as the index of a book, the gazetteer for an atlas, the telephone directory for a community, the directory of students in a school, and the periodic table of the elements. Search engines help users find infor-

Card Catalog

The **traditional card catalog** is a cabinet of small file drawers containing cards for every book in the library. The card catalog also has cards for filmstrips, records, movies, or other materials the library has. On the front of each drawer are letters that show what part of the alphabet that drawer contains.

There are three cards for each book, arranged alphabetically in the catalog. An **author card**, a **title card**, and a **subject card** will help you find the book you need. You will use different cards according to the kinds of information you already know about the book.

Author Cards If you know the author of the book, you can look in the card catalog under the author's last name. To find a book by James Muirden, for example, you would look in the drawer that covers the letter *M*.

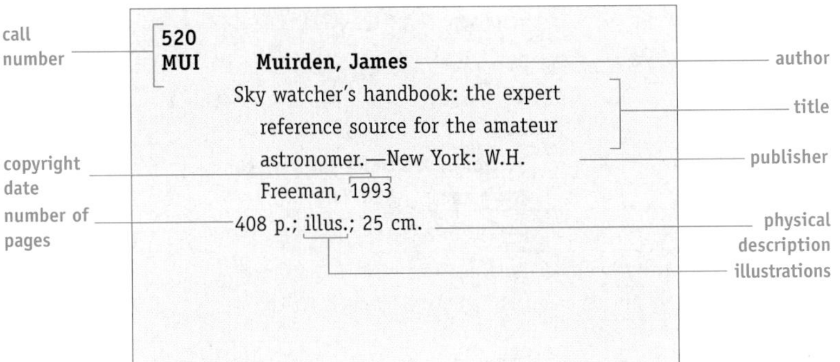

Title Cards If you know the title of a book but not its author, you can find the book by looking up the first word in the title (except *a, an,* and *the*). To find *Sky Watcher's Handbook*, look in the drawer containing the letter *S*.

REACHING ALL STUDENTS

Advanced Learners

Students can also locate useful books by scanning the shelves. If they know the call number of one book, they can scan the titles on books to either side of it to see if they might be useful. Or, if they wanted to look at whatever books the library had on a particular subject, they could find the call number of one title and scan the shelves in that section. For example, if they were considering writing a report on birds and they knew that most of their information would come from the school library, they could scan the shelves in the 598 section to see what was available. Have students try this method and report on how well it worked for them.

mation on the Internet. Most computer operating systems use a combination of files and folders to organize information. Discuss how well these methods work and what is comparable to them for the books and materials owned by a library.

Consolidate Skills

Through Guided Practice

Have students create a directory of students in the classroom. Consider various ways to organize it: alphabetically by last name or by first name, geographically by where students sit, numerically by telephone number, or some other method. Consider whether various methods might be more useful for specific purposes. A new teacher learning the names of the students, for example, might want a seating chart.

Apply to Communication

Through Independent Writing

Ask students to write a short essay comparing traditional and online cata-

HOME WORK

Assign students to identify the drawer in the catalog shown in the text in which they would find the author card, the title card, and the subject card for each of three different books that they select.

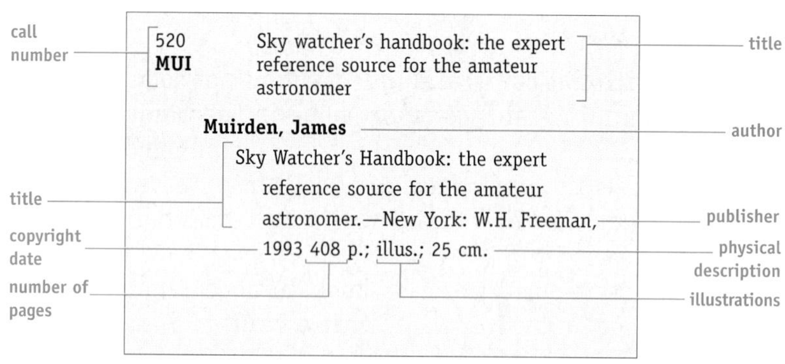

Subject Cards When gathering information for a report, you will use subject cards more than author or title cards. If your subject were astronomy, you would look under *A* in the card catalog. There you would find cards for all of the books about astronomy available in your library.

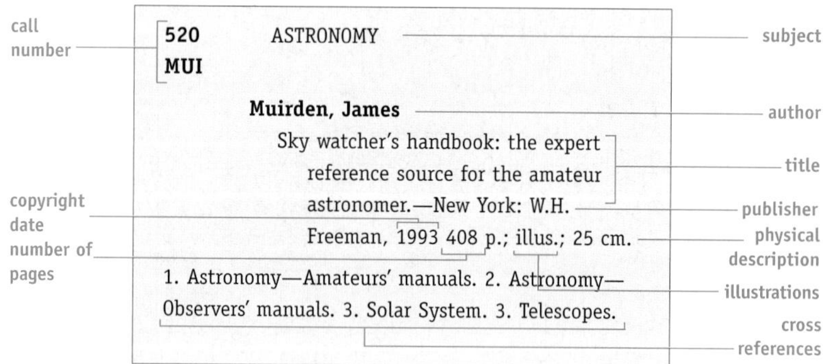

Guide Cards Guide cards are blank cards with words or a letter printed at the top. These cards are arranged in alphabetical order in each file drawer of the card catalog. Using guide cards will help you find author, title, and subject cards quickly.

logs. Students should note the relative advantages of each and express their preference for one over the other.

Transfer to Everyday Life

By Investigating Libraries

Make a list on the board of all the libraries students can think of in your community. Besides libraries in schools and public libraries, they might consider libraries in businesses, religious centers, and museums. Ask for volunteers to check each library to see whether it uses the Dewey decimal system or some other system and whether it has a traditional or an online catalog, or both. Students should share their findings with the class.

Pull It All Together

By Sharing

Ask students to describe ways they have found books in a library. They should mention using a catalog, but also discuss other methods: searching the shelves in specific sections, looking

Online Catalog

The **online catalog** is a computerized card catalog. While the traditional card catalog is usually limited to providing information on books, and only a few other types of materials, most online catalogs usually catalog all the materials available in a library or media center. You use it by entering the title, author, or subject of the book you are looking for. The computer will then display the results of your search. Some online catalogs can also tell if the material you are looking for is held by the library or media center you are in, whether it is currently available to check out, and what other libraries may have it. In some libraries, if a book is out on loan, you can even request that it be put on hold for you when it is returned.

SEARCH RESULTS FROM ONLINE CATALOG	
AUTHOR	Muirden, James
TITLE	Sky Watcher's Handbook: the expert reference source for the amateur astronomer /James Muirden.
EDITION	1st ed.
PUBLISHED	New York: W.H. Freeman, c1993
DESCRIPTION	viii, 408 p.: illus.; 25 cm.
CALL NUMBER	520 MUI
NOTES	Basic guide to searching the night sky. Star charts.
SUBJECTS	Astronomy—Amateurs' manuals. Astronomy—Observers' manuals.

COMPUTER TIP

When the library's online catalog displays the results of a search, instead of taking notes by hand, you can print out the information you need using the Print command. This will save you time and ensure that the information you are using to find a book is accurate.

FYI

Printing The Print dialogue box includes a pop-up menu labeled Options. Under this selection the user can turn the background printing feature on or off. Background printing allows the user to print one document while using the computer for other things. While this is usually very convenient, it may slow down both the printing and the operation of the computer.

How to Use with Windows™ To print a document, open the File menu and select Print. Or, you can press Control-P.

How to Use with Macintosh™ To print a document, open the File menu and select Print. Or, you can press Command-P.

randomly, and asking friends or librarians for help. Point out two of the advantages of using a catalog: one can do it without help and it is systematic.

Check Understanding

By Evaluating

Ask students if they feel comfortable finding books in a library. If some students do not, ask other students who do to work with them until they have more confidence.

PRACTICE YOUR SKILLS Answers

Searching Online Catalogs

1. Nonfiction books about birds commonly have call numbers in the 598 classification.
2. The works of Shakespeare commonly have call numbers in 822.33 section.
3. The *Diary of Anne Frank* commonly has a call number in the 812.5 classification. It may also have a call number in the Biography classification.

Using the Card Catalog

1. N-Ph
2. Br-Ch
3. Pi-R
4. M
5. B-Bo
6. Cu-D
7. U-V
8. Ci-Cr
9. N-Ph
10. S-Sq

Strategies for Finding Books

- Find out if the library has the book you want by finding the author card, the title card, or the subject card in the card catalog or by looking it up on the online catalog.
- Read the card or screen to see if the book is likely to contain the information you need. Check the copyright date to see how current the information is.
- On a slip of paper, copy the call number, the title, and the name of the author for each book you want to find, or print out the information.
- Use the call number to find each book. The first line of the call number tells which section of the library or media center to look in.

F or FIC	fiction section
B or 920	biography section
Dewey number	nonfiction section

Then find each book on the shelves by looking for its call number, located on the spine.

PRACTICE YOUR SKILLS

Searching Online Catalogs

Using the online catalog in your local public or school library or media center, find call numbers for the following books.

1. a nonfiction book about birds

2. a play by William Shakespeare

3. *The Diary of Anne Frank*

4. a biography of Thomas Jefferson

LESSON 3 *(pages C509–C519)*

OBJECTIVES

- To use general and specialized references, including encyclopedias, specialized encyclopedias, biographical references, atlases, almanacs and yearbooks, and specialized dictionaries to find information
- To use the *Readers' Guide to Periodical Literature* to find magazine articles

Create Interest

List on the board all of the specialized reference books that students can think of. Then ask them to think of ones they wish someone would develop. Students interested in calligraphy might want a book demonstrating and describing all existing writing systems in the world. Students who can hum a song but cannot recall its title might want an index to musical tunes

Using the Card Catalog

Write the letter or letters of the drawer in which you would find each of the following in the card catalog.

EXAMPLE *Old Yeller*
ANSWER N-Ph

1. otters
2. caves
3. Babe Ruth
4. Mexico
5. Black Hawk
6. the meaning of dreams
7. unidentified flying objects
8. *The Cloister and the Hearth*
9. Sandra Day O'Connor
10. *The Sea Around Us*

A	Cu-D	J-L	S-Sq
B-Bo	E-F	M	St-T
Br-Ch	G-Ha	N-Ph	U-V
Ci-Cr	He-I	Pi-R	W-Z

Writing Catalog Cards

Write an author card, a title card, and a subject card using the following information.

Football, 23 centimeters, published in New York by Children's Press, Dewey decimal number 796.33, copyright date 1995, written by Ray Broekel, 48 pages with illustrations.

Using Reference Materials

Reference books, such as encyclopedias, dictionaries, atlases, and almanacs, are kept in a separate section of the library. Usually these books cannot be checked out. There are often study tables set up in this section so that you can use the books while you are in the library.

Most libraries also have a section for nonprint materials such as audiotapes, CDs, DVDs, and videos. These can be found either in the reference section or in their own separate media section.

Writing Catalog Cards

Author Card
796.33 Broekel, Ray
Football.
New York: Children's Press
[1995] 48 p.; illus.; 23 cm.

Title Card
796.33 Football.
Broekel, Ray
New York: Children's Press
[1995] 48 p.; illus.; 23 cm.

Subject Card
796.33 Football
Broekel, Ray
Football.
New York: Children's Press
[1995] 48 p.; illus.; 23 cm.

according to whether each of the first sixteen notes go up or down from the one preceding it. Students curious about foreign phrases might want a dictionary of foreign phrases commonly used by English speakers. Point out that all of these reference books currently exist.

Guide Instruction

By Modeling Strategies

Borrow volumes of the *Readers' Guide to Periodical Literature* and bring them to class. Have students work with a partner to look up topics that interest them and to figure out how to read the entries. You could also have all students look up a topic on which interest has changed sharply over the years covered in the volumes. For example, students may be curious how the number of entries on computers changed during the 1980s.

REACHING ALL STUDENTS

Struggling Learners

If students have difficulty interpreting the entries in the *Readers' Guide to Periodical Literature,* have them design their own entry forms. Their forms need to include all of the information that a potential reader would need to locate the article, and the information needs to be as condensed as possible. Then have students compare their forms with the one actually used and discuss any differences in class.

Readers' Guide to Periodical Literature

Magazines are published more frequently than almanacs and yearbooks. For this reason they are excellent sources of current information. *The Readers' Guide to Periodical Literature* is an index that will help you find magazine articles on subjects of interest. It includes a comprehensive list of magazines.

Each edition of the *Readers' Guide* has a date on its spine. The date tells you the time period covered in the volume. The following entries are from the February 1999 edition.

SUBJECT ENTRY — **ELECTRONIC JOURNALS** See Electronic magazines
ELECTRONIC MAGAZINES
See also
Estronet (Website)
Salon (Periodical)
Slate (Periodical)
The electronic word [Issues in science and technology Website] K. Finneran. *Issues in Science and Technology* v15 no1 p30 Fall '98
Thank God AOL is not like Fortune magazine. S. Alsop. il *Fortune* v138 no10 p277-8 N 23 '98
Try some teamwork [Smart computing's Website; editorial] il *Smart Computing* v9 no10 p108 O '98

SUBJECT ENTRY — **ELECTRONIC MAIL SYSTEMS**
See also
Computer bulletin boards
Eudora (Computer program)
Free electronic mail systems
Instant messaging (Internet)
Junk E-mail
PocketMail (Electronic mail devices)
United States Postal Service—Automation
Unified messaging systems
Voice mail systems
E-mail addiction. G. Kawasaki. il or *Forbes* v162 no14 p128 D 28 '98
E-mail: write protection? [Wesley College case] P. A. Zirkel. *Phi Delta Kappan* v79 no8 p631-2 Ap '98
E-phones connect. S. K. Kirschner. il *Popular Science* v253 no2 p62-5 Ag '98
Going online: America Online's new E-mail tools. A. Phelps. il *Smart Computing* v9 no11 50 N '98
Grandparenting by E-mail. P. S. Estess. il *New Choices* v38 no8 p67 O '98

Consolidate Skills
Through Guided Practice
Give each student the name of a specific reference book to find in the library and to learn how to use. Have each student show two other students how to use the book.

Apply to Communication
Through Independent Writing
Have each student write an introduction to using the reference book they explored in the previous activity. Students should describe the book, explain how it is organized and how to use it, and suggest who might be most interested in using it.

Transfer to Everyday Life
By Considering Questions
Have students make a list of questions that come up during a day. They should include both questions that arise during a class, such as, "What caused the Korean War?" as well as questions that arise informally, such as, "Is a peanut really a nut?" Each student should bring a list of five questions to

Following are some results from a search of the online version of the *Readers' Guide* for the subject of electronic mail.

TITLE
E-mail addiction
PERSONAL AUTHOR
Kawasaki,-Guy, 1954-
SOURCE
Forbes. v. 162 no14 Dec. 28 1998 p. 128

TITLE
Going online: America Onlines's new E-mail tools
PERSONAL AUTHOR
Phelps,-Alan
SOURCE
Smart-Computing. v. 9 no11 Nov. 1998 p. 50

TITLE
Grandparenting by E-mail
PERSONAL AUTHOR
Estess,-Patricia-Schiff
SOURCE
New-Choices. v. 38 no8 Oct. 1998 p. 67

TITLE
E-phones connect
PERSONAL AUTHOR
Kirschner,-Suzanne-Kantra
SOURCE
Popular-Science. v. 253 no2 Aug. 1998 p. 62-5

TITLE
E-mail: write protection?
OTHER TITLES
Augmented title: Wesley College case
PERSONAL AUTHOR
Zirkel,-Perry-A
SOURCE
Phi-Delta-Kappan. v. 79 no8 Apr. 1998 p. 631-2

YOUR IDEAS
For Using the *Readers' Guide to Periodical Literature*

class. Divide students into small groups, and have each group suggest reference books that might answer the questions.

Pull It All Together

By Sharing

Ask students to share what they have learned about libraries and media centers in studying this chapter. Review how libraries are organized, how to use card catalogs, how to find periodical literature, and how to use specialized reference books.

Check Understanding

By Evaluating the Literary Excerpt

Compare the types of information described in "The First Alexandrian Library" with the types of information found in your school library or in your local public library. Both have materials on many subjects. While the Library at Alexandria had no books, films, or computers, modern libraries rarely have papyrus scrolls.

PRACTICE YOUR SKILLS Sample Answers

1. Electronic Magazines
2. page 108
3. Electronic Mail Systems
4. Electronic Magazines, Electronic Journals
5. Fall '98
6. vol. 9
7. Electronic Mail Systems
8. G. Kawasaki
9. "The Electronic Word" and "Try Some Teamwork"
10. 6

HOME WORK

Have students select a topic that interests them and find and copy down three entries about their topic in the *Readers' Guide to Periodical Literature.*

Each entry in the *Readers' Guide* provides all the information you need to locate articles on a particular subject. Notice how the information is listed in the following print and online entries on electronic mail.

SUBJECT

ELECTRONIC MAIL SYSTEMS

ARTICLE	AUTHOR	ILLUSTRATED	MAGAZINE	VOLUME	PAGE	DATE
E-mail addiction.	G. Kawasaki.	il	Forbes	v162 no14	p128	D 28 '98

TITLE

SUBJECT — E-mail addiction

ARTICLE — **PERSONAL AUTHOR**

AUTHOR — Kawasaki,-Guy, 1954-

SOURCE

MAGAZINE — Forbes. v. 162 no14 Dec. 28 1998 p. 128

VOLUME

DATE

PAGE

PRACTICE YOUR SKILLS

Using the Readers' Guide

Use the entries from the *Readers' Guide* on page C510 to answer the following questions.

1. What subject is the article "Try some teamwork" about?
2. On what page in *Smart Computing* magazine does this article appear?
3. Under what heading does the article "Grandparenting by E-mail" by P. S. Estess appear?
4. What subject headings would you look under to find information about electronic magazines?
5. What is the date of the magazine in which an article by K. Finneran appears?
6. What volume of *Smart Computing* magazine contains the article about America Online's new features?

7. What subject heading would you look under to find information about electronic mail systems?
8. Who is the author of the article "E-mail addiction"?
9. What are the titles of two magazine articles written about electronic magazines?
10. How many of the magazine articles listed in the entries contain illustrations?

Encyclopedias

Encyclopedias contain general information on a wide variety of subjects. The information is arranged in alphabetical order by subject. Guide letters on the spine help you find the right volume. Inside every volume are guide words at the top of each page to direct you to your subject.

Most encyclopedias provide an index in a separate volume or at the end of the last volume. The index tells if your subject is discussed in more than one volume or if it is listed under another name.

Online and CD-ROM encyclopedias are arranged in the same manner as printed encyclopedias—alphabetical—but there are no guide words, nor index. Instead, in order to find information on a particular subject, you enter the subject in a search box. The program will then show you the results of your search. Some programs will also give you short movies, a list of related topics, and links to Internet sites about your subject.

PRINT *Collier's Encyclopedia*
Compton's Pictured Encyclopedia
Encyclopedia Americana
Encyclopedia Britannica
World Book Encyclopedia

CD-ROM *Encarta Encyclopedia Deluxe Edition*
The World Book Multimedia Encyclopedia Deluxe Edition
Compton's Interactive Encyclopedia

GETTING STUDENTS INVOLVED

Reciprocal Teaching

Divide the class into groups of two or three students. Assign each group a range of numbers in the Dewey decimal system, such as 300 to 399. Then students should explore the reference books in the school library in that range. Each group should report on one or a few of the books they think would be most useful to their classmates. They should also describe the most unusual reference book they found. Have groups share their findings with the class.

INTEGRATING TECHNOLOGY

Internet

Have the class compile a list of reference works available on the Internet. You may have students specialize in particular subject areas or types of materials. Have each student find at least five works, and write a brief description of how each might be useful. An excellent starting point for finding reference books is the WWW Virtual Library at http://vlib.org/Overview.html. Utrecht University in the Netherlands has one of the best sources of links to atlases and maps on the Internet at http://oddens.geog.uu.nl/index.html. A Web of Online Dictionaries, based at Bucknell University and including links to online dictionaries in over 400 languages and hundreds of specialized dictionaries, is at http://www.facstaff.bucknell.edu/rbeard/diction.html.

ONLINE *Encyclopedia Britannica Online,* **http://www.britannica.com**
The Concise Columbia Electronic Encyclopedia, **http://www.encyclopedia.com**

Specialized Encyclopedias

Specialized encyclopedias focus on one particular subject. They provide more information about a subject than general encyclopedias do. Specialized encyclopedias are also arranged in alphabetical order for easy reference. Just like general encyclopedias, specialized encyclopedias come in print, online, and CD-ROM versions. Following are some specialized encyclopedias.

PRINT *International Wildlife Encyclopedia*
Encyclopedia of American Cars
Encyclopedia of Card Tricks
Encyclopedia for American Facts and Dates
The McGraw-Hill Encyclopedia of Science and Technology
Encyclopedia of Tropical Fish

ONLINE *Encyclopedia Smithsonian,* http://www.si.edu/resource/faq/start.html
The World eText Library, http://www.netlibrary.net/WorldReferenceE.html

General Biographical References

Biographical references are works that give information about the lives of famous people, past and present. Some provide only a paragraph of facts, such as birth date, education, family, occupation, and awards. Others contain long articles about each person in the volume. Following are some well-known biographical references.

PRINT	*Current Biography* *Who's Who in America* *Webster's Biographical Dictionary* *Dictionary of American Biography* *American Men and Women of Science*
CD-ROM	*Her Heritage: A Biographical Encyclopedia of Famous American Women*
ONLINE	*Biography*, **http://www.biography.com**

PRACTICE YOUR SKILLS

Using General Biographical References

Using a biographical reference book, match the famous American cartoonists in the first column with the comic strip character they created in the second column.

1. C. C. Beck	*Captain America*
2. Jim Davis	*Peanuts*
3. Al Capp	*Little Orphan Annie*
4. Jack Kirby	*Captain Marvel*
5. Alex Raymond	*Dennis the Menace*
6. Harold Gray	*Popeye*
7. Hank Ketcham	*Doonesbury*
8. Charles Schultz	*L'il Abner*
9. Elzie C. Segar	*Flash Gordon*
10. Gary Trudeau	*Garfield*

Atlases

Atlases are collections of maps. They usually include many different kinds of maps, some showing climate, some showing population density. In addition, many atlases include charts

PRACTICE YOUR SKILLS Answers

1. Captain Marvel
2. Garfield
3. L'il Abner
4. Captain America
5. Flash Gordon
6. Little Orphan Annie
7. Dennis the Menace
8. Peanuts
9. Popeye
10. Doonesbury

HOME WORK

Assign students to use a biographical reference book to find out more information about five people of their choice. For each individual, students should list the year of birth and one or more accomplishments.

USING STUDENTS' STRENGTHS

Multiple Intelligences: Spatial

Atlases can cover almost any topic in which spatial distribution is significant. They can cover microscopic areas, such as cells; immense areas, such as the solar system; or imaginary areas, such as the mythical land of Middle Earth. In addition, some atlases include significant amounts of text to explain what is shown on the map. Encourage students to find maps about a topic of personal interest, whether it is college football or classical composers. Make a list of the diversity of topics on which students can find maps or atlases.

with facts about mountains, deserts, rivers, oceans, and natural resources. The table of contents and the index of each atlas directs you to the information you need. Following are some popular atlases.

PRINT	*Collier's World Atlas and Gazetteer* *Hammond's Medallion World Atlas* *Rand McNally International World Atlas* *Goode's World Atlas* *The National Geographic Atlas of the World*
ONLINE	*U.S. Geological Survey,* **http://www.nationalatlas.gov/mapit.html**

Almanacs and Yearbooks

Almanacs and **yearbooks** are published once a year. For this reason they contain much up-to-date information. They cover a wide variety of subjects, such as famous people, unusual achievements, the economy, politics, countries, and sports. Following are some of the most popular almanacs and yearbooks.

PRINT	*Information Please Almanac* *World Almanac and Book of Facts* *Hammond's Almanac*
CD-ROM	*Guinness Book of World Records*
ONLINE	*The Old Farmer's Almanac,* **http://www.almanac.com**

Specialized Dictionaries

Specialized dictionaries contain entries about one specific subject. Some, for example, are limited to mathematics. Others may be limited to abbreviations. One kind of dictionary, called a thesaurus, includes only synonyms. The following list shows the variety of specialized dictionaries.

PRINT	*The New Roget's Thesaurus in Dictionary Form* *Webster's New Dictionary of Synonyms* *Abbreviations Dictionary* *Dictionary of American History*
CD-ROM	*Oxford English Dictionary*
ONLINE	English and foreign language dictionaries, http://www.dictionary.com
	Roget's Thesaurus, http://www.thesaurus.com
	Compton's Illustrated Science Dictionary

COMPUTER TIP

Some libraries are linked to online databases. These databases contain all types of information. Libraries that are linked to the Internet have access to almost unlimited amounts of information sources. You can search for a topic by entering a keyword or phrase. The computer will display the results of your search and you can print the information.

PRACTICE YOUR SKILLS

Using Specialized Reference Materials

Following is a list of library resources. Number a piece of paper from 1 to 10. Then write the best source for answering each question.

specialized encyclopedia	atlas
biographical reference	almanac
specialized dictionary	

1. In what part of Alaska is the capital located?

2. When and where was actor-comedian Bill Cosby born?

GETTING STUDENTS INVOLVED

Cooperative Learning

Divide the class into small groups. Each group should make a list of ten trivia questions that they can answer using resources in the school library. Compile the lists into one and then distribute them to the teams. Give each team two days to find the answers to all of the questions. Teams must identify the source they used to find the answers.

FYI

Online Searches Encourage students to try different keywords and combinations of keywords when searching an online database. They will want to find a balance between keywords that are so general that they include many items that are not relevant and keywords that are too narrow to include all useful items.

Practice Your Skills Answers

1. atlas
2. biographical reference
3. specialized dictionary
4. specialized encyclopedia
5. specialized dictionary
6. atlas
7. almanac
8. biographical reference
9. atlas
10. specialized dictionary

3. What does the term *fielder's choice* mean in baseball?
4. What is a harvest moon?
5. What does the term *staccato* mean in music?
6. What river flows through the Grand Canyon?
7. What policy for naming hurricanes was adopted in 1979?
8. For what sport is Michelle Kwan known?
9. What are the chief crops grown in Indiana?
10. What does the term *Manifest Destiny* mean in American history?

Finding Facts in Reference Materials

Use the library's reference materials to find the answers to the ten questions listed above.

Vertical Files

The **vertical file** is a collection of leaflets, catalogs, pamphlets, newspaper clippings, and brochures kept in filing cabinets. Inside the file drawers, items are arranged in alphabetical order according to subject.

Microforms

Another useful reference source that can be found in many libraries is newspapers. Your library will probably have the most recent editions of local and major national papers as well as a few specialized papers. Because they take up so much space and can be delicate, older editions of papers are usually stored in **microform:** either **microfilm** (a reel of film) or **microfiche** (a sheet of film). You can view these types of film by using a special projection machine. The films are usually cataloged in books similar to the *Readers' Guide to Periodical Literature* *(See page C510)*. Once you have found a film with information on your topic in the guide, you can use a projection machine to view the appropriate pages of the archived newspaper. You can also scan or print what you are viewing.

Recorded Materials

Most libraries have a section where the recorded materials are kept. These usually include audiotapes, CDs and records, videos and DVDs, CD-ROMs and other software. If your library has an online catalog, you will find these materials indexed there. If your library uses a card catalog, you will find these materials indexed there or in a separate, smaller card catalog near where the materials are stored.

Some of the recorded materials may be borrowed and others can only be used in the library. Many libraries and media centers have listening, viewing, and computer rooms where these types of materials can be used.

Time Out to Reflect

You have seen that some information in a library or media center is in print form, while other information is in electronic form. Each format has its own advantages. What advantages did you find in using the Internet to gather information instead of going to print or bound materials? Were there any advantages to looking in books instead of going online? In what situations would each form of information be most useful? Record your reflections in your **journal**.

HOME WORK

Have students list two topics they would expect to find in each of the five types of library resources listed in the activity.

EXPANDING THE LESSON

Using Technology

You will find additional **instructional** and **practice** materials for this chapter at http://www.bkenglish.com.

A Writer's Guide to Electronic Publishing

The Internet offers many ways to do research, including the World Wide Web, E-mail, and much more. Together with the resources in your local library or media center, you can gather a large amount of data to help you create a well-developed project or report.

Once you've organized your material, ask yourself: What's the best way to present this information?

Years ago your choices might have been limited to using text from a typewriter, photos and glue, and construction paper. But now electronic publishing offers choices such as desktop publishing (creating printed documents on your computer), audio and video recordings, and even online publishing on the World Wide Web (creating your own Website).

Not every type of electronic publishing is right for every project. Each method has advantages and disadvantages. You will need to choose the method that best suits your topic and project. Ask yourself:

- Is my project **visual?** For example, perhaps you're doing a report on backyard insects. Video would be a good choice for this topic.
- Is **sound** an important part of this project? Suppose you're putting together an opinion poll, and you plan to interview many people. An audio recording could work very well in this situation.
- Could my project **branch off** into many sections? Perhaps you're preparing a presentation that addresses different aspects of your community service club. This topic could make an effective Website.

Once you decide which publishing method is right for your project, let your imagination go!

Desktop Publishing

The computer is a powerful tool that gives you the ability to create everything from party invitations and banners to newsletters and illustrated reports. Many software programs deliver word-processing and graphic arts capabilities that once belonged only to professional printers and designers. Armed with the knowledge of how to operate your software, you simply need to add some sound research and a healthy helping of creativity to create an exciting paper.

Word-Processing Magic

The written word is the basis of almost every project. Using a standard word-processing program, such as Microsoft Word, makes all aspects of the writing process easier. Use a word-processing program to do the following:

- create an outline
- create charts and graphs
- save multiple versions of your work
- revise your manuscript
- proofread your spelling, grammar, and punctuation
- produce a polished final draft document

Fascinating Fonts

Once your written material is revised and edited, it's fun to experiment with type as a way to enhance the content of your written message. Different styles of type are called **fonts** or **typefaces.** Most word-processing programs feature more than 30 different font choices. You'll find them listed in the Format menu under Font.

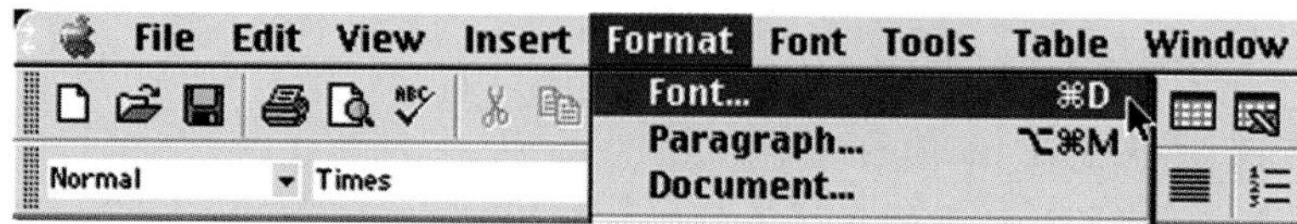

Font choices may also be located on the toolbar at the top left of your screen.

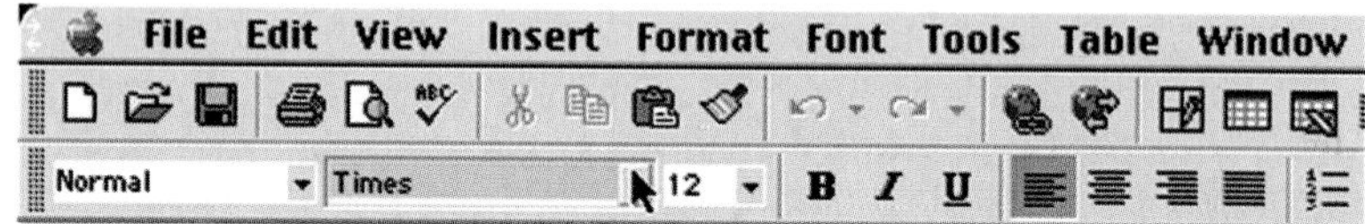

Although each typeface, or font, has its own distinguishing characteristics, most fall into one of two categories: serif typefaces or sans serif typefaces. A **serif** is a small curve or line added to the end of some of the letter strokes. A typeface that includes these small added curves is called a **serif** typeface. A font without them is referred to as **sans serif,** or without serifs. *Sans* is the French word for "without."

> Times New Roman is a serif typeface.
> Arial is a sans serif typeface.

In general sans serif fonts have a sharp look and are better for shorter pieces of writing, such as headings and titles. Serif typefaces work well as body copy.

Of all the typefaces, serif or sans serif, which is best? In many cases that decision depends on your project. Each font has a personality of its own and makes a different impression on the reader. For example:

> *This is French Script MT and might be fun to use in an invitation to a special birthday party.*
>
> **This is Playbill and would look great on a poster advertising a performance by the Drama Club.**
>
> **This is Stencil and would be a great way to say "Top Secret" on a letter to a friend.**

As fun as they are, these three typefaces are probably inappropriate for a school report or term paper. Specialized fonts are great for unique projects (posters, invitations, and personal correspondence) but less appropriate for writing assignments for school.

Since most school writing is considered formal, good font choices include Times New Roman, Arial, Helvetica, or Bookman Antiqua. These type styles are fairly plain and straightforward. They allow the reader to focus on the meaning of your words instead of being distracted by the way they appear on the page.

With so many fonts to choose from, you may be tempted to include a dozen or so in your document. Be careful! Text printed *in* multiple fonts *can* be extremely *confusing* **to read.** The whole idea of different typefaces is to enhance and clarify your message, not the other way around!

A Sizable Choice

Another way to add emphasis to your writing is to adjust the size of the type. Type size is measured in points. One inch is equal to 72 points. Therefore, 72-point type would have letters that measure one-inch high. To change the point size of your type, open the Format menu and click Font.

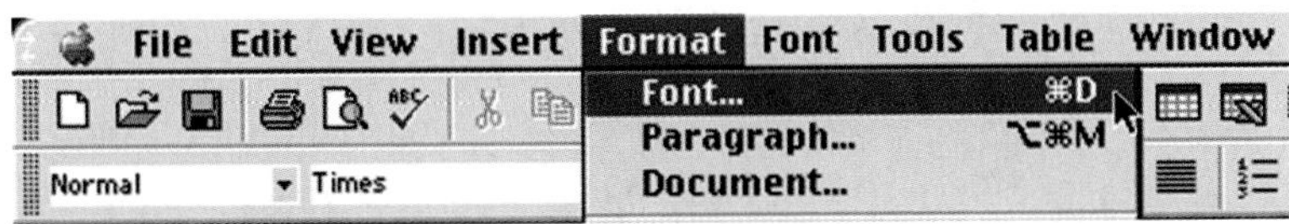

You can also use the small number box in the center of the toolbar at the top of your screen.

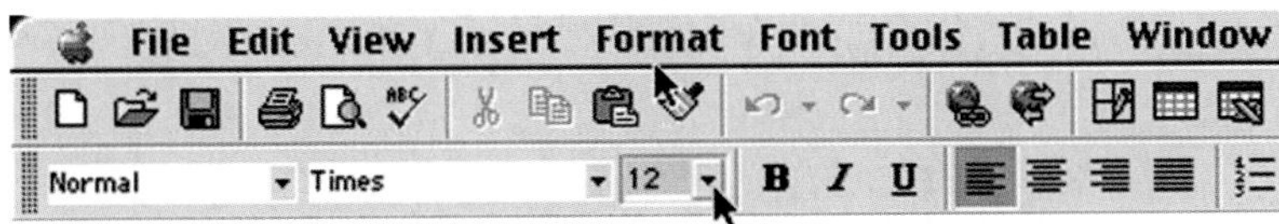

For most school and business writing projects, 10 or 12 point is the best type size for the main body copy of your text. However, it's very effective to change the type size for titles, headings, and subheadings to give the reader a clear understanding of how your information is organized. For example, look at how the type in the subheading "A Sizable Choice" on page C523 is different from the rest of the type on that page, indicating the beginning of a new section.

Another way to add emphasis is to apply a style to the type, such as **bold**, *italics,* or underline. Styles are also found in the Format menu under Font.

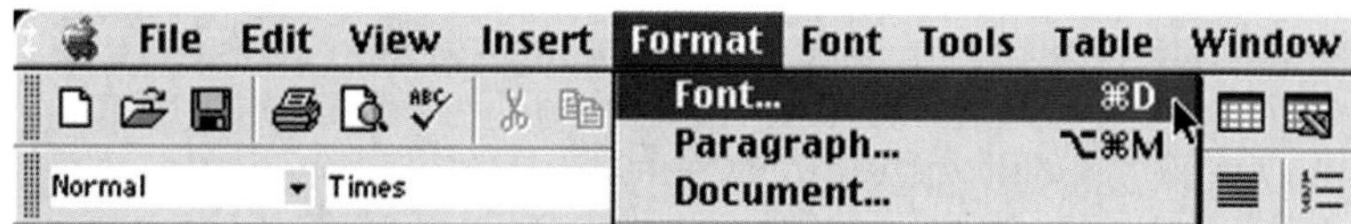

You can also look for them in the top center section of the toolbar on your screen abbreviated as **B** for bold, *I* for italics, and U for underline.

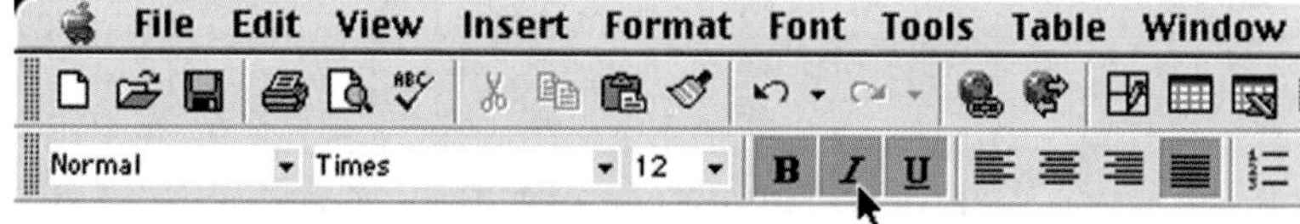

Here's one more suggestion—**color.** If you have access to a color printer, you may want to consider using colored type to set your headings apart from the rest of the body copy. Red, blue, or other dark colors work best. Avoid yellow or other light shades that might fade out and be difficult to read.

Like choosing fonts, the trick with applying type sizes, styles, and colors is to use them sparingly and consistently throughout your work. In other words, all the body copy should be in one style and size of type, all the headings should be in another, and so on. If you pepper your copy with too many fonts, type sizes, styles, and colors, your final product could end up looking more like a patchwork quilt than a polished report.

Layout Help from Your Computer

One way to organize the information in your document is to use one of the preset page layouts provided by your word-processing program. All you have to do is write your document using capital letters for main headings, and uppercase and lowercase letters for subheadings. Set the headings apart from the body copy with returns. Then open the Format menu and click the Autoformat heading. Your copy will probably look like this:

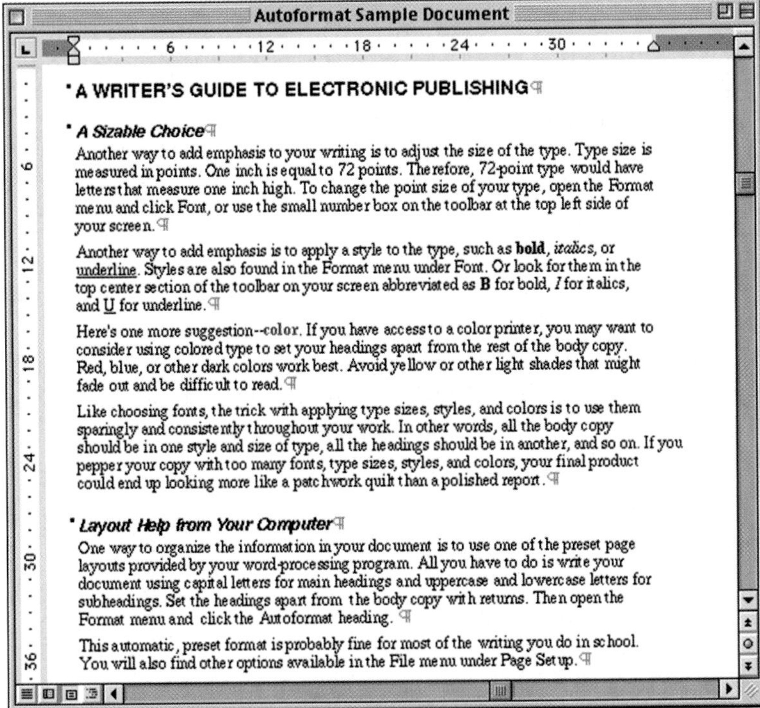

Autoformat Sample Document

A WRITER'S GUIDE TO ELECTRONIC PUBLISHING

A Sizable Choice

Another way to add emphasis to your writing is to adjust the size of the type. Type size is measured in points. One inch is equal to 72 points. Therefore, 72-point type would have letters that measure one inch high. To change the point size of your type, open the Format menu and click Font, or use the small number box on the toolbar at the top left side of your screen.

Another way to add emphasis is to apply a style to the type, such as **bold**, *italics*, or underline. Styles are also found in the Format menu under Font. Or look for them in the top center section of the toolbar on your screen abbreviated as **B** for bold, *I* for italics, and U for underline.

Here's one more suggestion--color. If you have access to a color printer, you may want to consider using colored type to set your headings apart from the rest of the body copy. Red, blue, or other dark colors work best. Avoid yellow or other light shades that might fade out and be difficult to read.

Like choosing fonts, the trick with applying type sizes, styles, and colors is to use them sparingly and consistently throughout your work. In other words, all the body copy should be in one style and size of type, all the headings should be in another, and so on. If you pepper your copy with too many fonts, type sizes, styles, and colors, your final product could end up looking more like a patchwork quilt than a polished report.

Layout Help from Your Computer

One way to organize the information in your document is to use one of the preset page layouts provided by your word-processing program. All you have to do is write your document using capital letters for main headings and uppercase and lowercase letters for subheadings. Set the headings apart from the body copy with returns. Then open the Format menu and click the Autoformat heading.

This automatic, preset format is probably fine for most of the writing you do in school. You will also find other options available in the File menu under Page Setup.

This automatic, preset format is probably fine for most of the writing you do in school. You'll also find other options available in the File menu under Page Setup. For example, you can create a document in the size of large or small index cards for note taking.

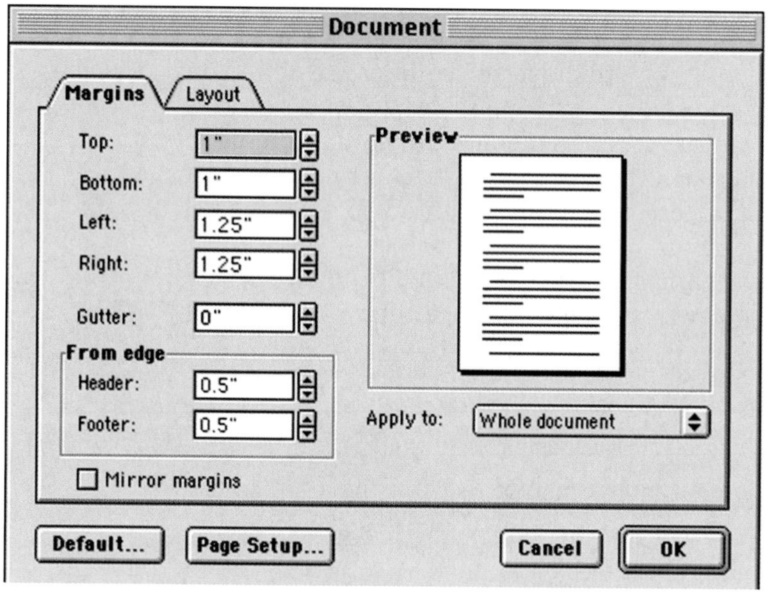

Here you can change the margins and indicate where you want to place headers and footers. **Headers** and **footers** are descriptive titles that automatically appear in a preset position at the top or bottom of each page without having to retype them each time. For example, you may wish to add the title of your project and the date as a header and page numbers as a footer.

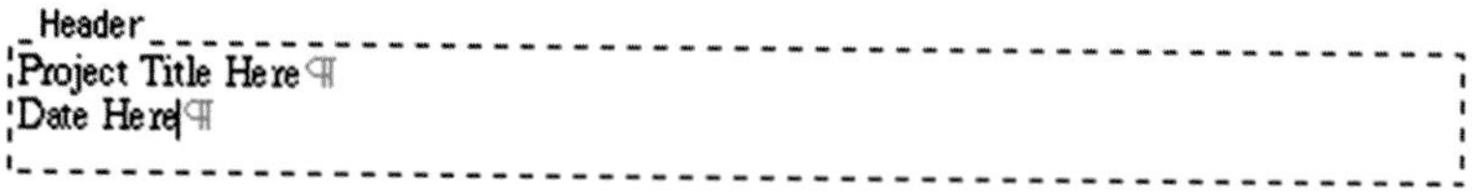

To insert a header or footer, go to View and click on Header and Footer. Note that page numbers may also be inserted by way of the Insert option on your menu bar.

Let's Get Graphic

The old saying "A picture is worth a thousand words" is particularly true when it comes to spicing up papers and reports. Desktop publishing programs (such as Adobe PhotoDeluxe Home Edition, Macromedia FreeHand, Microsoft PhotoDraw, and

Microsoft PowerPoint) give you the ability to include photographs, illustrations, and charts in your work that can express your ideas more clearly and concisely than words alone.

The key to using graphics effectively is to make sure each one conveys a message of importance. Don't use graphics just for decoration. Be sure they add something meaningful, or you'll actually take away from your written message.

Drawings Many paint and draw programs allow you to create or import (bring in from another program) an illustration into your document. Drawings can help illustrate concepts that are difficult to describe, such as mechanical parts or procedures. Cartoons can also add a nice touch. If you use them sparingly, they can lighten up an otherwise dry, technical report.

Clip Art Another kind of drawing is called **clip art**. These simple, black-and-white or color line pictures are often included in desktop publishing or word-processing programs. Pre-drawn clip art usually is not very good for illustrative purposes, but it does work well as graphic icons that can help guide your reader through various parts of a long report.

For example, suppose you are writing a report on the top arts programs in the United States. You might choose the following clip art for each of the sections:

When you introduce the section of your report that deals with music, you might use the music icon like the large size pictured above. Then, in the headers of all the following sections that deal with music, you might use a smaller version of the icon that looks like this:

Using clip art as icons in this way lets your readers know at a glance which part of the report they are reading.

Charts and Graphs If your project, or part of your project, deals with comparing numbers and statistics, one of the best ways to communicate this information is by using charts and graphs. Programs such as Microsoft PowerPoint allow you to create bar graphs, pie charts, and line graphs that can communicate fractions, figures, and measurements much more powerfully than written descriptions.

Photographs When you flip quickly through a book or a magazine, what catches your eye? Probably photographs. Most of us are naturally curious and want to see what we are reading about. Photos are the perfect companions to written work. With the widespread availability of digital cameras and scanners, adding photos to your project is an easy and effective way to enhance your content.

Using a digital camera or a scanner, you can load photos directly into your computer. Another option is to shoot photographs with a regular camera, but when you have them developed, request that they be returned to you as "pictures on disc," which you can open on your computer screen.

Photographic images are stored as bits of data in an electronic file. Once you have the photos in your computer, you can use a graphics program such as Adobe PhotoDeluxe Home Edition to manipulate the images in a variety of ways and create amazing visual effects. You can crop, or cut, elements out of the photo, add special filters and colors, combine elements of two different pictures into one—the possibilities are endless.

After you have inserted the edited photo into your document, be careful when you print out your final draft. Standard printers often don't reproduce photographs well. You may want to take your document on disk to a professional printing company and have it printed out on a high-resolution printer to make sure you get the best quality.

Captions and Titles While it's true that a single photo can say a great deal, some pictures still need a little explanation in order to have the strongest impact on your reader. Whenever you include an illustration or photograph in a document, also include a simple caption or title for each image.

Add captions in a slightly smaller type size than the body copy and preferably in a sans serif typeface. Use the caption to add information that isn't immediately apparent in the photo. If there are people in the picture, tell us who they are. If the photo features an odd-looking structure, tell us what it is. Be smart with your captions. Don't tell the reader the obvious. Give him or her a reason to read your caption.

For example, suppose you are doing a report about Mt. Everest and you include a dramatic photograph of its snowy peak.

WEAK CAPTION	The summit of Mt. Everest is very high and treacherous.
STRONG CAPTION	At its summit, Mt. Everest soars to 29,028 feet, making it the tallest mountain in the world.

Stand-Alone Graphics Occasionally you may include well-known graphics or logos in a story or report. These graphics convey powerful messages on their own and don't require captions. Examples of these logos or symbols include:

You may also want to design your own logos and scan them into your work.

Nonprint Media—Audio and Video

The world we live in is becoming increasingly multimedia-savvy. The power of the spoken word and the visual image is widely recognized for the impact it carries. Many businesses rely on multimedia presentations to market their products or convey messages to consumers and employees. Exciting opportunities exist for people who can produce clear, concise messages in audio and visual formats.

Pre-Production—Put It on Paper First

Although the final presentation of your subject material may be an audiotape or a video, your project needs to begin on paper first. When you write down your ideas, you do four things:

- Organize your thoughts.
- Narrow your focus.
- Isolate the main messages.
- Identify possible production problems.

Grabbing a tape recorder or camcorder and then running off to record your project is a sure-fire way to create an unorganized mess. This helter-skelter collection of shots and sound bites probably takes hours longer to unravel and fix than if you had taken the time to plan your production in the first place. Resist the urge to record immediately! You will be glad you did.

Concept Outline The first task is to write a short, one-page document that describes the basic idea of the project. Ideally this should be three paragraphs—one paragraph each describing the beginning, the middle, and the end. Do not go forward until you have clearly identified these three important parts of your project.

Brief Next ask yourself, "What is the purpose of this video or audiotape? Who is the audience? What is the result I hope to achieve when this group of people sees or hears my presentation? Do I want them to be informed about something? Motivated to do something? Excited about something?" Write three paragraphs that describe the point of your project: how it will be used, who the intended audience is, and what you hope to achieve with the presentation. This is your **brief**.

Treatment The next phase of the writing process fleshes out the ideas you expressed in your outline and brief. The **treatment** is several pages long. It contains descriptions of the characters, dialogue, and settings, and describes the presentation in order, scene by scene. Include in your treatment descriptions of the mood and the tone of your piece. Is it upbeat and whimsical, or dark and scary? If your project is a video, set the stage by describing the overall look and feel of the production.

Script Now you are ready to go to script. The **script** is the blueprint for your production, similar to a blueprint for a house. Everything that is mentioned in the script is what will wind up in the audio recording or on the screen. On the other hand, anything that is left out of the script will likely be overlooked and omitted from the final production.

For an audio recording, the script contains all narration, dialogue, music, and sound effects. For a videotape, it contains all of these elements plus descriptions of the characters, any sets, props, or costumes, plus all camera shots and movements, special visual effects, and onscreen titles or graphic elements. In short the audio script includes everything that is heard, and the video script covers everything that is seen and heard.

Storyboard For video productions, it's also helpful to create **storyboards**—simple frame-by-frame sketches with explanatory notes jotted underneath—that paint a visual picture of what the video will look like from start to finish.

The final stages of pre-production include putting together all of the elements you will need before you begin recording your audiotape or shooting your video. Here's a general checklist.

Pre-Production Checklist

Audiotape Tasks

- ✓ Arrange for audio recording equipment
- ✓ Cast narrator/actors
- ✓ Find music (secure permission)
- ✓ Arrange for sound effects
- ✓ Set up recording schedule
- ✓ Coordinate all cast and crew
- ✓ Arrange for transportation if needed
- ✓ Rehearse all voice talent

Videotape Tasks

- ✓ Arrange for video equipment (including lighting and sound recording equipment)
- ✓ Cast narrator/host/actors
- ✓ Find music (secure permission)
- ✓ Arrange for sound/visual effects
- ✓ Set up shooting schedule
- ✓ Coordinate all cast and crew
- ✓ Arrange for transportation if needed
- ✓ Set up shooting locations (secure permission)
- ✓ Arrange for costumes, props, sets
- ✓ Arrange for make-up if needed
- ✓ Rehearse all on-camera talent

Video Production Schedule Tucked into the list of pre-production tasks is "Set up recording/shooting schedule." For videotaping, this means much more than just deciding what day and time you will begin shooting.

During the video production phase of your project, the idea is to shoot everything that your script calls for in the final production. Often the most efficient way to do this is what is called "out-of-sequence" filming. This means that, rather than shoot scenes sequentially (in the order that they appear in the script), you shoot them in the order that is most convenient. Later you will edit them together in the correct order in post-production.

For example, your video might begin and end in the main character's office. Rather than shoot the first office scene, then move the cast and crew to the next location, then later at the end of the day return to the office, it might be easier to shoot both office scenes back-to-back. This will save a great deal of time and effort involved in moving people, lights, and props back and forth.

Lighting may be a factor in the order in which you shoot your scenes. For example, scenes 3, 4, and 7 might take place in the daytime, and scenes 1, 2, 5, and 6 might take place at night. To take into account all of these factors, you will need to plan your shooting schedule very carefully. The difference between a smooth shoot day and chaos is a well thought-out shooting schedule.

Finally, for video or audio recording, it's also a good idea to bring your team together for a pre-production meeting before you begin. This is your chance to have everyone read through the script, go over time schedules, review the responsibilities of each person involved, plus answer any questions or discuss possible problems before you begin rolling tape. Pre-production meetings are worth their weight in gold for reducing stress levels and headaches during production.

Production—We're Rolling!

At last, you've completed all your preparation. Now it's time to roll tape.

Audio Production The better the recording equipment, the higher-quality sound recording you will be able to achieve. The most convenient format for student audio recording is the audiocassette—a high-quality tape in a plastic case that you simply drop inside your cassette recorder.

If you are using an audiocassette recorder, use an external microphone rather than the built-in microphone on the tape recorder for best results. To increase the quality of your production, consider the following suggestions:

- Select a high-quality, low-noise tape stock.
- Choose a quiet place to do your recording. Look for a quiet room with carpeting, soft furniture, and a door you can close firmly. Hang a sign outside the door that says, "Quiet Please—Recording in Progress" so you will not be disturbed in the middle of your session.
- Do a voice check before you begin recording so you know whether the sound level on the recorder is set correctly.
- Lay the script pages out side-by-side to eliminate the rustling sound of turning pages.
- If music is part of your production, cue up the correct cut and practice turning it on and fading the volume up and down at the appropriate parts. Do a sound check on the music volume before you start. Do the same with any sound effects.

Video Production As with audio recording, there are a number of different formats to choose from for video recording.

Here are some common video formats.

Video 8	A format sometimes referred to as a camcorder, the Video 8 shoots 8-millimeter videotape. It produces a good quality picture and hi-fi sound. With special cable attachments, you can play the tape back through your VCR or television.
High 8	A compact and lightweight format, High 8 is much more expensive than Video 8, but the quality of sound and picture is excellent. High 8 video can be played back on a TV or VCR using special cable attachments.
Betacam	This professional standard video delivers top-quality sound and pictures. Most news crews shoot Betacam video. Betacam tape can be played back only on a Betacam tape deck.

Ideally you will have ironed out issues regarding shooting when you wrote your production schedule, back in the pre-production phase. This will leave you free during production to focus on your production values, your camera shots, and your actors' performances.

Production value is another way of saying how polished and professional your project turns out. There are many ways to increase the production value of your presentation. Some of the easiest ways include the following:

- Use a tripod to keep the camera steady. Nothing screams "Amateur!" louder than shaky, hand-held camera shots. If you can't get your hands on a tripod, lean against something sturdy, such as a tree or the side of a car, to keep your subjects from bouncing around in the frame.
- Use sufficient light. If your audience can't see what's happening, they will quickly lose interest in your show. The best way to light a subject is from one side at a 45-degree angle with the light

shining in a downward direction. Supplement this with a slightly less powerful light from the other side and even from behind your subject to avoid unsightly shadows.

- Check your focus frequently. Don't wait until your entire production is nearly finished to check whether the shots are clear. Sometimes the manual focus on some cameras is more reliable than the auto-focus feature. Experiment with your camera using both methods *before* your shoot day to see which gives you better results.
- Use an external microphone. The built-in microphone on the camera will only pick up sounds that are very close by. If you want to record sounds that are farther off, try using an external microphone that can plug into the video recorder. Poor sound quality can greatly lessen the production values of your video.

Next think about *how* you shoot your video. One way to keep your production lively and interesting is to vary your camera shots. The next time you watch a television show or movie, keep a little notepad handy. Every time you notice a different camera move or cut, make a hash mark on your notepad. At the end of 15 minutes, count the hash marks. You may be amazed to find out how many shots were used!

To hold the interest of your audience, use a variety of camera shots, angles, and moves. Check your local library or media center for good books on camera techniques that describe when and how to use various shots—from long shots to close-ups, from low angles to overhead shots. As a rule, every time you change camera shots, change your angle slightly as well. This way when the shots are edited together, you can avoid accidentally putting two nearly identical shots side-by-side, which creates an upsetting jarring motion called a "jump cut."

Do some research on framing techniques as well to make sure you frame your subjects properly and avoid cutting people's heads off on the screen. Also try to learn about ways to move the camera in order to keep your audience eager and interested.

For example, three common but effective camera moves include panning, tracking, and zooming. **Panning** means moving the camera smoothly from one side of the scene to another. Panning works well in an establishing shot to help direct your audience to the setting where the action takes place.

Tracking means moving the camera from one place to another in a smooth action as well, but in tracking the camera parallels the action, such as moving alongside a character as he or she walks down the street. It's called tracking because in professional filmmaking, the camera and the operator are rolled forward or backward on a small set of train tracks alongside the actor or actress.

Zooming means moving the camera lens forward or back, rather than the camera. By touching the zoom button, you can move in on a small detail that you'd like to emphasize, or you can pull out to reveal something.

The important factor in any kind of camera move is to keep the action moving and, in most cases, slow and steady. But, use camera movement sparingly. You want to keep your audience eager and interested, not dizzy and sick!

Another good way to keep your presentation moving is to use frequent cuts. While the actual cuts will be done during post-production, you need to plan for them in production. Professional filmmakers use the word *coverage* for making sure they have enough choices for shots. You can create coverage for your production by planning shots such as the following:

establishing shot	This shot sets up where the action of the story will take place. For example, if your story takes place inside a classroom, you may want to begin with an establishing shot of the outside of the school.

reaction shot	It's a good idea to get shots of all on-camera talent even if one person does not have any dialogue but is listening to, or reacting to, another character. This gives you the chance to break away from the character who is speaking to show how his or her words are affecting other people in the scene.
cutaway shot	The cutaway shot is a shot of something that is not included in the original scene, but is somehow related to it. Cutaways are used to connect two subjects. For example, the first shot may be of a person falling off a boat. The second shot could be a cutaway of a shark swimming deep below the water.

If you are adventurous, you may want to try some simple special effects. For instance, dry ice can create smoke effects. You can also have your actors freeze; then stop the camera, remove an object from the set, and restart the camera. This technique will make objects seem to disappear as if by magic. Other effects can be achieved using false backdrops, colored lights, and filters. Just use your imagination.

Post-Production—The Magic of Editing

Without access to a sound mixing board, it's difficult to do post-production on audio recordings. However, there's a great amount of creative control you can have over your video project in post-production using your camera and your VCR.

Once all of your videotaping is complete, it's time to create the **final cut**—that is, your choice of the shots you wish to keep and the shots you wish to discard. The idea, of course, is to keep only your very best shots in the final production. Be choosy and select the footage with only the best composition, lighting, focus, and performance to tell your story.

There are three basic editing techniques.

in-camera editing	This process means you edit as you shoot. In other words, you need to shoot all your scenes in the correct sequence and in the proper length that you want them to appear. This is the most difficult editing process because it leaves no room for error.
insert editing	In insert editing you transfer all your footage to a new video. Then, on your VCR, you record over any scenes that you don't want with scenes that you do want in the final version.
assemble editing	This process involves electronically copying your shots from the original source tape in your camera onto a new blank tape, called the edited master, in the order that you want the shots to appear. This method provides the most creative control.

In the best scenario, it's ideal to have three machines available—the camera, a recording VCR for transferring images, and a post-production machine or computer program for adding effects. These effects might include a dissolve from one shot to another instead of an abrupt cut. A **dissolve** is the soft fading of one shot into another. Dissolves are useful when you wish to give the impression that time has passed between two scenes. A long, slow dissolve that comes up from black into a shot, or from a shot down to black, is called a **fade** and is used to open or close a show.

In addition to assembling the program, post-production is the time to add titles to the opening of your program and credits to the end of the show. Computer programs, such as Adobe Premiere, can help you do this. Some cameras are also equipped to generate titles. If you don't have any electronic means to produce titles, you can always mount your camera on a high tripod and focus it downward on well-lit pages of text and graphics placed on the floor. Then edit the text frames into the program.

Post-production is also the time to add voiceover narration and music. Voiceovers and background music should be recorded separately and then edited into the program on a separate sound track once the entire show is edited together. Video editing programs for your computer, such as Adobe Premiere, allow you to mix music and voices with your edited video. Some VCRs will also allow you to add sound tracks.

After post-production editing, your video production is ready to present to your audience.

Publishing on the World Wide Web

The World Wide Web is an exciting part of the Internet where you can visit thousands of Websites and communicate with other people all over the world via E-mail. You can also become a part of the exciting Web community by building and publishing a Website of your own.

Scoping Out Your Site

The Web is a unique medium with distinctive features that make it different from any other form of communication. The Web offers the following.

- universal access to everyone
- interactive communication
- the ability to use photographs, illustrations, animation, sound, and video
- unlimited space
- unlimited branching capabilities
- the ability to link your site with other Websites

If you are going to publish on the Web, it makes sense to take advantage of all of these features. In other words, it's possible to take any written composition, save it in a format that can be displayed in a Web browser, upload it to a server, and leave it at that. But how interesting is it to look at a solid page of text on your computer screen?

Just like planning a video, you need to plan your Website. Don't just throw text and graphics together up on a screen. The idea is to make your site interesting enough that visitors will want to stay, explore, and come back to your site again—and that takes thought and planning.

Back to the Drawing Board

Again, you need to capture your thoughts and ideas on paper before you publish anything. Start with a summary that states the purpose of your Website and the audience you hope to attract. Describe in a paragraph the look and feel you think your site will need in order to accomplish this purpose and hold your audience's attention.

Make a list of the content you plan to include in your Website. Don't forget to consider any graphics, animation, video, or sound you may want to include.

Next, go on a World Wide Web field trip. Ask your friends and teachers for the URLs of their favorite Websites. URL stands for Uniform Resource Locator. Visit these sites and bookmark the ones you like. Then ask yourself, "Do I like this site? Why or why not?" Determine which sites are visually appealing to you and why. Which sites are easy to navigate, and why? Print out the pages you like best, and write notes on your reactions.

On the other hand, which sites are boring and why? Print out a few of these pages as well, and keep notes on how you feel about them. Chances are the sites you like best will have clean, easy-to-read layouts, be well written, contain visually stimulating graphic elements, and have understandable **interfaces** that make it simple to find your way around.

One sure kiss of death for any Website is long, continuous blocks of text. Scrolling through page after page of text is extremely boring. Plan to break up long passages of information into manageable sections. What will be the various sections of your site? Will there be separate sections for editorial content? News? Humor? Feedback? What sections will be updated periodically and how often?

Pick up your drawing pencil and make a few rough sketches. How do you picture the "home" page of your site? What will the icons and buttons look like? Then give careful thought to how the pages will connect to each other, starting with the home page. Your plan for connecting the pages is called a **site map.**

Because the Web is an interactive medium, navigation is critical. Decide how users will get from one page to another. Will you put in a navigation bar across the top of the page or down the side? Will there be a top or home page at the beginning of each section?

Once you have planned the content, organized your material into sections, and designed your navigation system, you are ready to begin creating Web pages.

Planning Your Pages

To turn text into Web pages, you need to translate the text into a special language that Web browsers can read.

- You can use the Save As HTML feature in the File menu of most word-processing programs. HTML stands for Hypertext Markup Language.
- You can import your text into a Web-building software program and add the code yourself, if you know how.
- You can use a software program such as Adobe PageMill that does the work for you. Web-building software programs are referred to as WYSIWYG (pronounced "Wiz-E-Wig"), which stands for What You See Is What You Get.

Web-building software also allows you to create links to other Web pages using a simple process called **drag and drop.** Be sure to read the directions that come with your software package for complete instructions.

Putting It All Together

Writing for the Web is different from writing for print. The Web is a fast medium. It's about experiences, not study time, so write accordingly. Keep your messages concise and to the point. Use short, punchy sentences. Break up your copy with clever subheads. Try not to exceed 500 to 600 words in any single article on any one page.

Compose your Web copy on a standard word-processing program. This will give you access to your formatting tools and spell-check features. Following the directions of your Web-building software, you can then import the completed text into the software program for placement on your Web page.

Next you will want to lay out your Web page and flow the text around some interesting graphics. Be sure to include blank space on the page as well. Blank space lets your page "breathe" and makes for a much more inviting experience.

You can use a variety of images on your Website, including charts, graphs, photos, clip art, and original illustrations. Collect graphics for the Web in exactly the same way you would get graphics for any desktop publishing project—scan in images, use a digital camera, or create your own graphics using a graphics software program.

You can also add audio files and video files (referred to as QuickTime Video) to your Website. These are fun and interesting additions. However, there are two drawbacks—audio and video files are time-consuming to prepare and take a long time for the user to load. Also, audio quality can be quite good on the Internet, but full-motion video is still not at the broadcast-quality level most people have come to expect.

As an alternative to video, consider animated graphics. Animated graphics are much easier to create using graphics software programs. These programs also allow you to compress the animations so that they load much faster than video files and still run smoothly on screen.

If you'd like to learn more about adding audio and video features, as well as graphics, to your Web pages, visit http://msc.pangea.org/tutorials/www/cap_5-eng.htm.

Going Live

Once all your pages are put together you are ready to go live on the World Wide Web, right? Not quite.

Before you upload your new Website, it's a good idea to test all your pages first, using common Web browsers such as Netscape's Navigator or Microsoft's Internet Explorer—browsers your visitors are likely to use. Open your pages on these browsers and look at them closely. Do the text and graphics appear the way you had designed them? Are all the page elements fitting neatly into the screen space, or do you need to tweak the copy or graphics a little to make them fit better?

Test all links on your page. Click on every page and be sure that it takes you to the site you originally intended. Click on all your navigation elements and buttons. Is everything working the way it's supposed to work? Make any corrections on your home or classroom computer before uploading your Website to a host server and going live to the world.

Your Web-building software program has built-in features that make uploading and adding files to your Website a snap. In fact, some of this software is even available free on the Internet and is easy to download right onto your home or classroom computer.

For more information on how to build and launch your own Website, check the Web. You'll find some great tips at http://www.hotwired.com/webmonkey/kids.

This Website even features a guided lesson plan called "Webmonkey for Kids" with step-by-step directions on how to create your own site. It also has information about useful software programs that schools and other educational institutions can download for free.

Here's one more shortcut to building a Website. If you or your school already has an Internet Service Provider (ISP), you may be entitled to a free Website as part of your service package. In fact, if you already have an E-mail address for correspondence, this address can be changed slightly to serve as the URL address of your Website. Call your ISP and ask about Website services included in your sign-up.

Finally, beware of small errors that can occur when you transmit your Website material to the Web. As soon as you have finished uploading your Website, open your browser, enter the URL address, and take your new site out for a test drive. Click on all your navigational buttons, links, animations, or any other multimedia features. Check to make sure all the pages are there and everything looks the way you planned it.

Does everything check out? Great. Now all you have to do is send an E-mail to everyone you know and invite each person to visit your brand new Website!

A Writer's Guide to Using the Internet

Have you heard people use the word *cyberspace* or the phrase *Information Superhighway?* These terms refer to the Internet—an intricate communication system made up of hundreds of thousands of computers all over the world that can "talk" to one another.

The Internet has been around for several decades. It started as a government project in 1969, when a group of scientists and engineers connected the computers of four universities. This connection gave them the ability to share research information by sending it back and forth to each other using their computers.

There was only one problem—the information was not organized in any way! Imagine if you went to the library to do some research for a school report and all the books were just piled together in the middle of the floor. How would you find anything?

The next step was to find a way that people could search through the Internet to find specific information. Over the next few years, several different methods were developed. One of the best is still the most popular search system used today. It's called the World Wide Web.

The Web is a network of computers *within* all of the computers that make up the Internet. This special network can deliver to your computer screen all kinds of information that you would find in books—text, photographs, and illustrations. The Web can also deliver multimedia content—sound clips (music and voice), animation (cartoons), and video.

Best of all, like the Internet, the World Wide Web comes over the same communication lines into personal computers all over the globe—including yours!

How Does the Internet Work?

The Internet is made up of literally thousands of networks all linked together around the globe. Each network consists of a group of computers that are connected to one another to exchange information. If one of these computers or networks fails, the information simply bypasses the disabled system and takes another route through a different network.

No one "owns" the Internet, nor is it managed in a central place. No agency regulates or censors the information on the Internet. Anyone can publish information on the Internet as he or she wishes.

In fact, the Internet offers such a vast wealth of information and experiences that sometimes it's described as the *Information Superhighway*. So how do you "get on" this highway? It's easy. Once you have a computer, a modem, and a telephone or cable line, all you need is a connection to the Internet.

The Cyberspace Connection

A company called an Internet Service Provider (ISP) connects your computer to the Internet. Examples of ISPs that provide direct access are AT&T, Microsoft Network, MediaOne, and Netcom. You can also get on the Internet indirectly through companies such as America Online (AOL), Prodigy, and CompuServe.

ISPs charge a flat monthly fee for their service. Unlike the telephone company, once you pay the monthly ISP fee, there are no long-distance charges for sending or receiving information on the Internet—no matter where your information is coming from, or going to, around the world! Once you are connected to the Information Super Highway, all you have to do is learn how to navigate it.

Alphabet Soup—Making Sense of All Those Letters!

Like physical highways the Information Superhighway has road signs that help you find your way around. These road signs are expressed in a series of letters that can seem confusing at first. You've already seen some of these different abbreviations—ISP and AOL. How do you make sense out of all these letters? Relax. It's not as complicated as it looks.

Each specific group of information on the World Wide Web is called a **Website** and has its own unique address. Think of it as a separate street address of a house in your neighborhood. This address is called the URL, which stands for Uniform Resource Locator. It's a kind of shorthand for where the information is located on the Web.

Here's a typical URL: **http://www.bkenglish.com.**

All addresses, or URLs, for the World Wide Web begin with **http://**. This stands for HyperText Transfer Protocol and is a programming description of how the information is being exchanged.

The next three letters are easy—**www.** They let you know that you're on the World Wide Web. The next part of the URL—**bkenglish**—is the name of the site you want to visit. And the last three letters, in this case **com**, indicate that this Website is sponsored by a commercial company. Here are other common endings of URLs you will find:

- "org" is short for organization, as in http://www.ipl.org, which is the URL of the Website for the Internet Public Library.
- "edu" stands for education, as in the Web address for the Virtual Reference Desk, http://thorplus.lib.purdue.edu/reference/index.html. This site features online dictionaries, telephone books, and other reference guides.
- "gov" represents government-sponsored Websites, such as http://www.whitehouse.gov, the Website for the White House in Washington, D.C.

To get to a Website, you use an interface called a **browser**. Two popular browsers are Netscape's Navigator and Microsoft's Internet Explorer. A browser is like a blank form where you fill in the information you are looking for. If you know the URL of the Website you want to explore, all you have to do is type it in the area marked Location, click Enter on your keyboard, and wait for the information to be delivered to your computer screen.

There are many other ways to find information on the Web. We'll talk more about these methods later in this guide.

Basic Internet Terminology

Here are some of the most frequently used words you will hear associated with the Internet.

address The unique code given to information on the Internet. This may also refer to an E-mail address.

bookmark A tool that lets you store your favorite URL addresses, allowing you one-click access to your favorite Web pages without retyping the URL each time.

browser Application software that supplies a graphic, interactive way to search, find, view, and manage information on the Internet.

cyberspace The collective realm of computer-aided communication.

download The transfer of programs or data stored on a remote computer to a storage device on your personal computer.

E-mail Electronic mail that can be sent all over the world from one computer to another.

FAQs The abbreviation for Frequently Asked Questions. This is a great resource to get information when visiting a new Website.

flaming	Using mean or abusive language in cyberspace. Flaming is considered to be in extremely poor taste and may be reported to your ISP.
home page	The start-up page of a Website.
keyword	A simplified term that serves as a subject reference when doing a search.
link	Short for *Hyperlink*. A link is a connection between one piece of information and another.
Net	Short for *Internet*.
netiquette	The responsible and considerate way for a user to conduct himself or herself on the Internet.
network	A system of interconnected computers.
online	To "be online" means to be connected to the Internet via a live modem connection.
real time	Information received and processed (or displayed) as it happens.
search engine	A computer program that locates documents based on keywords that the user enters.
spam	Electronic junk mail.
surf	A casual reference to browsing on the Internet. To "surf the Web" means to spend time discovering and exploring new Websites.
Website	A page of information or a collection of pages that is being electronically published from one of the computers in the World Wide Web.

Why Use the Internet?

By the end of the 1990s, the Internet had experienced incredible growth. An estimated 196 million people were using the Internet worldwide, spending an average of 8.8 hours a week online. By 2003, this number is estimated to increase to more than 500 million people who will be surfing the Web. Why? What does the Internet offer that makes so many people want to go online? And what are the advantages of using the Internet for writers in particular?

The World at Your Fingertips

The Internet offers an amazing amount of knowledge and experiences at the touch of your computer keyboard. For writers it's a great way to get ideas and do in-depth research. You'll find thousands upon thousands of Websites offering a mind-boggling array of subjects. You can explore the Web as a way to jumpstart your creativity or tap into unlimited information.

The Internet also lets you communicate with experts whom you might not otherwise have access to. You can connect with other people all over the world who have the same interests you do—maybe even find a new writing partner.

In short, the Internet is an invaluable tool for creating great writing. In this section we'll explore just some of these exciting advantages.

Just an E Away

One of the most popular features of the Internet is electronic mail, or E-mail for short. Unlike traditional mail (nicknamed "snail mail" by tech-savvy people), E-mail messages are practically instantaneous. It's so convenient that by 1999, 46 percent of Americans were sending or receiving E-mail every day.

E-mail is a fun and easy way to keep in touch with friends and relatives. You can send anything from a lengthy family newsletter to a quick question or "news flash." E-mail is also appropriate for formal correspondence, such as requesting information from a museum. In this case it's a good idea to follow up with a hard copy in the traditional mail.

Have you ever teamed up with another student or maybe a group of students in your class to work on a project together? With E-mail you can collaborate with other students in other states or even other countries. Many schools are taking advantage of E-mail to pair a class in for example, Houston, Texas, to work on a cooperative project with a class in Seattle, Washington, or maybe as far away as Sydney, Australia.

For writers E-mail is an especially valuable tool. It's a great way to communicate with people who are experts in their fields. Many times, well-known authorities, who are difficult to reach by phone or in person, will respond to questions and requests for information via E-mail. It comes in particularly handy when the person you would like to communicate with lives in another part of the world. It eliminates the expense of long-distance phone calls plus awkward problems due to different time zones.

An easy way to locate experts in a particular area is to visit Websites about that subject. Many times these Websites will list an E-mail address where you can send questions.

Another way writers can use E-mail is to gather information and make contacts. E-mail queries can be sent out to many people in a single click by simply adding multiple addresses to the same message. For example, suppose you are writing a paper about raising exotic fish. With one click you can send out an E-mail to 30 friends and associates that asks, "Do you know anyone who has exotic fish?" Chances are at least a few of the people you ask will have one or two contacts they can provide—and think how much faster corresponding by E-mail is than making 30 phone calls!

You can learn more about sending E-mail on pages C560–C564.

Picture This

Whatever you write will probably have more impact if it's accompanied by some sort of visual. Many sites on the World Wide Web offer photos, illustrations, and clip art that can be downloaded and integrated into your work. Sometimes there are fees for using this artwork, but many times it's free.

Another way to illustrate your writing is to take your own photos, turn them into electronic images, and integrate them into your work. One way to do this is to use a digital camera and download the images directly into your computer. If you don't have a digital camera, you can also take pictures using a regular camera. When you have the photos developed, ask the developer if you can have them returned to you either on disc or via E-mail.

Another option is to use a scanner, a device that looks somewhat like a copy machine. You place the photo on the glass, and the image is scanned into your computer.

Once you have an image in your computer, you can add it to a report or article in a number of ways—for example, on the cover page as a graphic or border design. There are even a number of photo-editing programs available that give you the ability to manipulate images in all sorts of creative ways.

Sometimes a graph or chart can help you illustrate your point more clearly. Using a program such as Microsoft PowerPoint, you can create all kinds of graphs and tables that you can incorporate into your writing project for extra emphasis.

One of the best advantages of photos, tables, charts, and artwork that are stored as electronic images is that you can also send them as E-mail attachments. Imagine—with a click of a button, you have numerous options.

- Share photos of your last soccer game instantly with friends and relatives anywhere in the world.
- Take your pen pals on a "virtual" tour of your home, school, or neighborhood.
- Swap pictures and graphs with writing partners across the globe and double your resources.

Online Help

Hundreds of Websites can help you with specific subjects you are probably studying right now. These sites cover a variety of topics in English, social studies, math, science, foreign languages, and more. Here's just a tiny sample of some of the sites waiting to help you:

- The Guide to Grammar and Writing (http://webster.commnet.edu/HP/pages/darling/grammar.htm)
- The Looney Bin—a light-hearted look at how to improve your study skills (http://www.geocities.com/Athens/3843/index.html)
- The Math Forum—interesting math challenges, featuring the whimsical "Ask Dr. Math" (http://forum.swarthmore.edu/students)
- The Guide to Experimental Science Projects (http://www.isd77.k12.mn.us/resources/cf/SciProjInter.html)
- The Smithsonian Institution—links to sites ranging from Aeronautics to Zoology (http://www.si.edu)

One cautionary note when surfing the Web:

- No matter how tempting, do not give out your name, address, telephone number, or school name to any site that may ask for this information.
- If you sense any inappropriate requests for information, notify your teacher and/or a parent.

Don't Believe Everything You Read

Wow, all this terrific information—just a click away. There's only one problem. Not all of it is credible or accurate.

When you check out a book from the library, a librarian or a committee of educators has already evaluated the book to make sure it's a reliable source of information, but remember, no one owns or regulates the Internet. Just because you read something online, doesn't mean it's true. How can you tell the difference? Here are a few guidelines on how to evaluate an online source.

- **Play the name game**
  First, find out who publishes the site. Does the URL end in ".com" (which means it's a commercial company)? If so, is it a large, reputable company, or one you've never heard of that might just be trying to sell you something? An educational site in which the URL ends in ".edu," such as a college or university, might be a more reliable choice. A site sponsored by a well-known organization with a URL that ends in ".org," such as the American Red Cross (http://www.crossnet.org), would also probably be a credible source.
- **Scope it out**
  Click around the site and get a feel for what it's like. Is the design clean and appealing? Is it easy to get around the site and find information? Are the sections clearly labeled? Does the site accept advertising? If you think the site seems disjointed or disorganized, or you just have a negative opinion of it, listen to your instincts and move on to another one.
- **Says who?**
  Suppose you find an article on the Web that seems chock-full of great information. The next question you need to ask yourself is, "Who is the author? Is the person an acknowledged expert on the subject?" If you don't recognize the author's name, you can do a search

on the Web, using the author's name as the keyword to get more information about him or her.

In some cases, an article won't list any author at all. If you don't find an author's name, be skeptical. A credible site clearly identifies its authors and usually lists the person's professional background and credentials.

- **Is this old news?**
If you are doing research on the pyramids, it's probably all right if the information wasn't posted yesterday. But if you're looking for information in quickly changing fields, such as science and politics, be sure to check the publication date before you accept the data as true.

- **Ask around**
Reliable Websites frequently provide E-mail addresses or links to authors and organizations connected to the content on the site. Send off a quick E-mail to a few of these sources, tell them what you are writing, and ask them: "Is this material accurate?"

Perhaps the best way to find out if the information on any Website or the information in any article (signed or unsigned) is accurate is to check it against another source—and the best source is your local library or media center.

Internet + Media Center = Information Powerhouse!

Although the Internet is a limitless treasure chest of information, remember that it's not catalogued. It can be tricky to locate the information you need, and sometimes that information is not reliable. The library is a well-organized storehouse of knowledge, but it has limited resources. If you use the Internet *and* your local media center, you've got everything you need to create well-researched articles, reports, and papers.

Use the Internet to

- get great ideas for topics to write about;
- gather information about your topic from companies, colleges and universities, and professional organizations;
- connect with recognized experts in your field of interest;
- connect with other people who are interested in the same subject and who can put you in touch with other sources.

Use the Media Center to

- find additional sources of information either in print or online;
- get background information on your topic;
- cross-check the accuracy and credibility of online information and authors.

I Don't Own a Computer

You can still access the Internet even if you don't have your own computer. Many schools have computer labs that are open after school and on weekends. Some schools will even allow students to use these labs even though they are not enrolled at that particular school. Many libraries are also equipped with computers and Internet connections.

Consider taking a computer course after school or even attending a computer camp. You'll find information about these programs listed at the library, the YMCA, and in parenting magazines.

Maybe you have a friend or neighbor with a computer that you can use in exchange for a service you might provide, such as baby-sitting or yard work.

How to Communicate on the Internet

E-mail is a great way of exchanging information with other people on the Internet. Here's how to use this useful form of communication, step-by-step.

Keep in Touch with E-mail

Any writer who has ever used E-mail in his or her work will agree that sending and receiving electronic messages is one of the most useful ways of gathering information and contacts for writing projects. It's fast, inexpensive, and fun!

Once you open your E-mail program, click on the command that says Compose Mail. This will open a new blank E-mail similar to the one pictured below. Next, fill in the blanks.

Type the person's E-mail address here. There is no central listing of E-mail addresses. If you don't have the person's address, the easiest way to get it is to call and ask for it. You can address an E-mail to one or several people, depending on the number of addresses you type in this space.

CC stands for courtesy copy. If you type additional E-mail addresses in this area, you can send a copy of the message to other people.

BCC stands for blind courtesy copy. By typing one or more E-mail addresses here, you can send a copy of the message to others without the original recipient knowing that other people have received the same message. Not all E-mail programs have this feature.

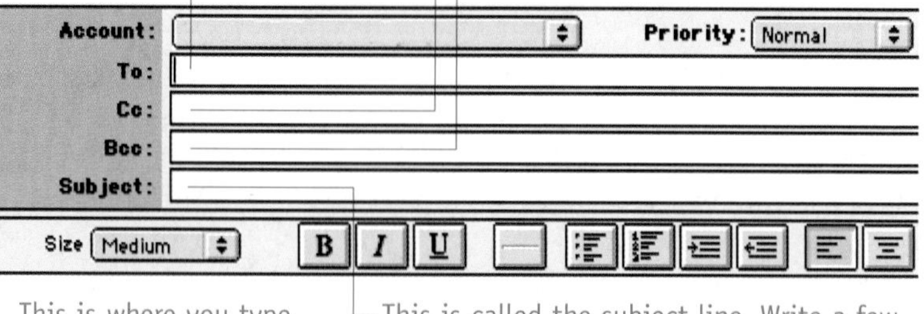

This is where you type your message.

This is called the subject line. Write a few brief words that best describe what your E-mail message is about.

Say It with Style

Like regular letters, E-mail can have a different tone and style depending on to whom you are writing. Usually informal E-mails, such as instant messages (IMs) to close friends, are light, brief, and to the point. In the case of more formal E-mails, such as a request for information from an expert or a museum, it's important to keep the following guidelines in mind.

- Make sure your message is clear and concise.
- Use proper grammar and punctuation.
- Check your spelling. (Some E-mail programs have their own spell-check function—use it!)
- Double-check the person's E-mail address to be sure you've typed it correctly.

Because E-mail is a fast medium designed for quick communication, E-mail users have developed a kind of shorthand that helps them write their messages even faster. Here are a few commonly used abbreviations that you may find in informal E-mail:

COMMON E-MAIL ABBREVIATIONS			
BRB	be right back	BTW	by the way
FYI	for your information	F2F	face-to-face
IMHO	in my humble opinion	IOW	in other words
LOL	laughing out loud	L8R	later
OIC	oh, I see	ROFL	rolling on the floor laughing

Are you sending the E-mail to a friend or relative? If so, would you like to add a touch of fun? Then you may want to explore **emoticons** (also know as "smileys")—little sideways faces made out of keyboard symbols that you add to your messages to express how you feel about something.

COMMON EMOTICONS

:) happy
:-D laughing
;-) winking
:-0 shocked
:-<> bored
:-# my lips are sealed
:(sad
:`-(crying
:-} smirking
:-/ skeptical
*<|:-) Santa Claus
8-) I'm wearing glasses

Attach a Little Something Extra

When you send E-mail, you can send other information along with your message. These are called **attachments.** Depending on your E-mail program's capabilities, you can attach documents, photos, illustrations—even sound and video files. Click Attach, and then find and double-click on the document or file on your computer that you wish to send.

After you have composed your message and added any attachments you want to include, click the Send button. Presto! Your message arrives in the other person's mailbox seconds later, whether that person lives right next door or on the other side of the world. Because there is usually no charge to send E-mail, it's a great way to save money on postage and long-distance telephone calls.

Follow Up

It's important to note that just because you've sent a message, you shouldn't automatically assume that the other person has received it. Internet Service Providers (ISPs) keep all messages that are sent until the recipient requests them. The person you sent your E-mail to might be away from his or her computer or may not check messages regularly.

Also, the Internet is still an imperfect science. From time to time, servers go down or other "hiccups" in electronic transmissions can occur, leaving your message stranded somewhere in cyberspace. If you don't get a reply in a reasonable amount of time, either resend your original E-mail message or call the person and let him or her know that your message is waiting.

You've Got Mail

When someone sends *you* an E-mail message, you have several options:

Reply: Click Reply, and you can automatically send back a new message without having to retype the person's E-mail address. (Be sure you keep a copy of the sender's E-mail address in your address book for future use.)

Forward: Suppose you receive a message that you would like to share with someone else. Click Forward, and you can send a copy of the message, plus include a few of your own comments, to another person.

Print: In some instances you may need to have a paper copy of the E-mail message. For example, if someone E-mails you directions to a party, click Print to take a hard copy of the instructions with you.

Store: Do you want to keep a message to refer to later? Some E-mail programs allow you to create folders to organize stored messages.

Delete: You can discard a message you no longer need just by clicking Delete. It's a good idea to throw messages away regularly to keep them from accumulating in your mailbox.

Mind Your Manners!

As in any social setting, there are a few guidelines to follow when you're talking to people online. This conduct is called **netiquette.** These suggestions will help you be considerate of others in cyberspace.

- Never use harsh or insulting language. This is called **flaming** and is considered rude. Derogatory words swapped back and forth in a continuing argument is called a **flamewar.** Avoid this situation.
- Type your messages using uppercase and lowercase letters. WRITING IN ALL CAPITAL LETTERS IS DIFFICULT TO READ AND IS REFERRED TO AS "SHOUTING."
- Respect other people's ideas and work. Don't forward a message or attach documents written by someone else without first asking the author's permission.
- Don't send spam. **Spamming** refers to sending messages to entire lists of people in your E-mail addresses for the purpose of selling something.
- Respect other people's privacy. The Internet is an enormous public forum, so be careful about what you write and post on the Internet that hundreds or thousands of people might see. Don't use your E-mail to spread rumors or gossip.

How to Do Research on the Internet

The Information Superhighway could be the best research partner you've ever had. It's fast, vast, and always available. But like any other highway, if you don't know your way around, it can also be confusing. It takes time to learn how to navigate the Net and zero in on the information you need. The best thing to do is practice early and often. Don't wait until the night before your paper is due to learn how to do research on the Internet!

Getting Started

Just as there are several different ways to get to your home or school, there are many different ways to arrive at the information you're looking for on the Internet.

CD-ROM Encyclopedia One way to begin is not on the Web at all. You might want to start your search by using a CD-ROM encyclopedia. These CD-ROMs start with an Internet directory. Click the topic that is closest to your subject. This will link you to a site that's likely to be a good starting point. From there, you can link to other resources suggested in the site.

Search Page Another good way to get information is to start on your browser's search page. Type a word or short phrase that describes what you're searching for. Then select the search tool you wish to use. Some of these tools, sometimes referred to as **search engines,** include:

Excite—http://www.excite.com
HotBot—http://www.hotbot.com
InfoSeek—http://www.infoseek.com
Lycos—http://www.lycos.com
WebCrawler—http://www.webcrawler.com
Yahoo!—http://www.yahoo.com

Search services usually list broad categories of subjects, plus they may offer other features, such as "Random Links," or "Top 25 Sites," and customization options. Each one also has a search field. Type in a word or short phrase, called a **keyword,** which describes your area of interest. Then click Search or press the Enter key on your keyboard. Seconds later a list of Websites known as "hits" will be displayed, all containing the word you specified in the search field. Scroll through the list and click the page you wish to view.

So far this sounds simple, doesn't it? The tricky part about doing a search on the Internet is that a single keyword may yield a hundred or more sites. Plus, you may find many topics you don't need. For example, suppose you are writing a science paper about the planet Saturn. If you type the word *Saturn* into the search field, you'll turn up some articles about the planet, but you'll also get articles about NASA's Saturn rockets and Saturn, the automobile company.

Search Smart!

Listed below are a few pointers on how to narrow your search, save time, and search *smart* on the Net.

1. The keyword or words that you enter have a lot to do with the accuracy of your search. Focus your search by adding the word "and" or the + sign followed by another descriptive word. For example, try "Saturn" again, but this time, add "Saturn + space." Adding a third word, "Saturn + space + rings" will narrow the field even more.

2. On the other hand, you can limit unwanted results by specifying information that you do *not* want the search engine to find. If you type "dolphins not football," you will get Websites about the animal that lives in the ocean rather than the football team that uses Miami as its home base.

3. Specify geographical areas using the word "near" between keywords as in "islands near Florida." This lets you focus on specific regions.
4. To broaden your search, add the word "or" between keywords; for example, "sailboats or catamarans."
5. Help the search engine recognize familiar phrases by putting words that go together in quotes such as "Tom and Jerry" or "bacon and eggs."
6. Sometimes the site you come up with is in the ballpark of what you are searching for, but it is not exactly what you need. Skim the text quickly anyway. It may give you ideas for more accurate keywords. There might also be links listed to other sites that are just the right resource you need.
7. Try out different search engines. Each service uses slightly different methods of searching, so you may get different results using the same keywords.
8. Check the spelling of the keywords you are using. A misspelled word can send a search engine in the wrong direction. Also, be careful how you use capital letters. By typing the word *Gold,* some search services will only bring up articles that include the word with a capital *G.*

Saving a Site for Later

You may want to keep a list handy of favorite Websites or sites you are currently using in a project. This will save you time because you can just click on the name of the site in your list and return to that page without having to retype the URL.

Different browsers have different names for this feature. For example, Netscape calls it a **bookmark**, while Microsoft's Internet Explorer calls it **favorites.**

Searching Out a Subject

Suppose you are writing a paper about dinosaurs, specifically Velociraptors—the really smart, agile dinosaurs depicted in the original film *Jurassic Park*. Here's an idea of one way to research this topic.

First, we'll select a search engine. We'll start with InfoSeek—at http://infoseek.go.com/. The first keyword we'll enter is "dinosaurs." The search engine found these sites:

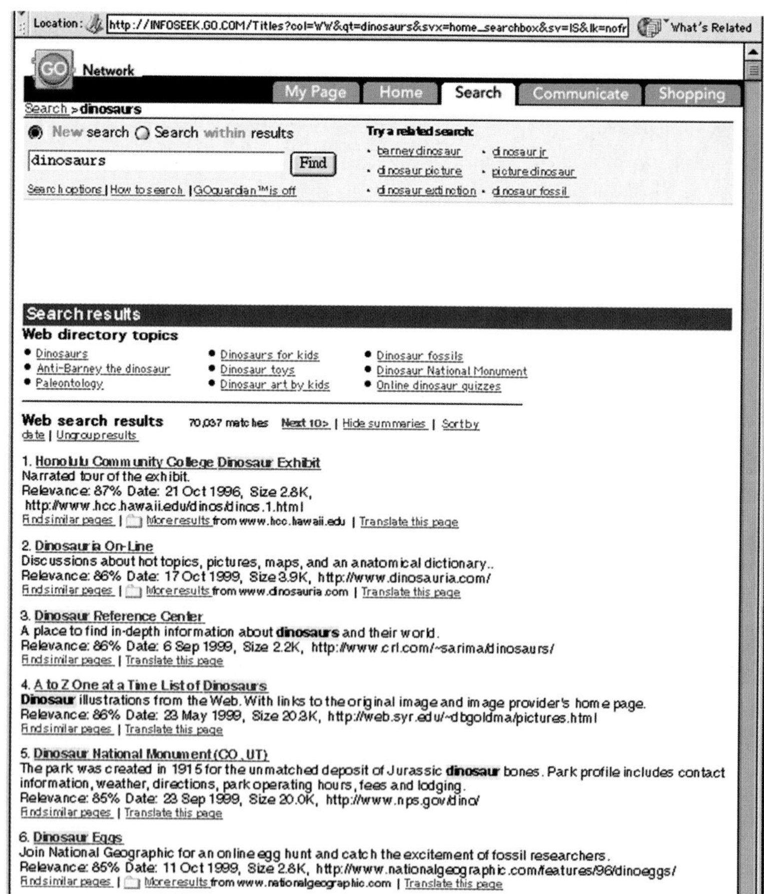

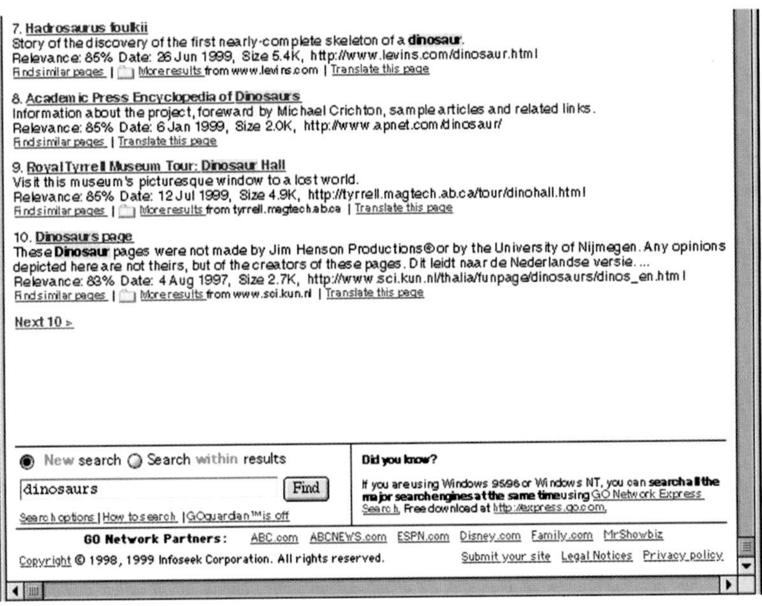

7. Hadrosaurus foulkii
Story of the discovery of the first nearly-complete skeleton of a **dinosaur**.
Relevance: 85% Date: 26 Jun 1999, Size 5.4K, http://www.levins.com/dinosaur.html
Find similar pages | More results from www.levins.com | Translate this page

8. Academic Press Encyclopedia of Dinosaurs
Information about the project, foreward by Michael Crichton, sample articles and related links.
Relevance: 85% Date: 6 Jan 1999, Size 2.0K, http://www.apnet.com/dinosaur/
Find similar pages | Translate this page

9. Royal Tyrrell Museum Tour: Dinosaur Hall
Visit this museum's picturesque window to a lost world.
Relevance: 85% Date: 12 Jul 1999, Size 4.9K, http://tyrrell.magtech.ab.ca/tour/dinohall.html
Find similar pages | More results from tyrrell.magtech.ab.ca | Translate this page

10. Dinosaurs page
These **Dinosaur** pages were not made by Jim Henson Productions® or by the University of Nijmegen. Any opinions depicted here are not theirs, but of the creators of these pages. Dit leidt naar de Nederlandse versie. ...
Relevance: 83% Date: 4 Aug 1997, Size 2.7K, http://www.sci.kun.nl/thalia/funpage/dinosaurs/dinos_en.html
Find similar pages | More results from www.sci.kun.nl | Translate this page

Next 10 >

New search Search within results
dinosaurs Find
Search options | How to search | GOguardian™ is off

Did you know?
If you are using Windows 95/98 or Windows NT, you can **search all the major search engines at the same time** using GO Network Express Search. Free download at http://express.go.com.

GO Network Partners: ABC.com ABCNEWS.com ESPN.com Disney.com Family.com MrShowbiz

Copyright © 1998, 1999 Infoseek Corporation. All rights reserved. Submit your site Legal Notices Privacy policy

Wow! Look at all these sites about dinosaurs. There aren't, however, any specific topics related to Velociraptors. By clicking on the words "next 10" at the bottom of the page, we can get another page of topics to look at.

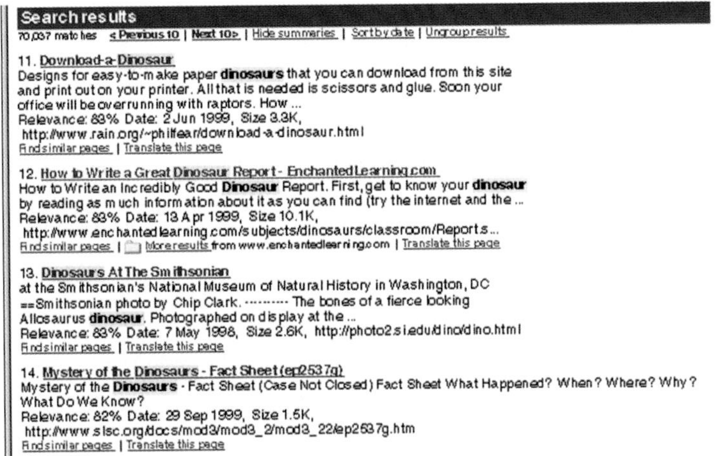

Search results
70,037 matches < Previous 10 | Next 10 > | Hide summaries | Sort by date | Ungroup results

11. Download-a-Dinosaur
Designs for easy-to-make paper **dinosaurs** that you can download from this site and print out on your printer. All that is needed is scissors and glue. Soon your office will be overrunning with raptors. How ...
Relevance: 83% Date: 2 Jun 1999, Size 3.3K,
http://www.rain.org/~philfear/download-a-dinosaur.html
Find similar pages | Translate this page

12. How to Write a Great Dinosaur Report - EnchantedLearning.com
How to Write an Incredibly Good **Dinosaur** Report. First, get to know your **dinosaur** by reading as much information about it as you can find (try the internet and the ...
Relevance: 83% Date: 13 Apr 1999, Size 10.1K,
http://www.enchantedlearning.com/subjects/dinosaurs/classroom/Reports...
Find similar pages | More results from www.enchantedlearning.com | Translate this page

13. Dinosaurs At The Smithsonian
at the Smithsonian's National Museum of Natural History in Washington, DC ==Smithsonian photo by Chip Clark. --------- The bones of a fierce looking Allosaurus **dinosaur**. Photographed on display at the ...
Relevance: 83% Date: 7 May 1998, Size 2.6K, http://photo2.si.edu/dino/dino.html
Find similar pages | Translate this page

14. Mystery of the Dinosaurs - Fact Sheet (ep2537g)
Mystery of the **Dinosaurs** - Fact Sheet (Case Not Closed) Fact Sheet What Happened? When? Where? Why? What Do We Know?
Relevance: 82% Date: 29 Sep 1999, Size 1.5K,
http://www.slsc.org/docs/mod3/mod3_2/mod3_22/ep2537g.htm
Find similar pages | Translate this page

15. Creation, Dinosaurs and thE Flood
Creation Explanation You have questions We have answers Ask your questions about Creation, Evolution, **Dinosaurs**, Noah's Flood here. Creation Science Workshops Seminars, Books and Videos November 11, 1999 ...
Relevance: 82% Date: 6 Oct 1999, Size 13.5K, http://www.sixdaycreation.com/
Find similar pages | Translate this page

16. Guide to Dinosaur Sites in Western Colorado and Eastern Utah
has moved to its new home at http://www.dinosaurweb.com/guide.htm Rocky Mountain West Electronic Publishing 739 Belford Avenue Grand Junction, Colorado 81501 USA 970-243-2431 ...
Relevance: 82% Date: 4 Jun 1999, Size 1.0K, http://www.rmwest.com/dinosaur/guide.htm
Find similar pages | Translate this page

17. The Queensland Museum Explorer
A virtual visit to Queensland's Museum of natural environment and cultural heritage.
Relevance: 82% Date: 26 Dec 1998, Size 1.3K, http://www.qmuseum.qld.gov.au/nature/dinowelcome.html
Find similar pages | Translate this page

18. Dinosaurs
The planet earth is VERY old, about 4,600 million years. (thats a lot of birthday candles!!!). * There was no life at all on earth for millions of years. * The first living things lived in the sea, they were so ...
Relevance: 82% Date: 23 May 1997, Size 6.7K, http://www.oink.demon.co.uk/topics/dinosaur.htm
Find similar pages | Translate this page

19. NMNH Dinosaur Homepage
Click "Welcome" to enter. Scientific illustrations by Frederick Berger
Relevance: 82% Date: 30 Sep 1998, Size 1.2K, http://www.nmnh.si.edu/paleo/dino/
Find similar pages | More results from www.nmnh.si.edu | Translate this page

20. MY DINOSAUR PAGE
Table of Contents General **Dinosaur** Information Specific **Dinosaurs** Museums and Parks Fossils Education General **Dinosaur** Information Barrett's Web Pointers Dino Russ's Lair **Dinosaur** Extinction: The Volcano ...
Relevance: 82% Date: 21 Sep 1999, Size 9.6K, http://www.eagle.ca/~matink/dinosaur.html
Find similar pages | More results from www.eagle.ca | Translate this page

< Previous 10 | Next 10 >

This page has a lot of dinosaur information, too, although there isn't anything specific about Velociraptors here either. But since you are writing a report about dinosaurs, the site "How to Write a Great Dinosaur Report" seems worth checking out.

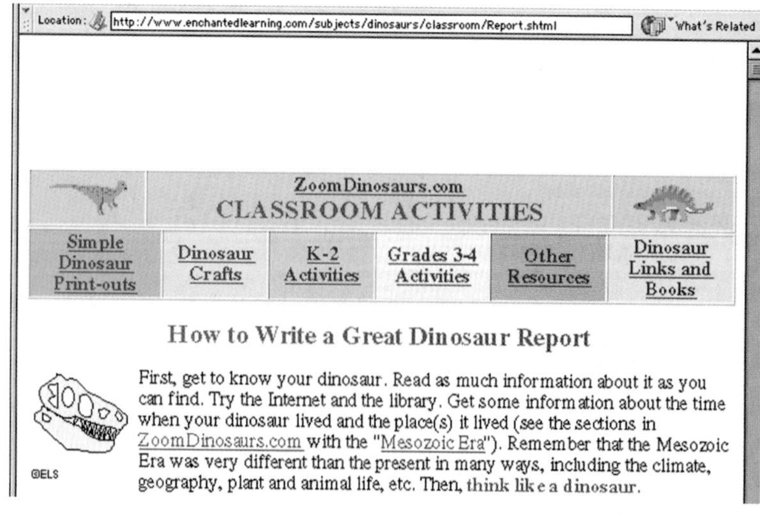

Location: http://www.enchantedlearning.com/subjects/dinosaurs/classroom/Report.shtml
What's Related
ZoomDinosaurs.com
CLASSROOM ACTIVITIES
Simple Dinosaur Print-outs
Dinosaur Crafts
K-2 Activities
Grades 3-4 Activities
Other Resources
Dinosaur Links and Books
How to Write a Great Dinosaur Report
First, get to know your dinosaur. Read as much information about it as you can find. Try the Internet and the library. Get some information about the time when your dinosaur lived and the place(s) it lived (see the sections in ZoomDinosaurs.com with the "Mesozoic Era"). Remember that the Mesozoic Era was very different than the present in many ways, including the climate, geography, plant and animal life, etc. Then, think like a dinosaur.
©ELS

For information on particular dinosaurs, try the Dinosaur Information Sheets and the Dinosaur and Paleontoloy Dictionary.

When you write your report, try to answer as many of the following questions as you can (not all of these things are known for all dinosaurs):

- What does its name mean? Often this will tell you something important or interesting about the dinosaur.
- What did your dinosaur look like? For example, how big was it, what shape was its body, were its legs long or short, did it have horns, plates, crests or claws, describe the teeth, head, neck, tail, etc. Draw a picture if you can. Remember that dinosaur weights are very hard to estimate and can vary widely from one reference to another.
- How did its anatomy affect its life? For example: a giant sauropod had to eat a lot but didn't have to worry much about protecting itself, a tiny dinosaur probably had to be fast to escape being eaten for dinner, an armored dinosaur didn't have to be fast, but did have to avoid being flipped over, etc.
- What did it eat and how did it get its food? Where was this dinosaur in the food chain?
- How did it walk (2 or 4 legs - slow or fast locomotion)?
- Is there anything special about this dinosaur? This can often be the best part of the report, taking you off on interesting topics. For example, how did blood get to a Brachiosaurus' head, what were Stegosaurus' plates used for, what was Parasaurolophus' unusual crest probably used for, or how did Spinosaurus use its sailback?
- What is known about your dinosaur's behavior, if anything? For example: Is there evidence of herding? Did it nurture its young? Have any nests or eggs been found? How did your dinosaur rate in terms of intelligence?
- How did it defend itself (and/or attack other animals)?
- What animals might have attacked it? Or what animals might it have preyed upon? (See the section on when your dinosaur lived during the Mesozoic Era to find some of its contemporaries.)
- What type of dinosaur was it (how is it classified and what dinosaurs is it closely related to)?
- When did it live? Was it an early dinosaur or one of the last before the K-T extinction.
- What was the Earth like at that time? What was your dinosaur's environment like and what other dinosaurs (and other interesting animals) lived in that environment? What did the Earth's continents look like at that time? (This information is available in the section called "Mesozoic Era.")
- Where have fossils been found? When were they first found? Are there just a few fragments or are there almost complete specimens?
- Who named the dinosaur? Is there anything interesting about that scientist?

Use your own words. Check your spelling and grammar. Define any technical terms (look them up in the Dinosaur Dictionary). And remember to think like a dinosaur.

References: When you write your bibliography, list all of your references. A format for each type of publication follows (there are different formats):

- **Web Site:** Author(s). *Title of Site or web page* . URL of site, copyright year listed.
- **Book:** Author(s). *Title of book* . Edition. Location of publisher: Name of Publisher, year of publication.
- **Encyclopedia:** *Title of encyclopedia* , volume of encyclopedia used. Location of publisher: Name of Publisher, year of publication, pages where the article is located.
- **Magazine or Journal:** Author(s). "Title of article." *Name of magazine* , Volume.issue (date): pages where the article is located.

Author(s) are listed last name first, first name or initials (as cited in the publication)

For example: Zoom Dinosaurs would be cited as follows:

Col, Jeananda. Zoom Dinosaurs. http://www.ZoomDinosaurs.com 1999.

We've found a number of good ideas for writing a report. This might be a page worth copying into a file on your computer or printing out. Listed in the text is also a reference to the Dinosaur and Paleontology Dictionary. (*Paleontology* is the science dealing with the life of past geological periods based on fossil remains.) This dictionary might have some information on Velociraptors, so we'll click here.

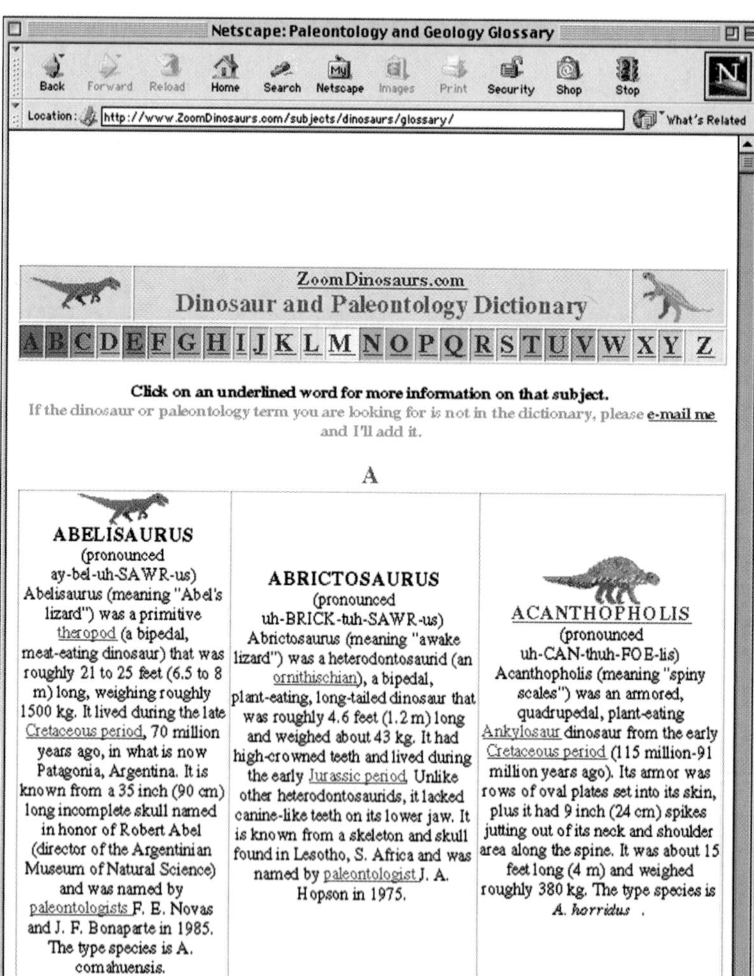

Here's the dictionary. We'll click on the letter "V" for Velociraptors.

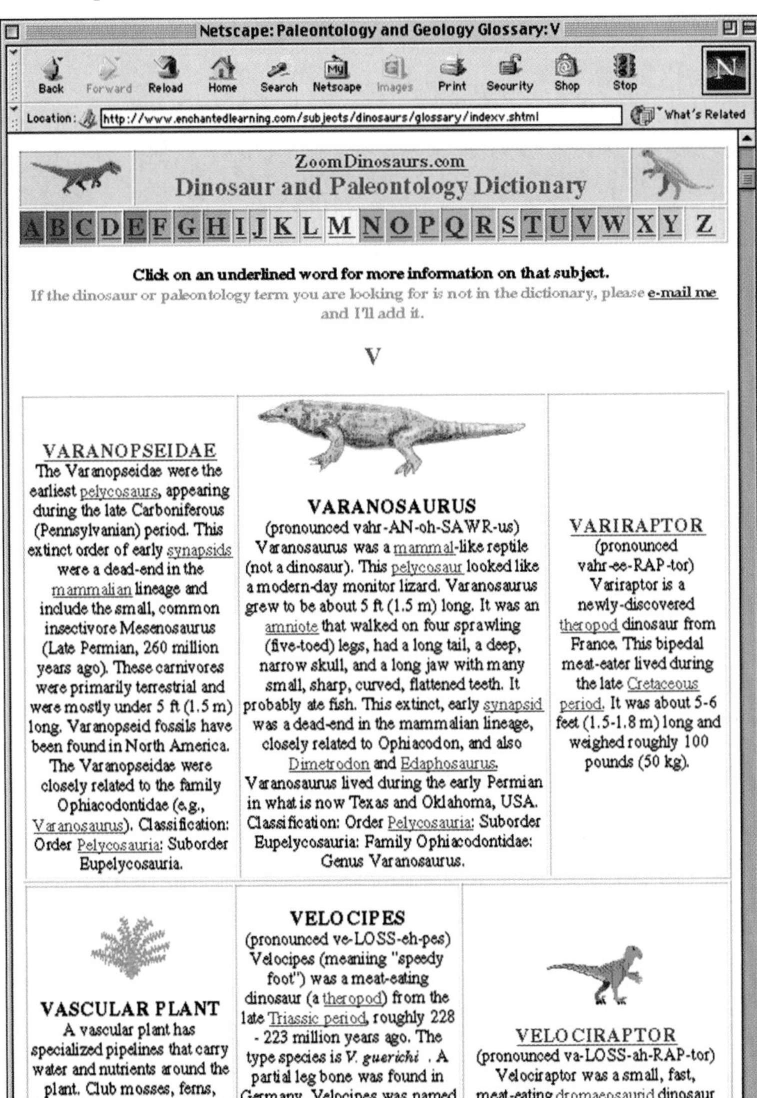
Netscape: Paleontology and Geology Glossary: V

Back Forward Reload Home Search Netscape Images Print Security Shop Stop

Location: http://www.enchantedlearning.com/subjects/dinosaurs/glossary/indexv.shtml What's Related

ZoomDinosaurs.com

Dinosaur and Paleontology Dictionary

A B C D E F G H I J K L M N O P Q R S T U V W X Y Z

Click on an underlined word for more information on that subject.

If the dinosaur or paleontology term you are looking for is not in the dictionary, please e-mail me and I'll add it.

V

VARANOPSEIDAE
The Varanopseidae were the earliest pelycosaurs, appearing during the late Carboniferous (Pennsylvanian) period. This extinct order of early synapsids were a dead-end in the mammalian lineage and include the small, common insectivore Mesenosaurus (Late Permian, 260 million years ago). These carnivores were primarily terrestrial and were mostly under 5 ft (1.5 m) long. Varanopseid fossils have been found in North America. The Varanopseidae were closely related to the family Ophiacodontidae (e.g., Varanosaurus). Classification: Order Pelycosauria: Suborder Eupelycosauria.

VARANOSAURUS
(pronounced vahr-AN-oh-SAWR-us)
Varanosaurus was a mammal-like reptile (not a dinosaur). This pelycosaur looked like a modern-day monitor lizard. Varanosaurus grew to be about 5 ft (1.5 m) long. It was an amniote that walked on four sprawling (five-toed) legs, had a long tail, a deep, narrow skull, and a long jaw with many small, sharp, curved, flattened teeth. It probably ate fish. This extinct, early synapsid was a dead-end in the mammalian lineage, closely related to Ophiacodon, and also Dimetrodon and Edaphosaurus. Varanosaurus lived during the early Permian in what is now Texas and Oklahoma, USA. Classification: Order Pelycosauria: Suborder Eupelycosauria: Family Ophiacodontidae: Genus Varanosaurus.

VARIRAPTOR
(pronounced vahr-ee-RAP-tor)
Variraptor is a newly-discovered theropod dinosaur from France. This bipedal meat-eater lived during the late Cretaceous period. It was about 5-6 feet (1.5-1.8 m) long and weighed roughly 100 pounds (50 kg).

VASCULAR PLANT
A vascular plant has specialized pipelines that carry water and nutrients around the plant. Club mosses, ferns, horsetails, gymnosperms, and flowering plants are vascular plants.

VELOCIPES
(pronounced ve-LOSS-eh-pes)
Velocipes (meaning "speedy foot") was a meat-eating dinosaur (a theropod) from the late Triassic period, roughly 228 - 223 million years ago. The type species is *V. guerichi* . A partial leg bone was found in Germany. Velocipes was named by paleontologist von Huene in 1932. This is doubtful genus due to insufficient fossil material.

VELOCIRAPTOR
(pronounced va-LOSS-ah-RAP-tor)
Velociraptor was a small, fast, meat-eating dromaeosaurid dinosaur from the Cretaceous period.

Here's a picture of our dinosaur—the Velociraptor. We'll click on the picture.

Location: http://www.EnchantedLearning.com/subjects/dinosaurs/dinos/Velociraptor.shtml What's Related

ZoomDinosaurs.com
ALL ABOUT DINOSAURS!

What is a Dinosaur? | Dino Info Sheets | Dinosaur Print-outs | Name That Dino | Biggest, Smallest, Oldest,... | Evolution of Dinosaurs | Dinos and Birds | Dino Myths

VELOCIRAPTOR
"Speedy Thief"

ANATOMY

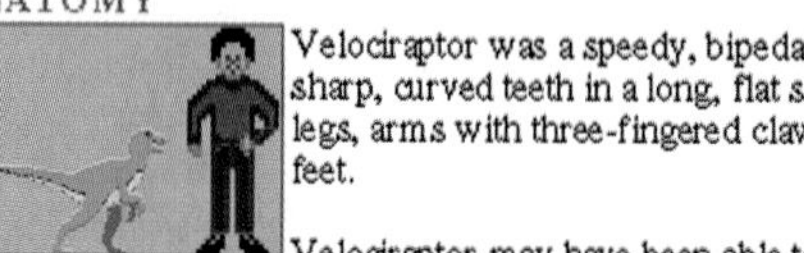

Velociraptor was a speedy, bipedal carnivore. It had about 30 very sharp, curved teeth in a long, flat snout, an s-shaped neck, long thin legs, arms with three-fingered clawed hands and four-toed clawed feet.

Velociraptor may have been able to run up to roughly 40 mph (60 km/hr) for short bursts.

Velociraptor was about 6 feet long (2 m), and 3 feet tall (1 m). It may have weighed about 15 to 33 pounds (7 to 15 kg). It had a stiff tail that worked as a counterbalance and let it make very quick turns.

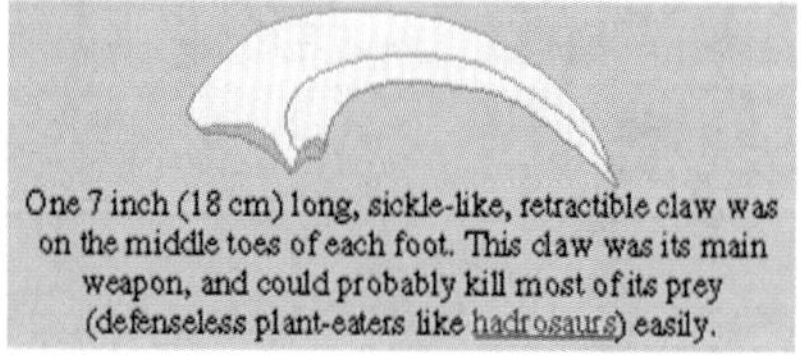

One 7 inch (18 cm) long, sickle-like, retractible claw was on the middle toes of each foot. This claw was its main weapon, and could probably kill most of its prey (defenseless plant-eaters like hadrosaurs) easily.

Velociraptor brains were very large in comparison to their body size (this is true for all the Dromaeosaurid dinosaurs, who were the most intelligent dinosaurs).

WHEN VELOCIRAPTOR LIVED

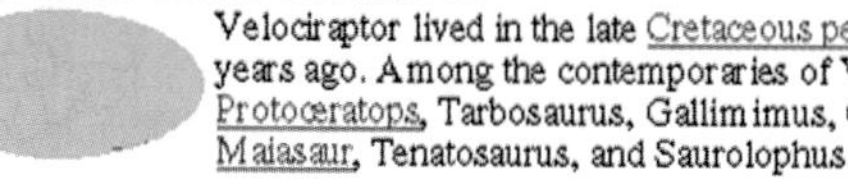

Velociraptor lived in the late Cretaceous period, about 85 - 80 million years ago. Among the contemporaries of Velociraptor were Protoceratops, Tarbosaurus, Gallimimus, Oviraptor, Anatosaurus, Maiasaur, Tenatosaurus, and Saurolophus.

BEHAVIOR
Velociraptor may have hunted in packs, attacking even very large animals. In 1971, fossils of a Velociraptor and a Protoceratops were found together. They died together; the Velociraptor was attacking the Protoceratops with its claws and the armored head of the Protoceratops had apparently pierced the chest of the Velociraptor.

Velociraptor, along with the other Dromaeosaurids, were the smartest dinosaurs, as calculated from their brain:body weight ratio. This made them very deadly predators.

INTELLIGENCE
Velociraptor was a dromaeosaurid, whose intelligence (as measured by its relative brain to body weight, or EQ) was the highest among the dinosaurs.

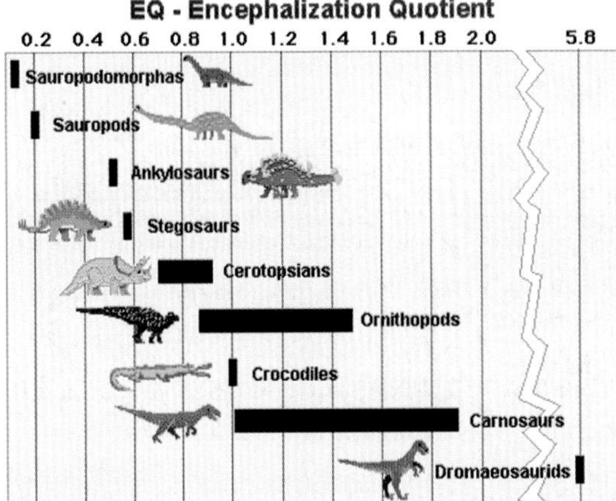

DIET
Velociraptor was a carnivore, a meat eater. It probably ate just about anything it could slash and tear apart. It may have hunted in packs. It ate Protoceratops (one was found fossilized with Velociraptor in a battle to the death) and probably ate many other plant-eaters, like hadrosaurs (duck-billed dinosaurs).

LOCOMOTION
Velociraptor walked on two slender legs; it was certainly among the fastest of the dinosaurs, considering its long legs and light weight. Velociraptor may have been able to run up to roughly 40 mph (60 km/hr) for short bursts. Velociraptor could probably jump also.

DISCOVERY OF FOSSILS
Velociraptor was first found and described by paleontologist H. F. Osborn in Mongolia in 1924. About a dozen Velociraptor fossils have been found, including one who died in a battle to the death with Protoceratops and two hatchling Velociraptor skulls that were found near an oviraptorid nest in Mongolia (they may have been a meal). Fossils have been found in Mongolia, Russia, and China.

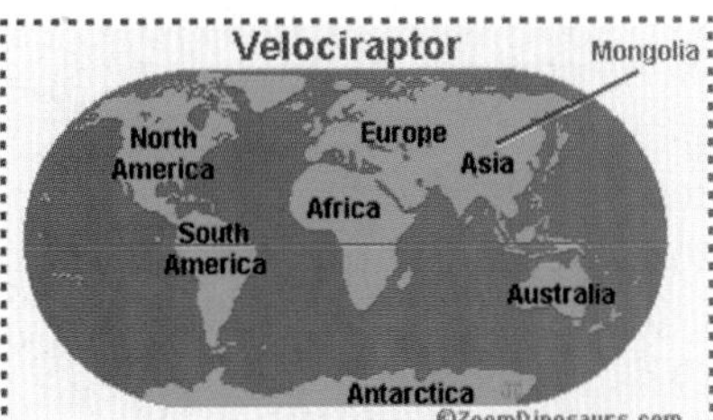

CLASSIFICATION
Velociraptor belonged to the:

- Kingdom Animalia (animals)
- Phylum Chordata (having a hollow nerve chord ending in a brain)
- Class Archosauria (diapsids with socket-set teeth, etc.)
- Order Saurischia - lizard-hipped dinosaurs
- Suborder Theropoda - bipedal carnivores
- Infraorder Coelurosauria - lightly-built fast-running predators with hollow bones and large brains
- Superfamily Maniraptoriformes - advanced coelurosaurs with a fused wrist bone
- Family Dromaeosauridae - the smartest dinosaurs. They were equipped with sickle-like foot claws. These included Velociraptor, Utahraptor, Saurornitholestes, and Dromaeosaurus).
- Genus Velociraptor
- species mongoliensis (the type species).

VELOCIRAPTOR ACTIVITIES

- Print out a K-3 level Velociraptor info page to color!
- A first-grade level Velociraptor addition activity print-out.
- A Velociraptor word hunt activity - A print-out for second and third graders.
- A Velociraptor Activity print-out for beginning readers (advanced first graders to second graders). Students read and follow the directions to complete a Cretaceous scene.
- A quiz about Velociraptor - Unscramble the answers and see how much you know this deadly little dinosaur! For grades 2-3.

VELOCIRAPTOR LINKS
Velociraptor found near Maiasaur skull in Montana (from Worldwide Museum of Natural History).

Information Sheets About Dinosaurs
(and Other Prehistoric Creatures)

Just click on an animal's name to go to that information sheet. If the dinosaur you're interested in isn't here, check the Dinosaur Dictionary or the list of dinosaur genera. Names with an asterisk (*) were not dinosaurs.
How to write a great dinosaur report.

This is great! Now we have an entire page of information about the Velociraptor, including its size, weight, intelligence, diet, behavior, environment—all sorts of interesting facts and figures about this ancient animal.

There's another way to do a search for a specific topic—get more specific! This time, let's try another search engine, HotBot.com.

In the search field, we'll type in two words—"dinosaur" and "Velociraptor." Then click Search.

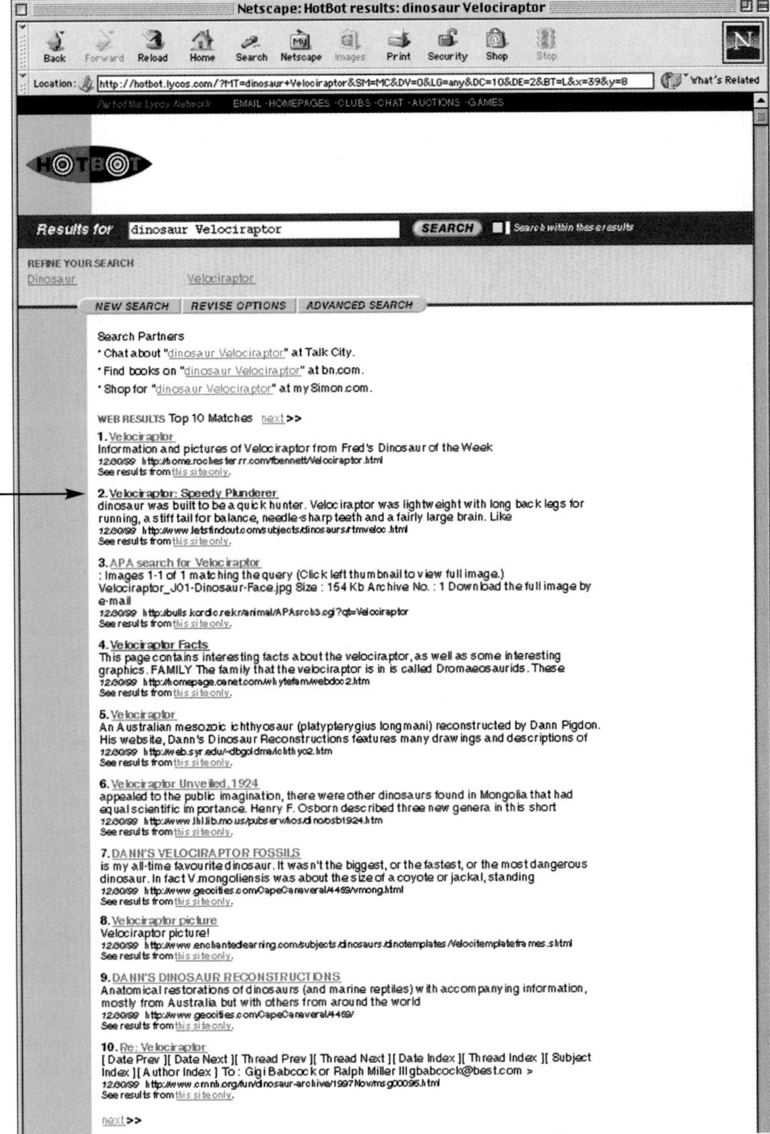

This article, Velociraptor: Speedy Plunderer, seems interesting. Let's check it out.

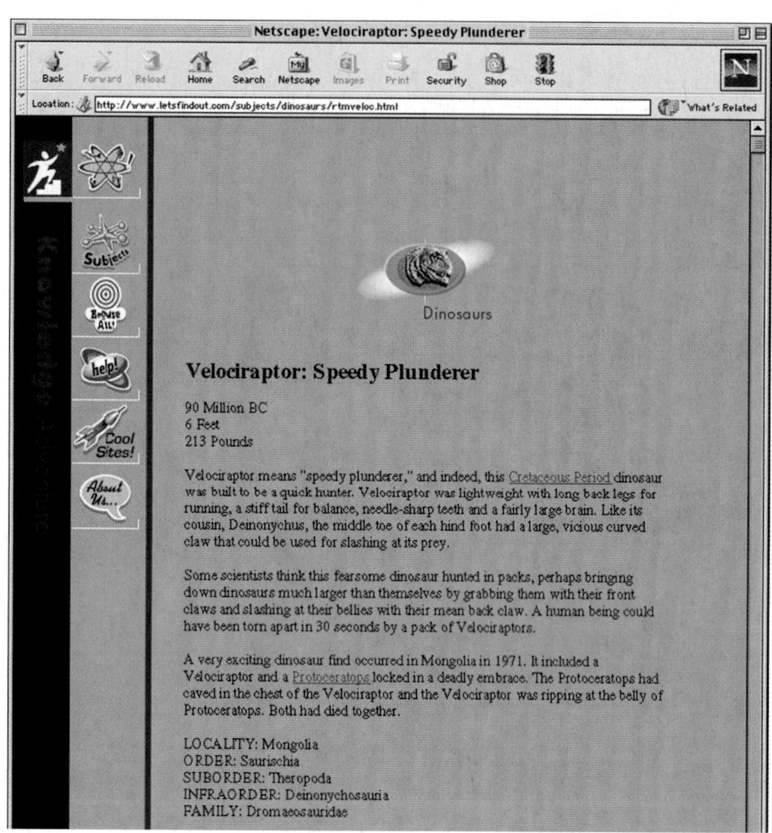

Again, we've found an entire page about this particular dinosaur, including information about an exciting dinosaur find in Mongolia in 1971. If we wanted to continue our search, we would click Back and return to the page of articles listed on HotBot.

Obviously we could go on and on. The important thing to remember is to use your imagination plus a little common sense. Just imagine you are a paleontologist yourself and doing your very own *Internet* dinosaur search!

LANGUAGE

Teaching Suggestions

Essential Knowledge and Skills

- Comparing his/her own perception of a spoken message with the perception of others
- Adapting spoken language such as word choice, diction, and usage to the audience, purpose, and occasion
- Capitalizing and punctuating correctly to clarify and enhance meaning, such as using sentence punctuation
- Employing standard English usage in writing for audiences, including subject-verb agreement
- Responding in constructive ways to others' writing
- Interpreting and evaluating the various ways visual image makers, such as illustrators, represent meaning

BLOCK SCHEDULING

- If your schedule requires that you cover the chapter in a **shorter time,** use the instruction on sentences and the Check Your Understanding and QuickCheck exercises.
- If you want to take advantage of **longer class time,** add these applications to writing: Connect to Writer's Craft, Connect to Speaking and Writing, Connect to the Writing Process, and Apply to Writing exercises.

CHAPTER 1

The Sentence

Directions

Write the letter of the term that correctly identifies the underlined word or words in each sentence.

EXAMPLE **1.** The <u>Pacific Ocean</u> is the largest body of water in the world.

1 A simple subject
B complete subject
C simple predicate
D complete predicate

ANSWER **1 A**

1. <u>The largest salt-water lake</u> is the Caspian Sea.
2. The <u>South Pole</u> and the <u>North Pole</u> are both icy.
3. Land and ice <u>form the South Pole</u>.
4. The <u>North Pole</u> is not land but is floating ice.
5. <u>From out of Egypt flows the Nile River.</u>
6. <u>The tallest mountain in the world.</u>
7. Mauna Loa in Hawaii <u>is known</u> as the biggest active volcano.
8. Hot deserts <u>cover</u> parts of northern Africa but <u>yield</u> to lush forests further south.
9. <u>Look at this map of the Ganges River in India.</u>
10. The Ganges River <u>possesses</u> the widest delta of all rivers.

IDENTIFYING COMMON STUMBLING BLOCKS

Following is a list of the most common errors students make when writing sentences.

Problem
- Sentence fragments

Solution
- Instruction, pp. L5–L6
- Practice, pp. L6–L7

Problem
- Correctly punctuating sentences

Solution
- Instruction, pp. L34–L35
- Practice, pp. L35–L37

1 **A** simple subject
B simple predicate
C complete subject
D complete predicate

2 **A** compound subject
B compound verb
C verb phrase
D inverted order

3 **A** complete subject
B verb phrase
C compound verb
D complete predicate

4 **A** complete subject
B simple subject
C compound subject
D complete predicate

5 **A** simple subject
B inverted order
C complete predicate
D natural order

6 **A** sentence fragment
B complete subject
C simple subject
D inverted order

7 **A** complete predicate
B verb phrase
C simple predicate
D compound verb

8 **A** complete predicate
B inverted order
C verb phrase
D compound verb

9 **A** sentence fragment
B complete subject
C imperative sentence
D complete predicate

10 **A** simple subject
B simple verb
C verb phrase
D natural order

A DIFFERENT DELIVERY SYSTEM

If you prefer, you can print the pretest from the BK English Test Bank located at http://www.bkenglish.com.

Using *the Pretest*

Assessing Prior Knowledge

The pretest will help you and your students assess where they stand in their basic understanding of sentences. The test indicates students' ability to distinguish sentences and sentence fragments and to identify the different kinds of sentences.

Customizing the Test

Use these questions to add or replace items for alternate versions of the test.

11. In Tibet at an altitude of over 1600 feet is the largest high plateau.

12. The Amazon River is wider and holds more water than the Nile.

13. Listen to this astonishing fact!

14. The Caspian Sea is a lake, not a sea.

11. **A** sentence fragment
B imperative sentence
C natural order
D inverted order

12. **A** simple verb
B compound verb
C verb phrase
D complete predicate

13. **A** exclamatory senetnce
B declarative sentence
C imperative sentence
D interrogative sentence

14. **A** inverted order
B compound verb
C complete predicate
D simple verb

ADDITIONAL RESOURCES

Language Skills Practice . . . . pages 1–15
Transparency Tools AW1, AW2
ESL Practice and Test Preparation . . . . . pages 85–87
Assessment: Pretest . . . . pages 16–29
Assessment: Chapter Test. . . . . pages 101–108

FOR YOUR INFORMATION

About Art Criticism

Edmund Burke Feldman was a noted art professor who gave his students the tools needed to understand and appreciate art. His model for art criticism begins with describing the work of art. The second stage is a formal analysis of the work. In the third stage, interpretation, the observer finds meaning in the work of art. Finally, in the fourth stage, evaluation, the observer forms judgments about the work of art in relation to other works.

To Stimulate Writing

Use the questions for art criticism as writing or discussion prompts.

Possible Answers:

Describe Images include a woman's face, the head and upper body of a black monkey, two dome-topped cacti, a few large leaves, and a tree, all with different textures.

Analyze I notice the woman's face first because it is in the center of the painting and is the clearest, most detailed image. Everything else in the painting is sort of blurred.

Interpret The person in the portrait is the artist herself. The cactus plants suggest both harshness and survival (because they can go a long time without water). The woman's face is serious. The colors are muted, and are soft and blurred except for the woman's face, which is warm and detailed. Overall, I think the artist is saying she can overcome difficulties and survive and flourish.

Judge Answers will vary.

Frida Kahlo, *Fulang-Chang and Me,* 1937.
Two-part ensemble (assembled after 1939). Part one: 1937, oil on composition board, 15 3/4 by 11 inches, painted mirror frame (added after 1939), 22 1/4 by 17 3/8 by 1 3/4 inches, including frame. The Museum of Modern Art, New York.

Describe What images do you recognize in the painting? If you could touch these images, what textures do you think you would feel?

Analyze What image do you notice first? What technique did the artist use to draw your attention to this image?

Interpret What does the word *Me* in the title tell you about the portrait? What do you think the artist's message is? What do the background images and facial expression tell you about the mood of the painting?

Judge Do you think the artist was successful in creating a clear mood for her painting? What aspect of the mood could a writer present differently?

At the end of this chapter, you will use this artwork to stimulate ideas for writing.

FOR DEVELOPING LANGUAGE SKILLS

LESSON 1 *(pages L5–L33)*

OBJECTIVES

- **To distinguish between sentences and sentence fragments**
- **To distinguish between simple and complete subjects**
- **To distinguish between simple and complete predicates**
- **To identify verb phrases, compound subjects, and compound verbs**

Create Interest

Write the following examples on the board.

- Usually eat a salad for lunch.
- The salad contains.

A Sentence

Before you even knew what a sentence was, you were talking in sentences. Because you listened to conversation daily, you were able to organize your words into a variety of sentences, too. You learned how to ask for things and how to tell about things. With practice you mastered the ability to communicate your complete thoughts to other people.

A **sentence** is a group of words that expresses a complete thought.

I ate a pizza for lunch today.
I had carrots and ranch dressing for a snack.
Raquel gave me a glass of lemonade.

The preceding examples are sentences. Because each expresses a complete thought, they will all be easily understood by anyone who hears them. Once in a while, of course, everyone includes an incomplete thought or two in writing or conversation.

A group of words that expresses an incomplete thought is called a **sentence fragment.**

Because a fragment is only a part of a sentence, some of the meaning of the sentence is lost, and listeners can misunderstand what is being said. The following groups of words are sentence fragments.

Pizza for lunch today.
Carrots and ranch dressing for a snack.
A glass of lemonade.

To form a complete sentence, you need to add the missing information.

FOR INCREASING STUDENT ACHIEVEMENT

REACHING ALL STUDENTS

Advanced Learners

Tell students that they can easily determine whether or not a question is a fragment by rewording the question as a statement and then identifying the subject and predicate. Complete the first example below with students. Then have students complete the last three examples on their own.

- Do you like salad with your meals? *You do like salad with your meals.* (subject is *You*; predicate is *Do like*)
- Will you choose this salad dressing?
- Are the carrots cooked or raw?
- Is celery an ingredient in that recipe?

Struggling Learners

Remind students that a sentence must express a complete thought. Have students listen to the following examples as you read them aloud. Students should decide whether or not each expresses a complete thought.

- Meatballs in my spaghetti.
- I add parmesan cheese to my pasta.
- The cheese is stuck together.
- Shaking the container to get the cheese out onto my plate.

Ask students if these examples express a complete thought. Have students suggest what is wrong with each example. Then have students add a missing subject or predicate to make each thought complete. Have students explain how the subject and the predicate work together to make a complete sentence.

Guide Instruction

By Connecting Ideas

Have students read a specific paragraph from their literature textbooks, taking note of the subjects and predicates the author uses. Have students identify the subjects and predicates in each sentence of the paragraph. Have students critique the author's use of particular predicates. How might other verbs have changed the paragraph?

Consolidate Ideas

Through Guided Practice

The **Check Your Understanding** exercises on pages L8, L9, and L11 will help students identify complete and simple subjects. Point out that a noun

USING STUDENTS' STRENGTHS

Multiple Intelligences: Linguistic

Have students work with a classmate or friend to audiotape one of their informal conversations. Students should then listen to the tape and write any sentence fragments from the conversation as complete sentences. Have students re-record the conversation using their complete sentences. Ask students how the conversation has changed.

A DIFFERENT APPROACH

Auditory

Have one student read each group of words in the **Check Your Understanding** activity aloud. Other students should listen for missing subjects or predicates without looking at the examples in their books. Listeners should decide whether to label each item *S* for a sentence or *F* for a fragment.

HOME WORK

Have students locate five sentence fragments in newspaper or magazine articles or in print advertisements. Have students bring their examples of the sentence fragments to class. They should also rewrite each sentence fragment as a complete sentence.

CONNECT TO SPEAKING AND WRITING

When you talk to a friend or a family member, you may speak faster and use informal speech. Sometimes people use fragments when they speak informally. When you are making a formal speech, speaking to an audience, or writing formally, remember to use complete sentences to make a better impression.

INFORMAL	Great pizza!
FORMAL	I think pizza is a delicious and healthful food.

You can learn more about sentence fragments on pages L291–L300.

PRACTICE YOUR SKILLS

Check Your Understanding

Recognizing Sentences

Health Topic **Label each group of words *S* if it is a sentence or *F* if it is a sentence fragment.**

1. Eating a healthful breakfast. ^is good for you. F
2. Green vegetables include broccoli, string beans, peas, and lettuce. S
3. Nutrients are necessary for your body. S
4. ^Nutrients help Your body grow. F
5. ^Growing requires a large Amount of energy. F
6. Try to eat a balanced diet. S
7. Foods belong in five basic food groups. S
8. Milk, yogurt, and cheese. ^provide calcium. F
9. You should not eat a lot of sweets. S
10. Good snack foods. ^are nuts and fruits. F

can be both a complete subject and a simple subject. Provide students with several examples such as the following:

- *Long's Book Store* also serves coffee.
- *Amelia* works at the coffee counter.

Tell students that usually the simple subject of a sentence is referred to simply as *the subject*.

Apply to Communication

Through Independent Writing

The **Communicate Your Ideas/Apply to Writing** activities on pages L7 and L12 prompt students to write a recipe to place on the Internet and to write a favorable book review about a book they have enjoyed. Ask students why their recipes should contain clear directions and complete sentences. Lead students to understand that clear directions are necessary to complete a recipe correctly and that complete sentences should always be used in

Connect to the Writing Process: Revising

Completing Sentences

11.–15. Add information to turn each of the sentence fragments from the exercise on the preceding page into a sentence. Remember to begin each sentence with a capital letter and to end it with a punctuation mark. [Answers may vary. See possible responses given above.]

Communicate Your Ideas

APPLY TO WRITING

Directions: ***Complete Sentences***

Imagine that you are going to write a recipe to place on the Internet. Decide what your recipe will be. Give reasons why someone would want to make this food. If the recipe is for a dish from another country, tell something about when people eat it in that country.

As you are writing your recipe, be sure to include a list of ingredients. Write the directions for making the recipe in complete sentences. Be sure they are in the correct order. Include the following sentence fragments, written correctly as sentences.

- Is delicious.
- Easy to make.
- Serves a lot.
- Great for parties.

TIMESAVER *QuickCheck*

Limit your evaluation of students' recipe directions to their use of complete sentences. In addition to using complete sentences throughout their directions, students should rewrite the four example fragments as complete sentences.

HOME STUDY

Have students rewrite a recipe from home. Students should bring to class a family recipe that contains fragments and rewrite the recipe with complete sentences. Have students then exchange favorite recipes with a classmate.

formal writing. When students write their book review, ask them what effect their choices of complete and simple subjects have upon their writing.

Transfer to Everyday Life

Identifying Complete and Simple Subjects in a News Report

Have students view a news report and identify as many complete and simple subjects as they can from the report. Have students share all of the complete and simple subjects that they were able to identify.

Pull It All Together

By Sharing

Have students share some of the subjects they chose for their book reviews. Point out how various types of subjects are effective. For example, some of students' subjects are complete and some may be simple. Have students

REACHING ALL STUDENTS

Advanced Learners

Point out to students that their choice of a subject has to agree with the verb they are using in a sentence. Provide students with the following example, and then have them choose subjects for the second and third sentences.

- **He buys** a book for me every year.
- ▢ **buy** many books every year.
- ▢ **buys** books from that store.

YOUR IDEAS

For Reaching All Students

Subjects and Predicates

A sentence has two main parts: a subject and a predicate.

The **subject** names the person, place, thing, or idea that the sentence is about.

The **predicate** tells something about the subject.

	SUBJECT	PREDICATE
PERSON	Jane	swims fast.
PLACE	The pool	is her domain.
THING	The watch	measures her times.
IDEA	A record	is her goal.

PRACTICE YOUR SKILLS

Check Your Understanding

Combining Subjects and Predicates

Sports Topic

Match each subject in the first column with a predicate in the second column. Then combine them to form five sentences that make sense. Be sure to begin each sentence with a capital letter and end each one with a period.

1. many athletes
2. two runners
3. the shuttle run
4. marathons
5. not many students

a. ^are usually twenty-six miles⊙ (4. Marathons)
b. ^think of sports as physical science⊙ (5. Not many students)
c. ^possess great speed⊙ (1. Many athletes)
d. ^is a difficult race⊙ (3. The shuttle run)
e. ^might compare their speeds⊙ (2. Two runners)

discuss the subjects they think are most interesting.

Check Understanding

By Identifying Subjects in a Picture Book

Provide students with a wide selection of short children's picture books, and have them identify the complete and simple subjects in each book. Students should write out the subjects and share them with a partner.

Complete Subjects

In the exercise on the preceding page, some subjects—such as *the shuttle run*—have more than one word. These subjects are complete subjects.

A **complete subject** includes all words used to identify the person, place, thing, or idea that the sentence is about.

To find a complete subject, ask yourself either, *Who or what is doing something?* or *About whom or what is some statement being made?*

complete subject
The birds in our backyard fly from tree to tree.

(Who or what is doing something in this sentence? *The birds in our backyard* is the complete subject.)

complete subject
The birds' nest in the yard is filled with baby birds.

(About whom or what is some statement being made? *The birds' nest in the yard* is the complete subject.)

Practice Your Skills

Check Your Understanding

Finding Complete Subjects

Science Topic **Write each complete subject.**

1. The wingspan of an albatross averages ten to twelve feet.
2. The nest of a golden eagle can weigh several tons.
3. The smallest hummingbird in the world weighs less than a dime.

USING STUDENTS' STRENGTHS

Multiple Intelligences: Musical

Review with students the syllables, or beats, in a three-line haiku. Tell them that the first line must contain five beats, the second line should have seven beats, and the third line should have five beats. Have students suggest ways in which this type of poetry has a musical quality. Provide students with the following haiku example. Then have them write their own haiku that contains at least one simple subject and one complete subject.

Birds in my backyard (contains a simple subject)
Fluttering by my window
The smallest bird flies. (contains a complete subject)

A DIFFERENT APPROACH

Visual

Have students choose five sentences from a book they are reading. Then have students create rebuses by rewriting each sentence, replacing the subject of the sentence with an illustration.

INTEGRATING TECHNOLOGY
Audio

Divide the class into four or five small groups. Provide each group with a tape recorder and an audiotape of a novel. Have each group listen to at least three minutes of the audiotape. As they listen, students should jot down as many simple subjects as they can identify from the story.

YOUR IDEAS
For Using Media in the Classroom

4. Small, colorful orioles nest in the same tree year after year.
5. Some eagles in South America feed on monkeys.
6. Owls in the forest see better at night than do most other animals.
7. Some wild ducks build their nests in treetops.
8. The largest bird's egg in the world belongs to the ostrich.
9. One type of penguin builds its nest out of rocks.
10. A female condor lays one egg every two years.

Simple Subjects

Most complete subjects include more than one word. Within each complete subject, however, there is one main word that clearly answers either, *Who or what is doing something?* or *About whom or what is some statement being made?* This main word is called the simple subject.

A **simple subject** is the main word in the complete subject.

In the following examples, the complete subject is in **bold** type, and the simple subjects are underlined.

The author of my favorite book talked at the conference.

(What is the main word in the complete subject? Who or what is doing something? The simple subject is *author.*)

The first speaker wrote many nonfiction books.

(What is the main word in the complete subject? Who or what is doing something? The simple subject is *speaker.*)

Grant's Used Bookstore on Brooks Road is closed on holidays.

(*Grant's Used Bookstore* is the simple subject even though it is three words. All three words are considered the name of one place.)

A complete subject and a simple subject can be the same.

Katharine writes in her journal every day.
Everyone read the assignment about whales.

Throughout the rest of this book, the simple subject will be called the subject.

Practice Your Skills

Check Your Understanding
Finding Complete and Simple Subjects

Social Science Topic

Write each complete subject. Then underline each simple subject.

1. People have been writing for a long time.
2. Writers found different useful surfaces to write on.
3. The ancient Egyptians made paper from reeds.
4. The fresh, flat reeds were pressed together.
5. Colonial Americans used parchment for important records.
6. The parchment for the Bill of Rights was made from linen fibers.
7. Modern paper is made from wood pulp.
8. Each new decade of science brings new and improved materials.
9. Computers are very important today.
10. Many writers rely heavily on the computer.

DEVELOPING WORKPLACE COMPETENCIES

Basic Skills: Reading

Provide each student with a copy of one page from the assembly instructions for a toy, a prefabricated bookshelf, or other assembly project. Have students read through the page and decide what the subjects are in some of the direction sentences. Ask students how their misunderstanding of any of the subjects might affect their ability to complete the projects. How might this affect their ability to follow directions and to complete projects for future employers?

HOME STUDY

Have students locate a book review in a newspaper, magazine, or journal. Then have students rewrite the review, substituting new subjects for the original subjects. Students should decide whether their new subjects will be complete or simple. Have students read their revised book reviews to the class.

YOUR IDEAS

For Home Study

Connect to the Writing Process: Drafting

Writing Complete Sentences

Add a complete subject to each sentence.

[Answers may vary. Possible responses are given.]

11. Mary's cousin is going to the library after school.

12. The library is across the street from the grocery store.

13. The store on the corner has a supply of magazines and newspapers.

14. Almost any subject can be used for a research project.

15. A number of people hook up to the Internet.

Communicate Your Ideas

APPLY TO WRITING

Book Review: *Using Complete and Simple Subjects*

Write a book review about a book you have enjoyed. In your review, praise the book and recommend it to your classmates. Remember to give a few details about the main character, the setting, and the plot. As a writer, you can place emphasis on what you are writing about by using the title of the book as the subject of your first sentence. For example, your book review might begin like this:

> The *Call of the Wild* by Jack London is one of the most exciting books I have ever read. The main character in this book survives many adventures. Author Jack London has carefully crafted many exciting scenes. Because the perspective is that of a dog, the author can share details with the reader that might not ordinarily be revealed to a person.

Complete Predicates

To express a complete thought, a sentence must have a subject and a predicate.

A **complete predicate** includes all the words that tell what the subject is doing or tell something about the subject.

To find a complete predicate, first find the subject. Then ask yourself, *What is the subject doing?* or *What is being said about the subject?*

complete predicate

Dinosaurs **roamed the earth.**

(The subject is *dinosaurs.* What did the dinosaurs do? *Roamed the earth* is the complete predicate.)

complete predicate

Mario **visited the dinosaur exhibit at the museum.**

(The subject is *Mario.* What is being said about Mario? *Visited the dinosaur exhibit at the museum* is the complete predicate.)

Practice Your Skills

Check Your Understanding

Finding Complete Predicates

Science Topic **Write each complete predicate.**

1. The dodo bird stood about three feet tall.
2. This mostly ash-gray bird weighed fifty pounds.
3. Its face had only a few feathers.
4. A strange tuft of curly feathers served as a tail.
5. Its huge beak extended as much as nine inches.

REACHING ALL STUDENTS

English Language Learners

Tell students that usually the predicate comes after the subject in English sentences. Provide students with several example sentences to demonstrate the common location of predicates. Then show students the following exception: *In the middle of the road was a large boulder.* Tell students that sentences like this one are called "inverted." Have students identify the subject and the predicate in the sentence.

A DIFFERENT APPROACH

Auditory

As an alternative to writing each complete predicate, have students work in pairs taking turns reading the sentences in the **Check Your Understanding** activity aloud. After one student reads the sentence, the other student should identify the complete predicate. Students should continue taking turns until they have completed the exercise.

HOME WORK

Have students locate three family photographs that they would not mind temporarily sharing with the class. Have students write a sentence, or "caption," to accompany each photograph. Students should underline the complete predicate in each of their sentences. Have students share their photographs and captions with the class.

6. This flightless bird had stubby wings of three or four black feathers.
7. The dodo lived on the island of Mauritius.
8. This island is located off the coast of Africa.
9. Its dinner consisted mainly of vegetables and fruit.
10. The female laid one big white egg a year.
11. The flightless dodo built its nest on the ground.
12. Portuguese sailors discovered the dodo in 1598.
13. The sailors took cats, dogs, and pigs to the island.
14. These animals destroyed many nests of the dodo.
15. The Dutch destroyed the dodo's forest habitat.
16. A resident of the island saw the last dodo bird around 1681.

Simple Predicates, or Verbs

Within each complete predicate, there is one main word or phrase that tells what the subject is doing, or that tells something about the subject. This main word or phrase is called the simple predicate, or verb.

A **simple predicate,** or **verb,** is the main word or phrase in the complete predicate.

Verbs that tell what a subject is doing are **action verbs.** Action verbs can show physical action, mental action, or ownership. In the following examples, the complete predicates are in **bold** type, and the simple predicates, or verbs, are underlined twice.

My brother **takes terrific photographs.**

(What is the main word in the complete predicate? What does the subject do? The simple predicate is *takes.*)

Marisa **dreamed about the photography contest.**

(What is the main word in the complete predicate? What did the subject do? The simple predicate is *dreamed*.)

Some verbs do not show action. These verbs tell something about a subject. The following common verb forms are used to make a statement about a subject.

COMMON VERBS THAT MAKE STATEMENTS				
am	is	are	was	were

The film **is on the table.**

His camera lens **was a gift from his grandmother.**

Just as a complete and simple subject can be the same, so can a complete predicate and a simple predicate.

The camera **broke.**

The lens **froze.**

You can learn about subject and verb agreement in Chapter 13.

CONNECT TO SPEAKING AND WRITING

When you speak or write, use verbs that will make your ideas exciting and interesting. The verbs should create a clear, colorful picture for your audience. Use action verbs rather than verbs that make a statement. Notice the difference among the verbs in the following sentences.

The flash of the camera **is** bright.

The flash of the camera **blinded** me.

The flash of the camera **startled** me. 

GETTING STUDENTS INVOLVED

Reciprocal Teaching

Have students who demonstrate an understanding of complete and simple predicates work with a less-proficient partner to work through the examples on this page. After students have read the examples, have them devise a method to help them remember the verbs in the chart.

YOUR IDEAS

For Mnemonic Devices

A DIFFERENT APPROACH

Kinesthetic

Write out the last two sentences from the **Practice Your Skills** activity on a large poster board. Each word should be large and visible. Have students cut apart each sentence, leaving each word on a separate card. Give the resulting twenty-one word cards to different students in the class. Have students work together, moving around the room to form sentences. After students have moved into positions that form complete sentences, have volunteers identify the complete predicates in each sentence.

PRACTICE YOUR SKILLS

Check Your Understanding

Finding Complete Predicates and Verbs

Science Topic

Write each complete predicate. Then underline each verb.

1. Your eyes have features like those of a camera.
2. The iris is a kind of shutter.
3. An automatic light meter controls the shutter.
4. The shutter opens wide in darkness.
5. It becomes very small in bright light.
6. The lens serves as a color filter.
7. The lens filters certain colors.
8. An eye changes its focus from near to far.
9. The cornea serves as a cover for the eye.
10. The eyelids and tears clean the cornea.

Connect to the Writing Process: Revising

Using Vivid Verbs

Rewrite the following sentences, replacing each verb with a more vivid verb. [Answers may vary. Possible responses are given.]

11. At the gallery I ~~saw~~ glimpsed photographs by Ansel Adams.
12. His photographs ~~show~~ capture images in black and white.
13. His photographs ~~are~~ illustrate power in stillness.
14. He ~~created~~ invented a new procedure for photographers.
15. Adams ~~mixed~~ combined technology, nature, and spirit.
16. He ~~used~~ varied filtration for dramatic contrasts in his photographs.
17. The photographer ~~changed~~ evolved into an artist.
18. Adams ~~caught~~ captured the spirit of the American West.

Communicate Your Ideas

APPLY TO WRITING

Description: ***Predicates***

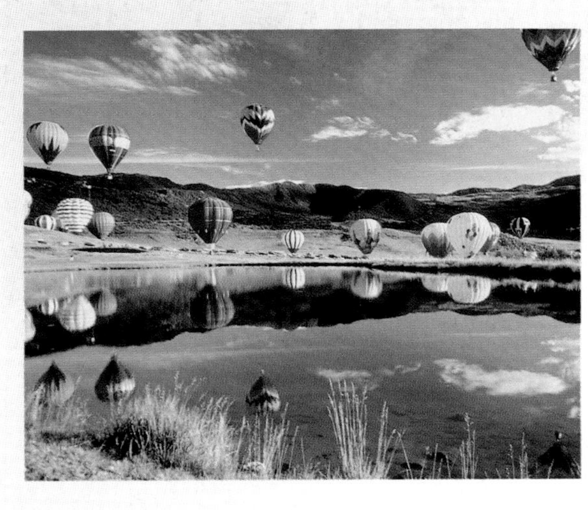

The fifth graders at a neighborhood school are holding a photography contest. You and several of your classmates have been asked to judge the contest. Write a description of the photograph for the other judges. Use vivid verbs in your description.

Verb Phrases

Sometimes a verb needs the help of other verbs, which are called **helping verbs,** or auxiliary verbs.

A **verb phrase** includes the main verb plus any helping, or auxiliary, verbs.

TIMESAVER *QuickCheck*

When evaluating students' writing, look for specific, vivid verbs they included in their descriptions of the photograph. Students should include at least five vivid verbs in their writing. The verbs should be appropriate to the scene in the photograph.

HOME STUDY

Have students attend a local photography contest to find out how the event is judged. If no contests are in your area, have students conduct their own school photography contest. They should solicit photography entries from other students in your school. Students should take note of how the judges describe and evaluate the entries. Have students list at least five vivid verbs used in the photography evaluations.

USING STUDENTS' STRENGTHS

Multiple Intelligences: Interpersonal

Have students work with a partner to make sentences using the words from the Common Helping Verbs chart. Each student should make at least five sentences using the verbs. The sentences must state something positive about their partner. Have students take turns coming up with positive sentences about one another that contain the helping verbs.

REACHING ALL STUDENTS

Advanced Learners

After students have completed the **Practice Your Skills** activity, have them revise each of the sentences by replacing the verb phrases with simple verbs without helping verbs. Provide students with the following example from the first sentence: *Artists **share** their thoughts and feelings about their subjects.* After students have completed the remaining items, have them explain how the tense of the verbs and meanings of the sentences have changed.

Here is a list of common helping verbs.

	COMMON HELPING VERBS
be	am, is, are, was, were, be, being, been
have	has, have, had
do	do, does, did
OTHERS	may, might, must, can, could, shall, should, will, would

The verb phrases in the following examples are underlined twice. The helping verbs are in bold type.

> The artist **is** painting the colorful landscape today.
>
> The artist **will be** sketching pictures of the hills.

You can learn about subject and verb agreement with verb phrases on pages L414–L415.

PRACTICE YOUR SKILLS

Check Your Understanding

Finding Verb Phrases

Art Topic **Write each verb phrase.**

1. Artists are sharing their thoughts and feelings about their subjects.
2. An artist could be drawing an imaginary scene.
3. Some artists have planned one painting for several years.
4. These artists will read a history of a place.
5. A few ambitious painters will live in the place.

6. New sculptors should begin with a good teacher.
7. They will learn the techniques of the masters.
8. Teachers may ask their students questions about their subject.
9. New artists will learn about line, color, and space.
10. Any good teacher will demand hard work.

Interrupted Verb Phrases

A verb phrase is often interrupted by one or more words. The verb phrases in the following examples are in **bold** type.

> We **should** never **have crossed** that desert.
> Some vegetables **will** not **grow** well in the desert.

To find the verb phrase in a question, turn the question around to make a statement.

> **Have** people **discovered** oil and natural gas beneath some deserts?
>
> (People *have discovered* oil and natural gas beneath some deserts.)

Throughout the rest of this book, a verb phrase will be called a verb.

CONNECT TO SPEAKING AND WRITING

Not and its contraction *n't* are never part of a verb phrase.

That camel **did** not **stop** at the oasis.

That camel **did**n't **stop** at the oasis.

When you are writing formally, avoid using the contraction *n't*. You can use it in speaking or in informal writing, however.

You can learn more about contractions on pages L625–L626.

REACHING ALL LEARNERS

Struggling Learners

Remind students that the word *not* is an adverb and is never part of a verb phrase. Have students make up five more sentences with verb phrases using the word *not*.

GETTING STUDENTS INVOLVED

Reciprocal Teaching

Divide the class in half. One by one, each student on side A creates a sentence containing a verb phrase and the word *not*. After listening to the sentence, a student from side B rewords the sentence without using the word *not*. If the student on side B rewords the sentence correctly without the word *not*, side B earns a point. If not, side A earns a point. Remind students that they must listen carefully in order to revise the sentences.

A DIFFERENT APPROACH

Visual

Rather than have students write out the exercises in **Practice Your Skills** individually, have them take turns coming to the board to complete the sentences. If time permits, have students write additional sentences with verb phrases.

HOME WORK

Have students find out more about deserts using the library, Internet, or other resources. They should then write two paragraphs about deserts. Students' paragraphs should contain at least five verb phrases. Allow students to read their competed desert paragraphs to the class and work together to identify the verb phrases.

PRACTICE YOUR SKILLS

Check Your Understanding

Finding Verb Phrases

Social Studies **Write each verb phrase.**

1. Camels are often used for desert travel.
2. Camels can travel for days with little food or water.
3. The hump on a camel's back is used for fat storage.
4. Arabian camels will often eat thorny plants.
5. They can carry heavy supplies.
6. A camel might live 40 years.
7. Camels have traveled up to 25 miles in one day.
8. They hardly ever act obstinate.
9. Have you ever ridden a camel?
10. Nomads didn't build permanent homes in the desert.
11. Early people could not live in deserts for very long.
12. Some Indians had settled in the Sonoran Desert.
13. They were soon learning techniques for good crops.
14. These Indians would sometimes dig canals with sticks and poles.
15. The canals would carry water to the settlements.

Connect to the Writing Process: Prewriting

Listing Verbs

You have just returned from a trip through the desert. Write a list of verbs that will tell your friends about your experiences. Assume these friends are interested in making the same trip. The verbs should tell them what you did.

Communicate Your Ideas

APPLY TO WRITING

Narrative Paragraph: *Verbs*

Use your list of verbs from the preceding exercise and write a paragraph for your friends that tells what you did on your trip to the desert last summer. Describe your experiences in the order they happened. When you have finished, underline the verbs you used. Brainstorm answers to the following questions before writing your first draft.

- Which desert did you visit last summer? Where is it located?
- What did you do first? What was your impression of this experience?
- What did you do second? Why was this experience important?
- What was the most amazing feature of the desert? Why?

IDENTIFYING COMMON STUMBLING BLOCKS

Problem

- Using nonstandard verb forms, such as *had brung* and *had went*

Solution

- Remind students that they must use the correct form of the verbs in verb phrases. Have students use the correct forms, *had brought* and *had gone* in two sentences.

YOUR IDEAS

For Using Verb Forms

REACHING ALL LEARNERS

Struggling Learners/Advanced Learners

Before completing **QuickCheck,** pair advanced learners with struggling learners to review ways of identifying subjects and verbs. Have students practice a few examples together in their paired groups. Then work through **QuickCheck** together.

Mixed Practice

Science Topic **Write the subject and verb in each sentence.**

1. Insects have great strength.
2. An ant, for example, moved a stone fifty-two times its own weight.
3. A beetle carried something on its back 850 times its own weight.
4. A person with similar strength could do great things.
5. Such an individual could probably pull a 14,000 pound trailer truck.
6. Scientists haven't overlooked the other unusual feats of insects either.
7. A mosquito can carry something twice as heavy as itself.
8. Some insects can fly hundreds of miles nonstop.
9. Butterflies in large swarms have flown from the United States to the island of Bermuda.
10. Sailors have also seen insects far out at sea.

Different Positions of Subjects

A sentence is in **natural order** when the subject comes before the verb.

In the following examples, each subject is underlined once, and each verb is underlined twice.

The Civil War lasted from 1861 until 1865.

This war caused many deaths.

When the verb or part of the verb phrase comes before the subject, the sentence is in **inverted order.**

To find the subject in such a sentence, turn the sentence around to its natural order.

INVERTED ORDER	From deep in the forest appeared the soldiers.
NATURAL ORDER	The soldiers appeared from deep in the forest.
INVERTED ORDER	Out of the dark night roared the thunder of a cannon.
NATURAL ORDER	The thunder of a cannon roared out of the dark night.

Questions are usually written in inverted order. To find the subject easily in a question, change the question into a statement.

QUESTION	Did differences arise between the North and the South?
STATEMENT	Differences did arise between the North and the South.
QUESTION	Was the North a place of large cities?
STATEMENT	The North was a place of large cities.

Sentences beginning with *there* or *here* are also in inverted order. To find the subject easily in such a sentence, turn it around to its natural order.

INVERTED ORDER	Here is an artifact from the Civil War.
NATURAL ORDER	An artifact from the Civil War is here.

USING STUDENTS' STRENGTHS

Multiple Intelligences: Linguistic

After reading the definitions and examples of natural and inverted order, have students look up the definitions of *natural* and *inverted* in a dictionary. Discuss how the textbook's explanations of these words compare with the dictionary's definitions. Have students provide examples of each term.

YOUR IDEAS

For Natural and Inverted Order

YOUR IDEAS
For Developing Workplace Competencies

INVERTED ORDER	There is a Civil War museum in Gettysburg, Pennsylvania.
NATURAL ORDER	A Civil War museum is in Gettysburg, Pennsylvania.
	(Sometimes *there* must be dropped for the sentence to make sense.)

You can learn about subject and verb agreement with inverted order on pages L421–L422.

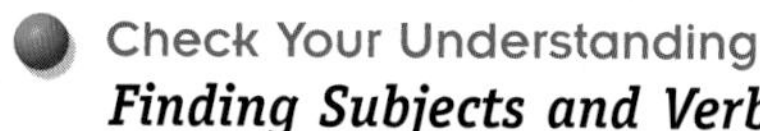

Check Your Understanding
Finding Subjects and Verbs

History Topic **Write the subject and verb in each sentence.**

1. For what reasons was the Civil War important?
2. There are economic, political, social, and emotional reasons.
3. Here is an explanation of the conflict.
4. In ruins was left the South's agriculture.
5. Did many people in the South survive starvation?
6. In the North were the winners with a strong industrial economy.
7. To the South moved some Northerners after the end of the war.
8. How did the free African Americans feel?
9. For all Americans there was the powerful federal government.
10. After four years of conflict came a time of reconstruction.

Connect to the Writing Process: Revising

Varying Sentence Beginnings

11.–15. Add interest to the following paragraph by changing five sentences into inverted order.

Answers may vary. Possible responses are given.

Seven states had left the United States of America
The Confederate States of America were formed.
by 1861. They formed the Confederate States of
America. The Confederate soldiers used cannons on
War was declared by President Abraham Lincoln.
Fort Sumter. President Abraham Lincoln declared war.
He called up troops to save the United States. Four
more states in the South joined the Confederacy. Many
leaders on both sides thought the South could win the
war. These leaders saw divisions in the country. Four
Not leaving the Union were four slave states. Divided were their
slave states did not leave the union. Their citizens
citizens during the Civil War. A short war was predicted incorrectly
were divided during the Civil War. Both sides incorrectly
by both sides.
predicted a short war.

Communicate Your Ideas

APPLY TO WRITING

Persuasive Paragraph: *Positions of Subjects*

The year is 1861, and Abraham Lincoln is president of the United States. You are a Northern industrialist. You want to convince a Southern plantation owner that slavery should no longer be allowed. Write a paragraph that expresses your belief. Try to persuade the Southern plantation owner to agree with you. In your argument be sure to vary the position of the subjects of your sentences to keep the owner's interest.

DEVELOPING WORKPLACE COMPETENCIES

Thinking Skills: Problem Solving

Ask students how the persuasive paragraph about slavery presents problems to solve. Both the issue of slavery and the writing task itself present issues and problems to solve. Discuss with students ways in which these problems might be solved. Then ask students to suggest ways that such problem-solving skills might be helpful in future careers. How might issues and task-oriented problems be dealt with in a positive manner? What types of problems might students face in their future careers, and how will they deal with them? How do students think persuasive writing helps them practice their problem-solving skills? Allow time for students to share their views on these topics.

INTEGRATING TECHNOLOGY

Computer

Have students use computers and word-processing software to create a list of at least ten sentences that contain the understood subject *you*. Students' sentences can be about a specific topic or various topics. After students have completed their sentences, have them exchange papers. Students should review each other's sentences for grammatical or spelling errors. They should correct these errors for their final paper.

Understood Subjects

When the subject of a sentence is not stated, the subject is an **understood *you*.**

The subject *you* is not stated in a command or a request.

COMMAND	(**you**) Wait for me in the library.
REQUEST	(**you**) Please check out that book for me.

PRACTICE YOUR SKILLS

Check Your Understanding

Finding Subjects and Verbs

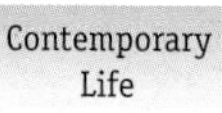

Write the subject and verb in each sentence. If the subject is an understood *you*, write *you* in parentheses.

1. Get ready for the modern public library. (you)
2. Please follow me on a tour. (you)
3. The public library offers a variety of adventures.
4. May I first show you the nonprint media?
5. Look at the videotapes, DVD disks, and microfilm. (you)
6. Please click on the computer's database. (you)
7. Do the icons identify clearly the library's holdings?
8. Take a right turn for the books and magazines. (you)
9. Please enjoy the fun of listening and viewing. (you)
10. Look for biographies behind the nonfiction section. (you)
11. Listen to a book on tape. (you)
12. The activity schedule is in the lobby.
13. Mark your calendar for the job fair. (you)
14. Do not forget your books. (you)
15. Come back for a longer visit. (you)

Connect to the Writing Process: Revising

***Using the Understood* You**

Rewrite the following instructions using the understood *you*.

First, ~~you should~~ decide on a research subject. Then, ~~you~~ look at the title of the book. Find ~~You find~~ the year of publication on the back of the title page. Next, ~~you should~~ read the table of contents. Note ~~You can note~~ the length of the chapters on your subject. ~~You might~~ Also ~~also~~ look at the list of the book's topics in the index. Then ~~you can often~~ read about the author. Last, ~~you can~~ make a decision about the usefulness of the book.

Communicate Your Ideas

APPLY TO WRITING

Directions: *Understood* You

Do you have a favorite place in the school media center or the public library? Write directions on how to get there for a person new to the school. Assume that the person knows nothing about the media center or the library. Use sentences with an understood *you* so that your directions are short and easy to follow. Before writing, think about these questions.

- Where will the map begin?
- What do I see as I walk this route?
- Where do I turn, and in what direction do I turn each time?

REACHING ALL STUDENTS

English Language Learners

Discuss with students who the *you* refers to in the **Connect to the Writing Process** paragraph. Who might *you* refer to in this paragraph? Have students volunteer responses. (The *you* refers to the reader in general.)

TIMESAVER *QuickCheck*

Remind students that their directions need to be concise and clear for their readers. Evaluate students' writing on how well they use the understood *you* and on the conciseness of their directions. Writing that accomplishes both of these goals should be considered excellent, while writing that achieves only one of these goals should be considered good.

USING STUDENTS' STRENGTHS

Multiple Intelligences: Linguistic

After they have completed the **QuickCheck** activity, have students write out responses to the questions and statements about making a speech. Students should write at least one response sentence for each of the ten items in **QuickCheck.**

YOUR IDEAS

For Writing Prompts

QuickCheck Mixed Practice

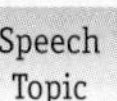

Speech Topic

Write the subject and verb in each sentence. If the subject is an understood *you,* write *you* in parentheses.

1. Have you ever given a speech?
2. Try it sometime. (You)
3. There are many opportunities for speeches.
4. Do not think of the experience as difficult or scary. (You)
5. To many speakers it is a thrill.
6. Prepare your information. (You)
7. Practice your delivery. (You)
8. At the end of the speech is a sense of accomplishment.
9. There is a speaker somewhere inside you.
10. Will you make a speech next week?

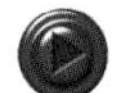

Compound Subjects

A **compound subject** is two or more subjects in one sentence that have the same verb and are joined by a conjunction.

In the following examples, each subject is underlined once and each verb is underlined twice.

ONE SUBJECT	Sacajawea joined the expedition.
COMPOUND SUBJECT	Lewis **and** Clark explored the West.
COMPOUND SUBJECT	Sacajawea, Lewis, **and** Clark traded horses with the Shoshone.

A pair of conjunctions such as *either/or, neither/nor,* or *both/and* may also join the parts of a compound subject.

Either Lewis **or** Clark had brought supplies.

You can learn about subject and verb agreement with compound subjects on pages L426–L427.

CONNECT TO WRITER'S CRAFT

Writers often combine two short sentences that have the same verb. The new sentence will have a compound subject. Combining sentences makes writing flow smoothly.

SEPARATE	**Lewis** traveled into new territory.
	Clark traveled into new territory.
COMBINED	**Lewis** and **Clark** traveled into new territory.

PRACTICE YOUR SKILLS

Check Your Understanding

Finding Compound Subjects

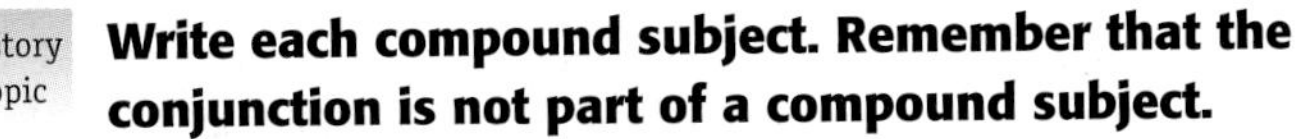

History Topic **Write each compound subject. Remember that the conjunction is not part of a compound subject.**

1. Meriwether Lewis and William Clark led an expedition.
2. President Jefferson and Congress sponsored the trip in 1804.
3. Science, profit, and politics were some of the reasons for the trip.
4. Neither Lewis nor Clark would go alone across the country.
5. New places and dangers challenged them.

USING STUDENTS' STRENGTHS

Multiple Intelligences: Spatial

Provide students with magazines that they can cut apart. Have students find photographs from the magazines to help them create sentences with compound subjects. The images from the photos will represent the subjects in their sentences. Students should glue down their images in the proper locations in their sentences and write out the remaining sentence text. Students should create at least three illustrated compound subject sentences.

YOUR IDEAS
For Reaching All Students

6. Two interpreters and expert frontiersmen joined the explorers.
7. The Rocky Mountains and the Pacific Ocean were their goals.
8. New travel routes and nature interested them.
9. Sacajawea, Cameahwait, and the Shoshone helped the men.
10. The two explorers and their group inspired westward travel.

Connect to the Writing Process: Revising
Writing Sentences with Compound Subjects

Combine each pair of sentences into one sentence with a compound subject. Use *and* or *or* to connect your subjects. [Answers may vary. Possible responses are given.]

11. Meriwether Lewis [and William Clark] had served in the army. ~~William Clark also was in the military.~~
12. Plants [and animals] were studied. ~~Animals were studied.~~
13. The Missouri River [and the Yellowstone River were] ~~was~~ explored. ~~The Yellowstone River was explored, too.~~
14. The Rocky Mountains [and the Cascade Range] were crossed. ~~The Cascade Range was crossed.~~
15. The Mandan people [and the Shoshone] helped the expedition. ~~The Shoshone also helped.~~

Compound Verbs

A **compound verb** is two or more verbs that have the same subject and are joined by a conjunction.

In the examples on the following page, each subject is underlined once, and each verb is underlined twice.

ONE VERB	The rabbit ate the food.
COMPOUND VERB	The rabbit ate the food and hopped away.

A sentence can include both a compound subject and a compound verb.

The rabbit and the squirrel scampered away and searched for food.

CONNECT TO WRITER'S CRAFT

Writers often combine two short sentences that have the same subject to make their writing smoother. The following sentences were combined with a compound verb.

SEPARATE	The squirrel **looked** around cautiously.
	The squirrel quickly **scurried** up the tree.
COMBINED	The squirrel **looked** around cautiously and quickly **scurried** up the tree.

PRACTICE YOUR SKILLS

Check Your Understanding

Finding Compound Verbs

Science Topic **Write each verb. Remember that a conjunction is not part of a compound verb.**

1. A school science project requires careful observation but prohibits dangerous experiments.
2. One eighth grader chose her pet, focused on nutrition, and wrote a hypothesis.
3. Nailah watched and collected data on her pet rabbit Brad.

REACHING ALL STUDENTS

Struggling Learners

Tell students that in order to combine sentences and form compound verbs, the sentences must have the same subject. Provide students with the following example to show how sentences with different subjects cannot be combined to form a sentence with a compound verb.

- The squirrel looked around cautiously.
- The cat quickly scurried up the tree.
- The squirrel and the cat looked around cautiously and quickly scurried up the tree.

Explain that the reader does not know which animal looked and which one scurried. Both animals did not look and scurry, so the new sentence does not express the original information correctly.

A DIFFERENT APPROACH

Tactile

After students have written out their responses to the **Practice Your Skills** activity, have them work with a partner to complete the activity in a different way. Students should use their fingers to trace the words on the page that are compound verbs. For items one through ten, students should read the sentence orally to their partner and trace over the verbs in each sentence with their fingers.

4. For three weeks she carefully measured and recorded Brad's food.
5. The baby rabbit ate quickly and did not see Nailah.
6. The rabbit either ate or slept in his big, cozy cage.
7. He ate and ate and gained weight.
8. Nailah added up the amount of food, calculated Brad's weight gain, and recorded her results.
9. Then Nailah fed Brad less food for three weeks but allowed exercise.
10. Fewer calories and exercise resulted in weight loss and more energy but did not make Brad happier.

Connect to the Writing Process: Revising

Writing Sentences with Compound Verbs

Combine each pair of sentences into one sentence with a compound verb. Use *and, or,* or *but* to connect verbs.

11. Scientists perform their own experiments. and ~~Scientists~~ observe the results.
12. They set up controls for their experiments. ~~They~~ and test their hypotheses.
13. Scientists take notes. and ~~They~~ write down their observations.
14. Some scientists mix or store chemicals in test tubes. ~~They store chemicals in test tubes also.~~
15. Archaeologists dig gently. and ~~They~~ look for artifacts.
16. They save each tiny bone. and ~~They~~ rebuild fossils.
17. Botanists plant seeds. and ~~They~~ develop new plants.
18. Gottleib Zinn went to Mexico. and ~~He~~ developed the zinnia.
19. Geologists analyze soil. but Some dig for minerals.
20. Gemologists cut jewels. and ~~They~~ appraise them.

 Mixed Practice

Contemporary Life **Write the subject and verb in each sentence.**

1. How many young people dream and wish for a vehicle?
2. Cars, trucks, motorcycles, and vans will take them home, deliver them to the movies, and let them cruise the open spaces.
3. A car costs money and gobbles extra cash.
4. The state requires a tag and registration and charges for both.
5. Then the state asks for proof of insurance and will not allow registration without it.
6. The insurance company charges people under twenty-five a high rate but will accept regular monthly payments.
7. A car owner buys gas, pays for oil, and worries about regular maintenance.
8. Of course, any reasonable person must buy and install a good sound system.
9. No one expects a ticket for a violation or plans for a large fine.
10. A car or truck provides many benefits but at a steep price.

EXPANDING THE LESSON

Using Technology

You will find additional **instructional** and **practice** materials for this chapter at http://www.bkenglish.com.

YOUR IDEAS

For Using Technology

LESSON 2 *(pages L34–L37)*

OBJECTIVES

- **To identify declarative, interrogative, imperative, and exclamatory sentences**
- **To use correct punctuation with various types of sentences**

Create Interest

Write these sentences with missing punctuation on the board:

- Have you ever studied geometry
- Take the book to your math teacher
- This geometry class is amazing
- I learned to measure the angles of a triangle

Ask students to tell what is similar and different about the sentences. Then, have students come to the board to add the correct punctuation to each sentence. Have students write additional sentences of various types with the correct end punctuation.

USING STUDENTS' STRENGTHS

Multiple Intelligences: Linguistic

Select a reading passage that includes many interrogative sentences. Read the passage aloud to students. Have students identify the interrogative sentences they hear. They should try to remember as many of the questions as possible. Write these interrogative sentences on the board as students recall them. Then have student volunteers rewrite each question as a declarative sentence.

Kinds of Sentences

All sentences can be grouped according to their purpose. A sentence can make a statement, ask a question, give a command, or express strong feeling. The punctuation mark that belongs at the end of a sentence is determined by the purpose of that sentence.

A **declarative sentence** makes a statement or expresses an opinion and ends with a period.

> One, three, and seven are prime numbers**.**
>
> (statement)
>
> Geometry is harder than algebra**.**
>
> (opinion)

An **interrogative sentence** asks a question and ends with a question mark.

> How is math important to your life**?**

An **imperative sentence** makes a request or gives a command and ends with either a period or an exclamation point.

> Answer problems 1–4 on page 63 of your mathematics book**.**
>
> (This imperative sentence ends with a period because it is a mild request.)
>
> Don't forget to study**!**
>
> (This sentence ends with an exclamation point because it is a strong command.)

Guide Instruction

By Modeling Strategies

Draw a four-column chart on the board with the following headings: *declarative (tell), exclamatory (exclaim), interrogative (ask),* and *imperative (demand)*. Explain each different type of sentence to the class. Write an example sentence for each type under the headings. Then have student volunteers come to the board to write another example of each sentence on the chart.

Consolidate Skills

Through Guided Practice

The **Check Your Understanding** activities on pages L35–L36 will help students identify various types of sentences. To help students understand the terms *declarative, interrogative, imperative*, and *exclamatory*, have them define the terms using a dictionary. Then have students come up with alternative meanings in their own words.

An **exclamatory sentence** expresses strong feelings and ends with an exclamation point.

What an interesting problem that is**!**

Connect to Speaking and Writing

You can sometimes use different kinds of sentences to express similar ideas.

I would like you to study math with me**.**
(declarative)

Will you study math with me**?**
(interrogative)

Please study math with me**.**
(imperative)

Oh, do I ever need your help with math**!**
(exclamatory)

Using different kinds of sentences will help you get the attention of your listener or reader.

Practice Your Skills

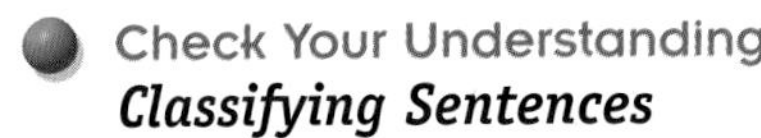

Check Your Understanding

Classifying Sentences

Math Topic

Write each sentence. Label each one using the following abbreviations. Then write the correct punctuation mark.

declarative = *d.* imperative = *imp.*
interrogative = *int.* exclamatory = *ex.*

1. Sometimes you have to use indirect measurement to calculate distances. declarative

2. Do you know how to use indirect measurement? interrogative

3. Suppose a six-foot fence casts an eight-foot shadow. imperative

Reaching All Students

English Language Learners

Tell students that the punctuation following a sentence depends on the kind of sentence and on the message or level of emotion expressed in the sentence. Review with students the various uses of periods and exclamation points. Point out that the emotion expressed in a sentence can determine whether it is declarative or exclamatory. Provide the following examples:

- I really need some help with algebra. (declarative if expressing little emotion)
- I really need some help with algebra! (exclamatory if expressing great emotion)

A Different Approach

Visual

Have students take turns writing the ten sentences from the **Practice Your Skills** activity on the board. Students should add the correct end punctuation. Beside each sentence, they should write either *declarative, interrogative, imperative*, or *exclamatory*.

Apply to Communication

Through Independent Writing

The **Communicate Your Ideas/Apply to Writing** activity on page L37 prompts students to write persuasive dialogue using different kinds of sentences and correct punctuation. Ask students how various kinds of sentences will make their dialogue more interesting to an audience.

Transfer to Everyday Life

Finding Exclamatory Sentences in Advertisements

Have students locate at least ten exclamatory sentences in advertisements. Students should look at billboards, television commercials, and magazine ads to find exclamatory sentences. Have students write down their ten sentences to share with class.

Pull It All Together

By Sharing

Have students work with a partner and exchange the persuasive dialogues

YOUR IDEAS

For Punctuating Sentences

SELECTION AMENDMENT
Description of change: excerpted
Rationale: to focus on the grammar skill

4. You know that a telephone pole casts a twenty-five-foot shadow⊙ declarative
5. About how high is the telephone pole**?** interrogative
6. Don't shake your head at me**!** exlamatory and imperative
7. You can use triangles to measure the fence post and then the telephone pole⊙ declarative
8. The shadows of the post and the pole are proportional⊙ declarative
9. Use cross products of the proportions to approximate the corresponding height of the telephone pole⊙ imperative
10. The telephone pole is approximately nineteen feet, six inches high⊙ declarative

Connect to the Writing Process: Editing
Punctuating Sentences

Dialogue in a story or play reveals the thoughts and feelings of the characters. To increase the interest of the reader or audience, dialogue should have different types of sentences. The sentences should be punctuated correctly to show how the dialogue is to be read or heard. Rewrite the following dialogue adapted from Mark Twain, using the correct end mark for each sentence.

Hastings: Henry, how would you like to go to London**?**
Henry: Thank you, no⊙
Hastings: Listen to me⊙I'm thinking of taking a month's option on the Gould and Curry Extension for the locators⊙
Henry: And—
Hastings: They want one million dollars for it⊙

they have written. Students should identify all four kinds of sentences in their partners' writing. Have students suggest ways in which the dialogue might be improved.

Check Understanding

Different Kinds of Sentences in Literature

Have students locate two examples of declarative, interrogative, imperative, and exclamatory sentences in a literary work. They might use a novel they are reading or find sentences in their literature textbook. Students should write down the eight sentences they find and share them with the class.

Henry: Not too much—if the claim works out the way it appears it may⊙

Hastings: I'm going to try to sell it to London interests, which means a trip there, and I want you to go with me, because you know more about these papers than I⊙

Henry: No, thanks⊙

Hastings: I'll make it well worth your while⊙I'll pay all your expenses and give you something over if I make the sale⊙

Henry: I have a job**!**

Hastings: I'll arrange for you to get a leave of absence⊙What do you say**?**

Henry: No⊙

Hastings: Why**?**

—*Walter Hackett,* The Million-Pound Bank Note

Communicate Your Ideas

APPLY TO WRITING

Persuasive Writing: *Dialogue*

Write a portion of dialogue for a scene in a play that a parent or other adult will see or read. Show one person trying to persuade someone else to do something that he or she does not want to do. Perhaps one of your characters wants to go the movies while the other character wants to go to the mall. To make the dialogue interesting, write different kinds of sentences. Make sure to use the correct punctuation for each kind of sentence.

TIMESAVER *QuickCheck*

Students' dialogues should contain at least one example each of declarative, imperative, interrogative, and exclamatory sentences. Students earn twenty points (awarded one time only for each) for the appropriate use of each kind of sentence and one point for correct punctuation of each of the four kinds of sentences, for a total of eighty-four points. Students earn an additional sixteen points for their dialogues actually being persuasive.

HOME STUDY

Have students write about a conversation they have had with a family member in which they were trying to persuade a parent, adult, or sibling in some way. Student should identify at least one interrogative sentence that was used in the persuasive conversation and discuss the function of that question to the conversation.

FOR REVIEWING SKILLS

Using *Sentence Diagraming*

Sentence diagraming helps students develop variety and style in their writing. In this activity, students will focus on diagraming subjects and verbs.

Sample Answers for *Sentence Diagraming:*

1. Cats | are sleeping

2. (you) | Be quiet

3. young / old (Both ... and) | are resting

4. (you) | Are watching

5. Cats | wake (and) leave

Sentence Diagraming

Diagraming Subjects and Verbs

A **sentence diagram** is a picture made up of lines and words. It can help you find and identify all the parts of a sentence.

Subjects and Verbs A baseline is a horizontal line that is the foundation of all sentence diagrams. A straight, vertical line separates the subject (or subjects) on the left from the verb (or verbs) on the right. Capital letters are included in the diagram, but punctuation is not. In the second example, notice that the whole verb phrase is written on the baseline.

People work.

People | work

Roy has been sleeping.

Roy | has been sleeping

Questions A question is diagramed as if it were a statement.

Has Dale arrived? (Dale has arrived.)

Dale | has arrived

Understood Subjects When the subject of a sentence is an understood *you,* as in a command or a request, place *you* in parentheses in the subject position.

Watch.

(you) | Watch

Compound Subjects and Verbs Place the parts of a compound subject or a compound verb on parallel horizontal lines. Then put the conjunction connecting each part on a broken line between them. In the first example, notice that the two conjunctions are written on either side of the broken line.

Both girls and boys attended.

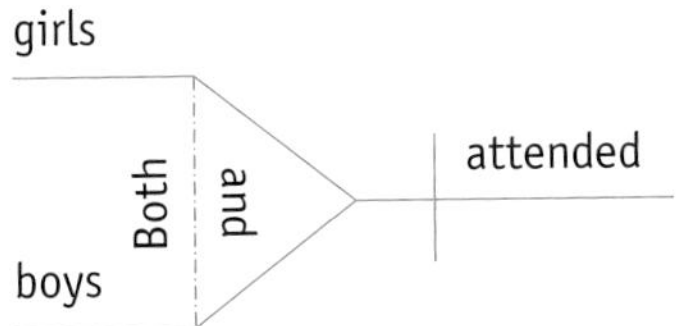

Karen and Bart dived or swam.

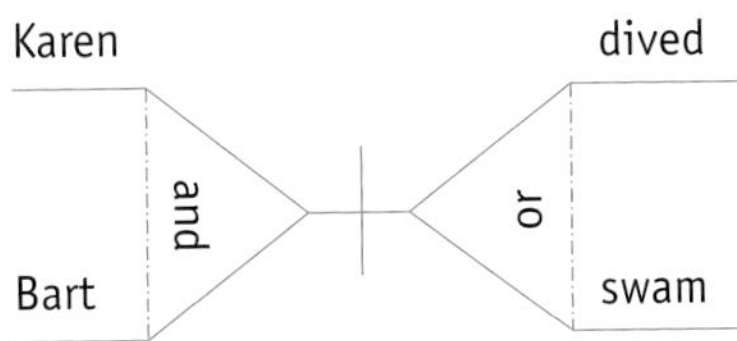

Practice Your Skills

Diagraming Subjects and Verbs

Diagram the following sentences or copy them. If your teacher tells you to copy them, draw one line under each subject and two lines under each verb. If the subject is an understood *you*, write *you* in parentheses.

1. Cats are sleeping.
2. Be quiet! (you)
3. Both young and old are resting.
4. Are you watching?
5. Cats wake and leave.
6. Elu and I are following and watching.
7. Elu, listen.
8. They are purring.
9. Do cats bite?
10. They might come and stay.

6. Elu | and | I | are following | and | watching

7. (you) | listen | Elu

8. They | are purring

9. cats | Do bite

10. They | might come | and | stay

Using *CheckPoint*

This feature on sentences can be used as further independent practice or as a cumulative review of the chapter. It covers finding subjects and verbs and writing different kinds of sentences.

CheckPoint

Finding Subjects and Verbs

Write the subject and verb in each sentence. Label each *S* for subject or *V* for verb.

1. Warm air (S) and moisture (S) rise (V) into the sky.
2. At a certain height, the warm air (S) cools (V).
3. At the cooler temperatures, the air (S) can't (V) hold all its moisture.
4. The extra moisture (S) then changes (V) into small drops of water or bits of ice.
5. From those droplets clouds (S) will (V) develop.
6. About 100,000,000 droplets (S) form (V) one large raindrop.
7. *Cirrus* (S), *stratus* (S), and *cumulus* (S) are (V) the names of the three main types of clouds.
8. Clouds (S) are always changing (V) their shapes.
9. Weather forecasters (S) can look (V) at clouds and learn (V) much about the day's weather.
10. Do you (S) see (V) any clouds in the sky today?

Finding Subjects and Verbs

Write the subjects and verbs in the following sentences. Label each *S* for subject or *V* for verb. If the subject is an understood *you*, write *you* in parentheses.

1. Stand (V) beside Barbara for the picture. (you) (S)
2. Amanda (S) does (V) not have a paper route anymore.
3. Sing (V) more softly. (you) (S)
4. At the aquarium one porpoise (S) blows (V) a horn and leaps (V) through a hoop.

5. From behind the door jumped a clown. [V: jumped; S: clown]
6. Wade has never ridden on a subway. [S: Wade; V: ridden]
7. Look for the clues in the mystery. (you) [V: Look; S: (you)]
8. On the top of the tent lay the compass. [V: lay; S: compass]
9. Mozart and Beethoven were famous composers. [S: Mozart, Beethoven; V: were]
10. Should the dogs go out now? [S: dogs; V: go]

Writing Sentences

Write sentences that follow the directions below. (The sentences may come in any order.) Write about one of the following topics or a topic of your choice: a race you have seen or a race you have participated in. [Answers may vary. Possible responses are given.]

1. Write a declarative sentence. The last race I was in was a sack race.
2. Write an interrogative sentence. Don't you think sack races are funny?
3. Write an imperative sentence. You should enter a sack race next time you have a chance.
4. Write an exclamatory sentence. They are hilarious!
5. Write a sentence with a subject of understood *you*. Think about it. (you)

Underline each subject once and each verb twice. Remember to add capital letters and end punctuation.

YOUR IDEAS

For Reviewing Sentences

Using *Language and Self-Expression*

Consider using this writing assignment to assess students' ability to use sentences correctly and effectively. You may want students to complete the assignment as part of a descriptive writing strand for their portfolios.

Prewriting

Suggest that students revisit their analysis of the painting that they did in *Making Visual Connections* on page L4.

Tell students that asking themselves questions like the ones below during prewriting may help them focus on why they chose to write about these particular people and things in their lives.

- Who are the people that are most important in your life?
- Do you spend any time with pets?
- What do you like to do in your free time?

FOR YOUR INFORMATION

About the Artwork

This self-portrait shows the artist with her pet monkey, Fulang-Chang. The artist added the painted frame around her self-portrait in 1939 after completing the original painting in 1937.

About the Artist

Mexican artist Frida Kahlo began painting at the age of 19, but she was not widely known as a painter until after her death. Her bold, stylized paintings have been called Surrealistic, a connection she denied. She produced some 200 paintings, most of which are self-portraits.

Language and *Self-Expression*

Frida Kahlo often painted her own portrait. She used personal elements such as her pets to show a side of herself. She chose colors to set the mood, such as neutral tones to show strength and the ability to survive difficult circumstances.

In your mind, picture your own portrait. Write a description, including the images as well as artistic elements such as color, shape, and space. Vary your sentences by using compound subjects and verbs and different kinds of sentences.

Prewriting List items, people, or pets that are important to you and help explain your personality. Next describe the mood of your self-portrait, and list several colors that support this mood. What kinds of lines and shapes would the portrait have?

Drafting Write a description that is three to four paragraphs long. Devote one paragraph to the images and another to the colors. You could explain the portrait's message or title in the last paragraph.

Revising Read all of your paper except the last paragraph to a classmate. Ask him or her to describe what the message or title might be. What are the differences between what your classmate predicted and what you wrote? Revise your description if necessary. Also check for variety in subjects and predicates and in the kinds of sentences.

Editing Check for errors in spelling, grammar, and punctuation.

Publishing Organize a "portrait reading" in which one person reads aloud someone else's portrait and the class uses clues to determine whose portrait it is.

The Sentence

A **sentence** is a group of words that expresses a complete thought.

A **sentence fragment** is a group of words that expresses an incomplete thought.

Subjects and Predicates

The **subject** names the person, place, thing, or idea that the sentence is about. *(page L8)*

A **simple subject** is the main word in the complete subject. *(pages L10–L11)*

A **compound subject** is two or more subjects in one sentence that have the same verb and are joined by a conjunction. *(pages L28–L29)*

The **predicate** tells something about the subject. *(page L8)*

A **simple predicate,** or **verb**, is the main word or phrase in the complete predicate. *(pages L14–L15)*

A **verb phrase** includes the main verb plus any helping, or auxiliary, verbs. *(pages L17–L18)*

A **compound verb** is two or more verbs that have the same subject and are joined by a conjunction. *(pages L30–L31)*

Kinds of Sentences

A **declarative sentence** makes a statement or expresses an opinion and ends with a period. *(page L34)*

An **interrogative sentence** asks a question and ends with a question mark. *(page L34)*

An **imperative sentence** makes a request or gives a command and ends with either a period or an exclamation point. *(page L34)*

An **exclamatory sentence** expresses strong feelings and ends with an exclamation point. *(page L35)*

Other Information About Sentences

Recognizing subjects in various positions *(pages L22–L24)*

Diagraming sentences *(pages L38–L39)*

Using *Another Look*

Another Look summarizes the terms defined in the chapter and provides cross-references to the specific pages on which they are explained. Consider having students use this feature prior to completing **CheckPoint** or taking the post-test. Students who can provide several examples of each term should be able to score well on either measurement.

Using *the Posttest*

Assessing Learning

The posttest will help you and your students assess where they stand in their ability to identify sentences and sentence fragments, as well as different kinds of sentences.

IDENTIFYING COMMON STUMBLING BLOCKS

Following is a list of the most common errors students make when using writing sentences.

Problem

- Sentence fragments

Practice

- Instruction, pp. L5–L6
- Practice, pp. L6–L7

Problem

- Correctly punctuating sentences

Solution

- Instruction, pp. L34–L35
- Practice, pp. L35–L37

Directions

Write the letter of the term that correctly identifies the underlined word or words in each sentence.

EXAMPLE **1.** Claude Monet <u>was a French Impressionist painter</u>.
A verb phrase
B complete predicate
C simple predicate
D compound verb

ANSWER **1 B**

1. <u>Throughout the gallery were hung priceless paintings.</u>

2. <u>Edvard Munch's most well-known painting</u> is *The Scream*.

3. The famous painter Paul Gauguin <u>worked as a stockbroker</u>.

4. Van Gogh <u>was born</u> in 1853 in the Netherlands.

5. In public buildings <u>Diego Rivera</u> painted a series of murals.

6. Salvador Dali <u>studied</u> and <u>painted</u> in Madrid and Paris.

7. <u>Rossetti</u> and <u>Alighieri</u> share the same first name: Dante.

8. <u>Dante Gabriel Rossetti</u> was an English painter and poet.

9. The famous poem *The Inferno* <u>was written</u> by Dante Alighieri.

10. <u>Where was Pablo Picasso born?</u>

A DIFFERENT DELIVERY SYSTEM

If you prefer, you can print the posttest from the BK English Test Bank located at http://www.bkenglish.com.

1 A simple subject
B inverted order
C complete subject
D sentence fragment

2 A compound subject
B complete subject
C verb phrase
D inverted order

3 A complete subject
B verb phrase
C compound verb
D complete predicate

4 A complete subject
B compound subject
C verb phrase
D complete predicate

5 A simple subject
B inverted order
C complete predicate
D compound subject

6 A compound verb
B complete predicate
C simple verb
D inverted order

7 A simple subject
B verb phrase
C compound subject
D compound verb

8 A verb phrase
B inverted order
C compound subject
D simple subject

9 A imperative sentence
B complete predicate
C verb phrase
D simple verb

10 A declarative sentence
B sentence fragment
C interrogative sentence
D simple subject

Customizing the Test

Use these questions to add or replace items for alternate versions of the test.

11. Frida Kahlo was a talented painter of vibrant, colorful portraits.

12. Injured seriously in a bus accident in 1925.

13. During her recovery from many operations, she began painting.

14. Kahlo and Diego Rivera, her mentor in art, later married.

15. In 1943 she received a position as professor of painting.

11. A simple verb
B imperative sentence
C complete predicate
D verb phrase

12. A simple verb
B inverted verb
C simple subject
D sentence fragment

13. A verb phrase
B compound verb
C complete subject
D simple verb

14. A inverted order
B compound subject
C complete predicate
D simple subject

15. A declarative sentence
B complete subject
C imperative sentence
D verb phrase

TEACHING SUGGESTIONS

Essential Knowledge and Skills

- Writing to inform such as to explain, describe, report, and narrate
- Writing to entertain such as to compose short stories
- Employing standard English usage in writing for audiences, including pronoun referents
- Writing with increasing accuracy when using pronoun case
- Evaluating how well his/her own writing achieves its purpose
- Taking notes from relevant and authoritative sources such as online searches
- Describing how illustrators' choice of style, elements, and media help to represent or extend the text's meaning

BLOCK SCHEDULING

- If your schedule requires that you cover the chapter in a **shorter time,** use the instruction on nouns and pronouns and the Check Your Understanding and QuickCheck exercises.
- If you want to take advantage of **longer class time,** add these applications to writing: Connect to Speaking and Writing, Connect to the Writing Process, and Apply to Writing exercises.

CHAPTER 2

Nouns and Pronouns

Directions

Read the passage and choose the word or words that correctly complete each sentence. Write the letter of the correct answer.

EXAMPLE Denim jeans are popular with all ages, and __(1)__ hang in almost everyone's closet.

1 **A** it
B they
C you
D we

ANSWER **1 B**

__(1)__ is a short history of denim jeans. __(2)__ are also called blue jeans or dungarees. In the mid-1800s in the __(3)__, the first jeans were designed for a __(4)__ of workers. The jeans were constructed as durable work clothes, and __(5)__ had reinforced seams. Small copper rivets reinforced points of stress on __(6)__ work clothes. My research tells __(7)__ that as time went on, other workers across the country bought __(8)__ blue jeans. Eventually, people in other countries started wearing __(9)__ as well. Nowadays, both men and women stock __(10)__ closets with jeans.

IDENTIFYING COMMON STUMBLING BLOCKS

Following is a list of the most common errors students make when using nouns and pronouns.

Problem
- Noncapitalization of proper nouns

Solution
- Instruction, pp. L54–L55
- Practice, pp. L55–L56

Problem
- Pronoun and antecedent agreement

Solution
- Instruction, pp. L57–L58
- Practice, pp. L58–L59

1 **A** This
B Them
C These
D Those

2 **A** Them
B We
C They
D That

3 **A** united states
B united States
C United states
D United States

4 **A** fleet
B batch
C crew
D herd

5 **A** we
B he
C it
D they

6 **A** this
B that
C these
D them

7 **A** me
B her
C him
D them

8 **A** himself
B themselves
C herself
D itself

9 **A** them
B they
C that
D you

10 **A** my
B our
C their
D your

A DIFFERENT DELIVERY SYSTEM

If you prefer, you can print the pretest from the BK English Test Bank located at http://www.bkenglish.com.

Using *the Pretest*

Assessing Prior Knowledge

The pretest will help you and your students assess where they stand in their basic understanding of nouns and pronouns. The test indicates students' ability to identify nouns and pronouns and to use them effectively in their own writing.

Customizing the Test

Use these questions to add or replace items for alternate versions of the test.

Many people want (11) jeans to have a designer label on the back pocket. They tell (12) that the right label will make them stand out in a (13). (14) will search the mall for hours looking for the perfect pair. They'll try on dozens of pairs before buying (15).

11. A mine
B theirs
C their
D this

12. A ourselves
B herself
C themselves
D itself

13. A swarm
B league
C flock
D crowd

14. A They
B Them
C It
D He

15. A everyone
B one
C few
D anyone

ADDITIONAL RESOURCES

Language Skills Practice . . . . pages 16–26
Transparency Tools FA1, AW3
ESL Practice and Test Preparation . . . . . pages 88–90
Assessment: Chapter Test. . . . . pages 109–116

MAKING VISUAL CONNECTIONS

For Language Development

Ask students what nouns or pronouns they would use to tell a friend about *Dream Catcher.* How would they use nouns and pronouns to tell about the shapes and colors in this artwork?

To Stimulate Writing

Use the questions for art criticism as writing or discussion prompts.

Possible Answers:

Describe The artist used twine, twigs or vines, leather, beads, and feathers.

Analyze The circle's shape dominates the art. Since the circle's center is transparent, you get the idea that something could move through the center. Also, the feathers are attached in a dangling manner that suggests they could sway in a breeze. The curved shaped of the feathers is liquid and in a way suggests movement.

Interpret The title tells me that art is a device to catch dreams. Since dreams are abstract, the meaning of the art is metaphorical. You can't physically catch dreams. The lines of the art are arranged like a net or spider web, which catches things. The dream catcher is a net for dreams.

Judge I think a dream catcher should be displayed somewhere where it can catch a breeze or near where a person sleeps or daydreams. I would hang it in the window of my room. There, it could catch the breeze if I opened the window. It would also be nearby when I slept, and it would be above the desk where I write my dreams in my journal.

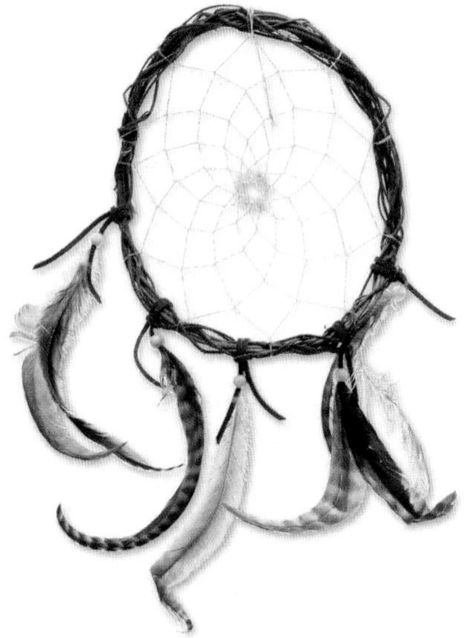

Sarochin Tollette, *Dream Catcher,* 1996.
Twined vines, leather, beads, feathers, mother-of-pearl, and artificial sinew, 9 by 7½ by 2½ inches.

Describe What are the materials the artist used to make this work of art?

Analyze What is the dominant shape in *Dream Catcher*? Describe the potential for movement in the work.

Interpret What does the title of the work, *Dream Catcher*, tell you about the purpose of the art? How do the lines of the artwork reinforce the title?

Judge Do you think *Dream Catcher* is meant to be displayed in, say, a glass case, or is it meant to be displayed somewhere such as in a doorway or window? Why do you think this? If *Dream Catcher* were yours, where would you display it? Why would you choose this particular location?

At the end of this chapter, you will use this artwork to stimulate ideas for writing.

FOR DEVELOPING LANGUAGE SKILLS

LESSON 1 *(pages L49–L56)*

OBJECTIVE

- **To identify nouns, concrete and abstract nouns, compound and collective nouns, and common and proper nouns**

Create Interest

Ask students if they have ever tried to speak with someone who spoke a language different from their own. What were the major ideas—things, people, places—that they tried to communicate? Have students name some words that they tried to express to the other person. Write the nouns on the board.

Nouns

There are thousands of words in English, but there are only eight **parts of speech.** A word's part of speech is determined by the job it does in a sentence. The same word may be used as a noun in one sentence and as an adjective in another sentence.

THE EIGHT PARTS OF SPEECH	
noun (names)	**adverb** (describes, limits)
pronoun (replaces)	**preposition** (relates)
verb (states action or being)	**conjunction** (connects)
adjective (describes, limits)	**interjection** (expresses strong feelings)

Suppose you were in another country and could not speak the language. The words that you would want to know first are those that name people, places, things, or ideas. These words are called nouns. The most frequently used part of speech is the noun.

A **noun** is a word that names a person, a place, a thing, or an idea.

NOUNS	
PEOPLE	girl, men, scientist, Dr. Taylor, meteorologist
PLACES	buildings, cities, Dallas, Atlantic Ocean
THINGS	rain, wind, trees, cotton, clouds, devices

FOR INCREASING STUDENT ACHIEVEMENT

REACHING ALL STUDENTS

Advanced Learners

After reviewing the eight parts of speech, have students identify the part of speech for each underlined word in the following sentences. Write the sentences on the board.

- Daniel wasn't feeling well, so we took him to the doctor. (pronoun)
- The snow began to fall heavily. (adverb)
- The infant crawled under the table. (preposition)
- Jessie likes to swim and fish. (conjunction)
- Kristi pounded on the drum. (verb)

Point out that nouns are used more frequently in English than any other part of speech.

Guide Instruction

By Modeling Strategies

Write the following words on the board: astronauts, woman, Denver, love. Ask students how the words are alike. (They are all nouns.) Then ask students how the words are different. Lead students to understand that there are several different kinds of nouns. *Astronauts* is a plural noun, *woman* is a singular noun, *Denver* is a proper noun, and *love* is an abstract noun. Have students name additional examples for each type of noun.

Consolidate Skills

Through Guided Practice

The **Check Your Understanding** exercises on pages L50, L53, and L55 as well as the **QuickCheck** on page L56 will help students identify nouns. Tell students that they can test to see whether or not a word is a noun by placing either *a, an* or *the* in front of it.

A DIFFERENT APPROACH

Kinesthetic

After students have completed **Check Your Understanding,** have them redo the exercise without using words. Have students read each sentence silently. Then ask a volunteer to act out silently one of the nouns from the sentences as other students try to guess. Continue until students have acted out and guessed all of the nouns.

HOME WORK

As a home work assignment, have students write ten additional sentences on the topic of science. They should underline all of the nouns in each sentence.

Ideas and Qualities	love, friendship, kindness, thoughtfulness courage, patriotism, faith, ideals, ambition

Notice in the examples on the preceding page that some nouns can be seen or touched. These nouns are called **concrete nouns.** Other nouns, called **abstract nouns,** cannot be seen or touched. They may be ideas, qualities, or characteristics. Examples of abstract nouns include nouns such as *faith, courage,* and *kindness.*

You can learn about forming plurals of nouns and possessive nouns on pages L617–L619 and L665–L670.

Connect to Speaking and Writing

When you speak or write, using specific nouns can add interest to your ideas. Notice the difference between the nouns in the following sentences.

The **animals** hid in their den during the **storm.**

The **foxes** hid in their den during the **hurricane.**

The **family** lost their crop of **vegetables.**

The **Jensen family** lost its crop of **potatoes.** 

Practice Your Skills

 Check Your Understanding

Finding Nouns

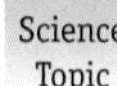

Write each noun. There are 30 nouns.

1. A hurricane begins over the ocean in hot regions of the world.

2. Strong winds whirl.

3. The sky becomes dark with clouds and rain begins to fall.

If it makes sense, the word is probably a noun. Tell students that this test does not work with some proper nouns and with dates. Practice the first example on page L50 together. Then have students use this test to complete the remaining exercises independently.

Apply to Communication

Through Independent Writing

The **Communicate Your Ideas** activities on pages L52 and L56 prompt students to write a description of a painting and an autobiographical paragraph. Ask students how their choices of nouns will differ between each writing assignment. Do they think the nouns used to describe the painting will differ greatly from the nouns in their autobiographical paragraph? Have students discuss the types of nouns they will use in each assignment.

4. A hurricane can blow down trees on the land.
5. These storms begin in the ocean.
6. Scientists called meteorologists predict the path of these storms.
7. An enormous amount of energy is used by a hurricane.
8. People may need faith and courage during a hurricane.
9. Cities in the path of a hurricane are given specific information.
10. Many different scientific devices forecast these destructive storms.

Connect to the Writing Process: Revising

Using Specific Nouns

Rewrite each sentence, replacing the underlined general nouns with more specific nouns. [Answers may vary. Possible responses are given.]

11. You should stock up on ~~supplies~~ food and water before a hurricane.
12. ~~The man~~ Dr. Kimble showed courage during the storm.
13. ~~Our neighbors~~ The Johnsons went to the shelter at a school.
14. A new ~~car~~ sport utility vehicle was crushed by a tree.
15. The police had to close ~~the street~~ Main Street because power lines were down.
16. ~~Rain~~ Torrents pounded the roof for hours.
17. The ~~water~~ flood rushed through the streets and overcame everything in its path.
18. A ~~wind~~ gust tore the roof off the airport hangar.
19. Many airplanes had damaged ~~parts~~ wings.
20. Students from the university sorted through the ~~mess~~ debris during the following week.

DEVELOPING WORKPLACE COMPETENCIES

Thinking Skills: Creative Thinking

After completing the exercise, have students imagine they are rescue workers helping during a hurricane. Have students write two paragraphs on their specific role and how they would help during the crisis. Students should read through their completed paragraphs and identify the specific nouns they used to describe their roles and tasks.

Transfer to Everyday Life

Identifying Nouns in a Magazine Advertisement

Provide students with magazines. Have students work with a partner to find examples of nouns in a magazine ad. Partners should make a list of at least four nouns they find. Have students share their completed lists with the class.

Pull It All Together

By Summarizing

Have students take turns summarizing the different types of nouns discussed in Lesson 1. Have students provide examples for each type of noun.

Check Understanding

Finding Nouns in Literature

Have students use their literature textbooks or a book they are currently reading to locate one example of each type of noun discussed in Lesson 1. Students should find examples of the following types of nouns: concrete,

TIMESAVER *QuickCheck*

Use peer evaluation to check students' writing. Have students exchange papers with a partner. Students should award one point for each concrete noun used to describe the painting by Janet Fish. Discuss results to see which student used the most concrete nouns in their writing. List some of these nouns on the board.

HOME STUDY

As a home study assignment, have students locate an additional work of fine art to describe. Students should write a description of the work using as many concrete nouns as possible. Have them share their art images and completed descriptions with the class. Discuss the effective concrete nouns student used in their writing.

FOR YOUR INFORMATION

About the Artist

Janet Fish, who was born in 1938, knew as a child that she wanted to be an artist. She was influenced by her mother, a sculptor, and by her grandfather, a painter. Although her earlier works were in the Abstract Expressionist style, she now prefers to paint realistic images. Fish says, "I chose to be faithful to what I can see."

Communicate Your Ideas

APPLY TO WRITING

Description: *Nouns*

Janet Fish. *Yellow Pad,* 1997.
Oil on canvas, 36 by 50 inches. The Columbus Museum, Columbus, GA. ©Janet Fish/Licensed by VAGA, New York, NY.

Write a vivid description of Janet Fish's *Yellow Pad* so that someone who has not seen the oil painting could recognize it in a museum. Be sure to use concrete nouns that show specific details rather than vague abstract nouns.

Compound and Collective Nouns

Sometimes a noun has more than one word. These kinds of nouns are called **compound nouns.** Compound nouns may be written as a single word *(baseball),* two words *(home run),* or with a hyphen *(T-shirt).* Always use a dictionary to check the spelling of a compound word.

abstract, compound, collective, common, proper.

COMPOUND NOUNS	
One Word	football, dugout, sideline
Two Words	first base, Super Bowl, jump ball
Hyphenated Words	good-bye, runner-up, warm-up

Other nouns, called **collective nouns,** name a group of people or things.

COMMON COLLECTIVE NOUNS			
band	congregation	flock	orchestra
class	crew	group	swarm
committee	crowd	herd	team
colony	family	league	tribe

Practice Your Skills

Check Your Understanding

Identifying Compound and Collective Nouns

General Interest

Make two columns. Label one column *Compound Nouns* and the other column *Collective Nouns.* Under the appropriate column, list each compound or collective noun.

1. The first lady (comp.) threw the first pitch.
2. The baseball (comp.) landed next to the pitcher.
3. The crowd (coll.) cheered.
4. Not a seat could be found at the ballpark (comp.).
5. The first batter hit the ball to the shortstop (comp.).
6. He was a new player in this league (coll.).

REACHING ALL STUDENTS

English Language Learners

After discussing the charts on this page, tell students that most collective nouns can be used as either singular or plural words. For example, the following uses for the collective noun *crew* are both correct:

- The crew like the new manager. (*crew* is plural)
- The crew likes the new manager. (*crew* is singular)

Have students make sentences for the following collective nouns, using them as both singular and plural: *committee, group, team, class, choir.*

A DIFFERENT APPROACH

Auditory

Draw a two-column chart on the board. Label one column *Compound Nouns* and the other column *Collective Nouns.* Read the first sentence from **Check Your Understanding** aloud as students listen. Have students decide whether the nouns in the sentence are compound or collective. Write each noun on the board in the appropriate column. Continue for each sentence.

HOME WORK

Have students write a paragraph about a sport they like. Using compound and collective nouns, students' paragraphs should explain the object of the game, the general rules of the game, and the environment in which the game is played.

GETTING STUDENTS INVOLVED

Cooperative Learning

After discussing the chart on this page, have students work together to suggest additional items that could be included. Have one student suggest a common noun for the first column. Then have another student suggest a proper noun to go with the first student's common noun. Have students write their nouns on the board in column form.

7. The team (coll.) tried to help him feel better.

8. They wanted to boost his self-esteem (comp.).

9. The next batter hit a home run (comp.).

10. The ball narrowly missed the foul line (comp.).

Connect to the Writing Process: Editing

Writing Compound Nouns

Write correctly the compound noun or nouns in each sentence. If a compound noun is correct, write *C*. Use a dictionary to check your spelling.

11. The band from the ~~highschool~~ high school played at halftime.

12. The stadium was packed with ~~well wishers~~ well-wishers.

13. A reporter covered the game for a newspaper. C

14. The ~~quarter back~~ quarterback took the field.

15. Our family waited for the ~~kick off~~ kickoff.

Common and Proper Nouns

A **common noun** names any person, place, or thing.

A **proper noun** names a particular person, place, or thing.

Proper nouns begin with a capital letter.

COMMON NOUNS	PROPER NOUNS
girl	Amy Clark
country	United States
book	*Hatchet*

As you can see from the chart, some proper nouns may be more than one word. Even though *United States* is two words, it is still the name of only one place.

You can learn more about capitalizing proper nouns in Chapter 15.

Practice Your Skills

Check Your Understanding

Distinguishing Between Common and Proper Nouns

Science Topic

Write each noun and label it *C* for common or *P* for proper. (A date is a noun.)

1. Daniel Bernoulli was a scientist.
2. Bernoulli was born in Switzerland.
3. His main interests were water and air.
4. Bernoulli's Principle was published in 1738.
5. This scientific principle helped Orville Wright and Wilbur Wright.
6. The Wright brothers used the principle to fly at Kitty Hawk in 1903.
7. As air blows faster across a wing, the wing lifts.
8. The velocity or speed of the air is generated by the plane's engine.
9. The first flight of 120 feet in North Carolina was powered by a twelve-horsepower engine.
10. By 1904, the Wright brothers had completed 105 flights.
11. In 1909, they created the Wright Company to build airplanes.
12. As a result of Bernoulli's Principle, two Americans became famous.

A DIFFERENT APPROACH

Tactile

Have students use their hands to create objects that are common nouns and proper nouns. For example, they might use fabric and cardboard to create a doll (common noun). They might create a doll that represents a specific person (proper noun). Have students share their creations of common and proper nouns with the class.

TIMESAVER *QuickCheck*

Encourage students to self-assess their papers after their autobiographies are completed. Tell them to especially check for capitalization of all proper nouns.

HOME STUDY

Before they begin writing, have students discuss their autobiography with a parent or other family member. Encourage students to incorporate suggestions from a family member into their papers.

INTEGRATING TECHNOLOGY

Internet

Have students work with a partner to search the Internet for additional information about how dams help us. Students might use the following words for their search: *Army Corps of Engineers, dams, Hoover Dam.* Have each pair summarize their findings in a paragraph to read aloud to the class. As students are reading their paragraphs aloud, have another student write any nouns they used on the board.

EXPANDING THE LESSON

Using Technology

You will find additional **instructional** and **practice** materials for this chapter at http:/www.bkenglish.com.

Communicate Your Ideas

APPLY TO WRITING

Autobiography: *Nouns*

You have been asked to write a brief autobiography for publication in a local newspaper. The newspaper editor has asked you to include the following information:

- full name
- place and date of birth
- your favorite book
- your school's name
- your favorite movie
- name of a person you admire

Write a brief paragraph about yourself for the newspaper, using both common and proper nouns. When you have finished, underline all the nouns that you used. Be sure to correctly capitalize proper nouns.

Finding Nouns

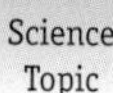

Science Topic **Write each noun.** (A date is a noun.)

1. In 1981, an experiment gave hope to the future of wildlife along Currant Creek in Wyoming.
2. The cattle had eaten all the grass and shrubs.
3. The creek was a muddy hole.
4. The answer was to build dams to form ponds.
5. The townspeople found two scientists with an idea.
6. They brought beavers to Currant Creek.
7. Because there were no trees left, men hauled in logs.
8. The busy beavers built several dams.
9. Soon grass and trees began to sprout.
10. Other states now use these hardworking animals.

LESSON 2 *(pages L57–L67)*

OBJECTIVES

- **To identify the antecedents of personal pronouns**
- **To distinguish among demonstrative, interrogative, personal, indefinite, reflexive, and intensive pronouns**

Create Interest

Tell students that pronouns help make the English language more interesting and more pleasurable to the ear. Have students imagine not having words to replace nouns in some sentences. Help students to realize that language would be boring and repetitious without pronouns. Have students make the following sentences more interesting by substituting pronouns for some of the nouns:

- President Roosevelt did not want the American people to know that Roosevelt had health problems.
- During the Depression, many people worried about people's jobs.

Pronouns

Now that you can recognize nouns, you can learn to identify pronouns.

A **pronoun** is a word that takes the place of one or more nouns.

Look at each pair of sentences below. Notice how pronouns save the second sentence of each pair from being boring and repetitious.

When Franklin Roosevelt was president, Franklin Roosevelt started many programs.

When Franklin Roosevelt was president, **he** started many programs.

Meg bought Roosevelt's biography, and she read the biography.

Meg bought Roosevelt's biography, and she read **it.**

Pronoun Antecedents

In the preceding examples, the pronouns *he* and *it* take the place of nouns. The word or group of words that a pronoun replaces, or refers to, is called its **antecedent.**

An antecedent usually comes before the pronoun. It may be in the same sentence as the pronoun or in another sentence. In the following examples, arrows point from the pronouns to their antecedents.

Roosevelt created many **programs. They** helped people.

(The antecedent is in the preceding sentence.)

REACHING ALL STUDENTS

Struggling Learners

Review with students the definition of a noun. Tell students that pronouns are words that are used instead of nouns. List the following examples of pronouns for students: *I, me, you, he, she, it, they.* Have students add other examples of pronouns to this list. Tell students that words such as *his, her, our, their* are examples of possessive pronouns. Ask students for additional examples of possessive pronouns.

IDENTIFYING COMMON STUMBLING BLOCKS

Problem

- Unclear pronoun referents

Solution

- Point out that the following sentence lacks clear pronoun reference.

  When Carrie gave Alice the book, she beamed with pleasure.

  Tell students that the reader does not know whether *she* refers to Carrie or Alice.
- Have students make the following vague pronoun references clearer:

  The contractors met with the owners of the house, and they told us what needed to be changed.

  The house and the garage were renovated, and it looks much better.

Guide Instruction

By Modeling Strategies

Use the following examples to show students how personal pronouns and antecedents refer to the same thing. Write the sentences on the board and use arrows to connect pronouns and their antecedents.

- Candace was reading the book about Roosevelt to herself. (*Candace* and *herself* both refer to *Candace.*)
- Candace said, "I enjoy reading about Roosevelt. I will write a book about him." (*Candace* and *I* both refer to *Candace. Roosevelt* and *him* both refer to *Roosevelt.*)

Consolidate Skills

Through Guided Practice

The **Check Your Understanding** exercises as well as the **QuickCheck** on page L67 will help students identify pronouns. Draw a graphic organizer such as a web on the board with the middle circled labeled *Pronouns*. Have students add circles around the origi-

A DIFFERENT APPROACH

Auditory

Have students complete the **Check Your Understanding** by reading each item to a partner. Students should work together to identify all of the pronouns. Discuss students' responses to items one through ten.

Eleanor Roosevelt told **her** husband about the sick children.

(The antecedent is in the same sentence.)

A pronoun can have more than one antecedent.

The **president** and **first lady** visited **their** family.

Sometimes more than one pronoun can refer to the same antecedent.

Franklin Roosevelt took **his** secretary with **him.**

PRACTICE YOUR SKILLS

Check Your Understanding

Finding Pronouns and Antecedents

History Topic **Write each pronoun. Beside each pronoun, write its antecedent.**

1. Franklin Roosevelt began his first term as president in 1933. Franklin Roosevelt
2. Roosevelt had been struck with polio in 1921, and he was confined to a wheelchair. Roosevelt
3. The campaign trail presented its challenges. trail
4. The president told the American people that the only thing we have to fear is fear itself. people, president
5. Eleanor Roosevelt also addressed the people and their problems. people
6. The voters were worried about their money and their futures. voters
7. Roosevelt and the citizens were tired of the Depression and its problems. Depression

nal one and list the various types of pronouns in Lesson 2. Have students give an example of each type of pronoun as they are included in the web.

Apply to Communication

Through Independent Writing

The **Communicate Your Ideas** activities on pages L63 and L67 prompt students to write a business letter and a biography. Ask students to think of ways that their business letters and biographies could be combined into one activity. For example, they might write a biography to send along with their business letters about Internet biographies. Allow time for students to give other suggestions.

Transfer to Everyday Life

Identifying Pronouns in a Business Letter

Provide students with a collection of business letters. These can be collected from home or be samples of student writing. Have students read through the letters and identify all of the pronouns in each letter. Discuss the pronouns

8. Fifteen proposals were sent to Congress, and it passed all of them. Congress; proposals
9. It was called the "New Deal." (no antecedent)
10. The New Deal did not end the Depression, but it did lessen the financial hardships of many Americans. New Deal
11. The New Deal was designed to make people feel better, and it did. New Deal
12. The Civilian Conservation Corps met its goal of creating 2.5 million jobs. Civilian Conservation Corps
13. Franklin Roosevelt helped Americans by restoring their confidence. Americans
14. Roosevelt was the only president to serve his country for more than two terms. Roosevelt

HOME WORK

Have students find an article from a newspaper or magazine. Students should rewrite the article, using nouns in the place of all the pronouns. The new articles should not contain any pronouns. Have students bring their newly written articles to the class and read them aloud. Have students discuss the repetitiousness of the new articles and comment on which version is more interesting.

Personal Pronouns

Of all the different kinds of pronouns, **personal pronouns** are used most often. There are first-person, second-person, and third-person pronouns. The following is a list of the singular and plural forms for each person.

PERSONAL PRONOUNS		
	Singular	Plural
FIRST PERSON (speaker)	I, me, my, mine	we, us, our, ours
SECOND PERSON (person spoken to)	you, your, yours	you, your, yours
THIRD PERSON (person or thing spoken about)	he, him, his, she, her, hers, it, its	they, them, their, theirs

students underlined in each letter.

Pull It All Together

By Summarizing

Have students take turns summarizing the information from Lesson 2. Each student should define one type of pronoun and give an example of each one. Students' examples should include the following types of pronouns: *personal, reflexive, intensive, indefinite, interrogative, demonstrative.*

Check Understanding

Naming Types of Pronouns

Have students identify the type of pronoun as you verbally give examples of each type. For example, after you say *each* one student should respond, *indefinite pronoun*. Continue with each student. Write on the board the different kinds of pronouns students have learned: personal, demonstrative, interrogative, indefinite, reflexive, and intensive. Then, as you call out examples, have students identify the type of pronoun.

YOUR IDEAS

For Pronouns

The following sentences show the ways in which personal pronouns are used.

FIRST-PERSON PRONOUNS	**I** must remember to take **my** book report with **me** to school tomorrow.
	We haven't seen **our** grades yet.
SECOND-PERSON PRONOUNS	**You** shouldn't try to read the book without **your** glasses.
	You may sit next to each other and share **your** notes.
THIRD-PERSON PRONOUNS	**He** told **her** that the book was **his.**
	They have taken **their** computer with **them** on **their** vacation.

Reflexive and Intensive Pronouns

You can add *–self* or *–selves* to some personal pronouns. These pronouns, called **reflexive** and **intensive pronouns,** are used to refer to or to emphasize a noun or another pronoun.

REFLEXIVE AND INTENSIVE PRONOUNS	
SINGULAR	myself, yourself, himself, herself, itself
PLURAL	ourselves, yourselves, themselves

Robert kept telling **himself** that he would finish the book of short stories.
(The reflexive pronoun *himself* refers to *Robert.*)

We committed **ourselves** to a successful book fair.
(The reflexive pronoun *ourselves* refers to *We.*)

The students **themselves** came up with the idea for a book fair.

(The intensive pronoun *themselves* emphasizes who came up with the idea. Intensive pronouns often come immediately after the antecedent.)

When you use reflexive or intensive pronouns, remember never to use them by themselves. They must always have an antecedent to refer to. Also, never use *hisself* or *theirselves.*

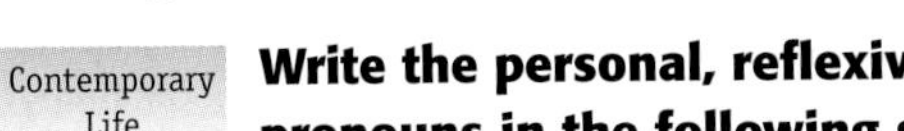

Check Your Understanding

Finding Personal Pronouns

Contemporary Life **Write the personal, reflexive, and intensive pronouns in the following sentences.**

1. I went to the book fair with my English class during third period.

2. Mr. Jenkins himself helped us pick out some books for our book reports.

3. He suggested that we choose books for young adults by well-known authors.

4. Christopher chose *The Outsiders* by S. E. Hinton for his report.

5. Did you know that S. E. Hinton is a woman?

6. She wrote *The Outsiders* in 1967, but it is still popular with middle-school students today.

7. Maya looked for a Walter Dean Myers book for herself because he is her favorite author.

8. She found several of them in a special display of works by African American authors.

A DIFFERENT APPROACH

Visual

As an alternative to the written exercises, have students work with partners to read through the items and identify each pronoun by pointing to it on the page of their textbooks.

HOME WORK

Have students locate a book by S. E. Hinton. Students should identify at least twenty personal pronouns in Hinton's writing. Have students bring their pronoun list and the example of Hinton's writing to class to share.

USING STUDENTS' STRENGTHS

Multiple Intelligences: Musical

Have students use a song already written or write a new song of their own. Students should read the lyrics of the song and identify any pronouns used in the lyrics. Have students count how many of each type of pronoun are used. Which type of pronoun is used the most in the song lyrics? Have students share their findings with the class.

9. They were next to some copies of *M. C. Higgins, the Great* by Virginia Hamilton.
10. Were you able to locate any novels by Anne McCaffrey for your report on science fiction?

Connect to the Writing Process: Revising

Using Personal Pronouns

Rewrite the following short biography, using personal pronouns to replace the overused common and proper nouns. [Answers may vary. Possible responses are given.]

Jules Verne was born in 1828, in Nantes, France. Jules Verne was a French writer. ~~Jules Verne~~ He studied law but eventually ~~Jules Verne~~ he began writing. Verne soon discovered that ~~Verne~~ he had an ability to write about imaginary journeys and other fantasies having to do with science. ~~Verne's~~ His writing became known as science fiction. Science fiction was invented by ~~Jules Verne~~ him. ~~Jules Verne~~ He wrote many stories. One story ~~Verne~~ he wrote was *Twenty Thousand Leagues Under the Sea*. ~~*Twenty Thousand Leagues Under the Sea*~~ It was made into a movie. The first movie version came out in 1916. Other movie versions came out in 1954 and 1993. Jules Verne mixed humor, adventure, and scientific discovery in a book called *Around the World in Eighty Days*. ~~*Around the World in Eighty Days*~~ It also became a movie.

Communicate Your Ideas

APPLY TO WRITING

Business Letter: *Personal Pronouns*

You have an idea for a series of biographies that could be written for the Internet. Then anyone doing research might find essential biographical information about specific people. Write a business letter to an appropriate company, proposing your idea. Use personal pronouns to keep your proposal interesting. When you have finished, underline the personal pronouns you used.

Indefinite Pronouns

Personal pronouns are not the only kind of pronouns. Another group of pronouns is called **indefinite pronouns.** They are called indefinite pronouns because they usually do not have a definite antecedent like personal pronouns do. Instead, indefinite pronouns usually refer to unnamed people or things.

COMMON INDEFINITE PRONOUNS		
all	either	none
another	everybody	no one
any	everyone	nothing
anybody	everything	one
anyone	few	several
anything	many	some
both	most	someone
each	neither	something

TIMESAVER *QuickCheck*

Have students exchange their completed business letters with a partner to assess their use of personal pronouns. Have students incorporate their partners' suggestions that they agree with into their letters.

HOME STUDY

Have students check the Internet for various sites that provide biographical information. Students might use different search engines to look up the names of famous people who are of interest to them. Have students share with the class their impressions of these sites and their opinions of the sites' usefulness.

A DIFFERENT APPROACH

Visual

Have students write each of the sentences from **Check Your Understanding** on the board. Then have other students replace each indefinite pronoun with a personal pronoun. Read and discuss the new sentences.

HOME WORK

Have students find five examples of indefinite pronouns from their school math textbooks or other books about math. Students should bring these examples of pronouns to class to share.

Did **anyone** notice **something** strange about the problem?

Can **anybody** take **all** of these calculators to the desk?

No one knew **anything** about the math problem.

You can learn about indefinite pronouns being used as adjectives on page 110.

Practice Your Skills

Check Your Understanding

Finding Indefinite Pronouns

Math Topic **Write each indefinite pronoun.**

1. Does anyone know about ratios and percents?
2. Nothing makes sense in the assignment.
3. Each seems to have the same idea.
4. Someone told me that ratios and percents are fractions.
5. No one, however, explained how fractions compare with whole numbers.
6. Everybody has had experience comparing a number such as 10 with 100.
7. Some claim to use ratios and percents every day.
8. Will anybody help clear up the confusion?
9. Several knew that 10 is one tenth of 100.
10. One suggested that 10 is 10 percent of 100.
11. The conclusions were accepted by all.
12. Both wanted to know the ratio of pencils to pens.
13. Someone counted 33 pencils and 11 pens.

14. The three-to-one ratio was guessed by few.

15. Most use special fractions in sports statistics.

16. Many are easier to answer with a calculator.

Demonstrative and Interrogative Pronouns

Demonstrative pronouns do what their name suggests. They demonstrate, or point out, people or things.

DEMONSTRATIVE PRONOUNS			
this	that	these	those

This is a beautiful house. **These** are the bedrooms.

That was a great idea! Lee already saw **those.**

This and *these* point to people or things that are near. *That* and *those* point to people or things that are farther away.

In the last chapter, you learned that interrogative sentences ask questions. **Interrogative pronouns** are used to ask questions.

INTERROGATIVE PRONOUNS				
what	which	who	whom	whose

What did you want?
Which did he choose?
Who will figure out the cost of lumber?
Whom did you choose to survey the property?
Whose are those work boots?

DEVELOPING WORKPLACE COMPETENCIES

Thinking Skills: Knowing How to Learn

Have students imagine they are starting a new job in an office. A few hours into their new position they realize they have several questions about how to operate some of the office equipment needed to complete various tasks. How will they ask these questions? To whom will they address the questions? Have students write out their questions and share them with the class. Discuss any interrogative pronouns students use in their sentences.

HOME WORK

Have students write three sentences using interrogative pronouns and three sentences using demonstrative pronouns. Have students share their sentences with the class.

PRACTICE YOUR SKILLS

Check Your Understanding
Finding Pronouns

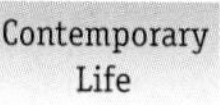

Write each demonstrative and interrogative pronoun. Label each one *D* for demonstrative or *I* for interrogative.

1. What (I) is the charitable organization building homes for families?
2. Who (I) communicates between the project and the headquarters of Habitat for Humanity?
3. These (D) are homes for families willing to do the work.
4. Who (I) works on the new homes besides the future owners?
5. Which (I) are the best resources for the personnel in the volunteer pool?
6. These (D) could include retirees, craftspersons, or students.
7. Who (I) is the former American president with Habitat for Humanity?
8. That (D) is Jimmy Carter.
9. Who (I) wants to call and volunteer?
10. This (D) could be a great challenge!

Connect to the Writing Process: Prewriting
Using Interrogative Pronouns

Choose someone you admire in your school, family, or neighborhood. Make a list of questions to ask this person about his or her life, work, interests, or achievements. Be sure to use a variety of interrogative pronouns in your questions.

Communicate Your Ideas

APPLY TO WRITING

Biography: *Pronouns*

Interview the person you selected in the previous activity, using the questions you have already listed. Then write what you have learned about him or her in a short paragraph for the school newspaper. Be sure to use a variety of pronouns.

Mixed Practice

Science Topic

Write each pronoun. Label each one *personal, reflexive, intensive, indefinite, demonstrative,* or *interrogative.*

1. What [interrogative] makes the dog special to Americans?
2. The canine is singled out from all the 4,236 other animals as our [personal] "best friend."
3. Many [indefinite] may not like the answer.
4. They [personal] are descended from wolves.
5. Despite their [personal] differences in size and shape, they [personal] are all from the same species.
6. You [personal] can see genetic differences for yourself [reflexive], but they [personal] themselves [intensive] are small.
7. Mature dogs—and wolves—can have puppies once they [personal] are fully mature adults.
8. It [personal] is a fact of science.
9. The next time you [personal] look into your [personal] dog's big eyes, think about the wolf.
10. That [demonstrative] is not something I [personal] will do.

TIMESAVER *QuickCheck*

Before students submit their paragraphs to the school newspaper, have the class evaluate them and choose the best three. The class should focus on the appropriate use of pronouns and choose the most interesting of these papers.

HOME STUDY

Have students compare their biographies with one they find in a newspaper article from home. Students should implement useful techniques from these articles into their own biographical writing.

EXPANDING THE LESSON

Using Technology

You will find additional **instructional** and **practice** materials for this chapter at http://www.bkenglish.com.

Using *CheckPoint*

This feature on nouns and pronouns can be used as further independent practice or as a cumulative review of the chapter. It covers the following types of nouns: compound, collective, common and proper. It also covers the following types of pronouns: personal, reflexive, intensive, indefinite, interrogative, and demonstrative.

CheckPoint

Finding Nouns

Write each noun. (A date is a noun.) You will find 25 nouns.

The first woman to become an astronomer was Maria Mitchell. She was born in Nantucket, which is an island off the coast of Massachusetts. For many years, even though she was working as a teacher, she spent much time studying the stars and galaxies with her father in their observatory. In 1847, she sighted a new comet. Later she received a great honor. A committee decided to give her name to the comet she had found. Eventually she became a professor at Vassar College. Maria Mitchell wrote about her own work and encouraged many students to study astronomy.

Finding Personal Pronouns and Antecedents

Write each personal pronoun. Then beside each one, write its antecedent.

owner

1. The pet store owner said to the customer, "I have a most unusual dog in my store."

owner

customer

2. "Would you be interested?" the owner asked the customer.

owner/customer

3. The owner pointed to a little brown dog near them.

customer

4. The owner looked at the customer and continued, "You will like this dog!"

dog

5. "It costs only ten dollars," the owner added.

dog

6. The dog heard the conversation and cried out, "Buy me!"

7. The dog pleaded to the customer, "I can cook and clean your house." (dog; dog)
8. Because the customer was so surprised to hear the dog talk, he asked the owner, "Why are you selling this dog?" (customer)
9. The customer added, "I have never heard a dog talk before!" (customer; owner; customer)
10. "Because," said the owner, "I can't stand a bragger!" (owner)

Writing Sentences

Write sentences that follow the directions below. (The sentences may come in any order.) Write about one of the following topics or a topic of your own choice: a favorite family activity or something enjoyable you do with a friend.

Write a sentence that . . .

1. includes a noun that names a person, a place, or a thing.
2. includes a noun that names an idea.
3. includes a common noun and a proper noun.
4. includes a collective noun.
5. includes a compound noun.
6. includes a personal pronoun and its antecedent.
7. includes a reflexive pronoun.
8. includes one or two indefinite pronouns.
9. includes a demonstrative pronoun.
10. includes an interrogative pronoun.

When you are finished, put an *N* over each noun and a *P* over each pronoun.

Sample Answers for *Writing Sentences:*

1. I (P) haven't seen my (P) friend (N) Brandy (N) in over a year (N).
2. Our (P) friendship (N), however, is still strong.
3. I (P) live in Richardson (N), but she (P) lives in another town (N).
4. A batch (N) of letters (N) from her (P) sits on my (P) desk (N).
5. We (P) exchange E-mails (N) nearly every weekday (N).
6. Brandy (N) signs her (P) E-mails (N) "Bran Muffin (N)," which (P) is her nickname (N).
7. She (P) doesn't take herself (P) too seriously.
8. Anybody (P) can see that she (P) is a friend (N) to everyone (P) she (P) meets.
9. These (P) are some (P) of her best qualities (N): loyalty (N), honesty (N), and compassion (N).
10. Who (P) wouldn't want to be her (P) friend (N)?

Using *Language and Self-Expression*

Consider using this writing assignment to assess students' ability to use nouns and pronouns correctly and effectively. You may want students to complete the assignment as part of a narrative writing strand of their portfolios.

Prewriting

Demonstrate how to use a cluster diagram for students who wish to use one in their prewriting stage. Draw the graphic organizer on the board and have several students suggest what they might write in each area of the organizer. Encourage students to include such a graphic organizer in the prewriting stage. Then show students how to make a sequence of events chart to detail the events in their stories. Remind students that these prewriting tools can be changed many times to meet their story needs, are meant for their own use, and should not be turned in.

FOR YOUR INFORMATION

About the Artwork

Several American Indian cultural groups, including the Sioux, Ojibwa, and Oneida peoples, have used dream catchers. According to one legend, the spirit of Spider twisted a twig into a circle and wove a web inside it. Spider told humans to hang the dream catcher over their beds. Good dreams would be caught in the webbing and would become part of the dreamer. Bad dreams would fly through the hole in the center.

Language and *Self-Expression*

In American Indian legend, the dream catcher is used to catch good dreams. Bad dreams pass through the hole in the center of the dream catcher. Some dream catchers are made of colorful materials, while others, like this one, use tones of earth and nature.

Write your own story about a dream catcher. Decide on a main character and create a difficult situation. Describe how the character overcomes the conflict by using a dream catcher.

Prewriting You may want to make a cluster diagram showing the character's name, personality traits, and the conflict he or she faces. Then make a sequence of events chart detailing the events of the story.

Drafting Use the sequence of events chart to tell your story and the cluster diagram to bring your character to life. Your first sentence should capture the tone of the story. Your concluding sentence should summarize the story.

Revising Ask a classmate to read your story aloud. As you listen, jot down notes for revision. Does your writing make you visualize the character and action clearly? Is the dream catcher vividly described? Add variety to your writing by using different kinds of nouns and by using pronouns where appropriate.

Editing Make sure each sentence expresses a complete thought. Make sure nouns, pronouns, and antecedents are used properly. Finally, check for correct capitalization of proper nouns.

Publishing Prepare a final copy of your story. Draw your own dream catcher. Write the title of your story on your drawing and use it as a cover page.

Another Look

Nouns and Pronouns

Types of Nouns

A **noun** is a word that names a person, a place, a thing, or an idea.

A **concrete noun** can be seen and touched. *(page L50)*
An **abstract noun** cannot be seen or touched. *(page L50)*
A **compound noun** is made of more than one word. They can be written as a single word, two words, or with a hyphen. *(pages L52–L53)*
A **collective noun** names a group of people or things. *(page L53)*
A **common noun** names any person, place, or thing and does not begin with a capital letter. *(page L54)*
A **proper noun** names a particular person, place, or thing. It begins with a capital letter. *(pages L54–L55)*

Types of Pronouns

A **pronoun** is a word that takes the place of one or more nouns.

An **antecedent** is the word or group of words that a pronoun replaces.

Personal pronouns are categorized as first-person, second-person, or third-person pronouns. *(pages L59–L60)*
Reflexive pronouns and **intensive pronouns** end in *–self* or *–selves* and are used to refer to a noun or another pronoun. *(pages L60–L61)*
Indefinite pronouns usually do not have a definite antecedent. *(pages L63–L64)*
Demonstrative pronouns point out people, places, and things. *(page L65)*
Interrogative pronouns are used to ask questions. *(page L65)*

Other Information About Nouns and Pronouns

Recognizing common collective nouns *(page L53)*
Recognizing common indefinite pronouns *(page L63)*

Using *Another Look*

Another Look summarizes the terms defined in the chapter and provides cross-references to the specific pages on which they are explained. Consider having students use this feature prior to completing **CheckPoint** or taking the posttest. Students who can provide several examples of each term should be able to score well on either measurement.

FOR ASSESSING LEARNING

Using *the Posttest*

Assessing Learning

The posttest will help you and your students assess where they stand in their ability to identify different kinds of nouns and pronouns.

IDENTIFYING COMMON STUMBLING BLOCKS

Following is a list of the most common errors students make when using nouns and pronouns.

Problem

- Noncapitalization of proper nouns

Solution

- For reteaching, use the chart on page L54.

Problem

- Pronoun and antecedent agreement

Solution

- For reteaching, use the explanatory copy printed in blue beside the examples on pages L57–L58.

Directions

Read the passage and decide which kind of noun or pronoun the underlined word in each sentence is. Write the letter of the correct answer.

EXAMPLE **1.** The student <u>jury</u> will listen to both sides of the dispute.

1 **A** antecedent
B abstract noun
C proper noun
D collective noun

ANSWER **1** **D**

1. <u>Katya</u> joined our school's teen court this semester.

2. <u>She</u> will meet after school with other members of the court.

3. First, they list the cases for the day on the <u>chalkboard</u>.

4. They will listen to the disputes and complaints of <u>students</u>.

5. The <u>group</u> will decide on a course of action for each situation.

6. <u>This</u> may be a recommendation for disciplinary action if the student is guilty.

7. We all know, however, that <u>someone</u> may be unjustly accused.

8. For these people, the teen court will prove their <u>innocence</u>.

9. The teen court has shown <u>itself</u> to be fair.

10. <u>Who</u> wants to volunteer for court next semester?

A DIFFERENT DELIVERY SYSTEM

If you prefer, you can print the pretest from the BK English Test Bank located at http://www.bkenglish.com.

1 A common noun
B collective noun
C proper noun
D compound noun

2 A indefinite pronoun
B reflexive pronoun
C personal pronoun
D antecedent

3 A compound noun
B collective noun
C proper noun
D abstract noun

4 A proper noun
B abstract noun
C pronoun
D common noun

5 A collective noun
B pronoun
C proper noun
D reflexive pronoun

6 A reflexive pronoun
B demonstrative pronoun
C indefinite pronoun
D interrogative pronoun

7 A indefinite pronoun
B demonstrative pronoun
C reflexive pronoun
D intensive pronoun

8 A pronoun
B collective noun
C concrete noun
D abstract noun

9 A demonstrative pronoun
B reflexive pronoun
C indefinite pronoun
D personal pronoun

10 A demonstrative pronoun
B personal pronoun
C interrogative pronoun
D intensive pronoun

Customizing the Test

Use these questions to add or replace items for alternate versions of the test.

11. Yesterday Katya heard a case involving forged notes.

12. Marshall had forged his mother's name but spelled it wrong.

13. He himself proved his guilt!

14. Another student accused her friend of stealing her backpack.

15. This person was just angry at her friend and later dropped the charge.

11. A proper noun
B concrete noun
C abstract noun
D compound noun

12. A proper noun
B common noun
C collective noun
D abstract noun

13. A interrogative pronoun
B personal pronoun
C indefinite pronoun
D intensive pronoun

14. A collective noun
B proper noun
C compound noun
D indefinite pronoun

15. A common noun
B intensive pronoun
C abstract noun
D demonstrative pronoun

TEACHING SUGGESTIONS

Essential Knowledge and Skills

- Adapting spoken language such as word choice, diction, and usage to the audience, purpose, and occasion
- Writing to express, discover, record, develop, reflect on ideas, and to problem solve
- Producing cohesive and coherent written texts by organizing ideas, using effective transitions, and choosing precise wording
- Using verb tenses appropriately and consistently such as present, past, future, perfect, and progressive
- Interpreting and evaluating the various ways visual image makers represent meaning

BLOCK SCHEDULING

- If your schedule requires that you cover the chapter in a **shorter time,** use the instruction on verbs and the Check Your Understanding and QuickCheck exercises.
- If you want to take advantage of **longer class time,** add these applications to writing: Connect to Writer's Craft, Connect to Speaking and Writing, Connect to the Writing Process, and Apply to Writing exercises.

CHAPTER 3

Verbs

Directions

Decide which words are linked by the underlined verb in each sentence. Write the letter of the correct answer.

EXAMPLE **1.** In the hot sun, sombreros <u>are</u> useful for shade.

1 A sun, shade
B sombreros, useful
C sombreros, shade
D sun, useful

ANSWER **1 B**

1. The charming beret <u>is</u> flat, round, and usually woolen.
2. Baseball caps <u>have been</u> popular on and off the field.
3. In sports, helmets <u>can be</u> life-saving headwear.
4. Men's silk top hats <u>must have been</u> expensive.
5. Bonnets with chin ribbons <u>were</u> once a necessity.
6. This felt fedora <u>will be</u> perfect with my outfit.
7. <u>Is</u> a crown the same thing as a tiara?
8. The most beautiful crown <u>is</u> a jeweled one.
9. The tiara <u>was</u> a headdress of the ancient Persians.
10. Today's tiara <u>is</u> a coronet of jewels or flowers.

IDENTIFYING COMMON STUMBLING BLOCKS

Following is a list of the most common errors students make when using verbs.

Problem
- Distinguishing between transitive and intransitive verbs

Solution
- Instruction, p. L80
- Practice, p. L81

Problem
- Distinguishing between linking and action verbs

Solution
- Instruction, p. L89
- Practice, p. L90

1
- **A** beret, usually woolen
- **B** charming, beret
- **C** beret, flat, round, woolen
- **D** beret, flat

2
- **A** caps, field
- **B** Baseball, popular
- **C** caps, popular
- **D** Baseball, popular

3
- **A** sports, life-saving
- **B** helmets, headwear
- **C** helmets, life-saving
- **D** sports, headwear

4
- **A** silk, expensive
- **B** top, expensive
- **C** Men's, expensive
- **D** top hats, expensive

5
- **A** ribbons, once
- **B** Bonnets, necessity
- **C** ribbons, necessity
- **D** Bonnets, once

6
- **A** fedora, outfit
- **B** This, outfit
- **C** This, perfect
- **D** fedora, perfect

7
- **A** crown, thing
- **B** crown, same
- **C** crown, tiara
- **D** same, tiara

8
- **A** crown, jeweled
- **B** crown, a
- **C** beautiful, jeweled
- **D** crown, one

9
- **A** tiara, Persians
- **B** tiara, headdress
- **C** tiara, a
- **D** The, Persians

10
- **A** Today's, flowers
- **B** tiara, a
- **C** tiara, coronet
- **D** tiara, jewels

A DIFFERENT DELIVERY SYSTEM

If you prefer, you can print the pretest from the BK English Test Bank located at http://www.bkenglish.com.

Using the Pretest

Assessing Prior Knowledge

The pretest will help you and your students assess where they stand in their basic understanding of action verbs and linking verbs. The test indicates students' ability to identify these verbs and to use them correctly in their own writing.

Customizing the Test

Use these questions to add or replace items for alternate versions of the test.

11. This lace scarf will be the perfect covering for my hair.

12. Your ski mask should have been much cheaper.

13. That red, scuffed bike helmet might be mine.

14. His kerchief could be a liner for that scratchy straw hat.

11.
- **A** scarf, perfect
- **B** This, perfect
- **C** lace, hair
- **D** scarf, covering

12.
- **A** mask, cheaper
- **B** mask, much
- **C** ski, much
- **D** Your, cheaper

13.
- **A** That, mine
- **B** scuffed, mine
- **C** helmet, mine
- **D** red, mine

14.
- **A** kerchief, liner
- **B** His, hat
- **C** kerchief, hat
- **D** His, liner

ADDITIONAL RESOURCES

Language Skills Practice . . . . pages 27–32
Transparency Tools FA2
ESL Practice and Test Preparation . . . . . pages 91–93
Assessment: Chapter Test. . . . . pages 117–122

MAKING VISUAL CONNECTIONS

To Stimulate Writing

Use the questions for art criticism as writing or discussion prompts.

Possible Answers:

Describe It looks like the artist used clay or stone. The artist smoothed the surface of the figurine and then carved cuts in repeated patterns on the hat and clothing.

Analyze I think the figurine is illustrating happiness and fun. The laughing mouth and the eyes closed in laughter help convey this impression. Also, the hands are held up in sort of a teasing or waving gesture, which contributes to the impression of fun and happiness.

Interpret When I first looked at the figurine, I smiled. It made me feel amused, like I might giggle. I think the artist wanted the viewer to feel happy thoughts when looking at the sculpture.

Judge I have seen another happy statue, the laughing Buddha. I've also seen figurines of people's heads. Some of these were African art, and some were European statues like *The Thinker*. This figurine is more memorable than the others because of its unusual facial expression and because it causes me to actually smile when I look at it. The other figurines I've seen are really nice, but they are not as striking.

Artist unknown. *Smiling Figurine,* ca. A.D. 6th to 9th century.
Limestone, approximately 19¾ by 12¾ by 4½ inches.

Describe What materials and tools were probably used to form this work of art? What did the artist do to the surface of the figurine?

Analyze What emotion do you think the artist wants this figurine to illustrate? Which characteristics express this emotion?

Interpret When you look at the figurine, how does it make you feel? What do you think the artist's purpose was in creating this figurine?

Judge What other sculptures or figurines have you seen before? What were their expressions? Is this figurine memorable compared to the others? Explain.

At the end of the chapter, you will use this artwork to stimulate writing ideas.

FOR DEVELOPING LANGUAGE SKILLS

LESSON 1 *(pages L77–L84)*

OBJECTIVES

- **To identify action verbs, helping verbs, and verb phrases**
- **To distinguish between transitive and intransitive verbs**

Create Interest

Write the following sentences on the board: *I tobble the art museum often; The sculpture swirties on a lovely pedestal; The music kriggles through the air.* Have students choose suitable words that make sense to replace the nonsense words. Tell students that the words they are choosing are verbs.

Action Verbs

A verb is a very important word in a sentence. In fact, without a verb a group of words cannot be a sentence. When organizing a sentence, remember that it is necessary to include a subject and a predicate. Without a verb, your predicate is incomplete.

A **verb** is a word used to express an action or a state of being.

Most of the verbs you are already familiar with are called action verbs because they show action or movement.

An **action verb** tells what action a subject is performing.

To find an action verb, first find the subject of the sentence. Then ask yourself, *What is the subject doing?* Some action verbs show physical action.

PHYSICAL ACTION — The band **played.**

(The subject is *band.* What did the band do? *Played* is the action verb.)

They **marched** across the field.

(The subject is *They.* What did they do? *Marched* is the action verb.)

Some action verbs show mental action. Others show ownership or possession.

MENTAL ACTION — I **forgot** the dancer's name.
I **know** the steps to that dance.

OWNERSHIP — Jeffrey **has** two paintings.
They **belong** to him.

FOR INCREASING STUDENT ACHIEVEMENT

USING STUDENTS' STRENGTHS

Multiple Intelligences: Kinesthetic

Have students use their bodies to demonstrate various action verbs. Ask them how they could use just their bodies to express the action verb *talked.* Have students take turns acting out different physical action verbs.

Guide Instruction

By Modeling Strategies

Tell students that most verbs are action verbs. If a physical or mental action is being performed, the verb is an action verb. Illustrate identifying action verbs using the following example: The sculptor chiseled a large marble block.

Tell students to determine if a verb is an action verb they should ask themselves, *The subject is doing or thinking what?* Because in the sentence the sculptor *chiseled,* and chiseled is a physical action, *chiseled* is an action verb.

Consolidate Skills

Through Guided Practice

The **Check Your Understanding** exercises as well as the **QuickCheck** on page L84 will help students identify action verbs and verb phrases. Tell students that they can test to see whether or not a word is an action verb by asking *What is the subject*

A DIFFERENT APPROACH

Kinesthetic

After students have written out their responses to the **Practice Your Skills** activities, have them act out the verbs used in each sentence for items 11 through 20. Tell students that while some of the words are mental actions, they can also portray these verbs in a charade-like fashion.

HOME WORK

Have students write down ten action verbs that reflect what they saw while watching a television program or commercials. Remind students that action verbs can be either physical or mental actions.

CONNECT TO SPEAKING AND WRITING

When you speak or write, the verbs you use show action in your sentences. You can use verbs to create vivid pictures for your audience. When you choose your verbs carefully, you can also help your audience hear what is happening.

Less Vivid	The race cars' tires **made loud noises** as the drivers **sped** around the track.
More Vivid	The race cars' tires **squealed** as the drivers **zoomed** around the track.

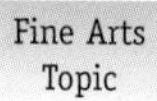

You can learn about regular and irregular verbs on pages L315–L324.

Practice Your Skills

Check Your Understanding

Finding Action Verbs

Fine Arts Topic **Write each action verb.**

1. Musicians, dancers, and artists create beautiful artwork for other people.
2. A dancer performs with his or her body.
3. An artist paints with his or her hands.
4. A musician plays an instrument.
5. These performers rarely forget their goal of entertainment.
6. Musicians and dancers practice every day.
7. Artists strive for perfection.
8. They often display their works in art shows.
9. These artists express themselves creatively in their respective crafts.
10. They believe in their art and in themselves.

doing or thinking? If the subject is performing a physical or mental action, then the verb is an action verb. Practice the first example on page L78 together. Then have students ask themselves the question to complete the remaining exercises independently.

Apply to Communication

Through Independent Writing

The **Communicate Your Ideas** activity on page L79 prompts students to write a narrative about an exciting event using action verbs. Ask students what characteristics make an interesting action verb? For example, which verb would be more interesting to students as readers: *ate* or *gobbled?* Have students provide additional examples of interesting action verbs that they might use in their narrative writing.

Transfer to Everyday Life

Identifying Action Verbs in Conversations

Have students carry a notepad and jot

Check Your Understanding

Finding Action Verbs

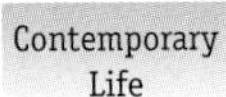

Write each action verb.

11. Once a year we attend a festival.

12. Glorious music reaches our ears.

13. Sometimes we listen to the lively music.

14. Flavorful scents lead to foods of many nations.

15. I taste these wonderful dishes.

16. The food melts in my mouth.

17. Next I count the number of craft booths.

18. Artists display jewelry, pottery, and paintings.

19. I search for the perfect item.

20. I enjoy this super event!

Connect to the Writing Process: Prewriting

Using Specific Verbs

Imagine that you have just returned from an exciting event, and you want to tell a classmate about it. Make a list of action verbs that show what you experienced at this event. Then list some activities and things you did while there. Match action verbs to each activity.

Communicate Your Ideas

APPLY TO WRITING

Narrative: *Verbs*

Refer to the list of action verbs and activities you made in the preceding activity. Write a narrative of the event so that your classmates will feel as if they had attended. Use a variety of exciting action verbs.

TIMESAVER *QuickCheck*

Tell students that their narrative writing will be evaluated on their effective use of action verbs. Give students 5 points for each action verb they use effectively and correctly in their writing.

YOUR IDEAS

For Action Verbs

down any action verbs they hear in conversations throughout a school day. Have students share some of the interesting action verbs that they heard and noted.

Pull It All Together

By Sharing

Have students share with the class some of the action verbs they used in their narrative writing about an exciting event. Write some of these interesting verbs on the board. Have listeners classify the verbs as transitive or intransitive.

Check Understanding

Identifying Action Verbs and Verb Phrases

Provide students with newspapers and have them read through several articles looking for action verbs and verb phrases. Students should create a two-column chart of action verbs and verb phrases and enter the verbs

REACHING ALL STUDENTS

English Language Learners

Some students may have difficulty understanding intransitive verbs. Remind them that intransitive verbs express action that is not directed at a specific person or thing. Have students use the *What?* or *Whom?* test to check whether a verb is transitive or intransitive. Encourage students to create a chart of transitive and intransitive verbs to help them distinguish between the two.

Transitive and Intransitive Verbs

Some action verbs are **transitive** because the action they express is directed at a person or thing. Other action verbs are **intransitive** because the action they express is not directed at a person or thing. To decide whether an action verb is transitive or intransitive, say the subject and verb. Then ask the question *What?* or *Whom?* A word that answers either question is called an **object.** An action verb that has an object is transitive. An action verb that does not have an object is intransitive.

TRANSITIVE — Marie **dropped** a beaker in the laboratory.
(Marie dropped what? *Beaker* is the object. Therefore, *dropped* is a transitive verb.)

Marie **told** us about her first day at work.
(Marie told what? Marie told whom? *Us* is the object. Therefore, *told* is a transitive verb.)

INTRANSITIVE — She **works** at a chemical company.
(She works what? She works whom? Because there is no object, *works* is an intransitive verb.)

A few verbs can be transitive in one sentence and intransitive in another sentence.

TRANSITIVE — The scientist **wrote** an experiment.
(The scientist wrote what? *Experiment* is the object.)

INTRANSITIVE — The scientist **wrote** slowly.
(The scientist wrote what or whom? There is no object.)

You can learn more about complements on pages L156–L185.

they found into the chart. Display students' completed charts in the classroom.

Practice Your Skills

Check Your Understanding

Understanding Transitive and Intransitive Verbs

Science Topic

Write the verb in each sentence. Label the verb *T* for transitive or *I* for intransitive.

1. Many companies use [T] organic compounds.

2. They make [T] CDs, athletic shoes, and videotapes with organic compounds.

3. An organic compound usually comes [I] from a carbon-based element.

4. In fact, more than 90 percent of all compounds include [T] carbon-based, organic elements.

5. As early as 1830, scientists made [T] artificial organic compounds in their laboratories.

6. Now artificial organic compounds number [I] in the millions.

7. Scientists discover [T] more and more organic compounds.

8. Companies create [T] new products all the time.

9. Their research progresses [I] slowly sometimes.

10. New products require [T] a great deal of testing.

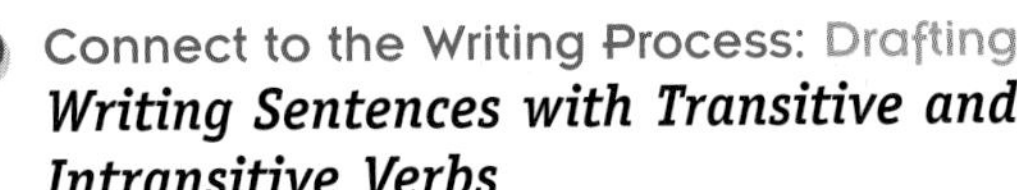

Connect to the Writing Process: Drafting

Writing Sentences with Transitive and Intransitive Verbs

Write a sentence in which each verb is either transitive or intransitive as indicated in parentheses. Focus on science.

11. combine (transitive)

12. invent (transitive)

13. create (transitive)

14. destroy (intransitive)

15. experiment (intransitive)

A DIFFERENT APPROACH

Auditory

Complete items one through ten of the **Practice Your Skills** exercises orally with students. Students should close their books and listen as you read each sentence. Ask students whether the verb in each sentence is transitive or intransitive.

HOME WORK

Have students write five sentences that contain transitive verbs and five sentences that contain intransitive verbs. Have students share some of their home work sentences the next day in class.

REACHING ALL STUDENTS

Advanced Learners

Have students work with partners. Provide each pair with a tape recorder and an audio version of a book. Have students listen to portions of the book, jotting down any verb phrases they hear. Encourage students to listen for unusual or interesting verb phrases. Have students share their verb phrases with the class.

USING STUDENTS' STRENGTHS

Multiple Intelligences: Linguistic

Have students rewrite the following questions as statements and identify the verb phrases in each sentence:

- Have you seen the new science book? (You have seen the new science book.)
- Do you like bugs? (You do like bugs.)
- Has he been to the bug exhibit? (He has been to the bug exhibit.)
- Can we take pictures at the exhibit? (We can take pictures at the exhibit.)

Helping Verbs

Sometimes an action verb or a linking verb is part of a verb phrase that includes **helping verbs,** or auxiliary verbs.

A **verb phrase** is made up of a main verb and one or more helping verbs.

The following is a list of common helping verbs.

COMMON HELPING VERBS	
be	am, is, are, was, were, be, being, been
have	has, have, had
do	do, does, did
OTHERS	may, might, must, can, could, shall, should, will, would

A verb phrase may have one or more helping verbs.

Those insects **are** distributing pollen.

Those bees **have been** gathering honey.

One or more words may interrupt a verb phrase. *Not* and its contraction *n't,* for example, often interrupt verb phrases.

New species of winged insects **have** suddenly appeared.

He **should**n't proceed without assistance.

To find the verb phrase in a question, turn the question into a statement.

QUESTION	Have you seen the ants' tunnels?
STATEMENT	You **have** seen the ants' tunnels.

Practice Your Skills

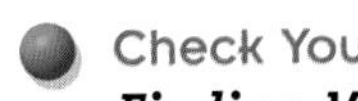

Check Your Understanding

Finding Verb Phrases

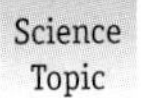

Science Topic

Write each verb phrase. Remember that a verb phrase may be interrupted by one or more words.

1. Have you ever counted the number of different bugs in a field at one time?
2. This would not have been an easy task.
3. Scientists have identified about five million different species of insects.
4. From one batch of eggs, some insects can produce two thousand identical offspring.
5. Ants have built some incredible underground cities with areas for specific activities.
6. Of course, all ants in a colony do not work every hour of every day.
7. Some ants will kidnap the workers from another tribe of ants.
8. According to scientists, a dragonfly can fly faster than fifty miles an hour.
9. Cockroaches have existed 265 million years longer than humans.
10. These insects actually have not changed very much in all that time.
11. Do you know today's temperature?
12. You can count the chirps of a single cricket for fourteen seconds.
13. Then you should add forty to the number of cricket chirps.
14. You will then have a nearly accurate Fahrenheit temperature.

A DIFFERENT APPROACH

Auditory

Have students work with partners to read each sentence in the **Practice Your Skills** exercise. Students should substitute new verb phrases for the ones in the book.

HOME WORK

Have students write five additional sentences about insects. Their sentences should all contain verb phrases. Have students underline the verb phrases on their home work papers.

INTEGRATING TECHNOLOGY

Internet

Have students find an article or information about the triathlon on the Internet. Students should print off the information and underline fifteen verbs and verb phrases in the article. Have students share their information and the verbs they identified with the class.

EXPANDING THE LESSON

Using Technology

You will find additional **instructional** and **practice** materials for this chapter at http:/www.bkenglish.com.

Mixed Practice

Sports Topic **Write the verb or verb phrase in each sentence.**

1. Runners have always called the marathon the great competitive sport.
2. Today many people across the country are racing in the triathlon.
3. This race includes a 2.4-mile swim, a 112-mile bicycle race, and a 26-mile run.
4. The competitors do swim the 2.4 miles in the choppy waters of the ocean.
5. According to records the triathlon started in Hawaii in 1978.
6. Only twelve athletes competed in that first triathlon.
7. This competition was first called the Iron Man Triathlon.
8. Over the years more and more women were joining the competition.
9. Within three years the triathlon had become a major event in the United States.
10. More than four thousand people from across the world started in the race that year.
11. Triathletes must be in excellent condition.
12. They will train every day for weeks, or even months, before a competition.
13. Competitors require strength and endurance.
14. Triathletes will usually compete against their previous records.
15. Many athletes will certainly reach their goals.

LESSON 2 *(pages L85–L91)*

OBJECTIVES

- **To identify linking verbs**
- **To distinguish between action verbs and linking verbs**

Create Interest

Write the following sentences on the board. Have students identify the problem with each sentence. Have students come to the board and rewrite each sentence using linking verbs.

- That chemistry test hard.
- The temperatures in the chemistry lab low.
- Our experiment completed yesterday.

Guide Instruction

By Connecting Ideas

Refer students to the charts of linking verbs on pages L85–L86 and L88. Tell students that they should become very familiar with these verbs that connect

Linking Verbs

Verbs that do not show action are called state-of-being verbs. These verbs make statements about a subject.

> The chemistry book **is** on the top shelf.
> Mason and Sharon **were** in the lab early.

State-of-being verbs are often used as linking verbs. This means that they join the subject to another word in the sentence.

A **linking verb** links the subject with another word in the sentence. The other word either renames or describes the subject.

> Christopher's favorite class **is** chemistry.
>
> (*Is* links *class* with *chemistry*. *Chemistry* renames the subject.)
>
> The temperatures in the lab **have been** very low.
>
> (*Have been* links *temperatures* with *low*. *Low* describes the temperatures—*the low temperatures.*)

The following is a list of common linking verbs. All the verbs in the list are forms of the verb *be.*

COMMON LINKING VERBS		
be	shall be	have been
is	will be	has been
am	can be	had been
are	could be	could have been

IDENTIFYING COMMON STUMBLING BLOCKS

Problem

- Using the incorrect verb tense when the subject and predicate are separated by an intervening prepositional phrase

Solution

- Direct students not to be distracted by a prepositional phrase that comes between the subject and the verb or verb phrase. Use the example sentence from page L85 to demonstrate a linking verb that comes directly after an intervening prepositional phrase: *The temperatures* in the lab *have been very low.* Tell students that if they took out the prepositional phrase, the subject *temperatures* agrees with the linking verb *have been.* Some students might be tempted to say "The temperatures in the lab *has been* very low."
- Have students choose correct linking verbs for the following sentences:

  The chapters in our chemistry book (are, is) interesting.

  The activities at the end of the chapter (have been, has been) difficult.

or link ideas in a sentence. Demonstrate how linking verbs are used in a sentence. Have students create sentences for some of the other linking verbs listed in the charts.

Consolidate Skills

Through Guided Practice

The **Check Your Understanding** exercises on pages L86–L87, L88–L89 and L90 will help students distinguish between action verbs and linking verbs. Practice the first example on page L86 together. Students should then complete the remaining exercises independently.

Apply to Communication

Through Independent Writing

The **Communicate Your Ideas** activity on page L91 prompts students to write a report based on their observations of a family. Remind students that the

A DIFFERENT APPROACH

Auditory

Have students make word cards that contain each of the 22 linking verbs/verb phrases from the chart on pages L85–L86. As you read the sentences in items one through ten, have students listen and point to the card that contains the linking verb for each sentence. Then have students show the cards with the correct linking verbs on them.

HOME WORK

Have students use their linking verb word cards from the above activity to write ten additional sentences about science. Each sentence should contain a linking verb.

was	should be	should have been
were	would be	may have been
	may be	might have been
	might be	must have been

CONNECT TO WRITER'S CRAFT

Professional writers choose strong and direct action verbs rather than state-of-being verbs to help keep their readers interested. Notice the difference between the verbs in the following sentences. Which sentence sounds the most interesting? Why?

The scientist **is** in the laboratory.

The scientist **works** in the laboratory.

The scientist **struggles** in the laboratory. 

PRACTICE YOUR SKILLS

Check Your Understanding

Finding Linking Verbs

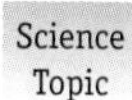

Science Topic **Write each linking verb. Then write the words that the verb links.**

1. A metal spoon and a red brick are solids. spoon, brick—solids

2. Every solid is a definite shape. solid—shape

3. For example, a brick is the same shape in or out of water. brick—shape

4. The tops of bricks are rectangles. tops—rectangles

5. Usually a solid will be the same shape under normal pressure. solid—shape

6. Water can be a solid, a liquid, or a gas. water—solid, liquid, gas

audience for their report is parents. Students should use action verbs to make their writing more interesting.

Transfer to Everyday Life

Identifying Linking Verbs in Comic Books

Provide students with copies of appropriate comic books. Tell students that although comic books are known for their action verbs, linking verbs can also be found in them. Have students work with a partner to identify at least ten linking verbs in their comic book.

Pull It All Together

By Sharing

Have students read their observation reports to the class. List the most common action verbs that students used as they observed families. As a class, create a line graph showing the five most common action verbs students used in their reports.

7. The water in the glass could have been an ice cube. water—cube
8. Steam from a tea kettle is a gas. steam—gas
9. Orange juice is a liquid. juice—liquid
10. An orange is a solid. orange—solid

Check Your Understanding

Writing Linking Verbs

Science Topic

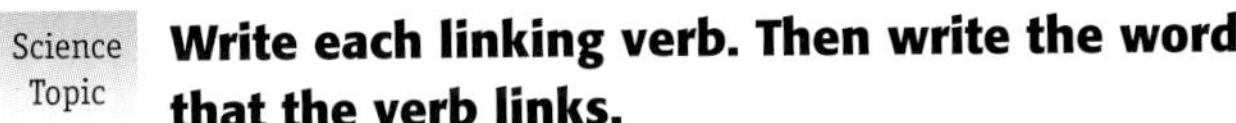

Write each linking verb. Then write the words that the verb links.

11. The sun is the star closest to Earth. sun—star
12. The sun must be a medium-sized star. sun—star
13. It should be a distance of ninety-three million miles away from Earth. It—distance
14. Earth is our home. Earth—home
15. Earth's rotation around the sun must be the cause of day and night. rotation—cause
16. In 365 days it will be another year. it—year
17. Without the sun, Earth would be a dark and cold place. Earth—place
18. The sun is Earth's source of light and heat. sun—source
19. The sun has been the subject of many Native American dances. sun—subject
20. Many early cultures were believers in the sun's importance in their lives. cultures—believers

Additional Linking Verbs

Forms of the verb *be* are not the only words that can be used as linking verbs. Additional linking verbs are listed in the box on the following page.

USING STUDENTS' STRENGTHS

Multiple Intelligences: Spatial

Have students use the sentences in the **Check Your Understanding** activity to create a ten-page children's picture book about the solar system. Each sentence from items 11 through 20 will represent a page in their books. For example, sentence 11 will appear on page 1, and so on. Have students illustrate their books using markers, watercolors, construction paper, or other art materials of their choosing.

DEVELOPING WORKPLACE COMPETENCIES

Basic Skills: Speaking

After discussing the definition of linking verbs, have students tell how the use of linking verbs is crucial to communicating effectively in the workplace. For example, how might an idea be misunderstood by a coworker if someone uses the linking verb *has been* instead of *had been*? Discuss with students other possible misunderstandings using linking verbs.

Check Understanding

Distinguishing Action Verbs from Linking Verbs

Ask students to summarize the difference between action verbs and linking verbs. Encourage them to provide examples of different types of action verbs and linking verbs as they define each.

A DIFFERENT APPROACH

Visual

Before students complete the **Practice Your Skills** activity, have them work in small groups to create large charts containing the linking verbs. Display the charts in different sections of the classroom. Tell students that the charts can be referenced as they complete the assignment. When students have completed the assignment, have them comment on the effectiveness of the charts.

HOME WORK

Have students find out more about painter Grant Wood. Students should complete their research as a three-day home work assignment. Have students write a two-paragraph paper about the artist. Students should underline all of the linking verbs in their completed papers.

ADDITIONAL LINKING VERBS			
appear	grow	seem	stay
become	look	smell	taste
feel	remain	sound	turn

Any of the verbs in the box can link a subject with a word that either renames or describes the subject.

That painter **became** the new teacher.

(*Teacher* renames the subject *painter*.)

Yesterday the future **felt** very bright.

(*Bright* describes the subject—*the bright future*.)

Like action verbs, these linking verbs can also have helping verbs.

The art teacher **is becoming** hoarse.
That painting **does look** beautiful.

PRACTICE YOUR SKILLS

Check Your Understanding

Finding Linking Verbs

Art Topic **Write each linking verb. Then write the words that each verb links.**

1. Grant Wood's *Parson Weems's Fable* has become a famous painting. *Parson Weems's Fable*—painting
2. The foreground scene appears familiar. scene—familiar
3. At the same time, it seems unusual. it—unusual

4. The smaller character looks shrunken. character–shrunken
5. Could the character be George Washington? character–George Washington
6. George Washington was the first president of the United States. George Washington–president
7. The house and lawn feel too perfect. house, lawn–perfect
8. The cherry trees appear exactly the same shape. trees–shape
9. The first cherry tree looks perfectly round at the top. tree–round
10. This famous painting remains a puzzle to many viewers. painting–puzzle

Linking Verb or Action Verb?

Some of the additional linking verbs you have just studied are not always used as linking verbs; they can also be used as action verbs. When you come across one of the verbs, ask yourself this question: *What is the verb doing in the sentence?* If the verb links a subject to a word that renames or describes it, it is a linking verb. If the verb is used to show action, it is an action verb.

LINKING VERB	The man in that picture **looked** happy.
	(*Looked* links *happy* and *man. Happy* describes the subject *man.* The sentence is about the *happy man.*)
ACTION VERB	For days the girl **looked** desperately for that calendar.
	(*Looked* shows action. It tells what the girl did. Also, there is no word in the sentence that renames or describes the subject.)

REACHING ALL STUDENTS

English Language Learners

Explain to students that the order in which linking verbs appear is fixed. For example, it is incorrect to say *I have could painted that work of art.* The order of *could have* must always be the same, just as the other linking verbs must be in their correct order. Tell students the sentence should be *I could have painted that work of art.* Encourage students to refer to their linking verb charts to check the order of the linking verbs in their speech and writing.

A DIFFERENT APPROACH

Auditory

Divide the class into two teams. As you read each sentence in the **Practice Your Skills** activity, have students from each team try to respond correctly by identifying the verbs as either action or linking. Teams score a point for each correct response.

HOME WORK

As a home work assignment, have students create a game that will help others identify action and linking verbs. Encourage students to use various types of materials, such as cardboard or wood to construct their games. Have students bring their completed games to class. Try some of the games as a whole group.

PRACTICE YOUR SKILLS

Check Your Understanding

Distinguishing Between Linking Verbs and Action Verbs

Contemporary Life

Write each verb. Then label each one *linking* or *action.*

1. The twenty-first century feels [linking] the same as the last century.
2. We turned [action] the page on our calendar.
3. Neither our experiences nor our feelings suddenly became [linking] different.
4. Our lives remain [linking] the same.
5. The outside air smells [linking] clean and fresh.
6. The food still tastes [linking] delicious.
7. We stay [action] in the same neighborhood.
8. No one suddenly grew [linking] anxious.
9. Everything appears [linking] normal.
10. Did you feel [action] the change from one century to another?

Connect to the Writing Process: Drafting

Writing Sentences

[Answers may vary. Possible responses are given.]

For each noun in the following list, write a sentence in which the noun is followed by an action verb. Then write another sentence, using the same noun with a linking verb.

11. citizens Citizens formed action committees. The citizens are proud.
12. downtown Our downtown confuses tourists. Your downtown is better.
13. pizza Pizza makes me happy. Pizza is not low in calories.
14. photograph The photograph reveals the truth. The photograph looks very old.
15. earthquake The earthquake shook the house. The earthquake was minor.

Communicate Your Ideas

APPLY TO WRITING

Observation Report: *Verbs*

Imagine that you are a social scientist interested in the family. Choose a public location such as an amusement park, a sporting event, or a fast-food restaurant where families go. Observe the action. Watch how the parents and the children behave. Write a brief report for parents that summarizes "family behavior" in a public place. Use action verbs to show the actual behavior. Use linking verbs to name the behaviors. Be prepared to identify each kind of verb.

TIMESAVER *QuickCheck*

Have students exchange their completed observation reports with a partner. Have students evaluate the papers by focusing on the action verbs and linking verbs used. Have students make constructive suggestions as to how the papers might be improved.

HOME STUDY

Have students write observation reports of their own families. Their intended audience for this report should be their own parents. Remind students to use action verbs and linking verbs in their reports.

EXPANDING THE LESSON

Using Technology

You will find additional **instructional** and **practice** materials for this chapter at http:/www.bkenglish.com.

FOR REVIEWING SKILLS

Using CheckPoint

This feature on verbs can be used as further independent practice or as a cumulative review of the chapter. It covers action verbs, linking verbs, and verb phrases.

CheckPoint

Finding Action and Linking Verbs

Write each verb or verb phrase. Then label each one *action* or *linking.*

1. The grocer weighed the cheese. action
2. The waves were pounding against the shore. action
3. The battery in our car is dead. linking
4. Over the weekend the ocean remained rough. linking
5. The heart of a normal adult will beat about 38 million times each year. action
6. Once again the computer was correct. linking
7. More than three hundred United States citizens have appeared on the stamps of other countries. action
8. Sodium in salt can contribute to high blood pressure. action
9. The roses near the house smell fragrant. linking
10. Benjamin Franklin was the founder of the first public library in the United States. linking

Finding the Verb

Write each verb or verb phrase. Then label each one *action* or *linking.*

The morning of August 24, A.D. 79, was (linking) normal in Pompeii, a beautiful little city in Italy. Everyone was talking (action) about that evening's sports contests. Mount Vesuvius, a nearby volcano, seemed (linking) peaceful. For 1,500 years the volcano had been (linking) inactive. Then around noon

action / action

it suddenly erupted. Hot rock and ash fell like rain from the sky. Huge clouds of ash, smoke, and poisonous gases grew dark and thick. People could not see the sun anymore. After eight days the volcano finally became quiet. Pompeii, however, had disappeared under twenty feet of ash and rock.

(Labels above verbs: erupted — action; fell — action; grew — linking; could not see — action; became — linking; had disappeared — action)

Writing Sentences

Write sentences that follow the directions below. (The sentences may come in any order.) Write about one of the following topics or a topic of your own choice: a pet or a wild animal. You could also write about an animal you would like to be and why.

Write a sentence that . . .

1. includes an action verb.
2. includes a linking verb.
3. includes a verb phrase.
4. includes an interrupted verb phrase.
5. includes *taste* as an action verb.
6. includes *taste* as a linking verb.
7. includes *look* as an action verb.
8. includes *look* as a linking verb.
9. includes *appear* as an action verb.
10. includes *appear* as a linking verb.

When you finish, underline each verb or verb phrase.

Sample Answers for *Writing Sentences:*

1. At one time, I raised rabbits.
2. They were adorable.
3. They could have won poster contests!
4. The did not bite or scratch.
5. Once the rabbits tasted fresh vegetables, they wouldn't eat their alfalfa.
6. The hay probably tastes bitter.
7. They looked through their wire cages whenever I came near.
8. They looked clean and fluffy.
9. One day, a litter of seven baby rabbits appeared.
10. With hairless skin and closed eyes, they appeared helpless.

Using *Language and Self-Expression*

Consider using this writing assignment to assess students' ability to use verbs correctly and effectively. You may want students to complete the assignment as part of a descriptive writing strand for their portfolios.

Prewriting

Suggest that students revisit their analysis of the sculpture that they did in *Making Visual Connections* on page L76.

Tell students that focusing on the expression and gestures of the sculpture will help them in the prewriting stage. Have students use the following questions as they complete their sketches of the artwork:

- What does the position of the arms express to the viewer?
- How does the expression on the figure's face make you feel?
- Are the lines in the sculpture smooth or rigid?

FOR YOUR INFORMATION

About the Artwork

This limestone figurine was discovered in the southern portion of Veracruz in Mexico. Archeologists believe that such figures are related to the gods of music, dance, and vegetation. The artist is unknown.

Language and *Self-Expression*

This carved figurine comes from Mexico. Some of the patterns on the hat and garment are symbols for ideas and beliefs. The crisscross lines on the hat, for example, stand for movement. Imagine what the figurine would be doing if it actually could move.

If an artist created a figurine of you, would there be symbols, colors, or particular textures? What would be the expression on your face? What impression would you want the figurine to make on viewers?

Prewriting Draw a rough sketch of a figurine representing you. Don't worry about your artistic talent. Instead focus on details like shape, line, color, symbols, and facial expression. If you are drawing in a single color, make notations about colors you would use.

Drafting Use your sketch as a visual prompt for descriptive writing. You might focus one paragraph on shape and line and another on facial expression and body language. Your conclusion could sum up the overall message of the figurine.

Revising Put the sketch out of sight. Now read your paragraphs. Does it create a vivid mental impression of the figurine and the ideas it conveys? Are your verbs colorful and accurate?

Editing Check your writing for correct spelling and punctuation. Be sure that each sentence expresses a complete thought.

Publishing Write a final copy and give it to your English teacher. If you take an art class, look for an opportunity to spend time drawing this figurine.

Another Look

Verbs

A **verb** is a word used to express an action or a state of being.

A **verb phrase** is made up of a main verb and one or more helping verbs.

Action Verbs

An **action verb** tells what action a subject is performing. *(page L77)*

A **transitive verb** is an action verb that expresses action directed at a person or thing. *(page L80)*

An **intransitive verb** is an action verb whose action is not directed at a person or thing. *(page L80)*

Helping Verbs

Helping (auxiliary) verbs are used with a main verb in a verb phrase. *(page L82)*

Linking Verbs

A **linking verb** links the subject with another word in the sentence. The other word either renames or describes the subject. *(pages L85–L86)*

Using *Another Look*

Another Look summarizes the terms defined in the chapter and provides cross-references to the specific pages on which they are explained. Consider having students use this feature prior to completing **CheckPoint** or taking the post-test. Students who can provide several examples of each term should be able to score well on either measurement.

Using *the Posttest*

Assessing Learning

The posttest will help you and your students assess where they stand in their ability to use and identify verbs.

IDENTIFYING COMMON STUMBLING BLOCKS

Following are the most common errors students make when using verbs.

Problem

- Wrong verb tense or verb form

Solution

- For reteaching, use the explanatory copy printed in blue beside the examples on page L80.

Problem

- Subject-verb agreement

Solution

- For reteaching, use the explanatory copy printed in blue beside the examples on page L89.

Directions

Decide which word receives the action of the underlined verb in each sentence. Write the letter of the correct answer. If the verb is intransitive, write *D*.

EXAMPLE **1.** Please sand these boards as thoroughly as possible.

1 **A** these
B possible
C boards
D intransitive verb

ANSWER **1 C**

1. Do not use those rusty nails.
2. I have been designing this entertainment stand for weeks.
3. The paint should dry for at least three hours.
4. The lumber store downtown is having a sale on cedar planks.
5. I will go to the lumber store for you this afternoon.
6. In shop class we are each building a cedar chest.
7. I will also put a durable lock on mine.
8. Marcos stayed in the shop room for several hours after school.
9. Mr. Mandell told us about the various projects.
10. I could hear the jigsaw from across the room.

A DIFFERENT DELIVERY SYSTEM

If you prefer, you can print the posttest from the BK English Test Bank located at http://www.bkenglish.com.

1 **A** those
B rusty
C nails
D intransitive verb

2 **A** stand
B entertainment
C weeks
D intransitive verb

3 **A** dry
B hours
C three
D intransitive verb

4 **A** downtown
B sale
C planks
D intransitive verb

5 **A** store
B afternoon
C lumber
D intransitive verb

6 **A** chest
B class
C cedar
D intransitive verb

7 **A** also
B lock
C mine
D intransitive verb

8 **A** room
B hours
C school
D intransitive verb

9 **A** various
B projects
C us
D intransitive verb

10 **A** hear
B jigsaw
C room
D intransitive verb

Customizing the Test

Use these questions to add or replace items for alternate versions of the test.

11. The woodworking class will start at noon this Saturday.
12. My dad and I are taking the class together.
13. He is spending more time with me lately.
14. We will each choose a different project for class.
15. I prefer small, detailed projects over large, easy ones.

11. A Saturday
B start
C noon
D intransitive verb

12. A I
B class
C together
D intransitive verb

13. A time
B me
C lately
D intransitive verb

14. A class
B project
C different
D intransitive verb

15. A ones
B small
C projects
D intransitive verb

TEACHING SUGGESTIONS

Essential Knowledge and Skills

- Writing to express, discover, record, develop, reflect on ideas, and to problem solve
- Employing standard English usage in writing for audiences, including parts of speech
- Using adjectives and adverbs appropriately to make writing vivid or precise
- Generating ideas and plans for writing by using prewriting strategies such as brainstorming, graphic organizers, notes, and logs
- Summarizing and organizing ideas gained from multiple sources in useful ways such as outlines and conceptual maps
- Interpreting and evaluating the various ways visual image makers represent meanings

BLOCK SCHEDULING

- If your schedule requires that you cover the chapter in a **shorter time,** use the instruction on adjectives and adverbs and the Check Your Understanding and QuickCheck exercises.
- If you want to take advantage of **longer class time,** add these applications to writing: Connect to Speaking and Writing, Connect to the Writing Process, and Apply to Writing exercises.

CHAPTER 4

Adjectives and Adverbs

Directions

Write the letter of the term that correctly identifies the underlined word in each sentence.

EXAMPLE **1.** Natalie has organized a <u>maid</u> service.

1 **A** adjective
B noun
C proper adjective
D adverb

ANSWER **1** **A**

1. Natalie is <u>very</u> efficient at cleaning.
2. She knows the proper way to clean a <u>Persian</u> rug.
3. She can turn <u>grimy</u>, moldy bathroom tiles into sparkling clean tiles within minutes.
4. Whether a table is made of <u>cherry</u> wood or metal, Natalie knows which cleaner to use.
5. Natalie does all her work on <u>Saturdays</u>.
6. Her dad drops her off at the client's house and picks her up <u>later</u>.
7. With her earnings Natalie buys the <u>best</u> cleaning supplies.
8. She has <u>some</u> money left over for the week.
9. In addition, she deposits <u>some</u> into her account.
10. <u>Gradually</u> Natalie is saving to buy a car.

IDENTIFYING COMMON STUMBLING BLOCKS

Following is a list of the most common errors students make when using adjectives and adverbs.

Problem
- Failure to capitalize proper adjectives

Solution
- Instruction, p. L106
- Practice, pp. L107–L108

Problem
- Faulty adverb forms

Solution
- Instruction, pp. L114–L115, L117
- Practice, pp. L115–L116, L118–L121

1. Adverb
2. Proper Adj
3. adjective
4. Adjective
5. proper noun
6. adverb
7. adjectve
8. adjectue

1 **A** adjective
B noun
C proper adjective
D adverb

2 **A** adjective
B noun
C proper adjective
D adverb

3 **A** adjective
B noun
C proper adjective
D adverb

4 **A** adjective
B noun
C proper adjective
D adverb

5 **A** adjective
B noun
C proper noun
D adverb

B noun
C pronoun
D adverb

9 **A** adjective
B noun
C pronoun
D adverb

10 **A** adjective
B noun
C proper adjective
D adverb

A DIFFERENT DELIVERY SYSTEM

If you prefer, you can print the pretest from the BK English Test Bank located at http://www.bkenglish.com.

Using *the Pretest*

Assessing Prior Knowledge

The pretest will help you and your students assess where they stand in their basic understanding of adjectives and adverbs.

Customizing the Test

Use these questions to add or replace items for alternate versions of the test.

11. Natalie worked faithfully at her weekend job throughout junior high and high school.
ver several years, she faithfully saved a reat deal of money.
fter graduation she started a home business.
She efficiently manages the money and work schedules while her employees do the "dirty work."

A adjective
B noun
C proper adjective
D adverb

2. **A** adjective
B noun
C pronoun
D adverb

13. **A** adjective
B noun
C proper adjective
D adverb

14. **A** adjective
B noun
C proper adjective
D adverb

ADDITIONAL RESOURCES

Language Skills Practice . . . . pages 33–40
Transparency Tools FA3, FA4
ESL Practice and Test Preparation . . . . . pages 94–96
Assessment: Chapter Test. . . . . pages 123–129

MAKING VISUAL CONNECTIONS

For Language Development

Focus on the name of the sculpture, *Family Group.* Ask students the following questions. What figures are in the sculpture? What colors, lines, and shapes make up the artwork? What message do they think the artist was trying to send based on the name of the artwork? As students respond, write down their answers. Then point out how many of their details were phrased as adjectives and adverbs.

To Stimulate Writing

Use the questions for art criticism as writing or discussion prompts.

Possible Answers:

Describe The lines of the sculpture are in three distinct directions: horizontal, vertical, and diagonal. The shapes have rounded edges and the three heads are round. The texture is smooth and clean.

Analyze Safe, simple, comforting, graceful, soft.

Interpret The sculpture's title, lines, shapes, and texture suggest a happy, ideal family.

Judge I would display the sculpture outside a shopping mall because many families go there, and this sculpture would remind them that they are special and belong together. I think my written description would better convince the two to buy the sculpture because my words describe the sculpture *and* the reasons why it is worth displaying.

Henry Moore, *Family Group,* 1951.
Bronze, 59¼ by 26½ inches. © Boltin Picture Library, Croton-on-Hudson, New York.

Describe Describe the elements of line, shape, and texture in this sculpture.

Analyze List several adjectives that describe the tone, or mood, of this work of art. What elements of the sculpture support this tone?

Interpret What ideas do you think the artist wanted to convey? How does the name of the sculpture support this message?

Judge Based on the message of the sculpture, where in your community would you display this sculpture? Why would you choose this location? Do you think the sculpture or your verbal description would better convince the town to purchase the sculpture? Explain your answer.

At the end of this chapter, you will use this artwork to stimulate ideas for writing.

FOR DEVELOPING LANGUAGE SKILLS

LESSON 1 *(pages L101–L113)*

OBJECTIVES

- To identify and use adjectives as modifiers of nouns and pronouns
- To identify proper adjectives and correctly capitalize them
- To distinguish between adjectives and nouns and adjectives and pronouns
- To use fresh, vivid adjectives in writing

Create Interest

Tell students that adjectives can be the most exciting part of reading. Adjectives tell us more about the subject

Adjectives

Imagine what writing would be like if the only parts of speech were nouns and verbs. It would be dull and lifeless! Fortunately, there are words that can change or add meaning to other words. These words are called modifiers**. Modifiers** describe other words. They add color and exactness to a sentence. One kind of modifier is an adjective.

An **adjective** is a word that modifies a noun or a pronoun.

An adjective answers the question *What kind of? Which one? How many?* or *How much?* about nouns and some pronouns. In the following examples, an arrow points to the noun or pronoun each adjective modifies.

WHAT KIND?	The **rough** seas upset the **rich** passengers.
WHICH ONE?	**These** ships are better than **that** one.
HOW MANY?	**Few** people liked the **two** ships.
HOW MUCH?	A **little** space would be a **great** relief.

CONNECT TO SPEAKING AND WRITING

When you speak or write, use adjectives to change the mood of a sentence. Note the difference the adjectives make in the following sentences.

It was a **cold** and **snowy** night.
It was a **moonlit** and **silvery** night.
It was a **dark** and **dreary** night.
It was a **starry** and **cloudless** night. 

FOR INCREASING STUDENT ACHIEVEMENT

USING STUDENTS' STRENGTHS

Multiple Intelligences: Linguistic

Have students play a word game often featured as a category on a popular TV quiz show. First, students think of an answer that combines an adjective and a noun that rhyme and have the same number of syllables. Then students write a question that calls for that answer.

- What is a plastic dessert? (a fake cake)
- What is an aqua slipper? (a blue shoe)

REACHING ALL STUDENTS

Struggling Learners

To help students further understand the definition of the word *adjective,* have them tell you about a time they have seen or have been on a ship. Write some of their responses on the board. Tell students that the words they used as descriptions are adjectives. Underline the adjectives in students' sentences on the board.

and the setting of a sentence or story than any other part of speech. Read the following literature model and point out the author's use of vivid adjectives to help readers see the action:

"Amy flashed an angry look, then turned her face again to the sea of wind-whipped cotton, turned hurriedly and took the cow-horn that hung on the wall and placed it to her lips. . . . The children came leaping in, racing and tumbling in tense, laughing competition—the three smaller ones getting under the feet of the three larger ones."

—Zora Neale Hurston, *Jonah's Gourd Vine*

(angry, wind-whipped, tense, laughing, three, smaller, three, larger, and, the)

Guide Instruction

By Modeling Strategies

Show students how to identify adjectives in a sentence by using the questions on page L101. Write the following sentences on the board.

A DIFFERENT APPROACH

Visual

Complete the first three items in **Practice Your Skills** as a class. Have three students come to the board and write items one through three on the board. Then have students model the strategies they use to identify adjectives and the words they modify in each sentence. Discuss students' responses. Then have the class complete the remaining items individually.

Practice Your Skills

Check Your Understanding

Finding Adjectives

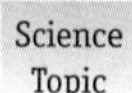
Science Topic

Write each adjective. Beside each one, write the word it modifies.

1. A channel runs through several islands off the coast of New Zealand. islands
2. The narrow and risky route is a shortcut for ships. route
3. On a stormy morning in 1871, the schooner *Brindle* approached the channel. morning
4. Suddenly a young porpoise jumped up in front of the ship. porpoise
5. The friendly porpoise swam near the ship. porpoise
6. It then led the ship safely through the deep waters. waters
7. For years the brave porpoise led ships through the channel—except for one ship, the *Penguin*. porpoise, ship
8. In 1903, a passenger on the *Penguin* shot the defenseless porpoise. porpoise
9. The porpoise survived, but it never again guided the *Penguin* through the dangerous channel. channel
10. In 1909, the *Penguin* sank in the channel with many casualties. casualties

Connect to the Writing Process: Revising

Using Specific Adjectives

Rewrite each sentence, filling in the blank with a specific adjective. The words in parentheses tell what kind of adjective to use. [Answers may vary. Possible responses are given.]

11. ■ (Three) groups of animals that make the ocean their home are dolphins, porpoises, and beluga whales. (How many?)

- It took a courageous person to sail rough, uncharted seas many years ago. (a, courageous, rough, uncharted, many)
- An Italian sailor decided to find new lands with his three ships. (An, Italian, new, three)
- The adventurous explorer received help from the Spanish king and queen. (The, adventurous, the, Spanish)

Use the questioning strategies to help students identify the adjectives in these sentences.

Consolidate Skills

Through Guided Practice

The **Check Your Understanding** exercises as well as the **QuickCheck** on pages L112–L113 will help students identify different types of adjectives. Tell students to use the questioning strategies explained on page L101 as they complete the exercises. Practice

12. Dolphins, porpoises and ▢ (beluga) whales are actually related to each other. (What kind?)

13. These animals will go to ▢ (great) lengths to help other dolphins that are wounded. (How much?)

14. The beluga whale lives in the ▢ (Arctic) waters near the North Pole. (What kind?)

15. ▢ (Beluga) whales are also called white whales. (What kind?)

Different Positions of Adjectives

Usually an adjective comes right before the noun or the pronoun it modifies. Sometimes, though, an adjective can follow the word it modifies. It can also follow a linking verb.

Before a Noun	The **brave, adventurous** explorer led an expedition through the jungle.
After a Noun	The explorer, **brave** and **adventurous,** led an expedition through the jungle.
After a Linking Verb	The explorer was **brave** and **adventurous.**

Connect to Writer's Craft

A writer often uses a variety of specific adjectives that will appeal to the reader's five senses.

See	**Gray** smoke billowed from the chimney.
Touch	The **warm** embers indicated recent campers.
Taste	Jo found an orange that was **sweet** and **juicy.**
Smell	A **tangy citrus** scent filled the room.
Hear	**Gruff** sounds of wolves reached us. 

USING STUDENTS' STRENGTHS

Multiple Intelligences: Kinesthetic

Write each word of the three example sentences from the middle of the page on a separate sheet of paper. Give each sheet of paper to a different student, then have students stand in the front of the class and form sentences with the words they are holding. Demonstrate the various positions of the adjectives by having students holding adjectives move around to different positions. Read the different sentences aloud.

the first example on page L102 together. Then have students use this strategy to complete the remaining exercises independently.

Apply to Communication

Through Independent Writing

The **Communicate Your Ideas** activities on pages L106, L108, and L112 prompt students to write a travel journal, an advertisement, and a comparison/contrast paragraph. Ask students how they think adjectives will improve these three different writing assignments and make them more interesting for readers. Students should be able to point out that communicating details about appearance and feelings will make their writing livelier and more interesting to readers.

DEVELOPING WORKPLACE COMPETENCIES

Basic Skills: Writing

Have students imagine they are scientists hired by a pharmaceutical company to investigate and report on a region never explored. The company would like to find plants that can be tested and used to create new medicines. How would students go about writing their reports? How would they describe the new region? How could they clearly explain the various kinds of plant life they see? Have students write their reports and then tell how the reports could be used by their employers.

PUNCTUATION WITH TWO ADJECTIVES

Sometimes you will write two adjectives together before or after the noun they describe. If those two adjectives are not connected by *and* or *or,* you might want to put a comma between them. To decide if a comma belongs or not, read the adjectives with the word *and* between them.

- If the adjectives make sense, use a comma to replace the *and*.
- If the adjectives do not make sense with the word *and* between them, do not add a comma.

COMMA NEEDED	The journey began on a **humid, hot** day. (A *humid and hot day* reads well.)
COMMA NOT NEEDED	They saw **several incredible** lands. (*Several and incredible lands* does not read well.)

Usually no comma is needed after a number and after an adjective that refers to size, shape, or age. For example, no commas are needed in the following sentence.

Six large ships had **large sunny decks.**

You can learn more about commas before nouns on pages L546–L547.

Articles

A, an, and *the* form a special group of adjectives called **articles.** *A* comes before words that begin with a consonant sound. *An* comes before words that begin with a vowel sound.

I picked up **a** microphone and made **an** announcement.

(*A* comes before a consonant sound such as *m,* and *an* comes before a vowel sound such as *a.*)

Transfer to Everyday Life

Identifying Adjectives in Literature

Have students find vivid, unusual adjectives in a passage from a short story or novel. Students should select a one-page passage from a favorite book and reread the selection, looking for adjectives. Students should keep a list of the adjectives in the passage and then share their three favorite adjectives with the class.

Pull It All Together

By Sharing

Have students share with the class some of the adjectives they used in their travel journal writing assignment. Write some of these interesting adjectives on the board. Have listeners use some of the adjectives in new sentences.

Check Understanding

Brainstorming Adjectives

Have students use their imaginations to take turns brainstorming adjectives. Write some of students' interesting

PRACTICE YOUR SKILLS

Check Your Understanding

Finding Adjectives

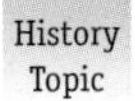

History Topic **Write each adjective. Beside each one, write the word it modifies.**

1. In 1519, Ferdinand Magellan, a courageous mariner, led five ships from Spain. mariner, ships
2. Magellan sailed across the broad Atlantic. Atlantic
3. He took the southern route along the eastern coast of South America. route, coast
4. His sailors, restless and weary, soon rebelled against the long and dangerous journey. sailors, journey
5. One ship left and returned to familiar waters. ship, waters
6. With four ships in 1520, Magellan found the narrow, dangerous passage to the Pacific. ships, passage
7. The sea captain expected to reach Asia in a few weeks, but the voyage lasted four months. captain, weeks, months
8. The crew, hungry and desperate, ate wooden sawdust and leather riggings. crew, sawdust, riggings
9. Magellan never finished the tragic journey. journey
10. He was killed in a brutal war in the Philippines. war

Connect to the Writing Process: Prewriting

Linking Specific Adjectives with Nouns

Imagine that you are going on a journey to another town, state, or country—or even just to the mall or a friend's house. Make a list of nouns that name the places along the way to your destination. Make sure you have at least five place names. Then make a list of adjectives that describe the places in your noun list. Try to include at least two adjectives for each noun. Be sure to make the adjectives as specific as possible.

A DIFFERENT APPROACH

Visual

As an alternative to writing out the **Practice Your Skills** exercises individually, complete the exercises together as a whole-group activity. Draw a two-column chart on the board, and have students use the chart to write their responses. They should write the adjectives in the left column and the words they modify in the right column.

responses on the board. Then choose some of the adjectives on the board for students to use in sentences. Call on individual students to create the sentences.

IDENTIFYING COMMON STUMBLING BLOCKS

Problem

- Overusing the same adjectives

Solution

- Point out that using the same adjective to apply to a number of different situations indicates a limited vocabulary and an inability to express oneself precisely.
- Give students a list of the following overused adjectives and have them use a thesaurus to find alternatives: *fine, good, excellent, funny, nice, interesting, cute, terrible.*

TIMESAVER QuickCheck

Have students self-evaluate their journal writing for use of vivid adjectives. Have students decide what criteria they will use to evaluate their writing.

HOME STUDY

Have students create illustrations to accompany their travel writing. The illustrations should enhance the adjectives they used to describe their travels.

Communicate Your Ideas

APPLY TO WRITING

Travel Journal: ***Specific Adjectives***

You have just returned from your journey and are ready to write about it. Use your list of nouns and adjectives from the activity on the preceding page to create a journal entry about your journey. Describe your journey in chronological, or time, order. Review your choice of adjectives. They should be vivid and specific so that you will be able to recall your travel experience years later. As you write your journal entry, be sure to include the following information.

- Date
- Destination
- Five places along the way
- Time of day at each place
- Vivid and specific adjectives

Proper Adjectives

Suppose you traveled to France on your journey. Did you know that the word *France* is a proper noun? That is because it is the name of a particular place. The word *French,* however, is a **proper adjective.** It is formed from the proper noun *France,* but it is used to modify a noun or a pronoun—the *French* city. A proper adjective always begins with a capital letter.

PROPER NOUNS AND ADJECTIVES		
Proper Nouns	Europe	America
Proper Adjectives	European explorer	American trade

Check Your Understanding

Finding Proper Adjectives

History Topic **Write each proper adjective. Beside each one, write the word it modifies.**

1. In 1497, John Cabot established the first British claim in North America. claim
2. The first permanent European settlement in the United States was in St. Augustine. settlement
3. In the early 1600s, English and Dutch colonists began settling New France. colonists
4. New York City began in 1612 with the arrival of Dutch ships on the Hudson River. ships
5. Swedish colonists settled Delaware and southern New Jersey. colonists
6. Farms in South Carolina were in the style of Spanish plantations. plantations
7. One of the first crops exported from the American colonies was cranberries. colonies
8. The Spanish government expanded its holdings in North America. government
9. La Salle claimed the Mississippi River valley for the French people. valley, people
10. Fur trade with various Native American tribes in the Americas was crucial to the Europeans. tribes

Connect to the Writing Process: Editing

Capitalizing Proper Adjectives

Rewrite the sentences, capitalizing each proper adjective.

11. Near 1630, english Puritans settled in New England.
12. The center of each puritan village was a meetinghouse.

USING STUDENTS' STRENGTHS

Multiple Intelligences: Linguistic

After discussing proper adjectives, have students take turns naming additional proper adjectives and writing them on the board. Remind students to capitalize the initial letters of proper adjectives. Then have students listen as you say the following words. Have them decide whether or not each is a proper adjective: *Emily, Irish, grocery store, Jack's Candy Shop, Swedish, Japanese.*

A DIFFERENT APPROACH

Auditory

Have students work with partners and read the **Practice Your Skills** exercises together. Students should work cooperatively to identify the proper adjectives in each sentence.

HOME WORK

Have students use newspapers to find ten sentences containing proper adjectives. Students should write out the complete sentences and underline the proper adjectives.

TIMESAVER *QuickCheck*

Have students exchange their completed advertisements with a partner to evaluate the use of proper adjectives. Have students critique each other's use of and capitalization of proper adjectives.

REACHING ALL STUDENTS

Advanced Learners

After discussing the function of adjectives and nouns and the sample sentences on this page, have students create additional examples of words that can be nouns or adjectives, depending on their function in a sentence. Write students' correct responses on the board.

13. Were there any scottish people on the *Mayflower?*

14. The architecture and windmills throughout colonial New York were a result of dutch influence.

15. King Philip's War was caused by disagreements over native american land.

Communicate Your Ideas

APPLY TO WRITING

Advertisement: ***Proper Adjectives***

Suppose you wanted to start a new, contemporary colony. Write an advertisement describing the location of the new colony, what people will find there, who the colony's leaders will be, the purpose of the colony, job opportunities, weather conditions, and any other information you think new settlers might need to know. Be sure to use a capital letter for each proper adjective.

Adjective or Noun?

A word's part of speech depends on how it is used in a sentence. *Street* and *water,* for example, can be either nouns or adjectives.

NOUN	The narrow **street** was crowded.
ADJECTIVE	**Street** cleaners are working near our apartment building.
NOUN	**Water** is important to our lives.
ADJECTIVE	A **water** plant is near my home.

Practice Your Skills

Check Your Understanding

Finding Adjectives

Science Topic **Write *adjective* or *noun* to identify each underlined word.**

1. A water (adj.) technician looks for contamination.
2. The technician collects and tests water (n.).
3. Water from a city well (n.) and local lakes is tested.
4. In the laboratory the well (adj.) water is examined carefully.
5. Workers may add a chemical (n.) to the water supply.
6. Technicians treat water with chemical (adj.) additives.
7. These technicians take courses in chemistry, mathematics, and biology (n.).
8. The biology (adj.) courses cover everything from basic cells to zoology.
9. A future (adj.) technician should also have mechanical skills.
10. A technician's job in the future (n.) will include maintenance duties and repairing water pumps.

Connect to the Writing Process: Drafting

Writing Sentences with Nouns and Adjectives

Write two sentences for each of the following words. Use the word as an adjective in the first sentence. Use the word as a noun in the second sentence. Then label the use of each one. [Answers may vary.]

11. past **14.** laboratory
12. job **15.** salary
13. work

A DIFFERENT APPROACH

Kinesthetic

Have students write the words *adjective* and *noun* on two separate word cards. Have students complete items one through ten of **Practice Your Skills** by holding up the correct responses to each item as you read the sentences aloud. Discuss students' responses to each sentence.

HOME WORK

Have students write five words that can be used as nouns or as adjectives depending on their function in a sentence. Students should then write sentences using each word as a noun and as an adjective.

Sample Answers for *Writing Sentences:*

11. For past (adj.) Christmases, we all came home. That was in the past (n.).
12. We need to have job (adj.) security. On Monday I start my new job (n.).
13. They wore new work (adj.) clothes. He loves his work (n.) as a teacher.
14. She is a laboratory (adj.) technician. I left her in the laboratory (n.).
15. That was a salary (adj.) issue. We will all be given a better salary (n.).

REACHING ALL STUDENTS

Struggling Learners

Tell students that the function of a word determines whether it is a pronoun or an adjective. Discuss the chart at the bottom of the page, then have students create sentences using each word as an adjective and as a pronoun. Tell students that possessive pronouns like *my, your, his,* and *her* will be discussed in a later chapter.

Adjective or Pronoun?

A word can be a pronoun in one sentence and an adjective in another sentence. For example, *this* is a pronoun if it stands alone and takes the place of a noun. *This* is an adjective if it modifies a noun or a pronoun.

ADJECTIVE	**This** number is a prime number. (*This* modifies *number.*)
PRONOUN	**This** is a prime number. (*This* replaces the noun *number.*)
ADJECTIVE	**Which** problem did you solve? (*Which* modifies *problem.*)
PRONOUN	**Which** did you solve? (*Which* replaces the noun *problem.*)

The following pronouns can be used as adjectives in a sentence.

WORDS USED AS PRONOUNS OR ADJECTIVES

DEMONSTRATIVE	INTERROGATIVE	INDEFINITE	
this	what	all	many
these	which	another	more
that	whose	any	most
those		both	neither
		each	other
		either	several
		few	some

The possessive pronouns *my, your, his, her, its, our,* and *their* are sometimes called **pronominal adjectives** because they answer the adjective question *Which one?* Throughout this book, however, these words will be considered pronouns.

PRACTICE YOUR SKILLS

Check Your Understanding

Distinguish Between Adjectives and Pronouns

Mathematics Topic **Label each underlined word as an *adjective* or a *pronoun*.**

1. What (adj.) rule is used for dividing rational numbers?
2. That (pron.) is the inverse operation for multiplying rational numbers.
3. What (pron.) did you say?
4. That (adj.) mathematical operation is very simple.
5. In fact, several (adj.) numbers can be multiplied or divided.
6. Because rational numbers can be used together, we include several (pron.) in our homework.
7. However, too many (adj.) numbers confuse some students.
8. Many (pron.) confuse the operations and the inverses.
9. Which (adj.) group do you belong to—the comfortable or the confused?
10. I don't know which (pron.).

Connect to the Writing Process: Drafting

Writing Sentences

Write two sentences for each of the following words. Use the word as an adjective in the first sentence. Use the word as a pronoun in the second sentence. Then label the use of each one. [Answers may vary. Possible responses are given.]

11. this — This (adj.) book is wonderful. This (pron.) is not what I expected.
12. which — Which (adj.) hat should I wear? Which (pron.) do you prefer?
13. both — Both (adj.) girls are coming with us. I am very fond of both (pron.).
14. some — Some (adj.) cookies are too sweet. Try some (pron.) before you go.
15. these — I love these (adj.) lazy weekends. Are these (pron.) your photographs?

HOME WORK

Have students write sentences using each of the underlined words in **Practice Your Skills.** If the word was originally used as a pronoun, have them write a sentence using it as an adjective and vice versa.

YOUR IDEAS

For Pronouns

TIMESAVER *QuickCheck*

Encourage students to use the same words as nouns, pronouns, and adjectives. Tell students that each correct use of these parts of speech will earn one point. Each incorrect use will result in a point being subtracted from their writing assignments.

Communicate Your Ideas

APPLY TO WRITING

Compare and Contrast Paragraphs: *Adjectives, Nouns, and Pronouns*

Think of two things, topics, that are alike in some ways and different in other ways. Examples from math include adding and subtracting or multiplying and dividing. Before writing, you may wish to use a chart similar to the following Venn diagram to help you organize your ideas.

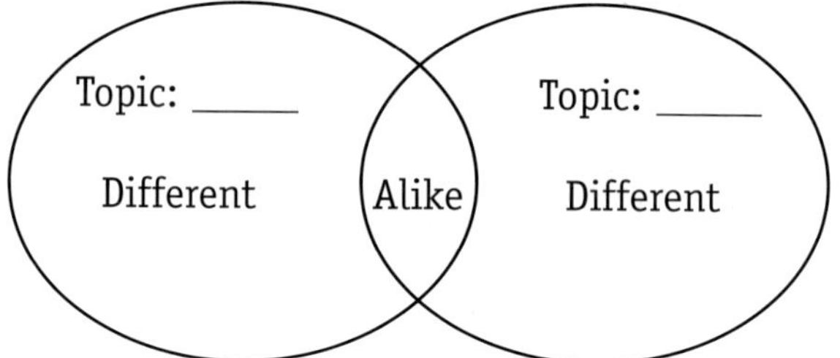

In the first paragraph, compare the two topics. Name as many ways as you can that tell how the two topics are alike. In the second paragraph, tell how they are different in a variety of ways. Use some of the same words as nouns, pronouns, and adjectives.

Mixed Practice

Science Topic **Write each adjective. Beside each one, write the word it modifies.**

1. Which animal is the oddest creature on Earth? animal, creature

2. The answer is easy. answer

3. It is the <u>Australian</u> platypus. platypus
4. The platypus is a <u>primitive</u> animal. animal
5. Unlike <u>most</u> kinds of mammals, however, the platypus lays eggs. kinds
6. The eggs have a <u>tough</u>, <u>leathery</u> covering. covering
7. <u>Baby</u> platypuses are <u>blind</u> and <u>helpless</u>. platypuses
8. The feet of the platypus are <u>unusual</u>. feet
9. They have webs for swimming, but they also have <u>hard</u> claws for digging. claws
10. The <u>back</u> legs of <u>male</u> platypuses have daggers made of bone. legs, platypuses
11. The daggers, <u>narrow</u> and <u>hollow</u>, are like the fangs of a rattlesnake. daggers
12. The platypus can shoot a <u>deadly</u> poison through the daggers. poison
13. A jab from one of <u>these</u> daggers can instantly kill an enemy. daggers
14. A platypus pokes around in <u>river</u> mud with a <u>broad</u> bill. mud, bill
15. This bill is <u>soft</u> and <u>flexible</u>. bill
16. A platypus eats worms, snails, and <u>tiny</u> shellfish. shellfish

EXPANDING THE LESSON USING TECHNOLOGY

You will find additional **instructional** and **practice** materials for this chapter at http://www.bkenglish.com.

YOUR IDEAS

For Adjectives

LESSON 2 *(pages L114–L121)*

OBJECTIVES

- **To identify adverbs as modifiers of verbs, adjectives, or other adverbs**
- **To use adverbs accurately and effectively in writing**

Create Interest

Ask students to brainstorm as many words as they can that end in *-ly.* Write students' ideas on the board. Point out that most of these words are adverbs. Explain that adverbs modify verbs, adjectives, and other adverbs. Have students use some of the adverbs on the board in complete sentences.

Guide Instruction

By Modeling Strategies

Show students how to identify adverbs in a sentence by using the questions at the bottom of page L114. Write the following sentences on the board. Use the questioning strategies to identify adverbs in these sentences with students:

GETTING STUDENTS INVOLVED

Collaborative Learning

Have students work collaboratively to use adverbs to describe educational computer games. Provide students with various educational computer games to play. After students have played the games for a period of time, have them work together to write a paragraph about the game. Encourage students to use adverbs and to underline them in their game descriptions.

REACHING ALL STUDENTS

Advanced Learners

Have students devise a questionnaire about the spending habits of people their age. Tell them to make their questions multiple choice, offering a range of answers using the adverbs *always, often, seldom,* and *never*. When they have administered the questionnaire to at least 25 people, have them tally their results and write up their conclusions.

Adverbs

Just as nouns and pronouns have adjective modifiers, verbs and adjectives also have modifiers. These modifiers are called adverbs. Adverbs make the meaning of verbs, adjectives, and other adverbs more precise.

An **adverb** is a word that modifies a verb, an adjective, or another adverb.

Many adverbs end in *–ly.*

Hold the rope **tightly** as you lower the bucket **slowly.**

The common adverbs in the following list, however, do not end in *–ly.*

COMMON ADVERBS			
again	far	never	soon
almost	fast	next	still
already	hard	not (n't)	then
also	here	now	there
always	just	often	too
down	late	quite	very
even	more	rather	well
ever	near	so	yet

Adverbs That Modify Verbs

Most adverbs modify verbs. To find these adverbs, ask yourself, *Where? When? How?* or *To what extent?* about each verb. A word that answers one of these questions is an

- She easily won the race. (*How?* easily)
- He often races on weekends. (*To what extent?* often)
- The race was completed quickly. (*How?* quickly)

Consolidate Skills

Through Guided Practice

The **Check Your Understanding** exercises on pages L115 and L118 as well as the **QuickChecks** on pages L120–L121 will help students identify adverbs. Tell students to use the questioning strategies explained on pages L114–115 as they complete the exercises. Practice the first example on page L115 together. Then have students complete the remaining exercises independently.

adverb. When it modifies a verb, an adverb can usually be placed anywhere in the sentence.

WHERE?	Last spring everyone gathered **outside** to watch the race.
WHEN?	**Sometimes** we race in the fall.
HOW?	She ran **quickly.**
TO WHAT EXTENT?	The sun **completely** disappeared.

More than one adverb can modify the same verb.

Ray **never** ran **fast.**

When there are helping verbs in addition to the main verb, an adverb modifies the entire verb phrase.

You should accept a compliment **graciously.**

An adverb sometimes interrupts a verb phrase in a statement or a question.

STATEMENT	I have **always** enjoyed running.
QUESTION	Did**n't** she know her competitors?

PRACTICE YOUR SKILLS

Check Your Understanding

Finding Adverbs

Literature Topic **Write each adverb and the word or words it modifies.**

1. Toni Cade Bambara's *Raymond's Run* always gives readers food for thought. gives

2. The girl in the story truly fears nothing. fears

REACHING ALL STUDENTS

English Language Learners

Tell students that they can identify adverbs that modify verbs by moving the adverbs to either the beginning or the end of the sentence. Explain that if the sentence still makes sense, the word being moved is an adverb. For example, *We accepted the invitation graciously* can be rewritten *Graciously, we accepted the invitation.* Have students use this strategy with other examples.

Apply to Communication

Through Independent Writing

The **Communicate Your Ideas** activity on page L120 prompts students to write an interpretive paragraph based on a painting. Ask students to list some of the adverbs they might use in their writing.

Transfer to Everyday Life

Identifying Adverbs in Conversation

Have students identify at least ten adverbs they use in conversations throughout one day. Students should write down any adverbs and the sentences in which they were used. Have students share their sentences with the class. Discuss the adverbs and the words they modify with the class.

Pull It All Together

By Sharing

Have students share with the class some of the adverbs they decided to use in their writing assignments about the family painting. Write some of the adverbs on the board. Have lis-

A DIFFERENT APPROACH

Auditory

Have students take turns completing **Practice Your Skills** aloud. Have one student read a sentence. Then have other students identify the adverbs and the words they modify. Encourage students to identify the adverbs and words being modified by listening to rather than by reading the sentences.

HOME WORK

Have students observe a member of their household for 30 minutes, noting the person's actions during that time. Then have the student write one paragraph summarizing the person's activities. Emphasize the use of adverbs in students' writing.

3. She, Squeaky, loudly tells everyone about her racing wins. tells

4. She works hard for her goals. works

5. The story is even told from Squeaky's point of view. is told

6. Squeaky does often seem bossy. does seem

7. The kids in the new neighborhood do not believe her. do believe

8. The same kid has always won this race. has won

9. Squeaky fiercely protects her physically challenged brother Raymond. protects

10. When Squeaky races, Raymond also prepares himself for the race. prepares

11. Even though he is not an official runner, he races. is

12. Squeaky proudly watches Raymond's commitment and achievements. watches

13. She suddenly decides something important. decides

14. Squeaky will now become Raymond's coach. will become

15. Squeaky's attitudes and goals do dramatically change from the beginning to the end of the story. do change

Connect to the Writing Process: Revising

Using Adverbs

Revise the following sentences by adding adverbs. Use adverbs that make each sentence's meaning more precise. After you have revised each sentence, underline the adverb. [Answers may vary. Possible responses are given.]

16. A tree limb fell and ^completely blocked the path of the runner.

17. She ^suddenly recovered her strength and determination.

18. Her opponent was ^rapidly gaining and looked as if she might win.

19. The girl ^badly wanted to win the race.

20. Who would cross the finish line ^first?

teners identify the words that the adverbs modify after hearing them in sentences from students' original writing.

Check Understanding

Identifying Adverbs and the Words They Modify

Have students create sentences containing adverbs. Write some of students' responses on the board. Call on individual students to come to the board and underline the words modified by the adverbs.

Adverbs That Modify Adjectives and Other Adverbs

Almost all adverbs modify verbs. However, occasionally an adverb, such as *quite, rather, so, somewhat,* and *very,* modifies an adjective or another adverb. Such an adverb usually comes immediately before the word it modifies.

MODIFYING AN ADJECTIVE — Inventors are **very** creative.

(*Creative* is an adjective. *Very* is an adverb that modifies *creative.* It tells how creative inventors are.)

MODIFYING AN ADVERB — The inventor worked **especially** fast.

(*Fast* is an adverb. *Especially* is an adverb that modifies *fast.* It tells how fast the inventor worked.)

You can learn more about using adjectives and adverbs in Chapter 14.

CONNECT TO SPEAKING AND WRITING

When you speak or write, you convey your ideas better when you use specific adverbs. Try to avoid repeating adverbs or using abstract adjectives in your writing or speech. The following sentences repeat the same adverbs and use a vague adjective.

VAGUE — Pedro is a **very very** good inventor.
Megan is **really** a **very sweet** person.

Spoken or written, the following sentences are more effective because the modifiers are more specific and less repetitive.

SPECIFIC — Pedro is a **creative** and **extremely intelligent** inventor.
Megan is a **generous** person. 

USING STUDENTS' STRENGTHS

Multiple Intelligences: Interpersonal

After discussing the examples in **Connect to Speaking and Writing,** have students write a letter. Their letters should describe another friend. Students should focus on their use of adverbs, making sure that they do not overuse particular adverbs such as *very* and *really.*

A DIFFERENT APPROACH

Visual

Have students complete **Practice Your Skills** independently by using their fingers to point to the correct responses. They should identify both the adverbs and the words they modify. Discuss students' responses after they have finished.

HOME WORK

Have students write five additional sentences about inventors. Each sentence should contain an adverb. Have students underline the adverbs in their sentences. They should draw a line to the word or words each adverb modifies.

PRACTICE YOUR SKILLS

Check Your Understanding

Finding Adverbs

Science Topic **Write each adverb and the word or words it modifies.**

1. Inventors are definitely curious about the way things work. curious
2. They are almost always creating with their imaginations. always, are creating
3. Inventors must work especially hard at solving problems. hard, must work
4. Their inventions are often amazing. amazing
5. A definitely important invention was Clarence Birdseye's quick-freeze food. important
6. He identified a very important need and found a surprisingly effective solution. important, effective
7. Inventors have been known to take things already useful and turn them into unusually important products. useful, important
8. Many have also found incredibly simple solutions to highly complex problems. simple, complex
9. Albert Einstein was overwhelmingly voted the most influential man of the twentieth century. was voted
10. Technology and science have quite dramatically advanced because of his theories. dramatically, have advanced
11. Einstein pushed his studies far beyond the boundaries of the principles of science and physics. beyond, pushed
12. The world now clearly understands the atom. understands, understands
13. The way light travels was explained easily. was explained
14. Einstein's theory of relativity unlocked the mysteries of the universe amazingly quickly. quickly, unlocked

15. His career was chosen rather easily because of his love for science and math. easily, was chosen

Connect to the Writing Process: Prewriting

Using Adverbs

Write sentences that follow each direction to describe the painting *Abuelitos Piscando Nopalitos* by Carmen Lomas Garza. Use adverbs to modify your verbs, adjectives, and other adverbs.

Carmen Lomas Garza. *Abuelitos Piscando Nopalitos (Grandparents Harvesting Cactus),* 1980.
Gouache painting, 11 by 14 inches. ©1980 Carmen Lomas Garza. Collection of Richard L. Bains and Amalia Mesa-Bains, San Francisco, CA.

16. Describe how sharp the cactus might be.

17. Describe how the man cuts the cactus.

18. Describe how the woman might feel if she were not using the knife and fork to cut the cactus.

19. Describe how sharp the tools must be.

20. Compare or contrast the speed of the harvesting done by the older woman and the young boy.

21. Compare or contrast how much sun the woman in the background will get with the man in the foreground.

USING STUDENTS' STRENGTHS

Multiple Intelligences: Linguistic

As an alternative activity, have students prepare their responses to items 16 through 21 as a speech. How might they write their responses, knowing that they will be spoken as opposed to written? Will their choices of adverbs and adjectives differ because they are writing a speech rather than merely writing sentences? Have students deliver their speeches about the painting to the class.

DEVELOPING WORKPLACE COMPETENCIES

Personal Qualities: Sociability

After discussing the painting, have students list some of the admirable personal qualities it demonstrates. Students should comment on such qualities as friendliness, politeness, understanding, adaptability, and empathy. Discuss with students how the characters in the painting demonstrate these personal attributes. Ask students why these are important qualities for people to possess. Discuss with students why these qualities would be highly valued in the workplace.

YOUR IDEAS

For Checking Comprehension

APPLY TO WRITING

Interpretive Paragraph: *Adverbs*

Using some of the sentences you wrote in the preceding activity, write a paragraph that tells what you think are the relationships of the family members in the painting. Are the family members kind and considerate? Do they care for each other? Use evidence from the painting to support your interpretation. Use adverbs to emphasize your ideas.

QuickCheck Mixed Practice

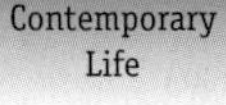

Contemporary Life **Write each adverb and the word or words it modifies.**

1. The Beatles have a very strong fan following. strong
2. Older listeners quite naturally listen to the music of their youth. naturally, listen
3. However, younger fans have also noticed the "Fab Four." noticed
4. Very likely the Beatles will have the best-selling recordings in the extremely long history of music. likely, will have, long
5. The early albums recently have been digitally remastered perfectly to CDs. have been digitally remastered
6. In fact, songs such as "Michelle" and "Yesterday" are especially clear compared to the records of the 1960s. clear
7. The Beatles are now accepted by a large audience. are accepte

8. Their music is commonly heard in commercials on television. is heard

9. This new popularity must surely please older adults. must please

10. They can easily share their music with their teenagers. can share

 Mixed Practice

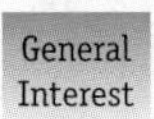

General Interest

Write each adjective and adverb. Beside each one, write the word or words that the adjective or adverb modifies.

1. Humans communicate in various (adj.) ways. ways

2. Words and actions are the main (adj.) means of human (adj.) communication. means, communication

3. Music has always (adv.) been a universal (adj.) method of communication. has been, method

4. People very (adv.) often (adv.) send messages through songs. often, send

5. Some people also (adv.) express their ideas and feelings through body (adj.) movements. express, movements

6. Others communicate more (adv.) through their facial (adj.) expressions. communicate expressions

7. Communication is especially (adv.) important (adj.) in groups. important, Communication

8. People must be extremely (adv.) careful (adj.) of other (adj.) people's (adj.) feelings. careful, People, people's, feelings

9. Good (adj.) communication (adj.) skills are developed gradually (adv.). communication, skills, are developed

10. People should be good (adj.) speakers and excellent (adj.) listeners. speakers, listeners

EXPANDING THE LESSON

Using Technology

You can find additional **instructional** and **practice** materials for this chapter at http://www.bkenglish.com.

GETTING STUDENTS INVOLVED

Reciprocal Teaching

Once students have completed the **QuickCheck** exercise, have them work in pairs to check their answers. Have them do so by identifying each question that the identified adjective or adverb answers. For example the adjective *main* in the second sentence answers the question "What kind?"

FOR REVIEWING SKILLS

Using *Sentence Diagraming*

Sentence diagraming helps students develop variety and style in their writing. In this activity, students will focus on diagraming sentences containing adjectives and adverbs.

Sample Answers for *Sentence Diagrams:*

1.
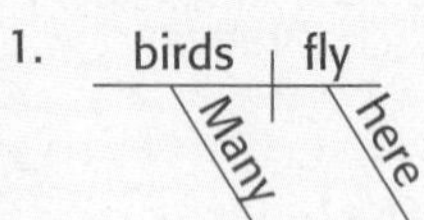

2.
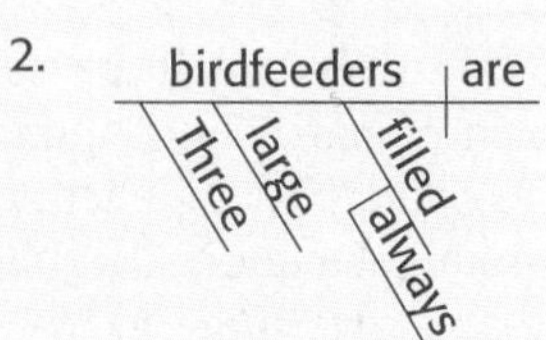

3.
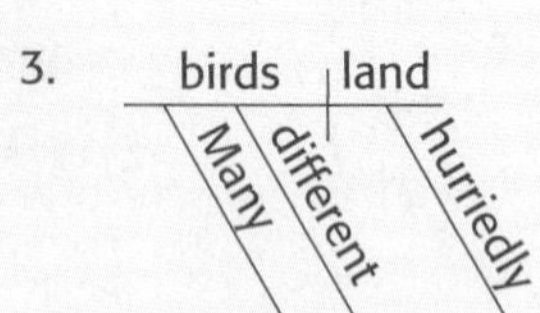

4.
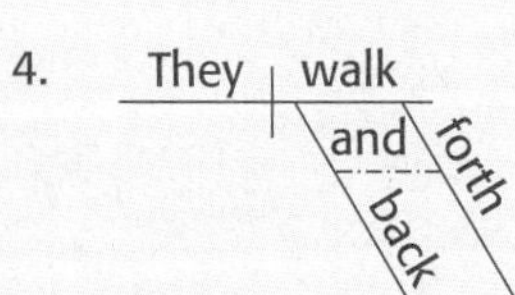

5.
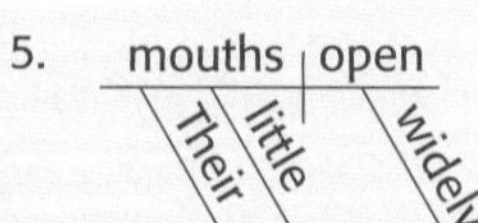

Sentence Diagraming

Diagraming Adjectives and Adverbs

Adjectives and **adverbs** are both diagramed on a slanted line below the words they modify.

The eager crowd is arriving.

crowd | is arriving
The
eager

Everyone looks excited.

Everyone | looks
excited

Ushers, helpful and efficient, mingle.

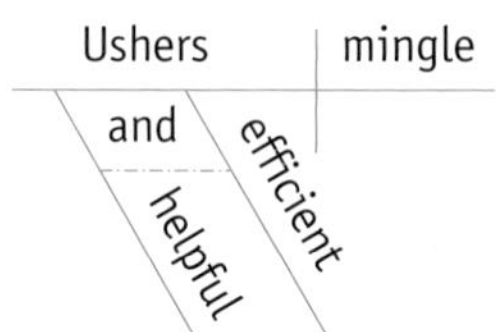

People are noisily talking.

People | are talking
noisily

The band concert starts soon.

concert | starts
The
band
soon

Adverbs That Modify Adjectives or Other Adverbs An adverb that modifies an adjective or other adverb is also connected to the word it modifies. It is written on a line parallel to the word it modifies.

A very costly error occurred quite recently.

error | occurred
A
costly
very
recently
quite

Too often these obviously careless mistakes happen.

mistakes | happen
these
careless
obviously
often
Too

PRACTICE YOUR SKILLS

Diagraming Adjectives and Adverbs

Diagram the following sentences or copy them. If you copy them, draw one line under each subject and two lines under each verb. Then label each modifier *adjective* or *adverb*.

1. Many [adj.] birds fly here [adv.].
2. Three [adj.] large [adj.] birdfeeders are always [adv.] filled [adj.].
3. Many [adj.] different [adj.] birds land hurriedly [adv.].
4. They walk back [adv.] and forth [adv.].
5. Their little [adj.] mouths open widely [adv.].
6. Suddenly [adv.] the dog barks loudly [adv.].
7. They fly away [adv.] very [adv.] quickly [adv.].
8. The very [adv.] curious [adj.] dog looks around [adv.].
9. It goes away [adv.] again [adv.].
10. Quite [adv.] soon [adv.] the hungry [adj.] birds will return.

6. dog | barks
the
Suddenly
loudly

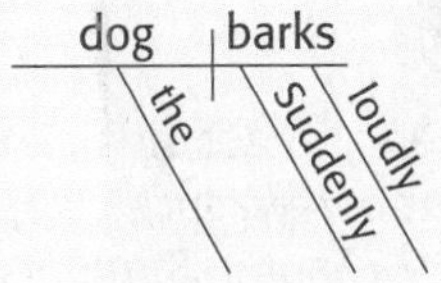

7. They | fly
away
quickly
very

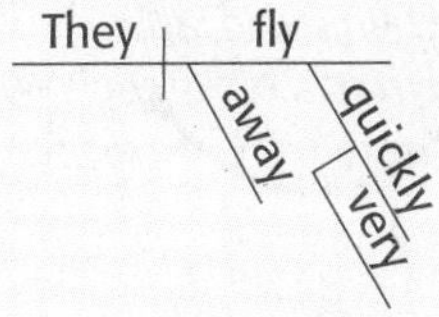

8. dog | looks
The
curious
very
around

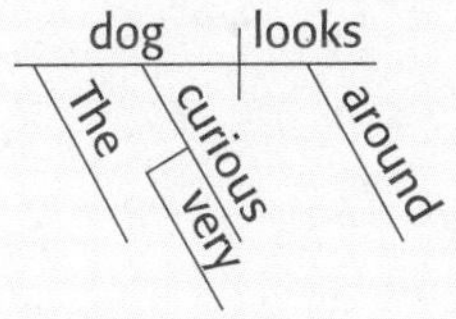

9. It | goes
away
again

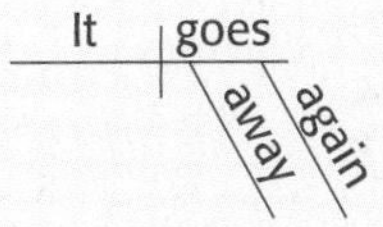

10. birds | will return
the
hungry
soon
Quite

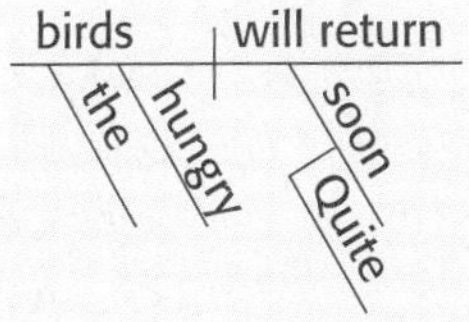

Using *CheckPoint*

This feature on adjectives and adverbs can be used as further independent practice or as a cumulative review of the chapter. Students identify adjectives and adverbs, identify the words modified by adjectives and adverbs, distinguish among different parts of speech, and write sentences that demonstrate proper usage.

CheckPoint

Finding Adjectives and Adverbs

Make two columns on your paper. Label the first column *Adjectives* and the second column *Adverbs.* Then in the proper column, write each adjective and adverb.

1. In 1883, a volcano on Krakatoa erupted suddenly [adv.].
2. This [adj.] eruption was the most [adv.] violent [adj.] explosion of modern [adj.] times.
3. Volcanic [adj.] ash soared fifty [adj.] miles into the atmosphere.
4. The ash constantly [adv.] circled the earth.
5. The dark [adj.] cloud of ash severely [adv.] blocked the sun.
6. In fact, the normal [adj.] amount of heat could not [adv.] reach the earth during the whole [adj.] next [adj.] year.
7. Weather [adj.] patterns changed throughout the world.
8. The northern [adj.] states were unusually [adv.] cold [adj.] in 1884.
9. That [adj.] year was "the year without a summer."
10. After forty [adj.] years the island of Krakatoa finally [adv.] became green [adj.] again [adv.].

Identifying Adjectives and Adverbs

Write each adjective and adverb. Then beside each one, write the word or words each one describes.

1. Words and actions are the main [means] means of human [communication] communication.
2. Animals also [have] have various [ways] ways to communicate.
3. Very [often] often [are] the songs of birds are messages.
4. Some [animals] animals communicate with body [movements] movements.
5. Communication is especially [important] important [Communication] in groups.

Distinguishing Among Different Parts of Speech

Write each underlined word. Then label each one *noun, pronoun,* or *adjective.*

1. Which (adj.) airplane (adj.) hangar is off limits to the public?
2. I have math (n.) after lunch (n.).
3. What (adj.) book did this (pron.) come from?
4. Party (adj.) decorations were hung across the barn (adj.) door.
5. Several (adj.) desserts were on the lunch (adj.) menu.
6. What (pron.) is the answer to the second math (adj.) problem?
7. I need a new picture (adj.) frame for this (adj.) photograph.
8. Which (pron.) would you prefer to fly, a glider (n.) or a jet?
9. Several (pron.) of my friends have been invited to the party (n.).
10. Did you paint the picture (n.) of the barn (n.)?

Writing Sentences

Write sentences that follow the directions below. (The sentences may come in any order.) Write about this topic or one of your own choice: a memorable dream you have had.

Write a sentence that . . .

1. includes two adjectives before a noun.
2. includes an adjective after a linking verb.
3. includes two adjectives after a noun.
4. includes a proper adjective.
5. includes an article.
6. includes *that* as an adjective.
7. includes *that* as a pronoun.
8. includes an adverb at the beginning of a sentence.
9. includes an adverb in the middle of a sentence.
10. includes an adverb at the end of a sentence.

Sample Answers for *Writing Sentences:*

1. My fluffy, brown dog is named Bear.
2. Bear is funny.
3. Bear, energetic and playful, stays in the backyard.
4. Once we were having a Texas barbecue in the backyard.
5. This backyard cookout used a charcoal fire in the grill.
6. That fire produced a spark that fell on dried leaves.
7. That attracted Bear's attention.
8. Quickly Bear stamped out the fire with his front paw.
9. We cheered loudly when we saw what he'd done.
10. Bear wagged his fluffy tail proudly.

Using *Language and Self-Expression*

Consider using this writing assignment to assess students' ability to use adjectives and adverbs correctly and effectively. You may want students to complete the assignment as part of a personal writing strand for their portfolios.

Prewriting

Suggest that students revisit their analysis of the sculpture that they did in *Making Visual Connections* on page L100.

Tell students that asking themselves questions like the ones below during prewriting may help them focus on what their own family will include.

- How many people will be in your family?
- Will your family include children?
- What role will the adults serve?
- What will be the responsibilities of individual family members?

FOR YOUR INFORMATION

About the Artwork

British sculptor Henry Moore created this bronze sculpture for the grounds of an English school. The interlocking figures have a graceful fluidity, with the child forming a "knot" where the arms of the parents flow together. The figures are familiar, yet somewhat abstract. Moore's belief in the essential dignity of the human form is evident in this sculpture, one of his first major works in bronze.

Language and *Self-Expression*

Henry Moore chose to include a man, a woman, and a child in his sculpture of a family. Other artists depict different groups. Raphael painted a mother and a baby in *The Grand-Duke's Madonna,* and Grant Wood painted a man and a woman in *American Gothic.* What portrayals of families have you seen?

When you are an adult, what will your own family include? Write a composition about your ideal family. Use adjectives and adverbs to make your writing sharp and interesting.

Prewriting You may want to make a cluster diagram showing the roles in your ideal family: husband, daughter, and even a cat!

Drafting Using your chart, write a description of the family you plan to have. Then explain why each role is important in this family. You could also explain why you chose to leave out a common role such as parent, if applicable.

Revising Make sure each paragraph has a clear topic sentence, and that every sentence supports that topic sentence. Divide a paragraph in two if it contains more than one main idea. Check for accurate and vivid adjectives and adverbs.

Editing Check your writing for correct spelling and grammar. Make sure each paragraph is indented and each sentence ends with the correct end mark.

Publishing Write a final copy for your English teacher. Keep a copy for yourself to read when you have formed your own family in the future.

Adjectives and Adverbs

An **adjective** is a word that modifies a noun or a pronoun.

An **adjective** answers the question *What kind of? Which one? How many?* or *How much? (page L101)*
A, an, and *the* form a special group of adjectives called **articles** *(page L104)*
A **proper adjective** is formed from a proper noun and begins with a capital letter. *(page L106)*

An **adverb** is a word that modifies a verb, an adjective, or another adverb. Many adverbs end in *–ly*.

An **adverb** answers the question *Where? When? How?* or *To what extent? (page L114)*

Positions of Adjectives and Adverbs

Usually an adjective comes *before* the noun or pronoun it modifies. *(page L103)*
Sometimes an adjective follows the noun or pronoun it modifies. *(page L103)*
An adjective can also follow a linking verb. *(page L103)*
When an adverb modifies a verb, the adverb can usually be placed anywhere in the sentence. *(page L115)*
An adverb sometimes interrupts a verb phrase in a statement or a question. *(page L115)*
When an adverb modifies an adjective or another adverb, the modifying adverb usually comes immediately before the word it modifies. *(page L117)*

Other Information About Adjectives and Adverbs

Using punctuation with two adjectives *(page L104)*
Recognizing words used as adjectives or pronouns *(page L110)*
Recognizing common adverbs *(page L114)*
Using demonstrative pronouns, interrogative pronouns, and indefinite pronouns *(page L110)*

Using *Another Look*

Another Look summarizes the terms defined in the chapter and provides cross-references to the specific pages on which they are explained. Consider having students use this feature prior to completing **CheckPoint** or taking the post-test. Students who can provide several examples of each term should be able to score well on either measurement.

FOR ASSESSING LEARNING

Using *the Posttest*

Assessing Learning

The posttest will help you and your students assess where they stand in their ability to use and identify adjectives and adverbs.

IDENTIFYING COMMON STUMBLING BLOCKS

Problem

- Failure to punctuate two consecutive adjectives correctly

Solution

- For reteaching, use the explanatory copy printed in blue beside the examples on page L104.

Problem

- Confusion with words used as pronouns or adjectives

Solution

- For reteaching, use the explanatory copy printed in blue beside the examples on page L110.

Directions

Read the passage and decide which word or words are modified by the underlined word or words. Write the letter of the correct answer.

EXAMPLE The <u>large</u> (1), carnivorous boa constrictor lives in South America.

1 **A** carnivorous
B areas
C boa constrictor
D South America

ANSWER **1 C**

<u>Usually</u> (1), all boas are called *boa constrictors* by people who don't know that there are about <u>sixty</u> (2) different species of boa. <u>Primarily</u> (3), boas live in trees. The rubber boa, however, is a <u>burrowing</u> (4) species, and the <u>western</u> (5) United States is its home. The length of adult boas varies from eight inches to over <u>fifteen</u> (6) feet long. <u>Most</u> (7) species of boa give birth to live young, not eggs. Boas live <u>mainly</u> (8) in warm areas of North and South America. A <u>hungry</u> (9) boa captures rats and birds by biting them. Then the boa <u>powerfully</u> (10) squeezes its prey until the prey can't breathe.

A DIFFERENT DELIVERY SYSTEM

If you prefer, you can print the posttest from the BK English Test Bank located at http://www.bkenglish.com.

1 **A** *boa constrictors*
B are called
C boas
D people

2 **A** different
B boa
C around
D species

3 **A** live
B boas
C trees
D species

4 **A** species
B rubber boa
C burrowing
D however

5 **A** home
B its
C is
D United States

6 **A** long
B length
C feet
D boas

7 **A** boa
B birth
C species
D live

8 **A** warm
B live
C areas
D North and South America

9 **A** A
B them
C captures
D boa

10 **A** squeezes
B boa
C until
D breathe

Customizing the Test

Use these questions to add or replace items for alternate versions of the test.

People enjoy creating scary (11) snake stories about the boa constrictor. Often (12) these stories describe a terrified person being squeezed to death by a huge (13) boa constrictor. Contrary to popular belief, boa constrictors are not (14) dangerous to humans. Although these snakes may grow ten or eleven feet long, they prefer to eat birds and small (15) mammals, not humans.

11. **A** stories
B boa constrictor
C creating
D about

12. **A** stories
B these
C describe
D terrified

13. **A** death
B boa constrictor
C squeezed
D huge

14. **A** boa constrictor
B humans
C dangerous
D are

15. **A** mammals
B humans
C birds
D not

TEACHING SUGGESTIONS

Essential Knowledge and Skills

- Connecting his/her own experiences, information, insights, and ideas with the experiences of others through speaking and listening
- Writing to inform such as to explain, describe, report, and narrate
- Using conjunctions to connect ideas meaningfully
- Employing standard English usage in writing for audiences, including subject-verb agreement, pronoun referents, and parts of speech
- Using prepositional phrases to elaborate written ideas
- Interpreting and evaluating the various ways visual image makers such as illustrators represent meanings

BLOCK SCHEDULING

- If your schedule requires that you cover the chapter in a **shorter time,** use the instruction on prepositions, conjunctions, interjections, and other parts of speech and the Check Your Understanding and QuickCheck exercises.
- If you want to take advantage of **longer class time,** add these applications to writing: Connect to Writer's Craft, Connect to the Writing Process, and Apply to Writing exercises.

CHAPTER 5

Other Parts of Speech and Review

Pretest

Directions

Write the letter of the term that correctly identifies the underlined word in each sentence.

EXAMPLE **1.** <u>Wow!</u> What pretty music that is.
1 A preposition
B noun
C conjunction
D interjection

ANSWER **1 D**

1. At the circus you <u>always</u> hear the calliope.
2. A calliope has a <u>keyboard</u> like one on a piano.
3. The keyboard is attached to <u>steam</u> whistles.
4. The calliope appeared in 1855 <u>and</u> was a hit.
5. <u>It</u> was first used for entertainment on riverboats.
6. <u>After</u> twenty years steamboats no longer used it.
7. Soon it found a home under the <u>circus</u> tent.
8. Even today the calliope <u>remains</u> the instrument commonly used by circuses and carnivals.
9. <u>Yippee!</u> We are going to the circus on Saturday.
10. Perhaps <u>I</u> will see a calliope up close.

IDENTIFYING COMMON STUMBLING BLOCKS

Following is a list of the most common errors students make when using prepositions, conjunctions, interjections, and other parts of speech.

Problem
- Difficulty distinguishing between prepositions and adverbs

Solution
- Instruction, p. L138
- Practice, pp. L138–L139

Problem
- Identifying parts of speech in a sentence

Solution
- Instruction, pp. L145–L146
- Practice, pp. L147–L148

1 A preposition
B verb
C adverb
D adjective

2 A noun
B adjective
C pronoun
D adverb

3 A verb
B adjective
C adverb
D noun

4 A interjection
B preposition
C adverb
D conjunction

5 A noun
B interjection
C verb
D pronoun

6 A interjection
B preposition
C conjunction
D adverb

7 A adjective
B noun
C adverb
D preposition

8 A verb
B adjective
C adverb
D preposition

9 A conjunction
B preposition
C verb
D interjection

10 A noun
B pronoun
C verb
D interjection

A DIFFERENT DELIVERY SYSTEM

If you prefer, you can print the pretest from the BK English Test Bank located at http://www.bkenglish.com.

Using *the Pretest*

Assessing Prior Knowledge

The pretest will help you and your students assess where they stand in their basic understanding of prepositions, conjunctions, interjections, and other parts of speech. The test indicates students' ability to identify parts of speech and to use them correctly in their own writing.

Customizing the Test

Use these questions to add or replace items for alternate versions of the test.

11. The calliope is a steam-whistle organ.

12. A boiler forces steam through a set of whistle pipes.

13. A keyboard or a cylinder functions by sending the steam to the correct pipes.

14. Whew! You can hear the shrill sound of the calliope miles away.

11. A noun
B adjective
C conjunction
D adverb

12. A adjective
B adverb
C conjunction
D preposition

13. A pronoun
B preposition
C conjunction
D interjection

14. A interjection
B preposition
C conjunction
D adverb

ADDITIONAL RESOURCES

Language Skills Practice . . . . pages 41–50
Transparency Tools FA5, AW4
ESL Practice and Test Preparation . . . . . pages 97–99
Assessment: Chapter Test. . . . . pages 130–136

MAKING VISUAL CONNECTIONS

For Language Development

Have students study *Master of Ceremonies* for a minute or two and focus on the objects and shapes in the artwork. Have students brainstorm some of the objects and shapes they noticed right away. Then have students write a paragraph detailing the position of objects in the artwork. Tell students to use as many prepositions as possible to tell, for example, that the woman's color palette is on her stomach or that the man's head is under his hat. Students should underline all of the prepositions in their paragraphs.

To Stimulate Writing

Use the questions for art criticism as writing or discussion prompts.

Possible Answers:

Describe I recognize a male and female performer and another female standing to the side. The male and female performer appear to be dancing, while the other female observes them.

Analyze The mood of the painting is frenetic and passionate, as if the performers were leaping with flames. The bright reds and yellows add to the vibrant mood of the painting.

Interpret I think the artist felt entranced by the intensity of the performance.

Judge If the artwork had a soundtrack to go with it, I would expect to hear lively sounds and an upbeat tempo for the performers to dance to. I do not think a soundtrack would be necessary since the painting already captures the excitement of the performance.

Miriam Schapiro. *Master of Ceremonies,* 1985.
Acrylic and fabric on canvas, 90 inches by 144 inches. Collection of Elaine and Stephen Wynn. Courtesy Steinbaum Krauss Gallery, New York. © Miriam Schapiro.

Describe What figures do you recognize in this artwork? What are they doing?

Analyze Describe the mood, or tone, the artist has created in this painting. How does color help create this mood? What else helps create this mood?

Interpret How do you think the artist felt about the subject of the artwork?

Judge What sounds do you think you would hear with *Master of Ceremonies* if the artwork had a soundtrack to go with it? Do you think such a soundtrack would be necessary?

At the end of this chapter, you will use the artwork as a visual aid to stimulate ideas for writing.

FOR DEVELOPING LANGUAGE SKILLS

LESSON 1 *(pages L133–L140)*

OBJECTIVES

- **To identify and use prepositions**
- **To identify and use prepositional phrases**
- **To distinguish between prepositions and adverbs**

Create Interest

Point out several different objects around the classroom. For example, have students describe the location of the board, their desks, shelves, pencils, art materials, and windows. Have students focus on the "location" words they are using such as *under, beside,*

Prepositions

If someone gives you directions, a preposition such as *beside, on,* or *under* could make all the difference in whether you find what you are looking for.

> Look for Kate's painting **beside** the desk.
> Look for Kate's painting **on** the desk.
> Look for Kate's painting **under** the desk.

A **preposition** is a word that shows the relationship between a noun or a pronoun and another word in a sentence.

The following is a list of common prepositions. Notice that some prepositions can be more than one word.

COMMON PREPOSITIONS			
about	below	inside	to
above	beneath	into	toward
according to	beside	like	under
across	between	near	underneath
after	beyond	of	until
against	by	off	up
along	down	on	upon
among	during	out of	up to
around	except	over	with
at	for	past	within
before	from	since	without
because of	in	through	
behind	in front of	throughout	

FOR INCREASING STUDENT ACHIEVEMENT

REACHING ALL STUDENTS

English Language Learners

Point out that prepositions help to clarify or explain relationships. After discussing the function of prepositions, have students identify the prepositions in the following sentences. Students should then explain how they know that these words are prepositions.

- Kelly put the paintbrush into the green paint. (into)
- She mixed the green paint with yellow paint before painting. (with, before)
- She looked out the window for inspiration. (out, for)

above, and *inside.* Tell students that these words are prepositions.

Guide Instruction

By Connecting Ideas

Write some of students' "location" sentences from **Create Interest** on the board. Point out that in each sentence the word that shows the relationship between a noun or a pronoun and another word is a preposition. Underline the prepositions in the sentences you wrote on the board. Ask students if other prepositions would also make sense in the sentences. Have students come to the board and rewrite the sentences using different prepositions.

Consolidate Skills

Through Guided Practice

The **Check Your Understanding** exercises will help students identify prepositions and prepositional phrases. Guide students through the first example in each exercise and discuss their responses.

A DIFFERENT APPROACH

Auditory

Have students complete the **Practice Your Skills** activity by reading the sentences and their responses aloud. Allow students to take turns discussing their responses.

HOME WORK

Have students write a paragraph about an art topic. Encourage students to use prepositions in their paragraphs. Students should underline the prepositions they use in their writing.

PRACTICE YOUR SKILLS

Check Your Understanding

Supplying Prepositions

Art Topic

Complete each sentence. Fill in the blank with a preposition that makes sense. [Answers may vary. Possible responses are given.]

1. To make a batik, use muslin, acrylic paint, paintbrushes, and white tempera paint (from) an applicator bottle.
2. Plan a design (around) the month of your birthday or another event.
3. Place a piece of muslin (on) a table.
4. Put newspapers (beneath) the muslin (for) the table's protection.
5. (With) the white tempera paint, draw a design (on) the muslin.
6. When the paint has dried, add water (to) the acrylic paint until it is thin and runny.
7. Carefully brush the paint (on) the muslin.
8. You can put different colors (under) each other and (over) each other.
9. Wait until the paint has dried, and then dip your muslin (into) water.
10. Rub (off) the tempera paint (from) the muslin and (before) your eyes you will behold a batik!

Prepositional Phrases

A preposition is usually part of a group of words called a prepositional phrase often part of a verb i.e. *turn on.*

Apply to Communication

Through Independent Writing

The **Communicate Your Ideas/Apply to Writing** activity on page L139 prompts students to write a narrative paragraph. Ask students to list some of the prepositions they might use to describe their journeys through their newly created computer world. Write some of students' responses on the board.

Transfer to Everyday Life

Searching for Prepositional Phrases on the Internet

Have students find five examples of prepositional phrases on the Internet. Students might focus their searches on travel, geographical, or scientific sites that often describe locations. Have students share their prepositional phrases with the class.

Pull It All Together

By Sharing

Have students share their narrative paragraphs with a partner after they

A **prepositional phrase** is a group of words made up of a preposition, its object, and any words that modify the object.

PREPOSITIONAL PHRASES

Did you speak **with the baseball players?**
(*Players* is the object of the preposition *with.*)

Within a few months, the season will be finished.
(*Months* is the object of the preposition *within.*)

The players **on the team** will be friends.
(*Team* is the object of the preposition *on.*)

A prepositional phrase can have more than one object. Such a phrase has a **compound object of a preposition.**

COMPOUND OBJECT OF A PREPOSITION

Boxes **of uniforms, bats, and balls** filled the dugout.

A sentence can have more than one prepositional phrase.

Before the game they rode **to the ball field.**

During the game some players go **into a frenzy around the dugout.**

CONNECT TO WRITER'S CRAFT

When you write, use prepositional phrases to add interest and appeal to your writing. You can use similes that begin with the preposition *like* to make unusual comparisons.

His swing was **like a clock's pendulum.**

She ran **like a gazelle.** 

You can learn more about prepositions in phrases on pages L189–L197.

GETTING STUDENTS INVOLVED

Cooperative Learning

After discussing prepositional phrases and reading through the example sentences, divide the class into two groups. Have the groups collaborate to create sentences with prepositional phrases. A student in one group should begin a sentence either with a prepositional phrase or some other part of a sentence. Then a student from the other group should complete the sentence. If the first student did not use a prepositional phrase, the second student must add one to the sentence starter. For example, the first student might say *My mother stood* and the second student might add *beside the fireplace.* Continue the activity until all students have participated.

have written their first drafts. Partners should make some constructive suggestions that could improve students' use of prepositions. Have students make improvements to their papers during the editing stage.

Check Understanding

Identifying Prepositions and Prepositional Phrases

Have students open any one of their textbooks and find four examples each of prepositions and prepositional phrases. Have some students write their example sentences on the board, underlining all prepositional phrases and circling prepositions.

A DIFFERENT APPROACH

Visual

Complete the first item in **Practice Your Skills** together. Write the sentence on the board and have students identify the prepositions and their objects. Continue by having students take turns writing the sentences and their responses on the board for items two through fifteen.

HOME WORK

Write the following sentence fragments on the board, and have students copy them for their home work assignment. Have students add prepositional phrases to complete the sentences.

- The baseball diamond was located ▢.
- ▢ the player stepped up.
- The batter looked ▢.
- ▢ the pitcher threw the ball.
- The ball sailed ▢.

PRACTICE YOUR SKILLS

Check Your Understanding

Finding Prepositional Phrases

Sports Topic **Write each prepositional phrase. Underline the preposition and circle its object.**

1. Baseball was originally played without any special equipment.
2. It was probably based on the English game of rounders.
3. In the early days, bases were tall stakes.
4. Many players ran into the stakes and were hurt.
5. Later the stakes were replaced with rocks.
6. Unfortunately, the rocks were also dangerous to the baseball players.
7. Eventually sandbags were placed at each base.
8. Early baseball bats were adapted from sticks.
9. In 1861, there was no limit for the length of a bat.
10. The diameter of a bat was restricted to $2\frac{1}{2}$ inches.
11. Baseballs in terrible condition were used.
12. For many years baseball was played without gloves.
13. The first baseball glove was developed by Charles Waite.
14. It was like an ordinary winter glove.
15. Catchers did not use masks until 1877.

Check Your Understanding

Finding Prepositional Phrases

Mathematics Topic **Write each prepositional phrase. Underline the preposition and circle its object.**

16. A discount store in your neighborhood sells souvenir baseballs and packs of baseball cards.

17. The store sells the packs of cards for $2.29 and sells the souvenir balls for $13.

18. Yesterday it sold a total of thirty-six packs of baseball cards and souvenir balls for $232.38.

19. Of the thirty-six items sold, fourteen were balls.

20. At a cost of $13 each, the ball sales totaled $182.

21. How many packs of baseball cards were sold?

22. What were the total sales for the baseball cards?

23. The salespeople sold a total of twenty-two packs of baseball cards for a net sale of $50.38.

24. The manager of the discount store has plans for more baseball products.

25. He will send an order to the baseball memorabilia distributor.

Connect to the Writing Process: Revising

Adding Prepositional Phrases

Complete each sentence. Fill in the blank with a prepositional phrase that completes the meaning of the sentence. [Answers may vary. Possible responses are given.]

26. The baseball player came ■. onto the field

27. He spoke ■. to the excited audience

28. The baseball player held the attention ■. of the crowd

29. The students crowded around their guest ■. of honor

30. The athlete shook hands ■. with everyone

31. He wrote his name ■. on posters

32. A few students played catch ■. with him

33. The athlete gave the students some tips ■. about hitting

34. He put his equipment ■. in his bag

35. The students thanked him ■. for coming

DEVELOPING WORKPLACE COMPETENCIES

Basic Skills: Writing

Have students imagine they work for a company that designs baseball fields. They are assigned the job of describing to a client how the baseball field will look, where it will be located, and how it will benefit the team and the fans. Have students write their client report, focusing on their use of prepositions to tell the client about the new baseball field. Have students share their completed papers with the class. Discuss students' effective use of prepositions.

REACHING ALL STUDENTS

Struggling Learners

After discussing how to distinguish a preposition from an adverb, point out that some words can be prepositions or adverbs depending on their function in the sentence. Tell students that the word's *function* in the sentence is the key to determining whether it is a preposition or an adverb. Point out that in most cases, if the word in question is at the end of the sentence, it is an adverb. Have students determine if the italicized words in the following sentences are prepositions or adverbs by listening as you read them aloud:

- Many students have used a computer *before.* (adverb)
- Some people learn to use a computer *before* they can type. (preposition)
- I learned to hook up the wires *behind* my computer. (preposition)
- If I do not learn this skill, I will be left *behind.* (adverb)

A DIFFERENT APPROACH

Auditory

Have students make letter cards, one with the letter *P* and the other with the letter *A*. As you read the sentences in **Practice Your Skills** aloud, have students hold up their letter cards to respond to each item. Repeat the underlined word so that students will know which word in the sentence should be identified. Discuss students' responses.

Preposition or Adverb?

Some words can be a preposition in one sentence and an adverb in another sentence. *Around,* for example, is a preposition when it is part of a prepositional phrase. *Around* is an adverb, however, when it stands alone and is not part of a prepositional phrase.

PREPOSITION	The student moved the cursor ***around*** *the computer screen.* (*Around the computer screen* is a prepositional phrase.)
ADVERB	Alana moved the cursor **around.** (*Around* is an adverb that tells where Alana moved the cursor. It is not part of a prepositional phrase, and it has no object.)

PRACTICE YOUR SKILLS

Check Your Understanding

Distinguishing Between Prepositions and Adverbs

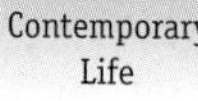

Label each underlined word *P* for *preposition* or *A* for *adverb*.

1. Many students had never seen a particular computer program before. (A)
2. Before (P) the first day of school, they had little experience with different word processing programs.
3. When they first are offered the "Help" option, they zip past. (A)
4. They have gone past (P) that key many times.
5. Through blank pages, error messages, and odd warning sounds, they stumble along. (A)

6. Many hope that a teacher will stop by. (A)
7. Others wait for their friends to come by (P) the computer lab.
8. Along (P) the way, they will swallow their pride.
9. They stay inside (A) until they learn the program.
10. The students will seek answers to their questions inside (P) the "Help"option.

Connect to the Writing Process: Prewriting
Using Prepositions and Adverbs

Imagine that you have been asked to design a computer program that takes younger children on a journey through an imaginary place. Think about the imaginary place and then write two sentences for each of the following words. The first sentence should use the word as a preposition. The second sentence should use the word as an adverb. Then label the use of each one.

11. over **13.** down **15.** across
12. without **14.** along **16.** through

Communicate Your Ideas

APPLY TO WRITING

Narrative Paragraph: *Prepositions and Adverbs*

Pretend that you really are going to write a computer program for younger children. Using some or all of the sentences from the preceding exercise, write a short imaginary story about a journey through an unfamiliar place. Think about what the journey will be like on a computer screen. Use prepositional phrases and adverbs to provide details about the journey.

TIMESAVER QuickCheck

Evaluate students' narrative paragraph by focusing on students' effective use of prepositions and adverbs. Also, point out how students might improve their writing by using different prepositions or adverbs.

HOME WORK

Have students create storyboard-like illustrations to show how their computer programs for young children will look. Show students how to draw frames in which to illustrate their computer programs before they begin their home work assignments. Each frame should represent a "page" or stage in the computer journey. Encourage students to use graphics that would be appealing to young children.

EXPANDING THE LESSON

Using Technology

You will find additional **instructional** and **practice** materials for this chapter at http://www.bkenglish.com.

 Mixed Practice

Science Topic **Write each prepositional phrase.**

1. Fireflies live in warm areas throughout the world.
2. During the daytime many fireflies eat plant pollen.
3. Fireflies lay their eggs on the ground.
4. Newly hatched fireflies burrow underneath the ground or hide within old stumps.
5. The red-and-green lights from one kind of firefly resemble traffic signals.
6. Scientists have recently learned much about firefly light.
7. The firefly's light comes from light organs on the underside of the abdomen.
8. The light of fireflies, according to scientists, is not hot.
9. This cool light is produced by chemical reactions inside the insect.
10. The firefly's light stops after a final chemical reaction.

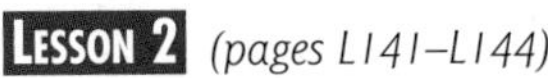

LESSON 2 *(pages L141–L144)*

OBJECTIVES

- **To identify conjunctions and use them correctly**
- **To identify interjections and use them effectively in writing**

Create Interest

Tell students that conjunctions are like extension cords: they "plug in" one section of a sentence to another. They are the "connectors," while an interjections is a word that expresses how one feels. Illustrate the function of conjunctions and interjections in the following sentences:

- My favorite writers are Charles Dickens *and* Frank McCourt.
- I enjoy reading McCourt's books, *but* I especially like listening to him speak.
- Wow, that reading by Frank McCourt made the book come alive.

Conjunctions and Interjections

A connecting word is called a conjunction. There are three kinds of conjunctions: coordinating, correlative, and subordinating.

A **conjunction** connects words or groups of words.

A **coordinating conjunction** is a single connecting word. The conjunctions in the following list are used to connect single words or groups of words.

COORDINATING CONJUNCTIONS			
and	but	or	yet

CONNECTING WORDS	*Jack London* **and** *Jamie Gilson* are good writers. (connects nouns)
	Have you ever heard of *him* **or** *her?* (connects pronouns)
	They *read* **and** *reviewed* their books. (connects verbs)
	Her book was *long* **but** *funny.* (connects adjectives)
	He wrote *slowly* **yet** *urgently.* (connects adverbs)
CONNECTING GROUPS OF WORDS	She looked *on the chair* **and** *under the chair.* (connects prepositional phrases)
	He *began the story* **but** *did not finish it.* (connects complete predicates)
	He should finish the story, **or** *it will be ruined.* (connects sentences)

GETTING STUDENTS INVOLVED

Reciprocal Teaching

Have students work together to review the chart of coordinating conjunctions. Students who understand clearly the function of the conjunctions should explain to other students how these parts of speech function in a sentence. Students should also provide example sentences.

Guide Instruction

By Modeling Strategies

Point out to students that interjections are not always accompanied by an exclamation point. Students should focus on the strong emotion expressed by words to decide whether or not they are interjections. Point out the interjections in the following examples:

- Oops! I picked up the wrong book. (Oops)
- Oh, where is that book? (Oh)
- Aha! There it is. (Aha)

Consolidate Skills

Through Guided Practice

The **Check Your Understanding** exercise on page L143 will help students identify conjunctions and interjections. Guide students through the first example and discuss their responses.

INTEGRATING TECHNOLOGY

Audio

Have students work with partners and use a tape recorder to record sentences containing correlative conjunctions. Encourage students to write out the sentences before they record them. Each pair should create at least ten sentences using *both/and, either/or,* and *neither/nor.* Place students' completed recordings at a learning center for students to listen to on their own.

Correlative conjunctions are pairs of conjunctions. Like coordinating conjunctions, correlative conjunctions connect words or groups of words.

CORRELATIVE CONJUNCTIONS		
both/and	either/or	neither/nor

CONNECTING WORDS

Both *Lois Duncan* **and** *Gary Paulsen* are writers.
(connects nouns)

That book is **neither** *good* **nor** *interesting.*
(connects adjectives)

CONNECTING GROUPS OF WORDS

The book is either *in the car* **or** *on the shelf.*
(connects prepositional phrases)

Either *we will read it now,* **or** *we will wait for the next semester.*
(connects sentences)

The third kind of conjunction is a subordinating conjunction. You can learn about subordinating conjunctions on pages L257–L258.

Words such as *ugh, whew,* and *wow* are interjections. All these words show strong emotions.

An **interjection** is a word that expresses strong feelings.

An interjection usually comes at the beginning of a sentence. It is followed by an exclamation point or a comma.

Ouch! That snack is hot.
Surprise! We were waiting for you.
Oh, I just remembered the dishes in the oven.

Apply to Communication

Through Independent Writing

The **Communicate Your Ideas/Apply to Writing** activity on page L144 prompts students to write a book review. Encourage students to use conjunctions and interjections that will keep their audience—teenagers—interested. Remind students, however, that overuse of these parts of speech will turn readers and viewers away.

Transfer to Everyday Life

Listening for Interjections in Speech

Have students listen to find six different interjections from conversations they hear throughout a day. Students should write down these interjections and share them with the class.

Pull It All Together

By Sharing

Have students share their book reviews with the class. Have the class as a whole critique each student's use of conjunctions and interjections. Peers should decide whether the

COMMON INTERJECTIONS			
aha	oh	ugh	yes
goodness	oops	well	yikes
hooray	ouch	wow	yippee

CONNECT TO WRITER'S CRAFT

Avoid using interjections too often. They lose their emphasis when you use too many of them. Try to save them for truly strong emotions so they will have a greater impact on your reader.

PRACTICE YOUR SKILLS

Check Your Understanding

Finding Conjunctions and Interjections

Literature Topic **Write and label each conjunction as *conj.* and each interjection as *inter.***

1. Wow (inter.)! Have you ever read Jack London's story "To Build a Fire"?
2. It is a chilling story of a man and (conj.) a dog in Alaska.
3. Oh (inter.), the story starts off calmly, but (conj.) soon the Yukon offers more than enough adventure.
4. Neither (conj.) the man nor (conj.) the dog is prepared for what happens next.
5. The temperature is 75°F below zero, but (conj.) the inexperienced man does not know how cold it is.
6. First the man gets his feet wet, and (conj.) then he is slow to get a fire going.
7. Ouch (inter.), the frostbite starts with sharp pain!

A DIFFERENT APPROACH

Visual

Have students write the **Practice Your Skills** exercises on the board. Students should point to each conjunction and interjection. Discuss students' responses. As an extension, have students supply new conjunctions or interjections that could also be used in the sentences.

HOME WORK

Have students find at least ten interjections in newspaper or magazine articles. The following day have students share with the class the interjections they located and describe how they were used in sentences.

reviews need more or fewer of these parts of speech.

Check Understanding

Defining Conjunction and Interjection

Have students write down their own definitions for the words *conjunction* and *interjection.* Then students should provide at least two examples of sentences containing these parts of speech. Have students read their responses to the class.

USING STUDENTS' STRENGTHS

Spatial

Have students illustrate their book reviews. Their illustrations should complement the information they provide in their sentences. Students should decide what medium they will use for their artwork. For example, they might decide that chalk will convey the information from the books they read better than paints could. Have students display their artwork with their completed book reports.

8. As he goes numb, both [conj.] the inexperienced man and [conj.] the loyal dog know they are in trouble.
9. Hurrah [inter.]! A match finally sparks, the fire blazes, and [conj.] they seem to be saved.
10. Alas [inter.], neither [conj.] the man nor [conj.] the dog will ever leave the cold Yukon.

Connect to the Writing Process: Prewriting

Using Conjunctions and Interjections

Plan a book report about your favorite book. To get your ideas flowing, follow the directions given below.

[Answers may vary. Possible responses are given.]

11. Use *both/and* to connect two proper nouns.
    Both Charles Ingalls and Caroline Ingalls were pioneers.
12. Use *or* to connect two prepositional phrases.
    Were their houses built of wood or of brick?
13. Use *either/or* to connect two subjects.
    Either family or friends would come to the woods to visit.
14. Use *but* to connect two adjectives.
    The book is old but enthralling.
15. Use *and* to connect two verbs.
    I would recommend you read it and study the history of the time.
16. Write a sentence that begins with *Yes!*
    Yes! I love the entire *Little House* series.
17. Write a sentence that begins with *Well*.
    Well, you should hurry and start your reading.

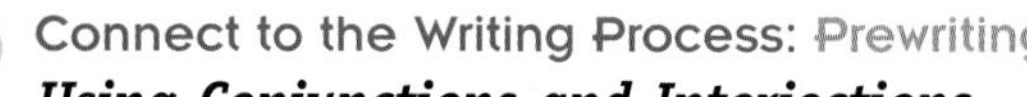

APPLY TO WRITING

Book Review: ***Conjunctions and Interjections***

Write a book review on your favorite book for a teen TV station. Be sure to summarize the book and to tell important events. You can discuss characters and story problems. Use the information you gathered in the preceding prewriting exercise to help you. Be sure to describe the events as they happened and to use conjunctions and interjections to keep your audience interested.

LESSON 3 *(pages L145–L149)*

OBJECTIVES

- **To review the eight parts of speech**
- **To identify the grammatical function of a particular word according to its use in a sentence**

Create Interest

Begin a *Part of Speech* chart on the board. The chart should include the name of the part of speech, a definition, and an example used in a sentence. If possible, have students use the same word as different parts of speech. Add to the chart as students complete the lesson.

Guide Instruction

By Modeling Strategies

Use the examples on pages L145–L146 as well as the following examples to help students review the eight parts of speech. Point out that a word's function in a sentence determines what part of speech it is.

Parts of Speech Review

This section reviews the eight parts of speech. Remember, though, that a word does not become a part of speech until it is used in a sentence. Suppose, for example, that someone asked you what part of speech the word *play* is. Before answering, you would have to see how *play* is used in a sentence because *play* can be used as three different parts of speech.

NOUN	I saw a **play**.
VERB	She can **play** that sport well.
ADJECTIVE	The toddler rode in her little **play** car.

To find a word's part of speech, ask yourself, *What is the word doing in this sentence?*

NOUN — Is the word naming a person, place, thing or idea?

> **Riley** saw two different **events** in the swimming **competition.**
> He has **faith** in the **Olympic Committee.**
> Where is the **Olympic Stadium?**

PRONOUN — Is the word taking the place of a noun?

> **This** is **his** present to **you.**
> The medal is **hers.**

VERB — Is the word showing action? Does it link the subject with another word in the sentence?

> The athlete **has competed** in the event.
> He **studied** his opponent's serve.
> The tennis ball **was** very light.

REACHING ALL STUDENTS

Advanced Learners

Have students explain the examples on pages L145–L146. Students should tell how a word's part of speech is determined. Then have students give additional examples of each part of speech. Their sentences should all pertain to the topic of the Olympics.

YOUR IDEAS

For Reviewing Parts of Speech

- She competed in gymnastics **competitions** when she was a **child.** (nouns)
- **She** practiced as the coach guided **her.** (pronouns)
- She **flipped** over the balance beam. (verb)
- She enjoyed the **uneven parallel** bars. (adjectives)
- The competitions were **thoroughly** exhausting. (adverb)
- She learned **from** her coach. (preposition)
- The coach taught her persistence **and** skill. (conjunction)
- **Yes!** She won twenty medals in her gymnastics career. (interjection)

Consolidate Skills

Through Guided Practice

The **Check Your Understanding** exercise on page L147 will help students determine parts of speech. Guide students through the first example and discuss their responses.

USING STUDENTS' STRENGTHS

Multiple Intelligences: Linguistic

Divide the class into two teams. Send one member from each team into the hallway. List all the parts of speech (except interjection) in a column on the board, and ask the class to choose a word for each part of speech. Write their choices beside the appropriate part of speech. When the students have returned to the classroom from the hallway, tell them that the object of the game is to write a sentence on the board using the eight words listed. Set a time limit. At the end of the time allowed, check the sentences. If all words have been used correctly, the team gets one point. Continue the game until all members of both teams have had the chance to write a sentence.

ADJECTIVE — Is the word modifying a noun or a pronoun? Does it answer the question *What kind? Which one? How many?* or *How much?*

The **college** coach seems **friendly.**

Almost everyone saw the **two** events.

ADVERB — Is the word modifying a verb, an adjective, or another adverb? Does it answer the question *How? When? Where?* or *To what extent?*

The **very** young girl ran **extremely** fast.

The archer won a gold medal **immediately.**

PREPOSITION — Is the word showing a relationship between a noun or a pronoun and another word in the sentence? Is it a part of a phrase?

Before *the race,* she asked advice ***from*** *the Olympic Committee.*

CONJUNCTION — Is the word connecting words or groups of words?

Bring your camera **and** some film.

Track is her favorite sport, **but** she is developing an interest in swimming.

INTERJECTION — Is the word expressing strong feeling?

Wow! Those runners are quick.

Well, they have had lots of practice!

Ouch! Did you see the jumper hit the bar?

Apply to Communication

Through Independent Writing

The **Communicate Your Ideas/Apply to Writing** activity on page L149 prompts students to write several paragraphs about a problem and how it was solved. Tell students to use all eight parts of speech at least two times each in their writing.

Transfer to Everyday Life

Identifying Parts of Speech in a Sports Article

Have students locate sports related articles in the library. Students should read the articles and identify the eight parts of speech in at least two paragraphs from the article. Have students copy two paragraphs from the articles and underline and label the parts of speech.

Pull It All Together

By Sharing

Have students share their problem and solution paragraphs with the class. Students should read their paragraphs aloud. Listeners should identify the

Check Your Understanding

Determining Parts of Speech

Sports Topic **Write each underlined word. Beside each one, write its part of speech: *noun, pronoun, verb, adjective, adverb, preposition, conjunction,* or *interjection.***

1. Wilma Rudolph was born on (preposition) June 23, 1940, in St. Bethlehem, Tennessee (noun).
2. At age four, she suffered (verb) attacks of (preposition) double pneumonia and scarlet fever.
3. After these illnesses she totally (adverb) lost the use of her left (adjective) leg.
4. For the next seven years, she could not (adverb) walk without (preposition) braces on her legs.
5. With enormous determination (noun) she painfully (adverb) exercised every day.
6. Wilma Rudolph even played (verb) basketball in her backyard (noun).
7. Incredible! (interjection) By high school she was a very healthy champion athlete.
8. During this time she broke records in both (conjunction) track and (conjunction) basketball.
9. In college she (pronoun) set world records as a sprinter and then set her eyes on the Olympics (noun).
10. In 1956, Rudolph was a (adjective) member of (preposition) the American Olympic 400-meter relay team.
11. Each member of the (adjective) team received (verb) a bronze medal.
12. In 1960, this courageous athlete became the first American (adjective) woman to win three (adjective) gold medals in track and field.

A DIFFERENT APPROACH

Auditory

Have students work with partners to read aloud the **Practice Your Skills** sentences. Partners should record their reading with a tape recorder. After reading each sentence, the students should repeat the underlined words in each sentence and identify the parts of speech. Have students trade completed recordings with another group. Groups should then critique the audiotaped responses for accuracy.

HOME WORK

Have students write ten additional sentences on a sports related topic. Students should underline two words in each sentence and identify the parts of speech of those underlined words.

problem and the solution in each paper. Then list on the board some examples of parts of speech from students' writing. Discuss these parts of speech and their function in the sentences.

Check Understanding

Distinguishing Parts of Speech

Have students work with a partner to identify the eight parts of speech in a selection from their literature textbooks or from a novel they are reading. When completed, partners should share with the class the parts of speech they identified.

USING STUDENTS' STRENGTHS

Multiple Intelligences: Linguistic

Have students use dictionaries to look up the ten italicized words in **Connect to the Writing Process.** Show students how the dictionary identifies a word and its parts of speech, depending on its function in a sentence. Use the first word *well* as an example and look it up together. Show students how the part-of-speech abbreviation next to the word identifies the word's function. Have students continue the activity independently.

13. She set an Olympic [adjective] record in [preposition] the 100-meter dash.

14. She [pronoun] also won [verb] the 200-meter race.

15. Before she retired from [preposition] competition, Wilma Rudolph had set numerous world records in the 100-meter and 200-meter races [noun].

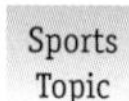

Check Your Understanding

Identifying Words as Different Parts of Speech

Sports Topic

Write each underlined word. Then write how each word is used, using the following abbreviations.

noun = *n.* verb = *v.* adjective = *adj.*

16. Can you name [v.] the greatest athlete of the twentieth century?

17. His name [n.] is respected by people around the world.

18. According to *Sports Illustrated*, the answer to this name [adj.] game is Muhammad Ali.

19. Tiger Woods plays the game of golf [n.].

20. He golfs [v.] in many major tournaments.

21. Do you know the brand of his golf [adj.] clubs?

22. Tara Lapinsky is skating [v.] professionally now.

23. She won a gold medal in figure [adj.] skating.

24. Her skating [adj.] days are far from over.

25. Which sport do you watch [v.]?

Connect to the Writing Process: Drafting

Writing Sentences

Write ten sentences, following the instructions for each given below. Remember that a part of speech depends on its use in a sentence. [Answers may vary. Possible responses are given.]

26. Use *well* as an adverb and an interjection.

He did well. Well, good for him.

27. Use *fight* as a noun and a verb.
They had a fight. Lets' not fight about it.

28. Use *around* as a preposition and an adverb.
It was around her waist. He drove around.

29. Use *more* as an adjective and an adverb.
I want more soup. They were more evenly matched.

30. Use *but* as a conjunction and a preposition.
I am young but I am strong. Nobody but Tom was there.

31. Use *one* as a pronoun and an adjective.
One of us must go. We have only one ticket.

32. Use *over* as an adverb and a preposition.
Please come over. Put the cover over the birdcage.

33. Use *run* as a noun and a verb.
He went for a run. I run every day.

34. Use *store* as a noun and an adjective.
They own the store. They are store owners.

35. Use *all* as a pronoun and an adjective.
Is that all? All students must attend school.

Communicate Your Ideas

APPLY TO WRITING

Problem and Solution: *Parts of Speech*

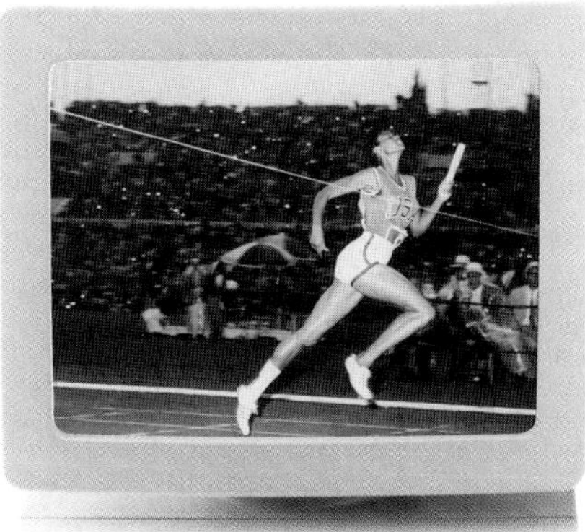

Wilma Rudolph overcame a physical problem to become an Olympic athlete. Every day people overcome problems to succeed at something. Think about a problem you have overcome or helped someone overcome. Then write several paragraphs telling about the problem and how it was solved. Pay careful attention to your word choice. Try to use as many parts of speech as you can.

HOME STUDY

Have students research to find out how other athletes such as Lance Armstrong and Jim Abbott overcame illness or physical limitations to go on to become champions in their sports.

FOR REVIEWING SKILLS

Using CheckPoint

This feature on prepositions, conjunctions, interjections, and other parts of speech can be used as further independent practice or as a cumulative review of the chapter. Students identify the eight parts of speech in sentences and write sentences that demonstrate their knowledge of the parts of speech.

CheckPoint

Finding Prepositions, Conjunctions, Interjections, and Prepositional Phrases

Write each sentence. Above the sentence, label each preposition *prep.*, each conjunction *conj.*, and each interjection *interj.* Then underline each prepositional phrase.

EXAMPLE Together Sam and Joey ran around the track.

conj. prep.

ANSWER Together Sam and Joey ran around the track.

1. The lawyers for the trial spoke slowly but precisely. (prep.: for; conj.: but)
2. After the rain the air seemed cooler, and the grass looked greener. (prep.: After; conj.: and)
3. Yikes! Did you see that worm crawl up my toe and leg? (interj.: Yikes; prep.: up; conj.: and)
4. Either sleet or snow is expected today. (conj.: Either, or)
5. The black walnut grows widely over the eastern half of the United States. (prep.: over, of)
6. Congratulations! Both your son and daughter have won. (interj.: Congratulations; conj.: and)
7. The surefooted horse walked along the steep mountain trail without any difficulty. (prep.: along, without)
8. In spite of their curiosity, neither Sam nor Earl has been inside the old mine or shack. (prep.: In spite of, inside; conj.: neither, nor, or)
9. Gosh! Amanda walked onto the stage and immediately forgot her lines. (interj.: Gosh; prep.: onto; conj.: and)
10. At that moment a huge dog dashed into our yard. (prep.: At, into)

Identifying Parts of Speech

Write each underlined word. Then, beside each one, write its part of speech: *noun, pronoun, verb, adjective, adverb, preposition, conjunction,* or *interjection.*

conj. noun adv.
1. David and Dora dawdled dreamily down the deck.

adj. noun noun
2. The brisk breeze blighted the bright blossoms.

adj. adv. prep.
3. Several sheep were sheared swiftly with sharp scissors.

adv. pron.
4. The humble hermit hummed happily on his hickory
noun
harmonica.

v. conj. pron.
5. The butler bought the butter, but he found it bitter.

interj. pron. v.
6. Ugh! I saw a slippery slug hug a beetle bug.

adj. adv. v.
7. Shellfish shells seldom sell.

noun v. adv.
8. Double-bubble gum bubbles beautifully.

adj. noun adj.
9. Wealthy Wanda wears Swiss wristwatches.

noun v. prep.
10. Sunshine shines softly on scenic seashores.

Writing Sentences

Write sentences that follow the directions below. Then label the use of each italicized word in the sentence.

1. Use *apple* as a noun and an adjective.
2. Use *turn* as a noun and a verb.
3. Use *both* as a pronoun and an adjective.
4. Use *in* as an adverb and a preposition.
5. Use *toy* as a noun and an adjective.
6. Use *each* as a pronoun and an adjective.
7. Use *down* as an adverb and a preposition.
8. Use *plant* as a noun, a verb, and an adjective.
9. Use *well* as a noun, an adverb, and an interjection.
10. Use *light* as a noun, a verb, and an adjective.

Sample Answers for *Writing Sentences:*

N
1. How many apples do we need for an
ADJ.
apple pie?

V
2. After you turn into the driveway, I'll take
N
my turn at driving.

ADJ.
3. Both puppies are cute, but I can't afford
PRO.
both.

ADV. PREP.
4. After you go in, sit in the waiting area.

N ADJ.
5. On Paul's list of toys, I see a toy truck listed.

PRO. ADJ.
6. Each will perform each experiment alone.

ADV. PREP.
7. Put the scissors down and then go down the hall to your sister.

V N
8. Where should we plant this new plant—in
ADJ.
the yard or in the wooden plant container.

INTERJ. N
9. Well, the well in the backyard provides
ADV.
pure water and is well situated.

N V
10. In this light I won't light a lamp, but I'll sit
ADJ.
by a light window.

Using Language and Self-Expression

Consider using this writing assignment to assess students' ability to use the eight parts of speech correctly and effectively. You may want students to complete the assignment as part of a creative writing strand for their portfolios.

Prewriting

Tell students that asking themselves questions like the ones below during prewriting may help them focus on the thoughts or emotions of an audience viewing this artwork.

- What does the man's expression convey to an audience?
- How do the colors used make you feel?
- What might the location and the shape of the palette on the woman's abdomen area represent?

Once students have considered these questions, have them focus on the graphic organizer they are constructing in this prewriting stage.

FOR YOUR INFORMATION

About the Artist

Miriam Schapiro (1923–). As a child, American artist Miriam Schapiro was encouraged by her parents to pursue her artistic gifts. She earned a master's degree in art from Iowa State University. Well-known for her Abstract Expressionist style, in the 1970s Schapiro and her husband, artist Paul Brach, moved to California, where she began creating large paint and fabric collages called "femmages." She felt that these artworks connected her to the women throughout the ages who produced unrecognized art forms through applied arts. Schapiro's bold, revolutionary work continues to inspire many audiences.

Language and Self-Expression

Miriam Schapiro's vivid painting *Master of Ceremonies* shows performers on stage. What kind of show might have inspired the artist? What elements of Schapiro's painting make you see or feel the spirit and energy of the show? What adjectives, adverbs, and nouns would adequately describe the excitement of seeing such a performance?

Write a poem eight to ten lines in length that expresses the emotions or thoughts you imagine for the audience members. The lines do not have to rhyme, and you do not have to write in complete sentences. More importantly, each line should convey a clear expression of an attitude or thought you imagine the audience to have.

Prewriting Draw a chart with eight columns on a sheet of paper, labeling each column with a part of speech. Brainstorm by writing as many words as possible to describe the emotions or thoughts of the audience. Write each word in the appropriate column.

Drafting Using your chart, write eight or ten lines of poetry. You may want to begin each line with a different part of speech and then use other words from your lists to express the idea fully.

Revising Read your poem aloud. Listen for the rhythm of the words in each line, and move or replace words to create the rhythm you like.

Editing Check your poem for correct spelling. Remember to capitalize the first word of each line of poetry.

Publishing Write and record a final version of your poem to read to your class. Use sound as well as words to express the emotion in your poem.

Another Look

Parts of Speech Review

A **noun** is a word that names a person, a place, a thing, or an idea.

A **pronoun** is a word that takes the place of one or more nouns.

A **verb** is a word used to express an action or a state of being.

An **adjective** is a word that modifies a noun or a pronoun.

An **adverb** is a word that modifies a verb, an adjective, or another adverb.

A **preposition** is a word that shows the relationship between a noun or a pronoun and another word in the sentence.

A **prepositional phrase** is a group of words made up of a preposition, its object, and any words that modify the object.

A **conjunction** connects words or groups of words.

An **interjection** is a word that expresses strong feelings.

Other Information About Prepositions, Conjunctions, and Interjections

Recognizing common prepositions *(page L133)*
Distinguishing between prepositions and adverbs *(page L138)*
Using coordinating and correlative conjunctions *(pages L141–L142)*
Recognizing common interjections *(page L143)*

Using *Another Look*

Another Look summarizes the terms defined in the chapter and provides cross-references to the specific pages on which they are explained. Consider having students use this feature prior to completing **CheckPoint** or taking the post-test. Students who can provide several examples of each term should do well on either measurement.

Using *The Posttest*

Assessing Learning

The posttest will help you and your students assess where they stand in their ability to identify the eight parts of speech.

IDENTIFYING COMMON STUMBLING BLOCKS

Following is a list of the most common errors students make when using different parts of speech.

Problem

- Difficulty distinguishing between prepositions and adverbs

Solution

- For reteaching, use the explanatory copy printed in blue beside the examples on page L138.

Problem

- Difficulty identifying parts of speech in a sentence

Solution

- For reteaching, use the explanatory copy printed in blue beside the examples on pages L145–L146.

Directions

Write the letter of the term that correctly identifies the underlined word or words in each sentence.

EXAMPLE **1.** Mathematicians use a variety <u>of</u> tools.

1 **A** adjective
B noun
C preposition
D conjunction

ANSWER **1** **C**

1. A protractor plots <u>and</u> measures angles.

2. The instrument with two pointed <u>arms</u> is a compass.

3. The compass <u>is used</u> for drawing circles or arcs.

4. A straightedge is the tool to use for drawing <u>straight</u> lines.

5. A ruler makes a handy <u>straightedge</u>.

6. <u>With</u> the ruler you can also measure lengths and widths.

7. For great lengths or distances, a tape measure is <u>also</u> useful.

8. A yardstick is the measuring instrument preferred by <u>many</u>.

9. We must <u>not</u> forget the calculator either.

10. In addition, most people also <u>like</u> a good eraser.

A DIFFERENT DELIVERY SYSTEM

If you prefer, you can print the posttest from the BK English Test Bank located at http://www.bkenglish.com.

1 **A** pronoun
B adverb
C conjunction
D adjective

2 **A** noun
B pronoun
C preposition
D adjective

3 **A** adverb
B interjection
C verb
D conjunction

4 **A** verb
B adverb
C noun
D adjective

5 **A** preposition
B noun
C verb
D conjunction

6 **A** interjection
B noun
C adjective
D preposition

7 **A** adverb
B adjective
C preposition
D noun

8 **A** preposition
B adjective
C pronoun
D adverb

9 **A** preposition
B conjunction
C adjective
D adverb

10 **A** preposition
B verb
C adjective
D adverb

Customizing the Test

Use these questions to add or replace items for alternate versions of the test. **11.** Using your compass, draw a circle. **12.** Using your straightedge, draw a straight line through the center of the circle. **13.** Measure the length of the line from the center of the circle to the edge of the circle. **14.** This measurement is the radius. **15.** Now carefully calculate the circumference of the circle.

11. **A** verb
B preposition
C adverb
D noun

12. **A** verb
B preposition
C pronoun
D interjection

13. **A** adverb
B adjective
C verb
D preposition

14. **A** pronoun
B interjection
C verb
D adjective

15. **A** adverb
B preposition
C interjection
D adjective

Teaching Suggestions

BLOCK SCHEDULING

- If your schedule requires that you cover the chapter in a **shorter time,** use the instruction on complements and the Check Your Understanding and Quick Check exercises.
- If you want to take advantage of **longer class time,** add these applications to writing: Connect to Speaking and Writing, Connect to the Writing Process, and Apply to Writing exercises.

Essential Knowledge and Skills

- Writing to inform such as to explain, describe, report, and narrate
- Writing to entertain such as to compose poems
- Producing cohesive and coherent written texts by organizing ideas, using effective transitions, and choosing precise wording
- Employing standard English usage in writing for audiences, including subject-verb agreement and parts of speech
- Evaluating how well his/her own writing achieves its purpose
- Selecting, organizing, or producing visuals to complement and extend meanings

CHAPTER 6

Complements

Pretest

Directions

Write the letter of the term that correctly identifies the underlined word in each sentence.

EXAMPLE **1.** I gave Grandpa a new snow <u>shovel</u> after the first snow of the season.

1 A direct object
B indirect object
C predicate nominative
D predicate adjective

ANSWER **1 A**

1. Have you ever thrown a <u>snowball</u>?
2. One snowball is several thousand <u>snowflakes</u>.
3. Since 1940, scientists have studied <u>snowflakes</u>.
4. They have offered the <u>public</u> interesting information about snowflakes.
5. Each snowflake is <u>unique</u>.
6. Snowflakes generally have eight <u>sides</u>.
7. Their patterns, however, are always <u>different</u>.
8. Scientists often give these different <u>patterns</u> names.
9. The smallest flakes are extremely <u>tiny</u>.
10. Snowflakes are probably the most beautiful <u>forms</u> in nature.

IDENTIFYING COMMON STUMBLING BLOCKS

Following is a list of the most common errors students make when using complements.

Problem
- Recognizing a predicate nominative in a question

Practice
- Instruction, pp. L168–L169
- Practice, pp. L170–L171

Problem
- Mistaking indirect objects for direct objects

Solution
- Instruction, pp. L163–L165
- Practice, pp. L165–L168

1 A direct object
B indirect object
C predicate nominative
D predicate adjective

2 A direct object
B indirect object
C predicate nominative
D predicate adjective

3 A direct object
B indirect object
C predicate nominative
D predicate adjective

4 A direct object
B indirect object
C predicate nominative
D predicate adjective

5 A direct object
B indirect object
C predicate nominative
D predicate adjective

6 A direct object
B indirect object
C predicate nominative
D predicate adjective

7 A direct object
B indirect object
C predicate nominative
D predicate adjective

8 A direct object
B indirect object
C predicate nominative
D predicate adjective

9 A direct object
B indirect object
C predicate nominative
D predicate adjective

10 A direct object
B indirect object
C predicate nominative
D predicate adjective

A DIFFERENT DELIVERY SYSTEM

If you prefer, you can print the pretest from the BK English Test Bank located at http://www.bkenglish.com.

Using *the Pretest*

Assessing Prior Knowledge

The pretest will help you and your students assess where they stand in their basic understanding of complements. The test indicates students' ability to distinguish direct objects from indirect objects and to identify predicate nominatives and predicate adjectives.

Customizing the Test

Use these questions to add or replace items for alternate versions of the test.

11. Temperature and water vapor affect the shape of snowflakes.

12. Particles of dust are sometimes the basis for snowflake crystals.

13. Other snowflakes are pure water vapor.

14. If the air is humid, snowflakes grow rapidly.

11. A direct object
B indirect object
C predicate nominative
D predicate adjective

12. A direct object
B indirect object
C predicate nominative
D predicate adjective

13. A direct object
B indirect object
C predicate nominative
D predicate adjective

14. A direct object
B indirect object
C predicate nominative
D predicate adjective

ADDITIONAL RESOURCES

Language Skills Practice	pages 51–56
Transparency Tools	FA6, AW5
ESL Practice and Test Preparation	pages 100–102
Assessment: Chapter Test	pages 137–143

MAKING VISUAL CONNECTIONS

For Language Development

Engage students in a discussion about the painting, asking them such questions as *How do the people make you feel as you watch them? What details contribute to the realism? Why do you think the artist showed this scene?* As students respond to your questions, write down their words and phrases. Point out how many of their details contain complements.

To Stimulate Writing

Use the questions for art criticism as writing or discussion prompts.

Possible Answers:

Describe The three basic colors in the palette are black, white, and red. Three people are playing dominoes. A woman is sewing.

Analyze Because red is such a contrast to black and white, it attracts the eye to the smoker's hat, the glass container, the oil lamp, the quilt, the cloth pile, and the stove.

Interpret The people look comfortable and relaxed; they are probably relatives. The woman wearing a cap looks like the grandmother. The woman who is smoking is the mother. The boy and girl are probably her children.

Judge I think the painting portrays the artist's vision of the scene more accurately than words could.

Horace Pippin. *Domino Players,* 1943.
Oil on composition board, 12¾ inches by 22 inches. © The Phillips Collection, Washington, D.C., Chester Dale Collection.

Describe What three basic colors make up the palette of the painting? What activities are depicted?

Analyze Which color is used the least? How does this color draw your attention to different areas of the painting?

Interpret What kind of relationship do you think the people in *Domino Players* share? What clues in the painting support your view of this relationship?

Judge Do you think a written description would portray the scene as clearly as the painting does? Why or why not?

At the end of this chapter, you will use the artwork to stimulate ideas for writing.

FOR DEVELOPING LANGUAGE SKILLS

LESSON 1 *(pages L159–L175)*

OBJECTIVES

- **To identify direct objects**
- **To identify indirect objects**
- **To identify predicate nominatives and predicate adjectives**

Create Interest

Explain that the word *complement* is similar to the word *complete.* Tell students that complements are the words that complete a sentence. Write the following sentences on the board, underlining the complements. Have students read the sentences and tell how the underlined complements help

Kinds of Complements

You know that every sentence has a subject and a verb.

Laura found. Paulo seems.

These groups of words have a subject and a verb, but each one needs another word to complete its meaning. This additional word is called a **complement,** or completer.

Laura found her **painting.**

Paulo seems **inspired.**

There are four kinds of complements. Direct objects and indirect objects always follow action verbs. Predicate nominatives and predicate adjectives always follow linking verbs and are called subject complements.

Direct Objects

A direct object is always a noun or a pronoun that follows an action verb.

A **direct object** is a noun or pronoun that answers the question *Whom?* or *What?* after an action verb.

To find a direct object, first find the subject and the action verb in a sentence. Then ask yourself *Whom?* or *What?* after the verb. The answer to either question will be a direct object. In the following examples, the subjects are underlined once, and the verbs are underlined twice.

DIRECT OBJECTS Mark will exhibit two **paintings.** (d.o.: paintings)

(Mark will exhibit what? *Paintings* is the direct object.)

FOR INCREASING STUDENT ACHIEVEMENT

REACHING ALL STUDENTS

Advanced Learners

Have students research object complements. Tell students that object complements complete the meaning of direct objects by identifying or describing them. Provide the following example sentence: *The people elected her president.* Students should define *object complements* and provide example sentences. Have students also consider why it is important to identify these types of complements in their own writing.

to complete the sentences. Have them read what the sentences would sound like without the complements.

- Sally creates beautiful paintings.
- She also teaches children to paint.
- Her classes are fun.

Guide Instruction

By Modeling Strategies

Copy the following graphic organizer onto poster board or chart paper. Tell students that the questions can be used to identify direct objects and indirect objects in sentences. Demonstrate how to use the questions by using randomly selected sentences from students' literature textbook. Display the chart in the classroom for future reference.

GETTING STUDENTS INVOLVED

Reciprocal Teaching

Have each student work with a partner and read pages L159–L160 together. Then have partners explain to each other the difference between a direct object and a compound direct object.

YOUR IDEAS

For Direct Objects

Carrie invited **them** to the museum. (d.o.: them)

(Carrie invited whom? *Them* is the direct object.)

To find the direct object in a question, change the question into a statement.

QUESTION	Did you view the exhibit?
STATEMENT	You did view the **exhibit.** (d.o.: exhibit)
	(You did view what? *Exhibit* is the direct object.)

A **compound direct object** consists of two or more direct objects following the same verb.

COMPOUND DIRECT OBJECT	Uncle Luke sells **paintings** and **sculptures.** (d.o.: paintings; d.o.: sculptures)
	(Uncle Luke sells what? The compound direct object is *paintings* and *sculptures.*)

You can learn about action verbs and transitive verbs on pages 77–80.

PRACTICE YOUR SKILLS

Check Your Understanding

Finding Direct Objects

Art Topic **Write the action verb in each sentence. Then beside it, write the direct object or compound direct object.**

1. As a young person, Marc Chagall loved Russia. Russia

2. The future painter studied the landscape, the buildings, and the people. landscape, buildings, people

To identify direct objects ask:	To identify indirect objects ask:
Whom? after the verb	*To whom?*
What? after the verb	*For whom?*
	To what?
	For what?

Consolidate Skills

Through Guided Practice

The **Check Your Understanding** exercises as well as the **QuickCheck** activities on pages L168 and L175 will help students identify and use complements. Complete the first item in each activity together. Then have students complete the remaining items independently.

3. He saw beauty in all these things. beauty
4. One day he drew a wonderful portrait of a man. portrait
5. Chagall drew more and more pictures. pictures
6. The young Russian had found his career. career
7. Later, he studied art in Paris. art
8. In Paris, Chagall joined the Cubism art movement. movement
9. He used bright colors and fantasy in his paintings. colors, fantasy
10. He met his future wife in Russia. wife
11. The couple made their home in Paris. home
12. Chagall's art contained many poetic images. images
13. He decorated the ceiling of the Paris Opera. ceiling
14. Later he designed many stained glass windows. windows
15. With bright colors and vivid images, he expressed his optimistic nature. nature

Check Your Understanding

Adding Direct Objects to Sentences

Art Topic

Write each sentence, adding a direct object after each action verb. In the following activity, you would use tracing paper to produce rubbings.

[Answers may vary. Possible responses are given.]

16. Have you ever made a ▢ with interesting textures? rubbing
17. You should gather ▢. materials
18. You should find ▢ with unusual and interesting textures. objects
19. First, you lay ▢ over your object. paper
20. Second, you rub the ▢ with a colored pencil or pastel. paper
21. Next, you choose the ▢ for your picture. rubbings
22. Then, you cut the ▢ out. shapes
23. Paint the ▢ for the background with watercolors. color

HOME WORK

Have students research another painter besides Marc Chagall. Students should write at least three paragraphs about the painter they research. Have student volunteers read their completed reports to the class. Write some of the students' sentences on the board and have students identify the direct objects.

Apply to Communication

Through Independent Writing

The **Communicate Your Ideas/Apply to Writing** activities on pages L162, L167, L172 and L174 prompt students to write sentences in response to a poem; a thank-you letter; an original poem; and a movie review. Ask students how their use of complements might make these various writing assignments more interesting and complete for readers.

Transfer to Everyday Life

Identifying Complements in Portfolio Writing Samples

Have students find examples of complements in writing samples from their own writing portfolios. Students can search through writing they have completed in the past and through current writing projects. Have students share some of the complements in their writing.

TIMESAVER *QuickCheck*

Evaluate students' writing according to the accuracy of their responses to the six objective questions about the poem "The Choice." Each correct response earns one point, for a total of six possible points.

HOME STUDY

Have students find another poem written by Dorothy Parker. Students should share their favorite Dorothy Parker poem with the class.

24. On the paper, you arrange the ■. shapes

25. Then you glue the ■ into a design. shapes

Connect to the Writing Process: Drafting

Writing Sentences with Direct Objects

Think about a time you visited an art museum, or imagine what an art museum is like. Write a sentence that answers each of the following questions. Then underline each direct object. [Answers may vary. Possible responses are given.]

26. What did you see at the museum? We saw paintings, drawings, and sculptures.

27. How many works of art did you see? We saw dozens of works of art.

28. Which painting did you like most? I liked *Washington Crossing the Delaware* most.

29. Which style of painting do you like the least? I like Cubism the least.

30. Do you like abstract images or traditional images? I like traditional images.

31. Which art medium looked easiest? Oil painting looked easiest.

32. What two mediums would you like to work in? I would choose clay or oils.

33. What kinds of colors do you prefer in art? I prefer stark, bold colors.

34. What is your favorite piece of art? My favorite piece of art is the Mona Lisa.

35. Which artist is your favorite? My favorite painter is Winslow Homer.

Communicate Your Ideas

APPLY TO WRITING

Writer's Craft: ***Analyzing the Use of Direct Objects***

Read the poem "The Choice" on the next page, and write a sentence to answer the questions that follow. Underline the direct object in each of your sentences. Note: This poem contrasts the appeal of two different men to the woman writing the poem. She refers to the first man as *he* and to the second man as *you*.

[Answers may vary. Possible responses are given.]

Pull It All Together

By Summarizing

Have students summarize the four types of complements explained in this chapter (direct objects, indirect objects, predicate nominations, predicate adjectives). Students should provide examples of each type of complement.

Check Understanding

Distinguishing Complements

Have students explain how they distinguish a direct object from an indirect object and a predicate adjective from a predicate nominative. Allow time for students to give examples of each type of complement.

The Choice

He'd have given me rolling lands,
 Houses of marble, and billowing farms,
Pearls, to trickle between my hands,
 Smoldering rubies, to circle my arms.
You—you'd only a lilting song,
 Only a melody, happy and high,
You were sudden and swift and strong,—
 Never a thought for another had I.

He'd have given me laces rare,
 Dresses that glimmered with frosty sheen,
Shining ribbons to wrap my hair,
 Horses to draw me, as fine as a queen.
You—you'd only to whistle low,
 Gaily I followed wherever you led.
I took you, and I let him go,—
 Somebody ought to examine my head!

—*Dorothy Parker,* "The Choice"

- What would the first man have given the speaker? What is the appeal of these things to the speaker?

 The first man wouild have given the speaker lands, marble houses, farms, pearls, rubies, laces, dresses, ribbons, and horses. These things would offer the speaker material wealth, comfort, and pleasure.

- What would the second man have given to the speaker? What is the appeal of these things to the speaker?

 The second man could offer the speaker only a happy song and an exciting personality. These things offered the speaker romance and adventure.

- Which man did the woman choose?

 The woman took the second man.

- What do you think the last line of the poem says that the woman feels now—happiness or regret?

 The woman found regret.

Indirect Objects

Like a direct object, an indirect object is a noun or pronoun that follows an action verb. To have an indirect object, a sentence must have a direct object.

YOUR IDEAS

For Using Poetry

REACHING ALL STUDENTS

English Language Learners

Remembering the correct word order, or sentence patterns, can be difficult for people learning a new language. Tell students who are learning English as a second language that when indirect objects are used in a sentence, the subjects, verbs, indirect objects, and direct objects should always appear in the following order: *Subject–Verb–Indirect Object–Direct Object.* Provide students with this example sentence: *I took Terry and Mike some books.* Label the parts of speech and the complements in the example sentence. Have students provide additional examples.

An **indirect object** is a noun or pronoun that answers the questions *To whom or For whom?* or *To what? or For what?* after an action verb.

To find an indirect object, first find the direct object. Then ask yourself, *To whom? For whom? To what?* or *For what?* about the direct object. The answer to any of these questions will be an indirect object. An indirect object always comes before a direct object.

INDIRECT OBJECTS

The guest speaker showed the **senators** (i.o.) the video (d.o.).

(*Video* is the direct object. The guest speaker showed the video to whom? *Senators* is the indirect object.)

The guide gave **everyone** (i.o.) a sample (d.o.).

(*Sample* is the direct object. The guide gave a sample to whom? *Everyone* is the indirect object.)

A **compound indirect object** consists of two or more indirect objects that follow the same verb.

COMPOUND INDIRECT OBJECT

I bought **Mandy** (i.o.) and **them** (i.o.) souvenirs (d.o.).

(I bought souvenirs for whom? The compound indirect object is *Mandy* and *them.*)

They showed **Jack** (i.o.) and **Tim** (i.o.) the souvenirs (d.o.).

(They showed the souvenirs to whom? The compound indirect object is *Jack* and *Tim.*)

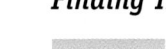

Connect to Speaking and Writing

When you speak and write, you can combine sentences by using direct objects and indirect objects. The combined sentences will have action verbs and will allow you to say and write more in fewer words and sentences. Your speaking and writing will flow and hold the attention of your audience. Notice how the twelve words in the first two sentences below can be combined to make one sentence of seven words.

I bought a gift of apples. I gave the apples to Mary.

I bought Mary a gift of apples.

Practice Your Skills

Check Your Understanding

Finding Indirect Objects

Contemporary Life **Write each indirect object.**

1. Fate has dealt Max Cleland an unusual life.

2. His parents promised the young boy from Georgia a college education.

3. At college, the United States Army granted the sophomore a commission in the Reserve Officer Training Corps.

4. In 1964, the Army gave the college graduate a commission in Vietnam.

5. A grenade during combat assigned Max a new role as a physically challenged veteran.

6. Life in a wheelchair handed the amputee new opportunities.

7. The people of Georgia gave the former political science major a job as a state legislator.

A Different Approach

Visual

Have different students write out the sentences from **Practice Your Skills** in large black letters on chart paper. Then have other students come up and circle and label, in a different color, the direct object and indirect object in each sentence.

Your Ideas

For Finding Direct Objects

YOUR IDEAS
For Indirect Objects

8. A few years later, President Carter sent the official an invitation to direct the U.S. Veterans Administration.

9. In recent years his home state has handed the amputee a seat in the U. S. Congress.

10. This remarkable man gives other people inspiration.

Check Your Understanding

Finding Compound Indirect Objects

General Interest **Write each compound indirect object.**

11. American expansion in the 1800s gave Alaska, Panama, and Hawaii economic growth.

12. Building the Panama Canal supplied Europe, the United States, and the rest of the world quicker travel routes.

13. The purchase of Alaska from Russia provided Americans and investors oil, gold, and copper resources for the future.

14. In the early 1800s, Hawaii offered missionaries and Americans wonderful economic opportunities.

15. Key location and rich soil brought the Hawaiian Islands and the Pacific region opportunities for trade.

16. The Pacific region provided the United States and other countries strategic ports.

17. The Hawaiians sold planters and businesses their land.

18. These beautiful islands give their people and businesses sugar cane and pineapples.

Communicate Your Ideas

APPLY TO WRITING

Business Letter: *Indirect Objects*

Imagine that you have just returned from a trip to Hawaii. Write a thank-you letter to a Hawaiian business from which you purchased something. Express your appreciation for either good service or a great product. Before writing, ask yourself the following questions to help choose your topic.

- What product might I purchase only in Hawaii?
- What would be special about a trip to Hawaii?
- Would I most appreciate a sailing, fishing, or dining experience on this island?

Keep the letter short by using action verbs, direct objects, and indirect objects.

TIMESAVER *QuickCheck*

Have students conduct peer evaluations of each other's letters. They should check each letter for correct business letter form and for correct use of action verbs, direct objects, and indirect objects. Students should decide which changes they will incorporate into their writing.

HOME STUDY

Have students write a thank-you letter to a local business or organization that has helped them or their families. For example, students might thank a local grocer for having special items on sale or thank a youth athletic association for providing coaches for their teams. Have students share some of their completed thank-you letters with the class.

IDENTIFYING COMMON STUMBLING BLOCKS

Problem

- Difficulty recalling the difference between a direct object and an indirect object

Solution

- Remind students that the indirect object always comes after the verb and before the direct object. Review the sentence pattern *S-V-I-O.* Tell students to use the question *To/For What or Whom?* to identify the indirect object.

Mixed Practice

General Interest **Write the object or objects in each sentence. Label the direct objects *d.o.* and the indirect objects *i.o.***

1. The teacher gave everyone (i.o.) a food guide (d.o.) from the health book.
2. Did you find Jesse (i.o.) and me (i.o.) a cookbook (d.o.)?
3. We are planning nutritious meals (d.o.).
4. We made them (i.o.) a fruit salad (d.o.) with fruit from the garden.
5. I made the family (i.o.) eggs (d.o.) and toast (d.o.) for breakfast.
6. Jesse gave Luis (i.o.) a glass (d.o.) of milk.
7. Will you lend me (i.o.) your recipe (d.o.) for that salad?
8. Mom showed Jesse (i.o.) and me (i.o.) the ingredients (d.o.) for the recipe.
9. Add this cucumber (d.o.) and tomato (d.o.).
10. We brought our teacher (i.o.) some delicious salad (d.o.) for her lunch.

Predicate Nominatives

A predicate nominative is a noun or a pronoun that follows a linking verb. A predicate nominative is also called a subject complement because it identifies, renames, or explains the subject of a sentence.

A **predicate nominative** is a noun or a pronoun that follows a linking verb and identifies, renames, or explains the subject.

To find a predicate nominative, you first must be able to recognize a linking verb.

COMMON LINKING VERBS	
***Be* Verbs**	is, am, are, was, were, be, being, been, shall be, will be, can be, should be, would be, may be, might be, has been, have been, had been
Others	appear, become, feel, grow, look, remain, seem, sound, stay, taste, turn

You can learn more about linking verbs on pages L85–L89.

To find a predicate nominative, first find the subject and the linking verb. Then find the noun or the pronoun that identifies, renames, or explains the subject. This word will be a predicate nominative.

Predicate Nominative

p.n.
He was the **actor** of the year.

(*Actor* renames the subject *he.*)

p.n.
That is my favorite **movie.**

(*Movie* renames the subject *that.*)

p.n.
Was that **they** in the movie?

(Change a question into a statement. *That was they in the movie. They* renames the subject *that.*)

p.n.
Might she be a famous **actress?**

(Change a question into a statement. *She might be a famous actress. Actress* renames the subject *she.*)

YOUR IDEAS

For Teaching Predicate Nominatives

A DIFFERENT APPROACH

Kinesthetic

Have students come to the board and take turns writing out sentences 1 through 20 from **Practice Your Skills.** Have students use their fingers to draw a line from the predicate or compound predicate in each sentence to the direct objects or compound direct objects. Discuss students' responses.

YOUR IDEAS

For Predicate Nominatives

A **compound predicate nominative** consists of two or more predicate nominatives following the same verb.

COMPOUND PREDICATE NOMINATIVES — The earliest actresses of television were **Lucille Ball** (p.n.) and **Imogene Coca.** (p.n.)

(The compound predicate nominative *Lucille Ball* and *Imogene Coca* renames the subjects *actresses.*)

PRACTICE YOUR SKILLS

Check Your Understanding

Finding Predicate Nominatives

General Interest **Write each predicate nominative.**

1. Television is the electronic transmission of images and sound.
2. An important period in television history was the early part of the 1950s.
3. Television production is the creation of a television show.
4. Former radio listeners became an audience of television viewers.
5. A television set was the new technology for homes.
6. All through the 1970s, television remained the main form of home entertainment.
7. Was that it in the home entertainment industry?
8. During the 1980s, videos became the new technological wonder.
9. Video systems became a new forum for games.
10. Video games are technology and entertainment.

Check Your Understanding

Supplying Predicate Nominatives

[Answers may vary. Possible responses are given.]

Contemporary Life

Write a predicate nominative that completes each sentence. Beside each predicate nominative, write the word it renames. (If you use a pronoun as a predicate nominative, use only *I, you, he, she, it, we,* or *they.*)

11. One of the most popular television shows today is ■. *ER* - one

12. Members of my family who like the show are ■ (Mom) and ■. Dad - members

13. Two reasons for its popularity are its ■ (interest) and its ■. action - reasons

14. Its appeal to young people is its ■. excitement - appeal

15. My favorite actor on the show always has been ■. Noah Wiley - actor

16. Was that ■ (Alan Alda - guest star) who was a guest star last week?

17. My favorite episodes are ■ (the premiere) and ■. the finale - episodes

18. Some of the sponsors are ■, ■, and ■. car, insurance, travel companies - sponsors

19. The writers of this show should be ■. young persons - writers

20. In another five years, I still will be a ■ (fan - I) of that show.

Connect to the Writing Process: Revising

Replacing Predicate Nominatives

Revise each sentence, replacing the underlined predicate nominative with a noun. [Answers may vary. Possible responses are given.]

21. The owner of the local TV station is <u>she</u>. Jone Smith

22. The stars of the early morning news show are <u>she</u> and <u>he</u>. Jane Summers John Levacy

23. Who are <u>they</u> in the studio? the actors

24. "It is <u>I</u>," said Gary Rogers. Gary

25. The executive producer of daytime programming is <u>he</u>. Joseph Grimes

A DIFFERENT APPROACH

Auditory

Have students close their eyes and listen as you read aloud the sentences in **Practice Your Skills.** After each sentence, pause and allow students to respond by identifying the predicate nominative.

REACHING ALL STUDENTS

Struggling Learners

Remind students that one way to identify predicate nominatives is to first look for the linking verbs. Have students identify the linking verbs in items 11 through 25 before they complete the **Check Your Understanding** and **Connect to the Writing Process** activities.

HOME WORK

Have students write five sentences containing predicate nominatives. The sentences should be about video games. These can be video games they have played or games they would like to create.

TIMESAVER *QuickCheck*

Have students self-evaluate their poems by reading them carefully. Tell students to consider the predicate nominatives they used in their self-descriptive poems. Would different predicate nominatives make their poems more correct? Might other adjectives make their poems more descriptive?

HOME STUDY

Have students research to find out more about the word *nominative,* including the word's origins, derivatives, and definitions. Students should share their findings with the class.

Communicate Your Ideas

APPLY TO WRITING

Poetry: *Predicate Nominatives*

Write a poem of at least eight lines and have each line begin with the phrase "I am." Use predicate nominatives to complete each line. You might include your various roles—"I am the first son of"—in your family, at school, and in your community. You also may name the things that you do, such as "I am a baseball player." Use adjectives to modify your predicate nominatives to create individual images and sounds in your poem.

Predicate Adjectives

A predicate adjective is an adjective that follows a linking verb. A predicate adjective is also called a subject complement because it modifies, or describes, the subject of the sentence.

> A **predicate adjective** is an adjective that follows a linking verb and modifies the subject.

To find a predicate adjective, first find the subject and the linking verb. Then find an adjective that follows the verb and describes the subject. This word will be the predicate adjective.

PREDICATE ADJECTIVES

That silent movie seems unusually **comical.** (p.a.)

(*Comical* describes the subject—the *comical movie.*)

Is that movie too **long?**

(Change a question into a statement. *That movie is too long. Long* describes the subject—the *long movie.*)

A **compound predicate adjective** consists of two or more predicate adjectives that follow the same verb.

COMPOUND PREDICATE ADJECTIVE — The theater was **clean** and **comfortable.**

(Both *clean* and *comfortable* describe the subject *theater.*)

PRACTICE YOUR SKILLS

Check Your Understanding

Finding Predicate Adjectives

General Interest **Write each predicate adjective. (Some sentences may have a compound predicate adjective.)**

1. Surprisingly, the costumes in the movie are colorful.
2. The dancer is amazingly graceful.
3. The eyes of the singer appeared especially beautiful and kind.
4. The music is soft but fast.
5. The actor sounded confident during his interview with the director.
6. Those questions seemed easy to him.
7. Some songs from the movie are incredibly rhythmical.

A DIFFERENT APPROACH

Kinesthetic

Have students complete their responses to the **Practice Your Skills** activity by pantomiming the predicate adjectives. Remind students that pantomime involves body gestures, expression, and movement. No speech or sound is used. Demonstrate by pantomiming the predicate adjective *colorful* from the first sentence. You might use your arms and body to generate a "rainbow" or pretend to be using many different "crayons" from a crayon box. Allow students to take turns completing the activity.

TIMESAVER *QuickCheck*

Evaluate students' movie reviews according to their clear opinion statements. Students should provide reasons for their opinions. Also, check to make sure students have underlined all of the predicate adjectives in their writing.

HOME STUDY

Focusing on the predicate adjectives they used in their movie reviews, have students create a movie poster for the movie they reviewed. Depending on the adjectives they used, students' posters could be positive or negative. Students can use paints, markers, pencils or whatever medium they feel is appropriate for their poster. Display the completed posters with students' movie reviews.

8. Over the past year, the actress has become quite popular.

9. Was that movie very good?

10. The characters seemed unusually fascinating and realistic.

Check Your Understanding
Supplying Predicate Adjectives

Literature Topic **Write a predicate adjective that completes each sentence.** [Answers may vary. Possible responses are given.]

11. Today English class became ■. exciting

12. The poetry assignment seemed ■. unusual

13. I wrote in my journal that the assigned poem is ■ and ■. disturbing complicated

14. All during class, the other students were ■ quiet and ■. attentive

15. The classroom atmosphere felt ■. electric

16. The teacher looked rather ■ when she read the poem aloud. nervous

Communicate Your Ideas

APPLY TO WRITING

Movie Review: ***Predicate Adjectives***

Write a movie review of your favorite movie for the school newspaper. State your opinion of the movie. Try to use vivid and specific predicate adjectives in your sentences to make your opinion clear to the reader. When you have finished your review, underline the predicate adjectives you used.

QuickCheck Mixed Practice

General Interest **Write the complement or complements in each sentence. Then label each one, using the following abbreviations.**

predicate adjective = *p.a.* indirect object = *i.o.*
predicate nominative = *p.n.* direct object = *d.o.*

1. The amusement park had its start [d.o.] in France during the eighteenth century.
2. Originally it was a place [p.n.] only for relaxation.
3. Park directors soon gave these parks [i.o.] games [d.o.] and rides [d.o.].
4. Around 1860, Coney Island became the biggest attraction [p.n.] in New York City.
5. It was fun [p.a.] for people of all ages.
6. Coney Island developed three parks [d.o.] within its borders.
7. Steeplechase Park was the most popular [p.a.] of those three.
8. Other cities were anxious [p.a.] for amusement parks of their own.
9. Soon cities across the country built new parks [d.o.].
10. The introduction of the theme park gave directors [i.o.] of parks new ideas [d.o.].

EXPANDING THE LESSON

Using Technology

You will find additional **instructional** and **practice** materials for this chapter at http://www.bkenglish.com.

YOUR IDEAS

For Reviewing Complements

Using *Sentence Patterns*

Most sentences students write will follow one of five different sentence patterns. An understanding of these sentence patterns will help students write correct sentences.

Sentence Patterns

Using Sentence Patterns

Good writers not only select the correct words, but also place them in the right order or in the right pattern. Following are examples of five basic sentence patterns.

PATTERN 1: S-V (subject–verb)

S V S V
Dogs bark. Many dogs bark at strangers.

PATTERN 2: S-V-O (subject–verb–direct object)

S V O
Students enjoy sports.

S V O
Most students at my school really enjoy team sports.

PATTERN 3: S-V-I-O (subject–verb–indirect object–direct object)

S V I O
Friends give us fruit.

S V I O
Several friends often give us fruit from their trees.

PATTERN 4: S-V-N (subject–verb–predicate nominative)

S V N
My collection is stamps.

S V N
My biggest collection is stamps from foreign lands.

PATTERN 5: S-V-A (subject–verb–predicate adjective)

S V A
Customers were restless.

S V A
The customers in the restaurant were very restless.

To find the pattern of a sentence, drop all the modifiers and the prepositional phrases.

S V N

~~The~~ Pentagon is ~~the largest office~~ building ~~in the world~~.

Practice Your Skills

Check Your Understanding

Write the sentence pattern of each sentence. Use the abbreviations beside each pattern on page L176.

1. The copper weather vane on the roof creaks. S-V
2. Students in the school annually hold an art exhibit. S-V-O
3. The waterfall near our camp sounded quite pleasant. S-V-A
4. My grandfather proudly showed the dinner guests his bowling trophies. S-V-I-O
5. The fireworks at the Fourth-of-July celebration brightly lit the dark sky. S-V-O
6. The old bed in the attic feels very lumpy. S-V-A
7. My next-door neighbor just became a reporter. S-V-N
8. The wind howled like a wolf last night. S-V
9. The autumn leaves suddenly turned very colorful. S-V-A
10. My little sister bought her best friend two goldfish. S-V-I-O

Expanding Sentences

Each of the following sentences follows a different sentence pattern. Expand each sentence by adding modifiers or prepositional phrases or both.

1. (S-V) Airplanes landed.
2. (S-V-O) Hikers found paths.
3. (S-V-I-O) Children told visitors stories.
4. (S-V-N) Winner was a friend.
5. (S-V-A) Weather is uncertain.

Sample Answers for *Sentence Patterns:*

1. Several airplanes landed within a few minutes.
2. The three hikers found all the paths on the map.
3. The older children told the Japanese visitors stories about local history.
4. The winner of the state lottery was an old friend of my Aunt Claire.
5. The weather predicted for tomorrow is highly uncertain.

Using *Sentence Diagraming*

Diagraming gives students a visual representation of the structure of a sentence. It can help them understand how the different parts of a sentence function.

Sample Answers for *Sentence Diagraming:*

1. 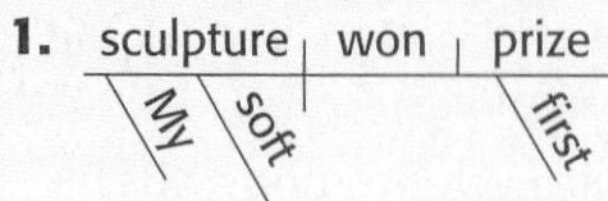

2. Dad | gave | stamps
me
some
new

3. collection | is \ hobby
A
doll
a
good

4. 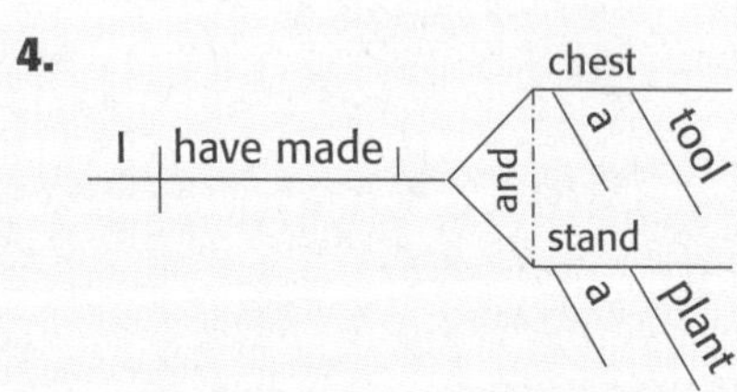

5. paintings | look \ real
Your
very

Sentence Diagraming

Diagraming Complements

The **sentence base** includes a subject, a verb, and sometimes a complement. Complements are diagramed on the baseline or are attached to it.

Direct Objects A direct object is placed on the baseline after the verb. The direct object and the verb are separated by a vertical line that stops at the baseline.

I have already read that book.

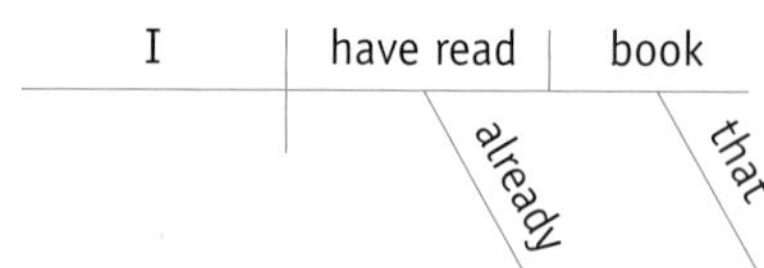

Compound Direct Objects Place the parts of a compound direct object on parallel horizontal lines. Then put the conjunction connecting each part on a broken vertical line between them.

Jonathon repaired the fence and gate.

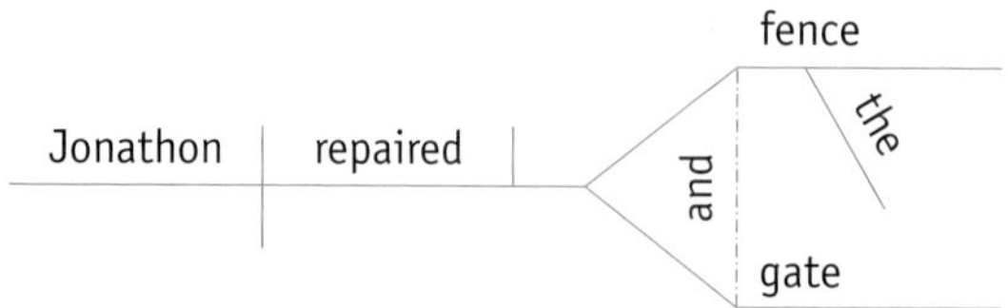

Indirect Objects An indirect object is diagramed on a horizontal line that is connected to the verb by a slanted line.

Give me a chance.

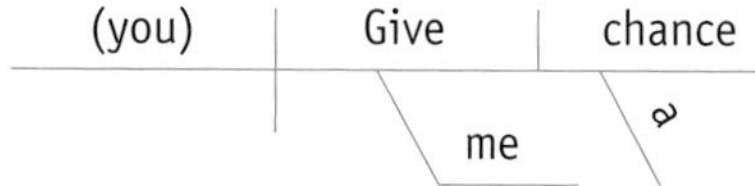

Subject Complements A predicate nominative or a predicate adjective is placed on the baseline after the verb. These subject complements are separated from the verb by a slanted line that points back toward the subject.

Alaska is the largest state.

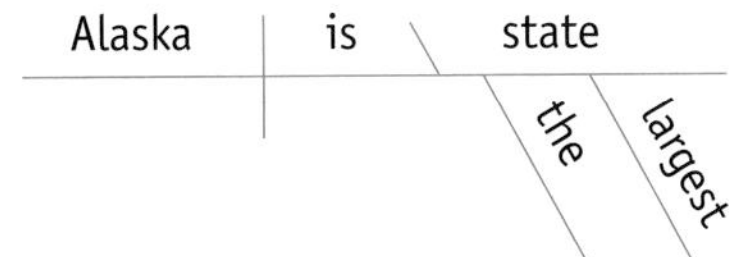

The morning air was quite damp.

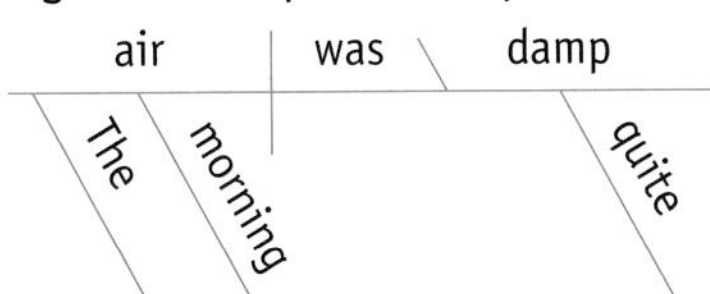

Diagraming Complements

Diagram the following sentences or copy them. If you copy them, draw one line under each subject and two lines under each verb. Label each complement using the abbreviations.

d.o. = direct object	*p.n.* = predicate nominative
i.o. = indirect object	*p.a.* = predicate adjective

1. My soft sculpture won first prize [d.o.].
2. Dad gave me [i.o.] some new stamps [d.o.].
3. A doll collection is a good hobby [p.n.].
4. I have made a tool chest [d.o.] and a plant stand [d.o.].
5. Your paintings look very real [p.a.].
6. Will you show Ben [i.o.] and me [i.o.] your coin collection [d.o.]?
7. Haven't you given him [i.o.] your old bottle caps [d.o.]?
8. Some old books are dusty [p.a.] and smelly [p.a.].
9. Play us [i.o.] another song [d.o.]. (you)
10. My favorite hobbies are the drums [p.n.] and art [p.n.].

6. you | Will show | collection; Ben and me; your; coin

7. you | Have given | caps; not; him; your; old; bottle

8. books | are \ dusty and smelly; Some; old

9. (you) | Play | song; us; another

10. hobbies | are \ drums and art; My; favorite; the

Using *CheckPoint*

This feature on complements can be used as further independent practice or as a cumulative review of the chapter. It covers identifying direct objects, indirect objects, predicate nominatives, and predicate adjectives. Students are also asked to write sentences using these four kinds of complements.

CheckPoint

Finding Direct and Indirect Objects

Write each complement. Then label each one *d.o.* for direct object or *i.o.* for indirect object. (Some sentences have a compound complement.)

1. Pitcher plants trap insects [d.o.] in their hollow leaves.
2. Each Mother's Day Ann serves her mother [i.o.] breakfast [d.o.].
3. Ayako feeds her turtle [i.o.] special food [d.o.].
4. Will you do a favor [d.o.] for me?
5. Before dinner, show Bruce [i.o.] and him [i.o.] the new calf [d.o.].
6. On his birthday José gave a card [d.o.] and a present [d.o.] to Rosa.
7. Orchids take their food [d.o.] and water [d.o.] from the air.
8. Brian likes most fresh vegetables [d.o.].
9. Our neighbors gave us [i.o.] a fan [d.o.] during the heat wave.
10. Wish me [i.o.] luck [d.o.].

Finding Subject Complements

Write each complement. Then label each one *p.n.* for predicate nominative or *p.a.* for predicate adjective. (Some sentences have a compound complement.)

1. The state flower of Alaska is the forget-me-not [p.n.].
2. Chinese food is certainly tasty [p.a.] and nutritious [p.a.].
3. Your fingerprints are different [p.a.] from everyone else's.
4. Did Mark become an officer [p.n.] in the Honor Society?
5. The harpies of Greek mythology were hideous monsters [p.n.].
6. The new band members are she [p.n.] and Carlos [p.n.].
7. The action in a hockey game is fast [p.a.] and furious [p.a.].

8. That must have been Shaniqua [p.n.] on the telephone.

9. In the moonlight the swamp looked ghostly [p.a.].

10. The winds of Antarctica are constant [p.a.] and violent [p.a.].

Identifying Complements

Write each complement. Then label each one *d.o.* for direct object, *i.o.* for indirect object, *p.n.* for predicate nominative, or *p.a.* for predicate adjective.

1. Yesterday my family bought a computer [d.o.].

2. The computer is a basic, no-frills model [p.n.].

3. We are, however, happy [p.a.] about our high-tech purchase.

4. Today we sent an Internet provider [i.o.] our application [d.o.].

5. Now we can send E-mails [d.o.] to all our friends.

6. Sharing the computer is a challenge [p.n.].

7. Everyone is eager [p.a.] for an hour or two at the keyboard.

8. My brother actually offered me [i.o.] ten dollars [d.o.] for my turn!

Writing Sentences

Write five sentences that follow the directions below. (The sentences may come in any order.) Write about one of the following topics or about a topic of your own choice: the funniest present you ever gave or received.

Write a sentence that . . .

1. includes a direct object.

2. includes an indirect object and a direct object.

3. includes a predicate nominative.

4. includes a predicate adjective.

5. includes a compound direct object.

When you have finished, underline and label each complement.

Sample Answers for *Writing Sentences:*

1. I gave a "white elephant" gift [d.o.] to Dion.

2. I gave him [i.o.] a gift certificate [d.o.] from a local clothing store.

3. The amount was a hundred dollars [p.n.].

4. The certificate, however, had expired [p.a.].

5. Dion took Fran [d.o.] and Zina [d.o.] to the store.

Using *Language and Self-Expression*

Consider using this writing assignment to assess students' ability to use complements correctly and effectively. You may want students to complete the assignment as part of a descriptive writing strand for their portfolios.

Prewriting

Tell students that brainstorming during the prewriting stage may help them focus on the people and events they wish to portray in their writing. Have students consider the following questions:

- When you hear the word *family,* who immediately comes to mind?
- What kinds of activities does your family do together?
- When you think of your family, in what scene or setting do you immediately imagine them?

FOR YOUR INFORMATION

About the Artist

Horace Pippin (1888–1946) was the grandson of slaves and the son of domestic workers who lived in New York. Pippin enjoyed drawing at a young age and, after losing the use of his right arm in World War I, began to paint as therapy for bouts of depression. In 1937 one of his paintings was discovered in the window of a shoe repair shop by art connoisseur Christian Brinton and artist N. C. Wyeth. Within a year four of Pippin's paintings were included in an exhibition of Folk artists at the Museum of Modern Art in New York City. Painting from memory and imagination, Pippin created landscapes, still lifes, and scenes from the war.

Language and *Self-Expression*

Horace Pippin grew up in the late 1800s and early 1900s in Goshen, New York. Besides antiwar paintings, he painted scenes of everyday activities in the lives of African Americans. *Domino Players* shows Pippin's own family at home.

Can you picture a scene of your own family relaxing at home? Who is in the scene? What is each person doing? If you painted the scene, what colors would you use? Write a descriptive composition about this family scene. Write as though you were looking at a painting and describing it as vividly as possible to someone over the telephone.

Prewriting Brainstorm a list of people to include in the scene and an activity for each person. What is the focal point of your family scene?

Drafting Use your list to write descriptions of your family members and their activities. You could describe the scene in order, from the least important to the most important. Use complements to help create a colorful mental image of the scene.

Revising Make sure each paragraph has a topic sentence and that all sentences clearly relate to their topic sentence. Read your paper aloud. Does it create a vivid mental image? How can you enhance the clarity or detail of this mental image?

Editing Check your writing for mistakes in spelling or punctuation. Make sure you have capitalized the names of people and places correctly.

Publishing Write a final copy for your English teacher. If you take an art class or have art supplies at home, you may want to use the materials to paint or draw the scene you described.

Another Look

Complements

A **direct object** is a noun or pronoun that answers the question *Whom?* or *What?* after an action verb. *(pages L159–L160)*
A **compound direct object** consists of two or more direct objects following the same verb. *(page L160)*
An **indirect object** is a noun or pronoun that answers the questions *To whom?*, *For whom?*, *To What?*, or *For what?* after an action verb. *(pages L163–L164)*
A **compound indirect object** consists of two or more indirect objects that follow the same verb. *(page L164)*
A **predicate nominative** is a noun or a pronoun that follows a linking verb and identifies, renames, or explains the subject. *(pages L168–L170)*
A **compound predicate nominative** consists of two or more predicate nominatives following the same verb. *(page L170)*
A **predicate adjective** is an adjective that follows a linking verb and modifies the subject. *(pages L172–L173)*
A **compound predicate adjective** consists of two or more predicate adjectives that follow the same verb. *(page L173)*

Position of Complements

A **direct object** is a noun or a pronoun that follows an action verb. *(page L159)*
An **indirect object** is a noun or a pronoun that follows an action verb and comes before a direct object. *(pages L163–L164)*
A **predicate nominative** is a noun or a pronoun that follows a linking verb. *(page L168)*
A **predicate adjective** is an adjective that follows a linking verb. *(page L172)*

Other Information About Complements

Recognizing predicate nominatives by finding linking verbs *(page L169)*
Recognizing predicate adjectives by finding linking verbs *(pages L172–L173)*

Using *Another Look*

Another Look summarizes the terms defined in the chapter and provides cross-references to the specific pages on which they are explained. Consider having students use this feature prior to completing **CheckPoint** or taking the post-test. Students who can provide several examples of each term should be able to score well on either measurement.

FOR ASSESSING LEARNING

Using *the Posttest*

Assessing Learning

The posttest will help you and your students assess where they stand in their ability to identify and use different kinds of complements.

IDENTIFYING COMMON STUMBLING BLOCKS

Following is a list of the most common errors students make when using complements.

Problem

- Identifying indirect objects incorrectly as direct objects

Solution

- For reteaching, use the explanatory copy printed in blue beside the examples on p. L166.

Problem

- Difficulty identifying predicate adjectives

Solution

- For reteaching, use the explanatory copy printed in blue beside the examples on pp. L172–L173.

Directions

Write the letter of the term that correctly identifies the underlined word in each sentence.

EXAMPLE **1.** My music instructor is teaching <u>me</u> the cello.

1 A direct object
B indirect object
C predicate nominative
D predicate adjective

ANSWER **1 B**

1. The cello is a stringed musical <u>instrument</u> of the violin family.
2. I like the deep, rich <u>voice</u> of the cello.
3. The sound of the cello is a beautiful <u>bass</u>.
4. Compared to the violin, the cello is quite <u>large</u>.
5. Someone told <u>me</u> the measurements of the cello.
6. The entire instrument is about forty-seven <u>inches</u> in length.
7. Nowadays, cellos have four <u>strings</u>.
8. The first cellos were a <u>product</u> of the sixteenth century.
9. Crafters often gave these early <u>cellos</u> five strings.
10. Cellos were <u>popular</u> in ensembles.

A DIFFERENT DELIVERY SYSTEM

If you prefer, you can print the posttest from the BK English Test Bank located at http://www.bkenglish.com.

1 A direct object
B indirect object
C predicate nominative
D predicate adjective

2 A direct object
B indirect object
C predicate nominative
D predicate adjective

3 A direct object
B indirect object
C predicate nominative
D predicate adjective

4 A direct object
B indirect object
C predicate nominative
D predicate adjective

5 A direct object
B indirect object
C predicate nominative
D predicate adjective

6 A direct object
B indirect object
C predicate nominative
D predicate adjective

7 A direct object
B indirect object
C predicate nominative
D predicate adjective

8 A direct object
B indirect object
C predicate nominative
D predicate adjective

9 A direct object
B indirect object
C predicate nominative
D predicate adjective

10 A direct object
B indirect object
C predicate nominative
D predicate adjective

Customizing the Test

Use these questions to add or replace items for alternate versions of the test.

11. I gave my music instructor my research report on the cello.

12. It was quite good, if I say so myself.

13. During the seventeenth century, the cello and the harpsichord were a popular combination.

14. Bach, Beethoven, Mozart, and other composers wrote beautiful scores for the cello.

15. One of the outstanding cellists of the twentieth century was Pablo Casals.

11. A direct object
B indirect object
C predicate nominative
D predicate adjective

12. A direct object
B indirect object
C predicate nominative
D predicate adjective

13. A direct object
B indirect object
C predicate nominative
D predicate adjective

14. A direct object
B indirect object
C predicate nominative
D predicate adjective

15. A direct object
B indirect object
C predicate nominative
D predicate adjective

TEACHING SUGGESTIONS

BLOCK SCHEDULING

- If your schedule requires that you cover the chapter in a **shorter time,** use the instruction on prepositional and appositive phrases and the Check Your Understanding and QuickCheck exercises.
- If you want to take advantage of **longer class time,** add these applications to writing: Connect to Writer's Craft, Connect to the Writing Process, and Apply to Writing exercises.

Essential Knowledge and Skills

- Writing to inform such as to explain, describe, report, and narrate
- Using prepositional phrases to elaborate written ideas
- Editing drafts for specific purposes such as to ensure standard usage, varied sentence structure, and appropriate word choice
- Corresponding with peers or others via E-mail
- Interpreting and evaluating the various ways visual image makers such as illustrators represent meanings

CHAPTER 7

Phrases

Directions

Write the letter of the term that correctly identifies the underlined word or words in each sentence.

EXAMPLE **1.** There are several species of large flightless birds.
1 **A** adjective phrase
B adverb phrase
C appositive
D appositive phrase

ANSWER **1 A**

1. The cassowary, a large bird, does not fly.
2. Cassowaries live in the rain forests of Australia and Malaysia.
3. The largest living birds, ostriches, are found in Africa.
4. Ostriches lay their eggs in holes in the sand.
5. The height of an ostrich can be eight feet.
6. Another flightless bird, the large, brownish rhea, lives in Africa.
7. The speed of a running rhea can surpass that of a horse.
8. The five-foot rhea feeds on plants and insects.
9. The emu is a fourth type of flightless bird.
10. Their large greenish eggs are hatched by the male.

IDENTIFYING COMMON STUMBLING BLOCKS

Following is a list of the most common errors students make when using prepositional phrases, appositives, and appositive phrases.

Problem
- Misplaced modifiers

Solution
- Instruction, p. L194
- Practice, p. L195

Problem
- Lack of commas with long introductory adverb phrases

Solution
- Instruction, p. L197
- Practice, pp. L198–L199

1 **A** adjective phrase
B adverb phrase
C appositive
D appositive phrase

2 **A** adjective phrase
B adverb phrase
C appositive
D appositive phrase

3 **A** adjective
B adverb phrase
C appositive
D appositive phrase

4 **A** adjective phrase
B adverb phrase
C appositive
D appositive phrase

5 **A** adjective phrase
B adverb phrase
C appositive
D appositive phrase

6 **A** adjective phrase
B adverb phrase
C appositive
D appositive phrase

7 **A** adjective phrase
B adverb phrase
C appositive
D appositive phrase

8 **A** adjective phrase
B adverb phrase
C appositive
D appositive phrase

9 **A** adjective phrase
B adverb phrase
C appositive
D appositive phrase

10 **A** adjective phrase
B adverb phrase
C appositive
D appositive phrase

A DIFFERENT DELIVERY SYSTEM

If you prefer, you can print the pretest from the BK English Test Bank located at http://www.bkenglish.com.

Using *the Pretest*

Assessing Prior Knowledge

The pretest will help you and your students assess where they stand in their basic understanding of phrases and appositives. The test indicates students' ability to identify adjective and adverb phrases, appositives, and appositive phrases.

Customizing the Test

Use these questions to add or replace items for alternate versions of the test.

11. Our science teacher, Ms. Randall, knows some interesting facts.

12. She told us about ostrich farms.

13. Ostrich meat, a low-fat and low-calorie meat, is considered a delicacy by some.

14. The fat content of ostrich meat is lower than that of chicken.

11. **A** adjective phrase
B adverb phrase
C appositive
D appositive phrase

12. **A** adjective phrase
B adverb phrase
C appositive
D appositive phrase

13. **A** adjective phrase
B adverb phrase
C appositive
D appositive phrase

14. **A** adjective phrase
B adverb phrase
C appositive
D appositive phrase

ADDITIONAL RESOURCES

Language Skills Practice . . . . pages 57–65
Transparency Tools FA7, AW6
ESL Practice and Test Preparation . . . . . pages 103–105
Assessment: Chapter Test. . . . . pages 144–148

MAKING VISUAL CONNECTIONS

For Language Development

To connect the fine art with the language concept presented in this chapter, ask students to brainstorm words and phrases they would use to describe this painting by Picasso. Have students consider the following questions as they think about their descriptive words and phrases: What color dominates the painting? What setting and subjects make up the painting? How would students describe the overall mood of the painting? Have students write a poem using some of the phrases they used to describe Picasso's work.

To Stimulate Writing

Use the questions for art criticism as writing or discussion prompts.

Possible Answers:

Describe The setting is a beach at night. Picasso used mainly dark, cool colors: blues, greens, blacks, with white highlights.

Analyze The whole scene is still. The only movement suggested is in the boy's hands. The people's shapes are vertical rectangles without arms or legs sticking out at angles.

Interpret The cold, dark colors and the people's body language create a mood of hopelessness and sadness.

Judge Yes, he was successful. He used colors and body language to effectively create a tragic scene. If I wrote about the mood and emotions in *The Tragedy,* I would write a short and poignant poem.

Pablo Picasso. *The Tragedy,* 1903.
Wood, 41½ inches by 27⅛ inches.

Chester Dale Collection.

Describe What is the setting in this painting? What colors has the artist used?

Analyze Overall, has Picasso created a sense of movement or of stillness? How did he use lines and shapes to create this effect?

Interpret What mood does Picasso create, using color and body language? What do you think has happened to these people?

Judge Do you think the artist was successful at creating a sense of tragedy? If you expressed the mood and emotions of *The Tragedy* in writing, would you write a poem or a story? Why?

At the end of this chapter, you will use the artwork to stimulate ideas for writing.

FOR DEVELOPING LANGUAGE SKILLS

LESSON 1 *(pages L189–L200)*

OBJECTIVES

- **To identify prepositional phrases, including adjective phrases and adverb phrases**
- **To identify and correct misplaced modifiers**
- **To punctuate adverb phrases**

Create Interest

Tell students that to understand prepositional phrases, they must be clear about the functions of prepositions, adjectives, and adverbs. Tell students that reviewing can be a part of "reminiscing." Have students give the definitions of these parts of speech. Have students reminisce by looking back

Prepositional Phrases

A **phrase** is a group of words that acts like a single part of speech. It does not have a subject or a verb. One kind of phrase is a prepositional phrase.

A **prepositional phrase** is a group of words that begins with a preposition, ends with a noun or a pronoun, and is used as an adjective or an adverb.

PREPOSITIONAL PHRASES	The woman **with the binoculars** is our guide.
	The lion leaped **over the stream.**

The following is a list of common prepositions.

COMMON PREPOSITIONS			
about	below	inside	to
above	beneath	into	toward
according to	beside	like	under
across	between	near	underneath
after	beyond	of	until
against	by	off	up
along	down	on	up to
among	during	out of	upon
around	except	over	with
at	for	past	within
because of	from	since	without
before	in	through	
behind	in front of	throughout	

You can learn more about prepositions on pages L133–L138.

FOR INCREASING STUDENT ACHIEVEMENT

GETTING STUDENTS INVOLVED

Cooperative Learning

Divide the class into two teams. Have a student from one side provide a sentence starter that includes a subject and a verb, such as *The little boy ran.* Then a student from the other side should end the sentence with a prepositional phrase, such as *down the hallway.* Continue the activity until all students have had a turn.

REACHING ALL STUDENTS

Advanced Learners

Have students use their textbooks or other research materials to find out about another part of the prepositional phrase, the *object of the preposition.* After students have completed their research, have them write an instructional lesson to present to the class that explains objects of prepositions and that provides examples. Students should also write a ten-item exercise for students to complete after the instruction.

through their writing portfolios to find places in which they had identified prepositions, adjectives, and adverbs.

Guide Instruction

By Connecting Ideas

Tell students that they must be able to identify parts of speech before they can identify phrases. Demonstrate how to identify prepositions, adjectives, and adverbs in the following sentence: *The talented musician enthusiastically played the song on his guitar.* (*talented*-adj.; *enthusiastically*-adv.; *on*-prep.) Then explain that the phrase—*on his guitar*—is a prepositional phrase.

Consolidate Skills

Through Guided Practice

The **Check Your Understanding** exercises as well as the **QuickCheck** activity on page L200 will help students identify and use prepositional phrases. Tell students that prepositional phrases always begin with a preposition and end with an object of the preposition.

A DIFFERENT APPROACH

Kinesthetic

Write each sentence from the **Practice Your Skills** paragraph on separate long strips of paper. Mix up the sentences and have students put them back in the correct order. Have students check their sentence order against the paragraph in their books. Then have students read aloud the prepositional phrases in the paragraph.

HOME WORK

After reading the paragraph on this page, have students create a three-dimensional model of the hotel described in the paragraph. Direct students to focus their attention on the prepositional phrases in the paragraph to help them build their models. Students should use various materials from home, such as cardboard, wood, tree branches, or sticks to build their hotel models.

PRACTICE YOUR SKILLS

Check Your Understanding

Finding Prepositional Phrases

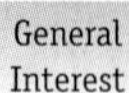

Write each prepositional phrase in the following paragraph.

A most unusual hotel is located in Africa. The hotel is not built on the ground. Instead, it is forty feet above the ground in the branches of a giant tree. Underneath the tree is a large salt deposit. During the evening the animals from the jungle come to the salt deposit for a lick. The guests at the hotel sit on the screened porch above the salt deposit. From their easy chairs, in comfort and safety, they can watch the wild animals.

Adjective Phrases

An adjective phrase is a prepositional phrase that is used like a single adjective.

Single Adjective	"Fiddler on the Roof" is a **long** CD.
Adjective Phrase	"Fiddler on the Roof" is a CD **with fourteen songs.**

An **adjective phrase** is a prepositional phrase that is used to modify a noun or a pronoun.

To guide instruction, complete the first item in each activity together. Then have students complete the remaining items independently.

Apply to Communication

Through Independent Writing

The **Communicate Your Ideas** activities on pages L193 and L199 prompt students to write a character sketch and an E-mail. Ask students how their use of prepositional phrases will make their writing more descriptive and clearer to their audience. What common prepositions might they use to describe someone and to write an E-mail?

Transfer to Everyday Life

Identifying Phrases in Speech

Have students find examples of prepositional phrases from a television program. Students should listen to a particular program and write down as many of these phrases as they can identify. Have students read their

An adjective phrase answers the question *Which one?* or *What kind?* just as a single adjective does.

WHICH ONE? The cassette **on the right** is hers.

I like the songs **on that CD.**

WHAT KIND? Dad prefers music **from the disco era.**

Mom has a car **without a CD player.**

A sentence can have more than one adjective phrase.

That kind **of song** is for parents **with young children.**

Friends and neighbors **from the community** came to the benefit **for the school band.**

Sometimes an adjective phrase may modify a noun or a pronoun in another phrase.

The show **about music of the past** was fascinating.

The section **on swing music across the ages** was cool.

CONNECT TO WRITER'S CRAFT

Writers always try to vary their sentences. One way writers accomplish this is to combine short sentences. Sometimes writers can combine short sentences with an adjective phrase.

Leo buys a lunch. Lunch is pizza and milk.

Leo buys a lunch **of pizza and milk.**

Jana emptied her purse. Her purse was full of coins.

Jana emptied her purse **of its coins.**

DEVELOPING WORKPLACE COMPETENCIES

Basic Skills: Writing

Ask students how communicating information like *which one* and *what kind* can be important in a business or trade. Have students provide examples of careers in which they would need to be specific about describing someone or something. Write some of students' examples and sentences on the board. Point out the adjective phrases used by students in their descriptions.

USING STUDENTS' STRENGTHS

Multiple Intelligences: Linguistic

After reading **Connect to Writer's Craft,** have students write five additional examples of short sentences that can be combined with an adjective phrase. Have students show how these sentences can be combined to make them more interesting.

sentences containing prepositional phrases aloud.

Pull It All Together

By Summarizing

Have students summarize the types of phrases discussed in Lesson 1: prepositional phrases, adjective phrases, adverb phrases. Have students create sentences containing each type of phrase and state their sentences aloud.

Check Understanding

Defining Different Kinds of Phrases

Without checking their textbooks, have students write their own definitions for the following words: *prepositional phrase, adjective phrase, adverb phrase.* Students should also write sentences containing these types of phrases. Discuss students' various definitions and example sentences.

A DIFFERENT APPROACH

Auditory

Discuss the musical topics in the **Check Your Understanding** activities. Have students identify the adjective phrases by taking turns singing the phrases aloud. If students are uncomfortable doing so, they may sing their responses to themselves. Discuss students' responses to each item.

HOME WORK

Have students find out more about Louis Armstrong and Richard Rodgers. Students should choose one of these people and write about him in a report. Their reports should be at least one page long and contain adjective phrases. Have students underline the adjective phrases in their reports.

PRACTICE YOUR SKILLS

Check Your Understanding

Finding Adjective Phrases

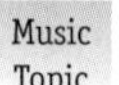

Music Topic **Write each adjective phrase.**

1. Louis Armstrong was a native of New Orleans.

2. He has been called the king of jazz trumpet players.

3. He joined the famous jazz band of Kid Ory.

4. However, this player of the trumpet preferred small bands.

5. A typical Armstrong recording is a mixture of voice and trumpet.

6. Armstrong's influence on jazz was enormous.

7. He played a variety of melodic variations.

8. Once he played a series of 250 high C notes in a row!

9. Some of his popular records include duets with Bessie Smith.

10. People outside jazz know Armstrong's "Hello, Dolly" and "Mack the Knife."

Check Your Understanding

Finding Adjectives Phrases

Music Topic **Write each adjective phrase. Then write the word it modifies.**

11. One musical by Richard Rodgers and Oscar Hammerstein is *Carousel.* musical

12. A carousel ride begins this story about two people and their friends. story

13. The person in front of the carousel attracts Julie's attention. person, front

14. Billy makes a sound like a loud microphone. sound

15. Julie rides the white horse on the carousel. horse

16. A carousel is another name for a merry-go-round. name

17. Billy loves Julie with the curly hair. Julie

18. Billy's death in a fight is sad. death

19. The Starkeeper in heaven sends Billy back home. Starkeeper

20. Billy must do something of value. something

Connect to the Writing Process: Revising

Combining Sentences Using Adjective Phrases

Combine each group of sentences into one sentence by using an adjective phrase. [Answers may vary. Possible reponses are given.]

21. Julie has brown hair~~. Her hair has~~ with curls.

22. She has an accent~~. The accent is~~ from New England.

23. She wears the same ~~clothes. She wears~~ combination of laced shoes and a frilly dress.

24. Julie is a happy person~~. She always has~~ with a smile on her face.

Communicate Your Ideas

APPLY TO WRITING

Character Sketch: ***Adjective Phrases***

Write a short, colorful description of a character for a young adult novel. Bring the character to life by describing physical and personal details of the person. The model for your character could be a friend, a neighbor, or a relative. To help make the character interesting, use adjective phrases.

IDENTIFYING COMMON STUMBLING BLOCKS

Problem

- Commas placed incorrectly before adjective phrases

Solution

- Remind students that no comma is necessary before an adjective phrase. Direct students to add a comma only if their combined sentences produce a compound sentence.
- Have students decide whether to use a comma in these sentences: *She has an accent and her accent is from New England. She has an accent from New England.*

INTEGRATING TECHNOLOGY

Computer

Have students use drawing or design software to create a replica of the person they described in their character sketch writing assignment. Students should focus on the adjectives they used to describe this person. Remind students that this character should be appealing to young adult readers.

TIMESAVER *QuickCheck*

To evaluate the work produced by students in the **Apply to Writing** activity, create a checklist that includes the following: includes a character that would be appealing to young adult readers; includes several adjective phrases; includes colorful descriptions; includes personal details of the person; and includes physical details. Check off each item on the checklist as *excellent, good, weak,* or *poor.*

GETTING STUDENTS INVOLVED

Cooperative Learning

Working with misplaced modifiers can be amusing and entertaining for students. After discussing this page, write the following additional sentences on the board and have students work together to correct the misplaced modifiers.

- With icing on top, the children loved eating the cake.
- The cook created the dish with enthusiasm.
- The monsters fascinated the teenagers with hairy eyeballs.
- Inside the cabinet, Sue saw her new sweater.
- Jason worked in a small store with little opportunity to get ahead.

Misplaced Adjective Phrases

An adjective phrase should be as close as possible to the word it describes. When a phrase is too far away from the word it describes, it is called a **misplaced modifier.** Sometimes a misplaced modifier confuses the meaning of a sentence. At other times, it makes the sentence sound silly.

MISPLACED MODIFIERS

The children laughed at Zany Mr. Science **in the audience.**
(Because the phrase is misplaced, the sentence seems to be saying that Zany Mr. Science is in the audience.)

In the glass jar, Tom studied the squirming bugs.
(Because of this misplaced modifier, Tom seems to be in the glass jar.)

In the dish, the bugs ate the food.
(Because of this misplaced modifier, the reader might think the bugs are in the dish.)

To correct a misplaced modifier, place the adjective phrase as close as possible to the word it describes.

CORRECT MODIFIERS

The children **in the audience** laughed at Zany Mr. Science.
(Now the children, not Zany Mr. Science, are in the audience.)

Tom studied the squirming bugs **in the glass jar.**
(Now the bugs, not Tom, are in the glass jar.)

The bugs ate the food **in the dish.**
(Now the food, not the bugs, is in the dish.)

PRACTICE YOUR SKILLS

Check Your Understanding

Identifying Misplaced Modifiers

Science Topic **If a sentence contains a misplaced modifier, write *I* for incorrect. If a sentence is correct as written, write *C*.**

1. The class visited the animals in the nature preserve. ~~In the nature preserve, the class visited the animals.~~ I
2. The science teacher taught a lesson about the different species. C
3. She explained the procedure of the trip. C
4. Maps of the woods were handed out to the students. ~~Maps were handed out to the students of the woods.~~ I
5. Matt saw a small gray mouse with a skinny tail. ~~With a skinny tail Matt saw a small gray mouse.~~ I
6. Glenda fed the squirrels peanuts from a jar. ~~Glenda fed peanuts to the squirrels from a jar.~~ I
7. A skunk on the path had a broad white stripe. ~~A skunk had a broad white stripe on the path.~~ I
8. Jen saw an American eagle with huge wings. ~~With huge wings Jen saw an American eagle.~~ I
9. Take that lunch basket with the wooden handles to Mr. Reynolds. ~~Take that lunch basket to Mr. Reynolds with the wooden handles.~~ I
10. We quickly ate our lunch of sandwiches and juice. C

Connect to the Writing Process: Revising

Correcting Misplaced Adjective Phrases

11.–17. Rewrite the incorrect sentences from the preceding exercise, placing each adjective phrase closer to the word it modifies. [Answers may vary. Possible responses given above.]

Adverb Phrases

An adverb phrase is a prepositional phrase that is used like a single adverb.

A DIFFERENT APPROACH

Visual

Have students create thumbnail sketches for each incorrect sentence in **Check Your Understanding.** Encourage students to focus their sketches on the sometimes humorous aspects caused by misplaced modifiers. Have students share some of their favorite sketches with the class.

HOME WORK

Have students write ten more humorous sentences containing misplaced modifiers. Students should also include a correct version of each sentence.

GETTING STUDENTS INVOLVED

Reciprocal Teaching

After discussing adverb phrases and the examples, have students work with partners to find examples of adverb phrases from their writing portfolios. Students should look through their portfolios and find a writing sample that their partners can read. Each partner should then identify adverb phrases in the other's writing. Have partners share some of their adverb phrases with the class.

YOUR IDEAS

For Teaching Adverb Phrases

SINGLE ADVERB	The artist spoke **softly.**
ADVERB PHRASE	The artist spoke **in a whisper.**

An **adverb phrase** is a prepositional phrase that is used mainly to modify a verb.

An adverb phrase usually answers the question *Where? When?* or *How?* just as a single adverb does. Occasionally, an adverb phrase answers the question *Why?*

WHERE?	The artists moved **to the valley.**
WHEN?	**On Monday** the artist began his clay pot.
HOW?	The artist worked **on a precise schedule.**
WHY?	He bought tools **for his new project.**

When an adverb phrase is placed with a verb phrase, it modifies the entire verb phrase.

For one hour the clay has been fired slowly.

Two adverb phrases can modify the same verb. Also notice that adverb phrases may appear anywhere in a sentence.

Before Friday I must bring clay **to the artist.**

The artist waited **for clay for five days.**

Once in a while, an adjective phrase may modify the object of the preposition of an adverb phrase.

The artist dropped her new pot **into a puddle of water.**

PUNCTUATION WITH ADVERB PHRASES	
If a short adverb phrase begins a sentence, usually no comma is needed. However, a comma should be placed after an introductory adverb phrase of four or more words, after two or more introductory phrases, or after a phrase that ends in a date.	
NO COMMA	**During the exhibit** you can see clay pots.
COMMA	**During the pottery exhibit,** you can see clay pots.
COMMA	**During the pottery exhibit at the museum,** you can see clay pots.
COMMA	**During 1999,** the museum had an exhibit of clay pots.

PRACTICE YOUR SKILLS

Check Your Understanding
Finding Adverb Phrases

Art Topic **Write each adverb phrase. Beside each one, write the word or words it modifies.**

1. Early settlers worked with clay. worked
2. They created their work without machinery. created
3. In the bright sunshine, they began their work. began
4. First they dumped raw clay onto a work surface. dumped
5. In the beginning the clay was shaped with the hands and fingers. was shaped
6. They turned and pressed the clay for a long time. turned, pressed
7. Artists made shapes with tools and with coils. made

USING STUDENTS' STRENGTHS

Multiple Intelligences: Logical

Discuss the Punctuation with Adverb Phrases chart. Have students devise some way that they and others can remember the information in the chart. Students might consider memory devices such as songs or rhyming poems. They might also use sketches, shorthand, or graphic organizers to help them remember the information. Have students share their memory devices with the class. Ask the class to choose a memory device and vote on the one that seems to work the best for them.

A DIFFERENT APPROACH

Kinesthetic

As an alternative to the **Check Your Understanding** activity, have students write the sentences on the board and circle the adverb phrases with their fingers. Then, for each sentence, have students create new adverb phrases that would make sense.

HOME WORK

Have students create picture books for young children by writing ten additional sentences containing adverb phrases. The topic of their sentences should be fairs, such as art fairs or county fairs they have attended. Each sentence will end up being a page in their books. Students should create an illustration for each page of their book. Have students share their completed books with younger children.

8. The potters fired their creations in an oven. fired
9. On occasion, the artists decorated their creations. decorated
10. Shards have been found during archaeological digs. have been found

Check Your Understanding

Finding Adverb Phrases

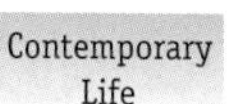

Write each adverb phrase. Beside each one, write the word or words it modifies.

11. Craft fairs are held each year in the park. are held
12. Spring brings many fairs to communities. brings
13. Fairs often begin before noon. begin
14. In one day people can view many crafts. can view
15. Some participants move past the stands slowly. move
16. People search for the best buys. search
17. Dancers and singers perform on the tiny stage. perform
18. The audience sits on chairs in front of the stage. sits
19. After the performance workers clean the stage. clean
20. By next week another fair will come to town. will come

Connect to the Writing Process: Editing

Writing Sentences: Punctuating Adverb Phrases

Rewrite each sentence, correctly punctuating the adverb phrases. If a sentence is correct, write *C*.

21. At the start of the 1950s‸ the United States enjoyed much prosperity.
22. During that decade Americans put World War II behind them. C
23. Through government support many men and women were going to college. C
24. Like the economy families were booming. C
25. With an increase in wages‸ Americans bought more.

26. With the savings from technological advances, companies were making more money.

27. According to economic experts, the United States turned into a country of consumers.

28. By 1955, computers were on the market.

29. In 15 years income jumped 46 percent. C

30. By the end of the decade, some people had color TVs.

Communicate Your Ideas

APPLY TO WRITING

E-mail: ***Adverb Phrases***

Write an E-mail to a friend about where you would like to go on your next school vacation. Describe your plans. For variety in your sentences, begin at least two sentences with an adverb phrase. Use commas as needed.

USING STUDENTS' STRENGTHS

Multiple Intelligences: Linguistic

Have students create a test that would evaluate students' understanding of using commas with adverb phrases. Students should decide what format the test should be. For example, they might choose to make their tests fill-in-the-blank, matching, or sentence completion format. Students should create an answer key for their tests. Check students' completed tests for accuracy before administering them to the class.

DEVELOPING WORKPLACE COMPETENCIES

Thinking Skills: Creative Thinking

Have students consider how they can be more effective and creative in their future careers by focusing on the words *where, when, how,* and *why.* How might students use these questioning words to create new solutions to problems or to find out important information? What inventions might they create by thinking about these words? Have students write a two- to three-paragraph paper explaining how they can use these four words effectively in the future.

GETTING STUDENTS INVOLVED

Reciprocal Teaching

Have students bring in copies of superhero comic books. Have students work with partners to identify adjective phrases and adverb phrases in the comic books. Students should explain to their partners why they selected particular phrases. If partners have difficulty identifying any prepositional phrases, students should work with them and help them to find the phrases. Have partners share two or three of their favorite prepositional phrases from the comic books with the class.

EXPANDING THE LESSON

Using Technology

You will find additional **instructional** and **practice** materials for this chapter at http://www.bkenglish.com.

Mixed Practice

Contemporary Life

Write each prepositional phrase. Then label each one *adj.* for adjective or *adv.* for adverb.

1. For family fun (adv.) you can go on a treasure hunt (adv.) in the United States (adj.).
2. Can you mine samples of gemstones (adj.) in America (adv.)?
3. At North Carolina's "gem mining" businesses (adv.), you might choose a bucket of dirt (adj.) from a specific gemstone mine (adv.).
4. Then you search for the stone (adv.) of your preference (adj.).
5. You shovel your dirt into a wooden flume (adv.) and water rushes through it (adv.).
6. You recognize flashes of colors (adj.).
7. Some stones might not look promising in rock form (adv.).
8. Cutting will unveil the color and beauty of the stones (adj.).
9. A dark brown stone might actually be cut into a ruby (adv.).
10. Many families have searched for samples (adv.) of garnets, sapphires, emeralds, and topazes (adj.).
11. There are also geological rewards for digging (adj.) in shale (adv.).
12. Families are digging for fossils (adv.) in different locations (adv.).
13. A trip to Wyoming (adj.) could yield souvenirs of fossils (adj.) of prehistoric plants or creatures (adj.).
14. The layers of rock (adj.) in this state (adj.) have revealed everything from palms (adj.) to alligators (adj.).
15. Any large fossils, however, are considered property of the state (adj.).

LESSON 2 *(pages L201–L205)*

OBJECTIVES

- **To identify appositives and appositive phrases**
- **To punctuate appositives and appositive phrases**

Create Interest

Review with students the meaning of *nouns* and *pronouns.* Have students list several nouns and pronouns. Then have students complete the following sentences, using nouns or pronouns. Tell students that the words they are filling in are appositives.

- My best friend, ■, came over on Saturday.
- We talked about our favorite hobby, ■.
- We ate a tasty snack, ■.

Appositives and Appositive Phrases

Sometimes a noun or pronoun is added immediately after another noun or pronoun to explain or identify the first noun or pronoun.

We talked about our common interest, **poetry.**

(*Poetry* explains what the common interest is.)

We student poets, **Ryan and I,** left early.

These identifying words are called appositives.

An **appositive** is a noun or a pronoun that identifies or explains another noun or pronoun in the sentence.

When an appositive has modifiers, it is called an **appositive phrase**.

Mr. Lewis, **the poetry club sponsor,** works hard.

Take this memo to Ms. Burns, **a poetry teacher.**

Sometimes a prepositional phrase may also be a part of an appositive phrase.

Haddam Middle School, **the school near the bus station,** is the location for the poetry contest.

PUNCTUATION WITH APPOSITIVES AND APPOSITIVE PHRASES

If the information in an appositive or appositive phrase is essential to the meaning of a sentence, no commas are needed. The information is essential if it identifies a person, place, or thing.

USING STUDENTS' STRENGTHS

Multiple Intelligences: Intrapersonal

Have students write a journal entry about themselves. They should use appositives and appositive phrases in their entries. Students might want to think about the following ideas to write their journal entries. *My favorite things; how I would describe myself; my talents; my favorite pastime; people I enjoy being around; how I feel today; what I think about the future; how I will reach my goals.* Have students share some of their appositives with the class.

Guide Instruction

By Modeling Strategies

Tell students that appositives and appositive phrases are easy to identify because they are nouns or pronouns and they always modify nouns or pronouns. Model the strategy for identifying appositives and appositive phrases by writing the following sentences on the board. Circle the appositives and draw arrows to the words they modify.

- Langston Hughes, a poet, wrote direct and simplistic poems. (a poet modifies Langston Hughes)
- Music, a central feature of Hughes's poetry, was an important part of the poet's life. (a central feature of Hughes's poetry modifies Music)
- The blues, a type of music, is evident in many of Hughes's poems. (a type of music modifies blues)

Consolidate Skills

Through Guided Practice

The **Check Your Understanding** exercise as well as the **QuickCheck** on page L205 will help students identify

IDENTIFYING COMMON STUMBLING BLOCKS

Problem

- Lack of commas with nonessential appositives and appositive phrases

Solution

- Point out that nonessential appositives and phrases can be taken out, or "separated from," the sentence and it will still make sense. These appositives are separated using commas at the beginning and at the end of the appositive or appositive phrase.
- Give students sentences like these and ask them to decide whether or not commas should be used with the appositives or appositive phrases:

  The novel *The Great Turkey Walk* tells of fifteen-year-old Simon's 900-mile walk to sell his turkeys. (no commas)

  The Great Turkey Walk by Kathleen Karr sounds like a great book. (*Walk*, by Kathleen Karr,)

  Simon's home state Missouri is his starting point. (state, Missouri,)

A comma is needed before and after an appositive or an appositive phrase if the information is not essential to the meaning of the sentence. You can usually tell if the information is essential or not essential by reading the sentence without the appositive. If the sentence makes sense without the appositive, then the appositive is not essential.

Essential	The poem **"Mother to Son"** was written by Langston Hughes. (If **"Mother to Son"** were dropped, the sentence would not make sense. Therefore, the appositive is essential and no commas are needed.)
Not Essential	"Mother to Son," **a poem by Langston Hughes,** is one of my teacher's favorite poems. (If the appositive phrase were dropped, the sentence would still make sense. Therefore, the appositive is not essential and needs a comma before and after it.)

You can learn more about using commas with appositives on page L567.

CONNECT TO WRITER'S CRAFT

When you write, you can use appositives to add information that will help make your writing clearer. When an appositive phrase is placed next to a noun, it can add clarity to your writing.

Langston Hughes lived in Harlem.

Langston Hughes**, an African American poet,** lived in Harlem.

appositives and appositive phrases. To guide instruction, complete the first item in each activity together. Then have students complete the remaining items independently.

Apply to Communication

Through Independent Writing

The **Communicate Your Ideas/Apply to Writing** activity on page L204 prompts students to write a friendly letter. Ask students to brainstorm some appositives and appositive phrases they might use to describe their friend to their grandmother. List some of these appositives and appositive phrases on the board. Leave the list on the board for students to refer to later as they complete the writing assignment.

PRACTICE YOUR SKILLS

Check Your Understanding

Finding Appositives and Appositive Phrases

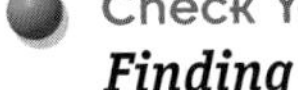

Write each appositive or appositive phrase.

1. Jazz in the 1920s inspired people such as Langston Hughes, an African American poet.
2. Writers and artists gathered in Harlem, a section of New York City.
3. The group in Harlem became a movement of African American culture, the Harlem Renaissance.
4. The Harlem Renaissance, a time of growth and achievement for African American writers, remains important today.
5. Two poets, Countee Cullen and Claude McKay, wrote of their experiences before coming to Harlem.
6. Langston Hughes, a poet, novelist, and playwright, published his first collection of poems in 1926.
7. This collection, *The Weary Blues,* would be followed by many other works.
8. Like Walt Whitman, his favorite poet, Hughes wrote about America.
9. Many readers also know the excellent writing of Zora Neale Hurston, a famous novelist from Florida.
10. Arna Bontemps, poet and novelist, was the historian of the Harlem Renaissance.
11. *God Sends Sunday,* Bontemps's first book, is considered by some people to be the last important novel of the Harlem Renaissance.
12. Another of Bontemps's books, *Story of the Negro,* won the Newbery Honor Book award in 1949.

A DIFFERENT APPROACH

Auditory

Before students write out their responses for **Check Your Understanding,** read the sentences aloud and have students listen for appositives and appositive phrases. Have students explain how they identify the appositives and appositive phrases after each response.

HOME WORK

Have students rewrite the sentences in **Check Your Understanding,** leaving out the appositives and appositive phrases. Students should also write a statement commenting on the effectiveness of the sentences without the appositives. Do they think the sentences are as interesting without the appositives? What did the appositives add to the sentences?

REACHING ALL STUDENTS

Struggling Learners

Remind students that only nonessential appositives—those not needed in the sentence—require commas. Show students, using the sentence in item 11, where to place the commas with nonessential appositives. Direct students to place a comma at the beginning of the nonessential appositive or appositive phrase and to place a comma at the end. Have students read each sentence with the appositive and without it to decide whether or not it is necessary to the sentence.

Transfer to Everyday Life

Identifying Appositives

Have students find five examples of appositives or appositive phrases in song lyrics. Provide students with appropriate lyrics to songs that contain appositives. The school music teacher or band leader might be a good source for appropriate sheet music. Have students write out the section of the lyrics containing the appositives. Discuss students' findings as a group.

Pull It All Together

By Sharing

Have students share their completed friendly letters with the class. Discuss the appositives and appositive phrases students used in their letters to their grandmothers.

Check Understanding

Distinguishing Between Appositives and Appositive Phrases

Have students jot down on a piece of paper the difference between an appositive and an appositive phrase.

TIMESAVER QuickCheck

Use the following checklist to evaluate students' friendly letters:

- Uses appositives to provide specific details
- Uses appositive phrases to provide specific details
- Punctuates appositives correctly
- Punctuates appositive phrases correctly

Connect to the Writing Process: Editing

Punctuating Appositives and Appositive Phrases

Rewrite each sentence, correctly punctuating the appositive or appositive phrase. If a sentence is correct, write C.

13. Georges Bizet,the composer,was born in Paris.
14. His reputation is based on the opera *Carmen.* C
15. Bizet,a child star,studied music at an early age.
16. At nineteen he won the Paris Conservatory's big prize,the Prix de Rome.
17. Bizet,a student of piano,preferred composing.
18. He became a hardworking composer in Rome,the capital of Italy.
19. Two of his early operas,*The Pearl Fishers* and *Djamileh*,were successful.
20. *Carmen*,one of the most popular operas ever,went on stage on March 3, 1875.
21. The opera,a showpiece for a bold soprano,first received mixed reviews.
22. Bizet,the composer of *Carmen*,did not live to enjoy the success of his famous opera.

Communicate Your Ideas

APPLY TO WRITING

Friendly Letter: *Appositives and Appositive Phrases*

A close friend of yours is going with you to spend the weekend at your grandmother's house. Your grandmother has never met your friend. Write a letter to your grandmother. Describe your friend. Use appositives and appositive phrases to provide specific details. Use commas with the appositives as necessary.

Then have students exchange papers. Students should volunteer answers that they feel are correct and complete. Allow time for discussion of students' responses.

Mixed Practice

Write the prepositional and appositive phrases. Write *P* for prepositions and *A* for appositive.

1. What do you know about the most powerful men in our history, the former presidents of the United States?
2. George Washington, the father of our country, reportedly had wooden false teeth.
3. The second president, John Quincy Adams, felt more comfortable working with ideas rather than with people.
4. Thomas Jefferson, the successor to Adams, was inaugurated in everyday street clothes.
5. General Andrew Jackson was defeated by John Quincy Adams, the son of the second president, in 1824.
6. Jackson, a self-made man and a war hero, won the 1828 election by a landslide.
7. The political party of President James K. Polk, the Democrats, pushed him into war with Mexico in 1846.
8. Abraham Lincoln defeated opponents Stephen A. Douglas, John Breckinridge, and John Bell.
9. Lincoln won a clear majority of the electoral votes, 180 out of 303.
10. When Lincoln was assassinated in 1865, Vice President Andrew Johnson, a former Democratic senator from Tennessee, became the President.

EXPANDING THE LESSON

Using Technology

You willl find additional **instructional** and **practice** materials for this chapter at http://www.bkenglish.com.

Using *Sentence Diagraming*

Sentence diagraming helps students develop variety and style in their writing. In this activity, students will focus on diagraming adjective phrases, adverb phrases, appositives, and appositive phrases.

Sample Answers for *Sentence Diagraming:*

1. 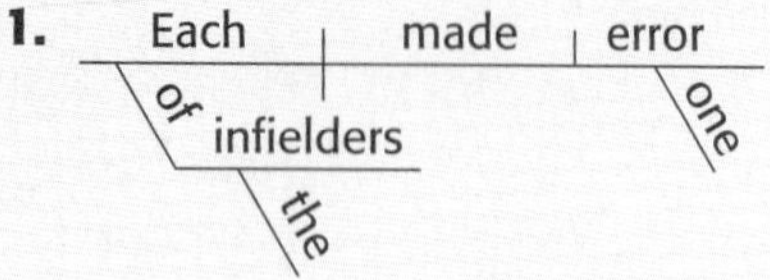

2. 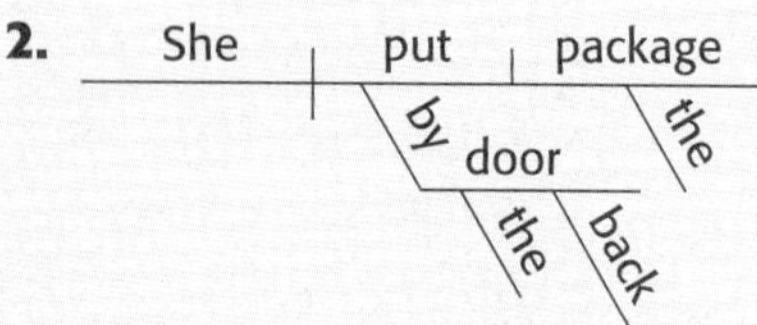

3. 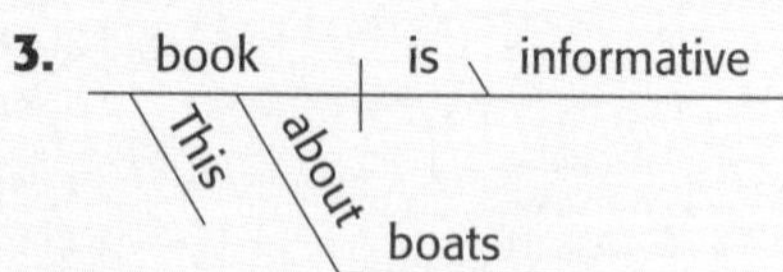

4. 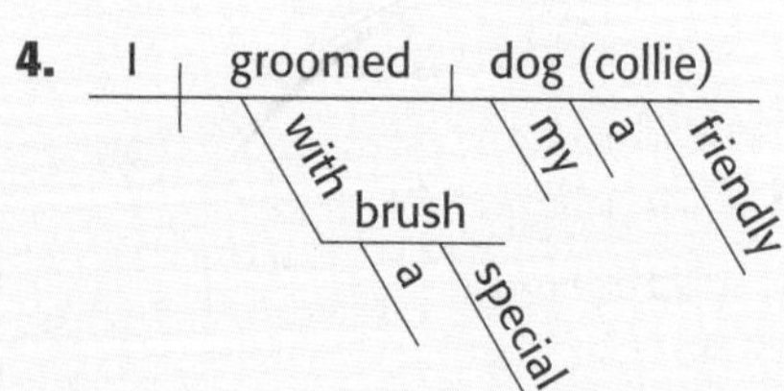

5. 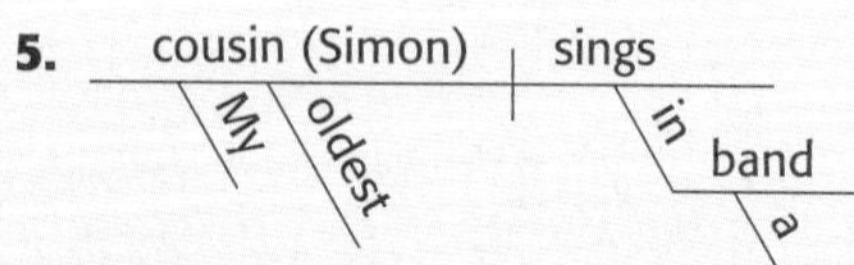

Sentence Diagraming

Diagraming Phrases

In a diagram, prepositional phrases are connected to the words they modify.

Adjective Phrases An adjective phrase is connected to the word it modifies. The preposition is placed on a connecting slanted line. The object of the preposition is placed on a horizontal line that is attached to the slanted line.

Your recipe for chicken is delicious.

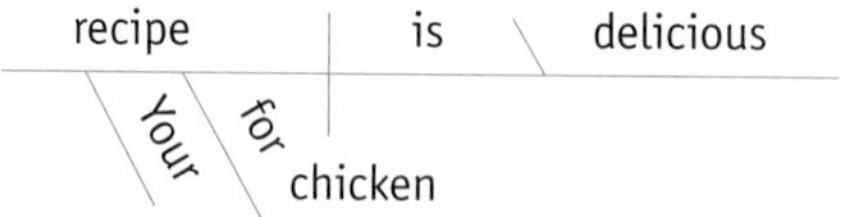

Sometimes an adjective phrase modifies the object of a preposition of another phrase.

Juanita waited by the swings in the park.

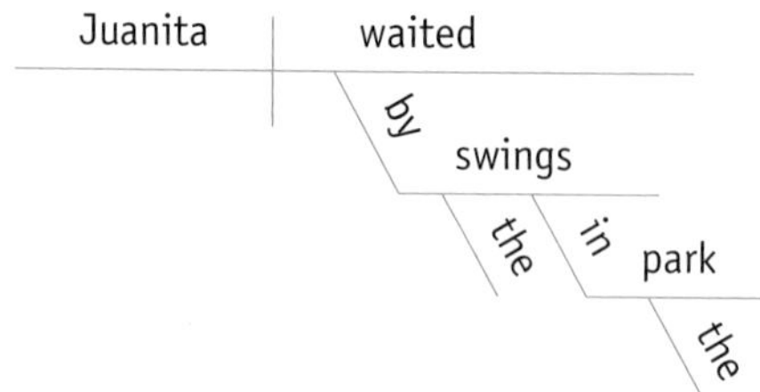

Adverb Phrases An adverb phrase is connected to the verb it modifies.

During the night we heard some strange noises.

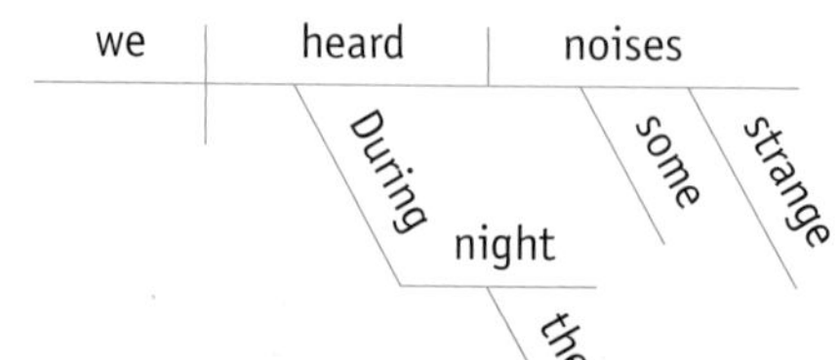

Appositives and Appositive Phrases An appositive or an appositive phrase is diagramed in parentheses next to the word it identifies or explains.

I chose Wendy, my best friend at school.

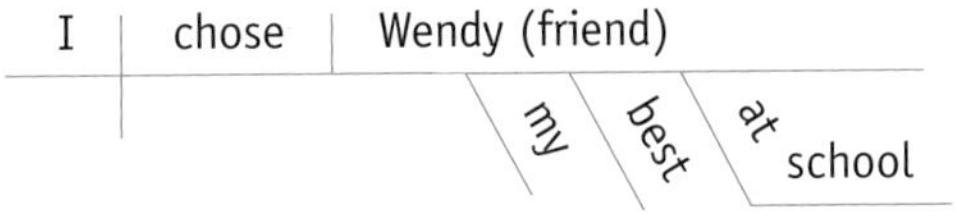

I | chose | Wendy (friend)
my
best
at
school

Jamul, the soloist in the musical, performed flawlessly.

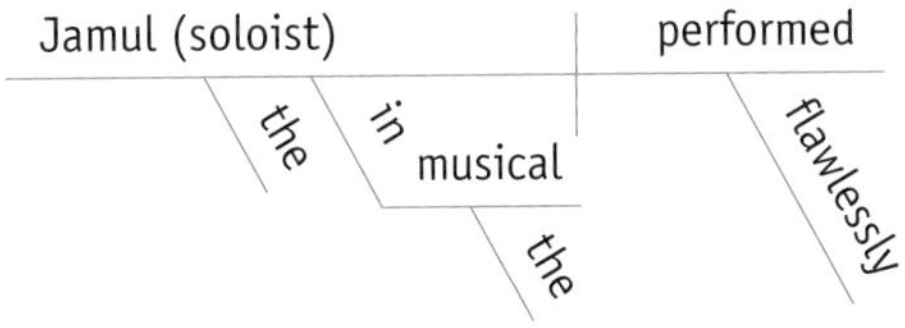

Jamul (soloist) | performed
the
in
musical
the
flawlessly

Practice Your Skills

Diagraming Phrases

Diagram the following sentences, or copy them. If you copy them, draw one line under each subject and two lines under each verb. Put parentheses around each phrase and label it *adjective, adverb,* or *appositive.*

1. Each (of the infielders) adj. made one error.
2. She put the package (by the back door) adv.
3. This book (about boats) adj. is informative.
4. I groomed my dog, (a friendly collie) app. (with a special brush) adv.
5. Simon, (my oldest cousin) app., sings (in a band) adv.

Using *CheckPoint*

This feature on phrases can be used to further independent practice or as a cumulative review of the chapter. It covers finding phrases, identifying the words modified by phrases and appositives, and writing sentences containing phrases and appositives.

CheckPoint

Finding Phrases

Write each prepositional phrase and each appositive phrase. Then label each one *adj.* for adjective, *adv.* for adverb, or *app.* for appositive.

1. The rain beat against our windows. (adv.)
2. The water below the cliff is deep and icy. (adj.)
3. During the first inning, Curt made a home run. (adv.)
4. With great speed Stephanie walked nervously past the old house. (adv.; adv.)
5. In the cave we searched for unusual crystals. (adv.; adv.)
6. The decision will affect many areas within the city. (adj.)
7. Leon found Hissy, his pet snake, in the kitchen. (app.; adv.)
8. The Choy family has moved into the new house with a two-car garage. (adv.; adj.)
9. This tree, a large oak, expels approximately seven gallons of water through its leaves in one day. (app.; adj.; adv.; adv.)
10. I painted the walls blue, my favorite of all colors. (app.; adj.)
11. Mrs. Gellar, the woman with all the cats, adopted a new kitten. (app.; adj.)
12. The reports in this basket have not been graded yet. (adj.)
13. The table in the southwest corner of the lunchroom is my favorite table. (adj.; adj.)
14. Mr. Richard Moon, the new language arts teacher, seems interesting. (app.)
15. This container of sandwiches should be taken to the party. (adj.; adv.)

Identifying Phrases

Write each phrase. Then write the word the phrase modifies or describes.

1. A private company started the Pony Express, a mail delivery system, in 1860. Pony Express/started
2. The company established a network of relay stations that were ten or fifteen miles apart. network
3. Pony Express riders carried United States mail by horseback between California and Missouri. carried/carried
4. At each station a rider transferred mail to a fresh horse. transferred/transferred
5. Each of the riders rode three horses. Each
6. Then a new rider at the next station took over. rider
7. The usual time for delivery, eight days, was not cheap. time/time
8. The cost of the service was very high. cost
9. The Pony Express lasted for only eighteen months. lasted
10. The completion of a faster delivery method, the first transcontinental telegraph line, abruptly ended the service. completion/method

Using Phrases

Write five sentences that follow the directions below. (The sentences may come in any order.) Write about one of the following topics or a topic of your own choice: how you earn money or how you would like to earn money.

Write a sentence that . . .

1. includes an adjective phrase.
2. includes an adverb phrase.
3. includes an introductory adverb phrase.
4. includes an appositive.
5. includes an appositive phrase.

When you have finished, underline and label each phrase. Then check for the correct punctuation of each sentence.

Sample Answers for *Using Phrases:*

1. A job in the world of music (adj.) is my dream.
2. I will work with the latest songs (adv.) from the best bands (adj.).
3. During my career (adv.) I will meet band members in person (adv.).
4. I already know everything about the job's subject matter (adj.), music (app.).
5. My ideal job, a disc jockey position (app.), is waiting in my future (adv.).

Using *Language and Self-Expression*

Consider using this writing assignment to assess students' ability to use phrases and appositives correctly and effectively. You may want students to complete the assignment as part of a persuasive writing strand for their portfolios.

Prewriting

Suggest that students revisit their analysis of the painting that they did in *Making Visual Connections* on page L188.

Tell students that reading magazines or journals with expertise in the area of their topic will help students in the prewriting stage. For example, students might research information on their topic in *National Geographic* or *Audubon* magazines. Researching will provide them with new information and additional ideas as they focus on their topic.

FOR YOUR INFORMATION

About the Artist

Pablo Picasso painted *The Tragedy* during his Blue Period (1901–1904), during which he used shades of blue to paint images of beggars and lonely people. This period was followed by his Rose Period (1905–1906), when he painted images of circus performers in shades of pink. Although he used warmer colors, these paintings continued to reflect a sense of isolation.

Language and *Self-Expression*

Pablo Picasso often used art to show feelings and emotions. As writers do, he created scenes that would engage viewers and compel them to study the work for clues to its meaning. What aspect of *The Tragedy* attracts your interest most?

Write an informative article for your school newspaper about a tragedy or serious problem that you believe deserves public awareness. It could be an environmental issue, such as endangered animals, scarce natural resources, or a hazardous area of your town or city. It could be a problem involving people you know or that you have heard about in the news. As you write, use prepositional phrases and appositive phrases to make your writing accurate and descriptive.

Prewriting Write your topic at the top of a piece of paper. Underneath, brainstorm answers to these questions: *Who? What? When? Where? Why? How?*

Drafting Write a draft of your article. Use the first paragraph to give an overview of the situation and the body paragraphs to explain it. The final paragraph could either call your readers to action or tell them where to get more information.

Revising Check your article for organization. Does each paragraph have a clear topic sentence? Does every sentence support or explain the topic sentence? Be sure to use a variety of phrases to make your writing come alive.

Editing Be sure that you have punctuated the appositive phrases correctly. Also perform your usual checks for correct spelling and capitalization.

Publishing Write a final copy for your English teacher. Submit another copy to your school newspaper.

Another Look

Phrases

An **adjective** is a word that modifies or describes a noun or a pronoun.

An **adverb** is a word that modifies or describes a verb, an adjective, or an adverb.

A **phrase** is a group of words that acts like a single part of speech. It does not have a subject or a verb.

Prepositional Phrases

A **prepositional phrase** is a group of words that begins with a preposition, ends with a noun or pronoun, and is used as an adjective or adverb. *(page L189)*

An **adjective phrase** is a prepositional phrase that is used to modify a noun or a pronoun. An adjective phrase answers the question *Which one?* or *What kind?* just as a single adjective does. *(pages L190–L192)*

An **adverb phrase** is a prepositional phrase that is mainly used to modify a verb. An adverb phrase usually answers the question *Where? When?* or *How?* just as a single adverb does. *(pages L195–L197)*

Appositives and Appositive Phrases

An **appositive** is a noun or a pronoun that identifies or explains another noun or pronoun in the sentence. *(page L201)*

When an appositive has modifiers, it is called an **appositive phrase.** *(page L201)*

Punctuation of Phrases

Punctuating adverb phrases *(page L197)*

Punctuating appositives and appositive phrases *(page L201–L202)*

Other Information About Phrases

Recognizing common prepositions *(page L189)*

Recognizing misplaced modifiers *(page L194)*

Using *Another Look*

Another Look summarizes the terms defined in the chapter and provides cross-references to the specific pages on which they are explained. Consider having students use this feature prior to completing **CheckPoint** or taking the post-test. Students who can provide several examples of each term should be able to score well on either measurement.

Using the Posttest

Assessing Learning

The posttest will help you and your students assess where they stand in their ability to identify and use prepositional phrases, appositives, and appositive phrases.

IDENTIFYING COMMON STUMBLING BLOCKS

Following are the most common errors students make when using phrases and appositives.

Problem

- Misplaced modifiers

Solution

- For reteaching, use the explanatory copy printed in blue beside the examples on page L194.

Problem

- Lack of commas with long introductory adverb phrases

Solution

- For reteaching, use the chart on page L197.

Directions

Write the letter of the word that the underlined phrase modifies or describes.

EXAMPLE **1.** For over 35 years Jane Goodall, an animal behaviorist (1), studied chimpanzees.

1 **A** studied
B Jane Goodall
C years
D chimpanzees

ANSWER **1** **B**

The scientist Jane Goodall was born in London (1) in 1934. In her twenties she began her life's work, the study of animals (2). She booked passage to Africa and began assisting an anthropologist, the now-famous Louis Leakey (3). She later established a field camp in the Gombe Stream Game Reserve (4). Goodall's subject of study, chimpanzees (5), became the focus of her life's work. During her years there (6), she made numerous significant observations about the behavior (7) of chimpanzees (8). They make sounds that are like language. They hunt, and they engage in warfare (9). Interestingly, chimpanzees also experience awe at natural wonders (10) like waterfalls.

A DIFFERENT DELIVERY SYSTEM

If you prefer, you can print the posttest from the BK English Test Bank located at http://www.bkenglish.com.

1 A Jane Goodall
B was born
C 1934
D scientist

2 A life's
B work
C began
D twenties

3 A assisting
B Africa
C passage
D anthropologist

4 A established
B She
C camp
D field

5 A subject
B Goodall's
C became
D focus

6 A she
B there
C made
D observataions

7 A significant
B observations
C chimpanzees
D made

8 A behavior
B observations
C made
D about

9 A hunt
B make
C engage
D they

10 A experience
B chimpanzees
C Interestingly
D awe

Customizing the Test

Use these questions to add or replace items for alternate versions of the test.

Jane Goodall wrote numerous books about her fascinating studies (11) of chimpanzees. One book, *The Chimpanzees of Gombe: Patterns of Behavior*, (12) was published in 1986. It summarizes a good deal of her work (13). Goodall also appeared occasionally on television shows (14). She became one of the foremost role models for young scientists (15) in the field.

11. A numerous
B Jane Goodall
C wrote
D books

12. A was
B published
C One
D book

13. A deal
B summarizes
C It
D good

14. A appeared
B Goodall
C occasionally
D also

15. A became
B models
C field
D foremost

TEACHING SUGGESTIONS

BLOCK SCHEDULING

- If your schedule requires that you cover the chapter in a **shorter time,** use the instruction on participles, gerunds, and infinitives and the Check Your Understanding and QuickCheck exercises.
- If you want to take advantage of **longer class time,** add these applications to writing: Connect to the Writing Process and Apply to Writing exercises.

Essential Knowledge and Skills

- Connnecting his/her own experiences, information, insights, and ideas with the experiences of others through speaking and listening
- Writing to inform such as to explain, describe, report, and narrate
- Writing to entertain such as to compose humorous poems or short stories
- Editing drafts for specific purposes such as to ensure standard usage, varied sentence structure, and appropriate word choice
- Responding in constructive ways to others' writing
- Evaluating how different media forms influence and inform

CHAPTER 8

Verbals and Verbal Phrases

Pretest

Directions

Write the letter of the term that correctly identifies the underlined word or words in each sentence.

EXAMPLE **1.** The Rhine River, flowing through western Europe, is like a road.

1 A prepositional phrase
B gerund phrase
C participial phrase
D infinitive phrase

ANSWER **1 C**

1. Our plans include crossing the Rio Grande.
2. I have learned to find many rivers on maps.
3. The Mississippi River flows from Minnesota to the Gulf of Mexico.
4. Stretching for 210 miles, the Thames is in England.
5. Find the flowing Congo River in Africa.
6. The Congo, known also as the Zaire, is very long.
7. To call the Missouri "Big Muddy" is to use its nickname.
8. Roaring, the waters of Niagara Falls crash down.
9. It is easy to find the Nile River on a map of Africa.
10. Many national parks are next to the Colorado River.

IDENTIFYING COMMON STUMBLING BLOCKS

Following is a list of the most common errors students make when using participles, gerunds, and infinitives.

Problem
- Misplaced participial phrases

Solution
- Instruction, p. L225
- Practice, p. L226

Problem
- Confusing gerunds with participles

Solution
- Instruction, p. L228
- Practice, p. L229

1 A prepositional phrase
B gerund phrase
C participial phrase
D infinitive phrase

2 A prepositional phrase
B gerund phrase
C participial phrase
D infinitive phrase

3 A prepositional phrase
B gerund phrase
C participial phrase
D infinitive phrase

4 A prepositional phrase
B gerund phrase
C participial phrase
D infinitive phrase

5 A gerund
B verb
C participial phrase
D participle

6 A prepositional phrase
B nonessential phrase
C essential phrase
D infinitive phrase

7 A prepositional phrase
B gerund phrase
C participial phrase
D infinitive phrase

8 A verb
B participle
C gerund
D participial phrase

9 A prepositional phrase
B gerund phrase
C participial phrase
D infinitive phrase

10 A prepositional phrase
B gerund phrase
C participial phrase
D infinitive phrase

A DIFFERENT DELIVERY SYSTEM

If you prefer, you can print the pretest from the BK English Test Bank located at http://www.bkenglish.com.

Using the Pretest

Assessing Prior Knowledge

The pretest will help you and your students assess where they stand in their basic understanding of participles, gerunds, and infinitives. The test measures students' ability to identify these elements and to use them correctly in their own writing.

Customizing the Test

Use these questions to add or replace items for alternate versions of the test.

11. To raft on the Colorado River is a desire of mine.

12. This map shows the Jordan River emptying into the Dead Sea.

13. Standing on the banks of the Mississippi, I watched a barge go by.

14. River water flows by gravity from one point to another.

11. A prepositional phrase
B gerund phrase
C participial phrase
D infinitive phrase

12. A prepositional phrase
B gerund phrase
C participial phrase
D infinitive phrase

13. A prepositional phrase
B gerund phrase
C participial phrase
D infinitive phrase

14. A prepositional phrase
B gerund phrase
C participial phrase
D infinitive phrase

ADDITIONAL RESOURCES

Language Skills Practice . . . . pages 66–75
Transparency Tools AW7, AW8
ESL Practice and Test Preparation . . . . . pages 106–108
Assessment: Chapter Test. . . . . pages 149–155

MAKING VISUAL CONNECTIONS

For Language Development

Discuss the name of the painting *Pictograph.* Ask students the following questions. Why do you think this artwork was given this particular name? Who do you think named the cave painting? What do you think the artist was trying to express in this work? Discuss students' responses.

To Stimulate Writing

Use the questions for art criticism as writing or discussion prompts.

Possible Answers:

Describe I recognize images of animals: horses, buffalo, and bison with horns. The artist used clear simple lines filled with varying degrees of shading; heavy shading is used to add emphasis to the horses' heads.

Analyze The unity of the artwork comes from the use of the same lines and shading throughout the whole painting. The simple use of line helps to achieve the unity because it keeps the images from getting too complicated, and no image is able to dominate the entire painting.

Interpret The theme of the work is probably hunting. I would title the painting *Images from the Hunt.*

Judge The images of horses and buffalo and the theme of hunting tell me that the artist values hunting for food. Hunting may be the most time-consuming and the most important activity of the day in this culture. I would display this painting in my dining room or in a nice restaurant.

Artist unknown, *Pictograph,* ca. 30,000 B.C.
Chauvet Grotto, France.

Describe What images do you recognize in the painting? In what way has the artist used line and color to create these images?

Analyze How does the artist create a sense of unity among so many images? Which artistic element seems the most important in achieving this unity? Why do you think so?

Interpret What is a possible theme for this work? If you gave the work a title based on its theme, what would you call it?

Judge What do the painting's images and theme tell you about the artist's culture and interests? If you displayed this artwork somewhere other than a museum, where would you put it? Do you think a written report would better communicate these details than the pictograph? Why or why not?

At the end of this chapter, you will use the artwork to stimulate ideas for writing.

FOR DEVELOPING LANGUAGE SKILLS

LESSON 1 *(pages L217–L226)*

OBJECTIVES

- **To identify and use participles and participial phrases**
- **To distinguish between participles and verbs**
- **To use participles and participial phrases accurately and effectively in writing**

Create Interest

Review the function of adjectives with students. Then tell them that participles help to add interest to a sentence, just as adjectives do. Participles also

Participles and Participial Phrases

A **verbal** looks like a verb. In fact, it is a verb form, but it acts like another part of speech—such as an adjective or a noun.

The following examples show the verbals *waiting* and *broken*. *Waiting* is a form of the verb *wait*. *Broken* is a form of the verb *break*. However, in the following sentences they act like adjectives, not verbs. Verbals that act like adjectives are called participles.

She helped the **waiting** customer.

The workers threw away the **broken** boxes.

There are three kinds of verbals: participles, gerunds, and infinitives. Often these verbals are linked with related words to form **verbal phrases.** Because all verbals are verb forms, they can add energy and liveliness to your writing.

A **participle** is a verb form that is used as an adjective.

The two forms of a participle are **present participles** and **past participles**. Present participles always end in *-ing*. Past participles usually end in *-ed* or *-d*. Some, however, have irregular endings, such as *-n, -t,* or *-en*.

VERB	PRESENT PARTICIPLE	PAST PARTICIPLE
look	looking	looked
fade	fading	faded
talk	talking	talked

FOR INCREASING STUDENT ACHIEVEMENT

REACHING ALL STUDENTS

Struggling Learners

To help students differentiate between participles and verbs, direct them to focus on the *function* of the word in the sentence and not on how the word *looks.* Tell students that participles look like verbs, but they do not serve the same purpose, or function. Have students identify the participles in the following sentence and explain why they are not verbs.

- Exhausted and bewildered, the Roanoke settlers finally ended their frightening voyage. (Exhausted, bewildered, frightening)

describe or tell the reader more about a particular noun or pronoun. Have students complete the following sentences, filling in each blank with a word ending in *-ing, -ed, -d, -n, -t,* or *-en.* Then have other students choose different words to complete the sentences. Discuss students' choices. Tell students that the words they supplied are participles.

- The ▒ mathematician rattled off the formula. (learned, fascinating, exciting, inspiring)
- This formula led to a (an) ▒ medical cure. (astounding, needed, proven)

Guide Instruction

By Modeling Strategies

Show students how to identify and use participial phrases by combining sentences. Write the following example on the board. Demonstrate how to combine the sentences by using a participle.

A DIFFERENT APPROACH

Auditory

Have a student read the first sentence in **Practice Your Skills** aloud and identify the participle. Discuss the correct response and how the participle was identified. Have students take turns reading each sentence aloud and modeling the strategies they use to identify participles. Then have students take turns reading the sentences, leaving out the participles. Students should comment on the sentences' effectiveness without the participles.

tear	tearing	torn
send	sending	sent

PRESENT PARTICIPLE	Everyone enjoys the **challenging** work.
PAST PARTICIPLES	The mathematician's **framed** diploma was a **prized** possession.

Like an adjective, a participle modifies a noun or a pronoun. Also like an adjective, it answers the question *Which one?* or *What kind?*

WHICH ONE?	The **humming** computer filled the air with sound.
	The **crowded** table is filled with reports.
WHAT KIND?	The **interesting** problem will be solved quickly.
	The **ruined** shipment must be replaced.

PRACTICE YOUR SKILLS

Check Your Understanding

Recognizing Participles

Mathematics Topic

Write each participle.

1. A New York City trucking company makes regular shipments to Boston, Hartford, Portland, and Albany.

2. The company's pressing problem is to find the best and safest routes.

- Nick concentrated on the math problem.
- He finally figured it out. (Concentrating on the math problem, Nick finally figured it out.)

Point out the participial phrase. (Concentrating on the math problem) Have students create additional examples.

Consolidate Skills

Through Guided Practice

The **Check Your Understanding** exercises will help students identify and use participles and participial phrases. Direct students to read each sentence in the exercises carefully and to remember that participles and participial phrases function as adjectives.

Complete the first item in each exercise together. Allow time for students to discuss any difficulties they might be having. Then have students complete the exercises independently.

3. The puzzled manager knows the driving distances between each pair of cities.
4. The manager interviews each experienced driver.
5. A young woman steps forward with a sharpened pencil.
6. The smiling driver asks for an atlas, some paper, and a ruler.
7. Let's make a map that shows the connected cities.
8. First, draw a point on the page for each of the designated cities.
9. Then draw lines between the scattered dots.
10. We can add together the lengths of the edges and find the solution to the confusing problem.

Check Your Understanding

Finding the Words Participles Describe

Mathematics Topic **Write each participle. Then write the word or words it modifies.**

11. My math teacher made an amazing statement. statement
12. Geometry is a needed skill for people of all ages. skill
13. Children play with building blocks. blocks
14. The differing shapes teach them about the world. shapes
15. Julie stacked many varied wood blocks as a child. blocks
16. Experienced architects and builders combine shapes in their structures. architects, builders
17. Cooks use a variety of different shapes in their baked goods. goods
18. Scientists study the shapes of living things. things
19. Her moving words inspired me. words
20. Dedicated teachers can make geometry fun. teachers

USING STUDENTS' STRENGTHS

Multiple Intelligences: Linguistic

After completing items eleven through twenty in **Check Your Understanding,** have students use a thesaurus to substitute the original participles in each sentence for new ones that would still make sense. Have students take turns writing their responses on the board. Discuss students' various responses.

HOME WORK

Have students write five sentences with participles. Students should then rewrite the same sentences without participles. Have students share their completed home work assignments with the class the following day.

Apply to Communication

Through Independent Writing

The **Communicate Your Ideas/Apply to Writing** activity on page L224 prompts students to write a historical narrative about the Roanoke colonists' disappearance. Students' stories should contain participles and participial phrases. In the prewriting stage, have students brainstorm some participles that would make their writing more intriguing and interesting.

Transfer to Everyday Life

Identifying Participles and Participial Phrases in History

Have students find examples of participles and participial phrases in passages from their history textbook or other historical texts in the library. Encourage students to read passages about the Roanoke settlers when

COMMON STUMBLING BLOCKS

Problem

- Distinguishing a participle from a verb

Solution

- Read the section on this page that demonstrates the difference between participles and verbs. Tell students that verbs *are* a part of speech, while participles only *serve as* a part of speech. Participles can be thought of as "disguised" verbs acting as adjectives.
- Have students rewrite the following sentences, changing the participles into verbs or verb phrases.

  I was motivated by my inspiring teacher.

  She showed me how to improve my disappointing grades.

Participle or Verb?

A participle is formed from a verb, but it cannot be used alone as a verb. To act as a verb, a participle needs a helping verb before it.

PARTICIPLE	Everyone clapped for the **prancing** horses.
VERB	The horses **were prancing** across the ring.
PARTICIPLE	The **banging** door was very noisy.
VERB	The door **was banging** all day.

PRACTICE YOUR SKILLS

Check Your Understanding

Distinguishing Between Participles and Verbs

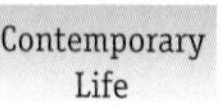

Contemporary Life

Write each underlined word. Then label each one as either *P* for participle or *V* for verb.

1. The writing [P] teacher made an assignment.
2. The class members are writing [V] furiously.
3. The whole class is working [V] on the same story.
4. One student writes about a working [P] actress.
5. At first, the actress likes the long auditioning [P] sessions.
6. She is auditioning [V] with hundreds of other actors.
7. Is her confidence suffering [V] as the acting parts go to others?
8. She did not deliver a suffering [P] performance.
9. Someday, she will not be standing [V] in line for parts.
10. She will win standing [P] ovations.

searching for their participles. Have students share their three favorite participles or participial phrases with the class.

Pull It All Together

By Summarizing

Have students summarize the definitions and functions of participles and participial phrases. Students should write out their responses and provide sentences with two examples of each term.

Check Understanding

Using Participles in Sentences

Have students use their imaginations to write five sentences containing participles. Write some of students' sentences on the board. Have students come to the board and underline the participles in each sentence.

Participial Phrases

Because a participle is a verb form, it has some of the features of a verb. It can have one or more complements. In addition, it can be modified by an adverb or an adverb phrase. A participle and any modifiers or complements form a participial phrase.

A **participial phrase** is a participle with its modifiers and complements—all working together as an adjective.

PARTICIPLE WITH AN ADVERB	The **very daring** explorers headed to the Americas.
PARTICIPLE WITH A PREPOSITIONAL PHRASE	Early settlers, **hoping for new lives,** soon followed.
PARTICIPLE WITH A COMPLEMENT	**Risking life and limb,** they left their homeland.

PUNCTUATION WITH PARTICIPIAL PHRASES

A participial phrase that comes at the beginning of a sentence is always followed by a comma.

Listening carefully, the colonists learned from the native people.

Participial phrases in the middle or at the end of a sentence may or may not need commas. If the information in the phrase is essential to the meaning of the sentence, no commas are needed. Information is essential if it identifies a person, place, or thing in the sentence.

If the information in a participial phrase is not essential to the sentence, commas must separate it from

REACHING ALL STUDENTS

English Language Learners

Remind students that phrases are groups of words that work together, but that do not express a complete thought, as a complete sentence does. Phrases might contain a subject and a verb, but they do not express a complete thought. Point out that participial phrases contain participles and do not express a complete thought. Have students use their literature books to identify three participial phrases.

REACHING ALL STUDENTS

Struggling Learners

Remind students that nonessential phrases, whether appositive or participial, require commas to separate them from the essential parts of a sentence. As with nonessential appositive phrases studied previously, direct students to consider a nonessential participial phrase as separated from the rest of the sentence by commas because it is not needed. Have students explain how they will determine whether commas should be used with participial phrases.

A DIFFERENT APPROACH

Visual

Complete items one through twenty of **Practice Your Skills** together as a whole-group activity. Have students write their responses on the board. Discuss students' responses and the correct use of commas with each participial phrase. For items eleven through twenty, have students also identify the part of speech of each word that is modified by a participial phrase.

the rest of the sentence. A participial phrase is not essential if it can be removed without changing the meaning of the sentence.

Essential	The crops **growing in that field** must be harvested. (Commas are not needed because the participial phrase is needed to identify which crops must be harvested.)
Nonessential	The corn, **growing ever taller,** will probably be sweet. (Commas are needed because the participial phrase could be removed from the sentence without changing the meaning: *The corn will probably be sweet.*)

To learn more about essential and nonessential phrases, see pages L201–L202.

Practice Your Skills

Check Your Understanding

Finding Participial Phrases

History Topic **Write each participial phrase. Then underline the participle.**

1. Remembering the thirteen colonies, most people think of the English as the early settlers of North America.

2. In the 1500s, Spanish conquistadors, searching for treasure, began the exploration of North America.
3. Finding gold and silver, the Spanish settled in the Americas even earlier than the English.

4. The city of St. Augustine, located on Florida's Atlantic coast, was a certain success.

5. Founded in 1564, St. Augustine became the oldest Spanish settlement of the United States.

6. The settlement, surrounded by a wooden fence, was a safe place for early settlers.

7. Later, the settlement had many streets lined with houses and stores.

8. Giving up its claim to Florida, Spain turned St. Augustine over to the English.

9. Refusing the English ways, many residents kept their Spanish customs.

10. Today many visitors searching for information about the past tour St. Augustine.

Check Your Understanding

Recognizing Participial Phrases as Modifiers

History Topic **Write each participial phrase. Then write the word it modifies.**

11. Have you been to Roanoke Island, located off the coast of North Carolina? Roanoke Island

12. In 1587, a band of English colonists, led by John White, settled there. band

13. The 117 colonists, including 17 women and 9 children, faced difficult winters. colonists

14. John White's daughter gave birth to a baby girl named Virginia Dare. girl

15. Seeking supplies and more colonists, John White sailed to England. John White

16. Delayed for three years, the Englishman found the island empty on his return. Englishman

HOME WORK

Have students create a map or 3-D representation of St. Augustine, based on the information provided in items one through ten. Students can choose the medium for their renderings. Encourage students to use various materials in their representations. Have students comment on the role of the participles in the sentences in helping them complete the project.

YOUR IDEAS

For Teaching Participial Phrases

TIMESAVER *QuickCheck*

Have students exchange their completed historical narratives with a partner. Partners should evaluate the narratives according to correct use of participles and participial phrases. Students should also check for correct use of commas with participial phrases.

HOME STUDY

Have students find out more about the mystery of the vanishing Roanoke Island settlers. Students should use primary and secondary source materials at the library to complete their assignments. Have students create five questions in the prewriting stage to direct their research. Students should present their reports to the class.

17. The only clue was the word *Croatoan* carved on a gatepost. word

18. White set out for that island, located about one hundred miles to the south. island

19. Sweeping into the area, a bad storm kept White on Roanoke Island instead. storm

20. Roanoke Island, deserted by the colonists, never offered further clues about their disappearance. Roanoke Island

Connect to the Writing Process: Prewriting

Writing Sentences with Participial Phrases

[Answers may vary. Possible responses are given.]

Use each of the following participial phrases to write a sentence about what you think may have happened to the Roanoke colonists. Be sure to use commas correctly.

21. Searching for food , the colonists wandered far from their settlement.

22. Hidden from sight , the Indians watched the colonists.

23. Seeking a clue , John White sailed to Croatoan Island.

24. Running swiftly , the Indians escaped White's men.

25. Locked in a steel-like grip , the colonists' leader was unable to break free.

Communicate Your Ideas

APPLY TO WRITING

Historical Narrative: ***Participial Phrases***

Using one or more of your sentences from the preceding exercise, write a story about what you think happened to the Roanoke colonists. Remember to end your story with a deserted island, as in the actual story. Use participial phrases to add vivid images to the story. Underline the participles and participial phrases you used.

Misplaced Participial Phrases

In the last chapter, you learned that an adjective phrase placed too far from the word it modifies is called a **misplaced modifier.** Since a participial phrase acts like an adjective, it also becomes a misplaced modifier if it is placed too far from the word it describes.

The travel agent called the people **looking for a hotel in Williamsburg.**

(A reader might think that in this sentence the people are looking for a hotel.)

Looking for a hotel in Williamsburg, the travel agent called the people.

(In this sentence the travel agent, not the people, is looking for a hotel.)

These examples have different meanings, but both make sense. Some misplaced modifiers, however, result in misunderstanding or even silliness—such as the following example.

MISPLACED MODIFIER	**Hanging on the wall of the old house in Williamsburg,** Ben saw a beautiful painting. (This sentence suggests that Ben, not the painting, was hanging on the wall.)

To correct a misplaced modifier, first decide what the intended meaning of the sentence is. Then find the word that should be modified. Place the phrase near that word.

CORRECT MODIFIER	Ben saw a beautiful painting **hanging on the wall of the old house in Williamsburg.** (Now the participial phrase is close to the word it is describing.)

GETTING STUDENTS INVOLVED

Cooperative Learning

After discussing misplaced modifiers, have students work with partners to create their own humorous sentences that contain misplaced participial phrases. Have partners take turns reading their sentences aloud. Then have other students tell how they would correct the misplaced modifiers.

YOUR IDEAS

For Teaching Misplaced Modifiers

A DIFFERENT APPROACH

Auditory

After students have completed **Practice Your Skills** independently, discuss the words that each correctly placed participial phrase modifies. Remind students that misplaced participial phrases modify the incorrect word. Discuss students' responses.

HOME WORK

Have students find five examples of sentences that contain misplaced participial phrases in newspapers, magazines, or their own writing. Students should write out each example and correct the errors.

PRACTICE YOUR SKILLS

Check Your Understanding

Identifying Misplaced Participial Phrases

General Interest **Write each participial phrase. Beside each phrase, write *C* if it is placed correctly or *I* if it is placed incorrectly.**

Walking around Williamsburg, Virginia, many people enjoy the sights.

1. ~~Many people enjoy the sights walking around Williamsburg, Virginia.~~ I

The tourists are seeking a glimpse of the past dating back to the 1770s.

2. ~~Dating back to the 1770s, the tourists are seeking a glimpse of the past.~~ I

Wearing authentic costumes, inhabitants of the old town reenact eighteenth-century life.

3. ~~Inhabitants of the old town reenact eighteenth-century life wearing authentic costumes.~~ I

Amateur historians can visit a variety of homes and shops made with logs and mortar.

4. ~~Made with logs and mortar, amateur historians can visit a variety of homes and shops.~~ I

5. They can smell bread baking in old ovens. C

The visitors can see colonial women working ancient looms by hand.

6. ~~Working ancient looms by hand, the visitors can see colonial women.~~ I

7. Made of cotton, the old-style dresses are not as colorful as today's fashions. C

People go up and down the streets, unpaved with asphalt.

8. ~~Unpaved with asphalt, people go up and down the streets.~~ I

9. Lacking electricity and large windows, the homes are like caves. C

10. ~~The visitors appreciate their cool hotel rooms exhausted after a day in Williamsburg.~~ I

Exhausted after a day in Williamsburg, the visitors appreciate their cool hotel rooms.

Connect to the Writing Process: Revising

Correcting Misplaced Participial Phrases

11.–17. Rewrite the incorrect sentences from the preceding exercise so that the misplaced participial phrases are placed correctly.

[Answers may vary. See possible responses given above.]

LESSON 2 *(pages L227–L232)*

OBJECTIVES

- **To identify gerunds and gerund phrases**
- **To distinguish between gerunds and participles**
- **To use gerunds accurately and effectively in writing**

Create Interest

Put the following quotation on the board and underline the gerund. Tell students that gerunds function as nouns. Have students create two additional examples of sentences containing gerunds.

"Shouting on the ball field never helped anyone except where it was one player calling to another to take the catch."

—Gil Hodges, former Dodgers baseball player

Gerunds and Gerund Phrases

Another verbal is a gerund. Like a present participle, a gerund also ends in *-ing*. However, unlike a participle, a gerund is used as a noun, not as an adjective.

A **gerund** is a verb form that is used as a noun.

A gerund is used in the same ways a noun is used.

SUBJECT	**Hiking** is great exercise. (*Hiking* tells what the sentence is about.)
DIRECT OBJECT	The campers enjoy **hiking.** (What do the campers enjoy? *Hiking* is the direct object.)
INDIRECT OBJECT	My grandparents give **hiking** all their attention. (They give what? *Attention* is the direct object. They give attention to what? *Hiking* is the indirect object.)
OBJECT OF A PREPOSITION	The hardest part of **hiking** is a steep, rocky trail. (*Hiking* is the object of the preposition *of.*)
PREDICATE NOMINATIVE	My brother's favorite activity is **hiking.** (*Hiking* renames the subject *activity.*)
APPOSITIVE	Terry has a new hobby, **hiking.** (*Hiking* identifies the hobby.)

GETTING STUDENTS INVOLVED

Cooperative Learning

Have students work collaboratively to write sentences containing a gerund used as a subject, direct object, indirect object, object of a preposition, predicate nominative, and adjective. One student should write a sentence containing a gerund, and the other student should decide how the gerund functions in the sentence. Partners should then exchange roles and continue the activity until they have written sentences for each type of gerund. Have groups share some of their sentences with the class.

Guide Instruction

By Connecting Ideas

Tell students that gerunds, like all words, must be judged on what they *do* and not on how they *appear.* Point out that gerunds, like participles, might look like verbs. Gerunds are verbals that end in *-ing.* Tell students that they must think about what words ending in *-ing* actually do to determine if they are gerunds or participles. Ask students how the underlined words function in the following sentences:

- Swimming is a good form of exercise. (gerund)
- Many people watched the swimming dolphin. (participle)

Consolidate Skills

Through Guided Practice

The **Check Your Understanding** exercises will help students identify gerunds and gerund phrases. Tell students to use questioning strategies as they complete the exercises. Students should ask themselves "How does this word that ends in *-ing* function in the

A DIFFERENT APPROACH

Kinesthetic

Have students take turns completing **Practice Your Skills** by pantomiming each gerund in items one through ten. First have one student read each sentence aloud. Then have another student pantomime the gerunds. Have students take turns until all of the gerunds have been identified.

HOME WORK

Have students rewrite items one through ten, substituting each gerund for another appropriate gerund. Allow time the following day for students to read some of their revised sentences aloud.

PRACTICE YOUR SKILLS

Check Your Understanding

Finding Gerunds

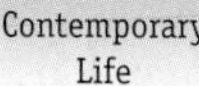

Write each gerund.

1. Exercising makes many people feel younger.
2. Directing is Matthew's passion.
3. The twins' favorite sport is bicycling.
4. Swimming provides hours of enjoyment.
5. More than anything else, Alicia loves dancing.
6. The thrill of skiing is fun for Amanda and Jim.
7. Traveling has always been a favorite activity for the Martinez family.
8. My favorite pastime, skating, is not difficult.
9. Racing is a wonderful sport for participants and observers.
10. The gymnast gives practicing his top priority.

Gerund or Participle?

Because a gerund and a participle both end in *-ing,* it is easy to confuse them. Remember that a gerund is used as a noun, and a participle is used as an adjective.

GERUND — Jessica's **writing** is quite good.

(*Writing* is used as a noun, the subject of the sentence.)

PARTICIPLE — The **writing** lessons were fantastic.

(*Writing* is an adjective that tells what kind of lessons.)

sentence? How is it used?" Practice the first example on page L228 together. Then have students complete the remaining exercises independently.

Apply to Communication

Through Independent Writing

The **Communicate Your Ideas/Apply to Writing** activity on page L232 prompts students to write a museum brochure. Ask students to brainstorm some "museum" gerunds, such as *painting,* that they might use in their writing. List these words on the board for students' future reference in this writing assignment.

Transfer to Everyday Life

Identify Gerunds in Product Directions or Assembly Instructions

Provide students with assembly instructions from a product such as an office chair or bookshelf. You can also provide students with directions for using products, such as appliances or electronics. Have students work with

PRACTICE YOUR SKILLS

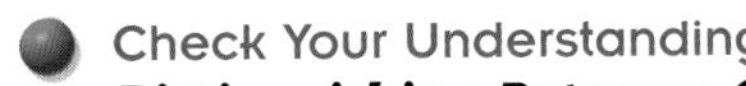

Check Your Understanding

Distinguishing Between Gerunds and Participles

Literature Topic **Write each underlined verbal. Label each one as either a *participle* or a *gerund.***

1. Today's reading assignment was fun.
2. The reading is "The Zodiacs" by Jay Neugeborn.
3. The main character wants a winning baseball team.
4. Winning is the main objective, so he recruits a star pitcher.
5. The pitching star is promised newspaper coverage and new uniforms.
6. The Zodiacs' pitching is excellent, but the hitting is average.
7. George's high batting average wins many games for the team.
8. The Zodiacs' luck runs out, however, when George's batting and pitching go haywire.
9. There is a running joke about George's temper.
10. George's running has improved.

Gerund Phrases

A gerund is often combined with modifiers and complements to form a gerund phrase.

A **gerund phrase** is a gerund with its modifiers and complements—all working together as a noun.

The examples on the following page show how a gerund phrase can be made up of several different groups of words.

REACHING ALL STUDENTS

Struggling Learners

After discussing the difference between gerunds and participles, remind students to focus on the *function* of the word in a sentence and not on the way the word *appears.* Have students tell how gerunds function and how participles function before they continue with the **Practice Your Skills** exercises. Write students' explanations on the board.

HOME WORK

After completing **Practice Your Skills,** have students write two paragraphs about a sports subject in which they are interested. They should include gerunds in their writing. Have students share their paragraphs with the class the next day. Identify and discuss gerunds students used effectively in their writing.

partners to identify at least five gerunds in these instructional materials. Students should write down any gerunds and the sentences in which they appear. Have students share their sentences with the class. Discuss the gerunds and the words they modify.

Pull It All Together

By Sharing

Have students share their museum brochures with the class. After students have shared their brochures, have other students identify the gerunds used in the brochures. List some of the gerunds on the board.

Check Understanding

Identify the Function of Gerunds

Have students identify each gerund and its function in the sentences below. They should label each gerund as functioning as a *subject, direct object, indirect object, object of a pre-*

USING STUDENTS' STRENGTHS

Multiple Intelligences: Linguistic

After discussing gerund phrases, have students explain how they can tell a gerund phrase from a participial phrase. Have students also provide examples of sentences containing each type of phrase. Discuss students' responses and write the most accurate responses on the board along with example sentences.

A DIFFERENT APPROACH

Auditory

Have students take turns reading the sentences in **Check Your Understanding** aloud. Then have other students identify each gerund phrase. Encourage listening students not to look at their textbooks as they listen for each sentence and response. After completing the exercise together, have students work independently to write out their responses.

HOME WORK

Have students find examples of gerund phrases from various sources at home. Encourage students to look in magazines, journals, books, game instructions, computer software, or television programs to find examples of gerund phrases. Have students share their phrases with the class and tell where they found most of the gerund phrases.

GERUND WITH AN ADJECTIVE	Jon's **colorful painting** won him many awards.
GERUND WITH AN ADVERB	**Painting expressively** creates superb results.
GERUND WITH A PREPOSITIONAL PHRASE	I always enjoy **painting on the beach.**
GERUND WITH A COMPLEMENT	**Painting natural scenes** relaxes me.

PRACTICE YOUR SKILLS

Check Your Understanding

Finding Gerund Phrases

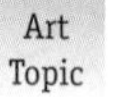

Art Topic **Write each gerund phrase.**

1. Learning about art is important.
2. Some artists enjoy interpreting the world around them.
3. Their understanding of colors is complex.
4. Artists see hues of both warm and cool coloring.
5. Landscape painting requires colors for atmosphere.
6. For example, cool and subtle colors may make for sad or peaceful viewing.
7. Choosing warm colors may attract viewers.
8. Using cool colors relaxes me.
9. Choosing the best colors for a subject is only one of the artist's skills.
10. Painting rapidly may provide only an impression of a subject.

position, predicate nominative, or *appositive.*

- Pitching takes a lot of skill. (subject)
- Jesse practices swimming with a trainer. (direct object)
- He also gives batting a lot of his attention. (indirect object)
- Valerie likes to exercise by swimming. (object of a preposition)
- Neil's favorite pastime is running. (predicate nominative)

Check Your Understanding

Completing Gerund Phrases

Art Topic **Write a gerund that can complete the gerund phrase in each sentence. Then use the following abbreviations to identify the other words in each gerund phrase.**

adjective = *adj.*	adverb = *adv.*
prepositional phrase = *p.p.*	complement = *c.*

11. ▢ the styles of famous artists sometimes helps young painters. (Imitating; c.)

12. Thousands of art students remember ▢ to the city's art museum. (going; p.p.)

13. ▢ pieces of art requires a great deal of attention. (Studying; c.)

14. ▢ through an exhibit is not advisable. (Hurrying; p.p.)

15. ▢ a long visit to an art gallery is a good idea. (Planning; c.)

16. The young artists concentrate on the details of ▢ on the walls. (paintings; p.p.)

17. Some ▢ creates strong feelings in the observer. (adj.; drawing)

18. Sometimes ▢ artwork simply brings back memories. (viewing; c.)

19. Often strong emotions affect clear ▢. (adj.; thinking)

20. ▢ the reason for a choice of subject, color, or setting is also helpful. (Imagining; c.)

21. Walking through a museum of art, many spend time ▢ the artists at work. (c.)

22. Those fascinated by the smooth, flawless surface of a statue might imagine ▢ marble like a sculptor. (imagining; carving; c.)

23. Statues might prompt images of ▢ in bronze. (p.p.; working)

24. Ancient pottery brings to mind visions of ▢ with clay and primitive tools. (p.p.; working)

25. ▢ perfectly is the challenge of every artist. (Creating; adv.)

DEVELOPING WORKPLACE COMPETENCIES

Basic Skills: Speaking

Have students imagine they are the curator of a major art, science, or historical museum. They are giving a speech to prospective employees about the museum, its functions, and its importance in the community. Have students write their speeches, using gerunds and gerund phrases to make their speeches more interesting to prospective employees. Students should present their completed speeches to the class.

TIMESAVER *QuickCheck*

Students might use some of the points they made in their speeches about a museum to make their brochures appealing and inviting. Evaluate students on their effective use of gerunds and gerund phrases and on their ability to focus on their audience, tourists.

Connect to the Writing Process: Prewriting
Writing Sentences with Gerunds and Gerund Phrases

26.–30. Write five sentences about a museum you have been to or heard about in your town or city. Use gerunds or gerund phrases as the subjects of at least three of your sentences. To form a gerund, you simply take an action verb and add *-ing.*

Communicate Your Ideas

APPLY TO WRITING

Museum Brochure: ***Gerunds and Gerund Phrases***

Using the sentences from the previous exercise, write a short brochure to attract tourists to a museum in your town or city. Focus on the exciting activities people might take part in at the museum. Try to write action-packed, vivid sentences to make people want to visit the museum. Be sure to include gerunds and gerund phrases in your writing.

LESSON 3 *(pages L233–L239)*

OBJECTIVES

- **To identify infinitives and infinitive phrases**
- **To distinguish between infinitives and prepositional phrases**
- **To use infinitives accurately and effectively in writing**

Create Interest

Ask students familiar with William Shakespeare's famous "To be, or not to be" soliloquy from *Hamlet* to recite or recall any of the passage with which they are familiar. Explain that the soliloquy contains many infinitives. Have students identify verbs preceded by the word *to* in the following excerpt from *Hamlet.* Point out that these are infinitives.

"To be, or not to be: that is the question: Whether 'tis nobler in the mind to suffer The slings and arrows of outrageous fortune, Or to take arms against a sea of troubles, And by opposing end them? To die:

Infinitives and Infinitive Phrases

The third kind of verbal is the infinitive. Infinitives are usually used as nouns, but can also be used as adjectives or adverbs.

An **infinitive** is a verb form that can be used as a noun, an adjective, or an adverb. The word *to* usually comes before an infinitive.

NOUN

To wait was the only choice during the gasoline shortage.

(*To wait* is the subject. It tells what the sentence is about.)

Jordan plans **to wait.**

(Jordan plans what? *To wait* is the direct object.)

ADJECTIVE

The best time **to wait** was in the morning.

(*To wait* describes *time.*)

Do you have a good reason **to wait?**

(*To wait* modifies *reason.*)

ADVERB

Jordan drove to the back of the line **to wait.**

(*To wait* modifies *drove;* it tells why Jordan drove to the back of the line.)

We always went to the gas station **to wait.**

(*To wait* tells why we went.)

GETTING STUDENTS INVOLVED

Cooperative Learning

After discussing the three types of infinitives, have students work with partners to write a story based on a historical topic. Students should use their history textbooks, the library, and the Internet to search for interesting information about their topic. Tell students that their stories should contain at least ten infinitives. Have partners share their stories with the class. Discuss the infinitives used in students' writing.

To sleep; No more; and, by a sleep
to say we end . . . "
—William Shakespeare, *Hamlet*

Guide Instruction

By Connecting Ideas

Tell students that infinitives, like participles and gerunds, are formed from verbs and are called *verbals.* Point out that infinitives do not function as verbs, but instead function as nouns, adjectives, or adverbs. Have students provide additional examples of each type of infinitive on page L233.

Consolidate Skills

Through Guided Practice

The **Check Your Understanding** exercises will help students identify infinitives and infinitive phrases. Remind students to look for the word *to* preceding verbs and to focus on the function of the words to identify infinitives. Practice the first example on page

A DIFFERENT APPROACH

Visual

Have students come to the board and rewrite the sentences from **Practice Your Skills.** Then have students use another color of chalk to circle each infinitive.

HOME WORK

Have students find out more about the gasoline shortage of the 1970s and write ten sentences containing infinitives. Encourage students to identify the U.S. president serving during this crisis and to discuss how the problem was resolved.

PRACTICE YOUR SKILLS

 Check Your Understanding

Finding Infinitives

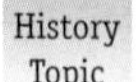

Write each infinitive.

1. In the 1970s, the gasoline shortage showed Americans the need to conserve.
2. Gas stations began to close.
3. Owners had little gasoline to sell.
4. This forced the price of gas to increase.
5. The number of cars on the road began to decrease.
6. People lined up at the pumps for hours to fill up.
7. Most Americans had big cars then, but they learned to conserve.
8. To drive was important for workers.
9. Oil prices were allowed to jump.
10. A new way of life was about to begin.

Infinitive or Prepositional Phrase?

Sometimes infinitives are confused with prepositional phrases that begin with *to*. Remember that an infinitive is the word *to* plus a verb form. A prepositional phrase is the word *to* plus a noun or pronoun.

INFINITIVE	That CD is fun **to play.** (The phrase ends with a verb form, *play*.)
PREPOSITIONAL PHRASE	Please bring the CD **to class.** (The phrase ends with a noun, *class*.)

L234 together. Then have students complete the remaining exercises independently.

Apply to Communication

Through Independent Writing

The **Communicate Your Ideas/Apply to Writing** activity on page L238 prompts students to write directions for a short comic or dramatic scene. Ask students how infinitives will help them in their directions to the actors. List some of students' infinitives on the board for future reference.

Transfer to Everyday Life

Identifying Infinitives in Literature

Have students search for infinitives and infinitive phrases in a work of literature that they have read and enjoyed in the past. If students do not have a copy of the literature, they should retrieve a copy from the library or other source. Direct students to find

PRACTICE YOUR SKILLS

Check Your Understanding

Distinguishing Between Infinitive and Prepositional Phrases

Music Topic **Write each underlined phrase. Then label it *I* for infinitive or *P* for prepositional phrase.**

1. From the age of four, Ludwig van Beethoven used many hours each day to practice. I
2. He went to lessons every day of the week except Sunday. P
3. At age eleven he was encouraged to compose. I
4. He was sent to the royal court to play. I
5. At the royal court, Bach's music became known to him. P
6. In 1792, Beethoven was sent to Vienna. P
7. The plan was for him to study. I
8. After Mozart died, Beethoven went to Haydn for lessons. P
9. Student and teacher started to argue. I
10. Beethoven was forced to stop his lessons. I

Infinitive Phrases

Like the other verbals, an infinitive can be combined with modifiers or complements to form an infinitive phrase.

An **infinitive phrase** is an infinitive with its modifiers and complements—all working together as a noun, an adjective, or an adverb.

An infinitive phrase can be made up of several different combinations of words.

USING STUDENTS' STRENGTHS

Multiple Intelligences: Musical

After completing **Practice Your Skills,** listen to music composed by Beethoven. Ask students to freewrite while they are listening on any topic that pops into their head. Then have students revise the piece, writing carefully with infinitives and prepositional phrases.

A DIFFERENT APPROACH

Kinesthetic

Have students complete **Practice Your Skills** by using their fingers to write the correct response to each sentence. They should identify each infinitive by forming an *I* and identify the prepositions by forming a *P* after each sentence. Discuss students' responses after they have finished.

at least ten sentences containing infinitives or infinitive phrases. Have students share their sentences with the class. Discuss the similarities and differences in students' findings.

Pull It All Together

By Summarizing

Have students summarize what they have learned about participles, gerunds, and infinitives. Students should compare and contrast these types of words and provide examples of each in sentences.

Check Understanding

Defining Infinitives and Infinitive Phrases

Have students write their own definitions for the words *infinitive* and *infinitive phrase.* Students should write example sentences containing infinitives and infinitive phrases. Have students exchange papers with partners

USING TECHNOLOGY

Audio

After discussing infinitive phrases, have students listen to an audio version of a novel and identify infinitives and infinitive phrases. Students should write down and share with class at least five examples of infinitives.

YOUR IDEAS

For Infinitive Phrases

INFINITIVE WITH AN ADVERB	She told us **to read thoughtfully.**
INFINITIVE WITH A PREPOSITIONAL PHRASE	We plan **to read around the clock.**
INFINITIVE WITH A COMPLEMENT	Don't hesitate **to open the book.**

PRACTICE YOUR SKILLS

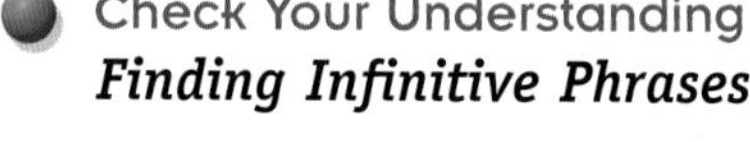

Check Your Understanding

Finding Infinitive Phrases

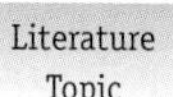

Literature Topic **Write each infinitive phrase.**

1. Many writers use infinitives to write their most famous lines.

2. The main character in Shakespeare's *Hamlet* says, "To be, or not to be; that is the question."

3. "To err is human, to forgive divine" is from Alexander Pope's "An Essay on Criticism."

4. Read the whole work to understand the meaning.

5. Be sure to give credit to the author.

6. I want to find the whole quotation for "ignorance is bliss."

7. You need to check Grey's works for this quotation.

8. To recite a quotation accurately is important.

9. Not all quotations are made to impress people.

10. On his return to Ohio, Senator John Sherman said, "I have come home to look after my fences."

and share their definitions and example sentences. Discuss students' responses as a class.

Check Your Understanding
Adding Infinitives

Contemporary Life

Write each sentence, adding an infinitive that makes sense. [Answers may vary. Possible responses are given.]

11. When were you taken ▢ your first play? to see

12. I'm trying ▢ the year. to see each show of

13. In New York, I had a chance ▢ the world of theater. to learn about

14. ▢ a show on Broadway is a rare treat. To see

15. Alex is ready ▢ his first play. to go to

16. He wants ▢ an interesting play. to see

17. One goal of a comedy is ▢ cheer. to bring

18. In contrast, a drama is meant ▢ a problem. to pose

19. Alex wants ▢ *My Fair Lady* or another musical. to see

20. A musical requires a person ▢ to the lyrics of the songs. to listen

21. The characters begin ▢ their ideas and problems in the lyrics. to voice

22. You must pay close attention ▢ the story. to understand

23. The crystal chandelier in *Phantom of the Opera* is amazing ▢. to see

24. The stage for *Les Miserables* is constructed on revolving sets ▢ the audience both sides of the story. to show

25. Musicals with such dramatic props and sets are sure ▢ Alex. to please

Connect to the Writing Process: Prewriting
Using Infinitives

26.–30. Write five sentences containing infinitives that a director might use in giving directions to an actor.

IDENTIFYING COMMON STUMBLING BLOCKS

Problem

- Split infinitives

Solution

- Tell students that when they write sentences containing infinitives, they should not put any words between the word *to* and the verb in their infinitives or infinitive phrases. Tell students that this sentence contains a split infinitive: *To carefully listen is important when learning a new skill.* The error can be corrected by placing the word *carefully* in another location in the sentence: *To listen carefully is important when learning a new skill.*
- Have students correct these split infinitives:

  I had to loudly speak to the audience.

  The audience was happy to graciously listen.

TIMESAVER *QuickCheck*

Have students create their own checklists to evaluate their comic or dramatic directions writing. Remind students that a key point of the assignment is to use infinitives and infinitive phrases effectively. Have students share their checklists with the class. Discuss the various elements on students' checklists. As a class, decide the checklist students should use to self-evaluate their writing.

Communicate Your Ideas

APPLY TO WRITING

Giving Directions: *Infinitives and Infinitive Phrases*

Try writing a short comic or dramatic scene to share with the class. The scene should have lots of action but no dialogue. Write the directions that the actors should follow as they silently act out the scene. You may use some of your sentences from the preceding exercise. Be sure to use infinitives and infinitive phrases, and be prepared to identify them. Before writing, answer the following questions.

- Who are your characters?
- From what directions do they enter and exit the stage?
- Where should they stand on stage?
- What do you wish for them to express without using words?

Mixed Practice

Art Topic

Write each underlined phrase. Then label each one a *participial phrase,* a *gerund phrase,* or an *infinitive phrase.*

1. Sofonisba Anguissola was to become a famous artist in Spain. infintive phrase

2. Born in the sixteenth century in Italy, she broke new ground. participial phrase

3. Back then, studying school subjects was usually not a part of a young girl's life. gerund phrase

4. The young woman went against the tradition of only boys studying art. gerund phrase

5. Back then, many people thought girls were meant to sew and to be good wives. infintive phrase

6. Like the boys, she learned to draw portraits. infintive phrase

7. Joining the boys in their classes, Anguissola studied many subjects. participial phrase

8. Her father was impressed by a portrait drawn by her. participial phrase

9. The king of Spain asked her to become a painter in his court. infintive phrase

10. She agreed to travel from Italy to Spain. infintive phrase

11. Wanting a portrait of themselves, people came to the new court artist. participial phrase

12. She liked most to paint children. infintive phrase

13. Offering a record of history, Anguissola's art shows how people lived hundreds of years ago. participial phrase

14. Nothing stopped her from becoming an artist. gerund phrase

15. Learning to be an artist helped Anguissola become successful. gerund phrase

EXPANDING THE LESSON

Using Technology

You will find additional **instructional** and **practice** materials for this chapter at http://www.bkenglish.com.

FOR REVIEWING SKILLS

Using *Sentence Diagraming*

Sentence diagraming helps students develop variety and style in their writing. In this activity, students will focus on diagraming sentences containing verbals and verbal phrases.

Sentence Diagraming

Diagraming Verbals and Verbal Phrases

Before diagraming a sentence with a verbal in it, you will have to determine how the verbal is used.

Participial Phrases A participial phrase is diagramed under the word it modifies. It is written in a curve. If the participial phrase has a complement it is diagramed after the participle. A vertical line separates the complement from the participle. A single participle is diagramed exactly the same way as the participle *making* is diagramed below—except that it has no complement or modifiers. The single participles *running* and *untied* are diagramed in the second example below.

Everyone watched the robin **making its nest.**

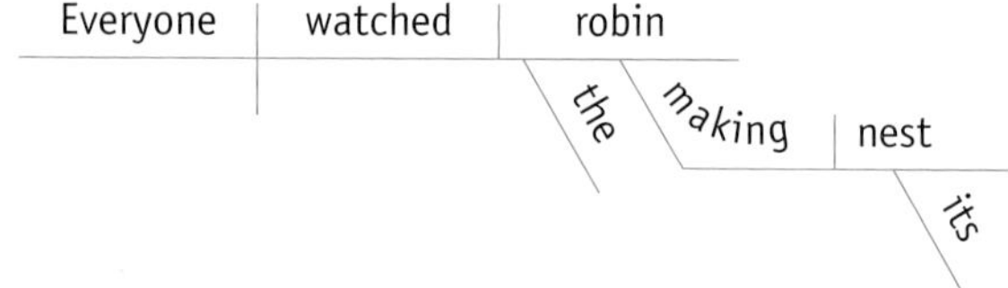

The **running** toddler tripped on his **untied** shoelaces.

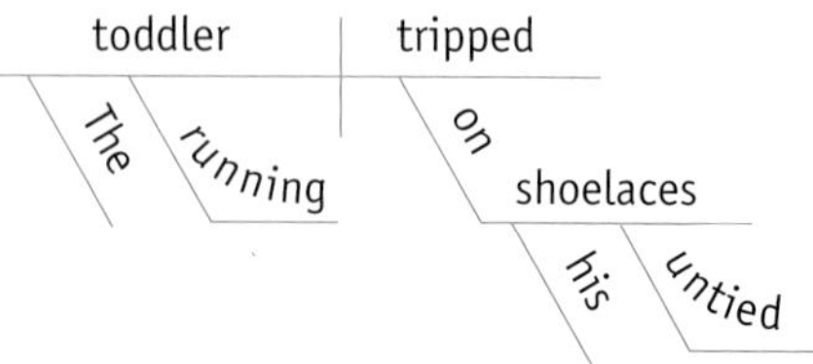

Gerund Phrases Because a gerund phrase is used as a noun, it can be diagramed in any noun position. The first gerund in the example below is used as a subject. Notice that the complement *popcorn* and the prepositional phrase *in a movie theater* are part of the gerund phrase. The second gerund phrase is used as an object of the preposition *of.* A single gerund is diagramed exactly the same way the gerunds *eating* and *enjoying* are diagramed below—except that they have no complements or modifiers. The single gerund *dancing* is diagramed in the second sentence below.

Eating popcorn in a movie theater is an important part of **enjoying the movie.**

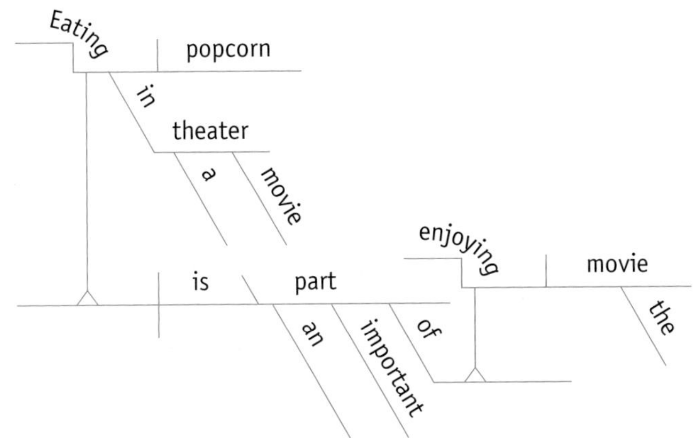

Dancing is a particularly good form of exercise.

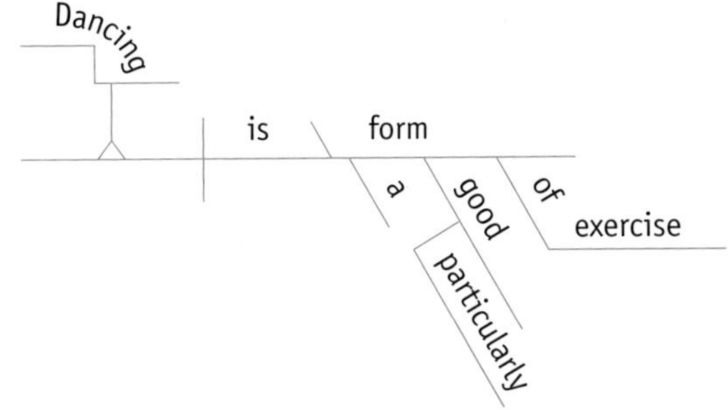

YOUR IDEAS

For Sentence Diagraming

Using *Sentence Diagraming*

Sentence diagraming helps students develop variety and style in their writing. In this activity, students will focus on diagraming adjective phrases, adverb phrases, appositives, and appositive phrases.

Sample Answers for *Sentence Diagraming:*

1. 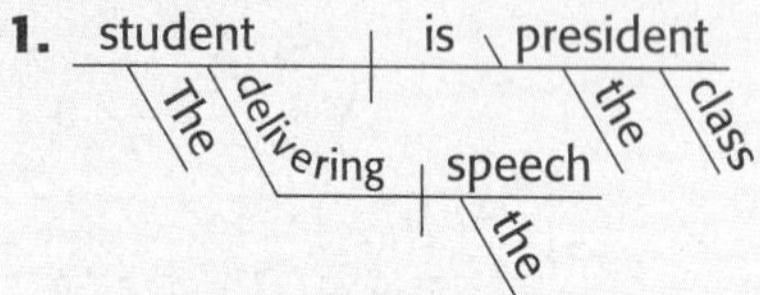

2. 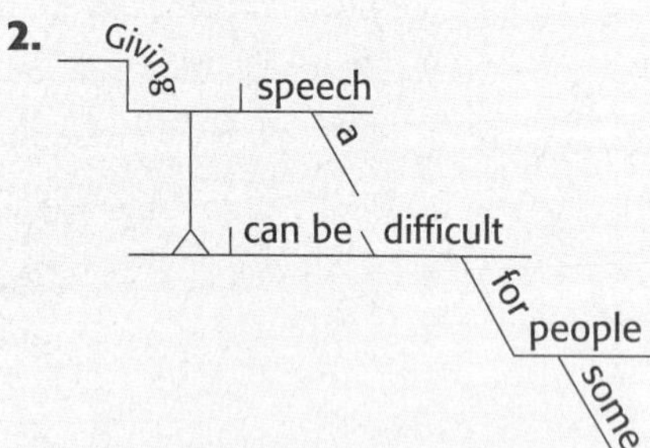

3. 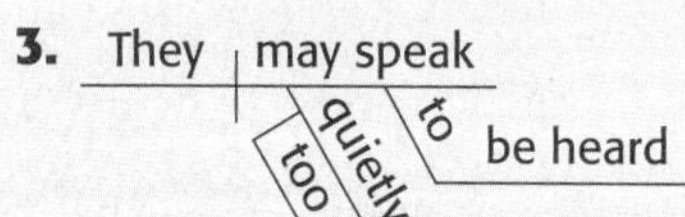

4. 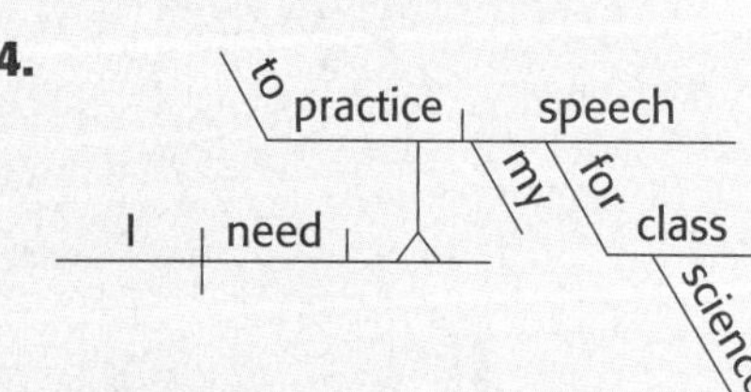

5. 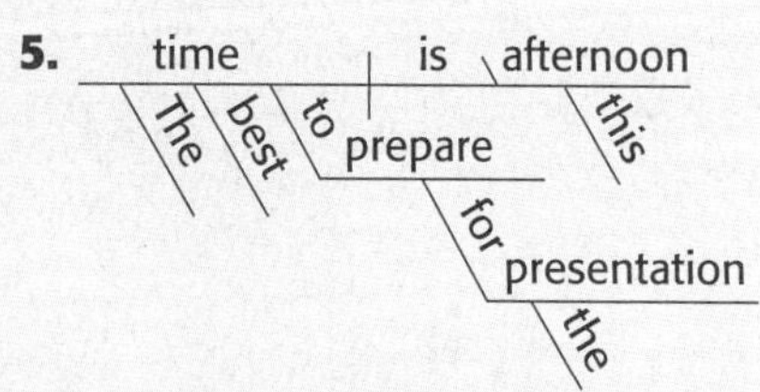

Infinitive Phrases Because an infinitive phrase may be used as an adjective, an adverb, or a noun, it is diagramed in several ways. The infinitive phrase in the first example below is used as a direct object. The infinitive phrase in the second example is used as an adjective. Single infinitives are diagramed exactly the same way *to identify* and *to use* are diagramed below—except that they have no complements or modifiers. The single infinitives *to study* and *to learn* are diagramed in the third example.

For a new badge I need **to identify ten constellations.**

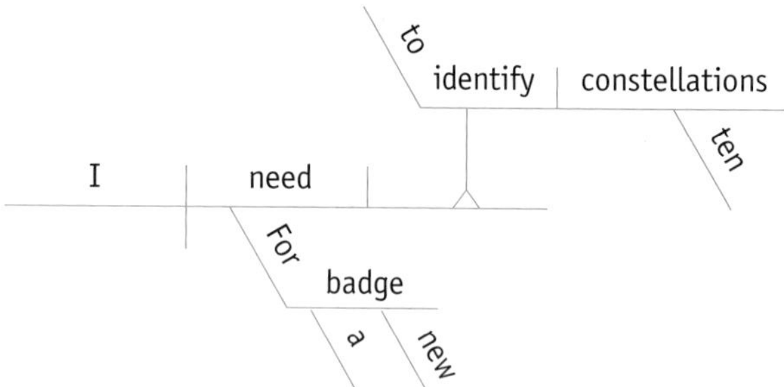

This is the best pencil **to use for the test.**

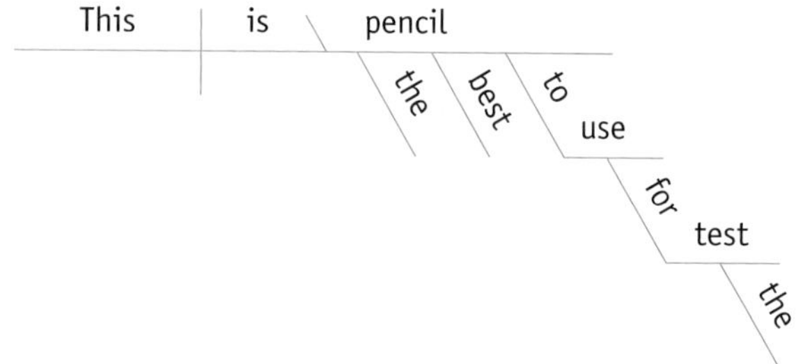

To study might be the only way **to learn.**

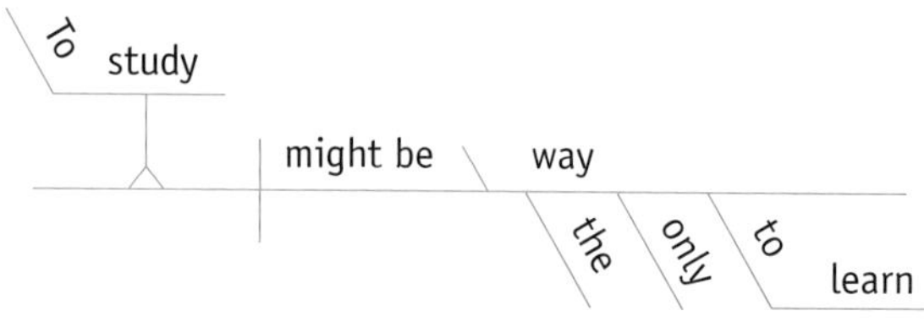

Diagraming Verbal Phrases

Diagram the following sentences or copy them. If you copy them, draw one line under each subject and two lines under each verb. Then put parentheses around each verbal phrase and label each one *part.* for participial, *ger.* for gerund, or *inf.* for infinitive.

1. The student (delivering the speech) [part.] is the class president.
2. (Giving a speech) [ger.] can be difficult for some people.
3. They may speak too quietly (to be heard) [inf.].
4. I need (to practice my speech for science class) [inf.].
5. The best time (to prepare for the presentation) [inf.] is this afternoon.
6. (Practicing a speech aloud) [ger.] is helpful.
7. (Turning on my stopwatch) [part.], I timed my speech.
8. I needed (to shorten my speech) [inf.].
9. (Shortening a speech) [ger.] is sometimes harder than (writing the material) [ger.].
10. My speech, (shortened to exactly ten minutes,) [part.] is now complete.

6.
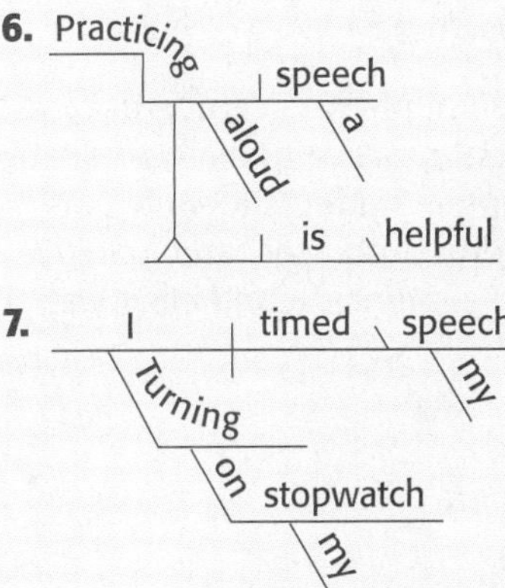

8.
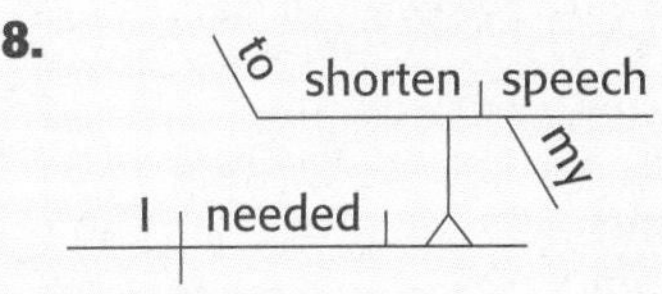

9.
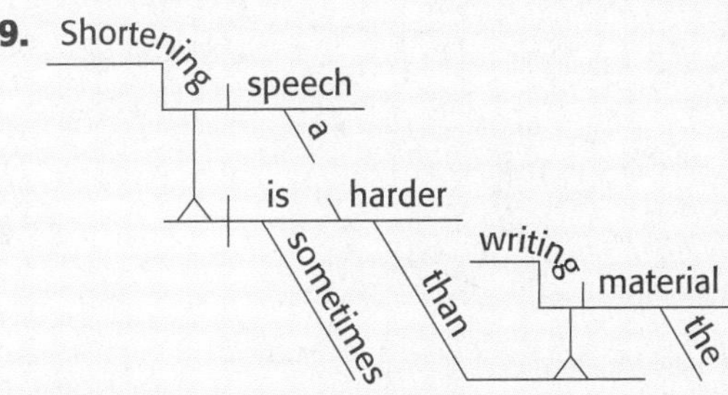

10.
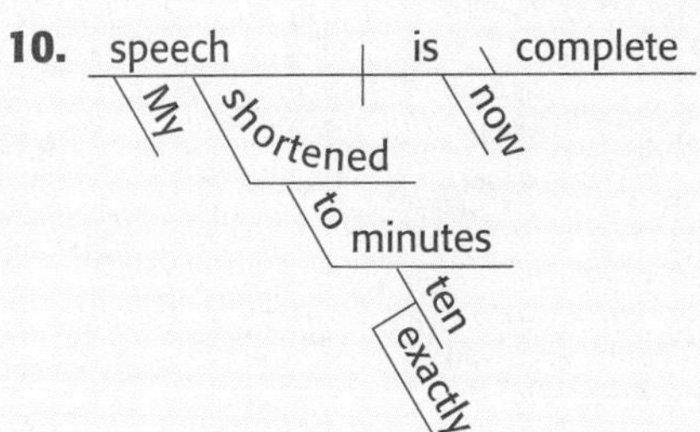

Using *CheckPoint*

This feature on verbal phrases can be used as further independent practice or as a cumulative review of the chapter. Students identify participial phrases, gerund phrases, and infinitive phrases and write sentences containing verbal phrases.

CheckPoint

Finding Participial Phrases and Infinitive Phrases

Write each participial phrase and infinitive phrase. Label each phrase *part.* for participial phrase or *inf.* for infinitive phrase.

1. The matador, facing the bull (part.), waved his red cape to challenge it (inf.).
2. Rising since noon (part.), the temperature is now 98 degrees.
3. These mittens, knit by my aunt (part.), are now too small to wear comfortably (inf.).
4. Using a telescope (part.), Galileo could see the rings around Saturn.
5. Sitting up (part.), Ginger began to beg for a dog biscuit (inf.).
6. The first steam locomotive to be built in the United States (inf.) was the *Tom Thumb,* built in 1830 (part.).
7. We had a wonderful campsite overlooking the lake (part.).
8. Drumming on the telephone pole (part.), the woodpecker dug a hole for its nest.
9. The sun's rays, focused through glass (part.), can start a fire.
10. The spaniel, barking ferociously (part.), raced through the tall grass to catch the rabbit (inf.).
11. The child carrying the Easter basket (part.) is my niece.
12. The gifts to wrap for the Christmas party (inf.) are on the table.
13. Drawn in black ink (part.), the sketch showed a teddy bear wearing overalls (part.).
14. The Valentine cards to distribute to my friends (inf.) are in my backpack.

Finding Gerund Phrases and Infinitive Phrases

Write each gerund phrase and infinitive phrase. Label each phrase *ger.* for gerund phrase or *inf.* for infinitive phrase.

1. I have found a new hobby, bird watching. (ger.)
2. To do this, sitting quietly near some trees is the first step. (inf.; ger.)
3. The hardest part is waiting patiently to catch glimpses of the birds. (ger.; inf.)
4. Seeing a bright red cardinal up close is worth the wait. (ger.)
5. I give watching the cardinal my complete attention. (ger.)
6. I love listening to the various chirps of birds. (ger.)
7. Besides looking through binoculars, I often perform another activity, recording birdsongs. (ger.; ger.)
8. I attract songbirds by putting birdseed nearby. (ger.)
9. To record their beauty, perhaps I will sketch them. (inf.)
10. Studying birds' habits and songs is an enjoyable hobby to practice regularly. (ger.; inf.)

Using Verbal Phrases

Write five sentences that follow the directions below.

1. Include the participial phrase *singing at the top of his lungs* at the beginning of a sentence.
2. Include the participial phrase *won by the girls' basketball team* in a sentence.
3. Include the gerund phrase *falling asleep at night* at the beginning of a sentence.
4. Include the infinitive phrase *to prevent the flu* at the beginning of a sentence.
5. Include the infinitive phrase *to see a rodeo* in a sentence.

When you have finished, underline and label each phrase. Then check for correct punctuation of each sentence.

Sample Answers for *Using Verbal Phrases:*

1. Singing at the top of his lungs, Marty worked happily. *Part.*
2. The exciting game, won by the girls' basketball team, drew a large crowd. *Part.*
3. Falling asleep at night is difficult for some people. *Ger.*
4. To prevent the flu is the purpose of the shot. *Inf.*
5. We drove for two hours to see a rodeo. *Inf.*

Using *Language and Self-Expression*

Consider using this writing assignment to assess students' ability to use verbals and verbal phrases correctly and effectively. You may want students to complete the assignment as part of an expository writing strand for their portfolios.

Prewriting

Suggest that students revisit their analysis of the painting that they did in *Making Visual Connections* on page L216.

Encourage students to use a graphic organizer to help them organize their thoughts in the prewriting stage. For example, students might use a word web with the word *food* in the center. Surrounding circles would contain the various functions of food and ideas about food in students' families and communities. Students should refer to their graphic organizers as they proceed with their writing.

FOR YOUR INFORMATION

About the Artwork

This collection of intricately detailed paintings and engravings was discovered at the Chauvet Grotto in southeastern France. It includes images of animals and human hands. The animals depicted include an owl and a panther, two species that had never before been seen in prehistoric artworks. The paintings are approximately 30,000 years old.

Language and *Self-Expression*

This cave painting was found in southeastern France. Scientists have dated it as being more than thirty thousand years old. At that time, people were nomadic and lived mainly by hunting and gathering food. What does the painting tell you about how and what they hunted?

What role does food play in our lives today? Write a report of your observations in your community, and imagine that your report will be read a thousand years from now. As you write, use verbals and verbal phrases to give your sentences variety. Then prepare your document to be added to a time capsule.

Prewriting To begin, write the word *food* at the top of a piece of paper. Under it, write down every idea that comes to you.

Drafting Use the information in your prewriting to explain the role of food in your community. Your first paragraph should list the main topics the body paragraphs will cover. The final paragraph should draw a conclusion about these topics.

Revising Be sure your sentence order makes sense. Also be sure you have included participial, gerund, and infinitive phrases.

Editing Check for correct punctuation of phrases. Make sure each paragraph is indented.

Publishing Write a final copy to read aloud to your class. Have the class brainstorm lists of items to accompany your document in a time capsule. As a group, discuss your conclusions about the role of food in your community and the importance of this information to future generations.

Verbals and Verbal Phrases

A **verbal** is a verb form that acts like another part of speech—such as an adjective or a noun.

Participles and Participial Phrases

A **participle** is a verb form that is used as an adjective. *(pages L217–L218)*
A **participial phrase** is a participle with its modifiers and complements all working together as an adjective. *(pages L221–L222)*
A participial phrase becomes a **misplaced modifier** if it is placed too far from the word it describes. *(page L225)*
An **essential participial phrase** identifies a person, place, or thing in the sentence. *(page L221)*
A **nonessential participial phrase** can be removed without changing the meaning of the sentence. *(page L222)*

Gerunds and Gerund Phrases

A **gerund** is a verb form that is used as a noun. *(page L227)*
A **gerund phrase** is a gerund with its modifiers and complements—all working together as a noun. *(pages L229–L230)*

Infinitives and Infinitive Phrases

An **infinitive** is a verb form that can be used as a noun, an adjective, or an adverb. The word *to* usually comes before an infinitive. *(page L233)*
An **infinitive phrase** is an infinitive with its modifiers and complements—all working together as a noun, an adjective, or an adverb. *(pages L235–L236)*

Punctuation with Participial Phrases

Using introductory phrases *(page L221)*
Recognizing essential participial phrases *(page L221)*
Recognizing nonessential participial phrases *(page L222)*

Other Information About Verbals and Verbal Phrases

Distinguishing between participles and verbs *(page L220)*
Distinguishing between gerunds and participles *(page L228)*
Distinguishing between infinitives and prepositional phrases *(page L234)*

Using *Another Look*

Another Look summarizes the terms defined in the chapter and provides cross-references to the specific pages on which they are explained. Consider having students use this feature prior to completing **CheckPoint** or taking the post-test. Students who can provide several examples of each term should be able to score well on either measurement.

FOR ASSESSING LEARNING

Using *the Posttest*

Assessing Learning

The posttest will help you and your students assess where they stand in their ability to use and identify verbals and verbal phrases.

IDENTIFYING COMMON STUMBLING BLOCKS

Problem

- Misplaced participial phrases

Solution

- For reteaching, use the explanatory copy printed in blue beside the examples on page L225.

Problem

- Confusing gerunds with participles

Solution

- For reteaching, use the explanatory copy printed in blue beside the examples on page L228.

Directions

Write the letter of the term that correctly identifies the underlined word or words in each sentence.

EXAMPLE **1.** Have you ever wanted to find out about the flesh-eating piranha?

1 **A** prepositional phrase
B gerund phrase
C participial phrase
D infinitive phrase

ANSWER **1 D**

1. Watching a program on television, I became intrigued by carnivorous fish.

2. Fascinated, I remained to watch the show in its entirety.

3. Eating flesh with razor-sharp teeth is how piranhas survive.

4. They are infamous for devouring their prey.

5. They sometimes follow the scent of blood to find their next meal.

6. Piranhas, traveling in groups, usually prey on other fish.

7. They can quickly reduce even a large animal to a skeleton.

8. One species of piranha, reaching a length of two feet, is one of the most dangerous.

9. Studying these dangerous fish fascinates me.

10. I went to the library to find out more about them.

A DIFFERENT DELIVERY SYSTEM

If you prefer, you can print the posttest from the BK English Test Bank located at http://www.bkenglish.com.

1	A prepositional phrase B gerund phrase <u>C</u> participial phrase D infinitive phrase	6	A prepositional phrase <u>B</u> nonessential phrase C essential phrase D infinitive phrase
2	A prepositional phrase B gerund phrase C participial phrase <u>D</u> infinitive phrase	7	<u>A</u> prepositional phrase B gerund phrase C participial phrase D infinitive phrase
3	A prepositional phrase <u>B</u> gerund phrase C participial phrase D infinitive phrase	8	A prepositional phrase B gerund phrase <u>C</u> participial phrase D infinitive phrase
4	A prepositional phrase <u>B</u> gerund phrase C participial phrase D infinitive phrase	9	A prepositional phrase <u>B</u> gerund phrase C participial phrase D infinitive phrase
5	A prepositional phrase B gerund phrase C participial phrase <u>D</u> infinitive phrase	10	<u>A</u> prepositional phrase B gerund phrase C participial phrase D infinitive phrase

Customizing the Test

Use these questions to add or replace items for alternate versions of the test.

11. <u>Searching in the library</u>, I found information about other carnivorous fish.

12. I would not want <u>to encounter a tiger fish in a river or ocean</u>.

13. <u>Protruding from their closed mouths</u> are dagger-like teeth.

14. The largest species of tiger fish may grow <u>to six feet long</u>!

15. <u>Found in African freshwaters and elsewhere</u>, tiger fish are fierce and combative.

11. **A** prepositional phrase
B gerund phrase
<u>C</u> participial phrase
D infinitive phrase

12. **A** prepositional phrase
B gerund phrase
C participial phrase
<u>D</u> infinitive phrase

13. **A** prepositional phrase
<u>B</u> gerund phrase
C participial phrase
D infinitive phrase

14. **<u>A</u>** prepositional phrase
B gerund phrase
C participial phrase
D infinitive phrase

15. **A** prepositional phrase
B gerund phrase
<u>C</u> participial phrase
D infinitive phrase

TEACHING SUGGESTIONS

BLOCK SCHEDULING

- If your schedule requires that you cover the chapter in a **shorter time,** use the instruction on independent and subordinate clauses, simple, compound, and complex sentences, and the Check Your Understanding and QuickCheck exercises.
- If you want to take advantage of **longer class time,** add these applications to writing: Connect to Writer's Craft, Connect to the Writing Process, and Apply to Writing exercises.

Essential Knowledge and Skills

- Writing to inform such as to explain, describe, report, and narrate
- Writing in complete sentences, varying the types such as compound and complex sentences, and using appropriately punctuated independent and dependent clauses
- Proofreading his/her own writing and that of others
- Responding in constructive ways to others' writing
- Interpreting and evaluating the various ways visual image makers represent meanings
- Selecting, organizing or producing visuals to complement and extend meaning

Clauses

Directions

Write the letter of the term that correctly identifies the underlined word or words in each sentence.

EXAMPLE **1.** I tell whoever will listen about strange inventions.

1 A adverb clause
B adjective clause
C noun clause
D simple sentence

ANSWER **1 C**

1. Because chickens peck at each other, someone invented chicken glasses.
2. The glasses, which extend to the back of a chicken's neck, protect its eyes.
3. Where you sleep is the place of another invention.
4. A clock has blocks that hang over your head.
5. When the alarm rings, the blocks fall on you.
6. You will want the following invention.
7. It's a hat that is attached to a parachute.
8. It comes with padded shoes that soften the landing.
9. A twirling spaghetti fork's handle that you can move with your thumb has a small wheel.
10. The fork spins around, and it rolls up the spaghetti.

IDENTIFYING COMMON STUMBLING BLOCKS

Following is a list of the most common errors students make when using clauses and simple, compound, and complex sentences.

Problem
- Lack of comma with an introductory adverb clause

Solution
- Instruction, pp. L256–L258
- Practice, p. L260

Problem
- Lack of comma with a compound sentence

Solution
- Instruction, pp. L271–L273
- Practice, pp. L274–L275

1
- **A** independent clause
- **B** adverb clause
- **C** complex sentence
- **D** adjective clause

2
- **A** adverb clause
- **B** noun clause
- **C** independent clause
- **D** adjective clause

3
- **A** noun clause
- **B** adjective clause
- **C** misplaced modifier
- **D** simple sentence

4
- **A** independent clause
- **B** noun clause
- **C** adverb clause
- **D** adjective clause

5
- **A** misplaced modifier
- **B** adjective clause
- **C** adverb clause
- **D** independent clause

6
- **A** simple sentence
- **B** complex sentence
- **C** subordinate clause
- **D** compound sentence

7
- **A** compound sentence
- **B** simple sentence
- **C** subordinate clause
- **D** complex sentence

8
- **A** noun clause
- **B** adverb clause
- **C** misplaced modifier
- **D** adjective clause

9
- **A** noun clause
- **B** misplaced modifier
- **C** simple sentence
- **D** adverb clause

10
- **A** simple sentence
- **B** subordinate clause
- **C** compound sentence
- **D** complex sentence

A DIFFERENT DELIVERY SYSTEM

If you prefer, you can print the pretest from the BK English Test Bank located at http://www.bkenglish.com.

Using *the Pretest*

Assessing Prior Knowledge

The pretest will help you and your students assess where they stand in their basic understanding of clauses and simple, compound, and complex sentences. The test measures students' ability to identify these elements and to use them correctly in their own writing.

Customizing the Test

Use these questions to add or replace items for alternate versions of the test.

11. The drinking straw that has several twists in it is a "crazy straw."

12. What I like are those socks with individual toes woven in them.

13. If you have not jumped on a pogo stick, you've missed a great invention!

14. The jogger that glows in the dark has special strips on her shoes.

11.
- **A** adjective clause
- **B** noun clause
- **C** misplaced modifier
- **D** adverb clause

12.
- **A** simple sentence
- **B** noun clause
- **C** adverb clause
- **D** adjective clause

13.
- **A** adverb clause
- **B** noun clause
- **C** adjective clause
- **D** independent clause

14.
- **A** independent clause
- **B** simple sentence
- **C** adverb clause
- **D** misplaced modifier

ADDITIONAL RESOURCES

Language Skills Practice . . . . pages 76–86
Transparency Tools FA8, FA9, AW9
ESL Practice and Test Preparation . . . . . pages 109–111
Assessment: Chapter Test. . . . . pages 156–163

MAKING VISUAL CONNECTIONS

For Language Development

Have students study the M. C. Escher artwork *Triangle System I A3 Type I.* Tell students to concentrate on the elements in the work and to think about what the figures might be doing in the artwork. What objects make up most of the painting? What do these figures look like? What do they appear to be doing?

To Stimulate Writing

Use the questions for art criticism as writing or discussion prompts.

Possible Answers:

Describe The image of a man is repeated. Escher used color to distinguish one man from another. The lines outlining each man are bold and clear, while the lines within each man are thinner.

Analyze The shapes form a mathematical pattern that is balanced across the picture. No single shape stands out as the focal point of the picture. Your eye may wander across the picture, picking out all the men of one color. Then you look some more and see all the men of another color.

Interpret The title makes me focus on the concept of the triangle. There is a faint background grid of triangles traced across the entire picture. Also, each set of three interlocking men forms a triangle.

Judge I think the triangle theme is subtle. There are no dominant, exact triangle shapes that attract your attention.

M.C. Escher, *Triangle System 1 A3 Type 1*, 1938.
Pencil, ink, and watercolor, 13 inches by 9½ inches.
Private collection.

Describe What image is repeated in this artwork? How has the artist used color and shape?

Analyze How do shape and color direct your attention to different images in the drawing? How has Escher created a sense of balance?

Interpret What does the title tell you about the images? What two different sets of triangles do you see? If you could give the artwork a title that reflects the work's meaning to you, what would it be?

Judge Do you think Escher's theme of triangles is obvious or subtle? Why do you think so?

At the end of this chapter, you will use the artwork to stimulate ideas for writing.

FOR DEVELOPING LANGUAGE SKILLS

LESSON 1 *(pages L253–L270)*

OBJECTIVES

- **To distinguish between independent clauses and subordinate clauses**
- **To identify adverb clauses, adjective clauses, and noun clauses**
- **To identify and correct misplaced adjective clauses**
- **To use adverb clauses and adjective clauses correctly and effectively in writing**

Create Interest

Have students look up the words *independent* and *subordinate* in a dictionary. Have two students write the definitions on the board. Tell students that

Independent and Subordinate Clauses

In this chapter you will learn about three kinds of sentences: simple, compound, and complex. However, before you can fully understand the different kinds of sentences, you must learn about groups of words called clauses.

A **clause** is a group of words that has a subject and a verb.

Notice that both a clause and a phrase are made up of a group of words. However, only a clause has a subject and a verb. In the following examples, the subject of the clause is underlined once. The verb is underlined twice.

PHRASE We will play **after halftime.**
CLAUSE We will play **after halftime is over.**

There are two kinds of clauses. One kind is called an independent, or main, clause.

An **independent (main) clause** can stand alone as a sentence because it expresses a complete thought.

When an independent clause stands by itself, it is called a **sentence.** It only becomes an independent clause when it appears in a sentence with another clause. In the following example, the clauses are joined with a comma and a conjunction.

independent clause — independent clause
Alicia hit the ball**, and** the crowd cheered.

Both of these clauses can stand alone as single sentences. This means that the two clauses are independent clauses.

Alicia hit the ball**.** The crowd cheered**.**

FOR INCREASING STUDENT ACHIEVEMENT

IDENTIFYING COMMON STUMBLING BLOCKS

Problem

- Inability to distinguish clauses from phrases

Solution

- Tell students that clauses are often confused with phrases in a sentence. Point out that phrases can never function separately from a sentence because they do not contain verbs. Tell students that a clause can function as a sentence if it is an independent clause. Subordinate clauses do not express a complete thought even though they have a subject and a verb.
- Have students identify the underlined sections of these sentences as *clauses* or *phrases.*

  Using the new bat, she hit a homerun. (phrase)

  I hoped to see a homerun when I went to the ballpark. (clause)

  The ball flew over the fence, and it landed in the crowd. (clause)

clauses, or special parts of a sentence, are either independent or subordinate. Tell students that all clauses have a subject and a verb. Some clauses express a complete thought, while other clauses do not express a complete thought. Tell students that they will learn how to distinguish between independent and subordinate clauses.

Guide Instruction

By Connecting Ideas

Show students how to identify clauses in the following sentences:

- I went to the Olympics with my friend Casey who skates.
- While she laughed hysterically, I fell down on the ice.

Tell students that these are clauses and not phrases because they contain both a subject and a verb. Phrases do not contain verbs. Review with students the definition of *phrase* and have them provide example sentences.

A DIFFERENT APPROACH

Auditory

Read each sentence in **Practice Your Skills** aloud as students listen. Discuss the correct responses. Have students share what strategies they used to identify the clauses in each sentence as independent or subordinate.

HOME WORK

After completing **Practice Your Skills,** have students find out more about the origins of a sport that they enjoy participating in or viewing. Students should write two paragraphs about the sport's origins. Then students should underline each clause and identify it as either independent or subordinate.

The second kind of clause is called a subordinate clause, or dependent clause. It has the name *dependent* because it depends on another clause to give it meaning. It cannot stand alone as a sentence.

A **subordinate (dependent) clause** cannot stand alone as a sentence because it does not express a complete thought.

Look at the following examples. Neither of the subordinate clauses expresses a complete thought—even though each has a subject and a verb.

subordinate clause | independent clause

After the game ended, the players left the field.

independent clause | subordinate clause

They enjoyed the game **that they watched last night.**

PRACTICE YOUR SKILLS

Check Your Understanding

Distinguishing Between Clauses

Sports Topic

Write each underlined clause. Then label it *independent* or *subordinate.*

1. Panels that the ancient Greeks carved show players using crooked sticks to hit a small object. subordinate

2. Field hockey was played in Europe during the Middle Ages, but the game was once outlawed in England. independent

3. Field hockey interfered with archery training, which was the basis of the national defense. subordinate

4. Even though field hockey was played worldwide after 1850, it did not become popular in the United States. subordinate

Consolidate Skills

Through Guided Practice

The **Check Your Understanding** exercise on page L254 will help students differentiate between independent and subordinate clauses. Have students tell the difference between these types of clauses before they begin the exercise. Complete the first item together. Then have students complete the exercise independently.

Transfer to Everyday Life

Identifying Clauses in Sports Articles

Have students find five examples of clauses in a sports article from a newspaper or sports magazine. Students should write out these sentences and underline the clauses. Have students read their sentences to the class. Discuss whether the clauses are independent or subordinate.

5. Although it became part of the Olympics in 1908, field hockey was not organized in the United States until 1926. independent
6. In that year Henry Greer arranged matches between teams that were made up of men from New York. subordinate
7. While it is not certain, the first men's field hockey match in the United States probably occurred in 1928. subordinate
8. Because the U.S. Olympic committee wanted an American team, it organized the men's hockey teams. subordinate
9. The teams formed the Field Hockey Association of America in 1930, and a team was sent to the 1932 Olympics. independent
10. Field hockey is now very popular among women, and many high schools and universities have a women's team. independent

Check Your Understanding

Identifying Subordinate Clauses

Sports Topic **Write the subordinate clause from each sentence.**

11. Field hockey is a sport that is usually played on grass or artificial turf.
12. Each team consists of eleven players who run strategic plays across the field.
13. The striker starts the game when he or she initiates a pass-back play.
14. After the striker hits the ball, it cannot immediately cross the centerline.
15. Before the ball is sent across the centerline, it must be touched by another player.

YOUR IDEAS

For Identifying Clauses

Pull It All Together

By Summarizing

Have students summarize the definitions for *independent clause* and *subordinate clause.* Students should write out their responses and provide sentences with examples of each term. Have students share their responses.

Check Understanding

Writing Sentences and Identifying Clauses

Have students write five sentences about any topic of their choosing and identify the clauses in each sentence as independent or subordinate. Have students share their sentences with the class.

Create Interest

Tell students that in this lesson they will be learning about the three different kinds of subordinate clauses: adverb clauses, adjective clauses, and noun clauses. Point out that each type of clause is named according to its function in a sentence. Review with students the functions of adverbs,

GETTING STUDENTS INVOLVED

Cooperative Learning

Before reading this page, have students work collaboratively with partners to tell what they think adverb clauses are and how they function in a sentence. Have each pair write a tentative definition for *adverb clause* and write an example sentence that contains what they believe to be an adverb clause. Have students read this page again and check their predictions for accuracy.

Uses of Subordinate Clauses

Like phrases, subordinate clauses can be used in several different ways. Subordinate clauses can be used as adverbs, adjectives, and nouns.

Adverb Clauses

A subordinate clause can be used the same way a single adverb or an adverb phrase is used. Such a clause is called an adverb clause.

SINGLE ADVERB	Let's meet **here.**
ADVERB PHRASE	Let's meet **at the music history museum.**
ADVERB CLAUSE	Let's meet **where we met last time.**

An **adverb clause** is a subordinate clause that is used mainly to modify a verb.

An adverb clause answers the adverb question *How? When? Where? Under what conditions?* or *Why?* Notice in each of the following examples that an adverb clause modifies the whole verb phrase.

HOW?	Adam described the old instruments **as if he had seen them all before.**
WHEN?	**When he saw the old harpsichord,** his mouth dropped open.
WHERE?	We will go **wherever the next concert is.**

adjectives, and nouns before discussing clauses.

Guide Instruction

By Modeling Strategies

Write these example sentences from the textbook on the board and model questioning strategies for distinguishing among adverb clauses, adjective clauses, and noun clauses. Show students how to use questioning to focus on the function of the clause to determine its type.

- When he saw the old harpsichord, his mouth dropped open. (adverb clause because it answers *When?*)
- Ken's home, which is blue and white, is new. (adjective clause because it answers *Which one?*)
- We'll read whatever poem is your favorite. (noun clause because it functions as a direct object.)

UNDER WHAT CONDITIONS	**If you have never seen a wooden flute,** go to the winds room immediately.
WHY?	We missed the first performance of the lute **because Anthony's watch had stopped.**

Subordinating Conjunctions

An adverb clause begins with a **subordinating conjunction.** A few of the subordinating conjunctions listed in the following box—such as *after, as, before,* and *until*—can also be used as prepositions. Remember that these words are subordinating conjunctions only if they are followed by a group of words with a subject and a verb.

COMMON SUBORDINATING CONJUNCTIONS			
after	as soon as	in order that	until
although	as though	since	when
as	because	so that	whenever
as far as	before	than	where
as if	even though	though	wherever
as long as	if	unless	while

***As soon as* the conductor arrives,** the concert will begin.

Bring your binoculars ***so that* you can see the musicians.**

The musicians prepare ***before* the concert begins.**

They arrange their music ***so that* it is easy to read.**

USING STUDENTS' STRENGTHS

Multiple Intelligences: Spatial

After discussing the **Common Subordinating Conjunctions** chart and the function of subordinating conjunctions, have students create an "illuminated" chart of subordinating conjunctions to display in the classroom. Tell students that illuminated pages are text pages that are adorned or decorated in ways that make them more appealing to readers. Use the example of illuminated manuscripts from the Middle Ages and provide students with images of these decorated pages. Provide students with large sheets of chart paper on which to create their illuminated charts.

Consolidate Skills

Through Guided Practice

The **Check Your Understanding** exercises on pages L259, L263, and L269–L270 as well as the **QuickCheck** on page L270 will help students identify and use clauses. Complete the first item in each exercise together, discussing and reviewing the major strategies students should use to complete the exercises. Then have students complete the remaining exercises independently.

Apply to Communication

Through Independent Writing

The **Communicate Your Ideas** activities on pages L260 and L265 prompt students to write a cause-and-effect explanation of a school rule and an informative report about a family member's childhood. Have students consider ways they will use different kinds of clauses to improve their writing. For example, ask students how adjective clauses can make their informative reports more descriptive.

A DIFFERENT APPROACH

Visual

Have students complete **Practice Your Skills** by referring to their illuminated charts from the previous activity. Students' decorated charts should be displayed around the room in places where students can easily read them. Students should choose subordinate conjunctions from the charts to complete items one through ten.

PUNCTUATION WITH ADVERB CLAUSES

Always place a comma after an adverb clause that comes at the beginning of a sentence.

Since the conductor has arrived, the concert can begin.

Practice Your Skills

Check Your Understanding

Supplying Subordinate Conjunctions

Music Topic

Complete each sentence by filling in the blank with a subordinating conjunction that makes the sentence's meaning clear.

1. Cristofori invented the piano around 1700 ■ (while) he worked for the Medici family in Florence, Italy.
2. ■ (Because) the piano is a popular instrument, more solo compositions have been written for it than any other instrument.
3. ■ (Because) it is so versatile, the piano is well liked by people of all ages.
4. The piano can make a wide variety of sounds ■ (even though) it is just one instrument.
5. ■ (Although) most pianos have eighty-eight keys, not all keyboards have that many.
6. ■ (When) a pianist presses a key, a felt hammer strikes a string.
7. A felt damper then is lifted ■ (so that) the sound of the string can ring out.
8. The damper is moved off the string ■ (as) the key is released.

How can they use adverb clauses to demonstrate cause and effect? Have students share their ideas.

Transfer to Everyday Life

Communicating Without Subordinate Clauses

Have students try to talk for a while without using any subordinate clauses. Remind students that every sentence they say must be a complete thought, or independent clause. After a while, students will realize that this task is almost impossible. Have students comment on the mundane nature of communicating without subordinate clauses.

Pull It All Together

By Sharing

Have students share their informative reports about a family member's childhood with partners. Working with their partners, have students identify the different types of clauses in their writing. Have each group share two

9. All the strings of a piano are made of steel [so that] they are strong enough to withstand the tension.

10. The tone is higher [when] the shorter strings are struck.

Check Your Understanding

Finding Adverb Clauses

History Topic **Write each adverb clause. Then identify the verb that each clause modifies.**

11. Most people move to America because they are seeking a better way of life.

12. Before 1865, most immigrants came from Europe after the conditions in their native countries became difficult.

13. Families immigrated because their governments treated them unfairly.

14. As soon as the Civil War ended, the flood of newcomers grew.

15. Even though many still immigrated from western Europe, a larger number from eastern and southern Europe sought the American Dream.

16. Immigration reached its peak before World War I started.

17. As though they had all heard the same stories, people from Mexico, China, and Japan joined the immigration.

18. Because many immigrants did not speak English, they did not blend easily into American society.

19. Long-time citizens considered the newcomers different because their cultures were unfamiliar.

20. The immigrants clustered together so that they would feel safe.

HOME WORK

Have students substitute the verb and adverb clause that modifies it with a verb and clause of their own for items 11 through 20.

YOUR IDEAS

For Adverb Clauses

clauses from their writing with the class.

Check Understanding

Identifying the Function of Clauses

Have students identify the various functions of adverb clauses, adjective clauses, and noun clauses. List students' responses on the board. Add any pertinent information that students do not recall. Discuss their responses and leave the information on the board for students reference as they complete Lesson 1.

GETTING STUDENTS INVOLVED

Reciprocal Teaching

After students have completed items 21 through 25 of **Connect to the Writing Process,** have them exchange papers with partners. Have partners edit each other's papers for correct sentence structure, spelling, capitalization, and correct punctuation of adverb clauses. Students should explain why they suggested particular changes to their partners' papers. Students should incorporate their partners' constructive edits into their writing.

TIMESAVER *QuickCheck*

Evaluate students' writing according to their ability to clearly explain a rule and its effects. Students should also provide support for their explanations. Check for appropriate use of adverb clauses, including correct punctuation.

HOME STUDY

Have students write a new rule that they think would be most important for a new society. Students should explain this rule, how it would be enforced, and the effects this new rule would have on a society. Students should underline any adverb clauses in their writing.

Connect to the Writing Process: Editing

Punctuating Adverb Clauses

Rewrite the following sentences, adding commas where needed. If a sentence is correct, write *C*.

21. Because she feels guilty about Myra,a classmate tells the story "Day of the Butterfly."

22. Until her illness keeps her from class,Myra is treated differently from the others.

23. Because Myra is sick,she does not come to school one day.

24. The class visits the hospital while Myra is a patient. C

25. When Myra does not return to school,the narrator wishes she had been kinder to the immigrant girl.

APPLY TO WRITING

Cause and Effect: ***Adverb Clauses***

Explain a school rule to a new student. First explain the cause of the rule. Then explain the effect of that rule. Use adverb clauses to show the relationship between the cause and effects. Your conclusion might state your opinion of the rule.

Adjective Clauses

You may recall that a single adjective or an adjective phrase is used to modify a noun or a pronoun. A subordinate clause can be used in the same way. Such a clause is called an **adjective clause.**

SINGLE ADJECTIVE	The 1950s was a **great** decade.
ADJECTIVE PHRASE	The 1950s was a decade **beyond our expectations.**
ADJECTIVE CLAUSE	The 1950s was a decade **that we will never forget.**

An adjective clause is a subordinate clause that is used to modify a noun or a pronoun.

An adjective clause answers the adjective question *Which one?* or *What kind?* Usually an adjective clause modifies the noun or pronoun directly in front of it.

WHICH ONE?	Ken's home, **which is blue and white,** is new.
WHAT KIND?	Cathy likes houses **that are close to the schools.**

Relative Pronouns

Most adjective clauses begin with a relative pronoun. A **relative pronoun** relates an adjective clause to the noun or the pronoun the clause modifies.

RELATIVE PRONOUNS				
who	whom	whose	which	that

USING STUDENTS' STRENGTHS

Multiple Intelligences: Linguistic

After discussing adjective clauses and the examples on this page, make a two-column chart on the board with the headings *Which one?* and *What kind?* Have students take turns writing example sentences that contain adjective clauses under the appropriate heading. The class should then identify the adjective clauses in each sentence. Have students also identify the words that are modified by the adjective clauses.

YOUR IDEAS

For Explaining Relative Pronouns

I just met Cindy, **who lives in the yellow house in our neighborhood.**

Barbara, **whose house is in that development,** hopes to make many friends.

Sometimes a relative pronoun simply begins an adjective clause. At other times, it is the subject of an adjective clause.

I haven't seen a house **that I like.**

I haven't seen a house **that is like yours.**

PUNCTUATION WITH ADJECTIVE CLAUSES

No punctuation is used with an adjective clause that contains information that is essential to identify a person, place, or thing in the sentence.

ESSENTIAL A vaccine **that will prevent the disease** was discovered in the laboratory.

A comma or commas, however, should set off an adjective clause that is nonessential. A clause is nonessential if it can be removed from the sentence without changing the basic meaning of the sentence. A clause is usually nonessential if it modifies a proper noun.

NONESSENTIAL The scientist, **who works in the laboratory,** found the cure.

The relative pronoun *that* is used in an essential clause, and *which* is usually used in a nonessential clause.

PRACTICE YOUR SKILLS

Check Your Understanding
Finding Adjective Clauses

History Topic **Write each adjective clause. Then underline the relative pronoun.**

1. The 1950s was the decade that established the United States as a world leader.
2. The men and women who played a role in World War II wanted to have families.
3. The American population, which was 150 million, boomed to more than 179 million.
4. The children of the families, who are now called Baby Boomers, fueled the economy.
5. Changes came to a country that enjoyed prosperity.
6. Polio, which had struck many children, became less of a threat.
7. Dr. Jonas Salk, who developed a polio vaccine, saved many children from the disease.
8. William Levitt developed Levittown, which was the first suburban development.
9. Much attention focused on the automobile, which became a necessity.
10. There were few homes that did not have a TV.

Check Your Understanding
Identifying the Words Adjective Clauses Describe

Art Topic **Write each adjective clause. Then write the word that each clause modifies.**

11. Some artists paint thousands of tiny dots that form images.
12. Georges Seurat, who painted in the late 1800s, used dots of different colors.

A DIFFERENT APPROACH

Visual

Have students complete **Practice Your Skills** by writing out each sentence. Then students should use a highlighter to identify each adjective clause. Students should use a different colored highlighter to identify the relative pronoun in each sentence. Discuss students' responses.

USING STUDENTS' STRENGTHS

Multiple Intelligences: Intrapersonal

After completing items 21 through 25, have students reflect on some experiences that grandparents or other older family members have shared with them. Have students write five sentences containing adjective clauses about these experiences. Remind students to use commas correctly with their adjective clauses.

HOME WORK

After completing **Practice Your Skills,** have students write five sentences about the United States during the 1950s. Each sentence should contain an adjective clause. Encourage students to use the library to find out more about this topic before beginning their home work sentences. The next day have students read their sentences aloud. As a class, identify the adjective clauses and the relative pronouns in students' sentences.

13. He studied art in museums where he learned about painters and their techniques.

14. First, Seurat made drawings that were in black-and-white.

15. He then turned to a new approach that used light and color.

16. He also stopped using lines, which give a boxed-in feeling.

17. His paintings were often on large canvases that took years to cover.

18. They portrayed people who were having fun outdoors.

19. People who were at home in the city were frequent subjects.

20. His most famous painting is *A Sunday on la Grande Jatte—1884,* which shows a day in the park.

Connect to the Writing Process: Editing

Punctuating Adjective Clauses

Write the following sentences, adding commas where needed. If sentence needs no commas, write *C* for correct.

21. My grandfather fought in World War II, which was fought in Europe, Asia, and Africa.

22. My grandmother, who worked in a factory, has vivid memories.

23. She remembers the families who raised their own gardens. C

24. The garden that grew next door was very large. C

25. These gardens, which were called Victory Gardens, gave citizens plenty of food.

Connect to the Writing Process: Drafting

Writing Sentences with Adjective Clauses

[Answers may vary. Possible responses are given.]

Add an independent clause to each adjective clause to make a complete sentence. Use commas where needed.

I finally revisted Pittsburgh, which was my home town.

26. which was my home town

They made an apartment house out of the school that I attended.

27. that I attended

I ran into my high school English teacher, who made the best cookies.

28. who made the best cookies

There are many friends and neighbors whom I still remember.

29. whom I still remember

I have a cousin from Pittsburgh who calls me every weekend.

30. who calls me every weekend

Communicate Your Ideas

APPLY TO WRITING

Informative Report: *Adjective Clauses*

Find out more about what life was like for a member of your family when he or she was a child. Then, in several paragraphs, write about his or her early life. Be sure to use adjective clauses to help make your sentences more descriptive.

Misplaced Adjective Clauses

Place an adjective clause as near as possible to the word it modifies. A clause that is too far away from the word it modifies is called a **misplaced modifier.**

MISPLACED Mandy sold the flowers **who runs the garden shop.**

CORRECT Mandy, **who runs the garden shop,** sold the flowers.

REACHING ALL STUDENTS

Struggling Learners

Before completing items 26 through 30, review independent clauses with students. Remind students that independent clauses can function as complete sentences. Complete the following example together before having students complete the exercise independently.

whom I talked to every day

Eddie was my friend whom I talked to every day.

DEVELOPING WORKPLACE COMPETENCIES

Basic Skills: Writing

Have students consider why it is important in everyday writing, and especially in the workplace, to be careful not to use misplaced adjective clauses. Discuss the following example: *We went with Ted to see the manager, who was being promoted.* If Ted is the one being promoted and not the manager, then the sentence should read *We went to see the manager with Ted, who was being promoted.* Have students provide additional examples of how misplaced adjective clauses might create misunderstandings and miscommunications in future careers.

A DIFFERENT APPROACH

Auditory

Complete items one through ten in **Practice Your Skills** together with students. Have students take turns reading each sentence and identifying them as *correct* or *incorrect.* Have students explain why or why not they chose a particular response.

PRACTICE YOUR SKILLS

Check Your Understanding

Recognizing Misplaced Adjective Clauses

General Interest **Write *C* if an adjective clause is placed correctly or *I* if an adjective clause is placed incorrectly.**

1. "Science is everywhere," Mrs. Lee told me, who is a true scientist. I "Science is everywhere," Mrs. Lee, who is a true scientist, told me.
2. My father, who is a chemist, agrees with this idea of Mrs. Lee. C
3. Looking up at the stars is an example of science that glow in the dark. I Looking up at the stars that glow in the dark is an example of science.
4. Energy has always interested me, which makes machinery work. I Energy, which makes machinery work, has always interested me.
5. The car that goes up a ramp in a parking garage illustrates motion. C
6. My mother uses chemistry to make cookies for the family, who is a wonderful baker. I My mother, who is a wonderful baker, uses chemistry to make cookies for the family.
7. The light from the sun, which shines brightly, reaches the flowers. C
8. The magnet entertained my brother that hung on the refrigerator. I The magnet that hung on the refrigerator entertained my brother.
9. My youngest sister that spins around loves her new wind-up toy. I My youngest sister loves her new wind-up toy that spins aro
10. "Where is the bee?" said my friend that is buzzing in my ear. I "Where is the bee that is buzzing in my ear?" said my friend.

Connect to the Writing Process: Revising

Correcting Sentences with Misplaced Adjective Clauses

11.–17. Rewrite the incorrect sentences from the preceding exercise, placing the adjective clauses correctly. Use commas where needed.

[Answers may vary. See possible responses given above.]

Noun Clauses

A subordinate clause can also be used like a single noun. Such a clause is called a noun clause.

SINGLE NOUN	Show us the **poem.**
NOUN CLAUSE	Show us **what you read.**

A **noun clause** is a subordinate clause that is used like a noun.

A noun clause can be used in the same ways that a noun can be used.

SUBJECT	**Whatever poem you choose** is fine with me. (*Whatever poem you choose* is what the sentence is about.)
DIRECT OBJECT	We'll read **whatever poem is your favorite.** (We'll read what? *Whatever poem is your favorite* is the direct object.)
INDIRECT OBJECT	Give **whoever reads first** your attention. (The direct object is *attention.* Give attention to whom? *Whoever reads first* becomes the indirect object.)
OBJECT OF A PREPOSITION	Matt was confused by **what the poem implied.** (*What the poem implied* is the object of the preposition *by.*)
PREDICATE NOMINATIVE	That poem is **what I expected.** (*What I expected* renames the subject, *poem.*)

HOME WORK

Have students prepare for the next section on noun clauses by reading pages L267 to L269. Students should write a few sentences explaining the difference between adjective clauses and noun clauses. Students should also tell the five different ways a noun clause can function in a sentence. Have students write five sentences demonstrating noun clauses functioning as subjects, direct objects, indirect objects, objects of prepositions, and predicate nominatives.

GETTING STUDENTS INVOLVED

Cooperative Learning

Have students work in small groups to create example sentences containing each type of noun clause. Write the headings *Subject, Direct Object, Indirect Object, Object of a Preposition,* and *Predicate Nominative* on the board. Have groups take turns sharing their sentences with the class. Have students write some of their sentences in the appropriate columns on the board.

All the words in the box can begin a noun clause.

COMMON INTRODUCTORY WORDS FOR NOUN CLAUSES		
how	when	whoever
if	where	whom
that	whether	whomever
what	which	whose
whatever	who	why

Remember that the words *who, whom, whose, which,* and *that* may also begin adjective clauses. Do not rely on the introductory words alone to identify a noun clause. Instead, decide how the subordinate clause is used in a sentence.

NOUN CLAUSE — I believe **that she will win the poetry contest.** (The clause is used as a direct object—I believe what?)

ADJECTIVE CLAUSE — The fact **that she will win the poetry contest** is widely known. (The clause is used to describe the noun *fact*—which fact?)

PRACTICE YOUR SKILLS

Check Your Understanding

Finding Noun Clauses

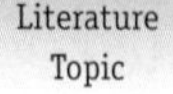

Literature Topic **Write each noun clause.**

1. Who wrote America's best-known poetry is an easy question.

2. Americans are often interested in what Robert Frost wrote.
3. Frost's poems state that human life is a struggle with nature and society.
4. He never forgot that his life was full of disappointment.
5. His family life was what is described as tragic.
6. He gave whatever he was writing his full attention.
7. Whoever reads "The Road Not Taken" must think.
8. His poems are about what we think during day-to-day events.
9. For Frost, life is what pleases and worries us.
10. The award-winning poet was not swayed by what other poets wrote.

Check Your Understanding

Identifying the Use of Noun Clauses

Literature Topic **Write each noun clause. Then label each one using the following abbreviations.**

subject = *s.* | object of a preposition = *o.p.*
direct object = *d.o.* | predicate nominative = *p.n.*
indirect object = *i.o.*

11. Why someone writes poetry is a personal matter. s.
12. Give whoever writes poetry high praise. i.o.
13. Poetry requires that you think like an artist. d.o.
14. The approach to your subject determines how well your poem will turn out. d.o.
15. Whatever subject you choose must be well thought out. s.
16. When you write poetry can also be important. s.
17. The value of a poem is also measured by what the reader gets from it. o.p.

A DIFFERENT APPROACH

Kinesthetic

Before writing out their responses to **Practice Your Skills,** have students read each sentence silently and trace a circle around all the noun clauses with their fingers. Students should complete items one through ten using this approach. After students write out their responses using pencil and paper, discuss their answers as a class.

HOME WORK

Have students write a descriptive paragraph about someone they respect. In their explanation of why they respect that person, students should use noun clauses.

REACHING ALL STUDENTS

Struggling Learners

Review with students the differences among adverb clauses, adjective clauses, and noun clauses. Remind students to think about how the clause functions in the sentence and to think about which words the clauses modify.

EXPANDING THE LESSON

Using Technology

You will find additional **instructional** and **practice** materials for this chapter at http://www.bkenglish.com.

s.

18. Whoever attempts to skim a poem is missing out.

p.n.

19. The speaker of your poem is whomever you wish.

20. In a narrative poem, a poet must relate whatever historical event is being told. d.o.

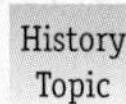

Mixed Practice

History Topic **Write each subordinate clause. Label each one as an *adverb clause,* an *adjective clause,* or a *noun clause.***

1. Many swimmers have crossed the English Channel, which is twenty-two miles wide. adjective clause

noun clause

2. Whoever accomplishes the feat is admired.

3. In 1961, Antonio Abertondo attempted something that no one else had ever done before. adjective clause

adjective clause

4. Abertondo, who was forty-two years old, swam across the channel and back without a stop.

adverb clause

5. When he arrived at Dover Beach, he was covered with grease for protection against the cold water.

6. He swam steadily for the next eighteen hours and fifty minutes until he reached the coast of France. adverb clause

7. Abertondo was not stopped by what the cold sea had to offer. noun clause

adverb clause

8. When he reached the English coast, he had been swimming for forty-three hours and fifteen minutes.

adjective clause

9. The last mile, which had taken him two hours, had been the hardest.

noun clause

10. Abertondo showed that he was a determined man.

LESSON 2 *(pages L271–L279)*

OBJECTIVES

- **To identify simple, compound, and complex sentences**
- **To correctly punctuate compound sentences**
- **To use simple, compound, and complex sentences accurately and effectively in writing**

Create Interest

Tell students that sentence variety makes reading more enjoyable. Have students read the following paragraph and comment on the lack of variety in the sentence types and suggest how they would improve the paragraph.

Kim caught a fish. Michael showed her how to reel it in. She scooped up the fish with a net. The fish was flopping around. Its eyes were big. Kim put the fish back into the water.

Kinds of Sentence Structure

The ability to recognize independent and subordinate clauses will help you understand sentence structure. There are three kinds of sentences: simple, compound, and complex. In the example sentences that follow, subjects are underlined once and verbs are underlined twice.

Simple and Compound Sentences

A **simple sentence** contains one independent clause.

Terry caught several fish in the mountain stream.

We cooked the fish over our campfire.

The cat pounced on the leftover fish.

A compound sentence is made up of two or more sentences. The sentences are usually joined by the conjunction *and, but, or,* or *yet*.

A **compound sentence** consists of two or more independent clauses.

Each independent clause in a compound sentence can stand alone as a separate sentence.

[independent clause] Kim has the tackle box, and [independent clause] Michael has the net.

[independent clause] Kim held the net, and [independent clause] Michael reeled in the fish.

[independent clause] The fishing party is ready, but [independent clause] the guide is not here.

GETTING STUDENTS INVOLVED

Reciprocal Teaching

After discussing the definitions and examples of simple and compound sentences, have students share their own summaries of what they learned from the page. Students who can distinguish between simple and compound sentences should work with students who are having difficulty. Students should provide examples for those students who cannot distinguish between simple and compound sentences. After sharing learning strategies and writing several example sentences together, have partners share with the class the explanations and learning strategies that helped them the most.

Guide Instruction

By Modeling Strategies

Tell students that they should use sentences of different types to make their writing more interesting and more appropriate for particular audiences. Explain that simple sentences contain one independent clause. Compound sentences contain two independent clauses joined by a semicolon or by a comma and a coordinating conjunction. Complex sentences contain an independent clause and one or more subordinate clauses. Demonstrate each type of sentence using these examples:

- The fish was jumping. (simple)
- The fish was jumping, and it came right out of the water. (compound)
- The fish was jumping as Kim took it out the water with the net. (complex)

A DIFFERENT APPROACH

Kinesthetic

Have students write the words *simple* and *compound* on two separate word cards. Complete **Practice Your Skills** by reading each sentence aloud and having students hold up the correct word card. Encourage students not to say the answers, but instead to hold up their cards identifying each type of sentence. Discuss students' correct and incorrect responses.

HOME WORK

Have students write ten sentences about a subject of their own choosing. They should write five simple sentences and five compound sentences. Have students share their sentences with the class the following day. Make sure students have used correct punctuation with their compound sentences.

PRACTICE YOUR SKILLS

Check Your Understanding

Recognizing Simple and Compound Sentences

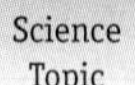

Label each sentence *simple* or *compound*.

1. Dogs cannot tell the difference between the colors red and green. simple
2. Moths usually fly at night, and butterflies fly during the day. compound
3. A lobster may easily grow a lost claw. simple
4. The brown pelican dives for fish, but the white pelican scoops fish from the water's surface. compound
5. The earthworm has no lungs. simple
6. The fastest land animal is the cheetah. simple
7. The walrus is a marine animal like a seal. simple
8. Many insects have feelers and wings, but spiders do not have either. compound
9. A grain of sand in the shell of an oyster may eventually become a pearl. simple
10. The animal brain is smaller, and it usually cannot reason. compound

Compound Sentence or Compound Verb?

Sometimes a simple sentence that has a compound verb is mistaken for a compound sentence. Notice the difference in the following sentences.

COMPOUND SENTENCE	The sailor untied the lines, and the ship moved away from the dock.

Consolidate Skills

Through Guided Practice

The **Check Your Understanding** exercises as well as the **QuickCheck** on page L279 will help students identify simple, compound, and complex sentences. Write the definitions and example sentences for each type of sentence on the board. Allow students to refer to them as they complete the exercises. Practice the first example together in each exercise. Then have students complete the remaining exercises independently.

Apply to Communication

Through Independent Writing

The **Communicate Your Ideas/Apply to Writing** activities on pages L275 and L278 prompt students to write a story and an analysis of a painting. Ask students how using the three types of sentences will make their analysis of a

COMPOUND VERB — The sailor untied the lines and jumped onto the ship.

PUNCTUATION WITH COMPOUND SENTENCES

There are several ways to connect the independent clauses in a compound sentence. One way is to join them with a comma and a coordinating conjunction.

We left the dock at 6:30**, but** Ian did not arrive until 7:00.

You can also join the independent clauses with a semicolon and no conjunction.

The fish were biting**;** everyone on the boat was catching big fish with each cast.

PRACTICE YOUR SKILLS

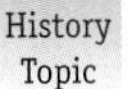

Check Your Understanding

Distinguishing Between Simple and Compound Sentences

History Topic **Label each sentence *simple* or *compound.***

1. In 1606, the Virginia Company of London requested and received a settlement charter for North America. simple

2. The company acted quickly, and more than 140 settlers left England. compound

3. The settlers had dreams of finding gold and setting up trade. simple

INTEGRATING TECHNOLOGY

Internet

Have students work with a partner to find examples of compound sentences at the following Internet site: http://www.historychannel.com.

Students should find examples of compound sentences joined by a comma and a coordinating conjunction and compound sentences joined by a semicolon. Have students share their findings with the class.

painting more interesting for their audience, older readers.

Transfer to Everyday Life

Comparing and Contrasting

Have students search for simple, compound, and complex sentences in a children's picture book and in a novel they are reading. Students should compare and contrast the types of sentences used in each book. After students have found examples of sentences in the books, discuss their findings and any general statements they can make about the majority of sentence types used in each book. For example, did the picture books contain more simple sentences or complex sentences? Did the novels contain more compound sentences than did the picture books? Discuss students' findings.

A DIFFERENT APPROACH

Visual

Have students complete items eleven through twenty of **Connect to the Writing Process** by writing the sentences on the board. Have students take turns coming to the board to correctly place commas, conjunctions, and semicolons. Discuss students' responses.

HOME WORK

Have students write ten sentences, some simple and some compound. The next day have students write two sentences on the board, checking for correct punctuation as a class.

4. In 1607, three ships entered Chesapeake Bay and sailed up the river. simple

5. Nearly one hundred people settled on a peninsula, and nature quickly tested them. compound

6. Only a few of the Jamestown colonists dug wells and cleared land for their spring gardens. simple

7. The rest searched for gold and hoped for wealth. simple

8. Disease and hunger devastated the colonists, and fewer than thirty-eight greeted the supply ships. compound

9. Captain John Smith took control and organized the survivors. simple

10. Jamestown survived another year, but the recovery was short-lived. compound

Connect to the Writing Process: Editing

Punctuating Compound Sentences

Rewrite each compound sentence, making sure that commas, conjunctions, and semicolons are used properly. If a sentence is punctuated correctly, write *C*.

11. Hunters and gatherers roamed the earth in early times,^ and no one settled in any one place.

12. Most people settled as farmers,^ but not all did.

13. The land of the Greeks became overcrowded, and some Greeks formed colonies overseas. C

14. Early on,^ Rome was a monarchy,^ but later on it became a republic.

15. The Roman Empire declined; Germanic tribes took over the western half of the former empire. C

16. Lords owned the manor during the Middle Ages,^ yet serfs worked the land.

17. The Middle Ages was a time of feudalism; people owed loyalty to the lord. C

Pull It All Together

By Summarizing

Have students summarize what they have learned about simple, compound, and complex sentences. Students should write the definition and an example sentence for each type of sentence. Have students share their responses with the class.

Check Understanding

Through Definition

Have students write definitions for *simple sentence, compound sentence,* and *complex sentence.* Students should write example sentences for each definition. Discuss students' responses as a class.

18. The Renaissance fostered growth for the arts,and artists developed new ways of painting.

19. The Age of Discovery brought Europeans to the Americas,but Native Americans had lived there for centuries.

20. Most colonists wanted independence,but a few remained loyal to Britain.

TIMESAVER *QuickCheck*

Evaluate students' writing according to their effective use of simple and compound sentences. Students should use coordinating conjunctions, commas, and semicolons correctly in their writing.

Communicate Your Ideas

APPLY TO WRITING

Story: ***Simple and Compound Sentences***

Think about your favorite time in history. What would it have been like to live at that time? Share your ideas with your classmates, and then write a story with you as the main character. Describe a typical day in your life in the period of history you have chosen. Use both simple and compound sentences in your story.

Complex Sentences

If you can recognize independent and subordinate clauses, you can also recognize complex sentences.

A **complex sentence** consists of one independent clause and one or more subordinate clauses.

adverb clause — independent clause

Since we have extra time, we can drive around the islands.

independent clause — adjective clause

I have already driven on the new road that opened last week.

A DIFFERENT APPROACH

Auditory

Read sentences one through fifteen of **Check Your Understanding** aloud and have students identify each one as simple, compound, or complex without looking in their textbooks. Students should explain why they chose their answers.

CONNECT TO WRITER'S CRAFT

When you write, think about your audience as you choose the kinds of sentences you use. Using simple sentences is most appropriate for a young audience. Compound and complex sentences are more difficult to understand, but they show the relationship between ideas. Notice the difference in the following sentences.

> The electric car was new**. We** did not have to recharge the battery.
>
> The electric car was new**, and** we did not have to recharge the battery.
>
> **Because** the electric car was new, we did not have to recharge the battery.

Check Your Understanding

Distinguishing Between Simple, Compound, and Complex Sentences

Science Topic **Label each sentence *simple, compound,* or *complex.***

1. The first steam-driven cars were unpopular because they were noisy and dirtied the air. complex
2. Early postal trucks were made so that a mule could be substituted for a failed engine. complex
3. Postal trucks have steering wheels on the right side. simple
4. An electric car gets its power from a battery, but the battery must constantly be recharged. compound
5. Electric cars are inexpensive to run and help protect our air. simple
6. Electric cars were popular in the 1890s and 1900s, but cars with gasoline engines soon replaced them. compound

7. Although people had hired vehicles for thousands of years, the word *taxicab* was not used until the 1800s. complex

8. Now in many large cities people cannot get around and cannot conduct their daily lives without taxicabs. simple

9. The longest bicycle, which was built for thirty-five people, was made in Denmark in 1976. complex

10. The bicycle weighed more than a ton, and it was seventy-two feet long. compound

11. All the riders had to work together and must have had enormous confidence in the person at the handlebars. simple

12. Some astronauts who went to the moon traveled in a lunar rover. complex

13. A lunar rover looks something like a jeep, but a rover's top and sides are completely open. compound

14. Since a lunar rover has no engine, it runs on power from a battery. complex

15. Science and history have both repeated and progressed at the same time. simple

Connect to the Writing Process: Drafting

Writing Different Kinds of Sentences

[Answers may vary. Possible responses are given.]

Following the directions below, write five sentences about a science experiment you once saw or tried.

16. Write a simple sentence about the person who performed the experiment. My teacher performed the experiment.

17. Write a compound sentence about what materials were used. He used oil and he added water to it.

18. Write a compound sentence about what happened during the experiment. The water sank to the bottom and the oil rose to the top.

HOME WORK

Starting with a simple sentence, have students build compound and complex sentences. First, they write a simple sentence. Second, they add to the simple sentence to write a compound sentence. Third, using the theme of the simple sentence they write a complex sentence.

FOR YOUR INFORMATION

About the Artist

Paul Klee (1879–1940). The simple style and joyous spirit of *Runner at the Goal* are typical of the work of Swiss artist Paul Klee. The son of a musician, Klee learned to play the violin well enough to become a professional musician but decided instead to become an artist. He described his work as "taking a line for a walk." Klee is considered one of the most intuitive artists of the 20th century.

19. Write a complex sentence about what you learned from the experiment. When I watched this experiment, I learned that oil and water do not mix.

20. Write any kind of sentence that tells about another experiment you would like to try. Label your sentence *simple, compound,* or *complex.*

I would like to try mixing water and dry ice. (simple sentence)

Communicate Your Ideas

APPLY TO WRITING

Analysis: *Simple, Compound, and Complex Sentences*

Paul Klee. *Runner at the Goal,* 1921.
Watercolor and gouache, 11⅞ by 9 inches. Solomon R. Guggenheim Museum, New York.

Write an analysis of *Runner at the Goal* by Paul Klee for someone older than you. Explain what is in the painting, how it is presented, and why it is presented that way. Use a combination of simple, compound, and complex sentences to express your ideas.

 Mixed Practice

Art Topic **Label each sentence *simple, compound,* or *complex.***

1. Charles Wilson Peale never saw a painting until he was a grown man. complex

2. He was a saddle maker by trade and lived in Annapolis, Maryland. simple

3. One day Peale went to Norfolk for supplies and saw paintings for the first time. simple

4. He did not like any of the paintings; they did not look realistic. compound

5. When he returned home, he took up painting with a great deal of energy and talent. complex

6. He took lessons in Boston and even went to London for more lessons. simple

7. After he had made some money from his paintings, he became a full-time painter. complex

8. Peale loved painting, but his enjoyment was not enough for him. compound

9. He taught his skills to his seventeen children and all his relatives and created a family of artists. simple

10. Charles Wilson Peale became the famous patriot artist who painted George Washington's portrait. complex

EXPANDING THE LESSON

Using Technology

You will find additional **instructional** and **practice** materials for this chapter at http://www.bkenglish.com.

Using *Sentence Diagraming*

Sentence diagraming helps students develop variety and style in their writing. In this activity, students will focus on diagraming clauses and simple, compound, and complex sentences.

Sentence Diagraming

Diagraming Sentences

All simple sentences have one baseline. Diagrams for compound and complex sentences, however, have two or more baselines. Each clause has its own baseline.

Compound Sentences These sentences are diagramed the way two simple sentences are. The baselines of the separate sentences, however, are joined by a broken line on which the conjunction is placed. The broken line connects the verbs.

Dad enjoys movies, but Mom prefers the theater.

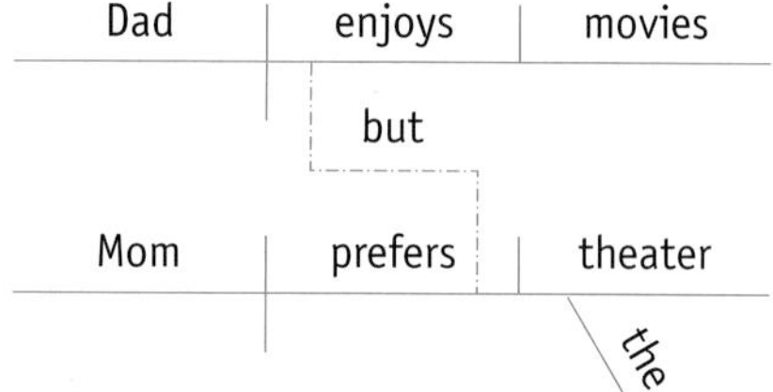

Complex Sentences In a complex sentence, an adverb clause is diagramed beneath the independent clause. The subordinating conjunction belongs on a broken line that connects the verb in the adverb clause to the word the clause modifies.

After I watch the movie, I am going to bed.

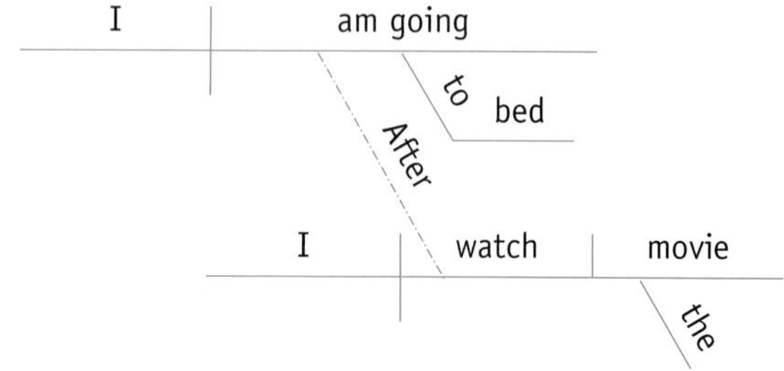

An adjective clause is also diagramed beneath the independent clause. The relative pronoun is connected by a broken line to the noun or the pronoun the clause modifies.

The dancer who is best is my friend.

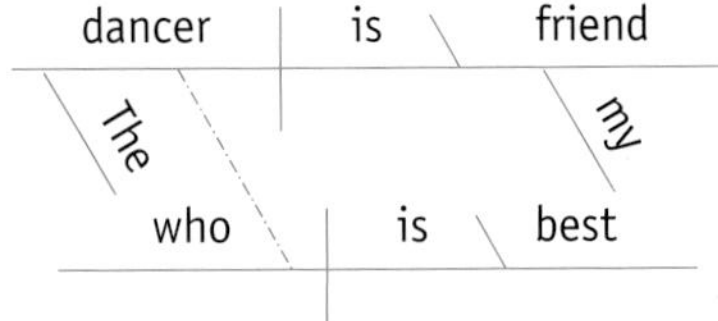

A noun clause is diagramed on a pedestal in the same place a single noun with the same function would be placed. The noun clause in the following diagram is the subject.

Whoever wrote the screenplay was brilliant.

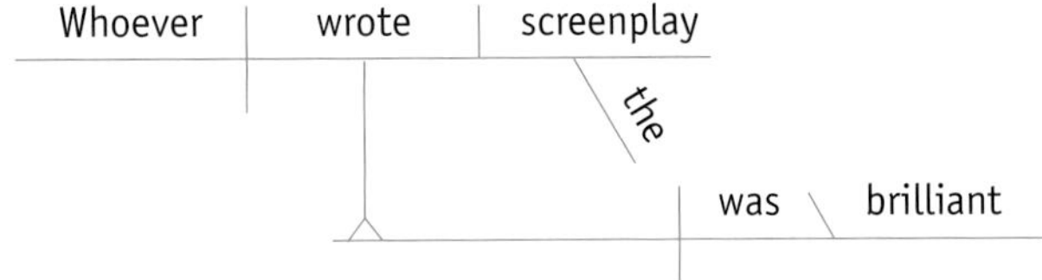

Practice Your Skills

Diagraming Sentences

Diagram the following sentences or copy them. If you copy them, draw one line under each subject and two lines under each verb. Put parentheses around each subordinate clause. Then label each subordinate clause *adv.* for adverb, *adj.* for adjective, or *n.* for *noun.*

1. A snail has no legs, but it does have a foot.
2. Rao will collect tickets, and Diane will usher.
3. (Before the rain started), I closed the car windows. adv.
4. (Why the cabin burned) is a mystery. n.
5. Mrs. O'Reilly, (who just moved here) will teach the new computer course. adj.

Sample Answers for *Sentence Diagraming:*

1.

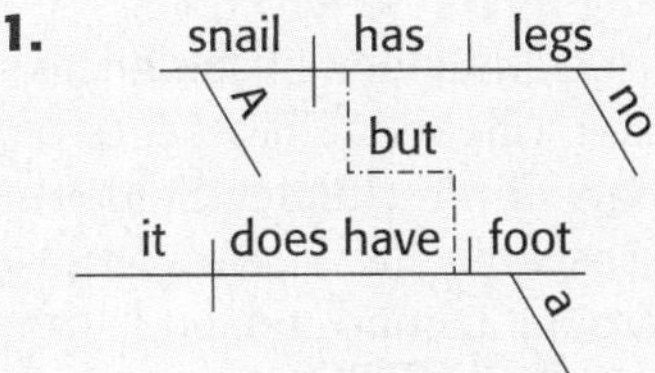

2. Rao | will collect | tickets — and — Diane | will usher

3. I | closed | windows — the — car — Before — rain | started — the

4. cabin | burned | Why — the — is — mystery — a

5. Mrs. O'Reilly | will teach | course — the — new — computer — who | moved — just — here

Using *CheckPoint*

This feature on clauses and kinds of sentences can be used as further independent practice or as a cumulative review of the chapter. Students identify adverb clauses, adjective clauses, and noun clauses and simple, compound, and complex sentences.

CheckPoint

Finding and Identifying Subordinate Clauses

Write each subordinate clause. Then next to each one, label it *adv.* for adverb, *adj.* for adjective, or *n.* for *noun.*

1. As soon as the bell rings, I will go to the cafeteria and eat lunch. adv.
2. Grandmother will give you whatever you want for your fourteenth birthday. n.
3. We must find the people whose car is blocking ours. adj.
4. Phina can't eat now because she has a swim meet in less than an hour. adv.
5. I laughed at how comical John's costume looked. n.
6. I know Mr. Myers, whom you mentioned in your note. adj.
7. When my dog doesn't recognize a visitor, she barks and growls menacingly. adv.
8. Whoever owns that beagle won three blue ribbons in last night's show. n.
9. Don't put the glass where it will get broken. adv.
10. The first baseball game that was a tie occurred in 1854. adj.
11. Because Terry was early, he got the best seat in the house. adv.
12. Measure the cloth before you cut it. adv.
13. The flan that Marisela made is delicious! adj.
14. After the fax arrived, Ms. Styles took it to the principal. adv.
15. Whatever made these marks in the dirt was quite heavy. n.

Identifying Kinds of Sentences

Label each sentence *simple, compound,* or *complex.*

1. If the ice on the south polar cap melted, the water would cover the Statue of Liberty up to her nose. complex
2. The waves crashed, and the sandpipers ran toward them. compound
3. Al climbed over the stone wall that bordered the farm. complex
4. The sphinx moth curls up its tongue and uses it as a pillow. simple
5. The center lost the ball, and five players fell on it. compound
6. We left early for the train station but had a flat tire. simple
7. A fly can walk upside down on a ceiling because it has special pads on each of its six feet. complex
8. Although the weather was bad, we kept playing. complex
9. Eskimos buy refrigerators so that food won't freeze. complex
10. A spider spins a web of silk that it makes inside its body. complex

Using Sentence Structure

Write sentences that follow the directions below. (The sentences may come in any order.) Write about one of the following topics or a topic of your choice: your idea of an ideal place to live or the best things about where you live now.

1. Write a simple sentence.
2. Write a complex sentence with an introductory adverb clause.
3. Write a complex sentence with an adjective clause.
4. Write a compound sentence.
5. Write a complex sentence with a noun clause.

When you have finished, label each sentence *simple, compound,* or *complex.* Then check the punctuation of each one.

Sample answers for *Using Sentence Structure:*

1. Living by the ocean would be wonderful. *(S. sentence)*
2. As the sun rose each morning, I would go for a swim. *(Cx. sentence with adv. clause)*
3. The beach that lies near my dream house would be a perfect recreation area. *(Cx. sentence with adj. clause)*
4. I could swim in the summer, and I could jog there in cooler months. *(Cd. sentence)*
5. I don't know when I will live in this dream. *(Cx. sentence with noun clause)*

Using *Language and Self-Expression*

Consider using this writing assignment to assess students' ability to use clauses correctly and effectively. You may want students to complete the assignment as part of a descriptive writing strand for their portfolios.

Prewriting

Suggest that students revisit their analysis of the painting that they did in *Making Visual Connections* on page L252.

Encourage students to use questioning strategies to help them organize their thoughts in the prewriting stage. For example, students might use the following questions to help them proceed with their writing:

- Who are the most important people in your life?
- What lessons have these people taught you?
- What symbols or objects have been an important part of these lessons?

FOR YOUR INFORMATION

About the Artist

M. C. Escher was the youngest child in a family with three boys. The son of a civil engineer, Escher studied literature and architecture before becoming a graphic artist. His artworks have become increasingly popular over the years because they combine humor and precision to create optical illusions and unexpected perspectives.

Language and *Self-Expression*

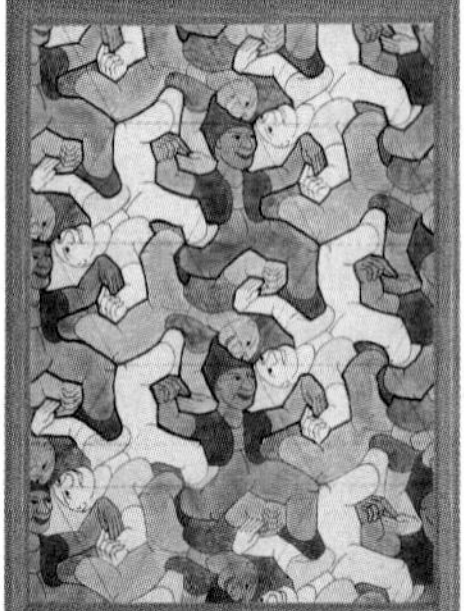

M. C. Escher became famous for his *tessellations*, which are patterns of shapes that fit together with no space in between. He used people, places, and objects he encountered as inspiration for his prints. Does the image in this print remind you of anything or anyone you have seen before?

If you created a tessellation out of an image that is meaningful to you, what would the image be? Write a description of this image and explain what it symbolizes to you. Using different kinds of clauses, describe the colors and textures you would use in a tessellation to create a greeting card using this image.

Prewriting Brainstorm for a list of people, objects, and symbols that are meaningful to you. Choose one to write about. Then brainstorm for colors, textures, or other elements you associate with this image.

Drafting Write a vivid description of your image and explain its meaning. First describe the artistic elements of shape, color, and so on. Then explain the symbolism of the image. You could end the description by giving the title of your image.

Revising Ask a friend to read your description and give you feedback. Is the image described precisely and clearly? Does the explanation of the symbolism make sense? Be sure you have used different kinds of clauses and sentences for variety.

Editing Check for errors in punctuation, spelling, and grammar.

Publishing Make a greeting card using the image you have described. With your classmates, hold a greeting card exposition to display your cards. Write a final copy of your description to give to your teacher.

Clauses

A **clause** is a group of words that has a subject and a verb.

An **independent (main) clause** can stand alone as a sentence because it expresses a complete thought. *(page L253)*

A **subordinate (dependent) clause** cannot stand alone as a sentence because it does not express a complete thought. *(page L254)*

Subordinate Clauses

An **adverb clause** is a subordinate clause that is used mainly to modify a verb. *(pages L256–L258)*

An **adjective clause** is a subordinate clause that is used to modify a noun or a pronoun. *(pages L260–L262)*

An adjective clause that is too far away from the word it modifies is called a **misplaced modifier.** *(page L265)*

A **noun clause** is a subordinate clause that is used like a noun. *(pages L267–L268)*

An **essential clause** contains information that is necessary to the meaning of the sentence. *(page L262)*

A **nonessential clause** can be removed from the sentence without changing the basic meaning of the sentence. *(page L262)*

Kinds of Sentence Structure

A **simple sentence** contains one independent clause. *(page L271)*

A **compound sentence** consists of two or more independent clauses. *(page L271)*

A **complex sentence** consists of one independent clause and one or more subordinate clauses. *(page L275)*

Other Information About Clauses

Punctuating adverb clauses *(page L258)*
Punctuating adjective clauses *(page L262)*
Distinguishing between a compound sentence and a compound verb *(pages L272–L273)*
Punctuating compound sentences *(page L273)*
List of common subordinating conjunctions *(page L257)*
List of relative pronouns *(page L261)*
List of common introductory words for noun clauses *(page L268)*

Using *Another Look*

Another Look summarizes the terms defined in the chapter and provides cross-references to the specific pages on which they are explained. Consider having students use this feature prior to completing **CheckPoint** or taking the posttest. Students who can provide several examples of each term should be able to score well on either measurement.

FOR ASSESSING LEARNING

Using *the Posttest*

Assessing Learning

The posttest will help you and your students assess where they stand in their ability to use and identify adverb clauses, adjective clauses, noun clauses, simple sentences, compound sentences, and complex sentences.

IDENTIFYING COMMON STUMBLING BLOCKS

Problem

- Lack of comma with an introductory adverb clause

Solution

- For reteaching, use the chart on page L258.

Problem

- Lack of comma with a compound sentence

Solution

- For reteaching, use the chart on page L273.

Directions

Write the letter of the term that correctly identifies the underlined words in each sentence.

EXAMPLE **1.** I study the stars whenever the night is clear.

1 A adverb clause
B adjective clause
C noun clause
D simple sentence

ANSWER **1 A**

1. Whoever gazes at the moon tends to be romantic.

2. The constellations that I recognize include the Big Dipper, the Little Dipper, and Orion.

3. Do not look directly at the sun or an eclipse.

4. I spotted the comet as soon as it appeared.

5. If you use a telescope, you can see many more details of the moon's surface.

6. When we studied asteroids, I made a three-dimensional model of an asteroid belt.

7. The moving model of the solar system is in the closet that I made as a child.

8. Whoever could name the planets in order from the sun received bonus points on the test.

9. I peered through the fog, but I could not see any stars tonight.

10. The students who enjoy astronomy may sign up for an extra-credit assignment.

1 A independent clause
B adverb clause
C noun clause
D adjective clause

2 A adverb clause
B noun clause
C independent clause
D adjective clause

3 A simple sentence
B complex sentence
C subordinate clause
D compound sentence

4 A independent clause
B noun clause
C adverb clause
D adjective clause

5 A misplaced modifier
B subordinate clause
C compound sentence
D complex sentence

6 A independent clause
B adverb clause
C noun clause
D adjective clause

7 A misplaced modifier
B simple sentence
C noun clause
D adverb clause

8 A noun clause
B adverb clause
C misplaced modifier
D adjective clause

9 A noun clause
B compound sentence
C simple sentence
D complex sentence

10 A noun clause
B adverb clause
C misplaced modifier
D adjective clause

A DIFFERENT DELIVERY SYSTEM

If you prefer, you can print the posttest from the BK English Test Bank located at http://www.bkenglish.com.

Customizing the Test

Use these questions to add or replace items for alternate versions of the test.

11. A solar eclipse occurs when the moon obscures the sun from the earth.

12. Whoever thought of the term "falling star" was confused.

13. What we call a falling star is actually a meteor that is entering the earth's atmosphere.

14. "Northern Lights" is a common term for the Aurora Borealis, which lights the night sky near the north pole.

11. A adjective clause
B noun clause
C misplaced modifier
D adverb clause

12. A misplaced modifier
B noun clause
C adverb clause
D adjective clause

13. A adverb clause
B noun clause
C adjective clause
D independent clause

14. A compound sentence
B complex sentence
C simple sentence
D subordinate clause

Teaching Suggestions

Block Scheduling

- If your schedule requires that you cover the chapter in a **shorter time,** use the instruction on fragments and run-ons and the Check Your Understanding and QuickCheck exercises.
- If you want to take advantage of **longer class time,** add these applications to writing: Connect to Writer's Craft, Connect to the Writing Process, and Apply to Writing exercises.

Essential Knowledge and Skills

- Writing to inform such as to explain, describe, report, and narrate
- Writing in complete sentences, varying the types such as compound and complex sentences, and using appropriately punctuated independent and dependent clauses
- Editing drafts for specific purposes such as to ensure standard usage, varied sentence structure, and appropriate word choice
- Analyzing published examples for models of writing
- Evaluating the purposes and effects of varying media such as film, print, and technology presentations

CHAPTER 10

Sentence Fragments and Run-ons

Directions

Read the passage. Write the letter of the best way to write each underlined section. If the underlined section contains no error, write *D*.

EXAMPLE **1.** One natural disaster being a hurricane.

1 **A** disaster, a hurricane.
B disaster is a hurricane.
C disaster. Being a hurricane.
D No error

ANSWER **1** **B**

Develops into a hurricane only when (1) conditions are perfect. To grow, hurricanes need (2) warm waters, high humidity, and high winds. Hurricanes can last up to two or three weeks but they weaken (3) if they travel over cold water or land. Hurricanes take place only in the Atlantic and Eastern Pacific. In the Northern Pacific and Philippines. Such storms (4) are called typhoons. In the Southern Pacific, they are called cyclones. (5)

IDENTIFYING COMMON STUMBLING BLOCKS

Following is a list of the most common errors students make involving sentence fragments and run-on sentences.

Problem
- Sentence fragments

Solution
- Instruction, p. L291
- Practice, p. L292

Problem
- Run-on sentences

Solution
- Instruction, pp. L301–L303
- Practice, pp. L304–L305

1 A A storm develops into a hurricane. Only when
  B A storm develops into a hurricane only when
  C Develops into a hurricane, only when
  D No error

2 A To grow. Hurricanes need
  B To grow. Hurricanes needing
  C To grow into hurricanes need
  D No error

3 **A** two or three weeks, but they weaken
  B two or three weeks. But they weaken
  C two or three weeks they weaken
  D No error

4 A In the Northern Pacific and Philippines are such storms
  B In the Northern Pacific and Philippines having such storm
  C In the Northern Pacific and Philippines, such storms
  D No error

5 A In the Southern Pacific. They are called cyclones.
  B They are called cyclones, which is in the Southern Pacific.
  C They are called, cyclones, in the Southern Pacific.
  D No error

A DIFFERENT DELIVERY SYSTEM

If you prefer, you can print the pretest from the BK English Test Bank located at http://www.bkenglish.com.

Using *the Pretest*

Assessing Prior Knowledge

The pretest will help you and your students assess where they stand in their basic understanding of fragments and run-ons.

Customizing the Test

Use these questions to add or replace items for alternate versions of the test.

Under the earth's crust. Lies (6) hot rock called magma. Pressure builds up under the surface it pushes the magma (7) upward. The magma reaches cracks in the crust. Now it is not called magma anymore it is called lava. (8) Sometimes the lava simply spills out. Other times it erupts with a huge fountain (9) of gas and dust.

6. A earth's crust. Lying
  B earth's crust lies
  C earth's crust lying
  D No error

7. **A** under the surface, and it pushes the magma
  B under the surface, it pushes the magma
  C under the surface and it pushing the magma
  D No error

8. **A** called magma anymore. It is called lava.
  B called magma anymore but lava.
  C called magma. Anymore it is called lava.
  D No error

9. A Other times it erupts. With a huge fountain
  B Other times. It erupts with a huge fountain
  C Other times it erupts, and with a huge fountain
  D No error

ADDITIONAL RESOURCES

Language Skills Practice . . . . pages 87–90
Transparency Tools FA10
ESL Practice and Test Preparation . . . . . pages 112–114
Assessment: Chapter Test. . . . . pages 164–170

MAKING VISUAL CONNECTIONS

For Language Development

Have students study the photographs of a galloping horse by Eadweard Muybridge. Tell students that the photographs were taken to prove that a horse's hooves are simultaneously off the ground during each stride. Have students write a paragraph telling whether *Horse Galloping* should be considered a work of art or a part of a scientific experiment. Remind students to use complete sentences and to avoid run-on sentences in their writing.

To Stimulate Writing

Use the questions for art criticism as writing or discussion prompts.

Sample Answers:

Describe The photographs show a horse and rider at full gallop.

Analyze The photographs show step-by-step the movements and positions involved in a gallop.

Interpret A writer might describe the movement in a step-by-step description. Vivid verbs could show how the movements differ from step to step. Making all the sentences the same—"The horse does this. The horse does that."—would be dull. Combining sentences and adding descriptive phrases and clauses would add interest.

Judge I would refer to the pictures because they show the motion involved in a horse's gallop.

Eadweard Muybridge. *Horse Galloping,* 1887.
Collotype print. George Eastman House, Rochester, New York.

Describe What is the subject of these photographs?

Analyze How does the photographer manage to convey the illusion of movement through this series of still photographs?

Interpret How might a writer describe the movement of the horse? Why would vivid verbs be important in the description? How could varying sentence length keep the description from being dull?

Judge If you truly wanted to understand the sensation of a horse galloping, would you refer to these pictures or to a written description? Why?

At the end of this chapter, you will use the artwork to stimulate ideas for writing.

FOR DEVELOPING LANGUAGE SKILLS

LESSON 1 *(pages L291–L300)*

OBJECTIVES

- **To identify sentence fragments, phrase fragments, and clause fragments**
- **To correct sentence fragments, phrase fragments, and clause fragments**

Create Interest

Have students gather examples of sentence fragments from advertisements, newspapers, Internet sites, or magazine articles. Have students display these fragments in class. Discuss the use of fragments in informal writing. Explain that fragments should never be used in formal writing, such as school

Sentence Fragments

You have learned that to express a complete thought, a sentence must have a subject and a verb. A group of words that does not have either a subject or a verb is called a sentence fragment.

A **sentence fragment** is a group of words that does not express a complete thought.

In the example sentences that follow, subjects are underlined once and verbs are underlined twice.

NO SUBJECT	Wrote an editorial about the traffic problem.
	(Who wrote an editorial?)
SENTENCE	Bob wrote an editorial about the traffic problem.
NO VERB	The new members of the city council.
	(What did they do?)
SENTENCE	The new members of the city council sponsored a seminar.

When you edit your writing, always check specifically for any missing subjects or missing verbs.

CONNECT TO WRITER'S CRAFT

Fragments are used in creative writing for dialogue or for suggesting an incomplete thought. In most writing, however, a fragment is very informal. It is not usually appropriate for school assignments or business letters.

FOR INCREASING STUDENT ACHIEVEMENT

IDENTIFYING COMMON STUMBLING BLOCKS

Problem

- Inability to distinguish complete sentences from fragments

Solution

- Tell students that a sentence is not complete unless it expresses a complete thought. If, after reading a sentence, a reader is left asking *Who or what did?* or *What did he, she, or they do?*, then the sentence is a fragment.
- Have students read the following sentences aloud and decide whether they are *sentences* or *fragments.*

  Using the newspaper as a resource for writing about the weather. (fragment)

  I also read about medical research. (sentence)

  The information the newspaper provided was correct and thorough. (sentence)

  By using this medical information. (fragment)

work, business letters, and job applications. Ask students why fragments might be used, for example, by advertisers. Discuss students' responses.

Guide Instruction

By Modeling Strategies

Show students how to identify and correct fragments using the following examples:

My friend Beck, who collects fire engines. (My friend Beck, who collects fire engines, is coming over today.)

About fire engines appeared on page one. (An article about fire engines appeared on page one.)

The photograph of the fire engine. (Beck saved the photograph of the fire engine.)

A DIFFERENT APPROACH

Auditory

Read each sentence in **Check Your Understanding** aloud as students listen and respond by saying either *sentence* or *sentence fragment.* Discuss the correct responses. Have students share the strategies they used to identify each item as a sentence or as a fragment.

PRACTICE YOUR SKILLS

Check Your Understanding

Distinguishing Between Sentences and Fragments

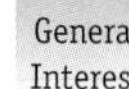

Label each group of words as a *sentence* or a *sentence fragment.*

1. The newspaper prints national and local news articles. S
2. Every city with a large population. [has at least one newspaper.] F
3. Most readers prefer delivery in the morning. S
4. Many people read the sports page first. S
5. Many people like to read the comics. S
6. [Newspapers] Contain informative articles about houses. F
7. The comics used to be printed in black-and-white. S
8. [Newspapers carry] Stories about famous and ordinary people. F
9. [Newspapers also] Provide information on manners, health, and movies. F
10. [The newspaper] Represents a terrific bargain for the cost. F

Connect to the Writing Process: Revising

Correcting Sentence Fragments

[Answers may vary. See possible responses given above.]

11.–15. Revise the sentence fragments from the preceding exercise to make complete sentences.

Communicate Your Ideas

APPLY TO WRITING

Analysis: *Complete Sentences*

Write a one-paragraph analysis of the types of articles found in a major section of your local newspaper. Use sentences to classify and describe the articles as news, feature, human interest, or editorial columns. Use specific details to make your analysis clear.

Remind students not to be fooled by the length of a fragment. A sentence is complete only if it contains a subject and a predicate that together express a complete thought.

Consolidate Skills

Through Guided Practice

The **Check Your Understanding** exercises will help students differentiate between complete sentences and fragments. Have students explain the difference between a sentence and a fragment. As part of their explanation, students should provide examples of phrase fragments and clause fragments. Complete the first item in each **Check Your Understanding** exercise together. Then have students complete the exercise independently.

Phrase Fragments

A complete sentence must have a subject and a verb. Because a phrase does not have either a subject or a verb, it can never stand alone as a sentence. When phrases are written alone, they result in **phrase fragments.**

The following examples of phrase fragments are in **bold** type. Notice that the fragments are capitalized and punctuated as if they were sentences.

PREPOSITIONAL PHRASE	Every morning I deliver the newspaper. **Onto the Johnsons' front porch.**
APPOSITIVE PHRASE	Every payday I will collect from Mr. Johnson. **The oldest customer on my paper route.**
PARTICIPIAL PHRASE	**Sitting on his front porch.** He always reads the newspaper.
INFINITIVE PHRASE	**To please Mr. Johnson.** I will deliver the newspaper on time.

PRACTICE YOUR SKILLS

Check Your Understanding

Distinguishing Between Sentences and Fragments

General Interest **Label each group of words as a *sentence* or a *phrase fragment.***

1. Comics are fun to read. S
2. To make people laugh. PF
3. Of a scene or a complete scene in the strip. PF
4. With exaggerated features and in common clothes. PF

DEVELOPING WORKPLACE COMPETENCIES

Thinking Skills: Decision Making

Have students consider how sentence fragments might cause confusion or indecisiveness in the workplace. Ask students: How might sentence fragments in business memorandums affect someone's ability to make clear decisions? Students should comment on the following memorandum and tell how it might affect the manager's, Ms. Moore's, ability to make a clear decision:

Ms. Moore:
Please let the Human Resources department know. For completing a job application. Whether applicants should use Form A or Form B. Sometimes applicants use Form B. Which form do you prefer? Often inconsistent. Hire people using Form A? Or using Form B? If you had to choose one.
Thank you,
B. Miller

Apply to Communication

Through Independent Writing

The **Communicate Your Ideas** activities on pages L292 and L300 prompt students to write an analysis of newspaper articles and an analysis of an author's use of clause fragments. Before students begin writing, have them consider what strategies they will use to avoid fragments in their own writing. How might they respond to a famous author's use of fragments? Allow time for students to share their responses.

Transfer to Everyday Life

Correcting Fragments in Newspaper Articles and Advertisements

Have students correct fragments they find in newspaper articles and advertisements. Students should include the fragments and write out their complete sentences on a separate sheet

GETTING STUDENTS INVOLVED

Reciprocal Teaching

After discussing the examples on pages L294–L295, have advanced learners write ten examples of phrase fragments. Then have these students work with struggling learners to correct and rewrite these fragments. Students should make sure that the corrected sentences express complete thoughts and contain correct punctuation. Have struggling learners explain the learning strategies or explanations that helped them the most.

5. A strip about families or animals will appeal to all ages. S
6. From a group of soldiers to talking pets. PF
7. Expressed many feelings besides humor. PF
8. Ranging from poking fun to social satire. PF
9. Charles Schulz was a comic-strip artist. S
10. Drew the comic strip called *Peanuts*. PF

Ways to Correct Phrase Fragments

Always look for phrase fragments when you edit your writing. If you find any, you can correct them by adding a subject and a verb to make the phrase into a separate sentence or by attaching a phrase to a related group of words that has a subject and a verb.

The following examples show how to correct the phrase fragments on the preceding page.

CORRECTED PREPOSITIONAL PHRASE FRAGMENTS	Every morning I deliver the newspaper. **It flies onto the Johnsons' front porch.** (subject and verb added)
	Every morning I deliver the newspaper **onto the Johnsons' front porch.** (attached to a sentence)
CORRECTED APPOSITIVE PHRASE FRAGMENTS	Every payday I will collect from Mr. Johnson. **He is the oldest customer on my paper route.** (subject and verb added)
	Every payday I will collect from Mr. Johnson, **the oldest customer on my paper route.** (attached to a sentence)

of paper. Have students read their fragments and corrected sentences to the class.

Pull It All Together

By Classifying

Have students classify the following fragments as *phrase fragments* or as *clause fragments.* Then have students correct each fragment.

To get better grades. Anthony studies hard. (phrase fragment; Anthony studies hard to get better grades.)

Before he studies. Anthony listens to classical music. (clause fragment; Before he studies Anthony listens to classical music.)

Anthony spends time swimming. Because he also enjoys competing in sports. (clause fragment; Because he also enjoys competing in sports, Anthony spends time swimming.)

CORRECTED PARTICIPIAL PHRASE FRAGMENTS	**He is sitting on his front porch.** He always reads the newspaper. (subject and verb added)
	Sitting on his front porch, he always reads the newspaper. (attached to a sentence)
CORRECTED INFINITIVE PHRASE FRAGMENT	**To please Mr. Johnson,** I will deliver the newspaper on time. (attached to a sentence)

PRACTICE YOUR SKILLS

Check Your Understanding

Distinguishing Between Sentences and Fragments

History Topic **Label each group of words as a *sentence* or a *phrase fragment.***

1. In the charter colonies of Connecticut and Rhode Island of the 1760s. PF
2. The colonists from these places elected their own representatives. S
3. From Great Britain an appointed governor. PF
4. Elected representatives passed their own legislation. S
5. The proprietary colonies of Maryland, Delaware, and Pennsylvania. PF
6. Depending on the authority of the delegated officials. PF
7. The people elected only the lower representatives. S
8. To live in the royal colonies of Georgia, Massachusetts, New Hampshire, New Jersey, North Carolina, and Virginia. PF

A DIFFERENT APPROACH

Kinesthetic

After students have written their responses to **Check Your Understanding,** have them stand as you read each sentence aloud. As students listen they should respond by using gestures. Tell students that thumbs up represents a *complete sentence,* and thumbs down represents a *sentence fragment.* Have students gesture the correct response as you read aloud items one through ten. Discuss why students chose particular responses.

Check Understanding

Writing Complete Sentences

Have students write a paragraph explaining how they avoid fragments in their own writing. Remind students to focus on writing complete sentences and using correct punctuation. Have students share their paragraphs with the class.

HOME WORK

First, have students review the lesson on phrase fragments. Then have students write a paragraph about a community program/service they feel is important to society.

9. Ruled directly by Great Britain all of the royal colonies. PF

10. With little or no say in their own government. PF

Connect to the Writing Process: Editing

Combining Sentences and Phrase Fragments

Add each phrase fragment to the first sentence to form a complete sentence.

11. The Dutch first settled New Netherland. Was later changed to New York. [and; its name]

12. The British captured New Netherland in 1684. Adding it to their royal colonies.

13. The Swedish lost control of Delaware. Lost to the Duke of York.

14. William Penn purchased Delaware from England. The proprietor of Pennsylvania. [and became]

15. English law obligated colonists. To remain loyal to their king.

Connect to the Writing Process: Revising

Correcting Phrase Fragments

Rewrite each phrase fragment to make a complete sentence. [Answers may vary. Possible responses are given.]

16. [Our democratic government is elected] By the people and for the people.

17. [I try to be active in] My own community.

18. [I believe in a society] With the same rights for everyone.

19. Depending on other people for leadership. [is all too easy.]

20. To enjoy the benefits of democracy. [we should all be participants in democracy.]

21. [Those who vote for this law are] Voting for personal rights.

22. To participate in the democratic process. [I will always vote.]

Clause Fragments

A subordinate clause often looks very much like a complete sentence because it has a subject and a verb. However, when it stands alone, it becomes a **clause fragment** because it does not express a complete thought.

The following examples in **bold** type are clause fragments. Notice that they are punctuated and capitalized as if they were complete sentences.

ADVERB CLAUSE FRAGMENTS	**When I design a product.** I list materials necessary to make it.
	Products are tested. **So that safety and longevity can be guaranteed.**
ADJECTIVE CLAUSE FRAGMENTS	Stella is the engineer. **Who is in charge of testing.**
	Is this the design for the seats? **That uses a great deal of plastic?**

PRACTICE YOUR SKILLS

Check Your Understanding

Distinguishing Between Sentences and Fragments

Science Topic **Label each group of words *S* for sentence or *CF* for clause fragment.**

1. Telephones last a long time and are durable. S
2. When you pick up the telephone. CF
3. Notice the materials it is made of. S
4. Because most of its parts are made of plastic. CF
5. Plastic is a modern material. S

A DIFFERENT APPROACH

Auditory

Before writing out their responses to **Check Your Understanding,** read items one through ten aloud. Students should respond by telling whether each item is a *sentence* or a *clause fragment.* Tell students that listening to sentences, rather than just reading them, can help them to distinguish complete sentences from fragments. Discuss students' responses and how listening helped them to distinguish sentences and fragments.

HOME WORK
Have students look through their writing portfolios and search for sentence fragments. As a home work assignment, students should correct their fragments and label them as *phrase fragments* or *clause fragments.*

6. Plastic is a synthetic polymer-based material. S
7. That can be easily molded into various shapes. CF
8. After they are manufactured from organic compounds. CF
9. If you notice ordinary things in your life. CF
10. That are made of synthetic polyethylene. CF
11. Check the tags on furniture. S
12. When you are at department stores. CF
13. Don't be surprised to see different plastics listed. S
14. Ask about the strength of contemporary fabrics. S
15. Who knows how durable a fabric is? S

Ways to Correct Clause Fragments

When you edit your written work, you can correct clause fragments in one of two ways. You can make the subordinate clause into an independent clause, or you can attach a clause fragment to a related sentence next to it.

Corrected Adverb Clause Fragments

When I design a product, I list the materials necessary to make it. (attached to a sentence)

Products are tested. **Safety and longevity can be guaranteed.** (made into an independent clause)

Corrected Adjective Clause Fragments

Stella is the engineer **who is in charge of testing.** (attached to a sentence)

Is this the design for the seats **that uses a great deal of plastic?** (attached to a sentence)

PRACTICE YOUR SKILLS

Check Your Understanding
Distinguishing Between Sentences and Fragments

History Topic **Label each group of words as a *sentence* or a *clause fragment.***

1. Before the Spanish explorers wandered throughout Florida. CF
2. A civilized, well-governed society inhabited the peninsula. S
3. The Seminoles, who settled in areas and farmed the land, were some of the earliest inhabitants of Florida. S
4. ~~Who settled in many areas and farmed the fertile land.~~ CF
5. The Seminoles left burial mounds and other artifacts. S
6. Which suggest the existence of some form of government. CF
7. The Native Americans had a loose confederation of tribes. S
8. ~~Where~~ in which different tribes were constantly trying to control each other. CF
9. Rules that gave power to the chief of each tribe were made to keep the confederation working. S
10. ~~That gave power to the chief of each tribe in the confederation.~~ CF

Connect to the Writing Process: Revising
Correcting Clause Fragments

11.–15. Rewrite the clause fragments from the preceding exercise to make complete sentences. Remember that you can attach a clause fragment to another sentence. [Answers may vary. See possible responses given above.]

HOME WORK

Have students create their own game to reinforce what they have learned about sentences and sentence fragments. Students can choose appropriate materials to construct their games. For example, they might use sentence cards and an illustrated game board to have participants distinguish between sentences and fragments. Have students explain their completed games to the class. Then spend a day trying out all of the various games. Discuss what made certain games effective and entertaining.

TIMESAVER *QuickCheck*

Evaluate students' responses to the five bulleted questions by focusing on their assessment of the literature model. Students should use complete sentences in their responses.

HOME STUDY

Have students locate "Rain, Rain, Go Away" or another short story by Isaac Asimov and identify other fragments in Asimov's writing. Ask students to provide possible reasons for Asimov's use of fragments in those particular sections of the stories.

SELECTION AMENDMENT
Description of change: excerpted
Rationale: to focus on the grammar skill

Communicate Your Ideas

APPLY TO WRITING

Writer's Craft: *Analyzing the Use of Clause Fragments*

Sometimes writers purposely use clause fragments to create a certain effect. In the following excerpt, a wife asks her husband a question. Notice the husband's response.

> "But why didn't you ever tell me?"
>
> "Because Tommie only told me this morning and because I thought he must have told you already and, to tell the absolute truth, because I thought you could just manage to drag out a normal existence even if you never found out."
>
> *—Isaac Asimov,* "Rain, Rain, Go Away"

- The husband's response begins with the word *because.* How many subordinate clauses are in his response? There are four subordinate clauses in his response. [See below.]
- Write each subordinate clause from his answer. How does each begin? The first three begin with the word *because*, the last with *even if.*
- Is there an independent clause in his answer? If so, what is it? There is no independent clause in his answer.
- What is the effect on the reader of so many subordinate clauses? It is confusing.
- What do you suppose would have happened if each subordinate clause had been followed by an independent clause? The sentence would be repetitive.

The four subordinate clauses: "Because Tommie only told me this morning"; "because I thought he must have told you already"; "because I thought you could just manage to drag out a normal existence"; "even if you never found out."

LESSON 2 *(pages L301–L305)*

OBJECTIVES

- **To identify and correct run-on sentences**
- **To distinguish between sentences, fragments, and run-ons**

Create Interest

Have students brainstorm words to describe how they feel, as readers, after reading the following examples. For example, do they feel confused or agitated? Write students' responses on the board.

I enjoy all kinds of music rock, classical, and bluegrass and I like to play different kinds of music when I'm with my friends after school and on weekends.

We use guitars and drums to play and we hope to get a recording contract from a big company but we need to practice some more before that can happen.

Run-on Sentences

A common mistake some writers make when they are writing too fast is to combine several thoughts and write them as one sentence. The result is a run-on sentence.

A **run-on sentence** is two or more sentences that are written together and are separated by a comma or no mark of punctuation at all.

Run-on sentences are usually written in either of two ways.

WITH A COMMA	The concert is beginning, it will be over by lunchtime.
WITH NO PUNCTUATION	Danny conducted the orchestra the musicians played very hard.

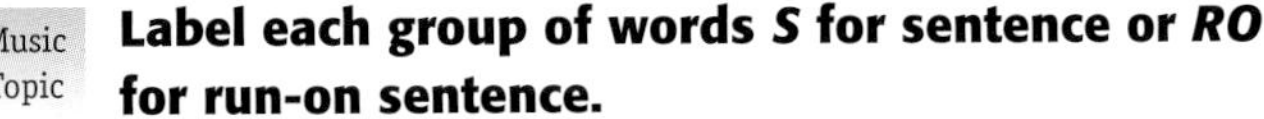

PRACTICE YOUR SKILLS

Check Your Understanding

Distinguishing Between Sentences and Run-on Sentences

Music Topic **Label each group of words *S* for sentence or *RO* for run-on sentence.**

1. Conductors direct an orchestra, chorus, or opera production. S
2. Conductors usually specialize in orchestral or choral conducting, each specialization shares many common elements. RO
3. They have a difficult job many jobs are rolled into one title. RO

A DIFFERENT APPROACH

Visual

Have students complete **Check Your Understanding** by taking turns writing their responses on the board. Have students read each item aloud and then write their responses, correcting any run-on sentence. Discuss students' responses after they have explained why a sentence is or is not a run-on sentence.

Guide Instruction

By Modeling Strategies

Write these example sentences on the board and model strategies for distinguishing sentences from run-on sentences. Show students how to separate the run-on sentences. Point out that sometimes run-on sentences contain correct punctuation, which makes them harder to identify.

Jack is interested in music and literature and he especially likes science fiction novels. (run-on; needs comma between *literature, and*)

I love to watch science fiction movies, but I do not like watching them alone. (sentence)

What kind of movies do you like and what kind of books do you enjoy reading? (run-on; needs comma between *like, and*)

Consolidate Skills

Through Guided Practice

The **Check Your Understanding** exercises as well as the **QuickCheck** on

HOME WORK

After discussing the models for correcting run-on sentences on pages L302–L303, have students write similar models for correcting other run-on sentences. Students should take two of the run-on sentences they identified in **Check Your Understanding** and correct them by creating separate sentences, by writing compound sentences, or by writing complex sentences as shown in the examples on these two pages.

4. They must study and memorize many thousands of measures of music. S

5. While conducting, they turn from the sheet music, they must be free to look at the orchestra or the chorus. RO

6. Conductors must rehearse with the performers they also have to find new music to perform. RO

7. They must be able to conduct a group and to know about each instrument. S

8. Conductors give advice they give orders. RO

9. They must be in excellent physical condition, they work like athletes. RO

10. Orchestra conductors use a baton choral conductors usually depend on their hands. RO

Ways to Correct Run-on Sentences

Basically there are three ways to correct a run-on sentence. You can turn it into two separate sentences, a single compound sentence, or a single complex sentence.

RUN-ON SENTENCES	The movie is beginning, it will be over by three o'clock.
	The aliens roamed outer space the creatures searched for food.
SEPARATE SENTENCES	The movie is beginning. It will be over by three o'clock.
	The aliens roamed outer space. The creatures searched for food.

page L305 will help students identify and correct run-on sentences. Complete the first item in each exercise together, discussing and reviewing the major strategies students should use to identify run-on sentences. Then have students complete the remaining exercises independently.

Transfer to Everyday Life

Identifying Run-ons in Speech
Have students make a list of five run-on sentences they hear in conversations throughout the day. Have students share their run-on sentences with the class. Discuss with students the reasons people use run-on sentences in speech, especially in informal conversations.

Pull It All Together

By Sharing
Have students share their strategies for identifying run-on sentences. Students should also show their partners how

COMPOUND SENTENCES

The movie is beginning, but it will be over by three o'clock.

(The two independent clauses are joined by a comma and the coordinating conjunction *but.*)

The aliens roamed outer space, and the creatures searched for food.

(The two independent clauses are joined by a comma and the coordinating conjunction *and.*)

COMPLEX SENTENCES

Because the movie is beginning, it will be over by three o'clock.

(The first independent clause is made into a subordinate clause with the addition of the subordinating conjunction *because.* The subordinate clause is joined to the independent clause with a comma.)

As the aliens roamed outer space, the creatures searched for food.

(The first independent clause is made into a subordinate clause with the addition of the subordinating conjunction *as.* The subordinate clause is joined to the independent clause with a comma.)

CONNECT TO WRITER'S CRAFT

Writers sometimes include run-on sentences to create a sense of constant movement or meandering in their writing. However, when writing formally, it is best to avoid run-on sentences.

YOUR IDEAS

For Correcting Run-on Sentences

to correct run-on sentences by correctly using commas or semicolons or by creating separate sentences.

Check Understanding

Defining Run-on Sentence

Have students write their own definition for *run-on sentence*. Students should also write a complete sentence and an example of a run-on sentence. Then have students compare their own definitions with the definition of *run-on sentence* on page L301 in their textbooks.

A DIFFERENT APPROACH

Auditory

Have students complete **Check Your Understanding** with a partner by reading each item aloud. Partners should decide whether each item is a sentence or a run-on sentence. When completed, call on various pairs to share their responses. Partners should be able to explain why they chose their particular responses.

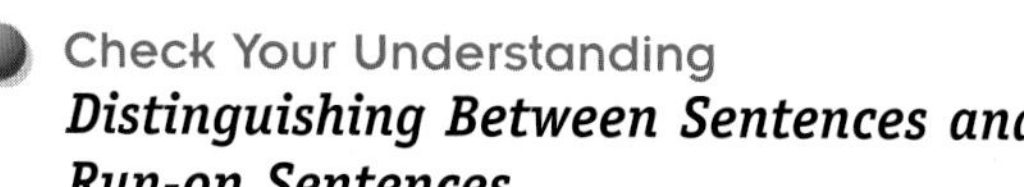

PRACTICE YOUR SKILLS

Check Your Understanding

Distinguishing Between Sentences and Run-on Sentences

Literature Topic **Label each group of words *S* for sentence or *RO* for run-on sentence.**

1. Science fiction has been a popular form of literature for many years, and many readers enjoy this special form of fantasy. RO
2. Science fiction allows writers to offer adventures in the future. S
3. The stories may tell of adventures on other planets. They may narrate stories of time travel or space travel. RO
4. Its setting in the future separates science fiction from historical fiction. S
5. Science fiction focuses on the future, and historical fiction looks to the past. RO
6. Usually a successful writer of science fiction knows a good deal of science, and the crafty writer often takes science to an extreme. RO
7. Of course, with the rapid advance in technology and science, this special type of literature has grown in the last fifty years. S
8. Some popular science fiction writers include Ray Bradbury, Kurt Vonnegut, and Isaac Asimov. There are hundreds of well-known writers. RO
9. This type of writing comes in many forms, and it is also very close to folklore. RO
10. Have you read any science fiction? Who is your favorite writer? RO

Connect to the Writing Process: Revising

Correcting Run-on Sentences

[Answers may vary. See possible answers given on previous page.]

11.–17. Rewrite the run-on sentences from the exercise on the preceding page to make complete sentences.

Mixed Practice

Literature Topic

Label each group of words *S* for sentence, *F* for fragment, or *RO* for run-on sentence.

1. John Milton is a famous British author of the seventeenth century. S
2. Milton wrote poetry, pamphlets, and drama he was blind for half of his life. RO
3. Before he left school and became a professional writer. F
4. All of his writing mixed religion and politics. S
5. He wrote several long works his most famous work is *Paradise Lost.* RO
6. Based on the Bible, the very long poem tells the story of the Garden of Eden. S
7. Having more than ten thousand lines and recited by the blind poet to his daughters for revision. F
8. "Lycidas" was written to commemorate a person who had drowned. S
9. A writer of booklets on education and literature who had many enemies and few friends. F
10. Blindness is a challenge that some people believe is impossible to overcome, John Milton's life proves just the opposite. RO

EXPANDING THE LESSON

Using Technology

You will find additional **instructional** and **practice** materials for this chapter at http://www.bkenglish.com.

FOR REVIEWING SKILLS

Using *CheckPoint*

This feature on sentence fragments and run-on sentences can be used as further independent practice or as a cumulative review of the chapter. Students identify and correct sentence fragments and run-on sentences.

CheckPoint

Correcting Sentence Fragments

Correct each sentence fragment. Add capital letters and punctuation marks where needed.

1. Beginning in the nineteenth century, Ice hockey was first played in eastern Canada.
2. We found a battered trunk, In the old red barn.
3. Before you go to bed, Please lock the front door.
4. Dad was in the yard, When the phone rang.
5. We could see the horses, Jumping over the fence.
6. Swimming for hours, We enjoyed our day at the beach.
7. I lost my purse, But found the car keys on the lawn.
8. The score was tied, Between Weston and Newton High.
9. In the museum, We saw our first mummy.
10. Six-day bicycle races were a fad, In the early 1900s.

Correcting Run-on Sentences

Correct each run-on sentence. Add capital letters, conjunctions, and punctuation marks where needed.

1. Duluth is about 2,000 miles from the Atlantic, its harbor is reached through the St. Lawrence Seaway. Duluth is about 2,000 miles from the Atlantic. Its harbor is reached through the St. Lawrence Seaway.
2. I always buy mysteries I love to read them. I always buy mysteries because I love to read them.
3. The winter Olympics were held in Japan in 1972, this was the first time these games had been held in Asia. When the winter Olympics were held in Japan in 1972, this was the first time these games had been held in Asia.
4. The American Revolution began in 1775 it ended in 1783. The American Revolution began in 1775, and it ended in 1783.
5. Most of the snakes in the United States are harmless, many of them benefit farmers. Most of the snakes in the United States are harmless, and many of them benefit farmers.

6. I eat a healthful diet I eat salads, fish, and vegetables. I eat a healthful diet. I eat salads, fish, and vegetables.

7. Alexander Hamilton's picture is on the ten-dollar bill, Andrew Jackson's is on the twenty. Alexander Hamilton's picture is on the ten-dollar bill, and Andrew Jackson's is on the twenty.

8. Bill lifts weights, he trains every day. Bill lifts weights. He trains every day.

9. The first Academy Awards® ceremony was held in 1927, only 250 people attended. The first Academy Awards® ceremony was held in 1927. Only 250 people attended.

10. Martin takes Latin he studies an hour a night. Martin takes Latin. He studies an hour a night.

Correcting Sentence Errors

Rewrite the following paragraph, correcting each sentence fragment and run-on sentence. Add capital letters, conjunctions, and punctuation marks where needed.

You may have a microwave oven in your home. But did you know that microwaves also carry television programs through space? When you call overseas. The call may be transmitted to a satellite by microwave. You may have seen towers with unusual satellite dishes these are microwave towers. Ships and airplanes may use microwaves. To detect objects around them. A radar dish on the ground beams microwaves they strike an object and bounce back.

Writing Sentences

[Answers may vary. Possible responses are given.]

Write five sentences that follow the directions below. Beware of sentence fragments and run-ons. Write about an important invention or about a topic of your choice.

1. Write a sentence that contains only a subject and a verb. Lightbulbs illuminate.

2. Write a sentence that consists of a simple sentence with an attached phrase. Light from lightbulbs is called white light.

3. Write a sentence that consists of a simple sentence with an attached clause. When you use a lightbulb, thank Thomas Edison.

4. Write a sentence containing the word *and* that is not a run-on sentence. He was a great inventor, and he benefited mankind.

5. Write a sentence containing the word *but* that is not a run-on sentence. He invented the phonograph, but he could not hear.

Sample Answers for *Correcting Sentence Errors:*

You may have a microwave oven in your home, but did you know that microwaves also carry television programs through space? When you call overseas, the call may be transmitted to a satellite by microwave. You may have seen towers with unusual satellite dishes. These are microwave towers. Ships and airplanes may use microwaves to detect objects around them. A radar dish on the ground beams microwaves. They strike an object and bounce back.

Using *Language and Self-Expression*

Consider using this writing assignment to assess students' ability to use clauses correctly and effectively. You may want students to complete the assignment as part of a descriptive writing strand for their portfolios.

Prewriting

Encourage students to use questioning strategies to help them organize their thoughts in the prewriting stage. For example, students might use the following questions to help them proceed with their writing:

What is the first thing you do when you wake up every morning?

How would you describe this activity to someone from another planet?

What words could you use to make your description clear to your readers?

FOR YOUR INFORMATION

About the Artist

During the 1860s and 1870s, Englishman Eadweard Muybridge (1830–1904) was recognized for his photographs of the Yosemite wilderness in the United States. In 1872 Leland Stanford hired Muybridge to settle a bet. He wanted to prove that as a horse gallops, all four of its hooves are simultaneously off the ground during each stride. To prove this, Muybridge produced a sequential series of photographs using several cameras. In 1879 Muybridge invented the zoopraxiscope, a machine that reproduced the motion of the galloping horse using the photographs. The machine was the forerunner of cinematography.

Language and *Self-Expression*

This famous series of photographs was commissioned as a way of answering the question "Does a running horse ever have all four hooves off the ground at once?" Galloping horses move so fast that stop-action photography seemed the only way to determine the answer. Muybridge set up a series of still cameras along the race track, each with a tripwire for the horse to set off as it ran by. At the time, the 1870s, this was a radically innovative way to study movement. Later, Muybridge found that if he projected the photographs in quick motion, they gave the illusion of motion.

Describing any movement step by step is a challenge. It requires breaking down the total motion into smaller units. Think of a movement you perform every day. Write a step-by-step description of the motions involved.

Prewriting Draw sketches of yourself doing the movement you chose. For each sketch write a verb or descriptive phrase that tells about the step.

Drafting Begin with a sentence that states the main idea of your description. Use your sketches to add details in step-by-step order.

Revising Reread your description, and replace dull words with more specific ones. Look for sentence fragments and run-ons, and correct them.

Editing Review your description, looking for errors in grammar, capitalization, punctuation, and spelling. Make any corrections that are necessary.

Publishing Prepare a final copy of your description. Share your paragraph with a classmate. See whether your classmate can follow the steps you wrote to imitate the movement.

Another Look

Sentence Fragments and Run-ons

A **sentence fragment** is a group of words that does not express a complete thought.

Phrase Fragments

Since a phrase does not have a subject and verb, it cannot stand alone as a sentence. When prepositional, appositive, participial, and infinitive phrases are written alone, they result in **phrase fragments.** *(pages L293–L295)*

Clause Fragments

A subordinate clause often looks very much like a complete sentence because it has a subject and verb. However, when it stands alone, it becomes a **clause fragment** because it does not express a complete thought. *(pages L297–L298)*

A **run-on sentence** is two or more sentences that are written together and are separated by a comma or no mark of punctuation at all.

Other Information About Sentence Fragments and Run-ons

Correcting phrase fragments *(pages L294–L295)*
Correcting clause fragments *(page L298)*
Correcting run-on sentences *(pages L302–L303)*

Using *Another Look*

Another Look summarizes the terms defined in the chapter and provides cross-references to the specific pages on which they are explained. Consider having students use this feature prior to completing **CheckPoint** or taking the post-test. Students who can provide several examples of each term should be able to score well on either measurement.

FOR ASSESSING LEARNING

Using *the Posttest*

Assessing Learning

The posttest will help you and your students assess where they stand in their ability to identify and correct sentence fragments and run-on sentences.

IDENTIFYING COMMON STUMBLING BLOCKS

Following is a list of the most common errors students make involving sentence fragments and run-on sentences.

Problem

- Sentence fragments

Solution

- For reteaching, use the explanatory copy printed in blue beside the examples on page L291.

Problem

- Run-on sentences

Solution

- For reteaching, use the explanatory copy printed in blue beside the examples on page L303.

Directions

Read the passage. Write the letter of the best way to write each underlined section. If the underlined section needs no change, write *D*.

EXAMPLE **1.** Because Norway has little farmland. Fishing is important there.

1 A Norway has little farmland, fishing is important there.

B Norway has little farmland because fishing is important there.

C Because Norway has little farmland, fishing is important there.

D Correct as is

ANSWER **1 C**

Norway is so mountainous. That the land **(1)** is hard to cultivate. People raise dairy cattle, and timber is an important product. The Lapps of the North raise reindeer. For their milk **(2)** and meat. Long ocean inlets they are called *fjords* slice **(3)** Norway's western coast. When farmland is available. It tends to be **(4)** at the heads of fjords. For the most part, however, the people of Norway live in cities. Oslo is the capital, and Bergen and Trondheim are two more big cities. **(5)**

1 **A** so mountainous, that the land
B so mountainous that the land
C so mountainous, the land
D No error

2 **A** raise reindeer for their milk
B raise reindeer and for their milk
C raise reindeer. Mainly for their milk
D No error

3 **A** inlets. They are called *fjords* slice
B inlets called *fjords* slicing
C inlets called *fjords* slice
D No error

4 **A** When farmland is available. Tending to be
B When farmland is available, it tends to be
C Farmland is available, it tends to be
D No error

5 **A** Oslo is the capital, Bergen and Trondheim are two more big cities.
B Oslo is the capital. And Bergen and Trondheim are two more big cities.
C Oslo, the capital, Bergen, and Trondheim, are two more big cities.
D No error

A DIFFERENT DELIVERY SYSTEM

If you prefer, you can print the posttest from the BK English Test Bank located at http://www.bkenglish.com.

Customizing the Test

Use these questions to add or replace items for alternate versions of the test.

Lapland is an enormous region of northern Europe. (6) Most of it lies within the Arctic Circle. Lapland is often considered part of Norway. But it also incorporates (7) parts of Sweden, Finland, and Russia. The climate is severe. Part of Lapland is forest most is tundra. (8)

6. **A** Lapland is an enormous region. Of northern Europe.
   B Lapland being an enormous region of northern Europe.
   C Lapland is an enormous region and of northern Europe.
   D No error
7. **A** part of Norway, but it also incorporates
   B part of Norway, also incorporating
   C part of Norway, also incorporating
   D No error
8. **A** Part of Lapland is forest. And most is tundra.
   B Part of Lapland is forest, most is tundra
   C Part of Lapland is forest, but most is tundra.
   D No error

Teaching Suggestions

Essential Knowledge and Skills

- Writing to inform such as to explain, describe, report, and narrate
- Using verb tenses appropriately and consistently such as present, past, future, perfect, and progressive
- Proofreading his/her own writing and that of others
- Responding in constructive ways to others' writing
- Interpreting important events and ideas gathered from graphics

BLOCK SCHEDULING

- If your schedule requires that you cover the chapter in a **shorter time,** use the instruction on principal parts of verbs, verb tenses, active voice and passive voice, and the Check Your Understanding and QuickCheck exercises.
- If you want to take advantage of **longer class time,** add these applications to writing: Connect to Speaking, Connect to the Writing Process, and Apply to Writing exercises.

CHAPTER 11

Using Verbs

Directions

Read the passage and choose the word or group of words that belongs in each underlined space. Write the letter of the correct answer.

EXAMPLE **1.** Oliver Wendell Holmes __(1)__ the name of two famous Americans.

1 **A** is being
B is
C have been
D will have been

ANSWER **1 B**

The first Holmes, Oliver Wendell Holmes, Senior, __(1)__ in 1809. He __(2)__ up in a wealthy and cultured New England home. In his youth Holmes __(3)__ his first poem, "Old Ironsides."

Holmes __(4)__ medicine, but his fame __(5)__ as a man of letters—a poet and speaker. His poem "The Chambered Nautilus" __(6)__ by students for generations.

After he __(7)__ at Harvard for some years, Oliver Wendell Holmes, Junior, __(8)__ to the Supreme Court in 1902. He __(9)__ as "The Great Dissenter" because of his eloquent dissents on many cases. His writings __(10)__ a series of lectures widely read today by law students.

IDENTIFYING COMMON STUMBLING BLOCKS

Following is a list of the most common errors students make when using verb forms and verb tenses.

Problem
- Wrong tense or verb form

Solution
- Instruction, pp. L315–L324
- Practice, pp. L317–L327

Problem
- Incorrect tense shift

Solution
- Instruction, p. L343
- Practice, p. L344

1 **A** was born
B born
C is borning
D borned

2 **A** grow
B growed
C grew
D has grown

3 **A** publish
B published
C was published
D had been published

4 **A** is practicing
B has practiced
C practice
D practiced

5 **A** was achieved
B achieved
C is achieving
D has achieved

6 **A** has read
B is read
C has been read
D reads

7 **A** having taught
B will have taught
C had taught
D teaches

8 **A** appoints
B was appointed
C appointed
D is appointing

9 **A** knew
B known
C had known
D was known

10 **A** were included
B are including
C include
D will include

A DIFFERENT DELIVERY SYSTEM

If you prefer, you can print the pretest from the BK English Test Bank located at http://www.bkenglish.com.

Using *the Pretest*

Assessing Prior Knowledge

The pretest will help you and your students assess where they stand in their basic understanding of principal parts of verbs, verb tenses, active voice, and passive voice.

Customizing the Test

Use these questions to add or replace items for alternate versions of the test.

A chambered nautilus (11) a kind of mollusk. It (12) its life in a small shell and (13) larger ones as it grows. Oliver Wendell Holmes, Senior, (14) this animal as a symbol in his poem. The chambered nautilus (15) human growth and self-betterment.

11. A be
B will be
C is
D has been

12. A begins
B has begun
C is beginning
D had begun

13. A builds
B building
C was built
D had built

14. A was using
B using
C used
D had been used

15. A was symbolizing
B symbolizes
C had symbolized
D symbolizing

ADDITIONAL RESOURCES

Language Skills Practice . . . . pages 91–102
Transparency Tools FA11, AW10, AW11, AW12
ESL Practice and Test Preparation . . . . . pages 115–117
Assessment: Chapter Test. . . . . pages 171–176

MAKING VISUAL CONNECTIONS

For Language Development

Have students name the games they recognize in the painting *Children's Games.* Ask them to share times when they have played similar games. Then have students brainstorm a list of verbs of various tenses to describe the action in the painting. List their responses on the board. Discuss the variety in the verbs listed by students and point out the various verb tenses.

To Stimulate Writing

Use the questions for art criticism as writing or discussion prompts.

Possible Answers:

Describe Children are playing many different games, including hoop games, tag, ball games, and so on.

Analyze The artist may have wanted to show the remarkable diversity of human play.

Interpret You might describe it by telling exactly what each figure is doing. You would have to use many different verbs to differentiate among the many different actions.

Judge A writer could also do an adequate job of describing this scene using vivid images, verbs, and adjectives. I would prefer to see these activities depicted in a painting, however, so I could see what the games look like.

Pieter Brueghel, the Elder. *Children's Games,* 1560.
Oil on oakwood, 47 inches by 64 inches. Kunsthistorisches Museum, Vienna, Austria.

Describe What kinds of activities are taking place in this painting?

Analyze Why do you suppose the artist included so many different activities instead of focusing on one?

Interpret If you were a writer faced with the scene in *Children's Games,* how would you describe it? Why would you need to use a variety of verbs?

Judge Do you think that a writer could do an adequate job of describing this scene so that a reader could picture it? Would you rather read about the activities or see them in a painting? Why?

At the end of this chapter, you will use the artwork as a visual aid for writing.

FOR DEVELOPING LANGUAGE SKILLS

LESSON 1 *(pages L315–L335)*

OBJECTIVES

- **To identify the principal parts of verbs**
- **To determine correct verb form**
- **To correct improperly used verbs**
- **To find principal parts of verbs in a dictionary**
- **To write sentences using correct verb forms**

Create Interest

Ask students which one of the eight parts of speech in English is used to express time. If necessary, list on the board the eight parts of speech from which students can choose. Students

The Principal Parts of Verbs

A verb not only shows action or tells something about its subject. It also tells when something happened.

PRESENT ACTION	Every day I **eat** a sandwich.
PAST ACTION	Yesterday I **ate** a sandwich.
FUTURE ACTION	Tomorrow I **will eat** a sandwich.

Different forms of a verb can express different times. A different form of a verb is called the **tense of a verb**. From the four main forms of a verb, called the principal parts, all the different forms of a verb are developed.

The **principal parts** of a verb are the present, the present participle, the past, and the past participle.

The principal parts of the verb *cook* follow. Notice that the present participle and the past participle must each have a helping verb when they are used as verbs.

PRESENT	I **cook** one night a week.
PRESENT PARTICIPLE	I *am* **cooking** tonight.
PAST	I **cooked** last week.
PAST PARTICIPLE	I *have* **cooked** two times this month.

You can find a list of helping verbs on page 82.

Regular Verbs

Most verbs form their past and past participle just like the verb *cook*—by adding *-ed* or *-d* to the present. These verbs are called regular verbs.

FOR INCREASING STUDENT ACHIEVEMENT

GETTING STUDENTS INVOLVED

Cooperative Learning

After discussing as a class the definitions and examples on this page, have students work with partners to create example sentences for each type of verb presented. Partners should create sentences using the present, past, and future parts of verbs as well as the past and present participles. Have partners share some of their sentences with the class.

should realize that verbs are used to express time: past, present, and future. Have students create sentences that express various actions and times using the following subjects:

- A boy and an ice cream cone
- An igloo
- A fishing hole in Alaska

Guide Instruction

By Modeling Strategies

Point out that whether students are using regular verbs or irregular verbs, they must choose the correct verb forms. Tell students that they have been choosing and using regular and irregular verb forms since they could speak and write. Tell students that irregular verb forms, once they are learned, will become a natural part of their speaking and writing. Demonstrate choosing correct verb forms using the following examples.

- She (is wondering, is wondered) if it will snow today.
- We (talking, talked) about the weather this morning.

REACHING ALL STUDENTS

English Language Learners

Students learning to speak English as a second language might have trouble pronouncing past-tense endings. Tell students that the *-ed* added to the base forms of verbs is sometimes pronounced like a *d* and sometimes pronounced like a *t.* Go over the following rules with students and have them practice the verb endings:

- When a verb ends in a voiced sound, the *-ed* is pronounced like a *d,* as in *cried, hammered,* and *hugged.*
- When a verb ends in a voiceless consonant, the *-ed* is pronounced like a *t,* as in *helped, watched,* and *wished.*
- When the base form of a verb ends in either *d* or *t,* the *-ed* is pronounced like a *d,* as in *weeded, pounded,* or *painted.*

A **regular verb** forms its past and past participle by adding *-ed* or *-d* to the present.

The principal parts of the verbs *wish, jump, wonder,* and *agree* are listed below. Notice that the present participle is formed by adding *-ing* to the present form. Also, as the rule says, the past is formed by adding *-ed* or *-d* to the present.

Present	Present Participle	Past	Past Participle
wish	(is) wishing	wished	(have) wished
jump	(is) jumping	jumped	(have) jumped
wonder	(is) wondering	wondered	(have) wondered
agree	(is) agreeing	agreed	(have) agreed

When you add *-ing* or *-ed* to verbs such as *taste, skip, cry,* and *picnic,* the spelling changes. If you are unsure of the spelling of a verb form, check the dictionary.

Present	Present Participle	Past	Past Participle
taste	(is) tasting	tasted	(have) tasted
skip	(is) skipping	skipped	(have) skipped
cry	(is) crying	cried	(have) cried
picnic	(is) picnicking	picnicked	(have) picnicked

When the present participle or past participle is used as a main verb, it is always joined with a helping verb.

I *am* waiting.	I *have* watched.
He *is* waiting.	She *has* watched.
They *are* waiting.	They *had* watched.

- I (am waiting, waited) for a bus right now.

Consolidate Skills

Through Guided Practice

The **Check Your Understanding** exercises as well as the **QuickChecks** on pages L327 and L335 will help students correctly use the principal parts of verbs. Guide students through the first item in each exercise. Vary instruction by reading some items aloud and writing some items on the board. Allow time for students to express their questions or concerns about the exercises. Then have students complete the exercises independently.

Apply to Communication

Through Independent Writing

The **Communicate Your Ideas** activities on pages L326 and L334 prompt students to write a note to a veterinarian and to write descriptions of three recreational activities. Ask students how the verbs they choose will make their writing more effective. Ask

PRACTICE YOUR SKILLS

Check Your Understanding

Writing the Principal Parts of Regular Verbs

Make four columns on your paper. Label them *present, present participle, past,* and *past participle.* Then write the four principal parts of each of the following regular verbs. Use *is* with the present participle and *have* with the past participle. Check a dictionary if you are unsure of the spelling of a verb form.

1. talk	**4.** jump	**7.** drop	**10.** suppose
2. ask	**5.** use	**8.** play	**11.** share
3. move	**6.** stop	**9.** knock	**12.** gaze

Connect to the Writing Process: Drafting

Writing Sentences with Regular Verbs

Write the principal parts of the following regular verbs. Then write a sentence using each of the principal parts of these verbs.

13. start **14.** row **15.** wrap

Irregular Verbs

A few verbs, called irregular verbs, form their past and past participle differently from regular verbs.

An **irregular verb** does not form its past and past participle by adding *-ed* or *-d* to the present.

Remember that the word *is* is not part of the present participle and the word *have* is not part of the past participle. Still, they have been added to the lists of irregular verbs on the following pages to remind you that all present participles

A DIFFERENT APPROACH

Visual

Complete **Check Your Understanding** together by drawing four columns on the board and labeling them *present, present participle, past,* and *past participle.* Have students write the principal parts for each item in the appropriate columns. Discuss students' responses. Have students share the strategies they used to decide what to write in each section of the chart. Leave the chart on the board for students to reference as they complete other exercises in this chapter.

Sample Answers for *Writing Sentences with Regular Verbs:*

13. She starts school tomorrow.
She is starting school tomorrow.
She started school yesturday.
She has started school already.

14. They row quickly through the water.
They are rowing quickly through the water.
They rowed quickly through the water.
They have rowed quickly through the water.

15. He wraps the gifts.
He is wrapping the gifts.
He wrapped the gifts.
He has wrapped the gifts.

students why it will be important for them to use correct verb forms with these two writing assignments.

Transfer to Everyday Life

Identifying Verb Tenses in Literature

Have students choose a novel or short story from which they can select a paragraph to analyze. Students should make a photocopy of the paragraph and underline each verb. Then students should identify the tense of each underlined verb. Discuss students' findings and the correct tenses of the identified verbs.

Pull It All Together

By Sharing

Have students share either their note to a veterinarian or their recreational activity descriptions with the class. After students have read their writing aloud, discuss some of the verbs students used. Write some of these verbs

REACHING ALL STUDENTS

Advanced Learners

After discussing the Group 1 chart of irregular verbs, have students write sentences for any three present participles and any three past participles from the list using the subjects *I, she,* and *they.* Students should realize that they must change the helping verb in each sentence to agree with the subject. Have students exchange their sentences with a partner to check for accuracy.

and past participles must have a form of one of these helping verbs when they are used as verbs in sentences.

Group 1 These irregular verbs have the same form for the present, the past, and the past participle.

Present	Present Participle	Past	Past Participle
burst	(is) bursting	burst	(have) burst
cost	(is) costing	cost	(have) cost
hit	(is) hitting	hit	(have) hit
put	(is) putting	put	(have) put
let	(is) letting	let	(have) let

Group 2 These irregular verbs have the same form for the past and the past participle.

Present	Present Participle	Past	Past Participle
bring	(is) bringing	brought	(have) brought
buy	(is) buying	bought	(have) bought
catch	(is) catching	caught	(have) caught
make	(is) making	made	(have) made
say	(is) saying	said	(have) said
leave	(is) leaving	left	(have) left
lose	(is) losing	lost	(have) lost
teach	(is) teaching	taught	(have) taught

on the board and have students identify the verb tenses.

Check Understanding

Providing Correct Verb Forms

Write the following sentences on the board. Have students provide an appropriate verb for each sentence. Discuss students' various responses.

- I always ▒ to the movie theater.
- Shawn ▒ with me this week.
- He ▒ the same movie last Friday.

PRACTICE YOUR SKILLS

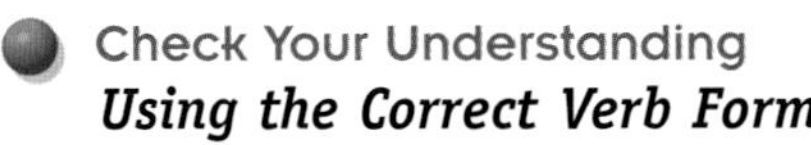

Check Your Understanding

Using the Correct Verb Form

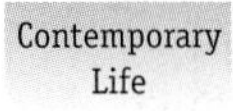

Contemporary Life

Label each underlined verb form *past* or *past participle.* Remember that a helping verb is used with a past participle.

1. All the newscasters said to expect a storm. past
2. The last two storms caught us by surprise. past
3. We have lost our electricity during the last three storms. past participle
4. The worst storm hit last January. past
5. Our experiences have taught us important lessons. past participle
6. One storm left us without power for three days. past
7. We have just put new batteries in our flashlights. past participle
8. Laura has brought in some firewood. past participle
9. Last time we made a fire to keep us warm. past
10. We have bought extra canned food. past participle

Connect to Speaking: Reading a Dialogue

Correcting Improperly Used Verbs

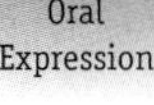

Oral Expression

Read the following dialogue aloud with a partner. As you read, correct any verb errors you find.

MARISOL: Has the rain let up yet?

ANNA: No, it ~~has~~ is still coming down. Have you ~~brung~~ brought your umbrella?

MARISOL: No, I ~~lose~~ lost it last week.

ANNA: That's the third umbrella your mother has ~~buyed~~ bought for you! Where were you when yesterday's storm ~~hitted~~ hit?

A DIFFERENT APPROACH

Auditory

Have students complete both **Practice Your Skills** exercises with a partner. Students should read aloud the sentences for items one through ten and identify the underlined verbs as *past* or *past participles.* For the **Connect to Speaking** exercises, have students record their readings of both the uncorrected version and the corrected version of the dialogue. Students might need to write out their corrected version before recording. Partners should contrast both readings of the dialogue.

HOME WORK

Have students find a dialogue excerpt from a play at the library or from the Internet. Students should photocopy a page and identify ten verbs and label them *past, present, past participle,* or *present participle.* Have students share their verbs and dialogues with the class.

YOUR IDEAS
For Irregular Verbs

MARISOL: The storm ~~catched~~ caught me by surprise. I ~~putted~~ put a bag over my head.

ANNA: I'll bet the rain ~~make~~ made you very wet, anyway. I hope this ~~had teached~~ has taught you to be more careful with your umbrellas.

MARISOL: My mother ~~sayed~~ said the same thing to me.

Group 3 These irregular verbs form the past participle by adding *-n* to the past tense.

PRESENT	PRESENT PARTICIPLE	PAST	PAST PARTICIPLE
break	(is) breaking	broke	(have) broken
choose	(is) choosing	chose	(have) chosen
freeze	(is) freezing	froze	(have) frozen
speak	(is) speaking	spoke	(have) spoken
steal	(is) stealing	stole	(have) stolen

Group 4 These irregular verbs form the past participle by adding *-n* to the present.

PRESENT	PRESENT PARTICIPLE	PAST	PAST PARTICIPLE
blow	(is) blowing	blew	(have) blown
draw	(is) drawing	drew	(have) drawn
drive	(is) driving	drove	(have) driven

give	(is) giving	gave	(have) given
grow	(is) growing	grew	(have) grown
know	(is) knowing	knew	(have) known
rise	(is) rising	rose	(have) risen
see	(is) seeing	saw	(have) seen
take	(is) taking	took	(have) taken
throw	(is) throwing	threw	(have) thrown

PRACTICE YOUR SKILLS

Check Your Understanding

Determining the Correct Verb Form

Contemporary Life **Write the correct verb form for each sentence.**

1. This snowstorm has (took, taken) us off guard.

2. The strong winds have (grew, grown) fiercer since yesterday morning.

3. The weather station just (gave, given) tomorrow's forecast.

4. It has (drew, drawn) a gloomy picture of the blizzard's devastation.

5. Winter has (stole, stolen) up on us this year.

6. I have never (knew, known) it to snow in October.

7. I nearly (froze, frozen) this morning!

8. A chilly wind has (blew, blown) all day.

9. I (saw, seen) very few people outdoors.

10. No one (drove, driven) on the icy streets.

A DIFFERENT APPROACH

Kinesthetic

Have students complete the **Check Your Understanding** activity by using their fingers to underline each correct response for items one through ten. After students have traced their responses, have them write out their answers.

HOME WORK

Have students create ten sentences similar to those in **Check Your Understanding.** They should create verb choices for each sentence as is done in items one through ten. The next day have students exchange their papers with a partner. Students should complete the sentences by choosing the correct verbs. Discuss students' sentences and responses.

A DIFFERENT APPROACH

Auditory

After students have completed items 11 through 25 individually, have them read their sentences aloud to themselves to check for correct verb forms. Point out that listening to their responses, rather than just writing them out, will help students choose the correct responses. Tell students that listening will help them realize when a response does not sound correct. Have students share their final responses.

Check Your Understanding

Using the Correct Verb Form

Contemporary Life **Write the correct past or past participle of each verb in parentheses.**

11. We have not (see) such a storm in ten years. have seen
12. The plaza fountain has (freeze) solid. has frozen
13. The snow has (drive) most people off the streets. has driven
14. It has (throw) the whole town into confusion. has thrown
15. The snowdrifts have (rise) higher than the tops of the cars. have risen
16. A snowplow has (broke) through the drifts on Central Avenue. has broken
17. It (take) the crew three hours to clear eight blocks. took
18. The radio has (give) us weather reports all day. has given
19. The mayor just (speak) and told us the latest emergency measures. spoke
20. Most people have (choose) to stay home anyway. have chosen

Connect to the Writing Process: Editing

Correcting Improperly Used Verbs

Write the following sentences, replacing any incorrect verb with the correct verb form. If a sentence is correct, write *C*.

21. The lake has froze over enough for skating. has frozen
22. Many families have took their children there. have taken
23. They knew the ice was safe. C
24. A few people have driven snowmobiles across the lake. C
25. I even seen a Shetland pony with bells and a small sleigh. have seen

Connect to Speaking: Delivering a Weather Report

Correcting Improperly Used Verbs

Oral Expression **Read the following weather report aloud to a classmate. As you read, correct verb errors.**

We're giving bad news and good news this afternoon. Yesterday's storm ~~blown~~ [blew] so hard that most of Rockridge lost its electrical power. Low temperatures froze water lines across the city. Many pipes ~~broken~~ [broke] last night. Wise drivers have ~~give~~ [given] up and are staying off the icy roads. However, we've ~~saw~~ [seen] some signs that our bad weather is ending. The temperature has ~~rose~~ [risen] ten degrees today. The sunshine is ~~shown~~ [shining] through.

Group 5 These irregular verbs form the past and past participle by changing a vowel. In these verbs the *i* in the present changes to an *a* in the past and to a *u* in the past participle.

Present	Present Participle	Past	Past Participle
begin	(is) beginning	began	(have) begun
drink	(is) drinking	drank	(have) drunk
ring	(is) ringing	rang	(have) rung
sing	(is) singing	sang	(have) sung
sink	(is) sinking	sank	(have) sunk
swim	(is) swimming	swam	(have) swum

HOME WORK

Have students write their own weather reports. Their reports should reflect the current or upcoming weather for their local area. Remind students to use correct verb forms in their weather reports. Students should underline all of the verbs in their reports. Have students share their completed reports with the class.

USING STUDENTS' STRENGTHS

Multiple Intelligences: Interpersonal

Have students write a letter to a friend using at least three present participles and three past participles from the Group 6 chart. Remind students to change the helping verbs as needed for subject-verb agreement. Students who wish to do so may share their letters with the class before sending them to a friend.

INTEGRATING TECHNOLOGY

Computers

Using the Group 1 through Group 6 charts for irregular verbs on pages L318 through L324, have students create tests that can be used to assess students' understanding of irregular verbs. Students should create their tests and answer keys on a computer. Remind students to vary the types of questions on the tests to make them more interesting and to assess different types of skills. Point out that they can include various types of exercises, such as sentence completion activities, verb choice items, matching, and sentence writing activities.

Group 6 These irregular verbs form the past and past participle in other ways.

Present	Present Participle	Past	Past Participle
come	(is) coming	came	(have) come
do	(is) doing	did	(have) done
eat	(is) eating	ate	(have) eaten
fall	(is) falling	fell	(have) fallen
go	(is) going	went	(have) gone
ride	(is) riding	rode	(have) ridden
run	(is) running	ran	(have) run
wear	(is) wearing	wore	(have) worn
write	(is) writing	wrote	(have) written

PRACTICE YOUR SKILLS

Check Your Understanding

Determining the Correct Verb Form

General Interest **Write the correct verb form for each sentence.**

1. All day the cattle (ate, eaten) the long grass beside the river.
2. They (drank, drunk) from the river, too.
3. Paco (rode, ridden) to the river.
4. He (sang, sung) out loudly, "Get along there!"
5. When he shouted, the anxious herd (ran, run) into the river.

6. Now most have (swam, <u>swum</u>) safely across.
7. However, one calf (<u>sank</u>, sunk) into the mud.
8. It has (fell, <u>fallen</u>) and cannot get to its feet.
9. Paco has (went, <u>gone</u>) to pull the calf up the bank.
10. His long day has (wore, <u>worn</u>) him out.

Check Your Understanding
Using the Correct Verb Form

Contemporary Life **Write the correct past or past participle of each verb in parentheses.**

11. Tom has (write) a letter to his brother. has written
12. We (begin) the cattle drive last month. began
13. We have (come) two hundred miles since then. have come
14. I have (wear) out the seat of my pants! have worn
15. I have (eat) too many cold suppers. have eaten
16. Two of our cowhands (fall) sick recently. fell
17. They (drink) some bad water. drank
18. We (do) go on without them. did
19. Sam Sparks (go) to Abilene for some extra help. went
20. Sam and three new cowhands (ride) up last night. rode

Check Your Understanding
Finding the Principal Parts of Verbs in a Dictionary

Look up each of the following irregular verbs in a dictionary. Then write the principal parts of each.

21. shrink	26. fly	31. wake	36. beat
22. pay	27. bleed	32. dive	37. hurt
23. fight	28. shake	33. hide	38. build
24. forget	29. stick	34. prove	39. lend
25. grow	30. tear	35. sleep	40. show

Sample Answers for *Finding the Principal Parts of Verbs in a Dictionary:*

Present	Present Participle	Past	Past Participle
21. shrink	(is) shrinking	shrank	(have) shrunk
22. pay	(is) paying	paid	(have) paid
23. fight	(is) fighting	fought	(have) fought
24. forget	(is) forgetting	forgot	(have) forgotten
25. grow	(is) growing	grew	(have) grown
26. fly	(is) flying	flew	(have) flown
27. bleed	(is) bleeding	bled	(have) bled
28. shake	(is) shaking	shook	(have) shaken
29. stick	(is) sticking	stuck	(have) stuck
30. tear	(is) tearing	tore	(have) torn
31. wake	(is) waking	woke	(have) woken
32. dive	(is) diving	dived or dove	(have) dived
33. hide	(is) hiding	hid	(have) hidden
34. prove	(is) proving	proved or proven	(have) proved or proven
35. sleep	(is) sleeping	slept	(have) slept
36. beat	(is) beating	beat	(have) beaten
37. hurt	(is) hurting	hurt	(have) hurt
38. build	(is) building	built	(have) built
39. lend	(is) lending	lent	(have) lent
40. show	(is) showing	shown	(have) shown

TIMESAVER *QuickCheck*

Have students self-evaluate their writing. They should proofread their veterinarian notes for correct use of all verb forms. If they are uncertain, refer students to the verb charts on pages L320 to L324 which contain the five verbs students use in this writing assignment.

HOME STUDY

Have students imagine they are the veterinarian from **Communicate Your Ideas/Apply to Writing.** They have examined the pet and they are writing a letter of response to report on the pet's condition. Have students write their response letters and check for correct use of verb forms.

Communicate Your Ideas

APPLY TO WRITING

Note: ***Verb Forms***

You need to send your pet to the veterinarian. If you don't have a pet, imagine that the one in the picture is yours. You cannot go with your pet, so you decide to write a note to the veterinarian. A useful note should give information about your pet's history, especially its health history. Use some of the following verbs as you write your note. [Answers may vary. Possible responses are given.]

- Past form of *see* I first saw a swelling in my cat's jaw last week.
- Past participle of *grow* It has grown a lot since then.
- Present participle of *begin* I am beginning to be very worried about him.
- Present participle form of *eat* Now he is not eating very much.
- Past participle of *done* I have done all I can to make him comfortable.

 Mixed Practice

Contemporary Life **Write the correct past or past participle of each verb in parentheses.**

1. Our community's older citizens have (see) [have seen] big changes in the last fifty years.
2. Once the Clearwater River (run) [ran] through a valley of farmland and forests.
3. People (swim) [swam] and fished there in the summer.
4. Then the city engineers (build) [built] a dam.
5. This (come) [came] about because we needed more power.
6. We got a modern power station, but we (lose) [lost] one fourth of our farmland.
7. The power (cost) [cost] us more than we realized then.
8. This cheap source of power (bring) [brought] more factories to our town.
9. The factories (let) [let] their waste products flow into the river.
10. The amount of pollution in the river has (rise) [has risen] steadily for twenty-five years.
11. More people (begin) [began] to move here to be close to work.
12. Our population has (grow) [has grown] by more than fifty percent.
13. New homes for everyone has (leave) [left] us with even less open land.
14. We have (drive) [have driven] almost all wildlife out of the region.
15. Our experience with the dam has (teach) [taught] us a valuable lesson.

EXPANDING THE LESSON

Using Technology

You will find additional **instructional** and **practice** materials for this chapter at http://www.bkenglish.com.

GETTING STUDENTS INVOLVED

Cooperative Learning

Have students work with partners to write eight sentences that correctly use all of the forms of *bring* and *take* shown in the chart. Students should check their sentences against the chart. Have groups share their completed sentences with the class.

 Six Problem Verbs

Telling some verbs apart can be as confusing as knowing when to use their principal parts.

bring and *take*

Bring indicates motion toward the speaker. *Take* indicates motion away from the speaker.

PRESENT	PRESENT PARTICIPLE	PAST	PAST PARTICIPLE
bring	(is) bringing	brought	(have) brought
take	(is) taking	took	(have) taken

BRING She **brings** us the newspaper every morning.

She **is bringing** us the newspaper now.

She **brought** us the newspaper yesterday at 6:00 A.M.

She **has brought** us the newspaper for two years now.

TAKE **Take** this newspaper to the Smith family.

Ryan **is taking** the newspaper to the Smith family today.

His brother **took** the newspaper to the Smith family yesterday.

Sometimes I **have taken** the newspaper to the Smith family.

PRACTICE YOUR SKILLS

Check Your Understanding
Using the Correct Verb

Oral Expression

Read the following sentences aloud to practice using the correct verb form. Be prepared to explain why each verb is correct.

1. The teacher brought in some giant sunflowers for us to paint. Bring indicates motion toward the speaker.
2. Please bring me the jar of yellow paint. Bring indicates motion toward the speaker.
3. If you are going past Maria, take her this new jar of paint. Take indicates motion away from the speaker.
4. Maria dropped the paint jar as she took it from me. Take indicates motion away from the speaker.
5. Kim is bringing some rags to wipe up the paint. Bring indicates motion toward the speaker.
6. Lila has taken away the broken glass. Take indicates motion away from the speaker.
7. Justin has brought us more yellow paint. Bring indicates motion toward the speaker.
8. Matthew took my small brush and gave me his wide one. Take indicates motion away from the speaker.
9. Jessie brought her painting here and left it. Bring indicates motion toward the speaker.
10. Laura is taking her painting to our teacher. Take indicates motion away from the speaker.

Check Your Understanding
Using the Correct Verb

Contemporary Life

Write the correct verb for each sentence.

11. Have all of you (brought, taken) your artwork to share with us today?
12. Angela is (bringing, taking) me a bracelet.
13. Please (bring, take) your statue to the display table over there.

HOME WORK

After completing items 11 through 20, have students write ten sentences about paintings, mosaics, sculptures, or other types of artwork they have made. Each sentence should use forms of the verbs *bring* or *take.* Students should check their sentences for correct verb forms.

YOUR IDEAS
For Problem Verbs

14. Deanna (brings, takes) a picture from Bill's hand.
15. Devon (brought, took) her painting to the bulletin board at the back of the room.
16. The twins (brought, took) in a mosaic to show us.
17. Sam is (bringing, taking) his sculpture to the art show downtown.
18. Emily often (brings, takes) me collages of seashells.
19. Please (bring, take) your mobile here.
20. Did someone (bring, take) the pastel chalk drawing from the table?

learn and *teach*

Learn means "to gain knowledge." *Teach* means "to instruct" or to "show how."

PRESENT	PRESENT PARTICIPLE	PAST	PAST PARTICIPLE
learn	(is) learning	learned	(have) learned
teach	(is) teaching	taught	(have) taught

LEARN
He **learns** best in the morning.
He **is learning** all the irregular verbs.
He **learned** two groups of verbs yesterday.
He **has learned** half of the verbs already.

TEACH
Teach me the new song.
She **is teaching** me several new songs.
She **taught** me one song yesterday.
She **has taught** me two songs already.

Practice Your Skills

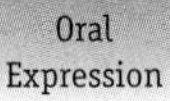

Check Your Understanding

Using the Correct Verb

Oral Expression **Read these sentences aloud to practice using the correct verb form. Be prepared to explain why each verb is correct.**

1. Mr. Klein teaches us art two days a week. Teach means to "instruct" or to "show how."
2. We learn to use a new technique each month. Learn means to "gain knowledge."
3. Last week we learned how to model clay figures. Learn means to "gain knowledge."
4. This week Mr. Klein is teaching us to apply glazes. Teach means to "instruct" or to "show how."
5. This morning he taught us how glazes change after they are fired. Teach means to "instruct" or to "show how."
6. I learned that pale glazes turn brilliant colors in the kiln. Learn means to "gain knowledge."
7. I am also learning from my friend Sara. Learn means to "gain knowledge."
8. Sara and her mother teach art classes after school. Teach means to "instruct" or to "show how."
9. She has taught me a lot about mixing colors. Teach means to "instruct" or to "show how."
10. Through practice I have learned how to make a rich turquoise. Learn means to "gain knowledge."

Check Your Understanding

Using the Correct Verb

Art Topic **Write the correct verb for each sentence.**

11. My research for art class is (learning, teaching) me a lot about Pueblo pottery.
12. I (learned, taught) that a Hopi artist, Nampeyo, was a modern pioneer in her field.
13. She (learned, taught) her three daughters about her work.

A DIFFERENT APPROACH

Visual

Complete **Check Your Understanding** items 11 through 20 as a class. Use one color of chalk to write the sentences on the board. Then, using a different color of chalk, have students take turns circling the correct verb choices. Discuss students' verb choices at the completion of the activity.

HOME WORK

Have students research to find out more about Nampeyo or another famous pottery artisan. Students should use the library and sources on the Internet to write a report about the potter they chose. Remind students to use correct verb forms in their reports. Encourage students to use the charts in Chapter 11 to check their verb forms for accuracy, especially when using irregular verbs. Have students share their reports with the class. Discuss students' use of correct verb forms.

GETTING STUDENTS INVOLVED

Reciprocal Teaching

After discussing the examples using *leave* and *let,* have students work with a partner to create sentences using the forms of *leave* and *let* in the chart. Have students explain to their partner why they chose a particular verb form in each of their eight sentences. If their partners are still having difficulty, students should help by demonstrating strategies they use to select the correct verb forms.

14. Each generation has (learned, taught) from the previous generation.
15. Many generations of potters have (learned, taught) their skills to their daughters and sons.
16. Even today expert potters (learn, teach) their apprentices about pots.
17. Some potters (learn, teach) to use old methods.
18. I am (learning, teaching) about pottery styles.
19. I (learned, taught) myself how to tell them apart.
20. I (learned, taught) that San Juan Pueblo is known for red-on-tan pottery.

leave and *let*

Leave means "to depart" or "to go away." *Let* means "to allow" or "to permit."

PRESENT	PRESENT PARTICIPLE	PAST	PAST PARTICIPLE
leave	(is) leaving	left	(have) left
let	(is) letting	let	(have) let

LEAVE **Leave** now before the storm.
She **is leaving** here in five minutes.
She **left** an hour ago.
She **has** never **left** this early before.

LET **Let** the dog inside.
He **is letting** the dog inside now.
He **let** the dog inside last week.
He **has let** the dog inside several times today.

Practice Your Skills

Check Your Understanding
Using the Correct Verb

Oral Expression

Read these sentences aloud to practice using the correct verb form. Be prepared to explain why each verb is correct.

1. The city is letting us use the fairgrounds for our art exhibit again. Let means to "allow" or to "permit."
2. They have left us more room than last year. Leave means to "depart" or to "go away."
3. The art teachers have let us choose our favorite artwork. Let means to "allow" or to "permit."
4. I let my friend Roberto hang his oil paintings with mine. Let means to "allow" or to "permit."
5. We always let a committee arrange the hall. Let means to "allow" or to "permit."
6. I worked on the exhibit so late that I left at 6:00 P.M. Leave means to "depart" or to "go away."
7. I have usually left around 3:00 P.M. Leave means to "depart" or to "go away."
8. I am leaving for the fairgrounds now. Leave means to "depart" or to "go away."
9. We are not letting anyone in until 9:00 A.M. Let means to "allow" or to "permit."
10. We are leaving the art on display through Sunday. Leave means to "depart" or to "go away."

Check Your Understanding
Using the Correct Verb

Contemporary Life

Write the correct verb for each sentence.

11. We have always (left, let) our teachers plan the show.
12. We are (leaving, letting) parents come on Friday for a preview.
13. I (left, let) a note about the show on the kitchen table for my parents.

DEVELOPING WORKPLACE COMPETENCIES

Basic Skills: Writing

Ask students why it is important for people in the workplace to use verbs correctly in communications. Have students provide examples of times they will be asked to produce written forms of communication in future careers. Reproduce the following business memorandum for each student. Have students correct forms of *bring, take, learn,* and *teach* that are used incorrectly.

Mr. Walsh:

I would like for Ms. Mullins to learn our department how to use the new computers. Will she take us the new computer books, or should we use the computer books we brung before? Ms. Mullins has learned us in the past, and she teached us a lot. I have also learnt how to use the new spreadsheet software.

Sincerely:

P. Kaplan

A DIFFERENT APPROACH

Kinesthetic

After students have written their responses to **Practice Your Skills,** have a few students write the *leave/let* chart from p. L332 on the board. Once the chart is completed, read each sentence from items 11 through 20 aloud. One at a time, students should respond by coming to the board and selecting the correct response from the chart. Students should use their fingers to point to the correct verb form.

HOME WORK

As a review, have students write one sentence for each problem verb using the present participle, the past tense, and the past participle.

TIMESAVER *QuickCheck*

Have students exchange their activity descriptions with a partner. Partners should check for clear descriptions and for correct verb forms. Students should mark any errors and write suggestions for improvements. After returning papers, students should make corrections to their own descriptions.

14. Did you (leave, let) your parents know the time?

15. My parents have just (left, let) the house.

16. Mr. Klein is (leaving, letting) the sixth graders hand out the catalogs.

17. I hope your parents aren't (leaving, letting) yet.

18. Don't (leave, let) until you've seen Elena's sculpture of the fox.

19. The crowd will (leave, let) you through.

20. Who (left, let) that sculpture on the table?

Connect to the Writing Process: Editing

Correcting Verb Usage

If an underlined verb is incorrect, write the correct verb. If an underlined verb is correct, write *C*.

21. The cat took me a dead mouse again! brought

22. Amy learned the cat to slip through the mail slot. taught

23. Someone bring that cat away from here. took

24. The cat jumped out the window and left the room. C

25. Don't you leave that cat back in the house again! let

Communicate Your Ideas

APPLY TO WRITING

Activity Descriptions: *Problem Verbs*

You are helping to write a catalog for the summer recreation program in your community. Many popular classes are being offered. Think of three possible classes and write descriptions of these activities. In your descriptions use at least one form of each of the six problem verbs *bring/take, learn/teach,* and *leave/let.*

 Mixed Practice

Contemporary Life

Write the correct verb for each sentence.

1. The ranger is (learning, teaching) us about the seashore.
2. The ranger says, "(Bring, Take) me that broken shell."
3. The broken shell was (left, let) on the rocks by a gull.
4. Gulls have (learned, taught) to break open shells.
5. A big wave washed over some kelp and (brought, took) it back out to sea.
6. The ranger will not (leave, let) us touch any tide pool creatures.
7. A small fish is (bringing, taking) its prey into the green seaweed.
8. A tern has (left, let) a trail of footprints across the wet sand.
9. I stood still to (leave, let) a crab scuttle quietly across the rocks.
10. The ranger (learned, taught) us to respect the life of the shore.

EXPANDING THE LESSON

Using Technology

You will find additional **instructional** and **practice** materials for this chapter at http://www.bkenglish.com.

LESSON 2 *(pages L336–L351)*

OBJECTIVES

- To identify verb tenses
- To correct shifts in verb tense
- To identify progressive verb forms
- To identify active voice and passive voice

Create Interest

Write the following passage about the painting *Mona Lisa* on the board and have students take note of the various underlined verb tenses. Tell students that the word *tense* comes from the Middle English word *tens* meaning time and from the Latin word *tempus.* Point out that verb tenses express actions at certain times. Discuss the author's use of tenses to express time.

"She is older than the rocks among which she sits; like the vampire, she has been dead many times, and learned the secrets of the grave; and has been a diver in deep seas, and keeps their fallen day about her; and trafficked for strange webs with

REACHING ALL STUDENTS

English Language Learners

Students who are learning English may have difficulty understanding how to form verb tenses. Some languages do not express the time of an action through verb tense, and others have more tenses or different tenses than does English. Allow students to share how time is expressed in their native languages. Compare students' methods for expressing time in their native languages with the way tenses are formed in English.

Verb Tense

Every verb has six tenses: the present, past, future, present perfect, past perfect, and future perfect.

The time expressed by a verb is called the **tense** of a verb.

In the following examples, the six tenses of *walk* are used to express action at different times.

PRESENT	Every day I **walk** five miles.
PAST	I **walked** five miles yesterday.
FUTURE	I **will walk** again tomorrow.
PRESENT PERFECT	For two years I **have walked** each morning.
PAST PERFECT	I **had** not **walked** much before that.
FUTURE PERFECT	I **will have walked** eight hundred miles by May.

 Uses of the Tenses

The examples of the different tenses of *walk* show that verbs in the English language have six tenses. All of these tenses can be formed from the principal parts of verbs—with the helping verbs *have, has, had, will,* and *shall.*

Present tense is used to express an action that is going on now. To form the present tense, use the present form (the first principal part of the verb) or add *-s* or *-es* to the present form.

PRESENT TENSE	I **paint** pictures. Michele **gives** tours.

Eastern merchants: and as Leda, was the mother of Helen of Troy, and, as Saint Anne, the mother of Mary; and all this has been to her but as the sound of lyres and flutes, and lives only in the delicacy with which it has molded the changing lineaments, and tinged the eyelids and the hands."

—Walter Pater, *Studies in the History of the Renaissance,* 1873

Guide Instruction

By Modeling Strategies

Use the example sentences on pages L336 to L338 to model strategies for choosing verb tenses to express time. For each of the six verb tenses, provide another sentence using a different verb. To check students' understanding, have them also provide additional example sentences for each verb tense discussed.

Past tense expresses an action that already took place or was completed in the past. To form the past tense of a regular verb, add *-ed* or *-d* to the present form.

To form the past of an irregular verb, check a dictionary for the past form or look for it on pages L317–L332.

Past Tense	I **painted** a picture last night.
	Michele **gave** a tour last night.

Future tense is used to express an action that will take place in the future. To form the future tense, use the helping verb *will* or *shall* with the present form.

Future Tense	I **shall paint** another picture tomorrow.
	Michele **will give** a tour at noon tomorrow.

You can learn more about the correct use of shall *and* will *on page L485.*

Present perfect tense expresses an action that was completed at some indefinite time in the past. It also expresses an action that started in the past and is still ongoing. To form the present perfect tense, add *has* or *have* to the past participle.

Present Perfect Tense	I **have painted** portraits of my family members.
	Michele **has given** tours for a long time.

Past perfect tense expresses an action that took place before some other action. To form the past perfect tense, add *had* to the past participle.

Past Perfect Tense	I **had painted** landscapes before I painted portraits.
	Michele took a break after she **had given** the tour.

USING STUDENTS' STRENGTHS

Multiple Intelligences: Linguistic

After discussing the verb tenses on pages L336–L338, have students reflect on short stories and novels they have read. Ask students what tense they think was used the most in telling the stories in these narratives. Have students look through short stories and novels in the classroom or in the library to find out which tense is used most often in narratives. Students should conclude that the past tense is used the most because it conveys what has happened; it tells about a particular series of events that occurred in the past. Have students imagine a storyteller or narrator using the present tense and the future tense to tell a story.

Consolidate Skills

Through Guided Practice

The **Check Your Understanding** exercises as well as the **QuickCheck** on page L351 will help students identify verb tenses, active voice, and passive voice. Complete the first item in each exercise together, discussing and reviewing the major strategies students should use to identify verb tenses and voice. Remind students to refer to the charts in this chapter if they have difficulties choosing correct verb forms or tenses. Have students complete the remaining exercises independently.

Transfer to Everyday Life

Identifying Verb Tense and Voice in Newspapers

Have students use the newspaper to identify sentences using the six verb tenses, active voice, and passive voice. Students should use highlighters to trace over the examples they find. Discuss students' examples. Ask

REACHING ALL STUDENTS

Struggling Learners

Point out to students that the future tense is formed differently than are the other verb tenses. The past, past perfect, present, present perfect, and future perfect tenses are all formed by making distinctive changes to the main verb's endings or to the verb's vowels. The future tense instead is formed by adding the words *will* or *shall* to the main verb, which remains unchanged. Have students practice forming the future tense of *skate, create, sing,* and *ride* and then using them in sentences.

Future perfect tense expresses an action that will take place before another future action or time. To form the future perfect tense, add *shall have* or *will have* to the past participle.

Future Perfect Tense	I **shall have painted** more than three new pictures by the end of the month.
	Michele **will have given** one hundred tours before her summer job ends.

CONNECT TO WRITER'S CRAFT

As a writer completes a résumé, it is necessary to use tenses correctly so that the reader does not misunderstand.

Incorrect	I will have refined my unique portrait style.
Correct	Before 2000 ends, I will have refined my unique portrait style.

Verb Conjugation

A **conjugation** lists all the singular and plural forms of a verb in its six tenses. The following is a conjugation of the irregular verb *give,* whose four principal parts are *give, giving, gave,* and *given.*

The present participle is used to conjugate only the progressive forms of verbs. Those verbs are covered on pages L345–L346.

CONJUGATION OF THE VERB *GIVE*

Present

Singular	Plural
I give	we give
you give	you give
he, she, it gives	they give

students if the verb choices are correct and if the voice used by the writer for a particular sentence is appropriate.

Pull It All Together

By Summarizing

Have students summarize their understanding of the following terms: *present, past, future, present perfect, past perfect, future perfect, active voice, passive voice.* Write correct responses on the board. Discuss examples of each term if students are having difficulties.

Check Understanding

Summarizing Verb Tense and Voice

Have students write a paragraph summarizing what they have learned about the six verb tenses. Students should also write a paragraph about active and passive voice. Students should provide example sentences that demonstrate their understanding of

Past	
Singular	**Plural**
I gave	we gave
you gave	you gave
he, she, it gave	they gave
Future	
Singular	**Plural**
I shall/will give	we shall/will give
you will give	you will give
he, she, it will give	they will give
Present Perfect	
Singular	**Plural**
I have given	we have given
you have given	you have given
he, she, it has given	they have given
Past Perfect	
Singular	**Plural**
I had given	we had given
you had given	you had given
he, she, it had given	they had given
Future Perfect	
Singular	**Plural**
I will/shall have given	we will/shall have given
you will have given	you will have given
he, she, it will have given	they will have given

YOUR IDEAS

For Conjugating Verbs

these concepts. Have students share their paragraphs and sentences with the class.

A DIFFERENT APPROACH

Auditory

Have students complete **Check Your Understanding** by working with partners. One student should read a sentence aloud while the other student listens. The listening student should say the correct response to the reader. Students should take turns completing the activity for items one through ten. When all groups are finished, discuss students' responses and check for accuracy.

HOME WORK

Have students create an activity similar to **Check Your Understanding** items 11 through 20. Students can choose to write the activity using paper and pencil or a computer. The topic for students' sentences can vary. Remind them to include one correct and one incorrect choice for each item. Have students exchange their exercises with a partner the following day. Have students complete the new exercises.

PRACTICE YOUR SKILLS

Check Your Understanding

Identifying Verb Tenses

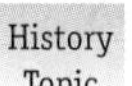

History Topic **Write the tense of each underlined verb.**

1. Hidden Cave lies within a hillside in the Nevada desert. present

2. Ancient people had stored their valuables in it more than 3,500 years ago. past perfect

3. Four boys rediscovered its entrance in 1927. past

4. "We will use this as a hideout," the boys decided. future

5. Years later an archaeologist heard that a miner had found old "junk" in a cave. past perfect

6. In 1940, S. M. and Georgetta Wheeler excavated the cave for the first time. past

7. Now three generations of archaeologists have looked for artifacts in the cave. present perfect

8. Heaps of unbroken artifacts have proved that the cave was not a dump site for junk. present perfect

9. Evidence suggests that the cave was a storage vault. present

10. After the artifacts have been studied, we will have learned much about these early people. future perfect

Check Your Understanding

Understanding Verb Tenses

Write the correct verb tense in parentheses for each sentence.

11. The excavation (had ended, have ended), and then the cave was opened to the public.

12. Archaeologists (has provided, provided) many artifacts for the museum.

13. Today the Churchill County Museum (offers, offered) free tours of the cave and the museum exhibit.

14. The museum (has trained, will have trained) local volunteers as tour guides.

15. The staff (decided, will decide) on two Saturdays each month for tours.

16. The museum (will schedule, will have scheduled) special tours for school groups.

17. The tour begins after visitors (have watched, had watched) a video history of the cave and its artifacts.

18. Comfortable clothing and sturdy walking shoes should be worn by visitors who (hike, hiked) one quarter of a mile uphill to the cave.

19. Young children should not come on the tour as they (will find, had found) the long, uphill hike much too difficult.

20. By the time this year ends, an expected 4,500 visitors (have toured, will have toured) Hidden Cave.

Connect to the Writing Process: Drafting

Using Verb Tenses

Write six sentences, using the tense of the verb indicated for each below. [Answers may vary. Sample responses are given.]

21. Present tense of *learn* I learn something new each day.

22. Past tense of *go* She went to school in Chicago.

23. Future tense of *bring* Will he bring the book?

24. Present perfect tense of *ride* He has ridden an elephant.

25. Past perfect tense of *sing* We had sung that chorus ten times.

26. Future perfect tense of *write* You will have written twenty pages by the time you finish.

YOUR IDEAS

For Teaching Verb Tenses

FOR YOUR INFORMATION

About the Artist

Realist artist Peter Hurd moved to New Mexico after living for many years in the East, where he studied with N.C. Wyeth. In addition to paintings and illustrations of rural New Mexican people, Hurd is known for his murals and portraits. His portrait of President Lyndon B. Johnson (1967) is in the National Portrait Gallery in Washington, D.C. The title of this painting refers to the feast day honoring Saint John, which is celebrated by Roman Catholics on December 27. Saint John is often portrayed with long, flowing hair like the girl in the painting. Three lights in the painting shine from the candle, the house, and the setting sun.

Communicate Your Ideas

APPLY TO WRITING

Journal Entry: *Verb Tenses*

Peter Hurd. *Eve of St. John,* 1960.
Tempera on board, 28 by 48 inches (71 by 48 inches). San Diego Museum of Art. Gift of Mr. and Mrs. Norton S. Walbridge. 1975:069.

Imagine that you are the girl in the picture or that you are her brother. Write a journal entry that tells what happened on that day. Think about what it must be like to live in a place like the one shown in the painting. Make up your own explanation for what the girl is doing with the candle.

- What might you have done that day?
- What are you planning to do tomorrow?

Remember that most journal writers tell about events in the order they happened. When you have finished your entry, underline six verbs that you used. In the margin beside each verb, label its tense.

Shifts in Tense

When you read a story, you quickly learn when it took place by noting the tense of the verbs. When you write, you pass on that same kind of information to your readers. Keep your tenses consistent as you write. For example, if you are telling a story that took place in the past, use the past tense of verbs. If you suddenly shift to the present, you probably will confuse your readers.

Avoid unnecessary shifts in tense within a sentence or within related sentences.

A shift in tense can occur within a sentence itself or within related sentences.

INCONSISTENT	After I **laid** (past) the blanket on the beach, the sun **goes** (present) behind a cloud.
CONSISTENT	As I **lay** (present) my blanket on the beach, the sun **goes** (present) behind a cloud.
CONSISTENT	After I **laid** (past) my blanket on the beach, the sun **went** (past) behind a cloud.
INCONSISTENT	I **wear** (present) my shirt and I **won't burn.** (future)
CONSISTENT	I **will wear** (future) my shirt and I **won't burn.** (future)
CONSISTENT	I **wear** (present) my shirt and I **don't burn.** (present)

IDENTIFYING COMMON STUMBLING BLOCKS

Problem

- Incorrect shift in verb tense

Solution

- Tell students that reading their writing aloud to themselves or to others will help them realize when they have made an incorrect shift in verb tense. Shifts in verb tense are not always obvious to writers as they are writing.
- Have students read the following sentences aloud to decide whether or not there is an incorrect shift in verb tense. Discuss students' responses.

  Jeremy caught the fish and reels in his catch.

  His father is proud and will be grinning as Jeremy reels in the fish.

  Jeremy finished just as his father sits up.

A DIFFERENT APPROACH

Kinesthetic

Complete the **Check Your Understanding** exercises together as a class. Have students think of ways to form the letters *S* and *C* using their arms, legs, head, and torso. Have students use these gestures to respond to the items as you read them aloud. Remind students not to call out the answers, but to instead gesture their responses.

HOME WORK

Ask students to write a paragraph that discusses a typical school day for them, from the point of view of the afternoon. The first sentences about the morning will be in the past, the afternoon will be in the present, and the evening will be in the future.

PRACTICE YOUR SKILLS

Check Your Understanding

Identifying Shifts in Verb Tense

Science Topic

Write *S* if a sentence contains a shift in verb tense. If a sentence is correct, write *C*.

1. Jupiter orbits the sun far beyond our planet, and Europa ~~circled~~ circles Jupiter. I

2. The astronomer Galileo discovered Europa in 1610 when he trained his homemade telescope on Jupiter. C

3. He saw three bright stars near this planet and ~~takes~~ took note of their positions. I

4. It astonished him when they ~~will appear~~ appeared in new positions the next night. I

5. He rightly concluded that these were moons, not stars. C

6. Today we have stronger telescopes, but we cannot see Europa clearly through telescopes. C

7. In the 1980s, the staff at the Jet Propulsion Laboratory developed a spacecraft that they ~~name~~ named *Galileo*. I

8. When NASA launched the *Galileo* spacecraft toward Jupiter in 1989, it ~~carries~~ carried the Hubble space telescope. I

9. A space telescope maintains a radio link to Earth and ~~transmitted~~ transmits images and data back to scientists. I

10. The *Galileo* sent back images that ~~will teach~~ have taught us facts about Europa. I

Connect to the Writing Process: Editing

Correcting Shifts in Tenses

11.–17. Rewrite the sentences in the preceding exercise that contain shifts in verb tense. [Answers may vary. See possible responses above.]

Communicate Your Ideas

APPLY TO WRITING

Informative Report: *Verb Tenses*

Imagine that you are a member of the crew of a spaceship that is exploring Jupiter and its moons. Write a short report for Mission Control back on Earth. Describe what you have seen and what conclusions you have drawn. Do some research to get ideas for what to write about. When you finish, read your report aloud to yourself or a classmate to identify any inappropriate shifts in tense.

Progressive Verb Forms

Each of the six tenses has a **progressive form.** These forms are used to express continuing or ongoing action. The progressive forms add a special meaning to verbs that the regular tenses do not. Notice the differences in meaning in the following examples.

PRESENT	She **runs.**
	(*Runs* shows that she can or does run.)
PRESENT PROGRESSIVE	She **is running.**
	(*Is running* shows that she is running right now.)

The use of progressive forms of verbs often brings a sense of excitement because something is happening right then and there. That is why sports announcers and radio commentators often use the progressive form when they describe something that is going on.

TIMESAVER *QuickCheck*

Have students work with partners to create checklists to evaluate their informative reports about Jupiter. Remind students to include criteria that they are focusing on in their writing. Students' checklists should include at least four items. Have groups share their checklists with the class. Then create one checklist that all students should use to evaluate their writing.

HOME STUDY

Have students find out more about how student progress is evaluated across the country. Students should research library sources and the Internet to find examples of testing and other methods of measuring student progress. Students should find out how the measuring devices are constructed and how they are administered. Have students write a report of their findings. Remind students to check their writing for correct use of verb tenses.

GETTING STUDENTS INVOLVED

Cooperative Learning

After discussing the six progressive verb forms, have students work with a partner to write a paragraph using each progressive form at least once. Students should take turns creating sentences about a topic of their choice. Have students read their paragraphs aloud to check for incorrect shifts in tense. Have groups share their paragraphs with the class. Write some of students' sentences using progressive forms on the board.

A DIFFERENT APPROACH

Visual

After writing out their responses to **Check Your Understanding,** have students take turns writing the sentences on the board using two different colors of chalk. Students should write each sentence in one color and identify the verb phrases with a different color. Discuss students' responses.

To form the progressive, add a form of the verb *be* to the present participle. Notice in the following examples that all of the progressive forms end in *-ing*.

Present Progressive	I am giving.
Past Progressive	I was giving.
Future Progressive	I will (shall) be giving.
Present Perfect Progressive	I have been giving.
Past Perfect Progressive	I had been giving.
Future Perfect Progressive	I will (shall) have been giving.

Practice Your Skills

Check Your Understanding

Identifying Progressive Verb Forms

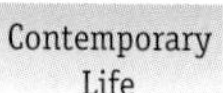

Write each verb phrase.

1. Lila has been enjoying gymnastics for years.

2. She was taking classes before her fourth birthday.

3. In June, she will have been performing on the bars for six years.

4. She has been improving in the last two years.

5. Until last year, she had been practicing at the gym.

6. Now she is taking lessons with a private coach.

7. She has been competing locally.

8. I was watching her yesterday.

9. Next month she will be going to a competition in Dallas.

10. Her family is supporting her dream.

Connect to the Writing Process: Drafting

Using Progressive Verb Forms

Write five sentences, using the indicated progressive form of each verb given below.

[Answers may vary. Sample responses are given.]

11. Past progressive of *watch* I was watching TV when it happened.

12. Future progressive of *wear* I will be wearing my new outfit.

13. Present perfect progressive of *read* I have been reading a wonderful book.

14. Past perfect progressive of *wonder* I had been wondering when you would arrive.

15. Future perfect progressive of *study* I will have been studying six hours when the clock strikes twelve.

Communicate Your Ideas

APPLY TO WRITING

Observation Log: ***Progressive Verbs***

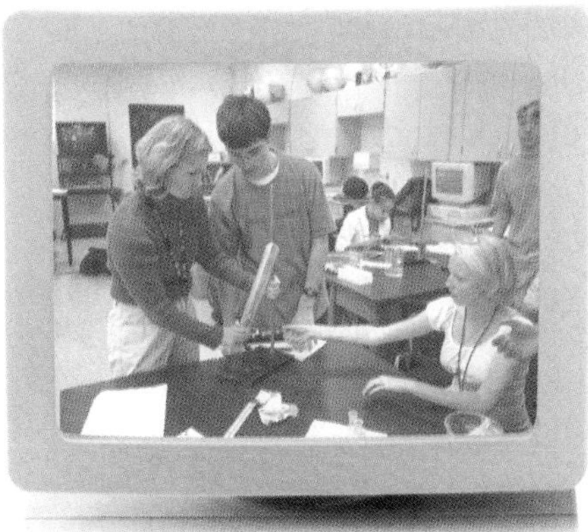

Look around the classroom and observe what is going on right now. Take notes about what you see. Then write an entry for a classroom observation log, explaining what you see and hear. Use progressive forms of verbs. When you have finished, compare your entry with a classmate's, and then bind all the entries together for a classroom observation log.

HOME WORK

After completing items eleven through fifteen in **Connect to the Writing Process,** have students write five additional sentences for home work, using different progressive verb forms than those indicated in the exercise. Students should use the same five main verbs listed.

TIMESAVER *QuickCheck*

After completing their observation logs, have students self-evaluate their writing for correct use of verb forms before including their writing in the classroom observation log. Encourage students to use the charts listed throughout Chapter 11 if they are having difficulties evaluating their writing.

USING STUDENTS' STRENGTHS

Multiple Intelligences: Linguistic

After discussing the examples on this page, have students create two sentences using the active voice and two sentences using the passive voice. Students should share their sentences with the class and explain what makes each sentence active or passive. Write some of students' sentences on the board.

Active Voice and Passive Voice

In addition to tense, a verb is in active voice or passive voice. Writers can use either the active voice or the passive voice to tell about an action.

The **active voice** indicates that the subject is performing the action.

The **passive voice** indicates that the action of the verb is being performed upon the subject.

ACTIVE VOICE	Mr. Takamoto **placed** the round stones in the garden.
PASSIVE VOICE	The round stones **were placed** in the garden by Mr. Takamoto.
ACTIVE VOICE	The wind **rattles** the tall stalks of bamboo.
PASSIVE VOICE	The tall stalks of bamboo **are rattled** by the wind.

A verb in the passive voice consists of a form of the verb *be* plus a past participle. The forms of *be* used for the passive voice are *is, are, was, were, has been, have been,* and *had been.* Study the following examples.

ACTIVE VOICE	The wind **blew** over the small pine on the hill. (*The wind* is performing the action.)
PASSIVE VOICE	The small pine on the hill **was blown** over by the wind. (The pine is receiving the action of the verb. *Was* is a form of the verb *be,* and *blown* is the past participle of *blow.*)

Use of Active Voice and Passive Voice

It is important to avoid the passive voice in your writing. Passive voice verbs are weak and wordy. When you write, use the active voice as much as possible. The active voice is more forceful and adds life to your writing. The only time the passive voice is more appropriate is when the doer of the action is unknown or unimportant.

PASSIVE VOICE Irises **were planted** beside the stream.

PRACTICE YOUR SKILLS

Check Your Understanding

Recognizing Active Voice and Passive Voice

Write the verb in each sentence and label it *active* or *passive*.

1. The art of gardens is honored by the Japanese. passive
2. In Japan most householders with land maintain a garden. active
3. The distinct features of Japanese gardens were developed ten centuries ago. passive
4. Tidy flower beds and straight paths give gardens an unnatural look. active
5. Japanese gardens are known for their natural settings. passive
6. Few brightly colored flowers grow in these gardens. active
7. Mostly, evergreens are planted there. passive
8. Many gardens contain ponds or waterfalls. active
9. The visitor is soothed by the sound of water. passive
10. The ideal garden provides a tranquil place for restful thoughts. active

DEVELOPING WORKPLACE COMPETENCIES

Basic Skills: Writing

Ask students which voice, active or passive, should be used most often in the workplace. Have students think of examples when they would use active voice and passive voice in the workplace. Students should conclude that active voice should be used in most cases because it is more direct and forceful. Passive voice sentences appear to be weak and wordy. Have students imagine they are employed by a large toy manufacturer. Have students write a short business proposal for a new toy. Students should check their writing to ensure they have used active voice.

TIMESAVER *QuickCheck*

Have students exchange their completed descriptive paragraphs with a partner. Partners should evaluate students' paragraphs according to appropriate use of active voice and passive voice. Students should include suggestions for improvements on the writing they are critiquing.

Connect to the Writing Process: Revising

Changing Verbs to Active Voice

Rewrite each sentence, changing the underlined verb from passive voice to active voice.

My family entered this year's county fair gardening competition.

11. This year's county fair gardening competition was entered by my family.

We created a Japanese-style garden.

12. A Japanese-style garden was created by us.

My sister drew the plan.

13. The plan was drawn by my sister.

My mother and I arranged the plants.

14. The plants were arranged by my mother and me.

The judges gave us second prize.

15. We were given second prize by the judges.

Communicate Your Ideas

APPLY TO WRITING

Descriptive Paragraph: *Active and Passive Voice*

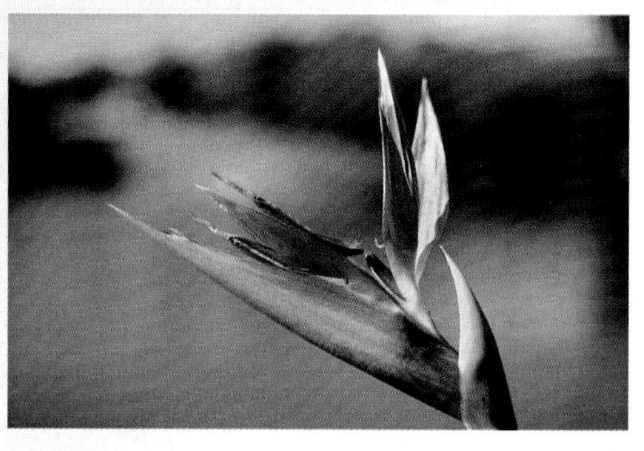

You are writing a descriptive paragraph for a garden book about an interesting and unusual plant. Give some facts about its history, its care, and its use. You may do research on a plant that exists or make up a plant to write about. Use the active voice to make your writing lively or use the passive voice if it is appropriate. Be ready to explain why you chose to use active or passive voice.

Mixed Practice

Art Topic

Rewrite each sentence, correcting any incorrect verb forms or shifts in tense. If the passive voice is used inappropriately, correct it. If it is appropriate, leave it as it is.

1. Artist Murakami Kagaku was born in 1888 and ~~dies~~ died in 1939.
2. He led a new movement in Japanese-style art for modern painters.
3. He ~~blends~~ blended Western art techniques with traditional Japanese methods and subjects.
4. By the time he was fourteen, he ~~is~~ was winning prizes for his work.
5. In his early years, he ~~works~~ worked in color.
6. Later he ~~becomes~~ became more interested in landscapes in ink.
7. He showed his deep appreciation for nature in his works.
8. A beautiful picture, *Autumn Willow,* was painted by him the year before he died.
9. Although it is very simple, it ~~held~~ holds your attention.
10. In it a tangle of pale ghostly branches ~~has been outlined~~ is outlined against a background of golden morning fog.

EXPANDING THE LESSON

Using Technology

You will find additional **instructional** and **practice** materials for this chapter at http://www.bkenglish.com.

YOUR IDEAS

For Active and Passive Voice

FOR REVIEWING SKILLS

Using CheckPoint

This feature on verb forms, active voice, and passive voice can be used as further independent practice or as a cumulative review of the chapter. Have students identify correct and incorrect verb forms, active voice, passive voice, and write sentences using correct verb forms.

CheckPoint

Using the Correct Verb Form

Write the correct verb form for each sentence.

1. On our trip to Florida, we (saw, ~~seen~~) several models of cities of the world at a theme park.
2. Luis (threw, ~~throwed~~) the ball to home plate.
3. I had never (~~swam~~, swum) in salt water before today.
4. Mom (~~knowed~~, knew) Dad in high school.
5. Have you ever (~~rode~~, ridden) in a helicopter?
6. Mom always (~~lies~~, lays) the mail by the door.
7. During the last three days, I (~~teached~~, taught) my sister how to ride a bike.
8. Several students have (~~wrote~~, written) poems for the school's fiftieth anniversary.
9. Have you (~~chose~~, chosen) a name for your dog yet?
10. I have already (~~ate~~, eaten) lunch.

Using the Correct Verb Form

Find and correct each verb form that is incorrectly used in the following sentences. If a sentence is correct, write *C*.

1. The sun finally ~~come~~ came out in the afternoon.
2. You should have seen the large audience at our play. C
3. These vines have ~~growed~~ grown three feet in one week.
4. Hurricane-force winds have ~~sank~~ sunk several boats at the town marina.
5. Who ~~drunk~~ drank all the milk?
6. I should have ~~took~~ taken a book with me to the doctor's office.

7. That basketball player has ~~stole~~ stolen the ball from the opposing team several times.
8. Yesterday we ~~begun~~ began math class with a surprise quiz.
9. Have you ~~gave~~ given a donation to that charity?
10. The stock market has fallen six points since yesterday. C

Identifying Verb Voice

Write each verb and label it *active* or *passive.*

1. After the play the curtain was slowly lowered. passive
2. Dr. Jonas Salk discovered the polio vaccine. active
3. Air-conditioning was invented in 1902 by Willis H. Carrier. passive
4. Darrell painted the garage last summer. active
5. Neil Armstrong made his walk on the moon in 1969. active
6. In right-handed people, motor control is ruled by the left half of the brain. passive
7. Cindy auditioned for the school play. active
8. Altitude is measured by an altimeter. passive
9. The beaver's dam was constructed in one evening. passive
10. Reds, greens, and blues form the picture in color television. active

Using Verbs Correctly

Write five sentences that follow the directions below.

Write a sentence that

1. includes the past tense of *write.*
2. includes the future tense of *rise.*
3. includes the past perfect tense of *speak.*
4. includes any forms of the verbs *bring* and *take.*
5. includes any forms of the verbs *learn* and *teach.*

Sample Answers for *Using Verbs Correctly:*

1. I wrote his address on a napkin.
2. Hot air will rise to the second floor.
3. He had spoken to his aunt about the dinner.
4. Joe took the tickets I brought with delight.
5. The puppy learned every command I taught her.

Using *Language and Self-Expression*

Consider using this writing assignment to assess students' ability to use verb forms and voice correctly and effectively. You may want students to complete the assignment as part of a descriptive writing strand for their portfolios.

Prewriting

Suggest that students revisit their analysis of the painting that they did in *Making Visual Connections* on page L314.

Encourage students to use questioning strategies to help them organize their thoughts in the prewriting stage. For example, students might use the following questions to help them proceed with their writing:

- What forms of play do you immediately recognize in the painting?
- How would you describe these activities to a young child who had never played them?
- What precise verbs can you use to make your descriptions clear?

FOR YOUR INFORMATION

About the Artist

Pieter Brueghel (1525(?)–1569). Known as Pieter Brueghel the Elder, the distinguished Flemish artist was an engraver, illustrator, printer, and painter. His elaborate landscapes, appreciated for their originality and craftswork, reveal a love of nature. Many of his paintings document peasant life. His works are often satirical or allegorical and show the paradoxes and ironies of the human condition.

Language and *Self-Expression*

Pieter Brueghel, the Elder, (he also had a famous son who was "the Younger") is known for his vibrant paintings of lively peasants at work and play. He worked in what is now Belgium in the 1500s. His paintings give audiences today a clear and fascinating picture of everyday activities from five hundred years ago.

Focus on a single section of the painting and look at two or three activities that are going on in that section. Try to describe what is happening. Use vivid, lively verbs and adjectives so that a reader will be able to picture the games being played.

Prewriting Choose the section of the painting on which you intend to focus. Brainstorm a list of verbs that name the actions of people in that section.

Drafting Use your list of verbs to write descriptions of the activities you have chosen. First write a sentence or two that introduces your description by telling the main idea behind the painting. Then write a separate paragraph for each activity.

Revising Reread your description, and make sure you have used the active voice throughout. Replace any verbs that are not specific enough with verbs that are more precise. Check to be sure you have not changed tenses awkwardly in mid-paragraph.

Editing Review your description, looking for errors in grammar, capitalization, punctuation, and spelling. Make any corrections that are necessary.

Publishing Prepare a final copy of your description. Exchange it with a classmate and see whether your classmate can identify the section of the painting you described.

Another Look

Using Verbs

The **principal parts** of a verb are the present, the present participle, the past, and the past participle.

A **regular verb** forms its past and past participle by adding *–ed* or *–d* to the present.

An **irregular verb** does not form its past and past participle by adding *–ed* or *–d* to the present.

Six Problem Verbs

Distinguishing *bring* and *take.* *(page L328)*
Distinguishing *learn* and *teach.* *(page L330)*
Distinguishing *leave* and *let.* *(page L332)*

The time expressed by a verb is called the **tense** of a verb. The six tenses are present, past, future, present perfect, past perfect, and future perfect.

Each of the six tenses has a **progressive form.** These forms are used to express continuing or ongoing action. *(page L345)*

Active Voice and Passive Voice

The **active voice** indicates that the subject is performing the action. *(pages L348–L349)*

The **passive voice** indicates that the action of the verb is being performed upon the subject. *(pages L348–L349)*

Other Information About Using Verbs

A **conjugation** lists all the singular and plural forms of a verb in its six tenses. *(page L338)*

Avoid unnecessary shifts in tense within a sentence or within related sentences. *(page L343)*

Using *Another Look*

Another Look summarizes the terms defined in the chapter and provides cross-references to the specific pages on which they are explained. Consider having students use this feature prior to completing **CheckPoint** or taking the posttest. Students who can provide several examples of each term should be able to score well on either measurement.

FOR ASSESSING LEARNING

Using *the Posttest*

Assessing Learning

The posttest will help you and your students assess where they stand in their ability to use verb forms correctly.

IDENTIFYING COMMON STUMBLING BLOCKS

Following is a list of the most common errors students make involving verb forms and verb tenses.

Problem

- Incorrect tense shift

Solution

- For reteaching, use the example sentences on page L343.

Problem

- Wrong tense or verb form

Solution

- For reteaching, use the charts on pages L316, L318, L320, L321, L323, and L324.

Directions

Read the passage and choose the word or group of words that belongs in each underlined space. Write the letter of the correct answer.

EXAMPLE **1.** Golda Meir __(1)__ one of the founders of the modern state of Israel.

1 A was
B has been
C have been
D will be

ANSWER **1 A**

Golda Meir __(1)__ as Israel's first and only female prime minister. She __(2)__ Goldie Mabovitch in Russia in 1898. She __(3)__ briefly in the United States. Then, in 1921, she __(4)__ to Palestine. Within a short time, she __(5)__ the labor movement. She __(6)__ as minister of labor in 1949. Later, she __(7)__ as minister of foreign affairs.

Meir __(8)__ prime minister in 1969. Although she __(9)__ after the 1973 Arab-Israeli War, she __(10)__ for her dedication to the goal of peace in the Middle East.

A DIFFERENT DELIVERY SYSTEM

If you prefer, you can print the posttest from the BK English Test Bank located at http://www.bkenglish.com.

1 A knew
<u>B</u> is known
C having been known
D was known

2 A born
B has been born
<u>C</u> was born
D is borning

3 A teached
<u>B</u> taught
C has taught
D is teaching

4 <u>A</u> moved
B moving
C moves
D has been moved

5 A is joining
B joins
C has been joined
<u>D</u> had joined

6 A chose
B choosed
<u>C</u> was chosen
D is choosing

7 A was served
B serving
C has served
<u>D</u> served

8 <u>A</u> was elected
B elected
C had elected
D is electing

9 A criticized
B was criticizing
<u>C</u> was criticized
D will have been criticized

10 A remembers
<u>B</u> will be remembered
C has remembered
D will remember

Customizing the Test

Use these questions to add or replace items for alternate versions of the test.

The 1973 Arab-Israeli War (<u>11</u>) as the Fourth Arab-Israeli War. It (<u>12</u>) with a surprise attack by Egyptian and Syrian forces on the Jewish holiday of Yom Kippur. The Israelis (<u>13</u>) back, but later they (<u>14</u>). An agreement (<u>15</u>) on January 18, 1974.

11. A known
B was knowed
<u>C</u> is known
D has been knowed

12. A begins
B has begun
<u>C</u> began
D had began

13. A force
<u>B</u> were forced
C was forced
D have been forced

14. A rallying
<u>B</u> rallied
C have rallied
D had been rallying

15. <u>A</u> was signed
B was signing
C signed
D has been signed

Teaching Suggestions

Essential Knowledge and Skills

- Writing to inform such as to explain, describe, report, and narrate
- Spelling frequently misspelled words correctly such as *their, they're,* and *there*
- Employing standard English usage for audiences, including subject-verb agreement, pronoun referents, and parts of speech
- Writing with increasing accuracy when using apostrophes in contractions
- Writing with increasing accuracy when using pronoun case
- Assessing how language, medium, and presentation contribute to the message

BLOCK SCHEDULING

- If your schedule requires that you cover the chapter in a **shorter time,** use the instruction on pronoun case and pronoun antecedents and the Check Your Understanding and QuickCheck exercises.
- If you want to take advantage of **longer class time,** add these applications to writing: Connect to Speaking and Writing, Connect to the Writing Process, and Apply to Writing exercises.

CHAPTER 12

Using Pronouns

Directions

Read the passage and choose the pronoun that belongs in each underlined space. Write the letter of the correct answer.

EXAMPLE Linda and __(1)__ took a ferry to Vashon Island.

1 A me
B I
C us
D him

ANSWER **1 B**

My cousins moved to Seattle, Washington, and last year I visited __(1)__ there for the first time. The skyline amazed __(2)__. __(3)__ is dominated by the Space Needle, a tall tower left over from the World's Fair in 1962. __(4)__ rotating restaurant is wonderful.

Seattle lies on Puget Sound, and __(5)__ there seems to love the water. Lake Washington runs along the east of the city. The most famous resident there may be Bill Gates, __(6)__ has a house near the water. My cousins took me out on __(7)__ powerboat, and __(8)__ passed many fabulous lakeshore homes.

I liked the market downtown. Fish vendors wrap fish for tourists, to __(9)__ they then toss the neatly packaged salmon. One man tossed a gigantic fish to my cousins and __(10)__. Luckily, we caught it!

IDENTIFYING COMMON STUMBLING BLOCKS

Following is a list of the most common errors students make when using pronouns.

Problem
- Incorrect pronoun case with compound subject

Solution
- Instruction, pp. L363–L364
- Practice, pp. L364–L365

Problem
- Vague pronoun antecedent

Solution
- Instruction, p. L394
- Practice, pp. L395–L397

1 A her
B them
C it
D they

2 A me
B I
C my
D mine

3 A He
B They
C We
D It

4 A It
B Her
C Its
D It's

5 A both
B many
C several
D everybody

6 A its
B whom
C who
D her

7 A their
B theirs
C they
D its

8 A us
B we
C he
D him

9 A who
B whose
C him
D whom

10 A me
B I
C we
D he

A DIFFERENT DELIVERY SYSTEM

If you prefer, you can print the pretest from the BK English Test Bank located at http://www.bkenglish.com.

Using *the Pretest*

Assessing Prior Knowledge

The pretest will help you and your students assess where they stand in their basic understanding of pronouns. The test measures students' ability to identify pronouns and to use them correctly in their writing.

Customizing the Test

Use these questions to add or replace items for alternate versions of the test.

The city of Seattle was named for a great Dwamish Indian chief (11) lived from 1786 until 1866. (12) once said, "Whatever happens to the beasts also happens to the man." This was a reminder to (13) it might concern that harming (14) land hurts every living thing. These words are still relevant to (15) today.

11. A he
B who
C whom
D his

12. A He
B Him
C We
D They

13. A who
B him
C whom
D they

14. A our
B theirs
C ours
D it's

15. A I
B we
C us
D they

ADDITIONAL RESOURCES

Language Skills Practice . . . . pages 103–114
Transparency Tools FA12, AW13, AW14
ESL Practice and Test Preparation . . . . . pages 118–120
Assessment: Chapter Test. . . . . pages 177–181

MAKING VISUAL CONNECTIONS

For Language Development

Have students study *Pianist and Checker Players* and think about the thoughts of the characters in the painting. After discussing the various elements of the artwork, have students write five sentences about the thoughts of the lady playing the piano. What might she be thinking about as she plays? What might she have thought about before she began playing the piano? What might her feelings be toward the children playing checkers? Have students read some of their completed sentences to the class. Point out any pronouns students used correctly in their writing.

To Stimulate Writing

Use the questions for art criticism as writing or discussion prompts.

Possible Answers:

Describe I see a woman playing a piano while two children are playing checkers. I see stripes, circles, and curves and reds and browns.

Analyze I feel cozy and comfortable viewing this scene. The dark, warm colors and repeated shapes contribute to the mood of the painting.

Interpret A writer could create the same mood by describing with words the cozy warmth of the scene.

Judge I think the painting more truly gives a sense of how a family in 1924 relaxed.

Henri Matisse. *Pianist and Checker Players,* 1924.
Oil on canvas, 29 by 36⅜ inches. Collection of Mr. and Mrs. Paul Mellon.
National Gallery of Art, Washington, D.C.

Describe What images do you see in this painting? What shapes and colors do you see?

Analyze What feelings do you have as you view the scene? How do the colors and shapes contribute to the mood of the painting?

Interpret The artist used the visual elements of color and shape to create a certain mood, or feel, for this painting. What writing elements could a writer use to create the same mood with words?

Judge This painting represents a typical 1924 family at leisure. A historical text would probably provide more factual details. Which would be the "truer picture" of the family? Explain your answer.

At the end of this chapter, you will use the artwork to stimulate ideas for writing.

FOR DEVELOPING LANGUAGE SKILLS

LESSON 1 *(pages L361–L387)*

OBJECTIVES

- **To identify pronouns**
- **To use pronoun case correctly**
- **To use pronouns as direct objects, indirect objects, and objects of prepositions**
- **To use possessive pronouns correctly**
- **To distinguish between possessive pronouns and contractions**
- **To use *who* and *whom* correctly**

The Cases of Personal Pronouns

Personal pronouns have different forms, called cases, depending on whether they are subjects, objects, or possessives in a sentence.

> **She** helped **him.**
> Rob helped **his** aunt.

Case is the form of a noun or pronoun that indicates its use in a sentence.

In English, there are three cases: the nominative case, the objective case, and the possessive case.

NOMINATIVE CASE (used for subjects and predicate nominatives)		
	SINGULAR	PLURAL
FIRST PERSON	I	we
SECOND PERSON	you	you
THIRD PERSON	he, she, it	they

OBJECTIVE CASE (used for direct objects, indirect objects, and objects of prepositions)		
	SINGULAR	PLURAL
FIRST PERSON	me	us
SECOND PERSON	you	you
THIRD PERSON	him, her, it	them

FOR INCREASING STUDENT ACHIEVEMENT

GETTING STUDENTS INVOLVED

Cooperative Learning

After discussing as a class the definitions and pronoun charts on pages L361 and L362, have students work together in groups of three or four to create example sentences for each type of pronoun presented. Each group should create sentences using the nominative, objective, and possessive cases. Have groups share some of their sentences with the class. Discuss their examples.

Create Interest

Write the following sentences on the board. Have students complete each one with a pronoun. Review with students words that are pronouns, such as *I, me, we, they, him, her.* Discuss students' responses to the sentence completions and take note of any incorrect uses of nominative case and objective case.

- ___ am afraid to ride on roller coasters.
- ___ decided to go with ___ on the Ferris wheel.
- ___ was more fun than ___ expected.
- ___ and ___ want to go back to the amusement park.

Guide Instruction

By Modeling Strategies

Before assigning the **Practice Your Skills** activity on page L362, discuss the pronoun case charts on pages L361–L362 with students. As you discuss each chart, write the following examples sentences on the board for students to read and review.

A DIFFERENT APPROACH

Visual

After completing **Practice Your Skills** independently, discuss students' responses as a class. Create a three-column chart on the board, with the headings *Nominative, Objective,* and *Possessive.* As you review items one through ten, have students come to the board and put their responses in the appropriate columns. Display the chart for students to refer to.

POSSESSIVE CASE
(used to show ownership or possession)

	SINGULAR	PLURAL
FIRST PERSON	my, mine	our, ours
SECOND PERSON	your, yours	your, yours
THIRD PERSON	his, her, hers, its	their, theirs

PRACTICE YOUR SKILLS

Check Your Understanding

Using Pronouns

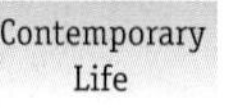

Write the pronoun or pronouns in each sentence. Label each pronoun *nominative, objective,* or *possessive.*

1. Our (poss.) family went to the amusement park and beach.
2. My (poss.) mother bought ride tickets for Melissa, Matt, and me (obj.).
3. Then she (nom.) and my (poss.) father went to relax on the beach.
4. Melissa asked us (obj.) to go on the roller coaster with her (obj.).
5. Matt said that he (nom.) always gets sick on the roller coaster.
6. He (nom.) saw some friends on the Ferris wheel and waved at them (obj.).
7. They (nom.) and Matt rode on the spaceship ride.
8. I (nom.) got a glimpse of their (poss.) faces as they (nom.) whirled around.

- *Nominative Case*
  They and I went to the park.
  Mother said that she could go with Matt.
  We met at the park's lemonade stand.
- *Objective Case*
  Sally wants us to meet her near the bumper cars.
  Mother also plans to take him and them.
  Jerry is giving me a ride.
- *Possessive Case*
  My favorite ride is the spaceship ride.
  Now his family is going to their car.
  The choice is yours.

Consolidate Skills

Through Guided Practice

The **Check Your Understanding** exercises as well as the **QuickChecks** on pages L371 and L379 will help students correctly use pronouns. Guide students through the first item in each exercise. Vary instruction by reading some items aloud and writing some

9. Later we (nom.) all went on the water slide.
10. It (nom.) is a favorite ride of mine (poss.)!

The Nominative Case

The personal pronouns in the following box are in the nominative case.

NOMINATIVE CASE		
	SINGULAR	PLURAL
FIRST PERSON	I	we
SECOND PERSON	you	you
THIRD PERSON	he, she, it	they

Pronouns in the nominative case are used in two ways.

The **nominative case** is used for subjects and predicate nominatives.

SUBJECT	**She** rescued the dog.
PREDICATE NOMINATIVE	The man in the blue suit is **he.**

You can learn more about personal pronouns on pages L59–L61.

Pronouns Used as Subjects

A subject names the person, place, or thing the sentence is about. Because the pronouns in the sentences at the top of the next page are used as subjects, the nominative case is used.

HOME WORK

Have students read this page independently and then write ten sentences using pronouns in the nominative case. Remind students that the pronouns in these sentences should be used as subjects or predicate nominatives.

YOUR IDEAS

For Pronouns

items on the board. Allow time for students to express their questions or concerns about the exercises. Then have students complete the exercises independently.

Apply to Communication

Through Independent Writing

The **Communicate Your Ideas** on pages L370, L379, and L385 activities prompt students to write a dialogue for a movie scene, a friendly letter, and a history magazine article. Ask students to compare and contrast the types of pronouns they will use in these three writing assignments. Have students brainstorm the types of pronouns that will be most prevalent in each writing assignment.

Transfer to Everyday Life

Identifying Pronouns and Voice in an Article

Have students choose an article to read from *National Geographic* magazine. After reading the entire article, students should close the magazine and try to recall the pronouns used in the article. Students should list these

GETTING STUDENTS INVOLVED

Reciprocal Teaching

After reading and discussing the instruction on nominative pronouns on pages L363 and L364, have advanced students work with students who are having difficulties. Advanced students should provide explanations and strategies that struggling students can use to identify and use subject pronouns. Write the following sentences on the board for students to use in their instruction.

- Casey and (I, me) play basketball. (I)
- (We, Us) are the team captains. (We)
- (He, Him) and Brad have scored the most points. (He)
- (Them, They) have earned college scholarships. (They)
- Can Brad and (me, I) shoot a few hoops? (I)
- Were the cheerleaders and (them, they) shouting before halftime? (they)

SUBJECTS	**I** decorated my room. Do **they** live in that apartment? (Turn a question into a statement: *They do live in that apartment.* Then it is easy to see that *they* is the subject.)

When a sentence has only one subject, choosing the correct pronoun is usually not a problem. If a sentence has a compound subject, however, it is easy to make a mistake.

COMPOUND SUBJECT	Mom and (I, me) painted the fence.

To find the correct pronoun, say the sentence as if each pronoun stood alone.

CORRECT	**I** painted the fence.
INCORRECT	**Me** painted the fence.

By separating the choices, you can see and hear which pronoun is correct. The nominative case *I* is the correct form to use.

CORRECT	Mom and **I** painted the fence.

You can learn more about finding the subject of a sentence on pages L22–L29.

PRACTICE YOUR SKILLS

 Check Your Understanding

Using Pronouns as Subject

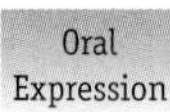

Read each sentence aloud, trying each pronoun separately. Then read the sentence aloud again, choosing the correct pronoun.

1. Her friends and (she, her) are in the band.

2. Ben's brother and (he, him) play trumpets.

pronouns and describe how they are used. Then students should tell whether the majority of the article was written in active voice or passive voice. Have students go back through the article to check their responses.

Pull It All Together

By Sharing

Have students share one of their writing samples from the **Communicate Your Ideas** activity with a partner. After students have read each other's writing, they should discuss the pronouns and the voice used in their writing. Have partners share some of the pronouns and examples of the voice used in their writing with the class.

Check Understanding

By Summarizing

Have students write a summary of the types of pronouns they recall from this chapter. They should provide examples that demonstrate how each pronoun

3. (They, Them) and French horns are brass instruments.

4. After a year Rosa and (I, me) were pretty good clarinet players.

5. After playing clarinets, (he, him) and Efrain switched to oboes.

6. Can Tyler or (I, me) play the tuba?

7. Weren't the boys and (she, her) at the last rehearsal?

8. Beatrice and (we, us) heard them last Saturday.

9. Can't you and (he, him) come to the next concert?

10. Vanessa and (they, them) sound terrific.

Check Your Understanding

Using Pronouns as Subjects

[Answers may vary. Possible responses are given.]

Contemporary Life **Complete each sentence by writing an appropriate pronoun. Do not use *you* or *it.***

11. His family and ours went to the band concert.

12. The musicians and he were outdoors in the plaza.

13. Weren't Rachel's sister and he playing in the band?

14. Why don't you and I spread our blankets over there?

15. Are your parents and his music lovers?

16. After a while, the tuba player and he showed up.

17. My aunt's friends and we found seats.

18. She and the other children raced around the bandstand.

19. Neither Rob nor I forgot a note.

20. At the end of the performance, the bandleader and he stood up to bow.

A DIFFERENT APPROACH

Auditory

Have students complete items 11 through 20 of **Check Your Understanding** in small groups. Students should take turns reading each sentence aloud and completing it with an appropriate response. When each group has finished, discuss their responses as a class.

HOME WORK

Have students write ten sentences similar to those in **Check Your Understanding.** Students should supply appropriate pronouns to complete their sentences. Students may choose one topic or random topics for their sentences.

is used. Then students should provide examples of sentences written in active voice and passive voice.

USING STUDENTS' STRENGTHS

Multiple Intelligences: Musical

Have students search the library or the Internet for music lyrics containing examples of predicate nominatives. Remind students that formal writing and speaking always use predicate nominatives correctly. Point out that some music styles like rock-and-roll and blues may not provide many examples of predicate nominatives due to their frequent use of informal English. Have students share their final examples with the class.

Pronouns Used as Predicate Nominatives

A **predicate nominative** is a word that follows a linking verb—such as *is, were,* or *has been*—and identifies or renames the subject. A pronoun used as a predicate nominative is in the nominative case.

PREDICATE NOMINATIVES	The best dancer is **he.**
	Are the two in costumes **they?**
	(Turn a question into a statement: *The two in costumes are they*. Then it is easy to see that *they* renames the subject.)

Check for the correct case of a pronoun in a compound predicate nominative by turning the sentence around to make the predicate nominative the subject. Then say each pronoun separately to learn which is correct.

PREDICATE NOMINATIVE	The musicians will be Brett and (she, her). Brett and (she, her) will be the musicians.
CORRECT	**She** will be a musician.
INCORRECT	**Her** will be a musician.
CORRECT	The musicians will be Brett and **she.**

Sometimes sentences with pronouns used as predicate nominatives *sound* wrong even though they are technically correct. When you write, you can avoid these awkward-sounding sentences by reversing them. Turn the predicate nominatives into the subjects.

AWKWARD	The best dancer is **he.**
BETTER	**He** is the best dancer.

AWKWARD	The two in costumes are **they.**
BETTER	**They** are the two in costumes.
AWKWARD	The musicians will be Brett and **she.**
BETTER	**She** and Brett will be the musicians.

CONNECT TO SPEAKING AND WRITING

Expressions like *It's me* or *That's her* are acceptable in informal speech. When you write, however, the required expressions are *It is I* and *That is she* because *I* and *she* are predicate nominatives.

You can learn more about predicate nominatives on pages L168–L170.

You can learn more about linking verbs on pages L85–L89.

PRACTICE YOUR SKILLS

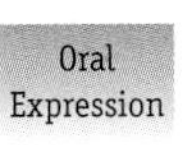

Check Your Understanding

Using Pronouns as Predicate Nominatives

Oral Expression

Turn each sentence around to make the predicate nominative the subject. Read each sentence aloud, trying each pronoun separately. Then read each sentence aloud again, choosing the correct pronoun.

1. The stars of the movie are Nate and (she, her).
2. I'm sure that the actor who played the role of Nekka was (he, him).
3. The giant slug is (she, her) or Michael Yee.
4. The grossest characters were (him, he) and the Vaxons.
5. The biggest fans of science-fiction movies are Brittany and (I, me).

A DIFFERENT APPROACH

Visual

Have students complete items 1 through 20 of **Practice Your Skills** by writing out the sentences as they appear in their textbooks including both pronoun choices. Students should then use a highlighter to circle the correct pronouns to complete each sentence. Discuss each sentence as students circle the correct pronoun.

HOME WORK

Have students write ten sentences similar to the ones in **Check Your Understanding.** Remind students to include two pronoun choices to complete each sentence. Have students exchange papers with a classmate the following day. Students should then answer each other's sentences. After students have completed the sentences, discuss the exercises and some of their responses.

6. The renters of the latest movie are the twins' parents and (they, them).
7. The biggest fans are Brian and (I, me).
8. Is the producer of this movie (she, her) or Jeff Ogawa?
9. The lucky winner of this year's Oscar might be (they, them).
10. The best actors of our own generation could be you and (I, me).

Check Your Understanding

Using Pronouns as Predicate Nominatives

Contemporary Life **Write the correct pronoun for each sentence.**

11. The masters of the universe will definitely be (we, us).
12. The sabotagers of the Juno mission were Nekko and (they, them).
13. The crew members who saw the explosions were the Jermiz and (I, me).
14. The Vaxons' foes have always been the Jermiz and (we, us).
15. Aren't their most cunning leaders (her, she) and the Pandit of Dreewald?
16. The enemies are Star-rover 2 and (he, him).
17. Are the allies of the slugs (they, them)?
18. Should the ambassador to Nekka be the Captain or (she, her)?
19. The Peacekeepers are (we, us) and the other inhabitants of Galaxy Four.
20. That is (they, them) on our radar screen.

Check Your Understanding

Supplying Pronouns in the Nominative Case

[Answers may vary. Possible responses are given.]

Contemporary Life

Complete each sentence by writing an appropriate pronoun. Do not use *you* or *it*.

21. The first ones in the movie theater will be José and ▪. she

22. That's ▪ at the head of the line. he

23. The movie's biggest fans are ▪. we

24. Where's Tanya? Daniel and ▪ promised to be here on time. she

25. My two oldest friends are Tanya and ▪. he

26. ▪ and Daniel will get a ride to the movie theater from their father. She

27. The last in line are ▪. they

28. Ryan and ▪ will come, too. she

29. Aaron, Maria, and ▪ know most of the lines by heart. I

30. Some of our friends and ▪ plan to buy the video of the movie. I

Connect to the Writing Process: Editing

Correcting Nominative Case Errors

If an underlined pronoun is in the wrong case, write it correctly. If it is in the correct case, write *C*.

31. José or ~~him~~ (he) will save us seats.

32. Are Brady and ~~her~~ (she) sitting over there?

33. Julia and ~~them~~ (they) are waving at us.

34. The ones with the best seats in the theater are the Green family and ~~us~~ (we).

35. Scott and they can't see the screen very well. C

36. Are ~~her~~ (she) and you buying the popcorn?

YOUR IDEAS

For Pronoun Cases

TIMESAVER *QuickCheck*

After students have written their dialogues, have them self-evaluate their writing for correct use of subject pronouns and predicate nominatives. Encourage students to check their use of pronouns against example sentences and definitions of these two types of pronouns on pages L363 and L366.

HOME STUDY

Have students find out more about dialogues and how they are written for plays. Students should use library and Internet sources to find out about a playwright of their choice. Students should tell how the playwright writes dialogue for his or her plays.

37. Will you and I get the ice cream sandwiches for José? C

38. Tanya and ~~Me~~ I will have our hands full with snacks for everyone.

39. The noisiest people in the crowded theater must be you and ~~him~~ he.

40. When the movie starts, neither José nor ~~her~~ she will say a word.

Connect to the Writing Process: Drafting

Writing Sentences with Pronouns

[Answers may vary. Sample responses are given.]

Write five sentences, following the instructions below.

41. Use *they* as a subject. They are the most important ones.

42. Use *Rosa and I* as a compound subject. Rosa and I raced to get there in time.

43. Use *Jeff and he* as a compound subject in a question. Are Jeff and he full members?

44. Use *he and I* as a compound predicate nominative. The coaches were he and I.

45. Use *she* as a predicate nominative in a question. Is the surprise guest she?

Communicate Your Ideas

APPLY TO WRITING

Dialogue: ***Pronouns in the Nominative Case***

You are making a movie for teenagers about two space explorers who crash on an inhabited planet. Someone who speaks the explorers' language takes them to the planet's leaders. Write dialogue for a scene in which the explorers and the leaders meet. Use at least three pronouns as subjects and three as predicate nominatives.

Mixed Practice
[Answers may vary. Possible responses are given.]

History Topic **Complete each sentence by writing an appropriate pronoun. Do not use *you* or *it*.**

1. The Blues and she were loyal to different emperors.
2. The Blues' allies were the Greens and he.
3. Neither Angelus nor they would join the Blues.
4. We talked our cousin out of joining the rebels.
5. When the Blues rioted, Justinian's advisors and he wanted to flee.
6. Theodora's supporters and she would rather die than flee.
7. My comrades and I fought the Blues and Greens.
8. The greatest leaders of Justinian's army had always been Belisarius and he.
9. He and the others fought for Empress Theodora.
10. After all, didn't she really rule Constantinople?

The Objective Case

The following personal pronouns are in the objective case.

OBJECTIVE CASE		
	SINGULAR	PLURAL
FIRST PERSON	me	us
SECOND PERSON	you	you
THIRD PERSON	him, her, it	them

EXPANDING THE LESSON

Using Technology

You will find additional **instructional** and **practice** materials for this chapter at http://www.bkenglish.com.

IDENTIFYING COMMON STUMBLING BLOCKS

Problem

- Using subject pronouns as object pronouns

Solution

- Tell students that subject pronouns should not be used as object pronouns unless the sentence contains a helping verb. Demonstrate the correct use of pronouns using the following examples:

  Dad gave Steve and (me, I) a ride to practice. Tell students the correct response is *me* because it is an object pronoun and because the verb *gave* is not a helping verb.

  The winner is (her, she). Tell students that the correct response is *she* because the sentence contains the helping verb *is.*

- Have students choose the correct pronouns in these examples:

  David answered the phone by saying, "This is (him, he)." (he)

  Can you give Linda and (she, her) and ride? (her)

  The teacher read him and (me, I) a story. (me)

  The next person in line was (me, I). (I)

The **objective case** is used for direct objects, indirect objects, and objects of prepositions.

DIRECT OBJECT	The Website interested **us.**
INDIRECT OBJECT	Mom gave **us** directions to the site.
OBJECT OF A PREPOSITION	She always shares interesting sites with **us.**

Pronouns Used as Direct and Indirect Objects

A **direct object** follows an action verb and answers the question *Whom?* or *What?*

DIRECT OBJECT

The Walkers invited **us.**
(Invited whom? *Us* is the direct object.)

Did you see **them?** (Turn a question into a statement: *You did see them.* You did see whom? *Them* is the direct object.)

An **indirect object** comes before a direct object and answers the question *To or for whom?* or *To or for what?*

INDIRECT OBJECT

Ms. Green gave **us** (i.o.) the assignment (d.o.).
(Ms. Green gave what? *Assignment* is the direct object. She gave the assignment to whom? *Us* is the indirect object.)

Did you give **her** (i.o.) the tickets (d.o.)?
(Turn a question into a statement: *You did give what? Tickets* is the direct object. Give the tickets to whom? *Her* is the indirect object.)

Check for the correct case of a compound object in the same way you check for the correct case of a compound subject. Say the nominative and objective case pronouns separately.

DIRECT OBJECT	Did Miguel thank Chris and (he, him)?
INCORRECT	Miguel did thank **he.**
CORRECT	Miguel did thank **him.**
CORRECT	Did Miguel thank Chris and **him?**
INDIRECT OBJECT	Mom handed Kim and (I, me) a gift.
INCORRECT	Mom handed **I** a gift.
CORRECT	Mom handed **me** a gift.
CORRECT	Mom handed Kim and **me** a gift.

You can learn more about direct objects and indirect objects on pages L159–L164.

PRACTICE YOUR SKILLS

Check Your Understanding

Using Pronouns as Direct and Indirect Objects

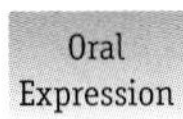
Oral Expression

Read each sentence aloud, trying each pronoun separately. Then read the sentence aloud again, choosing the correct pronoun.

1. My mother showed Sarah and (I, me) our new brothers.

2. The doctors had given Dad and (she, her) some sad news about Sam.

3. Because of an unusual condition, Sam's legs would never support (he, him).

4. The news from the doctors shocked my family and (I, me) at first.

5. His inability to use his legs did give him and (we, us) problems sometimes.

A DIFFERENT APPROACH

Kinesthetic

Before completing **Practice Your Skills,** have students use their fingers to underline the correct response for items one through fifteen. After pointing out each response with their fingers, students should read their responses aloud to a partner. Discuss students' responses and write some of the examples on the board.

HOME WORK

After completing **Check Your Understanding,** have students find out more about special athletes like Sam. Students should search *Sports Illustrated* magazine and other sources to find out about athletes who have overcome physical obstacles to compete in athletics and to succeed. For example, Lance Armstrong overcame cancer to win the Tour de France in 1999. Have students write a report about their special athlete. Remind students to check for correct pronoun usage in their writing.

Check Your Understanding

Using Pronouns as Direct and Indirect Objects

Contemporary Life **Write the correct pronoun for each sentence.**

6. My parents took my brothers, sister, and (I, me) to the mountains.

7. My mother's father had taught her two sisters and (she, her) the sport of skiing.

8. Sam was very excited because our parents bought (he, him) a special toboggan.

9. First, Mom showed Sam and (we, us) the basics of skiing.

10. Then Dad showed (he, him) the principles of sit-skiing.

11. In no time at all, we joined the other skiers and (they, them) at the top of the hill.

12. Dad told Mom and (we, us) about Sam's skill on the slopes.

13. I didn't remind (he, him) about the need to shift his weight.

14. Because of his skill, Sam made Sarah and (I, me) a little jealous.

15. He gave Stevie, me, and (she, her) rides on the toboggan.

16. Afterwards, a horse-drawn sleigh took Sam and (we, us) back to the lodge.

17. A waiter offered (we, us) some hot chocolate.

18. Sarah didn't want any, so he brought (she, her) hot cider instead.

19. The fireplace warmed up Sam and (me, I).

20. Stevie saw (us, we) and sat down also.

Pronouns Used as Objects of Prepositions

A **prepositional phrase** begins with a preposition, such as *with, to, by,* or *for.* A prepositional phrase ends with the object of a preposition. A pronoun used as an object of a preposition is in the objective case.

OBJECTS OF PREPOSITIONS	Did David talk to **them?** (*To them* is the prepositional phrase.)
	Nicole mailed the tickets to **us.** (*To us* is the prepositional phrase.)

You can find a list of prepositions on page L133.

CONNECT TO SPEAKING AND WRITING

People sometimes make a common mistake when they use the preposition *between.* When people try to sound formal or correct, they often use nominative case pronouns after *between.* However, all pronouns used as objects of prepositions must be in the objective case. In this case, what sounds more natural is correct.

INCORRECT	The argument was *between* **she** and **I.**
CORRECT	The argument was *between* **her** and **me.**

PRACTICE YOUR SKILLS

Check Your Understanding

Using Pronouns as Objects of Prepositions

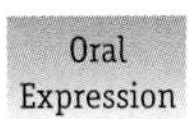

Oral Expression

Read the following sentences aloud to practice saying the underlined pronouns and hearing them used correctly. Be prepared to explain why each pronoun is correct. The answer in each case is that a pronoun used as an object of a preposition is in the objective case.

1. Grandma showed some old photos to Alex and me.
2. We looked at our grandpa and her when they were teenagers.

REACHING ALL STUDENTS

Struggling Learners

To reinforce **Connect to Speaking and Writing,** have students choose the correct pronoun in the following sentences that use the word *between.*

The judge chose between (him, he) and (me, I). (him, me)

Between (her, she) and (him, he), they finished the pie. (her, him)

The secret was between Nick and (me, I). (me)

INTEGRATING TECHNOLOGY

Computers

Have students complete items 11 through 20 of **Check Your Understanding** using computers to type and print out their responses. Students should type the complete sentences with their pronoun choices. Remind students to check for correct spelling, capitalization, and punctuation in their sentences.

3. We laughed together at their friends and them.
4. Their clothes seem really weird to our friends and us today.
5. The skirts on her friends and her looked like beach umbrellas.
6. They wore several petticoats under them.
7. She pointed out the plaid shirts on Grandpa and them.
8. We hunted for Grandma and him in their graduation picture.
9. We finally saw Grandpa between his friend Howie and her.
10. They gave their block sweaters to Nancy and me for a costume party.

Check Your Understanding

Using Pronouns as Objects of Prepositions

General Interest **Write the correct pronoun for each sentence.**

11. We talked to Grandpa and (she, her) about their parties.
12. No party in the neighborhood could start without Nancy and (I, me).
13. Grandpa remarked to (we, us) that the boys usually brought food.
14. Grandma did not agree with (he, him) about that fact.
15. One summer our parents gave a tape player to my sister and (I, me).
16. My uncle bought new tapes for my cousin and (we, us).

17. We would dance to (they, them) every afternoon after school.

18. Everyone danced to the fast songs except Howie and (he, him).

19. "I could eat all afternoon," Grandpa said to Alex and (she, her).

20. If I didn't keep an eye on (they, them), the food would vanish.

Check Your Understanding

Supplying Pronouns in the Objective Case

[Answers may vary. Possible responses are given.]

Contemporary Life

Complete each sentence by writing an appropriate pronoun. Do not use *you* or *it*.

21. Baby-sitting was a good job during the summer for my sister and ■. me

22. Mrs. Spencer had called the two of ■. us

23. She has four children and needed a trustworthy sitter for ■. them

24. The Spencers told our parents and ■ us the date and time.

25. We had the telephone numbers of their friends and ■. them

26. "Put Bradley's toy elephant in bed with ■ him," said his mother.

27. She introduced the children and ■ us to one another before she left.

28. She said, "Make sure you have all of ■ them in bed by nine."

29. Linda read a book to Bradley and ■. them

30. Everything went very well that night for Linda and ■. me

YOUR IDEAS

For Choosing the Correct Pronoun

HOME WORK

Have students record examples of pronouns in the objective case they hear throughout the day. After writing out the sentence, they should indicate whether the usage is correct or not.

Connect to the Writing Process: Drafting

Writing Sentences with Pronouns

[Answers may vary. Possible responses are given.]

Write five sentences following the instructions below.

No one noticed Dad and me at the door.

31. Include *Dad and me* as a compound direct object.

Are you going to include Sarah and us?

32. Include *Sarah and us* as a compound direct object in a question.

The committee will award Zack or him the scholarship.

33. Include *Zack or him* as a compound indirect object.

Are you planning to give the team members and them a second chance?

34. Include the *team members and them* as a compound indirect object in a question.

I hope the school does not have to choose between Allison and her.

35. Include *Alison and her* as a compound object of a preposition.

Connect to the Writing Process: Editing

Using Pronouns in the Objective Case

Rewrite the following paragraph, correcting all pronouns in the wrong case.

The children played happily with Linda and ~~I~~ me until nine o'clock. Then Linda told Bradley and ~~they~~ them that it was bedtime. First ~~her~~ she and I took Bunnie and Bonnie into the bathroom. They brushed their teeth. Then I read Bradley a story. He sat between his little sister Becky and ~~I~~ me. Linda asked for help, and I left ~~they~~ them for a minute. When I came back, Bradley had gone into the kitchen with Becky. He had found some crayons and was using ~~they~~ them on his and Becky's arms. I took the crayons away from Becky and ~~he~~ him. Bunnie got out of bed and sat in the sooty fireplace. "If the Spencers ask ~~we~~ us again," I said, "you and ~~me~~ I are unavailable."

Communicate Your Ideas

APPLY TO WRITING

Friendly Letter: ***Pronouns in the Objective Case***

Imagine that you're trying to get a summer job taking care of a seven-year-old girl and a four-year-old boy for four hours a day. Write a letter to the children's parents, telling them you want the job. Be specific about some things you would do to keep the children entertained. Keep in mind that the difference in their ages means that they won't always enjoy the same activities! Use pronouns as direct objects, indirect objects, and objects of prepositions in your letter. When you have finished, underline the pronouns you used.

Mixed Practice

[Answers may vary. Possible responses are given.]

Contemporary Life

Complete each sentence by writing an appropriate pronoun. Do not use *you* or *it*.

1. Mom took Jordan and ■ (me) to the mall.
2. Can anyone see a parking space for ■ (us)?
3. I waited for Jordan and ■ (her) at the top of the escalator.
4. ■ (We) spotted Eric's dad and Eric in the sportswear department.
5. We know their whole family and ■ (him) from Little League games.
6. Eric's brother hangs around with my friend Adam and ■ (me).

TIMESAVER QuickCheck

Have students use two forms of evaluation to check their child care letters. After completing the first draft of their letters, students should have a parent or another adult in their family read their letters to comment on content. Do the adults think the activities and proposals sound appropriate for caring for two young children? The adults should critique and comment on the letters' contents. Then students should have a classmate check their letters for correct grammar, letter form, spelling, capitalization, punctuation, and pronoun usage. Students should implement the adult and peer improvements into their writing before drafting their final letters.

USING STUDENTS' STRENGTHS

Multiple Intelligences: Linguistic

After discussing possessive pronouns, slowly read aloud each line of the following poem by Henry Wadsworth Longfellow. Have students identify all of the pronouns in the poem. Students should distinguish between those pronouns that are possessive and those which are not possessive.

Nature
As a fond mother, when the day is o'er,
Leads by the hand her little child to bed,
Half willing, half reluctant to be led,
And leave his broken playthings on the floor,
Still gazing at them through the open door,
Nor wholly reassured and comforted
By promises of others in their stead,
Which, though more splendid, may not please him more;
So nature deals with us, and takes away
Our playthings one by one, and by the hand
Leads us to rest so gently, that we go
Scarce knowing if we wish to go or stay,
Being too full of sleep to understand
How far the unknown transcends the what we know.

(Possessive pronouns: *her, his, their, Our*; pronouns: *them, others, him, us, we*)

7. The clerk brought out some sweatpants for Eric and ▢ (me).
8. Eric stood between Jordan and ▢ (me) as we looked in the mirror.
9. Are those pants too large for Jordan or ▢ (him)?
10. Mom and ▢ (I) liked the pants on Eric and Jordan.

The Possessive Case

The following personal pronouns are in the possessive case.

POSSESSIVE CASE		
	SINGULAR	PLURAL
FIRST PERSON	my, mine	our, ours
SECOND PERSON	your, yours	your, yours
THIRD PERSON	his, her, hers, its	their, theirs

The **possessive case** is used to show ownership or possession.

Possessive pronouns can be divided into two groups: (1) those that are used like adjectives to modify nouns and (2) those that are used alone.

USES OF POSSESSIVE PRONOUNS	
USED LIKE ADJECTIVES	my, your, his, her, its, our, their
USED ALONE	mine, yours, his, hers, its, ours, theirs

Pronouns used as adjectives are sometimes called possessive adjectives.

My hat is here, but **yours** is over there.

Her sweater is yellow, and **mine** is green.

Apostrophes are used with possessive nouns, but they are never used with possessive forms of personal pronouns.

POSSESSIVE NOUN	Is this **Jessica's** coat?
POSSESSIVE PRONOUN	Is this coat **hers?** (not *her's*)

You can learn about apostrophes with possessive nouns on pages L617–L619.

PRACTICE YOUR SKILLS

Check Your Understanding

Using Possessive Pronouns

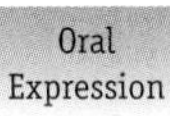

Oral Expression **Read each sentence aloud, trying each pronoun separately. Then read the sentence aloud again, choosing the correct pronoun.**

1. I am writing (my, mine) report on an animal's use of tools.

2. What are you writing (your, yours) on?

3. Lin's report is on gorillas, and so is (my, mine).

4. Miguel is doing (him, his) on animal communication.

5. Kevin and Mali are planning (their, theirs) presentations together.

6. Leah has offered us (her, hers) book on African apes.

7. Can Anna, Rick, and I pool (our, ours) source materials?

8. Kayla's report is done, but Wes and I need two more days for (our, ours).

A DIFFERENT APPROACH

Auditory

Have students work in groups of three or four to complete items 1 through 20 of **Practice Your Skills.** Students should take turns reading each sentence aloud and choosing the correct pronoun to complete each sentence. Students should be able to explain why they chose a particular pronoun for each sentence. Discuss students' responses when each small group has finished.

HOME WORK

Have students write fifteen sentences that correctly use possessive pronouns. Students may choose the topic for their sentences. Remind students not to confuse possessive pronouns with contractions. Have students share their sentences with the class the following day.

YOUR IDEAS

For Possessive Pronouns

9. Have Pedro and Matt finished (their, theirs) yet?

10. This book is losing (it, its) cover.

Check Your Understanding

Using Possessive Pronouns

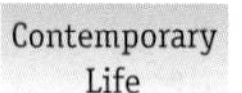

Write the correct pronoun for each sentence.

11. Are you ready with (your, yours) presentation?

12. I rehearsed (my, mine) until midnight.

13. Juan and Matt are showing slides with (his, theirs).

14. Sita and I have made maps for (our, ours).

15. Julia has written out (her, hers) notes on large file cards.

16. The twins found much of (theirs, their) material on the Internet.

17. I dried (my, mine) model outside, and the neighbor's dog stepped on it.

18. The dog left (it, its) muddy footprints all along one side.

19. Susannah, it will be (our, ours) turn in a few more minutes.

20. My throat is dry. How about (your, yours)?

Connect to the Writing Process: Editing

Correcting Possessive Pronouns

Write each underlined pronoun. If it is correct, write *C*. If it is incorrect, write it correctly.

21. I studied Paki the gorilla and her baby. C

22. We had left the two of them alone in ~~theirs~~ their cage.

23. For some reason Paki was neglecting that baby of ~~her.~~ hers

24. Eventually we separated Kishina and ~~hers~~ her mother.

25. We put Kishina in our nursery for human contact. C

Possessive Pronoun or Contraction?

Sometimes some contractions are confused with personal pronouns because they sound alike.

POSSESSIVE PRONOUNS AND CONTRACTIONS	
Possessive Pronouns	its, your, their, theirs
Contractions	it's (it is), you're (you are), they're (they are), there's (there is)

The best way to separate these words in your mind is to say the two words that a contraction stands for.

Possessive Pronoun or Contraction?	Is (**you're, your**) coat here?
Incorrect	Is **you are** coat here?
Correct	Is **your** coat here?

You can learn more about contractions on page L625.

Connect to Speaking and Writing

When you speak, some contractions and possessive pronouns sound the same. When you write, you have to know which one to use. One of the most frequent mistakes is writing *it's* for *its.* Notice that no possessive pronoun has an apostrophe. When you aren't sure whether to write *it's* or *its,* mentally substitute the word *his.* If *his* makes sense, then write *its.*

The dog knocked over **its** dish.

The dog knocked over **his** dish. 

GETTING STUDENTS INVOLVED

Reciprocal Teaching

After discussing strategies to distinguish possessive pronouns from contractions, have students work with partners to make sure they both can use these strategies. Partners should write six sentences that demonstrate the difference between possessive pronouns and contractions. When completed, have students share their sentences and strategies that help them distinguish between the two.

A DIFFERENT APPROACH

Visual

Have students complete items one through fifteen of **Check Your Understanding** by writing the sentences on the board. Students should take turns writing the sentences in one color of chalk and the correct pronouns in another color of chalk. Discuss each item as students complete them on the board.

HOME WORK

After completing **Check Your Understanding,** have students write ten additional sentences using possessive pronouns and contractions correctly. Students' sentences should be about archaeology. Tell students they can get information for their sentences from such sources as archaeological magazines or television programs on *The Discovery Channel* or *The Learning Channel.*

Practice Your Skills

Check Your Understanding

Using Possessive Pronouns and Contractions

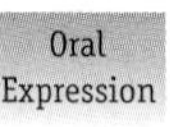

Read the following sentences aloud. Identify each word as a possessive pronoun or a contraction. If you aren't sure, test the word in one of the ways you have learned about.

1. Which boat in the harbor is yours? [poss. pron.: yours]
2. It's the one with the bold red stripe. [con.: It's]
3. When is your boat leaving? [poss. pron.: your]
4. Aren't you afraid you're going to be late? [con.: you're]
5. No, there's still an hour before it's time to go. [con.: there's; con.: it's]
6. Look, there's Zach! Where are your sisters? [con.: there's; poss. pron.: your]
7. They're buying their tickets for the boat ride. [con.: They're; poss. pron.: their]
8. Didn't you bring your camera? [poss. pron.: your]
9. No, I lost its case, so I plan to use theirs. [poss. pron.: its; poss. pron.: theirs]
10. You're going to have a great time on your tour. [con.: You're; poss. pron.: your]

Check Your Understanding

Distinguishing Between Possessive Pronouns and Contractions

Contemporary Life

Write the correct word in parentheses for each sentence.

11. There's the island of Crete on (<u>your</u>, you're) left.
12. (Theirs, <u>There's</u>) the place where the Minoans lived.
13. (<u>Their</u>, They're) cities and palaces fell into ruins.
14. (Your, <u>You're</u>) going to tour the ruins of Knossos.
15. (Its, <u>It's</u>) been partially excavated.

Communicate Your Ideas

APPLY TO WRITING

Magazine Article: *Pronouns*

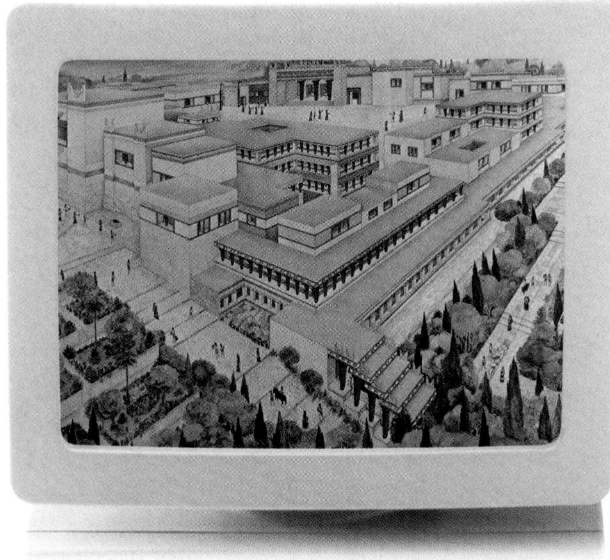

The Palace of Knossos on Crete might have looked like this three thousand years ago. Imagine that you are writing an article for a history magazine. You want to explain what it must have been like to live in this place and time. Make comparisons to your own life to help your readers understand the similarities and differences. (You can find out more about ancient Crete by doing research in reference books or on the Internet.) Use at least six different pronouns in your article. When you have finished, underline the pronouns and label them *nominative, objective,* or *possessive.*

TIMESAVER *QuickCheck*

Have students self-evaluate their completed magazine articles by creating a three-column chart with the headings *Nominative, Objective,* and *Possessive.* Students should list each pronoun they use in their articles in the appropriate column in the chart to check for correct pronoun usage.

IDENTIFYING COMMON STUMBLING BLOCKS

Problem

- Confusing the *whose* and *who's*

Solution

- Tell students that *whose* is a pronoun and should not be confused with the contraction *who's.* Explain that *who's* is the contraction for the words *who is* or *who has.*
- To check for correct usage, have students substitute *who is* or *who has* for *who's* or *whose* in sentences and choose the one that makes sense. For example, students can check the following sentence by reading it *"Who's (who is) going with us?"* Have students choose the correct word to complete these sentences.

  (Whose, Who's) shoes are in the gym? (Whose)

  I asked, "(Whose, Who's) left their shoes in the gym?" (Who's)

  I know (whose, who's) shoes those are. (whose)

  (Whose, Who's) picking up the shoes? (Who's)

Pronoun Problem: *Who* or *Whom?*

Who and *whom* can be used as interrogative pronouns. Like personal pronouns, these pronouns also have case.

Who is in the nominative case and can be the subject.

Subject	**Who** decorated the classroom for the party?

Whom is in the objective case and can be used as a direct object or as an object of a preposition.

Direct Object	**Whom** did you see during the school trip?
	(Turn a question into a statement. *You did see whom during the school trip. Whom* is the direct object.)
Object of a Preposition	From **whom** did you receive those magazines?
	(*From whom* is a prepositional phrase.)

Whose can be used as an interrogative pronoun also. It always shows possession.

Whose is this backpack on the floor?

(*Whose* modifies *backpack.*)

Looking at all the backpacks, we didn't know **whose** were **whose!**

(*Whose* is used as a subject and then as a predicate nominative.)

You can learn more about interrogative pronouns on page L65.

Practice Your Skills

Check Your Understanding

Using* Who *and* Whom *Correctly

Contemporary Life

Complete each sentence, using the interrogative pronouns *who, whom,* or *whose* correctly.

1. [Who] needs a ride to the game?
2. To [whom] did you give the game schedule?
3. [Who] will be shortstop in this game?
4. [Whom] is the coach considering as catcher?
5. This glove belongs to [whom]?
6. [Whose] is that bat?
7. [Whom] did they choose for their team captain this year?
8. [Who] has seen Ben's cap?
9. [Whose] is that jacket under the top row of the bleachers?
10. [Whom] do you expect at the game?

Connect to the Writing Process: Editing

Correcting Sentences with Interrogative Pronouns

Rewrite each sentence, correcting the interrogative pronoun. If the pronoun is correct, write *C*.

11. ~~Who~~ Whom did the coach send into the batting box first?
12. ~~Whom~~ Who came up to bat with the bases loaded in the final inning?
13. For ~~who~~ whom were the fans cheering?
14. Whose fly ball did Jeff catch? C
15. ~~Whom~~ Who tagged out Katie?

A DIFFERENT APPROACH

Auditory

Have students complete items one through fifteen of **Practice Your Skills** by taking turns reading the sentences aloud. Students should choose the correct interrogative pronoun to complete each sentence. Students should also identify each pronoun they choose as *nominative, objective,* or *possessive.* Discuss students' responses.

HOME WORK

Have students identify the pronouns *who, whom,* and *whose* in a story or novel they are reading. Students should read a passage and identify at least ten of these pronouns. Have students share their sentences and pronouns the following day.

LESSON 2 *(pages L388–L397)*

OBJECTIVES

- **To make pronouns and their antecedents agree**
- **To make personal pronouns and indefinite pronouns agree**
- **To correct unclear or missing antecedents**

Create Interest

Write the following sentences on the board. Have students identify what is wrong with each sentence. Students should come to the board and correct each sentence. Point out that the errors are in agreement between pronouns and their antecedents.

- Ava bought some flowers. They placed them in a vase. (She)
- The flowers were fresh. It looked nice in the vase. (They)
- Ava gave their own cat a bath. (her)
- The cat licked their wet paws. (its)

REACHING ALL STUDENTS

English Language Learners

Students who are learning English as a second language may have difficulty understanding pronoun and antecedent agreement, including gender and number. Have students make a list of English pronouns along with their equivalents in the students' first languages. Students should take note of how English pronouns change to accommodate differences in gender and number.

Pronouns and Their Antecedents

The word or group of words that a pronoun refers to or replaces is called the pronoun's **antecedent.** In the following sentences, *Maria* is the antecedent of *her,* and *Waltons* is the antecedent of *they.*

PRONOUNS AND ANTECEDENTS

Maria raised **her** hand and volunteered.

The **Waltons** are our neighbors. **They** are planning a garage sale.

Because a pronoun and its antecedent both refer to the same person, place, or thing, they must be in agreement.

A pronoun must agree in number and gender with its antecedent.

Number is the term used to indicate whether a noun or pronoun is singular (one) or plural (more than one). A pronoun must be singular if its antecedent is singular. It must be plural if its antecedent is plural.

SINGULAR **Luis** is preparing **his** presentation for the meeting.

PLURAL The **teachers** have turned in **their** grades for the semester.

The personal pronouns *you, your,* and *yours* can be either singular or plural.

Gender tells whether a noun or a personal pronoun is masculine, feminine, or neuter. A personal pronoun must also agree with its antecedent in gender. The chart on the next page lists personal pronouns according to their gender.

Guide Instruction

By Modeling Strategies

Use the instruction and example sentences on pages L388 to L389 to model strategies for choosing correct pronouns and antecedents. Use these additional example sentences to demonstrate pronoun and antecedent agreement:

- Bob put on his shoes.
- I would like to change my clothes.
- The boys all changed their shoes.
- We carried our shoes to the gym.

Consolidate Skills

Through Guided Practice

The **Check Your Understanding** exercises as well as the **QuickCheck** on page L397 will help students use pronouns and their antecedents correctly. Complete the first item in each exercise together, discussing and reviewing the major strategies students should

GENDER OF PERSONAL PRONOUNS	
Masculine	he, him, his
Feminine	she, her, hers
Neuter	it, its

Things and places are neuter in gender. Unless animals are given proper names, they are usually also considered neuter.

Masculine	**Brian** forgot **his** sneakers.
Feminine	**Amy** gave **her** cat a bath.
Neuter	Wash the **car** and wax **it.**

The plural pronouns *them* and *their* have no gender. They can have masculine, feminine, or neuter antecedents. Their antecedents may also be combinations of masculine and feminine.

The three **women** presented **their** report to the board.

The **men** and **women** on the board compared **their** notes.

Practice Your Skills

Check Your Understanding

Making Pronouns and Their Antecedents Agree

History Topic **Complete each sentence by writing an appropriate pronoun.**

1. We cut or arrange [our] hair in the styles of our culture.

2. Native Americans wore [their] hair in various ways.

3. Most of them wore [their] hair long.

YOUR IDEAS

For Presenting Gendered Pronouns

use to make pronouns and their antecedents agree. Have students complete the remaining exercises independently.

Apply to Communication

Through Independent Writing

The **Communicate Your Ideas** activities on pages L393 and L396 prompt students to write a letter and to analyze the pronouns used by James Thurber in a paragraph. Ask students to consider whether their own pronoun usage will differ from the pronouns used by an established author. Have students brainstorm the types of pronouns they will use in their letters.

Transfer to Everyday Life

Identifying Correct Pronoun and Antecedent Agreement

Have students use newspapers to identify sentences that use correct pronoun and antecedent agreement. Students should read an article and highlight at least five examples of pronouns and antecedents that agree.

A DIFFERENT APPROACH

Visual

After completing **Check Your Understanding,** have students share their responses by writing the sentences on large sheets of chart paper. Students should take turns displaying their responses on the chart paper. Discuss the correct responses and have students share strategies they used to make sure the pronouns and antecedents agreed.

HOME WORK

Ask students to return to the **Check Your Understanding** exercise, substituting plural pronouns for singular ones and singular pronouns for plural ones.

4. Sometimes a man's braids had fur woven into ▢. (them)

5. The feathers in the hair of a man showed ▢ status as a warrior. (his)

6. Some men wore ▢ hair long and loose. (their)

7. A man of a warrior tribe might shave ▢ head. (his)

8. His skull was bare except for a stiff crest down ▢ center. (its)

9. Many men stiffened ▢ crests with deer quills or paint. (their)

10. The hairstyle of a Hopi woman showed whether ▢ was married. (she)

Indefinite Pronouns as Antecedents

An indefinite pronoun can be the antecedent of a personal pronoun. Some indefinite pronouns are singular, and others are plural. Still other indefinite pronouns may be either singular or plural.

When one of the following indefinite pronouns is the antecedent of a personal pronoun, the personal pronoun must be singular.

SINGULAR INDEFINITE PRONOUNS			
anybody	either	neither	one
anyone	everybody	nobody	somebody
each	everyone	no one	someone

SINGULAR **One** of the boys can't open **his** locker.

Someone in the girls' chorus forgot **her** music.

Have students share their highlighted examples with the class.

Pull It All Together

By Summarizing

Have students write a paragraph explaining how to make pronouns agree with their antecedents. Students should discuss number and gender and provide at least five example sentences demonstrating pronoun and antecedent agreement.

Check Understanding

Defining Antecedents

Have students write a definition that explains what antecedents are and how they should be used with pronouns. Students should also write five example sentences demonstrating correct pronoun and antecedent agreement. Have students take turns writing one of their examples on the board. Discuss students' responses.

Sometimes the gender of a singular indefinite pronoun is not indicated in the sentence. Standard English solves this problem by using *his or her.*

> **Everyone** must finish **his or her** homework.

Although sentences like the previous one are correct, some may sound awkward. You can often eliminate awkwardness by rewriting a sentence in the plural form.

> All **students** must finish **their** homework.

When one of the following indefinite pronouns is the antecedent of a personal pronoun, the personal pronoun is plural.

PLURAL INDEFINITE PRONOUNS			
both	few	many	several

> PLURAL **Several** of the women offered **their** help.
> **Both** of my brothers lost **their** keys.

When one of the following indefinite pronouns is the antecedent of a personal pronoun, that pronoun can be either singular or plural.

SINGULAR OR PLURAL INDEFINITE PRONOUNS				
all	any	most	none	some

A personal pronoun used with one of these indefinite antecedents agrees in number and gender with the object of the preposition that follows it.

> SINGULAR **All** of the **art** was returned to **its** owner.
> PLURAL **Some** of the **players** wore **their** uniforms.

YOUR IDEAS

For Indefinite Pronouns

A DIFFERENT APPROACH

Visual

Have students make pronoun word cards before they begin **Check Your Understanding.** Students should write each pronoun they can think of on a separate index card. Then read each sentence aloud. Students should look through their word cards and decide whether or not they have a word card that could correctly complete the sentence. If so, students should stand up and display their card. Discuss students' correct responses.

HOME WORK

Have students create an activity or game to reinforce what they have learned about indefinite pronouns. Students can choose the topic for their activity or game. Remind students to refer to pages L390–L391 to guide them as they construct their activities or games. Have students share their completed activities the following day.

PRACTICE YOUR SKILLS

Check Your Understanding

Making Personal Pronouns Agree with Indefinite Pronouns

Contemporary Life **Complete each sentence by writing an appropriate pronoun.**

1. Everyone contributed ■ ideas for the mural. his or her — We all contributed our ideas for the mural.
2. Several of the students submitted ■ designs. their
3. Many asked ■ families for donations of supplies. their
4. Some of the merchants let us paint on ■ walls. their
5. One of the girls said ■ would transfer the sketch to the wall. she
6. A few of us brought ladders from ■ homes. our
7. Part of the wall should remain ■ original color. its
8. No one wore ■ good clothes to the work party. his or her — We all wore old clothes to the work party.
9. Some of the painters wore ■ coveralls. their
10. Neither of the boys remembered ■ paintbrush. his
11. Someone on our crew left the lid off ■ paint can. his or her — Someone on our crew left the lid off a paint can.
12. Both of the merchants came out of ■ shops. their
13. None of the workers left until ■ had cleaned up. he or she — We all stayed until we had cleaned up.
14. If some of the paint gets smudged, we can paint over ■ later. it
15. Will anyone bring ■ camera tomorrow? his or her — Will anyone bring a camera tomorrow?

Connect to the Writing Process: Drafting

Writing Sentences to Eliminate Awkward Constructions

[Answers may vary. See possible responses given above.]

16.–19. Find sentences in the preceding exercise that you completed with *his or her.* Rewrite these sentences in the plural form.

Communicate Your Ideas

APPLY TO WRITING

Friendly Letter: ***Personal Pronouns and Antecedents***

Traveling photographer Solomon Butcher took this photograph of the Shore family, Nebraska pioneers, in the 1880s. Having your picture taken was a rare and special event on the prairie. Imagine you are part of this family. Write a letter to a relative describing the day you had your picture taken. Tell what your family members did to get ready. Tell what the photographer did. Use at least five personal pronouns and make sure that they agree with their antecedents.

TIMESAVER *QuickCheck*

Have students exchange their completed letters with a classmate. Students should read to make sure that at least five personal pronouns have been used and that these pronouns agree with their antecedents. Have students write down any suggestions for improvements. After returning letters, students should implement constructive suggestions into their letters.

DEVELOPING WORKPLACE COMPETENCIES

Basic Skills: Writing

Discuss with students how the misuse of pronouns and their antecedents can cause problems or miscommunications in the workplace. Have students brainstorm the kinds of problems that might arise in various occupations from the use of missing or unclear antecedents. Students should then write a short E-mail or letter to a future colleague. Students should check their writing for correct pronoun and antecedent agreement. Have students share their writing with the class.

Unclear or Missing Antecedents

The meaning of your writing and speaking can become confusing if the pronouns you have used do not have clear antecedents.

Every personal pronoun should clearly refer to a specific antecedent.

UNCLEAR	I didn't go to the concert because **you** couldn't get a ticket.
	(*You* is incorrect because it does not refer to the *I* who is speaking. Instead, it appears to refer to the listener *you*.)
CLEAR	I didn't go to the concert because **I** couldn't get a ticket.
UNCLEAR	Nicholas told Scott **he** could get the tickets.
	(Who could get the tickets—Nicholas or Scott? The pronoun *he* has two possible antecedents.)
CLEAR	Nicholas agreed that Scott could get the tickets. Scott was reassured that Nicholas could get the tickets.
MISSING	My brother is a musician, but I know nothing about **it.**
	(What does *it* refer to? The antecedent is missing.)
CLEAR	My brother is a musician, but I know nothing about **music.**

PRACTICE YOUR SKILLS

Check Your Understanding

Correcting Unclear or Missing Antecedents

Contemporary Life

Write *I* for each antecedent that is unclear or missing and *C* for each antecedent that is used correctly.

Because reservations are needed, we can't go to the aquarium on Monday.

1. ~~We can't go to the aquarium Monday because you need reservations.~~ I

Many people have Monday off so the museum will be busier than usual on that day.

2. ~~Many people have Monday off, so it will be busier than usual.~~ I

When Julia and Amy set the date, Amy promised to buy the tickets.

3. ~~When Julia and Amy set the date, she promised to buy the tickets.~~ I

When he was in Monterey, Paul bought tickets for Mark.

4. ~~Paul bought tickets for Mark when he was in Monterey.~~ I

I could take the bus, but I must have the exact change.

5. ~~I could take the bus, but you must have the exact change.~~ I

You can obtain the aquarium schedule by calling 555-1029.

6. ~~The aquarium schedule can be obtained by contacting it at 555-1029.~~ I

I am looking forward to seeing the jellyfish I read about in the newspaper.

7. ~~I read a newspaper article about the jellyfish, and I am looking forward to it~~. I

All of the birds are from our own bay area.

8. The aquarium staff recently finished the new display of marshland birds. ~~All of them are from our own area~~.

Ashley's parents are marine biologists so she knows a lot about marine biology.

9. ~~Ashley's parents are marine biologists, so she knows a lot about it~~. I

10. When a seal looks into my eyes, it probably asks itself what kind of creature I am. C

Connect to the Writing Process: Revising

Correcting Sentences with Unclear or Missing Antecedents

[Answers may vary. See possible responses given above.]

11.–19. Rewrite the incorrect sentences from the preceding exercise, making the antecedents clear.

A DIFFERENT APPROACH

Kinesthetic

Complete items one through ten of **Check Your Understanding** together as a class. Have students use their bodies to form the letters *I* and *C.* Have students use these gestures to respond to the items as you read them aloud. Remind students not to call out the answers.

HOME STUDY

Have students read the entire short story "The Dog That Bit People" by James Thurber. Then have students share some of the pronouns Thurber correctly uses in his story. Have students write some example sentences from the story on the board.

SELECTION AMENDMENT
Description of change: excerpted
Rationale: to focus on the grammar skill

Communicate Your Ideas

APPLY TO WRITING

Writer's Craft: *Analyzing the Use of Pronouns and Their Antecedents*

Careful writers keep personal pronouns in agreement with their antecedents and make sure their antecedents are clear. In this paragraph James Thurber describes Muggs, a bad-tempered family dog. Read the paragraph and then follow the directions.

> Nobody ever had mice exactly like the mice we had that month. . . . They were so friendly that one night when my mother entertained at dinner the Friraliras, a club she and my father had belonged to for twenty years, she put down a lot of little dishes with food in them on the pantry floor so that the mice would be satisfied with that and wouldn't come into the dining room. Muggs stayed out in the pantry with the mice, . . . growling to himself—not at the mice, but about all the people in the next room that he would have liked to get at. Mother slipped out into the pantry once to see how everything was going.
>
> —*James Thurber,* "The Dog That Bit People"

- Write the underlined personal pronouns in the paragraph. Beside each one, write its antecedent. They: mice; she: my mother; them: dishes; he: Muggs
- The second sentence contains the phrase *my mother.* There is no antecedent for *my.* Whom does *my* refer to? How do you know? My refers to the author. We know this because the piece is being told in the first person.
- Notice the word *we* in the first sentence. Whom might *we* refer to? We refers to the whole community—the whole neighborhood, town, or city.

- The first sentence contains an indefinite pronoun. What is it? What effect does that word have on your understanding of the situation? The use of the indefinite pronoun nobody in the first sentence generalizes and emphasizes the size of the problem.

Mixed Practice

General Interest

Write the correct pronoun for each sentence.

1. (Who, Whom) knows why women's shirts often button differently from men's?

2. We can find the answer to (our, your) question in the thirteenth century.

3. In those days, everyone had lots of buttons on (their, her or his) clothes.

4. A woman's dress might have scores of buttons on (her, it).

5. For many men and women, (your, their) right hand was the more skillful one.

6. A man dressed himself, so (his, their) coat overlapped from left to right.

7. A rich woman, on the other hand, had maids to dress (her, them).

8. Right-handed maids did (her, their) work more easily when garments overlapped right to left.

9. (Who, Whom) is dressed by maids today?

10. Few of the manufacturers design (its, their) shirts for today's women.

EXPANDING THE LESSON

Using Technology

You will find additional **instructional** and **practice** materials for this chapter at http://www.bkenglish.com.

FOR REVIEWING SKILLS

Using *CheckPoint*

This feature on pronouns can be used as further independent practice or as a cumulative review of the chapter. Students choose correct pronouns, correct pronoun errors, make pronouns and antecedents agree, and write sentences using pronouns.

CheckPoint

Using Pronouns in the Correct Case

Write the correct word in parentheses.

1. Althea and (she, her) are equal partners in the delivery service.
2. During the Boston Tea Party, some of the ships in the harbor lost (its, their) cargo.
3. Should the tickets be sent to you or (he, him)?
4. (Who, Whom) did you just introduce to Ryan?
5. Was that (he, him) on the subway?
6. Give Daniel or (she, her) the money from the car wash.
7. The director chose David and (she, her) for the leads.
8. (They're, Their) work on the project was excellent.
9. Either of the women will give (her, their) report.
10. The volleyball game will be played between our relatives and (they, them).

Correcting Pronoun Errors

Write each sentence and correct any error in the use of pronouns. If a sentence is correct, write *C*.

1. The final decision must be made by Ellen and ~~he~~ him.
2. ~~Who~~ Whom did you choose for the lead in the play?
3. Clara and ~~him~~ he will be school monitors this term.
4. Isn't that she by the side of the pool? C
5. Tell Ana and ~~they~~ them about the play.
6. Mr. Brown and his wife have sold ~~they're~~ their farm.
7. Ruth gave Lily and ~~she~~ her matching sweaters.

8. To whom am I speaking? C
9. With Roscoe and ~~he~~ [him] as my helpers, we cleaned the house.
10. You must sign ~~you're~~ [your] name on this line.

Making Pronouns Agree with Antecedents

Write the pronoun that correctly completes each sentence.

1. Both of the girls must give ▢ [their] speeches today.
2. Amanda has gone to the movies with ▢ [her] friends.
3. Mr. and Mrs. Ruiz are away on ▢ [their] vacation.
4. One of the female plaintiffs will plead ▢ [her] own case.
5. All of the beach has white sand covering ▢ [it].
6. The pony ran quickly to ▢ [its] mother.
7. Most of the apples have worms in ▢ [them].
8. Lloyd couldn't find ▢ [his] hockey stick anywhere.
9. Several of the chorus members will sing ▢ [their] own songs.
10. Everyone on the boys' relay team has ▢ [his] racing time.

Using Pronouns Correctly

Write ten sentences that follow the directions below.

Write a sentence that . . .

1. includes *Bill and I* as subjects.
2. includes *him and her* as direct objects.
3. includes the prepositional phrase *between you and me.*
4. includes the words *your* and *you're.*
5. includes the words *their* and *they're.*
6. includes *who.*
7. includes *whom.*
8. includes *nobody* as the subject.
9. includes *some of the bread* as the subject.
10. includes *some of the papers* as the subject.

Sample Answers for *Using Pronouns Correctly:*

1. Bill and I started our own business.
2. We invited him and her to the party.
3. Jake sat between you and me.
4. You're going to lose your umbrella.
5. They're too worried about their looks.
6. Who finished the test first?
7. Whom did you take to the dance?
8. Nobody knows that teacher's first name.
9. Some of the bread seems moldy.
10. Some of the papers are under the table.

Using *Language and Self-Expression*

Consider using this writing assignment to assess students' ability to use pronouns correctly and effectively.

Prewriting

Encourage students to use questioning strategies to help them organize their thoughts in the prewriting stage. For example, students might use the following questions to help them proceed with their writing:

- What activities have you or your family taken part in that are similar to those depicted in the painting?
- How would you describe the mood of your family members while they participated in these activities?
- What pronouns can you use in your descriptions?

FOR YOUR INFORMATION

About the Artist

As a young man in France, Henri Matisse abandoned the study of law to devote himself to art. He experimented with using color in a more spontaneous way. He sought to emphasize the flatness of a picture plane, as well as the purity of line, decorative pattern, and color. Discovering that he could make certain colors glow and vibrate against one another, Matisse continued to experiment with color and light, stripping his paintings to their bare essentials and choosing strong colors to create striking effects.

Disabled by arthritis in the last years of his life, Matisse was able to continue creating art through collage. His artworks include sculpture, printmaking, stained glass, and drawing.

Language and *Self-Expression*

This colorful painting from 1924 shows a typical family at leisure. Henri Matisse, one of the most significant artists of the twentieth century, often used color to express a mood or feeling. Both the warm red colors and the repeated shapes contribute to the feeling of unity in this family scene.

If you were to write a description of your family relaxing, what written images would you include? How would you tie those images together to create a unified whole? Write a one-page description of your family at leisure. What is each person doing? Are you all in the same room, or are you all in separate spaces? Write your description in the first person, using the pronoun *I*. Include your feelings about the scene you are describing.

Prewriting Write down the name of every person in your family. Then list typical leisure activities for each person. Don't forget to include yourself.

Drafting Use your list to write your description. If you are all together, you might begin by naming the room you are in and then describing each person. If you are all in separate places, take one at a time and describe the place, person, and activity.

Revising Reread your description to see whether you have created a unified description of your family. Think of transitional words or phrases to help your description flow better.

Editing Review your work, looking for errors in pronoun–antecedent agreement, punctuation, and spelling. Make any corrections needed.

Publishing Prepare a neat final copy of your description. Share it with your family.

Another Look

Using Pronouns

Case is the form of a noun or pronoun that indicates its use in a sentence.

The **nominative case** is used for subjects and predicate nominatives.

The **objective case** is used for direct objects, indirect objects, and objects of prepositions.

The **possessive case** is used to show ownership or possession.

Pronouns and Their Antecedents

A **pronoun** must agree in number and gender with its antecedent. *(page L388)*

Every **personal pronoun** should clearly refer to a specific antecedent. *(page L394)*

Other Information About Pronouns

Recognizing pronouns used as subjects *(pages L363–L364)*
Recognizing pronouns used as predicate nominatives *(pages L366–L367)*
Recognizing pronouns used as direct and indirect objects *(pages L372–L373)*
Recognizing pronouns used as objects of prepositions *(page L375)*
Determining possessive pronoun or contraction *(page L383)*
Using *who* or *whom* *(page L386)*

Using *Another Look*

Another Look summarizes the terms defined in the chapter and provides cross-references to the specific pages on which they are explained. Consider having students use this feature prior to completing **CheckPoint** or taking the posttest. Students who can provide several examples of each term should be able to score well on either measurement.

FOR ASSESSING LEARNING

Using *the Posttest*

Assessing Learning

The posttest will help you and your students assess where they stand in their ability to use pronouns correctly.

IDENTIFYING COMMON STUMBLING BLOCKS

Following is a list of the most common errors students make when using pronouns.

Problem

- Incorrect pronoun case with compound subject

Solution

- For reteaching, use the explanatory copy printed in blue beside the examples on pages L363–L364.

Problem

- Vague pronoun antecedent

Solution

- For reteaching, use the explanatory copy printed in blue beside the examples on page L394.

Directions

Read the passage and choose the pronoun that belongs in each underlined space. Write the letter of the correct answer.

EXAMPLE Have (1) ever heard of Sirimavo Bandaranaike?

1 A you
B your
C us
D them

ANSWER **1 A**

When Sirimavo Bandaranaike's husband was assassinated in 1959, (1) took over as Sri Lanka's prime minister. That made (2) the first female prime minister the world had ever seen. The position was (3) for five years and then for seven more years in the 1970s. In 1994, (4) succeeded (5) own daughter as prime minister when the younger woman became president.

(6) of the people in Sri Lanka are Sinhalese, (7) are Buddhist by tradition. A smaller percentage are Tamil, of Hindu background.

Civil wars have torn apart this small nation, (8) is a bloody and violent history. First Tamil guerrillas attack government forces, and then the government forces push (9) back. This back-and-forth fighting has gone on as long as (10) remembers.

A DIFFERENT DELIVERY SYSTEM

If you prefer, you can print the posttest from the BK English Test Bank located at http://www.bkenglish.com.

1 **A** he
B she
C it
D her

2 **A** she
B he
C her
D it

3 **A** her
B hers
C it's
D our

4 **A** she
B her
C it
D we

5 **A** hers
B she
C her
D his

6 **A** One
B Most
C Neither
D Each

7 **A** whose
B who's
C whom
D who

8 **A** whom
B whose
C who
D who's

9 **A** him
B it
C they
D them

10 **A** anyone
B several
C many
D they

Customizing the Test

Use these questions to add or replace items for alternate versions of the test.

When the monsoons hit Sri Lanka annually, (11) bring with (12) destruction on a huge scale. Monsoons are winds that are dry in winter and wet in summer. The summer monsoons terrify Sri Lankans, many of (13) live on flat plains that are subject to flooding. (14) quite common for thousands to lose (15) lives during the seasonal flooding.

11. **A** he
B they
C their
D it

12. **A** them
B their
C they're
D it

13. **A** who
B him
C whom
D they

14. **A** It
B Its
C He's
D It's

15. **A** they
B theirs
C their
D his

TEACHING SUGGESTIONS

Assessing Prior Knowledge
Pretest (pages L404–L405)

Making Visual Connections
(page L406)

Developing Language Skills
Agreement of Subjects and Verbs (pages L407–L425)
Other Agreement Problems (pages L426–L439)

Reviewing Language Skills
CheckPoint (pages L440–L441)
Language and Self-Expression (page L442)
Another Look (page L443)

Assessing Learning
Posttest (pages L444–L445)

BLOCK SCHEDULING

- If your schedule requires that you cover the chapter in a **shorter time,** use the instruction on subject-verb agreement and the Check Your Understanding and QuickCheck exercises.
- If you want to take advantage of **longer class time,** add these applications to writing: Connect to Speaking and Writing, Connect to the Writing Process, and Apply to Writing exercises.

Essential Knowledge and Skills

- Adapting spoken language such as word choice, diction, and usage to the audience, purpose, and occasion
- Generating criteria to evaluate his/her own oral presentations and the presentations of others
- Writing to entertain such as to compose humorous poems or short stories
- Employing standard English usage in writing for audiences, including subject-verb agreement
- Writing with increased accuracy when using apostrophes in contractions such as doesn't

CHAPTER 13

Subject and Verb Agreement

Directions

Write the letter of the best way to write the underlined word or words in each sentence. If an underlined part contains no error, write *D.*

EXAMPLE **1.** The wild turkey <u>are found</u> only in the New World.

1 A is found
B were found
C found
D No error

ANSWER **1 A**

1. A grouse, a quail, or a pheasant <u>are</u> a close relative of the turkey.
2. There <u>was</u> turkeys in Mexico long ago.
3. Turkeys in the United States today <u>come</u> from these Mexican birds.
4. The feathers of a male bird <u>is</u> greenish brown.
5. Each of the males <u>have</u> a flock of females.
6. The flock <u>wanders</u> in the woods during the day.
7. At night males and females <u>roost</u> in trees.
8. Neither a female nor a young male <u>gobble</u>.
9. Adult males with bristly beards <u>make</u> that sound.
10. <u>Hasn't</u> you heard gobbling in the woods?

IDENTIFYING COMMON STUMBLING BLOCKS

Following is a list of the most common errors students make involving subject-verb agreement.

Problem

- Lack of subject-verb agreement with contractions ending in *-n't*

Solution

- Instruction, pp. L416–L417
- Practice, pp. L417–L418

Problem

- Lack of subject-verb agreement with compound subjects

Solution

- Instruction, pp. L426–L427
- Practice, pp. L427–L429

1
- **A** is
- **B** were
- **C** are being
- **D** No error

2
- **A** is
- **B** were
- **C** was being
- **D** No error

3
- **A** comes
- **B** coming
- **C** is coming
- **D** No error

4
- **A** is being
- **B** am
- **C** are
- **D** No error

5
- **A** are having
- **B** have had
- **C** has
- **D** No error

6
- **A** wandering
- **B** wander
- **C** were wandering
- **D** No error

7
- **A** roosts
- **B** is roosted
- **C** was roosting
- **D** No error

8
- **A** were gobbling
- **B** are gobbling
- **C** gobbles
- **D** No error

9
- **A** makes
- **B** is making
- **C** has made
- **D** No error

10
- **A** Haven't
- **B** Isn't
- **C** Has
- **D** No error

A DIFFERENT DELIVERY SYSTEM

If you prefer, you can print the pretest from the BK English Test Bank located at http://www.bkenglish.com.

Using *the Pretest*

Assessing Prior Knowledge

The pretest will help you and your students assess where they stand in their basic understanding of subject-verb agreement. The test measures students' ability to use subjects and verbs correctly in their writing.

Customizing the Test

Use these questions to add or replace items for alternate versions of the test.

11. The wild turkey eat berries, insects, shoots, and seeds.

12. I has seen several turkeys at my stepfather's farm.

13. My family enjoy their gobbling and clucking.

14. Our Labrador retriever and Irish setter looks nervous at the sound.

11.
- **A** are eating
- **B** eats
- **C** have eaten
- **D** No error

12.
- **A** have seen
- **B** has been seen
- **C** is seeing
- **D** No error

13.
- **A** have enjoyed
- **B** enjoys
- **C** are enjoying
- **D** No error

14.
- **A** look
- **B** is looking
- **C** has looked
- **D** No error

ADDITIONAL RESOURCES

Language Skills Practice . . . . pages 115–130
Transparency Tools FA13
ESL Practice and Test Preparation . . . . . pages 121–123
Assessment: Chapter Test. . . . . pages 182–185

MAKING VISUAL CONNECTIONS

For Language Development

Have students view *Church Picnic Story Quilt* for a full minute without responding verbally. Have students focus on the materials used to make the quilt: fabric and acrylic on cotton canvas. Then have students brainstorm sentences to describe how the quilt would probably feel to the touch. Write some of students' sentences on the board. Discuss the subject-verb agreement in students' sentences.

To Stimulate Writing

Use the questions for art criticism as writing or discussion prompts.

Possible Answers:

Describe The quilt pictures a group of church members having a picnic outdoors on a lawn.

Analyze The story is of a group of people who attend the same church and hold an annual Sunday School picnic. Details in the clothing, landscape, and picnic foods help to place the viewer in a particular time and place.

Interpret The story probably explains who the people are and what is happening in the scene.

Judge The artwork tells its own story. The artwork gives the viewer a starting point for imagining his/her own story.

Faith Ringgold. *Church Picnic Story Quilt,* 1988.
Tie-dyed, printed fabrics, acrylic on canvas, 76 by 76 inches. Collection of the High Museum, Atlanta, Georgia. © 1988 Faith Ringgold.

Describe	Who is pictured in this quilt? What is happening?
Analyze	What story does this artwork tell? How has the artist captured a particular place and time?
Interpret	The artist framed her painted cloth with a written story. What would you expect the story to tell?
Judge	Do you need to read the story to appreciate the artwork? Is the painted quilt meaningful on its own? Explain your answer.

At the end of the chapter, you will use the artwork as a visual aid for writing.

FOR DEVELOPING LANGUAGE SKILLS

LESSON 1 *(pages L407–L425)*

OBJECTIVES

- **To identify the number of nouns, pronouns, and verbs**
- **To make subjects and verbs agree**
- **To make subjects and contractions agree**
- **To make interrupted subjects and verbs agree**
- **To make subjects and verbs in inverted order agree**
- **To write sentences using subject and verb agreement**

Agreement of Subjects and Verbs

You would never think of wearing two shoes that did not match. Subjects and verbs must go together, just like a pair of shoes. The subject and verb in *A dog barks* and *Dogs bark* go together. *Dogs barks* does not go together. Subjects and verbs match when there is **agreement** between them.

A verb must agree with its subject in number.

Number

As you may recall, **number** is the term used to indicate whether a word is *singular*—meaning "one"—or *plural*—meaning "more than one." Nouns, pronouns, and verbs all have number.

The Number of Nouns and Pronouns

The plural of most nouns is formed by adding *-s* or *-es* to the singular form. A few nouns, however, form their plurals in other ways. A dictionary always lists irregular plurals.

	NOUNS		
SINGULAR	monkey	church	mouse
PLURAL	monkey**s**	church**es**	m**ice**

Pronouns also have number. For example, *I, he, she,* and *it* are singular, and *we* and *they* are plural. *You* can be singular or plural.

FOR INCREASING STUDENT ACHIEVEMENT

GETTING STUDENTS INVOLVED

Cooperative Learning

Have students work together with partners to brainstorm a list of nouns and pronouns. Partners should then write both the singular and plural of each word from their list. Encourage students to use dictionaries to check for irregular plurals if they are having difficulties. Discuss each group's examples and list some of them on the board.

Create Interest

Write the following sentences on the board. Have students decide what is wrong with each sentence and correct the errors.

The tadpole were small when I first got it. (was)

Little tadpoles has long tails. (have)

The tails helps them swim. (help)

I now has a full-grown African clawed frog. (have)

Guide Instruction

By Connecting Ideas

Remind students that they have previously studied verbs in Chapter 3 and Chapter 11. Review with students some of the verb charts from Chapter 11. Tell students that as they choose appropriate verbs for their sentences, they also must consider the subjects and make sure that the subjects and verbs agree in number. Use the following examples to demonstrate agreement in number:

A DIFFERENT APPROACH

Auditory

After students complete **Practice Your Skills** independently, have them provide the other form of each word orally. For example, if the singular is given, students should provide the plural and vice versa. Write students' singular and plural words on the board.

HOME WORK

Have students write twenty additional nouns and pronouns in both their singular and plural forms. Have students share some of their words with the class the following day.

PRACTICE YOUR SKILLS

Check Your Understanding

Determining the Number of Nouns and Pronouns

Label each word *singular* or *plural.*

1. we P
2. it S
3. men P
4. day S
5. he S
6. feet P
7. star S
8. she S
9. they P
10. pearl S
11. boxes P
12. birds P
13. teeth P
14. cities P
15. calves P
16. colors P
17. teacher S
18. sweater S
19. glasses P
20. elevator S

The Number of Verbs

Most present-tense verbs ending in *-s* or *-es* are singular. Plural forms in the present tense do not end in *-s* or *-es.*

	Singular		Plural
A bird	eat**s**.	Birds	eat.
	sleep**s**.		sleep.
	fl**ies**.		fly.

Be, have, and *do* have special singular and plural forms in the present tense. *Be* also has special forms in the past tense. The chart at the top of the next page shows the special forms of *be, have,* and *do.*

African clawed frogs do not (lives, live) on land. (live)

They (stay, stays) in the water for all of their lives. (stay)

My frog (is, are) big enough to eat shrimp pellets now. (is)

Katy (feed, feeds) the frog in the aquarium. (feeds)

Consolidate Skills

Through Guided Practice

The **Check Your Understanding** exercises as well as the **QuickChecks** on pages L413 and L425 will help students with subject and verb agreement. Guide students through the first item in each exercise. Discuss students' responses. Then have students complete the exercises independently.

Apply to Communication

Through Independent Writing

The **Communicate Your Ideas/Apply to Writing** activities on pages L412 and L424 prompt students to write a descriptive paragraph about an animal

FORMS OF *BE, HAVE,* AND *DO*

	SINGULAR	PLURAL
be	is (present)	are (present)
	was (past)	were (past)
have	has	have
do	does	do

In the following examples, each subject is underlined once and each verb is underlined twice.

SINGULAR	The bird is a robin.
	A robin has a red breast.
	The robin was in a tree.
PLURAL	The birds are robins.
	Robins have red breasts.
	The robins were in a tree.

Check Your Understanding

Determining the Number of Verbs

Write each verb and label it *singular* or *plural*.

1. falcons travel P
2. pigeons fly P
3. it is S
4. eagles soar P
5. we observe P
6. an ostrich runs S
7. a cheetah speeds S
8. cheetahs race P
9. snails were P
10. a robin appears S
11. we care P
12. I arrive S

and an analysis of a memoir. Ask students what strategies they plan to use to make sure that their subjects and verbs agree in their writing. Write some of students' suggestions on the board. Remind students as they complete their writing to refer to the instruction and examples in Chapter 13 if they are having difficulties with subject and verb agreement.

Transfer to Everyday Life

Checking of Subject and Verb Agreement in Writing Portfolios

Have students choose a writing sample from their own writing portfolios. Students should read through their writing sample, looking for correct subject and verb agreement. If they need help doing so, have students exchange papers with a partner. Students should correct any errors in agreement.

YOUR IDEAS

For Subject and Verb Agreement

Singular and Plural Subjects

Since nouns, pronouns, and verbs all have number, the number of a verb must agree with the number of its noun or pronoun subject.

A singular subject takes a singular verb.

A plural subject takes a plural verb.

To make a verb agree with its subject, ask yourself two questions: *What is the subject?* and *Is the subject singular or plural?* Then choose the correct verb form.

SINGULAR — That man coaches a softball team each Saturday.

She was on the team.

PLURAL — Those men coach a softball team each Saturday.

They were on the team.

CONNECT TO SPEAKING AND WRITING

Keeping in mind the rules you just studied will help you remember how to make subjects and verbs agree. Even the most experienced speakers and writers sometimes get confused. One question that you can ask to clear up your own confusion about subjects and verbs is this: *What do you do when the subject and predicate nominative are joined by a linking verb?* You know the answer: *Make the verb agree with the subject.*

The solution is longer study halls.

(*Is* agrees with *solution,* not *halls.*)

Longer study halls are the solution.

(*Are* agrees with *halls,* not *solution.*)

Pull It All Together

By Sharing

Have students share one of their writing samples from **Communicate Your Ideas/Apply to Writing** with a partner. After students have read each other's writing, they should check for correct subject and verb agreement. Students should correct any errors in their writing.

Check Understanding

By Choosing Verbs That Agree in Number

Have students choose the correct verbs to complete the following sentences. Discuss students' responses. Students should explain why they chose a particular verb.

I (raise, raises) a pet rabbit. (raise)

Soon I will (show, shows) my rabbit at the fair. (show)

Rabbits (is, are) interesting animals to watch. (are)

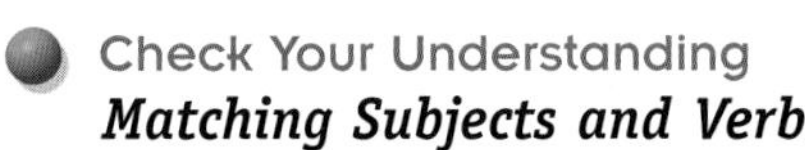

Practice Your Skills

Check Your Understanding

Matching Subjects and Verbs

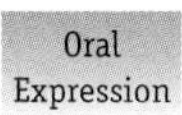

Oral Expression

Read each sentence aloud. Decide whether the subject is singular or plural, and then choose the verb that agrees with the subject.

1. Frogs (was, were) on the earth fifty million years before dinosaurs.

2. A close relative of the frog (is, are) the toad.

3. These small creatures (has, have) huge appetites.

4. A toad (eats, eat) about one hundred insects every day.

5. Toads (catches, catch) insects with their long, sticky tongues.

6. The longest leap by a frog (was, were) more than seventeen feet.

7. Many people (collects, collect) frog figures.

8. One frog balloon (was, were) huge.

9. People (runs, run) frog farms in marshes and swamps.

10. Frogs' legs (is, are) popular appetizers in some restaurants.

Check Your Understanding

Making Subjects and Verbs Agree

Write each word or words in the *Subjects* column that agrees in number with the verb in the *Verbs* column.

	Subjects	Verbs
11.	stores, house, monuments, shed	stands —house, shed
12.	friends, Luisa, Dad, leader	talks—Luisa, Dad, leader
13.	minerals, rocks, metal, gem	is —metal, gem

A DIFFERENT APPROACH

Visual

Have students complete items one through ten of **Check Your Understanding** by taking turns writing their responses on large sheets of chart paper. Students should use one marker to circle singular subjects and use a different marker to circle plural subjects. Then students should choose the correct verb as they write out each sentence. Have students read their completed sentences aloud.

HOME WORK

Have students write complete sentences with the subjects and verbs in the **Check Your Understanding** exercise on Making Subjects and Verbs Agree.

They (wriggle, wriggles) their noses when they (eat, eats). (wriggle; eat)

TIMESAVER QuickCheck

Have students exchange papers to check for subject and verb agreement.

HOME STUDY

After students have written their descriptive paragraphs, have them use various art materials to illustrate their papers. Have students attach their paragraphs to the bottom of their artwork. Remind students to check for subject and verb agreement in their writing before they prepare their final draft.

14.	planes, kites, pilot, flag	fly —planes, kites
15.	puppy, kittens, baby, men	sleeps—puppy, baby
16.	cars, boat, bicycle, train	moves—boat, bicycle, train
17.	leaves, bark, plants, tree	grow—leaves, plants
18.	Mother, artists, guard, teachers	study—artists, teachers
19.	stars, diamond, light, silver	twinkle—stars
20.	tadpoles, Alex, rabbits, child	hop—tadpoles, rabbits

Connect to the Writing Process: Editing

Making Subjects and Verbs Agree

Science Topic

Write each sentence, changing the verb to agree with the subject. If the verb in a sentence is correct, write *C*.

21. Red-spotted toads ~~lives~~ live in the desert.

22. They make sounds like the chirp of a cricket. C

23. Rocks ~~provides~~ provide cool shelters for them on hot days.

24. A summer thunderstorm ~~bring~~ brings them out.

25. A toad's diet consists mostly of insects. C

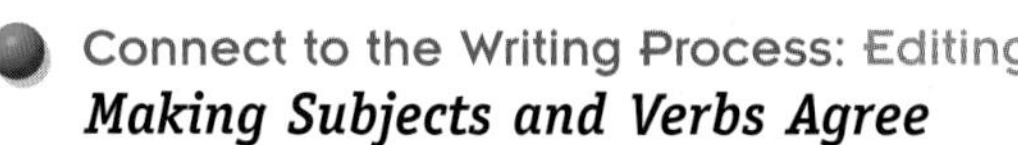

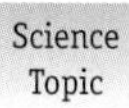

Communicate Your Ideas

APPLY TO WRITING

Descriptive Paragraph: ***Subject and Verb Agreement***

Your class is planning a booklet called "Interesting *B*'s." Think about an interesting bird, butterfly, or bug you have seen. Write a paragraph that describes the animal for the booklet. Be sure to explain how the animal looks and behaves. When you have finished, check that your subject and verb agree in each sentence.

 Mixed Practice

Art Topic **Write the appropriate form of the verb in parentheses.**

1. Alonzo Clemens (has, have) a brain disorder.

2. Many everyday activities (is, are) hard for him.

3. Nevertheless, he (make, makes) extraordinary animal sculptures.

4. This unusual artist (is, are) able to sculpt any animal he sees.

5. A very short glimpse (tells, tell) him all he needs to know.

6. Clemens's unusual memory (stores, store) every small detail.

7. Every muscle (stands, stand) out as in real life.

8. He (make, makes) wax sculptures in less than twenty minutes.

9. His unique talent (helps, help) him succeed.

10. Doctors (calls, call) people with his kind of memory *savants*.

11. *Savant* (come, comes) from the French word *savoir*.

12. *Savoir* (means, mean) "to know."

EXPANDING THE LESSON

Using Technology

You will find additional **instructional** and **practice** materials for this chapter at http://www.bkenglish.com.

REACHING ALL STUDENTS

Advanced Learners

Have students prepare an oral presentation that explains and demonstrates how to make verb phrases agree with their subjects. When preparing their presentations, students should make sure that their word choice, diction, and usage are appropriate for their audience, purpose, and occasion. The audience for their presentations will be their classmates. The purpose is to instruct fellow classmates. Have students present their completed lessons to the class.

Common Agreement Problems

Certain problems in making subjects and verbs agree arise more often than others. The following are some of the most common problems.

Verb Phrases

A **verb phrase** is the main verb plus one or more helping verbs. If a sentence has a verb phrase, the first helping verb must agree in number with the subject. In all of the following examples, subjects are underlined once, verbs are underlined twice, and the first helping verb is in bold type.

SINGULAR Mom **is** driving today.

(*Mom* and the helping verb *is* agree because they are both singular.)

PLURAL We **have** been taking the early bus.

(*We* and the first helping verb *have* agree because they are both plural.)

The first helping verb must agree in number with the subject.

The following is a list of singular and plural forms of common helping verbs.

	COMMON HELPING VERBS
SINGULAR	am, is, was, has, does
PLURAL	are, were, have, do

SINGULAR Angie **was** waiting for the bus.

Briana **does** have a ride.

PLURAL The buses **have** been running late today.

The twins **are** riding their bikes.

Practice Your Skills

Check Your Understanding

Making Subjects and Verbs Agree

History Topic **Write each subject. Then write the helping verb in parentheses that agrees with the subject.**

1. Automobiles (does, do) have a long and interesting history.
2. Inventors (has, have) been tinkering with vehicles for centuries.
3. A steam carriage (was, were) built in France in 1770.
4. Its passengers (was, were) barreling along at 2.5 mph.
5. An early steam carriage (has, have) been discovered recently.
6. A regular steam bus route (was, were) established in Britain by 1836.
7. Unfortunately, the railroad companies (was, were) opposed to the competition.
8. Laws (was, were) passed against the buses.
9. A man (was, were) required to walk in front of each bus.
10. Red danger flags (was, were) waved by the men.

A DIFFERENT APPROACH

Auditory

Complete items one through ten of **Check Your Understanding** by reading each sentence aloud. Students should choose the correct verb to complete each sentence. Students should be able to explain why they chose a particular verb.

HOME WORK

After completing items eleven through twenty of **Connect to the Writing Process,** have students write two similar activities to be completed by classmates. Students should write ten similar exercises that focus on the same skills as those in their textbooks. Have students exchange papers the following day. After students have completed the new exercises written by their partners and discuss their responses. Write some of students' exercises on the board.

Connect to the Writing Process: Drafting
Making Subjects and Verbs Agree

Choose the verb form in parentheses that agrees with each subject. Then write a complete sentence for each item. [Answers may vary. Possible responses are given.]

11. Today's cars (has, have) ■. Today's cars have powerful engines.

12. Most bicyclists (is, are) ■. Most bicyclists are physically fit.

13. Our neighbors' daughter (was, were) ■. Our neighbor's daughter was working at home.

14. The weather (is, are) becoming ■. The weather is becoming hot and humid.

15. The children (was, were) looking ■. The children were looking for buried treasure.

Connect to the Writing Process: Editing
Making Subjects and Verbs Agree

Rewrite the sentences in which the subjects and verbs do not agree. If a sentence is correct, write *C.*

16. The Japanese transit system ~~have~~ has become one of the world's best.

17. The railway lines ~~has~~ have been linking more and more cities together.

18. The first high-speed trains were launched in Japan in 1964. C

19. Today's passengers ~~is~~ are traveling at speeds around 140 mph.

20. Engineers ~~has~~ have steadily improved the bullet trains.

Doesn't or *Don't?*

When contractions are used, agreement with a subject can be confusing. To check for agreement, always say the individual words of any contraction.

The verb part of a contraction must agree in number with the subject.

INCORRECT	This piece **do**n't fit into the puzzle.
	(This piece *do* not fit into the puzzle.)
CORRECT	This piece **does**n't fit into the puzzle.
	(*Does* agrees with *piece*.)
INCORRECT	They **does**n't enjoy puzzles.
	(They *does* not enjoy puzzles.)
CORRECT	They **do**n't enjoy puzzles.
	(*Do* agrees with *they*.)

The preceding rule applies to all contractions. Remember which contractions are singular and which are plural.

	CONTRACTIONS
SINGULAR	**does**n't, **is**n't, **was**n't, **has**n't
PLURAL	**do**n't, **are**n't, **were**n't, **have**n't

You can learn more about contractions on page L625.

PRACTICE YOUR SKILLS

Check Your Understanding

Making Subjects and Contractions Agree

Contemporary Life

Write the contraction in parentheses that agrees with the subject.

1. Many Americans (hasn't, haven't) been to Canada.
2. We (doesn't, don't) need passports.
3. The Canadian dollar (isn't, aren't) the same as the U.S. dollar.

GETTING STUDENTS INVOLVED

Cooperative Learning

Have students work in groups of three or four to supply subjects for each verb in the contractions chart. Students should recreate the chart and write a subject that agrees with each verb listed in the chart. Remind students to share responsibilities in their groups and to contribute equally to the activity. Discuss each group's subjects when they have completed their charts.

A DIFFERENT APPROACH

Auditory

After students have written out their responses to **Check Your Understanding,** have them take turns reading their complete sentences aloud. Students should read each contraction as two words to check for subject-verb agreement. Then students should read the complete sentence with the correct verb choice.

HOME WORK

Have students write ten sentences on a topic of their choice that demonstrate correct subject and verb agreement with verb contractions ending in *-n't.* Tell students not to use subject/verb contractions, such as *she's, I'm,* or *he'll.* Have students share their sentences with the class the following day.

4. Danielle (wasn't, weren't) aware that Quebec is a city and a province.
5. Quebec City (don't, doesn't) lie too far from the Maine border.
6. Amy's family (wasn't, weren't) from Quebec.
7. Her parents (isn't, aren't) able to speak French.
8. They (wasn't, weren't) of French heritage.
9. Amy (hasn't, haven't) studied French yet.
10. She (isn't, aren't) able to speak or understand the language easily.

Connect to the Writing Process: Drafting

Making Subjects and Contractions Agree

[Answers may vary. Possible responses are given.]

Use each of the following word combinations to write a sentence.

11. don't want I really don't want a second helping.
12. aren't here Fran and Marci aren't here at school today.
13. wasn't lost The puppy wasn't lost after all.
14. haven't stopped The neighbors haven't stopped complaining about the noise.
15. isn't waiting Mike isn't waiting at the bus stop.

Interrupting Words

Words, such as prepositional phrases, can come between a subject and its verb. When this happens, a mistake in agreement is easy to make. Sometimes the verb is mistakenly made to agree with a word that is closer to it, rather than with the subject.

The agreement of a verb with its subject is not changed by any interrupting words.

In the following examples, notice that each subject and verb agree in number—despite the words that come between them. The best way to find the correct agreement in these sentences is to mentally take out all of the prepositional phrases. Then it is easy to see the remaining subject and verb.

SINGULAR The juice from these oranges is sour.

(*Is* agrees with the subject *juice,* not with the object of the preposition *oranges*—even though *oranges* is closer to the verb.)

PLURAL The fruits in this beverage are oranges and raspberries.

(*Are* agrees with the subject *fruits,* not with the object of the preposition *beverage*—even though *beverage* is closer to the verb.

Compound prepositions, such as *in addition to, as well as,* and *along with,* often begin interrupting phrases. Make sure the verb always agrees with the subject, not the object of the preposition.

Blackberry pie, as well as several other desserts, was on the menu.

(*Was* agrees with the subject *pie*—not with *desserts,* the object of the preposition *as well as.*)

Cinnamon and mocha ice cream flavors, in addition to vanilla, were available.

(*Were* agrees with the subject *flavors*—not with *vanilla,* the object of the preposition *in addition to.*)

You can learn more about prepositional phrases on pages L189–L197.

COMMON STUMBLING BLOCKS

Problem

- Subject and verb agreement when a sentence contains intervening adjective phrases

Solution

- Tell students that sometimes an adjective phrase comes between a subject and a verb. Point out that adjective phrases that interrupt subjects and verbs should not be considered when trying to make subjects and verbs agree. Tell students to read the sentence without the phrase to choose the verb that agrees.
- Have students choose the correct verbs in these examples:

  The young boy, tired from walking with the others, (sit, sits) down along the trail. (sits)

  Each book, written by different authors, (tell, tells) about the Trail of Tears. (tells)

  The Native Americans, eager to share their story, (write, writes) down their personal accounts. (write)

A DIFFERENT APPROACH

Auditory

Complete **Check Your Understanding** by having students read each sentence aloud. Have students take turns choosing the correct verb to complete each sentence. After students identify the correct verb, they should also identify the subject. Discuss how each subject agrees with each verb identified.

PRACTICE YOUR SKILLS

Check Your Understanding

Making Interrupted Subjects and Verbs Agree

Art Topic

Write each subject. Then write the verb form in parentheses that agrees with the subject.

1. The Museum of American Arts and Crafts (cover, covers) an entire block.
2. The cases in the Native American Hall (holds, hold) many ancient craft items.
3. The display of Native American baskets (has, have) been recently added.
4. The materials in the baskets (is, are) mostly plant stems or split reeds.
5. Different techniques of weaving (was, were) used to make baskets, mats, and bags.
6. Experts in Native American art (says, say) the women did most of the weaving.
7. Women of the far North (was, were) known for their delicate baskets.
8. Expert needlework with colored silks (creates, create) pretty patterns.
9. Cradles for children (was, were) woven by the men in some regions.
10. The plaque next to some unusual items (identifies, identify) them as fishing baskets.

Connect to the Writing Process: Editing

Making Interrupted Subjects and Verbs Agree

Rewrite each sentence, using the correct verb form. If a verb form is correct, write *C*.

11. The Native Americans of Arizona ~~keeps~~ keep the art of basketry alive.

12. Most baskets of the Southwest ~~comes~~ come from the Hopi and the Papago.

13. The Hopi people of Second Mesa make coiled bowls and decorative plaques. C

14. Common materials for basket-making ~~is~~ are rabbit brush and sumac.

15. A pattern of diamonds sometimes represents butterfly wings. C

Inverted Order

In a sentence's natural order, the subject comes before the verb. However, in a sentence in **inverted order,** the verb or part of the verb phrase comes before the subject. A verb always agrees with its subject, whether the sentence is in natural order or in inverted order.

The subject and the verb of an inverted sentence must agree in number.

To find the subject of an inverted sentence, turn the sentence around to its natural order.

INVERTED ORDER	On the glacier were two penguins.
NATURAL ORDER	Two penguins were on the glacier.
QUESTION	Can these large birds fly?
NATURAL ORDER	These large birds can fly.
SENTENCE BEGINNING WITH *HERE*	Here is the penguins' nesting colony.
NATURAL ORDER	The penguins' nesting colony is here.

YOUR IDEAS

For Teaching Subjects and Verbs in Inverted Order

REACHING ALL STUDENTS

Struggling Learners

To reinforce **Connect to Speaking and Writing,** have students choose the correct word to complete the following sentences.

(There's, There are) places I would like to visit. (There are)

(There's, There are) a good example of a landmark. (There's)

(There's, There are) my travel agent's office. (There's)

(There's, There are) students who learned about the Alamo. (There are)

HOME WORK

Have students look in newspapers or magazines for ten sentences in which the subject comes after the verb or verb phrase. Students should write down each sentence and circle the subjects and the verbs or verb phrases. Have students share their inverted order sentences the following day. Discuss how the subjects and verbs agree in these sentences.

SENTENCE BEGINNING WITH *THERE*	There were no babies in the nest.
NATURAL ORDER	No babies were in the nest.
	(Sometimes *here* or *there* must be dropped to make a sentence sound right.)

Remember that the words *here* and *there* are never the subject of a sentence.

CONNECT TO SPEAKING AND WRITING

"Think before you speak" is an especially good policy when you begin sentences with the contractions *there're* (*there are*) and *there's* (*there is*). A common mistake is to use a sentence such as "There's more people using public transportation" because you didn't pause to think about the meaning of the contraction. Your mental ear can tell you that "There is people" sounds wrong before you utter the words.

PRACTICE YOUR SKILLS

Check Your Understanding

Making Subjects and Verbs in Inverted Order Agree

History Topic **Write each subject. Then write the verb form in parentheses that agrees with the subject.**

1. There (is, was) a national historical landmark in San Angelo, Texas.
2. Here (is, are) the best preserved frontier outpost in the United States.
3. At the top of that pole (fly, flies) the Lone Star flag.

4. (Was, Were) this fort established before or after the Civil War?

5. Not far from the fort (was, were) the junction of two rivers.

6. (Wasn't, Weren't) Fort Concho established in 1867?

7. There (was, were) many cavalry and infantry units stationed here.

8. Among the companies (was, were) the Buffalo Soldiers.

9. (Wasn't, Weren't) that the name the Native Americans gave the African American soldiers?

10. There (is, are) a buffalo on the crest of the Tenth Cavalry today.

Connect to the Writing Process: Drafting

Writing Sentences Using Subject and Verb Agreement

[Answers may vary. Possible responses are given.]

Write five sentences, following the instructions below.

The students in our school come from many different backgrounds.

11. Write a sentence that includes *the students in our school* as the subject. Use a present-tense verb.

The street by my home is a great place to play ball.

12. Write a sentence that includes *the street by my home* as the subject. Use a present-tense verb.

There were sitting in the courtroom many judges.

13. Write a sentence in inverted order that includes the verb phrase *were sitting.*

Has Felix graduated yet?

14. Write a question that begins with *Has.*

There are too many noodles in my soup.

15. Write a sentence that begins with *There are.*

Connect to the Writing Process: Editing

Making Interrupted or Inverted-Order Subjects and Verbs Agree

Rewrite each sentence, using the correct verb form. If a verb form is correct, write C.

16. Twenty-three buildings on the site ~~has~~ have been restored.

INTEGRATING TECHNOLOGY

Computers

Have students complete items one through twenty of **Practice Your Skills** using computers to type and print out their responses. Students should type complete sentences with their correct responses. Remind students to check for correct spelling, capitalization, and punctuation in their sentences.

TIMESAVER *QuickCheck*

Have students exchange their analyses with a partner to evaluate their responses. Students should explain why they chose a particular response to each question or task. Students should come to a consensus on their analyses to produce one final draft.

SELECTION AMENDMENT
Description of change: excerpted
Rationale: to focus on the grammar skill

17. In the enlisted men's barracks ~~are~~ is stored the equipment of the infantry soldiers.
18. There is an outstanding living history program at Fort Concho. C
19. ~~Isn't~~ Aren't there historical reenactments at the fort on weekends?
20. Volunteers from the community dress in authentic historical costumes. C

Communicate Your Ideas

APPLY TO WRITING

Writer's Craft: *Analyzing Subject-Verb Agreement*

When there are several shifts between singular and plural subjects within a paragraph, writers must stay alert to keep their verbs in agreement. The following passage is from a memoir written by a woman who lived in the Southwest in the late 1800s. Read the paragraph and then follow the directions.

> We (S) were walking single file, John first, I next, and Mother bringing up the rear. We had gone a little way, when mother called John. I had stepped right over a snake (S) that was crawling across our path. It (S) was not a rattle snake, however, tho' quite as exciting. As we (S) were returning, we (S) were startled by the real thing. On the opposite side of a bush—his head at least two feet in the air—was a rattler (S)—coiled ready to strike. Mother and I stood guard until John secured a shovel to kill it.
>
> —*Sadie Martin,* My Desert Memories

- Write the underlined verbs and verb phrases in the passage. Then write the subject that each one agrees with. See responses on the previous page.
- Find the verb phrase *was crawling*. Why did the writer choose the singular verb *was* instead of the plural verb *were*? The number of the verb must agree with the number of the subject.
- Which sentence is in inverted order? Why do you think the writer chose to put the subject near the end of the sentence?

The sixth, or next-to-the-last sentence, is in inverted order. The writer chose to put the subject at the end of this sentence to increase the sense of suspense—and surprise.

Mixed Practice

Contemporary Life **Write the appropriate form of the verb in parentheses.**

1. (Doesn't, Don't) this game take hours to play?
2. The objects of the game (is, are) to find the secret chamber and locate the treasure chest.
3. There (is, are) a gold-and-silver crown inside the chest.
4. Here (is, are) the first of your choices.
5. Which one of these doors (seem, seems) the most promising?
6. Behind one of the doors (is, are) the first important clue.
7. There (is, are) many misleading clues, however.
8. (Isn't, Aren't) there hazards to look out for?
9. Sometimes the long corridors of the castle (doesn't, don't) go anywhere.
10. At the end of some passages (is, are) trapdoors into the dungeons.

EXPANDING THE LESSON

Using Technology

You will find additional **instructional** and **practice** materials for this chapter at http://www.bkenglish.com.

LESSON 2 *(pages L426–L439)*

OBJECTIVES

- **To make verbs agree with compound subjects**
- **To make verbs agree with collective nouns**
- **To make verbs agree with *you* and *I***
- **To make verbs agree with indefinite pronouns**

Create Interest

Ask students what strategies they would use to identify the correct verb in each of the following sentences. Tell students that each sentence presents a special agreement problem that will be discussed in this lesson.

Neither the boys nor Sarah (talk, talks) during class. (talks)

David and Linda (is, are) studying. (are)

The team (is, are) playing in the Sugar Bowl. (is)

REACHING ALL STUDENTS

English Language Learners

Students who are learning English may have difficulty understanding compound subjects and how they should agree with verbs. Have students use a dictionary to write out the definition for *compound*. Also, review examples of compound sentences to reinforce the concept of *compound* as representing two things. Use the following examples to show students how to make verbs agree with compound subjects.

English and French (is, are) beautiful languages. (are)

Neither I nor my friends (know, knows) how to speak French. (know)

The children and the teacher (learn, learns) a new language. (learn)

Other Agreement Problems

Certain other subjects and verbs require special attention as well.

Compound Subjects

A **compound subject** is two or more subjects that have the same verb. A compound subject is usually joined by the conjunction *and* or *or,* but a compound subject can also be joined by the pairs of conjunctions *and/or, both/and, either/or,* or *neither/nor.* When you write a sentence with a compound subject, you need to remember two agreement rules.

When subjects are joined by *and* or *both/and,* the verb is usually plural.

And indicates more than one. When a subject is more than one, it is plural. The verb, therefore, must also be plural to agree with the subject.

PLURAL VERB	Jordan **and** Hannah **are** sketching the lake in their sketch diaries.
	Both the tablet **and** the pencils belong to Hannah.

When a compound subject is joined by *or, either/or,* or *neither/nor,* agreement between the subject and the verb follows a different rule.

When subjects are joined by *or, either/or,* or *neither/nor,* the verb agrees with the closer subject.

Neil and I (play, plays) football. (play)

You three girls (sing, sings) beautifully. (sing)

Most of the food (is, are) gone. (is)

Guide Instruction

By Modeling Strategies

Use the instruction and the example sentences throughout this lesson to model strategies for choosing correct verbs in special circumstances. After presenting the instruction, have students create example sentences to demonstrate subject and verb agreement in these special circumstances. Complete the sentences that students suggest by writing them on the board and demonstrating strategies for selecting the correct forms of verbs.

SINGULAR VERB	**Either** Julia **or** the teacher **has** left this tablet behind. (The verb is singular because *teacher,* the subject closer to it, is singular.)
PLURAL VERB	Charcoals **or** pastels **are** best for this purpose. (The verb is plural because *pastels,* the subject closer to it, is plural.)

This rule is especially important to keep in mind when one subject is singular and the other is plural.

SINGULAR VERB	**Neither** the two boys **nor** Sarah **has** brought an easel. (The verb is singular because *Sarah,* the subject closer to it, is singular.)
PLURAL VERB	**Neither** the tree **nor** the ducklings **were** in Sarah's picture. (The verb is plural because *ducklings,* the subject closer to it, is plural.)

PRACTICE YOUR SKILLS

Check Your Understanding

Making Verbs Agree with Compound Subjects

Contemporary Life **Write the correct form of the verb in parentheses.**

1. Ronnie and Christine (is, are) eating at Carmen's Café.

2. Neither Paul nor his parents (has, have) eaten there before.

A DIFFERENT APPROACH

Auditory

After writing out their responses to items one through twenty of **Practice Your Skills,** have students read each sentence aloud, substituting each original compound subject for a new compound subject. Students should check to make sure that the verb agrees with the new compound subject they use in the sentence. Discuss each item as students complete the activity.

Consolidate Skills

Through Guided Practice

The **Check Your Understanding** exercises as well as the **QuickChecks** on pages L432 and L439 will help students with subject-verb agreement in special circumstances. Complete the first item in each exercise together, discussing and reviewing the major strategies students should use to make subjects and verbs agree in sentences with compound subjects, with collective nouns, with the subjects *you* or *I*, and with indefinite pronouns. Have students complete the remaining exercises independently.

Apply to Communication

Through Independent Writing

The **Communicate Your Ideas/Apply to Writing** activities on pages L431 and L438 prompt students to write a review of a musical performance and a dialogue for a short scene. When their writing is completed, ask students to share some of the strategies they used

HOME WORK

After completing **Connect to the Writing Process,** have students write ten new sentences that demonstrate subject-verb agreement with compound subjects. Remind students that each sentence must contain a compound subject. Refer students to the instruction on pages L426 and L427 if they are having problems choosing compound subjects for their sentences.

3. The twins and their cousin (is, <u>are</u>) meeting them here.

4. Neither the counter nor the tables (<u>has</u>, have) room for a party of five.

5. Both Emily and Nita (eats, <u>eat</u>) here often.

6. Either Carmen or Sunny (<u>waits</u>, wait) on the tables.

7. Salsa and chips (was, <u>were</u>) brought to the table.

8. Both the chili and burrito (costs, <u>cost</u>) $3.50.

9. Neither the bean burrito nor the cheese enchilada (<u>contains</u>, contain) meat.

10. Beef, chicken, or cheese (<u>is</u>, are) used in the enchiladas.

11. Both Carmen and Joshua (cooks, <u>cook</u>) during the lunch hour.

12. Two *rellenos* or the combination plate (<u>is</u>, are) what Brandon wants.

13. Neither April nor her cousin (<u>likes</u>, like) the shrimp dishes.

14. Rice, beans, and a salad (comes, <u>come</u>) with all the dinners.

15. A soup or salad (<u>is</u>, are) included in the price of the dinner.

16. Either Lola or the twins (<u>orders</u>, order) chicken with mole sauce.

17. Onions and garlic (was, <u>were</u>) added to this sauce.

18. Crushed chiles or hot sauce (make, <u>makes</u>) this dish extra spicy.

19. Either custard or fried bananas (<u>follows</u>, follow) the dinner.

20. Does Nita or Emily (wants, <u>want</u>) dessert?

to make sure their subjects and verbs agreed in each sentence. Point out some of the special problem subjects that students used in their sentences and discuss how they agree with the verbs students selected.

Transfer to Everyday Life

Identifying Sentences with Special Subjects in Literature

Have students use their literature textbooks or a novel they are reading to identify sentences that contain the following special subjects: compound subjects, collective nouns, *you* or *I* as subjects, and indefinite pronouns. Students should photocopy or write out an example of each type of special subject. Students should also underline the subjects and verbs in all of their sentences. Have students share their findings with the class. Discuss how the subjects and verbs agree in the sentences.

Connect to the Writing Process: Editing

Making Verbs Agree with Compound Subjects

Rewrite each sentence, using the correct verb form. If a verb form is correct, write *C*.

21. Sonia and her friends ~~wants~~ want to grab a snack.

22. Either Chinese food or Mexican food ~~are~~ is fine with her.

23. Neither Melissa nor the boys walks far. C

24. Minh and Sonia discuss their food choices. C

25. Neither Broadway nor Third Avenue ~~have~~ has a Chinese restaurant.

26. Hamburgers or a pizza ~~sound~~ sounds great to Juan.

27. The two drive-ins and the Food Court ~~has~~ have good burgers.

28. Either take-out orders or table service ~~are~~ is available at the Shanghai Palace.

29. Neither the Shanghai Palace nor the two Mexican restaurants requires reservations. C

30. A taco or a bag of fries ~~are~~ is Katya's choice.

Collective Nouns

In Chapter 2 you learned that a **collective noun** names a group of people or things.

COMMON COLLECTIVE NOUNS			
band	congregation	flock	orchestra
class	crew	group	swarm
committee	crowd	herd	team
colony	family	league	tribe

YOUR IDEAS

For Collective Nouns

Pull It All Together

By Summarizing

Have students write a paragraph telling how to make verbs agree with the following problem subjects: compound subjects, collective nouns, *you* or *I* as subjects, and indefinite pronouns. Students should explain how they choose verbs in sentences that contain each of these special subjects.

Check Understanding

Summarizing Subject and Verb Agreement

Have students write a paragraph summarizing how they make subjects and verbs agree in sentences they are writing. Remind students to discuss special circumstances and problem subjects in their summaries. Have students share their paragraphs with the class.

USING STUDENTS' STRENGTHS

Multiple Intelligences: Linguistic

Have students write a humorous poem or short story using at least three collective nouns. Have students check for correct agreement between their collective nouns and verbs. Encourage students to share their humorous writing with a partner and to check each other's writing for subject-verb agreement.

How a collective noun is used determines its agreement with the verb.

Use a singular verb with a collective-noun subject that is thought of as a unit. Use a plural verb with a collective-noun subject that is thought of as individual units.

> The team **is playing** in the Memorial Day game.
>
> (The team as a whole—as one unit—is playing in the game. Therefore, the verb is singular.)
>
> The team **are** unable to agree on new uniforms.
>
> (The individuals on the team are acting separately. Therefore, the verb is plural.)

To make the second sentence clearer—and less awkward—you could add the word *members* after *team*.

> The team members **are** unable to agree on new uniforms.

PRACTICE YOUR SKILLS

Check Your Understanding

Making Verbs Agree with Collective Nouns

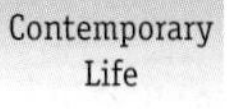

Contemporary Life

Write the correct form of the verb in parentheses.

1. The crowd (is, are) the largest of the season.
2. The orchestra (was, were) tuning up their instruments.
3. The band (was, were) in their new uniforms.
4. The audience (was, were) filing out through the emergency exits.

5. The team (<u>heads</u>, head) to the new restaurant.
6. The Yien family (meet, <u>meets</u>) us there.
7. The committee (<u>has</u>, have) been holding its meetings before the show.
8. The ant colony (<u>was</u>, were) discovered by an usher.
9. The group in those seats (has, <u>have</u>) jumped out of the way.
10. A pest-control crew (have, <u>has</u>) been called.

Connect to the Writing Process: Editing
Making Verbs Agree with Collective Nouns

Rewrite each sentence, using the correct verb form. If a verb form is correct, write *C*.

11. The Scout Troop ~~have~~ has eighteen members.
12. The flock were scattered by the barking dogs. C
13. The congregation ~~was~~ were shaking the pastor's hand.
14. The public ~~was~~ were sending letters to the editor of the newspaper.
15. The league ~~are~~ is holding tryouts next week.

Communicate Your Ideas

APPLY TO WRITING

Review: ***Subject and Verb Agreement***

Write a review of a musical production or performance for your school newspaper. It can be one that you have seen live or one that you have seen on TV. In your review, use at least three of these words as the subject of a sentence: *orchestra, band, cast, crew, audience,* or *public.* Use at least one compound subject joined by *either/or* or *neither/nor.*

TIMESAVER *QuickCheck*

Have students exchange their completed reviews with a partner. Students should check for subject-verb agreement and check to make sure students have used the assigned collective-noun subjects. Students should also check for correct use of compound subjects. Students should write any suggestions for improvement on the papers they are evaluating.

EXPANDING THE LESSON

Using Technology

You will find additional **instructional** and **practice** materials for this chapter at http://www.bkenglish.com.

Mixed Practice

Contemporary Life

Write each verb. If a verb does not agree with the subject, write the correct form of the verb. If a verb is correct, write *C*.

1. Amanda, Jeff, and Jordan ~~is~~ are on the same Little League team.
2. The team ~~are~~ is called the Giants.
3. The league ~~are~~ is made up of eight teams from the Garden Grove area.
4. Either Jordan's team or his brother's team ~~were~~ was the winners of the championship.
5. Jeff, Amanda, or Kai ~~are~~ is pitching in the first inning.
6. The team ~~has~~ have invited their parents to the play-offs.
7. Jeff's family always watches him. C
8. Amanda's mother or Jeff's parents ~~is~~ are taking videos of the game.
9. Neither Jeff nor his two best friends ~~has~~ have made it into the all-star game.
10. Don't your sister or your cousins play for Little League? C
11. Sherry and Rick ~~plays~~ play for Connie Mack.
12. Evening or late afternoon ~~are~~ is the time for the games.
13. The team has new uniforms this season. C
14. Blue and yellow ~~was~~ were the colors.
15. ~~Doesn't~~ Don't the new uniforms and caps look great?

Agreement Problems with Pronouns

When certain pronouns are used as subjects, they can present some subject-verb agreement problems.

You and *I* as Subjects

The pronouns *you* and *I* do not follow the rules for agreement that you just learned. *You* is always used with a plural verb—whether *you* refers to one person or more than one person.

PLURAL VERBS	Martina, you are an excellent poet.
	Students, you write very well.
	You have many good ideas.

Although *I* refers to one person, it takes a plural verb. The only exceptions are the *be* forms *am* and *was*.

PLURAL VERBS	I write poetry.
	I have Dickinson's *Collected Poems*.
	I like Dickinson's poetry style.
SINGULAR VERBS	I am a poet.
	I was in the Corner Book Shop yesterday.

Remember that whenever *I* is part of a compound subject connected with *and*, the *be* verbs become plural, just as they would with any compound subject.

Jordan **and** I are poets.

Miriam **and** I were the readers of the poems.

GETTING STUDENTS INVOLVED

Reciprocal Teaching

Have students work in groups of three or four to write ten sentences that demonstrate subject-verb agreement using the special subjects *you* and *I*. Remind students that they should make sure that these special subjects agree with the verbs they choose in their sentences. While working together in their groups, students should explain to other group members what they have learned from the instruction in the textbook and contribute to writing their group's sentences. Students who understand the instruction on this page should teach students who are struggling. Have groups share their sentences with the class.

A DIFFERENT APPROACH

Visual

Have students complete items one through fifteen of **Practice Your Skills** by writing their sentences in pencil and using a colored marker to write the correct verb choice for each sentence. Then have students use a black marker to draw an arrow from the verb to the subject with which it agrees. Tell students that focusing on the subjects and verbs by using different colors will help them check for subject-verb agreement. Discuss students' responses as they take turns holding up their sentences.

HOME WORK

After completing **Practice Your Skills,** have students write a paragraph about a memorable experience in their lives that involved music. The experience can involve their performing or listening to music. Tell students to use *you* and *I* as subjects at least twice. When they have completed their paragraphs and have checked all sentences for subject-verb agreement, have students draw an arrow from each verb to the subject with which it agrees.

PRACTICE YOUR SKILLS

Check Your Understanding

***Making Verbs Agree with* You *and* I**

Contemporary Life

Write the correct form of the verb in parentheses.

1. I (intends, intend) to rehearse my parts of the performance.
2. Marisa, you (sounds, sound) a little flat.
3. You two boys (has, have) to sing louder.
4. I (don't, doesn't) hear you singing, Angela.
5. You (was, were) a little slow at the start of the first song.
6. I (was, were) thinking about the rhythm.
7. You (come, comes) in with the response immediately.
8. Boys, you (sings, sing) that line more loudly than the other line.
9. (Hasn't, Haven't) you and Beth learned your parts?
10. Mr. Jamison and I (am, are) scheduling an extra rehearsal on Friday.

Connect to the Writing Process: Editing

***Making Verbs Agree with* You *and* I**

Rewrite each sentence, using the correct verb form. If a verb form is correct, write *C*.

11. I ~~were~~ was out front in the audience.
12. You ~~has~~ have all deserved those cheers.
13. I applaud your best performance ever. C
14. You three ~~waits~~ wait here for the curtain call.
15. I ~~expects~~ expect good reviews in tomorrow's newspaper.

Indefinite Pronouns

An indefinite pronoun can be the subject of a sentence. Some indefinite pronouns are singular, some are plural, and some can be either singular or plural.

A verb must agree in number with an indefinite pronoun used as a subject.

The following is a list of common indefinite pronouns.

COMMON INDEFINITE PRONOUNS	
Singular	anybody, anyone, each, either, everybody, everyone, neither, nobody, no one, one, somebody, someone
Plural	both, few, many, several
Singular/Plural	all, any, most, none, some

SINGULAR Someone **has** called you on the telephone two times.

(*Has* agrees with the singular indefinite pronoun *someone.*)

Neither of the messages is very clear.

(*Is* agrees with the singular indefinite pronoun *neither,* not with the object of the preposition *message.*)

PLURAL Both **are** ringing.

(*Are* agrees with the plural indefinite pronoun *both.*)

COMMON STUMBLING BLOCKS

Problem

- Using the pronouns *you* and *they* as indefinite pronouns

Solution

- Tell students that sometimes writers use the words *you* and *they* incorrectly, as in the following sentence: *At the library, they help you find books.* Tell students that the words *they* and *you* should not be used as indefinite pronouns. Instead, the sentence should be rewritten as *At the library, librarians help people find books.*
- Have students correct the indefinite pronoun errors in the following sentences:

  They have some nice dresses in that store. (There are)

  In that store, you can get a good deal. (one)

USING STUDENTS' STRENGTHS

Multiple Intelligences: Linguistic

Have students write ten sentences that will help other students practice using the indefinite pronouns *all, any, most, none,* and *some*. Refer students to the instruction on page L435 if they need help. Remind students to provide two verb choices for each sentence. When completed, have students exchange papers and complete the exercises.

Few of the calls were for me.

(*Were* agrees with the plural indefinite pronoun *few,* not with the object of the preposition *calls.*)

All, any, most, none, and *some* can be either singular or plural. The number of each of these pronouns is determined by the object of the preposition that follows it.

SINGULAR All of his **communication** was by phone.

(Since *communication* is singular, *was* is also singular.)

PLURAL All of the **calls** were in the morning.

(Since *calls* is plural, *were* is also plural.)

You can learn more about indefinite pronouns on pages L63–L64.

PRACTICE YOUR SKILLS

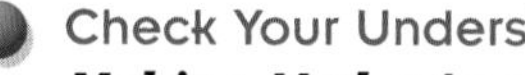

Check Your Understanding

Making Verbs Agree with Indefinite Pronouns

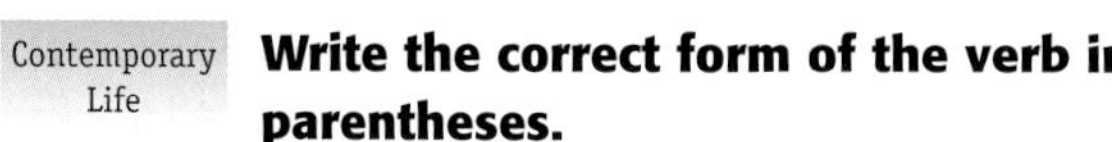

Contemporary Life **Write the correct form of the verb in parentheses.**

1. Everyone in my homeroom (was, were) present yesterday.
2. All of the math classes (has, have) the same assignment.
3. Each of the crossing guards (wears, wear) a badge.
4. Neither of the boys on the bicycles (have, has) left yet.

5. All of the broken glass (has, have) been cleared from the walkway.
6. Several of the students (was, were) on their way to the cafeteria.
7. None of the milk (was, were) delivered on time.
8. One of my friends always (brings, bring) her own lunch.
9. Many of the teachers (dislike, dislikes) cafeteria duty.
10. Anyone with a lunch ticket (gets, get) food first.

Connect to the Writing Process: Editing

Making Verbs Agree with Indefinite Pronouns

Find the six verbs that do not agree with their subjects. Then correct and rewrite each sentence that contains an incorrect verb.

~~Do~~ Does anyone know about nutrients and vitamins? Both ~~is~~ are required for a healthy body. Nutrients are found in food. A body uses nutrients for energy. Every one of the body's parts wears out a little each day. Most of the cells ~~is~~ are constantly being restored by the nutrients in our foods.

Vitamins are necessary to the body. Many of our essential vitamins ~~comes~~ come from one or more servings of fresh fruit per day. Grapefruit and oranges furnish vitamin C. Either ~~are~~ is also a source of vitamin A, calcium, and iron. Dairy products are rich in calcium, too. Nobody stays healthy without at least 800 milligrams of calcium per day. Most of the calcium ~~are~~ is used for bones and teeth. Lean meat provides important minerals, too.

YOUR IDEAS

For Verb-Pronoun Agreement

TIMESAVER *QuickCheck*

Check students' dialogues to make sure they have correctly used indefinite pronouns. Make sure that students have not used the subjects *you* and *I* as indefinite pronouns. Meet with students one-on-one to discuss their use of indefinite pronouns and subject and verb agreement in their writing. Have students correct any errors in their dialogues.

HOME STUDY

Have students choose a topic to write about by viewing the photograph on this page. For example, students can write about snakes or the clothes the people are wearing in the photograph. After students write a paragraph, they should check their writing for subject and verb agreement.

Communicate Your Ideas

APPLY TO WRITING

Dialogue for a Play: *Making Verbs Agree with Pronouns*

Bring this scene to life. Imagine that the people in this picture have begun to speak.

- Who is the man in the picture?
- What do you think he is saying about the snake?
- Are there questions the students might be asking him or one another, or remarks they might be making?

Write a short dialogue for these people in the form of a play. Use at least two indefinite pronouns as subjects, along with the pronouns *I* and *you*.

 Mixed Practice

Contemporary Life

Write the appropriate form of the verb in parentheses.

1. I (has, have) to help my family clean the garage today.

2. (Does, Do) you want some of this junk?

3. Most of it (is, are) no longer useful to us.

4. No one (wants, want) those old stacks of magazines.

5. All of them (is, are) going to the recycling center.

6. (Does, Do) anyone want these rackets?

7. Several (is, are) missing strings.

8. (Is, Are) you keeping those two dusty green skateboards?

9. Both (seems, seem) to have jammed wheels.

10. I (was, were) fixing them last week.

11. Most of this camping equipment (is, are) in good shape.

12. Perhaps someone (has, have) a use for it.

13. I (am, are) donating the sleeping bag and the tent to the thrift store.

14. Domingo, you (has, have) been a great help.

15. Everyone (deserves, deserve) the rest of the day off.

EXPANDING THE LESSON

Using Technology

You will find additional **instructional** and **practice** materials for this chapter at http://www.bkenglish.com.

Using *CheckPoint*

This feature on subject and verb agreement can be used as further independent practice or as a cumulative review of the chapter. Students choose verbs that agree with subjects, correct subject and verb agreement errors, and write sentences using subject and verb agreement.

CheckPoint

Making Subjects and Verbs Agree

Write the verb form in parentheses that agrees with each subject.

1. The weight of those rocks (is, are) about five hundred pounds.
2. None of these instructions (makes, make) sense.
3. The common length of most lightning bolts (is, are) about half a mile.
4. (Is, Are) you trying out for the track team?
5. The boys in the shop (plays, play) baseball at lunchtime.
6. You (hasn't, haven't) received mail today.
7. As the football flies through the uprights, the crowd (cheers, cheer).
8. Some swans (carries, carry) their young on their backs.
9. A few of my friends (has, have) called about the party.
10. There (is, are) twelve letters in the Hawaiian alphabet.

Making Subjects and Verbs Agree

Find and write the verbs that do not agree with their subjects. Then write each sentence correctly. If the sentence is correct, write *C*.

1. The rich mud of drained swamps ~~make~~ makes good farmland.
2. Neither Don nor Chris ~~were~~ was chosen as an actor.
3. No one on the front steps was waiting for a bus. C
4. ~~Have~~ Has one of the actors forgotten his lines?
5. There are 35 million digestive glands in the stomach. C
6. ~~Don't~~ Doesn't Jerry have his jacket with him?

7. You ~~was~~ were smiling in the photograph.
8. Each of the Miller children ~~have~~ has a calf and a pig.
9. Does your family like Thanksgiving? C
10. The grandfather clock ~~chime~~ chimes beautifully.

Editing for Subject and Verb Agreement

Write the following paragraphs, correcting each verb that does not agree with its subject.

> Trees are green plants. A tree, like other green plants, ~~have~~ has roots, stems, leaves, and seeds. Trees, however, are the oldest of all plants. Some of the sequoia trees of the Northwestern United States ~~is~~ are more than 4,000 years old. These giants were here before Columbus.
>
> The age of trees ~~are~~ is recorded in their rings. There ~~is~~ are rings in the cross section of most kinds of tree trunks. Each of the rings ~~represent~~ represents one year of the tree's life.

Using Subject Verb Agreement

Using the present tense, write five sentences that follow the directions below.

Write a sentence that . . .

1. begins with the word *Doesn't.*
2. begins with the word *There.*
3. includes *my brother and sister* as the subject.
4. includes *either Brad or his brothers* as the subject.
5. includes *band* as the subject.

Sample Answers for *Subject Verb Agreement:*

1. Doesn't the cloud look fluffy?
2. There are two cartons of milk on the table.
3. My brother and sister like to sing.
4. Either Brad or his brothers have the tickets.
5. The band plays in unison.

Using *Language and Self-Expression*

Consider using this writing assignment to assess students' ability to use subjects and verbs correctly and effectively. You may want students to complete the assignment as part of a narrative writing strand for their portfolios.

Prewriting

Encourage students to use questioning strategies to help them organize their thoughts in the prewriting stage. Students might use the following questions to help them proceed with their writing:

- What activities do you see depicted in the quilt?
- What expressions and feelings might the characters in the quilt have?
- What might have happened the day before and the day after these events took place?

FOR YOUR INFORMATION

About the Artist

Growing up in Harlem in New York City, Faith Ringgold learned about fabrics from her mother, a clothing designer. After studying art, Ringgold taught in New York City schools. She is known for her story quilts, her large soft sculptures, and artworks that reflect her childhood memories and her African American heritage.

Language and *Self-Expression*

Faith Ringgold uses paint and fabric to create her detailed story quilt collages. Here she shows an event from her childhood in images. The images are surrounded by the story told in words.

Use Ringgold's painted quilt to write your own story about the day pictured. Tell who is at the picnic and explain what they are doing. One way to organize your story might be in space order, tracing the groups of people clockwise from the top left to the bottom left and discussing each group as you observe them. Another way to organize might be in time order, telling how the picnic began and what happened to get it to the point pictured on the quilt.

Prewriting Decide how you will organize your story—in space order or in time order. Look closely at the painting and make a list of vivid verbs that describe some of the actions you see.

Drafting Use your list and organizing plan to write the story. Begin with a paragraph that introduces the setting and main characters. Continue using the organization you chose. End with a paragraph that sums up your story.

Revising Check your story to make sure you have used a variety of sentence types.

Editing Review your work, looking for errors in subject-verb agreement, punctuation, and spelling. Make any corrections needed.

Publishing Prepare a final copy of your story. Publish it by including it in a notebook of class stories.

Subject and Verb Agreement

Agreement

A verb must agree with its subject in number. *(page L407)*
A singular subject takes a singular verb. *(page L410)*
A plural subject takes a plural verb. *(page L410)*

Common Agreement Problems

The first helping verb must agree in number with the subject. *(page L414)*
The verb part of a contraction must agree in number with the subject. *(pages L416–L417)*
The agreement of a verb with its subject is not changed by any interrupting words. *(pages L418–L419)*
The subject and the verb of an inverted sentence must agree in number. *(pages L421–L422)*

Other Agreement Problems

When subjects are joined by *and* or *both/and,* the verb is usually plural. *(page L426)*
When subjects are joined by *or, either/or,* or *neither/nor,* the verb agrees with the closer subject. *(pages L426–L427)*
Use a singular verb with a collective-noun subject that is thought of as a unit. Use a plural verb with a collective-noun subject that is thought of as individual units. *(page L430)*

Agreement Problems with Pronouns

Use a plural verb with *you* whether it refers to one person or more than one person. *(page L433)*
Except for the forms of *be, am* and *was,* use a plural verb with *I.* *(page L433)*
A verb must agree in number with an indefinite pronoun used as a subject. *(pages L435–L436)*

Other Information About Subject-Verb Agreement

Recognizing the number of nouns and pronouns *(page L407)*
Using forms of *be, have,* and *do* *(pages L408–L409)*

Using *Another Look*

Another Look summarizes the terms defined in the chapter and provides cross-references to the specific pages on which they are explained. Consider having students use this feature prior to completing **CheckPoint** or taking the posttest. Students who can provide several examples of each term should be able to score well on either measurement.

FOR ASSESSING LEARNING

Using *the Posttest*

Assessing Learning

The posttest will help you and your students assess where they stand in their ability to make subjects and verbs agree.

IDENTIFYING COMMON STUMBLING BLOCKS

Following is a list of the most common errors students make involving subject and verb agreement.

Problem

- Lack of subject-verb agreement with contractions ending in *-n't*

Solution

- For reteaching, use the explanatory copy and examples on pages L416–L417.

Problem

- Lack of subject-verb agreement with compound subjects

Solution

- For reteaching, use the explanatory copy and examples on pages L426–L427.

Directions

Write the letter of the best way to write each underlined word or words. If an underlined part contains no error, write D.

EXAMPLE **1.** The Gothic fiction of the Romantic era <u>are related</u> to today's detective and horror stories.

1 **A** relate
B is related
C have been related
D No error

ANSWER **1** **B**

1. Mary Shelley and Bram Stoker <u>was</u> novelists in the Gothic tradition.

2. <u>Wasn't</u> they writing nearly a century apart?

3. There <u>was</u> several movies based on their novels.

4. Mary Shelley's famous novel about a scientist and his creation <u>resemble</u> science fiction.

5. Some of the best Gothic writers <u>was</u> women.

6. My mother's book club <u>admires</u> Ann Radcliffe.

7. Neither she nor Mary Shelley <u>are</u> particularly well known.

8. However, both <u>have given</u> us classics in the genre.

9. <u>Hasn't</u> you read *The Mysteries of Udolpho?*

10. That Radcliffe novel from the late eighteenth century still <u>seem</u> scary today.

A DIFFERENT DELIVERY SYSTEM

If you prefer, you can print the posttest from the BK English Test Bank located at http://www.bkenglish.com.

1 A is
B were
C has been
D No error

2 A Weren't
B Was
C Hasn't
D No error

3 A has been
B is
C were
D No error

4 A resembles
B are resembling
C have resembled
D No error

5 A is
B were
C has been
D No error

6 A admire
B are admiring
C were admired
D No error

7 A are being
B were
C is
D No error

8 A is giving
B gives
C has given
D No error

9 A Has
B Haven't
C Doesn't
D No error

10 A seems
B are seeming
C have seemed
D No error

Customizing the Test

Use these questions to add or replace items for alternate versions of the test.

11. Among American writers, Edgar Allan Poe are considered one of the best Gothic storytellers.

12. Either "The Fall of the House of Usher" or "The Telltale Heart" have terrified many a reader.

13. In the first story, a brother and sister is united in death.

14. In the second, a murderer confess suddenly because of a strange, ticking sound.

11. **A** is considered
B consider
C have been considered
D No error

12. **A** terrify
B are terrifying
C has terrified
D No error

13. **A** are united
B unites
C has been united
D No error

14. **A** have confessed
B confesses
C are confessing
D No error

TEACHING SUGGESTIONS

BLOCK SCHEDULING

- If your schedule requires that you cover the chapter in a **shorter time,** use the instruction on adjectives, adverbs, and problem modifiers and the Check Your Understanding and QuickCheck exercises.
- If you want to take advantage of **longer class time,** add these applications to writing: Connect to Speaking and Writing, Connect to the Writing Process, and Apply to Writing exercises.

Essential Knowledge and Skills

- Writing to influence such as to persuade, argue, and request
- Choosing the appropriate form for his/her own purpose for writing letters
- Producing cohesive and coherent written texts by organizing ideas, using effective transitions, and choosing precise wording
- Spelling frequently misspelled words correctly such as *their, they're,* and *there*
- Uses resources to find correct spellings
- Using adjectives (comparative and superlative forms) and adverbs appropriately to make writing vivid or precise
- Comparing and contrasting print, visual, and electronic media with written story

CHAPTER 14

Using Adjectives and Adverbs

Directions

Read the passage and choose the word or group of words that belongs in each underlined space. Write the letter of the correct answer.

EXAMPLE Jupiter is the __(1)__ planet in our solar system.

1 **A** large
B larger
C largest
D most largest

ANSWER **1** **C**

Mercury is by far the __(1)__ of the planets. It speeds around the sun in __(2)__ time than it takes for a single growing season on Earth. Mercury does not have __(3)__ air to trap heat, so it is very cold at night. Venus, which is not as close to the sun, is hotter than __(4)__ planet.

Nothing __(5)__ live on Saturn—it has no water or oxygen. Saturn's day is ten hours long—far __(6)__ than ours on Earth. Its trip around the sun, however, takes twenty-nine years. Even at that pace, Saturn revolves __(7)__ than Uranus, Neptune, or Pluto. Those planets travel __(8)__ distances than Saturn, so it makes sense that they are __(9)__. Pluto moves at a pretty __(10)__ speed, given that it is the farthest planet from the sun.

IDENTIFYING COMMON STUMBLING BLOCKS

Following is a list of the most common errors students make when using adjectives and adverbs.

Problem
- Faulty comparative and superlative forms

Solution
- Instruction, pp. L449–L452, L454–L455
- Practice, pp. L450, L452–L458

Problem
- Double comparisons and double negatives

Solution
- Instruction, pp. L461, L463
- Practice, pp. L462–L464

1 A swiftest
B swifter
C most swift
D swift

2 A least
B less
C little
D leastest

3 A no
B none
C any
D nothing

4 A other
B anyone else
C any
D any other

5 A can
B can't
C doesn't
D cannot

6 A more shorter
B short
C shorter
D shortest

7 A rapidly
B more rapidly
C most rapidly
D more rapidlier

8 A long
B longer
C longest
D more long

9 A the most slowest
B more slower
C slowest
D slower

10 A better
B well
C best
D good

A DIFFERENT DELIVERY SYSTEM

If you prefer, you can print the pretest from the BK English Test Bank located at http://www.bkenglish.com.

Using *the Pretest*

Assessing Prior Knowledge

The pretest will help you and your students assess where they stand in their basic understanding of modifier use.

Customizing the Test

Use these questions to add or replace items for alternate versions of the test.

Mars is (11) in many ways to Earth than (12) planet is. In size, though, it is (13) smaller. That means that its gravity pulls (14) than gravity on Earth. Although Mars has water and air, it is not designed to support life as (15) as Earth can.

11. A close
B closer
C closest
D more closer

12. A any
B any other
C other
D all

13. A many
B more
C most
D much

14. A hard
B less hard
C least hard
D little harder

15. A well
B good
C better
D best

ADDITIONAL RESOURCES

Language Skills Practice . . . . pages 131–135
Transparency Tools FA14
ESL Practice and Test Preparation . . . . . pages 124–126
Assessment: Chapter Test. . . . . pages 186–189

MAKING VISUAL CONNECTIONS

For Language Development

Have students study the family depicted in *Portrait of Amilcare, Minerva, and Astrubale Anguissola.* What comparisons can students make about the people in the painting? For example, who is the tallest person in the painting? the youngest? the oldest? What colors are the brightest? What fabrics are smoother than other fabrics in the painting? Have students write four sentences that compare elements in the painting. Write some of students' sentences on the board.

To Stimulate Writing

Use the questions for art criticism as writing or discussion prompts.

Possible Answers:

Describe The foreground shows a man, two children, and a dog. The background seems to show some ruins and a mountain.

Analyze The viewer's eye is drawn to the hands of the subjects, which lead the eye across a diagonal. The man and boy are actually holding hands, and the man's hand is on the boy's shoulder. The way that the children are looking at each other and the father seems to connect them in a familial way.

Interpret She might write a character sketch or biography.

Judge Answers will vary.

Sofonisba Anguissola. *Portrait of Amilcare, Minerva, and Astrubale Anguissola,* ca. 1559.
Oil on canvas, $61\frac{13}{16}$ inches by $48\frac{1}{32}$ inches.
Nivaagards Malerisammling, Niva, Denmark.

Describe What is in the foreground of this painting? What is in the background?

Analyze How did the artist use the subjects' hands and eyes to connect them? How can you tell that this is a family?

Interpret In this painting an artist represents her family. Imagine she were a writer instead. What writing form might she use to convey the same information?

Judge A painting allows you to draw your own conclusions about a subject's personality. A written work might plant images in your head about the subject's character and attitude. What would you use to gain an overall impression of a person, a painted portrait, or a written character sketch? Why?

At the end of the chapter, you will use this artwork as a visual aid for writing.

FOR DEVELOPING LANGUAGE SKILLS

LESSON 1 *(pages L449–L458)*

OBJECTIVES

- **To identify the three degrees of comparison**
- **To form correct comparisons**
- **To use the correct form of modifiers**

Create Interest

Write the following sentences on the board. Have students decide what is wrong with each sentence and correct the errors. Tell students that they will learn how to make correct comparisons in Chapter 14.

The bear can run quickest than the sloth. (more quickly)

Comparison of Adjectives and Adverbs

When you write, you often compare one thing with another. Adjectives and adverbs generally have three forms that are used for comparisons. These forms are called degrees of comparison.

Most adjectives and adverbs have three degrees of comparison: the positive, the comparative, and the superlative.

The **positive degree** is used when no comparison is being made.

Adjective	The tiger is **big.**
Adverb	A giraffe runs **swiftly.**

The **comparative degree** is used when two people, things, or actions are being compared.

Adjective	Obviously, an elephant is even **bigger** than a tiger.
Adverb	A giraffe can run **more swiftly** than a zebra.

The **superlative degree** is used when more than two people, things, or actions are being compared.

Adjective	The blue whale is the **biggest** animal of all.
Adverb	Of all animals, the cheetah runs **most swiftly.**

You can learn more about adjectives and adverbs in Chapter 4.

FOR INCREASING STUDENT ACHIEVEMENT

REACHING ALL STUDENTS

English Language Learners

Students who are learning English may have trouble knowing when to use *more* and *most* with adjectives and adverbs. They also might have difficulty when adding the endings *-er* and *-est.* Tell students that *-er* and *-est* are generally added to shorter adjectives and adverbs. *More* and *most* are generally used before longer adjectives and adverbs. Have students practice saying the following sets of words: *warm, warmer, warmest; happy, happier, happiest; delicious, more delicious, most delicious.* Then have students make similar list of words to practice on their own.

A polar bear is the most whitest animal at our zoo. (whitest)

That monkey is the cheerfullest one I've ever seen. (most cheerful)

We arrived at the zoo more earlier than you did. (earlier)

Guide Instruction

By Modeling Strategies

Using the charts on pages L451–L452, demonstrate how to form comparisons using one-syllable, two-syllable, and three-syllable modifiers. Use the instruction on these pages to present strategies students should use to form comparisons. Tell students that some spellings of the original modifiers change and some do not change. Use the following examples in addition to the examples in the textbook:

My grades were (more high, higher) this semester than last semester. (*higher* because *high* is a one-syllable modifier)

A DIFFERENT APPROACH

Kinesthetic

Before completing **Practice Your Skills,** have the class create body gestures or movements to represent the following words: *positive, comparative, superlative.* After deciding on gestures, read each sentence aloud as students respond with the appropriate gesture. Students should use the gestures to identify each underlined adjective or adverb in items one through ten.

HOME WORK

After completing **Practice Your Skills,** have students write ten sentences about the local weather as home work. Students should use positive, comparative, and superlative comparisons in their sentences. The following day, write some of students' sentences on the board and discuss their comparisons.

PRACTICE YOUR SKILLS

Check Your Understanding

Identifying Degrees of Comparison

General Interest **Label each underlined adjective or adverb *P* for positive, *C* for comparative, or *S* for superlative.**

1. This winter has been the rainiest (sup. adj.) winter of the last ten years.
2. I would gladly (pos. adv.) never see another winter like that one.
3. The days are growing longer (comp. adj.) now that spring is here.
4. The winds have been blowing more gently (comp. adv.) today than yesterday.
5. Yesterday must have been the warmest (sup. adj.) day of the year.
6. It was hazier (comp. adj.) this morning than it was yesterday.
7. The haze has been burning off more slowly (comp. adv.) this month than last.
8. Today will be muggy (pos. adj.).
9. Monday was the clearest (sup. adj.) day of the week.
10. Next week's weather should be drier (comp. adj.) than this week's weather.

Regular Comparison

Most adjectives and adverbs form the comparative and superlative degrees in a regular manner. The form often depends on the number of syllables in the modifier.

Add *-er* to form the comparative degree and *-est* to form the superlative degree of one-syllable modifiers.

She is (sillier, more silly) than her sister. (*sillier* because *silly* is a two-syllable modifier)

That is the (most beautiful, beautifullest) flower I've ever seen. (*most beautiful* because *beautiful* is a three-syllable modifier)

Consolidate Skills

Through Guided Practice

The **Check Your Understanding** exercises as well as the **QuickCheck** on page L458 will help students form correct comparisons using adjectives and adverbs. Have students brainstorm some adjectives and adverbs that they have used in the past to make comparisons. Write some of students' responses on the board and discuss ways to use these modifiers in sentences. Then guide students through the first item in each exercise. Have students complete the exercises independently.

ONE-SYLLABLE MODIFIERS			
	POSITIVE	COMPARATIVE	SUPERLATIVE
ADJECTIVE	bright	bright**er**	bright**est**
	sad	sadd**er**	sadd**est**
ADVERB	soon	soon**er**	soon**est**

A spelling change sometimes occurs when *-er* or *-est* is added to certain modifiers, such as *sad*. Check the spelling in the dictionary if you are not sure of it.

Many two-syllable modifiers are formed exactly like one-syllable modifiers. A few two-syllable modifiers, however, would be difficult to pronounce if *-er* or *-est* was added. "Usefuler" and "usefulest," for instance, sound awkward. For such two-syllable modifiers, *more* and *most* are used to form the comparative and superlative forms. Also, *more* and *most* are usually used with adverbs ending in *-ly*.

Use *-er* or *more* to form the comparative degree and *-est* or *most* to form the superlative degree of two-syllable modifiers.

TWO-SYLLABLE MODIFIERS			
	POSITIVE	COMPARATIVE	SUPERLATIVE
ADJECTIVE	funny	funni**er**	funni**est**
	cheerful	**more** cheerful	**most** cheerful
ADVERBS	early	earli**er**	earli**est**
	quickly	**more** quickly	**most** quickly

Notice that a spelling change occurs in modifiers that end in *y*, such as *funny* and *early*. The *y* changes to *i* before *-er* or *-est* is added.

USING TECHNOLOGY

Video

Have students find four examples of comparative adjectives or adverbs in television advertising. Students should view television commercials and write down the comparative forms used in the advertisements. They should identify the products being advertised. Have students share their comparative forms with the class.

Apply to Communication

Through Independent Writing

The **Communicate Your Ideas/Apply to Writing** activity on pages L457–L458 prompts students to write a persuasive letter. Ask students how they might use comparisons and modifiers to make their persuasive letter more convincing. In what situations might they use the superlative form to make a point? Ask students what precise wording they could use to make their writing more persuasive. Discuss students' plans for using comparisons in their writing.

Transfer to Everyday Life

Identifying Comparisons in News Articles and News Reports

Have students use news articles and news reports to identify at least three comparisons. Students should write down the sentences that contain the comparisons and read them aloud to the class. Students should also sum-

YOUR IDEAS

For Forming Regular and Irregular Comparisons

CONNECT TO SPEAKING AND WRITING

Many two-syllable modifiers are heard so often that you automatically know which comparative form to use. Occasionally both forms may sound right. That may be because the comparative degrees of some two-syllable modifiers—such as *handsome, common,* and *lovely*—are correctly written either way. Consult an unabridged dictionary whenever you are in doubt about a comparative form. If you have a choice, choose the form that sounds best in the sentence you are writing.

All modifiers with three or more syllables form their comparative and superlative degrees by using *more* and *most.*

Use *more* to form the comparative degree and *most* to form the superlative degree of modifiers with three or more syllables.

THREE-SYLLABLE MODIFIERS			
	POSITIVE	COMPARATIVE	SUPERLATIVE
ADJECTIVE	difficult	**more** difficult	**most** difficult
ADVERB	frequently	**more** frequently	**most** frequently

PRACTICE YOUR SKILLS

Check Your Understanding

Forming Regular Comparisons

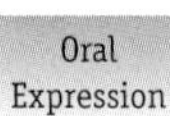

Read each sentence aloud, trying each form in parentheses. Choose the correct form and then read the sentence aloud again.

1. Pyrotechnicians have one of the (thrillingest, most thrilling) jobs available.

marize how the comparisons were used in articles. Discuss students' examples and how effective the comparisons were in the news articles.

Pull It All Together

By Sharing

Have students share their writing samples from **Communicate Your Ideas/ Apply to Writing** with the class. After students have read their writing aloud, have the class critique each students' use of positive, comparative, and superlative modifiers. List some examples on the board and have students point out any errors that need to be corrected.

Check Understanding

By Summarizing

Have students summarize the strategies they use to form positive, comparative, and superlative comparisons. Remind students to include examples with one- , two- , and three-syllable modifiers and irregular modifiers.

2. Creating fireworks displays is (<u>riskier</u>, more risky) than most other jobs.

3. Independence Day is the (<u>busiest</u>, most busy) day of the year for pyrotechnicians.

4. Each year they stage (beautifuler, <u>more beautiful</u>) displays than the year before.

5. Displays in the past were (dangerouser, <u>more dangerous</u>) than displays are now.

6. The experts lit a fuse and ran away (<u>faster</u>, more fast) than the speed of fire.

7. Today, launching rockets is (<u>safer</u>, more safe) than it was fifty years ago.

8. Computerized control panels allow the technicians to stand (<u>farther</u>, more far) away.

9. The (<u>latest</u>, most late) technology times each explosion down to a millisecond.

10. The (creativest, <u>most creative</u>) task is planning the displays.

Check Your Understanding

Forming Comparative and Superlative Modifiers

Write each modifier. Then write its comparative and superlative forms.

11. restless	**18.** late	**25.** hard
12. safe	**19.** pretty	**26.** fast
13. narrow	**20.** dark	**27.** often
14. wonderful	**21.** happy	**28.** high
15. carefully	**22.** athletic	**29.** easily
16. smart	**23.** slowly	**30.** lovely
17. loudly	**24.** obedient	

A DIFFERENT APPROACH

Visual

Have students complete items eleven through thirty of **Check Your Understanding** by taking turns writing their responses on the board. Write the headings *Positive, Comparative,* and *Superlative* on the board. Students should write the positive, comparative, and superlative forms of each word in the appropriate column. Have students use some of the modifiers in sentences when they have completed the exercise.

Sample Answers:

11. restless	more restless	most restless
12. safe	safer	safest
13. narrow	narrower	narrowest
14. wonderful	more wonderful	most wonderful
15. carefully	more carefully	most carefully
16. smart	smarter	smartest
17. loudly	more loudly	most loudly
18. late	later	latest
19. pretty	prettier	prettiest
20. dark	darker	darkest
21. happy	happier	happiest
22. athletic	more athletic	most athletic
23. slowly	more slowly	most slowly
24. obedient	more obedient	most obedient
25. hard	harder	hardest
26. fast	faster	fastest
27. often	more often	most often
28. high	higher	highest
29. easily	more easily	most easily
30. lovely	more lovely	most lovely

USING STUDENTS' STRENGTHS

Multiple Intelligences: Spatial

After students have written their responses for items 31 through 35 of **Check Your Understanding,** have them illustrate two of their sentences. Tell students that their pyrotechnics illustrations can be in a style of their choice, such as abstract or realistic. Display students' completed illustrations in the classroom with the appropriate comparative sentences.

REACHING ALL STUDENTS

Struggling Learners

Have students create eight sentences using the words in the irregular modifiers chart. Students should write sentences using the comparative and superlative forms of the words in the chart. Tell students that they will become more familiar with these forms as they use them more frequently. Have students share some of their sentences with the class.

Check Your Understanding

Using the Correct Form of Modifiers

General Interest **Write the correct modifier in each sentence.**

31. Pyrotechnicians are (more skillful, most skillful) than you might think.

32. The (more scientific, most scientific) part of their jobs is making the fireworks.

33. Their knowledge of chemistry is (deeper, deepest) than that of most people.

34. Colors of today glow (redder, reddest) than before.

35. Colors are (brighter, brightest) than ever.

Irregular Comparison

A few adjectives and adverbs are compared in an irregular manner. You should learn the comparative and superlative forms of the following modifiers so that you can use them correctly in your writing.

IRREGULAR MODIFIERS

Positive	Comparative	Superlative
bad/badly	worse	worst
good/well	better	best
little	less	least
much/many	more	most

Positive	Yesterday's storm was **bad.**
Comparative	It was **worse** than the storm last week.
Superlative	In fact, it was the **worst** storm of the summer.

Connect to Speaking and Writing

You will never hear a careful speaker call something "the most unique" of its kind. There are no degrees of comparison for some adjectives—such as *unique, universal, perfect, infinite*—and their adverb forms. The words themselves describe a quality of being complete or perfect. If you think about the meanings of words like these, you'll recognize that they need no modifiers before them.

Practice Your Skills

Check Your Understanding

Forming Irregular Comparisons

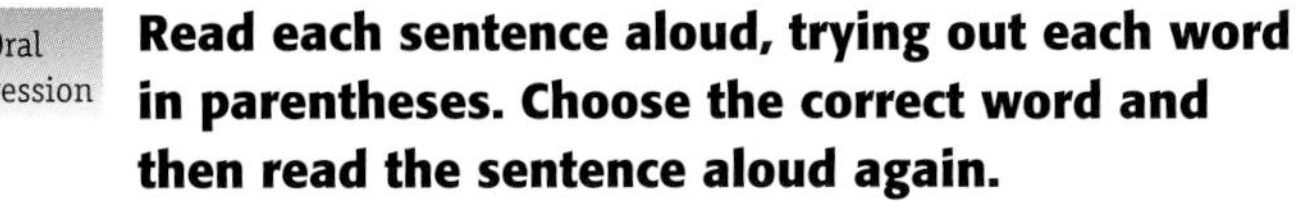

Oral Expression **Read each sentence aloud, trying out each word in parentheses. Choose the correct word and then read the sentence aloud again.**

1. Medieval people didn't have (much, many) variety in their winter diets.

2. For (much, many) months there was no fresh meat or fish.

3. The winter was the (worse, worst) time of the year for fishing.

4. There was very (little, less) fodder for farm animals.

5. (More, Most) peasants sold or slaughtered their stock in the fall.

6. It was (good, better) to do this than to have the animals starve.

7. Beef and pork kept (bad, badly) even in cold climates.

A Different Approach

Auditory

Have students work in small groups to complete items one through twenty-five in **Practice Your Skills.** Students should take turns in their groups reading each item aloud and responding with the correct answer. Group members should decide whether or not each response is correct and tell why it is correct or why it is not.

HOME WORK

Have students write ten sentences. These sentences should include comparative and superlative modifiers. Tell students to vary their use of comparative and superlative modifiers throughout their ten sentences.

8. The (better, best) solution was to salt or dry meats.
9. Vegetables were (less, least) important in the diet than meat.
10. Only dried beans and some root vegetables stored (well, best).

Check Your Understanding

Supplying the Correct Form of Modifiers

History Topic **Read the first sentence in each group. Then write the comparative and superlative forms of the underlined modifier in the two sentences below it.**

11. Vegetables were not a good source of natural salt.
    Cooked meat was a better source.
    Raw meat was the best source but it was unsafe to eat.
12. Many people preferred the brine salt from salt springs.
    More people could afford seawater salt.
    Most people bought cheaper salt from the mines.
13. Preserving fish by drying worked well.
    It worked better in drier climates.
    It worked best in areas that were both dry and windy.
14. Dried meat was not too bad for the people's health.
    Heavily salted meat was worse for them.
    Heavily salted half-spoiled meat was worst of all.
15. A little fresh game usually appeared on the menus of the wealthy.
    A craftsperson's menu contained less meat.
    A peasant's menu contained the least meat of all.

Connect to the Writing Process: Editing

Correcting the Form of Modifiers

If the underlined adjective or adverb in a sentence is incorrect, replace it with the correct word. If it is correct, write *C*.

16. The wealthy liked elaborate dishes ~~better~~ best of all.

17. Their cooks used sauces far ~~much~~ more than we do today.

18. Sauces made meats taste ~~least~~ less salty than they would have otherwise.

19. Some of the sauces were much like today's curries. C

20. Meats were the basis of ~~more~~ most dishes on a banquet menu.

21. ~~Much~~ Many different meats were served in one course.

22. The roasts of fresh meat would taste ~~better~~ good to us today.

23. Cod liver pastries might not be as ~~worse~~ bad as they sound.

24. One of the ~~less~~ least appealing dishes of all was simmered eels.

25. I can't imagine anything ~~worst~~ worse than songbirds cooked whole.

Communicate Your Ideas

APPLY TO WRITING

Persuasive Letter: ***Forms of Modifiers***

Suppose that a scientist has made time travel possible. The scientist has given you a choice of which time period you would like to live in—right now, in

TIMESAVER *QuickCheck*

Have students exchange their persuasive letters with a partner. Students should read their partners' writing, evaluating the use of comparative and superlative modifiers. Students should also check for clear and effective arguments in the persuasive letters. Have students discuss ways to improve their writing with their partners.

EXPANDING THE LESSON

Using Technology

You will find additional **instructional** and **practice** materials for this chapter at http://www.bkenglish.com.

medieval times, or one hundred years in the future. Write a letter to the scientist. Persuade the scientist to let you settle in the time period you prefer. Tell why you think that era would be better for you than the other two. Use both comparative and superlative forms of adjectives and adverbs. Be prepared to identify the forms you used.

Mixed Practice

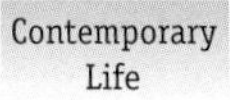

Find and write each incorrect modifier. Then write it correctly. If a sentence is correct, write *C*.

1. The landmarks tour is the ~~better~~ best thing to do on a Sunday.
2. The courthouse is the ~~most old~~ oldest building in the city.
3. The ~~more~~ most famous landmark in the county is the mission.
4. Rancho de los Alamedas was ~~largest~~ larger than the mission property.
5. There were ~~many~~ more people on the ranches than in the village.
6. The village's ~~faster~~ fastest growth took place after 1865.
7. Frame houses were built more often than brick houses. C
8. Wood cost ~~lesser~~ less than bricks after the railroad came through.
9. The Morrison house is the ~~more~~ most interesting one on the whole tour.
10. It was ~~most~~ more expensive to build than any other house of its time.

LESSON 2 *(pages L459–L467)*

OBJECTIVES
- **To use *other* and *else* correctly in comparisons**
- **To identify and correct double comparisons**
- **To identify and correct double negatives**
- **To use *good* and *well* correctly**

Create Interest
Have students read the following sentences and comment on them. Students should decide whether they sound correct or not. Tell students that they will learn about problem modifiers such as these in Lesson 2.

- This test is the most hardest one I've ever taken. (double comparison)
- That is the most brightest light I've ever seen. (double comparison)
- He didn't take no books home. (double negative)
- I hadn't had no lunch yet. (double negative)

Problems with Modifiers

Once you know how to form the comparative and superlative forms of modifiers, there are a few problems you should watch out for when you use them in your writing.

Other and *Else*

Do not make the mistake of comparing one thing with itself when it is part of a group. You can avoid this by adding the word *other* or *else* to your comparison.

Add *other* or *else* when comparing a member of a group with the rest of the group.

INCORRECT Dan is taller than any student in the eighth grade.
(Dan is being compared to all the students in the eighth grade. This means he is also being compared to himself because he is in the eighth grade, too.)

CORRECT Dan is taller than any **other** student in the eighth grade.
(Now he is being compared only with the other students, not with himself.)

INCORRECT Beth runs faster than anyone in her class.
(Since Beth is in the class, she is also being compared with herself.)

CORRECT Beth runs faster than anyone **else** in her class.
(Now she is being compared only to the rest of the class, not to herself.)

REACHING ALL STUDENTS

Struggling Learners
Tell students that the mistake of comparing one thing with itself when it is part of a group can be difficult to identify. Point out that students can correct these mistakes by simply adding *other* or *else* to their comparisons. Reinforce students' understanding of this error by correcting the following errors together.

- I played worse than anyone in the band. (worse than anyone else)
- Lindsay is smarter than any student in the class. (smarter than any other student)
- She was more tired than any person in the group. (more tired than any other person)

Guide Instruction

By Modeling Strategies

Use the instruction and the example sentences throughout this lesson to model strategies for forming comparisons in special circumstances, such as when using *other, else, good,* and *well.* After presenting the instruction, have students create example sentences that demonstrate correct comparisons in these special circumstances. Write some of students' sentences on the board and demonstrate strategies for using *other, else, good,* and *well* and for avoiding double comparisons and double negatives.

Consolidate Skills

Through Guided Practice

The **Check Your Understanding** exercises as well as the **QuickCheck** on page L467 will help students use *other, else, good,* and *well* correctly and will help them avoid double comparisons and double negatives. Complete the first item in each

A DIFFERENT APPROACH

Auditory

After writing out their responses to items one through ten of **Practice Your Skills,** have students read each sentence aloud, supplying the correct response. Discuss each item as students complete the activity. Students should be able to explain why they chose a particular response.

CONNECT TO SPEAKING AND WRITING

When you are speaking, get into the habit of saying *than*—not *then*—when you make comparisons. Pronouncing the word correctly will help you to remember to write *than* rather than *then.*

PRACTICE YOUR SKILLS

Check Your Understanding

Using* Other *and* Else *Correctly

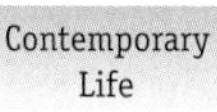

Write the word or words in parentheses that make the most sense in each sentence.

1. I know more about dogs than (anyone, anyone else) in my class does.
2. I like Labradors better than (any, any other) dog I've seen.
3. A Labrador is smarter than (any, any other) spaniel or Dalmatian.
4. Our dog Ginger would rather be with me than (anyone, anyone else) in our family.
5. Ginger prefers Skippers to (any, any other) pet food she's eaten.
6. She'd rather eat our sandwiches than (any, any other) dog food we give her.
7. She barks more at the new meter reader than at (anyone, anyone else).
8. Our neighbor's cat is meaner than (any, any other) dog in our neighborhood.
9. The cat prefers our yard to (anywhere, anywhere else) on the block.
10. Ginger dislikes that cat more than (any, any other) cat she's ever met.

exercise together and discuss the correct response. Have students complete the remaining exercises independently.

Apply to Communication

Through Independent Writing

The **Communicate Your Ideas/Apply to Writing** activity on page L466 prompts students to write a personal assessment using comparisons. Have students brainstorm some of their own activities that they might compare. Then have students list modifiers they can use in their comparisons. Discuss students' responses.

Transfer to Everyday Life

Identifying Correct Comparisons in Literature

Have students use their literature textbooks or a novel they are reading to identify sentences that contain correct comparisons. Students should find at least five examples of comparisons using problem modifiers, such as

Connect to the Writing Process: Editing

***Correcting Comparisons with* Other *and* Else**

Rewrite each incorrect sentence. If a sentence is already correct, write *C*.

11. Fish are easier to care for than any animal in the pet shop. C

12. Kahn's Pet Store has more kinds of fish than any ^other shop in town.

13. An angelfish is much prettier than any goldfish. C

14. The animals are healthier here than anywhere ^else I've been.

15. The puppy likes the rubber bone better than any ^other toy he has.

16. I want this puppy more than any ^other puppy I've seen.

Double Comparisons

Use only one method to form the comparative or the superlative of a modifier. Using *-er* and *more* together, for example, produces a **double comparison,** which is incorrect.

Do not use both *-er* and *more* to form the comparative degree, or both *-est* and *most* to form the superlative degree.

DOUBLE COMPARISON	Can you work **more quicklier?**
CORRECT	Can you work **more quickly?**
DOUBLE COMPARISON	This project is the **most hardest** one we've worked on.
CORRECT	This project is the **hardest** one we've worked on.

HOME WORK

Have students read **Connect to Speaking and Writing** for home work. Students should then write a paragraph explaining the difference between *than* and *then*. Students should use each word correctly in a sentence.

REACHING ALL STUDENTS

Advanced Learners

Have students write a humorous poem that contains double comparisons. Tell students that although double comparisons are incorrect, they can be amusing. After students have written their poems with double comparisons, have them write the same poem and correct the double comparisons. Have students comment on which version of the poem they like the best.

other, else, good, and well and that avoid double comparisons and double negatives.

Pull It All Together

By Summarizing

Have students write a paragraph telling how to avoid double comparisons and double negatives in their writing. Students should provide examples of these problems with modifiers and demonstrate how to correct them.

Check Understanding

Summarizing

Have students write five sentences using the following words: *other, else, good, well, no.* Students should use either comparative or superlative forms in their sentences. Have students write some of their sentences on the board.

HOME WORK

Have students peruse a newspaper article for double comparisons. They should make corrections when necessary.

Practice Your Skills

Check Your Understanding

Identifying Double Comparisons

Science Topic **Write *I* if a sentence contains double comparisons. Write *C* if a sentence is correct.**

1. There were no flowers among the world's ~~most~~ earliest plants. I

2. Bees are attracted to the ~~most~~ lightest flowers on plants. I

3. Orchid blossoms last ~~more~~ longer than those of most other plants. I

4. Succulents can live in a drier climate than many other plants. C

5. A ten-ton saguaro cactus is ~~more~~ taller than many trees. I

6. Among the ~~most~~ oddest plants are those that feed on insects. I

7. The eucalyptus is the ~~most~~ tallest Australian tree. I

8. The ~~most~~ rarest forget-me-not is found on only one Pacific Island. I

9. Sequoias are ~~more~~ older than any other American trees. I

10. The plant with the longest life span is the yucca. C

Connect to the Writing Process: Editing

Correcting Double Comparisons

11.–18. Rewrite the incorrect sentences from the preceding exercise so that there are no double comparisons. [See answers given above.]

Double Negatives

The following is a list of common negative words.

COMMON NEGATIVES		
no	nobody	none
not	no one	never
-n't	nothing	hardly

Two negative words should not be used together to express the same idea. When they are, the result is a **double negative.**

Avoid using a double negative.

DOUBLE NEGATIVE	We did**n't** swim **no** laps today.
CORRECT	We did**n't** swim any laps today.
CORRECT	We swam **no** laps today.
DOUBLE NEGATIVE	Carmen did**n't** **hardly** practice last week.
CORRECT	Carmen **hardly** practiced last week.

PRACTICE YOUR SKILLS

Check Your Understanding

Identifying Double Negatives

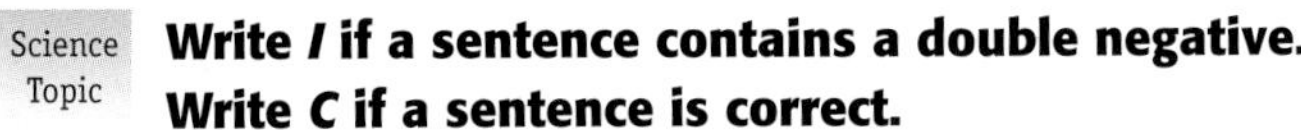

Science Topic **Write *I* if a sentence contains a double negative. Write *C* if a sentence is correct.**

1. Many people ~~don't~~ know nothing about turtles. I

2. Hardly anything was known about the Rancho del Oso Park turtles. C

REACHING ALL STUDENTS

English Language Learners

Point out to students learning English that sometimes two or more negatives can correctly appear in the same sentence. Tell students that it is incorrect to have two negatives in a sentence only when they express the same idea. Show students how two negatives can be used correctly in the same sentence by using the following examples:

- Eve could not paint well and was not happy about that.
- I didn't want to go and I wasn't going to change my mind.
- He couldn't get it through his head; he was never going to be a good singer.

USING STUDENTS' STRENGTHS

Multiple Intelligences: Linguistic

After discussing the instruction and examples for using *good* and *well* correctly, have students write a short story using these words. Remind students that a short story is a narrative with a beginning, a middle, and an end. Have students underline sentences in which they correctly use *good* and *well*. Have students share their stories with the class. Discuss their use of *good* and *well*.

3. Researchers ~~hadn't~~ had never been able to track the turtles' movements. I

4. They ~~couldn't~~ could see no reason against equipping turtles with beepers on their backs. I

5. The transistors on their backs didn't ~~hardly~~ bother the turtles at all. I

6. A turtle doesn't like anything better than basking on a sunny log. C

7. Female turtles don't like ~~no one~~ anyone near their nests. I

8. Their nests ~~couldn't~~ could never be found by most researchers. I

9. Even with beepers, the researchers still couldn't ~~hardly~~ track the turtles. I

10. They don't know how young turtles find their way to water. C

Connect to the Writing Process: Editing

Correcting Double Negatives

11.–17. Rewrite the incorrect sentences from the preceding exercise so that there are no double negatives. [See answers given above.]

Good or *Well?*

Good is always used as an adjective. *Well* is usually used as an adverb. However, when *well* means "in good health," it is used as an adjective. Remember that adjectives can follow linking verbs.

ADJECTIVE	The story was **good.**
	(*Good* is a predicate adjective that describes *story*.)

ADVERB Michael read the story **well.**

(*Well* is an adverb that tells how Michael read.)

ADJECTIVE I don't feel **well** today.

(In this sentence *well* means "in good health.")

You can learn more about predicate adjectives and linking verbs on pages L103–L104.

Check Your Understanding

***Using* Good *and* Well**

Contemporary Life **Write either *good* or *well* to correctly complete each sentence.**

1. Ted swims well.
2. The warm water at the beach felt good.
3. The loud pounding of the surf sounds good to me.
4. Dad's cold is gone, so he finally feels well.
5. Sandy surfs well.
6. Our car worked well on the way to the beach.
7. Ice cream tastes good on a warm day.
8. After eating the greasy fried food, Bert did not feel well.
9. I did well at my first diving lesson with my new coach.
10. The popcorn from the boardwalk stand smelled good.

A DIFFERENT APPROACH

Visual

Have students write the words *good* and *well* on two separate index cards. Then, as you read each sentence in **Practice Your Skills** aloud, have students hold up the card with the word that completes the sentence correctly.

TIMESAVER *QuickCheck*

Have students exchange their assessments with a partner. Partners should check for correct comparisons and make any suggestions for improvement. As a class, discuss ways in which students evaluated their partner's writing.

Connect to the Writing Process: Editing

Correcting Errors with **Good** *or* **Well**

Rewrite the following sentences if they contain errors with *good* or *well*. If a sentence is correct, write *C*.

11. Can young children learn to swim ~~good~~ well?

12. Many good instructors say *yes.* C

13. Why should little children swim ~~good~~ well?

14. Some youngsters swim well, and that makes pools safer for them. C

15. Children who cannot swim ~~good~~ well die every year.

Communicate Your Ideas

APPLY TO WRITING

A Personal Assessment: ***Problem Modifiers***

Write an assessment for yourself of the progress you've made in the last year in one of your activities. Describe the activity and compare the skills you had before to the ones you have now. When you have finished, check to make sure you have used all modifiers correctly.

Mixed Practice

Science Topic

Find the error in each sentence. Then write the sentence correctly.

1. The anaconda is longer and bigger than any other kind of snake.

2. The cobra is one of the three ~~most~~ largest snakes.

3. Rattlesnakes are the most ~~deadliest~~ deadly snakes in the far West.
4. You won't ~~never~~ ever see copperheads in the western states.
5. There aren't ~~no~~ any snakes at all in Iceland and Ireland.
6. Cobra family members are more common in Australia than any other snake.
7. The ~~most~~ greatest number of snake species live in the tropics.
8. Snakes don't eat ~~nothing~~ anything but animal food.
9. Snakes that hunt in the daytime can see ~~good~~ well.
10. A snake's sense of smell is better than that of almost any other animal.
11. The ~~most~~ fastest snake of all is probably the black mamba of Africa.
12. The snake that is smaller than any other snake is the Braminy blind snake.
13. Young snakes shed their skins more ~~oftener~~ often than old snakes.
14. Most snakes cannot focus their eyes ~~good~~ well.
15. Snakes actually move ~~most~~ more slowly than many other animals.

EXPANDING THE LESSON

Using Technology

You will find additional **instructional** and **practice** materials for this chapter at http://www.bkenglish.com.

FOR REVIEWING SKILLS

Using CheckPoint

This feature on modifiers can be used as further independent practice or as a cumulative review of the chapter. Students choose correct modifiers, correct errors with modifiers, and write sentences using modifiers.

Sample Answers for *Forming the Comparison of Modifiers:*

1. Karen uses her money more wisely than Sam does.
2. This knife is keener than that one.
3. That was the best dessert I ever tasted.
4. Sometimes a calculator is more useful than a computer.
5. Her costume is scarier than yours.
6. This box contains the most food.
7. That road is the smoothest one in the county.
8. He made each step more cautiously than the last.
9. The accident occurred on the most dangerous highway in the state.
10. This chair is more comfortable than that one.

CheckPoint

Using the Correct Form of Modifiers

Write the correct word or words in parentheses.

1. Your book report sounded (good, well).
2. Which shines (more, most) brightly, gold or silver?
3. Craig didn't know (nothing, anything) about the ring.
4. My three aunts held the baby, but Aunt Carrie was the (more, most) nervous.
5. Is Daniel (taller, more taller) than you?
6. There aren't (no, any) seats left in the theater.
7. Which of these three snakes is the (deadlier, deadliest)?
8. Susan worked harder than (anyone, anyone else) on the committee.
9. Who made the (wiser, wisest) choice, Jerry or Pat?
10. Which television set has the (worse, worst) picture, mine or yours?

Correcting Errors with Modifiers

Write the following sentences, correcting each error. If a sentence is correct, write *C*.

1. Which of the six New England states is ~~smaller~~ smallest?
2. There aren't ~~no~~ any oars in this boat.
3. In some science fiction stories, spaceships travel ~~more~~ faster than the speed of light.
4. I don't know who was ~~coldest~~ colder, you or I.
5. Of the two cars, this one is more reliable. C
6. Haven't you seen ~~none~~ any of my pictures?

7. That tree is healthier than any other tree in the garden.
8. Our twelve-year-old dog doesn't see very ~~good~~ well.
9. This coat looks ~~more~~ better on you than on me.
10. I did well on my lifesaving test at the YMCA. C

Forming the Comparison of Modifiers

Write the form indicated below for each modifier. Then use that form in a sentence.

1. the comparative of *wisely* more wisely
2. the comparative of *keen* keener
3. the superlative of *good* best
4. the comparative of *useful* more useful
5. the comparative of *scary* scarier
6. the superlative of *much* most
7. the superlative of *smooth* smoothest
8. the comparative of *cautiously* more cautiously
9. the superlative of *dangerous* most dangerous
10. the comparative of *comfortable* more comfortable

Using Adjectives and Adverbs

Write ten sentences that follow the directions below.

Write a sentence that . . .

1. compares two friends.
2. compares three desserts.
3. uses a form of *large* to compare three states.
4. uses a form of *easily* to compare two chores.
5. uses a form of *good* to compare two movies.
6. uses a form of *little* to compare three school subjects.
7. uses *other* in a comparison.
8. uses *else* in a comparison.

Sample Answers for *Using Adjectives and Adverbs:*

1. June is taller than Rita.
2. Of the cake, pie, and sorbet, the cake is the richest dessert.
3. Of Texas, Maine, and Alaska, Alaska is the largest state.
4. I did the raking more easily than I did the mowing.
5. Was *Long Day* better than *After School?*
6. Of my math, science, and English homework, math takes the least time.
7. The prize pig was fatter than any other pig in the competition.
8. I am a better writer than anyone else in my class.

Using *Language and Self-Expression*

Consider using this writing assignment to assess students' ability to use modifiers correctly and effectively. You may want students to complete the assignment as part of an expository writing strand for their portfolios.

Prewriting

Encourage students to use questioning strategies in addition to the graphic organizer to help them organize their thoughts in the prewriting stage. For example, students might use the following questions to help them proceed with their writing:

- What might the father be thinking?
- What thoughts and feelings might the children in the painting have?
- What might have happened in the characters' lives right before the portrait was painted?

FOR YOUR INFORMATION

About the Artist

Italian artist Sofonisba Anguissola was the first woman of the Renaissance to become internationally known. While in her twenties, Anguissola became court painter to King Philip II of Spain. As a lady-in-waiting in the court of Philip II, Anguissola painted portraits of the royal family that exemplify the lively Italian Renaissance tradition of straightforward realism. Her success was important to many gifted women who came after her, in Italy and throughout Europe.

Language and *Self-Expression*

Sofonisba Anguissola was a Renaissance painter whose parents allowed her to study art at a time when few women were educated. She painted this portrait of her father, sister, brother, and dog around the year 1559.

Write a character sketch that compares and contrasts the three people in the painting. Use the subjects' names—Amilcare (father), Minerva (sister), and Astrubale (brother)—in your sketch.

Prewriting Make a chart using the subjects' names as headings: *Amilcare, Minerva,* and *Astrubale.* List details you derive from the painting and from your imagination, such as appearance, behavior, likes, and dislikes. Write words or phrases that describe each of the three characters or that compare each with one or both of the others.

Drafting Use your chart to compose a character sketch that describes, compares, and contrasts the three characters. Begin with a paragraph that introduces the three people. Add paragraphs that describe each one individually and compare and contrast each with one or both of the others.

Revising Reread your sketch or have a classmate read it. Make sure that your transitions are smooth and that your details are sharp and convincing.

Editing Review your work, looking for errors in adjective and adverb use, capitalization, and punctuation. Make any corrections needed.

Publishing Prepare a final copy of your character sketch. Share it by reading it aloud as your classmates look at the portrait.

Another Look

Using Adjectives and Adverbs

Comparison of Adjectives and Adverbs

Most adjectives and adverbs have three degrees of comparison: the **positive,** the **comparative,** and the **superlative.** *(page L449)*

Add *-er* to form the comparative degree and *-est* to form the superlative degree of one-syllable modifiers. *(pages L450–L451)*

Use *more* to form the comparative degree and *most* to form the superlative degree of modifiers with three or more syllables. *(page L452)*

Irregular Comparison

A few adjectives and adverbs are compared in an irregular manner. *(page L454)*

IRREGULAR MODIFIERS		
Positive	Comparative	Superlative
bad/badly	worse	worst
good/well	better	best
little	less	least
much/many	more	most

Problems with Modifiers

Add *other* or *else* when comparing a member of the group with the rest of the group. *(page L459)*

Do not use both *-er* and *more* to form the comparative degree, or both *-est* and *most* to form the superlative degree. *(page L461)*

Avoid using a double negative. *(page L463)*

Good is always used as an adjective. *Well* is usually used as an adverb. *(pages L464–L465)*

Using *Another Look*

Another Look summarizes the terms defined in the chapter and provides cross-references to the specific pages on which they are explained. Consider having students use this feature prior to completing **CheckPoint** or taking the post-test. Students who can provide several examples of each term should be able to score well on either measurement.

Using *the Posttest*

Assessing Learning

The posttest will help you and your students assess where they stand in their ability to use modifiers correctly when making comparisons.

IDENTIFYING COMMON STUMBLING BLOCKS

Following is a list of the most common errors students make when using adjectives and adverbs.

Problem

- Faulty comparative and superlative forms

Solution

- For reteaching, use the explanatory copy and examples on pages L449–L452 and L454–L455.

Problem

- Double comparisons and double negatives

Solution

- For reteaching, use the explanatory copy and examples on pages L461 and L463.

Directions

Read the passage and choose the word or group of words that belongs in each underlined space. Write the letter of the correct answer.

EXAMPLE Is swimming __(1)__ for your lungs than running is?

1 **A** good
B better
C best
D more better

ANSWER **1** **B**

Aerobic conditioning has become one of the __(1)__ of all forms of exercise. Nobody __(2)__ go without some form of aerobics. Some aerobic exercises are cycling, dancing, jogging, rope jumping, swimming, tennis, and basketball. Of these, rope jumping may be the __(3)__. It doesn't require fancy shoes or equipment, and it takes up __(4)__ room than __(5)__ sport.

Warming up is __(6)__ no matter what exercise you do. If you are jumping rope, begin by jogging in place until your heart beats __(7)__ than it does at rest. Then do some warm-up jumps before proceeding to your basic jumps. You are doing __(8)__ if you can jump seventy-five jumps per minute. However, even if you jump __(9)__ than __(10)__ in your class, you are still helping your heart and lungs.

A DIFFERENT DELIVERY SYSTEM

If you prefer, you can print the posttest from the BK English Test Bank located at http://www.bkenglish.com.

1 A popular
B more popular
<u>C</u> most popular
D popularest

2 A shouldn't
<u>B</u> should
C cannot
D doesn't

3 A cheap
B cheaper
<u>C</u> cheapest
D most cheapest

4 A little
<u>B</u> less
C lesser
D least

5 A any
B other
<u>C</u> any other
D anybody else

6 <u>A</u> good
B well
C better
D best

7 A fast
B more fast
C fastest
<u>D</u> faster

8 A good
<u>B</u> well
C finely
D more better

9 A the most slowest
B more slower
C slowest
<u>D</u> slower

10 A anyone
B any other
<u>C</u> anyone else
D everyone

Customizing the Test

Use these questions to add or replace items for alternate versions of the test.

Swimming may be the (11) aerobic exercise of all. When you swim regularly, your muscles grow (12) and your endurance gets (13). It's (14) to add laps to your workout gradually, until you can swim continuously for thirty minutes. As another point in its favor, swimming hardly (15) causes injuries.

11. A good
B better
<u>C</u> best
D bestest

12. A strongly
<u>B</u> stronger
C strongest
D most strong

13. A gooder
<u>B</u> better
C best
D well

14. <u>A</u> good
B well
C bestest
D more good

15. A doesn't
B never
<u>C</u> ever
D won't

Using *the Writer's Glossary of Usage*

Direct students in how to use the Writer's Glossary of Usage to look up troublesome words throughout the year as they write, speak, and complete assignments. Students should refer to this glossary as they are writing, editing, and revising any writing assignments.

A Writer's Glossary of Usage

While the last four chapters dealt with the basic elements of usage, this section covers specific areas of difficulty. As you study A Writer's Glossary of Usage, pay attention to the various levels of language, including standard English and nonstandard English.

Standard English refers to the rules and conventions of usage most often accepted and used by English-speaking people throughout the world. **Nonstandard English** does not follow these conventions. The differences in regions and dialect, including current slang, account for the variations in nonstandard English. Using nonstandard English, although not wrong, is unacceptable in certain circumstances. Because nonstandard English lacks uniformity, be sure to use standard English when you write or speak in formal situations, such as in school assignments.

You will also notice references to formal and informal English in the glossary. **Formal English** follows conventional rules for grammar, usage, and mechanics. Business letters, technical reports, and well-written compositions are typical examples of formal English usage. In magazines, newspapers, and fiction, however, informal English is often used. Although it follows the conventions of standard English, **informal English** often includes words and phrases that would sound inappropriate in a formal piece of writing.

So that you can use this glossary more easily, the words appear in alphabetical order.

a, an Use *a* before words beginning with consonant sounds and *an* before words beginning with vowel sounds.

> Matt has **a** soccer game tonight.
> He'll have to eat **an** early dinner.

accept, except *Accept* is a verb that means "to receive with consent." *Except* is usually a preposition that means "but" or "other than."

> I will **accept** Jennifer's invitation to the dance.
>
> I would call her tonight to tell her **except** I have to study for a test.

affect, effect *Affect* is a verb that means "to influence" or "to act upon." *Effect* is usually a noun that means "a result" or "an influence." As a verb, *effect* means "to accomplish" or "to produce."

> How did the news **affect** Rachel?
>
> It had a pleasing **effect** on her.
>
> I'm glad it **effected** a positive improvement in her attitude.

ain't This contraction is nonstandard English. Avoid it in your writing.

> NONSTANDARD It **ain't** going to rain today.
> STANDARD It **isn't** going to rain today.

all ready, already *All ready* means "completely ready." *Already* means "previously."

> If we are **all ready,** we'll leave for the football game.
>
> Jan **already** said that she is waiting for us.

DEVELOPING WORKPLACE COMPETENCIES

Basic Skills: Speaking and Writing

Tell students that in this section, they will learn how to distinguish between—and among—words that are often confused. They will also learn how to distinguish between standard English usage and nonstandard English usage. Have students list on the board particular writing tasks in which formal English should be used (formal invitations; novels, short stories, and most poems; newspaper and magazine articles; business, memoranda, and letters; resumes and job applications; school assignments). Ask students when it would be acceptable to use nonstandard English (informal invitations; letters to close friends and family members; personal diaries and journals; some poems; some humorous writing). Help students come to the conclusion that in most workplace situations that call for speaking and writing, they should use standard (formal) English.

A DIFFERENT APPROACH

Auditory

Point out to students that *effect* is seldom used as a verb. Students usually confuse the verb *affect,* "to cause a change," with the noun *effect,* "result." To help students distinguish between the two words, have them use this strategy: They should remember to say aloud the phrase *the effect.* Only nouns can follow the definite article *the,* and the *e* in *the* reminds us that the noun *effect* begins with the letter *e.*

HOME WORK

Tell students that they can check a dictionary if they are unsure of standard and nonstandard English. For example, assign students to use a dictionary at home to look up *anywheres* and *anywhere.* What does the dictionary tell about these words? Students should also look up nonstandard words, such as *ain't* and *alot.* Have students read any usage notes given in the dictionary with these nonstandard words. Students should explain in their own words why these words should not be used.

a lot People very often write these two words incorrectly as one. There is no such word as "alot." *A lot,* even as two words, should be avoided in formal writing.

INFORMAL	You'll have **a lot** of fun at the springs.
FORMAL	You'll have **a great deal** of fun at the springs.

among, between These words are both prepositions. *Among* is used when referring to three or more people or things. *Between* is used when referring to two people or things.

Please divide your time **among** the whole family.

Tomorrow we can have a talk just **between** you and me.

amount, number *Amount* refers to a singular word. *Number* refers to a plural word.

The **amount** of time Lenny spent on the computer last week is more than the **number** of hours he worked on his homework.

anywhere, everywhere, nowhere, somewhere Do not add *–s* to any of these words.

Don't go **anywhere** until I return.

We went **nowhere** on Saturday.

I looked **everywhere** for my glasses.

at Do not use *at* after *where.*

NONSTANDARD	**Where** they're **at** really isn't our business.
STANDARD	**Where** they are really isn't our business.

PRACTICE YOUR SKILLS

Check Your Understanding

Finding the Correct Word

General Interest **Write the word in parentheses that correctly completes each sentence.**

1. The (affect, effect) of the nursing profession on our society is tremendous.
2. The (amount, number) of care and compassion nurses give cannot be measured.
3. (A great deal, a lot) of emphasis is placed on patient care.
4. The bond (among, between) a nurse and a patient is usually a special one.
5. Nurses often make their own decisions (accept, except) in situations that require a doctor's order.
6. Many people used to (accept, except) nursing as suitable for women only.
7. (All ready, Already) that stereotype has lessened.
8. (A, An) increase in men choosing nursing as a career has resulted.
9. The professional status of nursing is recognized (among, between) the entire medical community.
10. It (ain't, isn't) surprising that nursing has earned the gratitude and respect of society.

Connect to the Writing Process: Editing

Recognizing Correct Usage

Write each underlined word. If the word is used correctly, write *C* beside it. If the word is used incorrectly, write the correct form of the word.

In the early 1800s, almost ~~nowheres~~ nowhere was nursing considered ~~a~~ an honorable profession. The person who

YOUR IDEAS

For Recognizing Correct Usage

MULTIPLE INTELLIGENCE

Auditory

Writers often interchange the words *may* and *might.* However, careful writers who want to make their writing clear and precise use these two words to express specific actions. Remind students that to make their writing more precise, *may* should be used mainly to express permission and *might* should be used mainly to express possibility. Discuss the following examples. Then have students write two additional example sentences using these words, and read them aloud.

- Yes, you may go with your friends today. (permission)
- I might go with my friends today. (possibility)

effected
~~affected~~ a change was Florence Nightingale. She was known as "The Lady with the Lamp" because she carried a lamp to light her way when she walked among ~~between~~ her patients at night. The C number of countries where she trained ~~at~~ included England, Egypt, and Germany. Rumors of the terrible medical conditions of the Crimean War in 1854 C affected her greatly. All ready ~~Already~~ to volunteer her nursing services, she was appointed to lead the entire reform effort. Her bravery and compassion established modern nursing as C a profession of honor.

bad, badly *Bad* is an adjective and often follows a linking verb. *Badly* is used as an adverb. In the first two examples, *tastes* is a linking verb.

NONSTANDARD	The food tastes **badly** to me.
STANDARD	The food tastes **bad** to me.
STANDARD	Mother **badly** wanted to throw it away.

You can learn more about using adjectives and adverbs in Chapter 4.

bring, take *Bring* indicates motion toward the speaker. *Take* indicates motion away from the speaker.

Won't you **bring** me a clean plate?
Yes, after I **take** the dirty one to the kitchen.

You can learn more about using bring *and* take *on page L328.*

can, may *Can* expresses ability. *May* expresses possibility or permission.

Holly **can** speak French fluently.
When she visits, **may** I ask her to teach me?

doesn't, don't *Doesn't* is singular and must agree with a singular subject. *Don't* is plural and must agree with a plural subject or with the singular pronouns *I* or *you*.

> The new singer **doesn't** have a large following yet.
> The new singers **don't** have a large following yet.

double negative Words such as *but* (when it means "only"), *hardly, never, no, none, no one, nobody, not* (and its contraction *n't*), *nothing, nowhere, only, barely,* and *scarcely* are all negatives.

NONSTANDARD	**Nothing never** upsets Katie.
STANDARD	**Nothing ever** upsets Katie.
STANDARD	**Nothing** upsets Katie.

You can learn more about double negatives on page L463.

fewer, less *Fewer* is plural and refers to things that can be counted. *Less* is singular and refers to quantities and qualities that cannot be counted.

> You will have **fewer** clothes after cleaning out your closet.
>
> It will take **less** effort to put everything back in order.

good, well *Good* is an adjective and often follows a linking verb. *Well* is an adverb and often follows an action verb. However, when *well* means "in good health" or "satisfactory," it is used as an adjective.

> Don't you think the band sounds **good?** (adjective)
>
> The lead guitarist plays **well.** (adverb)
>
> I'm glad I felt **well** enough to attend the concert.
>
> (adjective meaning "in good health")

You can learn more about using good *and* well *on pages L464–L465.*

REACHING ALL STUDENTS

English Language Learners

Unlike in other languages, in English two negative words cannot be used to express the same idea. Tell students that two negative words actually can be used in the same sentence as long as they do not express the same idea. Help students differentiate between the two using the following examples. Then have students write four example sentences using negatives correctly.

- You can't not take me to the movies. (incorrect; double negative expressing the same idea)
- You are not a good driver, so you can't take me to the movies. (correct; two negatives used in the same sentence to express two different ideas)

GETTING STUDENTS INVOLVED

Reciprocal Teaching

Remind students not to substitute *of* for *have* when they use the word *could,* such as saying "could of" when they mean "could have." Tell students that "could of" is nonstandard English and should be avoided in speaking and writing. Have students practice in pairs by completing the following sentences:

- I (could of, could have) won that spelling bee. (could have)
- If Terri would have practiced in pairs more, she (could of, could have) aced the competition. (could have)

have, of Never substitute *of* for the verb *have.* When speaking, many people make a contraction of *have.* For example, they might say, "We should've gone." Because *'ve* sounds like *of, of* is often mistakenly substituted for *have* in writing.

NONSTANDARD	Tell them they should **of** waited for us.
STANDARD	Tell them they should **have** waited for us.

in, into Use *into* when you want to express motion from one place to another.

The stained glass window **in** the cathedral is beautiful.
Can you see it when you first walk **into** the vestibule?

its, it's *Its* is a possessive pronoun and means "belonging to it." *It's* is a contraction for *it is.*

To learn about **its** significance, we studied a unit on the flag.

It's surprising how much we already knew about **its** history.

CONNECT TO SPEAKING AND WRITING

A contraction, which **always** contains an apostrophe, stands for two words. When trying to decide correct usage between the possessive pronoun *its* and the contraction *it's* (it is), simply say the two words *it is* in the sentence. The correct usage will immediately become obvious. This hint applies to other possessive pronouns and contractions found in the glossary, such as *their/they're* (they are), *whose/who's* (who is) and *your/you're* (you are). Remember also that an apostrophe **never** appears in a possessive pronoun.

It's a symbol of freedom.

It is a symbol of freedom. 

Practice Your Skills

Check Your Understanding
Finding the Correct Word

Literature Topic **Write the word in parentheses that correctly completes each sentence.**

1. There are (fewer, less) tellers of tall tales today than there used to be.
2. If writers write a tall tale (good, well), they (can, may) make us laugh.
3. (Its, It's) "tongue-in-cheek" type of narration (doesn't, don't) usually make us think deeply.
4. Tall tales (doesn't, don't) usually have complicated stories because the plot is of (fewer, less) importance than the humor.
5. It does, however, (bring, take) us entertainment and often (brings, takes) us back to the days of the Old West.
6. Although writers (can, may) use a variety of humorous techniques, certainly one of them is exaggeration.
7. An unexpected fall is a (good, well) way to create slapstick.
8. Someone carelessly falling headfirst (in, into) a huge bucket of paint is one example of slapstick humor.
9. When a person (bad, badly) mispronounces a word by reversing its syllables, (its, it's) called a spoonerism.
10. Another technique, situation comedy, has a character react differently than we (would have, would of) expected.

USING STUDENTS' STRENGTHS

Multiple Intelligences: Linguistic

Tell students that "logged on" in Carl Sandburg's literature excerpt does not mean to "log on to a computer." The expression means that Paul Bunyan was a worker in the logging industry in Oregon. Have students think of and share similar examples of how language is influenced by technology.

SELECTION AMENDMENT
Description of change: excerpted
Rationale: to focus on the grammar skill

Connect to the Writing Process: Revising

Writing Negatives Correctly

Rewrite each sentence so that there are no double negatives.

11. Before the frontier days, almost no one ~~never~~ ever heard a tall tale.

12. Tall tales hadn't ~~hardly~~ been written at that time.

13. Of course, tall tales don't ~~never~~ ever tell a straight story.

14. In most tall tales, scarcely ~~no one~~ anyone speaks without using dialect.

15. Naturally, not ~~none~~ one of these stories is believed.

Communicate Your Ideas

APPLY TO WRITING

Writer's Craft: *Analyzing a Tall Tale*

Writers often create humor through the images they create. In the excerpt below from Carl Sandburg's "Paul Bunyan of the North Woods," notice the comic situation and the exaggeration used. Picture in your mind the scene described in this tall tale about Paul Bunyan, one of the American Northwest's legendary heroes of the lumber camps. Carefully read the excerpt, then write a paragraph that describes the scene. Explain how its humor is achieved. Include the correct form of at least five of the following words: *a/an; affect/effect; amount/number; good/well; its, it's.*

> Paul logged on the Little Gimlet in Oregon one winter. The cook stove at that camp covered an acre of ground. They fastened the side of a hog on each

snowshoe and four men used to skate on the griddle while the cook flipped the pancakes. The eating table was three miles long; elevators carried the cakes to the ends of the table where boys on bicycles rode back and forth on a path down the center of the table dropping the cakes where called for.

—*Carl Sandburg,* "Paul Bunyan of the North Woods"

learn, teach *Learn* means "to gain knowledge." *Teach* means "to instruct" or "to show how."

I will **learn** how to play the piano this year.

Will you **teach** me how to play the piano after our last class is over?

You can learn more about using the verbs learn *and* teach *on page L330.*

leave, let *Leave* means "to depart" or "to go away from." *Let* means "to allow" or "to permit."

NONSTANDARD	Will you **leave** me finish the dishes?
STANDARD	Will you **let** me finish the dishes?
STANDARD	I won't **leave** until you're through cleaning the kitchen.

You can learn more about using the verbs leave *and* let *on page L332.*

lie, lay *Lie* means "to rest or recline." *Lie* is never followed by a direct object. Its principal parts are *lie, lying, lay,* and *lain. Lay* means "to put or set (something) down." *Lay* is usually followed by a direct object. Its principal parts are *lay, laying, laid,* and *laid.*

LIE When I want to think quietly, I **lie** on the beach.
I wish I were **lying** there today.
Last week I **lay** near the pier.
I have **lain** there peacefully many times.

IDENTIFYING COMMON STUMBLING BLOCKS

Problem

- Using *lay* and *lie* correctly

Solution

- Have students ask themselves the following questions:

  What meaning do I intend? Is it "to be in a lying position," or is it "to put something down?"

  What is the time expressed by the verb and which principal part is required to express this time?

Also, warn students against two common misconceptions about *lay* and *lie.* Inanimate objects, not just people and animals, can be in a lying position. The other misconception is that because an inanimate object in a lying position must have been put there, one should use *lay,* the verb "to put." Regardless of its having once "been put down," the object *lies* (not *lays*) there.

LAY **Lay** the books on the desk.
(*Books* is the direct object.)

Are you **laying** the books on the corner of your desk at school?

When one student **laid** some books on the corner, they fell.

I have carefully **laid** my books in the middle of my desk.

You can learn more about using problem verbs on pages L328–L332.

passed, past *Passed* is the past tense of the verb *pass.* As a noun *past* means "a time gone by." As an adjective *past* means "just gone" or "elapsed." As a preposition *past* means "beyond."

The surveyors often **passed** this street.
(*passed* as a verb)

In the **past** our property was surveyed only when father decided to plant trees.
(*past* as a noun)

In the **past** two hours, they have walked **past** our house twice.
(*past* as an adjective and then as a preposition)

rise, raise *Rise* means "to move upward" or "to get up." *Rise* is never followed by a direct object. Its principal parts are *rise, rising, rose,* and *risen. Raise* means "to lift (something) up," "to increase," or "to grow something." *Raise* is usually followed by a direct object. Its principal parts are *raise, raising, raised,* and *raised.*

Mother always said that we should **rise** and shine in the morning.
I would always **raise** the sheet over my head.
(*Sheet* is the direct object.)

CONNECT TO SPEAKING AND WRITING

To avoid confusion between these two verbs and their principal parts, notice that all principal parts of *raise* retain the same *a* spelling as the base word: r**a**ise, r**a**ising, r**a**ised, and r**a**ised. For the word *rise,* neither the base word nor any of its principal parts contain the letter *a.*

shall, will Formal English uses *shall* with first person pronouns and *will* with second and third person pronouns. Today *shall* and *will* are used interchangeably with *I* and *we,* except that *shall* is used with *I* and *we* for questions.

> **Shall** we have lunch together?
> Yes, Elizabeth **will** join us also.
> I **will** be fifteen minutes late.

sit, set *Sit* means "to rest in an upright position." *Sit* is never followed by a direct object. Its principal parts are *sit, sitting, sat,* and *sat. Set* means "to put or place (something)." *Set* is usually followed by a direct object. Its principal parts are *set, setting, set,* and *set.*

> I'll **set** the time for the luncheon.
> (*Time* is the direct object.)
>
> Please **sit** down and relax while waiting for the team to arrive.
> (no direct object)

than, then *Than* is a subordinating conjunction and is used for comparisons. *Then* is an adverb and means "at that time" or "next."

NONSTANDARD	Did you meet the new quarterback who is taller **then** the coach?
STANDARD	After the coach acknowledged that Jim was taller **than** he was, the coach **then** introduced the other players.

IDENTIFYING COMMON STUMBLING BLOCKS

Problem

- Distinguishing between *than* and *then* in speech.

Solution

- Tell students to accentuate the *an* in *than* as they say the word. Have students practice saying these two words aloud and use them in the following sentences. Students should have partners listen and decide which word they are using.

  She is faster than he is.

  We went to the race, and then we sat down.

  Then the twenty-yard dash started.

  I am more grateful than she is that the race is over.

GETTING STUDENTS INVOLVED

Reciprocal Teaching

Tell students that although it is correct to use *that* or *who* to refer to people in their writing, careful writers should be more precise and use the word *who* when referring to people. Use the following examples. Students should form pairs and decide together which word sounds more precise.

- She is the person (that, who) read the most books. (who)
- The librarian was the one (that, who) held the contest. (who)
- That is the girl (that, who) gets the prize. (who)

that, which, who As relative pronouns, *that* refers to people, animals, or things; *which* refers to animals or things; and *who* refers to people.

> The books **that** I found in the attic were very old.
>
> The photo album, **which** was in the trunk, contained faded pictures.
>
> I thought it must have belonged to my aunt, **who** used to live with us.

PRACTICE YOUR SKILLS

Check Your Understanding

Finding the Correct Word

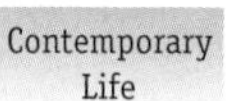

Contemporary Life

Write the word in parentheses that correctly completes each sentence.

1. Band is an elective course (that, which, who) offers a variety of musical instruction.
2. (Learning, Teaching) to play a musical instrument attracts many students to band classes.
3. Usually the band director (leaves, lets) students choose the musical instrument they want to play.
4. (Passed, Past) experience with an instrument can also affect the selection.
5. To (raise, rise) their level of performance, students often take private music lessons.
6. The key to a successful band program (lays, lies) in student and parent awareness of its benefits.
7. The responsibilities and dedication to band (shall, will) prepare students for many real-life experiences.
8. (Learning, Teaching) band requires extensive training in methods and techniques.

9. Most band directors (set, sit) high standards for the school programs.

10. They also (lay, lie) down certain rules about the care of instruments.

Connect to the Writing Process: Editing

Recognizing Correct Usage

Write each underlined word. If the word is used correctly, write *C* beside it. If the word is used incorrectly, write the correct form of the word.

Students learn [C] that band practice often requires more practice ~~then~~ [than] many sports. They sometimes ~~raise~~ [rise] early to attend rehearsals before school. Band performances, ~~who~~ [which] are played on various wind and percussion instruments, are popular events. When the band director raises [C] the baton, it then [C] signals the start of the program. Before a marching performance, band members ~~that~~ [who] have passed [C] inspection experience relief. Many parents experience pride when the school band marches ~~passed~~ [past] them in a parade. During a concert program, students must sit [C] attentively and watch for the band director's cues, which [C] set [C] the music's tempo. Performances at elementary schools ~~shall~~ [will] often help recruit future members. An active band program ~~lies~~ [lays] the foundation for success in the high school band. Lifelong appreciation of music lies [C] at the heart of the band program.

YOUR IDEAS

For Recognizing Correct Usage

IDENTIFYING COMMON STUMBLING BLOCKS

Problem

- Using *to* at the end of sentences

Solution

- Tell students that careful writers avoid using prepositions at the end of sentences. The word *to* when used as a preposition rather than an infinitive should never end a sentence. For example, students should never say or write "Where are you going to?" Instead, they should say or write "Where are you going?" Have students correct the following sentences.

  Which paragraph are we supposed to read to? (To which paragraph are we supposed to read?)

  Whom did you give the gift to? (To whom did you give the gift?)

Problem

- Saying *at* after *where* when making a statement or asking about location

Solution

- They should say "Where is my notebook?" rather than "Where is my notebook at?" Have students correct the following sentences for practice.

  Where does the trail start at? (Where does the trail start?)

  He asked where he was supposed to be at. (He asked where he was supposed to be.)

their, there, they're *Their* is a possessive pronoun. *There* is usually an adverb, but sometimes it begins an inverted sentence. *They're* is a contraction for *they are.*

Can we get **their** autographs?
There is usually time before the game.
They're in a hurry today because the bus was late.

theirs, there's *Theirs* is a possessive pronoun. *There's* is a contraction for *there is.*

Our breakfast is delicious; I wonder if **theirs** is also.
If **there's** time, I'll ask them before we leave.

them, those Never use *them* as a subject or a modifier.

NONSTANDARD	**Them** are the new neighbors. (subject)
STANDARD	**Those** are the new neighbors.
NONSTANDARD	Have you met **them** people? (adjective)
STANDARD	Have you met **those** people?

this here, that there Avoid using *here* or *there* in addition to *this* or *that.*

NONSTANDARD	I like **that there** frozen dessert.
STANDARD	I like **that** frozen dessert.

to, too, two *To* is a preposition. *To* also begins an infinitive. *Too* is an adverb that modifies a verb, an adjective, or another adverb. *Two* is a number.

Is Daniel going **to** the backyard **to** jump on the trampoline? (preposition, infinitive)

It's **too** late; only **two** can jump at one time. (adverb, number)

He can participate **too** when one person gets down. (adverb)

use to, used to Be sure to add the *d* to use.

NONSTANDARD	When I was younger, I **use to** jump rope.
STANDARD	When I was younger, I **used to** jump rope.

way, ways Do not substitute *ways* for *way* when referring to a distance.

NONSTANDARD	She drove a long **ways** to buy groceries.
STANDARD	She drove a long **way** to buy groceries.

where Do not substitute *where* for *that.*

NONSTANDARD	Did you read **where** school starts earlier?
STANDARD	Did you read **that** school starts earlier?

who, whom *Who,* a pronoun in the nominative case, is used as either a subject or a predicate nominative. *Whom,* a pronoun in the objective case, is used as a direct object, an indirect object, or an object of a preposition.

Who gave you the new bicycle?
(subject)

From **whom** did your sister buy it?
(object of a preposition)

whose, who's *Whose* is a possessive pronoun. *Who's* is a contraction for *who is.*

Whose party are you going to attend?
Who's going to take you home?

your, you're *Your* is a possessive pronoun. *You're* is a contraction for *you are.*

Your idea is the best.
We think **you're** going to win first place.

YOUR IDEAS
For Checking Understanding

PRACTICE YOUR SKILLS

Check Your Understanding
Finding the Correct Word

Contemporary Life

Write the word in parentheses that correctly completes each sentence.

1. When (your, you're) in eighth grade, you might go on a special class trip.
2. Parents and students (who, whom) express interest are invited (to, too, two) an informational meeting.
3. At (this, this here) meeting, a video usually describes the trip.
4. Most class trips are designed (to, too, two) provide students with insight into a subject (their, there, they're) currently studying.
5. The nation's capital is one of (them, those) popular and relevant sites.
6. (Theirs, There's) usually a need for parent chaperones for the trip (to, too, two).
7. (Theirs, There's) is an important job because they assist students (who, whom) are traveling without family.
8. Some students are not (use to, used to) being a long (way, ways) from home.
9. Teachers usually give at least one or (to, too, two) assignments that connect the class trip to studies.
10. (Your, You're) assignment might range from answering specific questions to keeping a journal.
11. (Whose, Who's) interested in touring our nation's Capitol building?
12. (Theirs, There's) an interesting story concerning the completion of the dome.

13. Is it true (where, that) the original wooden dome was considered to be (to, too, two) small for the structure?

14. Architect Thomas Walter provided a new design for (that, that there) dome in 1854.

15. In (your, you're) journals you might document when the Statue of Freedom was finally placed on top of the completed dome.

Connect to the Writing Process: Revising

Recognizing Correct Usage

Write each underlined word. If the word is used correctly, write *C* beside it. If the word is used incorrectly, write the correct form of the word.

Many students are looking forward to ~~they're~~ their trip to the nation's capital. Headphones, cassettes, books, and games make the bus ride there enjoyable too. ~~Whose~~ Who's going to room together and ~~who's~~ whose travel "buddy" you'll be is important. Those not from a large city will notice ~~where~~ that the traffic in Washington is bad. ~~Theirs~~ There's a variety of tours available. ~~Your~~ You're sure to enjoy a dinner cruise on the Potomac River. On the walking tour in the National Mall, your guide will point out famous landmarks. ~~Too~~ Two important sites that you should not miss are the Smithsonian Institute and the National Gallery of Art. There are also many statues in the Hall of Presidents in ~~that there~~ that Capitol building. Interesting facts will be revealed to you, for example from ~~who~~ whom the United States received the gift of cherry trees.

Communicate Your Ideas

APPLY TO WRITING

Explanatory Paragraph: *Correct Usage*

In the Lincoln Memorial, the words of the "Gettysburg Address" are inscribed on a tablet. Spoken by President Lincoln at the dedication ceremony on the battlefield of Gettysburg, the words were a tribute to those who had lost their lives in battle. Read the excerpt carefully, and then follow the instructions below.

> Four score and seven years ago our fathers brought forth on this continent, a new nation, conceived in Liberty, and dedicated to the proposition that all men are created equal. . . .
>
> We have come to dedicate a portion of that field, as a final resting place for those who here gave their lives. . . .
>
> –*Abraham Lincoln,* "Gettysburg Address"

Imagine you are doing peer tutoring for a student who has difficulty with the correct use of the words *to, that, who,* and *their.* Write a paragraph and explain why these four words, some of which appear more than once, are used correctly.

Mixed Practice

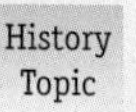

Write the word in parentheses that correctly completes each sentence.

1. Many history lessons await students (<u>who</u>, whom) visit Washington, D.C.

SELECTION AMENDMENT
Description of change: excerpted
Rationale: to focus on the grammar skill

2. The (amount, number) of information that (can, may) be learned is substantial.

3. Three of the most historic sites you (can, may) want to visit are located on the National Mall.

4. In 1848, workers (lay, laid) the cornerstone for Washington Monument, after the project (passed, past) government approval.

5. (Its, It's) in the shape of an obelisk, a design that (use to, used to) be prevalent in ancient Egypt.

6. From the top of (this, this here) monument, a view of the city (lays, lies) before you.

7. (Than, Then) you might visit the Jefferson Memorial, dedicated to the main author of the Declaration of Independence.

8. Built in the classic tradition, (its, it's) design is similar to that of Monticello, Jefferson's home.

9. A large statue of Jefferson and excerpts from his many writings are (in, into) the memorial.

10. (Nowhere, Nowheres) can you find a better view of the cherry trees in bloom.

11. Thirty-six is the (amount, number) of marble columns included in the memorial dedicated to Abraham Lincoln.

12. They represent the thirty-six states (already, all ready) in the Union when Lincoln was President.

13. The names of all the states (accept, except) Alaska and Hawaii are written above the columns.

14. (Them, Those) two names appear on a plaque located on the front steps of the memorial.

15. (Their, There, They're) are so many interesting buildings in Washington, don't feel (bad, badly) if you miss one.

Teaching Suggestions

Essential Knowledge and Skills

- Writing to inform such as to explain, describe, report, and narrate
- Capitalizing correctly to clarify and enhance meaning such as capitalizing titles
- Selecting and using reference materials and resources as needed for writing, revising, and editing final drafts
- Applying criteria to evaluate writing
- Organizing prior knowledge about a topic in a variety of ways such as by producing a graphic organizer
- Identify challenges faced by published authors and strategies they use to compose various types of text

BLOCK SCHEDULING

- If your schedule requires that you cover the chapter in a **shorter time,** use the instruction on capitalization and the Check Your Understanding and QuickCheck exercises.
- If you want to take advantage of **longer class time,** add these applications to writing: Connect to Speaking and Writing, Connect to the Writing Process, and Apply to Writing exercises.

Capital Letters

Directions

Read the passage and decide which underlined word should be capitalized. Write the letter of the correct answer.

EXAMPLE Mohandas Gandhi was an important indian national and spiritual leader. (1)

1 A Important
B Indian
C National
D Leader

ANSWER 1 B

Gandhi was born to a hindu family in the year (1) 1869. He was educated abroad and became a lawyer in south (2) Africa. on his return to India, he worked on campaigns for workers' rights (3). At the time, the country was controlled by the British government in a rule known as the "raj." (4) Gandhi joined the major political party, the Indian National congress. (5)

IDENTIFYING COMMON STUMBLING BLOCKS

Following is a list of the most common capitalization errors students make in their writing.

Problem
- Noncapitalization of proper nouns

Solution
- Instruction, pp. L500–L516
- Practice, pp. L501–L519

Problem
- Noncapitalization of proper adjectives

Solution
- Instruction, p. L520
- Practice, pp. L521–L522

1 A Born
B Hindu
C Family
D Year

2 A Educated
B Abroad
C Lawyer
D South

3 A On
B Campaigns
C Workers'
D Rights

4 A Country
B Government
C Rule
D "Raj"

5 A Political
B Party
C The
D Congress

A DIFFERENT DELIVERY SYSTEM

If you prefer, you can print the pretest from the BK English Test Bank located at http://www.bkenglish.com.

Using the Pretest

Assessing Prior Knowledge

The pretest will help you and your students assess where they stand in their basic understanding of capitalization. The test measures students' ability to identify capitalization errors in a paragraph.

Customizing the Test

Use these questions to add or replace items for alternate versions of the test.

With members of the Khilafat Movement, an alliance of muslims, Gandhi adopted a program of noncooperation (6) against the British. His crusade of civil disobedience led to the Salt march (7) of 1930. salt was taxed by the British, and its private manufacture (8) was illegal. Gandhi led his followers two hundred miles from his ashram, or temple, to the sea at dandi (9) to make salt.

6. A Alliance
B Muslims
C Program
D Non-cooperation

7. A Crusade
B Civil
C Disobedience
D March

8. A Salt
B Taxed
C Private
D Manufacture

9. A Miles
B Ashram
C Sea
D Dandi

ADDITIONAL RESOURCES

Language Skills Practice . . . . pages 136–145
Transparency Tools AW15
ESL Practice and Test Preparation . . . . . pages 127–129
Assessment: Chapter Test. . . . . pages 190–193

MAKING VISUAL CONNECTIONS

For Language Development

Have students study the photograph collage *Stephen Spender, Mas St. Jerome II.* After viewing and discussing the artwork, have students brainstorm a list of words to describe it. List students' responses on the board. Point out any proper nouns, proper adjectives, or other words that should be capitalized. Have students write a short paragraph describing the artwork. Students should use descriptive words from the board in their paragraphs. Have students share their paragraphs by reading them aloud.

To Stimulate Writing

Use the questions for art criticism as writing or discussion prompts.

Possible Answers:

Describe The features of the poet that stand out most in the portrait are his eyes, nose, mouth, and hat.

Analyze I think the artist created a collage rather than using a single portrait because he wanted to focus on different features of the subject's face.

Interpret A biography might focus on different aspects of a subject's life, also allowing you to see the subject from various angles.

Judge I would like to read some of the poet's poems to learn some of the thoughts behind the eyes portrayed in the collage.

David Hockney. *Stephen Spender, Mas St. Jerome II,* 1985. Photographic collage, 20½ inches by 20¼ inches. © David Hockney, 1990.

Describe What features of the subject stand out most in this portrait?

Analyze Why do you think the artist created this collage rather than shooting a single portrait?

Interpret This portrait allows you to see the subject from all angles. How could a biography do the same thing?

Judge Having seen this portrait of the poet Stephen Spender, would you like to learn more about him? Would you prefer to see more pictures of him, read some poems by him, or read a biography of him? Why?

At the end of this chapter, you will use the artwork to stimulate ideas for writing.

FOR DEVELOPING LANGUAGE SKILLS

LESSON 1 *(pages L497–L519)*

OBJECTIVE

- **To capitalize the first word in a sentence, the word *I*, proper nouns and their abbreviations, proper names**

Create Interest

Put the following words on the board: *may, china, turkey, pat, bill.* Ask students for brief, general definitions of each word and a sentence illustrating its use. Then write these words on the board: *May, China, Turkey, Pat, Bill.* Ask students what happens to the meaning of each word when it is

Rules of Capital Letters

Capital letters can be as important to writing as the words themselves. The correct use of capital letters makes what you write easy to follow and understand.

First Words

A capital letter clearly marks the beginning of a new idea—whether that idea is in a sentence, a line of poetry, a letter, or an outline.

Sentences and Poetry

A capital letter always tells readers that a new sentence or a new line of poetry has begun.

Capitalize the first word of a sentence and the first word of a line of poetry.

SENTENCE	**T**here are about twenty-five species of apples.
LINES OF POETRY	**O**f Jonathan Chapman **T**wo things are known, **T**hat he loved apples, **T**hat he walked alone. – *Stephen Vincent Benét,* "Johnny Appleseed"

Some modern poets purposely misuse capital letters or do not use any capitals at all in their poetry. When you quote such a poem, copy it exactly as the poet wrote it.

FOR INCREASING STUDENT ACHIEVEMENT

REACHING ALL STUDENTS

English Language Learners

Students who are learning English as a second language may have trouble knowing when to use capital letters. Have students share the kinds of words that are capitalized in their native languages. Discuss how these rules for capitalization are similar to or different from the rules for capitalization in English. Then have students keep a list of English words that should be capitalized in their journals. As the class discusses the kinds of words that should be capitalized, students should write these words and the rules for capitalization in their journals for future reference.

SELECTION AMENDMENT
Description of change: excerpted
Rationale: to focus on the grammar skill

capitalized. Have them use each capitalized word in a new sentence. Then students should name other words that change their meanings when they are capitalized. Encourage students to quickly flip through a dictionary for ideas.

Guide Instruction

By Connecting Ideas

Put the two sentences below on the board and point out that the second sentence is much more interesting than the first because specific proper nouns have been substituted for general common nouns. Remind students that using proper nouns correctly requires knowledge of the rules of capitalization.

- An area in the southeast region of the country was explored by a man long ago.
- Florida, in the southeast region of the United States, was explored by Juan Ponce de León in 1513.

USING STUDENTS' STRENGTHS

Multiple Intelligences: Interpersonal

Review with students the parts of a friendly letter and a business letter, including the heading, inside address (business only), salutation or greeting, body, closing, and signature. Highlight for students the places where capitalization generally occurs. Then have each student write a friendly or business letter to another student in the class.

Parts of Letters

Certain parts of a letter stand out because they begin with a capital letter.

Capitalize the first word in the greeting of a letter and the first word in the closing of a letter.

GREETINGS AND CLOSINGS	
Greeting	**D**ear Mr. Chapman,
Closing	**S**incerely yours,

Outlines

Capital letters make parts of an outline stand out.

Capitalize the first word of each item in an outline and the letters that begin major subsections of the outline.

I. **A**pple production in the U. S.

II. **H**ow apple trees and apples are used
  A. **F**oods and beverages prepared from apples
  B. **T**he uses of apple wood
    1. **U**ses in manufacturing
    2. **U**se for smoking meats
  C. **O**rnamental uses of trees

The Pronoun *I*

The pronoun *I* is always capitalized.

Capitalize the pronoun *I*, both alone and in contractions.

Consolidate Skills

Through Guided Practice

The **Check Your Understanding** exercises and the **QuickCheck** on page L519 will help students capitalize words correctly. Have students consider the types of words that should be capitalized, such as the names of places and the first word in a sentence. List students' examples on the board. Then guide students through the first item in each exercise. Have students complete the exercises independently.

Apply to Communication

Through Independent Writing

The **Communicate Your Ideas/Apply to Writing** activities on pages L500, L506, L512 and L518 prompt students to write a letter to a friend, a biographical questionnaire, a news story, and an analysis of author Eudora Welty's use of capitalization. Ask students how they will use capitalization in these various types of writing. How might incorrect capitalization in their

ALONE	Yesterday **I** bought a pound of apples.
CONTRACTION	Today **I**'m going to make a pie.

You can learn about using capital letters with direct quotations on page L597.

PRACTICE YOUR SKILLS

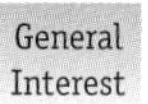

Check Your Understanding

***Capitalizing First Words and* I**

General Interest **Write the words and letters that should be capitalized.**

1. Red ~~red~~ sky at morning,
Sailors ~~sailors~~ take warning.
Red ~~red~~ sky at night,
Sailors ~~sailors~~ delight.

2. I. Weather ~~weather~~ lore
   a. Natural ~~natural~~ signs of weather changes
      1. Changes ~~changes~~ in animal behavior
      2. Environmental ~~environmental~~ changes
   b. Superstitions ~~superstitions~~ about the weather

3. Dear ~~dear~~ Anna,

My ~~my~~ uncle has been letting me help at the weather station, so I'm ~~i'm~~ having a wonderful time. When I come home, I'll ~~i'll~~ tell you all about it.

Your ~~your~~ friend,

Katy

A DIFFERENT APPROACH

Visual

Have students complete items one through three of **Practice Your Skills** by writing their responses in pencil. Students should then use a black marker to write each letter that should be capitalized. Tell students that focusing in this way on the capitalized letters will help them to remember capitalization rules.

writing affect their readers? Discuss students' responses.

Transfer to Everyday Life

Identifying Capitalization in a Travel Brochure or Magazine

Have students use travel brochures or travel magazines to identify ten examples of correct capitalization. Students should include various types of capital letters, such as the names of cities and countries, names of buildings and monuments, and first words in sentences. Have students share their lists with the class.

Pull It All Together

By Sharing

Have students share one of their writing samples from the **Communicate Your Ideas/Apply to Writing** activity with a partner. Students should work with their partner to check for correct capitalization in their writing.

HOME WORK

After completing **Connect to the Writing Process,** have students write a similar paragraph about a day when they did not have school. Students should check for correct capitalization in their sentences. Have students share some of their sentences on the board the following day. Discuss their use of capitalization.

TIMESAVER *QuickCheck*

Have students create a checklist of words that should be capitalized in their writing. Students should use the checklist to evaluate their letters.

Connect to the Writing Process: Editing

Correcting Errors in Capitalization

Rewrite the following paragraph, adding capital letters where needed.

~~there~~ There is no school today. I wonder what ~~i~~ I should do. ~~for~~ For several days ~~i've~~ I've been meaning to write to my grandparents. I think ~~i~~ I will do that. ~~sooner~~ Sooner or later, though, ~~i'll~~ I'll have to give the dog a bath. ~~there's~~ There's also that new magazine ~~i've~~ I've been wanting to read. ~~oh~~ Oh, well. ~~i~~ I think ~~i~~ I will just sit down for a while and rest until ~~i~~ I make up my mind.

Communicate Your Ideas

APPLY TO WRITING

Letter: ***Capital Letters for First Words and* I**

Find a short poem you like. Write a letter to a friend, telling him or her why the poem appeals to you. Quote some lines from the poem to get your point across. Be sure that you correctly capitalize the word *I*, the greeting and closing of your letter, the first word in each sentence, and the first word in each line of the poem.

Proper Nouns

A **proper noun** is the name of a particular person, place, thing, or idea. A proper noun begins with a capital letter.

Check Understanding

By Summarizing

Have students summarize the strategies they use to decide whether or not a word should be capitalized. Students should include at least three rules for capitalization in their summaries. Have students share their summaries with the class and write some of their rules for capitalization on the board.

COMMON AND PROPER NOUNS	
COMMON NOUNS	boy, park, cat
PROPER NOUNS	**D**aniel **L**opez, **B**ig **B**end **N**ational **P**ark, **S**moky

Capitalize proper nouns and their abbreviations.

Study the following rules for capitalizing proper nouns. Then refer to them when you edit your writing.

Names of persons and animals should be capitalized. Also capitalize the initials that stand for people's names.

NAMES OF PERSONS AND ANIMALS	
PERSONS	**K**ayla, **V. H. T**ang, **J**ames **R. R**icco, **J**r.
ANIMALS	**M**ax, **G**inger, **M**eatloaf, **M**iss **K**itty

You can learn more about nouns on pages L49–L55. You can learn about punctuating people's titles on page L540.

PRACTICE YOUR SKILLS

Check Your Understanding

Capitalizing the Names of Persons and Animals

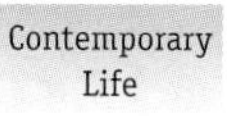
Contemporary Life

Write correctly each word that should be capitalized.

1. My real name is ~~hee sook park~~ Hee Sook Park, but my friends call me ~~suki.~~ Suki

2. I have a dog named ~~grumpy~~ Grumpy and a cat named ~~sneezy.~~ Sneezy

GETTING STUDENTS INVOLVED

Cooperative Learning

Have students work with partners to decide which words in the following list should be capitalized: *david, mr. edwards, st. augustine, president kennedy, dr. conley.* Students should be able to tell why they capitalized particular words.

USING TECHNOLOGY

Computers

After discussing the rules for capitalizing geographical names, have students search the Internet for capitalized names of places on maps. Students should search the Internet using words such as *Rand McNally* or *National Geographic.* Once students have located a map, they should print out the map and highlight at least five names of places that are correctly capitalized. Have students share their place names with the class.

3. My street was named after the explorer ~~ferdinand magellan~~. Ferdinand Magellan

4. My best friend's full name is ~~jacob joseph venturi~~. Jacob Joseph Venturi

5. He dreams of owning a horse called ~~silver blaze~~. Silver Blaze

6. I met my friend ~~rachel berg~~ at camp. Rachel Berg

7. She wants to sing like ~~judy garland~~, a well-known singer from long ago. Judy Garland

8. My friend ~~taylor johnson~~ lives next door. Taylor Johnson

9. Everybody calls her ~~t. j.~~ T. J.

10. My favorite author is ~~e. p.~~ clearwater. E. P.

Geographical names, which name particular places and bodies of waters, are capitalized. Do not capitalize prepositions, articles, or the conjunction *and* in geographical names or other proper nouns.

GEOGRAPHICAL NAMES	
STREETS, HIGHWAYS	**A**very **R**oad (**R**d.), **O**hio **T**urnpike (**T**pk.), **R**oute (**R**t.) 128, **F**ifty-sixth **S**treet (**S**t.) (The second part of a hyphenated numbered street is not capitalized.)
CITIES, STATES	**L**os **A**ngeles, **C**alifornia (**CA**) **P**lano, **T**exas (**TX**)
COUNTIES, PARISHES	**M**edina **C**ounty (**C**o.), **A**cadia **P**arish
COUNTRIES	**U**nited **S**tates of **A**merica (**U.S.A.**), **C**zech **R**epublic, **E**gypt, **B**razil
CONTINENTS	**N**orth **A**merica, **A**frica, **A**ntarctica

World Regions	**W**estern **H**emisphere, **P**acific **R**im, **N**orth **P**ole
Islands	**S**outh **P**adre **I**sland, **L**ong **I**sland
Mountains	**R**ocky **M**ountains, **M**ount (**M**t.) **H**ood
Forests and Parks	**S**uperior **N**ational **F**orest, **G**reat **B**asin **N**ational **P**ark
Bodies of Water	**M**ississippi **R**iver, **L**ake **O**ntario, **P**acific **O**cean, **G**ulf of **M**exico
Sections of the Country	the **S**outh, the **W**est **C**oast, **N**ew **E**ngland (Simple compass directions are not capitalized. *Go **s**outh on Main Street.*)

Words such as *street, lake, ocean,* and *mountain* are capitalized only when they are part of a proper noun.

> We live near some **m**ountains, but they are small compared to the **R**ocky **M**ountains.

Connect to Speaking and Writing

In geography class you might say a sentence like this:

> The isthmus of Panama lies between the **A**tlantic **O**cean and the **P**acific **O**cean.

You can shorten the sentence by changing it to the following:

> The isthmus of Panama lies between the **A**tlantic and the **P**acific oceans.

Notice that in the second sentence the word *oceans* is not capitalized because it is no longer a part of a proper name. You're saying that the isthmus lies between the two oceans known as the Atlantic and the Pacific.

GETTING STUDENTS INVOLVED

Cooperative Learning

Have teams of students play a geography game, using the names of cities, states, countries, mountains, bodies of water and so forth. The first player names a geographical location and feature and tells which letters are capitalized; the second player must then use the last letter of the word used by the first player as the first letter of his or her word. This player must also indicate which word or words are capitalized. If the second player cannot perform these two tasks, he or she is out. The team that has the most players left at the end of the game wins.

A DIFFERENT APPROACH

Visual

After students have completed items one through ten of **Check Your Understanding,** provide them with maps and globes. Have students locate these geographical places listed in the activity: *Denver, Niagara Falls, Indian Ocean, U.S.A., Lake Michigan.* Students should use their fingers to point to the places as they are identified.

HOME WORK

Have students write sentences using at least fifteen geographical names. Students should provide some factual information in the sentences about the geographical places. Remind students to check their writing for correct capitalization.

PRACTICE YOUR SKILLS

Check Your Understanding

Using Capital Letters in Geographical Names

Write *a* or *b* to indicate which item is correctly capitalized.

1. **a.** a park in Denver
   b. a Park in Denver
2. **a.** Moosehead lake
   b. Moosehead Lake
3. **a.** niagara falls
   b. Niagara Falls
4. **a.** Indian ocean
   b. Indian Ocean
5. **a.** the Frozen North
   b. the frozen North
6. **a.** a store on Forty-fifth Street
   b. a store on Forty-Fifth street
7. **a.** made in the u.s.a.
   b. made in the U.S.A.
8. **a.** a port on lake Michigan
   b. a port on Lake Michigan
9. **a.** 1411 north Chestnut Drive
   b. 1411 North Chestnut Drive
10. **a.** shelter island
    b. Shelter Island

Check Your Understanding

Capitalizing Proper Nouns and Their Abbreviations

History Topic **Write correctly each word that should be capitalized.**

11. In ~~in~~ 1812, Robert Stuart ~~robert stuart~~ led settlers across the ~~continental divide.~~ Continental Divide

12. ~~this~~ This group may have crossed near ~~south pass~~ South Pass, today known as an important gateway to the ~~west~~ West.

13. ~~a~~ A trapper's meeting place was established on the ~~green river~~ Green River.

14. ~~john coulter~~ John Coulter explored the area of ~~wyoming~~ Wyoming that later became ~~yellowstone national park~~ Yellowstone National Park.

15. ~~esther hobart morris~~ Esther Hobart Morris of ~~tioga county~~ Tioga County, in ~~new york~~ New York, was another early settler in ~~wyoming~~ Wyoming.

Connect to the Writing Process: Drafting

Writing Sentences with Proper Nouns and Abbreviations

Write an answer to each question. Respond in complete sentences and include details to make your answers as specific as possible. [Answers may vary. Possible answers are given.]

16. Who are the principal and vice principal of your school? Ms. Carlotta Louis and Mr. Dan Blake

17. On what street and in what city is your school located? Greene Boulevard in Los Angeles

18. What is your address? 25 Locust Street

19. What are the names of some pets that live in your neighborhood? Kelly, Lucky, Button

20. What park or parks in the United States have you visited? Glacier National Park, Twin Creeks Park

21. What place in your community was named after a person? Whom was it named after? Our school was named after President Thomas Jefferson

22. In what region of the country do you live? the Northeast

23. What is the largest mountain or mountain range in your region? Mt. Washington

24. What body of water do you live near? Lake Erie

25. What countries are neighbors of the United States? Canada and Mexico

USING STUDENTS' STRENGTHS

Multiple Intelligences: Spatial

Have students work together to create a large map that includes at least thirty geographical names. Their map can depict a real or an imaginary place. Students should construct their map on large mural paper using paints, colorful markers, and crayons. Remind students to capitalize the proper names of places on their map. Display the completed map in the classroom or hallway.

TIMESAVER *QuickCheck*

Have students self-evaluate their questionnaires before distributing them to classmates. Students should check for correct capitalization of proper names and geographical places. Students should also make sure they have capitalized the word *I* and the first word of each sentence.

HOME STUDY

Have students locate a product questionnaire or a political questionnaire that they or a family member might have received in the mail. Students should evaluate the questionnaire for its use of capitalization. Students should correct any capitalization errors. Have students share their questionnaires with the class. Discuss some of the correct and incorrect uses of capitalization in the questionnaires.

Connect to the Writing Process: Editing

Correcting Proper Nouns and Their Abbreviations

Rewrite the following paragraph, adding capital letters where needed.

The third-largest country in the world is ~~china~~ China. On the east, it is bounded by the ~~yellow sea~~ Yellow Sea, the ~~east china sea~~ East China Sea, and the ~~west china sea~~ West China Sea. All three are part of the ~~pacific ocean~~ Pacific Ocean. Also to ~~china's~~ China's east lie ~~japan~~ Japan, ~~korea~~ Korea, and the ~~philippine islands~~ Philippine Islands. The ~~himalaya mountains~~ Himalaya Mountains form a boundary between the ~~qing zang plateau~~ Qing Zang Plateau and the countries of ~~nepal~~ Nepal, ~~india~~ India, and ~~bangladesh~~ Bangladesh. The highest mountain in the ~~himalayas, mt. everest~~ Himalayas, Mt. Everest, is actually on the ~~nepal-tibet~~ Nepal-Tibet side of the border.

Communicate Your Ideas

APPLY TO WRITING

Questionnaire: ***Proper Nouns and Their Abbreviations***

Create a biographical questionnaire for your classmates to fill out. Ask questions about the people and places in their lives. Ask, for example, where they were born, where they live now, and whether they have pets. Exchange questionnaires with another student and write responses to the one you receive.

Nouns of historical importance should be capitalized. Capitalize the names of historical events, periods, and documents.

HISTORIC NAMES	
Events	the **F**rench **R**evolution, the **B**attle of **H**astings, **W**orld **W**ar II (**WWII**)
Periods of Time	the **V**ictorian **E**ra, the **S**pace **A**ge, the **D**ark **A**ges
Documents	the **D**eclaration of **I**ndependence, the **A**rticles of **C**onfederation, the **M**ayflower **C**ompact

Do not capitalize prepositions such as *of* in the names of events and documents.

Names of groups and businesses begin with capital letters. These include the names of organizations, businesses, institutions, teams, and government bodies and agencies.

NAMES OF GROUPS	
Organizations	**L**ittle **L**eague, the **N**ational **O**rganization for **W**omen (**NOW**), **A**merican **M**edical **A**ssociation (**AMA**)
Businesses	**C**asper's **M**arket, **F. R**osenberg & **C**ompany (**C**o.), the **W**estward **C**orporation (**C**orp.)
Institutions	**G**lover **M**emorial **H**ospital, **W**ayne **M**iddle **S**chool, the **U**niversity of **C**alifornia at **L**os **A**ngeles (**UCLA**)
Teams	the **D**allas **C**owboys, the **B**ayside **T**igers, the **M**innesota **T**wins
Government Bodies and Agencies	the **S**enate, **C**ongress, the **F**ederal **T**rade **C**ommission (**FTC**)
Political Parties	**D**emocratic **P**arty, a **R**epublican, a **D**emocrat

REACHING ALL STUDENTS

Struggling Learners

To reinforce the capitalization rules for historic names and names of groups, have students write sentences using at least ten of the capitalized words from the two charts on this page. Remind students to also capitalize the word *I* and the first word in each sentence. Have students share one of their sentences by writing it on the board. Discuss students' examples and reasons for capitalizing certain words.

A DIFFERENT APPROACH

Kinesthetic

Before students complete **Practice Your Skills** independently, work through the first three sentences together. As you read each word in the sentences aloud, students should use a "thumbs up" to identify words that should be capitalized and a "thumbs down" for words that should not be capitalized. Students should hold their thumbs up or down to respond as you read each word aloud.

HOME WORK

Have students write ten sentences that contain capitalization errors that can be corrected the following day by a classmate. Have students exchange papers the next day and correct each capitalization error they find.

PRACTICE YOUR SKILLS

Check Your Understanding

Using Capital Letters for Proper Names

General Interest **Write correctly each word that should be capitalized. If a sentence is correct, write *C*.**

1. The two houses of ~~congress~~ Congress are the ~~senate~~ Senate and the ~~house of representatives~~. House of Representatives
2. Many ~~cornell university~~ Cornell University graduates have served in the ~~peace corps~~. Peace Corps
3. The ~~smithsonian institution~~ Smithsonian Institution is our nation's most famous museum.
4. The ~~boston tea party~~ Boston Tea Party was one of the acts of rebellion that led to the ~~american revolution~~. American Revolution
5. The ~~dallas cowboys~~ Dallas Cowboys defeated the ~~buffalo bills~~ Buffalo Bills by a score of 14–0.
6. The prosperous 1920s were known as the ~~roaring twenties~~. Roaring Twenties
7. The ~~bill of rights~~ Bill of Rights is the name given to the first ten amendments of the ~~u. s. constitution~~. U. S. Constitution
8. The names of ~~britain's~~ Britain's two main political parties are the ~~conservative party~~ Conservative Party and the ~~labour party~~. Labour Party
9. Many stores in shopping malls are part of national chains. C
10. A fire at the ~~triangle shirtwaist factory~~ Triangle Shirtwaist Factory in 1911 created support for the ~~international ladies' garment workers union~~. International Ladies' Garment Workers Union

Specific time periods and events begin with capital letters. Capitalize the days of the week, the months of the year, civil and religious holidays, and special events. Also capitalize the abbreviations used in giving dates and the time of day.

TIME PERIODS AND EVENTS	
DAYS, MONTHS	**M**onday (**M**on.), **T**uesday (**T**ues.), **F**ebruary (**F**eb.), **M**arch (**M**ar.)
HOLIDAYS	**M**artin **L**uther **K**ing **D**ay, **P**residents' **D**ay, the **F**ourth of **J**uly
SPECIAL EVENTS	the **N**ew **Y**ork **M**arathon, the **F**estival of **R**oses
TIME ABBREVIATIONS	**A.D.** 466, 100 **B.C.**, 6:30 **A.M.**, 9:00 **P.M.**

Do not capitalize the seasons of the year unless they are part of a specific name.

> Each **s**ummer the library runs a special reading program.
> Here is a flyer about the library's **S**ummer **F**estival of **B**ooks.

You can learn more about punctuating abbreviations on pages L539–L541.

PRACTICE YOUR SKILLS

Check Your Understanding

Using Capital Letters for Specific Time Periods and Events

Write *a* or *b* to indicate which item is correctly capitalized.

1. **a.** an Independence Day celebration
b. an Independence Day Celebration

2. **a.** the last Saturday in August
b. the last saturday in August

3. **a.** the New York world's fair of 1939
b. the New York World's Fair of 1939

IDENTIFYING COMMON STUMBLING BLOCKS

Problem

- Capitalizing the seasons of the year

Solution

- Tell students that the seasons of the year should not be capitalized, unless they are the first word in a sentence or part of a proper name or title.
- Have students decide whether or not *spring, summer, winter, fall,* and *autumn* should be capitalized in these examples. Students should be able to explain their choices.

I wish it were summer. (summer)

autumn is my mom's favorite time of year. (Autumn)

Lindsay will attend college this fall. (fall)

That book is titled *The winter of Our Discontent.* (Winter)

The spring carnival is always fun. (spring)

A DIFFERENT APPROACH

Auditory

Have students work in small groups to complete items eleven through twenty in **Check Your Understanding.** Students should take turns reading each item aloud and responding with the correct answer. Group members should decide whether or not each response is correct and tell why or why not. When all groups are finished, discuss some of their responses.

4. **a.** a mother's day surprise
b. a Mother's Day surprise

5. **a.** a 9:00 a.m. class
b. a 9:00 A.M. class

6. **a.** the Rose Bowl parade
b. the Rose bowl Parade

7. **a.** in approximately 200 B.C.
b. in approximately 200 b.c.

8. **a.** february 14, Valentine's day
b. February 14, Valentine's Day

9. **a.** the beginning of National Book Week
b. the beginning of National Book week

10. **a.** at 4:30 P.M. next Friday
b. at 4:30 p.m. next Friday

Check Your Understanding

Capitalizing Proper Names

General Interest **Write correctly each word that should be capitalized.**

11. A very ancient law code, the code of hammurabi, was created before 1750 b.c. (Code of Hammurabi; B.C.)

12. The gilded age was a period of gross materialism in the 1870s. (Gilded Age)

13. We celebrate labor day on the first monday in september. (Labor Day; Monday; September)

14. Until 1953, armistice day was celebrated in november to commemorate the end of world war I. (Armistice Day; November; World War I)

15. In june, the red earth pow wow is held in oklahoma city. (June; Red Earth Pow Wow; Oklahoma City)

16. The u.s. marine corps band played in a concert on presidents' day. (U.S. Marine Corps Band; Presidents' Day)

17. Our town holds its may day celebration every spring. (May Day)

18. The ~~emoryville environment club~~ Emoryville Environment Club sent for information from the ~~u.s. department of forestry~~ U.S. Department of Forestry.

19. The delicatessen on ~~vine street~~ Vine Street is very busy just before each baseball game.

20. The ~~redwing bicycle company~~ Redwing Bicycle Company sponsored a team called the ~~rockets~~ Rockets in last summer's little league games.

Connect to the Writing Process: Drafting

Writing Sentences with Proper Nouns

[Answers may vary. Possible responses are given.]

Answer the following questions, using complete sentences.

21. At what time do you go to bed at night?
I go to bed at 11:00 P.M.

22. What school did you attend in the first grade?
I attended Public School No. 16.

23. Where does your family shop for groceries?
We shop for groceries at Safeway.

24. What sports team or teams do you enjoy watching?
I enjoy watching the Yankees.

25. Which holiday is your favorite? When is it celebrated?
My favorite holiday is Christmas, on December 25.

Connect to the Writing Process: Editing

Correcting Sentences with Proper Nouns

Rewrite the following paragraph, adding capital letters where needed.

The ~~american civil war~~ American Civil War came to a weary end in the spring of 1865. By ~~march~~ March the ~~confederates~~ Confederates were outnumbered 2–1 by the ~~union~~ Union troops. Then, on ~~april~~ April 1, General ~~sheridan's~~ Sheridan's victory in the ~~battle of five forks~~ Battle of Five Forks spurred ~~ulysses s. grant~~ Ulysses S. Grant to conquer ~~petersburg~~ Petersburg and ~~richmond~~ Richmond. The ~~army of the potomac~~ Army of the Potomac closed in on

DEVELOPING WORKPLACE COMPETENCIES

Basic Skills: Writing

Point out to students that the noncapitalization of proper nouns is one of the most common and serious errors found in writing in the workplace. Ask students why it might be especially important in this environment to take special care in making sure that proper nouns are capitalized. Students should note that proper nouns indicate important things, such as a person's name as well as his or her title or rank.

TIMESAVER *QuickCheck*

Give students these strategies with which to edit their news stories

- Make sure to capitalize the first letter of each sentence.
- Check to be sure you have appropriately capitalized proper nouns.
- Double check the capitalization of historical events, businesses, and government organizations.

the ~~confederates~~ Confederates. They were starving because the ~~confederate commissary department~~ Confederate Commissary Department could not get supplies through the ~~union~~ Union lines. At 5:00 ~~p.m~~ P.M. on ~~april~~ April 7, ~~grant~~ Grant sent ~~robert e. lee~~ Robert E. Lee a note. The note asked him to surrender. On ~~april~~ April 9, ~~lee~~ Lee and ~~grant~~ Grant met and agreed upon the terms of surrender shortly before 4:00 ~~p.m.~~ P.M.

Communicate Your Ideas

APPLY TO WRITING

News Story: ***Proper Nouns***

Imagine that you were present at a big annual parade in your community commemorating local historical events. Write a news story for your local paper about the event. Include the following information.

- the name of the parade and when it took place
- what historical events were represented by the parade participants
- what organizations participated in the parade
- what businesses and government agencies sponsored or created floats for the parade

After you have finished, check to make sure you used capital letters correctly.

Names of nationalities and races should be capitalized.

NATIONALITIES AND RACES	
NATIONALITIES	a **N**igerian, a **S**eminole, a **C**anadian
RACES	**C**aucasian, **H**ispanic

Religions, religious references, and religious holidays and holy days begin with capital letters.

RELIGIOUS NAMES	
RELIGIONS	**C**atholicism, **B**uddhism, **J**udaism, **I**slam
RELIGIOUS HOLIDAYS AND HOLY DAYS	**H**anukkah, **C**hristmas, **R**amadan, **E**piphany, **Y**om **K**ippur, **P**alm **S**unday, **S**t. **M**ichael's **D**ay
RELIGIOUS REFERENCES	**G**od, the **A**lmighty, the **O**ld **T**estament, the **T**almud, the **K**oran, the **V**edas

The word *god* is not capitalized when it refers to polytheistic gods. Their proper names, however, are capitalized.

> The Greek **g**od who gave fire to mortals was **P**rometheus.

USING STUDENTS' STRENGTHS

Multiple Intelligences: Linguistic

After discussing the capitalization rules for names of nationalities and races, have students look for additional examples in their geography or social studies textbooks. Students should write at least ten example sentences in which nationalities or races are correctly capitalized. Have students share their examples with the class by writing a few correctly capitalized names on the board. Point out any instances in which students actually used correctly capitalized proper adjectives, such as *Chinese writer.* Tell students that they will learn about capitalizing proper adjectives later in Chapter 15.

A DIFFERENT APPROACH

Visual

Before having students complete **Practice Your Skills** independently, allow time for them to share religious terms, holidays, or names with which they are familiar. Have students write some of these words on the board. Students should decide whether or not the words should be capitalized.

HOME WORK

Have students identify correctly capitalized religious terms in the faith or religion section of the newspaper. Students should cut out an article and highlight each correctly capitalized religious name, holiday, or term in the article.

PRACTICE YOUR SKILLS

Check Your Understanding

Using Capital Letters Correctly

General Interest **Write correctly each word that should be capitalized.**

1. On ~~ash wednesday~~, ~~christians~~ begin the period called ~~lent.~~
   Ash Wednesday Christians Lent
2. They prepare for ~~easter.~~
   Easter
3. On the day called ~~qing ming~~, the ~~chinese~~ visit cemeteries.
   Qing Ming Chinese
4. Some ~~buddhists~~ make pilgrimages to honor the ~~buddha~~ during ~~magha puja.~~
   Buddhists Buddha Magha Puja
5. In the city of ~~caracas~~, the children of ~~venezuela~~ roller-skate to the daily "~~christmas carol mass~~" between ~~december~~ 16 and 24.
   Caracas Venezuela Christmas Carol Mass December
6. On the ~~jewish~~ holiday ~~purim,~~ a family member reads aloud the ~~*book of esther.*~~
   Jewish Purim *Book of Esther*
7. The ~~muslims~~ celebrate ~~awwal muharram.~~
   Muslims Awwal Muharram
8. This is the day that the religion of ~~islam~~ began.
   Islam

Names of planets, moons, stars, and constellations are capitalized. Do not capitalize the words *sun* and *moon*.

ASTRONOMICAL NAMES	
PLANETS AND MOONS	**M**ercury, **U**ranus, **N**eptune, **G**anymede
STARS	the **N**orth **S**tar, **S**irus, **C**anopus
CONSTELLATIONS	**B**ig **D**ipper, **O**rion, **U**rsa **M**ajor

Do not capitalize *earth* if *the* comes before it.

CAPITAL	Is Venus larger or smaller than **E**arth?
NO CAPITAL	Six billion people live on *the* earth.

Languages and specific school courses followed by a number are capitalized.

LANGUAGES AND SCHOOL COURSES	
LANGUAGES	**E**nglish, **T**urkish, **R**ussian, **S**panish, **F**rench
COMPUTER LANGUAGES	**J**ava, **C**obal, **V**isual **B**asic
NUMBERED COURSES	**A**rt II, **A**lgebra I, **B**iology II

Course names such as *history, math, science,* and *physical education* are not capitalized.

Other proper nouns should also begin with capital letters.

OTHER PROPER NOUNS	
AWARDS	**N**obel **P**eace **P**rize, **W**orld **C**up, **G**rammy **A**ward
BRAND NAMES	**U**ltrasheen shampoo, **S**unrise orange juice, **R**oadrunner vans (The product itself—such as *shampoo, orange juice,* and *vans*—is not capitalized.)
BRIDGES, BUILDINGS	**B**rooklyn **B**ridge, **E**mpire **S**tate **B**uilding, **W**orld **T**rade **C**enter, **W**indsor **C**astle
MONUMENTS, MEMORIALS	**G**ateway **A**rch, **P**earl **H**arbor **M**emorial, **W**ashington **M**onument

REACHING ALL STUDENTS

Advanced Learners

After discussing the capitalization of brand names, have students research magazine advertisements and television commercials to find examples of product names and brand names that are not capitalized. Students should provide an example of such an ad or product label and explain why they think the name was not capitalized. Have students present their findings to the class.

HOME WORK

Kinesthetic

Ask students to peruse the science section of the newspaper or a science magazine like *Nature*. Have students choose an article and edit it for proper capitalization.

TECHNOLOGICAL TERMS	the **I**nternet, the **W**eb, **W**orld **W**ide **W**eb, **W**eb page, **E**-mail
VEHICLES	the ***Q**ueen **M**ary, **A**pollo **V**, **A**ir **F**orce **O**ne* (Also italicize, or underline, the names of vehicles.)

PRACTICE YOUR SKILLS

Check Your Understanding

Capitalizing Proper Nouns

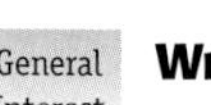

General Interest

Write *a* or *b* to indicate the sentence in each pair that is correctly written.

1. a. In our Astronomy class, we will take a field trip to the yerkes observatory.
b. In our astronomy class, we will take a field trip to the Yerkes Observatory.

2. a. One of the *apollo* spacecraft carried the first astronauts to walk on the Moon.
b. One of the *Apollo* spacecraft carried the first astronauts to walk on the moon.

3. a. I could see the planet Venus through my new Star Gazer telescope.
b. I could see the Planet Venus through my new Star Gazer Telescope.

4. a. The *Voyager* spacecraft was the first to photograph Jupiter's moon Europa.
b. The *Voyager* Spacecraft was the first to photograph Jupiter's Moon Europa.

5. a. In science class we learned about physicists who had won the Nobel Prize.
b. In Science Class we learned about physicists who had won the nobel prize.

Check Your Understanding
Using Capital Letters

Write the following items, using capital letters where needed.

6. the classroom for ~~geometry 1~~ Geometry I

7. the planet ~~neptune~~ Neptune

8. the ~~golden gate bridge~~ Golden Gate Bridge

9. the flight of the ~~*spirit of st. louis*~~ *Spirit of St. Louis*

10. the ~~pulitzer prize~~ Pulitzer Prize

Connect to the Writing Process: Editing
Using Capital Letters Correctly

Rewrite the following sentences, adding capital letters where needed.

11. On ~~october~~ October 1, 1847, ~~maria mitchell~~ Maria Mitchell discovered the comet ~~mitchell~~ Mitchell 1847VI.

12. From the roof of the ~~pacific bank~~ Pacific Bank, she observed the new comet.

13. It was just north of the ~~north star.~~ North Star

14. In 1858, her friends gave her an ~~alvan clark~~ Alvan Clark telescope.

15. In 1859, she was awarded the ~~medal of merit~~ Medal of Merit.

16. ~~mitchell~~ Mitchell wrote reports on ~~jupiter~~ Jupiter and ~~saturn~~ Saturn and their satellites.

17. She became the first woman director of the ~~vassar college observatory.~~ Vassar College Observatory

18. ~~mitchell's~~ Mitchell's name is often mentioned in ~~astronomy~~ Astronomy 101.

19. The ~~maria mitchell observatory~~ Maria Mitchell Observatory on ~~nantucket island~~ Nantucket Island was founded in her memory.

20. Does the observatory have a web page on the ~~world wide web~~? World Wide Web

YOUR IDEAS

For Using Capital Letters Correctly

TIMESAVER *QuickCheck*

Evaluate students' writing by checking for accurate comprehension of the literature model and for complete responses to the three analysis questions. Students should realize in their analyses that Welty capitalized the words *Little Store* for emphasis, to bestow importance, and because, as a child, it seemed the proper name of the place she often visited.

SELECTION AMENDMENT
Description of change: excerpted
Rationale: to focus on the grammar skill

Communicate Your Ideas

APPLY TO WRITING

Writer's Craft: *Analyzing the Use of Capital Letters*

Writers sometimes use capital letters to give a private nickname to a person, place, or thing. They do this to show its importance to them or their characters. Read this excerpt by Eudora Welty and then answer the questions that follow. [Answers may vary. Possible responses are given.]

> My mother considered herself pretty well prepared in her kitchen and pantry for any emergency that, in her words, might choose to present itself. But if she should, all of a sudden, need another lemon or find she was out of bread, all she had to do was call out, "Quick! Who'd like to run to the Little Store for me?"
>
> I would.
>
> She'd count out the change into my hand, and I was away. I'll bet the nickel that would be left over that all over the country, for those of my day, the neighborhood grocery played a similar part in our growing up.
>
> Our store had its name—it was that of the grocer who owned it, whom I'll call Mr. Sessions—but "the Little Store" was what we called it at home.
>
> *–Eudora Welty,* "The Little Store"

- If you heard someone say "the Little Store," would you consider the phrase a proper noun? Why or why not? I probably would not consider the phrase a proper noun because it sounds so common—not like a formal name.
- Why does Welty treat the name "the Little Store" as if it were a proper noun? She has chosen to treat the name as if it were a proper noun because she is describing a family custom.
- Why do you think a writer might use capital letters and refer to a character as "the Pest" or "the Brain"? Capitalizing the nickname of a character can emphasize that character's personality and actions.

Mixed Practice

General Interest

Write each word that should begin with a capital letter. Then answer as many of the questions as you can.

Thomas Jefferson **1.** ~~who~~ Who wrote the ~~declaration of independence~~ Declaration of Independence?

a hockey Team **2.** ~~who~~ Who wins the ~~stanley cup~~ Stanley Cup, a football team or a hockey team?

Charles Lindbergh **3.** ~~who~~ Who was the first person to fly solo across the ~~atlantic ocean~~? Atlantic Ocean

President Abraham Lincoln **4.** ~~who~~ Who was in the ~~white house~~ White House when the ~~emancipation proclamation~~ Emancipation Proclamation was issued in 1863?

Martin Luther King, Jr. **5.** ~~who~~ Who won the ~~nobel peace prize~~ Nobel Peace Prize in 1964, ~~martin luther king, jr.~~ Martin Luther King, Jr., or ~~john f. kennedy~~? John F. Kennedy

John Glenn **6.** ~~who~~ Who was the first ~~american~~ American to orbit the earth, ~~john glenn~~ John Glenn or ~~alan shepard~~? Alan Shepard

Boston **7.** ~~who~~ Who won the first ~~world series~~ World Series, ~~new york~~ New York or ~~boston~~? Boston

the U.S.S.R. **8.** ~~which~~ Which country launched ~~sputnik~~ Sputnik I, the world's first artificial satellite?

Janus **9.** ~~who~~ Who was the two-faced mythical god that the month of ~~january~~ January was named after?

Joseph Stalin **10.** ~~who~~ Who led the ~~soviet union~~ Soviet Union during ~~world war~~ World War II, ~~joseph stalin~~ Joseph Stalin or ~~karl marx~~? Karl Marx

the Incas **11.** ~~who~~ Who once ruled ~~peru~~ Peru, the ~~aztecs~~ Aztecs or the ~~incas~~ Incas?

Kristi Yamaguchi **12.** ~~who~~ Who won a gold medal in figure skating in the 1992 ~~winter olympics~~ Winter Olympics in ~~albertville, france~~? Albertville, France

Florence Nightingale **13.** ~~who~~ Who accomplished important health reforms during the ~~crimean war~~? Crimean War

British Prime Minister Tony Blair **14.** ~~who~~ Who lives at 10 ~~downing street~~ Downing Street in ~~london~~ London?

Jonah **15.** ~~who~~ Who in the ~~bible~~ Bible was swallowed by a whale?

USING STUDENTS' STRENGTHS

Multiple Intelligences: Linguistic

Have students develop their own list of trivia questions by using an almanac, encyclopedia, or another resource book. Have them model their questions after the ones in the **QuickCheck.** Compile the questions and give students the chance to answer them, correctly capitalizing both the questions and the answers for extra credit.

EXPANDING THE LESSON

Using Technology

You will find additional **instructional** and **practice** materials for this chapter at http://www.bkenglish.com.

LESSON 2 *(pages L520–L527)*

OBJECTIVE

- **To capitalize proper adjectives, titles used with the names of persons, titles of written works, and titles of works of art**

Create Interest

Have students explain how they would properly capitalize the titles of written works and works of art. Have students come to the board two at a time and write the titles of their favorite film, television program, book, or work of art. Discuss students' uses of capital letters and point out any capitalization errors that should be corrected. Tell students that they will learn to properly capitalize these items in Lesson 2.

Guide Instruction

By Modeling Strategies

Using students' titles from the previous activity, demonstrate how to correct

GETTING STUDENTS INVOLVED

Collaborative Learning

Have students look through cookbooks to find recipes with proper nouns and adjectives that may or may not be capitalized. Students should write out a recipe that includes at least one proper noun or proper adjective. Students should bring their recipe to class and share them with other students. Students should then work together to come up with a menu for a new restaurant which includes the dishes for which students brought in recipes.

Other Uses of Capital Letters

There are other uses for capital letters in addition to the ones you have already learned about. Some proper adjectives are capitalized. The titles of certain people and works of art are also capitalized.

Proper Adjectives

Like proper nouns, most proper adjectives begin with a capital letter.

Capitalize most proper adjectives.

PROPER NOUNS AND ADJECTIVES

PROPER NOUNS	PROPER ADJECTIVES
Asia	**A**sian art
Canada	**C**anadian provinces
Rome	**R**oman baths
Copernicus	**C**opernican theory
South **A**merica	**S**outh **A**merican rivers
Florida	**F**lorida oranges

CONNECT TO SPEAKING AND WRITING

A cookbook may refer to both *French food* and *french fries.* Some words or phrases from proper nouns become so common that they are written entirely in lowercase letters. Some examples are *brussels sprouts, dutch oven, india ink, manila envelope, plaster of paris,* and *venetian blinds.* When you use words like these, check a dictionary to see whether you should use a capital letter or not.

the capitalization errors in the list of films, programs, books, and artworks on the board. Tell students that titles are often tricky to capitalize. Point out that the first and last words in titles are always capitalized, as are any nouns, pronouns, verbs, adjectives, adverbs, long prepositions, and subordinating conjunctions. Articles, coordinating conjunctions, and the *to* in infinitives are always lowercase. Demonstrate by using students' titles.

Consolidate Skills

Through Guided Practice

The **Check Your Understanding** exercises and the **QuickCheck** will help students capitalize proper adjectives and titles of works correctly. After discussing the student instruction before each activity and after completing several examples together, guide students through the first item in each exercise. Then have students complete the exercises independently.

PRACTICE YOUR SKILLS

Check Your Understanding PRACTICE YOUR SKILLS

Capitalizing Proper Adjectives

Write *a* or *b* to indicate which item is correctly capitalized. You may use a dictionary.

1. a. new england seafood
b. New England seafood

2. a. an australian movie
b. an Australian movie

3. a. victorian literature
b. Victorian literature

4. a. Italian scientists
b. italian scientists

5. a. American History
b. American history

6. a. congressional committee
b. Congressional committee

7. a. British seaports
b. british seaports

8. a. a french restaurant
b. a French restaurant

9. a. european countries
b. European countries

10. a. an alaskan winter
b. an Alaskan winter

Connect to the Writing Process: Drafting

Writing Sentences with Proper Adjectives

[Answers may vary. Possible responses are given.]

Write a sentence to answer each question. Use a proper adjective in each sentence.

11. What type of ethnic cooking is your favorite?
Mexican cooking is my favorite.

12. Which region of America would you like to visit?
I would like to visit the Southwest.

YOUR IDEAS

For Capitalizing Proper Adjectives

Apply to Communication

Through Independent Writing

The **Communicate Your Ideas/Apply to Writing** activity on page L527 prompts students to write a list of titles of written works, music, and videos they would take with them to the South Pole. Ask students how they will use capitalization in their titles. Discuss students' responses.

Transfer to Everyday Life

Identifying Capitalization in Titles of Musical Works

Have students look through their own record, CD, or audiocassette music collection at home. As an alternative activity, have students find music titles in a local store. Students should find at least five correctly capitalized titles of musical works. They should also find five incorrectly capitalized musical titles. Remind students that the title of a collection, such as a CD title, should be italicized. The title of a song should be within quotation marks. Students, however, should focus primarily on the use of capitalization in the musical titles. Students should write the titles

USING STUDENTS' STRENGTHS

Multiple Intelligences: Logical

On the board create a chart that divides rules for titles into two columns: *Capitalize* and *Do Not Capitalize.* As you cover the specific rules on pages L522–L526, write the rule and an example in the correct column of the chart.

I have read Native American folktales.
13. What kind of ethnic folktales have you read?
I would like to visit the Inca ruins in Peru.
14. What kind of ruins do you think would be interesting to visit?
I would like to know more about the customs of the Native American tribes.
15. What kind of ethnic customs would you like to know more about?

Connect to the Writing Process: Editing

Correcting Sentences with Proper Adjectives

Rewrite each sentence, adding capital letters where needed.

16. ~~what~~ What replaced the ~~julian~~ Julian calendar?
17. ~~who~~ Who was the last ~~hawaiian~~ Hawaiian royal ruler?
18. ~~what~~ What is the ~~british~~ British term for *elevator?*
19. ~~why~~ Why isn't ~~basque~~ Basque a true ~~spanish~~ Spanish language?
20. ~~what~~ What bodies of water lie off the ~~vietnamese~~ Vietnamese coast?

Titles

Capital letters are used in the titles of people, written works, and other works of art.

Capitalize the titles of people and works of art.

Titles Used with Names of Persons

Capitalize a title showing office, rank, or profession when it comes before a person's name. The same title is usually not capitalized when it follows a name.

BEFORE A NAME	That woman is **C**olonel Hanks.
AFTER A NAME	When was Ann promoted to **c**olonel?

down, correct those that are incorrect, and share their titles with the class.

Pull It All Together

By Sharing

Have students share their list of titles from the **Communicate Your Ideas/ Apply to Writing** activity with an E-mail friend or pen pal. Students should include their list of titles in a letter or E-mail after checking with a class partner for correct capitalization. Students should also tell their partners why they chose these particular titles.

Check Understanding

By Summarizing

Have students summarize the strategies they use to decide whether or not a word should be capitalized in a proper adjective, the title of a literary work, musical composition, or work of art. Students should include at least

Titles Used in Direct Address

A noun of **direct address** is used to call someone by name. Capitalize a title used alone, instead of a name, in direct address.

Direct Address	What is your opinion, **P**rofessor?
	What, **S**enator, do you think about a possible tax increase?

You can learn more about commas with titles used in direct address on page L562.

Titles Showing Family Relationships

Capitalize titles showing family relationships when the titles come before people's names. Capitalize the titles, also, when they are used instead of names or used in direct address.

Used Before a Name	Is **U**ncle David staying for dinner?
Used as a Name	Yesterday **M**om helped with my homework.
Used In Direct Address	Thanks for the ride, **D**ad.

When a possessive noun or pronoun comes before a title showing a family relationship, do not capitalize the title—unless it is considered part of the person's name.

No Capital	*My* **a**unt is talking to *Linda's* **u**ncle.
Capital	Is *your* **A**unt Harriet from Arizona visiting?

You can learn about the use of possessive nouns with apostrophes on pages L617–L619 and about the use of possessive pronouns on pages L621–L622.

YOUR IDEAS
For Capitalizing Titles

three rules for capitalization in their summaries. Have students share their summaries with the class. Write some of their rules for capitalization on the board.

A DIFFERENT APPROACH

Visual

Complete **Connect to the Writing Process** as a class. Have two students use black markers to write the three paragraphs on large chart paper. Then call on various students to take turns correcting the capitalization errors in the paragraphs. Have students use a red marker to correct the capitalization errors.

HOME WORK

As a home work assignment, have students read about capitalizing titles used with the names of persons. Have students provide ten examples of titles that should be capitalized. Students' examples should be written in complete sentences.

PRACTICE YOUR SKILLS

Check Your Understanding

Capitalizing Titles Used with Names of People

Contemporary Life **Write correctly each word that should be capitalized.**

1. ~~have~~ Have you seen the governor of our state on television?
2. ~~i~~ I think, ~~sis~~ Sis, that we should visit the capital.
3. ~~can~~ Can ~~carmen's~~ Carmen's mother arrange a tour for us, ~~mom~~ Mom?
4. ~~she~~ She knows the representative from ~~hidalgo~~ Hidalgo county.
5. ~~let's~~ Let's ask ~~dad~~ Dad if we can go.
6. ~~last~~ Last fall ~~grandma solano~~ Grandma Solano invited us to ~~austin~~ Austin.
7. ~~we~~ We can stay at my ~~aunt rose's~~ Aunt Rose's house in ~~johnson city~~ Johnson City.
8. ~~my~~ My uncle was a student at the ~~university of texas~~ University of Texas.
9. ~~i~~ I think ~~ambassador smith~~ Ambassador Smith graduated from that university, too.
10. Isn't ~~senator hutchison~~ Senator Hutchison from your county?

Connect to the Writing Process: Editing

Correcting Titles Used with Names of People

Rewrite the following paragraphs, adding capital letters where needed.

Tyler asked, "Is there something special we can do for ~~grandma's~~ Grandma's birthday, ~~dad~~ Dad?"

In no time, ~~mom~~ Mom, ~~dad~~ Dad, my brother, and I were planning a surprise party. Fortunately, ~~aunt elena~~ Aunt Elena brought the food, and my ~~uncle joe~~ Uncle Joe supervised the barbecue.

We invited ~~captain yee~~ Captain Yee. He is ~~grandpa's~~ Grandpa's best friend. His wife is mrs. anna yee. ~~mrs. anna yee~~ Mrs. Anna Yee. My grandmother had gone to school with ~~mayor vaz~~ Mayor Vaz, so we asked her to come too. ~~grandma's~~ Grandma's neighbor, ~~rabbi joshua weiss~~ Rabbi Joshua Weiss, brought his band to provide the music.

Altogether, it was a wonderful party. Grandma was especially surprised to see ~~uncle tony~~ Uncle Tony. He had flown in from ~~chicago~~ Chicago.

Titles of Written Works and Other Works of Art

Capitalize the first word, the last word, and all important words in the titles of books, newspapers, magazines, stories, poems, movies, plays, musical compositions, and other works of art. Do not capitalize a short preposition, a coordinating conjunction, or an article unless it is the first or last word in a title.

BOOKS AND CHAPTER TITLES	I am reading the chapter "**P**eople and **L**and" in our textbook ***T**he **G**eography of the **W**orld.*
SHORT STORIES	Have you read Arthur Conan Doyle's story "**T**he **H**ound of the **B**askervilles"?
POEMS	Edgar Allan Poe wrote a poem called "**T**o **M**y **M**other."
MAGAZINES AND MAGAZINE ARTICLES	He found the facts in an article called "**A**re **C**ats **S**mart?" in *Discover* magazine.

USING STUDENTS' STRENGTHS

Multiple Intelligences: Intrapersonal

Tell students that song titles are capitalized and placed within quotation marks just as poems are. Have students list as many song titles as they can think of in two minutes. After the time is up, have students check their titles for correct capitalization. Remind students that the first and last words in song titles should always be capitalized. Ask students to identify the articles, coordinating conjunctions, and short prepositions that they did not capitalize. Have students write some of their song titles on the board, including correct capitalization and quotation marks.

A DIFFERENT APPROACH

Visual

Have students choose an item from **Practice Your Skills** to write out on large sentence strips. Students should use brightly colored markers to write out their title. Students may also choose to illustrate their titles. Remind students to correctly capitalize their titles. Display students' completed titles in the classroom.

Newspapers and Newspaper Articles	My sister wrote "**N**ew **D**igs for **D**inosaur **B**ones" for the ***V**alley **B**anner.* (The word *the* is not usually capitalized before the title of a newspaper.)
Television Series	She tapes the ***W**ild **W**orld* programs to watch later.
Musical Compositions	Have you heard **B**eethoven's **F**ifth **S**ymphony?
Movies	Most people are surprised by the ending of ***C**itizen **K**ane.*

You can learn about the punctuation of titles on page L540.

Practice Your Skills

Check Your Understanding

Capitalizing Titles of Things

General Interest **Write *C* if an item is correctly capitalized. Write *I* if it is incorrectly capitalized.**

1. a newspaper named ~~The~~ the *Oakland Daily times* I
2. a newspaper article entitled "It's a ~~dog's life~~ Dog's Life" I
3. Thurber's short story "The Night the Ghost Got In" C
4. the Western song "~~home on the range~~ Home on the Range" I
5. Shakespeare's play ~~the~~ *The Taming of the Shrew* I
6. Shelley's poem "Ode to the ~~west wind~~ West Wind" I
7. Debussy's composition *sonata for piano and cello* *Sonata for Piano and Cello* I
8. a book called *The ABC's of the Human Body* C
9. the TV series *the adventures of sherlock holmes* *The Adventures of Sherlock Holmes* I
10. the movie *Back to the Future* C

Connect to the Writing Process: Editing
Capitalizing Titles

11.–17. Rewrite the incorrect sentences from the preceding exercise, adding capital letters where needed. [See answers given on previous page.]

Communicate Your Ideas

APPLY TO WRITING

List: ***Other Uses of Capital Letters***

Imagine that you are going to stay at the South Pole for several months. You can take along books, videos, music CDs, and magazines to entertain yourself. List the titles of ten of these items you would take with you. Make sure you use capital letters correctly.

Mixed Practice

General Interest

Write correctly each word that should be capitalized. Then answer as many of the questions as you can.

1. ~~what~~ What were ~~lewis~~ Lewis and ~~clark~~ Clark sent to explore, the ~~mississippi river~~ Mississippi River or the ~~louisiana territory~~ Louisiana Territory? — the Louisiana Territory

2. ~~was~~ Was the famous painter ~~picasso~~ Picasso ~~french~~ French or ~~spanish~~ Spanish? — Spanish

3. ~~what~~ What is the name of the author of ~~*dr. jekyll and mr. hyde,*~~ *Dr. Jekyll and Mr. Hyde* ~~mark twain~~ Mark Twain, or ~~robert louis stevenson~~ Robert Louis Stevenson? — Robert Louis Stevenson

4. ~~what~~ What time is it in ~~los angeles~~ Los Angeles when it is 1:00 ~~p.m.~~ P.M. in ~~new york city~~ New York City? — 10:00 A.M.

5. ~~what~~ What is the name of ~~dorothy's~~ Dorothy's dog in the movie ~~*the wizard of oz,*~~ *The Wizard of Oz* ~~toto~~ Toto or ~~lassie~~ Lassie? — Toto

TIMESAVER QuickCheck

Instead of grading this exercise as you would a writing assignment, read it quickly for sense, underlining capital letters as you go. If students have correctly capitalized titles, give them a total number of points you have allotted; if they have missed opportunities to capitalize, lower the number of points accordingly.

EXPANDING THE LESSON

Using Technology

You will find additional **instructional** and **practice** materials for this chapter at http://www.bkenglish.com.

FOR REVIEWING SKILLS

Using *CheckPoint*

This feature on capitalization can be used as further independent practice or as a cumulative review of the chapter. Students choose words to capitalize in sentences, correct capitalization errors in a paragraph, and write sentences using correct capitalization.

CheckPoint

Using Capital Letters

Write each word that should begin with a capital letter.

[Underlined words should be capitalized.]

1. saturn has twenty moons, but earth has only one.
2. the supertanker *seawise giant* can carry a total load of over 560,000 tons.
3. do your mom and dad subscribe to the *tribune*?
4. the aardvark, an african mammal, eats termites.
5. the month of july was named after julius caesar.
6. does haver's hardware store rent clark tools, uncle ed?
7. the united states air force academy is located in colorado springs.
8. tasmania, a small island, is south of australia.
9. the song "happy birthday to you" was written by two sisters in 1936.
10. the red sea separates egypt from saudi arabia.

Using Capital Letters

Write each word that should begin with a capital letter.

[Underlined words should be capitalized.]

1. if all the world's ice melted, cities such as london and paris would be underwater.
2. is your brother taking algebra II or geometry?
3. medieval knights were specially trained soldiers.
4. uncle george and aunt martha live in the south.
5. the temperature on venus is hotter than it is on mercury, the planet closest to the sun.
6. i memorized "casey at the bat," a poem by ernest l. thayer.

Editing for Proper Capitalization

Write each word that should begin with a capital letter. Do not include words that are already capitalized.

[Underlined words should be capitalized.]

Early in the morning of monday, april 15, 1912, the *titanic*, a great ocean liner, struck an iceberg and sank off the coast of newfoundland. The ship was on a voyage from england to new york city.

In 1985, the ship was discovered on the floor of the atlantic ocean. Finding the ship had been a joint effort of the united states and france. Using sonar, a french research ship scanned the ocean bottom. When the wreck was found, scientists from the woods hole oceanographic institute in massachussetts sent down a submersible underwater sled named *argo*. Attached to the sled were lights and television cameras. After seventy-three years the great ship had been found in its resting place.

Writing Sentences

At the library or media center, find and write a one-sentence fact about each of the following topics. Each fact should include a proper noun, a proper adjective, or a title.

1. geography
2. government official
3. the presidency
4. astronomy
5. national business
6. brand name
7. holidays
8. social studies
9. space exploration
10. languages

Sample Answers for *Writing Sentences:*

1. Colorado is the home of Pike's Peak.
2. Our local representative is Assemblyman Martin A. Luster.
3. Andrew Johnson succeeded Abraham Lincoln on April 15, 1865.
4. Jupiter is the largest planet.
5. Seattle is the site of Boeing Aircraft's head-quarters.
6. The year 1999 may well be considered the year of Pokémon.
7. On Memorial Day, flags should fly at half-staff until noon.
8. The Black Hawk War took place in 1832.
9. The most recent mission to Mars was a failure.
10. The official languages on Cyprus are Greek and Turkish.

Using *Language and Self-Expression*

Consider using this writing assignment to assess students' ability to capitalize words correctly. You may want students to complete the assignment as part of an expository writing strand for their portfolios.

Prewriting

Suggest that students revisit their analysis of the photograph collage that they did in *Making Visual Connections* on page L496.

Encourage students to use questioning strategies in addition to the graphic organizer to help them organize their thoughts in the prewriting stage. For example, students might use the following questions to help them proceed with their writing:

- What would people want to know about this person?
- What have been this person's major accomplishments?
- Would my report be more interesting if I started from the present and worked back in the person's life, telling about his or her birth and childhood at the end of my report?

FOR YOUR INFORMATION

About the Artist

David Hockney is a noted British artist. He is a painter, a printer, a graphic designer, a photographer, and a stage designer. His early paintings were considered Pop Art by many and are said to have started the Pop movement in England in the late 1950s. In the 1980s he began experimenting with photography, creating photographic collages and using photocopiers in his artworks.

Language and *Self-Expression*

David Hockney began his career as a Pop artist, a painter of popular objects. He began working with photography in the 1980s, and this portrait of Stephen Spender was made in 1990, when the poet was eighty years old.

Think of a poet or novelist about whom you would like to know more. Do research to learn about the person you chose. Use your notes to write a brief biography, trying to look at your subject from different angles, as David Hockney did in his portrait.

Prewriting Take notes from reference resources. Use your notes to make an outline like the one below.

I. Birth and Childhood
   A.
   B.
II. Training and Early Work
   A.
   B.
III. Accomplishments and Legacy
   A.
   B.

Drafting Use your notes and outline to write a short biography. As you write think about viewing your subject from diffrent angles.

Revising Read your biography critically, looking for places you might add or delete details. Make sure your transitions are clear.

Editing Review your work, looking for errors in grammar, capitalization, punctuation, and spelling. Make any corrections that are necessary.

Publishing Recopy your biography neatly. Publish it by sharing it with your classmates.

Capital Letters

Capitalizing First Words and *I*

Capitalize the first word of a sentence and the first word of a line of poetry. *(page L497)*
Capitalize the first word in the greeting of a letter and the first word in the closing of a letter. *(page L498)*
Capitalize the first word of each item in an outline and the letters that begin major subsections of the outline. *(page L498)*
Capitalize the pronoun *I*, both alone and in contractions. *(pages L498–L499)*

Capitalizing Proper Nouns

Capitalize proper nouns and their abbreviations. *(page L501)*
Capitalize the following:
Names of persons and animals *(page L501)*
Geographical names *(pages L502–L503)*
Nouns of historical importance *(pages L506–L507)*
Names of groups and businesses *(page L507)*
Specific time periods and events *(pages L508–L509)*
Names of nationalities and races *(page L513)*
Religions, religious references, and religious holidays and holy days *(page L513)*
Names of planets, moons, stars, and constellations *(pages L514–L515)*
Languages and school courses *(page L515)*
Other proper nouns *(pages L515–L516)*

Other Uses of Capital Letters

Capitalize most proper adjectives. *(page L520)*

Capitalizing Titles

Capitalize the titles of people and works of art. *(pages L525–L526)*

Using *Another Look*

Another Look summarizes the terms defined in the chapter and provides cross-references to the specific pages on which they are explained. Consider having students use this feature prior to completing **CheckPoint** or taking the posttest. Students who can provide several examples of each term should be able to score well on either measurement.

Using *the Posttest*

Assessing Learning

The posttest will help you and your students assess where they stand in their ability to capitalize words correctly.

IDENTIFYING COMMON STUMBLING BLOCKS

Following is a list of the most common capitalization errors students make in their writing.

Problem

- Noncapitalization of proper nouns

Solution

- For reteaching, use the examples on pages L501–L503, L507, L509, and L513–L516.

Problem

- Noncapitalization of proper adjectives

Solution

- For reteaching, use the examples on page L520.

Directions

Read the passage and decide which underlined word should be capitalized. Write the letter of the correct answer.

EXAMPLE Eileen Collins was born and raised in the town of elmira, New York. (1)

1 **A** Born
B Raised
C Town
D Elmira

ANSWER **1 D**

The space shuttle *columbia* has flown several missions and been piloted by several commanders. (1) Other female astronauts include Valentina Tereshkova, who orbited earth in a capsule (2) in 1963. Sally Ride, who blasted off in the year 1983, was the first american woman in space. (3) However, Air Force lieutenant Colonel Eileen Collins was our first female space shuttle pilot. (4) As a girl, Collins loved *Star trek* and other science fiction, but it was reading about famous women aviators that led her to get her license to fly. (5)

A DIFFERENT DELIVERY SYSTEM

If you prefer, you can print the posttest from the BK English Test Bank located at http://www.bkenglish.com.

1 **A** *Columbia*
B Missions
C Piloted
D Commanders

2 **A** Female
B Astronauts
C Earth
D Capsule

3 **A** Year
B American
C Woman
D Space

4 **A** Lieutenant
B Space
C Shuttle
D Pilot

5 **A** *Trek*
B Science Fiction
C Aviators
D License

Customizing the Test

Use these questions to add or replace items for alternate versions of the test.

After getting a degree in math and economics from Syracuse University, (6) Collins joined the Air force for pilot training. She became an aircraft commander and instructor in cargo jets at Travis Air Force base (7). As a recent graduate of Test Pilot School, she was chosen for the (8) astronaut program at NASA in july of 1991. In 1995, she piloted a shuttle to rendezvous with the russian Space Station *Mir* as (9) it circled the earth.

6. **A** Degree
B Economics
C Force
D Training

7. **A** Aircraft
B Commander
C Cargo
D Base

8. **A** Graduate
B Astronaut
C Program
D July

9. **A** Shuttle
B Rendezvous
C Russian
D Earth

TEACHING SUGGESTIONS

Essential Knowledge and Skills

- Writing to express, discover, record, develop, reflect on ideas, and to problem solve
- Punctuating correctly to clarify and enhance meaning
- Proofreading his/her own writing and that of others
- Applying criteria to evaluate writing
- Interpreting and evaluating the various ways visual image makers such as illustrators, documentary filmmakers, and political cartoonists represent meanings

BLOCK SCHEDULING

- If your schedule requires that you cover the chapter in a **shorter time,** use the instruction on end marks and commas and the Check Your Understanding and QuickCheck exercises.
- If you want to take advantage of **longer class time,** add these applications to writing: Connect to Speaking and Writing, Connect to the Writing Process, and Apply to Writing exercises.

CHAPTER 16

End Marks and Commas

Pretest

Directions

Read the passage. Write the letter of the best way to write each underlined part. If the underlined part contains no error, write *D*.

EXAMPLE Derek who is a racing fan (1) told me about an incredible race.

1 **A** Derek who is a racing fan,
B Derek, who is a racing fan,
C Derek, who is a racing fan
D No error

ANSWER **1 B**

On February 12 1908 (1) a difficult automobile race was in progress. Six cars left New York for Paris in a route that included the United States, Japan, Russia, Poland, Germany and part of France (2). Met by blizzards and other dangers (3) the racers nevertheless kept (4) on. The German entry reached Paris five months later, and the (5) American entry followed Although (6) the German car came in first, it was (7) given a penalty. As a result of this decision (8) the American car won. The car a Thomas Flyer (9) had gone 13,400 miles in 168 days. What a race that was (10)

IDENTIFYING COMMON STUMBLING BLOCKS

Following is a list of the most common errors students make when using end marks and commas in their writing.

Problem
- Lack of comma with introductory elements

Solution
- Instruction, pp. L553–L554
- Practice, pp. L555–L556

Problem
- Lack of comma to set off parenthetical expressions

Solution
- Instruction, pp. L564–L565
- Practice, pp. L565–L566

1 A On February 12, 1908,
B On February 12 1908,
C On February 12, 1908
D No error

2 A Germany, and, part of France
B Germany and, part of France
C Germany, and part of France
D No error

3 A blizzards, and other dangers,
B blizzards, and other dangers
C blizzards and other dangers,
D No error

4 A racers, nevertheless, kept,
B racers nevertheless, kept
C racers, nevertheless kept
D No error

5 A later and the
B later and, the
C later, and, the
D No error

6 A followed, Although
B followed. Although
C followed. Although,
D No error

7 A came in, first, it was
B came in first it was
C came in, first it was
D No error

8 A result, of this decision,
B result, of this decision
C result of this decision,
D No error

9 A car, a Thomas Flyer,
B car a Thomas Flyer,
C car, a Thomas Flyer
D No error

10 A was!
B was.
C was?
D No error

A DIFFERENT DELIVERY SYSTEM

If you prefer, you can print the pretest from the BK English Test Bank located at http://www.bkenglish.com.

Using *the Pretest*

Assessing Prior Knowledge

The pretest will help you and your students assess where they stand in their basic understanding of end marks and commas.

Customizing the Test

Use these questions to add or replace items for alternate versions of the test.

Car racing is popular but not all (11) races involve cars. Horse racing which is my grandfather's favorite (12) is also popular. People with a fun, quirky sense (13) of humor have been known to race frogs snails and (14) roaches (15)

11. A popular, but not all,
B popular but not all,
C popular, but not all
D No error

12. A racing, which is my grandfather's favorite,
B racing, which is my grandfather's favorite
C racing which is my grandfather's favorite,
D No error

13. A a fun quirky sense,
B a fun, quirky, sense
C a fun quirky, sense
D No error

14. A frogs snails, and
B frogs, snails, and
C frogs, snails, and,
D No error

15. A roaches!
B roaches?
C roaches,
D No error

ADDITIONAL RESOURCES

Language Skills Practice . . . . pages 146–162
Transparency Tools AW16
ESL Practice and Test Preparation . . . . . pages 130–132
Assessment: Chapter Test. . . . . pages 194–200

MAKING VISUAL CONNECTIONS

For Language Development

Ask students about the shapes, curves, lines, and shadows in the sculpture *Mother and Child.* Have students write sentences on the board to describe these elements as they see them. As students write, point out how they have used end marks and commas to make their sentences clear and complete.

To Stimulate Writing

Use the questions for art criticism as writing or discussion prompts.

Possible Answers:

Describe The artist used wood for this sculpture. The outside edge of the sculpture is nearly a rectangle with straight lines. The face, neck, baby's head, and lower arm are all made of round or curved lines that are soft and gentle.

Analyze The repetition of the curved lines creates a sense of peace and harmony. The round head of the baby is especially peaceful-looking, because the lines are curved. The line that runs from below the baby's head up into the center of the raised arm suggests movement to me.

Interpret The mood of this sculpture is warm, safe, and peaceful. The title, *Mother and Child,* strengthens the mood. We think of a mother and child as a peaceful image.

Judge For the most part, I think the artist was successful in creating a clear mood, but one thing is a little confusing. Why is the mother looking up with her arm over her head? A writer could help clarify this.

Elizabeth Catlett,
Mother and Child, 1971.
Cedar, height 26 inches. © 2001 Elizabeth Catlett, licensed by VAGA, New York.

Describe	What material did the artist use to make this sculpture? What kind of lines and texture does the sculpture have?
Analyze	How did the artist use line to create a sense of unity in the art? Do any of the lines suggest movement to you? Explain.
Interpret	What mood has the artist created with her use of line and texture?
Judge	Do you think the artist was successful in creating a definite mood for the art? Why or why not? How could a writer present this mood differently?

At the end of this chapter, you will use the artwork to stimulate ideas for writing.

FOR DEVELOPING LANGUAGE SKILLS

LESSON 1 *(pages L537–L541)*

OBJECTIVES

- **To use periods, question marks, and exclamation marks correctly at the end of sentences**
- **To use periods correctly in abbreviations and in outlines**

Create Interest

Write the following paragraph on the board and have students comment on their immediate reaction. How does the lack of punctuation or incorrect punctuation affect them as readers? Discuss the paragraph's end mark errors.

End Marks

You may recall that the purpose of a sentence determines its end mark.

Place a **period** after a statement, after an opinion, and after a command or request made in a normal tone of voice.

PERIODS I want to be a forest ranger**.**
(statement)
The wilderness is peaceful**.**
(opinion)
Sign up for the career workshop**.**
(command)

Place a **question mark** after a sentence that asks a question.

QUESTION MARK Would you like to work outdoors**?**

Place an **exclamation point** after a sentence that expresses strong feeling or after a command or request that expresses great excitement.

EXCLAMATION POINTS The fire is spreading through the woods**!**
Listen to that roar**!**

You can learn more about the kinds of sentences on pages L34–L35.

You can learn about using end marks with direct quotations on pages L600–L601.

FOR INCREASING STUDENT ACHIEVEMENT

REACHING ALL STUDENTS

English Language Learners

Spanish-speaking students who are learning English may have trouble knowing when to use question marks and exclamation marks and knowing where to place these end marks. In Spanish, these marks are placed both at the beginning of sentences (written upside down) and at the end of sentences. Remind students that in English, these marks are written only at the end of sentences and are never written with the dots on the top. Have students practice writing sentences using exclamation marks and question marks at the end of sentences.

DEVELOPING WORKPLACE COMPETENCIES

Basic Skills: Writing

After reviewing the correct use of end marks, have students brainstorm reasons for using end marks in business letters. List some of students' responses on the board. Ask students what problems might occur if end marks in a business letter are incorrect. Construct a business letter with students on the board. Have students check for correct use of end marks.

Wow. I don't know how the firefighters made it out of that fire? They came charging out of the burning house! with hoses axes battering rams and wet blankets that they used to wrap the victims These firefighters deserve a medal for their bravery. After the whole ordeal was over my mother and I were relieved?

Guide Instruction

By Connecting Ideas

Demonstrate and review with students how to correct the errors in punctuation throughout the previous paragraph. Tell students that just as capitalization and spelling errors can be confusing to readers, end mark errors can cause just as much frustration.

Work with students to correct the paragraph as shown:

Wow! I don't know how the firefighters made it out of that fire! (or .) *They came charging out of the burning house with hoses, axes, battering rams, and wet blankets that they used to wrap the victims. These firefighters deserve a medal for their bravery.*

IDENTIFYING COMMON STUMBLING BLOCKS

Problem

- Overusing exclamation points

Solution

- Tell students that if they are unsure whether to use an exclamation point or a period after a command, use the period. The exclamation point should be used only rarely. If used too often, it loses its power to impress the reader.

PRACTICE YOUR SKILLS

Check Your Understanding
Using End Marks

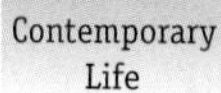

Contemporary Life **Write the correct end mark for each sentence.**

1. Should we take the train or the bus to Rock Island?
2. I think trains are more comfortable than buses⊙
3. The bus, however, is faster⊙
4. Where do I buy a ticket?
5. Go over to that booth⊙
6. The line has twenty-five people in it⊙
7. We'll miss the train!
8. Don't panic⊙
9. The train doesn't leave for another hour⊙
10. That's a relief!

Connect to the Writing Process: Editing
Adding End Marks to Sentences

Rewrite the following paragraphs, adding the correct end marks where needed.

Do you think electric cars are a new development? Think again! The first practical electric cars were on the roads by the late 1880s⊙By 1917, more than eleven million people per year in the United States were traveling by electric cars⊙Does this fact puzzle you? If it does, you're probably thinking along the wrong lines⊙ You're thinking of electric automobiles⊙The electric cars of the past were actually streetcars, or trolleys⊙

After the whole ordeal was over, my mother and I were relieved.

Consolidate Skills

Through Guided Practice

The **Check Your Understanding** exercises will help students use end marks correctly. Review the instruction on end marks before completing the exercises. Guide students through the first item in each exercise. Discuss students' responses and any difficulties they might have using end marks. Have students complete the exercises independently.

Apply to Communication

Through Independent Writing

The **Communicate Your Ideas/Apply to Writing** activities on pages L539 and L543 prompt students to write an advertisement and an outline that could be used to describe the location of their school. Ask students how end marks and punctuation will play a

Trolleys can run only on tracks⊙They are powered by electricity⊙Where does the power come from**?** The trolleys are connected to overhead lines that conduct electricity⊙Unfortunately, their need to run on tracks limits their use⊙That's why inventors are trying to perfect electric automobiles⊙These cars don't pollute the environment, and they can be run on electricity generated from water, solar power, and windpower⊙ Perhaps in a few decades, you won't have to step on the gas to start a car⊙You'll just switch on the power⊙

Communicate Your Ideas

APPLY TO WRITING

Advertisement: *End Marks*

Write copy for an advertising brochure to get customers interested in a new model of electric car. Address some of the questions customers might have about the car. Call their attention to its special features. Encourage them to test-drive the new car themselves. As you write, use questions, exclamations, statements, and commands to capture the attention of your readers.

Other Uses of Periods

Periods are used in other places besides the ends of sentences.

HOME WORK

After completing **Connect to the Writing Process,** have students write a similar paragraph about another transportation topic. Students should check for correct use of end marks after each sentence. Have students share some of their sentences on the board the following day. Discuss their use of end marks.

TIMESAVER *QuickCheck*

Have students work with partners to create a checklist of end marks they should use at the end of their sentences. Students should also decide how to evaluate the persuasive writing techniques used in their advertisements. For example, students might want to make sure they include clear arguments and support for their claims. Students should use the checklists to evaluate their advertisements.

crucial role in each of these writing assignments. Which writing task do students think will use the most exclamation marks? Which one will contain the most question marks? Which one will use periods frequently with numerals? For example, students should be able to point out that their outlines will use periods with numerals and their advertisements might use a lot of exclamation marks. Discuss students' responses.

Transfer to Everyday Life

Identifying End Marks in Writing Portfolios

Have students identify correct use of end marks in a writing sample from their own writing portfolios. Students should choose a completed writing sample that contains good examples of the correct use of periods, question marks, and exclamation marks. Have students share some of their examples with the class.

GETTING STUDENTS' INVOLVED

Cooperative Learning

After discussing the chart of common abbreviations on this page, have students work with partners to decide how they would abbreviate the words in the following list: *Doctor Edwards, Dellwood Avenue, Mister Ramsey, Saturday, Monday, 3000 years before Christ, August, February, Misses Black.* Students should be able to tell why they abbreviated the words as they did.

REACHING ALL STUDENTS

Struggling Learners

Have students unfamiliar with the terms in this chart make their own flashcards with the abbreviation on the front and its complete meaning on the back.

With Abbreviations

Abbreviations are brief ways of writing words. They are handy shortcuts when you are writing messages or taking notes in class. Most abbreviations, however, should not be used in formal writing such as letters, stories, or reports.

Use a period with most abbreviations.

The following is a list of common abbreviations. For the spelling and the punctuation of other abbreviations, look in a dictionary. Most dictionaries have a special section that lists abbreviations.

COMMON ABBREVIATIONS	
DAYS	Sun. Mon. Tues. Wed. Thurs. Fri. Sat.
MONTHS	Jan. Feb. Mar. Apr. Aug. Sept. Oct. Nov. Dec. (May, June, and July should not be abbreviated.)
ADDRESSES	Ave. Blvd. Dr. Hwy. Pl. Rd. Rt. St. Apt.
TITLES WITH NAMES	Mr. Mrs. Ms. Dr. Rev. Gen. Sgt. Lt. Jr. Sr. Pres.
INITIALS FOR NAMES	R. L. Rosen Kenneth A. Brevik L. Elizabeth Page
TIMES WITH NUMBERS	6:45 A.M. (*ante meridiem*—before noon) 9:00 P.M. (*post meridiem*—after noon) (A colon (:) goes between the hours and the minutes when time is written in numbers.) 2000 B.C. (before Christ) A.D. 650 (*anno Domini*—in the year of the Lord)
COMPANIES	Assoc. Co. Corp. Dept. Inc. Ltd.

Pull It All Together

By Sharing

Have students share one of their writing samples from the **Communicate Your Ideas/Apply to Writing** activity on page L543 with an E-mail friend or pen pal. After checking for correct use of end marks, students should send their writing sample in the form of a letter or E-mail.

Check Understanding

By Punctuating a Paragraph

Provide students with a copy of a story or a magazine article from which you have deleted all of the end marks. Make sure to keep a copy of the original. Have students read the story aloud and suggest end punctuation for each sentence. If students have difficulty interpreting any of the sentences without end punctuation, take the opportunity to point out the importance of such punctuation in written

Some organizations are known by abbreviations that stand for their full names. The majority of these abbreviations do not use periods. In addition, a few other common abbreviations do not include periods. Always check a dictionary if you are not sure whether an abbreviation needs periods.

ABBREVIATIONS WITHOUT PERIODS	
UN = United Nations	CD = compact disc
CIA = Central Intelligence Agency	ATM = automated teller machine
IQ = Intelligence Quotient	FAX = facsimile
km = kilometer	l = liter

Today almost everyone uses the post office's two-letter state abbreviations. These abbreviations do not include periods. A list of these state abbreviations usually can be found in the front of a telephone book. Here are a few examples.

STATE ABBREVIATIONS		
AL = Alabama	MD = Maryland	OH = Ohio
AK = Alaska	NV = Nevada	TX = Texas
HI = Hawaii	NY = New York	UT = Utah

CONNECT TO SPEAKING AND WRITING

When a sentence ends with an abbreviation ending in a period, use only one period. It serves as both the period for the abbreviation and the end mark for the sentence.

The man in the brown suit is Michael Alvarez, Jr.

USING TECHNOLOGY

Computers

After discussing the rules for forming abbreviations, have students search the Internet for additional abbreviations, such as in the names of government organizations, clubs, state names, and places. Students should print out and highlight at least ten abbreviations they find on the Internet. They should then write sentences using each abbreviation they find.

communication. Have students check their results against the original, consulting the rules and discussing any discrepancies.

REACHING ALL STUDENTS

Struggling Learners

Give students the following strategies for making an outline and have them point out how these strategies are used in their outlines.

- Center the title above the outline
- Every item of the outline must have at least two items (I and II, A and B, 1 and 2)
- Put a period after each numeral and letter
- Indent each new level of the outline
- All items of one kind (e.g., Roman numerals, capital letters, Arabic numerals) should line up with each other
- Capitalize the first word of each item

With Outlines

In an outline, periods set apart the letters and numbers from the text that follows.

Use a period after each number or letter that shows a division in an outline.

I. Routes to Oregon in the early 1800s
  A. Oregon Trail blazed in 1812 by fur traders
    1. Steamship from St. Louis to Independence
    2. Covered wagons to plains and Rockies
  B. The journey around Cape Horn
II. New routes to California

Practice Your Skills

Check Your Understanding

Writing Abbreviations

Write the correct abbreviation in parentheses for each item.

1. Monday (Mon. *or* Mon)
2. September (Septr. *or* Sept.)
3. centimeter (cm *or* cm.)
4. Mister (Mr *or* Mr.)
5. quart (qt. *or* qt)
6. post meridiem (PM *or* P.M.)
7. Route (Rt. *or* Rt)
8. United Nations (UN *or* U.N.)
9. before Christ (b.c. *or* B.C.)
10. Michigan (MI. *or* MI)

Connect to the Writing Process: Editing
Using Periods

Rewrite the following items, adding periods where needed.

Fri., Sept. 8, 2000
11. Fri, Sept 8, 2000
Abrams and Patel, Inc.
12. Abrams and Patel, Inc
Rev. R. J. Wong
13. Rev R J Wong
a new CD by P. J. Smith
14. a new CD by P J Smith
Ms. Elizabeth C. Boxer
15. Ms Elizabeth C Boxer
Sun., July 17, at Moore Corp.
16. Sun, July 17, at Moore Corp
Dr. Lee T. Silveira, Jr.
17. Dr Lee T Silveira Jr
a PTA meeting at 6 P.M. at 640 North Ave.
18. a PTA meeting at 6 PM at 640 North Ave
A.D. 250
19. AD 250
1121 Soquel Dr., Aptos, CA 95006
20. 1121 Soquel Dr, Aptos, CA 95006
B.C.
21. 962 BC
781 First St.
22. 781 First St
Wed., Feb. 16, 2000
23. Wed, Feb 16, 2000
Sgt. D. Francis O'Neill
24. Sgt D Francis O'Neill
a UN report dated Aug. 5
25. a UN report dated Aug 5

Communicate Your Ideas

APPLY TO WRITING

Outline: ***End Marks***

Create an outline that you could use to write a description of your school. Plan to give information about your school's location, size, grade levels, students, and kinds of classes offered. Remember to use periods where they are needed in your outline.

Sample Answer for *Apply to Writing:*

Thomas Jefferson Public High School

I. Location
  A. Corner of Grand Street and Phipps Drive
  B. Milford Center, Alaska
II. Student body
  A. Size–4,000 students
  B. Grade levels–8th–12th grades
III. Classes Taught
  A. Fast-Track
    1. Language arts
    2. Foreign languages
    3. Global Studies
    4. Sciences
    5. Mathematics
  B. Mainstream
    1. Language arts
    2. Foreign languages
    etc.

LESSON 2 (pages L544–L575)

OBJECTIVES

- **To use commas correctly with items in a series, with adjectives before a noun, with compound sentences, with introductory elements, with dates and addresses, and with letters**
- **To use commas to correctly enclose direct address, parenthetical expressions, appositives, and nonessential elements**

Create Interest

Put the following sentences on the board:

- *Add the flour slowly, stirring the mixture constantly.*
- *Add the flour, slowly stirring the mixture constantly.*

Ask students to comment on how the comma influences their interpretation of the recipe instructions. Students should be able to point out that in the first sentence, the comma tells the

A DIFFERENT APPROACH

Tactile

Fill a shoe box with several small items, such as erasers, pencils, cotton balls, paper clips, and chalk. Cover the box with the lid. Have students take turns putting their hands into the box without looking at the items. Students should try to guess what items they are feeling in the box. Students should then write one sentence describing all of the items they felt. Remind students to use commas to separate each item in their list as they write their sentence.

Commas That Separate

Commas keep similar items from running into each other and prevent misunderstanding by the reader.

Items in a Series

A **series** is three or more similar words or groups of words listed one after another. Commas are used to separate the items in a series.

Use commas to separate items in a series.

WORDS	We saw crabs**,** pelicans**,** and sandpipers. (nouns)
	Their new sailboat is lean**,** sleek**,** and swift. (adjectives)
	We found seashells**,** starfish**,** and seaweed. (compound words)
GROUPS OF WORDS	We will pack a lunch**,** walk to the dunes**,** and look for shells. (complete predicates)
	Paul is either on the beach**,** in the bait shop**,** or on his way to the pier. (prepositional phrases)

If a conjunction such as *and* or *or* connects all the items in a series, no commas are needed.

> Swimming and boating and hiking are fun beach activities.

You can learn about using commas with direct quotations on page L599.

cook to add the flour slowly. In the second sentence, because of the location of the comma, the cook will probably add all the flour at once and then stir slowly, perhaps resulting in a lumpy mixture. Tell students that these two sentences demonstrate the importance of using a comma to separate various parts of a sentence.

Guide Instruction

By Connecting Ideas

Tell students that commas are the most frequently used and misused mark of internal punctuation. In general, commas function within sentences to indicate pauses and to separate elements. Omitting needed commas or inserting needless commas can confuse readers, as demonstrated in the **Create Interest** recipe instructions.

Consolidate Skills

Through Guided Practice

The **Check Your Understanding** and **QuickCheck** exercises in this lesson will help students use commas correctly. Guide students through the first

PRACTICE YOUR SKILLS

Check Your Understanding

Using Commas in a Series

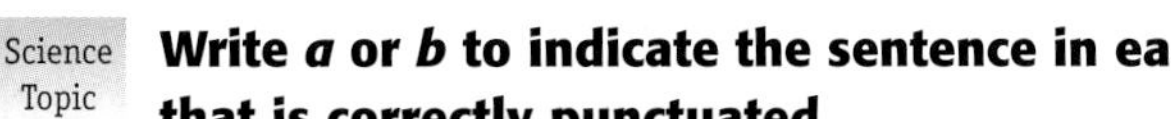

Science Topic

Write *a* or *b* to indicate the sentence in each pair that is correctly punctuated.

1. a. Cape Hatteras Cape Lookout Assateague Island, and Cape Cod are the names of four national seashores on the East coast.
<u>b</u>. Cape Hatteras, Cape Lookout, Assateague Island, and Cape Cod are the names of four national seashores on the East coast.

2. <u>a</u>. Waves wash over the beach, pick up sand, and drag the sand back into the sea.
b. Waves wash over the beach, pick up sand, and, drag the sand back into the sea.

3. a. The driftwood was dry smooth and silvery.
<u>b</u>. The driftwood was dry, smooth, and silvery.

4. <u>a</u>. Look for rocks or worn pebbles or sand dunes.
b. Look for rocks, or worn pebbles, or sand dunes.

5. a. Scrubby plants grow near dunes, next to the seawall, and up the face, of the cliff.
<u>b</u>. Scrubby plants grow near the dunes, next to the seawall, and up the face of the cliff.

Connect to the Writing Process: Editing

Using Commas in a Series

Rewrite the following sentences, adding commas where needed. If a sentence is correctly punctuated, write *C*.

6. A sandpiper scurries along the beach‸probes the wet sand‸and pulls out a mole crab.

7. The strange body of the mole crab is smooth‸shiny‸and pale.

8. What lives in tide pools‸under rocks‸and in the sand?

IDENTIFYING COMMON STUMBLING BLOCKS

Problem

- Omitting the comma before the conjunction that links items in a series

Solution

- Tell students that although some writers omit the comma before the coordinating conjunction in a series, that final comma is never wrong. It helps the reader see the last two items as separate. Tell students that consistently using a comma before the coordinating conjunction will ensure that their writing is clear.

item in each exercise by dictating the sentence to students, pausing slightly at each point that requires a comma. Have students identify the correct location for the commas. Discuss students' responses and any difficulties they might have using commas. Have students complete the exercises independently.

Apply to Communication

Through Independent Writing

The **Communicate Your Ideas/Apply to Writing** activities prompt students to write a journal entry, a personal history, an informative report, an invitation, and game directions. Ask students how commas will play a crucial role in each of these writing assignments. How might commas placed incorrectly create problems for readers? Discuss students' responses.

Transfer to Everyday Life

Identifying Comma Errors

Have students search newspapers, advertisements, restaurant menus, and billboards for errors made in the use

TIMESAVER *QuickCheck*

Have students self-evaluate their journal entries for correct use of commas in a series. Students should check for correct placement of the commas between items they list in their journal and be sure they use a comma before the last *and* in their lists.

YOUR IDEAS

For Using Journals

9. You might see a ghost shrimp or an oliveshell snail or a razor clam in the sand. C
10. Earwigs and flies and mole crickets hide under wood. C
11. The highest monthly tide rises up past the rockweed zone, past the barnacle zone, and up to the periwinkle zone.
12. A barnacle may fall prey to a starfish, a marine worm, or a carnivorous snail.
13. Sea hares swim to the shore, browse on the seaweed, and lay stringy eggs.
14. A beadlet anemone may be green, red, or amber.
15. Starfish eat little mollusks and shore worms and brittle stars. C

Communicate Your Ideas

APPLY TO WRITING

Journal Entry: ***Commas in a Series***

Sit quietly and observe the wildlife in a vacant lot or natural area near your home. Then write a journal entry that tells about the variety of plants and animals you observe. Use words in a series in at least four sentences. Describe how creatures look, where they are, and how they behave.

Adjectives Before a Noun

You have just learned that commas are needed between three or more adjectives in a series. If you have only two adjectives before a noun, however, you may or may not need a comma.

A comma is needed between two adjectives if it is replacing the word *and* between the two adjectives.

of commas. In addition to sharing their examples with the class, students should also be prepared to explain why confusion arises and how the message can be corrected with a comma or commas. For example, in the sentence *Our muffin choices include chocolate chip, blueberry, raisin and bran,* it looks as if there are only three choices rather than four. If the restaurant offers four choices, the menu should read *Our muffin choices include chocolate chip, blueberry, raisin, and bran.*

Pull It All Together

By Summarizing

Have students use the following editing checklist to summarize the chapter's main points about commas. As an alternative to giving students these guidelines, have them compose their own editing checklist.

- Check each *and* and *or* to see if it comes before the last item in a series of three or more words or phrases. Be sure that each item in a

I read new, unusual facts about Juana Briones de Miranda. (The facts were new *and* unusual.)

Use a comma sometimes to separate two adjectives that precede a noun and are not joined by a conjunction.

Sometimes a comma is not needed between two adjectives. To decide if a comma is needed, read the sentence with the word *and* between the two adjectives. If the sentence makes sense, use a comma. If it sounds awkward, do not.

Comma Needed	She was a strong, remarkable woman. (*A strong and remarkable woman* reads well.)
Comma Not Needed	She was a strong pioneer woman. (Since *a strong and pioneer woman* sounds awkward, no comma is used.)

Usually, no comma is used after a number or after an adjective that refers to size, shape, or age.

ADJECTIVE EXPRESSIONS	
six E-mail messages	a young black cat

Practice Your Skills

Check Your Understanding

Using Commas with Adjectives

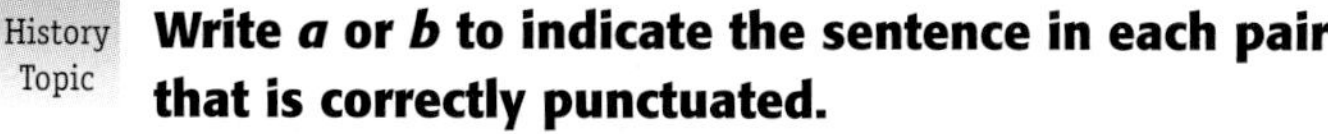

History Topic **Write *a* or *b* to indicate the sentence in each pair that is correctly punctuated.**

1. **a.** Juana's parents were brave Spanish colonists.
b. Juana's parents were brave, Spanish colonists.

2. **a.** They lived in a small unimportant town.
b. They lived in a small, unimportant town.

REACHING ALL STUDENTS

Struggling Learners

To reinforce the use of commas with adjectives before a noun, have students practice using the *and* test with the following examples after discussing the instruction on these pages.

- I have some wonderful interesting news. (wonderful, interesting)
- It was a long dull article. (long, dull)
- She wore two beautiful bracelets. (two beautiful)

A DIFFERENT APPROACH

Auditory

Read the sentences in **Practice Your Skills** aloud. After listening to the sentences, students should use a "thumbs up" to identify the correct sentence and a "thumbs down" to identify an incorrect sentence.

series except the last is followed by a comma.

- Look at every sentence that contains one of the conjunctions *and, but,* and *or.* If the group of words before and after the conjunction each functions as a complete sentence, you have a compound sentence. Make sure to use a comma before a conjunction.
- Check each sentence that does not begin with a subject to see whether it opens with an introductory element (a word or phrase that tells when, where, how, or why the main action of the sentence occurs). This introductory element should be followed by a comma, separating it from the main part of the sentence.

Check Understanding

By Applying Editing Strategies

Have students apply the editing checklist strategies from **Pull It All Together** to a writing assignment of

Sample Answers for *Writing Sentences Using Commas with Adjectives:*

6. I live in a large brick apartment building.

7. My best friend is a gentle, soft-spoken person.

8. My high school put on an amazing amateur performance of *Grease* last year.

9. I spent last Sunday doing a long, difficult home work assignment.

10. The nightly news program has hardly any important world news.

3. **a.** Today this town is the large urban city of San Francisco.
b. Today this town is the large, urban city of San Francisco.

4. **a.** Juana married a young rash soldier.
b. Juana married a young, rash soldier.

5. **a.** She had seven children with her husband.
b. She had seven, children with her husband.

Connect to the Writing Process: Drafting

Writing Sentences Using Commas with Adjectives

Write sentences that describe the items listed below. Use two or more adjectives before a noun in each sentence.

6. the place you live

7. your closest friend

8. a great performance

9. a day last week

10. a movie or TV show

Connect to the Writing Process: Editing

Using Commas with Adjectives

Write the following sentences, adding commas where needed. If a sentence is correct, write *C*.

11. Juana Briones bought a vast^fertile rancho south of San Francisco.

12. She was a clever^practical businesswoman.

13. She held onto her land through two dramatic changes in government. C

14. This was an unusual^resourceful accomplishment.

15. Juana was also a sincere^kind woman.

16. She raised five orphaned children. C

17. She was also an unselfish^fearless nurse.

18. She took care of the community of Bolinas during a deadly smallpox epidemic. C

their choice—either one from this chapter or one from their portfolio. Students can evaluate their own papers for these errors, or they can use the strategies to suggest ways a partner can edit his or her piece of writing.

19. One popular, eloquent journalist described her as a Clara Barton.

20. A memorial to her stands in a small popular park in San Francisco. C

Communicate Your Ideas

APPLY TO WRITING

Personal History: ***Commas That Separate***

Interview a family member to find out about an ancestor of yours who struggled through hard times. Then write a paragraph to share with your classmates. Describe the person and what he or she accomplished. Use commas to separate items in a series or to separate adjectives before a noun.

 Mixed Practice

General Interest **Rewrite the following sentences, adding commas where needed.**

1. The most valuable animals in the Old West were the hardy, dependable burros.

2. They plodded steadily across deserts, over mountains, and through high creeks.

3. They could survive long journeys in which food, water, and rest were scarce.

4. The ranchers, miners, and soldiers all praised burros.

5. Is the burro the strongest, bravest domestic animal?

6. Burros have soft, trustful eyes.

7. However, a burro will fight a wild stallion, a bull, or even a grizzly bear.

TIMESAVER *QuickCheck*

Have students exchange their completed paragraphs with a partner. Students should check for correct use of commas in a series and commas with adjectives before nouns. Have students correct any errors they find before writing their final drafts.

HOME STUDY

After students have interviewed a family member, have them find out as much as they can about their ancestors. Students should find out where their ancestors lived, when they came to the United States, and what types of jobs they held. Students should write several paragraphs about their ancestors. Remind students to check for correct use of commas and end marks.

IDENTIFYING COMMON STUMBLING BLOCKS

Problem

- Using commas incorrectly in compound sentences

Solution

- Tell students that compound sentences have two subjects and two verbs. A comma must be used in a compound sentence or it is considered a run-on sentence. Remind students that the comma should always be placed right before the coordinating conjunction. Remind students that coordinating conjunctions are "joining" words like *and, but, or, nor, for, so, yet.*
- Have students decide where to place the commas in the following sentences. Remind students to locate the subjects and verbs before deciding where to place commas.

  The summer brings many grasshoppers so my father bought me a net. (grasshoppers, so)

  The net was long but I was strong enough to hold it. (long, but)

  I caught many insects yet many jumped right out of the net. (insects, yet)

8. These creatures quickly recognize danger,dodge it fast,and keep their heads.

9. A threatened burro will halt,turn around,and kick.

10. A burro's hooves are hard,sharp,and very dangerous.

Compound Sentences

A comma and a conjunction often separate the independent clauses in a compound sentence. *And, but, or, nor,* and *yet* are commonly used conjunctions.

Use a comma to separate the independent clauses of a compound sentence if the clauses are joined by a conjunction.

In the following examples, notice that the comma comes before the conjunction.

> Many animals are plant eaters, and a few plants are animal eaters.
>
> Most soils nourish plants, but the soil in bogs may lack nitrogen.

Keep in mind the difference between a compound sentence and a simple sentence that has a compound verb.

COMPOUND SENTENCE	Bog plants attract insects, and the insects provide necessary nutrients. (A comma is needed because there are two sets of subjects and verbs.)
COMPOUND VERB	Bog plants attract insects and get nutrients from them. (No comma is needed with a compound verb.)

Using a comma and a conjunction together is one way to correct a run-on sentence.

RUN-ON SENTENCE	Carnivorous plants can survive without insects, they grow better with insects in their diet.
CORRECTED COMPOUND SENTENCE	Carnivorous plants can survive without insects, **but** they grow better with insects in their diet.

You can learn more about compound sentences on pages L271–L273.

You can learn about other ways to correct run-on sentences on pages L302–L303.

PRACTICE YOUR SKILLS

Check Your Understanding

Using Commas with Compound Sentences

Science Topic **Write *C* if a sentence is punctuated correctly. Write *I* if a sentence is punctuated incorrectly. Remember that a compound sentence needs a comma, but a compound verb does not.**

1. The cobra lily is the best-known carnivorous plant in the United States^and it is found in California and Oregon. I

2. It is also known as the California pitcher plant^and its scientific name is *Darlington californica.* I

3. It has a hooded head and looks like a colorful speckled snake. C

4. The roof of its hood is called a *dome*^and its forked tongue is called a *fishtail.* I

5. The dome has windows^and these let in light. I

6. Insects are attracted by the light and do not realize it is a trap. C

7. The pitcher and tongue produce nectar and attract many different insects. C

A DIFFERENT APPROACH

Auditory

Have students complete items one through ten in **Practice Your Skills** by working in small groups. Students should take turns reading each item aloud and deciding where commas should be placed. Group members should decide whether or not each response is correct and tell why or why not.

HOME WORK

Have students complete the **Apply to Writing** activity as home work. Remind students to correctly form compound sentences for each topic. Students should use each of the following coordinating conjunctions at least once in their sentences: *and, but, or, for, nor, so, yet*. Students should then place commas correctly in their compound sentences.

TIMESAVER *QuickCheck*

After completing **Apply to Writing,** have students exchange their reports with a partner. Students should read their partners' writing, evaluating the use of commas. Have students share with their partner ways to improve their writing and to correct any comma errors.

8. Insects fly inside the pitcher and then are unable to escape. C

9. They may fly up toward the light, but then they slip down into the pitcher. I

10. The water at the bottom dampens their wings, and they are unable to fly out. I

Connect to the Writing Process: Editing
Punctuating Compound Sentences

11.–16. Rewrite each incorrect sentence from the preceding exercise, adding commas where needed.
[See responses given above.]

Communicate Your Ideas

APPLY TO WRITING

Informative Report: ***Compound Sentences***

The photograph on the preceding page shows a Madagascar orchid, known botanically as *Angraecum sequipedal.* It has many interesting characteristics, and there is a remarkable story about this plant and Charles Darwin. Find out more about the Madagascar orchid and report your findings for your science teacher. Use at least four compound sentences in your report. Be sure you have used commas where they are needed. If you are unable to find information about this orchid, describe another plant that you find fascinating.

Introductory Elements

A comma follows certain words and groups of words at the beginning of a sentence.

Use a comma after certain introductory elements.

A comma sometimes separates an interjection from the rest of a sentence. Words like *no, now, oh, well, why,* and *yes* can be used as interjections.

WORDS	**Yes,** I really do enjoy hiking.
	Well, my last hike was a real disaster!

An interjection can also be followed by an exclamation point.

INTERJECTION	**Oh!** I almost forgot my compass.

A comma follows two or more prepositional phrases that come at the beginning of a sentence. A comma also follows one introductory prepositional phrase that has four or more words.

PREPOSITIONAL PHRASES	**With a map in my pocket,** I started out. (two prepositional phrases)

USING STUDENTS' STRENGTHS

Multiple Intelligences: Linguistic

After discussing the instruction on pages L553–L554, have students add introductory elements with commas to the following sentences. Students' introductory elements will vary, but suggestions have been provided.

- I was ready to hike. (With my compass in hand, I was ready to hike.)
- Up the hill we went. (Although we forgot our granola, up the hill we went.)
- My boot string snapped! (Oh, my boot string snapped!)

YOUR IDEAS

For Teaching Introductory Elements

	Inside the dense forest, the trail forked in two directions. (one prepositional phrase with four words)

You can learn more about prepositional phrases on pages L189–L197.

A comma follows a participial phrase that comes at the beginning of a sentence.

PARTICIPIAL PHRASES	**Looking at my map,** I could not find this fork. **Bubbling and murmuring,** the stream rushed down the hillside.

You can learn more about participial phrases on pages L217–L225.

A comma follows an infinitive phrase that comes at the beginning of a sentence.

INFINITIVE PHRASES	**To make up my mind,** I decided to flip a coin. **To take me to my destination,** the trail had to cross the stream.

You can learn more about infinitive phrases on pages L233–L236.

A comma follows an adverb clause when it comes at the beginning of a sentence.

ADVERB CLAUSES	**If I chose the right fork,** I'd be at the ranger station in an hour. **When I set out on my journey,** the sun was in the east.

You can learn more about adverb clauses on pages L256–L258.

PRACTICE YOUR SKILLS

Check Your Understanding
Identifying Introductory Elements

Contemporary Life

Identify and write the word or words that serve as the introductory element in each sentence. Be prepared to tell where you would insert a comma.

1. Looking back on my hike, I didn't make too many mistakes.
2. For my last birthday, my family had given me sturdy hiking boots.
3. To prepare for my hike, I had packed a map and compass.
4. To protect me from sudden storms, a garbage bag went into my pack.
5. Well, maybe it was a mistake to go hiking alone.
6. If I had hiked with Emily, she might have kept us on the right path.
7. During the previous year, our hiking group had taken that route only twice.
8. Between the two of us, we might have figured out our location.
9. Seeing a steam that deep, Emily would not have tried to cross it.
10. When I slipped on the stones, my pack fell off.

Connect to the Writing Process: Drafting
Writing Sentences with Introductory Elements

Write five sentences, following the directions for each given below. [Answers may vary. Possible responses are given.]

11. Begin a sentence with the interjection *no.*
    No, I'm not going to the party.
12. Begin a sentence with a long prepositional phrase.
    After a week of exams, I'm tired.

A DIFFERENT APPROACH

Visual

Before having students complete **Practice Your Skills** independently, allow time for them to share any hiking or camping experiences they may have had. Have students write sentences about their adventures on the board. Students should decide whether or not the sentences have any introductory elements or if they require commas.

HOME WORK

Have students use newspapers to identify commas used correctly with introductory elements, compound sentences, and items in a series. Students should cut out an article and highlight each correctly used comma in the article.

YOUR IDEAS

For Home Work

To get caught up on my sleep, I will even forgo a party.

13. Begin a sentence with an infinitive phrase.

Looking ahead to tomorrow, I'll feel more energetic than I do today.

14. Begin a sentence with a participial phrase.

If you don't mind, I'm going home now.

15. Begin a sentence with an adverb clause.

Connect to the Writing Process: Editing

Using Commas with Introductory Elements

Rewrite each sentence, adding commas where needed.

16. As soon as my pack fell into the stream I jumped in after it.

17. Rapidly rushing down the mountain the stream carried my knapsack away.

18. Oh what a disaster it was to lose my compass and map of the terrain!

19. Preparing us for this situation our hike leader had given us good advice.

20. To find your way back to civilization follow a stream downhill.

21. Squelching along in wet boots I followed the stream.

22. After I had hiked for an hour the ground became soft and mushy.

23. No I did not try to cross the bog.

24. At the end of the day two rangers found me.

25. Boy was I glad I'd checked in with them before I started out!

Commonly Used Commas

You will use some commas more often than others. On the following pages are some examples of the most common uses of commas.

With Dates and Addresses

Commas are commonly used between the parts of a date or an address.

Use commas to separate elements in dates and addresses.

In the following examples, notice that when a date or an address comes within a sentence, another comma is used at the end to separate it from the rest of the sentence.

DATES On Tuesday, December 7, 1999, our voyage began.
(No comma is used between the month and the day, but a comma is used after the year to separate the date from the rest of the sentence.)

We arrived home in January 2001.
(No comma is used between the month and the year if no day is given.)

ADDRESSES Write to us in care of Anna Melon, 791 Reata Lane, Arizona City, Arizona 85223, until March 4.
(No comma is used between the state and the ZIP Code, but a comma is used after the ZIP code to separate the address from the rest of the sentence.

We live at 18 Elgin Street **in** Boston, Massachusetts.
(A preposition can take the place of a comma between parts of an address.)

In Letters

Commas are commonly used after parts of a letter.

REACHING ALL STUDENTS

Struggling Learners

Have students search newspapers, magazines, or textbooks to find examples of commas used with dates and addresses. Students should provide an example of comma uses and explain why they think the commas were used correctly in each example. Have students present their findings to the class.

Advanced Learners

Tell students that when only the month or seasons and the year of a date is given, no comma is necessary, as in January 1996 and winter 2000.

A DIFFERENT APPROACH

Auditory

Read the first two sentences in **Check Your Understanding** aloud to students, pausing slightly at each comma and not pausing where commas should be but are not. Have students choose the correct answer based on what they hear. Follow the same procedure for the rest of the sentences.

Use a comma after the salutation of a friendly letter and after the closing of all letters.

OPENINGS AND CLOSINGS		
Openings	Dear Aunt Chris,	Dear Dad,
Closings	Yours truly,	Sincerely yours,

Practice Your Skills

Check Your Understanding

Using Commas That Separate

General Interest

Write *a* or *b* to indicate the sentence in each pair that is correctly punctuated. Be prepared to explain why the other sentence is not correct.

1. **a.** On May 1, 1884, construction was begun in Chicago, Illinois, on the first American skyscraper.

b. On May 1 1884, construction was begun in Chicago, Illinois on the first American skyscraper. There should be commas after "May 1" and after "Illinois."

2. **a.** The National Baseball Hall of Fame and Museum is at 25 Main Street, Cooperstown, NY 13326.

b. The National Baseball Hall of Fame and Museum is at 25 Main Street, Cooperstown, NY, 13326.

There should not be a comma between the abbreviation of the state's name and the ZIP c

3. **a.** In December 1886, Josephine Cochrane of Shelbyville, Illinois, patented a dishwasher.

b. In December 1886, Josephine Cochrane of Shelbyville, Illinois patented a dishwasher.

There should be a comma following the name of the state.

4. a. On March 10 1876, Alexander Graham Bell's home at 5 Exeter Place Boston, Massachusetts was the site of the first successful phone call.

b. On March 10, 1876, Alexander Graham Bell's home at 5 Exeter Place, Boston, Massachusetts, was the site of the first successful phone call.

There should be commas after "March 10," "5 Exeter Place," and "Massachusetts."

5. a. Dear Lily,

We stayed at this park. I can't wait to tell you about it.

Your friend,
Amanda

b. Dear Lily.

We stayed at this park. I can't wait to tell you about it.

Your friend.
Amanda

There should be a comma, not a period, after the letter's opening and after its closing.

Connect to the Writing Process: Drafting

Writing Sentences Using Commas

Write each sentence, adding a city and state or a month, date, and year in each blank. Use commas where needed.

6. The newspaper was dated ■. June 25, 1940

7. ■ is a place I'd like to spend a vacation. New York, New York,

8. After ■ the warranty runs out. January 1, 2002,

9. The plane stops at ■ on its way to Boston, MA. Chicago, Illinois,

10. On ■ I was born in ■. Savannah, Georgia September 17, 1988,

Connect to the Writing Process: Editing

Using Commas That Separate

Rewrite each sentence, adding commas where needed.

11. San Francisco's famous cable cars were first put into service on August 1,1893.

12. In 1872 the first mail-order house was established at 825 North Clark Street,Chicago,Illinois.

YOUR IDEAS

For Writing Letters Using Commas

TIMESAVER *QuickCheck*

Evaluate students' writing by checking for accurate letter form and correct use of commas with compound sentences, adjectives before nouns, introductory elements, dates and addresses, and in a series. Check students' use of end marks. Have students correct any errors in their final drafts.

13. On December 25, 1777, Captain Cook landed on Christmas Island.

14. Before August 1, 1958, a first-class stamp cost only three cents.

15. On May 30, 1793, the first daily newspaper in America was published in Philadelphia, Pennsylvania.

16. President George Washington went to Philadelphia, Pennsylvania, on April 22, 1793, to visit the first American circus.

17. On December 11, 1882, the Bijou Theater at 545 Washington Street in Boston, Massachusetts, became the first theater with electric lights.

18. In October 1797, the first parachute jump was made from a hot-air balloon over Paris, France.

19. The first hotel elevator was installed on August 23, 1859, in the Fifth Avenue Hotel in New York City.

20. You can write to 123 North Center Street, Mount Olive, North Carolina 28365 to find out about the North Carolina Pickle Festival.

Communicate Your Ideas

APPLY TO WRITING

Invitation: *Commas That Separate*

Imagine that your family is going to have a special celebration. You are allowed to invite one friend to this special family party. Write an invitation to your friend, describing the celebration. Give your friend details about the location and date of the party. When you have finished, check to make sure that you have used commas correctly.

Mixed Practice

Science Topic **Rewrite each sentence, adding commas where needed.**

1. While I was researching skateboards, I found an interesting old newspaper story.

2. In the June 29, 1999, edition of the *Mercury,* there was an article on skateboarding.

3. Some scientists in San Francisco, California, filmed skateboarders in action.

4. As they studied the film, they noticed some rules of science at work.

5. To be a good skater, you have to follow safety rules.

6. Yes, skateboarding is not only a sport but a science.

7. When you balance on a skateboard, there are three forces at work.

8. The weight of the rider is one force, and gravity is another.

9. Pushing up against the skateboard, the ground also acts as a force.

10. According to the laws of physics, these three forces must balance out to zero.

11. When one force changes, the others must also be adjusted.

12. If they want to jump high, skaters have to be going fast.

13. Before they roll onto a ramp, the skaters crouch.

14. At the beginning of a ramp, the skaters rise suddenly.

15. The action is called *pumping,* and it increases the skaters' speed.

YOUR IDEAS

For Checking Your Understanding

USING STUDENTS' STRENGTHS

Multiple Intelligences: Linguistic

Have students look through drama scenes or plays that they locate in the library or classroom. Students should look specifically for scenes in which the actors use direct address. When students have located examples, they should write them down, making sure to include correct use of commas around the nouns of direct address. Have students share their scenes with the class.

Commas That Enclose

Commas are used to enclose some expressions that interrupt the main idea of a sentence. When you read a sentence aloud, you naturally pause before and after an interrupting expression. Commas are placed where these pauses would occur. If you take interrupters enclosed by commas out of a sentence, the sentence will still make sense.

Direct Address

In conversation people are often addressed by name. This kind of interrupter is called a **noun of direct address.** Since nouns of direct address interrupt the flow of a sentence, they should be set off by commas.

Use commas to set off nouns of direct address.

The community picnic**, Brian,** will start at 11:00 A.M.
(The noun of direct address, *Brian,* could be removed.)

Please help me**, Dana and James,** pack the car.
(More than one noun can be included in direct address. *Dana and James* could be removed.)

Close the door, **kids,** behind us.
(Direct address might include a noun that is not a proper noun.)

In the following examples, only one comma is needed because the noun of direct address comes at the beginning or at the end of the sentence.

Mom, where is our ice chest?
May we borrow your canvas chairs**, Mrs. Anders?**

Practice Your Skills

Check Your Understanding
Using Commas with Direct Address

Contemporary Life **Write the word or words that should be set off by a comma or commas.**

1. Tell me, Reverend Dixon, where to find the grill.
2. Let me give you a hand with the cooler, Brandon.
3. Wait, Isaac, and I'll give you some plates to carry.
4. Do you need help moving the tables, Mrs. Aylard?
5. Yes, Tyler, I can use your help.
6. Mr. Mott is here, Dad, and is looking for you.
7. The food, Giselle, should be put out on the tables.
8. Tell Mom, Matt, that we brought more hamburgers.
9. No, Spot, get your nose out of that basket!
10. Hey, Jenna, catch that dog!

Connect to the Writing Process: Drafting
Writing Sentences: Using Commas with Direct Address

Write five sentences, following the directions for each given below. [Answers may vary. Possible responses are given.]

Thank you for coming, Mr. Suarez.
11. Include *Mr. Suarez* as a term of direct address at the end of a sentence.
Chris, I love this gift!
12. Include *Chris* as a term of direct address at the beginning of a sentence.
I'm up here, Mom, in the attic.
13. Include *Mom* as a term of direct address in the middle of a sentence.
I'd love to help you, Mrs. Toland, if you'll let me.
14. Include *Ms. Toland* as a term of direct address in the middle of a sentence.
Dion, you're a clown!
15. Include *Dion* as a term of direct address anywhere in a sentence.

A DIFFERENT APPROACH
Auditory

Have students work with partners to complete **Check Your Understanding**. The first student should read the first sentence aloud, pausing where commas should be placed. The second student should write down the sentence, placing commas where they belong. Students should continue to switch roles, one reading and one writing, until they complete the exercise.

GETTING STUDENTS INVOLVED

Cooperative Learning

Have students work in small groups to write the parenthetical expressions from the chart on long strips of paper. Then have students come to the board and write sentences about a subject of their choosing. For each sentence, have one student choose a parenthetical expression strip that could be inserted into the sentence. The student should then tell where commas should be placed in the new sentence. Continue the activity until all of the parenthetical expressions have been used correctly.

Connect to the Writing Process: Editing

Using Commas with Direct Address

Rewrite each sentence, adding commas where needed.

16. Please‸Mrs. Hernandez‸may I have another helping?

17. Surely‸Ryan‸you aren't going to eat all that.

18. Well‸Lonnie‸you ate at least three hot dogs.

19. Excuse me‸sir‸but have you seen a little boy with red hair?

20. Oh‸Angelica‸your brother is with your mom.

21. Hey‸Hector‸do you want to play softball?

22. Did you bring your bat and ball‸Emma?

23. Did you find Justin‸Mary?

24. Come on‸Sis‸we're going to play ball.

25. Jorge and Adriana‸will you play the infield?

Parenthetical Expressions

One type of interrupter is called a **parenthetical expression.** The following parenthetical expressions should be enclosed in commas.

COMMON PARENTHETICAL EXPRESSIONS		
after all	for instance	of course
at any rate	generally speaking	on the contrary
by the way	on the other hand	to tell the truth
however	in fact	nevertheless
for example	in my opinion	I believe (guess, hope, know)
consequently	moreover	

Use commas to set off parenthetical expressions.

Soccer**, in fact,** is preferred to baseball in many countries.
(*In fact,* could be removed without affecting the meaning of the sentence.)

In the following examples, only one comma is needed because the parenthetical expression comes at the beginning or at the end of the sentence.

In my opinion, soccer is more fun than baseball.
Soccer is a much more active game**, at any rate.**

CONNECT TO SPEAKING AND WRITING

When the words *I believe, I hope,* or *I think* appear at the beginning of a sentence, they are never parenthetical. In a sentence that begins with *I, I* is always the subject or part of the subject. Note the difference between these two sentences.

I hope John will come tomorrow.
John will come tomorrow**, I hope.**

In the second sentence, the subject is *John* and the main idea is that John is coming. *I hope* is only an afterthought.

PRACTICE YOUR SKILLS

Check Your Understanding
Using Commas with Parenthetical Expressions

Sports Topic **Write *I* if a parenthetical expression is incorrectly punctuated. Write *C* if it is correctly punctuated.**

1. To tell the truth, the Masters Golf Tournament isn't very interesting to me. C

2. Golf, I suspect is more fun for the player than the spectator. I

YOUR IDEAS
For Using Commas with Parenthetical Expressions

A DIFFERENT APPROACH

Visual

Complete **Connect to the Writing Process: Drafting** as a class. Have students use black markers to write out their sentences with parenthetical expressions on one large sheet of mural paper. Then have students use red markers to add commas correctly to each sentence. Then discuss all of the parenthetical expressions and commas on the large "sentence collage."

3. Golf requires considerable skill of course. I
4. This sport after all, requires the ability to aim very accurately. I
5. Without a doubt, players must know exactly how to strike a ball. C
6. Tennis matches on the other hand, fascinate me. I
7. Consequently I prefer to watch a Davis Cup match. I
8. Tennis, in my opinion, requires the same kind of coordination that golf does. C
9. In addition tennis players must have great reflexes. I
10. Generally speaking, you must be able to react almost instinctively. C

Connect to the Writing Process: Editing

Using Commas with Parenthetical Expressions

11.–16. Rewrite the incorrect sentences from the preceding exercise, adding commas where needed. [See responses given above.]

Connect to the Writing Process: Drafting

Writing Sentences with Parenthetical Expressions

[Answers may vary. Possible responses are given.]

Write five sentences, following the directions for each. Express some of your own opinions or observations.

17. Use the expression *in my opinion* in the middle of a sentence. That dog, in my opinion, could do with a bath!
18. Use the expression *As a rule* at the beginning of a sentence. As a rule, I watch football on Monday nights.
19. Use the expression *I believe* at the end of a sentence. Matt is from Kansas, I believe.
20. Use the expression *by the way* in the middle of a sentence. Give me a call, by the way, if you need more information.
21. Use the expression *of course* anywhere in a sentence. Mary, of course, always gets an *A*.

Appositives

An **appositive** renames, or explains, a noun or pronoun in the sentence. Usually an appositive comes immediately after that noun or pronoun and is written with modifiers. Because they interrupt the sentence, appositives should be set off by commas.

Use commas to set off most appositives and their modifiers.

> Texas**, my home state,** has an interesting history.
> (The appositive, *my home state,* could be removed.)

In the following example, only one comma is needed because the appositive comes at the end of the sentence.

> La Salle established Fort St. Louis**, the first French settlement here.**

Commas are *not* used if an appositive identifies a person or thing by clarifying, or naming, which one or ones are meant.

> A street has been named after the explorer **La Salle.**

You can learn more about appositives on pages L201–L202.

PRACTICE YOUR SKILLS

Check Your Understanding
Classifying Appositives

History Topic **Identify the appositive in each sentence. Then tell if it is necessary or unnecessary.**

1. The Caddo, a Native American group, lived in East Texas. unnecessary
2. They were the leaders of the Caddo Confederacy, a group that included the Wichita and Waco nations. unnecessary

GETTING STUDENTS INVOLVED

Collaborative Learning

Have pairs of students work together to match a noun with an appositive from the list below. Remind students to punctuate their sentences correctly.

Nouns	**Appositives**
Rome	the Greek god of the ocean
Beethoven	the world's most popular sport
Poseidon	the German composer
Kimono	the capital of Italy
Soccer	a loose robe tied with a sash

YOUR IDEAS
For Using Commas with Appositives

3. Cabeza de Vaca, a Spanish explorer, was shipwrecked on the Texas coast in 1528. unnecessary
4. His companion Estevanico was probably the first African American seen by Native Americans. necessary
5. In 1689, Mexican explorer Alonso de Leon found Ft. St. Louis abandoned. necessary
6. A city grew up around San Antonio Mission, one of many missions established in the early 1700s. unnecessary
7. Spain's claim to Texas was surrendered to the newly independent nation Mexico. necessary
8. Stephen Austin, spokesman for three hundred families, received permission to settle in Texas. unnecessary
9. In 1821, the families began settling in a region near the Brazos, a river in northern Texas. unnecessary
10. By 1835, about 25,000 colonists, mostly immigrants from the United States, occupied the region. unnecessary

Connect to the Writing Process: Editing
Using Commas with Appositives

Rewrite each sentence, adding commas where needed. If a sentence is correct, write *C*.

11. Mexico's dictator, Santa Anna, forbade further colonization.
12. In 1835, Anglo-American Texans captured San Antonio, a Mexican stronghold.
13. Members of the Convention of 1836, a revolutionary group, signed the Texas Declaration of Independence.
14. Texas was declared an independent republic on March 2, 1836, Sam Houston's birthday.
15. Mexican forces recaptured San Antonio in the Battle of the Alamo, one of the best-known events in Texas history.

16. Commander-in-Chief Sam Houston defeated the Mexican army and captured Santa Anna in 1836. C

17. In 1845 James Knox Polk, the president of the United States, signed a law making Texas our twenty-eighth state.

18. The Rio Grande, a river that flows into the Gulf of Mexico, was established as the Mexico-Texas boundary in 1846.

19. Confederacy supporters, mostly colonists from the South, caused Texas to secede during the Civil War.

20. Republican Edmund Davis became governor in 1870, and Texas was readmitted to the Union.

Mixed Practice

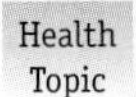

Rewrite the following paragraphs, adding commas where needed.

Noise can be harmful to your health. In fact, loud sounds can cause earaches, and persistent noise can give some people headaches. Worst of all, however, it can cause hearing loss in some people.

Measured in units called decibels, noise can be monitored. A classroom discussion, one type of ordinary conversation, hovers around 60 decibels. Popular music, however, can reach 110–120 decibels. Any noise over 70 decibels, by the way, can be dangerous.

For more information about noise, write to the Noise Center of the League for the Hard of Hearing, at 71 West 23rd Street, New York, New York 10010-4162.

USING STUDENTS' STRENGTHS

Multiple Intelligences: Musical

Listen to a piece of composed music with the students, either classical or jazz. Ask students to listen for the rests and pauses in the piece, and compare them to commas in a sentence.

REACHING ALL STUDENTS

Struggling Learners

Remind students that commas are used to separate clauses and phrases that are not needed from the rest of the sentence. Tell students that any phrase or clause that is essential to the meaning of the sentence should not be separated by commas. Discuss the examples on these pages. Then have students write additional examples on the board to check for understanding.

Nonessential Elements

Like parenthetical expressions, entire phrases and clauses can interrupt a sentence. Moreover, some of these phrases and clauses are not essential, or necessary, to the sentence.

A **nonessential** phrase or clause can be removed from a sentence, and the sentence would still make complete sense. A comma goes before and after a nonessential phrase or clause to show that the phrase could be removed.

Use commas to set off nonessential participial phrases and nonessential clauses.

A participial phrase is nonessential if it provides extra, unnecessary information.

Nonessential Participial Phrase	Outdoor games**, played in most cultures,** are enjoyed by old and young alike.

If the nonessential participial phrase were dropped, the main idea of the sentence would not be changed.

Outdoor games are enjoyed by old and young alike.

You can learn more about participial phrases on pages L217–L225.

Likewise, an adjective clause is nonessential if it provides extra, unnecessary information.

Nonessential Adjective Clause	Tug-of-war**, which is played in many cultures,** can be a team sport or a two-player contest.

If the nonessential adjective clause were dropped, the basic meaning of the sentence would not be changed.

Tug-of-war can be a team sport or a two-player contest.

You can learn more about adjective clauses on pages L260–L265.

A participial phrase or an adjective clause is sometimes essential. If an essential phrase or clause were dropped, the meaning of the sentence would be incomplete. **Essential** phrases and clauses usually identify a person, place, or thing and answer the question *Which one?* When a phrase or clause is essential, no commas are used.

Essential Participial Phrase	Games **played in the ancient world** were often taken seriously. (Without the phrase, the sentence would read *Games were often taken seriously.* The reader would not know which games.)
Essential Adjective Clauses	Adults in ancient cultures participated in sports **that developed necessary skills.** (Without the clause, the sentence would read *Adults in ancient cultures participated in sports.* The reader would not know which sports are meant.)
	Ancient hunters enjoyed games **that developed marksmanship.** (Without the clause, the sentence would read *Ancient hunters enjoyed games.* The reader would not know which games are meant.)

Practice Your Skills

Check Your Understanding

Identifying Essential and Nonessential Elements

General Interest **Write *E* if the underlined words in a sentence are essential or *N* if they are nonessential. Be prepared to explain your answer.**

1. People living in today's world seldom recognize the value of board games. E

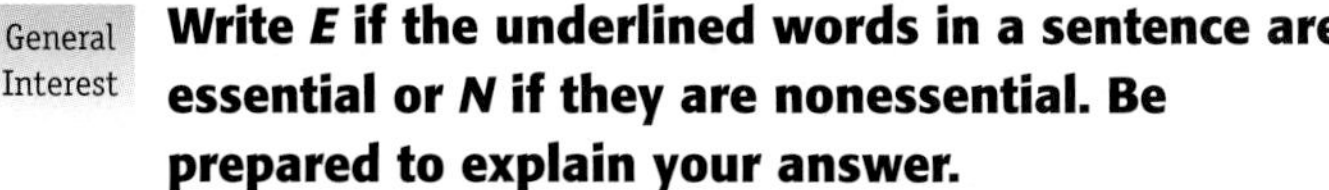

2. *Chaturanga,* developed in seventh-century India, taught players to think ahead. N

YOUR IDEAS

For Using Commas with Nonessential Elements

A DIFFERENT APPROACH

Auditory

Complete **Practice Your Skills** by having students state whether the correct response for each item is *E* for essential elements or *N* for nonessential elements. Read each sentence aloud and have individual students respond. Discuss students' responses.

HOME WORK

Have students find examples of commas used with nonessential elements in a literature textbook or a novel they are reading. Students should write out at least three examples and share them with the class the following day.

3. A great leader who commanded armies had to be able to anticipate the future. E

4. This complex game, renamed *chess* by the Europeans, was very popular in medieval times. N

5. The Europeans substituted the word *king* for the word *shah,* which was used by the Persians for their ruler. N

6. The word *checkmate* comes from *shat-mat,* which means "the shah is helpless." N

7. A similar battle-tactics game is *Go,* brought to Japan from China. N

8. Until A.D. 1600, students studying in military schools were required to play *Go.* E

9. The game *Wari,* which is also called by other names, is a game of strategy in Africa. N

10. Each player tries to capture the stones that sit in the other player's compartments. E

Check Your Understanding
Classifying Nonessential Elements

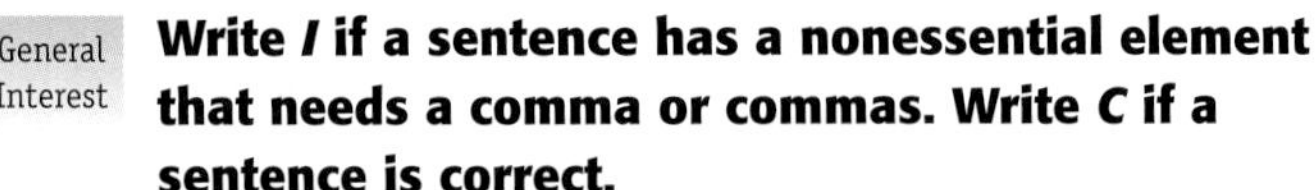

General Interest **Write *I* if a sentence has a nonessential element that needs a comma or commas. Write *C* if a sentence is correct.**

11. Nine Men's Morris, little known in the United States, is one of the oldest games in the world. I

12. Archeologists have found a Nine Men's Morris board that was used in Egypt in 1400 B.C. C

13. Each player gets nine men, which look like checkers. I

14. Checkers was created from backgammon pieces and the board used for chess. C

15. Polish checkers,which is one of many variations,is played on a board of one hundred squares. I

16. Few people have heard of the game of *halma*,which gets its name from the Greek word for "jump." I

17. A new variation of it was developed in 1880 in Sweden,where it became very popular. I

18. People who play the game in the United States call it *Chinese checkers.* C

19. From England comes the hunt game Fox and Geese, which was a favorite of Queen Victoria. I

20. The fox,which gets the first turn in the game,has only one game piece. I

Connect to the Writing Process: Editing

Using Commas with Nonessential Elements

21.–26. Rewrite the incorrect sentences from the preceding exercise, adding commas where needed.

[See responses given above.]

Connect to the Writing Process: Drafting

Writing Sentences Using Commas with Nonessential Elements

[Answers may vary. Possible responses are given.]

Follow the directions to write five sentences about some games that you know. Add commas where needed.

Chinese checkers, played often at my house, is my brother's favorite board game.

27. Write a sentence with the participial phrase *played often at my house* in the middle.

Chess, taught to me by my parents, has always been my first love.

28. Write a sentence with the participial phrase *taught to me by my parents* in the middle.

Someone always initiates a game of *Monopoly* over the holidays, providing hours of enjoyment.

29. Write a sentence with the participial phrase *providing hours of enjoyment* at the end.

The part about Charades that I enjoy most is acting out an obscure movie title.

30. Write a sentence with the adjective clause *that I enjoy most* in it.

Hearts, which I learned as a young child, is a good family card game.

31. Write a sentence with the adjective clause *which I learned as a young child* in it.

YOUR IDEAS

For Using Games

TIMESAVER *QuickCheck*

Before writing their final draft of game instructions, have students share their game ideas and instructions with friends or family members outside the classroom. The friend or family member should evaluate the game for its clear directions and for its entertainment qualities. Have students make any suggested improvements to their games before writing their final drafts.

HOME STUDY

Have students locate different game instructions either from home or at the library and evaluate the instructions for their clarity. Students should bring these game instructions to class and discuss how they are written. Have students and class members suggest ways that the directions might be improved. Students should also check the instructions for correct use of commas.

Communicate Your Ideas

APPLY TO WRITING

Directions: ***Commas That Enclose***

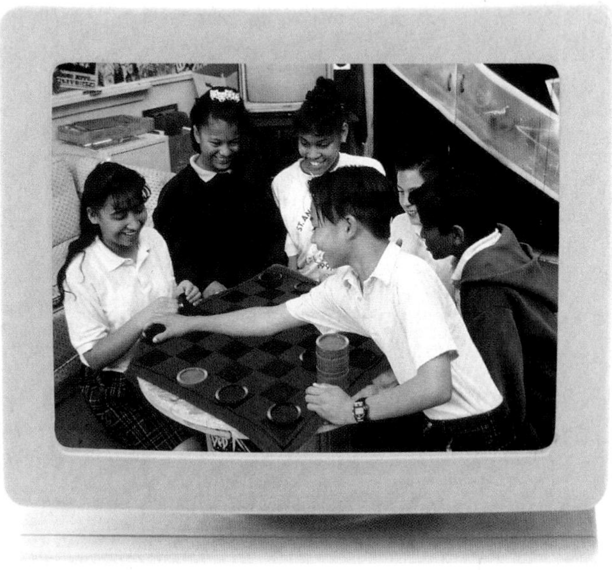

Your class is putting together a book of games for middle school students. Write brief directions for a board game that you enjoy or for an imaginary board game. Be sure to include answers to the following questions.

- How do the pieces move?
- What is the goal of the game?
- What strategies can players use to win?

As you write the directions, try to include some essential and nonessential elements. When you have finished, check to make sure that you have used commas correctly.

 Mixed Practice

Contemporary Life

Rewrite the following paragraphs, adding commas where needed.

I can walk to the Westside Pool which is quite near my home. Consequently my friend Scott and I go there often in the summer. Whitney and Ryan bicycling over from their own homes often meet us there.

As far as we're concerned the best time to get there is 9:00 A.M. The pool which gets very crowded by noon is almost empty in the morning. Little children aren't there because they must be brought by their parents who have errands to do in the morning. The lifeguard a friend of Ryan's sister lets us play games that aren't allowed in a crowded pool. We don't have to worry about splashing or running into other swimmers.

For example we have made up our own form of water polo which is played with two people on each side. Our ball borrowed from my little sister is a soft beach ball. What is most fun about our game in my opinion is changing the rules. Our most important rule which never changes is that the team who scores a goal gets to make up one new rule.

EXPANDING THE LESSON

Using Technology

Use Barrett Kendall ancillary instructional and practice materials located at http://www.bkenglish.com.

YOUR IDEAS

For Using Technology

FOR REVIEWING SKILLS

Using *CheckPoint*

This feature on end marks and commas can be used as further independent practice or as a cumulative review of the chapter. Students add end marks and commas to sentences, correct end mark and comma errors, and write sentences using end marks and commas correctly.

CheckPoint

Using End Marks and Commas Correctly

Write each sentence, adding end marks and commas where needed.

1. The fascinating, famous magician Houdini was born in Wisconsin.
2. Queens, workers, and drones are three classes of bees.
3. On the calendar several dates were circled, but I didn't know why.
4. To begin the game on time, the players will have to be here soon.
5. Before Columbus traveled to the Americas, tomatoes and corn were unknown in Europe.
6. On August 1, 1918, the Pirates and the Braves played twenty scoreless innings.
7. The first cold spell, of course, killed our plants.
8. Does Mark collect editions of the novel *Robin Hood*?
9. Watch out, Pam, for those rocks!
10. Pluto, which is the smallest planet in the solar system, is slightly smaller than the moon.

Using End Marks and Commas Correctly

Write each sentence, adding end marks and commas where needed. If a sentence does not need any changes, write *C*.

1. A star, of course, shines for millions of years.
2. To finish her test quickly, Amanda wrote less neatly than usual.
3. On the beach at Atlantic City, we found unusual shells.

4. My brother Sam pitches for the varsity team. C
5. *Black Beauty* is about a horse and is set in England. C
6. Air contains three gases: oxygen, nitrogen, and argon.
7. Write to Pride and Sons, 4290 Peach Tree Pkwy., Atlanta, GA 30341 for a free catalog.
8. Philadelphia, Benjamin Franklin's birthplace, is one of the country's major convention centers.
9. Standing on the stage, the mayor read the short, startling proclamation.
10. Did Liz bring the eggs, milk, cheese, and English muffins?

Using Commas

Write sentences that follow the directions below.

Write a sentence that . . .

1. includes a series of nouns.
2. includes two adjectives before a noun.
3. has two independent clauses joined by a coordinating conjunction.
4. includes a participial phrase at the beginning.
5. includes an adverbial clause at the beginning.
6. includes direct address.
7. includes a parenthetical expression.
8. includes an appositive.
9. includes a nonessential adjective clause.
10. includes a street number and name, city, state, and ZIP code.

Sample Answers for *Using Commas:*

1. I like pepperoni, mushrooms, and onions on my pizza.
2. Thin, flaky crust is my preference.
3. Alex works in a pizza parlor, and he gets free pizza.
4. Making pizza daily, Alex soon lost his appetite for pizza.
5. After he finishes his shift, Alex often brings me a pizza.
6. I was wondering, Amy, if you'd like to go out for pizza on Friday.
7. We would, of course, pay for this pizza!
8. Paul's Pizza Palace, the place where Alex works, would be a good place to go.
9. Alex, who is working on Friday, can make our pizza himself.
10. Meet me at 2435 Fulton Ave., Terrence, OK, 78726.

Using *Language and Self-Expression*

Consider using this writing assignment to assess students' ability to use end marks and commas correctly.

Prewriting

Encourage students to use graphic organizers like the ones below to help them organize their thoughts in the prewriting stage. For example, students might start with the following ideas and add their own ideas to help them proceed with their writing:

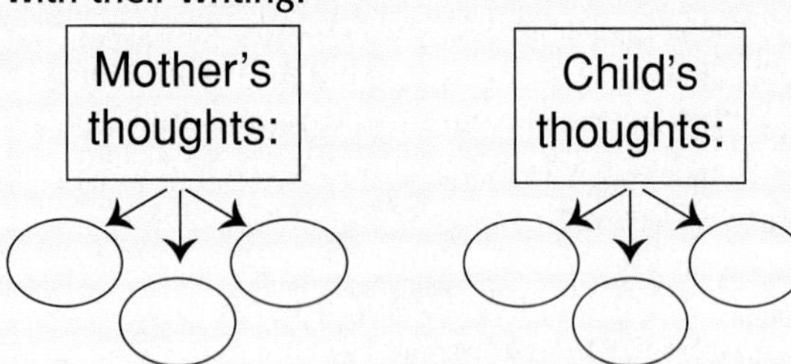

FOR YOUR INFORMATION

About the Artist

Elizabeth Catlett is widely known for her sculpture and graphic art, which often depicts her African American heritage. Born in Washington, D.C., Catlett began her art training at Howard University and continued at the University of Iowa, where Grant Wood encouraged her work in sculpture. In the 1940s, she moved to Mexico to work on a project, and she eventually became a Mexican citizen. In 1958, Catlett became the first woman professor of art at the National Autonomous University of Mexico. Her art has been influenced by the Mexican muralists, pre-Columbian sculpture, and African art.

Language and *Self-Expression*

The artist Elizabeth Catlett has used hard cedar wood to create a sculpture that looks soft and perhaps even warm. She has managed to show a mood and emotions in her sculpture even though she has not carved an expression on the mother's face.

Imagine that you are the mother in this sculpture. Write an entry in a journal or diary and describe how you are feeling and what you are thinking. If your classmates read the diary entry, would they agree that these thoughts and emotions are believable for this sculpture?

Prewriting Brainstorm a list of emotions and thoughts that might be in your mind if you were the woman in *Mother and Child*. Keep in mind the mood that the artist created with line and texture.

Drafting Using the list you made, write a diary entry describing what is going through your mind as you hold your child. You could give structure to your paper by describing an event that caused these thoughts and emotions.

Revising Read through your diary entry and make sure that each paragraph is focused on one main idea. Did you use a variety of end marks for your sentences, as appropriate?

Editing Check your sentences for mistakes in end punctuation or in comma usage. Make sure each paragraph is indented.

Publishing Write a final copy of your diary entry and read it to your classmates. As a class, discuss which aspect of your description was an especially good explanation of the mood of the sculpture.

Another Look

End Marks and Commas

End Marks

Place a **period (.)** after a statement, after an opinion, and after a command or request made in a normal tone of voice. *(page L537)*

Place a **question mark (?)** after a sentence that asks a question. *(page L537)*

Place an **exclamation point (!)** after a sentence that expresses strong feeling or after a command or request that expresses great excitement. *(page L537)*

Use a period with most abbreviations. *(pages L540–L541)*

Use a period after each number or letter that shows a division in an outline. *(page L542)*

Using Commas That Separate

Use commas to separate items in a series. *(page L544)*

A comma is needed between two adjectives if it is replacing the word *and* between the two adjectives. *(pages L546–L547)*

Use a comma to separate the independent clauses of a compound sentence if the clauses are joined by a conjunction. *(pages L550–L551)*

Use a comma after certain introductory elements. *(pages L553–L555)*

Use a comma to separate elements in dates and addresses. *(page L557)*

Use a comma after the salutation of a friendly letter and after the closing of all letters. *(page L558)*

Using Commas That Enclose

Use commas to set off nouns of direct address. *(page L562)*

Use commas to set off parenthetical expressions. *(pages L564–L565)*

Use commas to set off most appositives and their modifiers. *(page L567)*

Use commas to set off nonessential participial phrases and nonessential clauses. *(pages L570–L571)*

Other Information About End Marks and Commas

Recognizing common abbreviations *(pages L540–L541)*

Using common parenthetical expressions *(page L564)*

Using *Another Look*

Another Look summarizes the terms defined in the chapter and provides cross-references to the specific pages on which they are explained. Consider having students use this feature prior to completing **CheckPoint** or taking the post-test. Students who can provide several examples of each term should be able to score well on either measurement.

FOR ASSESSING LEARNING

Using *the Posttest*

Assessing Learning

The posttest will help you and your students assess where they stand in their ability to use end marks and commas correctly.

IDENTIFYING COMMON STUMBLING BLOCKS

Following is a list of the most common errors students make when using end marks and commas in their writing.

Problem

- Lack of comma with introductory elements

Solution

- For reteaching, use the examples on pages L553–L554.

Problem

- Lack of comma to set off parenthetical expressions

Solution

- For reteaching, use the examples on pages L564–L565.

Directions

Read the passage. Write the letter of the best way to write each underlined part. If the underlined part contains no error, write *D.*

EXAMPLE Did you know that Albert Einstein was not born a United States <u>citizen</u> (1)

1 **A** citizen,
B citizen.
C citizen?
D No error

ANSWER **1** **C**

Einstein, a <u>world-famous mathematician</u> (1) was born in Bavaria in 1879. He acquired Swiss nationality <u>in 1901 and</u> (2) he began working at the Swiss patent office the next year. Einstein <u>was however also</u> (3) publishing papers in physics. He became famous for his theories of <u>relativity and won</u> (4) the 1921 Nobel Prize for physics. To educate others about his <u>theories Einstein</u> (5) held some teaching positions. These positions were in <u>Switzerland Prague</u> (6) and Germany. After Hitler's rise to <u>power Einstein</u> (7) came to the United States. He lectured at Princeton University in <u>Princeton NJ</u> (8). This <u>brilliant creative</u> (9) man became a U.S. citizen in 1940. He is my <u>hero</u> (10)

A DIFFERENT DELIVERY SYSTEM

If you prefer, you can print the posttest from the BK English Test Bank located at http://www.bkenglish.com.

1 **A** world-famous, mathematician
B world-famous, mathematician,
C world-famous mathematician,
D No error

2 **A** in 1901 and,
B in 1901, and
C in 1901, and,
D No error

3 **A** was, however, also
B was however, also
C was, however also
D No error

4 **A** relativity, and won
B relativity and, won
C relativity, and, won
D No error

5 **A** theories, Einstein
B theories, Einstein,
C theories Einstein,
D No error

6 **A** Switzerland, Prague,
B Switzerland Prague,
C Switzerland, Prague
D No error

7 **A** power Einstein,
B power, Einstein,
C power, Einstein
D No error

8 **A** Princeton N.J.
B Princeton, NJ.
C Princeton, NJ
D No error

9 **A** brilliant, creative
B brilliant, creative,
C brilliant creative,
D No error

10 **A** hero?
B hero!
C hero,
D No error

Customizing the Test

Use these questions to add or replace items for alternate versions of the test.

To warn the president that Germany might make an atomic bomb Einstein (11) wrote to Roosevelt. After World War II Einstein (12) supported the international control of atomic weapons. Einstein wrote several works including *About Zionism* and (13) *Why War*. The latter work *Why War* (14) was written with Sigmund Freud.

11. A bomb Einstein,
B bomb, Einstein,
C bomb, Einstein
D No error

12. A World War II, Einstein
B World War II, Einstein,
C World War II Einstein,
D No error

13. A *Zionism,* and
B *Zionism,* and,
C *Zionism* and,
D No error

14. A work, *Why War*
B work, *Why War,*
C work *Why War,*
D No error

Teaching Suggestions

Assessing Prior Knowledge
Pretest *(pages L582–L583)*

Making Visual Connections
(page L584)

Developing Language Skills
Italics (Underlining)
Quotation Marks
(pages L585–L607)

Reviewing Language Skills
CheckPoint *(pages L608–L609)*
Language and Self-Expression *(page L610)*
Another Look *(page L611)*

Assessing Learning
Posttest *(pages L612–L613)*

Essential Knowledge and Skills

- Writing to inform such as to explain, describe, report, and narrate
- Capitalizing and punctuating correctly to clarify and enhance meaning such as capitalizing titles and sentence punctuation
- Generating ideas and plans for writing by using prewriting strategies
- Applying criteria to evaluate writing
- Analyzing published examples as models for writing
- Interpreting important events and ideas gathered from maps, charts, graphics, video segments, or technology presentations

BLOCK SCHEDULING

- If your schedule requires that you cover the chapter in a **shorter time,** use the instruction on italics and quotation marks and the Check Your Understanding and QuickCheck exercises.
- If you want to take advantage of **longer class time,** add these applications to writing: Connect to Writer's Craft, Connect to Speaking and Writing, Connect to The Writing Process, and Apply to Writing exercises.

CHAPTER 17

Italics and Quotation Marks

Pretest

Directions

Read the passage and choose the best way to write each underlined part. Write the letter of the correct answer. If the underlined part contains no error, write *D*.

EXAMPLE Jo saw the cricket and exclaimed wow (1)

1 **A** exclaimed, "Wow"!
B exclaimed, "Wow!"
C exclaimed "Wow!"
D No error

ANSWER 1 **B**

Jo said I (1) learned crickets are like grasshoppers." (2)

Well, (3) I always thought," said Jamal that (4) crickets and grasshoppers were the same."

No she replied but (5) they are related. I looked up cricket and (6) *grasshopper* in "Encyclopedia Britannica." (7)

"Are there different kinds of crickets?" Jamal asked (8)

Jo replied there (9) are four main types of crickets."

Yes he agreed (10) "I think I heard that."

IDENTIFYING COMMON STUMBLING BLOCKS

Following is a list of the most common errors students make when using italics and quotation marks in their writing.

Problem
- Lack of italics or underlining with names of newspapers

Solution
- Instruction, p. L586
- Practice, pp. L587–L588

Problem
- Lack of punctuation to separate a direct quotation

Solution
- Instruction, pp. L593–L595
- Practice, pp. L595–L596

1 A said, "I
B said. "I
C said, I
D No error

2 A grasshoppers".
B grasshoppers.
C grasshoppers,"
D No error

3 A *Well,*
B "Well,"
C "Well,
D No error

4 A Jamal, "That
B Jamal, "that
C Jamal "that
D No error

5 A "No," she replied, "but
B "No," she replied, "But
C "No" she replied, "but
D No error

6 A cricket and
B "cricket" and
C *cricket* and
D No error

7 A Encyclopedia Britannica.
B *Encyclopedia Britannica.*
C "Encyclopedia Britannica."
D No error

8 A Jamal asked.
B Jamal asked?
C Jamal asked."
D No error

9 A replied "There
B replied, "There
C replied, "there
D No error

10 A "Yes," he agreed,
B "Yes" he agreed,
C Yes, "he agreed,"
D No error

A DIFFERENT DELIVERY SYSTEM

If you prefer, you can print the pretest from the BK English Test Bank located at http://www.bkenglish.com.

Using *the Pretest*

Assessing Prior Knowledge

The pretest will help you and your students assess where they stand in their basic understanding of italics and quotation marks and their use in writing.

Customizing the Test

Use these questions to add or replace items for alternate versions of the test.

Jo said Although (11) the word "insect" (12) gives me chills, I don't kill insects." She paused, and then continued. "When I find a cricket in my house, for example, I do something I read about in "Friendly Earth" magazine (13). I trap the cricket under an overturned glass, then I slide a piece of paper under the glass. Then I take the cricket in the glass outside and let it go!" (14)

11. A said, "Although
B said," Although
C said "Although
D No error

12. A *"insect"*
B *insect*
C Insect
D No error

13. A *Friendly Earth* magazine
B "Friendly Earth magazine"
C Friendly Earth magazine
D No error

14. A go!".
B go!
C go"!
D No error

ADDITIONAL RESOURCES

Language Skills Practice	pages 163–172
Transparency Tools	AW17
ESL Practice and Test Preparation	pages 133–135
Assessment: Chapter Test	pages 201–204

MAKING VISUAL CONNECTIONS

For Language Development

Have students look at the comic strip *Heartless. Brainless. Cowardly. All of the Above.* Write the title of the comic strip on the board, including the italics, periods, and correct capitalization. Explain that the italics (or underlining) are used to correctly write the title of the comic strip. Have students locate additional comic strips in the newspaper and write the titles correctly using italics or underlining.

To Stimulate Writing

Use the questions for art criticism as writing or discussion prompts.

Possible Answers:

Describe I recognize the Tin Man, the Scarecrow, and the Cowardly Lion from *The Wizard of Oz*. The artist used black ink to outline and shade the shapes of the characters.

Analyze No, the use of color and space does not make one character stand out. In fact, they all look equal and balanced because they are the same color and size, and are evenly spaced across the page. I focus on the fourth character because the artist wrote "TERRORIST" on his hat, which expresses the cartoon's message.

Interpret The cartoon's message is that terrorists are heartless, brainless, and cowardly. The word *TERRORIST* on the fourth character's cap tied everything together for me and showed me that the message is actually serious, not funny.

Judge Answers will vary.

Ben Sargent, "Heartless, Brainless, Cowardly, All of the Above," April 30, 1995.
Cartoon for the Austin American-Statesman.

Describe Do you recognize the first three characters? What film has characters like these? The artist has used only one color of ink—black—but how has he used the black ink to create the cartoon? What word is written on the hat of the fourth character?

Analyze Does the artist's use of color and space make one figure stand out more than another? How does the artist focus your attention on one character? Which character is it?

Interpret What is the cartoon's message? Which part of the cartoon made the message "click" for you?

Judge How could a writer express the same message? Which do you think most people would pay more attention to, the cartoon or a piece of writing? Why do you think so?

At the end of this chapter, you will use the artwork to stimulate ideas for writing.

FOR DEVELOPING LANGUAGE SKILLS

LESSON 1 *(pages L585–L607)*

OBJECTIVES

- **To use italics (or underlining) correctly**
- **To use quotation marks correctly**

Create Interest

Write the following sentences on the board and ask students where they would place quotation marks. Tell students that in this chapter, they will learn how to use quotation marks correctly and where to place them.

Italics (Underlining)

When certain titles, letters, numbers, and words appear in a book, they are printed in italics. *Italic print, a special kind that slants to the right, is the kind used in this sentence.* Since you cannot write in italics, you should substitute underlining wherever italics are needed. If you use a computer, you can print in italics. To do this, first highlight the words you want to italicize. Then use the command for italics.

ITALICS	Have you ever read the book *Dragonwings* by Laurence Yep?
UNDERLINING	Have you ever read the book _Dragonwings_ by Laurence Yep?

Certain letters, numbers, words, and titles should be italicized or underlined.

Italicize (or underline) letters, numbers, and words when they are used to represent themselves.

LETTERS	His _I_'s look like _L_'s.
NUMBERS	Does your telephone number have a *3* in it?
WORDS	The word *paint* can be a noun, adjective, or verb.

In the first example, notice that only the *I* and the *L* are underlined (or italicized), not the apostrophe or the *s*.

You can learn about the use of apostrophes on pages L617–L629.

Italicize (underline) the titles of long written or musical works that are published as a single unit. Also italicize (underline) the titles of paintings and sculptures and the names of vehicles.

FOR INCREASING STUDENT ACHIEVEMENT

INTEGRATING TECHNOLOGY

Computers

After discussing the use of italics in titles and with words, letters, and numbers used to represent themselves, have students write the following sentences using a computer. Students should practice typing the sentences with the appropriate items in italics.

- Beck learned to write the number *5* and the letter *B* at preschool.
- Neil's favorite books are *The Castle* and *Motorcycle Racing Today.*
- Lindsay had some trouble spelling *exuberant* on her paper.
- I enjoy reading the *Wall Street Journal.*
- Sam wanted to see the play *Les Miserables* in New York City.

- I exclaimed, I will be the winner!
- You are sure to win, my mother remarked, if you practice.

Guide Instruction

By Connecting Ideas

Tell students that not only will they learn to use quotation marks correctly to indicate speech and titles of works, but they will also learn how to correctly use italics or underlining to indicate titles. Ask students where they have seen italics used in the past. List a few of the students' examples on the board. Point out those titles that should be in italics and those that should be within quotation marks.

Consolidate Skills

Through Guided Practice

The **Check Your Understanding** and **QuickCheck** exercises in this lesson will help students use italics and quotation marks correctly. Review the instruction on italics and quotation marks before completing each exercise. Guide students through the first

YOUR IDEAS

For Using Italics

The rule on the preceding page applies to long, separately published works that include books, magazines, newspapers, full-length plays, movies, and very long poems. Long musical works include operas, symphonies, ballets, and album or CD titles. Names of vehicles include the proper names of airplanes, ships, trains, and spacecraft. The titles of radio and television series are also italicized (or underlined).

Books	After I have finished reading *Robinson Crusoe,* I'm going to read Hatchet.
Magazines	I used *National Geographic* magazine for my research.
Newspapers	The Chicago Tribune is delivered to our house every day. (The word *the* is not usually considered part of the title of a newspaper or magazine.)
Plays, Movies	In 1999, *Titanic* won the Academy Award for the best picture. *Cats* is one of the longest-running Broadway musicals.
TV Series	One of the longest-running TV series is 60 Minutes.
Works of Art	Edward Hopper painted *Railroad Sunset*.
Names of Vehicles	An Agatha Christie mystery is set on the train the Orient Express. (The word *the* is not considered part of the title of a vehicle.)

You can learn about the capitalization of titles on pages L522–L526.

item in each exercise. Discuss students' responses and any difficulties they might have using italics or quotation marks. Have students complete the exercises independently.

Apply to Communication

Through Independent Writing

The **Communicate Your Ideas/Apply to Writing** activities prompt students to write a paragraph about an interview, a bibliography, a comic strip, and an analysis of a novel excerpt. Ask students how they plan to use italics or underlining and quotation marks in these particular writing tasks. For example, what part will quotation marks play in their bibliography? How will they use quotation marks in a comic strip? Discuss students' responses.

PRACTICE YOUR SKILLS

Check Your Understanding

Using Italics (Underlining)

Write *a* or *b* to indicate the item in each pair that is correctly underlined. Remember that in newspapers and magazines, the word the is not considered part of the title.

1. **a.** the Greek word chron
   b. the Greek word chron
2. **a.** the painting Washington Crossing the Delaware
   b. the painting Washington Crossing the Delaware
3. **a.** the newspaper the Miami Herald
   b. the newspaper the Miami Herald
4. **a.** the film The Bridge on the River Kwai
   b. the film The Bridge on the River Kwai
5. **a.** the word happiness
   b. the word happiness
6. **a.** the number 2
   b. the number 2
7. **a.** the book The Outsiders
   b. the book The Outsiders
8. **a.** Good Housekeeping magazine
   b. Good Housekeeping magazine

Connect to the Writing Process: Editing

Using Italics (Underlining) Correctly

Rewrite each sentence, underlining where needed.

9. The 1961 Newbery Medal book was Island of the Blue Dolphins.
10. John Paul Jones sailed on a ship called the Bonhomme Richard.

A DIFFERENT APPROACH

Kinesthetic

Have students complete the **Practice Your Skills** exercise by using a computer. Students should type out each item and italicize the appropriate sections. For items one through eight, students should type out only the correct response with italics. Have students print out their responses and share them with the class.

HOME WORK

Have students write out five titles that require italics (or underlining). Then have students use each title in a complete sentence.

Transfer to Everyday Life

Identifying Italics and Quotation Marks in Literature

Have students find examples of italics and quotation marks used correctly in selections from their literature textbooks. Have students share some of their examples with the class.

Pull It All Together

By Sharing

Have students share one of their writing samples from the **Communicate Your Ideas/Apply to Writing** activity with a partner. After checking for correct use of italics or underlining and quotation marks, students should incorporate any improvements suggested by their partners into their writing.

Check Understanding

By Summarizing

Have students summarize how to use italics (or underlining) and quotation marks correctly. Students should write a paragraph explaining how to refer-

TIMESAVER *QuickCheck*

Have students use the list on page L586 to check their use of italics (or underlining) with titles they use in their writing. After students have conducted their interviews, they should check their writing for correct use of italics with their titles before writing the final draft of their paragraphs.

11. The words broccoli and zucchini both have two c's.

12. The smallest plane ever built was called the Stits Skybaby; it was half as long as an average car.

13. The word quark was taken from the book Ulysses.

14. The most successful newsmagazines are Time and Newsweek.

15. The word unquestionably contains all five vowels and the letter y.

16. Bertolt Brecht wrote The Threepenny Opera.

17. The numbers 3, 5, and 7 are prime numbers.

18. During the Old English period, storytellers recited long poems such as Beowulf.

19. The radio play Sorry, Wrong Number is a classic mystery.

20. The musical titled Man of La Mancha is based on the Spanish novel Don Quixote.

21. Russian astronaut Valentina V. Tereshkova rode in a spacecraft called Vostok 5 in 1963.

22. One of the many words people use for the rolls of dust that collect under furniture is dust bunnies.

Communicate Your Ideas

APPLY TO WRITING

Interview: ***Italics (Underlining)***

Interview one of your classmates to find out his or her favorite book, magazine, movie, and TV series. Ask why he or she likes each favorite. Then write a paragraph naming and describing your classmate's favorites for a classroom book of favorites. Be sure to italicize or underline each title correctly.

ence titles of various works and direct speech. Students should provide at least three examples of using quotation marks in different situations, such as with titles, with direct address, and when quoting long passages.

Quotation Marks

Quotation marks (" ") always come in pairs. They are used to enclose certain titles, and they are used to enclose a person's exact words. Quotation marks are very important. Without them, for example, a conversation between people in a story would be difficult to read or understand.

Quotation Marks with Titles

Many titles are italicized (or underlined), but some titles are enclosed in quotation marks. Long works are italicized (or underlined). However, many of these long works are made up of smaller parts. A book, for example, might contain short stories, poems, or titled chapters. The titles of these smaller parts are enclosed in quotation marks.

Use quotation marks to enclose the titles of chapters, articles, stories, one-act plays, short poems, and songs.

Chapters in Books	Our assignment is to read the chapter "The Disappearing Frontier" in our history book, *American History.*
Articles in Magazines and Newspapers	The lead story in this week's Newsweek is "DNA Solves Crimes." The Sunday *Salem News* had a feature called "Garbage Gardening."
Short Stories in Books and Magazines	I liked the short story "The Ransom of Red Chief" in our literature book Discoveries. Did you read the story "Ticket to Saturn" in the last issue of *Galaxy* magazine?

GETTING STUDENTS INVOLVED

Collaborative Learning

Provide students with copies of newspapers, magazines, and professional journals. Have students work in small groups to find at least ten examples of titles within italics and ten examples of titles within quotation marks. Remind students that they can refer to the list on page L586 to see which titles should be italicized. Also, remind students that smaller sections or pieces of works and less substantial works are usually within quotation marks, such as chapter titles taken from novels, article titles taken from magazines, and song titles taken from CDs, as per the list on this page. Have each group share some of their titles by writing them on the board.

A DIFFERENT APPROACH

Visual

To reinforce the use of italics and quotation marks, have students complete items one through fifteen in **Check Your Understanding** by writing them on the board. Have students take turns writing the correct responses on the board by using underlining or quotation marks.

SHORT POEMS	I memorized the poem "O Pioneers" from the book From Sea to Shining Sea.
SONGS	The old song "All You Need Is Love" is my mother's favorite.

PRACTICE YOUR SKILLS

Check Your Understanding

Using Quotation Marks

General Interest

Write *C* if quotation marks and underlining are used correctly. Write *I* if the punctuation is used incorrectly.

1. ~~*Does Your Chewing Gum Lose Its Flavor on the Bedpost Overnight*~~ "Does Your Chewing Gum Lose Its Flavor on the Bedpost Overnight" was once a popular song. I
2. John McCrae wrote the patriotic ~~"poem In Flanders Fields"~~ poem "In Flanders Fields" during World War I. I
3. The song ~~*The Lonely Goatherd*~~ "The Lonely Goatherd" was written for the Broadway musical ~~"The Sound of Music."~~ *The Sound of Music* I
4. My favorite chapter in the book *The Wind in the Willows* is called "The Further Adventures of Toad." C
5. The newspaper article "A Fair to Remember" described events at the Ohio State Fair. C
6. The article ~~*Breaking the Record*~~ "Breaking the Record" was in the September issue of ~~"Sports Illustrated."~~ *Sports Illustrated* I
7. ~~Escape from the Sea~~ "Escape from the Sea" is the first chapter in the novel *Agents of Destiny*. I
8. In our textbook *Discovering Literature,* we read the poem "The Base Stealer" by Robert Francis. C
9. ~~*Drought Predicted*~~ "Drought Predicted" was today's lead story in our newspaper, the ~~"Des Moines Register."~~ *Des Moines Register* I

10. "Those Were the Days" was the theme song for the long-running television series *All in the Family.* C

11. This month's issue of *National Geographic* includes an article titled ~~*The Brothers Grimm*~~. "The Brothers Grimm."

"The Star-Spangled Banner"

12. ~~*The Star-Spangled Banner*~~ was written by Francis Scott Key.

"Pentium or the K6: The Microchip War,"

13. My brother's article, ~~*Pentium or the K6: The Microchip War*~~, will appear in the July issue of ~~"Wired"~~ magazine. *Wired*

14. My favorite chapter in *Moby Dick* is "Ahab's Leg." C

15. Our local newspaper, the *Miami Herald*, published an article titled "More Growth Expected" in today's issue. C

Connect to the Writing Process: Editing

Correcting Punctuation of Titles

16.–24. Rewrite the incorrectly punctuated items from the preceding exercise, using underlining and quotation marks correctly. [See responses given above.]

Connect to the Writing Process: Drafting

Writing Sentences with Titles

Write sentences that answer the following questions.

The title of my literature textbook is *Modern Literature.*

25. What is the title of your literature textbook?

My favorite poem in the book is "Pied Beauty."

26. What is the title of your favorite poem in the book?

The title of my math book is *Basic Principles of Math.*

27. What is the name of your math book?

The math chapter is called "Fractions."

28. What is the title of the chapter you just completed in math?

My favorite CD is *Bryan White* and my favorite song on it is "Still Life."

29. What is the title of your favorite CD and your favorite song on the CD?

HOME WORK

Have students write a short summary of a novel they have recently read. The summary should include the title and chapter names important to understanding the book.

TIMESAVER *QuickCheck*

Evaluate students' bibliographies by checking for correct use of italics (or underlining) and quotation marks. Students' annotated descriptions should be written in complete sentences.

HOME STUDY

Have students find examples of bibliographies from other sources, such as nonfiction works or magazine articles. Students should share the bibliographies and discuss the use of italics and quotation marks in reference titles.

Communicate Your Ideas

APPLY TO WRITING

Bibliography: *Titles*

Imagine that you are collecting materials to publish in an anthology about the sea. Your plan is to reprint magazine articles, poems, stories, songs, and chapters from books about the sea. Create a bibliography of at least five materials that you might include in your book. Be sure to give complete information about the materials. For example, list not only a poem but the name of a book where you found it. Remember to use italics (or underlining) and quotation marks correctly.

Mixed Practice

General Interest

Rewrite each sentence, using quotation marks and italics (underlining) where needed.

1. The word nevermore appears ten times in the poem ~~The Raven~~. "The Raven"
2. The Oxford English Dictionary lists 194 meanings for the word set.
3. The tune of ~~Happy Birthday to You~~ "Happy Birthday to You" was written by two sisters, Mildred and Patty Hill.
4. Rod McKuen said he rewrote his book The Sound of Solitude thirty-four times.
5. The TV series I Love Lucy has remained popular since the 1950s.
6. My favorite painting is van Gogh's Sunflowers.
7. Some buildings give the floor just after the twelfth floor the number 14 because of superstitions about the number 13.
8. The article ~~An Underground Railroad in Boston~~ "An Underground Railroad in Boston" was a feature in Scientific American magazine in 1849.
9. The word chortled first appeared in the poem ~~Jabberwocky~~ by Lewis Carroll. "Jabberwocky"
10. An article in the Chicago Tribune described an exhibit of artifacts recovered from the Titanic.

Quotation Marks with Direct Quotations

Quotation marks are used to enclose a **direct quotation,** the exact words of a person.

YOUR IDEAS

For Presenting Italics and Quotation Marks

EXPANDING THE LESSON

Using Technology

Use Barrett Kendall ancillary instructional and practice materials located at http://www.bkenglish.com.

REACHING ALL STUDENTS

Advanced Learners

Remind students that indirect quotations do not use quotation marks. Have students rewrite the following indirect quotations so that they require quotation marks. Students should add quotation marks in the appropriate places.

- He said he wanted to go to Alaska. (He said, "I want to go to Alaska.")
- Juanita replied that to go to Alaska, we will need to save money. ("To go to Alaska," replied Juanita, "we will need to save money.")
- I said I would love to go to Alaska, too. ("I would love to go to Alaska, too," I said.)

Use quotation marks to enclose a person's exact words.

Scott said, "I rowed across the harbor."
"The sea was very calm," he added.

Quotation marks do not enclose an **indirect quotation,** a rephrasing of a person's exact words.

Scott said he rowed across the harbor.
He added that the sea was very calm.

CONNECT TO SPEAKING AND WRITING

An indirect quotation, whether written or spoken, often contains the word *that.* Sometimes the word *that* helps clarify meaning. The meaning of the following two sentences is the same.

Rosa said **that** she enjoys the beach.
Rosa said she enjoys the beach.

A direct quotation that is a single sentence can be written in various ways. It can appear before or after a speaker tag such as *she answered* or *he stated.* It can also be interrupted by a speaker tag. In every case, quotation marks enclose only the person's exact words—not the speaker tag.

BEFORE	"The tide comes in at six o'clock tonight," he said.
AFTER	He said, "The tide comes in at six o'clock tonight."
INTERRUPTED	"The tide," he said, "comes in at six o'clock tonight."
	(Two sets of quotation marks are needed because the speaker tag interrupts the direct quotation.)

Use only one set of quotation marks to set off two or more sentences in a direct quotation if the sentences are not interrupted by a speaker tag.

> He said, **"**The tide tonight comes in at six. The ship will sail then.**"**
>
> (Quotation marks come only before *The* and after *then.*)

PRACTICE YOUR SKILLS

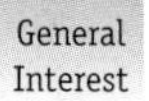

Check Your Understanding

Using Quotation Marks with Direct Quotations

General Interest **Write *a* or *b* to indicate the item in each pair that uses quotation marks correctly.**

1. a. "The earliest ancestor of bubble gum was a gum created in 1906," said Ken.

b. "The earliest ancestor of bubble gum was a gum created in 1906, said Ken."

2. a. He continued, Unfortunately, the gum had a lot of problems.

b. He continued, "Unfortunately, the gum had a lot of problems."

3. a. His friend, Victoria, asked him what he meant by that.

b. His friend, Victoria, asked him "what he meant by that."

4. a. He told her that the gum was too sticky and brittle.

b. He told her "that the gum was too sticky and brittle."

5. a. "Besides," he added, "it had a terrible name."

b. "Besides, he added, it had a terrible name."

A DIFFERENT APPROACH

Auditory

Have students complete **Check Your Understanding** with a partner. Partners should read each item aloud to each other and choose the correct responses. Discuss the correct responses with the class and have students write each correct sentence on the board.

HOME WORK

Have students write ten sentences that contain quotation marks. Students' sentences can be about a topic of their choice. Have students share some of their sentences using quotation marks correctly the following day.

Connect to the Writing Process: Editing

Using Quotation Marks with Direct Quotations

Rewrite each sentence, adding or taking out quotation marks where needed. If you are using a quotation mark to enclose a group of words that ends with a comma or a period, put the quotation marks *after* the comma or period.

6. Ken explained ~~"that~~ that the original name of the gum was Blibber-Blubber."
7. "In ~~1928~~ 1928," Ken continued, ~~the~~ "the gum company was still working on a formula for bubble gum."
8. "This is the story I read about ~~Blibber-Blubber,~~ Blibber-Blubber," Ken went on. ~~A~~ "A young man named Walter Diemer kept experimenting with different mixes. Then one day he found the perfect mix."
9. "When Diemer found the correct ~~formula,~~ formula," Ken said with a smile, ~~he~~ "he started dancing all over his office."
10. ~~"Unfortunately~~ "Unfortunately," Ken added, ~~"the~~ "the gum wouldn't work the next ~~day.~~ day."
11. "So, he experimented for another four months until the formula was just ~~right,~~ right," said ~~Ken."~~ Ken.
12. Eve asked Ken ~~"what~~ what color the first bubble gum ~~was."~~ was.
13. ~~"Ken~~ Ken smiled and said, ~~There's~~ "There's a funny story about ~~that."~~ that. Diemer made the gum pink because pink was the only food coloring he had on ~~hand.~~ hand."
14. "So that's why bubble gum is usually ~~pink,~~ pink," Ken ~~concluded."~~ concluded.
15. "I think I have seen bubble gum in other colors as ~~well,~~ well," Eve said.

Capital Letters with Direct Quotations

You know that a capital letter begins a sentence. It is natural, therefore, for a capital letter to begin a direct quotation.

Begin each sentence of a direct quotation with a capital letter.

"**L**ast summer we went to Minnesota," she said.
She said, "**L**ast summer we went to Minnesota."
"**L**ast summer," she said, "we went to Minnesota."

Notice that in the last example the word *we* does not begin with a capital letter because it is in the middle of a one-sentence direct quotation. In the following examples, however, a capital letter is used to begin a new sentence.

She said, "**L**ast summer we went to Minnesota. **I**t was an interesting trip."

"**L**ast summer we went to Minnesota," she said. "**I**t was an interesting trip."

Practice Your Skills

Check Your Understanding
Using Capital Letters with Direct Quotations

Contemporary Life

Write *a* or *b* to indicate the item in each pair that is correctly capitalized.

1. **a.** "We saw some gigantic wooden statues along the roadside in Minnesota!" exclaimed Angelica.
b. "we saw some gigantic wooden statues along the roadside in Minnesota!" Exclaimed Angelica.

2. **a.** "There are many statues of Paul Bunyan in Minnesota," said Ty. "did you see any of them?"
b. "There are many statues of Paul Bunyan in Minnesota," said Ty. "Did you see any of them?"

REACHING ALL STUDENTS

Struggling Learners

Have struggling learners work with advanced learners to complete the following examples focusing on capital letters with quotation marks. Advanced learners should explain to struggling students how capital letters should be used with quotation marks. Students should refer to the instruction on this page.

- "I would love to travel out West," said Tyson, "And see the Grand Canyon." ("I would love to travel out West," said Tyson, "and see the Grand Canyon.")
- "Have you ever visited Yellowstone National Park?" Asked Mary. ("Have you ever visited Yellowstone National Park?" asked Mary.)
- "no, I have never been there," Replied Alice, "But I am planning to go this summer." ("No, I have never been there," replied Alice, "but I am planning to go this summer.")

HOME WORK

Have students write ten sentences using quotation marks. Tell them to insert capitalization errors into their sentences, and also to write a separate, correct answer key. The next day, have students exchange their incorrect sentences with a partner. Partners should correct all errors, which can then be compared against the answer key.

3. **a.** “We saw Paul Bunyan frequently,” Angelica responded, “along with Babe the Blue Ox.”
   b. “We saw Paul Bunyan frequently,” Angelica responded, “Along with Babe the Blue Ox.”
4. **a.** She remarked, “one of the funniest statues we saw was a huge mouse and cheese near Lindstrom, Minnesota.”
   b. She remarked, “One of the funniest statues we saw was a huge mouse and cheese near Lindstrom, Minnesota.”
5. **a.** “the most impressive statue,” added Angelica, “Was the enormous wooden one of Smokey the Bear at International Falls.”
   b. “The most impressive statue,” added Angelica, “was the enormous wooden one of Smokey the Bear at International Falls.”

Connect to the Writing Process: Editing

Using Capital Letters with Direct Quotations

Rewrite each sentence, adding capital letters where needed.

6. “~~wasn't~~ Wasn't Smokey the Bear just a cartoon character?” James asked.
7. “~~no~~ No, he was also a real bear,” Ms. Low responded.
8. “~~rangers~~ Rangers rescued him,” she continued, “in New Mexico.”
9. Tony asked, “~~why~~ Why did Smokey need to be rescued?”
10. Ms. Low answered, “~~he~~ He was orphaned in a forest fire. ~~the~~ The rangers found him clinging to a charred tree.”
11. “~~when~~ When his burns healed,” continued Ms. Low, “he was taken to the National Zoo in Washington, D.C.”
12. “~~this~~ This young bear became the international symbol in a campaign to fight forest fires,” she added.

Commas with Direct Quotations

Commas are used to separate direct quotations from speaker tags.

Use a comma to separate a direct quotation from a speaker tag. Place the comma inside the closing quotation marks if the quotation comes first in the sentence. Place the comma immediately after the speaker tag if the speaker tag comes first.

> "A penny saved is a penny earned**,**" said Ben Franklin.
> Ben Franklin said**,** "A penny saved is a penny earned."
> "A penny saved**,**" said Ben Franklin**,** "is a penny earned."

In the third sentence, two commas are needed to separate the speaker tag from the direct quotation—one before the speaker tag and one after it.

Practice Your Skills

Check Your Understanding

Using Commas with Direct Quotations

General Interest

Write *C* if commas are used correctly in a sentence. Write *I* if commas are used incorrectly.

1. Mark Twain ~~said~~ said, "If you tell the truth, you don't have to remember anything." I

2. "Prejudice is an unwillingness to be confused by facts," ~~facts",~~ remarked H. L. Mencken. I

3. "False words are not only evil in themselves," Plato told his ~~students~~ students, "but they infect the soul with evil." I

4. A Spanish proverb ~~says~~ says, "Those who give quickly, give twice." I

DEVELOPING WORKPLACE COMPETENCIES

Basic Skills: Writing

Remind students that direct quotations represent a speaker's exact words. Ask students how recognizing direct quotations in the workplace will be important in their future careers. Help students to understand that when repeating or representing someone's exact words, it is important to be precise and accurate. Misquoting someone's exact words can create misunderstandings and misrepresentations.

A DIFFERENT APPROACH

Kinesthetic

Have students write out the ten sentences in **Check Your Understanding** separately on large sentence strips or on long mural paper using thick black markers. Students should not include the commas in these sentences. Then cut several large commas out of red construction paper. Apply masking tape to the back of each large comma and place them on several students' arms. As some students hold up the sentences, have the "comma" students move to the place in which the commas should be inserted in the sentences. Discuss the "comma" students' positions in the sentences and their relationship to the quotation marks.

5. "The weak can be ~~terrible~~" terrible," commented Rabindranath Tagore, "because they try furiously to be strong." I

6. Picasso once said, "Art is a lie which makes us see the truth." C

7. "Those who have the power to control themselves are the most powerful of all people," wrote Seneca. C

8. "The art of ~~writing~~" writing," said Mary Heaton Vorse, "is the act of applying the seat of the pants to the seat of the chair." I

9. "Tell me what company you keep," wrote Miguel de Cervantes, "and I'll tell you who you are." C

10. "Civility costs ~~nothing~~", nothing," remarked Mary Wortley ~~Montagu~~ Montagu, "and buys everything." I

Connect to the Writing Process: Editing

Using Commas with Direct Quotations

[See responses given above.]

11.–17. Rewrite the incorrectly punctuated sentences from the preceding exercise, using commas correctly.

End Marks with Direct Quotations

A period is used at the end of a sentence—whether it is a regular sentence or a direct quotation. The period goes *inside* the closing quotation marks when the quotation ends the sentence.

Place a period inside the closing quotation marks when the end of the quotation comes at the end of the sentence.

She said, "The storm has grown much fiercer**.**"

"The storm," she said, "has grown much fiercer**.**"

Usually question marks and exclamation points, like periods, go inside the closing quotation marks.

> He yelled, "The lightning struck nearby**!**"
> She asked, "Where did it strike**?**"
>
> (In both examples, the end marks go *inside* the closing quotation marks.)

When a question mark or exclamation point comes just before a speaker tag, the mark is still placed inside the closing quotation marks.

> "The lightning hit a tree**!**" Chris exclaimed.
> "Did it hit the pine on the hill**?**" asked Hannah.

Check Your Understanding

Using End Marks with Direct Quotations

General Interest **Write *a* or *b* to indicate the item in each pair that is punctuated correctly.**

1. a. Mr. Ott said, "Some legends tell about dragons".
b. Mr. Ott said, "Some legends tell about dragons."

2. a. "Do you mean fire-breathing dragons?" asked Liz.
b. "Do you mean fire-breathing dragons," asked Liz?

3. a. "Yes, Mr. Ott answered, "and there is an iguana that resembles that kind of dragon"
b. "Yes," Mr. Ott answered, "and there is an iguana that resembles that kind of dragon."

4. a. "That iguana is about four feet long." he added
b. "That iguana is about four feet long," he added.

5. a. "I hope I never run into one in my neighborhood!" Jeff exclaimed.
b. "I hope I never run into one in my neighborhood," Jeff exclaimed!

A DIFFERENT APPROACH

Visual

Have students complete the **Check Your Understanding** exercise with a partner. Each pair should write out their sentences using pencil. Then they should write the quotation marks and end marks in red pen or red marker to make them stand out. Discuss students' responses.

HOME WORK

Have students read the instructions about using end marks with quotation marks as a home work assignment. Students should then write ten sentences that demonstrate what they learned from the instructions. Have students share their examples the following day. Discuss students' responses and correct any errors as a class.

TIMESAVER *QuickCheck*

Have students use the instruction on pages L600–L601 to check their quotations for correct use of end marks. Encourage students to ask a classmate for assistance if they are still unsure about the placement of their end marks and quotation marks.

HOME STUDY

Have students find additional examples of quotation marks and end marks used correctly and incorrectly in comic strips, written interviews, and advertisements.

Connect to the Writing Process: Editing

Using End Marks with Direct Quotations

Language Arts Topic **Rewrite each sentence, adding periods, question marks, and exclamation points where needed.**

6. Bria said, "My topic is the Middle Ages in ~~England"~~ England."
7. Ms. Rayburn asked, "Who were the educated people at that ~~time"~~ time?"
8. "The priests were the educated ones," responded Bria, "and they wrote in Latin or ~~Greek"~~ Greek."
9. "Why didn't they use ~~English"~~ English?" asked ~~Nelson~~ Nelson. "Didn't most people speak ~~English"~~ English?"
10. "The common people spoke English," Bria explained, "but scholars looked down on ~~it"~~ it."

Communicate Your Ideas

APPLY TO WRITING

Comic Strip: *End Marks in Quotations*

Find a comic strip. Change the speech inside the balloons into direct quotations with speaker tags. For example: "Why are you always so mean to me?" Charlie Brown asked Lucy. Be sure you use end marks correctly in your quotations.

Mixed Practice

Science Topic **Rewrite the following quotations, adding quotation marks, commas, end marks, and capital letters where needed.**

1. ~~how~~ "How much of the earth is covered by ocean ~~water~~ water?" asked Mr. ~~Ames~~ Ames.

2. ~~More~~ "More than half the earth is ~~covered~~ covered," Tracy ~~answered~~ answered.
3. Mr. Ames ~~responded ocean~~ responded, "Ocean water actually covers three fourths of the earth's ~~surface~~ surface."
4. ~~that~~ "That doesn't leave much room for ~~land~~ land!" Brad ~~exclaimed~~ exclaimed.
5. ~~how~~ "How deep is the deepest ~~ocean~~ ocean?" Julie ~~asked~~ asked.
6. ~~the~~ "The average depth of the world's ~~oceans~~ oceans," Mr. Ames ~~replied is~~ replied, "is about three ~~miles~~ miles."
7. Brad ~~asked how~~ asked, "How high can waves ~~get~~ get?"
8. Mr. Ames ~~answered in~~ answered, "In a severe storm, some waves are forty-nine feet high. ~~they~~ They travel at fifty miles an ~~hour~~ hour."

Other Uses of Quotation Marks

What you have just learned about punctuating direct quotations can now be applied in the following situations.

Writing Dialogue

A **dialogue** is a conversation between two or more persons. The way it is written shows who is speaking.

When writing dialogue, begin a new paragraph each time the speaker changes.

In the following dialogue between Miguel and Lisa, a new paragraph begins each time the speaker changes.

> Miguel asked, "How long have you been helping at the computer club?"
>
> "I started last year," Lisa answered.
>
> "I'm thinking of joining the club, but I don't know if I should," he told her.
>
> Lisa answered, "Oh, I think you should. It's fun."

YOUR IDEAS

For Using End Marks with Quotation Marks

HOME WORK

Writing Dialogue

Ask students to reconstruct a dialogue they either encountered or had themselves that day. In addition to the dialogue, have students write at least one introductory sentence that explains the context of the dialogue.

Practice Your Skills

Check Your Understanding

Reading Dialogue

Oral Expression **Read aloud the following dialogue between Miguel and Lisa. Identify each place where a new paragraph should begin.**

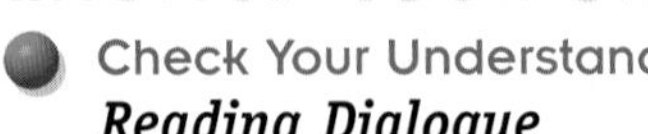

Miguel asked, "Do you need to have a computer at home to be a member?" ¶ "You don't have to," Lisa answered. ¶ "That's good because I don't have one. I am going to get one soon for my birthday," he told her. ¶ Lisa added, "I don't have one of my own either. I use my sister's."

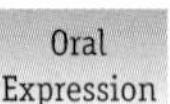

Connect to the Writing Process: Editing

Correcting the Paragraphing in a Dialogue

[See responses given above.]

Rewrite the preceding dialogue correctly, beginning a new paragraph each time the speaker changes.

Communicate Your Ideas

APPLY TO WRITING

Writer's Craft: ***Analyzing Dialogue***

You will notice, as you read short stories and novels, that writers usually put brief descriptions of a character's actions in the same paragraph with the direct quotations. In the following excerpt from a novel, the narrator describes the efforts of his father, a teacher, to lure a goat off the schoolhouse fire escape. Billy Joe, one of the father's pupils, has gone to get goat bait.

"They gave me some stuff for the goat to eat," Billy Joe said.

"What have you got?"

He opened the bag and peeped. "Got some turnips here and some broccoli and a pretty good bunch of carrots."

"Broccoli?" my father said. "I hate that stuff. I don't think that even a goat could choke down broccoli. Let's try the carrots."

"Here you go." He offered to toss the bag up to him.

"Just the carrots," he said. "The paper makes too much noise. Don't want to scare him off."

–Fred Chappell, Brighten the Corner Where You Are

The author makes this clear by alternating the paragraphs of dialogue between the father and Billy Joe.

- As you can see, the pronoun *he* is used for both characters. How can you tell which character is speaking or acting?

Billy Joe speaks first, which is indicated by the use of his name.

- Who speaks first? How can you tell?
- Who finishes the dialogue? The father finishes the dialogue.
- What would happen if the paragraph beginning with the word *broccoli* were missing?
  We would not know which of the characters was speaking next.

Quoting Long Passages

When you write a report, sometimes you need to support your own points with quotations by experts in a certain field. If any of those quotations are more than a paragraph long, there is a special way to write them.

When quoting a passage of more than one paragraph, place quotation marks at the beginning of each paragraph—but at the end of *only* the last paragraph.

YOUR IDEAS
For Writing Dialogue

SELECTION AMENDMENT
Description of change: excerpted
Rationale: to focus on the grammar skill

GETTING STUDENTS INVOLVED

Reciprocal Teaching

Have students work with partners to search for examples of quotation marks used with long passages. Students should use their literature textbooks to find examples. Have students explain to their partners how the quotation marks are used with long passages and when ending quotation marks should be used in long passages. Students should provide their partners with clear examples.

You omit the closing quotation marks at the end of each paragraph except the last one as a signal to a reader that the quotation is continuing. Look at the following example.

> "Goats were probably first used as domestic animals in Asia, about nine thousand years ago. Today there are about five species of goats, including both wild and domesticated ones.
>
> "Among the domestic goats, there are more than two hundred breeds. A few, like the Angora and Kashmiri goats, are grown for their soft fleece, which is woven into fabric. The rest are used for meat and milk."

CONNECT TO WRITER'S CRAFT

A long quoted passage may also be set off from the rest of the text by indenting both the left and right margins. If you are using a computer, you can also set the passage in smaller type. When you use this method of quoting a long passage, no quotation marks are needed.

PRACTICE YOUR SKILLS

Check Your Understanding

Quoting Long Passages

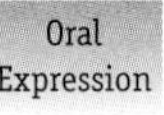

In a report on how to improve one's study skills, a student quotes the following passage. Add quotation marks correctly.

"To
~~To~~ help remember facts, try to make a connection with something you already know. Suppose you wanted to remember that warm air rises. If you live in a house with more than one story, you know that the top floor is the hottest place. The basement is the coolest. Use these facts to recall that warm air rises.

"Another ~~Another~~ good idea is to count the items you need to remember. That way, you'll always know whether you have remembered the whole list or left something out.

"It's ~~It is~~ also smart to break a long list into shorter parts. It is easier to learn two or three items at a time. If you need to memorize six things, memorize the first three, then memorize the last three. Finally, put the whole list together." ~~together.~~

QuickCheck Mixed Practice

General Interest

Rewrite each sentence, adding underlining, quotation marks, commas, capital letters, and end marks where needed. Remember that only a sentence with a speaker tag should be considered a direct quotation.

1. "Too ~~too~~ often we enjoy the comfort of opinion without the discomfort of thought," ~~thought~~ said John F. Kennedy. ~~Kennedy~~
2. The ~~the~~ article called "A Persistent Rebel," ~~A Persistent Rebel~~ in American History magazine told about Elizabeth Blackwell. ~~Blackwell~~
3. My favorite song from the musical My Fair Lady is ~~The Rain in Spain.~~ "The Rain in Spain."
4. "Education ~~Education~~ costs money," ~~money,~~ observed St. Claus Moser, "but, then, ~~but then~~ so does ignorance." ~~ignorance~~
5. Carl Sandburg's book Slabs of the Sunburnt West contains his poem ~~Primer Lesson~~ "Primer Lesson."
6. Alfred Adler once remarked, "It ~~remarked it~~ is easier to fight for one's principles than to live up to them." ~~them~~
7. "How ~~how~~ many r's are in the word *February*?" ~~February~~ asked Ty. ~~Ty~~

A DIFFERENT APPROACH

Tactile

Write out the three paragraphs from **Practice Your Skills** on large mural paper. Then have students use modeling clay, such as Play-Doh, to make sets of quotation marks. Students should form the beginning quotation marks and the ending quotation marks in the correct direction. One way to help students remember the direction is to tell them the beginning quotes look like *6*s and the ending quotes look like *9*s. The number *6* comes before the number *9.* Have students work together to place their clay quotation marks in the correct places within the paragraph mural.

EXPANDING THE LESSON

Using Technology

Use Barrett Kendall ancillary instructional and practice materials located at http://www.bkenglish.com.

Using *CheckPoint*

This feature on italics (underlining) and quotation marks can be used as further independent practice or as a cumulative review of the chapter. Students add underlining and quotation marks to titles, add quotation marks to direct address, and write sentences using quotation marks correctly.

CheckPoint

Punctuating Titles

Write each sentence, adding quotation marks and underlining where needed.

1. Is *Phantom of the Opera* a classic horror film?
2. In our textbook *New Poetry*, I read the poem "Dreams."
3. The word *typewriter* uses only the top row of letters on a typewriter.
4. Guy de Maupassant's short story "The Necklace" is tragic.
5. Charles Lindbergh's plane, *Spirit of St. Louis*, had no radio receiver or transmitter.
6. I read the article "Sports Greats" in this issue of *Life*.
7. The shortest word containing all five vowels is *eunoia*.
8. *Twelve Angry Men*, a three-act play, is also a movie.
9. "The Rain in Spain" is one song from *My Fair Lady*.
10. Sarah Bernhardt, a French actress, once played the prince's part in Shakespeare's *Hamlet*.

Punctuating Direct Quotations

Write each direct quotation, adding capital letters, quotation marks, and other punctuation marks where needed.

1. "~~what~~ What time do you want to get up?" Mom asked.
2. "~~a~~ A baby gazelle can outrun a horse," he explained.
3. "~~this~~ This book," Mom said, "must be returned to the library."
4. "~~you're~~ You're out!" shouted the umpire.
5. Dad asked, "~~do~~ Do we have another gallon of paint?"
6. "~~the~~ The coach asked, "~~which~~ Which is the third-most popular sport?"

7. The ~~the~~ humpback whale Mr. Keating said often covers more than four thousand miles in a single year
8. Karen cried out I've burned my finger!
9. Mr. Andrews said The ~~the~~ bell just rang Everyone ~~everyone~~ is dismissed
10. I just finished lunch she said It ~~it~~ was delicious

Punctuating Direct Quotations

Write each direct quotation, adding quotation marks, other punctuation marks, and capital letters where needed.

1. A ~~a~~ female whale weighs as much as thirty elephants he stated
2. Have ~~have~~ you ever visited New York City? Pat asked
3. Ms. Marsh said The ~~the~~ piano pieces by Mozart were composed for pianos with only five octaves
4. I smell smoke! Shelley screamed
5. Mrs. Jones asked Who ~~who~~ is going on the field trip?
6. Lobsters ~~lobsters~~ are so small at birth he explained that hundreds could fit in the palm of your hand
7. Andrew exclaimed I just won a free trip to Mexico!
8. Work ~~work~~ on your book reports They ~~they~~ are due on Friday Mrs. Keaton stated
9. Thomas Edison invented the electric voting machine she said It ~~it~~ was never used until twenty-three years later.
10. Ben asked Are ~~are~~ you cold? Shall ~~shall~~ I turn up the heat?

Using Quotation Marks

Follow the directions below.

1. Write an imaginary dialogue between you and your favorite singer or actor. Punctuate the dialogue correctly.
2. After an introductory paragraph, quote a long passage from a nonfiction book.

Possible Answers for *Using Quotation Marks:*

1.

I was in the mall when I saw my favorite actress, Natalie Portman. I went up to her with a smile.

"Hi," I said, "Aren't you Natalie Portman?"

"Yes, I am," she said. "I'm here in the mall promoting my latest movie."

"I am," I said, "one of your biggest fans. I even made a Website about you!"

"That's really nice," she said. "Do many people visit the site?"

"Hundreds of people visit!" I exclaimed. "It lists all the movies you have done, including *Star Trek 1—The First Episode*: *The Phantom Menace*."

Just then someone called Natalie to come to a photo shoot. I waved.

"Thanks for talking with me, and good luck!" I said.

2.

There are special words that artists use to talk about their work. The words *line* and *shape* refer to parts of the artwork. The word *composition* refers to the work of art. In "The Language of Art," Robyn Montana Turner writes, "Artists plan the composition of their artworks to help them communicate their ideas and feelings. This painting of a vibrant scene shows how artist Vincent Van Gogh felt about the sunrise.

"Special words, such as *line* and *shape* or *pattern* and *rhythm,* help artists talk about their compositions. Line and shape are two of the elements of art, or basic parts and symbols of artworks."

Using *Language and Self-Expression*

Consider using this writing assignment to assess students' ability to use italics (underlining) and quotation marks correctly. You may want students to complete the assignment as part of an expository writing strand for their portfolios.

Prewriting

Suggest that students revisit their analysis of the comic strip that they did in *Making Visual Connections* on page L584.

Encourage students to use questions like the ones below to help them organize their thoughts in the prewriting stage. For example, students might start with the following ideas and add their own ideas to help them proceed with their writing:

- What do I find humorous in the comic strip?
- What serious comments is the artist also making?
- How would I change the words or artwork?

FOR YOUR INFORMATION

About the Artist

Ben Sargent (1948–). Award-winning editorial cartoonist Ben Sargent was born in Amarillo, Texas. After graduating from the University of Texas at Austin, he worked as a reporter for five years. Sargent began drawing editorial cartoons for the *Austin American-Statesman* in 1974. He won a Pulitzer Prize for his work in 1982. Sargent's cartoons are distributed nationally by Universal Press Syndicate.

Language and *Self-Expression*

Ben Sargent, who drew this cartoon, is an editorial cartoonist. This type of cartoonist expresses opinions and messages through pictures instead of articles. The humor of the pictures often causes people to pay attention to the message when they might not read a whole article about the topic. Did you enjoy looking at this cartoon?

If you could change the label on the hat of the fourth character, what would you change it to? Write an editorial column in which you explain what your cartoon would mean. Imagine your audience as the readers of your school newspaper.

Prewriting Brainstorm for a list of words that would make sense used as the label on the fourth character's hat in this cartoon. You might focus on character traits that you dislike ("LIAR," for example). Then circle the word that gives you the most ideas.

Drafting Using the word you chose from your prewriting, write an editorial column explaining why this type of person is heartless, brainless, and cowardly. Interview friends and quote them in your article to show support or opposition for your opinion.

Revising Make sure your article expresses a clear opinion about the topic. Also, make sure you have used direct quotes from at least one other person.

Editing Check for mistakes in italics (underlining) and quotation marks. Make any corrections that are necessary.

Publishing Write a final copy and submit it to the school newspaper.

Another Look

Italics and Quotation Marks

Italics (Underlining)

Italicize (or underline) letters, numbers, and words when they are used to represent themselves. *(page L585)*

Italicize (or underline) the titles of long written or musical works that are published as a single unit. Also italicize (underline) the titles of paintings and sculptures and the names of vehicles. *(pages L585–L586)*

Quotation Marks

Use quotation marks to enclose the titles of chapters, articles, stories, one-act plays, short poems, and songs. *(pages L589–L590)*

Use quotation marks to enclose a person's exact words. *(page L594)*

Begin each sentence of a direct quotation with a capital letter. *(page L597)*

Use a comma to separate a direct quotation from a speaker tag. Place the comma inside the closing quotation marks if the quotation comes first in the sentence. Place the comma immediately after the speaker tag if the speaker tag comes first. *(page L599)*

Place a period inside the closing quotation marks when the end of the quotation comes at the end of the sentence. *(page L600)*

When writing dialogue, begin a new paragraph each time the speaker changes. *(pages L603–L604)*

When quoting a passage of more than one paragraph, place quotation marks at the beginning of each paragraph—but at the end of *only* the last paragraph. *(pages L605–L606)*

Other Information About Italics and Quotation Marks

Writing indirect quotations *(page L594)*

Using end marks with direct quotations *(pages L600–L601)*

Using *Another Look*

Another Look summarizes the terms defined in the chapter and provides cross-references to the specific pages on which they are explained. Consider having students use this feature prior to completing **CheckPoint** or taking the posttest. Students who can provide several examples of each term should be able to score well on either measurement.

FOR ASSESSING LEARNING

Using *the Posttest*

Assessing Learning

The posttest will help you and your students assess where they stand in their ability to use italics and quotation marks correctly.

IDENTIFYING COMMON STUMBLING BLOCKS

Following is a list of the most common errors students make when using italics (underlining) and quotation marks in their writing.

Problem

- Lack of italics or underlining with names of newspapers

Solution

- For reteaching, use the explanatory copy printed in blue beside the examples on page L586.

Problem

- Lack of comma to separate a direct quotation

Solution

- For reteaching, use the explanatory copy and examples on pages L593–L595.

Directions

Read the passage and choose the best way to write each underlined part. Write the letter of the correct answer. If the underlined part contains no error, write *D.*

EXAMPLE **1.** "We are having a block party said Mom. (1)

1 **A** party," said
B party", said
C party" said
D No error

ANSWER **1 A**

Mr. Cyr read about block parties in the article Know Your Neighbors (1). On our street all addresses start with 2's or 4s (2). Mom said that (3) Mr. Cyr is in charge.

"Let's enter the cake-baking contest said (4) Bonnie.

"Will a police officer speak about safety asked Lon (5)

"The article," continued Mr. Cyr says (6) that all neighbors should know each other.

I asked, "Does that increase safety? (7)

Yes answered (8) Mr. Cyr.

A sign on our street now reads Crime Watch Area (9).

No one wants to say, Help! I've been robbed! (10)

A DIFFERENT DELIVERY SYSTEM

If you prefer, you can print the posttest from the BK English Test Bank located at http://www.bkenglish.com.

1 A *Know Your Neighbors.*
B "Know Your Neighbors."
C "Know Your Neighbors."
D No error

2 A "2"'s or "4"'s
B *2*s or *4*s
C "2s" or "4s"
D No error

3 A said, "That
B said, that,
C said "that
D No error

4 A contest." Said
B contest", said
C contest," said
D No error

5 A safety" asked Lon?
B safety?" asked Lon.
C safety"? asked Lon!
D No error

6 A Mr. Cyr "says
B Mr. Cyr, "says
C Mr. Cyr, "Says
D No error

7 A safety?"
B safety"?
C safety?".
D No error

8 A Yes, answered
B "Yes," answered
C Yes, "Answered
D No error

9 A *Crime Watch Area.*
B *"Crime Watch Area."*
C "Crime Watch Area."
D No error

10 A "Help! I've been robbed!"
B "Help! I've been robbed"!
C *Help! I've been robbed!*
D No error

Customizing the Test

Use these questions to add or replace items for alternate versions of the test.

"What's so special about your street asked (11) Jordan.

I replied, "For one thing, we watch for suspicious people or activity (12)

"Another thing we do I continued (13) "is pick up mail and newspapers for a neighbor who is out of town."

Our neighborhood was named in the article "Safest Neighborhoods." (14)

11. A street?" asked
B street"? asked
C street? asked"
D No error

12. A activity".
B activity.".
C activity."
D No error

13. A do," I continued,
B do" I continued,
C do," I continued
D No error

14. A *Safest Neighborhoods*
B *"Safest Neighborhoods"*
C *"Safest Neighborhoods"*
D No error

Teaching Suggestions

BLOCK SCHEDULING

- If your schedule requires that you cover the chapter in a **shorter time,** use the instruction on apostrophes, semicolons, colons, and hyphens and the Check Your Understanding and QuickCheck exercises.
- If you want to take advantage of **longer class time,** add these applications to writing: Connect to Speaking and Writing, Connect to the Writing Process, and Apply to Writing exercises.

Essential Knowledge and Skills

- Writing to inform such as to explain, describe, report, and narrate
- Punctuating correctly to clarify and enhance meaning such as using hyphens, semicolons, colons, and possessives
- Writing with increasing accuracy when using apostrophes in contractions and possessives
- Proofreading his/her own writing and that of others
- Selecting and using reference materials and resources as needed for writing, revising, and editing final drafts
- Applying criteria to evaluate writing

CHAPTER 18

Other Punctuation

Pretest

Directions

Each sentence is missing one type of punctuation. Write the letter of the punctuation that correctly completes each sentence.

EXAMPLE **1.** The following holidays are my favorites Hanukkah, Thanksgiving, and the Fourth of July.

1 A apostrophe
B semicolon
C colon
D hyphen

ANSWER **1 C**

1. Do you wear red on Valentines Day?
2. We set up a self serve buffet on the Fourth of July.
3. Everyones house is decorated for Christmas.
4. I sent Easter cards to Topeka, Kansas Duluth, Minnesota and Salt Lake City, Utah.
5. Doesnt anyone in your family like eggnog?
6. How many *as* are in *Kwanzaa*?
7. My most memorable birthday party was in 99.
8. I always stay up at least until midnight on New Year's Eve I sleep late the next day.
9. I need the following gift wrap, boxes, and tape.
10. It is twenty two days until April Fool's Day.

IDENTIFYING COMMON STUMBLING BLOCKS

Following is a list of the most common errors students make when using apostrophes, semicolons, colons, and hyphens in their writing.

Problem
- Incorrectly adding apostrophes

Solution
- Instruction, pp. L621–L622
- Practice, p. L622

Problem
- Lack of an apostrophe in the contraction *it's*

Solution
- Instruction, p. L625
- Practice, pp. L626–L627

1 <u>**A**</u> apostrophe
B semicolon
C colon
D hyphen

2 **A** apostrophe
B semicolon
C colon
<u>**D**</u> hyphen

3 <u>**A**</u> apostrophe
B semicolon
C colon
D hyphen

4 **A** apostrophe
<u>**B**</u> semicolon
C colon
D hyphen

5 <u>**A**</u> apostrophe
B semicolon
C colon
D hyphen

6 <u>**A**</u> apostrophe
B semicolon
C colon
D hyphen

7 <u>**A**</u> apostrophe
B semicolon
C colon
D hyphen

8 **A** apostrophe
<u>**B**</u> semicolon
C colon
D hyphen

9 **A** apostrophe
B semicolon
<u>**C**</u> colon
D hyphen

10 **A** apostrophe
B semicolon
C colon
<u>**D**</u> hyphen

A DIFFERENT DELIVERY SYSTEM

If you prefer, you can print the pretest from the BK English Test Bank located at http://www.bkenglish.com.

Using *the Pretest*

Assessing Prior Knowledge

The pretest will help you and your students assess where they stand in their basic understanding of apostrophes, semicolons, colons, and hyphens.

Customizing the Test

Use these questions to add or replace items for alternate versions of the test.

11. My great grandmother was born in Mexico.

12. I wrote, "Dear City Hall I would like to be on the holiday decorating committee."

13. I bake cakes for holidays, birthdays, and parties and I make quite a bit of money.

14. I hung the piñata within the childrens reach.

15. The two girls favorite holiday is Christmas.

11. **A** apostrophe
B semicolon
C colon
<u>**D**</u> hyphen

12. **A** apostrophe
B semicolon
<u>**C**</u> colon
D hyphen

13. **A** apostrophe
<u>**B**</u> semicolon
C colon
D hyphen

14. <u>**A**</u> apostrophe
B semicolon
C colon
D hyphen

15. <u>**A**</u> apostrophe
B semicolon
C colon
D hyphen

ADDITIONAL RESOURCES

Language Skills Practice . . . . pages 173–184
Transparency Tools AW18
ESL Practice and Test Preparation . . . . . pages 136–138
Assessment: Chapter Test. . . . . pages 205–209

MAKING VISUAL CONNECTIONS

For Language Development

Have students study *Harlem Renaissance Party: Bitter Nest, Part II.* Then discuss the use of punctuation in the title of the artwork. Ask students how the artist's use of a colon and comma affect the viewer's understanding of the work. Have students write a sentence or two discussing their impression of the title and the artist's use of the colon and comma.

To Stimulate Writing

Use the questions for art criticism as writing or discussion prompts.

Possible Answers:

Describe This artwork is made of fabric, stitching, and probably paint (for the party scene). It looks like a quilt. Triangles and rectangles are used the most.

Analyze The color blue draws your attention to the center, and therefore the party scene. The large rectangle shape of the party scene dominates all the small triangles that surround it.

Interpret The word *Renaissance* in the title isn't really clear to me, but it makes me think of art or literature. The woman standing up with the colorful dress and mask might be telling a story to the others. The title also mentions a "Bitter Nest." I wish I had more explanation of what is bitter—is it the party or the story that the woman is telling? The last part of the title, *Part II,* tells me that this is probably part of a series of scenes.

Judge Answers will vary.

Faith Ringgold, *Harlem Renaissance Party: Bitter Nest, Part II,* 1988.
Acrylic on canvas, printed, tie-dyed, and pieced fabric, 94 inches by 82 inches. © 1988 Faith Ringgold, Inc.

Describe What materials did the artist use to create this artwork? What shapes are used most?

Analyze What is the center of interest in this artwork? How did the artist use shape and color to draw your attention there?

Interpret What kind of event does this artwork show? What does the title tell you about this event?

Judge How is this quilt different from most quilts? How is this artist's work similar to the work of a writer?

At the end of this chapter, you will use the artwork to stimulate ideas for writing.

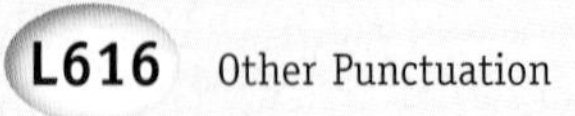

FOR DEVELOPING LANGUAGE SKILLS

LESSON 1 *(pages L617–L647)*

OBJECTIVES

- **To use apostrophes, semicolons, colons, and hyphens correctly**
- **To use apostrophes to show possession and to form contractions**
- **To use semicolons with compound sentences, conjunctive adverbs, and transitional words**
- **To use hyphens with divided words and with certain numbers, fractions, and some compound nouns**

Create Interest

Have students read and comment on the following sentences that contain

Apostrophes

An apostrophe is used to show possession. It is also used to form a contraction.

Apostrophes to Show Possession

You see apostrophes used most often to show that a person or thing owns or has something.

Paul**'s** shirt = the shirt that belongs to Paul

the shirt**'s** buttons = the buttons that the shirt has

The Possessive Forms of Singular Nouns

To form the possessive of a singular noun, write the noun but do not add or omit any letter. Then add an apostrophe and an *s*.

Add *'s* to form the possessive of a singular noun.

Nick + ***'s*** = Nick**'s**	Is that Nick**'s** green backpack?
backpack + ***'s*** = backpack**'s**	The backpack**'s** zipper is broken.
teacher + ***'s*** = teacher**'s**	That notebook is the teacher**'s**.
class +***'s*** = class**'s**	The class**'s** assignment is on the board.
box + ***'s*** = box**'s**	The box**'s** flaps were torn.

FOR INCREASING STUDENT ACHIEVEMENT

REACHING ALL STUDENTS

Struggling Learners

Tell students that the possessive apostrophe shows readers meaning in a visual way. For example, there is no way to distinguish among forms such as *horses, horse's,* and *horses'* merely by listening. Although they have distinctively different meanings, they are all pronounced the same. Remind students that when they write and when they read, they should focus on the location of apostrophes for meaning. Have students practice reading and telling the meaning of each sentence below.

- The horses have hooves.
- The horse's hoof was sore.
- The horses' hooves were sore.

errors. Ask students how the errors affect their ability to easily read and understand the sentences.

- Nicks is the best backpack. (Nick's)
- The dogs sleds were ready to go. (dogs')
- The sisters names were Judy and Meredith. (sisters')
- Jamess articles are interesting to read. (James's)

Guide Instruction

By Connecting Ideas

Ask students to list times they have seen apostrophes, semicolons, colons, and hyphens used in signs, advertisements, and commercials. Ask students to share any incorrect or informal uses of these punctuation marks that they can recall. Tell students that punctuation marks can sometimes add an element of humor or informality to an advertisement or street sign. Share the following message that was posted on a sign in a construction zone in Lancaster, Ohio: "People Working.

A DIFFERENT APPROACH

Kinesthetic

Have students complete **Practice Your Skills** with a computer. Students should type out each item and insert apostrophes in the appropriate locations. Have students print out their responses and share them with the class.

HOME WORK

Have students write out ten possessive words that require apostrophes. Students should then use each word in a complete sentence.

Practice Your Skills

Check Your Understanding

Forming Possessive Singular Nouns

Rewrite the following expressions, using the possessive form.

1. ~~core of an apple~~ an apple's core
2. ~~song of a bird~~ a bird's song
3. ~~sister of Rose~~ Rose's sister
4. ~~job of my mother~~ my mother's job
5. ~~edge of a river~~ a river's edge
6. ~~fender of a bus~~ a bus's fender
7. ~~chair of a dentist~~ a dentist's chair
8. ~~handbook of a scout~~ a scout's handbook
9. ~~cubs of a lioness~~ a lioness's cubs
10. ~~bat belonging to James~~ James's bat

Connect to the Writing Process: Drafting

Writing Sentences with Possessive Singular Nouns

[Answers may vary. Possible responses are given.]

11.–15. Write five sentences, using five of the possessive phrases you formed in the preceding exercise.

11. An apple's core has seeds.
12. We're listening to a bird's song.
13. Rose's sister is older than Rose.
14. A dentist's chair is comfortable.
15. James's bat is made out of aluminum.

The Possessive Forms of Plural Nouns

There are two rules to follow when forming the possessive of plural nouns.

Add only an apostrophe to form the possessive of a plural noun that ends in *s.*

boys + **'** = boys**'** The two boys**'** pets are dogs.
dogs + **'** = dogs**'** The dogs**'** tails are bushy.

Add *'s* to form the possessive of a plural noun that does not end in *s.*

men + **'s** = men**'s** The men**'s** cars are red.
sheep + **'s** = sheep**'s** The sheep**'s** coats are wool.

Give 'em a Break." Ask students how most drivers would respond to this sign. Does the sign sound more friendly and more likely to get a positive response in drivers than one that read "Slow Down! Construction Work Ahead"? Have students comment on the use of the apostrophe with *em* in the sign to represent the word *them.*

Have students share any other uses of these punctuation marks they have seen.

Consolidate Skills

Through Guided Practice

The **Check Your Understanding** and **QuickCheck** exercises will help students use apostrophes, semicolons, colons, and hyphens correctly. Review the instruction before completing each exercise. Guide students through the first item in each exercise. Discuss students' responses and any difficulties they might have. Have students complete the exercises independently.

Deciding which rule to follow is easy if you take two steps. First, write the plural of the noun—as it is. Second, look at the ending of the word. If the word ends in an *s,* add only an apostrophe. If it does not end in *s,* add an apostrophe and an *s.*

FORMING THE PLURAL OF NOUNS

PLURAL	ENDING	ADD	POSSESSIVE
lions	*s*	'	lions**'** roars
cats	*s*	'	cats**'** whiskers
mice	no *s*	's	mice**'s** tails
deer	no *s*	's	deer**'s** antlers

CONNECT TO WRITER'S CRAFT

Have you ever seen a sign that advertised "Orange's and Peach's"? The sign should have said "Oranges and Peaches." The sign maker got confused and used *'s* to form the plurals of nouns. Do not use an apostrophe to form the plural of a noun.

PRACTICE YOUR SKILLS

Check Your Understanding

Forming Possessive Plural Nouns

Rewrite the following expressions, using the possessive form.

1. ~~work of students~~ students' work
2. ~~lease of two years~~ two years' lease
3. ~~farm of grandparents~~ grandparents' farm
4. ~~cars of women~~ women's cars
5. ~~barking of dogs~~ dogs' barking
6. ~~honks of geese~~ geese's honking
7. ~~worth of six dollars~~ six dollars' worth
8. ~~first names of men~~ men's first names
9. ~~harnesses of oxen~~ oxen's harnesses
10. ~~ideas of both girls~~ both girls' ideas

REACHING ALL STUDENTS

English Language Learners

Students who are learning English might have difficulty deciding how to use the apostrophe and *-s* with some plural nouns, such as those ending in *-y.* Tell students that the plural possessive of nouns ending in *-y* is based on the plural form of the noun. Students should first decide how to spell the plural of the noun, such as *flies* is the plural of *fly.* Then they can decide on the plural possessive spelling *flies'.* Have students practice with the following words: *boy/boys/boys'; spy/spies/spies'; story/stories/stories'.*

Apply to Communication

Through Independent Writing

The **Communicate Your Ideas/ Apply to Writing** activities prompt students to write a character sketch, a paragraph for a tourist guidebook, a summary of social studies or science facts they have learned recently, and a descriptive paragraph about their favorite meal. Ask students how they might use colons in a tourist guidebook or in a menu describing their favorite meal. Why might apostrophes be important when they write their character sketches? Discuss students' responses.

Transfer to Everyday Life

Identifying Apostrophes, Semicolons, Colons, and Hyphens in News Magazine Articles

Have students find examples of apostrophes, semicolons, colons, and hyphens used correctly in news magazine articles, such as *Time* or

A DIFFERENT APPROACH

Visual

To reinforce the use of apostrophes with possessive nouns, have students complete **Check Your Understanding** by writing their answers on the board.

Check Your Understanding

Forming Singular and Plural Possessive Nouns

Decide whether each underlined noun is singular or plural. Then write its correct possessive form.

11. job of my sister — sister's
12. names of my sisters — sisters'
13. age of the child — child's
14. ages of the children — children's
15. price of the dress — dress's
16. prices of the dresses — dresses'
17. notice of one month — month's
18. notice of two months — months'
19. den of the wolf — wolf's
20. leader of the wolves — wolves'

Connect to the Writing Process: Drafting

Writing Sentences with Possessive Nouns

21.–25. Write five sentences about your school. Use a possessive noun in each sentence. You might use the possessive forms of nouns such as *school, class, classes, student, students, teacher, teachers, girls, boys, locker, lockers,* and *eighth graders.*

Connect to the Writing Process: Editing

Correcting Sentences with Possessive Nouns

Rewrite each sentence, correcting the possessive form. If the possessive form is correct, write *C*.

26. ~~Charlenes'~~ Charlene's library book is about the history of domesticated animals.

27. People's first domesticated animal was the dog. C

28. ~~Dogs's~~ Dogs' instincts attracted them to ~~human's~~ humans' leftovers.

29. ~~Sheeps'~~ Sheep's meat helped people survive when there were few animals to hunt.

30. Tending sheep was often children's work. C

31. According to many experts' conclusions, cattle were next to be tamed. C

U.S. News and World Report. Have students share some of their examples with the class.

Pull It All Together

By Sharing

Have students share one of their writing samples listed in the **Communicate Your Ideas/Apply to Writing** with you individually. After checking for correct use of punctuation, including apostrophes, semicolons, colons, and hyphens, discuss with students any improvements they might make to their writing.

Check Understanding

By Writing Examples

Have students write sentences using apostrophes, semicolons, colons, and hyphens correctly. Students should write at least two sentences for each type of punctuation mark. Students should provide various examples of using these punctuation marks in

32. A cattle ~~herds'~~ herd's meat could feed an entire community.

33. ~~Cows's~~ Cows' milk could also nourish humans.

34. With ~~oxens'~~ oxen's help, people could move heavy objects and plow larger areas.

35. These animals' hard work made civilization possible. C

The Possessive Forms of Pronouns

Personal pronouns do not use an apostrophe to show possession the way nouns do. Instead, they change their form.

	POSSESSIVE PERSONAL PRONOUNS
SINGULAR	my, mine, your, yours, his, her, hers, its
PLURAL	our, ours, your, yours, their, theirs

Do not add an apostrophe to form the possessive of a personal pronoun.

PERSONAL PRONOUNS	The bicycle is **hers.** The spider spun **its** web.

Indefinite pronouns, however, form the possessive by adding *'s.*

	COMMON INDEFINITE PRONOUNS
SINGULAR	anybody, anyone, each, either, everybody, everyone, neither, nobody, no one, one, somebody, someone
PLURAL	both, few, many, several

GETTING STUDENTS INVOLVED

Cooperative Learning

Have students work with a partner and choose ten pronouns from the two charts on this page. Students should work together to write a short story using these ten pronouns correctly. Remind students that personal possessive pronouns do not use apostrophes, but the indefinite possessive pronouns do require apostrophes. Have groups share their short stories with the class.

different situations, such as apostrophes with possessive nouns and contractions, semicolons with compound sentences, colons with lists, and hyphens with divided words.

YOUR IDEAS

For Using Possessive Pronouns

Add 's to form the possessive of an indefinite singular pronoun.

INDEFINITE PRONOUNS	She asked for everyone**'s** opinion.
	Someone**'s** wallet was found on the floor.

PRACTICE YOUR SKILLS

Check Your Understanding

Using Possessive Pronouns

Rewrite the following expressions, using the possessive form of each underlined pronoun.

1. bike belonging to him his bike
2. house belonging to us our house
3. coat of anybody anybody's coat
4. sister of you your sister
5. watch belonging to her her watch
6. front wheel of it its front wheel
7. bedroom belonging to me my bedroom
8. first choice of no one no one's first choice
9. good idea of someone someone's good idea
10. skateboards belonging to them their skateboards

Connect to the Writing Process: Drafting

Writing Sentences with Possessive Pronouns

[Answers may vary. Possible responses are given.]

Write five sentences, following the directions for each given below. Use a possessive pronoun in each sentence.

11. Describe your favorite article of clothing. My leather jacket is my favorite article of clothing.
12. Name the favorite song of you and your friends. Our favorite song right now is "I Want to Know."
13. Write a sentence giving the names of three well-known singers. Ricky Martin, Lauren Hill, and Jewel are my three favorite singers.
14. Write a question asking if a book belongs to anyone. Is this anyone's book?
15. Write a question asking if you can borrow a jacket from a friend. May I borrow your jacket?

Connect to the Writing Process: Editing

Correcting Sentences with Possessive Pronouns

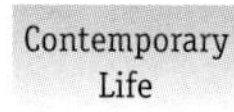

Rewrite each sentence, using the correct possessive pronoun. If a sentence is correct write *C.*

16. I have been working very hard on our school's Website. C

17. ~~It's~~ Its name is School Daze.

18. ~~Everyones~~ Everyone's suggestions have been both thoughtful and useful.

19. The idea for the design was ~~her's~~ hers.

20. I have spent my time organizing more than twenty volunteers. C

21. Tony and Emma have offered ~~they're~~ their help.

22. I am using one of James's articles and two of ~~your's~~ yours.

23. Have you finished your work on the new Internet links for homework? C

24. Did you ask for anybody's help? C

25. I've seen other sites, and I think ~~ours'~~ ours is the best one available.

Communicate Your Ideas

APPLY TO WRITING

Character Sketch: ***Possessive Nouns and Pronouns***

Imagine that your class is having a substitute teacher for a day. Write a paragraph for that teacher describing someone in the classroom. Gives facts about the person and about his or her likes and dislikes. Be sure to use possessive nouns and possessive pronouns in your sentences.

HOME WORK

Ask students to write a description of the room or environment they are sitting in as they write the assignment. Have students use at least ten pronouns, whether personal or indefinite in their writing.

TIMESAVER *QuickCheck*

Have students self-evaluate their character sketches by proofreading them after they are finished writing. Remind students to use apostrophes with possessive nouns but not to use apostrophes with possessive pronouns.

YOUR IDEAS
For Checking Your Understanding

Mixed Practice

Art Topic **Write the possessive form of each phrase in parentheses.**

1. I enjoy ~~(the class of Ms. Tahaku)~~ Mr. Tahaku's in Japanese brush painting.
2. We use only black ink and brushes for ~~(the drawings belonging to us)~~ our drawings.
3. My teacher was taught the art by ~~(the uncle belonging to her)~~ her uncle.
4. Brush painting has been practiced in ~~(the family of my teacher)~~ my teacher's family for many generations.
5. ~~(The techniques of the painters)~~ The painters' techniques were inspired by ancient thinkers.
6. ~~(The goals of the thinkers)~~ The thinkers' goals were to have an uncluttered mind and to appreciate the simple beauty of nature.
7. The painters want ~~(the work that belongs to them)~~ their work to suggest a great deal in just a few brush strokes.
8. To do ~~(the job of it)~~ its job, each brush stroke must be graceful and perfectly placed.
9. A famous painting of a misty mountain is ~~(a favorite of everyone)~~ everyone's favorite.
10. ~~(The skill of the painter)~~ The painter's skill captures the peaceful splendor of the mountain.
11. I wrote a poem about ~~(the beauty of the mountain)~~ the mountain's beauty.
12. I used haiku to express ~~(the thoughts belonging to me)~~ my thoughts.

Apostrophes with Contractions

Besides showing possession, an apostrophe is used in contractions. Two or more words are combined to form a contraction. The apostrophe replaces one or more missing letters.

CONTRACTIONS	
is n~~o~~t = is**n't**	let ~~u~~s = let'**s**
who ~~i~~s = who'**s**	there ~~i~~s = there'**s**
I ~~a~~m = I'**m**	o~~f the~~ clock = **o'**clock
he ~~i~~s *or* ~~ha~~s = he'**s**	she ~~ha~~d *or* ~~woul~~d = she'**d**

Use an apostrophe in a contraction to show where one or more letters have been omitted.

Do not confuse contractions with possessive pronouns, which have no apostrophe. When you are wondering whether to use an apostrophe, mentally say the individual words of a contraction.

CONTRACTIONS	it**'s** = it is
	you**'re** = you are
	they**'re** = they are
	there**'s** = there is or there has
	who**'s** = who is or who has
POSSESSIVE PRONOUN	its = belonging to it
	your/yours (belonging to you)
	their/theirs (belonging to them)
	whose (belonging to whom?)

REACHING ALL STUDENTS

Struggling Learners

For students who have trouble distinguishing between a contraction and a possessive pronoun, remind them that a contraction can always be written out as two individual words without losing any meaning. A possessive pronoun is not short for two words, but a complete word itself.

A DIFFERENT APPROACH

Visual

For items 21 through 32 in **Check Your Understanding,** have students come to the board to write out each correct response. Have the class read and discuss each sentence as it is completed. Students should be able to explain why they chose a particular response.

CONNECT TO SPEAKING AND WRITING

In everyday speech you probably make contractions using nouns. You may say, "Aaron's waiting in the car" instead of "Aaron is waiting in the car" or "The dog's chewed up your mitt" instead of "The dog has chewed up your mitt." When you write, these colloquial contractions are appropriate only in realistic story dialogue. They aren't acceptable in any form of formal writing.

PRACTICE YOUR SKILLS

Check Your Understanding

Writing Contractions

Write the contraction for each pair of words.

1. have not haven't
2. did not didn't
3. that is that's
4. are not aren't
5. who is who's
6. is not isn't
7. let us let's
8. I am I'm
9. she is she's
10. was not wasn't
11. we will we'll
12. I have I've
13. it is it's
14. do not don't
15. they are they're
16. you have you've
17. would not wouldn't
18. you are you're
19. we are we're
20. there is there's

Check Your Understanding

Distinguishing Between Contractions and Possessive Pronouns

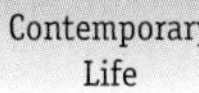

Write the correct word in parentheses.

21. (Who's, Whose) ready to go?

22. (Who's, Whose) name is on the class list for the first bus?

23. (It's, its) going to be late because (it's, its) tires needed more air.

24. (They're, Their) leaving now because (they're, their) bus has arrived.

25. (There's, Theirs) another bus arriving behind (there's, theirs).

26. (You're, your) going to be left behind if you don't find (you're, your) bus.

27. I can't tell (who's, whose) bus this is or (who's, whose) driving it.

28. I can see (it's, its) number; (it's, its) the bus for your group.

29. (There's, Theirs) plenty of time to find a seat.

30. Wait until others have found (there's, theirs).

31. If (you're, your) not saving that seat, put (you're, your) backpack on the floor.

32. Now that they've found (they're, their) seats, (they're, their) ready to leave.

Connect to the Writing Process: Editing

Correcting Sentences with Contractions

Rewrite each sentence, using the correct contraction or possessive pronoun. If a sentence is correct, write *C*.

33. ~~Their~~ They're getting off the bus now.

34. It's time for everyone to choose a partner. C

35. ~~Your~~ You're starting your tour of the wildlife park now.

36. ~~Theirs~~ There's a new trail here I'd like to try.

37. ~~Their~~ They're starting a clean-up program on this trail.

38. A class comes and cleans ~~it's~~ its part of the trail.

39. Your class can take part in the program. C

40. Its a great idea; ~~lets~~ let's do it!

HOME WORK

Have students write ten sentences that use contractions correctly. Students' sentences should be about the topic of wildlife trails or national parks.

YOUR IDEAS
For Using Apostrophes

 Apostrophes with Certain Plurals

To prevent confusion, certain items form their plurals by adding *'s*.

Add *'s* to form the plural of lowercase letters, some capital letters, and some words used as words that might otherwise be misread.

Lowercase Letters	My *u***'s** and *i***'s** look too much alike.
Capital Letters	How many *A***'s** did you write on your paper?
Words Used as Words	Our *hi***'s** echoed down the hallway. (Without the apostrophe, you might think that the word was *his*.)

Remember that the numbers, letters, symbols, and words used as words are themselves italicized (underlined) but that the apostrophe and the *s* are not.

The plurals of most other capital letters, symbols, numerals, and words used as words can be formed by adding just an *s*.

Capital Letters	How many *T*s did you have in your answers for the test?
Symbols	I used *s to mark the important information.
Numerals	There are three *2*s in her phone number.
Words Used as Words	Don't use too many *and*s in your sentences.

You can learn more about using apostrophes for plurals on page L672.

Apostrophes in Certain Dates

An apostrophe is also used when numbers are dropped from a date.

Use an apostrophe to show that numbers have been left out of a date.

My sister will graduate from college in ′06. (2006)

The Blizzard of ′88 was a major disaster in the Northeast. (1888)

The apostrophe is not used to form the plural of years in a decade. Add just an *s*.

I listen to some old bands from the 1960s.

PRACTICE YOUR SKILLS

Check Your Understanding

Using Apostrophes

Rewrite each phrase, adding an apostrophe where needed.

1. the Stock Market Crash of ~~29~~ ′29
2. a word with three ~~*as*~~ *a*′s in it
3. people born in the 1980s
4. the Spirit of ~~76~~ ′76
5. an address with three *6*s
6. two ~~*rs*~~ *r*′s in *February*
7. replace *and*s with &s
8. the ~~*ha-has*~~ *ha ha*′s for laughter
9. too many ~~*likes*~~ *like*′s in his sentences
10. learning one's *ABC*s

REACHING ALL STUDENTS

Struggling Learners

To reinforce the use of apostrophes with dates, have students use their social studies textbooks to find additional examples. Discuss the instruction on this page and then have students find at least ten more examples of apostrophes used correctly with dates in their social studies books. When finished, have students share some of their examples with the class.

A DIFFERENT APPROACH

Visual

Have students complete the **QuickCheck** with a partner. Each pair should write out their sentences using pencil. Then they should add the apostrophes in red pen or red marker to make them stand out. Discuss students' responses.

EXPANDING THE LESSON

Using Technology

Use Barrett Kendall ancillary instructional and practice materials located at http://www.bkenglish.com.

Mixed Practice

General Interest **Write each word that is missing an apostrophe and add the apostrophe in the proper place.**

1. Polar ~~bears~~ bears' fur is not white but clear, and their skins are black.
2. The Statue of ~~Libertys~~ Liberty's tablet is two feet thick.
3. There are two ~~*es*~~ *c*'s and two ~~*ms*~~ *m*'s in the word *accommodate.*
4. Ours was the first nation to declare its independence from Great ~~Britains~~ Britain's empire.
5. Cats were well known in ancient Egypt, but ~~theyre~~ they're never once mentioned in the Bible.
6. Whenever you see one of these #s, ~~youre~~ you're likely to call it the "number sign" or the "pound sign."
7. The country of Nauru ~~doesnt~~ doesn't have an official capital city; however, its government is based in Yaren.
8. During the Gold Rush, many of the first ~~49ers~~ '49ers came from Mexico, Peru, and Chile.
9. Congress ~~didnt~~ didn't remember to vote to admit Ohio to the Union until the 1950s.
10. ~~Its~~ It's possible to housebreak an armadillo.
11. Young children sometimes cannot tell the difference between ~~*bs*~~ and ~~*ds*~~. *b*'s *d*'s
12. A ~~states~~ state's population determines its number of representatives in Congress.

Semicolons

A semicolon (;) most often signals a pause between the parts of a compound sentence.

Semicolons with Compound Sentences

A **compound sentence** has two or more independent clauses. These clauses can be joined by a comma and a coordinating conjunction or by a semicolon.

Use a semicolon between the clauses of a compound sentence that are not joined by a coordinating conjunction. Coordinating conjunctions include *and, but, or,* and *yet.*

COMMA AND COORDINATING CONJUNCTION	My sister's hair is red**, but** mine is blond.
	My father's ancestors came from Ireland**, and** my mother's ancestors were Swedish.
SEMICOLON	My sister's hair is red**;** mine is blond.
	My father's ancestors came from Ireland**;** my mother's ancestors were Swedish.

You can learn more about compound sentences on pages L271–L273.

CONNECT TO WRITER'S CRAFT

You can use a semicolon to correct a run-on sentence.

RUN-ON	Everyone in my family is tall, my brother, for example, is six feet tall.
CORRECT	Everyone in my family is tall**;** my brother, for example, is six feet tall.

You can learn more about run-on sentences on pages L301–L303.

GETTING STUDENTS INVOLVED

Collaborative Learning

Have students work with partners to find ten compound sentences in literature excerpts from their literature textbooks. Students should work together to rewrite each compound sentence using semicolons. Remind students that the semicolon replaces the comma and the conjunction in compound sentences. Have groups share their new sentences with the class by writing some on the board.

A DIFFERENT APPROACH

Auditory

Complete **Check Your Understanding** by reading each sentence aloud, and noting the location of the commas and semicolons. Say "semicolon" as you come to each semicolon and "comma" as you come to each comma. Have students tell whether each sentence is correct or incorrect.

HOME WORK

Have students create five different compound sentences using commas. Then have students rewrite these sentences replacing the comma with a colon.

PRACTICE YOUR SKILLS

Check Your Understanding

Using Commas and Semicolons with Compound Sentences

Science Topic **Write *C* if a sentence is punctuated correctly. Write *I* if a sentence is punctuated incorrectly.**

1. Our bodies are made up of cells, and different types of cells have different functions. C

2. A control center is at the heart of each cell, it is called a nucleus. I [cell;]

3. Each nucleus contains forty-six threadlike parts; and these are our chromosomes. I [parts,]

4. These chromosomes are very small, but there is something else even tinier. C

5. Each chromosome is made up of thousands of genes, a gene is too small to be seen. I [genes;]

6. Our bodies are made up of many types of protein; genes carry the commands to make this protein. C

7. Genes come in pairs, we have one pair of genes for each of our physical characteristics. I [pairs;]

8. One pair of genes determines the color of our hair, another pair determines the color of our eyes. I [hair;]

9. Brothers and sisters have the same parents, yet only identical twins have the same genes. C

10. There are thousands of genes in a chromosome; and there are billions of possible combinations of the genes from just two parents. I [chromosome,]

Connect to the Writing Process: Editing

Punctuating Compound Sentences

11.–16. Rewrite the incorrectly punctuated sentences from the preceding exercise, using commas and semicolons correctly. [See answers given above.]

Semicolons with Conjunctive Adverbs and Transitional Words

Another way to combine independent clauses in a compound sentence is to use a semicolon along with one of the following conjunctive adverbs or transitional words.

COMMON CONJUNCTIVE ADVERBS		
accordingly	furthermore	otherwise
also	hence	similarly
besides	however	still
consequently	instead	therefore
finally	nevertheless	thus

COMMON TRANSITIONAL WORDS		
as a result	in addition	in other words
for example	in fact	on the other hand

Use a semicolon between clauses in a compound sentence that are joined by certain conjunctive adverbs or transitional words.

Notice in the following examples that the conjunctive adverb *therefore* and the transitional words *in fact* are preceded by a semicolon and followed by a comma.

> Kim practiced repeatedly**; therefore,** she played well at the recital.
>
> She had worried about stage fright**; in fact,** she performed calmly.

USING STUDENTS' STRENGTHS

Multiple Intelligences: Linguistic

Divide students into small groups and have them choose five words from the charts on this page to use in sentences. Students should work together to write sentences with these conjunctive adverbs and transitional words and make sure they use semicolons correctly. Have each group choose a member to write one of their sentences on the board to share with the class. Discuss groups' responses.

A DIFFERENT APPROACH

Visual

Have students write out each sentence in **Check Your Understanding** in pencil. Then have students use a red pen or marker to correct each incorrect sentence. Students should also use the red pen or marker to write *C* if the sentence is correct as is. Have students share their responses with a partner.

CONNECT TO WRITER'S CRAFT

Some of the conjunctive adverbs and transitional words shown in the box can also be used as parenthetical expressions within a single clause. When you use them as parenthetical expressions, you use commas—not a semicolon—to set them off.

JOINING CLAUSES	I play the guitar**; however,** I have never performed in public.
WITHIN A CLAUSE	My brother**, however,** has played in several concerts. 

You can learn more about punctuating parenthetical expressions on pages L564–L565.

PRACTICE YOUR SKILLS

Check Your Understanding

Punctuating Sentences

Science Topic **Write *C* if a sentence is punctuated correctly. Write *I* if a sentence is punctuated incorrectly.**

1. Your body needs special cells to fight germs; ~~otherwise~~ otherwise, you would be overcome by viruses and bacteria. I

2. Every ~~day;~~ day, in fact, your body makes billions of white blood cells. I

3. These defender cells travel throughout your bloodstream; consequently, they can attack germs anywhere in your body. C

4. Some white cells will attack any germ along the ~~way,~~ way; however, these cells often die quickly. I

5. Other white cells attack only a specific type of ~~germ,~~ germ; in fact, they carry special weapons called antibodies. I

6. Antibodies stick to the germs; in ~~addition~~ addition, other defenders destroy damaged cells. I

7. Antibodies are very strong; furthermore, they even have a kind of memory. C

8. They will, in other words, attack that kind of germ the next time. C

9. Your defender ~~cells;~~ cells, however, sometimes need help from outside the body. I

10. Vaccinations are harmless germs; consequently, your cells make antibodies against them. C

Connect to the Writing Process: Editing

Correcting Compound Sentences

11.–16. Rewrite the incorrect sentences from the preceding exercise, using commas and semicolons correctly. [See responses given above.]

Connect to the Writing Process: Drafting

Writing Sentences

[Answers may vary. Sample responses are given.]

Write five sentences, following the directions for each given below.

17. Write a compound sentence joined by a comma and the conjunction *and*.
She wants to come with us, and she doesn't know how to swim.

18. Write a compound sentence joined by a semicolon.
Larry is a great swimmer; he's on the team.

19. Write a compound sentence joined by *however*.
We should have won the race; however, the judges thought the other team was better.

20. Write a compound sentence joined by *in fact*.
She's a terrific pitcher; in fact, she excels at every sport she plays.

Semicolons to Avoid Confusion

Occasionally a semicolon will be used in place of a comma to eliminate any possible confusion in a sentence.

Use a semicolon instead of a comma between the clauses of a compound sentence if there are commas within a clause.

HOME WORK

Ask students to find an article of interest to them and rewrite one paragraph, inserting conjunctive adverbs and transitional words to make compound sentences. Remind students to punctuate these new sentences correctly.

YOUR IDEAS

For Using Semicolons

In the following sentences, the first independent clause in a compound sentence has commas in it. Therefore, a semicolon is used between that clause and the second clause.

> Matt grew healthy tomatoes, lettuce, and peppers; but his melons were a failure.
>
> In the Southern states, summers are hot, dry, and long; and this climate is ideal for growing melons.

CONNECT TO WRITER'S CRAFT

If a compound sentence still seems confusing, even when you use a semicolon, you may be better off rewriting it as two or more sentences.

> Summers are hot, dry, and long in the Southern states. This climate is ideal for growing melons. 

A semicolon also can take the place of a comma in certain sentences that consist of only one independent clause.

Use a semicolon instead of a comma between the items in a series if the items themselves contain commas.

In the following examples, a comma is needed between the cities and states. Normally a comma also would be placed between each item in a series. If all of those commas were put in, however, the second sentence would become very confusing to read. Therefore, semicolons are used between the items in a series when the items themselves contain commas.

SENTENCE WITH NO SERIES	They stayed in Jacksonville, Florida, and two other large cities.
SENTENCE WITH A SERIES	They stayed in Jacksonville, Florida; Albany, Georgia; and Mobile, Alabama.

You can learn more about items in a series on page L544.

PRACTICE YOUR SKILLS

Check Your Understanding

Using Semicolons to Avoid Confusion

Geography Topic

Write *C* if a sentence is punctuated correctly.
Write *I* if a sentence is punctuated incorrectly.

1. The three largest cities in the United States are ~~New York City New York, Los Angeles California, and Chicago Illinois.~~ I
New York City, New York; Los Angeles, California; and Chicago, Illinois.
2. New York City has many art galleries, museums, and ~~colleges,~~ its opera and ballet companies are famous. I colleges;
3. The four island boroughs of New York City are Manhattan, Brooklyn, Queens, and ~~Staten Island, and~~ only the Bronx is on the mainland. I Staten Island;
4. Los Angeles is a national center of manufacturing, finance, and ~~transportation and~~ its mass media industry is one of the largest in the world. I transportation;
5. The Los Angeles metropolitan area, which includes Long Beach, covers an area of more than 460 square miles. C
6. Los Angeles's museums include the County Museum of Natural History, with exhibits relating to California history; the Southwest Museum, where Native American arts are on display; and the California Museum of Science and Industry. C
7. Chicago was the birthplace of a modern school of ~~architecture, and~~ the city has buildings designed by great architects such as Frank Lloyd Wright, Louis Henry Sullivan, and William Le Baron Jenney. I architecture;
8. Chicago is home to the Cubs, a baseball ~~team, the~~ White Sox, a baseball ~~team, and~~ the Bulls, a basketball team. I team; the ... team; and

HOME WORK

Have students write a paragraph about an interesting city they have visited or about which they have read. Tell students to use apostrophes and semicolons in their writing. Refer students to pages L617, L631 and L633 to check their use of these punctuation marks.

TIMESAVER *QuickCheck*

Have students exchange their guidebook paragraphs with a partner. Students should check the paragraphs for correct use of semicolons. Also, students should make suggestions to improve the paragraph and to make it more interesting.

HOME STUDY

Have students bring to class any tourist guidebooks for cities or landmarks that they find interesting. Have students share any additional photographs, mementos, or information they have about the places. Ask students to share their experiences if they have visited the cities or landmarks.

Connect to the Writing Process: Editing

Punctuating Sentences with Semicolons

[See responses given on previous page.]

9.–14. Rewrite the incorrectly punctuated sentences from the preceding exercise.

Communicate Your Ideas

APPLY TO WRITING

Guidebook Paragraph: *Semicolons*

The photograph shows the Carson, Pirie, Scott Building in Chicago, Illinois. It was designed by architect Louis Henri Sullivan and erected in 1899. Find out more about Sullivan and the Chicago School of Architecture. Then use the facts you learn to write a paragraph for a Chicago guidebook for tourists. Use at least two sentences that contain semicolons in your paragraph.

Colons

A colon (**:**) is used most often to introduce a list of items.

Use a colon before most lists of items, especially when the list comes after an expression like *the following.*

Notice that commas are used between the items in each series.

> I am very interested in three subjects**:** biology, geography, and geology.
>
> The test will cover the following periods**:** the Jurassic, the Triassic, and the Permian.

You can learn more about commas with items in a series on page L544.

A colon is not needed between a verb and its complement or directly after a preposition.

INCORRECT	The earth's four main layers include**:** the inner core, outer core, mantle, and crust.
CORRECT	The earth's four main layers include the inner core, outer core, mantle, and crust.
CORRECT	The earth consists of four main layers**:** the inner core, outer core, mantle, and crust.
INCORRECT	The earth's mantle consists mainly of**:** silicon dioxide, magnesium oxide, and iron oxide.
CORRECT	The earth's mantle consists mainly of silicon dioxide, magnesium oxide, and iron oxide.
CORRECT	The earth's mantle consists mainly of three materials**:** silicon dioxide, magnesium oxide, and iron oxide.

DEVELOPING WORKPLACE COMPETENCIES

Basic Skills: Writing

Tell students that the salutation of business letters can contain either a comma or a colon. Although either punctuation mark is correct, more contemporary business letters are using colons in salutations. However, remind students that they should still use a comma in the closing of their business letters. Ask students which example of salutations and closings below is correct:

- Dear Mrs. Keller:
  Yours truly,
- Dear Mrs. Keller:
  Yours truly:

YOUR IDEAS
For Using Colons

There are a few other situations that require colons.

Use a colon to write hours and minutes, Biblical chapters and verses, and salutations in business letters.

COLON USAGE	
Hours and Minutes	6:30 A.M.
Biblical Chapters and Verses	Job 28:18
Salutations in Business Letters	Dear Sir:

Practice Your Skills

Check Your Understanding
Using Colons

General Interest

Write C if a sentence is punctuated correctly. Write *I* if a sentence is punctuated incorrectly.

1. In the past ten years, my family has lived in three ~~cities~~ cities: Memphis, Charlottesville, and Atlanta. I
2. The movie at Cinema II starts at ~~720~~ 7:20 P.M. I
3. The minister read from John 10:9. C
4. Animals with horns include these six: giraffes, deer, cattle, antelopes, sheep, and goats. C
5. California borders three other ~~states~~ states: Arizona, Nevada, and Oregon. I
6. We are waiting for~~:~~ Pat, Dylan, Chico, and Charlene. I
7. By 1944, Americans could buy the following frozen foods: meats, vegetables, fish, and dairy products. C
8. The bus stops here at ~~230~~ 2:30 and ~~430~~ 4:30. I
9. The three most heavily consumed food items in the United States are milk, potatoes, and beef. C
10. Dear ~~Ms. Anderson~~ Ms. Anderson:
    I am writing to apply for a summer job. I

Connect to the Writing Process: Editing

Correcting Sentences with Colons

11.–16. Rewrite the incorrect sentences from the preceding exercise, punctuating them correctly.

[See responses given on the previous page.]

Communicate Your Ideas

APPLY TO WRITING

Summary: ***Colons***

As a study aid for yourself, write a summary of the most important facts you have been studying recently in your science or social studies class. Include at least three lists that are introduced by colons.

Mixed Practice

General Interest **Rewrite each sentence, adding semicolons or colons where needed.**

1. Fruits that are purple include blueberries, plums, and ~~figs~~ figs; but no fruits are a true blue color.
2. A green color is a sign of ripeness in the following ~~fruits~~ fruits: kiwis, limes, and honeydew melons.
3. Some color names come from the names of ~~fruit~~ fruit: peach, apricot, orange, melon, and lime green.
4. A painter's palette may contain violet, rose, lavender, pink, buttercup, and ~~goldenrod,~~ goldenrod; and a garden may contain flowers with the same names.
5. The green violet has green ~~petals, otherwise~~ petals; otherwise, most violets are violet or purple.

TIMESAVER *QuickCheck*

After writing their summaries, have students refer to the instruction on pages L639–L640 to check their use of colons with lists. Remind students not to use colons immediately after verbs or prepositions.

EXPANDING THE LESSON

Using Technology

Use Barrett Kendall ancillary instructional and practice materials located at http://www.bkenglish.com.

USING STUDENTS' STRENGTHS

Multiple Intelligences: Linguistic

Have students turn to an excerpt in their literature textbooks or use a page from a novel they are reading. Tell students to check the hyphens at the end of each line to see if the words are divided correctly. Students should use a dictionary for correct word divisions. Discuss students' findings.

Hyphens

A hyphen **(-)** is used to divide words and is also part of the spelling of certain words.

Hyphens with Divided Words

Occasionally it is necessary to divide a word at the end of a line to keep the right margin even.

Use a hyphen to divide a word at the end of a line.

The following are some guidlines for dividing a word at the end of a line.

GUIDELINES FOR DIVIDING WORDS

1. Divide words only between syllables.

pro·duc·tion:	pro-duction or produc-tion

2. Never divide a one-syllable word.

Do Not Break	dine	cheap	strength

3. Do not divide a word after the first letter.

Do Not Break	omit	able	enough

4. Divide hyphenated words only after the hyphens.

sister-in-law	maid-of-honor	side-by-side

If you are not certain about where the syllable breaks in a word are, look up the word in a dictionary.

Practice Your Skills

Check Your Understanding
Using Hyphens to Divide Words

Add a hyphen or hyphens to show where each word can be correctly divided. If a word should not be divided, write *no* after the word.

1. occasion (oc-ca-sion)
2. summer (sum-mer)
3. evict (no)
4. milk (no)
5. sponge (no)
6. prince (no)
7. around (no)
8. middle (mid-dle)
9. question (ques-tion)
10. silent (si-lent)
11. repeat (re-peat)
12. fleet (no)
13. amazement (amaze-ment)
14. ocean (no)
15. aboard (no)

Connect to the Writing Process: Editing
Correcting Sentences with Hyphens

Rewrite the following paragraph, correcting the incorrect use of hyphens. If a word can be hyphenated, move the hyphen to an appropriate place. If a word cannot be hyphenated, write it as one word.

The hour of the day is determined ~~a-~~ ac-
~~ccording~~ cording to the position of the sun. This ~~me-~~ means
~~ans~~ that clocks in different regions ~~sh-~~ show
~~ow~~ different hours at the same moment in ~~ti-~~ time
~~me~~. Up until the 1800s, it was never necessary for Americans to know exactly what ~~h-~~ hour
~~our~~ it was in places far from their own homes.
In those days, travel was so slow and ~~unr-~~ unre-
~~eliable~~ liable that people measured long trips in
days, not in hours. They were ~~wil-~~ will-

A Different Approach

Visual

Have students write out the **Connect to the Writing Process** paragraph on large mural paper or chart paper. They should write the original paragraph in black marker. Then have students take turns using red marker to come up and correct the hyphenation errors in the paragraph.

INTEGRATING TECHNOLOGY

Computers

Have students use computers to type the example sentences in the instruction on these pages. Have students practice typing hyphens and tell them to take note of words that might hyphenate automatically as they type. Tell students that some word processing software programs allow users to disable the end-of-line hyphenation so that words are never hyphenated at the ends of lines. Have students practice doing this on the computer.

~~ling~~ ing to set their watches according to the ~~cl-~~ clocks
~~ocks~~ where they were. Since there ~~were-~~ weren't
~~n't~~ any time zones in the United States, ~~tr-~~ trav-
~~avelers~~ elers did not reset their watches by an
hour at a time as they traveled west or ~~ea-~~ east
~~st~~. Instead, they found themselves ~~gai-~~ gain-
~~ning~~ ing or losing five minutes at one ~~res-~~ rest-
~~ting~~ ing place or fifteen at another. With the ~~co-~~ com-
~~ming~~ ing of railroads and rapid travel, ~~howe-~~ how-
~~ver,~~ ever, Americans found that it was necessary
for train station clocks to agree with ~~ot-~~ oth-
~~her~~ er clocks in a region for the times of ~~arr-~~ ar-
~~ivals~~ rivals and departures.

Other Uses of Hyphens

A hyphen is used in spelling certain words, as well as in certain numbers, fractions, and compound nouns.

Hyphens with Certain Numbers

A hyphen is used in most numbers when they are written out in a report or story.

Use a hyphen when writing out the numbers twenty-one through ninety-nine.

"Sixty-four" is the answer to the math problem.
Twenty-five problems were on the test.

If a number is the first word of a sentence, it must *always* be written out.

There were **164** students taking the test.

One hundred sixty-four students were taking the test.

Hyphens with Certain Fractions

When a fraction is used as an adjective, it is written with a hyphen.

Use a hyphen when writing out a fraction used as an adjective.

HYPHEN — A **three-fourths** majority is needed to pass the amendment. (*Three-fourths* is an adjective that describes *majority*.)

NO HYPHEN — **Three fourths** of the members were present. (*Three fourths* is a noun used as the subject.)

Hyphens with Some Compound Nouns

A compound noun is a noun that is made up of two or more words. The words in a compound may be written in one of three ways: (1) together as one word, (2) as two separate words, or (3) as two words joined with a hyphen.

Use a hyphen to separate the parts of some compound words.

YOUR IDEAS
For Using Hyphens

A DIFFERENT APPROACH

Auditory

Complete **Practice Your Skills** with students by reading each item aloud. Students should explain where hyphens should be inserted in each item. Encourage students to check their responses in a dictionary.

COMPOUND WORDS	
One Word	birdlike, worldwide, crossroads, supermarket, grandmother
Two Words	all right, grocery store, dump truck, air conditioning
Hyphenated	great-grandmother, first-class, cross-examine

You can learn more about compound nouns on pages L52–L53.

Practice Your Skills

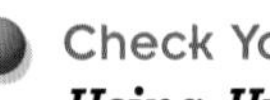

Check Your Understanding

Using Hyphens

Rewrite each phrase, adding hyphens where needed. If a phrase does not need a hyphen, write *C*. Use a dictionary to look up words you are unsure of.

1. the ~~twenty four~~ twenty-four members of the steering committee
2. a noisy jack-in-the-box C
3. three eighths of an apple pie C
4. a ~~trade in~~ trade-in on a sports car
5. a children's ~~merry go round~~ merry-go-round
6. a ~~mosquito free~~ mosquito-free campground
7. a ~~one tenth~~ one-tenth share of the profits
8. the ~~fifty first~~ fifty-first skydiver
9. a milelong causeway C
10. a ~~makebelieve~~ make-believe prairie schooner

Communicate Your Ideas

APPLY TO WRITING

Descriptive Paragraph: *Hyphens*

What would a meal made of your favorite foods consist of? Write a description to share with your parents. Use vivid adjectives to describe the appearance, taste, and smell of the dishes on the menu. Use at least three words that contain hyphens.

Mixed Practice

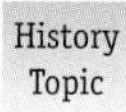

Rewrite the following paragraphs, adding apostrophes, semicolons, colons, and hyphens where needed.

Streetcars were a very common sight in the early 1900s. Maybe ~~youve~~ you've seen them in photographs or films. Perhaps ~~youve~~ you've actually ridden on one.

A ~~streetcars~~ streetcar's power came from electricity. ~~Europes~~ Europe's streetcars were powered by two overhead ~~wires~~ wires; however, most early streetcars in the United States were powered by one wire and one electrified track. Europe got its first streetcar system in ~~1881~~ 1881; the United States followed four years later.

Streetcars are used today in the following European ~~countries~~ countries: Germany, Austria, and Switzerland. They are almost extinct in the United States. A few lines have been revived in such cities as ~~Portland, Oregon,~~ Portland, Oregon; ~~Buffalo, New York, and Sacramento California~~ Buffalo, New York; and Sacramento, California.

TIMESAVER *QuickCheck*

Have students check their use of hyphenation in their descriptive paragraphs by using a dictionary. Students should correct any errors in hyphenation before they write the final draft of their papers.

EXPANDING THE LESSON

Using Technology

Use Barrett Kendall ancillary instructional and practice materials located at http://www.bkenglish.com.

Using *CheckPoint*

This feature on apostrophes, semicolons, colons, and hyphens can be used as further independent practice or as a cumulative review of the chapter. Students add correct punctuation to sentences, identify punctuation errors, and write sentences using these punctuation marks correctly.

CheckPoint

Punctuating Correctly

Write each sentence, adding apostrophes, semicolons, colons, and hyphens where needed. If a sentence is correct, write C.

1. Some restaurants serve frogs' legs.
2. Theirs can't be the house with the shutters.
3. Turtles have no teeth; instead, they have sharp beaks.
4. A honeybee's stinger has a hook at the end.
5. "A one-fifth share of the profits sounds good to me," said the board member whom we had just elected.
6. We steamed twenty-five ears of corn as part of someone's catering order.
7. Dad travels to many cities: Tulsa, Oklahoma; Tucson, Arizona; Las Vegas, Nevada; and Detroit, Michigan.
8. Vermont was not one of the original thirteen colonies; it became the fourteenth state in 1791.
9. Women's coats are on sale at the mall.
10. Do you know the following computer terms: *bit, byte,* and *bug?*

Punctuating Correctly

Write each sentence, adding apostrophes, semicolons, colons, and hyphens where needed. If a sentence is correct, write C.

1. Thirty-five billion pounds of potatoes are consumed by Americans each year. C
2. An elephant's trunk is actually its nose and upper lip. C
3. After eight hours' work, Mom finished her painting.

4. Tendons connect muscles to bones, ligaments link the bones of ankles, knees, and elbows.
5. We'll have to take the early train in order to get to everyone's appointments on time.
6. I missed the bus, otherwise, I had a wonderful day.
7. My parents' birthday present to me was a down vest stitched with a pattern of s's.
8. I wrote down the time of the sunrise, 6:17 A.M., the time of the sunset, 7:20 P.M., and the day's average temperature.
9. A small plane has three main controls: a throttle lever, a control column, and a rudder bar.
10. The men's soccer team is practicing for the Olympics. C

Using Punctuation Marks

Write sentences that follow the directions below.

Write a sentence that . . .

1. includes the possessive form of the noun *uncle.*
2. includes the possessive form of the noun *grandparents.*
3. includes the possessive form of the noun *children.*
4. includes the possessive form of the pronoun *no one.*
5. includes the words *you're* and *your.*
6. includes the plural of *no.*
7. includes two independent clauses joined by only a semicolon.
8. includes the word *nevertheless* between two independent clauses in a compound sentence.
9. includes a series of dates (day, month, and year).
10. includes *two-thirds* as an adjective.

When you are finished, make sure you have used all punctuation correctly.

Sample Answers for *Using Punctuation Marks:*

1. My uncle's hobby is collecting old coins.
2. My grandparents' farmhouse was built in the 1920s.
3. The children's toys were scattered across the floor.
4. It is no one's fault that the bread burned.
5. May I borrow your bicycle while you're in dance class?
6. I keep asking for things from my parents, but I keep getting *no's* in response.
7. I wash and mend my clothing weekly; I am known for my impeccable appearance.
8. Last summmer I promised myself I would get a job this summer; nevertheless, I am taking the summer off.
9. The birthdays in my family are on June 9, 1962; May 4, 1964; February 24, 1985; and December 4, 1988.
10. Use a two-thirds portion of that powdered drink mix instead of the entire amount recommended.

Using *Language and Self-Expression*

Consider using this writing assignment to assess students' ability to use apostrophes, semicolons, colons, and hyphens correctly. You may want students to complete the assignment as part of a narrative writing strand for their portfolios.

Prewriting

Suggest that students revisit their analysis of the quilt that they did in *Making Visual Connections* on page L616.

Encourage students to use questions like the ones below to help them organize their thoughts in the prewriting stage. For example, students might start with the following ideas and add their own ideas to help them proceed with their writing:

- What would I do if I had a quilt like this one: sleep with it or display it in my home?
- What story might the words around the quilt tell?
- If I wrote a story about this quilt, how would it start? How would it end?

FOR YOUR INFORMATION

About the Artist

As a young girl growing up in Harlem, New York City, Faith Ringgold wanted to be an artist. She studied art in school and later taught art in New York City schools. Ringgold is most famous for her story quilts, which tell about her childhood memories and her African American heritage. She also creates soft-sculpture figures, many of which represent cultural and personal heroes.

Language and *Self-Expression*

Faith Ringgold created this artwork to portray a group of artists who formed a community in New York City in the early 1900s. They would meet to share ideas and materials for creating art. Ringgold wrote a story along the borders of the quilt. What do you think the story is about?

Write a story that could be placed along the borders of this quilt. You could write about the people in the artists' group, or you could explain what events are behind the phrase *Bitter Nest* in the title of the art. Plan to have a storytelling session with your class in which you read your story aloud.

Prewriting Think of names for the characters in your story; a time and place for the action; and the events for the beginning, middle, and end.

Drafting Use your ideas from prewriting to write the first draft of your story and to give it a title. You might want to begin the story in the middle of an action scene to grab your readers' attention. You could reveal the meaning of the title at the end. Use apostrophes, semicolons, colons, and hyphens to make your sentences interesting.

Revising Read aloud your first and last paragraphs to a partner. Ask him or her how they relate to each other. Then have your partner read the entire story and give you feedback on it. Make sure you have used punctuation correctly.

Editing Check your story for mistakes in punctuation and spelling. Make sure each paragraph is indented.

Publishing Write a final copy of your story to read aloud in your class's storytelling session.

Another Look

Other Punctuation

Apostrophes

Add *'s* to form the possessive of a singular noun. *(page L617)*
Add only an apostrophe to form the possessive of a plural noun that ends in *s*. *(page L618)*
Add *'s* to form the possessive of a plural noun that does not end in *s*. *(pages L618–L619)*
Do not add an apostrophe to form the possessive of a personal pronoun. *(page L621)*
Use an apostrophe in a contraction to show where one or more letters have been omitted. *(page L625)*

Semicolons and Colons

Use a semicolon between the clauses of a compound sentence that are not joined by a coordinating conjunction. *(page L631)*
Use a semicolon between clauses in a compound sentence that are joined by certain conjunctive adverbs or transitional words. *(page L633)*
Use a semicolon instead of a comma between the items in a series if the items themselves contain commas. *(page L636)*
Use a colon before most lists of items, especially when the list comes after an expression like *the following*. *(page L639)*
Use a colon to write hours and minutes, Biblical chapters and verses, and salutations in business letters. *(page L640)*

Hyphens

Use a hyphen to divide a word at the end of a line. *(page L642)*
Use a hyphen when writing out the numbers twenty-one through ninety-nine. *(page L644)*
Use a hyphen when writing out a fraction used as an adjective. *(page L645)*
Use a hyphen to separate the parts of some compound words. *(pages L645–L646)*

Other Information About Punctuation

Using apostrophes *(pages L617–L629)*
Using semicolons and colons *(pages L631–L640)*
Using hyphens *(pages L642–L646)*

Using *Another Look*

Another Look summarizes the terms defined in the chapter and provides cross-references to the specific pages on which they are explained. Consider having students use this feature prior to completing **CheckPoint** or taking the posttest. Students who can provide several examples of each term should be able to score well on either measurement.

FOR ASSESSING LEARNING

Using *the Posttest*

Assessing Learning

The posttest will help you and your students assess where they stand in their ability to use apostrophes, semicolons, colons, and hyphens correctly.

IDENTIFYING COMMON STUMBLING BLOCKS

Following is a list of the most common errors students make when using apostrophes, semicolons, colons, and hyphens in their writing.

Problem

- Incorrectly adding apostrophes

Solution

- For reteaching, use the explanatory copy and examples on pages L621–L622.

Problem

- Lack of an apostrophe in the contraction *it's*

Solution

- For reteaching, use the explanatory copy and examples on page L625.

Directions

Each sentence is missing one type of punctuation. Write the letter of the punctuation that correctly completes each sentence.

EXAMPLE **1** The new puppys bed is lined with fleece.

1 **A** apostrophe
B semicolon
C colon
D hyphen

ANSWER **1** **A**

1. The pet stores shelves were filled with items I wanted for my pets.

2. At this store, youre allowed to bring your pet inside.

3. I didn't bring Whiskers, my older cat, or Bobtail, my younger cat but I did bring Rascal, my dog.

4. An announcement came over the loudspeaker saying that the store would stay open until 830 tonight.

5. I walked through the store with a basket I gradually filled the basket with items.

6. I remembered that my two cats scratching post was broken.

7. I asked someones help in getting a new scratching post from a high shelf.

8. After paying the cashier, I was down to my last dollar however, I was glad I had made the purchases.

9. I had bought the following items dog biscuits, catnip, a scratching post, and chew toys.

10. The narrow receipt caused words to be divided at the end of each line; for example, *customer* was written as *cus tomer.*

A DIFFERENT DELIVERY SYSTEM

If you prefer, you can print the posttest from the BK English Test Bank located at http://www.bkenglish.com.

1 **A** apostrophe
B semicolon
C colon
D hyphen

2 **A** apostrophe
B semicolon
C colon
D hyphen

3 **A** apostrophe
B semicolon
C colon
D hyphen

4 **A** apostrophe
B semicolon
C colon
D hyphen

5 **A** apostrophe
B semicolon
C colon
D hyphen

6 **A** apostrophe
B semicolon
C colon
D hyphen

7 **A** apostrophe
B semicolon
C colon
D hyphen

8 **A** apostrophe
B semicolon
C colon
D hyphen

9 **A** apostrophe
B semicolon
C colon
D hyphen

10 **A** apostrophe
B semicolon
C colon
D hyphen

Customizing the Test

Use these questions to add or replace items for alternate versions of the test.

11. My pets affection made the purchases worthwhile.

12. The ever affectionate Whiskers purred.

13. Rascal's responses were these barking, jumping, and licking.

14. I was glad I hadnt forgotten to get something special for each of them.

15. Everyones pet deserves loving treatment.

11. **A** apostrophe
B semicolon
C colon
D hyphen

12. **A** apostrophe
B semicolon
C colon
D hyphen

13. **A** apostrophe
B semicolon
C colon
D hyphen

14. **A** apostrophe
B semicolon
C colon
D hyphen

15. **A** apostrophe
B semicolon
C colon
D hyphen

A Writer's Guide to Citing Sources

When you write a report, you sometimes use other people's research to help you make your own point. If you paraphrase or quote the ideas of another person, you must include a note called a **citation** that gives credit to the original source.

Parenthetical citations are brief notes in parentheses right after the words or ideas you have borrowed. They give the reader enough information to identify the source in a list of works cited at the end of your report. Refer to the following examples to help you use parenthetical citations correctly.

BOOK BY ONE AUTHOR	Give author's last name and page number(s): (Chambers 197–198).
BOOK BY MORE THAN ONE AUTHOR	Give all of the authors' names and page number(s): (Bradbury, Clarke, Murray, Sagan, and Sullivan 36).
ARTICLE WITH AUTHOR NAMED	Give author's last name and page number(s): (Jakosky 648).
ARTICLE WITH AUTHOR UNNAMED	Give a shortened form of the title of the article (unless full title is already short) and page number(s): ("Mars" 54).
ARTICLE IN A REFERENCE WORK; AUTHOR UNNAMED	Give title (full or shortened) and page number(s); if the article is a single page from an encyclopedia arranged alphabetically, no page number is necessary: ("Mars").

Parenthetical citations should be as close as possible to the words or ideas being credited. Place them at the end of a phrase, clause, or sentence so that you will not interrupt the flow of the sentence.

A **works-cited page** is an alphabetical listing of all the sources you have used to write your report. It appears at the end of your report and provides complete information about each source. On a works-cited page, sources are alphabetized by the author's last name or by the title if there is no author listed. Page numbers are usually given for articles but not for books. Use the following examples for help in compiling a works-cited page.

General Reference Works	Carr, Michael H. "Mars." Encyclopedia Americana. 1999 ed.
Books by One Author	Chambers, Paul. Life on Mars: The Complete Story. New York: Sterling Press, 1999.
Books by Two or More Authors	Bradbury, Ray, Arthur C. Clarke, Bruce Murray, Carl Sagan, and Walter Sullivan. Mars and the Mind of Man. New York: Harper & Row, 1973.
Articles in Magazines	Jakosky, Bruce. "Water, Climate, and Life." Science 29 Jan. 1999: 648.
Articles in Newspapers	Wilford, John Noble. "Another Meteorite May Show Life on Mars, Scientists Report." New York Times 19 Mar. 1999, A4.
Article from a CD-ROM	Visions of Mars. CD-ROM. Moab: Andromeda Software, 1996.
Article from an Online Database with a Print Version	"Mars Climate Orbiter Declared Dead." Astronomy Now 24 Sept. 1999: 13 pars. 6 Oct. 1999 <www.astronomynow.com/mars/mco/990924/index.html>.
Online Material with No Print Version	Hardin, Mary. "New Mars Images: No Evidence of Ancient Ocean Shorelines." NASA News. 6 Oct. 1999 <liftoff.msfc.nasa.gov/news/article2.html>.

TEACHING SUGGESTIONS

Essential Knowledge and Skills

- Spelling derivatives correctly by applying the spellings of bases and affixes
- Spelling frequently misspelled words correctly
- Using resources to find correct spellings
- Spelling accurately in final drafts
- Generating ideas and plans for writing by using prewriting strategies such as brainstorming, graphic organizers, notes, and logs
- Selecting and using reference materials and resources as needed for writing, revising, and editing final drafts
- Applying criteria to evaluate writing

BLOCK SCHEDULING

- If your schedule requires that you cover the chapter in a **shorter time,** use the instruction on spelling strategies and spelling generalizations and the Check Your Understanding and QuickCheck exercises.
- If you want to take advantage of **longer class time,** add these applications to writing: Word Alerts, Connect to the Writing Process, and Apply to Writing exercises.

CHAPTER 19

Spelling Correctly

Directions

Read the passage and write the letter of the answer that correctly spells each underlined word. If the underlined word is correct, write *D*.

EXAMPLE An intresting (1) skill is ventriloquy.

1 A interesting
B inturesting
C interresting
D No error

ANSWER **1 A**

It is hard to believe (1) that the voice of a skilled ventriloquist's puppet comes from the human purformer (2). Yet learning to speak without moveing (3) your lips does not present much difficulty (4). Only five letters—*b, f, m, p,* and *v*—requir (5) lip movement. You can avoid words with troublsome (6) letters, or a similar (7) sound, such as an *n* for an *m*, can be used. A majorety (8) of the audience won't notise (9). If you practice (10) often, you can become a ventriloquist.

IDENTIFYING COMMON STUMBLING BLOCKS

Following is a list of the most common spelling errors students make when writing.

Problem
- Spelling words containing *ei* and *ie*

Solution
- Instruction, pp. L662–L663
- Practice, pp. L664–L665

Problem
- Doubling a final consonant before adding a suffix

Solution
- Instruction, pp. L682–L683
- Practice, pp. L683–L684

1 A beleive
B believ
C beelieve
D No error

2 A performur
B preformer
C performer
D No error

3 A mooving
B moving
C moveng
D No error

4 A difficulte
B dificulty
C difficultie
D No error

5 A reqire
B require
C reequire
D No error

6 **A** troublesome
B trublesome
C troublesume
D No error

7 A simular
B simelar
C similer
D No error

8 A majarity
B mejority
C majority
D No error

9 **A** notice
B notuce
C notuse
D No error

10 A practise
B practis
C practus
D No error

A DIFFERENT DELIVERY SYSTEM

If you prefer, you can print the pretest from the BK English Test Bank located at http://www.bkenglish.com.

Using *the Pretest*

Assessing Prior Knowledge

The pretest will help you and your students assess where they stand in their ability to spell commonly misspelled words.

Customizing the Test

Use these questions to add or replace items for alternate versions of the test.

Through the years, ventriloquists have used <u>their</u> (11) puppets to entertain and educate. The great <u>sucess</u> (12) of *Sesame Street* illustrates this point. That <u>particuler</u> (13) program has <u>benefitted</u> (14) many children. Whether used to bring a smile or <u>stimulate</u> (15) a mind, ventriloquism brings pleasure to many.

11. A thier
B there
C theire
D No error

12. A succes
B success
C sukcess
D No error

13. A perticuler
B partikular
C particular
D No error

14. **A** benefited
B benifited
C benifitted
D No error

15. A stimulat
B stemulate
C stemulat
D No error

ADDITIONAL RESOURCES

Language Skills Practice . . . . pages 185–189
Transparency Tools AW19
Assessment: Chapter Test. . . . . pages 210–213
Assessment: End of Course Test. . . . . . . pages 230–243

Strategies for Learning to Spell

The senses of hearing, sight, and touch are useful tools for learning to spell correctly. Try this five-step strategy that helps many people spell unfamiliar words.

1 Auditory

Say the word aloud. Answer these questions.

- Where have I heard or read the word before?
- What was the context in which I heard or read the word?

2 Visual

Look at the word. Answer these questions.

- Does this word divide into parts? Is it a compound word? Does it have a prefix or a suffix?
- Does this word look like any other word I know? Could it be part of a word family I would recognize?

3 Auditory

Spell the word to yourself. Answer these questions.

- How is each sound spelled?
- Are there any surprises? Does the word follow spelling rules I know, or does it break the rules?

4 Visual/Kinesthetic

Write the word as you look at it. Answer these questions.

- Have I written the word clearly?
- Are my letters formed correctly?

5 Visual/Kinesthetic

Cover up the word. Visualize it. Write it. Answer this question.

- Did I write the word correctly?
- If the answer is no, return to step 1.

FOR DEVELOPING LANGUAGE SKILLS

LESSON 1 *(pages L659–L687)*

OBJECTIVES

- **To recognize and correctly spell commonly misspelled words**
- **To recognize and use spelling patterns**
- **To use spelling generalizations to spell plurals correctly**
- **To use knowledge of prefixes and suffixes to spell words correctly**

Create Interest

Write the following sets of words on the board. Have students identify the word that is spelled correctly in each set. Discuss students' responses as they check their spellings in a dictionary.

Spelling Strategies

Misspelled words, whether in a composition for school or in a letter to a friend, call attention to themselves. Unfortunately, that means they are likely to distract readers from the thoughts being expressed. This chapter will introduce you to strategies and generalizations to help you improve your spelling.

STRATEGY **Use a dictionary.** If you're not sure how to spell a word, or if a word doesn't "look right," check its spelling in a dictionary. Don't rely on guessing to help you spell accurately.

STRATEGY **Proofread your writing carefully.** If you use a computer, do not rely on your word processing program to catch spelling errors. When you type the word *strait,* the computer can't know that you really meant to type *straight, strait, trait,* or even *strain.*

PRACTICE YOUR SKILLS

Check Your Understanding
Recognizing Misspelled Words

Write the letter of the misspelled word in each set. Then write the word correctly.

1. (a) absence (b) villain (c) ~~sergent~~ sergeant
2. (a) exceed (b) ~~occured~~ occurred (c) vacuum
3. (a) ~~picniced~~ picnicked (b) receipt (c) leisurely
4. (a) ~~exshaust~~ exhaust (b) gauge (c) fascinate
5. (a) cemetery (b) ~~fourty~~ forty (c) foreign
6. (a) echoes (b) specialty (c) ~~privelege~~ privilege

FOR INCREASING STUDENT ACHIEVEMENT

DEVELOPING WORKPLACE COMPETENCIES

Basic Skills: Writing

Discuss with students the importance of being able to spell correctly on job applications and in their future careers. Ask students to list professions in which spelling is crucial, such as nursing or pharmacy. Spelling errors in these jobs could lead to life-threatening mistakes. Have students use spelling strategies to learn to spell the following workplace words: *resumé, application, applicant, employee, employer, workplace, career, memorandum, knowledgeable, business, diploma, responsible, dependable.*

• wer'e	we're	w'ere
• foreign	foriegn	forign
• speek	speke	speak
• university	unaversity	univirsity

Guide Instruction

By Connecting Ideas

Ask students to share any spelling strategies, such as mnemonic devices, that they use to help them spell difficult words. Write some of these strategies on the board. To get students started, tell them that one way to remember the correct spelling for the head of a school is to say "A *principal* is a *pal*." The *pal* will remind them to use the *-al* ending rather than the *-le* ending in *principle.*

Consolidate Skills

Through Guided Practice

The **Check Your Understanding** exercises as well as the **QuickChecks** will

A DIFFERENT APPROACH

Auditory

Have students complete **Practice Your Skills** by pronouncing the words to themselves. Then have students look up the words in a dictionary to read the respellings that the dictionary offers. Tell students that these dictionary respellings will help them with pronunciations if they have difficulty pronouncing words. Also, tell students that different dictionaries use different types of respellings and that they can refer to the dictionaries' pronunciation keys to help them use the respellings.

HOME WORK

Have students use a dictionary to look up and write out ten respellings for words that they frequently misspell. Students should then use each word in a complete sentence.

7. (a) achievement (b) ~~likeble~~ likeable (c) quotation
8. (a) ~~prefered~~ preferred (b) discipline (c) procedure
9. (a) ~~existance~~ existence (b) condemn (c) conscience

STRATEGY **Be sure you are pronouncing words correctly.** "Swallowing" syllables or adding extra syllables can cause you to misspell a word.

PRACTICE YOUR SKILLS

Check Your Understanding

Pronouncing Words

Oral Expression **Practice saying each syllable in the following words to help you spell the words correctly.**

1. re•al•is•tic
2. cus•to•mar•y
3. re•cur•rence
4. nu•cle•ar
5. in•ter•fere
6. coun•ter•feit
7. Ant•arc•ti•ca
8. se•cur•i•ty
9. nat•ur•al•ly
10. di•a•per
11. ex•pe•di•tion
12. prac•ti•cal•ly
13. va•ca•tion
14. res•i•dence
15. equal•ly
16. pre•de•ter•mine
17. de•fi•cient
18. par•lia•ment
19. guar•an•tee
20. qual•i•fi•ca•tion

STRATEGY **Make up mnemonic devices.** Look for memorable small words or word patterns in difficult words: "It is un**clear** to me what nu**clear** energy is" or "The first *two* syllables of *Antarctica* begin with *a*'s followed by *two*

help students use spelling strategies and spell words correctly. Review the instruction before completing each exercise. Guide students through the first item in each exercise. Discuss students' responses and any difficulties they might have. Have students complete the exercises independently.

Apply to Communication

Through Independent Writing

The **Communicate Your Ideas/Apply to Writing** activities on pages L676 and L686 prompt students to write a journal entry and an advertisement. Ask students how spelling will be relevant or important in each type of writing. For example, would correct spelling be more important in a journal entry or in an advertisement? Discuss students' responses.

Transfer to Everyday Life

Identifying Spelling Errors in Print

Have students find examples of misspelled words from newspapers,

consonants." Inventing a sentence like "**Re**placing **cur**tains **ren**ovates **ce**llars" can help you remember the letter groups in *recurrence*.

STRATEGY **Keep a spelling journal.** Use it to record the words you have had trouble spelling. Here are some suggestions for organizing your spelling journal.

- Write the word correctly.
- Write the word again, underlining or circling the part of the word that gave you trouble.
- Write a tip that will help you remember how to spell the word in the future.

stationery	*stationery*	*A writer writes on stationery. (An artist needs a stationary model.)*
accidentally	*accidentally*	*The first and last consonants are doubled; the consonants in the middle are single.*

USING STUDENTS' STRENGTHS

Multiple Intelligences: Intrapersonal

Ask students what words they have difficulty spelling. Have students reflect on reasons why they continually misspell these words. Then have students begin a spelling journal in which they write down words they misspell or confuse on a regular basis. Students should use their spelling journals on a continuing basis whenever they write or are confronted with difficult spellings. Remind students that these journals are for their own personal use. No one else will use them or read them. Students should include spellings, definitions, pronunciations, and example sentences in their spelling journals.

books, or magazines. Students should provide the correct spelling for each word. Have students share some of their examples with the class and tell why or how some of the errors might have occurred.

Pull It All Together

By Sharing

Have students share one of their writing samples from **Communicate Your Ideas/Apply to Writing** with a partner. Students should check for correct spelling, using a dictionary if necessary. Students should proofread the writing and make corrections before writing final drafts.

Check Understanding

By Holding a Spelling Bee

Have students study the lists of words in this chapter and other lists of commonly misspelled words. Allow a week

INTEGRATING TECHNOLOGY

Computers

Ask students if they have ever used the spell check on their word processing program or if they have used a hand-held computerized spelling dictionary. Allow students to share their experiences. Ask students if these resources are correct and useful in every writing situation. Students should realize that these resources are not useful, for example, for words that are homonyms. The computer does not know whether your particular sentence requires the word *waste* or *waist, principal* or *principle, not* or *knot.* Caution students that while using such resources, they need to realize that the meaning of the word, and not just a correctly spelled word, is important in their writing. They must be sure they are using the correct word and that it is spelled correctly.

Spelling Generalizations

Some people are naturally good spellers. They can "see" the correct spelling of a word in their minds, or they can "hear" the word, remembering how the syllables sound. There are those who spell most easily when they can write or type a word. There are also those for whom spelling is very difficult, no matter what method they use. If you are not a naturally good speller, learning some generalizations should make spelling easier for you.

Spelling Patterns

Some spelling generalizations are based on the patterns of letters in words. You can find certain common patterns in words spelled with *ie* or *ei* and in words that end with the *seed* sound.

Words with *ie* and *ei*

Words with *ie* and *ei* often cause confusion. Use the following familiar rhyme to help you spell such words.

Put *i* before *e*
Except after *c*
Or when it sounds like long *a*
As in *neighbor* and *weigh.*

When you spell words with *ie* or *ei, i* frequently comes before *e* except when the letters follow c or when they stand for the long *a* sound.

or so for them to study the words. Then have a class spelling bee. Have students take turns spelling each word you say aloud. Students are eliminated when they misspell a word. Afterwards, have the winner describe how he or she prepared for the spelling bee and share any spelling strategies that are especially helpful.

The following examples show this generalization.

IE AND *EI*			
I* Before *E	belief	achieve	niece
	piece	field	brief
Except After *C*	ceiling	conceit	deceive
	perceive	receipt	receive
Sounds Like *A*	eight	reins	sleigh
	veil	weight	feign

These words do not follow the pattern.

EXCEPTIONS			
either	foreign	height	ancient
sufficient	species	forfeit	conscience
glacier	weird	their	leisure

When you look at exceptions to spelling generalizations, ask yourself if you can see patterns in them. For example, you might notice that *c* is followed by *ie* in words like *ancient, conscience,* and *sufficient*. Figuring out that *ie* follows *c* in the suffixes *–cient* and *–cience* can help you spell similar words.

Words Ending in *–cede, –ceed,* or *–sede*

Some other words that cause problems are those that end with a "seed" sound. This sound can be spelled *–cede, –ceed,* or *–sede*. Most words that end with this sound are spelled *–cede*.

In all but four words that end with the "seed" sound, this sound is spelled *–cede*.

REACHING ALL STUDENTS

English Language Learners

Students whose first language uses a more phonetic spelling system than English will have some difficulty learning to spell English words correctly. For example, in English the sound for */s/* can be spelled *s* (as in set), *c* (as in cent), *sc* (as in scene), *ss* (as in cross), *st* (as in listen), and *ps* (as is psalm). Some vowel sounds can have as many as twenty possible spellings. Tell students that by using the spelling strategies and generalizations in this chapter, they will gain a better understanding of English spellings. Encourage students to use their spelling journals to record troublesome words and those they use frequently.

A DIFFERENT APPROACH

Auditory

As students complete **Practice Your Skills,** have them spell each word aloud to themselves after they have written it. Have students add any words they have difficulty with to their spelling journals.

-*CEDE*			
precede	recede	concede	intercede

You'll have no trouble spelling these words if you memorize the four exceptions.

-*CEED* AND -*SEDE*			
exceed	proceed	succeed	supersede

Practice Your Skills

Check Your Understanding

Identifying Spelling Patterns

Write each word correctly, adding *ie* or *ei*.

1. r ■ gn (ei)
2. shr ■ k (ie)
3. ■ ghty (ei)
4. th ■ f (ie)
5. br ■ f (ie)
6. p ■ rce (ie)
7. pr ■ st (ie)
8. h ■ ght (ei)
9. sh ■ ld (ie)
10. w ■ ghty (ei)
11. forf ■ t (ei)
12. rel ■ ve (ie)
13. c ■ ling (ei)
14. retr ■ ve (ie)
15. for ■ gn (ei)
16. n ■ ghborhood (ei)
17. front ■ r (ie)
18. n ■ ther (ei)
19. effic ■ nt (ie)
20. consc ■ nce (ie)

Write each word, adding *–sede, –ceed,* or *–cede.*

21. re ■ (cede)
22. ex ■ (ceed)
23. ac ■ (cede)
24. se ■ (cede)
25. pre ■ (cede)
26. suc ■ (ceed)
27. pro ■ (ceed)
28. con ■ (cede)
29. inter ■ (cede)
30. super ■ (sede)

 Connect to the Writing Process: Editing

Using Spelling Patterns

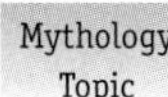
Mythology Topic

Find and rewrite the ten words that have been spelled incorrectly.

An ~~anceint~~ ancient Greek myth tells the story of Jason and the Golden Fleece. His uncle had agreed to act briefly as king. Then he would ~~conceed~~ concede the throne when Jason was old enough to ~~regn~~ reign. His deceitful uncle wasn't ready to ~~yeild~~ yield the crown, however. To get Jason out of the way, his uncle ~~succeded~~ succeeded in persuading him to go on a quest to the ~~neghboring~~ neighboring kingdom of Colchis. Jason was determined to ~~retreive~~ retrieve the Golden Fleece from there. He believed his family was its heirs. He ~~proceded~~ proceeded to have a ship built. Then, to the ~~releif~~ relief of his uncle, Jason ~~wieghed~~ weighed anchor and set out on the voyage.

 Plurals

The following generalizations will help you spell the plurals of nouns correctly. When in doubt, check a dictionary.

Regular Nouns

To form the plural of most nouns, simply add *s.*

MOST NOUNS				
SINGULAR	moon	moth	nova	age
PLURAL	moons	moths	novas	ages

HOME WORK

Have students write down the ten misspelled words from **Connect to the Writing Process.** Students should use each word in a sentence. Discuss students' sentences the following day.

YOUR IDEAS

For Spelling Plurals

REACHING ALL STUDENTS

Struggling Learners

Tell students that the plural forms of last names are often spelled incorrectly. Writers often incorrectly add apostrophes to form the plural of last names when all they need to add is an *s* or *es.* By adding an apostrophe, writers incorrectly form a possessive proper noun when they intend to write a plural noun. Have students use a phone directory or a directory from the Internet to find ten last names. Then have students write the plural of these names as in the following examples: *the Mullins family = the Mullinses; the Torres family = the Torreses; the Barkley family = the Barkleys.*

If a noun ends in *s, ch, sh, x,* or *z,* add *es* to form the plural.

	S, CH, SH, X, OR *Z*				
SINGULAR	lens	pea**ch**	blu**sh**	bo**x**	chint**z**
PLURAL	lens**es**	peach**es**	blush**es**	box**es**	chintz**es**

Follow the same generalizations to make proper nouns plural.

the Garcia family = the Garcia**s**
the James family = the James**es**
the Walsh family = the Walsh**es**

An apostrophe is never used to make the plural form of proper nouns. It is used to show possession.

Nouns Ending in *y*

Add *s* to form plurals of nouns ending in a vowel and *y.*

	VOWELS AND *Y*			
SINGULAR	decoy	alley	delay	chimney
PLURAL	decoy**s**	alley**s**	delay**s**	chimney**s**

Change the *y* to *i* and add *es* to a noun ending in a consonant and *y.*

CONSONANTS AND *Y*				
SINGULAR	gala**xy**	recove**ry**	pad**dy**	balco**ny**
PLURAL	gala**xies**	recove**ries**	pad**dies**	balco**nies**

PRACTICE YOUR SKILLS

Check Your Understanding
Forming Plurals

Write the plural form of each noun.

1.	~~hitch~~ hitches	**11.**	~~nursery~~ nurseries
2.	~~loss~~ losses	**12.**	~~sketch~~ sketches
3.	~~factory~~ factories	**13.**	~~brick~~ bricks
4.	~~essay~~ essays	**14.**	~~barbecue~~ barbecues
5.	~~ploy~~ ploys	**15.**	~~hoax~~ hoaxes
6.	~~duplex~~ duplexes	**16.**	~~waltz~~ waltzes
7.	~~flash~~ flashes	**17.**	~~injury~~ injuries
8.	~~history~~ histories	**18.**	~~kidney~~ kidneys
9.	~~focus~~ foci/focuses	**19.**	~~atlas~~ atlases
10.	~~mouth~~ mouths	**20.**	~~Holmes~~ Holmeses

Connect to the Writing Process: Editing
Spelling Plural Nouns

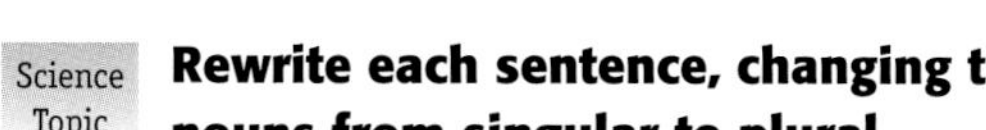

Science Topic **Rewrite each sentence, changing the underlined nouns from singular to plural.**

21. The diet of ancient people included many ~~variety~~ varieties of ~~berry~~ berries from ~~bush~~ bushes in the wild.

HOME WORK

After students have completed items one through twenty of **Practice Your Skills,** have them write the plural possessive form of each word. Remind students that they have already written the plural form and they now will use apostrophes and the letter *s* (and in some cases *es*) to show possession. Complete the first example together before students start their home work assignment. Have students add the word *the* and another noun, after each plural possessive noun, as in the following example: *the hitch's knot.*

22. They foraged for the ~~bulb~~ bulbs of ~~lily~~ lilies, ~~tulip~~ tulips, and other ~~plant~~ plants.

23. Necessary ~~starch~~ starches were also provided by cassava ~~root~~ roots and ~~salsify~~ salsify.

24. Successful ~~search~~ searches for food would have turned up tiny ~~bunch~~ bunches of wild ~~grape~~ grapes.

25. ~~Gourd~~ Gourds, used both as food and ~~container~~ containers, were a welcome addition to the pantry.

26. The first ~~agriculturist~~ agriculturists probably cultivated root ~~plant~~ plants like ~~turnip~~ turnips and ~~radish~~ radishes.

27. Today's different ~~barley~~ barleys are the ~~descendant~~ descendants of the first wild ~~grass~~ grasses.

28. The ~~seed~~ seeds of some plants might be considered ~~delicacy~~ delicacies.

29. The large ~~seed~~ seeds of ~~pumpkin~~ pumpkins, ~~sunflower~~ sunflowers and ~~lotus~~ lotuses are eaten as ~~snack~~ snacks today.

30. Modern ~~cook~~ cooks often sprinkle baked ~~good~~ goods with the ~~seed~~ seed of ~~poppy~~ poppies and sesame ~~flower~~ flowers.

Nouns Ending in *o*

Add *s* to form the plural of a noun ending with a vowel and *o*.

VOWELS AND O				
SINGULAR	rat**io**	cam**eo**	embr**yo**	tab**oo**
PLURAL	ratio**s**	cameo**s**	embryo**s**	taboo**s**

Add *s* to form the plural of musical terms ending in *o.*

MUSICAL TERMS WITH *O*				
Singular	trio	soprano	piccolo	tango
Plural	trio**s**	soprano**s**	piccolo**s**	tango**s**

Add *s* to form the plural of words that were borrowed from the Spanish language.

SPANISH WORDS				
Singular	lasso	rodeo	pinto	presidio
Plural	lasso**s**	rodeo**s**	pinto**s**	presidio**s**

The plurals of nouns ending in a consonant and *o* do not follow a regular pattern.

CONSONANTS AND *O*				
Singular	yo-yo	silo	veto	echo
Plural	yo-yo**s**	silo**s**	veto**es**	echo**es**

When you are not sure how to form the plural of a word that ends in *o,* consult a dictionary. Sometimes you will find that either spelling is acceptable. In this case, use the first form given. If the dictionary does not give a plural form, the plural is usually formed by adding *s.*

INTEGRATING TECHNOLOGY

Computers

Have students choose ten words from the lists on pages L665–L669 to write on the computer. Students should use the singular and plural forms of each word in a sentence. Students should take note as to when the word processing program alerts them to misspelled words. Have students spell a few words incorrectly and see if the computer alerts them to the misspelled words. Then have students correct the words and proofread their final sentences.

HOME WORK

Have students write ten sentences using the twenty words from the list in **Checking Your Understanding.** Tell students to study the spelling of each singular and plural form of the words. Test the students the following day on the spelling of each word, both singular and plural forms.

Nouns Ending in *f* or *fe*

To form the plural of some nouns ending in f or fe, just add s.

F OR *FE*				
Singular	belief	staff	giraffe	carafes
Plural	**beliefs**	**staffs**	**giraffes**	**carafes**

For some nouns ending in *f* or *fe,* change the *f* to *v* and add *es* or *s.*

F OR *FE* TO *V*				
Singular	calf	scarf	thief	life
Plural	**calves**	**scarves**	**thieves**	**lives**

Because there is no sure way to tell which generalization applies, consult a dictionary to check the plural form of a word that ends with *f* or *fe.*

Practice Your Skills

Check Your Understanding

Forming Plurals

Write the plural form of each noun.

potatoes **1.** potato	loaves **6.** loaf	chefs **11.** chef	curios **16.** curio
altos **2.** alto	oafs **7.** oaf	armadillos **12.** armadillo	carafes **17.** carafe
knives **3.** knife	dwarfs/dwarves **8.** dwarf	skiffs **13.** skiff	foodstuffs **18.** foodstuff
tacos **4.** taco	kazoos **9.** kazoo	portfolios **14.** portfolio	yourselves **19.** yourself
gulfs **5.** gulf	concerti/concertos **10.** concerto	patios **15.** patio	tariffs **20.** tariff

Connect to the Writing Process: Editing

Spelling Plural Nouns

General Interest **Rewrite this paragraph, changing the underlined nouns from singular to plural.**

These ~~photo~~ photos of ancient Roman houses are ~~memento~~ mementos/mementoes of our trip to Italy. The buildings' ~~roof~~ roofs have been replaced. The ~~fresco~~ frescoes have been restored to suggest how they looked centuries ago. Most homes had central ~~patio~~ patios. ~~Motif~~ Motifs about nature were popular in their art. My favorite fresco shows houses on ~~cliff~~ cliffs above the sea. I also saw a harbor scene with busy ~~wharf~~ wharves/wharfs and small ~~skiff~~ skiffs. I could almost hear the ~~echo~~ echoes/echos of the past.

Compound Words

Most compound nouns are made plural by adding an *s* or *es* at the end. However, it sometimes makes more sense to add the ending to the first word.

The letter *s* or *es* is added to the end of most compound nouns.

COMPOUND NOUNS		
SINGULAR	teammate	dragonfly
	tryout	bathing suit
PLURAL	teammate**s**	dragonfl**ies**
	tryout**s**	bathing suit**s**

When the *main* word in a compound noun appears first, that word is made plural.

REACHING ALL STUDENTS

Advanced Learners

After discussing the plural forms of two- and three-word compounds, have students form the plurals of each of the following words and use each plural form in a sentence:

mother-in-law (mothers-in-law)
man-of-war (men-of-war)
court martial (courts martial)
secretary-general (secretaries-general)

YOUR IDEAS
For Using Apostrophes in Plurals

EXCEPTIONS		
SINGULAR	father-in-law attorney general	part of speech passerby
PLURAL	father**s**-in-law attorney**s** general	part**s** of speech passer**s**by

Numerals, Letters, Symbols, and Words as Words

To form the plurals of most numerals, letters, symbols, and words used as words, add an *s.*

Those *8***s** look too much like *B***s.**
The 1870**s** and 1880**s** were called the Gilded Age.
Proofreaders' *#***s** tell printers to add space.

To prevent confusion, it's best to use an apostrophe and *s* with lowercase letters, some capital letters, and some words used as words. However, when you use this method to create the plural of italicized letters or words, you do not italicize the apostrophe and *s*.

How do you pronounce the *o***'s** in *footstool?*
There are a lot of *I***'s** in his conversation.
These two *theirs***'s** should be *they're***'s.**

Remember to use the apostrophe when writing letters as plurals to avoid confusion in content. Otherwise, plural letters might be mistaken for words such as is, as, and us.

INCORRECT	*Is*	*As*	*Us*
CORRECT	*I*'s	*A*'s	*U*'s
INCORRECT	*is*	*as*	*us*
CORRECT	*i*'s	*a*'s	*u*'s

You can learn about the use of italics on pages L585–L586.

Practice Your Skills

Check Your Understanding
Forming Plurals

Write the plural form of each noun.

1. ~~12~~ 12s
2. ~~member at large~~ members at large
3. ~~handout~~ handouts
4. ~~*ABC*~~ *ABCs*
5. ~~son-in-law~~ sons-in-law
6. ~~solar system~~ solar systems
7. ~~*hurray*~~ *hurray's*
8. ~~snackbar~~ snackbars
9. ~~1930~~ 1930s
10. ~~*e*~~ *e's*
11. ~~+~~ +s
12. ~~boiling point~~ boiling points
13. ~~forget-me-not~~ forget-me-nots
14. ~~*pro* and *con*~~ *pros* and *cons*
15. ~~assistant coach~~ assistant coaches
16. ~~pilot-in-command~~ pilots-in-command
17. ~~*p* and *q*~~ *p's* and *q's*
18. ~~1400~~ 1400s
19. ~~play-off~~ play-offs
20. ~~*R*~~ *Rs*

Connect to the Writing Process: Editing
Spelling Plural Nouns

General Interest **Write the underlined items as plurals.**

21. The ~~center of balance~~ centers of balance in men and women are in different parts of their bodies.
22. The only word with six ~~*i*~~ *i's* and no other vowels is *indivisibility*.
23. In German, *zwei* means "two," but you will hear *zwo* when Germans give addresses with ~~2~~ 2s in them.
24. ~~*A*~~ *A's* were first called *alephs*.
25. Our speech is full of ~~*and*~~ *and's*, ~~*of*~~ *of's*, and ~~*in*~~ *in's*.
26. The ~~cost of living~~ costs of living in Hong Kong and Tokyo are high.
27. ~~*Gee*~~ *Gee's* and ~~*haw*~~ *haw's* tell sled dogs to turn left or right.

A DIFFERENT APPROACH

Auditory

Have students complete items one through twenty of **Check Your Understanding** with a partner. Each pair should write out their words and spell them aloud to check their spelling. Students should take turns completing the items. Discuss their responses. Ask students how spelling the words aloud helped them to check their spellings.

GETTING STUDENTS INVOLVED

Collaborative Learning

Discuss the unconventional plural forms on this page. Have students work with partners to spell the plural forms of the words listed below. Encourage partners to use dictionaries to check their spellings. Have groups take turns writing their correctly spelled words on the board. Discuss the words' meanings and have students use them in sentences.

datum (data)
matrix (matrices)
analysis (analyses)
media (medium)
metamorphosis (metamorphoses)
bacteria (bacterium)

28. The two ~~runner-up~~ runners-up in Olympic competitions receive silver and bronze medals.

29. The ~~1900~~ 1900s have been referred to as the Age of Anxiety.

30. Most legal documents must be signed in the presence of lawyers or ~~notary public.~~ notaries public

Other Plural Forms

Irregular plurals are not formed by adding *s* or *es*.

IRREGULAR PLURALS		
foot, fe**e**t	woman, wom**e**n	child, child**ren**
goose, g**ee**se	mouse, m**ic**e	die, dice

Some nouns have the same form for singular and plural.

SAME SINGULAR AND PLURAL		
Swiss	sheep	pliers
moose	species	politics

PRACTICE YOUR SKILLS

Check Your Understanding

Forming Plurals

Write the plural form of each noun.

1. ~~square foot~~ square feet
2. ~~series~~ series
3. ~~musk ox~~ musk oxen
4. ~~toothbrush~~ toothbrushes
5. ~~measles~~ measles
6. ~~pants~~ pants
7. ~~walrus~~ walruses
8. ~~nobleman~~ noblemen

9. homework ~~homework~~
10. trout ~~trout~~
11. eyeteeth ~~eyetooth~~
12. schoolchildren ~~schoolchild~~
13. physics ~~physics~~
14. dormice ~~dormouse~~
15. equipment ~~equipment~~
16. advice ~~advice~~
17. snow geese ~~snow goose~~
18. lice ~~louse~~
19. mongooses ~~mongoose~~
20. policewomen ~~policewoman~~

Connect to the Writing Process: Editing

Spelling Plural Nouns

Literature Topic

Rewrite each sentence, changing the underlined nouns from singular to plural. If the plural form of a word is the same as the singular, simply write the word again as it is written.

21. John Steinbeck wrote the novel *Of ~~Mouse~~ Mice and ~~Man~~ Men*.

22. Farley Mowat wrote *~~Person~~ People of the Deer* about an Inuit group's struggle to survive.

23. Thornton Wilder's play *The Skin of Our ~~Tooth~~ Teeth* won a Pulitzer Prize.

24. *The Earth Beneath Sky Bear's ~~Foot~~ Feet* is a collection of Native American nature poems.

25. *Hamadi & the Stolen ~~Cattle~~ Cattle* is a children's story by an African author.

26. Euripides's play *The Trojan ~~Woman~~ Women* is about the brutality of war.

27. Folktales of the Canadian north have been collected in *The Girl Who Dreamed Only ~~Goose~~ Geese*.

28. One of Gertrude Atherton's most popular books was *Black ~~Ox~~ Oxen*.

29. *The ~~Child~~ Children of Sanchez* is a famous book about a poor family in Mexico.

30. *How the ~~Irish~~ Irish Saved Civilization* is a book about European history.

YOUR IDEAS

For Unconventional Plural Forms

TIMESAVER *QuickCheck*

Have students self-evaluate their journal entries by using a dictionary and by referring to their spelling journals. Students should correct any spelling errors before completing their journal entries.

Communicate Your Ideas

APPLY TO WRITING

Journal Entry: *Plurals*

Among the first European settlers in the Old West were pioneers from Mexico and Spain. Many established great ranches in the rolling foothills of California. Put yourself in the place of a first-time visitor to those shores. Consider the above photograph of a California ranch and the countryside. What are your impressions of the region's wildlife and of home life on a ranch? Record your thoughts in a journal. Use at least ten plural nouns in your entry. Try to use at least one word from Spanish and at least one noun with an irregular plural.

Mixed Practice

Write the plural form of each word. Use a dictionary whenever necessary.

1. ~~proof~~ proofs
2. ~~rancho~~ ranchos
3. ~~relish~~ relishes
4. ~~lullaby~~ lullabies
5. ~~pathway~~ pathways
6. ~~batch~~ batches
7. ~~echo~~ echoes/echos
8. ~~hockey~~ hockey
9. ~~Jones~~ Joneses
10. ~~leaf~~ leaves
11. ~~right of way~~ rights-of-way
12. ~~strike out~~ strike-outs
13. ~~video~~ videos
14. ~~20~~ 20s
15. ~~twenty~~ twenties
16. ~~good bye~~ good-byes
17. ~~cello~~ cellos/celli
18. ~~hoof~~ hooves/hoofs
19. ~~buoy~~ buoys
20. ~~prefix~~ prefixes

Prefixes and Suffixes

A **prefix** is one or more syllables placed in front of a base word to form a new word. When you add a prefix, the spelling of the base word does not change.

in + sincere = **in**sincere	**im** + patient = **im**patient
pre + caution = **pre**caution	**over** + rated = **over**rated
dis + honest = **dis**honest	**mis** + heard = **mis**heard
re + arrange = **re**arrange	**un** + noticed = **un**noticed
ir + resistible = **ir**resistible	**il** + legible = **il**legible

Occasionally, it is necessary to add a hyphen after a prefix to avoid confusing your reader. Check a dictionary if you are in doubt.

HYPHENATED PREFIXES	
re-cover	**semi**-independent

USING STUDENTS' STRENGTHS

Multiple Intelligences: Linguistic

Divide students into small groups and have them choose five words from **QuickCheck** to use in sentences. Students should work together to write sentences using both the singular and plural forms of the words they have chosen. Have each group choose a member to write one of their sentences on the board to share with the class. Discuss the groups' responses.

GETTING STUDENTS INVOLVED

Reciprocal Teaching

Have students who understand the function of prefixes and suffixes work with students who are having difficulty. Have students use the prefixes and suffixes listed on pages L677 and L678 to write new words using these affixes. Students should refer to the dictionary to check their spellings.

It's easy to leave out one of the *r*'s in *irresistible* or *overrated* if you forget that the words are created by adding prefixes to base words. Neither changes when you combine the two. If you're not sure whether a word has double letters in the beginning, ask yourself whether it could be one of these prefix-base word combinations.

A **suffix** is one or more syllables placed after a base word to change its part of speech and possibly also its meaning. In many cases, especially when the base word ends in a consonant, you simply add the suffix.

SUFFIXES	
eager + **ness** = eager**ness**	right + **ful** = right**ful**
treat + **ment** = treat**ment**	vague + **ly** = vague**ly**

In other cases, however, you must change the spelling of the base word before you add the suffix.

Words Ending in *e*

Drop the final e before a suffix that begins with a vowel.

VOWELS AND *E*	
pause + **ing** = paus**ing**	size + **able** = siz**able**
narrate + **ion** = narrat**ion**	universe + **al** = univers**al**

Keep the final e in words that end in *ce* or *ge* if the suffix begins with an *a* or *o.* The *e* keeps the sound of the *c* or *g* soft before these vowels.

CE AND *GE*
manage + **able** = manage**able**
replace + **able** = replace**able**
advantage + **ous** = advantage**ous**
notice + **able** = notice**able**
knowledge + **able** = knowledge**able**

Keep the final *e* when adding a suffix that begins with a consonant.

	CONSONANTS AND *E*
EXAMPLES	peace + **ful** = peace**ful**
	amuse + **ment** = amuse**ment**
	hope + **less** = hope**less**
	wise + **ly** = wise**ly**
	same + **ness** = same**ness**
EXCEPTIONS	wise + **dom** = wis**dom**
	judge + **ment** = judg**ment**
	true + **ly** = tru**ly**
	argue + **ment** = argu**ment**
	awe + **ful** = aw**ful**

Word Alert: If any of these examples or their exceptions is very difficult for you, take the time now to create your own mnemonic aid.

Jan **u**sually **d**oesn't **g**reet **m**y **e**xceptionally **n**ervous **t**iger. = judgment

Millie **i**s **l**osing **e**very **a**fternoon **g**ym **e**vent. = mileage

YOUR IDEAS

For Using Prefixes and Suffixes

HOME WORK

Ask students to write two words for each prefix and suffix introduced on pages L677–L679.

Practice Your Skills

Check Your Understanding

Adding Suffixes

Combine the base words and suffixes. Remember to make any necessary spelling changes.

1. ~~rotate + ion~~ rotation
2. ~~dense + ly~~ densely
3. ~~admire + er~~ admirer
4. ~~true + ly~~ truly
5. ~~rhyme + ing~~ rhyming
6. ~~continue + al~~ continual
7. ~~solve + able~~ solvable
8. ~~tense + ion~~ tension
9. ~~spire + al~~ spiral
10. ~~mature + ity~~ maturity
11. ~~idle + ness~~ idleness
12. ~~judge + ment~~ judgment
13. ~~blue + ish~~ bluish
14. ~~separate + ion~~ separation
15. ~~courage + ous~~ courageous
16. ~~pronounce + able~~ pronounceable
17. ~~settle + ment~~ settlement
18. ~~endure + ance~~ endurance
19. ~~adore + able~~ adorable
20. ~~knowledge + able~~ knowledgeable

Connect to the Writing Process: Editing

Spelling Words with Prefixes and Suffixes

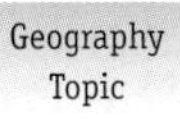

Rewrite the underlined words in the following paragraphs, correctly spelling those that are incorrect.

The singing sands of the Bay of Laig in Scotland are <u>remarkable</u>. If you walk on the sand, it emits sounds with <u>~~noticably~~</u> noticeably strong <u>~~resemblences~~</u> resemblances to the string instruments of an orchestra. The <u>tuneful</u> sounds range from basses to sopranos.

Scientists have <u>~~carefuly~~</u> carefully <u>investigated</u> the mystery and found the answer. Tiny grains of <u>unpolished</u> quartz have the ~~noteable~~ notable ability to transfer vibrations. This means that the sand ~~naturaly~~ naturally produces ~~contineuous~~ continuous sounds. Interestingly, laboratory experimentation has shown that the transmission can be interrupted when the sand is not ~~completly~~ completely clean.

Words Ending in *y*

To add a suffix to most words ending in a vowel and *y,* keep the *y.*

VOWELS AND *Y*	
Examples	play + **able** = play**able**
	mislay + **ing** = mislay**ing**
	enjoy + **ment** = enjoy**ment**
	replay + **ed** = replay**ed**
Exceptions	day + **ly** = dai**ly** gay + **ly** = gai**ly**

To add a suffix to most words ending in a consonant and *y,* change the *y* to *i* before adding the suffix. However, do not drop the *y* when adding *–ing.*

CONSONANTS AND *Y*	
Examples	envy + **able** = env**iable**
	bounty + **ful** = bount**iful**
	thrifty + **ly** = thrift**ily**
	dreary + **ness** = drear**iness**
	mercy + **ful** = merc**iful**
Exception	identify + **ing** = identif**ying**

REACHING ALL STUDENTS

Struggling Learners

After discussing adding suffixes to words ending in *y*, have students use dictionaries to add suffixes to the following words: *dry, joy, convey, copy, display, deny.* Remind students that not every suffix will make sense at the end of each word, so they must first choose a suffix that makes sense and then decide how to spell the new word. Have students share some of their words with the class.

USING STUDENTS' STRENGTHS

Multiple Intelligences: Musical

Tell students that condition two in the list for deciding whether to double final consonants depends on one's ability to identify stressed syllables. This skill, often related to musical skills, will help students spell words correctly. Have students stand as they practice pronouncing the words listed on these pages aloud, clapping out the syllables. Have students clap *and* stomp their feet for each stressed syllable. Tell students that by listening for the rhythm and stressed syllables of words, they can decide which consonants to double.

One-syllable words that end in *y* pronounced long *i* do not change their spellings when the suffixes *–ness* or *–ing* are added. They *do* change their spellings when the suffix *–ed* is added.

shy + **ness** = shy**ness**	dry + **ed** = dr**ied**
dry + **ness** = dry**ness**	pry + **ed** = pr**ied**
sly + **ness** = sly**ness**	spy + **ed** = sp**ied**

Doubling the Final Consonant

Sometimes the final consonant in a word is doubled before a suffix is added.

Double the final consonant in a word before adding a suffix only when all three of the following conditions are met:

(1) The suffix begins with a vowel.
(2) The base word has only one syllable *or* is stressed on the last syllable.
(3) The base word ends in one consonant preceded by a vowel.

	DOUBLE CONSONANTS
ONE-SYLLABLE WORDS	plot + **ing** = plo**tt**ing char + **ed** =cha**rr**ed trap + **er** =tra**pp**er mad + **est** = ma**dd**est
FINAL SYLLABLE STRESSED	befit + **ing** = befi**tt**ing transfer + **ed** = transfe**rr**ed rebut + **al** = rebu**tt**al recur + **ence** = recu**rr**ence

Don't double the final *r* in words that end in *fer* when you add the suffix *–ence* or *–able.* Notice how the pronunciation of the base word changes when the suffix is added. This is your clue that only one *r* is needed.

FINAL *R*
refer + **ence** = refe**r**ence
infer + **ence** = infe**r**ence
defer + **ence** = defe**r**ence
transfer + **able** = transfe**r**able

Be sure not to double the final letter if it is preceded by two vowels.

TWO VOWELS	
creep + **ing** = cree**p**ing	seat + **ed** = sea**t**ed
train + **er** = trai**n**er	proud + **est** = prou**d**est

PRACTICE YOUR SKILLS

Check Your Understanding
Adding Suffixes

Combine the base words and suffixes. Remember to make any necessary spelling changes.

1. ~~deter + ed~~ deterred
2. ~~cram + ed~~ crammed
3. ~~day + ly~~ daily
4. ~~weak + en~~ weaken
5. ~~plenty + ful~~ plentiful
6. ~~unnecessary + ly~~ unnecessarily
7. ~~strut + ing~~ strutting

A DIFFERENT APPROACH
Auditory

Have students complete the items in **Check Your Understanding** aloud. Students should take turns saying each word, listening for the stressed syllable in each word. If students find it helpful, they should clap out the syllables of each word.

HOME WORK

After students have corrected the spelling errors in **Connect to the Writing Process,** have them create new sentences for each word they corrected. Have students share their sentences with the class the following day.

8. ~~comply + ance~~ compliance
9. ~~hot + est~~ hottest
10. ~~snob + ism~~ snobbism
11. ~~timid + est~~ timidest
12. ~~annoy + ance~~ annoyance
13. ~~trek + ed~~ trekked
14. ~~employ + able~~ employable
15. ~~infer + ing~~ inferring
16. ~~study + ing~~ studying
17. ~~survey + ing~~ surveying
18. ~~justify + able~~ justifiably
19. ~~incur + ing~~ incurring
20. ~~drowsy + ness~~ drowsiness
21. ~~confer + ence~~ conference
22. ~~drain + ed~~ drained

Connect to the Writing Process: Editing

Spelling Words with Prefixes and Suffixes

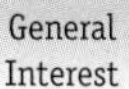

Rewrite the underlined words in the following paragraph, correctly spelling those that are incorrect.

We take household ~~applyances~~ appliances for granted. We don't ordinarily give any thought to their ~~fascinateing~~ fascinating history. Among the ~~earilest~~ earliest "irons," for example, were the glass linen smoothers. They were used by tenth-century Vikings. Later, European servants ~~wearyly~~ wearily ~~emploied~~ employed flat mallets to beat fabric smooth. By the 1500s, the exhausted servants were clumsily using flat metal boxes filled with hot charcoal. These ~~primateive~~ primitive contraptions were ~~undeniablely~~ undeniably dangerous to use. They sometimes ~~chared~~ charred and ~~spoilled~~ spoiled the linen. When stoves replaced open fireplaces, these fabric smoothers could be made of solid cast iron. They were readily ~~heatted~~ heated on the stove. They cooled quickly once off the stove and required ~~heatting~~ heating over and over again. By the late 1800s, the dreary ~~busyness~~ business of ironing was made ~~easyier~~ easier by the development of fuel-powered irons. Gasoline, alcohol, and gas irons were ~~fited~~ fitted with long tubes. The tubes were connected to fuel tanks. They stayed hotter longer, but they were ~~necessarilly~~ necessarily awkward to use.

YOUR IDEAS

For Adding Suffixes

TIMESAVER *QuickCheck*

Have students exchange their advertisements with a partner. Students should use a dictionary to check the spelling in their partners' papers. Remind students to check the spellings of those words ending in suffixes especially carefully. Once papers are returned, students should correct their own spelling errors.

Communicate Your Ideas

APPLY TO WRITING

Advertisement: *Suffixes*

Write an advertisement for a kitchen appliance. Choose an appliance, describe it, and explain why someone should have one. Make your advertisement convincing. Use at least five of the following words with suffixes in your ad.

- handy + *er, est,* or *ly*
- rely + *able* or *ance*
- dirty + *er* or *est*
- equip + *ed* or *ing*
- day + *ly*
- plug + *ed* or *ing*
- sturdy + *er, est,* or *ly*
- cook + *ed* or *ing*

Mixed Practice

Add the prefix and/or suffix to each base word and write the new word.

1. ~~ideal + ly~~ ideally
2. ~~trek + ed~~ trekked
3. ~~argue + ment~~ argument
4. ~~re + play + able~~ replayable
5. ~~out + wit + ing~~ outwitting
6. ~~transfer + able~~ transferable
7. ~~value + able~~ valuable
8. ~~rely + ance~~ reliance
9. ~~change + able~~ changeable
10. ~~terse + ly~~ tersely
11. ~~admire + ation~~ admiration
12. ~~duty + ful~~ dutiful
13. ~~service + able~~ serviceable
14. ~~refer + ing~~ referring
15. ~~ally + ance~~ alliance
16. ~~ir + response + ible~~ irresponsible
17. ~~program + ed~~ programmed
18. ~~un + necessary + ly~~ unnecessarily
19. ~~occur + ence~~ occurrence
20. ~~dis + advantage + ous~~ disadvantageous

WORDS TO MASTER

Make it your goal to learn to spell these fifty words this year. Use them in your writing and practice writing them until spelling them comes automatically.

a**cc**el**er**ate
a**cc**e**ss**ory
a**cc**o**mm**odate
a**cc**u**m**ulate
a**cqu**aintance
admi**tt**ance
advi**sa**ble
alli**a**nce
apprecia**ti**on
a**sc**end
carb**ure**tor
circ**ui**t
c**oi**ncidence
co**mm**i**ttee**
conc**ei**t
conse**que**nce
conven**ie**nce
counterf**ei**t
defend**a**nt
def**ia**nce
di**ss**atisfied
effic**ie**nt
exist**e**nce
e**xqu**isite
furl**ough**
hy**gi**ene
ingred**ie**nt
inter**cede**
i**rr**egul**a**r
l**ia**ble
man**eu**ver
mi**sc**e**ll**an**eous**
notic**ea**ble
o**cc**u**rr**ence
pa**gea**nt
paral**y**sis
physics
pneumonia
po**ss**ibi**li**ty
pre**ci**pitation
prefe**r**ence
recr**ui**t
regre**tt**able
s**ie**ge
station**a**ry
station**e**ry
su**cc**e**ss**ion
ta**riff**
tempor**ary**
vac**uu**m

EXPANDING THE LESSON

Using Technology

Use Barrett Kendall ancillary instructional and practice materials located at http://www.bkenglish.com.

FOR REVIEWING SKILLS

Using CheckPoint

This feature on spelling can be used as further independent practice or as a cumulative review of the chapter. Students choose correctly spelled words from a list.

CheckPoint

Applying Spelling Generalizations

Write the letter of the misspelled word in each group. Then write the word, spelling it correctly.

1.	(A) ~~calfs~~ calves	(B) sheriffs	(C) dollar signs
2.	(A) sharing	(B) ~~appling~~ applying	(C) receive
3.	(A) busily	(B) foreign	(C) ~~hankerchief~~ handkerchief
4.	(A) solos	(B) ~~mouses~~ mice	(C) discouraged
5.	(A) ~~desparate~~ desperate	(B) Internet	(C) resentful
6.	(A) ~~sleig~~ sleigh	(B) portraying	(C) happiest
7.	(A) proofs	(B) ~~complexs~~ complexes	(C) casually
8.	(A) trader	(B) misplace	(C) ~~horrifyed~~ horrified
9.	(A) ~~plainess~~ plainness	(B) kangaroos	(C) hastily
10.	(A) singular	(B) ~~nineth~~ ninth	(C) commanders-in-chief
11.	(A) ambushes	(B) sameness	(C) ~~mistatement~~ misstatement
12.	(A) ~~vetos~~ vetoes	(B) succeed	(C) carrying
13.	(A) joys	(B) ~~puppyes~~ puppies	(C) blitzes
14.	(A) ~~yeild~~ yield	(B) insane	(C) placement
15.	(A) ~~altoes~~ altos	(B) field	(C) craftiness
16.	(A) replied	(B) intersect	(C) ~~unatural~~ unnatural
17.	(A) pigment	(B) ~~speceis~~ species	(C) dissatisfied
18.	(A) assured	(B) realize	(C) ~~poletics~~ politics
19.	(A) ~~wierd~~ weird	(B) ranches	(C) efficient
20.	(A) ~~dutyful~~ dutiful	(B) finally	(C) blindness

Another Look

Spelling Correctly

Spelling Patterns *(pages L662–L664)*

When you spell words with *ie* or *ei*, *i* frequently comes before *e*, except when the letters follow *c* or when they stand for the long *a* sound.

The "seed" sound at the end of a word is spelled *cede* except for these four words: *exceed, proceed, succeed, supersede.*

Plurals *(pages L665–L674)*

If a noun ends in *s*, *ch*, *sh*, *x*, or *z*, add *es* to form the plural.

Add *s* to form the plural of a noun ending in a vowel and *y*.

Change the *y* to *i* and add *es* to a noun ending in a consonant and *y*.

Add *s* to form the plural of a noun ending in a vowel and *o*, musical terms ending in *o*, and words borrowed from the Spanish language that end in *o*.

The plurals of nouns ending in a consonant and *o* do not follow a regular pattern. They end in *s* or *es*.

To form the plural of some nouns ending in *f* or *fe*, just add *s*.

For some nouns ending in *f* or *fe*, change the *f* to *v* and add *es* or *s*.

The letter *s* or *es* is added to the end of most compound nouns. When the main word in a compound noun appears first, that word is made plural.

To form the plurals of most numerals, letters, symbols, and words used as words, add an *s*.

Irregular plurals are not formed by adding *s* or *es*.

Some nouns have the same form for singular and plural.

Prefixes and Suffixes *(pages L677–L683)*

When you place a suffix after a base word, especially when the base word ends in a consonant, you simply add the suffix.

Drop the final *e* before adding a suffix that begins with a vowel.

Keep the final *e* when the suffix begins with a consonant or when the base word ends in *ce* or *ge* if the suffix begins with an *a* or *o*.

Keep the *y* when adding a suffix to most words that end in a vowel and *y*. Change *y* to *i* when adding a suffix to words that end in a consonant and *y*. However, do not drop the *y* when adding the suffix *ing*.

Don't double the final *r* in words that end in *fer* when you add the suffix *ence* and *able*.

Using *Another Look*

Another Look summarizes the concepts explained in the chapter and provides cross-references to the specific pages on which they are explained. Consider having students use this feature prior to completing **CheckPoint** or taking the posttest. Students who can provide several examples of each concept should be able to score well on either measurement.

Using *the Posttest*

Assessing Learning

The posttest will help you and your students assess where they stand in their ability to use spelling strategies and generalizations to spell words correctly.

IDENTIFYING COMMON STUMBLING BLOCKS

Following is a list of the most common spelling errors students make when writing.

Problem

- Spelling words containing *ei* and *ie*

Solution

- For reteaching, use the charts on pages L662–L663.

Problem

- Doubling a final consonant before adding a suffix

Solution

- For reteaching, use the charts on pages L682–L683.

Directions

Write the letter of the answer that correctly spells the underlined word. If the underlined word is correct, write *D*.

EXAMPLE What <u>activitees</u> (1) do you enjoy most at the beach?

1 **A** activeties
B actevities
C activities
D No error

ANSWER **1 C**

If you are <u>adventurous</u> (1), try <u>rideing</u> (2) the swift-moving waves at the beach with a surfboard. A fast-paced volleyball game can also provide both <u>eggercise</u> (3) and <u>excitment</u> (4). On the other hand, a <u>skillful</u> (5) cast of a net might bring a reward of live bait. <u>Nothing</u> (6) is more challenging than battling the surf to reel in a fish. All ages can <u>injoy</u> (7) the task of building a mighty sandcastle before the tide <u>washes</u> (8) it away. With so many exciting things to do, it's almost <u>imposible</u> (9) to <u>expereince</u> (10) boredom at the beach.

A DIFFERENT DELIVERY SYSTEM

If you prefer, you can print the posttest from the BK English Test Bank located at http://www.bkenglish.com.

1 **A** adventureous
B aventurous
C adventureus
D No error

2 **A** ridding
B rideng
C riding
D No error

3 **A** exersize
B exercise
C egercise
D No error

4 **A** exsitement
B excitement
C excitemint
D No error

5 **A** skillfull
B skillfule
C skilfull
D No error

6 **A** Nuthing
B No thing
C Notthing
D No error

7 **A** enjoy
B ennjoy
C innjoy
D No error

8 **A** washs
B waches
C wasches
D No error

9 **A** impossable
B imposable
C impossible
D No error

10 **A** experience
B experiense
C expereinse
D No error

Customizing the Test

Use these questions to add or replace items for alternate versions of the test.

For beachgoers who enjoy peace and quiet, take a liesurely (11) stroll along the shore. Even watching the sailboats (12) glide across the water is soothing. Collecting seashells or diging (13) for sand crabs can provide hours of relaxashun (14). No matter what your lifestyle, a visit to the seashore brings entertainmint (15).

11. A leisurely
B leisurly
C leisurlie
D No error

12. A sailsboat
B saleboats
C salesboat
D No error

13. A digeng
B digginng
C digging
D No error

14. A relaxashion
B relaxation
C reelaxation
D No error

15. A intertainment
B intertainmint
C entertainment
D No error

GETTING STUDENTS INVOLVED

Collaborative Learning

Have the following assignment on the board as students enter the classroom. Have them read and complete the assignment.

You have to get an A on your next history test in order to pass the course and to graduate. How will you study for the test? What strategies and study skills will you use to make sure you get an A on the test and are able to graduate? Share some of your strategies in a paragraph.

Tell students that in this section, they will learn how to study. The section will provide them with some useful and very practical ways to approach their studies so that they will comprehend what they are learning and better remember important concepts. Have students go over their study strategies with a partner. Then each group should compile one list of effective study strategies and share them with the class.

A Study Guide for Academic Success

Academic success depends a great deal on preparation. You must be familiar with the material presented in textbooks and in the classroom; you must also be aware of various test-taking strategies. In some ways, preparing for a test is like learning to play a musical instrument. You cannot simply pick up an instrument and play it well. You must first learn all the necessary skills. If you learn certain strategies and apply helpful pointers, you can become better at playing an instrument or taking tests. Also, the more practice you have, the better prepared you are to play a difficult piece of music or take an important test.

In the following chapter you will become familiar with the different kinds of questions asked on standardized tests. Pay close attention to the "rules" for each type of question and the strategies used to master them. These lessons and practice exercises will help you develop your test-taking skills.

Keep in mind that the abilities you acquire in this chapter will carry over into homework and daily classroom assignments—and even into areas outside of school. Learning how to read for various information and how to approach different kinds of questions and problems will sharpen the critical thinking skills you use when you participate in classroom discussions, learn any new skill, and make important life decisions.

Learning Study Skills

Applying good study habits helps you in taking tests as well as in completing daily classroom assignments. Begin to improve your study habits by using the following strategies.

Strategies for Effective Studying

- Choose an area that is well lighted and quiet.
- Equip your study area with everything you need for reading and writing, including a dictionary and a thesaurus.
- Keep an assignment book for recording assignments and due dates.
- Allow plenty of time for studying. Begin your reading and writing assignments early.
- Adjust your reading rate to suit your purpose.

Adjusting Reading Rate to Purpose

Your reading rate is the speed at which you read. Depending on your purpose in reading, you may appropriately choose to read certain materials quickly or slowly, using the techniques of scanning, skimming, or close reading.

For example, if your purpose is to get a quick impression of the contents of a newspaper, you should scan the headlines. If you want to learn the main ideas of a certain article, you should skim it. On the other hand, if your purpose is to learn new facts or understand details, you may choose to read the article closely.

Whether you are reading a newspaper, an article in a periodical, or a textbook, you can read with greater effectiveness and efficiency if you adjust your reading rate to suit your purpose in reading the material.

YOUR IDEAS

For Teaching Study Skills

USING STUDENTS' STRENGTHS

Multiple Intelligences: Spatial

To help students decide when they might use each method of reading, create a reading chart on the board with three columns. The headings for the chart should be *Scan, Skim, Close Reading.* Have students brainstorm specific reading tasks in which they would use each reading method. List students' suggestions in the appropriate column. For example, students might use skimming to find out the major news events of the day when reading a newspaper. Students would scan, skim, and use close reading to study for a science test using their textbooks. Have students add additional examples to the chart.

Scanning

Scanning is reading to get a general impression and to prepare for learning about a subject. To scan, you should read the title, headings, subheadings, picture captions, words and phrases in boldface or italics, and any focus questions. Using this method you can quickly determine what the reading is about and what questions to keep in mind. Scanning is also a way to familiarize yourself with everything a book has to offer. Scan the table of contents, appendix, glossary, and index of a book before reading.

Skimming

After scanning a chapter, section, or article, you should quickly read, or skim, the introduction, the topic sentence of each paragraph, and the conclusion. **Skimming** is reading to identify quickly the purpose, thesis, main ideas, and supporting ideas of a selection.

Close Reading

Close reading is for locating specific information, following the logic of an argument, or comprehending the meaning or significance of information. After scanning the selection or chapter, read it more slowly, word for word.

Reading a Textbook

In studying a textbook, the techniques of scanning, skimming, and close reading are combined in the **SQ3R** study strategy. This method helps you to understand and remember what you read. The *S* in *SQ3R* stands for *Survey,* the *Q* for *Question,* and the *3R* for *Read, Recite,* and *Review.*

THE SQ3R STUDY STRATEGY	
SURVEY	First get a general idea of what the selection is about by scanning titles, subtitles, and words that are set off in a different type or color. Also look at maps, tables, charts, and other illustrations. Then read the introduction and conclusion or summary.
QUESTION	Decide what questions you should be able to answer after reading the selection. You can do this by turning the headings and subheadings into questions or by looking at any study questions in the book.
READ	Now read the selection. As you read, try to answer your questions. In addition, find the main idea in each section and look for important information that is not included in your questions. After reading, review the important points in the selection and take notes.
RECITE	Answer each question in your own words by reciting or writing the answers.
REVIEW	Answer the questions again without looking at your notes or at the selection. Continue reviewing until you answer each question correctly.

Taking Notes

Taking notes when reading a textbook or listening to a lecture will help you identify and remember important points. Three methods of taking notes are the informal outline, the graphic organizer, and the summary.

DEVELOPING WORKPLACE COMPETENCIES

Basic Skills: Reading

Have students brainstorm careers that would require a great amount of reading. Students might suggest writers, researchers, doctors, teachers, journalists, engineers, bankers, attorneys, social workers, and editors. Ask students to identify specific tasks in each person's job that would require scanning, skimming, and close reading. For example, a newspaper editor would use close reading to proofread an article they are writing for the next day's newspaper.

YOUR IDEAS
For Outlines

In an **informal outline,** you use words and phrases to record main ideas and significant details. Notes in this form are helpful in studying for an objective test because they emphasize specific facts.

In a **graphic organizer,** words and phrases are arranged in a visual pattern to indicate the relationships between main ideas and supporting details. This is an excellent tool for studying information for an objective test, for an open-ended assessment, or for writing an essay. The visual organizer allows you instantly to see important information and the relationships between ideas.

In a **summary** you use sentences to express important ideas in your own words. A summary should not simply restate the ideas presented in the textbook or lecture. Instead, a good summary should express relationships between ideas and draw conclusions. For this reason summaries are useful in preparing for an essay test.

In the following passage, the essential information for understanding the work of Leonardo da Vinci is underlined. Following the passage are examples of notes in an informal outline, a graphic organizer, and a summary form.

MODEL: Essential Information

Leonardo da Vinci, an Italian man of the Renaissance, is believed to be one of the greatest artists of all time. He was also, however, a genius in many other areas of study. Because his notebooks survived, we know that he laid out plans for hundreds of inventions and machines. Among them are designs for a flying machine, a helicopter, a parachute, a movable bridge, artillery, an alarm clock, and revolving stages. He was fascinated by anatomy and produced the first accurate drawings of the human body. However, he is probably most famous for his paintings, such as *The Last Supper.* His work inspired many other artists—among them another giant of the Renaissance, Michaelangelo.

INFORMAL OUTLINE:

Leonardo da Vinci

- Great Renaissance artist and inventor
- Sketched plans for hundreds of inventions and machines
- Created the first accurate drawings of the human anatomy
- Most famous for his paintings
- Inspired Michaelangelo

GRAPHIC ORGANIZER:

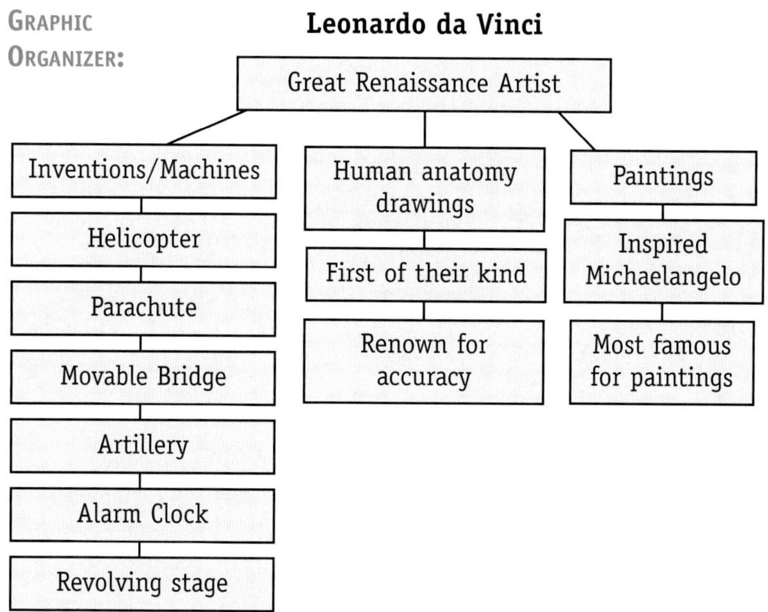

SUMMARY:

Leonardo da Vinci

Leonardo da Vinci was a great Renaissance artist and a great scientist, laying out plans for many inventions and machines. His scientific work was also concerned with accurate drawings of the anatomy of the human body. He influenced other greats like Michaelangelo.

USING STUDENTS' STRENGTHS

Multiple Intelligences: Logical

After discussing graphic organizers and studying the example on this page, have students construct a graphic organizer for a topic they are currently studying in science. Tell students that they can use visual organizers, such as webs, flow charts, graphs, tree diagrams, or tables to help them see what they are trying to organize in their heads for any subject matter. Remind students that graphic organizers are especially helpful in the prewriting stage when they are writing.

Whichever note-taking method you use, the following strategies will help you make those notes clear and well organized.

Strategies for Taking Notes

- Label your notes with the title and page numbers of the chapter or the topic and date of the lecture.
- Record only the main ideas and important details.
- Use the titles, subtitles, and words in special type to help you select the most important information.
- Use your own words; do not copy word for word.
- Use as few words as possible.

Taking Standardized Tests

A standardized test measures your academic progress, skills, and achievement in such a way that results can be compared with those of other students who have taken the same test. Standardized tests that assess your ability to use language—or verbal—skills include vocabulary tests, analogy tests, sentence-completion tests, reading tests, and tests of standard written English.

The best way to do well on standardized tests is to work consistently on your school subjects throughout the year, to read as much as possible from a variety of sources, and to learn the strategies of test taking. In addition, when you take standardized tests, apply the following strategies.

Strategies for Taking Standardized Tests

- Read the test directions carefully, always taking time to answer the sample questions to be sure you understand what the test requires.
- Relax. Although you can expect to be a little nervous, concentrate on doing the best you can.
- Preview the whole test quickly by skimming to get an overview of the kinds of questions on the test.
- Plan your time carefully, allotting a certain amount of time to each part of the test.
- Answer first the questions you find easiest. Skip hard questions, coming back to them later if you have time.
- Read and reread all choices before you choose an answer. If you are not sure of the answer, try to eliminate choices that are obviously wrong. Educated guessing often helps.
- If you have time, check your answers. Be sure you have not made a mistake in marking your answer sheet.

INTEGRATING TECHNOLOGY

Computers

Ask students to list the kinds of standardized tests they might have taken. Students might not recall the names of the tests, but they should recall taking tests that included multiple-choice questions, comprehension questions, analogies, synonyms and antonyms, and fill-in-the-blank questions. Tell students that in the future they might be taking the ACT or SAT as part of their college entrance exams and that many employers also administer tests to job applicants. Have students share some of the strategies they have used in the past to complete their tests successfully.

Then have students use computers to practice taking standardized tests by using ACT or SAT practice software. Such programs are available in most libraries.

Vocabulary Tests

One kind of vocabulary test asks you to find **antonyms**—words most nearly opposite in meaning. For instance, in the following test item, you must find the antonym for *slumber* among the five choices.

SLUMBER: (A) dream (B) hibernate (C) snore (D) awaken (E) sleep

(The answer is *(D)* because *awaken* is an antonym for *slumber.* The other choices are wrong for various reasons. The word *sleep* is a synonym for *slumber,* not an antonym. None of the other three choices means the opposite of *slumber.*)

COMPLEX: (A) mysterious (B) complicated (C) simple (D) fancy (E) harmless

(The answer is *(C)* because *simple* is the opposite of *complex.* The word *complicated* is a synonym for *complex,* and the other words do not have the opposite meaning of *complex.*)

Synonym items have the same format as antonym items, but instead of choosing the answer that means the opposite of the word in capital letters, you choose the word that means the same. For example, in the following item, the answer is *(D) stray,* which means the same as *wander.*

WANDER: (A) tempt (B) ask (C) hide
(D) stray (E) walk

(The answer is *(D)* because *stray* has close to the same meaning as *wander.* The word *walk* is related to *wander* in that when one wanders, one is usually walking, but it is not the same meaning. The words *hide, tempt,* and *ask* do not have the same meaning as *wander.*)

DESCEND: (A) agree (B) climb (C) struggle
(D) defend (E) fall

(The answer is *(E)* because the word *fall* is close to the same meaning as *descend.* The word *climb* means the opposite of *descend,* and the other words do not have the same meaning.)

Always consider every choice carefully. You can often figure out the meaning of a word by using a prefix, a root, or a suffix as a clue.

YOUR IDEAS

For Antonyms and Synonyms

A DIFFERENT APPROACH

Auditory

Tell students that although during actual tests it would not be appropriate to voice the test questions and their responses aloud, practicing or preparing for a test should involve auditory practice. Listening to their own answers can help students recognize errors in their responses. Have students work with partners to complete **Practice Your Skills** items one through ten. Partners should take turns reading each item and their responses aloud.

PRACTICE YOUR SKILLS

Check Your Understanding

Recognizing Antonyms

Write the letter of the word that is most nearly opposite in meaning to the word in capital letters.

1. STURDY:
(A) strong (B) unhealthy (C) weak
(D) faithful (E) upright

2. SPECIFIC:
(A) qualified (B) general (C) difficult
(D) trained (E) precise

3. NOTABLE:
(A) princely (B) special (C) unimportant
(D) official (E) smart

4. BENEFICIAL:
(A) friendly (B) dishonest (C) expensive
(D) reliable (E) harmful

5. INCOMPETENT:
(A) unreliable (B) capable (C) unbroken
(D) significant (E) unstable

Check Your Understanding

Recognizing Synonyms

Write the letter of the word that is most nearly the same in meaning as the word in capital letters.

6. ORNAMENTAL:
(A) bright (B) ugly (C) useful
(D) decorative (E) fancy

7. VARIETY:
(A) store (B) value (C) amusement
(D) assortment (E) collection

8. FREQUENTLY:
(A) often (B) rarely (C) seldom
(D) cheaply (E) sometimes

9. RADIANT:
(A) enjoyable (B) clever (C) dull
(D) glowing (E) warm

10. COMMOTION:
(A) calmness (B) swiftness (C) sympathy
(D) boredom (E) disturbance

Analogies

Analogy questions test your skill at figuring out relationships between words. The first step is to decide how the given words—the first, capitalized pair of words—are related to each other. The next step is to decide which other pair has the same kind of relationship as the given pair.

The punctuation in an analogy question stands for the words *is to* and *as*.

STALE : FRESH : : old : new

The above example reads, "Stale *is to* fresh as old *is to* new." That is, *stale* has the same relationship to *fresh* as *old* has to *new*. *Stale* is the opposite of *fresh*, just as *old* is the opposite of *new*. Explaining an analogy to yourself in one sentence can help you to figure out the answer. In the following item, for example, you might say to yourself, "One kind of tree is an oak."

TREE : OAK : :
(A) deer : buffalo (B) fever : virus
(C) music : jazz (D) plumber : wrench
(E) rose : flower

(The answer, *(C) music : jazz,* expresses the same category-to-item relationship)

USING STUDENTS' STRENGTHS

Multiple Intelligences: Logical

Tell students that they can improve their analogy skills by first improving their vocabulary. Provide students with vocabulary-building software to strengthen their vocabulary skills. Then have students practice identifying the relationship between two items. By being familiar with vocabulary and relationships, students will be successful at completing analogies. Have students practice by completing the following analogies:

1. lion: carnivorous
   diamond: ▪ (hard)
2. peas: vegetable
   gold: ▪ (metal)
3. hurricane: destruction
   reading: ▪ (knowledge)

GETTING STUDENTS INVOLVED

Cooperative Learning

In groups have students use this analogy chart to write an example of each type of analogy. Using the chart, each group should end up with eight different analogies. Have students look in other resource materials to locate other types of analogies not listed. Have each group share their findings with the class. Then as a class, write analogies for these new types.

Keep in mind that the word order in an analogy is very important. If the given pair of words in the analogy expresses a part-to-whole order, for example, the words in the correct answer should also be taken in order of part to whole.

Some analogies are written in sentence form.

> Rapid is to slow as raw is to ▒.
> (A) bitter (B) cooked (C) hard
> (D) quick (E) cold
>
> (The first two italicized words are antonyms. Therefore, the correct answer is *(B) cooked,* the opposite of *raw.*)

Knowing some of the common types of analogies, like those in the following chart, will help you figure out word relationships.

COMMON TYPES OF ANALOGIES

Analogy	Example
word : synonym	slim : slender
word : antonym	exciting : dull
part : whole	wing : airplane
cause : effect	drought : famine
worker : tool	carpenter : hammer
worker : product	baker : bread
item : purpose	ruler : measure
item : category	robin : bird

Practice Your Skills

Check Your Understanding
Recognizing Analogies

Write the letter of the word pair that has the same relationship as the word pair in capital letters.

1. ADD: SUBTRACT : :
(A) possesss : have
(B) fly : soar
(C) arrive : leave
(D) laugh : smile
(E) shock : surprise

2. NEVER: ALWAYS : :
(A) gradually : steeply
(B) powerfully : strongly
(C) bravely : boldly
(D) kindly : politely
(E) often : frequently

3. HOUR: DAY : :
(A) second : minute
(B) clock : hand
(C) week : minute
(D) watch : time
(E) day : sun

4. PLUMBER : WRENCH : :
(A) building : wire
(B) key : locksmith
(C) carpenter : hammer
(D) pipe : plumber
(E) tractor : farmer

5. TIGHTEN : LOOSEN : :
(A) distrust : doubt
(B) empty : fill
(C) employ : hire
(D) hold : grasp
(E) laugh : happy

Check Your Understanding
Completing Analogies

Complete the analogy with the choice that correctly completes the second pair.

6. Refrigerator is to food as wallet is to ▒.
(A) money (B) cold (C) pocket
(D) handbag (E) purse

USING STUDENTS' STRENGTHS

Multiple Intelligences: Logical

Remind students that sentence-completion questions test their reading comprehension and their ability to complete sentences logically. In order to comprehend sentences, they must be able to identify the relationship between the first and the last parts of sentences. Have students practice this skill by writing sentences using the following words: *however, and, because, therefore, thereafter, either/or, neither/nor, not only/but also.*

YOUR IDEAS
For Sentence Completion

7. Hand is to foot as arm is to ■.
(A) leg (B) finger (C) elbow
(D) wrist (E) shoulder

8. Look is to see as listen is to ■.
(A) say (B) silent (C) hear
(D) watch (E) noise

9. Jeans is to tuxedo as cabin is to ■.
(A) wood (B) material (C) palace
(D) small (E) dormitory

10. Smooth is to satin as rough is to ■.
(A) velvet (B) tan (C) difficult
(D) sandpaper (E) cotton

Sentence-Completion Tests

Sentence-completion tests measure your ability to comprehend what you read and to use context correctly. Each item consists of a sentence with one or more words missing. First read the entire sentence. Then read the answer choices and select the one that completes the sentence in a way that makes the most sense. For example, in the following item, read the sentence and then find the word that most appropriately completes the sentence.

Dr. Sawyer's mechanical servant Robbie is the ideal use of ■.
(A) friendship (B) automation (C) gasoline
(D) nurses (E) hospitals

The answer is *(B) automation.* The clue *mechanical servant* tells you that the use of *automation* is a robot Dr. Sawyer uses for assistance.

Some sentence-completion questions have two blanks in the same sentence, with each answer choice including two words. Find the correct answer in this example.

While all the other members of the jury thought the man was ▒, a single ▒ held on to her "not guilty" vote.
(A) friendly . . . witness (B) guilty . . . juror
(C) mean . . . officer (D) innocent . . . defense lawyer
(E) nice . . . judge

The answer is *(B) guilty . . . juror.* The other choices do not fit the context. A *juror* sits on a jury, and since the other members found the man guilty, the single *juror* had to have found him not guilty.

Practice Your Skills

Check Your Understanding
Completing Sentences

Write the letter of the word that best completes each of the following sentences.

1. Kathleen is reading the ▒ of Thomas Edison because she is interested in his life as well as in his inventions.
(A) encyclopedia (B) scientific papers
(C) calculations (D) biography
(E) paperback

2. Be sure to save your ▒; it will show when you bought your sweater and how much you paid for it.
(A) receipt (B) bag (C) tag
(D) wish list (E) wallet

3. James was nicknamed "Stretch" because he was so lean and ▒.
(A) hunched (B) rubbery (C) short
(D) chunky (E) lanky

4. "I can't ■ the outcome of the game," the coach said, "but I can tell you that our players are ready to put up a good fight."
(A) decide (B) overcome (C) predict
(D) dream (E) wish

5. Superman didn't even ■ when the boulder came tumbling down on him; he just stood there, hands on hips, unmoved.
(A) celebrate (B) jump (C) hunch
(D) crawl (E) flinch

Check Your Understanding

Completing Sentences with Two Blanks

Write the letter of the words that best complete each of the following sentences.

6. After ■ accidents, a new school law was passed that ■ skateboards on school grounds.
(A) a few . . . encourages
(B) some . . . requires
(C) several . . .prohibits
(D) numerous . . . permits
(E) too many . . . allows

7. In areas of high ■, such as the Rocky Mountains, the air is thin and breathing is ■.
(A) rainfall . . . shallow (B) elevation . . .difficult
(C) scenery . . . easy (D) sea level . . . humid
(E) trees . . . delightful

8. When you fill out the order form, ■ the size and color of the T-shirt you want so your order can be filled ■.
(A) name exactly . . . slowly
(B) reduce . . . incorrectly
(C) leave out . . . mysteriously
(D) pick out . . . quickly
(E) specify . . . accurately

9. The train sat ■ out in the middle of nowhere, while the ■ passengers wondered if it would ever move again.
(A) stationary . . . anxious
(B) heavy . . . giddy
(C) loaded . . . thrilled
(D) rotating . . . worried
(E) gliding . . . hungry

10. Carneval, a large ■ in Brazil, is famous for its showy samba dances and its costumes with many ■ colors.
(A) ceremony . . . brown (B) boat . . . dull
(C) celebration . . . brilliant (D) parade . . . white
(E) funeral . . . feathered

Reading Comprehension Tests

Reading tests assess your ability to understand and analyze written passages. The information you need to answer the test questions may be either directly stated or implied in the passage. You must study, analyze, and interpret a passage in order to answer the questions that follow it. The following strategies will help you answer questions on reading tests.

Strategies for Reading Comprehension Test Questions

- Begin by skimming the questions that follow the passage.
- Read the passage carefully and closely. Notice the main ideas, organization, style, and key words.
- Study all possible answers. Avoid choosing one answer the moment you think it is a reasonable choice.
- Use only the information in the passage when you answer the questions. Do not rely on your own knowledge or ideas on this kind of test.

USING STUDENTS' STRENGTHS

Multiple Intelligences: Linguistic

Remind students that they should never choose an answer for a reading comprehension item until they have *completely* read each answer choice. Also, tell students that they should read the questions *before* they read the short passage. By focusing on the questions first, students will be able to recall key points in the passage that they will need to know for their responses.

USING STUDENTS' STRENGTHS

Multiple Intelligences: Logical

Have students read the questions on pages L711 and L712 *before* they read the passage on Nelson Mandela. Remind students to read through the sample test questions to focus on the key elements of the passage. Then direct students to read the passage. Discuss students' responses.

Most reading questions will focus on one or more of the following characteristics of a written passage.

- **Main idea** At least one question will usually focus on the central idea of the passage. Remember that the main idea of a passage covers all sections of the passage—not just one section or paragraph.
- **Supporting details** Questions about supporting details test your ability to identify the statements in the passage that back up the main idea.
- **Implied meanings** In some passages not all information is directly stated. Some questions ask you to interpret information that the author has merely implied.
- **Purpose and Tone** Questions on purpose and tone require that you interpret or analyze the author's purpose in writing and the author's attitude toward his or her subject.

PRACTICE YOUR SKILLS

Check Your Understanding

Reading for Comprehension

Read the following passage and write the letter of each correct answer.

Nelson Mandela, a leader in the African National Congress, dared to resist apartheid. The apartheid system divided South Africa's people into groups based on race—white South Africans and black South

Africans. The apartheid laws said that each group must live, learn, work, and play separately. A major problem with apartheid was that white South Africans had the best land, jobs, schools, and opportunities. Apartheid made discrimation the law.

Nonwhite people fought the laws, using violence when necessary. Armed troops of the white government broke up the rallies, killed protesters, and imprisoned anti-apartheid leaders.

Nelson Mandela was sentenced to life in prison, and even from there, he inspired his South African followers. For ten thousand days—until 1990—he remained in prison. He became a symbol for the hardship his people endured.

1. The best title for this passage is
   (A) The History of South Africa.
   (B) Nelson Mandela's Jail Sentence.
   (C) Nelson Mandela's Struggle with Apartheid.
   (D) Apartheid by the White Man.
   (E) Prisons in South Africa.

2. The purpose of paragraph 1 is
   (A) to define apartheid.
   (B) to give biographical information on Mandela.
   (C) to argue against apartheid.
   (D) to explain the consequences of prison.
   (E) to explain why Mandela was imprisoned.

3. The passage indicates that the nonwhite people
(A) worked peacefully with the government.
(B) lived separately, but attended the same schools as whites.
(C) discriminated against whites.
(D) spent considerable time in prison.
(E) resisted the government with violence.

4. This passage would most likely appear in
(A) a front-page newspaper article.
(B) a book on the important people of our times.
(C) a book on the history of the United States.
(D) a textbook on the history of African art.
(E) the conclusion of a book entitled *Separate but Equal.*

5. The main purpose of paragraph 3 is
(A) to show the importance of prison.
(B) to explain the prison sentences in South Africa.
(C) to define apartheid.
(D) to explain the effects of Mandela's life on others.
(E) to set up the central conflict between the two races.

The Double Passage

You may also be asked to read two paired passages, called the **double passage,** and answer questions about each passage individually and about how the two passages relate to each other. The two passages may present similar or opposing views or may complement each other in various ways. A brief introduction preceding the passages may help you anticipate the relationship between them.

All of the questions follow the second passage. The first few questions relate to Passage 1, the next few questions relate to Passage 2, and the final questions relate to both passages. You may find it helpful to read Passage 1 first and then immediately find and answer those questions related only to Passage 1. Then read Passage 2 and answer the remaining questions.

Practice Your Skills

Check Your Understanding

Reading for Double Passage Comprehension

The following passages are about the Native American battles with the white settlers. The first passage is the recollection of the 1896 Battle of Little Big Horn by Wooden Leg, a Northern Cheyenne. The second is an 1877 surrender speech by Chief Joseph of the Nez Percé tribe. Read each passage and answer the questions that follow.

Passage 1

In my sleep I dreamed that a great crowd of people were making lots of noise. Something in the noise startled me. I found myself wide awake, sitting up and listening. My brother too awakened, and we both jumped to our feet. A great commotion was going on among the camps. We heard shooting. We hurried out from the trees so we might see as well as hear.

The shooting was somewhere at the upper part of the camp circles. It looked as if all of the Indians there were running away toward the hills to the westward or down toward the village. Women were screaming and men were letting out war cries. Through it all we could hear old men calling: "Soldiers are here! Young men, go out and fight them."

REACHING ALL STUDENTS

Struggling Learners

Tell students that as they are reading the test questions, they must be sure to differentiate between the two passages. They must read the test questions carefully to see which passage is being referenced in each question. Remind students to read the test questions *before* they read either passage. Their ability to concentrate and focus as they read will determine their success with this type of test. Provide students with additional examples of double-passage questions to practice. The library is a good source for test-taking booklets and sample standardized tests. Also, most libraries now have sample test-taking software for students to borrow. Have students practice taking reading comprehension tests and comment on their skills after practicing this skill for a period of time.

Passage 2

I am tired of fighting. Our chiefs are killed. Looking Glass is dead. Toohoolhoolzote is dead. The old men are all dead.

It is the young men who say yes and no. He who led on the young men is dead. It is cold and we have no blankets. The little children are freezing to death.

My people, some of them, have run away to the hills, and have no blankets, no food; no one knows where they are—perhaps freezing to death.

I want to have time to look for my children and see how many I can find. Maybe I shall find them among the dead.

Hear me, my chiefs. I am tired; my heart is sick and sad.

From where the sun now stands I will fight no more forever.

1. According to the author of Passage 1, which of the following best explains the reason the young men were called to fight?

(A) A crowd of people were having a celebration on their property.
(B) Their fellow Indians were being attacked.
(C) Women carrying babies were running.
(D) The tribe elders forced them into battle.
(E) They were startled by loud noise.

2. The purpose of Passage 1 is to
   (A) argue for the Cheyenne tribe's victory at Little Big Horn.
   (B) describe all the events of the battle of Little Big Horn.
   (C) complain about the white settlers.
   (D) show the importance of Indian fighting.
   (E) tell the story of Wooden Leg's experience of this day.

3. According to the Chief Joseph in Passage 2, which of the following best describes the purpose of his speech?
   (A) to argue for equality
   (B) to demonstrate the dominance of the white settlers
   (C) to explain the reasons for his surrender
   (D) to show how tired he is
   (E) to encourage other tribes to keep fighting

4. The details of Passage 2 show Chief Joseph's
   (A) gaiety.
   (B) sorrow.
   (C) forcefulness.
   (D) relief.
   (E) energy.

5. Which of the following attitudes is expressed by both authors?
   (A) The white men who fought the Native Americans caused turmoil.
   (B) The white man and the Native American can live happily in peace.
   (C) Fighting is the best way to defend yourself against invaders.
   (D) Surrender saves the women and the children.
   (E) Native Americans were more violent than the white settlers.

GETTING STUDENTS INVOLVED

Reciprocal Teaching

Ask students how they think they would prepare for a test of this type. What study skills or learning strategies would they use to study for a test in which they had to identify and correct errors in spelling, usage, grammar, punctuation, mechanics, and capitalization. List some of students' responses on the board. Tell students that by studying their English textbooks and by writing frequently, they can prepare for such tests.

YOUR IDEAS
For Standard Written English Tests

Tests of Standard Written English

Objective tests of standard written English assess your knowledge of language skills used for writing. They contain sentences with underlined words, phrases, and punctuation. The underlined parts will contain errors in grammar, usage, mechanics, vocabulary, and spelling. You are asked to find the error in each sentence, or, on some tests, to identify the best way to revise a sentence or passage.

Finding Errors

The most familiar way to test grammar, usage, capitalization, punctuation, word choice, and spelling is through finding errors in a sentence. A typical test item of this is a sentence with five underlined choices. Four of the choices suggest possible errors in the sentence. The fifth states that there is no error. Read the following sentence and identify the error, if there is one.

> The people (A) of Haiti (B) won their Independence (C) from France (D) in 1804.
>
> (The answer is *C*. The word *independence* should not be capitalized.)

The following list identifies some of the errors you should look for on a test of standard written English.

- lack of agreement between subject and verb
- lack of agreement between pronoun and antecedent
- incorrect spelling or use of a word
- missing, misplaced, or unnecessary punctuation
- missing or unnecessary capitalization
- misused or misplaced italics or quotation marks

Sometimes you will find a sentence that contains no error. Be careful, however, before you choose *E* as the answer. It is easy to overlook a mistake, since common errors are the kind generally included on this type of test.

Remember that the parts of a sentence that are not underlined are presumed to be correct. You can use clues in the correct parts of the sentence to help you search for errors in the underlined parts.

Practice Your Skills

Check Your Understanding

Recognizing Errors in Writing

Write the letter of the underlined word or punctuation mark that is incorrect. If the sentence contains no error, write *E*.

(1) In the year(A) 1919,(B) the native(C) people of India,(D) longed for their independence. **(2)** After nearly two and a half centuries of British(A) rule, they were ready to fight,(C) and live as free people in their(B) own land. **(3)** A small,(D) quiet man named Mohandas(A) Gandhi(B) spoke out for Freedom.(C) **(4)** "There is a better way,"(D) he said, "than choosing violence,(A) or terrorism."(B) **(5)** He taught(C) his fellow Indians(D) the principles of peaceful,(A) non-violent protest!(B) **(6)** "I know",(C) he said, "non-violence(D) is a weapon for the brave and the courageous."(A) **(7)** It takes patience(B) to let angry people,(C) attack you and(D) not attack them in return.(A) **(8)** "How difficult it is to follow this grand(B) law of love,"(C) he said, "but are not all great, and

GETTING STUDENTS INVOLVED

Reciprocal Teaching

Have students write ten items for a sentence-correction test. Remind students that their answer choices must contain only one correct answer. Students should proofread their completed tests before writing their final draft. Remind students to underline the section of each sentence on which test takers should focus. Have students exchange tests and answer each others' questions.

good things difficult to do?" **(9)** The world began to notice and be impressed with this man's courage and principles. **(10)** He was called Mahatma, or "Great Soul," by the millions who followed and love him.

Ⓓ A B E C D A B C Ⓓ

Sentence-Correction Questions

Sentence-correction questions assess your ability to recognize appropriate phrasing. Instead of locating an error in a sentence, you must select the most appropriate and effective way to write the sentence.

In this kind of question, a part of the sentence is underlined. The sentence is then followed by five different ways of writing the underlined part. The first way shown, *(A)*, simply repeats the original underlined portion. The other four give alternative ways of writing the underlined part. The choices may involve grammar, usage, capitalization, punctuation, or word choice. Be sure that the answer you choose does not change the meaning of the original sentence.

Look at the following example.

The statue Venus of Milo is displayed in a french museum.

(A) *Venus of milo* is displayed in a french museum.
(B) *Venus of Milo,* is displayed in a french museum.
(C) *Venus of Milo* is displayed in a French museum.
(D) *Venus of Milo* is displayed, in a french museum.
(E) *Venus of Milo* is displayed in a French Museum.

(The answer is (C). *Venus of Milo* is a proper noun and should be capitalized. *French* should also be capitalized.)

Practice Your Skills

Check Your Understanding
Correcting Sentences

Write the letter of the correct way, or the best way, of phrasing the underlined part of each sentence.

1. Modern paper is made from wood containing acids that release, and decay slowly.
(A) wood containing acids that release, and decay slowly.
(B) wood containing acids that release and decay slowly.
(C) wood, containing Acids that release and decay slowly.
(D) wood containing acids that release, and decay, slowly.
(E) wood containing acids that release and decay, slowly.

2. The ancient Egyptians made paper from tree bark and some of it still exists.
(A) tree bark and some of it still exists.
(B) tree bark, and some of it, still exists.
(C) Tree Bark, and some of it still exists.
(D) Tree Bark and some of it still exists.
(E) tree bark, and some of it still exists.

3. The Chinese first wrote on silk but then someone invented paper.
(A) Chinese first wrote on silk but then
(B) chinese, first wrote on silk but then
(C) Chinese, first wrote on silk, but then
(D) chinese first wrote on silk but then
(E) Chinese first wrote on silk, but then

REACHING ALL STUDENTS

Struggling Learners

Remind students that they must read test questions carefully. Tell students that if they misread the questions, they are almost sure to answer the questions incorrectly. Often one word can change the entire meaning of a question. Have students read the following questions and explain the difference between the two.

Which of these planets is close to Earth?

Which of these planets is not close to Earth?

YOUR IDEAS

For Revision-in-Context

4. The Chinese paper was made of bark and rags, that was mixed and placed over a frame.
   (A) bark and rags, that was mixed and placed
   (B) bark and rags that were mixed and placed
   (C) bark and rags, that are mixed and placed
   (D) bark and rags that were mixed, and placed
   (E) bark, and rags, that are mixed and placed
5. Eventually a paper mill opened in Spain and the art of paper making spread.
   (A) paper mill opened in Spain and the art of paper making
   (B) paper mill opened in spain and the art of paper-making
   (C) paper mill opened in Spain, and the art of papermaking
   (D) Paper Mill opened in Spain and the art of paper making
   (E) paper mill opened, in Spain, and the art of paper-making

Revision-in-Context

Another type of multiple-choice question that appears on some standardized tests is called revision-in-context. These questions are based on a short passage that is meant to represent an early draft of student writing. The questions following the reading ask you to choose the best revision of a sentence, a group of sentences, or the essay as a whole. This type of test assesses your reading comprehension, your composing skills, and your understanding of the conventions of standard written English.

Check Your Understanding
Correcting Sentences

Carefully read the following passage, which is an early draft of an essay about the book *Uncle Tom's Cabin* by Harriet Beecher Stowe. Write the letter of the correct answer next to each number.

(1) The novel *Uncle Tom's Cabin* by Harriet Beecher Stowe made many people in the 1860s very uncomfortable. **(2)** It told the story of the lives of slaves in the South. **(3)** Many of the slaves were shown in a positive way, and the white slave owners were shown in a negative way. **(4)** Stowe wanted to tell the people of the United States, both in the North and the South, that slavery was wrong. **(5)** Stowe's father was a minister. **(6)** This gave her the idea to use religion for her argument by making some of the slaves full of Christian goodness and faith. **(7)** The black characters were shown with a lot of sympathy, and the book really made a big difference in the way people saw slavery at that time. **(8)** When Abraham Lincoln met Mrs. Stowe, he said to her, "So, you're the little woman who wrote the book that started this great war!" **(9)** Whether she started the war or not, she did a good job of persuading people against slavery.

USING STUDENTS' STRENGTHS

Multiple Intelligences: Intrapersonal

Have students share test-taking experiences in which they were especially nervous or anxious. Why do students think they were worried about these tests? List some of students' reasons on the board. In most cases, students will say that being unprepared was the most common reason for test-taking anxiety. Tell students that they can relieve this type of stress by being better prepared for tests. Have students list some steps they will take in preparing for their next test.

1. Sentence 1 can best be described as a(n):
(A) elaboration
(B) analysis
(C) topic sentence
(D) conclusion

2. If you were to rewrite sentence 3, which of the following would be the best choice?
(A) Slaves were shown in a positive way. White slave owners were shown in a negative way.
(B) The slaves were shown in a positive way, while the white slave owners were shown in a negative way.
(C) A lot of the slaves were shown in a positive way, and the white slave owners were shown in a negative way.
(D) Consequently, many of the slaves were shown in a positive way, and instead, the white slave owners were shown in a negative way.

3. What is the purpose of sentence 4 in this composition?
(A) to restate the opening sentence
(B) to interest the reader in the story
(C) to analyze the author's purpose
(D) to summarize the plot of the novel
(E) to offer evidence for sentence 3

4. Sentence 6 can best be described as
(A) a summary.
(B) an introduction.
(C) an analysis.
(D) a conclusion.
(E) a topic sentence.

5. Which of the following is the best revision of sentence 7?

(A) The black characters were shown with a lot of sympathy, and the book made a big difference in the way people saw slavery at that time.

(B) The black characters were really shown sympathetically, and the book made a difference in the way people saw slavery at the time.

(C) The black characters were really nice. Stowe's book made a lot of difference in the way people saw slavery at the time.

(D) Because the black characters are really nice, the book made people see slavery really differently.

(E) The black characters were shown sympathetically. The book made a difference in the way people saw slavery at the time.

6. Sentence 8 refers back to which of the following sentences?

(A) sentence 1

(B) sentence 2

(C) sentence 5

(D) sentence 6

USING STUDENTS' STRENGTHS

Multiple Intelligences: Spatial

Tell students that using time wisely is one of the best ways to ensure completing essay test questions successfully. Remind students that, as in any writing assignment, they should use the stages of the writing process to manage their time and to help them organize their thoughts. Lead students through the instruction on the following four pages that demonstrates how students use the stages of the writing process to complete essay test questions. As you read and discuss each writing stage, have students write a sample essay question and response of their own. Tell students that they will complete a sample timed essay test using these strategies at the end of this section.

Taking Essay Tests

Essay tests are designed to assess both your understanding of important ideas and your ability to see connections, or relationships, between these ideas. To do well, you must be able to organize your thoughts quickly and to express them logically and clearly.

Kinds of Essay Questions

Always begin an essay test by carefully reading the instructions for all the questions on the test. Then, as you reread the instructions for your first question, look for key words, such as those listed in the following box. Such key words will tell you precisely what kind of question you are being asked to answer.

KINDS OF ESSAY QUESTIONS	
Analyze	Separate into parts and examine each part.
Compare	Point out similarities.
Contrast	Point out differences.
Define	Clarify meaning.
Discuss	Examine in detail.
Evaluate	Give your opinion.
Explain	Tell how, what, or why.
Illustrate	Give examples.
Summarize	Briefly review main points.
Trace	Show development or progress.

As you read the instructions, jot down everything that is required in your answer or circle key words and underline key phrases in the instructions, as in the following example.

The women's suffrage movement in the late 1800s had several key women leaders. Explain the life of one of the leaders of this movement. Write four paragraphs that describe her life, giving specific examples of how she was an influence on women's right to vote.

PRACTICE YOUR SKILLS

Check Your Understanding
Interpreting Essay Test Items

Write the key direction word in each item. Then write one sentence explaining what the question asks you to do.

EXAMPLE Explain how a seed becomes a flower.

POSSIBLE ANSWER *Explain*—Tell how how a seed develops and what is necessary for this to occur.

1. In your own words, define *electromagnetic* field.
2. How does the appearance of a cougar compare with that of a jaguar?
3. Briefly summarize one of the articles in *National Geographic.*
4. Shakespeare wrote, "To be or not to be. That is the question." Discuss his meaning.
5. Evaluate one of Edgar Allan Poe's short stories.
6. Explain how the planets revolve around the sun.
7. In a five paragraph essay, contrast 1969 space technology with today's.
8. Discuss the reasons you believe other people should read your favorite book.

YOUR IDEAS
For Taking Essay Tests

9. Evaluate your school's decision to make after-school study hall required.
10. Illustrate the reasons for or against a movie rating system.

Writing an Effective Essay Answer

The steps in writing a well-constructed essay are the same for an essay test as for a written assignment. The only difference is that in a test situation you have a strict time limit for writing. As a result, you need to plan how much time you will spend writing each answer and how much time you will devote to each step in the writing process. As a rule of thumb, for every five minutes of writing, allow two minutes for planning and organizing and one minute for revising and editing.

Prewriting — Writing Process

Begin planning your answer by brainstorming for main ideas and supporting details. Then organize your main ideas into a simple informal outline. Your outline will help you present your ideas in a logical order, cover all your main points, and avoid omitting important details.

INFORMAL OUTLINE:

Indian Writing Systems

1. Mayan glyphs used as a calendar
2. Aztec pictographs kept records
3. Inca quipu knots kept count of crops

You can also plan your answer by using a graphic organizer to indicate the relationships between your main ideas and supporting details.

GRAPHIC ORGANIZER:

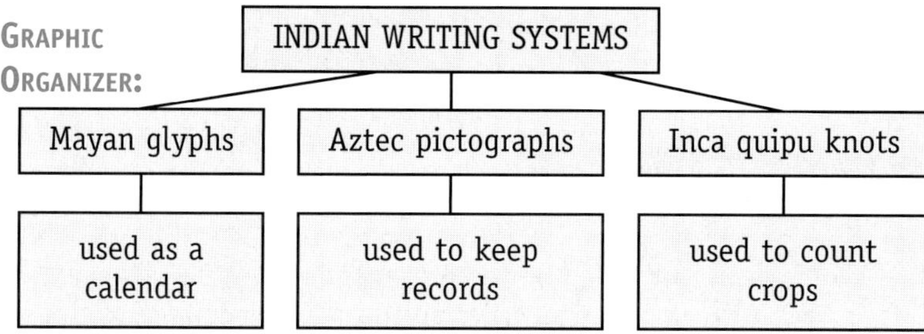

Your next step is to write a statement that states your main idea and covers all your supporting ideas. Often you can write a suitable main idea statement by rewording the test question.

ESSAY QUESTION: Compare and contrast the types of Indian writing systems and their purposes.

MAIN IDEA STATEMENT: There are many types of Indian writing systems and many purposes for these systems.

Drafting

Writing Process

As you write your essay answer, keep the following strategies in mind.

Strategies for Writing an Essay Answer

- Write an introduction that includes the main idea statement.
- Follow the order of your outline. Write one paragraph for each main point, beginning with a topic sentence.
- Be specific. Support each main point by using supporting details such as facts and examples.

YOUR IDEAS

For Graphic Organizers

GETTING STUDENTS INVOLVED

Reciprocal Teaching

Tell students that the more tests they take and the more they use test-taking strategies, the more comfortable they will become with taking tests. Timed tests are usually the form most feared by students. By practicing this form frequently, students can become more prepared for timed tests. Have students make a list of strategies they will use the next time they prepare for a timed test. Have students share their strategies with the class.

- Use transitions to connect your ideas and examples.
- End with a strong concluding statement that summarizes your main idea statement.
- Write clearly and legibly because you will not have time to copy your work.

MODEL: Essay Test Answer

In the United States today, we use a Roman alphabet to write our ideas and keep records. Of course, we have computers today, but we have had paper for writing for a very long time. Before the arrival of the Europeans, Indians had different systems for writing. There are many types of Indian writing systems and many different purposes for these systems. The most highly developed systems came from the Maya, the Aztec, and the Inca.

MAIN IDEA STATEMENT:

Mayan writing contained symbols called glyphs, which were carved in stone and on bark paper. They used these glyphs to create a calendar that is considered by some to be more accurate than those of the ancient Egyptians, Greeks, or Romans.

Aztec writing was made up of pictures called pictographs. These pictographs were used mainly to keep records. Even the Spanish explorers learned to read Aztec writing.

The Inca had a system of tying knots on a string called a *quipu*. The quipu used the decimal system, much as we do. The knots at the end stood for 1, those farther up each counted for 10, and those still higher up stood for 100. Crop records and population information were recorded by this method.

These systems had their own complex rules that the people of each group learned to use.

CONCLUDING STATEMENT: Records of all types have always been important to society. How we keep records will change as technology and our needs change.

Revising

Writing Process

Leave time to revise and edit your essay answer. To keep your paper as neat as possible, use proofreading symbols to mark any corrections or revisions. As you revise, think of the following questions.

- Did you follow the instructions completely?
- Did you interpret the question accurately?
- Did you begin with a main idea statement?
- Did you include facts, examples, or other supporting details?
- Did you sequence your ideas and examples logically in paragraphs according to your informal outline?
- Did you use transitions to connect ideas and examples?
- Did you end with a strong concluding statement that summarizes your main idea?

Editing

Writing Process

After you have made any necessary revisions, quickly read your essay to check for mistakes in spelling, usage, or punctuation. As you edit, check your work for accuracy in the following areas:

- agreement between subjects and verbs *(Chapter 13)*

YOUR IDEAS
For the Writing Process

- forms of comparative and superlative adjectives and adverbs *(pages L449–L454)*
- capitalization of proper nouns and proper adjectives *(pages L500–L520)*
- use of commas *(pages L544–L571)*
- use of apostrophes *(pages L617–L629)*
- division of words at the end of a line *(page L642)*

Timed Writing

Throughout your school years, you will be tested on your ability to organize your thoughts quickly and to express them in a limited time. Your teacher may ask you to write a twenty-minute, two-hundred-word essay that will then be judged on how thoroughly you covered the topic and organized your essay. To complete such an assignment, you should consider organizing your time in the following way.

5 minutes: Brainstorm and organize ideas.

12 minutes: Write a draft.

3 minutes: Revise your work and edit it for mistakes.

The more you practice writing under time constraints, the better you will be able to apply these effective writing strategies during timed tests.

Strategies for Timed Test

- Listen carefully to instructions. Find out if you may write notes or an outline on your paper or in the examination book.
- Find out if you should erase mistakes or cross them out by neatly drawing a line through them.
- Plan your time, keeping in mind your time limit.

Communicate Your Ideas

APPLY TO WRITING

Prewriting, Drafting, Revising, Editing: *Timed Writing*

Many people argue that too much television is not good for students' grades. Other people think that television has positive benefits that can help you in your studies and other ways. Write an essay that explains the effects television has on your grades. Be sure to include both the positive and negative effects of television.

Give yourself twenty minutes to write an answer for the essay question. Begin by writing a list of important points or using a graphic organizer. Be sure to write a strong main idea statement. As you draft your essay, follow the Strategies for Writing an Essay Answer on pages *L727–L728*. Remember that it is important to revise and edit your essay answer.

EFFECTS OF TELEVISION ON GRADES

POSITIVE

NEGATIVE

YOUR IDEAS
For Proofreading

Proofreading Symbols

Symbol	Meaning	Example
∧	insert	We ∧ ~~completed~~ an ∧ journey. (went on; eventful)
∧,	insert comma	Meg enjoys hiking, skiing ∧, and skating.
⊙	insert period	Gary took the bus to Atlanta ⊙
ℊ	delete	Refer ~~back~~ to your notes.
¶	new paragraph	¶ Finally Balboa saw the Pacific.
no ¶	no paragraph	no ¶ The dachsund trotted away.
. . . .	let it stand	I appreciated her sincere honesty.
#	add space	She will be allright in a moment.
⁀	close up	The airplane waited on the run way.
∿	transpose	They only have two dollars left.
≡	capital letter	We later moved to the south.
/	lowercase letter	His favorite subject was Science.
(sp)	spell out	I ate 2 oranges
∨̈ ∨̈	insert quotes	I hope you can join us, said my brother.
=	insert hyphen	I attended a school related event.
∨̓	insert apostrophe	The ravenous dog ate the cats food.
⟲	move copy	I usually on Fridays go to the movies.

GLOSSARY

A

Abbreviation shortened form of a word.

Abstract noun noun that cannot be seen or touched, such as an idea, quality, or characteristic.

Action verb verb that tells what action a subject is performing.

Active voice voice the verb is in when it expresses that the subject is performing the action.

Adjective word that modifies a noun or a pronoun.

Adjective clause subordinate clause used to modify a noun or pronoun.

Adjective phrase prepositional phrase that modifies a noun or a pronoun.

Adverb word that modifies a verb, an adjective, or another adverb.

Adverb clause subordinate clause that is used mainly to modify a verb.

Adverb phrase prepositional phrase that is used mainly to modify a verb.

Analogy logical relationship between a pair of words.

Antecedent word or group of words to which a pronoun refers.

Antonym word that means the opposite of another word.

Appositive noun or pronoun that identifies or explains another noun or pronoun in a sentence.

Audience person or persons who will read your work or hear your speech.

B

Bandwagon statement appeal that leads the reader to believe that everyone is using a certain product.

Brainstorming act of writing down everything that comes to mind about a subject.

Business letter writing form that uses formal language and contains six parts: the heading, inside address, salutation, body, closing, and signature.

C

Case form of a noun or a pronoun that indicates its use in a sentence. In English there are three cases: the nominative case, the objective case, and the possessive case.

Chronological order the order in which events occur.

Citation note that gives credit to the source of another person's paraphrased or quoted ideas.

Clarity the quality of being clear.

Clause group of words that has a subject and a verb.

Clustering visual strategy a writer uses to organize ideas and details connected to the subject.

Coherence logical and smooth flow of ideas connected with clear transitions.

Collective noun names a group of people or things.

Colloquialism informal phrase or colorful expression not meant to be taken literally but understood to have particular non-literal meaning.

Complement word needed to complete the meaning of a group of words.

Complete predicate all the words that tell what the subject is doing or that tell something about the subject.

Complete subject all the words used to identify the person, place, thing, or idea that the sentence is about.

Complex sentence sentence that contains a dependent and an independent clause.

Composition writing form that presents and develops one main idea.

Compound noun a single noun comprised of several words.

Compound sentence consists of two simple sentences, usually joined by a comma and the coordinating conjunction *and, but, or,* or *yet*.

Compound subject two or more subjects in a sentence that have the same verb and are joined by a conjunction.

Compound verb two or more verbs in one sentence that have the same subject and are joined by a conjunction.

Conclusion a strong ending added to a paragraph or composition that summarizes the major points, refers to the main idea, and adds an insight.

Concrete noun person, place, or thing that can be seen or touched.

Conjunction word that joins together sentences, clauses, phrases, or other words.

Contraction word that combines two words into one and uses an apostrophe to replace one or more missing letters.

Coordinating conjunction single connecting word used to join words or groups of words.

Creative writing writing style in which the writer creates characters, events, and images within stories, plays, or poems to express feelings, perceptions, and points of view.

D

Declarative sentence a statement or expression of an opinion. It ends with a period.

Demonstrative pronoun word that substitutes for a noun and points out persons and things.

Denotation literal meaning of a word.

Descriptive writing writing that creates in words a vivid picture of a person, an object, or a scene.

Dialogue conversation between two or more persons.

GLOSSARY

Direct object noun or a pronoun that answers the question *Whom?* or *What?* after an action verb.

Direct quotation passage, sentence, or words stated exactly as the person wrote or said them.

Drafting stage of the writing process in which the writer draws ideas together on paper forming a beginning, a middle, and an ending.

Double negative use of two negative words to express an idea when only one is needed.

E

Editing stage of the writing process in which the writer polishes his or her work by correcting errors in grammar, usage, mechanics, and spelling.

Elaboration addition of explanatory or descriptive information such as supporting details, facts, and examples.

Electronic publishing electronic forms of publishing one's work, including desktop publishing, audio and video recordings, and on-line publishing on the World Wide Web

E-mail electronic mail that can be sent all over the world from one computer to another.

Essay composition of three or more paragraphs that presents and develops one main idea.

Exclamatory sentence expression of strong feeling. It ends with an exclamation point.

F

Facts statements that can be proven.

Fiction prose works of literature, such as short stories and novels, which are partly or totally imaginary.

Fragment group of words that does not express a complete thought.

Freewriting prewriting technique of nonstop writing that encourages the flow of ideas.

Friendly letter writing form that contains a heading, salutation, body, closing, and signature.

G

Gerund verb form ending in *–ing* that is used as a noun.

Glittering generality word or phrase that most people associate with virtue and goodness that is used to trick people into feeling positively about a subject.

H

Helping verb auxiliary verb that helps the main verb to make up a verb phrase.

I

Imperative sentence a request or command. It ends with either a period or an exclamation point.

Indefinite pronoun word that substitutes for a noun and

GLOSSARY

refers to unnamed persons or things.

Independent clause group of words that can stand alone as a sentence because it expresses a complete thought.

Indirect object noun or a pronoun that answers the question *To* or *from whom?* or *To* or *for what?* after an action verb.

Infinitive verb form that usually begins with *to* and can be used as a noun, adjective, or adverb.

Informative writing writing that provides facts and information or explains by giving examples and directions.

Interjection word that expresses strong feeling.

Internet global network of computers that are connected to one another with high-speed data lines and regular telephone lines.

Interrogative pronoun word that is used to ask a question.

Interrogative sentence a question. It ends with a question mark.

Intransitive verb action verb that does not pass the action from a doer to a receiver.

Irregular verb verb that does not form its past and past participle by adding *–ed* to the present.

J

Jargon specialized vocabulary used by a particular group of people.

L

Linking verb verb that links the subject with another word that renames or describes the subject.

Literary analysis interpretation of a work of literature supported with appropriate details and quotations from the work.

Loaded words words carefully chosen to appeal to one's hopes or fears rather than to reason or logic.

M

Modifier word that changes or adds meaning to other words.

N

Narrative writing writing that tells a real or an imaginary story with a clear beginning, middle, and ending.

Network a system of interconnected computers.

Nonessential phrase phrase or clause that can be removed from a sentence without changing the meaning of the sentence.

Nonfiction prose work that contains facts about real people or events.

Nonstandard English less formal language used by people of varying regions and dialects; not appropriate for use in writing.

Noun word that names a person, place, thing, or idea.

Noun clause a subordinate clause used like a noun.

O

Object word that answers the question *What?* or *Whom?*

Occasion motivation for composing; the factor that prompts communication.

Online connected to the Internet via a line modem connection.

Opinion belief or judgment that cannot be proven.

Order of importance order in which evidence is arranged from least to most (or most to least) pertinent.

Outline information about a subject organized into main topics and subtopics.

P

Paragraph group of related sentences that present and develop one main idea.

Parody humorous imitation of a serious work.

Participial phrase participle that works together with its modifier and complement as an adjective.

Participle verb form that is used as an adjective.

Passive voice the voice a verb is in when it expresses that the action of the verb is being performed upon the subject.

Personal pronoun word that renames a particular person or group of people.

Personification giving human qualities to non-human subjects.

Persuasive writing writing that expresses an opinion and uses facts, examples, and reasons to convince readers.

Play piece of writing to be performed on a stage by actors.

Plot sequence of events leading to the outcome or point of the story; contains a climax or high point, a resolution, and an outcome or ending.

Possessive pronoun pronoun used to show ownership or possession.

Predicate word that tells something about the subject.

Predicate adjective adjective that follows a linking verb and modifies the subject.

Predicate nominative noun or a pronoun that follows a linking verb and identifies, renames, or explains the subject.

Prefix one or more syllables placed in front of a base word to form a new word.

Preposition word that shows the relationship between a noun or a pronoun and another word in the sentence.

Prepositional phrase group of words made up of a preposition, its object, and modifiers.

Prewriting invention stage of the writing process in which the writer plans for drafting based on the subject, audience, occasion, and purpose for writing.

Principal parts of a verb the *present*, the *past*, and the *past participle*. The principal parts help to form the tenses of verbs.

Pronoun word that takes the place of one or more nouns.

Proofreading carefully rereading and making corrections in grammar, usage, spelling, and mechanics in a piece of writing.

Publishing stage of the writing process in which the writer may choose to share the work with an audience.

Purpose reason for writing or speaking on a given subject.

R

Reflexive pronoun pronoun formed by adding *–self* or *–selves* to a personal pronoun; it is used to refer to or emphasize a noun or pronoun.

Regular verb verb that forms its past and past participle by adding *–ed* or *–d* to the present.

Relative pronoun pronoun that relates an adjective clause to the noun or pronoun the clause modifies.

Report a composition that uses information from books, magazines, and other sources.

Revising stage in the writing process in which the writer rethinks what is written and reworks it to increase its clarity, smoothness, and power.

Root part of the word that carries its basic meaning.

Run-on sentence two or more sentences that are written as one sentence and are separated by a comma or have no mark of punctuation at all.

S

Sentence group of words that expresses a complete thought.

Sentence fragment group of words that does not express a complete thought.

Sequential order the order in which details are arranged according to when they take place or when they are done.

Setting environment (location and time) in which the action takes place.

Short story well-developed story about characters facing a conflict or problem.

Simple predicate the main word or phrase in the complete predicate.

Simple sentence sentence that has one subject and one verb.

Simple subject the main word in a complete subject.

Slang nonstandard English expressions that are developed and used by particular groups.

Spatial order order in which details are arranged according to their location.

Standard English proper form of the language that follows a set pattern of rules and conventions.

Style visual or verbal expression that is distinctive to an artist or writer.

Subject names the person, place, thing, or idea that a

sentence is about; the topic of a composition.

Subordinate clause group of words that cannot stand alone as a sentence because it does not express a complete thought.

Subordinating conjunction single connecting word that introduces a dependent clause.

Suffix one or more syllables placed after a base word to change its part of speech and possibly its meaning.

Supporting sentences sentences that explain or prove the topic sentence with specific details, facts, examples, or reasons.

Synonym word that has nearly the same meaning as another word.

T

Tense the form a verb takes to show time. The six tenses are the *present*, *past*, *future*, *present perfect*, *past perfect*, and *future perfect*.

Testimonial persuasive strategy in which a famous person encourages the purchase of a certain product.

Thesaurus online or print reference that gives synonyms for words.

Topic sentence sentence that states the main idea of the paragraph.

Transitions words and phrases that show how ideas are related.

U

Understood subject a subject of a sentence that is not stated.

Unity combination or ordering of parts in a composition so that all the sentences or paragraphs work together as a whole to support one main idea.

V

Verb word that expresses an action or state of being.

Verbal verb form that acts like another part of speech, such as an adjective or noun.

Verb phrase main verb plus one or more helping verbs.

Voice the particular sound and rhythm of the language the writer uses (closely related to *tone*).

W

World Wide Web a network of computers within the Internet capable of delivering multimedia content and text over communication lines into personal computers all over the globe.

Writing process recursive stages that a writer proceeds through in his or her own way when developing ideas and discovering the best way to express them.

INDEX

Note: Italic page numbers indicate skill sets.

INDEX

Note: Italic page numbers indicate skill sets.

Note: Italic page numbers indicate skill sets.

INDEX

Note: Italic page numbers indicate skill sets.

Note: Italic page numbers indicate skill sets.

INDEX

Note: Italic page numbers indicate skill sets.

INDEX

Note: Italic page numbers indicate skill sets.

Note: Italic page numbers indicate skill sets.

Note: Italic page numbers indicate skill sets.

Note: Italic page numbers indicate skill sets.

INDEX

Note: Italic page numbers indicate skill sets.

INDEX

Note: Italic page numbers indicate skill sets.

S

Note: Italic page numbers indicate skill sets.

INDEX

Note: Italic page numbers indicate skill sets.

INDEX

Note: Italic page numbers indicate skill sets.

Note: Italic page numbers indicate skill sets.

Note: Italic page numbers indicate skill sets.

INDEX

ACKNOWLEDGMENTS

Barrett Kendall Publishing has made every effort to trace the ownership of all copyrighted selections in this book and to make full acknowledgment of their use. Grateful acknowledgment is made to the following authors, publishers, agents, and individuals for their permission to reprint copyrighted material.

Composition

C3: From *Eighth Book of Junior Authors and Illustrators.* **C45:** From *Writing Down the Bones: Freeing the Writer Within,* by Natalie Goldberg, © 1986. Reprinted by arrangement with Shambhala Publications, Inc., Boston, www.shambhala.com. **C73:** Reprinted with permission of Pocket Books, a Division of Simon & Schuster, from *The Miracle of Language* by Richard Lederer. Copyright © 1991 by Richard Lederer. **C99:** Excerpt, as submitted, from *Pilgrim at Tinker Creek* by Annie Dillard. Copyright © 1974 by Annie Dillard. Reprinted by permission of HarperCollins Publishers, Inc. **C127:** From *The House on Mango Street.* Copyright © 1984 by Sandra Cisneros. Published by Vintage Books, a division of Random House, Inc., and in hardcover by Alfred A. Knopf in 1994. Reprinted by permission of Susan Bergholz Literary Services, New York. All rights reserved. **C155:** "May," pp. 15-26, from *Rascal* by Sterling North, copyright © 1963 by Sterling North, renewed © 1991 by David S. North and Arielle North Olson, text. Used by permission of Dutton Children's Books, a division of Punguin Putnam Inc. **C189:** "E.B. White" from *Pauses: Autobiographical Reflections of 101 Creators of Children's Books,* by Lee Bennet Hopkins. HarperCollins Publishers. **C194:** "Thank You, M'am" © Langston Hughes. **C229:** "Like Scales" by Julia Mishkin. © Julia Mishkin. **C239:** © 1999 Time, Inc. Reprinted by permission. **C277:** From *Living Out Loud* by Anna Quindlen. Copyright © 1987 by Anna Quindlen. Reprinted by permission of Random House, Inc. **C305:** From *A Couple of Kooks and Other Stories About Love* by Cynthia Rylant. Copyright © 1990 by Cynthia Rylant. Reprinted by permission of Orchard Books, New York. **C341:** By William Carlos Williams, from *Collected Poems: 1909-1939,* Volume I. Copyright © 1938 by New Directions Publishing Corp. Reprinted by permission of New Directions Publishing Corp. **C345:** "Birth of a Legend" by Stephen Lyons. From www.pbs.org/wgbh/nova/lochness/legend.html. **C405:** By permission of Jerry Greenfield. © Jerry Greenfield. **C416:** From www.altculture.com/aentries/b/benjerry.html. **C426:** From *Collected Poems* by Langston Hughes. Copyright © 1994 by the Estate of Langston Hughes. Reprinted by permission of Alfred A. Knopf, a Division of Random House Inc. **C439:** Reprinted with permission of Pocket Books, a Division of Simon & Schuster, from *The Miracle of Language* by Richard Lederer. Copyright © 1991 by Richard Lederer. **C469:** Three page excerpt from *The Mother Tongue* by Bill Bryson. Copyright © 1990 by Bill Bryson. Reprinted by permission of HarperCollins Publishers, Inc. William Morrow. **C474, C475, C478-C480, C484, C486, C488:** Copyright © 1998 by Houghton Mifflin Company. Reproduced by permission from *The American Heritage Student Dictionary.* **C495:** "The First Alexandrian Library" and "The Legacy of Alexandria" written by Lee Schultheiss, reprinted from www.alexandriaproject.org with permission. **C528:** *Readers' Guide to Periodical Literature,* February 1999, Volume 98, No. 12, "Electronic Journals" through "Grandparenting by email." Copyright © 1999 by the H.W. Wilson Company. Material reproduced with permission of the publisher.

Language

L36: Excerpt from *The Million-Pound Bank Note* is reprinted by permission from *Radio Plays for Young People,* by Walter Hackett. Copyright © 1950 by Plays, Inc., Publishers, Boston, MA, USA. **L163:** "The Choice," copyright 1926, copyright renewed 1954 by Dorothy Parker, from *The Portable Dorothy Parker* by Dorothy Parker. Used by permission of Viking Penguin, a division of Penguin Putnam Inc. **L396:** From "The Dog That Bit People," from the book *My Life and Hard Times.* Copyright © 1933, 1961 by James Thurber. Reprinted by arrangement with Rosemary A. Thurber and the Barbara Hogenson Agency. **L497:** "Johnny Appleseed" by Stephen Vincent Benet. From *A Book of Americans* by Rosemary and Stephen Vincent Benet. Copyright © 1933 by Stephen Vincent Benet. Copyright renewed © 1961 by Rosemary Carr Benet. Reprinted by permission of Brandt & Brandt Literary Agents, Inc. **L518:** From *The Eye of the Story: Selected Essays and Reviews,* by Eudora Welty. © 1975 by Eudora Welty. Reprinted by permission of Random House, Inc.

PHOTO CREDITS

Key: (t) top, (c) center, (b) bottom, (l) left, (r) right.

Composition

C5: © Charles & Josette Lenars/Corbis.**C21:** © Gail Mooney/Corbis. **C48:** © Romare Bearden Foundation/Licensed by VAGA, New York, NY. **C99:** © Buddy Mays/Corbis. **C102:** © Maurizio Lanini/Corbis. **C130: (l)** © Jan Butchofsky-Houser/Corbis; **(r)** © Fran Antmann. **C134:** © Kennan Ward/Corbis. **C165:** © Jeffry W. Myers/Corbis. **C184:** © Mary Ann McDonald/Corbis. **C189:** © Bettmann/Corbis. **C192:** © Gail Mooney/Corbis. **C236:** © Tony Arruza/Corbis. **C240, C241:** © 1999 Time, Inc. Reprinted by permission. **C273:** © Mark Gibson/Corbis. **C277:** © Bettmann/Corbis. **C281:** © David C. Kennedy/Black Star/PictureQuest. **C299: (l)** © Sally A. Morgan/Corbis; **(r)** © Ian Harwood/Corbis. **C301:** © Doug Menuez/Photodisc. **C310:** © Fran Antmann. **C341:** Courtesy Brewster Arts Ltd. © 2001 Leonora Carrington/Artists Rights Society (ARS), New York. **C349:** © Ralph White/Corbis. **C377:** © Bettmann/Corbis. **C381:** © Kevin Fleming/Corbis. **C384:** © Jim Lukoski/Black Star/PictureQuest. **C405:** © Richard T. Nowitz/Corbis. **C407: (l)** © Kevin Horan/Stock Boston/PictureQuest; **(r)** © Tony Freeman/PhotoEdit/PictureQuest. **C445: (t), (b)** © Fran Antmann. **C497:** © David Lees/Corbis. **C501:** © Michael Freeman/Corbis.

Language

L4, L42: The Museum of Modern Art, New York. Mary Sklar Bequest. Photograph © 1996 The Museum of Modern Art, New York. © Fiduciario en el Fideicomiso relativo a los Museos Diego Rivera y Frida Kahlo. Reproduction authorized by the Bank of Mexico, Mexico City. Av. 5 de Mayo No. 2, Col. Centro 06059, Mexico, D.F. **L17:** Jay S. Simon/Tony Stone Images. **L21:** Paul Wakefield/Tony Stone Images. **L52:** Photo by Beth Phillips, courtesy DC Moore Gallery, NY. **L91:**

SuperStock. **L100, L126:** © Boltin Picture Library, Croton-on-Hudson, New York. **L149:** © Bettmann/Corbis. **L167:** Chad Ehlers/Tony Stone Images. **L188, L210:** © 1996 Board of Trustees, National Gallery of Art, Washington, D.C. Chester Dale Collection. © 2001 Estate of Pablo Picasso/Artists Rights Society (ARS), New York. **L199:** Jess Stock/Tony Stone Images. **L216, L246:** © Jean Clottes, Ministere de la Culture/Sygma. **L232:** Texas Department of Commerce/Tourism. **L238:** Michael Stuckey/Comstock, Inc. **L252, L284:** All M.C. Escher works © Cordon Art B.V., Baarn, Holland. All rights reserved. **L278:** Photograph by David Heald, © The Solomon R. Guggenheim Foundation, New York. **L314, L354:** Photograph by Erich Lessing/Art Resource, New York. **L326:** Garneau/Prevost/SuperStock. **L342:** San Diego Museum of Art. Gift of Mr. and Mrs. Norton S. Walbridge. 1975:069. **L347:** © Bob Daemmrich. **L350:** Barrett Kendall photo by Laurie O'Meara. **L360, L400:** Collection of Mr. and Mrs. Paul Mellon. Photograph © 1996 Board of Trustees, National Gallery of Art, Washington, D.C. © 2001 Succession H. Matisse, Paris/Artists Rights Society (ARS), New York. **L385:** Courtesy http://dilos.com. **L393:** Nebraska State Historical Society. **L396:** From "The Dog That Bit People," from the book *My Life and Hard Times*. Copyright © 1933, 1961 by James Thurber. Reprinted by arrangement with Rosemary A. Thurber and the Barbara Hogenson Agency. **L406, L442:** Collection of the High Museum, Atlanta, Georgia. Gift of Don and Jill Childress through the 20th Century Art Acquisition Fund, © 1988 Faith Ringgold. Photograph by Gamma I. **L448, L470:** Erich Lessing/Art Resource, NY. **L512:** Bob Daemmrich/Stock Boston. **L552:** Courtesy of Bill Schneider, Countryside Orchids. **L574:** Stephen McBrady/PhotoEdit. **L592:** Tom Benoit/SuperStock. **L638:** © Bettmann/Corbis. **L676:** Davis Barber/PhotoEdit.

Teacher's Notes

Teacher's Notes

Teacher's Notes

Teacher's Notes

Teacher's Notes

Teacher's Notes

Teacher's Notes